THE CAMBRIDGE HISTORY OF
CHRISTIANITY

*

Constantine to *c.* 600

This volume in the *Cambridge History of Christianity* presents the 'golden age' of patristic Christianity. After episodes of persecution by the Roman government, Christianity emerged as a licit religion enjoying imperial patronage and eventually became the favoured religion of the empire. The articles in this volume discuss the rapid transformation of Christianity during late antiquity, giving specific consideration to artistic, social, literary, philosophical, political, inter-religious and cultural aspects. The volume moves away from simple dichotomies and reductive schematisations (e.g., 'heresy v. orthodoxy') toward an inclusive description of the diverse practices and theories that made up Christianity at this time. While proportional attention is given to the emergence of the Great Church within the Roman empire, other topics are treated as well – such as the development of Christian communities outside the empire.

AUGUSTINE CASIDAY is Lecturer in Historical Theology, Department of Theology and Religious Studies, University of Wales, Lampeter. He is author of *Evagrius Ponticus* (2006) and *Tradition and Theology in St John Cassian* (2006) and assistant editor of *The Cambridge History of Early Christian Literature* (2004).

FREDERICK W. NORRIS is Professor Emeritus of World Christianity, Emmanuel School of Religion. He is author of over 200 articles, associate editor with Everett Ferguson of the *Encylopedia of early Christianity* (1990, second edition 1997) and co-editor with A. Malherbe and J. Thompson of *The Early Church in its Context* (1998).

THE CAMBRIDGE HISTORY OF
CHRISTIANITY

The *Cambridge History of Christianity* offers a comprehensive chronological account of the development of Christianity in all its aspects – theological, intellectual, social, political, regional, global – from its beginnings to the present day. Each volume makes a substantial contribution in its own right to the scholarship of its period and the complete *History* constitutes a major work of academic reference. Far from being merely a history of Western European Christianity and its offshoots, the *History* aims to provide a global perspective. Eastern and Coptic Christianity are given full consideration from the early period onwards, and later, African, Far Eastern, New World, South Asian and other non-European developments in Christianity receive proper coverage. The volumes cover popular piety and non-formal expressions of Christian faith and treat the sociology of Christian formation, worship and devotion in a broad cultural context. The question of relations between Christianity and other major faiths is also kept in sight throughout. The *History* will provide an invaluable resource for scholars and students alike.

List of volumes:

Origins to Constantine
EDITED BY MARGARET M. MITCHELL AND
FRANCES M. YOUNG

Constantine to c. 600
EDITED BY AUGUSTINE CASIDAY AND FREDERICK W.
NORRIS

Early Medieval Christianity c. 600–c. 1100
EDITED BY THOMAS NOBLE AND JULIA SMITH

Christianity in Western Europe c. 1100–c. 1500
EDITED BY MIRI RUBIN AND WALTER SIMON

Eastern Christianity
EDITED BY MICHAEL ANGOLD

Reform and Expansion 1500–1660
EDITED BY RONNIE PO-CHIA HSIA

Enlightenment, Reawakening and Revolution 1660–1815
EDITED BY STEWART J. BROWN AND TIMOTHY TACKETT

World Christianities c. 1815–1914
EDITED BY BRIAN STANLEY AND SHERIDAN GILLEY

World Christianities c. 1914–c. 2000
EDITED BY HUGH McLEOD

THE CAMBRIDGE
HISTORY OF
CHRISTIANITY

★

VOLUME 2
Constantine to *c.* 600

★

Edited by
AUGUSTINE CASIDAY
and
FREDERICK W. NORRIS

CAMBRIDGE
UNIVERSITY PRESS

CAMBRIDGE UNIVERSITY PRESS
Cambridge, New York, Melbourne, Madrid, Cape Town, Singapore, São Paulo

Cambridge University Press
The Edinburgh Building, Cambridge CB2 8RU, UK

Published in the United States of America by Cambridge University Press, New York

www.cambridge.org
Information on this title: www.cambridge.org/9780521812443

© Cambridge University Press 2007

First published 2007

Printed in the United Kingdom at the University Press, Cambridge

A catalogue record for this publication is available from the British Library

Library of Congress Cataloguing in Publication data
Constantine to c. 600 / edited by Augustine Casiday and Frederick W. Norris.
p.   cm. – (The Cambridge history of Christianity ; v. 2)
Includes bibliographical references and index.
ISBN-13: 978-0-521-81244-3 (hardback)
ISBN-10: 0-521-81244-5 (hardback)
1. Church history – Primitive and early church, c. 300–600.   I. Casiday, Augustine.   II. Norris,
Frederick W., 1941–   III. Title.   IV. Series.
BR200.C66   2007
270.2 – dc22   2006100088

ISBN 978-0-521-81244-3 hardback

Contents

Contents

Contents

Maps

Contributors

KHALED ANATOLIOS, Weston Jesuit School of Theology

PAUL M. BLOWERS, Emmanuel School of Religion

BEAT BRENK, Università di Roma I 'La Sapienza' and emeritus, Universität Basel

ALAN BROWN, Trinity College, Cambridge

DAVID BUNDY, Fuller Theological Seminary

AUGUSTINE CASIDAY, University of Wales, Lampeter

H. A. DRAKE, University of California, Santa Barbara

MARILYN DUNN, University of Glasgow

MARK EDWARDS, Christ Church, Oxford

GEORGIA FRANK, Colgate University

DAVID FRANKFURTER, University of New Hampshire

ROWAN A. GREER, emeritus, Yale Divinity School

DAVID G. HUNTER, Iowa State University

ANNA LEONE, University of Durham

SAMUEL N. C. LIEU, Macquarie University

WINRICH LÖHR, Universität Hamburg

J. REBECCA LYMAN, emerita, Church Divinity School of the Pacific

BRONWEN NEIL, Australian Catholic University, McAuley Campus

FREDERICK W. NORRIS, emeritus, Emmanuel School of Religion

KENNETH PENNINGTON, The Catholic University of America

CLAUDIA RAPP, University of California, Los Angeles

SAMUEL RUBENSON, Lund University

MICHELE RENEE SALZMAN, University of California, Riverside

KNUT SCHÄFERDIEK, emeritus, Rheinische Friedrich-Wilhelms-Universität Bonn

BRYAN D. SPINKS, Institute of Sacred Music, Yale University

GUY G. STROUMSA, The Hebrew University of Jerusalem

FRANK R. TROMBLEY, Cardiff University

KARL-HEINZ UTHEMANN, emeritus, Vrije Universiteit Amsterdam

RAYMOND VAN DAM, University of Michigan

Abbreviations

AB: *Analecta Bollandiana*
ACO: Acta Conciliorum Œcumenicorum
ACW: Ancient Christian Writers
AJP: *American journal of philology*
ANRW: *Aufstieg und Niedergang der römischen Welt*
ATR: *Anglican theological review*
BAR: British Archaeological Reports
BASP: *Bulletin of the American Society of Papyrologists*
BCTH: *Bulletin du Comité des Travaux Historiques et Scientifiques*
BETL: Bibliotheca ephemeridum theologicarum lovaniensium
BHG: *Bibliotheca Hagiographica Graeca*
BHO: *Bibliotheca Hagiographica Orientalis*
BSNAF: *Bulletin de la Société Nationale des Antiquaires de France*
BZAW: Beihefte zur Zeitschrift für die alttestamentliche Wissenschaft
CCSG: Corpus Christianorum Series Graeca
CCSL: Corpus Christianorum Series Latina
CIL: *Corpus Inscriptionum Latinarum*
CJ: *Codex Justinianus*
CMC: *Cologne Mani-Codex* (P. Colon. inv. nr. 4780)
CollÉFR: Collection de l'École française de Rome
CPG: *Clavis Patrum Graecorum*
CRAI: *Comptes rendus des séances de l'Académie des Inscriptions et Belles Lettres*
CSCO: Corpus Scriptorum Christianorum Orientalium
CSEL: Corpus Scriptorum Ecclesiasticorum Latinorum
CTh: *Codex Theodosianus*
DACL: *Dictionnaire d'archéologie chrétienne et de liturgie*
DK: Diels, H. and W. Kranz, eds., *Die Fragmente der Vorsokratiker*
DOP: *Dumbarton Oaks Papers*
DSp: *Dictionnaire de spiritualité ascétique et mystique, doctrine et histoire*
Ep(p).: Letter(s)
FOTC: Fathers of the Church
GCS: Griechischen christlichen Schriftsteller
GNO: Gregorii Nysseni Opera
GRBS: *Greek, Roman and Byzantine studies*

H.E.:   *Historia ecclesiastica (Church history)*
H.L.:   Palladius, *Historia Lausiaca*
Hom.:   homily, -ies
HTR: *Harvard theological review*
IGRR: *Inscriptiones Graecae ad res Romanas pertinentes*
ILCV: *Inscriptiones Latinae Christianae Veteres*
ILS: *Inscriptiones Latinae Selectae*
Ins.Chr.:   Inscriptiones Christianae urbis Romae septimo saeculo antiquiores
JAAR: *Journal of the American Academy of Religion*
JbAC: *Jahrbuch für Antike und Christentum*
JECS: *Journal of early Christian studies*
JRS: *Journal of Roman studies*
JTS: *Journal of theological studies*
LCL: Loeb Classical Library
LXX: Septuagint
Mansi: J. D. Mansi, ed., *Sanctorum conciliorum et decretorum collectio nova*
MEFRA: *Mélanges de l'École française de Rome, antiquité*
MGH aa: Monumenta Germaniae Historica – auctores antiquissimi
MGH leg: Monumenta Germaniae Historica – leges
MGH scr.mer.:   Monumenta Germaniae Historica – scriptores rerum
   merovingicarum
NHC: Nag Hammadi Codex
NPNF: Select Library of Nicene and Post Nicene Fathers of the Church
OCA: *Orientalia Christiana Analecta*
OECT: Oxford Early Christian Texts
Or.:   *Orations*
PG: Patrologia Graeca
PL: Patrologia Latina
PLRE: *Prosopography of the Later Roman Empire*
PO: Patrologia Orientalis
Proc. Brit. Acad.:   *Proceedings of the British Academy*
Proc. Cambr. Phil. Soc.:   *Proceedings of the Cambridge Philosophical Society*
Proc. Royal Anthro. Instit.:   *Proceedings of the Royal Anthropological Institute of Great Britain*
   and Ireland
PTS: Patristische Texte und Studien
RAC: *Reallexikon für Antike und Christentum*
RE: *Realencyklopädie für protestantische Theologie und Kirche*
REL: *Revue des études latines*
RendPontAcc: *Atti della Pontificia accademia romana di archeologia, Rendiconti*
RHE: *Revue d'histoire ecclésiastique*
SA: Studia Anselmiana
SC: Sources chrétiennes
SEA: Studia ephemeridis 'Augustinianum'
SEG: Supplementum Epigraphicum Graecum
SH: Subsidia Hagiographica

SP: *Studia Patristica*
SPA: *Studien der Patristischen Arbeitsgemeinschaft*
ST: Studi e Testi
ThPh: *Theologie und Philosophie*
TRE: *Theologische Realenzyklopädie*
TU: Texte und Untersuchungen
VChr: *Vigiliae Christianae*
WSA: Works of St Augustine
ZAC: *Zeitschrift für antikes Christentum*
ZÄS: *Zeitschrift für Ägyptische Sprache und Alterthumskunde*
ZKG: *Zeitschrift für Kirchengeschichte*
ZNTW: *Zeitschrift für die neutestamentliche Wissenschaft*
ZPE: *Zeitschrift für Papyrologie und Epigrafik*
ZPT: *Zeitschrift für Philosophie und Theologie*

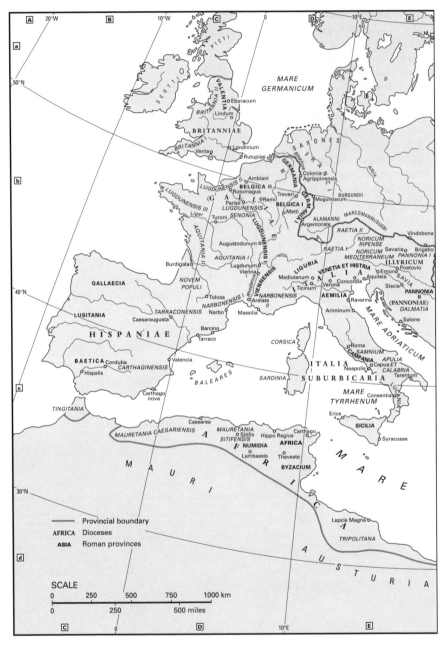

Map 1 The Roman empire, *c.* 400

Map 1 (*cont.*)

xvii

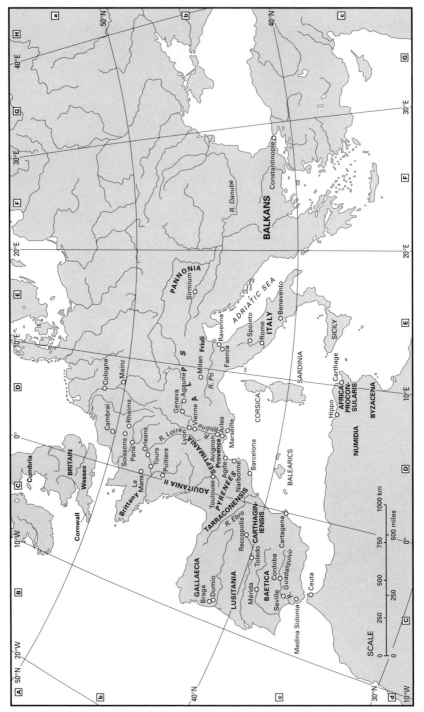

Map 2 Rome and the West, c. 600

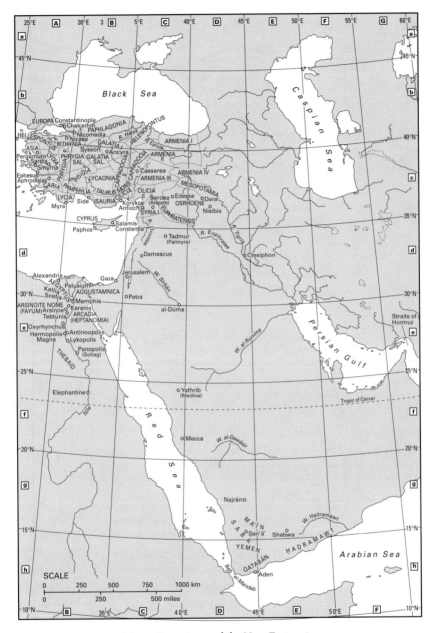

Map 3 Byzantium and the Near East, *c.* 600

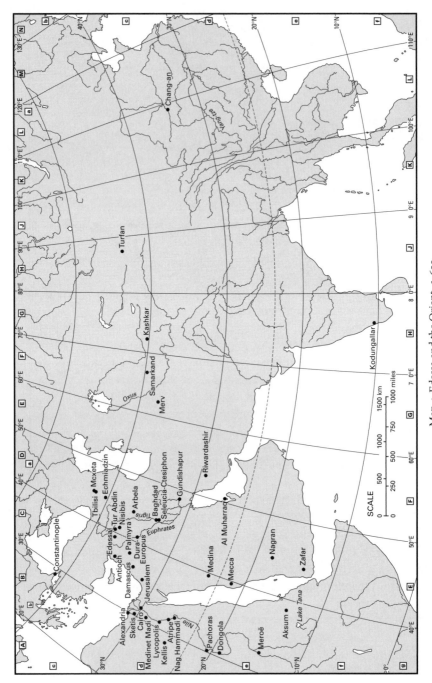

Map 4 Edessa and the Orient, c. 600

Introduction

AUGUSTINE CASIDAY AND FREDERICK W. NORRIS

The chapters in this volume of the *Cambridge History of Christianity* present the 'golden age' of patristic Christianity. After episodes of persecution by the Roman government, Christianity emerged as a licit religion enjoying imperial patronage and eventually became the favoured religion of the empire. It was during this period (*c.* 300–600) that the so-called Great Church emerges in the midst, as it were, of a great and vibrant flourishing of Christianities; the stories of the Great Church, the anonymous masses within it and indeed the countless numbers beyond it are retold in these pages.

Christianity was rapidly transformed during this period, and these transformations will be considered under several headings; artistic (ch. 29), cultural (chs. 12, 26–8), inter-religious (chs. 5, 1–11), literary (ch. 13), philosophical (chs. 10, 18–19), political (chs. 14–17), social (chs. 6–9, 17, 20–5) and, of course, theological aspects (chs. 18–20) are specifically considered. This coverage is in keeping with the multidisciplinary character of modern research into this time period, widely known now as 'late antiquity'. Accordingly, chapters in the book have been contributed by specialists in doctrinal theology, historical theology, social history, art history, liturgics, archaeology, philosophy, comparative religion, and philology.

Also in keeping with contemporary standards in the study of late ancient Christianity, the presentation in this volume moves away from simple dichotomies and reductive schematisations (e.g., 'heresy v. orthodoxy') and toward an inclusive description of the diverse practices and theories that made up Christianity during the period under consideration. Our coverage of Christianity therefore aims at inclusiveness insofar as surviving evidence allows (and, again, the wide range of expertise among the contributors promotes the consideration of correspondingly broad-based evidence). Thus, while proportional attention is given to the emergence of the Great Church within the Roman empire, other topics are also treated – such as divergent beliefs and practices within Christian communities inside the empire, as well as the development of Christian communities outside the empire.

In the West, the foundation of much European culture was laid by Christians as they began to take on much of the Greek and Latin heritage of the region and their faith and practices began to evolve accordingly (ch. 1). Many of the features that came to serve the papacy well in the middle ages and beyond made their appearance during this period. Standard features of Western Christianity (e.g., the biblical canon and its interpretation, the creeds and the roles of bishops, councils and monasticism within the Christian community) reached a level of maturity during this era that justifies speaking of the development of a larger 'narrative'. As is indicated in following chapters on Christianity in the West, bishops and society, lay devotion, pastoral care and discipline and gender, marriage and celibacy, the developing tale of late ancient Christianity featured attractive views of culture, family and friendship.

It is important to note, however, that simultaneously there were developing various understandings of faith and the institutions to serve the Christian West. From the late fourth century onwards, Germanic invaders brought into the later Roman empire their native cultures and religions – and, in some cases, strong Arian churches the origins of which are traced to the conversion of various central European Goths (see ch. 2). With the support of Germanic kings and societies, for whom a strong and unified religious presence was desirable (as for the Roman emperors and their communities), diverse and sometimes competing churches took their place in the Christian history of Europe and North Africa. These competitions often resulted in political involvement or interference, depending on one's position. Had the Arian invaders not been so successful in promoting their faith, established Western Christianity might have taken much longer to attain its imperial form throughout the entire Roman empire. Only later did the Great Church find ways to convert, or to suppress, these Arian Christians. Some communities who were declared heretical (like the Donatist communities in North Africa – see chs. 1 and 9) survived till near the end of our period, or even beyond, and their own stories evolved accordingly. In other cases, where regional Christianities emerged, Christianity was indigenised within a non-Roman culture (as within Celtic societies in the British Isles); these groups too were eventually absorbed into the Great Church.

The westward migration of Christians from central and Eastern Europe was obviously important as it brought divergent creeds into Western Europe and contributed in other ways to the social history of Christianity in the West. The movement of populations, or even individuals, played a significant part in the history of Christianity generally. From St Paul's missionary aspiration to visit Spain to Athanasius of Alexandria's exiles in Western Europe (not to mention the humbler but no less important journeys of mail carriers), these patterns of travel linked the whole of Europe and allowed Christians to promote their faith and practices broadly.

In Eastern Europe and the Near East, other narratives of Christianity developed (ch. 2). Relations between church leaders in the East and in the West were complex and often strained. The patriarchs in the East frequently looked to the papacy for its consistent adherence to proper faith, and treated it not infrequently as an appellate court when an Eastern synod reached a decision unfavourable to certain of the participants in the struggle. But the popes sometimes found themselves unable to act because they were hopelessly embroiled in political circumstance, and in any case not all of Rome's determinations were endorsed in the Christian East. On the other hand, the bishops of Rome occasionally dissented from the decisions of conciliar majorities, particularly when Rome's own position was challenged. Questions of doctrine and practice – regarding Trinity, Christology, salvation, canon law, local worship and lay piety – were hotly debated around the Mediterranean basin.

These debates occurred not simply inside halls of power and within synods of bishops, but also in fish markets and the public baths. In fact, civil and ecclesiastical politics had begun to intertwine at the local level long before any emperor became personally involved, but with Constantine's political ascent the importance of his Christianity for the divine safekeeping of the empire came to occupy the place that sacrifices to the gods had held for earlier emperors. Even though Constantine did not fully establish any Christianity as the single religion of his empire, showed no profound commitment to Christian virtues and even continued to support various pagan leaders and their religions, the favour he showered on Christians (not least through economic privileges and beneficence) put the empire's traditional religions at a great disadvantage. The programme of building grand churches – seen in Constantine's own works, that of such bishops as Ambrose in Milan, and finally the lavish construction efforts of Justinian throughout the empire – signalled the higher standing of Christians and the appeal of promoting Christianity to those of wealth and societal position. Architecture, liturgy and art as well as the capture of Hellenistic rhetorical and literary forms found the ear and the eye of upper classes who often judged the newer religion in terms of their own culture (see especially chs. 13 and 29). Attempts to justify philosophically Christian claims placed Christian conversation within another major cultural stream (ch. 10).

But of course not every powerful patron favoured Christianity. The emperor Julian (*regn.* 360–3) attempted to revive paganism by drawing on moral features taken from the 'Nazarenes' whom he so hated and, had he but lived longer, the stories of Christianity would have been remarkably different. But his death in battle, perhaps perpetrated by some of his Christian troops, foiled his plans. Theodosius II (401–50) set the final terms for Christian establishment by implementing measures in his legal code against heretical groups and traditional religions. Yet deeper investigation has revealed that, in various places, practitioners of traditional religions and marginalised Christian groups alike survived despite their outlawed status (see particularly chs. 6–7). Hagiography and inscriptions unmistakably illustrate how many bishops continued to struggle with pagan communities and influences (e.g., in North Africa: see ch. 9). We have long known of their efforts in writing against classical Greek and Roman paganism as well as groups like the Manichaeans (ch. 11); but more research findings show that, with bishops needing to give almost weekly attention to other religions' hidden festivals and secretive worship, no Christian group had completely eliminated its competitors, even towards the end of this period.

It also needs to be noted that the Christianisation of the Roman Empire itself was often a tumultuous and divisive business and it sometimes contributed to problems with neighbouring Christian populations. For example, in the Eastern Mediterranean, where Christian factions struggled against each other with alacrity and where the early Byzantines who established the Christianity of Constantinople exerted great pressure on its Christian opponents through taxation and bias in the courts, all the rival Christian communities were weakened. They proved to be no match for the seventh-century invasions of Islam.

The *Cambridge History of Christianity* includes by design significant coverage of Christian developments in the East and in the Orient – subject areas that are sometimes overlooked in surveys of this kind. Such coverage is entirely appropriate, not least because Christianity is, and from its early days has been, a missionary faith with global aspirations. And yet too often the earliest Christian developments outside of the Mediterranean world go unremarked. This is regrettable, though partly understandable, owing to the relative paucity of evidence and the fact that surviving literary and documentary evidence exists in multiple oriental languages. Even so, from the age explored in this book, Christianity enters into the history of a great many civilisations around the world and treatment of these communities in this early epoch helps set the stage for the treatment of 'world Christianity' in subsequent volumes.

For example, in Africa, Ethiopian Christianity is in many ways the great survivor and its roots run deep. Like Christianity in Nubia, it flourished along the Nile and soon showed significant levels of cultural flourishing; but, unlike Nubian Christianity, Christianity in Ethiopia survives to the modern period. In Egypt, where Christianity still survives (albeit as a marginalised and frequently oppressed community), before the end of this era Coptic theologians had already begun to articulate an identity that would sustain them for centuries.

In Asia Minor, Armenia and Georgia forged their national identities along with their Christian identity. Syria was home to vibrant and creative theologians for centuries. Christians also lived and practised their faith in Persia, present day Iraq, and India well before Constantine came to power. Though deeply persecuted in Persia, their numbers grew there and in fact throughout the region. In the meantime, a form of Christianity had made inroads among Arabs, at least in Palestine and Yemen and probably even deeper within Arabia. Yet even before Mohammed arose, some sixth-century Palestinian Christian Arabs were supporting Persia against Byzantine Christians.

We also have indications that at least one monk entered China during the sixth century. The warm greetings expressed by the Chinese emperor near the beginning of the seventh century give evidence that the monk's message of Christianity had caught the curiosity of this leader and seems to have allowed him to relate to it as a fascinating, different expression of 'The Way'.

To summarise, in this volume we deliberately move away from relating the story of Christianity with exclusive reference to the single imperial narrative and toward allowing these other Christianities to appear in their own rights. Even though many of them disappeared from history before the great missionary expansion of the nineteenth century, they are an important part of the rich flourishing of Christian religious and cultural expression that characterised our period. In many of these chapters (as, in fact, in much of this introduction), our attention is naturally drawn to instances of conflict – but we also need to be aware that interactions within and between communities were not always conflictual; they could be, and sometimes were, mutually enriching.

PART I

*

CHRISTIANITY: REGIONAL DEVELOPMENTS

Western Christianities

WINRICH LÖHR

The story of Western Christianities from Constantine to the close of the sixth century is one of both expansion and the formation of diverse Christianities. The expansion is slow and difficult to trace: at the beginning of the fourth century, the Western regions of the Roman empire were much less Christianised than the East, only an estimated 2 per cent of the population.[1] Although the progress can be tentatively gauged from the archaeological and epigraphic records or from the multiplication of episcopal sees, a general picture is difficult to establish. The countryside presumably resisted Christianisation (if it ever became completely Christian) far longer than the urban population; missionary efforts by bishops or monks (if they occurred) changed little. The Christianisation of Western aristocracies, on the other hand, has been comparatively well studied. Only in the second half of the fourth century did Christianity develop a message attuned to the ideology and value-system of the social elite that would attract many of them.[2]

Christian diversity is partly due to major political transformations within the later Roman empire. Perhaps the most important of them was the growing split between the Western and the Eastern parts of the empire. After the death of Constantine, the political division of the empire responded to administrative expediency and the military exigencies of almost uninterrupted warfare on the Rhenish, Danubian and Persian borders. The political centre shifted to the East, to Constantinople. During the fifth century, various German nations filled the power vacuum in the West. Their Homoian churches punctuated the map of Roman Christianities in Italy, Gaul, Spain and North Africa.[3] With

---

1 See Y. Modéran, 'La conversion de Constantin', 5.
2 See now M. R. Salzman, *The Making of a Christian Aristocracy*.
3 If the problematic term 'Western Christianities' is taken geographically, it must also include non-Roman and non-Latin-speaking Christianities. Although the impact of these Christianities must be mentioned here, Germanic and Celtic Christianities are treated at length in ch. 2. The existence of Latin-speaking enclaves in the East (e.g., monasteries in Jerusalem) should also be noted.

some regional exceptions, the West also saw substantial economic decline during the fifth and sixth centuries.

Other significant changes resulted from the religious policies of many of Constantine's Christian successors. Some, like Constantius II or – most impressively – Justinian, were deeply engaged in theological controversies because they believed that doctrinal unity grounded peace and prosperity. But ambitious attempts at establishing doctrinal unity on the part of Constantius II, Zeno or Justinian led ultimately to fragmentation into schismatic Christianities. Confronted with interventionist emperors, bishops like Hosius of Cordova in the fourth century, or Pope Gelasius in the fifth century, protested (not least when the emperors backed their opponents). From the sixth century onwards, the Ostrogothic, Visigothic, Burgundian and Merovingian kings partly emulated the Christian emperors' religious policies. Since their kingdoms were smaller and more homogenous, they had less difficulty controlling churches.

Another important factor in this period is the position of the Church of Rome, which increasingly advanced and confirmed its pre-eminence in the West and even attempted to assert itself further abroad. Pope Julius (*sed.* 337–52) asserted the right to review synodical judgments of other, Eastern, churches; the Western Council of Serdica endorsed his action. Pope Innocent I (*sed.* 402– 17) said Peter was the origin of both *apostolatus* and *episcopatus* and demanded that in disciplinary matters all Western churches must follow the Roman church. Pope Leo (*sed.* 440–61) built upon elements of the Petrine ideology already available in formulating the mystical and legal claim that the pope is Peter's deputy. In 495, a Roman synod acclaimed Pope Gelasius (*sed.* 492–96) *vicarius Christi.*[4] Roman Petrine ideology clashed with rival concepts: Justinian conceived of the church as a hierarchically structured body centred on the five patriarchates of Rome, Constantinople, Alexandria, Antioch and Jerusalem – an idea Rome denied.[5] With no clear-cut boundary established between Western and Eastern Christianities, from the late fourth century onwards, Rome and Constantinople competed for authority over the Balkan provinces, particularly Illyricum, where the variations of political and ecclesiastical geography were especially complex. During the episcopates of Popes Siricius (*sed.* 384–99) and Innocent (*sed.* 402–17), Rome claimed supra-metropolitan authority in Illyricum orientale, centred in Thessalonica. Even if the

---

4 Synod of Serdica, cc. 3 and 4 (Joannou, ed., *Discipline générale antique*, 1.2: 162–4); Innocent, *Letter* 2.1 (PL 20: 470); Gelasius, *Letter* 30,15 (ed. Thiel, 447); E. Caspar, *Geschichte des Papsttums*, 1: 427–31; R. Lorenz, *Das vierte bis sechste Jahrhundert*, 82–4; W. Ullmann, *Gelasius I.*

5 See R. Schieffer, 'Der Papst als Patriarch'.

'vicariate of Thessalonica' lapsed under Pope Leo and his successors, Rome still supported the autonomy of the Illyrian churches against Constantinople.[6]

These, then, are the themes that were in evidence across the Christian West throughout the period under consideration: political transformation and the formation of competing orthodoxies, the Christianisation of Western aristocracies, and the interplay between political and ecclesiastical structures.

Schism and the emergence of Nicene orthodoxy

When Constantine died in 337, he left his sons to rule: Constantine II in the Western prefecture (Britain, Gaul, Spain); Constans in Italy, Africa, Illyricum and Moesia; Constantius II in the East and the diocese of Thrace. Constantine II granted amnesty to some Eastern bishops whom his father had exiled from their sees, among them Athanasius of Alexandria and Marcellus of Ancyra. But their return raised difficulties and soon they were expelled again. Athanasius and Marcellus headed for Rome and appealed to Pope Julius to overturn their condemnations by Eastern councils. After a Roman synod had absolved both of them, Athanasius involved Constans. The Western emperor proposed to his brother Constantius II that they assemble Eastern and Western bishops in a council.

Nearly ninety Western and about eighty Eastern bishops arrived in Serdica (modern Sofia) for that purpose in 342 or 343, but the two parties never met in one council and the Eastern bishops – who rejected any revision of their synodical decrees – eventually withdrew.[7] The Western council continued under the presidency of Hosius of Cordova and eventually issued twenty-one canons. Two diverging creeds were formulated: the Western delegates signed one they viewed as a valid interpretation of the Nicene faith and defended Marcellus of Ancyra's theology; the Eastern bishops circulated one which rejected that position (the so-called fourth Antiochene formula).[8] The failure at Serdica exacerbated an existing rivalry between the emperors. Constans eventually threatened Constantius II with military aggression if he did not allow Athanasius to return to Alexandria. The Eastern emperor, whose army was fighting Persia, yielded.[9] But when he became sole ruler in 350, Constantius

---

6 The issues involved are complex. For some illumination, see C. Pietri, 'La géographie de l'Illyricum ecclésiastique'. Pietri cautions against attempts to describe the interactions between local churches in late antiquity in terms more attuned to the analysis of the foreign policies of modern states.

7 T. D. Barnes, *Athanasius and Constantius*, 71–81.

8 See J. N. D. Kelly, *Early Christian creeds*, 274–9; J. Ulrich, *Die Anfänge*, 26–109.

9 Rufinus, *H.E.* 10.20.

tried to heal the rift through creating a common creedal formula. This novel attempt at formulating an explicit orthodoxy led to an intense period of formulating compromise creeds: the second formula of Sirmium (the so-called 'blasphemy of Sirmium', 357); the third formula of Sirmium (358); the fourth formula of Sirmium (359); the formula of Rimini and the formula of Seleucia (359); and the formula of Constantinople (360).[10]

Hosius of Cordova and Liberius of Rome were caught up in Constantius' ambitious religious policy. The emperor suspected Athanasius of high treason and therefore had him condemned by synods in Arles (353) and Milan (355). The Milanese bishop Dionysius – like Eusebius of Vercelli and Lucifer of Calaris (Cagliari) – refused to join the condemnation, and was exiled and succeeded by the Cappadocian Auxentius. Hosius, too, refused to sign the Arles-Milan synodical decision but was probably left unharmed. During the summer of 357 Constantius called a small synod of bishops – possibly under Hosius' leadership – to his residence at Sirmium to heal the theological rift through a compromise formula of faith. The resultant second Sirmian formula outlawed any use of *ousia*-language (e.g., *homousios, homoiousios*).[11] Five Western bishops (Hosius, Potamius of Lisbon, and three Illyrians: Valens of Mursa, Ursacius of Singidunum and Germinius of Sirmium) subscribed to the formula. When the aged Hosius returned to Spain and propagated the second Sirmian formula, however, he met resistance in his home province, the Baetica. Meanwhile, Liberius of Rome criticised the condemnations of Athanasius at Arles and Milan and was therefore exiled to Beroia, Thrace. His senior clergy had sworn to support him. But the imperial resolve carried the day and Liberius was eventually replaced by Felix II. Felix proved unpopular, but in any case after two years Liberius was obliged to endorse both Athanasius' condemnation and the second Sirmian formula. Constantius then allowed him to return on the condition that he and Felix share the episcopal throne. The political compromise failed and public unrest ensued. Liberius and Hosius probably signed the creed in order to further the cause of ecclesiastical peace and unity.[12] Notwithstanding their support, the second Sirmian creed was contested in both East and West, and eventually withdrawn.

---

10 Kelly, *Early Christian creeds*, 283–95.
11 Hilary of Poitiers, *De synodis* 11.
12 Already at Serdica it was Hosius of Cordova who was most interested in reaching a compromise. The authenticity of the relevant letters of Liberius and his subscription to the second Sirmian formula have been conclusively established by H. C. Brennecke, *Hilarius von Poitiers*.

Even so, the emperor's ambitious policy of ecclesiastical reunification reached its planned climax with the double synod of Rimini (Italy) and Seleucia (Cilicia) in 359, one of ancient Christianity's largest councils. In the first session, a majority of the over 400 assembled bishops rejected the proposed 'Homoian'[13] creed and endorsed the Nicene faith – the first time this was done by a large number of Western bishops. In the second session, political pressure and the desire to end the schism of Serdica prevailed and Western bishops were moved to rescind their previous opposition. They re-established union with the Eastern churches by unanimously accepting the new, 'Homoian', formula of faith,[14] supplemented by a series of anti-Arian anathemas. A Western delegation from Rimini confirmed this outcome by accepting a (slightly variant) Homoian creed in Constantinople during a meeting with Constantius himself on New Year's Eve.[15] And yet, significantly, the see of Rome was not involved at Rimini.

Hilary of Poitiers, whose pamphlet warfare had attacked Constantius' policy, sharply blamed the emperor and his episcopal advisers for pressurising Western bishops at Rimini to relinquish Nicene orthodoxy and embrace Arian heresy. Liberius of Rome sent letters to other Western bishops concerning the acceptance of Homoian baptisms.[16] Die-hard clergy in Spain, Gaul and even Rome (such as Lucifer of Calaris – after whom they were dubbed 'Luciferians' – and Gregory, bishop of Elvira) broke communion with fellow bishops who participated in the reversal at Rimini. Jerome famously commented on the Council of Rimini-Seleucia-Constantinople: 'The whole world cried in anguish and was bewildered that it should be Arian!'[17] For Jerome, as for Hilary, Homoian orthodoxy had been imposed by deceit on the Western episcopate.[18]

This first attempt at an empire-wide creedal orthodoxy soon faced problems. Constantius died in 361 and after the interlude of Julian's reign (361–3) the few defenders of Homoian orthodoxy in the West – such as Auxentius of Milan, Germinius of Sirmium, Valens of Mursa and Ursacius of

---

13 The 'Homoian' creed says that the Son is 'like' (Greek: *homoios*) the Father; it rejects the Nicene position that the Son is of the same substance as the Father (*homoousios tô patri*).

14 This formula had first been accepted by a delegation of fourteen Western bishops at Nicaea, Thrace on 10 October 359; the bishops had been sent by the council to Constantinople in order to ask the emperor for the dismissal of the council.

15 See W. A. Löhr, *Entstehung*; H. C. Brennecke, *Studien*.

16 PL 84: 631.

17 Jerome, *Altercatio Luciferiani et Orthodoxi* 19 (SC 473: 158), 'ingemuit totus orbis, et Arianum se esse miratus est'.

18 See Y.-M. Duval, 'La manœuvre frauduleuse de Rimini'.

Singidunum – became marginalised.[19] Julian's Christian successors, the emperor-brothers Valentinian I (*regn.* 364–75) and Valens (*regn.* 364–78) seem to have favoured different theological orthodoxies: Valentinian lent measured support to Nicene faith in the West, whereas in the East Valens defended the Homoian episcopate established by the synod of Constantinople (360). Although a slow rapprochement between the Western and Eastern churches seemed possible, it was doubtful whether it could be achieved by Homoian orthodoxy. If a common creed was necessary, why not return to the venerable Nicene formula, interpreting it to overcome the resistance of most Eastern bishops?

In the West, Hilary of Poitiers failed to oust the Homoian Auxentius from Milan,[20] but Damasus of Rome and particularly Ambrose, the new bishop of Milan, championed Nicene orthodoxy.[21] However, the intransigent Roman support for the schismatic Nicene church of Paulinus in Antioch disturbed Eastern bishops like Meletius of Antioch and Basil of Caesarea, who proposed a compromise interpretation of the Nicene Creed. Under Theodosius I (*regn.* 379–95) unity of a kind was restored with synods in Antioch (379), Aquileia (381), Constantinople (381 – the Second Ecumenical Council; 382) and Rome (382) that endorsed Nicene orthodoxy – but the Western and Eastern bishops never assembled in one council. The Western churches reaffirmed the Nicene Creed without explicitly accepting the Eastern interpretation of the term *homousios* ('consubstantial').[22] On 28 February 380, Theodosius proclaimed the new orthodoxy by an edict that jointly cited Damasus of Rome and Peter of Alexandria as guardians of orthodox faith.[23] The end of the fourth century saw the empire's churches united in formal adherence to Nicene orthodoxy – without, however, having reached an agreement on its interpretation.

Nicene orthodoxy and Western Christianities: Defence and construction

Upon Theodosius' death on 17 January 395, the empire was again divided among the emperor's sons, who either were minors or otherwise powerless.

---

19 See M. Meslin, *Les ariens d'Occident*.

20 See Hilary's *Contra Auxentium* (PL 10: 609–18).

21 See D. H. Williams, *Ambrose of Milan*; C. Markschies, *Ambrosius von Mailand*; Y.-M. Duval, *L'extirpation de l'arianisme*.

22 Whereas Western Nicene theology spoke of one substance (*una substantia*) and three persons (*personae*), Eastern Nicene theology taught one being (*ousia*) and three hypostases. The terminological difference remained unresolved. See A. de Halleux, '"Hypostase" et "personne"'.

23 *CTh* 16.1.2 (SC 497: 114–15).

In the West, princesses like Galla Placidia and powerful generals, such as the Vandal Stilicho or the Roman Aetius, determined policy. Although formal imperial unity remained, the Eastern and the Western halves grew apart. Whereas the Eastern Empire was eventually secured, the disintegrating Western empire (its last emperor, Nepos, died in 480) saw the establishment of various Germanic kingdoms. The most remarkable new ruler was Theoderic who – after service as a Roman general and a consul – founded an Ostrogothic kingdom in Italy and, from 511 until his death in 526, also ruled the Visigothic kingdom in southern Gaul and Spain. At its height Theoderic's rule formed the radiating centre of a new assemblage of Germanic polities on old Western imperial territory.

An important consequence of the Western empire's dissolution was the rivalry of two Christian orthodoxies. Both emerged through the successive attempts by Constantius and Theodosius to integrate the churches of the Roman empire. The Germanic churches retained their traditional Homoian orthodoxy first adopted by Ulfilas, the bishop of a group of Goths living on Roman territory, a signatory of the Constantinopolitan creed of 360.[24] In the provinces of Italy, Gaul, Spain and North Africa, by contrast, the Roman Christianities adhered to Nicene orthodoxy. Yet the Catholic (Nicene) Christianities in the Western provinces had to deal with the Homoian Christianities of their Germanic overlords; the relations between the two Christianities varied from toleration (particularly in Italy and Gaul) to intermittent, sometimes severe, persecution (particularly in North Africa).

Despite the slow disintegration of the Western empire, the Western Catholic Christianities influenced the on-going formulation and construction of Nicene orthodoxy in the East. The Roman church took the lead for the West with varying success in the shifting alliances between Eastern bishops and patriarchs. In the early phase, Rome sided with Cyril of Alexandria against Nestorius of Constantinople; Pope Sixtus (*sed.* 432–40) erected the impressive S. Maria Maggiore dedicated to the *dei genetrix* (Greek: *theotokos*). But the miaphysite position[25] of Dioscorus of Alexandria (Cyril's successor) and archimandrite Eutyches led to a rift between Rome and Alexandria. When in 449 Theodosius II seemed to favour Dioscorus and Eutyches and wanted to convene a general council, Pope Leo (*sed.* 440–61) addressed his famous Tome to Flavian of Constantinople; in it, he refuted Eutyches' extreme miaphysite position at considerable length.[26] At the so-called 'Robber Council' of Ephesus in August 449,

---

24 See ch. 2, below.
25 See ch. 19, below.
26 ACO 2.2.1. 24–33.

Dioscorus terrorised the assembled bishops into submission. Leo's *Tome* was not read out and Flavian of Constantinople was deposed, but before he was dragged away by soldiers he passed a written appeal to the Roman delegation. The deacon Hilary was probably the only Roman legate who was able to make his way back to Rome. When in 461 Hilary succeeded Leo as pope, he caused an inscription to be made in the baptistery of the Lateran church in gratitude for his safe return.[27]

The 'Robber Council' was a serious setback for Rome. In August 450, however, Theodosius was succeeded by the general Marcian (who was married to the emperor's sister, Pulcheria). Marcian and Pulcheria, determined to reverse the religious policy of their predecessor, convoked a new council in October 451, which met at Chalcedon so the emperor could attend. More than 500 bishops attended, but the West was represented merely by a three-person Roman delegation and two bishops from Africa. The synod's Christological definition attempted to bring the Christological language from Leo's Tome in line with Cyril's second letter against Nestorius.[28] But many Eastern bishops still opposed Nicaeno-Chalcedonian orthodoxy and particularly resented the Tome. The Roman position towards this council remained ambivalent. On the one hand Rome defended Chalcedon's Christological definition and the 'Tome of Leo'. On the other hand, Rome stridently opposed canon 28, which – citing canon 3 of the Council of Constantinople (381) – attempted to establish Constantinople, the New Rome, on an equal footing with the Old Rome, on the grounds that both were capitals and imperial residences.[29] For Rome, the authority of its bishop was based on the pope's being the successor and, indeed, deputy (*vicarius*) of the apostle Peter. Pope Leo insisted on canon 6 of the Council of Nicaea, which he interpreted as confirming the unique position of his own see.[30]

The aftermath of Chalcedon and the Acacian schism

As schisms within the churches of the Nicene tradition broke out after Chalcedon, the emperors and bishops of Constantinople faced the consequences. They tried to re-integrate Nicaeno-Chalcedonian Christianity

---

27 *ILCV* 980. The inscription is dedicated to St John the Evangelist, at whose shrine in Ephesus Hilary had prayed for help. See A. Mandouze, *Prosopographie*, II.I: 989–92; H. Chadwick, *The church in ancient society*, 558–67.

28 This episode is discussed by K.-H. Uthemann in ch. 19, below.

29 Joannou, ed., *Discipline générale antique*, I.I: 90–3.

30 Caspar, *Geschichte des Papsttums*, I: 522f., 527–31.

by conceding some ground to Miaphysite opposition without abrogating Chalcedon's Christological definition. In the autumn of 482, Emperor Zeno (*regn.* 474–91) addressed a letter to the Alexandrian church that proposed a compromise formula drafted by Acacius of Constantinople. This declaration (the so-called *Henotikon*, or 'Formula of Union') insisted on the unique authority of Nicaea's creed, anathematised Nestorius and Eutyches as heretics and canonised Cyril's third letter to Nestorius.[31] On the basis of the *Henotikon*, Acacius sought to restore communion with the Miaphysite patriarch of Alexandria, Peter Mongus, and subsequently with the new Miaphysite bishop of Antioch, Peter the Fuller, when the latter had succeeded Calandion, who had been ousted from his see for defending the Chalcedonian definition. For Rome, however, Peter Mongus was a condemned heretic and an opponent of Chalcedonian faith and therefore such overtures were simply not acceptable. In July 484, a Roman synod chaired by Pope Felix III (*sed.* 483–92) deposed Peter Mongus as well as Acacius of Constantinople. A year later, a Roman synod excommunicated Peter of Antioch as well.[32]

Rome's resistance against the emperor's policy of enforced doctrinal compromise was sustained in the context of a deepening political divide between East and West. From 493, Theoderic, king of the Ostrogoths, established his court in Ravenna. Although he was officially subordinated to Constantinople, Ostrogothic kings ruled Italy for the next thirty years; their reign guaranteed political stability as well as a measure of prosperity and even some cultural flourishing. Although Theoderic wanted his rule to be recognised by the Eastern emperor, he did not care for too much influence of the imperial court in Italy. In Rome itself, the church and the senate disagreed on how best to deal with the schism: Pope Gelasius (*sed.* 492–6), the successor of Felix, defended the Roman position rigorously and even requested that Acacius' name be deleted from the diptychs in the Eastern churches.[33]

Attitudes in Rome subsequently changed. In 497, the Roman *princeps senatus*, the patrician Festus, in company with two Italian bishops, led an embassy to the emperor.[34] The delegation brought Theoderic's request to the emperor for official recognition as king, as well as a letter from Pope Anastasius (*sed.* 496–8) that noted his election and pleaded for Acacius' name no longer

---

31 E. Schwartz, *Publizistische Sammlungen*, 197f. – see further ch. 19.
32 See *Collectio Veronensis* 5, *Collectio Berolinensis* 26 (ed. Schwartz, *Publizistische Sammlungen*, 6–7, 76); *Collectio Avellana* 99, 70 (CSEL 35: 453.2–12, 155–61); see further ibid., 207f.
33 *Collectio Veronensis* 12 (ed. Schwartz, *Publizistische Sammlungen*, 49–55); see further ibid., 219–26.
34 See C. Pietri, 'Aristocratie et société cléricale', 1039–40.

to be commemorated.[35] During the negotiations with two ambassadors from the Alexandrian church (*apokrisarioi*), the Roman delegation even raised hopes that the pope might accept the *Henotikon*.[36] But when Festus and his delegation returned to Rome, Anastasius had died, the peace initiative disappeared and the situation in Rome was deteriorating, for two popes were elected in 498. One, Laurentius, seemed to adopt a conciliatory stance; the other, Symmachus (*sed*. 498–514), continued Gelasius' policy. After a protracted stand-off and skirmishes on the streets of Rome, Symmachus eventually prevailed. In 506, Theoderic recognised him as the legitimate pope; Symmachus' position against Constantinople may have helped.

Shortly thereafter, politics once more motivated efforts to re-establish communion. The new Eastern emperor Justin (*regn*. 518–27)[37] and Justinian (*regn*. 527–65), his nephew and successor, saw restored ecclesiastical unity as important for reviving the empire's ancient glory, and circumstances favoured reconciliation. Justin therefore forced John of Constantinople to accept the conditions set out by Pope Hormisdas, Symmachus' successor. Following a brief period of negotiations, in the spring of 519 Rome and Constantinople were again in communion: John was obliged to accept Hormisdas' formula that condemned, among others, Acacius, Peter Mongus, and Peter the Fuller. The papal formula also joined Chalcedon in condemning Eutyches and Dioscorus, and it confirmed 'all those letters which Pope Leo had written about the orthodox faith'. Moreover, John accepted Hormisdas' demand of erasing those excommunicated by Rome from his church's diptychs.[38]

Theoderic did not welcome Justin's new religious policy. His suspicion fell on Boethius, the Master of the Offices in Ravenna since 522, who had enjoyed warm relations with the court in Constantinople. Boethius was a learned lay theologian, who endorsed a version of Nicaeno-Chalcedonian orthodoxy amenable to compromise with the Miaphysite position.[39] These connections may have alarmed Theoderic, who had Boethius arrested, incarcerated in Pavia (where he penned his *Consolation of philosophy* and was intermittently tortured) and ultimately executed on charges of treason and sorcery. And

---

35 Anastasius, *Letter* I (ed. Thiel, 615–23).
36 *Collectio Avellana* 102.13 (CSEL 35: 472.9–16); see E. Schwartz, *Publizistische Sammlungen*, 226–30.
37 For Justin's religious policy, see K. Rosen, 'Iustinus I', 766–9 (bibliography).
38 *Collectio Avellana*, 159; Appendix IIII (CSEL 35: 607–10; 800–1); see A. Grillmeier, *Jesus der Christus*, II.1: 364–8.
39 H. Chadwick, *Boethius*, 46–66; Boethius is only the outstanding exemplar of a contemporary Roman aristocratic culture that began to develop an interest in theology: see Pietri, 'Aristocratie et société cléricale', 1030–3.

when Justin deprived eastern Homoian 'heretics' of their churches, Theoderic reacted swiftly and sharply. He dispatched Pope John I as the head of a delegation to Constantinople, threatening retaliatory measures against Catholics in Italy if the Eastern Homoians did not get back their churches and if the forced conversions to Nicene Christianity of Homoians were not overturned.[40] Theoderic was dissatisfied and when the delegation returned to Ravenna he arrested the pope for disloyalty. John died in prison and was buried as a martyr. Theoderic prepared reprisals against the Catholic churches in Ravenna, but before carrying them out he himself died on 30 August 526.

Schism in the West: Vigilius and the Fifth Ecumenical Council

Justinian, who wanted to succeed where his predecessors had failed, promoted Nicaeno-Chalcedonian orthodoxy in dialogue with Miaphysites, and sought support from Pope John II (*sed.* 533–5) for this project.[41] In 535, the new bishop of Constantinople, Anthimus, offered to re-establish communion with the Miaphysites and to welcome the *Henotikon*. When in the spring of 536 Pope Agapetus I (*sed.* 535–6) went to Constantinople on a political mission for the Ostrogothic king Theodahad, the pope forced Anthimus' resignation on canonical grounds and ordained his successor, Menas – the first papal ordination of an Eastern bishop.[42] Justinian and Menas proved their orthodoxy to the pope by presenting an enlarged version of Hormisdas' formula. Agapetus responded by continuing John II's support for Justinian.[43]

If on this occasion pope and emperor found common ground, problems underlying their alliance became evident under Pope Vigilius (*sed.* 537–55). Vigilius had an aristocratic background (his father was a praetorian prefect of Italy, his brother a prefect of Rome) and exemplified the trend towards the 'aristocratisation' of the papacy.[44] Having spent time as Roman ambassador to Constantinople, he seemed destined to enrol in Justinian's programme. But problems emerged between pope and emperor when Justinian took it in

40 *Liber Pontificalis* 55 (ed. Duchesne, 1: 275); Anonymus Valesianus c. 88 (ed. König, 92). The details of Theoderic's demands are unclear; see J. Moorhead, *Theoderic in Italy*, 235–42.
41 *Codex Justinianus* 1.1.6, 8 (ed. Krüger, 7–8, 10–12); *Collectio Avellana* 84 (CSEL 35: 320–8); ACO 4.2: 206–10. For Justinian's religious policy, see E. Schwartz, *Vigiliusbriefe* (bibliography); C. Capizzi, *Giustiniano I*; K.-L. Noethlichs, 'Iustinianus (Kaiser)', 688–701; Chadwick, *The church in ancient society*, 612–27; K.-H. Uthemann, 'Kaiser Justinian'; C. Sotinel, 'Emperors and popes'.
42 Liberatus, *Breviarium* 21 (ACO 2.5: 135–6).
43 *Collectio Avellana* 91 (CSEL 35: 342–7).
44 E. Wirbelauer, 'Die Nachfolgerbestimmung', 433–4; PLRE 2: 1166.

hand to work out a theological position that adequately defended Nicaeno-Chalcedonian orthodoxy without succumbing to 'Nestorianism' or conceding too much to the radical Miaphysites. Imperial edicts were the vehicles for his theology, and he obliged the bishops to subscribe to them. In 544/5 the emperor published a dogmatic treatise condemning the 'Three Chapters'.[45] This treatise circulated among the Eastern churches and in Africa, and was presented to the papal ambassador. The four Eastern patriarchs subscribed, despite strong misgivings. Rome's ambassador in Constantinople protested and suspended communion with Menas. Justinian ordered Vigilius to Constantinople. After being arrested by Roman soldiers, the pope departed Rome on an imperial ship on 22 November 545, just before the Ostrogoths started a second (and ultimately successful) siege of the city.

Vigilius had been informed about widespread opposition in Rome, Africa, Sardinia, Greece and Illyria to Justinian's condemnation of the 'Three Chapters'. Accordingly, the negotiations that began after his arrival in Constantinople on 25 January 547 were unsuccessful. The pope and the patriarch excommunicated each other; but six months later they were reconciled and the pope secretly communicated to the emperor his willingness to condemn the 'Three Chapters', which may indicate that his earlier resistance to the emperor's religious policy was ambivalent at best.[46] He convened a meeting of seventy bishops, chiefly Westerners, to sound out their opinions, but quickly broke off the talks. Justinian's *magister officiorum* requested the bishops' opinions within a week. One of the bishops, the formidable African Facundus of Hermiane, hastily prepared his defence of the 'Three Chapters' from excerpts of a larger treatise.[47] Facundus eventually returned to Byzacena (Africa), went into hiding and from there continued resisting Justinian for the next fifteen years. Meanwhile, Vigilius sent Menas a letter (the so-called *Iudicatum*, dated 11 April 548) that condemned the 'Three Chapters' while insisting on the validity of Chalcedon.[48]

The *Iudicatum* precipitated open schism in the West. Did Vigilius concede too much to Chalcedon's enemies? The primate of Dacia, Benenatus, was deposed for supporting it; an African synod formally excommunicated the pope; the bishop of Arles and papal vicar in Gaul, Aurelian, demanded an explanation. The emperor tried to suppress the resistance and summoned

45 The treatise is not extant, but the quotations are collected by E.Schwartz, *Kirchenpolitik*, 73–81. For the 'Three Chapters', cf. ch. 4.
46 ACO 4.1: 187–8.
47 Facundus, *Defence of the Three Chapters*, pref. (SC 471: 140–3).
48 For fragments of the *Iudicatum*, see ACO 4.1: 11–12; Collectio Avellana 299–303 (CSEL 35: 316–17).

Reparatus of Carthage, Firmus of Tipasa and two bishops from Byzacena to Constantinople. Reparatus was deposed, exiled and replaced by his own *apocrisiarius*, Primosus. Firmus yielded to the pressure but died on the journey home. Of the two Byzacene bishops one, Primasius, became primate of Byzacena after having condemned the 'Three Chapters'. The controversy continued. Justinian's re-conquest of Africa – aimed at liberating Catholics from the yoke of Homoians – resulted in more persecution. Eventually, however, Justinian's policy succeeded and African Christianity was united in its adherence to the new orthodoxy.[49]

As for Vigilius, he was permitted to withdraw the *Iudicatum* in 550 – on the condition that he had to assure the emperor of his loyalty regarding the condemnation of the 'Three Chapters' through a secret written oath.[50] The following July, Justinian issued a further edict against the 'Three Chapters' and published it in all the main churches of Constantinople.[51] The pope, assuming that the theological question should be resolved by a synod, or at least by written responses from Western bishops, required the removal of the edict.[52] He was supported in this by all the Western bishops who had remained in Constantinople (such as Datius of Milan). Meanwhile the situation in the capital had become so tense that Vigilius and his followers left the palace of Galla Placidia and sought refuge in the church of Sts Peter and Paul. On 14 August 551, Vigilius drafted the excommunication of Theodore of Caesarea (whom he considered behind the emperor's policy), his followers, and also Menas of Constantinople and his bishops.[53] For the time being, however, the pope held back his decree. The emperor dispatched soldiers to arrest him in the church. Vigilius clung to the altar columns and, when they tried to drag the old man away, the edifice burst and tumbling fragments nearly killed him. The pathetic scene aroused the sympathy of bystanders and the soldiers had to withdraw.[54] The pope returned to the palace where he was now virtually a prisoner. Two days before Christmas 551, Vigilius escaped to Chalcedon where he found asylum in the church of St Euphemia, where

---

49 Victor of Tunnuna, *chron.* 551, 552, 555, 556 (MGH aa II: 202–5); Victor himself, an ardent defender of the 'Three Chapters', suffered successive exiles in places as diverse as the Balearic isles and Alexandria. See Y. Modéran, 'Die Kirchen und die byzantinische Rückeroberung'.
50 ACO 4.1: 198–9: The pope promised to denounce to the emperor all supporters of the Three Chapters; in turn the emperor pledged to defend the honour and the privileges of the see of Rome.
51 E. Schwartz, *Drei dogmatische Schriften*, 72–III.
52 Schwartz, *Vigiliusbriefe*, 2.4ff.
53 Ibid., 10–15.
54 Ibid. 4.15ff; 22.8ff.

the Fourth Ecumenical Council had met a century earlier. The pope finally published the excommunication of Menas and Theodore, but they and other prominent Eastern bishops responded by solemnly declaring their allegiance to the four ecumenical councils and all letters (including those of Pope Leo) written concerning the orthodox faith and by declaring null and void anything written against the 'Three Chapters'.[55] Vigilius lifted his ban against the Eastern bishops, and returned to the capital.

Justinian, however, now wanted a council to complete ecclesiastical reunification. The council opened in the hall of the Hagia Sophia on 5 May 553; about 150 bishops were present, but not Pope Vigilius. Only a few handpicked Western bishops attended. Complying with the emperor's request, Vigilius and his supporters worked in a parallel meeting on a lengthy theological declaration they completed by 14 May 553. The resulting *Constitutum* censured sixty excerpts (*capitula*) from Theodore of Mopsuestia's writings, but did not denounce the man himself.[56] The *Constitutum* also refrained from personally condemning Theodoret of Cyrus, while assuring the emperor that any of his writings containing Nestorian or Eutychian errors stood condemned. As regards the letter of Ibas of Edessa, the *Constitutum* argued that Chalcedon had found it orthodox.

By not denouncing the 'Three Chapters', the pope broke his agreement with the emperor. Justinian's council ignored the *Constitutum*. In the seventh session, an imperial official revealed the full extent of the pope's secret commitment to Justinian's religious policy. The emperor ordered the removal of his name from the diptychs. The assembled bishops endorsed the emperor's letter.[57] In the final session of the council (2 June 553), all bishops subscribed to a lengthy *sententia synodica* together with fourteen anathemas including the condemnation of the 'Three Chapters'.[58] Opposing African bishops were exiled. Vigilius capitulated and on 23 February 554 published a second *Constitutum* endorsing the substance of the council's decisions: the condemnation of Theodore of Mopsuestia's and Theodoret of Cyrus' writings; an anathema against Theodore himself; and the denunciation of Ibas' letter, now declared a forgery.[59] Vigilius was thoroughly discredited but allowed to return to Rome; he died en route in Sicily on 7 June 555.

---

55 *Collectio Avellana* 83.3–9 (CSEL 35: 230–2).
56 *Collectio Avellana* 83 (CSEL 35: 230–320).
57 ACO 4.1: 202.
58 ACO 4.1: 207–20, 240–4. As to the council's other theological decisions, see chs. 2 and 19, below.
59 ACO 4.2: 138–68.

His deacon Pelagius succeeded him. Appointed by the emperor and pro-tected by his troops, Pelagius was ordained at Easter 556 by only two bishops. Although Pelagius proclaimed his allegiance to the four ecumenical coun-cils and apologised for his involvement in the 'Three Chapters' controversy, war-torn Italy resisted him, especially the metropolitans of Milan and Aquileia. A schism resulted. During the Lombard occupation, the bishop of Milan moved to Genoa, while the bishop of Aquileia withdrew to the isle of Grado. Relations between Milan and Rome were not re-established until 572, between Grado and Rome in 607. A rival metropolitan who continued to oppose Rome and the council of 553 was ordained in Lombard territory, in Aquileia. The council was similarly ignored in Visigothic Spain. The situation persisted for nearly a century and a half. Shortly before 700, the schism ended, like that of the Homoian Christianities of the Goths, the Suebians and the Vandals before. The remnant of an imperial religious policy that had failed was finally laid to rest by a synod in Pavia.[60]

Italy

Our picture of the expansion of Christianity in late antique Italy is only sketchy. Only sixteen Italian bishops attended a council in Rome in 313. A substantial growth in numbers can be assumed for the fifth century; at the close of the sixth century the number of 250 episcopal sees seems to be realistic, a fifth of them in the northern parts. Christian penetration of the countryside intensified in the fifth century: rural monasticism apparently played a role. The political instability that accompanied the dissolution of Theoderic's Ostrogothic king-dom in the sixth century, particularly the invasion of the Lombards, seems to have partly retarded the Christianisation of the countryside.[61]

The civil diocese of Italy was divided into *Italia suburbicaria* with Rome as its centre and in the north *Italia annonaria* with Milan as its centre. For the bishops of *Italia suburbicaria* the Roman bishop was the metropolitan. During the fourth century Milan became the ecclesiastical centre of *Italia annonaria*. When, however, the residence of the emperor was moved from Milan to Ravenna at the beginning of the fifth century, Milan lost its prominent position. In the longer run this resulted in a tripartition of ecclesiastical *Italia annonaria* with Milan, Ravenna and Aquileia as metropolitan sees.[62]

60 R. Markus, *Gregory the Great*, 125–42.
61 E. Pack, 'Italia I', 1166–8 (statistics of episcopal sees), 1177–82 (spread of rural Christianity).
62 Ibid., 1168–73.

The episcopate of Damasus (366–84) neatly illustrates the emergence of Rome as the pre-eminent church of Western Christianities.[63] Its beginnings were difficult enough: the schism between Liberius and Felix II was dividing the church. Two parties arose after Liberius' death (24 September 366): one, perhaps the minority, ordained Ursinus in the *Basilica Iuli* in Trastevere; their opponents elected Damasus in S. Lorenzo in Lucina.[64] Damasus gained possession of the Lateran church where he was ordained bishop of Rome in early October. He had the urban prefect Viventius expel Ursinus and two of his deacons, but they were liberated by the people and sought refuge in the *Basilica Liberii* on the Esquiline Hill. On 26 October, Damasus' supporters – an armed rabble of clergy, charioteers, arena orderlies and gravediggers (*fossores*) – besieged the church, set fire to it and massacred 160 men and women. Further unedifying episodes in the conflict with Ursinus overshadowed the rest of his episcopate. Several Roman synods and the Council of Aquileia (381) dealt with these problems, and Damasus appealed to the secular authorities to curtail the Ursinians. In 373, a certain Isaac accused Damasus of murder, among other things. The emperor Valentinian, convinced that this was false, terminated the judicial proceedings. In 378, a Roman synod acquitted Damasus and also made detailed proposals for ecclesiastical jurisdiction that enhanced the bishop of Rome's position among the churches of Italy and the Western empire. It further suggested that the pope should be exempted from the urban prefect's jurisdiction.[65]

Papal elections remained problematical in the following centuries: if the clergy (presbyters and deacons) could not agree on a candidate, there existed no fixed procedure to resolve the conflict. Schisms were the result. The most severe of these was probably the so-called 'Laurentian schism' at the close of the fifth century (see above).[66] The politicisation of papal elections confirms in a more general way the growing prestige and importance of the episcopate in late antiquity. On the one hand there was the local scene with an easily manipulated plebs, a powerful if seldom unanimous Christian aristocracy and an often-assertive clergy.[67] On the other hand, there were various regional and transregional powers: Roman / Byzantine emperors, their various plenipotentiaries, and Germanic kings.

---

63 See C. Carletti, 'Damaso I, santo'.
64 See A. Lippold, 'Ursinus'; A. Coskun, 'Der Praefect Maximinus' (with updated bibliography).
65 Pietri, *Roma Christiana*, I: 741–8.
66 See E. Wirbelauer, *Zwei Päpste*.
67 L. Pietri et al., 'Peuple chrétien ou plebs'.

Despite fierce opposition, Damasus was an energetic bishop and a devoted (if ruthless) leader of his riotous flock. He disseminated the Christian message through all media available, to increase the influence of his see and to promote ecclesiastical unity. By the second half of the fourth century, Christianity began to penetrate the highest levels of Roman society, and in the last decade of the century large numbers of Roman aristocrats became Christians.[68] The period from 370 until the end of the fifth century was the golden age of Christian euergetism in Rome, as the largesse of Christian aristocrats gradually replaced imperial donations.[69] The *tituli* (churches whose clergy were charged with pastoral care of the growing Christian population) that were founded were provided with liturgical apparatus (e.g., vestments, vessels), but more significantly with landed property in and around Rome, in Italy, in Sicily and even as far away as North Africa and Illyricum. These are the beginnings of the *patrimonium* of the Roman church whose administration must have been quite difficult during the troubled times of the fifth and sixth centuries.[70] Its revenues paid for the upkeep of the buildings and the stipends of the clergy. During the time of Damasus, a pagan aristocrat could joke about the papacy as an attractive career option.[71]

This new patronage enabled Damasus and his successors to carry forward an ambitious building programme that transformed the urban landscape. Rome first benefited from Constantine's munificence in 315,[72] and for several decades imperially sponsored projects outclassed papal efforts. The popes began to establish a network of *tituli*. The beginnings were modest, with a few small churches like the *titulus Silvestri*, the *titulus Marci* or the two basilicas erected possibly by Pope Julius I. The building activity continued under Pope Liberius with a basilica on the Esquiline Hill, and intensified under Pope Damasus and his successors. Damasus decorated the apse of S. Anastasia and built a baptistery in St Peter as well as the *titulus Damasi* (S. Lorenzo in Damasi),[73] the *titulus Fasciolae* (SS Nereo ed Achilleo), and the *titulus Pudentis* (S. Pudenziana) which were probably erected during his episcopate. The foundation of churches continued during the fifth century, despite a difficult economic situation, a

68 See ch. 8, below.
69 C. Pietri, 'Euergétisme'.
70 The extant correspondence of Gregory the Great (590–604) gives us some insight into the management of the *patrimonium*; see Markus, *Gregory the Great*, 112–24.
71 Jerome, *Against John* 8. And yet, in the middle of the fourth century, the *patrimonium* yielded no more than 10% of the income of the super-rich, see Pietri, 'Euergétisme', 822–3.
72 See V. Fiocchi Nicolai, *Strutture funerarie*, H. Brandenburg, *Ancient churches of Rome*, and the discussion in ch. 29, below.
73 C. Pietri, 'Damase', 47.

shrinking urban population, famines and even the plundering of the city.[74] During the episcopates of Coelestin I (422–32) and Sixtus III (432–40) the Christian transformation of the old city was resumed on an even larger scale. The great basilicas of S. Sabina, S. Pietro in Vincoli and S. Lorenzo in Lucina were created, as were the celebrated Lateran baptistery and the monumental S. Maria Maggiore. The impressive Constantinian *fastigium* of the Lateran church, destroyed by the Goths in 410, was restored. All the while, the church profited again and again from aristocratic donations.[75]

The growing network of *tituli* (about twenty-six churches by the end of the fifth century) facilitated catechesis and pastoral care within the city; the plebs became the *populus Dei*. Damasus also fostered the cult of the saints: with the assistance of able presbyters like Theodore, Verus and Leo, he provided almost all the important Christian cemeteries on the roads into Rome with oratories for venerating the saints. He refurbished the great *martyria* (martyr-basilicas) of Constantine and integrated them into his new network of Roman sainthood. They were adorned with splendid inscriptions carrying metrical epigrams composed by the pope himself. Their distinctive lettering was crafted by an accomplished artist, the librarian Furius Dionysius Filocalus, and his disciples.[76] The Christianisation of urban space was complemented by a corresponding Christianisation of time: it was in Rome, during Constantine's reign, that the birth of Jesus Christ was first celebrated on 25 December, the date of the pagan feast commemorating the birth of the sun god (*sol invictus*). The new feast spread and, by 386, it had arrived in Antioch.[77] Moreover, the Christian year was now filled with the *dies natales* of Roman martyrs. By the mid-fifth century, Rome had become a Christian city that attracted pilgrims from all the empire and beyond.[78] The pagan city of the mythical founder twins Romulus and Remus had become the Christian city of the apostles and martyrs Peter and Paul, joined in concord. Rome's transformation from pagan to Christian city set the precedent for other cities in Italy, Gaul and Africa.

In Christianising Rome, Damasus and his successors were supported by hierarchically structured clergy who – partly emulating the model of the military and the imperial bureaucracy – combined rigorous training from an early age with the possibility of rising through the ranks of a prescribed

---

74 Rome was besieged, sacked or occupied by the Visigoths in 410, by the Vandals in 455, by the Suebian Rikimer in 472, by the Ostrogoths in 537, and again in 545 . . .
75 F. Guidobaldi, 'Roma', 79–83. See further ch. 8, below.
76 See A. Ferrua, *Epigrammata Damasiana* and J. Fontaine, *Naissance de la poésie*, 111–25.
77 M. Wallraff, *Christus Verus Sol*, 174–90.
78 See C. Pietri, *Roma Christiana*, I: 617–24.

cursus.[79] The major clerical orders were the prestigious college of seven deacons, each being responsible for one of the seven regions of Rome,[80] and the far more numerous college of presbyters attached to the urban titular churches. The two *scholae* of notaries (*notarii*) and advocates (*defensores*) became the backbone of the emerging ecclesiastical administration, especially from the sixth century.[81] The popes and their apparatus increasingly relied on well-ordered archives and libraries, which served, in effect, as the bureaucratic memory of the Roman see. The Roman church was not alone in this respect, but the scope and quality of the Roman archives were such that they invited consultation when difficult cases of church administration and discipline arose elsewhere.

Rome also played its role in the development of a Western theological tradition. Under Damasus' predecessor Liberius Marius, Victorinus, a renowned teacher of rhetoric, had converted to Christianity.[82] In constant dialogue with Gnostic and Neoplatonic thought, he formulated his remarkable Trinitarian theology in treatises and hymns.[83] But Damasus' episcopate was a watershed. The pope himself sponsored the first-rate scholarship of Jerome.[84] Aware of the defects of the Old Latin versions of the Bible, he asked Jerome to revise them. The result (some twenty years on, and with the help of further translators) was the so-called Vulgate, the most important Western translation of the Bible before the Reformation.[85] Damasus' episcopate also saw Latin become the Roman church's liturgical language.[86] Theological works in Greek, particularly the series of biblical commentaries and other theological writings by Origen and Didymus the Blind, were translated and made accessible to learned clergy and aristocratic Romans. Jerome initiated the project and was eventually joined by Rufinus of Aquileia. From 393, however, their collaboration came to a halt with the eruption of the Origenist Controversy; their relationship, too, was irretrievably damaged. For the next fifteen years Jerome and Rufinus fought an embittered literary battle, which did not abate after Rufinus had

---

79 Despite c. 10 of the Western council of Serdica, this *cursus honorum* was not strictly adhered to in other Western Christianities, for example in the African churches; see Leo, *Letter* 12 (PL 54: 645–56) with C. Lepelley, 'Saint Léon le Grand', 427.

80 The division of Rome into ecclesiastical regions is first attested in the *Catalogus Liberianus* which attributes it to Pope Fabian (236–50); see *Liber Pontificalis* (ed. Duchesne, I: 5) and cf. Eusebius, *H.E.* 6.43.11.

81 C. Sotinel, 'Le personnel episcopal'.

82 Augustine, *Confessions* 8.2–4.

83 See P. Hadot, *Marius Victorinus*; M. Tardieu, *Recherches sur la formation de l'Apocalypse de Zostrien*.

84 Jerome, *Letter* 123.9; J. N. D. Kelly, *Jerome*, 83.

85 Kelly, *Jerome*, 85–90.

86 Th. Klauser, 'Der Übergang der römischen Kirche'.

left Rome for Palestine in 397. Jerome's friends Marcella and Pammachius convinced Pope Anastasius (*sed.* 399–402) to condemn Origen's teaching.

From 380 to 410, the salons of the Christian Roman aristocracy probably buzzed with theological argument. Jerome's exegetical work had found intellectual support and informed feedback in a kind of upper-class female graduate seminar made up of ascetic women like Paula and Marcella, some of whom could read scripture in the original languages. In 397, Jerome claimed that 1 Corinthians 1.26 no longer held true for Rome: now there were many learned and noble monks.[87] Urban monasticism flourished in Rome and fierce controversies raged about what made for a truly Christian way of life. Not everyone endorsed Jerome's views. Jovinian, a lapsed ascetic, denied the superiority of an ascetic lifestyle and Mary's perpetual virginity. Jovinian was not only condemned by Roman and Milanese synods and exiled by the emperor, he also provoked Jerome's embarrassing *Against Jovinian*.[88] Another spiritual guide for the Roman aristocracy was the British ascetic Pelagius. He apparently feared the demoralising effects of Augustine's doctrine of grace as related in his *Confessions*. For Pelagius and his followers, free will – the inalienable faculty to choose – is identical with the divine grace that empowers Christian asceticism.[89] Theological controversy erupted with Jerome and Augustine attacking Pelagius. After 411, the debate was carried on in North Africa, in southern Italy and Sicily, in Palestine, and again in Rome; throughout the fifth century, Augustine's doctrine of grace continued to be debated in the monasteries of southern Gaul. When the Council of Orange (529) defined a moderate position concerning Augustine's teaching on grace and predestination, it collaborated with the pope and his theologians. Outstanding theologians on the throne of Peter were the exception rather than the rule: Leo (*sed.* 440–61), as we have noted, played an important role in the Christological controversy and was a prolific preacher; Gelasius (*sed.* 492–6) defined the distinction between episcopal and royal power,[90] and wrote against the Miaphysites; Gregory the Great (*sed.* 590–604) was a preacher, able administrator and missionary strategist, and penned a commentary on Job and a handbook for church leaders.

Of the Italian churches, only Milan rivalled the prestige of Rome – and that, briefly. During the episcopate of Ambrose (374–97), Milan's influence reached its pinnacle. Ambrose was one of the earliest aristocratic bishops (his father

---

87 Jerome, *Letter* 66.4; see S. Rebenich, *Hieronymus*, 154–80.
88 Y.-M. Duval, *L'affaire Jovinien*.
89 Y.-M. Duval, 'Pélage en son temps', *SP* 38 (2001): 95–118. J.-M. Salamito, *Les virtuoses et la multitude*, argues that Pelagian spirituality was attuned to the social values of the Roman aristocracy.
90 See ch. 17, below.

having been a prefect of Gaul, he himself a governor of the provinces Liguria and Aemilia). In 374, he succeeded the Homoian bishop Auxentius. Ambrose was media-savvy and as determined as any pope. A prolific preacher and writer and author of hymns, he appears to have rivalled Constantine – and surpassed Damasus – with his church building.[91] As we have already noted, Damasus' and Ambrose's Nicene 'roll back' in Italy and Illyricum had marginalised Homoian orthodoxy. After councils in Aquileia, Rome and Constantinople (381/2), the Nicene side prevailed – backed by the emperor Theodosius I himself. Milan became the local stage for the great struggle.

The emperor Gratian, who was confronting the usurper Magnus Maximus in Gaul in 383, was killed there by a traitor. Maximus plotted to gain legitimacy by acting as Valentinian II's guardian. Ambrose and the leading men around Valentinian's mother, Justina, conspired to keep emperor and court in Milan. He succeeded, but the court's stay in Milan led to problems. Justina and many around her, including the soldiers, professed the Homoian orthodoxy of the Constantinopolitan council of 360. In March 385, Ambrose was summoned before the consistory in the imperial palace. There, he was required to give the Homoian Christians a small church outside the city walls (*Basilica Portiana*). Ambrose refused. This was the prologue to the famous 'basilica quarrel' in 386 which pitted Ambrose and his flock against the court and its soldiers.[92] An imperial decree of 23 January 386 guaranteed all Homoian Christians the right of assembly and threatened any opponents with capital punishment.[93] But, for Ambrose, Nicene and Homoian Christianities could not co-exist in Milan. When the court attempted to confiscate the *Basilica Portiana*, Ambrose and his people occupied the church until the troops were withdrawn. The situation escalated again during Easter week when the court sent soldiers to requisition a church inside the city. Ambrose emerged as a strong demagogue: without openly opposing the emperor, he manipulated the populace to keep control of the churches.[94] Meanwhile, the Christian laity strengthened their resolve by singing hymns and psalms, among them Augustine's mother Monica.[95] At length, Ambrose and his people prevailed. When Maximus finally marched on Italy in 387, Valentinian II and his court withdrew from Milan to Illyricum. Maximus embraced Nicene orthodoxy, as

---

91 B. Brenk discusses this further in ch. 29.
92 I follow the reconstruction by G. Nauroy, 'Le fouet et le miel'.
93 *CTh* 16.1.4; the law was later abolished: *CTh* 16.5.15.
94 N. McLynn, *Ambrose of Milan*.
95 Augustine, *Confessions* 9.7.15; in that passage, he also claims that at this time Ambrose introduced hymns 'sung after the custom of the eastern churches' (trans. H. Chadwick). See further Fontaine, *Naissance de la poésie*.

did Theodosius I, who in the following year defeated and killed the usurper. Thereafter, Ambrose was uncontested in his city. During the conflict, Ambrose had already rehearsed the attitude, slogans and formulae with which he would defend the authority of the bishop in matters of church discipline against Theodosius a few years later.[96]

During Ambrose's episcopate, Milan became an intellectual centre of Western Christendom. Augustine arrived in 384, to take up a professorship in rhetoric. Hoping for a career in political administration, he cultivated friendships with high-ranking court officials. He came in contact with a circle of Platonists – both Christian and pagan – with crucial consequences for his spiritual and intellectual development. Under their influence, he studied Platonist books (presumably Plotinus') in Marius Victorinus' Latin translation.[97] After Augustine converted to ascetic Christian philosophy in 386, he retired with his friends to Cassiciacum, an estate near Milan. There he developed his brand of Christian Platonism. One of the Milanese Christian Platonists whom Augustine contacted was Simplician, a learned priest, who had befriended Marius Victorinus in Rome during the 350s and encouraged him to make his Christian faith public. Simplician was also a spiritual father to Ambrose and, in 394, succeeded Ambrose as bishop.

The flowering of Milanese intellectual culture had apparently ended by the close of the fourth century. The imperial court moved to Ravenna. In about 430 it became a metropolitan see. Splendid new churches there began to testify to the newly acquired prestige. One of its bishops, Peter Chrysologus (d. 450), was renowned for his preaching. Whereas Milan suffered heavily under successive invasions of Goths, Alani and Huns, Ravenna became the Ostrogothic capital of Theoderic from 493 and, after the eclipse of Ostrogothic rule, towards the end of the sixth century the residence of the plenipotentiary ('exarch') of the emperor in Constantinople.

Gaul

Gallic Christianity (like Spanish Christianity) fully emerged into history during the second half of the fourth century. We can infer the rapid expansion of Gallic Christianity from the growing number of episcopal sees. In 314, sixteen bishops from Gaul attended the Council of Arles. By the beginning of the fifth century there were perhaps more than 100 Gallic bishoprics.[98] The

---

96 See ch. 7, below.
97 S. Lancel, *Saint Augustin*, 123–6.
98 For the following, see É. Demougeot, 'Gallia I'.

impact of the Germanic invasions and the subsequent eclipse of Roman rule in that century are difficult to assess.[99] We cannot suggest a picture of general decline and overlook indications of numerical and geographical expansion of Christianity in some regions. On the other hand, the life of many churches was severely interrupted, especially in northern Gaul. Whether incomplete episcopal lists testify to real vacancies is, however, unclear. Pursuing the establishment of an autonomous kingdom, the Visigothic king Euric (*regn.* 466–84) prevented the Catholic churches from filling vacant sees. Sidonius Apollinaris, bishop of Clermont, complains in a letter written in 475 to Bishop Basilius of Aix that, among others, the sees of Bordeaux, Périgueux, Limoges and Auch remained vacant. According to Sidonius, Euric threatened the very survival of Christianity. Sidonius himself was (briefly) exiled, as was another theologian from southern Gaul, Faustus of Riez.[100] Euric's successor, Alaric II (*regn.* 484–507), adopted a different religious policy, envisaging peaceful co-existence between the Nicene Church (particularly the senatorial aristocracy) and the Homoian Church of their Visigothic lords – precisely the arrangement that Ambrose had rejected in Milan. In 506, Alaric II issued the so-called 'Breviary of Alaric', a codification of Roman law. Much of the Roman church legislation from *Codex Theodosianus* 16 was adopted, except of course for laws outlawing Homoian heresy. Alaric II thus attempted to integrate Roman Nicene Christianity into his kingdom.[101]

The co-ordination of local Gallic churches led to conflict in the fifth century, in conjunction with late ancient power politics. Only the consolidation of new centres of political power in the sixth century, particularly Merovingian rule in Gaul and Visigothic rule in Spain, allowed for the consolidation of church organisation on a similar scale. Synods and councils were important in defining ecclesiastical structures and norms. In the fifth and early sixth centuries, metropolitan bishops (particularly the bishop of Arles) intermittently convened them; subsequently, Merovingian and Visigothic kings increasingly used synods to integrate their kingdoms' churches. The most serious controversy to arise in this process concerned the primacy of Arles.[102] The city's importance was in the first instance political. In the late fourth century, the praetorian prefecture of Gaul moved from Trier to Arles. When in 406/7 the Vandals, Alans and Sueves invaded Roman Gaul, many members of the Roman

---

99 See ibid. 920–3.
100 Sidonius Apollinaris, *Letter* 7.6 (ed. Loyen, III: 42–6).
101 For an analysis of Visigothic religious policy, see K. Schäferdiek, *Die Kirche*, 27–31, 42–55; H. Wolfram, *History of the Goths*, 197–202.
102 See G. Langgärtner, *Die Gallienpolitik*.

aristocracy of northern Gaul fled to Arles. And when, in 416–18, the emperor established the council of the seven Gallic provinces (which became the political basis for the provincial aristocracy), the council assembled at Arles.[103]

The bishop of Arles's chief rival at the close of the fourth century was the bishop of Vienne. In 398 the synod of Turin attempted a compromise. Primacy concerning the province of Viennensis should belong to the metropolitan bishop; if the sees of Vienne and Arles continued quarrelling, the problem should be resolved by basically partitioning the province.[104] But this ruling did not settle things: Patroclus of Arles appealed to Pope Zosimus (417/18) to establish the primacy of his see. Zosimus declared that no Gallic clergy should travel to Rome without obtaining an official letter of recommendation (*epistula formata*) from the bishop of Arles. Moreover, Zosimus informed the Gallic churches that the metropolitan bishop of Arles had the authority to ordain bishops in the provinces of Viennensis and Narbonnensis I and II (including Alpes Maritimae), effectively establishing Arles as a Roman vicariate in southern Gaul.[105] The pope's promotion of Arles had limited success: one bishop, Hilarius of Narbonne, capitulated, but others, like Simplicius of Vienne and Proculus of Marseille, ignored the decision.

Zosimus' successors, Boniface I and Leo I, failed to confirm Arles's primacy. Pope Leo I (*sed.* 440–61) clashed with Hilary of Arles (*sed.* 430–49) over these issues. Hilary owed his elevation to the bishopric to the political and military elite. He continued the work of the synod of Turin by formulating conciliar legislation that provided the Gallic churches with structure and discipline conforming to the fathers' statutes. In 439, 441 and 442 he assembled synods of bishops (mainly from the Viennensis, Narbonnensis II and Alpes Maritimae) that confirmed Arles' supra-metropolitan authority, particularly in the matter of ordaining bishops. Apparently enlisting the support of the prefect, Hilary travelled far and wide in southern Gaul, hastily ordaining bishops.[106] He employed military force to enter cities whose churches resisted him.[107] His fellow bishops in southern Gaul seem to have welcomed his zeal for church discipline, but when he proceeded against the bishop of Besançon, Chelidonius, he met with stiff resistance. When Hilary deposed him, Chelidonius appealed to Rome and was rehabilitated by Pope Leo in 445. Leo censured Hilary for his high-handedness and denied both his metropolitan and supra-metropolitan

---

103 F. Prinz, *Frühes Mönchtum*, 48f.; P. Heather, 'Senators and senates', 202–3.
104 Concilium Taurinense A.398 c.2 (CCSL 148: 55–6).
105 Zosimus, *Letter* 1 (PL 20: 642–5) with Langgärtner, *Gallienpolitik*, 26–52.
106 Leo, *Letter* 10.6 (PL 54: 633–4). See R. W. Mathisen, 'Hilarius, Germanus, and Lupus'.
107 Leo, *Letter* 10.6 (PL 54: 633–4). See M. Heinzelmann, *Bischofsherrschaft*, 77–84.

rights.[108] Leo's intervention was confirmed by an imperial decree that underlined Roman authority over Western regional Christianities.[109] After Ravennius had succeeded Hilary at Arles, Leo acted upon the decree of Turin (398) and partitioned the province between Vienne and Arles. When the Western empire ended in 476, however, and Arles fell to the Visigothic kingdom centred in Toulouse, the struggle between the sees of Vienne and Arles over metropolitan rights in Burgundy continued.

In 506, Caesarius, a monk from Lérins who was bishop of Arles,[110] presided over the Council of Agde, the first general council in one of the newly formed Germanic kingdoms. Alaric II assembled the council to complete the incorporation of the Nicene Catholic Church into his kingdom. The Council of Agde passed numerous canons that repeated and developed earlier conciliar legislation, concerning clerical life, admittance to ordination, bishops' authority, the administration of church property, rules for monks and nuns and various liturgical matters; every year thereafter a council was to be held, with the participation of the bishops from Visigothic Spain.[111] The Council of Agde established an autonomous Catholic (Nicene) Church on Visigothic territory subject to the Visigothic king. But the following year, war broke out. The attacks of Franks and Burgundians reduced Visigothic power dramatically. The Ostrogoths intervened to stop the Burgundian advance and subsequently the metropolitan see of Arles, together with Visigothic Provence, came under the rule of Theoderic, the Ostrogothic king. The praetorian prefecture – abolished in 476/7 – was revived, with the prefect residing once more in Arles. In 514 Pope Symmachus made Caesarius of Arles his vicar in both Gaul and Spain. Although it is unclear how much real power this appointment implied, it is possible that in this way the pope tried to respond to the newly emerging political and ecclesiastical geography.[112]

After King Chlodowech, a Frankish Catholic, annexed Visigothic Aquitania, he adopted Alaric's innovative religious policy and convened a council in Orléans (July 511),[113] which thirty-two bishops attended under the presidency of the bishop of Bordeaux. The king set the council's agenda and validated its thirty-one canons, which dealt mainly with practical matters: church asylum for slaves and criminals (cc. 1–3), ordination of slaves to clerical office (c. 8),

---

108 Leo, *Letter* 10.7 (PL 54: 634–5); Mathisen, 'Hilarius, Germanus, and Lupus', interprets this affair as another instance of aristocratic infighting over episcopal sees.
109 *Nov. Val.* 17, dated 8 July 445 (ed. Mommsen, CTh II: 103).
110 See W. Klingshirn, *Caesarius of Arles*.
111 *Concilia Galliae a.314–a.506* (CCSL 148: 189–228). See Schäferdiek, *Die Kirche*, 55–67.
112 Symmachus, *Letter* 16 (ed. Thiel, 728–9). See Schäferdiek, *Die Kirche*, 73f.
113 *Concilia Galliae a.511–a.695* (CCSL 148a: 3–19); see O. Pontal, *Synoden*, 23–34.

excommunication of delinquent priests and deacons (c. 9), subordination of abbots to their bishops and monks to their abbots (c. 19), administration of church property and church revenues (cc. 14–16). Canon 10 facilitated the integration of the newly formed church under Frankish rule: the 'heretical' clergy of the Homoian Visigothic churches were received into the Merovingian Catholic Church by a simple imposition of hands; Catholics could use re-consecrated Homoian buildings.

In the recently formed Burgundian kingdom, too, the church required organisation at the national level. First steps were made when King Sigismund, formerly a Homoian Christian, became a Catholic. A council assembled in Epao, probably in September 517.[114] Two metropolitan bishops, Avitus of Vienne (an accomplished writer and theologian) and Viventiolus of Lyon, issued the invitations. Twenty-two bishops and a priest (the delegate from Avignon) attended, together with laymen. Avitus was keen to avoid open conflict between Homoian and Catholic churches. So several of the forty canons that were issued concerned the relations between them: conversion from Homoian to Catholic Christianity is facilitated (c. 16); if senior Catholic clergy attend Homoian clergy's parties, they are suspended from communion for a year, while for the same offence junior clergy will be flogged (c. 15); Catholics can claim only those Homoian basilicas previously taken from them (c. 33).[115]

The Ostrogoths defeated the Burgundians again in 523, expanding their rule north of the river Durance (until *c.* 530). For the first time in over half a century, the metropolitan province of Arles was reunited under one rule. Caesarius seized the opportunity to assert his metropolitan rights by holding a series of councils. Their dual function was to formulate standards for aspects of church life and discipline, and to serve as tribunals for the clergy. The synod of Arles (524) issued rules for ordaining clergy in response to the increased number of parishes. The Council of Carpentras (527) disciplined a senior bishop (a decision confirmed by Pope Felix IV) and strengthened rural parishes. The Council of Vaisson in November 529 granted deacons and priests a greater role in preaching and teaching, a decision (again, prompted by the increasing number of parishes) meant to relieve overworked bishops.[116]

From Burgundy, the bishop of Vienne resisted his busy colleague and rival in Arles. In 528, he quarrelled with Caesarius over Augustine's contested doctrine of divine predestination. The consensus view, as discussed in Gaul throughout

---

114 The precise location of this ancient town is unclear: see Pontal, *Synoden*, 36.
115 *Concilia Galliae a.511–a.695* (CCSL 148a: 22–37); see Pontal, *Synoden*, 34–46.
116 *Concilia Galliae a.511–a.695* (CCSL 148a: 43–6, 47–52, 77–81); see Pontal, *Synoden*, 52–3, 54–5, 56–8.

the fifth century (particularly in the monasteries of Marseille and Lérins), favoured a rejection of strictly predestinarian views. Now, in the first quarter of the sixth century, the question was mooted again in Gaul, but also in North Africa and Rome by the so-called 'Scythian monks'. The bishop of Vienne convened a synod in Valence that censured Caesarius' position. Caesarius responded by assembling a synod in Orange (July 529). Fourteen bishops and eight aristocratic laymen attended. The synod issued twenty-five canons, framed by a brief preface and a definition of faith.[117] It defined a moderate Augustinianism that stressed prevenient grace without undermining Christian moral effort. Part of the synod's decisions had probably been prepared in Rome. Pope Boniface confirmed its orthodoxy in 531.

The days of Ostrogothic dominion in Provence were numbered. After defeating the Burgundians in 534, the Franks annexed the province in 536 and Arles fell under Merovingian rule. Caesarius found himself sidelined as the ecclesiastical centre of power shifted northwards: Merovingian Gaul was partitioned among kings who resided in Orléans, Paris, Reims and Soissons. The bishops from these realms assembled for supra-provincial councils – such as the Council of Orléans (533), the Fifth Council of Orléans (549) and the first council of Mâcon (581–3) – to continue the legislative work of the first council of Orléans (511). Other councils were restricted to bishops from within a given realm. When Chlotar II reunited Gaul, bishops from all over Gaul assembled at two councils in Paris (614) and in Clichy (626/7). Merovingian kings often convoked these councils; the conciliar and political interplay was accordingly complex.[118]

In addition to ecclesiastical law, late ancient Gallic Christianity also bequeathed to the early middle ages an ideal of episcopal sainthood that offered a novel Christian way to preserve the ancient aristocracy's prestige. Energetic bishops who hailed from an aristocratic background, like Hilary or Caesarius of Arles (to name but two),[119] belonged to this new type of ecclesiastical leadership.[120] An important aspect of this new ideal was its adaptation of Christian ascetic values. Asceticism had long been important in Gaul: the

---

117 *Concilia Galliae a.511–a.695* (CCSL 148a: 53–76); see Pontal, *Synoden*, 61–71.
118 See J. Gaudemet and B. Basdevant in SC 353, esp. 33–43.
119 The percentage of members of the senatorial aristocracy among Gallic bishops of the fifth and sixth centuries is difficult to estimate. For a concise analysis of recruitment patterns, see C. Rapp, *Holy bishops*, 192–5. The general trend is visible to a lesser degree also in Italy and elsewhere; see ibid., 188–95, C. Lepelley, 'Le patronat episcopal' and A. Demandt, *Die Spätantike*, 445–52.
120 See Heinzelmann, *Bischofsherrschaft* and, more recently, B. Beaujard, 'L'evêque dans la cité'.

Life of Anthony was probably addressed to a monastic audience in Gaul. But the future development of episcopal asceticism in Gaul was foreshadowed by domestic hagiography. The first embodiment of native Christian asceticism in Gaul was Martin of Tours, whose *Life*, published in 397 by Sulpicius of Severus, became a late ancient 'bestseller'. Martin combined his episcopacy with an ascetic life and his monastery at Marmoutiers (near Tours) attracted aristocrats who later became bishops.[121]

Some time before 410, Honoratus founded the famous island monastery of Lérins after an ascetic pilgrimage into the East. The monastery soon developed into a nursery for future bishops:[122] Honoratus himself served as bishop of Arles (*c.* 427); his cousin Hilary, whom we have already mentioned, followed in his steps. Later in the fifth century, two abbots of Lérins, Maximus and Faustus, became bishops of Riez. Faustus, a formidable theologian, came from Britain. Following Lérins's theological tradition, he interpreted Augustine's predestinarianism to safeguard the freedom of the will in ascetic life. Salvian of Marseille (*c.* 400–80), author of the *De gubernatione Dei*, was also probably a monk at Lérins before becoming a priest. Vincent of Lérins (d. before 450), who famously defined orthodoxy as 'that which has been believed everywhere, always and by all' (*quod ubique quod semper quod ab omnibus*),[123] also lived there as a priest. Lérins was a laboratory where the values of Eastern monasticism were transformed into an ascetic charisma that enabled some to become efficient church leaders.

These new bishops were able and ambitious administrators; sometimes they assumed the responsibilities of civil authorities, for example, by organising the distribution of donations from the faithful to those in need. Thus, Venantius Fortunatus' tribute to Bishop Carentius of Cologne (d. 565/7): 'You are food for the poor.'[124] Among the important obligations for bishops, conciliar legislation stipulates caring for the poor, ransoming captives and disbursing grain during famines. Under Merovingian rule, bishops were expected to intercede for the downtrodden before the king and his ministers. Bishops occasionally organised the building of a dam or military fortifications (as in the case of Nicetius of Trier, who died after 561).[125] Some of the most talented provincial

---

121 Sulpicius Severus, *Life of Martin* 10.8 (SC 133: 274); see Heinzelmann, *Bischofsherrschaft*, 194.
122 For the following, see Prinz, *Frühes Mönchtum*, 47–87; S. Pricoco, *L'isola dei santi*, with a useful prosopography on pp. 40–59.
123 Vincent, *Commonitorium* 2.5 (CCSL 64: 149).
124 Venantius Fortunatus, *Carm.* 3.14 (MGH aa 4.1: 68.19); see Th. Sternberg, *Orientalium more secutus*, 43.
125 Sternberg, *Orientalium more secutus*, 41f.; on Nicetius, see ibid., 21.

Roman aristocrats found a new role as ascetic contemplation replaced the life of cultured philosophical *otium*, and the pursuit of a military or civil career was transposed into the strenuous regime of an ascetic bishop. Ascetic values provided motivation for organised charity, and the bishop's house became its focus.[126] Some were still interested in organising monastic life after they became bishops. Caesarius of Arles stands beside Augustine as the most important monastic legislator of the Latin West before Benedict of Nursia.

Spain

As with Gaul, the watershed for Christianity in Spain was the invasion of various Germanic nations from 406/7. In 409, the Vandals, Alans and Sueves crossed the Pyrenees and wrought havoc in the provinces of Roman Spain. Only Tarraconnensis remained under Roman rule. Between 416 and 418, victorious Visigothic forces (now Roman allies) repelled the Alans and the Siling Vandals. In 429 the Vandals left Spain for North Africa. In two invasions (468 and 472/3), the Visigothic king Euric brought Spain (with the exception of the Suevian kingdom and the Basque north) completely under Visigothic rule.

It is difficult to determine how far the metropolitan structure envisioned by the Council of Nicaea was realised in Roman Spain. We do know, how-ever, that nineteen bishops and twenty-four priests from thirty-seven local churches attended the Council of Elvira (*c.* 306), most of them from the southern provinces. We have some information about synods at the turn of the fourth–fifth centuries, but then, nothing. Councils meet again in the sixth-century Visigothic kingdom (e.g., the Council of Tarragona, 516). As for administrative structure, Pope Hormisdas granted the metropolitan bishop of Seville oversight of the ecclesiastical provinces of Baetica and Lusitania in 520.[127]

In the first half of the sixth century, Nicene Catholics and Homoian Chris-tianities co-existed peacefully under Visigothic rule. The Homoian Church intermittently attempted to convert Roman provincials; the Catholic Church in the Suevian kingdom was left in peace although it sometimes may have been hindered in its synodical activity. Around 555, the Suevian king Chararic was converted to Nicene Christianity by Martin, a monk who came from Pannonia and went on to found the monastery of Dumio in Galicia before becoming

---

126 Ibid., 52–104; see also R. Nürnberg, *Askese als sozialer Impuls.*
127 T. Ulbert, 'Hispania I', 629–31.

the metropolitan bishop of Braga.[128] The king's conversion integrated church and kingdom, a process that was furthered by two synods at Braga (561, 572).

After the Visigoths had conquered the Suevian kingdom (585) the process continued under Visigothic rule – but with an important difference: Catholics under Visigothic rule experienced persecution. In 579, Hermenegild, the son of King Leowigild, started an insurrection. Hermenegild's residence was Seville; he was married to a Catholic Merovingian princess. Probably under the influence of his wife and Leander of Seville, Hermenegild became a Catholic and sought an alliance with Constantinople. When Hermenegild was defeated in 584 and refused to return to Homoian Christianity in prison, Leowigild began persecuting the Catholics in his kingdom.[129] He aimed at converting them to Homoian orthodoxy,[130] to integrate church and kingdom. In 580, he called a council in Toledo that permitted the reception of Catholics into the Homoian church without re-baptising them. Many laypeople seem to have been won over, but the Catholic clergy stood firm, with very few exceptions. Leowigild abandoned the persecution before dying in 586. The following year his successor, Rekkared, converted to Catholic Christianity and in 589 the Third Council of Toledo obliged the whole Visigothic kingdom to convert likewise. Rekkared's conversion thus achieved Leowigild's political aims.[131]

The conversion of Western aristocrats to Christianity – and specifically, to Christian *asceticism* – produced many remarkable personalities. The most controversial was probably Priscillian of Avila.[132] Born before 350 into a rich (possibly senatorial) family and baptised as an adult, he preached a more serious, ascetic Christianity and called for a deeper awareness of baptism's significance and the devil's operations. Priscillian's exhortation to strict Christianity appealed to Christian men and women of his own class, and probably beyond. Priscillian's urban followers went on retreats, periods of intense exploration of the scriptures (including apocryphal writings) and spiritual instruction spent in country houses to prepare themselves for the great feasts of the Christian year. Bishops in southern Spain, particularly those of Ossonuba (Faro) and Emerita (Merida), first raised the alarm. Priscillian was suspected of Gnostic or Manichaean heresy, of black magic and superstition. His movement spread into Galicia and, crossing the Pyrenees, southern Gaul (Aquitania). A synod in Saragossa (380) criticised Priscillian but apparently avoided condemnation. The

---

128 For his work on ecclesiastical law, see ch. 16, below.
129 Schäferdiek, *Die Kirche*, 140–57.
130 Leowigild was apparently prepared to envisage a terminological rapprochement with Nicene Christianity; see ibid., 188f.
131 Schäferdiek, *Die Kirche*, 157–92.
132 See H. Chadwick, *Priscillian*; V. Burrus, *The making of a heretic*.

next year, Priscillian became bishop of Avila. His metropolitan bishop, Hydatius of Emerita, sought Ambrose's help in securing an imperial rescript banning Priscillian as a heretic. Priscillian's requests for a hearing from Ambrose and Pope Damasus failed, but he did get Gratian's rescript rescinded.

One of Priscillian's enemies, Bishop Ithacius of Ossonuba, fled to Trier after the proconsul of Lusitania started proceedings against him for calumny. Influenced by Ithacius, the usurper Maximus ordered a synod in Bordeaux to investigate the charges against Priscillian. But before the synod finished its work, Priscillian appealed to Maximus. Maximus had Priscillian and four of his supporters tried, convicted and executed on charges of sorcery,[133] making him the first Christian heretic publicly executed in late antiquity. In Spain, two of Priscillian's followers were also executed, while others were exiled or had their property confiscated. A split developed. Some Gallic bishops refused to commune with Felix, bishop of Trier, because Ithacius took part in his ordination. The charismatic Martin of Tours criticised Priscillian's execution and regretted reversing his initial decision to shun Felix. Pope Siricius and Ambrose of Milan were likewise critical.[134] Meanwhile, in Spain (particularly in Galicia), Priscillian was honoured as a martyr. Even so, a council in Toledo anathematised Priscillian and his writings (400). All but four of the bishops present subscribed to the anathema. The leading bishop of Galicia, Symposius of Astorga, and his son and coadjutor Dictinnius, who propagated the cult of Priscillian, yielded under pressure, but they and the bishops they had ordained were allowed to retain their offices.[135] But even after Toledo, the Priscillianist schism persisted, particularly in the south. For instance, the first council of Braga in 561 issued seventeen chapters against the Priscillianist heresy, most of which repeated or developed earlier accusations,[136] and there were still Priscillianists in the seventh century.

Africa

More than any other region, late ancient African Christianity suffered much persecution, internal strife and schism – and yet no other region was in many

---

133 Sulpicius Severus, *Chronica* 2.51 (SC 441: 344–6). The date of Priscillian's execution is controversial, Chadwick, *Priscillian*, 132–8, argues for the summer of 386 as the most probable date; T. D. Barnes, 'Ambrose and the basilicas', 294–5, proposes winter 384–5.

134 Sulpicius Severus, *Chronica* 2.50 (SC 441: 342–3); *Dialogus* 12–13 (CSEL 1: 210–11); *Collectio Avellana* 40 (CSEL 35: 90–1); Ambrose, *Letter* 30.12 (CSEL 821: 214–15). See Chadwick, *Priscillian*, 145–8, 151–2.

135 See Chadwick, *Priscillian*, 234–9, with analysis: 170–88. For the other work of the Council of Toledo, see now A. Weckwerth, *Das erste Konzil von Toledo*.

136 J. Vives, ed., *Concilios Visigóticos*, 67–9.

respects so vital for the future of Christianity in the West, as the towering genius of Augustine alone assured. Africa is usually considered the most 'Christianised' region of the Western empire. There were about 250 episcopal sees in all Roman Africa around the year 300; by the early fifth century, the number had soared to 650.[137] During the fourth century the majority of the (often only superficially) Romanised population apparently became Christian.[138] At the beginning of the fifth century, Christianity even attracted some indigenous Berbers.[139] The Catholic Church was organised into six ecclesiastical provinces: Tripolitana, Byzacena, Africa Proconsularis, Numidia, Mauretania Sitifensis, and Mauretania Caesariensis. The most senior bishop presided at provincial synods; the bishop of Carthage, the primate of the African church, usually convened general councils.

During the fourth century, the Donatist schism (see below) disturbed any prospect for general councils.[140] When Constans resumed the anti-Donatist policy of his father Constantine, the Catholics celebrated the newly enforced unity with provincial synods and a general council in Carthage between 345 and 348.[141] The resurgence of Donatism, particularly under the emperor Julian, made life difficult for Catholics, but conciliar activity of the minority church resumed in the late fourth century when Donatism again came under pressure. The heyday of African conciliar activity occurred under the formidable Aurelius of Carthage (sed. 390–430). Supported by Theodosius' anti-pagan legislation, he transformed Carthage into a Christian city. The majority of urban basilicas in Carthage appeared during his episcopate. Augustine, Aurelius' colleague and friend, requested donations in several sermons to finance a new basilica there.[142] The first council in Carthage under Aurelius (393) confirmed the African church's organisational structure; it also decreed that every year the bishop of Carthage should inform other churches about the date of Easter and that a plenary council of the African churches should meet annually. General councils met again in 397, 399, 401, 402 (at Milevis, Numidia), 403, 404 and 405, but such regular travel was onerous for the bishops. Therefore the council of 407 decreed that, henceforth, general councils would only

---

137 The African churches were, however, criticised for having bishops even in obscure little villages by Leo, *Letter* 12.10 (PL 54: 654). Moreover, at the beginning of the fifth century the Catholic–Donatist struggles apparently led to the competitive establishment of dioceses; see the comments of S. Lancel at SC 195: 123–30.

138 See esp. the wealth of information in A. Schindler, 'Afrika I', 644, 652 (number of sees).

139 Modéran, *Les Maures et l'Afrique romaine*.

140 See C. Munier, 'Carthage V. Councils'.

141 *Concilia Africae a.345–a.525* (CCSL 149: 3–10).

142 L. Ennabli, *Carthage*, 148–9; 15–44 (dossier of texts).

convene as necessary.[143] Apart from co-ordinating the Catholic strategy against Donatism, these councils formulated a body of ecclesiastical law to unify the African churches in such matters as the biblical canon, clerical discipline and the fight against paganism. Important parts of this conciliar legislation were collected in the canons of Dionysius Exiguus.[144]

Influenced by Augustine, other African councils denounced Pelagian heresy: two synods at Milevis and Carthage in 416 were followed by a plenary council in Carthage on 1 May 418. As in the case of the Donatists shortly before (see below), the African bishops won imperial support: Honorius issued the anti-Pelagian decree on 30 April 418. But relations with Rome were not always harmonious. In May 419, a general council of 217 bishops with Aurelius presiding dealt with the case of Apiarius, a priest from Sicca Veneria. Apiarius had appealed to Rome against his excommunication and Pope Zosimus had accepted his appeal, citing as Nicene canons 3 and 4 of the Council of Serdica. The African council readmitted the delinquent priest, but referred to the sees of Constantinople, Antioch and Alexandria about the authenticity of the canons cited.[145] African churches were prepared to defend their autonomy and to reject Roman interference.[146]

The situation repeated itself some years later, with precisely the same results. A second council expelled Apiarius (424/5); the bishops from the council wrote a letter demanding that Rome stop interfering and even formulated a canon that explicitly prohibited appeals to Rome. During the Vandal occupation, in c. 445, Pope Leo I tried to intervene in the affairs of the churches at Mauretania Caesariana. Among other things, he enjoined the African bishops to submit a full report about all issues of the churches and the concord of the bishops to the pope – but this demand was probably never met. In any case, we know that when some sixty African bishops assembled in Carthage during 525 (after the Vandal persecution), they duly reiterated the canon of 424/5.[147]

In the fourth century, African Christianity was split by the Donatist schism, which (like the Melitian schism in Egypt) followed from events during the Great Persecution.[148] When a certain Caecilian was elected and ordained as

143 *Concilia Africae* (CCSL 149: 269–70; 215).
144 No acts or conciliar legislation survive from Donatist councils.
145 *Concilia Africae* (CCSL 149: 89–165; 94).
146 Already the plenary African council of 1 May 418 had been explicit in this respect; see *Concilia Africae* (CCSL 149: 227).
147 *Concilia Africae* (CCSL 149: 169–72, 266); Leo, *Letter* 12.13 (PL 54: 656). See Lepelley, 'Saint Léon le Grand'.
148 G. Bonner, *St. Augustine of Hippo*, 237–311; E. Grasmück, *Coercitio*; Schindler, 'Afrika I', 654–68; S. Lancel, 'Donatistae'. A collection of the relevant sources with commentary

bishop (c. 308), opponents within his church rejected him. A group of Numidian bishops supported Caecilian's enemies. About seventy Numidians assembled at a synod in a private home in Carthage. They excommunicated Caecilian, in part because one of his three consecrators, Felix of Aphthugni, was allegedly a *traditor* (i.e., someone who surrendered Bibles and liturgical books to the authorities), and they replaced him by a certain Maiorinus.[149] Maiorinus soon died and was succeeded by Donatus of Casae Nigrae – apparently an enemy of Caecilian.

Although there were *traditores* among the Numidian bishops who triggered the schism, the Donatists styled themselves the pure church of the martyrs, the one whose sacraments were valid. According to the Donatists, Caecilian's church was defiled, its clergy illegitimate. For them, Caecilian's invalid ordination spread like a contagion through the whole Catholic Church, invalidating every other ordination or baptism in the community.[150] As the only 'true church', the Donatists expected the emperor to hand over church buildings and church property to them. Constantine, however, backed the Catholics. In April 313 the Donatists sent Constantine a *libellus* detailing the charges against Caecilian and requested judges from Gaul to decide the matter.[151] Constantine assembled a tribunal of nineteen bishops (three from Gaul, the rest from Italy, with Pope Miltiades as the chair) who rejected the charges against Caecilian on 4 October 313. But the Donatists appealed and Constantine assembled another tribunal in Arles (August 314). Bishops from all parts of his Western empire were to take part. Caecilian attended the council, as did four Donatist bishops. The Donatist party failed again, but persisted. So Constantine summoned bishops to Milan and, in autumn 316, Caecilian was vindicated a third time.[152]

At this point, Constantine ordered a reunion of the two sides. One source complains of attempts at bribing Donatists, violence from the police and the military and the forceful profanation of Carthage churches.[153] Outside Carthage, the imperial order was probably ignored. In 321, the emperor

---

is provided by J.-L. Maier, *Le dossier du Donatisme*. For the early phase, see T. D. Barnes, *Constantine and Eusebius*, 54–61, with dissident proposals.

149 Optatus, *Against Parmenian* 1.17–20 (SC 412: 208–17); Augustine, *Letter* 43.2.3 (CSEL 34²: 86–7). In 315, an investigation ordered by Constantine cleared Felix of Aphthugni of the charge of *traditio*.

150 See B. Kriegbaum, *Kirche der Traditoren*.

151 Eusebius, *H.E.* 10.5.15–17, 10.6.1–5, 10.7.1–2; Augustine, *Letter* 88.2 (CSEL 34: 408); Optatus, *Against Parmenian* 1.22 (SC 412: 220–3).

152 Augustine, *Against Cresconius* 3.71.82 (CSEL 52: 487); *Letter* 43.7.20 (CSEL 34²: 102).

153 Augustine, *Letters* 88.3, 93.4.14 and 105.2.9 (CSEL 34²: 408–9; 458–9; 601–2); *c. litt. Petil.* 2.92.205 (CSEL 52: 129–30); *Sermo de passione sancti Donati episcopi Abiocalensis* (in Maier, *Dossier du Donatisme*, I: 201–11). See K. Schäferdiek, 'Der Sermo de passione sanctorum Donati et Advocati'.

reluctantly granted toleration; he however guaranteed privileges only to the Catholics.[154] Emboldened by Constantine's seeming lack of interest, the Donatists persecuted Catholics, particularly in the Donatist stronghold of Numidia, by occupying a Catholic church in Constantia (where Constantine had financed a new Catholic basilica) and illegally subjecting Catholic clergy to public duties. The result was bloodshed.

During the summer of 347, the emperor Constans revived the order to dissolve the Donatist church. Its buildings and properties were confiscated; bishops who refused conversion were exiled.[155] The Donatist church was substantially weakened and Donatus of Carthage exiled. This second attempt at forced reunification succeeded, but it also reinforced Donatist opposition against the emperor. Whereas under Constantine Caecilian and his party were the target, now the emperor became the enemy. Rumours had spread; two imperial commissioners who had come to offer relief to the poor were said to have demanded sacrifice before the emperor's image. Donatus raised the famous question, 'What has the emperor to do with the church?'[156] Already in Carthage, the edict led to martyrdoms and riots. Marculus, a member of a Donatist delegation to the imperial commissioner, was arrested and died in custody. A martyr cult developed.[157]

During Julian's short reign (361–3), the situation was reversed. Now the Donatists were supported by the imperial authorities and revenged themselves by occupying churches and committing atrocities.[158] A militant group arose within the Donatist church, the so-called *circumcelliones*,[159] who roamed the countryside, plundered the great estates in search for food and terrorised the Catholics. Confrontation also occurred at the intellectual level. On the Donatist side, Parmenian of Carthage claimed that only the sacraments (especially baptism) of the true church were valid. Moreover, he attacked Catholics for involving the military. Optatus of Milevis answered Parmenian's arguments:

---

154 Augustine, *brev. Coll.* 22.40 (CCSL 149A: 303); *Corpus Optati* 9 (Maier, *Dossier du Donatisme*, 241–2). But see *CTh* 16.5.1 (SC 497: 226).

155 Optatus, *Against the Donatists* 2.15; 3.1; *Passio Marculi* 3 (Maier, *Dossier du Donatisme*, 278–9); Augustine, *Against Cresconius* 3.50.55. See Grasmück, *Coercitio*, 117–18. A small Donatist church emerged in Rome.

156 Optatus, *Against the Donatists* 3.3.

157 *Passio Marculi* (Maier, *Dossier du Donatisme*, 275–91); Augustine, *c. litt. Petil.* 2.20.46 (CSEL 52: 46–7) and *Against Cresconius* 3.49.54 (CSEL 52: 461–2). For the cult of the martyrs in Africa, see Y. Duval, *Loca Sanctorum Africae*; for the cult of Marculus, see ibid. II: 705. See also L. Grig, *Making martyrs*.

158 Grasmück, *Coercitio*, 132–9.

159 According to Augustine, *Enarr. in ps.* 132.3, *circumcelliones* are so named because they roam around martyrs' shrines (*quia circum cellas vagantur*). A careful discussion of the *circumcelliones* can be found in Schindler, 'Afrika I', 662–5, 8; Shaw, 'Circumcelliones'.

only the *universal* church is the true church. As for the military response, Donatists brought it upon themselves.[160]

The *circumcelliones'* religious war was mixed with rebellion against the conditions of the rural underclass. Donatists were similarly implicated in the revolts of the Berber chiefs Firmus (372–5) and Gildo (397–8). Responding to Firmus' revolt, the imperial government resumed legislation against the Donatists: re-baptism was outlawed and the confiscation of Donatist property was renewed (*CTh* 16.6.1 and 2). Legal repression of Donatists continued with Theodosius' anti-heretical legislation and – after some interruption – was resumed under Honorius. From 393, African general councils under Aurelius attempted a conciliatory strategy of re-unification: Donatist bishops with their flocks were encouraged to join the Catholic Church (which was suffering from a severe clergy shortage). Catholics planned to send delegations to Donatists to convince them that their schism made no sense. This 'softly, softly' approach was partly inspired by the tireless Augustine who spared no effort (and no ink!) to heal the schism; his numerous anti-Donatist writings addressed almost every historical or theological aspect of the schism.

Despite some local advances, these peace initiatives were generally rejected by Donatists. Finally, in 404, the synod of Carthage dispatched a delegation to the emperor to ask for protection against the Donatists and to demand that Theodosius' anti-heretical legislation be implemented.[161] The request was granted and corresponding laws were published (*CTh* 16.5.38, 16.6.3–5, 16.11.2). This led to further violence and imperial support subsequently faltered. But in 410 the emperor called for a council to settle the matter through debate. The council sat from 1–8 June 411, in Carthage, under the chairmanship of Marcellinus, a Catholic *tribunus* and friend of Augustine.[162] The debate was acrimonious; predictably, Marcellinus favoured the Catholics. His edict issued on 26 June was severe: the churches of Donatist bishops who refused to join the Catholic Church were confiscated. Landowners who did not suppress the *circumcelliones* lost their estates.[163] A Donatist appeal only resulted in a more severe law, issued on 30 January 412: a heavy fine was now levied against Donatists of every social class, graded according to rank; masters were enjoined to admonish their slaves and beat their tenants (*coloni*) to make them submit. Recalcitrant clergy were exiled, their churches taken over. A similar

---

160 See Optatus, *Against the Donatists*.
161 *Concilia Africae* (CCSL 149), 211–14.
162 See the magisterial edition by S. Lancel (SC 194, 195, 224, 373).
163 *Gesta collationis Carthaginis* 3 init. (SC 224: 972–9).

law was issued on 17 June 414.[164] These laws indicate that Donatism was not confined to the lower classes.[165] These measures had some success. There are few sources for the Vandal occupation (430 to 533) and correspondingly little information about a continuing Donatist tradition. After the Byzantine re-conquest, however, Donatism seems to disappear.[166]

We have mentioned the Vandal occupation. Africa was the last region to experience the great migration of various German nations. In 429, Geiseric the Vandal king crossed the straits of Gibraltar with his Vandals and some Alans, numbering altogether about 80,000.[167] Military resistance was mostly ineffective; parts of Mauretania Sitifensis and Numidia were occupied. In 442, after having finally conquered Proconsularis (with Carthage, its capital), Byzacena and Tripolitana, Geiseric established autonomous Vandal rule. After 455, the Vandal kingdom expanded further and it throve for nearly eighty years. In none of the Germanic kingdoms in late antiquity was the persecution of Catholics as severe as under the rule of the Homoian Vandals.[168] The persecution was, however, not uniform. In Geiseric's view, Proconsularis was the Vandalian heartland, where he wished to eradicate Catholic Christianity, and persecution there was accordingly fierce.[169] To create a religiously integrated kingdom, Geiseric and his successors applied basically the same methods as Christian Roman emperors. Until 457, Catholic bishops were driven from their churches. The bishop of Carthage was exiled.[170] In Numidia and Byzacena Catholic clergy were watched closely. After 457, persecution intensified: ordinations were outlawed, liturgical vessels and holy books taken, religious assemblies forbidden.[171]

Political expediency dictated intermittent lulls in persecution. For instance, it was probably for the sake of a rapprochement with Valentinian III that Geiseric allowed Deogratias to be ordained bishop of Carthage in 454. By contrast, failed imperial attempts to destroy the Vandal kingdom (in 460 and

164 *CTh* 16.5.52 and 54 (SC 497: 306–9, 312–17); R. Delmaire has argued that the first law actually followed the second one; see SC 497: 488–92.
165 See C. Lepelley, 'Les sénateurs Donatistes'. Petilianus, Donatist bishop of Cirta, was a *vir clarissimus*; see Mandouze, *Prosopographie*, 855–68.
166 See Lancel, 'Donatistae', 621–2.
167 For the following, see Y. Modéran, 'Afrika und die Verfolgung durch die Wandalen'.
168 The most important source for the Vandal persecution until 484 is the *History of the Vandal persecution* by the African bishop Victor of Vita, now available in S. Lancel's magisterial edition.
169 Modéran, 'Afrika und die Verfolgung durch die Wandalen', 273f.
170 Victor of Vita, *History*, 1.15 (ed. Lancel, 103–4).
171 Ibid., 1.29 and 39–40 (ed. Lancel, 110, 114–15). See Modéran, 'Afrika und die Verfolgung durch die Wandalen', 274–5.

468) resulted in renewed persecution. In 474, Emperor Zeno concluded a treaty with Geiseric. As a consequence the Catholic clergy of Carthage returned from exile and the Catholic *basilica Fausti* was reopened. But these temporary relaxations represented no fundamental change in the Vandal religious policy of integrating Homoian Christianity in Proconsularis.

Geiseric's son and successor Huneric granted Zeno's request to allow the ordination of a Catholic bishop (Eugenius) for Carthage, but he demanded in return religious freedom for the Homoian churches; otherwise, he threatened to exile Catholic bishops and clergy into Berber territory. He soon deported about 5,000 bishops and clergy to the Berber tribes of southwest Numidia.[172] Monasteries, too, were targeted. In February 484, he staged a conference for Catholic and Homoian bishops to debate. The result was the expected conclusion and Huneric modelled his edict on the 412 anti-heretical laws: the Catholic Church was outlawed in Vandal Africa and Catholics were required to convert to Homoian Christianity.[173] Bishops were exiled to remote parts of the Vandal kingdom. Thus, in thirty years, the number of Catholic bishops in Proconsularis was reduced from 164 to 54.[174]

Under Gunthamund (*regn.* 484–96) and Thrasamund (*regn.* 496–523), persecution somewhat abated and Catholic bishops returned. But new ordinations of bishops were not allowed and, when the African Catholics dared to contravene their ruler's injunction in 508, about 120 bishops were exiled, half of them to Sardinia. The spiritual leader of the exiles there was Fulgentius of Ruspe, a monk and accomplished theologian of noble birth. In 515, King Thrasamund summoned Fulgentius to defend his Catholic faith. He did so by writing several anti-Arian treatises.[175] Finally Thrasamund's successor Hilderic (through his mother a grandson of Emperor Valentinian III) proclaimed religious tolerance – just ten years before the Vandal kingdom fell.[176]

Despite all this, local churches in Numidia and Byzacena functioned as before.[177] Monasticism apparently flourished; the monks even sheltered persecuted leaders.[178] During this time, African Catholics sought support from across the Mediterranean, particularly from Rome and Italy. The

---

172 Victor of Vita, *History*, 2.3 and 26–37 (ed. Lancel, 123–4, 133–9).
173 Ibid., 3.3–14 (ed. Lancel, 175–81).
174 See the *Notitia provinciarum et civitatium Africae* 1 (in Lancel's *Victor of Vita*, 252–4) and Victor of Vita, *History*, 1.29 (ibid., 110). See the analysis of Modéran, 'Afrika und die Verfolgung durch die Wandalen', 276f.
175 Ferrandus, *Vita Fulgentii* 44–8 (PL 65: 139–41).
176 Victor of Tunnuna, *chron.* 523 (MGH aa II: 197); Ferrandus, *Vita Fulgentii* 55 (PL 65: 145).
177 Modéran, 'Afrika und die Verfolgung durch die Wandalen', 286.
178 Ibid., 289.

martyrs of Africa even made their appeals in the dreams of Mediterranean Christians: it was allegedly a visitation by the martyred bishop Laetus that prompted Justinian to begin the *reconquista* of the African territories.[179] The re-constitution of the Catholic Church in Africa under Byzantine rule faced difficulties; the ecclesiastical provinces demanded greater autonomy. As in other Western Christianities, bishops assumed administrative functions. The archaeological record testifies to Justinian's impressive rebuilding of Roman African cities, including their basilicas.[180] At the dawn of the seventh century, Justinian's aggressive Christianity and military necessities prompted intensified missionary efforts among the Berbers.[181]

Bibliography

PRIMARY SOURCES

Ambrose. *Letters* (CSEL 821–4)
Anonymus Valesianus, in I. König, ed., *Aus der Zeit Theoderichs des Großen* (Darmstadt, 1997)
Augustine. *Against Cresconius* (CSEL 52)
  Against the letters of Petilian (CSEL 52)
  Confessions, ed. J. J. O'Donnell (Oxford, 1992)
  Enarrationes in psalmos (CCSL 38, 39, 40)
  Letters (CSEL 34$^{1-2}$, 44, 57, 58)
Codex Justinianus (*CJ*). Ed. P. Krüger, *Corpus iuris civilis* (Berlin, 1929^{11})
Codex Theodosianus (*CTh*). Eds. T. Mommsen and P. Meyer, *theodosiani libri XVI cum constitutionibus Sirmondianis: et leges novellae ad Theodosianum pertinentes*, 2 vols. in 3 (Berlin, 1954^2); for *CTh* 16, see now SC 497
Collectio Avellana (CSEL 35)
Concilia Africae a.345–a.525 (CCSL 149)
Concilia Galliae a.314–a.506 (CCSL 148)
Concilia Galliae a.511–a.695 (CCSL 148a)
Eusebius of Caesarea. *H.E.* (GCS *Eusebius Werke*, II)
Facundus of Hermiane. *Defence of the Three Chapters* (SC 471)
Ferrandus. *Vita Fulgentii* (PL 65)
Gaudemet, J. and B. Basdevant, eds. *Les canons des conciles Mérovingiens (VIe–VIIe siècles)* (SC 353, 354)
Gesta collationis Carthaginis (SC 194, 195, 224, 373)
Hilary of Poitiers. *Contra Auxentium* (PL 10)
  De synodis (PL 10)
Innocent. *Letters* (PL 20)

179 Victor of Tunnuna, *chron.* 534 (MGH aa II: 198).
180 The evidence is summed up by Modéran, 'Die Kirchen und die byzantinische Rückeroberung', 759–61.
181 Modéran, *Les Maures et l'Afrique romaine*, 645–62.

Jerome. *Against John* (PL 23)
  Altercatio Luciferiani et Orthodoxi (SC 473)
  Letters (CSEL 54, 55, 56)
Joannou, P. P., ed. *Discipline générale antique (IVe–IXe s.)* (Rome, 1962–3)
Leo. *Letters* (PL 54)
Liber Pontificalis, ed. L. Duchesne (Paris, 1886, 1892); supplementary volume, ed. C. Vogel (Paris, 1957)
Liberatus. *Breviarium* (ACO 2.5)
Liberius of Rome. *Letters* (PL 84)
Maier, J.-L. *Le dossier du Donatisme* (Berlin, 1987–9)
Optatus. *Against the Donatists* (SC 412, 413)
  Against Parmenian (SC 412)
Rufinus. *H.E.* (GCS *Eusebius Werke*, II)
Sidonius Apollinaris. *Letters*. Ed. A. Loyen, *Sidoine Apollinaire, correspondance* (Paris, 1970; reprint 2003)
Sulpicius Severus. *Chronica* (SC 441)
  Dialogus (CSEL 1)
  Life of Martin (SC 133)
Thiel, A., ed. *Epistolae Romanorum Pontificum genuinae* (Brunsberg, 1868), I
Venantius Fortunatus. *Carmina* (MGH aa 4.1)
Victor of Tunnuna. *Chronicon* (MGH aa II)
Victor of Vita. *History of the Vandal persecution*. Ed. S. Lancel, *Victor de Vita. Histoire de la persécution Vandale en Afrique. La passion des sept martyrs. Registre des provinces et des cités afriques* (Paris, 2002)
Vincent. *Commonitorium* (CCSL 64)
Vives, J., ed. *Concilios Visigóticos e Hispano-Romanos* (Madrid, 1963)
Zosimus. *Letters* (PL 20)

SECONDARY SOURCES

Barnes, T. D. 'Ambrose and the basilicas of Milan in 385 and 386', *ZAC* 4 (2000): 282–99
  Athanasius and Constantius (Cambridge, MA, 1993)
  Constantine and Eusebius (Cambridge, MA, 1981)
Beaujard, B. 'L'évêque dans la cité en Gaule aux Ve et VIe siècles', in C. Lepelley, ed., *La fin de la cité antique et le début de la cité médiévale* (Bari, 1996), 127–45
Bonner, G. *St. Augustine of Hippo. Life and controversies* (Norwich, 1986²)
Brandenburg, H. *The ancient churches of Rome* (Turnhout, 2005)
Brennecke, H. C. *Hilarius von Poitiers und die Bischofsopposition gegen Konstantius II*, PTS 26 (Berlin, 1984)
  Studien zur Geschichte der Homöer (Tübingen, 1988)
Burrus, V. *The making of a heretic. Gender, authority and the Priscillianist controversy* (Berkeley, CA, 1995)
Capizzi, C. *Giustiniano I tra politica e religione* (Messina, 1998²)
Carletti, C. 'Damaso I, santo', in *Enciclopedia dei papi* (Rome, 2000), I: 349–72
Caspar, E. *Geschichte des Papsttums* (Tübingen, 1930)

Chadwick, H. *Boethius* (Oxford, 1990)

The church in ancient society: From Galilee to Gregory the Great (Oxford, 2001)

Priscillian of Avila (Oxford, 1976)

Coskun, A. 'Der Praefect Maximinus, der Jude Isaak und der Strafprozeß gegen Bischof Damasus von Rom', *JbAC* 46 (2003)

Demandt, A. *Die Spätantike* (Munich, 1989)

Demougeot, É. 'Gallia I', *RAC* 8 (1972): 899–902

Duval, Y. *Loca sanctorum Africae. Le culte des martyrs en Afrique du IVe au VIIe siècle*, CollÉFR 58 (Rome, 1982)

'La manœuvre frauduleuse de Rimini', in *Hilaire et son temps*, Études augustiniennes (Paris, 1969), 51–103

'Pélage en son temps', *SP* 38 (2001): 95–118

Duval, Y.-M. *L'affaire Jovinien*, Studia Ephemiridis Augustinianum 83 (Rome, 2003)

L'extirpation de l'arianisme en Italie du nord et en Occident (Ashgate, 1998)

Ennabli, L. *Carthage. Une métropole chrétienne du IVe à la fin du VIIe siècle* (Paris, 1997)

Ferrua, A. *Epigrammata Damasiana* (Rome, 1942)

Fiocchi Nicolai, V. *Strutture funerarie ed edifici di culto paleocristiani di Roma dal IV al VI secolo* (Vatican, 2001)

Fontaine, J. *Naissance de la poésie dans l'occident chrétien* (Paris, 1981)

Grasmück, E. *Coercitio. Staat und Kirche im Donatistenstreit* (Bonn, 1964)

Grig, L. *Making martyrs in late antiquity* (London, 2004)

Grillmeier, A. *Jesus der Christus im Glauben der Kirche*, II.1 (Freiburg, 1986)

Guidobaldi, F. 'Roma. Il tessuto abitativo, le "domus" ed i "tituli"', in A. Carandini, L. Cracco Ruggini and A. Giardina, eds., *Storia di Roma. III: L'età tardoantica. II: I luoghi e le culture* (Turin, 1993), 69–83

Hadot, P. *Marius Victorinus. Recherches sur sa vie et ses œuvres* (Paris, 1971)

Halleux, A. de. '"Hypostase" et "personne" dans la formation du dogme trinitaire', *Revue d'histoire ecclésiastique* 79 (1984): 311–69, 623–70; reprinted in A. de Halleux, *Patrologie et oecuménisme. Recueil d'études* (Louvain, 1990), 113–214

Heather, P. 'Senators and senates', in A. Cameron and P. Garnsey, eds., *The Cambridge ancient history* (Cambridge, 1998), XIII: 184–210 at 202–3

Heinzelmann, M. *Bischofsherrschaft in Gallien* (Munich, 1976)

Kelly, J. N. D. *Early Christian creeds* (New York, 1995^3)

Jerome. His life, writings, and controversies (London, 1998^2)

Klauser, Th. 'Der Übergang der römischen Kirche von der griechischen zur lateinischen Liturgiesprache,' in *Gesammelte Arbeiten zur Liturgiegeschichte, Kirchengeschichte und christlichen Archäologie* (Münster, 1974), 184–94

Klingshirn, W. *Caesarius of Arles* (Cambridge, 1994)

Kriegbaum, B. *Kirche der Traditoren oder Kirche der Märtyrer? Die Vorgeschichte des Donatismus* (Innsbruck, 1986)

Lancel, S. 'Donatistae', in *Augustinus-Lexikon* (1996–2000), II: 606–38

Saint Augustin (Paris, 1999)

Langgärtner, G. *Die Gallienpolitik der Päpste im 5. und 6. Jahrhundert* (Bonn, 1964)

Lepelley, C. 'Le patronat épiscopal aux IVe et Ve siècles', in E. Rebillard and C. Sotinel, eds., *L'évêque dans la cité du IVe au Ve siècle* (Rome, 1998), 17–33

'Saint Léon le Grand et l'église maurétanienne', in *Aspects de l'Afrique romaine* (Bari, 2001), 415–31

'Les sénateurs Donatistes', in *Aspects de l'Afrique romaine* (Bari, 2001), 345–56

Lippold, A. 'Ursinus,' *RE* Supplement x (1965): 1141–8

Löhr, W. A. *Die Entstehung der homöischen und homöusianischen Kirchenparteien* (Bonn, 1986)

Lorenz, R. *Das vierte bis sechste Jahrhundert (Westen)* (Göttingen, 1970)

McLynn, N. *Ambrose of Milan* (Berkeley, CA, 1994)

Mandouze, A. *Prosopographie chrétienne du bas-empire: Prosopographie de l'Afrique chrétienne (303–533)* (Paris, 1982)

Markschies, C. *Ambrosius von Mailand und die Trinitätstheologie* (Tübingen, 1995)

Markus, R. *Gregory the Great and his world* (Cambridge, 1997)

Mathisen, R. W. 'Hilarius, Germanus, and Lupus: The aristocratic background of the Chelidonius affair', *Phoenix* 33 (1979), 160–9

Meslin, M. *Les ariens d'Occident* (Paris, 1967)

Modéran, Y. 'Afrika und die Verfolgung durch die Wandalen', in L. Pietri et al., eds., *Geschichte des Christentums* (Freiburg, 2005), iii: 264–99

'La conversion de Constantin et la christianisation de l'empire romain', at http://aphgcaen.free.fr/conferences/moderan.htm.

'Die Kirchen und die byzantinische Rückeroberung. A. Afrika', in L. Pietri et al., eds., *Geschichte des Christentums* (Freiburg, 2005), iii: 749–66

Les Maures et l'Afrique romaine (IVᵉ–VIIᵉ siècle) (Rome, 2003)

Moorhead, J. *Theoderic in Italy* (Oxford, 1992)

Munier, C. 'Carthage V. Councils', in *Encyclopedia of the early church* (1992), i: 146–8

Nauroy, G. 'Le fouet et le miel. Le combat d'Ambroise en 386', in *Ambroise de Milan. Écriture et esthétique d'une exégèse pastorale* (Bern, 2003), 33–189

Noethlichs, K.-L. 'Iustinianus (Kaiser)', *RAC* 19 (2001): 668–773

Nürnberg, R. *Askese als sozialer Impuls* (Bonn, 1988)

Pack, E. 'Italia I,' *RAC* 18 (1998): 1049–202

Pietri, C. 'Aristocratie et société cléricale dans l'Italie chrétienne au temps d'Odoacre et de Théodore', in C. Pietri, ed., *Christiana respublica* (Rome, 1997), ii: 1007–57

'Damase, évêque de Rome', in C. Pietri, ed., *Christiana respublica* (Rome, 1997), i: 31–58

'Euergétisme et richesses ecclésiastiques dans l'Italie du IVᵉ à la fin du Vᵉ siècles: L'éxemple romain', in C. Pietri, ed., *Christiana respublica* (Rome, 1997), ii: 813–33

'La géographie de l'Illyricum ecclésiastique et ses rélations avec l'église de Rome (Vᵉ–VIᵉ siècles)', in C. Pietri, ed., *Christiana respublica* (Rome, 1997), i: 547–88

Roma Christiana Recherches sur l'église de Rome, son organisation, sa politique, son idéologie de Miltiade à Sixte III (311–440) (Rome, 1976)

Pietri, L., Y. Duval and C. Pietri, 'Peuple chrétien ou plebs: Le rôle des laïcs dans les élections ecclésiastiques en Occident', in C. Pietri, ed., *Christiana respublica* (Rome, 1997), ii: 1059–81

Pontal, O. *Die Synoden im Merowingerreich* (Paderborn, 1986)

Pricoco, S. *L'isola dei santi. Il cenobio di Lerino e le origini del monachesimo gallico* (Rome, 1978)

Prinz, F. *Frühes Mönchtum im Frankenreich* (Darmstadt, 1988²)

Rapp, C. *Holy bishops in late antiquity* (Berkeley, CA, 2005)

Rebenich, S. *Hieronymus und sein Kreis* (Stuttgart, 1992)

Rosen, K. 'Iustinus I (Kaiser)', *RAC* 19 (2001): 763–78

Salamito, J.-M. *Les virtuoses et la multitude. Aspects sociaux de la controverse entre Augustin et les pélagiens* (Paris, 2005)

Salzman, M. R. *The making of a Christian aristocracy. Social and religious change in the Western Roman empire* (Cambridge, MA, 2002)

Schäferdiek, K. *Die Kirche in den Reichen der Westgoten und Suewen bis zur Errichtung der westgotischen katholischen Staatskirche* (Berlin, 1967)

'Der Sermo de passione sanctorum Donati et Advocati als donatistisches Selbstzeugnis', in *Oecumenica et patristica. Festschrift W. Schneemelcher* (Stuttgart / Geneva, 1989), 175–98

Schieffer, R. 'Der Papst als Patriarch von Rom', in M. Maccarone, ed., *Il primato del vescovo di Roma nel primo millennio. Ricerche e testimonianze* (Vatican, 1991), 433–51

Schindler, A. 'Afrika I', in *Theologische Realenzyklopädie* (1977), I: 640–700

Schwartz, E. *Drei dogmatische Schriften Justinians* (Munich, 1939)

Publizistische Sammlungen zum Acacianischen Schisma, Abhandlungen der Bayerischen Akademie der Wissenschaften N.F. 10 (Munich, 1934)

I. Vigiliusbriefe, II Zur Kirchenpolitik Iustinians, Sitzungsberichte der Bayerischen Akademie der Wissenschaften 1940, Nr. 2 (Munich, 1940)

Shaw, B. D. 'Who were the Circumcelliones?' in A. H. Merrills, ed., *Vandals, Romans and Berbers* (Aldershot, 2004), 227–58

Sotinel, C. 'Emperors and popes in the sixth century', in M. Maas, ed., *The Cambridge companion to the age of Justinian* (Cambridge, 2005), 267–90

'Le personnel episcopal', in E. Rebillard and C. Sotinel, eds., *L'évêque dans la cité du IVe siècle* (Rome, 1998), 105–26

Sternberg, Th. *Orientalium more secutus. Räume und Institutionen der Caritas im Gallien des 5. bis 7. Jahrhunderts* (Münster, 1991)

Tardieu, M. *Recherches sur la formation de l'Apocalypse de Zostrien et les sources de Marius Victorinus* (Bures-sur-Yvette, 1996)

Ulbert, T. 'Hispania I', *RAC* 15 (1991): 607–46

Ullmann, W. *Gelasius I (492–496)* (Stuttgart, 1981)

Ulrich, J. *Die Anfänge der abendländischen Rezeption des Nizänums*, PTS 39 (Berlin, 1994)

Uthemann, K.-H. 'Kaiser Justinian als Kirchenpolitiker und Theologe', in *Christus, Kosmos, Diatribe* (Berlin, 2005), 257–331

Wallraff, M. *Christus Verus Sol* (Münster, 2001)

Weckwerth, A. *Das erste Konzil von Toledo* (Münster, 2004)

Williams, D. H. *Ambrose of Milan and the end of the Nicene–Arian conflicts* (Oxford, 1995)

Wirbelauer, E. 'Die Nachfolgerbestimmung im römischen Bistum (3.–6. Jahrhundert)', *Klio* 76 (1994): 388–437

Zwei Päpste in Rom (Munich, 1993)

Wolfram, H. *History of the Goths* (Berkeley, CA, 1988)

2

Germanic and Celtic Christianities

KNUT SCHÄFERDIEK

Gothic and other early Germanic Christianities

Christianity began to spread in the Germanic world during the latter part of the third century among the Goths, who arrived in the region to the north of the Black Sea in the 230s. By the year 270, they had split to form two peoples, the Greutungi or Ostrogoths between the Don and the Dniestr and the Tervingi between the Dniestr and the Olt. It is there, in what is today's Moldavia and eastern Romania, that Gothic Christianity is to be found for the first time.[1] It started with a group of Christians who had been abducted during a Gothic invasion of the Roman province of Cappadocia (Inner Anatolia) in 257. These Christians were able to preserve their Christian faith and pass it on to their descendants, who became assimilated into their Gothic environment; this was possible because they obviously succeeded in building up a formal Christian community. A bishopric was even created for Gothia, the area occupied by the Tervingian Goths, which was represented at the Council of Nicaea in 325 by a bishop named Theophilus. Early Gothic Christianity consisted, therefore, not of Christianised Goths but of Gothicised Christians. In addition to the descendants of the Cappadocian founders, it probably also included other Christians of Roman origin. From the period around 370, a series of names of Gothic Christians has come down to us, and most of them are not of Germanic origin.

In 332 Constantine the Great succeeded in winning the Tervingian Goths as federates to the Roman empire, a development that was also to benefit the Christians among them. On the occasion of a Gothic legation to the imperial court, probably in 336, the reader Ulfila was consecrated bishop for the Christians in the land of the Goths, possibly as the successor to Theophilus. His consecrator was Eusebius of Nicomedia who was closely connected with

1 K. Schäferdiek, 'Die Anfänge des Christentums bei den Goten und der sog. gotische Arianismus'.

52

Constantine's court. Although Ulfila bore a Gothic name – 'little wolf' – he was in fact a descendant of those Cappadocian Christians who had been abducted in 257. He had clearly received a sound Christian education and, in addition to Gothic, knew Latin and Greek. Since Gothic Christians were regarded as sympathising with the Romans, disruptions in the Gothic–Roman relationship posed a threat to them and, during the 340s, a disruption of this kind eventually led to persecution. Ulfila and a larger number of Christians were driven out and resettled by the emperor Constantius in the Roman border region near Nicopolis ad Istrum (in the vicinity of Veliko Tărnovo in Bulgaria), where they established a small Gothic ethnic group under the religious and political leadership of Ulfila. As late as the mid-sixth century they were still found there as so-called *Gothi minores*. It was probably during this second phase of activity that Ulfila translated large parts of the Bible into Gothic, which in fact was the first translation of the Bible into the language of an oral culture. For this purpose he developed a Gothic alphabet, and he undoubtedly also set up a school in order to familiarise clergymen with the use of that new medium. Only fragments of Ulfila's Gothic translation remain. At the same time, he was involved in the theological debates of his time and joined the group of Homoians that formed in the years after 357. Their opponents discredited them as 'Arians', but the emperors Constantius and Valens favoured them as orthodox. By this time, it is likely that Ulfila was no longer active in Gothia; but even after his group had been driven out, a Christian diaspora church, now headed by a group of presbyters, remained there. When the Goths broke off their alliance with the Roman empire in 369, the Christian Goths had to suffer renewed persecution. They were asked to prove their ethnic Gothic identity by taking part in pagan rites, and many suffered martyrdom because they refused to comply. Both instances of persecution among the Goths are exceptional events in the history of Germanic Christianisation due to the fact that early Gothic Christianity did not originate among the ruling classes.

Soon after 369, the leader of one of the Tervingian tribes, Fritigern, sought Roman support during an internal struggle among the Goths and, along with his subjects, he therefore adopted the emperor's religion. These events opened a new chapter in the history of Gothic Christianisation. The emperor now launched a missionary effort in order to put Fritigern's decision into practice, and a rudimentary church organisation was set up within his sphere of power. In 375, however, with the invasion of the Huns, the Tervingian nation dissolved, and the majority of the Tervingi requested resettlement in Roman territory. With the approval of the East Roman emperor Valens, they crossed the Danube in 376, as did groups of Greutingi, and shortly afterwards the Christian Fritigern became their leader. Their resettlement on Roman territory, however, was delayed: the subsidies they had been promised were not forthcoming and so for several years the Goths roamed the Balkan peninsula, plundering as they went. At the same time they formed a new ethnic group. Ulfila's Goths did not join this new Gothic nation, which in the sixth century became known as the Visigoths. It was not until 382 that Theodosius the Great succeeded in stabilising the situation and settling the intruders in the border region on the Danube as federates.

Since crossing over into the Roman empire, these Goths had been regarded as Christians. The rudimentary church organisation set up shortly before the Hunic invasion had weathered the confusion and survived, adapting to the circumstances of a people on the move. This entailed the ability of the clergy to identify with the Goths. Indeed, in recruiting personnel, it is likely that the original imperial mission had drawn upon clergymen who had been trained in the Ulfilanian Gothic community. They taught the future Visigoths not only the Gothic liturgy and the Gothic Bible, but also the Homoian creed that defined the official orthodoxy in the eastern empire during the reign of Valens. Together with Ulfila's Goths, the Visigoths continued to adhere to it even after Theodosius the Great had brought about a swing to the Nicene Creed in 379. Both Gothic churches were subordinate to the patriarchate of Constantinople, which was at this time in its formative period. In 380, the Homoian bishop Demophilus of Constantinople was removed from his see and replaced by a Nicene primate. The Gothic churches, however, remained in communion with him, thus rejecting the change of official religious policy. Precedence was apparently given to personal over institutional allegiances. As a consequence of this, the Gothic Christians were henceforth deemed 'Arian'. They defined themselves as Catholics, and their opponents, the Nicenes, as 'the Romans' (Romani). But allegiance to the insignificant Arian community of Constantinople, racked as it was by internal disputes, cannot have held for long. The Arian churches were subsequently autonomous, the church of the North African Vandal kingdom even having its own patriarch.

At the end of the fourth century, a Gothic group on the Crimean Bosporus (Strait of Kerch), with its own king, adopted Catholic Christianity and saw to it that a bishop was consecrated for them by the bishop of Constantinople, John Chrysostom. The newly consecrated bishop's name, Unila, was Germanic. Nothing further is known with respect to the Christianisation of the numerous Goths resident in the Crimea, whose language was still attested as late as the sixteenth century. The Goths on the Taman peninsula, who had requested a bishop from the emperor Justinian in 548/9, had by then been Christians for a considerable time.

The history of the dissemination of Gothic Arian Christianity can only be painted in broad strokes. It spread in both the West and the East. In 408, the Visigoths moved westwards and, as federates of the Western Roman empire, settled in Aquitania in 418. Subsequently they extended their sphere of power as far as the river Loire and across substantial parts of Spain. Their bond with the empire was broken off in 475. They passed on their Arian Christianity to several other Germanic peoples living in the West.

The first of these were the Vandals. Having invaded the Roman empire in 406/7, they spent the period of 409–29 in southern Spain, before crossing to North Africa in 429. In the north of what is now eastern Algeria, Tunisia and Libya, they established an independent Vandal kingdom, but, while still in Spain, they had adopted Gothic Arian Christianity.

The Burgundians, another Germanic nation, had settled in the upper Rhine area during the early fifth century. After suffering disastrous defeat there at the hands of the Huns in 436, they were settled as Roman federates in Savoy several years later, and subsequently managed to extend their dominance into what was to become Burgundy. Although they had been exposed to Catholic influences at an early stage, they became Arians around the mid-fifth century. This conversion to Gothic Arianism was probably connected with the re-establishment by King Gundiok of a Burgundian kingship, since an older royal dynasty expired in consequence of the defeat of 436. Gundiok was descended from Visigothic nobility and thus was an Arian.

Around the year 450, the Suevi (who invaded Spain in 408 and settled in Galicia in 411 as federates) already had a Catholic king in the person of Rechiar, but from 466 they came again under Visigoth influence and Gothic Arian Christianity was adopted.

As the last example shows, there was probably an active missionary policy on the part of the Arian Visigoths, aiming at the establishment of a commonwealth of Germanic Arian Christianities. However, this policy was not universally successful. For example, in the late fifth century the Visigoths signally failed in their attempt to win over the aspiring Frankish king Clovis. In 507, Aquitania was conquered by the Franks. The Visigoths and their Arian church were driven back into Spain and the remaining Arian communities in Aquitania were assimilated into the Catholic Church.

Sixth-century Ostrogothic tradition claims that the Visigoths transmitted their version of Christianity to the Ostrogoths and the Gepids, another Gothic people, for reasons of ethnic closeness. This, however, is obviously not correct:

the Visigoths had already departed into the Western empire by the early fifth century. After the Huns crushed the vast Ostrogothic kingdom between the Don and the Dniestr in 375/6, a new Ostrogothic nation formed north of the lower Danube, within the area under Hunic control. It is probable that Tervingi who had remained north of the Danube in 376 were also assimilated into this grouping. After the fall of the Hunic domination, these Ostrogoths settled in Pannonia, between the rivers Drava and Sava, in 456/7, as federates of the Romans. In 473, most of them left these bases and crossed the Balkan peninsula before establishing themselves under their king Theoderic the Great in Italy during 488, with the approval of the emperor Zeno. It is fair to assume that Arian Christianity had taken root among them while they were in Pannonia. Around 1940 a folded tablet of lead, now lost, was discovered in an Ostrogothic burial site at Hács Béndekpuszta (in the county of Somogy, Hungary), dating from the late fifth or early sixth century.[2] It bore the Gothic text of John 17.11 ff.

It is possible that early Ostrogothic Christianity is related to Tervingian Christianity, since there were Christians among the Tervingi who had remained in the area under Hunic control. At the same time, however, Gothic influences from the Danubian border region of the East Roman empire may also be assumed. Such influences are suggested by the Gothic translation of an early fifth-century Greek *calendarium* that probably originated from the Arian community of Constantinople. A single leaf of it has been preserved in the Ostrogothic tradition.[3]

In the sixth century, the Gepids were also Arian Christians. Following the demise of the Hunic domination (454/5), they formed a kingdom between the river Tisa and the Carpathian mountains, but there is no record of their Christianisation.

Sources do not sufficiently confirm the assumption that Gothic Arianism in the sixth century also embraced the Skiri in the western part of the Hungarian plain, the Heruli in southern Moravia and the Rugi in Lower Austria, and even entered southern Germany.

The Lombards were latecomers to the commonwealth of Germanic Arian Christianities. In the second quarter of the sixth century, the centre of the area ruled and settled by them shifted from Bohemia and Lower Austria to Pannonia. By the late 540s, at least a part of their ruling classes was regarded as being Catholic. Within a grave in Bezenye (county Győr-Moson-Sopron,

---

2 Piergiuseppe Scardigli, 'Das Bleitäfelchen von Hács-Béndekpuszta'.
3 Knut Schäferdiek, 'Gotische Literatur. § 3. Das Kalenderfragment'.

Hungary), a pair of fibulas dating from the end of their Pannonian period was found bearing a runic inscription that includes the word *segun* (blessing).[4] It derives directly or indirectly from the Latin *signum*, sign (of the cross) and is commonly interpreted as an indication of Christian influence. Since the 560s, King Alboin had been seeking to associate himself with the tradition of Ostrogothic Arian Christianity. The motive for this must have been a political one, namely his wish to succeed to the Ostrogothic domination of Italy that had been destroyed by the emperor Justinian. This eventually came about in 568, when the Lombards invaded the country and subsequently conquered large parts of it. Gold foil crosses sewn onto cloth and laid upon the dead are frequently found within Lombard graves in Italy,[5] but these, while indeed providing evidence for the spread of Christianity, can hardly serve to distinguish between Arian and Catholic faith. From the outset, Arian Christianity met with opposition among the Lombards. On the one hand, pagan elements survived for some considerable time, while on the other, Catholic influences were apparent from a very early stage. Even in the 580s, King Authari deemed it necessary to prevent Lombard children from receiving a Catholic baptism, whereas his successor Agilulf had his own son baptised a Catholic.

According to the Homoian doctrine of the Arian churches, God the Son is like God the Father: both are God. This does not, however, rule out a subordination of the Son in relation to the Father. Homoian theology rejected the use of the term 'substance' and consequently also the Nicene expression *homousios* (*consubstantialis*). Furthermore, it did not regard the Holy Ghost as being God. In the liturgy, the difference between the Arian and Catholic doctrines found expression in the form of the doxology. In the Arian version, the wording is 'Glory (be) to the Father through the Son in the Holy Ghost', whereas the Catholic version is 'Glory (be) to the Father and the Son and the Holy Ghost'. Furthermore, the Arian practice of re-baptising those who converted from other Christian groups, a practice that originated in the Eastern tradition, caused offence in the West since the Western Catholic Church was traditionally satisfied if the convert had already been baptised by invoking the Trinity in a formally correct manner. It even recognised Arian baptism. But in usual church practice and people's everyday religious lives, there can scarcely have been much to distinguish Arians from Catholics.

Due to the fact that Gothic Arianism spread as it did, it has often been suggested that the Arian creed was specifically adapted to the culture of the

---

4 Stephan Opitz, *Südgermanische Runeninschriften*, 11.
5 Horst Wolfgang Böhme, 'Goldblattkreuze'.

Germanic nations. But there is no real proof of this.[6] Only the Gothic liturgy and the Gothic Bible – the only properly Germanic elements in so-called Germanic Arianism – could be cited as evidence for a Germanic acculturation of Arian Christianity. These, however, should not be interpreted as conscious responses to the needs of a Germanic cultural context, but must rather be understood as a characteristic consequence of the linguistic pluralism of the Eastern churches. After some time, Latin seems to have established itself alongside the Gothic language in the Arian church service, as is indicated by Gothic–Latin manuscripts of biblical texts and the adaptation of a Latin evangelistary according to a Gothic model.

The commonwealth of Germanic Arian Christianities did not enjoy a long history. Its demise, like its rise, is closely linked to the realities of late antique power politics. The Vandals and the Ostrogoths lost their political existence and consequently also their ethnic identity in 534 and 553, respectively, when the Byzantines re-conquered North Africa and Italy. The Gepids suffered the same fate in 567 with the advance of the pagan Avars. As a consequence, the Arian Christianities of the Vandals and the Gepids disappeared. In Italy, on the other hand, a certain continuity linking Ostrogothic and Lombard Arianism can be assumed.

In the case of the Burgundians, Arian Christianity was extinguished in 517 following the accession to power of King Sigismund, who was already a Catholic. In the Spanish Suevic kingdom, the conversion of King Chararich in 555 set in motion the transition to the Catholic faith. In the Visigoth kingdom, King Rekkared converted to Catholicism in 587, and the general conversion was carried out at the Third Council of Toledo in 589 by representatives of the ruling classes, among them several Arian bishops.

Catholic influences had begun to accompany Lombard Arianism at a very early stage. Lombard Arianism's decline during the course of the seventh century stretched over a considerable period and was completed during the time of King Percatrit (671–88). At the end of the sixth and the beginning of the seventh century, Queen Theodolinda, who was descended from the Bavarian ducal dynasty and was thus Catholic, was married first to King Authari and then to King Agilulf. She and the so-called Bavarian dynasty of the Lombard kings who can be traced back to her did much to hasten the erosion of Lombard Arianism. Although the political conditions under which the rejection of Arianism took place in the individual kingdoms varied considerably, the common background

---

6 For ideologically motivated views on Gothic Arianism, cf. Hanns Christof Brennecke, 'Der sog. germanische Arianismus als, arteigenes' Christentum'.

was a progressive acculturation to an environment in which Roman Catholics were far superior in numbers.

Celtic Christianities

Christianity reached Roman Britain during the third century at the latest. Traces of the new religion can be seen in archaeological finds from Roman times. In 314, three British bishops were signatories at the Council of Arles. In the late fourth century, the Christian layman and theologian Pelagius came from Britain to Rome, and in 429, after Roman rule had ended, Bishop Germanus of Auxerre made his way to Britain with the intention of fending off Pelagian tendencies. Although later hagiographical tradition claims that Germanus was influential in the development of the spiritual life of Celtic Christianity, there is no reason for associating both Patrick and the British abbot Illtud with him. Even as the time of the Romans was drawing to a close, the Christianisation of Britain was not yet complete; indeed, in remote Cornwall it may only just have got under way. In the second half of the fifth century, the invasion of the Anglo-Saxons caused the Britons to withdraw westwards, some of them even as far as Armorica on the mainland, which soon also came to be named Brittany. Writing in the sixth century, the Briton Gildas lamented the slide of both secular and religious leaders into moral decadence and called on them to repent. Gildas' lament, however, has to be read as part of his theological interpretation of the fate of Britain as a divine trial, and should therefore not be given too much significance.

British Christianity in fact even managed to gain ground during the period immediately after the end of Roman rule, crossing the former Roman frontier of Hadrian's Wall. The archaeological record provides at least sketchy indications that British Christianity spread to the Clyde and the Tay, but the density of its dissemination and the degree of church organisation it achieved remain unknown.

During the fifth century, the British bishop Ninian was active in Candida Casa (Whithorn [Galloway]). In the eighth century, it is recorded that he had been educated in Rome, erected a stone church in Whithorn (for which archaeological evidence exists)[7] and was buried there in the episcopal church. No doubt his alleged Roman education did not enter the hagiographical tradition until Anglian times. It rendered him acceptable to the Anglian Church, in which British bishops were generally held to be non-canonical. Furthermore,

7 Peter Hill, *Whithorn and St. Ninian*.

it is claimed that Ninian converted the southern Picts, another tradition that must be assumed to be of Anglian origin. Before 685, the southern Picts had been under Anglian rule for some time, and the abbot-bishop of Abercorn (West Lothian) was in charge of their ecclesiastical affairs. In this situation, it was possible to defend the British Christianity of the Picts between Tay and Forth against the suspicion of irregularity by claiming that it had been established by Ninian, who was recognised by the Anglian church. The Christian British ruler Coroticus, who had been excommunicated by Patrick, was seen as being lord of Dumbarton as early as the seventh century. However, this identification – which could be interpreted as evidence for the dissemination of Christianity in Strathclyde during the fifth century – remains disputed. St Kentigern, who according to the *Annales Cambriae* died in 612, was active there at a later time, but a mass of legends obscures the picture we have of him.

British Christianity also became established in Ireland, primarily in Leinster, during the initial third of the fifth century. The Roman bishop Coelestine dispatched Palladius to Irish Christians in 431, but nothing more is known with regard to this mission. Since the seventh century, the Briton Patrick has been regarded as having been the founder of the Irish church.[8] The question as to what forces drove Christianisation forward outside the area of his missionary activity remains unanswered. At the age of fifteen, Patrick was carried off by Irish pirates from Britain to Ireland into slavery, but managed to escape back to his homeland six years later. A dream vision after his return summoned him to preach the gospel in Ireland and this he later did, having been ordained bishop in the British church. Unlike Palladius, he was not called to minister to Christians but rather to pagans. It is not clear whether prior to his ordination he also spent some time in Gaul. He himself states that he was temporarily absent from Britain. The differing biographical details concerning a lengthy stay on the mainland as given in the lives of Patrick by Tírechán and Muirchú (seventh century) only serve to complete the hagiographic portrait of the saint. The exact period during which he worked is disputed. Not only do the Irish annals offer differing dates for his death, but also their claim that he began his work in 432 can be seen simply as a later attempt to provide a chronological connection with the mission of Palladius. He was active in northern Ireland, but again the precise whereabouts of his activities cannot be determined. Patrick's work was met with hostility and he was forced to 'buy' his freedom of movement by

8 The only reliable sources are Patrick's own writings (SC 249); see also R. P. C. Hanson, *The life and writings of the historical Saint Patrick*.

making gifts to tribal kings and judges. His mission was aimed at all levels of society, including serfs. It also found resonance in the nobility and even among the families of tribal kings, but there is no evidence that any kings were themselves persuaded by it. The training of his helpers and clergy for their tasks was undertaken by Patrick in person.

A number of those converted by St Patrick led an ascetic life as 'monks' and 'virgins of Christ'. This did not, however, amount to the early foundation of monasteries; the group of ascetics remained a part of the bishops' congregation that was traditionally the basic element of ecclesiastical organisation. Each of these bishoprics was probably defined through allocation to one of the numerous small kingdoms (*túatha* (sing. *túath*)).

In the course of the sixth century, however, the Celtic churches were taken over by coenobitic monasticism, though its arrival and spread in the British Isles cannot be traced with any certainty. Illtud, a figure shrouded in legend, founded the Llantwit Major monastery (Glamorgan) as early as the late fifth century. The British monasteries of the sixth century include St Davids (Pembroke), Dol (Brittany) and Llancafarn (Glamorgan), and their founders, David, Samson and Cadoc, are thought to have been pupils of Illtud.

In Ireland, the convent of Kildare in Leinster, which – through the association of a monks' community – became a double monastery, was created at the early date of around 500. Its foundation is attributed to St Bridget. A number of notable monasteries were founded in the mid-sixth century: from a monastic school founded by Finnian, there emerged the monastery of Clonard (Meath). One of the country's largest monasteries was Clonmacnois (Offaly), established in central Ireland by Ciáran, and Comgall founded the monastery of Bangor (Down) at Belfast Lough, which was known for its strict rules.

The characteristic ideal of ascetic pilgrimage for the sake of Christ (*peregrinatio pro Christo*) is impressively embodied by the northern Irish monk Columban (Colum Cille, 'Dove of the Church'). In 563, he travelled from Ireland to the Scottish part of the Irish kingdom Dál Ríata, which lay on both sides of the North Channel (Antrim on the Irish side and Argyll, with the offshore islands, on the Scottish side). He established an influential monastery on the island of Iona (Inner Hebrides), and it was also from there that, with the agreement of the Pictish king Bruide mac Maelchon, he undertook missionary work among the northern Picts. Columban's close relationship to the kings of Dál Ríata also throws light on the political significance of Irish monasticism.[9] Motivated by the *peregrinatio* idea, Columban the Younger set off from Bangor around

---

9 P. Ní Chatháin, 'Columba'.

590 to the Frankish kingdom and founded there the monastery of Luxeuil in Burgundy.[10] He is often regarded as having paved the way for Irish missionary activity on the mainland. But the impact of this Irish mission tends to be overrated. The true significance of Columban's historical mission to the continent rather lies in his attracting from the very beginning a considerable following from among the Frankish nobility. As a result of this, Luxeuil became the starting point for an important movement of monastic renewal (the first in a long series of similar movements in later centuries) within the Frankish kingdom. This movement – which is often called 'Iro-Frankish' – was in fact no longer dependent on Irish monks.

The emergence of a dense net of monasteries created the framework for the blossoming of Irish Christian-monastic culture. It radiated throughout the whole of Western Europe. At the same time, the dissemination of monasticism had important consequences for local ecclesiastical organisation. Monasteries began to be involved in pastoral care, and more and more priests joined the monastic movement. Transcending political boundaries, groups of monasteries formed around those monastic centres that enjoyed a high reputation. These groups were characteristically called *paruchiae*, a term that originally referred either to an ecclesiastical province under a metropolitan bishop or to the diocese of a bishop. In some cases, at least, monastic *paruchiae* took the place of bishoprics. In the course of this process, the abbots, who frequently were either themselves also ordained bishops or who delegated the sacramental tasks of a bishop to a monk who was ordained bishop, took over the running of the church. In the British church, however, the organisation remained in the hands of bishops, many of whom lived in monastic communities and carried out their offices from monasteries. Early in the seventh century, seven British bishops confronted Augustine of Canterbury and refused to acknowledge the precedence that he claimed.

A number of characteristically Celtic church customs became controversial at this time, particularly the manner in which the date of Easter was calculated. The British and Irish followed their own traditions for this, traditions unknown elsewhere in Western Christianities. The issue came into focus at the beginning of the seventh century, when Augustine of Canterbury unsuccessfully asked the British bishops to abandon their method of calculating the date of Easter. Similarly, in the Frankish kingdom, Columban of Luxeuil met with hostility because of his Irish practice. The determination of the date of Easter is based on so-called Easter cycles. A cycle of this kind is a series of years following

10 K. Schäferdiek, 'Columbans Wirken im Frankenreich (591–612)'.

the completion of which the virtual spring full moon necessary for calculating the determination of Easter again falls on the same date as it did in the first year of the cycle that has just expired. The churches on the continent and in southern England used a cycle of nineteen years, whereas the British and Irish used one consisting of eighty-four years. In addition, other parameters for the dating of Easter were fixed differently. In most years, therefore, the Easter dates were divergent. Furthermore, when the situation arose, the Celts also held Easter on the day of the spring full moon itself and not on the following Sunday at the earliest, as was usual elsewhere. Outside the Celtic churches, this was considered not only a divergence in ritual but a heresy. It was seen (in fact, wrongly) as a renewal of the old Christian Quartodeciman practice of the second century. These differences were not resolved until the abandonment of Celtic practice, which occurred much later, during the period from about the middle of the seventh to the middle of the eighth century.

The beginning of Frankish and Anglian Christianities

The conversions of Clovis, king of the Franks, in the late fifth century, and of the Kentish king Æthelberht, in the last years of the sixth century, came to assume fundamental significance for the further development of Christianities in the West.

The Franks, a confederation of Germanic tribes, had emerged east of the lower Rhine in the third century. Following the fall of the Roman Rhine border at the beginning of the fifth century, they settled on Roman territory. Around the mid-fifth century, the Frankish settlement reached the river Somme, and in its course new political units with their own kings replaced the old tribes. Clovis initially ruled one such small kingdom, with its centre in Tournai, from 481/2. Only a few years later he had conquered the last remaining region still under Roman rule in northern Gaul. In this way, he extended his rule beyond the area of continuous Frankish settlements as far south as the river Loire, that is, into a zone in which the continuity of Roman Christianity had never been disrupted. He transferred his centre of power into this zone, first to Soissons and later to Paris.

Upon Clovis' accession to power, the metropolitan bishop Remigius of Reims had already attempted to impress on the king the virtues and duties of a Christian ruler and had offered him the co-operation of the Catholic episcopate. A more direct influence on Clovis was that of his wife Chrotechildis, who was Catholic despite being a niece of the Arian king of the Burgundians, Gundobad.

For Clovis, the religious debate between Christianity and paganism turned on the question as to which God was the stronger one, a concern that since the days of Constantine had generally occupied pagan rulers in considering a conversion to the new faith. After an unexpected victory in a battle that appeared to have already been lost, Clovis thought that he could answer the question in Christ's favour. The scales were finally tipped by an encounter with the cult of St Martin of Tours. This must have been an overwhelming experience for the king: St. Martin subsequently became the patron saint of Clovis and the Merovingian dynasty to which he belonged. Having consulted the leaders of his army, upon whose loyalty he was dependent, Clovis was baptised by Bishop Remigius in Reims at Christmas 498 or 499, together with numerous members of his army.[11]

On the occasion of his baptism, Clovis received a message of congratulation from Avitus of Vienne, the leading bishop of the time in the Burgundian kingdom. Avitus' letter indicates that Clovis regarded his baptism as constituting a new religious legitimisation of his rule. Later, in West Frankish and French tradition, the anointment by Remigius – a traditional part of the baptismal rites – was interpreted as being an anointment as a king.

No less than the Catholics surrounding Clovis, the Arians also hoped to win him over. His decision in favour of the Catholic side has often been seen as having a purely political rationale. One aim that held considerable political significance for him was the elimination of his most powerful political opponent in Gaul, the Visigothic kingdom. It is often claimed that his decision in favour of Catholic Christianity enabled him to enlist the support of Catholic Christians under Visigothic rule. However, the idea of the Catholic elite in the Visigoth kingdom sympathising with the Frankish opponent rests solely on Gregory of Tours's biased narrative. There are no facts to support it. Clovis' decision gained its significance from his transformation of the Frankish confederation into a powerful Frankish kingdom by ruthlessly eliminating all rival Frankish kings. This kingdom was able to achieve and, despite its weaknesses, retain a position of supremacy in Europe for a considerable period of time.

The comprehensive political re-mapping of Western Europe that resulted from the rise of various Germanic kingdoms brought about ecclesiastical fragmentation. Regional churches with their own traditions with regard to ecclesiastical law and liturgy emerged. During 511, Clovis summoned a council to meet at Orléans and its canons testify to the sovereignty in ecclesiastical

---

11 The alternative date of 507/8 is far less probable; cf. Dieter Geuenich, 'Chlodwigs Alemannenschlacht(en) und Taufe'.

affairs now claimed by the king and recognised by the bishops. In this way, the church of the Frankish kingdom came to constitute a new ecclesiastical unit. The Catholic bishops in the Visigothic kingdom had already embarked on a similar course and with the approval of the Arian king Alarich II, whom they included in their prayers, had presented themselves as a new autonomous church at the Council of Agde in 506. At the Third Council of Toledo in 589, the Spanish-Visigothic church also made its appearance as an autonomous body. The development of the Celtic church is another instance of the fragmentation of Western Christendom. In its wake, the significance of Rome's ecclesiastical position was, in fact, diminished.

However, it is already possible to discern the beginnings of a countervailing development in 664 at the so-called synod of Whitby, during the Northumbrian dispute over the date of Easter. King Oswiu of Northumbria decided that following the Roman model in matters of ecclesiastical practice was indispensable. For Oswiu, this was not the solution of a theoretical conflict of norms, but an issue of personal religious commitment to the more powerful patron, in this case St Peter, as a witness to Roman tradition. This orientation towards the Roman model was only the first stage in a protracted process that led, via the Bonifatian church reform in the Carolingian kingdom of the eighth century, to the formation of a Western Christianity centred on the papacy in Rome.

Remigius of Reims created the bishoprics of Arras and Tournai while Clovis (d. 511) was still alive, but this attempt to make inroads into the area of pagan Frankish settlement north of the river Somme was premature. It was not yet possible to maintain either of the bishoprics. Frankish Christianisation was initially limited to the ruling class close to the king and to those Franks living in the zone of Roman Christian continuity within the Merovingian kingdom. However, Christianity appears to have emerged relatively early in the southern German peripheral lands of the Frankish kingdom. The Bavarian dynasty of the Agilolfingians that was set up by the Franks in the mid-sixth century was probably Christian from the outset. Gold foil crosses of Lombard type are to be found in southern German burial sites dating from as early as the first half of the seventh century, providing indications of temporary Christian influences from Italy. In the early seventh century, in the vicinity of Bregenz on the eastern side of Lake Constance, Columban of Luxeuil encountered Alemans who were apparently baptised but were taking part in pagan celebrations.

Both in the pagan heartland of the Frankish kingdom and in its periphery, Christianity did not become established on a broad basis until the seventh century. The process of Christianisation was long in duration and to a considerable extent went hand in hand with the expansion, intensification and represen-tation of political power. The sources describing Clovis' change of religion show at an early stage the transferral to Christianity of the political and social functions of pre-Christian religion in securing a successful and prosperous life in this world. Some scholars have interpreted this process as a Germanisation of Christianity,[12] but this notion is not particularly helpful for understanding what had happened. Functional pre-Christian to Christian continuity is a gen-eral phenomenon in the history of the rise of Christianity, and can similarly be observed in other Christianities of the antique and late antique world. Moreover, the term 'Germanisation' suggests the mistaken romantic idea that nations are natural entities providing an unchanging setting for historical developments.[13]

In Britain, new political units were created in those areas that were con-quered during the course of the fifth century by invading Germanic tribes generally known as Anglo-Saxons. In the sixth century, a number of small kingdoms emerged. Among them, Kent in southern England obtained a posi-tion of supremacy in the late sixth century. The marriage of the Kentish king Æthelberht to the Merovingian princess Bertha, daughter of the Frankish king Charibert I and great-granddaughter of Clovis, indicates the existence of relations with the continent. A certain Frankish bishop called Liuthard was part of Bertha's entourage. He reconstructed a church located to the east of Canterbury that dated from Roman times (and is still standing today) for the holding of church services and dedicated it to the Merovingian patron St Martin of Tours.

However, the Christianisation of Kent was not due to the Frankish bishop Liuthard, but rather began with an initiative of Pope Gregory the Great. He planned and launched a long-distance mission to Anglo-Saxon England, a novel enterprise without precedent in the history of late antique Christianities. A legend has been spun around his motives for doing so,[14] but he had certainly received information from Kent. In 596, he dispatched to England a group of Roman monks under the direction of the abbot Augustine. At the same time,

12 James C. Russell, *The Germanization of early medieval Christianity*.
13 Cf. Patrick J. Geary, *The myth of nations*.
14 Cf. *The earliest Life of Gregory the Great, by an anonymous monk of Whitby* 9 (ed. Colgrave, 90–3): Gregory met young Anglians at the Roman slave market and considered the names of their people, their king, and their kingdom a call to mission: *Anguli* – *Angeli Dei* (Anglians – God's angels), *Aelli* – *Alleluja. Laus enim Dei esse debet illic* (Ælle (king of Deira) – Hallelujah, the praise of God should be said there), *Deire* – *De ira Dei confugientes ad fidem* (Deira (between Humber and Tees) – from the wrath of God they take refuge to faith). For a slightly different version, see Bede, *Ecclesiastical history* 3.1 (eds. Colgrave and Mynors, 132–5).

he requested support for his mission from the Merovingian kings, asking them to supply Frankish clergymen to serve as interpreters for Augustine and his men. Augustine himself appears to have been ordained bishop by a Frankish bishop while on his way to Kent. The group landed in Kent in 597. Based in Canterbury, they set about their work and, by Christmas of that same year, Æthelberht and a large number of Kentish people had already received baptism. As the see for the bishopric, Augustine made use of a former Romano-British church in Canterbury. Like the episcopal church of Rome (today, S. Giovanni in Laterano) it was dedicated to the Saviour (Christ Church). He also founded a monastery dedicated to St Peter for the monastic cathedral clergy, which provided the basis for further work.

In 601, Gregory sent additional helpers to Kent who brought with them a very ambitious plan to renew the Britannic church according to a preconceived ideal. Augustine was to create a church province for the whole of England, with Canterbury and York as its centres. The British bishops were also to be included. Furthermore, Gregory demanded from the king that the pagan cult be suppressed and its shrines destroyed. However, a second letter that followed close on the heels of the first one amended these demands. It contains Gregory's much-quoted missionary instruction to Augustine and recommends a persuasive rather than coercive method as the right strategy. Temples were to be transformed into churches and sacrificial festivals into the days of saints and martyrs.

It is, however, doubtful whether this instruction had much impact on missionary practice. About twenty-five years later King Edwin of Northumbria converted to Christianity under Kentish influence. As a result of this, an apparently well-known centre of pagan worship in Goodmanham (East Riding) was burnt down and not replaced by a church. In early medieval mission, the destruction of pagan shrines remained commonplace. The fact that Christian churches were erected on sites that were formerly occupied by a pagan cult centre marked a disruption of traditional pagan religion and a new beginning and is thus a sign of religious discontinuity rather than continuity.

The involvement of Frankish clergy in the early Roman mission to Kent had a lasting impact. These Franks were probably responsible for bringing to England a group of elementary Christian loan words shared by the English and German languages. They include, for example, the word *church* (Scottish *kirk*, Old English *cirice*, German *Kirche* [Old High German *kirihha*], from the vulgar Latin **cirica*).

Although Augustine's actual achievements were modest in comparison to Gregory's ambitious plans, they were still remarkable. Augustine managed to extend his Kentish base by establishing a second bishopric in Rochester. Moreover, he was able to win over King Sæberht of Essex, who was related to Æthelberht, and with his help also to build a church dedicated to St Paul in London (the first predecessor of St Paul's Cathedral) and set up a bishopric there.[15] Augustine did not live to see the collapse of the mission in Essex, following the death of Kings Æthelberht and Sæberht around 618. Nor did he see how the continued existence of the Kentish church was for a time jeopardised by a pagan reaction. Ultimately the Kentish church was able to hold its ground. This brought lasting consequences for the shape of English Christianity, even though, in the broader perspective, Canterbury was to recede in significance as compared to other forces involved in the dramatic seventh-century history of Anglo-Saxon Christianisation.

References

PRIMARY SOURCES

Bede. *Ecclesiastical history*. Eds. Bertram Colgrave and R. A. B. Mynors, *Bede's ecclesiastical history of the English people* (Oxford, 1969)
The earliest Life of Gregory the Great, by an anonymous monk of Whitby, ed. Bertram Colgrave (Cambridge, 1985)
Patrick. *Confession and letter to Coroticus* (SC 249)

SECONDARY SOURCES

Böhme, Horst Wolfgang. 'Goldblattkreuze', in *Reallexikon der germanischen Altertumskunde* (Berlin, 1998), XII: 312–18
Brennecke, Hanns Christof. 'Der sog. germanische Arianismus als, arteigenes' Christentum,' in Thomas Kaufmann and Harry Oelke, eds., *Evangelische Kirchenhistoriker im 'Dritten Reich'* (Gütersloh, 2002), 310–29
Charles-Edwards, Thomas Mowbray. *Early Christian Ireland* (Cambridge, 2000)
Cusack, Carole M. *The rise of Christianity in Northern Europe 300–1000* (London, 1998)
Dumville, David N., ed. *Saint Patrick* (Woodbridge, 1993)
Fletcher, Richard. *The conversion of Europe: From paganism to Christianity 371–1386 AD* (London, 1997)
Geary, Patrick J. *The myth of nations. The medieval origins of Europe* (Princeton, 2002)
Geuenich, Dieter. 'Chlodwigs Alemannenschlacht(en) und Taufe', in *Die Franken und die Alemannen bis zur 'Schlacht bei Zülpich' (496/97)* (Berlin/New York, 1998), 423–37
Hanson, R. P. C. *The life and writings of the historical Saint Patrick* (New York, 1983)

---

15 In 2003, the undisturbed burial site of a Saxon ruler was discovered at Prittlewell (Southend-on-Sea, Essex); it is probably King Sæberht who was buried there. The grave goods included two gold foil crosses as hitherto only found in Lombard Italy and southern Germany. For the time being, the information is on the home page of the Museum of London Archaeology Service (www.molas.org.uk).

Hill, Peter. *Whithorn and St. Ninian: The excavation of a monastic town 1984–91* (Stroud, 1995)

Hughes, Kathleen. *The church in early Irish society* (London, 1966; reprint: 1980)

Jedin, Hubert and John Dolan. *Handbook of church history* (London, 1980)

Lexikon des Mittelalters (Munich, 1980–98) (with numerous informative contributions)

Mayr-Harting, Henry. *The coming of Christianity to Anglo-Saxon England* (London, 1991[3])

Ní Chatháin, Próinséas. 'Columba', *Theologische Realenzyklopädie* (Berlin, 1981), VIII: 154–9

Opitz, Stephan. *Südgermanische Runeninschriften im älteren Futhark aus der Merowingerzeit* (Kirchzarten, 1980[2])

Pearce, Susan Mary, ed. *The early church in western Britain and Ireland*, BAR British series 102 (Oxford, 1982)

Russell, James C. *The Germanization of early medieval Christianity: A sociohistorical approach to religious transformation* (Oxford, 1994)

Scardigli, Piergiuseppe. 'Das Bleitäfelchen von Hács-Béndekpuszta', in Wilhelm Streitberg, ed., *Die gotische Bibel* (Heidelberg, 2000[7]), 507–15

Schäferdiek, Knut. 'Die Anfänge des Christentums bei den Goten und der sog. gotische Arianismus', *ZKG* 112 (2001): 295–310

'Columbans Wirken im Frankenreich (591–612)', in Heinz Löwe ed., *Die Iren und Europa im früheren Mittelalter* (Stuttgart, 1982), I: 171–201 (= Schäferdiek, Knut, *Schwellenzeit* (Berlin/New York, 1996), 349–79)

'Germanenmission', *Reallexikon für Antike und Christentum* 10 (Berlin, 1978): 492–548

'Gotische Literatur. § 3. Das Kalenderfragment', *Reallexikon der germanischen Altertumskunde* (1998[2]), XII: 451–3

Thomas, Antony Charles. *The early Christian archaeology of north Britain* (London, 1971)

Christianity in Roman Britain to AD 500 (London, 1981)

Wallace-Hadrill, John Michael. *The Frankish church* (Oxford, 1983)

3

Greek Christianities

FREDERICK W. NORRIS

Apologists and, perhaps, a few believers dreamed that their religion might be politically favoured, but most Christians had experienced too many political nightmares to cherish such hopes. The emperor Diocletian's persecution (303–11) had given no hint of what was in store. He was a convinced follower of traditional religions, one who made no momentous military plans without discovering the will of the gods. The pagan priests warned that his whole campaign against the Persians was endangered because they could not read the gods' signs while there were Christians in the court. That such people were at court indicates their rise within Roman political and cultural circles; that they could be dismissed and persecuted shows how tenuous their positions were. All of them were expendable. Lactantius' personal reflections tell us of the palace intrigue, but a Coptic martyrology speaks of high-ranking Christian families in Antioch, members of the city council and generals in the legions based outside the city, who were exiled and put to death in Egypt. These persons were both religiously and politically too strong to be left within Diocletian's base of supplies and troops for eastern battles.[1]

Constantine did not choose Christianity because it brought him a majority of those within his rule. The reasons for his inclusion of that faith in the 313 decision of Milan about religious toleration are multiple and ambiguous. His vision at the Milvian Bridge provided a view of the Christian god who gave him victory. Yet his killing members of his own family indicates that he did not understand much about the virtues demanded by his new faith. The 'Edict of Milan' concerned toleration, meaning only that Christians were now included

---

1 *Acta martyrum*, ed. Hyvernat; D. L. O'Leary, *The Saints of Egypt*, 79–80, 101–3, 135–6; H. Delehay, 'Les martyrs d'Égypt'. Because the texts are in Bohairic, a late version of Coptic, they might be medieval challenges to Muslim rulers, or fictionalised attacks by Miaphysite Christians on Chalcedonian Roman rulers after 451, but some dates, places and names fit the Diocletian persecution.

among the authorised religions. Previous pagan emperors were somewhat curious about Christianity; some had persecuted it. But none of them had converted or had worked to make the religion officially sanctioned.

Christians and those who worshipped within other Hellenistic religions were shocked by the results of his choice. Lactantius (c. 250–c. 325) and Eusebius of Caesarea (c. 260–c. 339) had prepared themselves and others to live within a hostile environment and prevail through patience and active care of each other and their neighbours. On the one hand many truths and important categories for understanding the culture were taken over as a part of Christian life and theology. On the other, resistance to Greco-Roman religions and much of the culture was also a necessary part of Christian existence. Now both Lactantius and Eusebius scrambled to revise their views in order to catch up with this new emperor.[2]

Constantine became the subject of fawning praise from Eusebius. The emperor supported the construction of large Christian buildings in a number of Eastern cities and gave money for other projects. His mother was instrumental in selecting holy sites, particularly in Jerusalem, to be hallowed by great churches. Yet, for the 'orthodox', problems resulted from Constantine's decision to delay baptism and his final acceptance of the sacrament at the hands of an 'Arian' bishop, though they welcomed him for providing a new future and relief from persecution. For worldwide Christianity, however, the consequences of his actions were not always so welcome. Because he favoured Christians in his empire and yet allowed other religions, he saw fit to write a cautioning letter to the Persian ruler urging him also to tolerate Christians in Persia. (As far as we know there was no such letter asking for mercy toward Roman citizens worshipping Greco-Roman gods or perhaps traders who kept their religions privately.) The result was horrid. Persians persecuted Christians even more fiercely because they deduced that Constantine saw himself as the protector of Christians even in Persia. What more evidence for a threat of internal revolution did any sensible ruler need?[3]

Strictly speaking, Christianity in any of its forms did not become the single established religion of the Roman empire under Constantine. Well after his

---

2 Eusebius' *Life of Constantine* is exultant in tone, far above his more sombre mood in the *H. E.* Lactantius' *Institutes* describes Diocletian's persecution, but primarily views the beginnings of Constantine's changes.

3 Constantine, *Epistle to Sapor* in Theodoret, *Ecclesiastical history* 1.25. For the persecutions of Persian Christians, see chapter 4, below.

conversion the emperor supported a priest of the Eleusian mystery. His coinage consistently depicted the sun god whom he may still have worshipped. The emperor had a statue of the pagan ascetic and healer, Apollonius of Tyana, in his palace. During his reign, however, Constantine sometimes destroyed pagan worship centres by having his troops defile the sacred places and tear off their doors. He thought of their worship as superstition.[4] In the end, it was his overwhelming economic support of Christianity, not his endorsement of any religious consequences of the legal status granted Christians, that weakened the worship of the Greco-Roman pantheon. The sacrifices and the upkeep for priests and temples were expensive. Mild toleration did not secure the needed monies.

Constantine's most stunning achievement was moving the capital of the empire from Rome in the West to his new city in the East. The reasons were many. A large population under Roman control inhabited the Eastern Mediterranean, and the empire's most dangerous enemy was Persia. Troops stationed at Constantinople could move to Syria even more quickly than when they were in Milan. Troubles within some of the eastern provinces occurred frequently and required a response. Thus, having the centre of the empire in the East was more efficient.

He founded his capital city in 324 on the site of the more ancient and less noteworthy Byzantium. Its position on the promontory was easily defended and linked to both land and sea. The new capital, the new Rome, Constantinople, would eventually claim prestige among Christians worldwide through its talented patriarchs, councils, theological literature, liturgical developments, art and architecture, as well as its many monasteries. It became so prominent that within the materials we have from late antiquity, it overshadowed most other eastern Christian centres. Christian emperors in Constantinople tried their hands at determining 'true Christianity'.

From the church's perspective, the city's new layout created in turning Byzantium into Constantinople was remarkable and thrilling. Pagan temples were excluded from the city. A grand Christian basilica, Hagia Sophia, and other churches were raised in prominent places in the metropolis. Constantine's request to Eusebius (331) that the bishop-scholar have fifty Bibles made for the churches in Constantinople indicates the seriousness of his intentions to promote Christianity.[5]

---

4 T. D. Barnes, *Constantine and Eusebius*, 208–12.
5 Eusebius, *Life of Constantine* 4.36; T. Mathews, *The early churches of Constantinople*, describes some of those churches.

Nicaea (325)

One of the earliest well-known theologians in our period was Arius (256–336), born in Libya, educated in Antioch under the martyr Lucian and adjudged an archheretic at Nicaea. He had been a deacon, then a priest serving at the Baucalis Church in Alexandria. In Alexandria, priests had the unusual distinction of selecting the bishop of the city (elsewhere, this role was reserved for other bishops), so Arius was in a very prominent position. As an interesting theologian, an influential preacher and a composer of songs he caused quite a stir. Philostorgius, a church historian sympathetic to Arius, said that the lyrics were written 'for the sea, for the mill, for the road and then set to music'.[6] Some of this poetry is partly included in his *Thalia*. He not only argued biblically and philosophically for his cause but also brilliantly contextualised his theology for the masses.

His view that the Son of God was a secondary divinity, not of the same nature as the Father, was persuasive to some. According to him, the Son did not exist before time. That left the monotheism of his Christianity intact; only the one high God, the Father, ruled. He developed an earlier theological tendency of subordinating the Son to the Father. While his project may have seemed new in the fourth-century philosophical setting, it appealed to some skilled rationalists as well as some simpler folk. Whatever salvation was, for these people it did not demand that Jesus Christ's divinity be of the same essence as that of the Father. Arianism grew in Alexandria among a number of Christians. Priests elsewhere in the empire agreed with Arius.[7]

After Alexander (d. 328), bishop of Alexandria when Arius' teaching emerged, had held a synod in the city during 318 in which one hundred Egyptian bishops condemned those views and withdrew Arius' ordination and that of his ordained followers in Egypt, Arius paid little attention to the decision; he appealed to friends in the eastern Mediterranean who had been students of Lucian in Antioch. Eusebius of Nicomedia (d. 342), one of those friends, supported Arius fully. The problems that arose from Arius' teachings were such that Constantine decided to intervene. He did so by calling for an assembly at Nicaea in 325 to resolve the disputes. With Nicaea, Constantine enlarged the conception of church councils to represent unifying decisions for all Christians in the empire. He supplied postal wagons to transport bishops to Nicaea, as well as food and lodging during their trips. While they were in the city he took care of their needs and provided a large building for their sessions.

6 A. Martin, *Athanase d'Alexandrie*, 189–91; Philostorgius, *H. E.* 2.2.
7 R. Williams, *Arius: Heresy and tradition*, esp. 95–178.

We know neither how many bishops attended the Nicene council (perhaps 220–50), nor exactly who presided. Ossius of Cordova, a Western bishop who advised Constantine, might have been the president but only eight Western bishops participated. A few leaders east of Antioch attended, including some Armenians, Jacob of Nisibis and John of Persia.[8] Ancyra had been the site proposed by bishops at an Antiochene synod during 324, but Nicaea was selected because it was closer to the West and nearby Nicomedia, then Constantine's political capital. He himself was active in the proceedings because he believed, as did many previous emperors, that a united religious pillar helped uphold the government. Early drafts of the Nicene Creed depended on baptismal creeds, perhaps most directly that of Jerusalem rather than Eusebius' Caesarean Creed. In any case the position of Alexander of Alexandria won the day. Constantine promulgated the twenty canons from the council that dealt especially with the life of the clergy and with the administration of baptism, ordination and eucharistic communion.[9] As for Arius, the dominant group at the council rejected him and he was sent away. But in 328, Constantine brought him back from exile in Illyricum. Synods in Tyre and Jerusalem during 335 declared him an orthodox Christian and acknowledged him once again as part of the clergy. Constantine demanded that the bishop of Constantinople accept Arius, but Arius died suddenly in 336.

When Alexander died, Athanasius, a presbyter, became bishop of Alexandria. He had been active before Nicaea in the battle against Arius, but after Nicaea he was probably the most important supporter of its decisions. Tenacious in his views, but also capable of developing them further, he wrote not only against Arius, but also in favour of what he considered the orthodox faith. Although he was tried for killing a man, the evidence being a severed hand, his 'secret service' found the man and presented him to the court alive with both hands. Exiled five times by emperors (335, 339–46, 356–61, 363, 365/6), when he was sent out of Egypt he used those opportunities to promote his teaching, particularly among Christian leaders in the West. He appeared to be the rock from which Nicene orthodoxy was hewn. During his time as bishop, he fought pagans as well as Arians.[10]

The Meletian schism was another Egyptian difficulty dealt with at Nicaea. Its leader, Meletius, agitated for a stricter policy about accepting into the church those who gave church material to Roman troops or sacrificed to the gods

---

8 See chapter 4, below.
9 *Decrees of the ecumenical councils*, ed. and trans. Tanner I: 1–4; J. N. D. Kelly, *Early Christian creeds*, 211–30.
10 Theodoret, *H. E.* 1.30; K. Anatolios, *Athanasius*.

during the Diocletian persecution. So he ordained a group of his followers as bishops to keep the 'pure' church alive. Peter, bishop of Alexandria, then excommunicated both him and his new bishops. But further persecution by the government had led to Peter being martyred and Meletius being sent off to the mines. When Meletius returned, he continued working to keep the uncontaminated line of bishops and followers in place. The Council of Nicaea decided that Meletian bishops could serve under Alexander of Alexandria, and take the place of any 'Catholic' bishop who died and left the bishopric vacant. But when Athanasius became bishop of Alexandria, this solution broke down and the Meletians continued their schismatic churches. They lasted throughout our period within both congregations and monasteries. In a number of ways this schism resembled that of the Donatists in North Africa, but apparently with much less violence involved.[11]

After Nicaea

Athanasius continued to battle for the Nicene cause. He also wrote a propagandistic *Life* of Anthony, one of the first monks in Egypt. For Athanasius Anthony stood against Arius, a questionable claim, but the rest of the *Life* seems trustworthy. Letters that Anthony wrote indicate his strong Trinitarian position. When he decided to abandon his former life, he made arrangements for his orphaned sister and went to the desert. As he left the village he passed monks already following that life at the edge of his village.[12] Indeed, some monks and nuns of the fourth century lived within cities not villages. In about 315, Amoun (d. c. 350) had gone from Alexandria to the desert around Mt Nitria in the Nile delta, leaving his wife from an arranged continent marriage. She stayed put and organised her urban household into a convent.[13]

Early Egyptian monasticism depended upon the social climate of the country. Farmers could be displaced from their fields because of weather or in some areas by raiding desert tribes. Monasteries early and late drew from the displaced as well as those well established. The call to the disciplined life of a monk, whether as an itinerant, a hermit or in a community (*koinobion*), attracted people who could neither read nor write. Yet educated people retreated to the quiet places in order to pursue investigations of what troubled them religiously. That early Egyptian monasticism was educationally and

---

11 R. Williams, 'Arius and the Meletian schism', has demonstrated that there is no proven connection between Arius and the Meletians.
12 See chapter 27, below.
13 J. Goehring, *Ascetics, society and the desert*, 122–3.

socially mixed provides an interesting context for its development. Monastic wisdom is not limited to giving special revelations to *hoi polloi*, although visions and good sense among the poor and informally educated is often present, as the *Sayings of the desert fathers* show.[14]

Nicenes under fire

By the end of Constantine's reign, the interweaving of government and church was well under way. Many Christians were relieved that persecution had ended; emperors were pleased to have a growing religious power that supported imperial political and military rule. Constantine's sons moved back and forth from Nicene to Arian sympathies, however, and thus left the sense of Christian unity quite unsettled.

The life of Nicene bishops after Nicaea could be difficult. During this period Cyril of Jerusalem (d. 387) was born into a Christian family in Palestinian Caesarea and rose through the ranks of Christian leadership. He was favoured by his metropolitan, Acacius, bishop of Caesarea (*sed.* 341–65). Early on, Acacius was an Arian and thought that Cyril leaned in that direction, so he was happy to put Cyril forward as a candidate for bishop of Jerusalem. Acacius eventually claimed to be Nicene, but ultimately returned to his previous view.[15] There is no evidence that Cyril ever was an Arian. Perhaps he quietly allowed Acacius to think that he was.[16]

His twenty-four catechetical lectures, given in Jerusalem probably in 350, offer an important glimpse into church life in the Holy City. In these lectures, presented during Lent primarily to baptismal candidates, Cyril first welcomes them while noting the need for secrecy as well as the demand for penance, prayer, self-discipline, forgiveness of others and reading the Bible in preparation for baptism. For him the whole process of salvation remains a mystery. The fourth lecture summarises Christian doctrine; the fifth deals with the beginnings and nature of faith. The next twelve use the Jerusalem Creed as an outline.

Acacius' confrontation with Cyril irrupted in 354–5 after Cyril had sold liturgical vessels to feed the poor. Acacius accused him of embezzlement, called a synod in Caesarea during 357 and insisted that Cyril explain himself. Cyril refused to attend because he did not trust Acacius, particularly after he had deceived him. The synod condemned Cyril; he went to Tarsus and was well treated there. The emperor restored him to the throne of Jerusalem in

14 *The sayings of the desert fathers*, trans. Ward.
15 Jerome, *Lives of illustrious men*, 98.
16 J. W. Drijvers, *Cyril of Jerusalem: Bishop and city*, 32–42.

359, but Acacius went to Constantinople the next year, denounced Cyril and got him removed again. Then in 361 the emperor Julian had Cyril reinstated in Jerusalem, most probably to ensure that there would be disruptions among Christians in the city where Christ died and was raised.[17]

Another defender of the Nicene faith was Serapion of Thmuis in Egypt (d. after 362), a confidant of Athanasius. Letters to him from Athanasius contain one of the first serious discussions of the Holy Spirit. Yet strikingly Serapion never uses *homoousios*, 'of the same nature', the Nicene technical term for describing the Son's relationship to the Father. He seems to have been influenced by some of Origen's statements about hell (Origen rejected the salvation of the devil),[18] for he thinks of it as a place where the lost are taught. He may also offer the first view of the growing Christian cult of relics.[19] He also fought against Manichaeans and showed signs of familiarity with their teachings. His work proved helpful to others in the refutation of this pagan religion or heresy, but sadly for all he had not read lengthy treatises, but only selections that left much of Manichaean doctrine unclear.[20]

The emperor Julian

The largest threat to the growing prestige and power of all Christianities appeared in the emperor Julian's attempt to revive paganism. Few, however, knew to watch the developing religious programmes of Julian (*regn.* 360–3). Basil of Caesarea (330–79) and Gregory of Nazianzus (*c.* 330–90) had studied with him in Athens; they both attacked him and his views. Julian had grown up in an atmosphere in which 'Christian' leaders were his enemies: their government had killed members of his family. He had no reason to think that he should adhere to Christian faith and practice. During his education in Ephesus, one of his mentors was a philosopher who had not given up on the ancient Greco-Roman pantheon; indeed he evidently saw the best philosophy tied to those gods. The Christian bishop in charge of Julian's studies may well have been a closet pagan, as were some important bishops elsewhere, like Pegasius, who only emerged publicly to express their allegiance to the ancient rites when Julian was proclaimed emperor.[21] Men with Hellenistic educations

---

17 See the translations *St. Cyril of Jerusalem's lectures on the Christian sacraments*, ed. Cross and *Saint Cyrille de Jérusalem: Catéchèse*, trans. Paulin; *Cyril of Jerusalem. Mystagogue*, trans. Doval, argues that the piece is Cyril's.

18 F. Norris, 'Origen'.

19 Jerome, *Lives of illustrious men* 99.

20 K. Fitschen, *Serapion von Thmuis*, 23–57, sees Serapion as a good witness for Egyptian Manichaeism, but Serapion does not seem to have known primary Manichaean texts, only summaries. See further chapter 11, below.

21 Julian, *Letter* 19.

and positions did not always convert to Christian faith when they were made bishops. Some took the posts and kept sacrificing privately to the traditional gods.

Julian sought to revitalise the Greco-Roman religions. He cast his interpretation of the toleration laws brilliantly. Because all religions should have equal opportunities for worship, as the 'Edict of Milan' had made clear, the renewal of traditional Hellenistic religion should have its chance. For the rebirth to proceed, temples would be rebuilt and opened. Yet to be reconstructed, each pagan community had the right to reclaim its site and particularly the expensive columns that had formed its temples. Julian well knew that such rebuilding required the destruction of many Christian edifices because both their sites and much of their building material had been taken from the pagans.[22]

Julian's assessment of Christianity changed only slightly during his reign and then primarily in relationship to features of Christian communities that he thought his revived religion needed. The Galileans, as he called Christians, failed miserably because they had no sacrifice at the heart of their worship. Talk of Christ assuming that function once for all was ludicrous. Even Judaism continued such offerings and thus was much more like Hellenistic faiths. Julian sent money and hired workers to rebuild the Temple in Jerusalem, but what was possibly a gas pocket created a large fire and the project was stopped. Had Julian lived longer he might well have begun again. He was a consequential man.

What intrigued him about Christians was their help for those in trouble: the poor, hungry, sick, disabled. Indeed he was angry that these ritually and theologically deficient groups took care not only of their own needy but almost any who were vulnerable. By Julian's estimation, unless his reform could better serve such folks than Christians did, it would die at birth.[23] There is no more powerful witness to the strength of Christian social activity in the mid-fourth century than Julian. He stands in the line of Maximinus Daia (d. 313), the imperial usurper, who had tried to stamp out the church in Syria and Egypt. Maximinus, too, had wanted to restore paganism and its priests, perhaps even create a pagan church.[24]

Julian also mounted what many then and some today would consider a sound argument against having any Christian on the rolls of public school teachers. Surely everyone understood that doing justice to any literature demanded that the values of those writings be accepted and passionately

---

22 *Ammianus Marcellinus*, trans. Rolfe, 22.5.2–4.
23 Julian, *Letter* 22.
24 Eusebius *H.E.* 8.14.7–9 and 9.9.11–12; P. Keresztes, 'From the Great Persecution to the Peace of Galerius'.

taught. No one could tutor Greek classics without espousing the philosophy and religion imbedded within them. Julian's point probably combined personal conviction with political opportunism.[25] These decisions put all Christian leaders on alert. Apollinaris the elder and his son Apollinaris (*c.* 315–92) of Christological fame – who taught that there could be no human mind or will in Christ because that would make him fallible – insisted that they would cast the Bible into Greek verse and dialogues. In this way, the importance of Hellenic and Hellenistic culture would sing in the minds and hearts of Christian children. Their communities had just as much right to Greek literature as did any of Julian's followers. A series of Christian theologians produced new apologies that attacked 'Julian the Apostate' with the most virulent rhetoric they could muster. The prospect of having their churches pulled down and their access to Greek *paideia* denied was terrifying. Some scholars have considered Gregory Nazianzen's two orations against Julian to be exceptionally skilled invective.[26] The hatred of Christians for Julian, however, is most clearly seen in how Sozomen dealt with the emperor's fatal campaign in Persia. He quoted the pagan Libanius who insisted that a Christian among his own troops killed Julian. The tale, true or not, was told with pride in some Christian circles.[27]

Cappadocians

Gregory the Wonderworker (*c.* 210–60), a former student of Origen in Caesarea, had worked in Cappadocia. He probably baptised Macrina the Elder, the grandmother of Basil the Great (d. 379), his brother Gregory of Nyssa (331/40–95) and their sister Macrina the Younger (*c.* 327–79/80). Eustathius of Sebaste (*c.* 300–*c.* 380) seems to have begun the first monastic communities in Asia Minor. He was also responsible for the first hospice and for a time had an influence on at least Basil.[28] The brothers Basil and Gregory and their friend Gregory Nazianzen 'the Theologian' (d. 390) became theologians of international consequence. They began their Christian education and care in solid families and the lively congregations to which they belonged.[29]

Gregory the Theologian's mother, Nonna, eventually converted his father, Gregory the Elder. The elder Gregory came from a wealthy family that belonged to the Hypsistarii, whose religion seems to have been formed from

---

25 *CTh* 13.3–5; Julian, *Letter* 22; for a pagan and two Christian views, see also *Emperor Julian*, trans. Lieu.
26 G. Kennedy, *Greek rhetoric*, 221–3.
27 Sozomen, *H.E.* 6.1; W. R. Chalmers, 'Eunapius, Ammianus Marcellanus and Zosimos'.
28 W. D. Hauschild, 'Eustathius von Sebaste'.
29 J. Pelikan, *Christianity and classical culture*.

Jewish, Persian and Greco-Roman elements. The family disowned him when Nonna led him to Christianity, but the child Gregory would have had personal experience with at least this type of paganism. Perhaps that was one reason why he turned to writing the incendiary orations against Julian and his reign,[30] and to warning Christians about all paganism. Late in life Gregory wrote a considerable amount of poetry, all of it meant to show Christians how to keep the faith and to claim Greek *paideia* as theirs. Close reading of his orations at various places shows how penetrating a logician he was. He consistently argued for the Trinity.[31] He was the second president of the Constantinopolitan council of 381, but he resigned under duress.

As might be expected with their connection to Gregory the Wonderworker, the Cappadocians were among the strongest defenders of Origen. Formerly numbered as the three men, without the sister of Basil and Gregory of Nyssa, they should now be spoken of as four. What we know of Macrina the Younger appears primarily in a treatise Gregory of Nyssa wrote to honour her as well as to offer her insights on the resurrection and suffering. In that work he constantly refers to Macrina as his teacher on those and other topics.[32] We have many letters from Basil and Gregory Nazianzen that tell us much about the issues of the day. All four of them are not understandable without paying attention to their appropriation and adjustment of Origenian themes. Although only one line directly names the *Philokalia* as selections from Origen assembled by Gregory Nazianzen and Basil, they were likely its editors. Both of them had read much of Origen's corpus, as can be seen in their writings. Basil prepared nine fascinating sermons on the six days of creation. The Theologian has only one oration that is focused primarily on the exegesis of a particular text, while Gregory of Nyssa commented on the *Song of Solomon*. Perhaps their biblical commentaries are few because Origen had written so much. Most of their efforts are either orations or thematic essays of various sizes.

The Theologian's greatest theological disagreement with the council of 381 was over its doctrine of the Holy Spirit. He insisted that the Spirit should be called 'God' in public worship. (Basil wrote against the Neo-Arians who were being attacked at the council and produced a fine volume on the Holy Spirit, but naming the Spirit 'God' in public was not his practice.) Within

30 Gregory Nazianzen, *Ors.* 4 and 5.
31 F. Norris, *Faith gives fullness to reasoning*; B. Daley, *Gregory of Nazianzus*.
32 E. Clark, 'The lady vanishes', suggests that Gregory of Nyssa sent up a trial balloon rather than offering information about his sister's theology. S. Elm, '*Virgins of God*', finds Macrina quite important, perhaps even influencing Basil the Great's grasp of monasticism since her ascetic community came first.

Gregory's writings is an oration on the priesthood that both John Chrysostom and Gregory the Great used for their musings on pastoral care. He was also concerned about the downtrodden. Another oration encouraged Christians to care for the poor and lepers because Jesus Christ died for them. Leprosy might be a punishment for sin, but it was a burden that only the most spiritually mature could bear.[33]

That latter piece provided the rationale and the fund-raising effort behind the great social project that Basil built outside Cappadocian Caesarea.[34] Basil's wealthy family owned land just beyond the city's limits, on which Basil built a monastery, a church, a bishop's residence and a hospice. In the beginning the hospice served primarily as a way station for pilgrims, but because it provided them with lodging, food and any necessary medical treatment it was already prepared to assist those in difficulty. During a widespread and severe famine in the region during the 370s, the hospice became a hospital for the needy. The emperor Valens (*regn.* 364–78), who had quarrelled with both Basil and his friend Gregory, eventually sent funds because he knew the hospice could efficiently help in ways his own administration could not. Thousands were served. The programme was so successful and thus so highly honoured that by the seventh century the bustling centre of Caesarea had moved out to Basil's compound. The ancient Roman city withered away.[35] The hospice became a model for hospitals elsewhere in the East.

Gregory of Nyssa authored a number of pieces mostly centred on theological problems. His attacks were most potent against Eunomius' claims that the Son was not of the same nature as the Father. Gregory of Nyssa went beyond the other Cappadocians. His spiritual insights are perhaps the deepest and, of all the Cappadocians, his were the most often followed in later history.[36]

Monasticism was a strong concern among this group. Both Basil and Gregory Nazianzen were celibate. They originally thought about building a small retreat in Pontus, but forsook that plan. Basil had left his studies in Athens early to visit monasteries in Egypt, Palestine, Syria, and perhaps along the Euphrates. Once threatened by a Roman official because he did not follow the emperor's commands, Basil replied that the threats were ridiculous: he had no money, his clothes were rags and his body nearly worn out, so what could the man take from him? Greek tradition has credited Basil with both

---

33 Gregory Nazianzen, *Or.* 14.
34 J. McGuckin, *St. Gregory of Nazianzus*, 147–55. Although it is probably the programmatic oration for the creation of Basil's centre, it is strong enough to stand on its own.
35 B. Daley, 'Building a new city'.
36 A. Meredith, *The Cappadocians*; M. Azkoul, *St. Gregory of Nyssa*.

monastic rules and common liturgies. Some are genuine. The Theologian entered the ascetic community of St Thecla near Seleucia when he thought he needed time for more rigorous contemplation. Women in the family were also involved. Basil's mother and his sister Macrina headed a convent that drew poorer women from the streets to better lives and purposefully treated all equally.

Neo-Arians

The great theological opponents of the Cappadocians were Aetius of Antioch (c. 300–70) and Eunomius of Cyzicus (c. 325–c. 395). Aetius was an accomplished logician and theologian whose positions formed the backbone of what is often called Neo-Arianism. He probably did not come from a Christian home and was originally trained as a goldsmith, but his curiosity and intellectual gifts led to his going beyond positions taught by Arius' friends in the metropolis. Aetius was ordained a deacon under Leontius of Antioch during 344–5. Involved in imperial political machinations, he was exiled in 354 because of his friendship with Caesar Gallus; later he was brought back by Julian the Apostate, Gallus' brother. Aetius left public life after the revolt of Procopius, a cousin of Julian. Following his death, Eunomius, his secretary, buried him in Constantinople. Aetius' philosophical and logical acuity can be seen in his collection of theological puzzles. They have led some to think of Neo-Arianism as entirely a philosophical-theological school, but a number of its participants were bishops, not singularly philosophers.[37]

Eunomius came from similarly humble circumstances in Cappadocia and first trained in secretarial skills (we have already mentioned that he served as Aetius' secretary). But he studied rhetoric at Constantinople, Antioch and Alexandria, where he began to work for Aetius. Most of the opponents of the Neo-Arians focused their attacks on Eunomius' later works. He was condemned at an Ancyran council in 358, yet was rehabilitated by a Constantinopolitan council in 360. Eudoxius, bishop of Constantinople, appointed him bishop of Cyzicus. Exiled by the emperor Valens in 369–70, he assumed leadership of the Neo-Arian group after Aetius' death. Eunomius' writings were not the tight conundrums of Aetius; rather, they were longer treatises. He even wrote commentary on scripture. His arguments have power and show traditional and biblical sources as their authorities.[38]

---

37 'The *Syntagmation* of Aetius the Anomean', ed. and trans. L. R. Wickham. Philostorgius' *H.E.* does not limit their leaders to philosophers.
38 *Eunomius: The extant works*, ed. and trans. Vaggione; R. P. Vaggione, *Eunomius of Cyzicus and the Nicene revolution*.

Epiphanius the Nicene

The incessant battles between Christianities from Nicaea to Constantinople I are clear in the case of Epiphanius of Salamis on Cyprus (c. 315–403), the great troubler of all he considered to be heretics. He repudiated theologians alive or dead, including Arius and Origen. Born in Eleutheropolis, Palestine, he saw himself as the arbiter of the faith throughout the Mediterranean basin. Epiphanius kept contacts with Palestine by founding a monastery in his hometown around 335 and showed particular interest in the see of Jerusalem. When he travelled from Salamis to Jerusalem in order to uproot Origenism in Palestinian monasteries, John of Jerusalem asked him to fill his pulpit. The visitor proceeded to attack the bishop who was sitting in his own sanctuary! Epiphanius' *Panarion*, a history of heresy written in the 370s, is tightly organised, probably too trusting of friends and too distrusting of enemies, but it does show how one influential bishop understood heresy and offers invaluable material. His works took positions that were ratified at Constantinople in 381. He even travelled uncanonically to the synod of the Oak near Chalcedon in 403 to participate in the condemnation of the Tall Brothers, Origenistic monks from Egypt, but when he discovered that the emperor intended to depose Chrysostom he fled and died on the journey home.[39]

Constantinople 381

Neither the council at Nicaea, nor the deaths of Arius or of Athanasius (373), established the predominance of one of these embattled groups. The conflict lasted much longer. Almost sixty years elapsed before the majority of Christians in the empire held to an anti-Arian stance.

The two emperors Gratian and Theodosius I called a council in Constantinople (381) to discuss a series of issues. A hundred and fifty Eastern bishops attended, including some Armenians, but the Pneumatomachian party, those who fought against the divinity of the Spirit, had left the gathering before the official sessions began. Meletius of Antioch was made the president of the council, in order to reinforce his claims to being the proper bishop of that city. (Fervently supported by Basil of Caesarea, his position had not been fully acknowledged by Alexandria and denied by Rome.) Followers of the former Nicene bishop Eustathius, deposed in 326 by Arians, contested Meletius' place and put forth Paulinus as their bishop.

---

39 Epiphanius, *The Panarion*, trans. Williams; *L'Hérésiologie chez Épiphanius*, trans. Pourkier; A. Louth, 'Palestine: Cyril of Jerusalem and Epiphanius'.

At Constantinople, Meletius installed Gregory Nazianzen as its bishop. When Meletius died suddenly, Gregory took the presidency. Peter of Alexandria attacked Gregory's right to the see because he had served as a bishop elsewhere and thus had been translated to Constantinople in violation of canonical law. Gregory protested that he had been ordained as bishop of Sasima during Basil's battles with the Arians, but had never served as its bishop. He had also helped his father as adjutant bishop in Nazianzus, but again had never been a full bishop. Yet Peter was persuasive – and Gregory was sensitive. Gregory resigned and lambasted councils for such decisions.[40] Nectarius succeeded him as both bishop of Constantinople and president of the council. An upper-class friend of Emperor Theodosius, he had to be quickly baptised. As a new Christian he was certainly no theologian like Gregory. His social status was his primary credential. Another serious problem beset the bishopric of Constantinople. Maximus the Cynic had been ordained unlawfully at Constantinople when Gregory Nazianzen was bishop. He had been sent to Constantinople by Peter of Alexandria, ostensibly to assist the aging Gregory, but more probably to give Alexandria a friend at Constantinople. He had been quite helpful and had earned Gregory's praise, but canon 4 of this council denounced Maximus as illicitly ordained.

The first canon insisted that the profession of faith from Nicaea 325 was inviolate. The Neo-Arians (or Anomeans) were anathematised, as were the Arians or Eudoxians. Each party was criticised for failing to accept the full divinity of Christ the Son of God, satisfying themselves with a subordinate divine nature of secondary rank. Also under condemnation were the Pneumatomachoi (or Semi-Arians), as well as Sabellians, Marcellians, Photinians and Apollinarians. Pneumatomachians did not think the divine nature of the Holy Spirit was the same as that of the Father. They accepted the fully divine nature of the Son and were sometimes derided as Semi-Arians. Sabellians, Marcellians and Photinians believed that the Son and the Holy Spirit were only modes of the Father, which had appeared for specific purposes (like creation or redemption) and then returned to the unity of God. Apollinarians insisted that Jesus Christ could never have had a human mind or will, as either of those attributes would have threatened the purpose of the incarnation; the divine nature provided the mind and will in Jesus.

Although we do not have any record of the actual proceedings at Constantinople, canon 1 did develop a specific position about Jesus Christ, affirming him to be a divine person of full divinity with the Father and one whose full

---

40 Gregory Nazianzen, *Carmina historica* XI, 1509–1949 (PG 37: 1134–66).

manhood had been assumed as well. In the discussion with the Apollinarians, Gregory Nazianzen had picked up a phrase from Origen to the effect that any part of the human not assumed in the incarnation would not be saved.[41] Canon 5 accepted the 'Tome of the Westerns', and also recognised Antiochenes who confessed 'one single Godhead of Father Son and Holy Spirit'. This Western book in question is lost, but it probably showed a type of agreement of these Eastern bishops with the West.[42]

There has been a continuing disagreement among scholars about the form of creed put forth by this council. What is usually taken as its creed only appears in the documents from the Council of Chalcedon (451).[43] The exact character of this definition of faith and its relationship to possible sources remain matters of debate. Some have suggested that the term 'Nicene' was taken to mean a larger whole than any specific creedal statement, so that the creed of 381 would indeed be a Nicaeno-Constantinopolitan creed. Others argue the creed was deliberately altered by the council, indeed that the Antioch council in 379 employed both the Old Roman Creed and the Creed of Jerusalem to fashion the creed adopted at Constantinople in 381. There is always the possibility that it was developed by this council from yet other creeds – or perhaps it was not adopted by the council at all.[44]

This council also adopted four canons. Canons 2–4 dealt with the structure of the church. (2) Diocesan bishops were to keep within their own provinces: Alexandria in Egypt, bishops of the East to the East except that they should acknowledge the rights of Antioch, Asia to Asia, Pontus to Pontus and Thrace to Thrace. (3) Constantinople as the new Rome should have recognition of honour right after Rome; and (4) Maximus was not Constantinople's bishop, as noted above. It is likely that the increasing incursions of Alexandria into other domains were the main cause of all three canons.[45] But after 381, the battle for hegemony among the significant sees continued: Rome had no lasting competitor in the West, although prominent bishops in Thessalonica and particularly Milan had exercised some influence as long as those cities were the residences of emperors. Now Constantinople's patriarch was nearly equal to the Roman pope because he was imbedded more deeply in Eastern

---

41 Origen, *Dialogue with Heracleides* 7; Gregory Nazianzen, *Letter* 101.
42 *Decrees of the ecumenical councils*, ed. and trans. Tanner I: 32.
43 ACO II.1, 2: 80.3–16.
44 W-D. Hauschild, 'Nicäno-Konstantinopolitanisches Glaubensbekenntnis', 143–79; R. Staats, *Das Glaubensbekenntnis*; A. M. Ritter, *Das Konzil von Konstantinopel und sein Symbol*, 132–208; L. Abramowski, 'Was hat das Nicaeno-Konstantinopolitanum (C) mit dem Konzil von Konstantinopel 381 zu tun?'.
45 *Decrees of the ecumenical councils*, ed. and trans. Tanner, I: 31–2.

political issues than the Italian leader and thus at times had more ecclesiastical power in the East. Even more upset than Rome by Constantinople's rise, Alexandria's bishops persisted in asserting their importance. Alexandria had a long Christian lineage, in legend beginning with Mark. It also had large political and economic importance, particularly as a major food source for the Eastern Mediterranean.

Theophilus of Alexandria

Theophilus, bishop of Alexandria (*sed*. 385–412), did not think that canon 2 of Constantinople 381 fully applied to him. He was energetic and decisive. When John Chrysostom, bishop of Constantinople, accepted the Tall Brothers – Egyptian Origenist monks, who along with Origen had been condemned by Theophilus at an Alexandrian council in 401 – Theophilus turned against John for meddling in his affairs. Sadly Chrysostom was an easy target since he had no taste for politics. His rigorous disciplines, which had weakened his health, ran counter to the lifestyles of elite Christians, whether they were bishops, laity, political leaders or even monks. He so alienated Theodosius II's wife, the empress Eudokia, by occasionally referring to her as Jezebel rising again, that she vigorously supported all of Theophilus' efforts to make John's hospitality to the Tall Brothers his final impolitic act.[46] John was condemned by the synod of the Oak (403), held in a suburb of Chalcedon and attended by thirty-six to forty-five Egyptian church leaders and monks who were amenable to Theophilus' views. When the people of Constantinople heard that their beloved preacher had been exiled, they demanded that he be brought back. An earthquake and fire in the city seemed like divine support for their anger. But upon John's return he once more insulted Eudokia and was sent away again. The struggle ended with his exile to, and death in, Asia Minor.[47] Thus two synods (i.e., local councils) held by Theophilus, one in his jurisdiction and one out of his jurisdiction, had shifted the balance of power and theology between the bishoprics of Constantinople and Alexandria.

Theophilus' activities within Egypt were momentous. Although he did not plan the destruction of the Sarapeum in Alexandria, a cultural disaster of stunning proportions since it included a grand library, Christians were responsible for the deed during his reign and may have reacted in response to his verbal attacks on pagans. Within the church he not only turned his attention against the Origenism of desert monasticism, but also built many

---

46 R. L. Wilken, *John Chrysostom and the Jews*, 97–127, 158–60, argues against John being a ruthless anti-Semite.
47 Kelly, *Golden Mouth*, 211–85.

churches in the city, much as Ambrose had done in Milan.[48] Upon his death in 412 he was succeeded by his nephew Cyril, who was to become the key figure in the Council of Ephesus (431).

Cyril and Nestorius

Cyril (c. 375–444) had probably been under his uncle Theophilus' tutelage from early manhood. Theophilus took him to the synod of the Oak in 403 where he learned how a skilled ecclesiastical politician could wreak havoc on his enemies. As was not unusual in Alexandria, there was bloodshed during his election to the bishopric in 412. He was soon at odds with pagans, Jews and the governor of Egypt, Orestes. Like his uncle, he was no stranger to controversy. He was, for example, implicated when the distinguished pagan philosopher Hypatia was killed by a Christian mob. Socrates Scholasticus, the church historian, said the event 'brought disgrace not only on Cyril but on the whole Alexandrian church'.[49] Cyril was not charged by the government, however, and certainly was unable to control such mobs.

Nestorius, bishop of Constantinople (428–31) and the other major figure in events leading up to the council of 432, was a Syrian who probably studied under Theodore of Mopsuestia (c. 350–428) in the monastery where he lived near Antioch. His preaching at the metropolis was sterling and gained him wide renown. In 428 the emperor Theodosius II called him to Constantinople as bishop, but Nestorius soon attacked what he saw in the teaching of other bishops. Developing positions held by Theodore, he wanted to make more of Christ's humanity. For him and his supporters the human Jesus was not an impersonal nature, but an active agent with a complete human mind and will. That human was united with Christ's divine nature in one person, but within the unity the man could act. Nestorius' chaplain insisted in a sermon that Mary was not the *theotokos* ('the mother of God') but the *christokos* ('the mother of Christ'); she did not give birth to God. Nestorius made no effort to reprimand him. The bishop and his chaplain were also convinced that they had inherited or created sufficient philosophical terms and theological reasons to save both the unity of one person and the co-decisiveness of the human nature. Much Greek popular piety was as greatly, perhaps more deeply, offended by 'demoting' Mary as it was by 'humanising' Christ. Proclus, later bishop at New Rome (434–46) and probably one of the local candidates for bishop when Nestorius was called, preached a homily at Constantinople in 428 repudiating Nestorius'

48 W. Löhr, 'Theophilus von Alexandrian'.
49 Socrates, H.E. 7.13–6, citing 7.15.

teachings. Portions of the sermon became important in the Christological debate; finally the whole sermon was included in the *Acta* of the Council of Ephesus (431). He also wrote a *Tome* for eastern churches in which he attacked the Christological positions of Antiochenes like Theodore and Nestorius.[50] Nestorius appealed to Rome but a synod there in 430, partially influenced by Cyril, condemned his teachings. At that point his only appeal was to the emperor Thedosius II.

Ephesus (431)

Theodosius took the appeal seriously and with his co-emperor Valentinian III and Pope Celestine I he called a council to meet at Ephesus in 431. Cyril, bishop of Alexandria (412–44), was furious at Nestorius and exchanged letters with him; one letter included his twelve anathemas against the bishop of Constantinople.[51] He came to Ephesus with his minions well before the arrival of the Roman legates or the Antiochene contingent, who had been delayed by floods. Assisted by Memnon, bishop of Ephesus, Cyril began proceedings against Nestorius. When the Western representatives arrived, they agreed with the decisions since the Roman synod had already condemned Nestorius. As a result, Nestorius was condemned and deposed. The documents from that council included Cyril's second letter to Nestorius, Nestorius' response and the creed of Nicaea (325). Cyril's third epistle, which closes with twelve anathemas against Nestorius' teachings, was included as well.

By the time John of Antioch (d. 441) reached the city with his supporters, he had been excommunicated and those who followed him lay under a similar threat. These West Syrians set up their own council and excommunicated both Cyril and Memnon.[52] Cyril and John were eventually reconciled, however, in 433. Theodoret of Cyrrhus and John drafted the union statement about 'Jesus Christ, the only begotten Son of God, perfect God and perfect man of rational soul and body' and Cyril endorsed the statement. That agreement meant that Cyril could be seen either as one who accepted a phrase from Apollinaris concerning 'one nature of the incarnate Logos' that reached him in a forgery under Athanasius' name, or as one who proclaimed the full humanity in

---

50 N. Constas, *Proclus of Constantinople.*
51 J. McGuckin, *St. Cyril of Alexandria*; S. Wessel, *Cyril of Alexandria and the Nestorian controversy*; F. McLeod, *The roles of Christ's humanity in salvation*, 226–66.
52 ACO 1.4: 33–6; 1.5: 119–24.

Jesus.[53] In the union talks with John of Antioch in 433, Cyril forsook his twelve anathemas against Nestorius.

After Ephesus, Nestorius retired to his former monastery in Antioch, but by 435 his books were being burned and by 436 he had been exiled to a desert oasis in Egypt. He lived long enough to write the *Tome of Hericleides*, which rebutted a series of the charges against him, but he was not heard. We only know that writing in a Syriac translation. He may have had news about the coming Council of Chalcedon (451) and appears to have died in that same year.

Nestorius was not the only casualty at Ephesus; also condemned were the Messalians (or Euchites), particularly in Pamphilia, who denied the importance of work or discipline so as to dedicate themselves fully to prayer. They had already been rejected by a synod in Constantinople in 426. If they signed a series of anathemas against Messalianism, then they would be accepted, both clergy and laity, into unity with the church. If not, they were heretics and should be particularly watched lest they try to hide in monasteries.[54]

The council also agreed that the bishops of Cyprus could ordain leaders without external interference. Finally the council sent a letter to bishops informing them of its decisions. Only five representatives from the West had come and 197 bishops signed it.[55] Bishops east of Antioch did not attend in any number. This council could be considered fully 'ecumenical' only if the Christian *Oikoumenê* consisted of primarily Eastern Mediterranean communities.

A sequel in Ephesus

Within thirty years, Ephesus was the site of another major synod. This synod was called in 449 to vindicate the teachings of Eutyches, a revered and leading monk ('archimandrite') in Constantinople, and his supporter Dioscorus, bishop of Alexandria (444–51) and former archdeacon to Cyril. Eutyches' position was that Christ has one divine nature and so it is called 'Miaphysitism' (from the Greek for 'single nature'). Dioscorus' view was more moderate than Eutyches' and it was based on Cyril's affirmation of the 'one nature of the incarnate Logos'. The synod may have been held in Ephesus because the city could be expected to uphold the emperor Theodosius II and bishop Cyril against Nestorius, much as Memnon, bishop of Ephesus, had done in 431.

---

53 *Decrees of the ecumenical councils*, ed. and trans. Tanner, 1: 69–70; H. M. Diepen, *Douze dialogues*, 13–24; I. Pásztori-Kupán, *Theodoret of Cyrus*, 14–18; see also chapter 19, below.
54 T. Graumann, *Die Kirche der Väter*, 255–419.
55 *Corpus notitiarum episcopatuum ecclesiae orientalis graecae*, eds. E. Garland and V. Lauraent, 36 and 5.

The synod itself was atrocious. Delegates were beaten; Flavian, the bishop of Constantinople, died from the wounds he sustained. The Egyptian contingent included monks who were entirely prepared to maim and kill for their understanding of the faith. The synod was never received as an ecumenical council. In fact, it was quickly denounced by Pope Leo I as a 'Robbers' Council' (*latrocinium*), a term that is still used to describe the synod today. Despite Eutyches' powerful connections – he was the godfather of Chrysaphius, the emperor's chamberlain – and his victory at Ephesus, he was decisively condemned for his Christology two years later in Chalcedon.

Chalcedon (451)

The emperor Marcian (*regn.* 540–7), with the support of his wife, Pulcheria, summoned a council in Nicaea in 451, but the council soon reconvened in Chalcedon, where it would be closer to Constantinople and the emperor. Leo I (*sed.* 440–61) opposed it because he considered his *Tome to Flavian* sufficient, believed recalcitrant bishops should repent and endorse it and thus avoid further bickering, and feared that more debate might further fracture the church. For him, the only business of the council should be bringing home exiled bishops. He was also greatly preoccupied by Attila the Hun ravaging the West. Yet Marcian's decision was made before he knew of Leo's misgivings. So Leo sent legates: the bishops Paschasinus, Lucentius and Julian, along with the priests Boniface and Basil. Paschasinus, Lucentius and Boniface eventually presided while Julian sat with the bishops.[56]

The Eastern Mediterranean bishops were the large majority, numbering between 500 and 600; entire Christian regions (such as Armenia and Ethiopia) were not represented.[57] In the sixth session, the 'definition of faith' was agreed upon and was declared as in force in the presence of the emperor and his retainers. Leo's *Tome* against Eutyches was specifically noted in the definition. Creeds from both Nicaea (325) and Constantinople (381) were confessed; letters of Cyril and the repudiation of Nestorius were once again ratified. The addition of some phrases in their confession in particular (e.g., 'the same truly God and truly man, of a rational soul and body; consubstantial with the Father as regards his divinity, and the same consubstantial with us as regards his humanity') were seen as supporting the faith already expressed at Nicaea and Constantinople. Dioscorus of Alexandria, who was one of the planners for

---

56 *Decrees of the ecumenical councils*, ed. and trans. Tanner, I: 77–82.
57 See chapter 4, below.

the council, was deposed and exiled to Gangra in Paphlagonia where he died in 454.[58]

The council issued twenty-seven canons of ecclesiastical law. What was in many ways the most significant decision of the council ('canon 28') was a resolution passed only in the sixteenth session.[59] It stipulated that, since Constantinople was the New Rome, its patriarch should receive the same privileges as the pope as bishop of 'Old Rome' and that Constantinople should be established as the second see in order of precedence. The papal legates refused it. Anatolius, bishop of Constantinople, defended it in a letter to the pope. The emperor wrote to Leo and asked for his approval of the council. Leo withheld his decision until 453. Then he accepted the council but not 'canon 28', claiming that it did not abide by the terms of canon 3 of Constantinople and that it failed to safeguard adequately the prerogatives of other ancient sees.[60]

The Chalcedonian canons provide indirect evidence of the problems and challenges that the church was facing. Constantinople's strong influence in the East was recognised by giving her bishop the right to ordain metropolitans in Pontus, Asia and Thrace, including the bishops working among non-Greek-speaking congregations in those regions. Other canons specified that monks were not to challenge bishops. No church leaders could take their cases to secular courts. Foreign monks, who had congregated in large numbers at the capital city, were to be expelled. Their empty monasteries in various places should not be made into secular hostelries. No priest could marry a heretic; virgins who took vows of chastity could not marry; only women over forty could be ordained as deaconesses. Economic administrators (rather than bishops) were to handle church funds. The poor who travelled from place to place ought to have letters of peace, not commendation. Quite apart from the threat of doctrinal error, a plethora of wrong practices had to be redressed. These regulations make it obvious that Christian communities took seriously living their faith – and failed to do so with some regularity.[61]

The mixed reception that would meet the theological decisions from Chalcedon was foreshadowed at the time of the council. The power of the Cyrillian bloc within the council is perhaps best seen in the measures that were

---

58 D. Stiernon, 'Dioscurus of Alexandria'.
59 Greek collections also include c. 29 (an epitome of session 19) and c. 30 (an epitome of session 4): ACO II: 467.18–21 and 467.31–468.6.
60 F. Hofmann, 'Der Kampf Päpste von Konzil und Dogma von Chalkedon'; *Decrees of the ecumenical councils*, ed. and trans. Tanner, I: 32 (Constantinople, canon 3).
61 *Decrees of the ecumenical councils*, ed. and trans. Tanner, I: 89, 91–4, 97–100 (Constantinople, Canons 4, 9, 11, 14, 16, 23, 24, 26, 28).

taken specifically to deal with Egypt, the region where they were dominant: Egyptians who did not sign or agree in substance with Leo's *Tome* were not censured when they insisted they had to wait until their elder bishops had agreed. This example of *Realpolitik* reveals a deep sense that Egypt was not turned toward the Chalcedonian solution; its leaders were carefully protecting their traditions.

After Chalcedon

The doctrinal result of Chalcedon (451) was a vigorous debate not dissimilar to that which followed Nicaea (325). It will be helpful to describe the three major groups that interacted against each other in the aftermath of Chalcedon – the Dyophysites (or 'Nestorians'), the Anti-Chalcedonians ('Miaphysites') and the Chalcedonians – as well as an imperially sponsored attempt to reconcile the factions.

Dyophysites

Dyophysites (sometimes called Nestorians, for their support of Nestorius) had been leaving the empire since the decision against them at Ephesus in 431 and subsequent Roman legislation in 435.[62] An earlier group of Antiochene theologians (sometimes, but perhaps misleadingly, called the 'School of Antioch') had emphasised the activity of the humanity in Jesus Christ and favoured a literalist approach to reading scripture, though it must be remembered that ancient literal interpretations were dissimilar to modern fundamentalist interpretations. Diodore, bishop of Tarsus by 382 (d. *c*. 390) and a significant figure at the Council of Constantinople (381), was one of the earliest leaders. He had studied philosophy in Athens and wrote intriguing commentaries on scripture in which he expressed serious misgivings about some allegorical interpretations. Origen was his foil. Fragments of his comments on Paul and his reconstructed interpretation of the Psalms show that he was much interested in the narratives of the Bible and in the Old Testament as a type of the New. Diodore attacked paganism, particularly the efforts of the emperor Julian. He supported Meletius (d. 381) as Nicene bishop of Antioch and stood against the teaching of the Arians and the Apollinarians, insisting that both did damage to the human nature of Jesus and, further, that the Arians made the divine nature of the Son a secondary creation. Although his legacy is fragmentary and possibly interpolated at places by Apollinarians, his views form the background of the

---

62 *CTh* 16.5.66 (SC 497: 366–9).

Christology that the Councils of Ephesus (431) and Chalcedon (451) rejected in condemning Nestorius.[63]

Theodore, bishop of Mopsuestia (392–428), was a student of Libanius, the famous pagan rhetor at Antioch. Syriac translations of Theodore's commentaries on the Nicene Creed, the Lord's Prayer, baptism and the eucharist demonstrate his support of the Nicene faith described at Constantinople in 381. He attacked Arians and Apollinarians for many of the same reasons as Diodore did and thus fell under suspicion from Cyril of Alexandria as a precursor of Nestorius. He also spoke about the actions of the divine Son and those of the 'assumed man' and insisted on grace as the category through which to understand the incarnation, rather than the body / soul analogy employed particularly by Cyril and the Miaphysites. That allowed him to read many Gospel passages more literally, yet it made his understanding of the unity of Jesus Christ's person seem insubstantial. His many scriptural commentaries, now often extant only in Syriac or Latin fragments, have been used continuously by East Syrian ('Nestorian') churches that also follow his Christology.[64] His writings were declared heretical at Ephesus (431) and Chalcedon (451), but not his person.

The last famous Greek-speaker among the Antiochenes was Theodoret, bishop of Cyrrhus (*sed. c.* 428–66). From family money he built bridges and public buildings there and fought both paganism and Arianism in his diocese. His histories of the church and of monastic leaders have offered significant understandings of both arenas. At Ephesus (431), he was a major representative of the Dyophysite position and experienced considerable difficulty there. He worked for the reconciliation between John of Antioch and Cyril of Alexandria in 433 by collaborating with John to draft the document eventually agreed upon. His *Eranistes* of 447 was primarily an attack on Cyril's Christology and led to his being kept in 'diocese arrest' as an obdurate trouble-maker.[65] The Robber Synod deposed and exiled him in 449, but the new emperor, Marcian, reinstated him in 450. After Chalcedon (451), where he was quite active, he wrote his *History of heresies*, which follows the chain of heretics from the first century up to Chalcedon in five books. After declaring both Eutyches and Nestorius heretics in the fourth book, he went on in the fifth book to proclaim the teachings of the true church. But Theodoret's status was still contested by

---

63 R. Abramowski, 'Der theologische Nachlass'; L. Abramowski, 'Streit um Diodor'; *Diodore of Tarsus*, trans. Hill.

64 R. Norris, *Manhood and Christ*; D. A. Zaharopoulos, *Theodore of Mopsuestia on the Bible*; McLeod, *The roles of Christ's humanity in salvation*. His work on the Minor Prophets exists in Greek.

65 I. P. Kupan, *Theodoret of Cyrus*.

his enemies, who were certain that the Antiochene position could no more be reconciled to the Chalcedon faith than the Nestorian could.

The Eastern Syrian Christians could nevertheless read the 451 declaration of faith as close enough to their positions that some of them argued it did not fit squarely with a full condemnation of Nestorius' teaching. Others opposed or carefully reinterpreted it.[66] Babai the Great (551–628) skilfully employed Syriac terminology to create a thicker explanation of the unity of divine and human in Jesus Christ, thus deepening positions similar to the Antiochene Christological views. There were also rejoinders to the allegations that they were 'Nestorians'. Timothy I of Baghdad, the *catholicos* of the church (780–823), acknowledged the importance of Nestorius' Christology, but insisted that Eastern Syrian views of Jesus Christ were even more dependent upon the works of Gregory Nazianzen the Theologian, who was also an important father for Byzantine Orthodoxy. The Eastern Syrians were also extremely active in propagating Christianity. Timothy oversaw the most widespread Christian church until the Portuguese and Spanish expansions of the fifteenth and sixteenth centuries. His communities spanned from Cyprus to China.[67]

Anti-Chalcedonians (Miaphysites)

Miaphysitism – the affirmation of only one full nature in Jesus Christ, and that divine – had appeared as early as Apollinaris (d. 392) and, although some of the leading Miaphysites had been condemned at Ephesus in 431, it continued. After Chalcedon, polemicising the council became an important common cause for them. Opposition to Chalcedon became dominant in some areas that were not represented at the council (e.g., Armenia and Ethiopia) and in some that were (e.g., Egypt). In Egypt, some polemics may have been first written in Greek in order to reach the opponents in their tongue, fragments from which survive in Coptic histories and hagiographies. These sources describe some figures who were charged with being Miaphysite. For example, the hagiography of Macarius of Tkôw tells us that he supported Dioscorus of Alexandria and would not accept either Leo's Tome or the decisions of Chalcedon. (Reverence for Dioscorus as a saintly teacher of the faith is a regular feature in Egyptian churches to this day.) Macarius insisted on what he understood as Athanasius' sense of the faith and Cyril of Alexandria's interpretation of it; he maintained that Pope Leo and Chalcedon had sold out to the heretic Nestorius. Stephen

---

66 See chapter 19, below.
67 G. Chediath, *Christology of Mar Babai*; L. Abramowski, 'Die Christologie Babais des Grossen'; T. Hurst, 'The epistles of Timothy I of Baghdad', 108; F. Norris, 'Timothy I of Baghdad'.

of Hnês focused particularly on the efforts of the emperor Justinian to force Chalcedonian faith on the entire empire. A series of such hagiographical writings connected the rejection of Leo's Tome and of Chalcedon to the lives of famous monastic saints.[68] Egyptian monasteries became havens of Cyrillian partisans, which in some cases made them bases for Miaphysites.

Monks who had tried to live away from life's bustle and conflict could find themselves providing places of safety for the theological allies who had been forced to leave their monasteries, but these secluded monasteries also served as places of refuge for those fleeing their homes for other reasons. The White Monastery in Upper Egypt, where Shenoute of Atripe was abbot from 433 to c. 450, provides a good example. It was in an out-of-the-way location, but when the Blemmys, horsemen of the desert west of the Nile, invaded the farmlands to their east, thousands fled west to the White Monastery for sanctuary. Efficient use of irrigation and skilled animal husbandry enabled the monastery to care for waves of the needy: perhaps as many as 4,000 monks were able to make provision for nearly 10,000 refugees. Shenoute and his monastery were vastly influential in Upper Egypt, not just as a hospice or hospital for those in distress. The largest of the complex's buildings still stands, giving us a sense of the sheer size occupied by the community. Even more than the material remains, however, it is the textual record, which speaks of the large numbers of monks (and nuns in a nearby convent), that indicates how much this community swayed Christians in – and probably beyond – the region.[69]

Shenoute was not untouched by theological concerns. In some accounts of Shenoute's life, there is a section about his accompanying Cyril of Alexandria to the council at Ephesus and confronting Nestorius in anger. If true, he slapped the 'archheretic' in the face; but, even if legendary, the story correctly indicates the abbot's view of Constantinople's bishop. His authority and passion ensured that the Coptic Church would keep closely, if not exactly, to Cyril's Christology. Accordingly, Shenoute maintained that no human subject acted on its own in Jesus Christ; the Logos was the subject of both lowly and divine thoughts and actions.[70]

Timothy Aelurus, bishop of Alexandria (457–60, 475–7), belonged to the anti-Chalcedonian party. His nickname *aelurus* – which can be translated as either 'the Cat' or 'the Weasel' and seems to refer to his short stature – indicates

---

68 D. Johnson, 'Anti-chalcedonian polemics', 221; Dioscorus, *A Panegyric on Macarius of Tkôw*, ed. Johnson; Stephen, bishop of Heracleolis Magna, *Panegyric on Apollo*.
69 R. Krawiec, *Shenoute and the women of the White Monastery*.
70 Besa, *Life of Shenoute*.

something of the ambivalence with which he was received. At Chalcedon, he supported the moderate positions of some Miaphysites against the extreme views of Eutyches, but still rejected Dyophysite positions.[71] Later, however, he anathematised both the council and its confession of faith.[72] He was the dominant power in Egypt until the emperor Leo. Leo had ascertained that Timothy rejected Dyophysite positions, and would not follow Apollinaris' exclusion of human mind and will in Jesus Christ, but the bishop stood firm on the miscarriage at Chalcedon. In late 459 or early 460, Leo had him deposed and exiled.[73]

Zeno's Henotikon

The emperor Zeno reigned from 474 to 491, but for a year out of power (475–6) during a revolt led by Basilicus, the brother of Emperor Leo I's widow. Zeno was an Isaurian who had put his troops at the disposal of Leo and thus won a place in Leo's heart. He is best known for two things. The first was political. During 488, he convinced Theodoric and his Ostrogoths to move from the East into Italy to battle for the kingdom of Odoacer. The movement of the Ostrogoths released the pressure of the Gothic threat on the Eastern part of the empire where Zeno ruled and gave the West a gift that it might well have refused.

Second, although Zeno himself supported Chalcedon, he was very interested in assuaging its anti-Chalcedonian opponents. So, with the assistance of Acacius, patriarch of Constantinople, he prepared a document aimed at reconciling the different factions, known as the Henotikon (482). Again, we find an emperor trying to use his power and prestige to solidify the Christian faith within the empire because he needed assistance from the Eastern provinces, this time the area in which Miaphysitism was strong. Acacius opened talks with Peter Mongus, patriarch of Alexandria. He proposed the condemnation of both Nestorius and his sense of two natures with the lack of a full union as well as Eutyches and his destruction of the humanity of Jesus. The basis of these unity conversations would be the 381 Niceno-Constantinopolitan Creed and Cyril's twelve anathemas of Nestorius, but the council of 451 should also be accepted.

At first it seemed that this plan would succeed when a number of anti-Chalcedonians supported it. Acacius added his praise of Peter Mongus as the patriarch of Alexandria. Because of that and because the Henotikon failed to

---

71 L. R. Wickham, 'Timothy Aelurus'.

72 Zacharias Rhetor, Ecclesiastical history 4.3.

73 P. T. R. Gray, The defense of Chalcedon, 22.

mention the *Tome* of Leo, however, Pope Felix III excommunicated Acacius in 484. The excommunication led to the Acacian schism, which lasted until 519, thirty years after Acacius' death in 489. Zeno's and Acacius' attempt at Christian unity crashed on the rocks of Roman sensitivity. They had hoped to finesse the difficulties within the *Henotikon* by not discussing definitions of 'nature' or 'union' in Jesus Christ.[74]

The major polemicist of the anti-Chalcedonian camp was Severus of Antioch (*c.* 465–538). His works, which were written originally in Greek but are primarily preserved in Syriac, are extremely important not only because of his own theology but also because they preserve numerous fragments from otherwise lost writings by his opponents. That group includes Chalcedonian supporters whom he attacks as well as the anti-Chalcedonians with whom he disagrees. He was a Miaphysite, who became bishop of the metropolis in 512. Most of the populace in Antioch were well pleased with his election.[75] He found no difficulty in accepting the first three councils: Nicaea (325), Constantinople (381) and Ephesus (431). For him Zeno's *Henotikon* was also orthodox, but in a homily he explicitly condemned Nestorius and Eutyches, Chalcedon (451), the *Tome* of Leo, and indeed anyone who confessed 'two natures after the union'. According to Severus, such a confession always implied the acceptance of two persons in Christ, which he abhorred as deeply heretical. He himself claimed the 'one nature' formula of Cyril.[76] During a synod held at Antioch in 513, he and the others present officially adopted these positions.[77] At both times the emperor Anastasius (*regn.* 491–518) expected him to withhold his negative judgment on Chalcedon, but he did not. Severus was therefore deposed in 518. He then returned to Alexandria where he had been educated and continued his writing career. The diversity of anti-Chalcedonian beliefs is illustrated by Severus' opposition to the Miaphysite Julian of Halicarnassus (*c.* 527) and to the Apthartodocetae, who held that Jesus' body had been incorruptible from birth.[78]

Philoxenus of Mabbug (*c.* 440–523), who also attended the synod of Antioch (513), was likewise a great supporter of the Miaphysite cause and a remarkable theologian. Philoxenus wrote exclusively in Syriac. Like Severus, he revered Cyril as a saint and a great teacher, and he called the birth of the Son 'the birth of God'. Nestorius, Eutyches and Chalcedon were heretical, and all Roman

---

74 P. T. R. Gray, 'The legacy of Chalcedon', 224–5.
75 Zacharias Rhetor, *Vita Severi* (PO 2: 241–2).
76 Severus, *Homily* 1 (Coptic) (PO 38: 261–3).
77 Severus, *Letter* 46 'To Hippocrates' (PO 12: 321).
78 A. Grillmeier, *Christ in Christian tradition*, II.1, 281–4; P. Allen and C. T. R. Hayward, *Severus of Antioch*.

popes from Leo I onward had been Nestorians.[79] Again like Severus, Philoxenus was sent into exile, and while exiled he died under suspicious circumstances, apparently from inhaled smoke. Another noteworthy Miaphysite was John Philoponos (fl. 520–70), whose accomplishments were evident in theology, philosophy and science. He accepted much Aristotelian realism even in theology, though he attacked the Stagarite's affirmation of the eternity of matter as argued by Proclus in his treatise *On the eternity of the world*. The first Christian physicist, Philoponos advanced new ideas about light and motion in ways that are comparable to themes that have been explored in twentieth-century physics. For example, he did not accept a physical dualism and he began to articulate a relational view of space and time.

Miaphysites enjoyed some high-level support during Justinian's reign (527–65),[80] thanks to the sympathy of the empress Theodora. She protected anti-Chalcedonian monks who came to the city, even when Illyrian soldiers in the city were strongly supporting Chalcedonians.[81] She also protected Theodosius, Miaphysite bishop of Alexandria (535–6), who had been forced out of his position and had taken up residence in Constantinople (536–66). Theodosius was displaced to make way for Paul of Tabennisi, the new Chalcedonian bishop. Chalcedonian bishops were officially in place in Constantinople, Jerusalem, Antioch and Alexandria, to underscore the apparent victory of the Chalcedonians. But even in Constantinople Theodosius never accepted Chalcedon, despite pressure from the emperor. He began to ordain bishops for a separate anti-Chalcedonian church in 538. One of them was Jacob Baradaeus (500–78). Perhaps the most effective of the anti-Chalcedonian missionaries, he travelled throughout the East clothed in rags (hence his nickname, which is derived from the Syriac for 'horse blanket'). His success was phenomenal and at the end of the sixth century there were Miaphysite churches in many places throughout the East which owed their existence to his efforts.[82] The empress Theodora was directly responsible for sending Miaphysite missionaries to Ethiopia, when Justinian became interested in dispatching Chalcedonian supporters there.[83] Perhaps she also had a hand in Justinian's decision to send John, bishop of Ephesus, also known as John of Asia (c. 507–89), a Miaphysite monk, historian and missionary, to serve as a missionary in Asia Minor.

---

79 Philoxenus, *Letter to the monks of Senoun* (CSCO 232: 38, 63); A. de Halleux, *Philoxène de Mabbog*; Gray, *The Defense of Chalcedon*, 36–8.
80 T. Torrance, *The ground and grammar of theology*, 60–1; U. M. Lang, *John Philoponus*; F. A. J. de Haas, *John Philoponus' new definition*.
81 B. Croke, 'Justinian's Constantinople', 73, 76.
82 See chapter 4, below.
83 See chapter 4, below.

John of Ephesus had spent a great deal of time among Miaphysite refugees in Constantinople before departing on his missionary efforts. He claimed to have converted 80,000 Eastern Christians to his views, many of them former Montanists. They were members of a movement that began in second-century Asia Minor whose leader possibly considered himself the Holy Spirit incarnate to bring new revelation. The Montanists had resisted what they saw as worldly intrusions into the church.[84] The number of converts to Miaphysite faith is probably too large, but John's claims of success are bolstered by the fact that during this time the Montanists were indeed enveloped by a larger group. In addition to promoting Miaphysite Christianity, John supplied information through his writings about important figures in the East.[85]

Chalcedonians

Although their cause enjoyed support from Roman popes and Constantinopolitan emperors, not all Chalcedonians were urban theologians from great sees. Symeon Stylites the Elder (c. 390–459), a Syrian, had supported Chalcedon when Pope Leo I sought his opinion on Christology. He was the first of the 'pillar saints' who pioneered a form of asceticism that was widely emulated. He mounted a column in a place northeast of Antioch and stayed there the rest of his life. The pillar was enlarged, but he was brought down only occasionally when others saw him collapse from sickness or cold weather. Food was sent up, excrement sent down. A large monastic complex grew up around him. As a holy man in a culture that highly honoured them, he converted people from far away who came to see him and even influenced the decisions of emperors: Theodosius II forsook his plan to give Antiochene synagogues back to the Jews when Symeon protested and threatened to come off his pillar.[86]

Other monks were more directly involved in the discussions than Symeon. The case of Nephalius of Alexandria showcases monastic involvement on both sides of the controversy. In 482, he participated as a Miaphysite in a revolt of about 30,000 monks against Chalcedonian rulers. He insisted on a robustly anti-Chalcedonian reading of Zeno's *Henotikon*, but by 507 he had come round to the Chalcedonian view and led a violent uprising of monks against anti-Chalcedonian monks who supported Severus of Antioch. Most knowledge about Nephalius' thinking comes from accusations against him and fragments. Our primary source is Severus' *Orationes ad Nephalium*, which does not however contain quotations from Nephalius' own works. It would

---

84 W. Tabbernee, *Montanist inscriptions and testimonia*.
85 J. van Ginkel, *John of Ephesus*; S. A. Harvey, *Asceticism and society in crisis*.
86 S. A. Harvey, 'The sense of a Stylite'.

appear that he carefully avoided any 'one nature' formula and developed suc-
cinct Dyophysite phrasing. Yet Nephalius warned that such a position stated
crudely could support a possible Nestorian reading. According to Severus, he
assembled a dossier to prove that Gregory Nazianzen, Proclus, John Chrysostom and even Cyril of Alexandria had employed language similar to his. Severus
was also highly critical of Nephalius' interpretation of biblical texts.[87]

Severus' polemics also preserve for us evidence of the work of John the
Grammarian of Caesarea. Between 515 and 518, he wrote an *Apology* that has
been lost, except for the forty-four fragments from it that are excerpted in
Severus' *Contra Grammaticum*. John employed the Cappadocian Trinitarian
terms *physis* ('nature') and *ousia* ('essence') in his Christology. He insisted
that Christ must be *homoousios* ('consubstantial') with both God and man for
salvation to be effective, but also insisted that this did not imply that there were
two separate sons. To characterise the unity of these two natures, he turns to
Cyril's insistence upon the divine Logos – but even as he borrows from Cyril
he corrects the harshest Cyrillian language of 'one nature' that came from
Apollinaris and so ensures a meaningful place for the human Jesus. In sum,
his Christology depends upon a Cyrillian interpretation of Chalcedon.[88]

Leontius of Jerusalem, who is to be distinguished from Leontius of Byzantium, was an extremely important Chalcedonian theologian of the sixth century. Between 528 and 544, he wrote his *Contra Monophysitas* and also his *Adversus
Nestorianos*.[89] His anti-Nestorian polemic is significant not least because it preserves in Greek some Nestorian sources, thus providing the only such evidence
from this period that is not in Syriac.[90] It seems plausible to suppose that his two
attacks against what he considered to be the extremes of contemporary theology were complemented by a third section, now lost, in which he explained
his own view. He expected Severus to be able to accept Chalcedon since he
considered that its formulations agreed in substance with Cyril. For his part,
Leontius was able to accept the proposition that 'one of the Trinity suffered'
(the so-called theopaschite formula), because the Word did indeed suffer in his
flesh. Both natures, he affirmed, are necessary in terms of salvation, because
the humanity must be divinised.[91]

Leontius of Byzantium (d. c. 543) had entered the monastic life between 510
and 520, but by 531 he was established in Constantinople as a representative

87 Gray, *The defense of Chalcedon*, 105–11; L. Labate, 'Nephalius'.
88 See chapter 19, below.
89 M. Richard, 'Léonce de Jérusalem et Léonce de Byzance'.
90 L. Abramowski, 'Ein nestorianischen Traktat'; D. Krausmueller, 'Leontius of Jerusalem'.
91 Gray, *The defense of Chalcedon*, 122–41; A. Grillmeier with T. Hainthaler, *Christ in Christian
    tradition*, II.2: 271–312; see also chapter 19, below.

of Palestinian and Chalcedonian positions during two synods there in 532 and 536. Although we know almost nothing of his background, we can conjecture that he was probably well educated and that he was familiar with the works of Diodore of Tarsus and Theodore of Mopsuestia. After 536, he went back to Palestine for a time but returned to Constantinople in 540. While in the city, he lived as a hermit attached to the monastery of the Akoimetoi, or the 'Sleepless Ones', who were solidly supporters of Chalcedonian Christology. Leontius was a creative theologian who claimed that the unity in Jesus Christ is by a 'hypostasis' (enhypostasis) that included two natures. His primary work was Libri III contra Nestorianos et Eutychianos (543–4). Leontius was also connected with sixth-century Origenism, which is a topic to which we shall return.[92]

The emperor Justinian

The long reign of the emperor Justinian (regn. 527–65) was marked by developments that deeply affected the church. As his armies won back large portions of the former empire and pushed its borders to new lengths by recovering North Africa and Italy as well as conquering various peoples along the Danube,[93] he constructed many churches in the newly conquered territories and in the older regions. In doing so, he extended the establishment of Christianity even beyond the accomplishments of Theodosius II.

His law code, revised and then published in 529, attempted to remove perceived inconsistencies in the Theodosian Code. Justinian's Code also included other novellas, a digest of commentaries, legal textbooks, and the institutes made up of works from Gaius and others. It became a standard for the development of canon law in the West throughout the medieval period. It also set the foundation for the Byzantine pattern of church–state relationships. They were not totally independent powers, but were intended to work together, the state overseeing human affairs and the church directing spiritual needs. Caesaropapism was a poor interpretation of the interplay.[94]

Another remarkable and enduring legacy from Justinian was Hagia Sophia, the magnificent cathedral that he had built in Constantinople between 532 and 537. It replaced Constantine's church of the same name, which had burned in the Nika revolt of 532. This massive structure, 68 by 76m with a height of

---

92 Grillmeier with Hainthaler, Christ in Christian tradition II.2: 181–229; M. Gockel, 'A dubious Christological formula?'; B. Daley, 'A richer union'; B. Daley, 'The Origenism of Leontius of Byzantium'.
93 A. D. Lee, 'The empire at war'; see also W. Pohl, 'Justinian and the barbarian kingdoms' and G. Greatrex, 'Byzantium and the East in the sixth century'. The latter focuses more on the Persian Wars.
94 See chapter 17, below.

55m at the dome, was the work of architects Anthemius of Tralles and Isidore of Miletus. Nothing like it had been conceived, let alone completed. Marble and mosaics were employed lavishly. Over 18,100kg of silver were used for fashioning its furnishings; its main altar was gold.[95] The glory of the liturgical metal work forged in Constantinople can still be seen in a group of vessels found at Sion and displayed at Dumbarton Oaks in Washington, D.C. The splendour of its liturgy influenced most churches throughout the Eastern Mediterranean.

Constantinople (553)

It was in the great hall of Hagia Sophia Cathedral that Justinian convened a council on 5 May 553. Two theological controversies needed to be redressed. The first was the need to reach a consensus about the Christological claims of Theodore of Mopsuestia, Theodoret and Ibas of Edessa; their works in question were called the 'Three Chapters'. Divergent responses to their writings were leading to further divisions within an already fractious situation. Another set of problems had emerged concerning the theology of Origen of Alexandria and several other authors who had been influenced by him. Whether the latter problems were settled in the Council of Constantinople as such, or in a preparatory session, is a matter of dispute, but it is undisputed that they were a major issue during Justinian's reign.

Origenism

The debates about Origenism in Justinian's time followed an earlier controversy at the end of the fourth century. Jerome (c. 342–420) set up a monastery in Bethlehem during 385 with the backing of a Roman multi-millionaire named Paula (347–404) and her daughter Eustochium. Paula sought to increase her faith through life in a nunnery, or perhaps a double monastery for men and women. By giving much of her enormous wealth to the church, she could dictate where and how the money was used and so avoid the never-ending pressure from those of her upper class and the government to keep her financial holdings in general circulation. In her case, a monastic vow was indeed liberation from many of the demands in her daily life.[96]

That she still controlled a considerable sum while she lived in the monastery becomes clear in noticing that she and her aristocratic 'nuns' still had servants.

---

95 R. L. Nice, *Saint Sophia in Istanbul*; T. Klauser, 'Hagia Sophia'; N. Teteriatnikov, *Mosaics of Hagia Sophia*.
96 S. Rebenich, *Jerome*; E. Clark, 'Ascetic renunciation and feminine advancement'.

These women stood at the top of a carefully structured community that in many ways kept the lower-class women doing the menial tasks. Wealthy women had been rather well educated and thus could be encouraged not only to read and comment on scripture but also to learn Hebrew. Jerome greatly enjoyed their company. Such contacts were not uncommon: John Chrysostom and Rufinus also had women friends of such education, means and refinement.[97]

Rufinus (c. 345–410) was from Aquileia but came to Egypt in 372. While in Egypt, he studied under Didymus the Blind in Alexandria, visited monks in the desert and met Melania the Elder (c. 342–410). Similarly to Paula, this immensely rich woman travelled with Rufinus to Palestine and set up a double monastery on the Mount of Olives. Origen was highly esteemed there. Rufinus had translated various works of Origen into Latin. But he became embroiled with Jerome in a fierce controversy over the works of Origen. Rufinus challenged Jerome's use of Origen's ideas in his early biblical commentaries and Jerome did not bear such challenges gladly. Jerome, on the other hand, attacked Rufinus' translation of Origen's *On first principles*, accusing him of mistranslating several passages and carefully leaving out suspect sections. Jerome's own translation is lost to us except for some equally suspect excerpts. The feud between Jerome and Rufinus, which was waged in monasteries built by moneyed women, indicates how battles over Origenism separated former friends and the role played in debates by powerful women who wielded great influence.

Evagrius of Pontus (345–99) had supported Gregory Nazianzen at Constantinople from 379 till Gregory's departure from the city, and was ordained a deacon by him. While in the city he became a popular promoter of Nicaeno-Constantinopolitan orthodoxy. After leaving Constantinople, he travelled to Jerusalem where he joined the monastery of Rufinus and Melania the Elder. By 383, he was in the desert of Nitria with others who honoured Origen and became a pupil of St Macarius. His theology, spirituality and ascetic advice were widely influential East and West. Palladius (c. 365–425), his student and an Eastern historian of monasticism, John Cassian (c. 360–435), who had travelled to Eastern monasteries and later founded two monasteries near Marseille, and Maximus the Confessor (c. 580–662), arguably the greatest Eastern theologian of his time, were all in his debt. Evagrius was also influential through his writings. The Origenism that was singled out at Constantinople (553) looked to those writings for its inspiration. The fifteen 'Origenistic' statements

---

97 E. Clark, *Jerome, Chrysostom and friends*.

anathematised do not necessarily belong to the council of 553, nor do they self-evidently represent Origen's own thinking; they do, however, owe their form and structure to Evagrius.[98]

Another earlier author whose name figures prominently in the sixth-century debates is Didymus the Blind (313–98), who from early childhood was unable to see, but was nevertheless a prolific theologian who dictated numerous works and was also appointed by Athanasius to head the Alexandrian cate-chetical school. He was a renowned teacher, and people like Rufinus, Jerome and perhaps Gregory Nazianzen came to Alexandria to consult him. Not much is left of his substantial corpus, since he was denounced by name along with Origen and Evagrius by anti-Origenists. Since so few of his writings sur-vive, it is difficult to know precisely what they found so objectionable about him. Didymus' writings may have included a detailed study of the Trinity and an attack on Eunomius.[99] He clearly strove to demonstrate that Origen's Trinitarian thought was acceptable. Jerome's translation of his On the Holy Spirit was the only extant work until 1941, when workmen discovered a cache of papyri codices while clearing rock-quarries in Toura (sixteen kilometres south of Cairo). The Toura papyri included evidence for Didymus' commen-taries on Job, Zechariah and Genesis.[100] His allegorical approach to scriptural interpretation probably contributed to his ultimate rejection by opponents of Origenism in the sixth century.

The 'Three Chapters'

The other burning issue of the day was the on-going dispute over Christol-ogy after Chalcedon. Justinian hoped to win the support of Egyptian church authorities, certainly for political reasons and probably for some theologi-cal ones, by clearly distancing the Chalcedonian party from any association with Nestorian Dyophysitism. In 538, he condemned the person and work of Theodore of Mopsuestia (d. 428), Theodoret of Cyrrhus' (d. 460) writings against Cyril of Alexandria (d. 444) and a letter from Ibas of Edessa (d. 457) to Maris, bishop of Persia, in which Ibas praised Nestorius. (The condemned writings are known collectively as the 'Three Chapters'.) Justinian thought some specific Christological developments suggested by Scythian monks and Palestinian theologians opened up a practical way to resolve the conflicts

98 G. Bunge, Evagrius Pontikos; E. Clark, The Origenist controversy; A. Casiday, Evagrius Ponticus.
99 B. Krämer, 'Didymos von Alexandrien'; R. Layton, Didymus the Blind and his circle.
100 Didymus, On Zachariah (SC 83–5); On Genesis (SC 233–44); commentaries on Ezekiel and Psalms 20–44 were also discovered at Toura, but their authorship is disputed.

between Miaphysites and Dyophysites.[101] In 548, Pope Vigilius also wrote a *Judgment* against the Three Chapters. But these condemnations were not well received: a plethora of Western bishops vigorously rejected Vigilius' opinion. Vigilius reversed his position and even excommunicated the bishops in the imperial party who held to the condemnations. Justinian eventually abandoned the denunciation of the 'Three Chapters' in 551. His intention had been to promote ecumenical unity, and the document was counter-productive.

The council

Tensions between the emperor and the pope were fraught even in planning the council. Pope Vigilius had wanted the council to take place in Italy or Sicily, but Justinian determined to hold it in Constantinople. Vigilius decided not to attend since most of the bishops would be from the East. Indeed, although Justinian invited equal representation from Rome, Constantinople, Alexandria, Antioch and Jerusalem, the West was underrepresented among the bishops at the council. The most significant Western delegation consisted in eight representatives from Roman North Africa.

The heavy representation of Eastern sees was consistent with the urgent necessity to restore good relations between the capital and Egypt. Justinian needed to mollify the Egyptians because Egypt had long supplied most of the empire's grain. If confrontations worsened, the ecclesiastical or civil leaders, or indeed the people at large, could threaten to disrupt the food supply, which would have disastrous consequences for the entire empire. The possibility was ominously real, because many Egyptians regarded the decision of Chalcedon as blasphemy.[102] They worried that Nestorius' supporters could mouth the confession while holding to their views of 'two natures after the union'. That hypothetical situation aside, Egyptians believed that an active human nature in Jesus Christ (along the lines propagated in Nestorian doctrine) would destroy the united person of Christ.

On the other side of the debate, Pope Vigilius would not brook any insistence on only one divine nature in Jesus Christ. He held Miaphysite doctrine to be heretical and demanded that Chalcedon (451) be recognised as the touchstone of orthodoxy. A mere nine days after the council opened, he published his *Constitution*, a document that nullified and superseded his *Judgment* of 548. Vigilius' *Constitution* enumerated sixty propositions of Theodore that were false, but the pope declined to anathematise him personally because Ephesus

---

101 Gray, 'The legacy of Chalcedon'.
102 O. Mazal, *Justinian I. und seine Zeit*.

(431) and Chalcedon (451) had not. It would have been unseemly to declare the dead to be heretic. In his view, both Theodoret and Ibas had been cleared at Chalcedon. The conciliar fathers thought otherwise, however, and they anathematised Theodore of Mopsuestia, both his person and his works, and condemned certain writings by Theodoret and Ibas of Edessa. Pope Vigilius naturally objected, but Justinian sent him into exile and continued to work for reconciliation on his own terms.

After Constantinople II

In terms of restoring Christian unity, Justinian's council was unsuccessful. Vigilius' sanguine call for all to rally to Chalcedon notwithstanding, there seemed little realistic prospect for reconciliation through a unified doctrinal statement. Even unity in diversity became problematic, in large measure due to the way that the council dealt with the person and writings of Origen (c. 185–c. 254). A Greek-speaking Egyptian, Origen is the only person who could rival Augustine as the early church's deepest and most wide-ranging theologian. He died as a result of wounds suffered during the Decian persecution, but since he suffered wounds and only subsequently died he was considered a 'confessor' rather than a 'martyr'. Perhaps his reputation would have fared better had he died in custody. In 553, Origen (among others) was condemned by name in the eleventh anathema of Constantinople II. That condemnation calls for comment. We have no certain evidence that he and his views were discussed. But it would not be surprising if his teachings had been a topic of concern, because his robust Christological comments could support parts of either Cyril's or Nestorius' doctrine. On the other hand, it could be that the inclusion of his name among those anathematised is a later interpolation, as are the fifteen anathemas against Origenism.[103] Because the name and at least select propositions drawn from the works of the greatest Greek theologian of antiquity were compromised at Constantinople II, subsequent Byzantine Christians were obliged to deal carefully with Origen. Their diminished recourse to Origen may well have hindered Greek theologians in circumstances where the breadth of theological resources available from his works could have been extremely useful.

---

103 *Decrees of the ecumenical councils*, ed. and trans. Tanner, 1: 105–6, does not include those fifteen anathemas; V. Grummel, *Les regestes des actes du patriarcat de Constantinople*, 1: 245; F. Diekamp, *Die origenistische Streitigkeiten*, 90; F. W. Murphy and P. Sherwood, *Constantinople II et Constantinople III*, 108–9.

Another deep problem concerned the East Syrian Christians, who refused to abandon the works of Antiochene theologians and preserved many of them by translating them into Syriac. By the condemnation of Nestorius in 431, they were already established outside the empire and they proved to be strongly missionary-orientated. Their lines of commerce opened onto the Silk Road and Syrians took Christianity with them as far as China.[104] The scope of their accomplishment is all the more astounding when we recall that the East Syrian churches could not regularly count on any help from the Roman empire, even from Antioch, the metropolis that spawned many of their views.

The great sees of Rome, Constantinople, Alexandria, Antioch and Jerusalem did not find harmony in the decisions of 553. It had seemed (perhaps not accidentally) in 538 that those sees were solidly Chalcedonian.[105] Justinian had hoped that his vision would be endorsed by the council and, through it, those powerful centres as well. Rome and Jerusalem stood solidly behind Constantinople (553), but disputes continued in the capital and raged in Antioch. Alexandria, the home of Athanasius, and with it Egypt were primarily anti-Chalcedonian. Not long into the seventh century, only Rome and Constantinople remained Christian powers. The other three fell into Muslim hands and their influence was drastically weakened in larger Christian circles.

Two events in the last half of the sixth century foreshadowed the eclipse of both anti-Chalcedonian and Chalcedonian Christianities in the East.[106] Between 566 and 568, the time seemed ripe for an attempt at agreement, much as it had in the 540s. When the anti-Chalcedonian patriarch Theodosius died in 566, he was given a large and gracious funeral in Constantinople.[107] He was succeeded by John Scholasticus. Around the same time, Jacob Baradaeus and John of Ephesus, the great anti-Chalcedonian missionaries, were concerned by schism within their ranks. Some anti-Chalcedonian theologians were insisting on the distinction of the three persons of the Trinity and subordinating the Son and the Holy Spirit to the Father in a way that was uncomfortably redolent of fourth-century Neo-Arianism. Jacob Baradaeus and John of Ephesus were frankly dismayed at the prospect of this recrudescent 'tritheism', particularly since the 'tritheists' were intent on spreading their view far and wide.[108] John Scholasticus held meetings with these two anti-Chalcedonian groups and was able to work out a carefully crafted position on which they could agree. His

---

104 See chapter 4, below.
105 Gray, The defense of Chalcedon, 60.
106 W. H. C. Frend, The rise of Christianity, 873–6.
107 Michael, Chronicon 10.1 (ed. and trans. Chabot, 283).
108 John of Ephesus, H.E. 3.3.10; Michael, Chronicon 10.7.

position was strong because the leader of the Miaphysite Armenian church had travelled to the Byzantine capital to accept John as a proper Christian. The Armenian *catholicos* was motivated not least because the Persian government was again attacking his church.

Patriarch John thus faced the difficult task of bringing anti-Chalcedonians and Chalcedonians together.[109] A number of anti-Chalcedonian theologians were willing to work toward union if the phrase 'out of two natures, one' and Cyril of Alexandria's twelve anathemas against Nestorius were received by Chalcedonians as canonical and if the rejection of Severus of Antioch in 536 by Constantinople's Home Synod was withdrawn. If the Chalcedonians were to comply with those requests, the anti-Chalcedonians would accept the incumbent Chalcedonian patriarch in Antioch and not press for their own candidate.

The emperor Justin II (*regn.* 565–8) appointed a skilled negotiator from the metropolis, John, to lead discussions with the Syrian anti-Chalcedonians. The conference was held in the monastery of Mar Zakai not far from the fortress of Callinicum on Syria's border with Persia. John's document held the terms of the agreement made between the parties within Constantinople. But the Syrian monks were passionate about their anti-Chalcedonian convictions. When John proclaimed the agreement, they demanded to see the letter and snatched it from his hands. The agreement reached in Constantinople featured neither a rejection of Leo's *Tome* nor Chalcedon's confession of faith, because at Constantinople they had carefully eschewed topics that could lead to quarrels. When the monks found that their foundational statements of faith were not included, they tore up the document and even threatened to anathematise their famed missionary Jacob Baradaeus, who had endorsed the statement in Constantinople. Such was the depth of attachment among rural anti-Chalcedonians to their tradition. The conference was over. John left without eating another meal and entered Persia for a different set of negotiations.

As a result of the failure at Mar Zakai, only key areas such as Constantinople, certain Greek-speaking regions west and north of the capital (in what is now Europe), Asia Minor and Palestine came primarily under the control of Chalcedonians. Even in those areas, however, there were pockets of anti-Chalcedonians. The anti-Chalcedonian group was the majority in both Syria and Egypt (though there were also Chalcedonians to be found in Egypt). The anti-Chalcedonian mission forged ahead well beyond the Byzantine empire, making inroads to the south into Nubia and to the east into Arabia and India. The failure to reconcile these theological disagreements left the 'Christian

109 Michael, *Chronicon* 10.3.

cause' in disarray by the end of the sixth century. Any given Christian region might well harbour deep resentment against the neighbouring area and refuse to provide assistance in the event of troubles from outside.

The second major event was a tragic military disaster. The Ghassanids, an alliance of Arab tribes, lived along the border between Palestine and Arabia. They had become Christians during the sixth century and adhered to a Miaphysite confession. Their bishop lived in Bostra, the Arab provinces' capital, and from 542 he was known as 'the bishop of the Arabs'. For the Roman empire, a treaty with the Ghassanids was desirable because they could control other Arabs who might invade Palestine. Roman interests in the Ghassanids could be even more direct. For example, the emperor Tiberius (*regn.* 578–82) was at war with Persia and, seeking more than protection from the south, invited al-Muhdhir, king of the Ghassanids, to the capital in 580. There, Tiberius encouraged al-Muhdhir to attack the Persians. The invasion planned for 580 was directed by Maurice, who at that time was a count (*comes*) but later became emperor (582–602).

Maurice was an ardent Chalcedonian and so entertained suspicions against the anti-Chalcedonian Ghassanids on religious grounds. Upon leading his troops to the Persian border, Maurice discovered that the bridge across the Euphrates had been destroyed. It is possible, though far from obvious, that al-Muhdhir was not certain that the Byzantines would ultimately support this venture and, playing both sides against the middle, had the bridge torn down. Maurice in any case concluded that al-Muhdhir was an enemy, so he had him arrested, tried and banished to Cyprus. His family swore that they would never again be forced into negotiations with Romans. They joined Persia in the war and began raids on Palestine. So out of wounded pride and understandable resentment, aggrieved Christian Arabs were already attacking Roman Palestine decades before the Muslim invasions of the seventh century.

Conclusion

The movement of large numbers of Christians from one place to another, as immigrants,[110] pilgrims,[111] monks, bishops and theologians, connected numerous local forms of Christianity across the Greek-speaking world (and beyond, as the writings of John Cassian, Egeria and the Piacenza Pilgrim remind us). By

---

110 See, for example, the discussion of Milan's position on major Roman thoroughfares in chapter 8, below.
111 Many pilgrims travelled to the holy sites of the East. The most famous was Egeria, who wrote a travelogue for the benefit of her monastic sisters, detailing the sites and services that she saw.

the end of the sixth century, nearly all Christians in the Mediterranean shared an organisation of bishops and presbyters as well as deacons (and sometimes deaconesses). Bishops had become powerful leaders in the church, but also in society at large. Synods and councils attempted to bring unity to the various Christianities, but these efforts were never fully successful. Monasticism in its numerous forms shaped countless Christian lives, either directly when people became monks or nuns or indirectly as secular Christians sought their advice. Monasteries were 'in the world, but not of the world' and sometimes they acted as staging grounds for those who tried to evangelise the surrounding areas.

Churches and monasteries were built in urban and rural locations alike, to provide fixed points for the daily lives of Greek Christians. The Eastern Romans were deeply fond of Christian art and architecture.[112] Large churches went up to indicate success in attaining social positions and accumulating wealth. Another major component of the artistic heritage of Greek Christians was their literature. Collections of prayers, liturgies and hymns circulated, and sometimes they were translated into regional languages. Theological treatises – some of which were in themselves beautiful works – were similarly rendered into different tongues to allow them to circulate. Even the great and divisive creeds that were formulated during this era can be considered cultural monuments.

Of the numerous councils held c. 300–600, most were strictly regional or local. The majority were never recognised as ecumenical, though some could be regarded as 'trial runs' in which significant positions and terms were aired.[113] What should be remembered about the five councils in this era that eventually came to be recognised as ecumenical (Nicaea in 325; Constantinople in 381; Ephesus in 431; Chalcedon in 451; Constantinople in 553) is, first, that they were directly under the influence of emperors who wanted their wishes fulfilled.[114] Second, the Christian leaders who attended these councils often wrangled at least as much over the ranking of their sees as over theological

112 Eusebius of Caesarea, H.E. 7.18, tells us that in his city there was a bronze statue of Jesus healing a woman, one of Christianity's early art treasures. Macarius Magnes says that the woman depicted is Berenice, or Veronica, and the statue was first in Edessa. Sozomen (H.E. 5.1) and John Malalas (Chronicle) both claim to have seen it. Eusebius also saw pictures of Peter and Paul, even Jesus himself, all painted in colours as former pagans had been accustomed to depict their gods. Kurt Weitzmann, The icon, depicts and describes four icons from our period, three attributed to Constantinople and found at the St Catherine Monastery in Sinai (plate 1, 40–1; plate 2, 42–3; plate 8, 54–5) and the fourth to Palestine (plate 7, 52–3). See further chapter 29, below.
113 See chapter 15, below.
114 See chapter 1, above.

issues. Alexandria continuously fought with Antioch and Constantinople, a feud which was somewhat simplified when Antiochene presbyters regularly became the bishops of New Rome. Third, Western attendance at these councils was always limited; not even the Church of Rome was consistently represented. Fourth, rarely were bishops from east of Antioch party to these discussions, and even when they were their numbers were small. As a result, their different languages and insights never were integrated in the formulations. After Ephesus, few representatives from beyond the Roman empire appeared at church councils. Some of them specifically rejected Chalcedon when they discovered what had been decided there. The anti-Chalcedonian churches in Syria and elsewhere held their own councils, on occasion contravening what was decided at the 'ecumenical' councils.[115] Fifth, perhaps the most important point to be emphasised is that the creeds, canons and decisions of these councils attained universal force only when they were received as normative by Christians in the Eastern Mediterranean, Europe, Egypt, Ethiopia and elsewhere.[116]

The emergence of the Great Church did not destroy the rich diversity of Christianity in the East, precisely because it was unable to enforce full unity. Even the major fractious parties had differences among themselves. Other churches existed around the Mediterranean: Apollinarians, who affirmed in Christ no human soul, mind or will; Messalians, who insisted upon the need for ceaseless prayer after baptism; Novatians, who were theologically orthodox, but puritanical in their dealings with those who failed during earlier persecutions and sacrificed to pagan gods; Theopaschites, who maintained that one of the Trinity was crucified; and others. This brief sampling in no way exhausts the diversity that would have been found in the Christian East and Orient. This is to say nothing of the religious diversity that existed beyond Christianity, when local pagan religions continued to exist even as Christians were making converts among rural peasants.[117]

There can be no doubt that the influence of emperors on the Christian religion changed it profoundly. In addition to promoting certain expressions of the faith and certain practices and framing laws that promoted the established positions of 'Catholic' and 'Orthodox' Christianity, patronage from the upper echelons of society also resulted in the foundation of justly famous buildings as well as the production of luxurious Bibles and the development of ornate and beautiful liturgies. Imperial power formed the Great Church. Establishment,

115 See chapter 4, below.
116 A. de Halleux, 'La réception du symbole œcuménique'.
117 See chapter 7, below.

however, had its dangers. The shift has not always been viewed as for the best, not least by those Christians in this period who were attacked by emperor or council. The persecuted who later ruled often proved to have sadly short memories and persecuted those who had no power. Christians have seldom felt strong apprehension about using force to get their will. The empowerment of specific Christian groups frequently resulted in other Christian groups being disenfranchised and, in some cases, vulnerable to non-Christians. The East Syrian church, driven out of the empire, suffered greatly at the hands of Persians, who thought of Christians as a fifth column. On other occasions, inter-Christian rivalry in effect drove the relatively powerless Christian faction into the arms of non-Christian forces. Justinianic Christianity had so alienated the anti-Chalcedonians and others whom they considered heretics that many Christians in the Middle East at first welcomed the invading Muslims as liberators. The Great Church has given many good gifts, but it has also asked for and received much disdain for glorying in establishment.

Bibliography

PRIMARY SOURCES

Acta martyrum: Les actes des martyrs de l'Égypte tirés des manuscrits coptes de la Bibliothèque Vaticane et du Musée Borgia, i, ed. H. Hyvernat (Paris, 1886–7)

Aetius, 'The *Syntagmation* of Aetius the Anomean', ed. and trans. L. R. Wickham, *JTS* N.S. 19 (1968): 532–69

Ammianus Marcellinus, trans. J. C. Rolfe, LCL (London, 1950–2)

Apophthegmata Patrum, systematic collection (SC 387, 474)

Besa: *Life of Shenoute*, trans. D. N. Bell (Kalamazoo, MI, 1983)

Codex Justinianus (CJ), ed. P. Krüger. *Corpus iuris civilis* (Berlin, 1929¹¹)

Codex Theodosianus (CTh), eds. T. Mommsen and P. Meyer. *Theodosiani libri XVI cum Constitutionibus Sirmondianis: et leges novellae ad Theodosianum pertinentes* (Berlin, 1954²); for CTh 16, see now SC 497.

Corpus notitiarum episcopatuum ecclesiae orientalis graecae, fasc. ii, part ii (Council of Ephesus), eds. E. Garland and V. Lauraent (Kadi-Koey, 1936)

St. Cyrille de Jérusalem: Catéchète, trans. A. Paulin (Paris, 1959)

Cyril of Jerusalem. *Mystagogue*, trans. A. Doval (Washington, DC, 2001)

St. Cyril of Jerusalem's lectures on the Christian sacraments, ed. F. L. Cross (Crestwood, NY, 1986)

Decrees of the ecumenical councils, i: Nicaea I to Lateran V (= *Conciliorum oecumenicorum decreta*, eds. G. Alberigo et al., with English translation), ed. and trans. Norman Tanner (London and Washington, DC, 1990)

Didymus the Blind. *On Genesis* (SC 233–4)

On Zachariah (SC 83–5)

Diodore of Tarsus. *Commentary on Psalms 1–51*, trans. R. D. Hill (Boston, MA, 2005)

Dioscorus. *A panegyric on Macarius of Tkôw*, ed. D. Johnson (CSCO 415–16)

Egeria. *Travels* (SC 296); G. Röwenkamp and D. Thönnes, *Itinerarium = Reisebericht Egeria. Mit Auszügen aus De locis sanctis = Die heiligen Stäaten / Petrus Diaconus*, Fontes Christiani 20 (Freiburg, 1995); N. Natalucci, *Egeria, Pellegrinaggio in Terra Santa* (Bologna, 1999); J. Wilkenson, *Egeria's Travels, newly translated (from the Latin) with supporting documents and notes* (Warminster, 1999³)

Epiphanius. *The Panarion*, trans. F. Williams (Leiden, 1997)

L'Hérésiologie chez Épiphanius de Salamine, trans. A. Pourkier (Paris, 1992)

Eunomius. *Eunomius: The extant works*, ed. and trans. R. P. Vaggione (Oxford, 1987)

Eusebius. *Historia ecclesiastica* (GCS – Eusebius Werke, II); *The history of the church from Christ to Constantine*, trans. G. A. Williamson, rev. edn. with intro. by A. Louth (New York, 1989)

Life of Constantine (GCS Eusebius Werke, I); trans. Averil Cameron and Stuart G. Hall. Eusebius. *Life of Constantine* (Oxford, 1999)

Gregory of Nazianzus. *Carmina historica* (PL 37: 969–1452); see also C. White, ed. and trans., *Gregory of Nazianzus. Autobiographical Poems* (Cambridge, 1996)

Letters (SC 208)

Orations (PL 35 and PL 36: 12–664); for Gregory's *Orations* 4 and 5, see SC 309; for *Oration* 14, see PL 35: 857–909

Jerome. *Lives of illustrious men* (TU 14.1)

John of Ephesus. *Historia ecclesiasticae pars tertia* (CSCO 105–6)

John Malalas. *Chronographia*, ed. J. Thurn (Berlin, 2000); trans. E. Jeffreys et al. (Melbourne, 1986). Johannes Thurn, ed., *Ioannis Malalae Chronographia*, Corpus Fontium Historiae Byzantinae (CFHB) 35 (Berlin/New York: Walter de Gruyter, 2000)

Julian. *Emperor Julian*, trans. S. Lieu, Translated Texts for Historians (Liverpool, 1986) *The Works of the emperor Julian*, trans. W. C. Wright, LCL (London, 1913)

Lactantius. *Divine institutes*, ed. E. Heck and Antoine Wlosok (Saur, 2005); trans. A. Bowen and P. Garnsey, Translated Texts for Historians (Liverpool, 2003)

Macarius the Egyptian, *Sämmtliche schriften*, ed. and trans. M. Jocham (Kempten, 1878)

Maximus Tyrius. *Dissertations*, ed. M. B. Trapp (Stuttgart, 1994)

Michael the Syrian. *Chronicon*, ed. and trans. J.-B. Chabot (Brussels, 1963)

Origen. *Dialogue with Heracleides* (SC 67)

Pausanius. *Description of Greece*, trans. W. H. S. Jones and R. Wycherley, LCL (London, 1918–35)

Philostorgius. *Historia ecclesiastica* (GCS: *Philostorgius Kirchengeschichte*)

Philoxenus. *Letter to the monks of Senoun* (CSCO 231–2)

The sayings of the desert fathers: The alphabetical collection, trans. B. Ward (Kalamazoo, MI, 1984)

Serapion of Thumis against the Manichees, ed. R. P. Casey (Cambridge, MA, 1931)

Severus of Antioch. *Cathedral homilies* (PO 4, 12, 16, 20, 22, 23, 25, 26, 29, 35, 36, 37, 38)

A collection of letters of Severus of Antioch (PO 12, 14)

Socrates. *Historia ecclesiastica* (GCS, N.F. 1: *Sokrates Kirchengeschichte*; SC 477, 493–)

Sozomen. *Historia ecclesiastica* (GCS, N.F. 4: *Sozomenus Kirchengeschichte*)

Stephen, bishop of Heracleopolis Magna. *A panegyric on Apollo, archimandrite of the monastery of Isaac* (CSCO 394–5)

Symeon the Younger. *La Vie ancienne de S. Syméon le jeune*, ed. P. van den Ven (Brussels, 1962)

Theodoret. *Ecclesiastical history* (GCS N.F. 5)

Zacharias Rhetor. *Ecclesiastical history* (CSCO 83–4, 87–8); *Die sogennante Kirchengeschichte des Zacharias Rhetor*, ed. K. Ahrens and G. Krüger (Leipzig, 1899)

Life of Severus (PO 2)

SECONDARY SOURCES

Abramowski, L. 'Die Christologie Babais des Grossen', in *Symposium Syriacum, Rome 1972* (Rome, 1974), 219–45

'Ein nestorianischen Traktat bei Leontius von Jerusalem', *OCA* 21 (1983): 57–83

'Streit um Diodor zwischen den beiden ephesianischen Konzilien', *ZKG* 66 (1955): 252–87

'Was hat das Nicaeno-Konstantinopolitanum (C) mit dem Konzil von Konstantinopel zu tun?', *ThPh* 67 (1992): 481–513

Abramowski, R. 'Der theologische Nachlass des Diodor von Tarsus', *ZNTW* 42 (1949): 19–69

Allen, P. and C. T. R. Haywood. *Severus of Antioch* (London, 2004)

Anatolios, K. *Athanasius* (London, 2004)

Azkoul, M. *St. Gregory of Nyssa and the tradition of the fathers* (Lewiston, NY, 1995)

Barnes, T. D. *Constantine and Eusebius* (Cambridge, MA, 1981)

di Berardino, A., ed. *Encyclopedia of the early church*, trans. A. Walford (Oxford, 1992)

Bunge, G. *Evagrius Pontikos, Praktikos oder Der Mönch* (Cologne, 1989)

Casiday, A. *Evagrius Ponticus* (London, 2006)

Chalmers, W. R. 'Eunapius, Ammianus Marcellanus and Zosimos, on Julian's Persian expedition', *Classical Quarterly* 10 (1960): 152–60

Chediath, G. *The Christology of Mar Babai the Great* (Kottayam, India, 1982)

Clark, E. 'Ascetic renunciation and feminine advancement: A paradox of late ancient Christianity', *ATR* 63 (1981): 240–75

Jerome, Chrysostom and friends (New York, 1979)

'The lady vanishes: Dilemmas of a feminist historian after the "Linguistic Turn"', *Church History* 67 (1998): 1–31

The Origenist controversy: The cultural construction of an early Christian debate (Princeton, 1992)

Constans, N. *Proclus of Constantinople and the cult of the Virgin in late antiquity: Homilies 1–5, texts and translations*, Supplements to *VChr* 56 (Leiden, 2003)

Croke, B. 'Justinian's Constantinople', in M. Maas, ed., *The Cambridge companion to the age of Justinian* (Cambridge, 2005), 60–86

Daley, B. 'Building a new city: The Cappadocian fathers and the rhetoric of philanthropy', *JECS* 7 (1999): 431–61

Gregory of Nazianzus (London, 2006)

'The Origenism of Leontius of Byzantium', *JTS* N.S. 27 (1976): 333–69

'A richer union: Leontius of Byzantium and the relationship of human and divine in Christ', *SP* 24 (1993): 239–65

Delehaye, H. 'Les martyrs d'Égypt', *Analecta Bollandiana* 40 (1922): 127–54

Diekamp, F. *Die origenistischen Streitigkeiten im 6. Jahrhundert und das 5. Allgemeine Konzil* (Münster, 1899)

Diepen, H. M. *Douze dialogues de christologie anciennes* (Rome, 1960)

Doval, A. J. *Cyril of Jerusalem, mystagogue* (Washington, D.C., 2001)

Drijvers, J. W. *Cyril of Jerusalem: Bishop and city* (Leiden, 2004)

Elm, S. *'Virgins of God': The making of asceticism in late antiquity* (Oxford, 1994)

Fitschen, K. *Serapion von Thumis: Echte und unechte Schriften sowie die Zeugnisse des Athanasius und andere*, PTS 37 (Berlin, 1992)

Frend, W. H. C. *The rise of Christianity* (Philadelphia, 1984)

Ginkel, J. van. *John of Ephesus. Historian of the sixth century* (Gröningen, 1995)

Gockel, M. 'A dubious Christological formula? Leontius of Byzantium and the anhypostasis-enhypostasis theory', *JTS* n.s. 51 (2000): 525–32

Goehring, J. *Ascetics, society and the desert: Studies in early Egyptian monasticism* (Harrisburg, PA, 1989)

Grant, R. M. *Eusebius as church historian* (Oxford, 1980)

Graumann, T. *Die Kirche der Väter: Vätertheologie und Väterbeweis in den Kirchen des Ostens bis zum Konzil von Ephesus 431* (Tübingen, 2002)

Gray, P. T. R. *The defense of Chalcedon in the East (451–553)* (Leiden, 1979)

'The legacy of Chalcedon: Christological problems and their significance', in M. Maas, ed., *The Cambridge companion to the age of Justinian* (Cambridge, 2005), 227–36

Greatrex, G. 'Byzantium and the East in the sixth century', in M. Maas, ed., *The Cambridge companion to the age of Justinian* (Cambridge, 2005), 477–509

Grillmeier, A. *Christ in Christian tradition*, I, trans. J. S. Bowden (Atlanta, 1975²)

Christ in Christian tradition, II. 1, trans. P. Allen and J. Cawte (Atlanta, 1987)

Grillmeier, A., with T. Hainthaler. *Christ in Christian tradition*, II.2, trans. P. Allen and J. Cawte (Atlanta, 1987)

Grummel, V. *Les regestes des actes du patriarcat de Constantinople*, I: Les actes des patriarches; fasc. I, Les regestes de 381 à 751 (Istanbul, 1932)

Haas, F. A. J. de *John Philoponus' new definition of prime matter: Aspects of its background in Neoplatonism and the ancient commentary tradition*, Philosophia Antiqua 69 (Leiden, 1997)

de Halleux, A. *Philoxène de Mabbog: Sa vie, ses écrits, sa théologie* (Louvain, 1960)

'La réception du symbole œcuménique, de Nicée à Chalcédoine', *Ephemerides theologicae Lovanienses* 61 (1985): 1–47; reprinted in A. de Halleux *Patrologie et Œcuménisme: Recueil d'études*, BETL 93 (Louvain, 1990), 25–67

Harvey, S. A. *Asceticism and society in crisis: John of Ephesus and the 'Lives of the Eastern saints'* (Berkeley, 1990)

'The sense of a Stylite: Perspectives on Simeon the Elder', *VChr* 42 (1988): 376–94

Hauschild, W.-D. 'Eustathius von Sebaste', *TRE* 9 (1982): 547–56

'Nicäno-Konstantinopolitanisches Glaubensbekenntnis', *TRE* 24 (1995): 444–56

Hofmann, F. 'Der Kampf Päpste von Konzil und Dogma von Chalkedon von Leo dem Grossen bis Hormisdas (451–519)', in A. Grillmeier and H. Bacht, eds., *Das Konzil von Chalkedon: Geschichte und Gegenwart im auftrag der theologischen Fakultät S. J. Sankt Georgen* (Würzburg, 1953), II: 13–94

Hurst, T. 'The epistles of Timothy I of Baghdad: A study in Christian–Muslim controversy', Ph.D. dissertation, The Catholic University of America, 1986

Johnson, D. 'Anti-chalcedonian polemics in Coptic texts, 451–641', in B. A. Pearons and J. E. Goehring, eds., *The roots of Egyptian Christianity* (Philadelphia, 1986), 216–34

Kelly, J. N. D. *Early Christian creeds* (London, 1972³)

Golden Mouth. The story of John Chrysostom: Ascetic, preacher, bishop (Ithaca, NY, 1996)

Kennedy, G. *Greek rhetoric under Christian emperors* (Princeton, 1983)

Keresztes, P. 'From the Great Persecution to the Peace of Galerius', *VChr* 37 (1983): 379–99

Klauser, T. 'Hagia Sophia', *RAC* 13: 107–18

Krämer, B. 'Didymos von Alexandrian', *TRE* 8 (1981): 1–746

Krausmueller, D. 'Leontius of Jerusalem, a theologian of the seventh century', *JTS* n.s. 52 (2001): 637–57

Krawiec, R. *Shenoute and the women of the White Monastery: Egyptian monasticism in late antiquity* (Oxford, 2002)

Kupan, I. P. *Theodoret of Cyrus* (London, 2006)

Labate, L. 'Nephalius', in A. di Berardino, ed., *Encyclopedia of the early church*

Lang, U. M. *John Philoponus and the controversies over Chalcedon in the sixth century: A study and translation of the Arbiter* (Louvain, 2001)

Layton, R. *Didymus the Blind and his circle in late antique Alexandria: Virtue and narrative in biblical scholarship* (Urbana, IL, 2004)

Lee, A. D. 'The empire at war', in M. Maas, ed., *The Cambridge companion to the age of Justinian* (Cambridge, 2005), 113–33

Löhr, W. 'Theophilus von Alexandrian', *TRE* 33 (2002): 364–8

Louth, A. 'Palestine: Cyril of Jerusalem and Epiphanius', in F. Young et al., eds., *The Cambridge History of Early Christian Literature* (Cambridge, 2004), 283–8

McGuckin, J. *St. Cyril of Alexandria: The Christological controversy: Its history, theology and texts* (Crestwood, NY, 2004)

St. Gregory of Nazianzus: An intellectual biography (Crestwood, NY, 2004)

McLeod, F. *The roles of Christ's humanity in salvation: Insights from Theodore of Mopsuestia* (Washington, D.C., 2005)

Mainstone, R. *Hagia Sophia: Architecture, structure and liturgy of Justinian's great church* (London, 1988)

Martin, A. *Athanase d'Alexandrie et l'église d'Egypte au IVᵉ siècle (328–375)* (Rome, 1996)

Mathews, T. *The early churches of Constantinople: Archaeology and liturgy* (University Park, MD, 1971)

Mazal, O. *Justinian I. und seine Zeit: Geschichte und Kultur des Byzantinischen Reiches im 6. Jahrhundert* (Cologne, 2001)

Meredith, A. *The Cappadocians* (London, 1995)

Murphy, F. W. and P. Sherwood. *Constantinople II et Constantinople III* (Paris, 1974)

Nice, R. L. *Saint Sophia in Istanbul: An architectural survey, installments I and II* (Washington, D.C., 1966, 1986)

Norris, F. 'Eusebius on Jesus as deceiver and sorcerer', in H. W. Attridge and G. Hata, eds., *Eusebius, Christianity and Judaism* (Leiden, 1992), 523–40

Faith gives fullness to reasoning: The five theological orations of Gregory of Nazianzen, trans. L. Wickham and F. Williams (Leiden, 1991)

'Origen', in P. Esler, ed., *The early Christian world* (London, 2000), 105–26

'Timothy I of Baghdad, *catholicos* of the East Syrian church 780–823', *International Bulletin of Missionary Research* 30 (July 2006): 133–6

Norris, R. *Manhood and Christ: A study of the Christology of Theodore of Mopsuestia* (Oxford, 1963)

O'Leary, D. L. *The saints of Egypt* (London, 1937; reprint: Amsterdam, 1974)

Pásztori-Kupán, I. *Theodoret of Cyrus* (London, 2006)

Pelikan, J. *Christianity and classical culture: The metamorphosis of natural theology in the Christian encounter with Hellenism* (New Haven, 1993)

Pohl, W. 'Justinian and the barbarian kingdoms', in M. Maas, ed., *The Cambridge companion to the age of Justinian* (Cambridge, 2005), 448–76

Rebenich, S. *Jerome* (London, 2002)

Richard, M. 'Léonce de Jérusalem et Léonce de Byzance', *Mélanges de science religieuse* 1 (1944): 35–88

Ritter, A. M. *Das Konzil von Konstantinopel und sein Symbol. Studien zur Geschichte und Theologie des II Ökumenischen Konzils*, Forschung zur Kirchen- und Dogmengeschichte 15 (Göttingen, 1965)

Simonetti, M. 'Acacius of Beroea', in A. di Berardino, ed., *Encyclopedia of the early church*

Staats, R. *Das Glaubensbekenntnis von Nizäa-Konstantinopel* (Darmstadt, 1996)

Stiernon, D. 'Dioscurus of Alexandria', 'Eutherius', in A. di Berardino, ed., *Encyclopedia of the early church*

Tabbernee, W. *Montanist inscriptions and testimonia: Epigraphic sources illustrating the history of Montanism*, Patristic Monograph Series 16 (Macon, GA, 1997)

Teteriatnikov, N. *Mosaics of Hagia Sophia, Istanbul: The Fossati restoration and the world of the Byzantine institute* (Washington, D.C., 1998)

Torrance, T. *The ground and grammar of theology* (Charlottesville, VA, 1980)

Trombley, F. *Hellenic religion and Christianization*, 2 vols. (Leiden, 1993–4)

Vaggione, R. P. *Eunomius of Cyzicus and the Nicene revolution* (Oxford, 2000)

Voicu, S. 'Basil of Seleucia', in A. di Berardino, ed., *Encyclopedia of the early church*

Weitzmann, K. *The icon: Holy images – sixth to fourteenth century* (New York, 1978)

Wessel, S. *Cyril of Alexandria and the Nestorian controversy: The making of a saint and of a heretic* (Oxford, 2004)

Wickham, L. R. 'Timothy Aelurus: Against the definition of the Council of Chalcedon', in C. Laga et al., eds., *After Chalcedon: Festschrift A. von Roey* (Louvain, 1985), 155–66

Wilken, R. L. *John Chrysostom and the Jews: Rhetoric and reality in the late fourth century* (Berkeley, 1988)

Williams, R. *Arius: Heresy and tradition* (London, 2001²)

'Arius and the Meletian schism', *JTS* n.s. 37 (1986): 35–52

Zaharopoulos, D. A. *Theodore of Mopsuestia on the Bible* (New York, 1989)

4

Early Asian and East African Christianities

DAVID BUNDY

Introduction

Christian communities evolved along the trade routes east of Antioch and south of Alexandria early in the Christian period as Christian merchants and soldiers plied their trades and told their stories. These were followed by priests and much later by organisational structures that have been, for historians, more recognisable as Christian churches. As modern migration studies indicate, migrants and merchants generally take their religion with them as they move. However, merchant missionaries do not keep good records of their religious lives and rarely recognise the cultural complexities, even contradictions, with which they live. As a result, the records of Christian communities in Asia generally begin when they attract the attention of administrators of church and state.

Early Asian Christians lived in very diverse contexts, contexts sometimes masked by the political unity imposed on diverse regions. National boundaries rarely reflected cultural boundaries, although over time differentiation took place. Differences of language, religion and ethnicity were easily recognisable by later historians. Larger cultural issues such as the understandings of death, pollution, embodiment (including poverty and asceticism), representation (including the functions of art), the understanding of power, and the factors of group identity have received less attention but were no less crucial.

Before and during this period, Christians came to live in most areas of Asia, including what is now eastern Turkey, Armenia, Georgia, Azerbaijan, Syria, Iraq, Iran, Afghanistan, Central Asia, China, Pakistan, the Arabian peninsula, Soqotra, the Persian Gulf and India. Christians generally had no access to political power in these regions (with the partial exceptions of Georgia and Armenia). In Byzantium, Christians by the end of the fourth century had co-opted the institutions of social, intellectual and political power. This did not happen in Asia. Christians lived alongside, often without access to, the structures of power. They were forced to develop their own institutions without state subsidies. Their faith sometimes brought opprobrium and death.

Another difference from the Byzantine-controlled Christian areas is found in the Asian Christian approach to the intellectual life. Where institutions of higher learning and research were developed, such as at Edessa, Nisibis, Merv and some monasteries of the Tur Abdin in what is now southern Turkey, theologians and their debates had a more central role. However, beyond those centres, Christianity was defined primarily by the liturgy, kinship structures, spirituality and ethics. Therefore the Bible (and reflection on the biblical texts), the liturgy, lives of saints, wisdom sayings and synodal acts appear to have been more central to Christian life. In theological texts west and south of the areas of direct Byzantine influence, there is less precision of theological language. It was not that the writers were less capable; they were merely not directly involved in the struggles for power that were prevalent in Byzantium.

Throughout Asia, there were problems posed by the relation of Christianity to other religious traditions. Sometimes it was a matter of definition. In much of northern Mesopotamia, Marcionism was for perhaps two centuries the dominant expression of the Christian tradition. It is unclear when Asian Christians came to understand themselves as totally distinct from Judaism. Mani and the Manichaeans certainly understood themselves in continuity with the Christian tradition and had their roots in earlier Christian/Jewish baptistic traditions in Parthia and India that knew and honoured the story of Jesus of Nazareth, seeing him in continuity with the Jewish prophets and Mani as a continuation of that tradition. Developing as it did outside the orbit of Roman Christianity, Manichaeism developed structures and theological traditions that were quite different. Mani's tradition and the other Asian baptistic traditions were never accepted by Western Christians who considered them to be heretical competitors. The relations with Zoroastrianism, Buddhism, Confucianism and other local religious traditions were more complicated and the evidence for that interaction generally more subtle.

Finally, a history of early Christianity in Asia or in East Africa during this period cannot be written in the same ways as histories of the Western church where practitioners and their texts, from the fourth century onward, entered privileged places in the imperial culture. In Asia and Africa, there is less, and more episodic, documentation – more, as it were, a series of vignettes than a complete record. The amount of documentation varies significantly. Syriac, Armenian and Georgian sources are extensive, while the extant sources for important Christian presences such as those of Soghdia, China and India are few and suggestive. Those for other places, including much of Central Asia and Tibet, are generally lost. Coptic and Ethiopic sources are more plentiful but generally of more recent date and more recently written and/or copied. Only a few Nubian sources have survived.

However, Christian texts and peoples were scattered throughout Asia and parts of non-Latin/Greek-speaking Eastern Africa by the beginning of the fourth century. In order to understand the complexities of that period, it is essential to begin with the texts and traditions that gave these groups their identities. We will therefore survey the developments in early northern Mesopotamia by focusing on materials suggestive of what one finds as the fourth century opens. Then after a brief discussion of the fourth century in Syria and Persia, which are more fully documented, the focus shifts to national or ethnic expressions of Christianity, the experience of each of which differed according to larger socio-political and economic developments.

The beginnings of Christianity in Asia: Shadowy origins

Scholarly theories and ancient myths of the origins of Asian Christianity have, since the fourth century, focused on Edessa (ancient and modern Urfa), a city where the Christian version of Aramaic known as Syriac was developed and where the first Armenian alphabet was apparently also created. While it is probable that there was a Christian presence in Edessa from the earliest days of Christianity, little can be known about that development. There are three primary theories: (1) the Thomas traditions; (2) the Abgar-Addai traditions; and (3) Jewish origins.

The Thomas traditions

There are two early texts that lend some credence to the theory that Thomas brought Christianity to Edessa, or to a variant of that theory. The *Acts of Thomas* are an account of Thomas the apostle of Jesus from perhaps the early third century (before 226), written in Syriac. Versions of the text survive in Syriac, Greek, Armenian, Arabic, Coptic and Ethiopic. The best textual witness is the earlier unrevised Greek version. Allusions to the text are found in a variety of Christian and Manichaean texts. Its internal references are to Western Asia and to India. Its closest known literary relationships are to Syriac Christian texts, although it would appear to have influenced later Buddhist traditions as well. This text is different from the *Gospel of Thomas*, an early gospel attributed to Thomas that circulated in early Syriac churches, as well as Western churches.

The Greek version of the *Acts of Thomas* contains 171 chapters concluding with the martyrdom of Thomas. Chapters 1–16 describe the division of mission territories among the disciples. Thomas is assigned to India, where he goes unwillingly as a slave. He preaches, performs exorcisms and healings, resurrects the dead, and converts royalty to an ascetic and celibate Christianity, culminating with the conversion of King Gundaphor, whose resources Thomas had given to the poor. Another king, Misdai, angered at Thomas because he had been converting women to celibacy, has him executed. The relics of the saint are used to heal and to convert people. The text ends with the transmission of the relics to Edessa by merchants.

While it is often impossible to distinguish fact from fiction, the text is an important witness to the evangelistic traditions of the early Asian churches, both in Syria and in what are now Pakistan, Afghanistan, north-east India, Iran and Iraq, the old Kushan and Persian empires. It provides hymns (*Hymn of the bride* and *Hymn of the pearl*) and contains significant liturgical information. Ablution and anointing are important features of Christian celebration. The oil invokes the Holy Spirit as the feminine aspect of God, using the term 'the merciful mother'. As one would expect from other Syriac sources, asceticism was an important, even an essential, virtue to be adopted by Christian converts. It also provides access to the early traditions of Asian Christian spirituality. The text clearly presents a developmental spirituality and theology (sometimes derogatorily labelled 'Gnostic' by Latin and Western Christian writers) not unlike that of Origen of Alexandria and Ephrem of Syria.[1]

Abgar and Addai

The second tradition has to do with a set of correspondence, known since the writing of the *Ecclesiastical history* (1.13; 2.6–7) of the fourth-century Palestinian writer Eusebius, purporting to be letters written by Jesus and King Abgar of Edessa. In the spurious letters, which are extant in Syriac, Greek and Armenian, Abgar asks Jesus to come to Edessa to heal him. Jesus refuses but promises that after his ascension he will send a disciple to heal him. According to Eusebius, Thomas sent Thaddaeus (in Syriac, Addai). A Syriac document entitled *The teaching of Addai* claims that Jesus sent a messenger, who became a healer and evangelist, to Edessa with a response. The messenger was said to have painted a portrait of Jesus that was viewed by the Spanish woman Egeria, a

---

1 J. N. Farquhar, 'The apostle Thomas in North India'; J. N. Farquhar, 'The apostle Thomas in South India'; A. Mingana, 'The early spread of the gospel in India'; A. Adam, *Die Psalmen des Thomas*; A.F. J. Klijn, *The Acts of Thomas*; P.-H. Poirier, *L'Hymne de la perle*; G. Quispel, *Makarius*; *Hymn of the pearl*, ed. and trans. Ferreira.

fourth-century visitor to Edessa. This text and a sequel, the *Acts of St. Mari the apostle*, which records the efforts of Addai's successor, are both probably from the fourth century. A liturgical text ascribed to these two foundational figures, the *Liturgy of Addai and Mari*, is a eucharistic anaphora that is still used in Syria and India as well as in Syriac Christian communities in the diaspora.[2] Bardaisan, the first known Syriac Christian theologian, suggests that after the conversion of Abgar VIII (*regn. c.* 177–212), social policy in Edessa changed. It has been suggested, on the basis of scant evidence, that Osrohoene became perhaps the first Christian nation. During the reign of Abgar VIII, Bardaisan flourished and served to protect the city.

Jewish connections

The third theory suggests that early Christianity in Syria developed within Jewish circles, as it did within the Roman empire.[3] This theory finds support in archaeological evidence, the apologetic literature against Judaism, and texts such as the *Chronicle of Arbela* that describes a Christian presence within the city of Arbela from about 100. It would appear that the traditions are correct in positing an Antiochene or Palestinian origin for Christianity, and certainly the Christianity that became dominant under the influence of Byzantium had its origins among converts within and from Judaism, as did Manichaeism. The role of Judaism in the development of Marcionite and Bardaisanite communities of Christians cannot be ascertained.

Second- and third-century evidence for Christianity in northern Mesopotamia

The extant documentation for Christianity in northern Mesopotamia before the fourth century is meagre, but suggestive. The fact that this was not a period during which large-scale public churches were built, as far as we know, has led some to discount the significance of the presence of Christianity in northern Mesopotamia before the fourth century. Most likely the references to Christian churches are to be understood as house churches on the model of the synagogue and church at Dura Europos, a Roman military city on the eastern border of the empire. Such is probably the case for the reference in *The chronicle of Edessa* where it is noted that a 'church of the Christians' was destroyed in a flood during 312. Earlier than this, building on linguistic traditions of Jewish

---

2 *The eucharistic prayer of Addai and Mari*, ed. and trans. Gelston.
3 Robert Murray, *Symbols of church and kingdom*; Jacob Neusner, *Aphrahat and Judaism*.

Aramaic, scholars had produced the first biblical translations into Syriac, texts that were already revised by the fourth century. The *Diatessaron* (a harmony of the four Gospels into one text) of Tatian, a second-century Greek or Syrian scholar, may well have been the earliest non-Marcionite Syriac Christian text to circulate in northern Mesopotamia. A Greek fragment of the *Diatessaron* was discovered in Dura Europos. Destroyed by the Persians in 256, the city contained a house church with evidence of both Syriac and Latin presence. There is no evidence relating to Christian communities at Palmyra, although given the connections to Samosata there probably were such.

Several other texts need to be mentioned. The first, and most important, is *The book of the laws of the countries*. This text contains a dialogue between Bardaisan and a student called Awida (perhaps a Marcionite), which was recorded by another student, Phillip. Bardaisan (*c.* 154–222), known in Latin sources as Bardesanes, was a Christian philosopher at the court of Abgar VIII, in Edessa, capital of Osrohoene. A description of him by Julius Africanus, made about 212, describes him as an able archer, but does not discuss his theology. During his lifetime he was recognised as a Christian theologian by Eusebius. Bardaisan, together with his son Harmonius and his disciples, created a significant corpus of original Syriac compositions, including Christian hymns and theological treatises. Because he was declared a heretic by later Christian theologians most of his works did not survive, except in quotations by his detractors, especially Ephrem of Syria and the author of *The book of the laws of the countries*. A fragment of a treatise on astronomy was preserved by George, bishop of the Arabs (*Patrologia Syriaca* 2: 612–15). His theology, mistakenly characterised by some as Gnostic, encouraged a developmental spirituality (similar to that of Clement of Alexandria) and used Greek and local philosophical and scientific traditions to articulate his faith and understanding of the cosmos. There are interesting parallels with the pseudo-Clement and the Thomas traditions. Ephrem (306–73) found Bardaisanite Christians to be serious competitors during the later fourth century.[4]

An early text of significance for Nisibis is a funerary inscription dated from before 216 from Asia Minor. It recounts the travels of Aberkios to Nisibis where he encountered Christians: 'My name is Aberkios, the disciple of the chaste

---

4 L. Dillemann, *Haute Mésopotamie orientale et pays adjacents*; H. J. W. Drijvers, *Bardaisan of Edessa*; H. J. W. Drijvers, *Cults and beliefs at Edessa*; H. J. W. Drijvers, *History and religion in late antique Syria*; H. J. W. Drijvers, *East of Antioch*; T. Jansma, *Natuur, lot en vrijheid*; G. Phillips, *The doctrine of Addai*; J. B. Segal, *Edessa the blessed city*; J. Teixidor, *Bardesane d'Édesse*. For an early description of Bardaisan, see Julius Africanus' *Kestoi* (ed. Vieillefond; English translation and commentary by Francis Thee: *Julius Africanus and the early Christian view of magic*).

pastor who pastures his flock on the mountains and in the plains . . . I saw the plain of Syria and all the villages, Nisibis across the Euphrates. Everywhere I found people with whom to speak . . . the faith preceded me everywhere.'[5] Unfortunately this text reveals nothing about the Christian community at Nisibis other than its existence.

Another important text is from the Byzantine emperor Julian (*Letter* 41), in which he describes the pogroms of his predecessors against Syrian Marcionite villages in an effort to eradicate this tradition against which Ephrem wrote during the late fourth century. The details of the Marcionite Christian evangelisation in northern Mesopotamia cannot be known. No Marcionite sources survived. However, these churches became a formidable social force in Western Asia until the establishment of imperial Byzantine Christianity in the region at the end of the fourth century. There is a large anti-Marcionite corpus in early Syriac literature. Among the important anti-Marcionite writers were Bardaisan, the pseudo-Ephremian *Commentary on the Lucan parables* (pseudo-Ephrem A), Adamantius (*The correct faith in God*) and the hymns and prose refutations of opponents by Ephrem of Syria.[6]

Finally, the *Chronicle of Arbela*, mentioned above, states that the second bishop of Arbela was martyred during the reign of the Parthian King Xosroes. This would suggest that a leadership structure was developed, at least on a city level, early in the second century.

Other texts are suggestive of the theological and spiritual ethos of early northern Mesopotamian Christianity, but there are no internal chronological markers and scholars are sharply divided as to the date and provenance of the documents. These include the *Odes of Solomon*, the *Gospel of Thomas*, the pseudo-Clementine corpus, the *Didache*, and the *Apology* attributed to Melito, as well as early Manichaean texts.

During the third century there was significant upheaval in northern Mesopotamia. Roman emperors, seeking to emulate the conquests of Alexander the Great, had already pushed their interests eastward. By the reign of the emperor Lucus Verus (165–6), the empire stretched eastward to envelop Nisibis. However, after 226, when the Sassanid empire replaced Parthian rule, the Persian emperors began to look westward. Shapur I (*regn.* 240–72) conquered Roman fortifications on the Limes (including Dura Europos, 256), Emesa, parts of Cilicia and even, albeit briefly, Antioch. In an effort to decrease the economic power of Roman northern Mesopotamia and to

---

5 D. Bundy, 'The life of Abercius'.
6 H. J. W. Drijvers, 'Marcionism in Syria'; D. Bundy, 'The Anti-Marcionite commentary'.

increase the productivity of Persia, many thousands of Greek and Syriac villages were deported en masse and resettled throughout Persia. The Christians among the exiles brought with them their ecclesiastical structures. In many of the new villages both Syriac and Greek churches were organised, which in turn attracted native Persians to the Christian faith. While Syriac and Greek Christians were taken into Persia, Manichaeans followed the Persian armies into the Roman empire and quite successfully established their version of Christianity within that context.

Another tendency of northern Mesopotamian Christianity is present from these earliest sources: that is, the struggle between adapting to the local intellectual and cultural traditions (Bardaisan) and the outright rejection of these (Thomas traditions, and later Ephrem). The religious vision is not uniform and is mediated through the experiences of the authors of individual texts. Even from the small number of extant texts, it is clear that any generalisations about the theological or social worldviews of early northern Mesopotamia are simplifications of the complex data.

The fourth century: The churches in northern Mesopotamia

The fourth century began with much of northern Mesopotamia firmly in the control of the Roman empire. Two of the cities, Edessa and Nisibis, had privileged status (perhaps to prevent the reconstitution of Palmyra or Nabatea) for trade between the Persian and Roman empires. The anonymous fourth-century northern Mesopotamian author of *Expositio totius mundi et gentium* (written *c.* 359) observed: 'They [Nisibeans] are rich and supplied with goods. They receive from the Persians all that they sell in the land of the Romans and that which they purchase, they in turn sell to them, except bronze and iron, because it is forbidden to give bronze and iron to enemies.'[7] Both the *Expositio* and Ephrem's *Hymns on Nicomedia* describe Nisibis as a prosperous city with busy shops, artisans and agriculturalists. From Ephrem it is known that there were also economic connections to the unsettled Arab populations to the south. The *Expositio* noted that '. . . they lead a good life'. The privileged economic position facilitated the churches of these cities becoming the most important of northern Mesopotamia.[8]

---

7 *Expositio totius mundi et gentium* 22 (SC 124: 157–7, with commentary: 235–9).
8 D. Bundy, 'Bishop Vologese'.

The favourable trade location proved less advantageous during the wars between Rome and Persia. According to some sources, the Persians besieged the city in 338 but were successfully resisted. Ephrem insisted that the leadership and prayers of Bishop Jacob of Nisibis were responsible for saving the city. The bishop's group was not the only religious presence. Religious life was generally governed by traditional seers and healers, professions that were derogatorily called 'magicians' or 'fortune tellers' by the Christians. A number of Christian groups were present: Marcionites, Bardaisanites, Arians, Manichaeans and Palutians (named after a Bishop Palut of Edessa who was recognised by the Nicene party). The faith of this last group would become the recognised version of Christianity during the reign of Constantine. There was also a significant Jewish presence. Other groups are named but the sources do not provide significant information as to their cultural identity or religious perspective.

While there was probably a Roman/Byzantine governmental and military presence in these cities, the Christian theologians do not mention it or the imperial cult until the emperor Julian (*regn.* 372/3) set up a statue of a golden calf in the central square of Edessa, as an insult to all sects of Christians and the Jews. During earlier periods there were apparently martyrs during imperial crackdowns on Christians. The narratives, dating to perhaps the fourth century, document martyrdoms in Edessa, specifically those of Sarbel and Barsamja, who were apparently killed during the persecution orchestrated by the Roman emperor Decius, and Gurja, Semma and Habib, who were, according to the text, martyred during the reign of the Roman emperor Diocletian.[9]

The only information extant about the life of Christians in the churches in northern Mesopotamia is about Nisibis and Edessa, as found in the writings of Ephrem. The churches were organised with a bishop at their head. At Nisibis the incumbents were Jacob of Nisibis (*sed. c.* 307/8–c. 338), Babou (d. 340), Vologese (*sed.* 341–61), and Abraham (*sed.* 361–?). At Edessa there was Bishop Palut, Bishop Aithallah who participated at Nicaea, and Bishop Barses under whom Ephrem may have served following his probable move to Edessa.

Jacob of Nisibis became a model of the good bishop in Syriac literature, as well as in the Armenian, Latin and Byzantine churches. The most important sources on Jacob are the writings of Ephrem of Syria (*Hymns on Nisibis* 13–16), who extolled his virtues but unfortunately provided no significant biographical or historical data. According to the *Chronicle* of Elias of Nisibis (975–1047), Jacob

---

9 S. E. Assemani, *Acta sanctorum martyrum*; W. Cureton, *Ancient Syriac Documents*.

was consecrated bishop in 308/9. According to the *Chronicle of Edessa*, he was the builder of the first church at Nisibis (*c.* 313–20), and a baptistery built beside that church was dedicated to his memory by his successor Vologese in 359. From various conciliar lists, it is certain that Jacob represented Nisibis at the Council of Nicaea. He was known as an anti-Arian. Works attributed to him by later chronicles and manuscripts, including homilies of Aphrahat, were not written by Jacob. Jacob became a prominent feature of the later hagiographical traditions.[10]

The spirituality of the church was heavily ascetic. Many if not all converts committed to a life of celibacy, which attracted more women than men. Ephrem lamented that the husbands often used this as an excuse to purchase concubines from the nearby Arab nomadic tribes. At least some of the church participants were organised into two orders, 'Sons of the Covenant' and 'Daughters of the Covenant'. The exact nature of these groups has perplexed scholars. It was not monasticism as it was later developed under the influence of Egyptian Christianity and Buddhism, but the groups appear to have been structured efforts to encourage the development of asceticism and spirituality. They may have functioned as diaconal clergy. Women were involved in social ministries, prayer and ascetical practices. They also provided music for the liturgy, although there is no evidence for further involvement.

The most important Byzantine Asian author of the fourth century was Ephrem of Syria.[11] He is the most important and reliable source for the history and culture of the church in northern Mesopotamia during the fourth century. Ephrem's influence on the entire Christian church can scarcely be overstated. His works were translated into Armenian, Georgian, Latin, old Slavonic, Greek, Arabic, Chinese, Coptic and Ethiopic. His influence on the Syriac-language churches was probably the single most determinative factor in their development. He influenced biblical interpretation, theological

---

10 P. Peeters, 'La Légende de Saint Jacques de Nisibe'; J.-M. Fiey, *Nisibe*; D. Bundy, 'Jacob of Nisibis as a model for the episcopacy'; D. Bundy 'Vision for the city'; Bundy, 'Bishop Vologese'.

11 Edmund Beck has prepared an extensive critical edition of the Syriac text of Ephrem's works, with German translation, for CSCO (see the bibliography, below, for details). Translations of other material, often with quite useful notes and contextual material, include S. Brock, *The harp of the Spirit*; S. Brock, *St. Ephrem the Syrian: Hymns on paradise*; C. W. Mitchell et al., *Prose refutations*; C. McCarthy, *St. Ephrem's commentary on Tatian's Diatessaron*; E. G. Mathews, Jr. and Joe Amar, trans., *St. Ephrem the Syrian: Prose works*; and K. McVey, trans., *Ephrem the Syrian: Hymns*. For additional information, see S. Brock, *The luminous eye*; S. Brock, *The Syriac fathers on prayer and the spiritual life*; S. Griffith, 'Ephraem, the deacon of Edessa'; S. Hidal, *Interpretatio Syriaca*; T. B. Mansour, *La pensée symbolique de Saint Ephrem le Syrien*; Murray, *Symbols of church and kingdom*; and W. L. Petersen, *The Diatessaron and Ephrem Syrus*.

method, the content of theology, the definition of orthodoxy, liturgy, and hymnody. His criticism of older intellectual and scientific traditions in Syria contributed to their eventual demise as viable methods of explaining the universe.

Ephrem was born in a Christian home and eventually joined the church, becoming a member of the 'Sons of the Covenant'. He was never ordained. The title of 'deacon' was given to him by later sources in an effort to make him part of the church hierarchy. Despite his fame and influence, little is known of his life. According to the later hagiographers who supply details otherwise unknown, he left Nisibis for Edessa after Nisibis was surrendered to the Persians by the emperor Jovian after the death of the emperor Julian in a campaign against the Persians in 363. According to these same sources, he died while organising and providing relief during a famine in 373.

Ephrem was a prolific writer. Among his writings were biblical commentaries, sermons and prose essays that were polemical in nature, and many hymns. The extant exegetical material includes the only complete commentary on the *Diatessaron*. There is also a commentary on Genesis that is probably authentic. The commentaries and excerpts from commentaries attributed to Ephrem in Syriac, Arabic, Armenian and Ethiopic are probably not authentic. The exegesis of the *Commentary on the Diatessaron* shows continuities with the earlier Syriac theological texts noted above and with the Alexandrian tradition of theological reflection. For example, asceticism is valued as reflective of and expeditious for the development of Christian spirituality. There are two levels of text: the historical narrative of the life and ministry of Jesus as well as a theological or symbolic level. Ephrem also understood nature to be revelatory of God and of God's intention for the creation.

The prose works include a number of sermons and the *Refutation of heresies*. In the *Refutation of heresies*, Ephrem criticises the approaches to spirituality and theology found among his religious competitors in Nisibis and Edessa. Those criticised include the Manichaeans, Marcionites, Bardaisanites and Arians. He insisted on the freedom of the will and the necessity for Christians to progress toward Christian perfection (*theosis* or sanctification). Ephrem criticised proponents of theological systems that allowed for, or appeared to allow for, either determinism or dualism. These theologies, he insisted, led to an understanding of God and human nature that did not allow for the transformation of persons into the image of God. In this he has parallels with Philo, the *Acts of Thomas*, Clement of Alexandria and Origen. Ephrem's relationship with Judaism is quite complex. While he accepted the Jewish people as the original people of God, and the Jewish scriptures as essential to Christian theology, he insisted that the Hebrew Bible was half as important as the New Testament. From the beginning Ephrem, like most Christians, was determinedly supersessionist, but the efforts of the emperor Julian to rebuild the Jewish Temple in Jerusalem radicalised Christian understandings of Judaism. After 363, Ephrem became virulently anti-Jewish, as did other Christian theologians within the sphere of Byzantine influence.

Ephrem's most popular compositions were the metrical poems he composed to be sung by choirs of women in the churches. They provide access to the religious vision of the fourth-century Christians. More than 450 hymns have survived. These were early organised into 'cycles' or collections of hymns around various themes. Already during his lifetime these were translated into Greek, and eventually into diverse languages including Latin, Armenian, Georgian, old Slavonic, Coptic, Ethiopic, Arabic and Chinese. The problems of authenticity are significant, as many sought to duplicate his artistry and to have their work passed off under his name. Ephrem is one of the very few Christian theologians to be honoured in all branches of the Christian church, through the centuries, as a teacher and saint.

The next generation of Syriac Christianity in Byzantine northern Mesopotamia was led by leaders such as Rabbula (d. 435) who were not afraid to use the power of the state and the mobs to enforce Christian orthodoxy. Born in Calcis to a pagan father and Christian mother, Rabbula converted to Christianity about 400. He was consecrated bishop of Edessa (411/12–35). As bishop he led a bloody campaign against the Jews, pagans and those considered heretics. He destroyed at least four pagan temples and a synagogue. Rabbula also destroyed at least 400 copies of the *Diatessaron* and replaced it with the separate Gospels in the Syriac Peshitta version to conform to the standards of the Western churches. His inflexible administrative style and harsh treatment of those with whom he disagreed won him many enemies. He did, however, organise food relief for the poor and built an infirmary for the care of the sick. He also apparently codified the monastic rules and established strict guidelines for the lifestyle of clergy, monks and laity.

The theologians of Edessa had normally been partisans of the East Syrian tradition that revered the teachings of Diodore of Tarsus and Theodore of Mopsuestia. At the Council of Ephesus (431), Rabbula continued this tradition by refusing to condemn Theodore and Nestorius. However, he changed his mind and became an enthusiastic and doctrinaire supporter of the politics and theological position of Cyril of Alexandria. He then banned the writings of Theodore of Mopsuestia and of Nestorius from Edessa. This put him even more at odds with significant segments of his clergy. His contentious and inflexible approach to issues destroyed the academic leadership role of Edessa and can be said to have permanently divided the Syrian church.[12]

The political struggles over control of the land and minds of northern Mesopotamia led to increased dependence on Greek Christian writers and / or the Greek language by the Syriac churches. For example the homilies of John Chrysostom were translated and widely used, as were biblical and theological texts of Cyril of Alexandria, Athanasius, Evagrius of Pontus and Philoxenus of Mabbug, among others. Philoxenus of Mabbug is exemplary of the struggles of intellectuals to create a theological identity in the midst of this cultural conflict. Philoxenus (Akhsenaya) was born in Persia and received his education at the theological school of Edessa. In that context he became, theologically, a West Syrian and a primary theologian of that tradition. In 485, he was consecrated bishop of Mabbug (Hieropolis) in Syria where he became an influential writer and church politician. His involvement in intrigues in Constantinople led to his arrest and exile in 519. He died in 523. His literary production was significant, and written only in Syriac. Among his writings were commentaries on the Gospels of John (prologue), Matthew and Luke. Large collections of homilies, liturgical texts and some letters survive. He also commissioned and led a new translation of the scriptures in an effort to achieve a Syriac version that more accurately reflected the Byzantine biblical text tradition.[13]

The changing religious politics of the Byzantine empire left subscribers to the previously pronounced 'truths' isolated and vulnerable. Thus the West Syrians (adherents of the Council of Ephesus, 431) were decimated by imperial persecution during the sixth century as well as by the plagues that ravaged the cities and pilgrimage sites. The survival of the tradition in the face of the Byzantine police was due to the mythical Jacob Baradaeus. Jacob (c. 500–78) was born in Tella, Syria, the son of a priest. He entered a monastery near Nisibis, and became a monk. With another monk, Sargis, he was sent in 527 to Constantinople to intercede for the non-Chalcedonians, where he appears to have come under the protection of the empress Theodora who shamelessly used him as a pawn in her quest for influence. He remained in Constantinople for fifteen years, before apparently being appointed nominal, and probably

12 G. G. Blum, *Rabbula von Edessa*; M. Black, 'Rabbula of Edessa and the Peshitta'; P. Peeters, 'La vie de Rabbula, évêque d'Edesse'.
13 A catalogue of the writings (including extant manuscript references) of Philoxenus, together with a study of relevant biographical material and an introduction to his theology, was established by André de Halleux, *Philoxène de Mabbog*. References to several editions (with translations) of Philoxenus' works will be found in the bibliography.

canonically illegal, bishop of Edessa, a position that he appears never to have claimed.

After leaving Constantinople, he spent the rest of his life as an undercover encourager and organiser of the West Syrian Miaphysite church. The name by which he is known, 'Baradaeus' (Syriac: *Burd'ano*) refers to the ragged clothes and rags he used to disguise himself. He reconstituted the hierarchy and priesthood of the West Syrians. The assertions of the oldest sources (100,000 ordinations of clergy are claimed!) are clear overstatements of his activities. Most of his appointments were canonically irregular; most of those appointed were staunch Miaphysites from the monasteries. However, the campaign was effective as he managed to secure the sympathy of the populace and elude the imperial police who were eager to stop his campaign against the Byzantine church.[14]

Thus the West Syrian church ended the sixth century alienated from the empire and its church with which it had worked so hard during earlier centuries to conform.

Early Christianity in Persia

The diffusion of Christianity throughout Persia was caused by various factors: migration/evangelisation along the trade routes; adaptation of Christian ideas within existing communities (which may be related to trade patterns); and the forced migration of entire Greek- and Syriac-speaking communities from northern Mesopotamia. By the fourth century this had resulted in a strong presence divided by three languages: Greek, Syriac and Persian.

Relations with the Mazdaean traditions deteriorated as conversions increased. Accusations of disloyalty to the regime led to martyrdoms. The Christian martyrdom texts of the early period insist on the loyalty of the Christians to the Persian kings (and there is no evidence that they were disloyal). The texts suggest that Christians were not always respectful of the Mazdaean altars and fire temples. Called before the judges, they were forced to choose between large fines, conversion from Christianity or martyrdom. The Christians, according to the texts, responded with theological arguments about the nature of God and salvation and chose martyrdom. The texts may or may not reflect particular legal processes and it is doubtful, given the

---

14 H. G. Kleyn, *Jacob Baradaeus*; E. Honigmann, *Évêques et évêchés monophysites*; D. Bundy, 'Jacob Baradaeus'.

numbers of Christians killed, that an individual trial was held for each. During what was called 'the great persecution', at least 35,000 were martyred. Most of the martyrdoms and most of the extant texts can be dated to the reign of Shapur II.[15]

The most important early Persian Christian author, in addition to the authors of the martyr texts, whose work is extant is Aphraates (Syriac: Aphrahat).[16] He wrote a series of twenty-three treatises between 325 and 345. The first ten, dated 337, deal with theological questions as well as the Christian lifestyle, with a focus on asceticism. The fourteenth treatise and the introduction to the collection are in the form of letters, that treatise being a letter to a synod of bishops. This synod may be the one sometimes dated to 325 that met under the presidency of Papa bar 'Aggai at Seleucia-Ctesiphon (325). The last nine treatises reflect the argument between Christians and Jews in Persia during the early fourth century. The final treatise, number 23, was composed during the winter of 344–5 at the beginning of the persecution of Christians (as well as of Manichaeans, Jews and Buddhists) by Shapur II.

The church reflected in the texts differs significantly from the dominant Greek and Latin churches of the early fourth century. The local structures focus around the 'Sons of the Covenant' and the 'Daughters of the Covenant'. These groups are composed of celibate baptised believers. They are to be radical in their asceticism, love of God and love of neighbour. These proto-monastic groups appear to have constituted a significant portion of the church in both the Persian empire and pre-Julian northern Mesopotamia. It is impossible to ascertain Aphraates' role in the Persian church. He was certainly in discussion with the bishops and an informed theologian, but there is no evidence that he was a bishop. The exegetical methods used to interpret the scriptures are closely related to the rabbinic traditions of Judaism. His theology is modestly Trinitarian, but without the support of the Greek philosophical structures developed in the Western churches.

The treatises, or 'Demonstrations' as they are sometimes called, were translated into Armenian and into Ethiopic, where they were circulated under the name of Jacob (sometimes specified as Jacob of Nisibis). While the name 'Jacob' may have been a baptismal or episcopal name, there is no evidence that the texts were written in Nisibis or by Jacob of Nisibis. They reflect a Persian perspective and knowledge of Persian life that would be of minimal concern

---

15 G. Wiessner, *Zur Märtyrerüberlieferung aus der Christenfolgung Schapurs II.*
16 Murray, *Symbols of church and kingdom*; Neusner, *Aphrahat and Judaism*; Jacob Neusner, 'The Jewish–Christian argument in fourth century Iran'; T. Baarda, *The Gospel quotations of Aphrahat the Persian sage.*

to a bishop in Nisibis, which was during the life of Jacob of Nisibis part of the Roman empire.

The adoption of Christianity as the 'glue of empire' within Byzantium had serious repercussions for Persian Christians. While they had earlier been persecuted because of their zealous evangelistic work and refusal to bow to governmental and Zoroastrian demands, they now became suspect as a possible 'fifth column' for the Roman/Byzantine empire whose emperors had long dreamed of expanding their realm to the boundaries of that of Alexander the Great. The first effort to deal with the problem was the Council of Seleucia-Ctesiphon (399/400).[17] This Council met under the presidency of Maruta of Maipherqat and ratified the negotiations that temporarily stopped the persecution of Christians in Persia. It also elected Isaac as bishop and catholicos of Seleucia-Ctesiphon. A decade later, another Council of Seleucia-Ctesiphon (410) approved a creed (not that of Nicaea) and a text thought by the participants to be the canons of Nicaea.[18] Under the leadership of Isaac and Maruta of Maipherqat, co-conveners of the council, the Persian church was reorganised and then declared its independence from the Byzantine church and from the bishop of Antioch. The issue refused to go away and the Council of Dadišo' (420) was convened at Marktabta' of Tayyaye' (not Seleucia-Ctesiphon). Catholicos Dadišo' called this council to clarify his own role in the Persian church. The council affirmed the primacy of the bishop of Seleucia-Ctesiphon and reaffirmed the independence of the Persian church from that of the Byzantine empire.

The office of the catholicos was often contested. Rivals competed before the governments and used synods of supportive bishops in their quests for power. At the Council of Seleucia-Ctesiphon (486), sometimes called the Council of Aqaq (Acacius), Catholicos Aqaq confirmed the nullification of the synod of Bet Lapat held by his rival Barsauma, adopted a creed, affirmed classical East Syrian theology, asserted the authority of the bishops over the monks, limited celibacy to the monks and forbade celibacy for the clergy. Once again it reaffirmed the independence of the Persian church from Byzantium.

In 489, the emperor Zeno closed the theological school at Edessa because of the sympathy of its faculty for the ideas of the Antiochene theologians, especially Theodore of Mopsuestia and Nestorius. The theological faculty

---

17 On this synod/council and those discussed below, see *Synodicon orientale*, ed. and trans. Chabot ; J.-M. Fiey, *Jalons pour une histoire de l'église en Iraq*; J. Labourt, *Le christianisme dans l'empire perse*; O. Brun, *Das Buch der Synhados*.

18 J. Gribomont, 'La symbole de foi de Séleucie-Ctésiphon'; A. de Halleux, 'La symbole des évêques perses au synode de Séleucie-Ctésiphon'.

was reconstituted at Nisibis at the invitation of its bishop. Led by two influential theologians, Narsai and Barsauma, both prolific writers and politically engaged, the school of Nisibis became a formidable intellectual centre for the Asian Christian churches. The theological schism with the churches under Byzantine intellectual control improved the security of the Persian churches in the Persian empire.[19]

The relations both between the churches and with the government can be seen in the case of Mar Aba I (d. 552). Mar Aba was born at Hale in Radan. He grew up as a Mazdaian but converted to Christianity. He received his intellectual formation at the theological school of Edessa. He travelled and continued his study of Greek in Palestine, Greece and Egypt. He returned to Nisibis as a professor. From Nisibis he was elected and served as catholicos of the East Syrian church (540–52). Dissatisfied with the school at Nisibis, he started a theological school at Seleucia-Ctesiphon. Throughout his career, Aba remained an active author, contributing works in various theological disciplines as well as translations from Greek into Syriac of works by Theodore of Mopsuestia and Nestorius.[20]

The period of his catholicate was made difficult both by tensions within the church and by the problems between Christians and the Persian government. He worked to heal the schisms in the church. The government sent him into exile in Azerbaijan, and from there he worked to lead the church. About 548, he escaped from detention in Azerbaijan and returned to Seleucia-Ctesiphon. He was imprisoned for about three years, was released in 551 and died within the year.

The synod of 554 formally adopted the commentary of Theodore of Mopsuestia on the Nicene Creed as an authoritative text for the Persian church. From this period onward, the East Syrian churches were generally Dyophysite, although theologians were rarely totally consistent in their theological language; of primary concern was the separation from Byzantium.

Theological ferment was a regular feature of the intellectual centre at Nisibis. Central to these controversies during the sixth century was Henana (Hadisbaia') from Adiabene (d. c. 610). Following study at the theological school at Nisibis under a certain Moses, Henana was appointed professor at the institution. He became convinced that the exegetical and theological traditions of Theodore of Mopsuestia should be revised in the light of the work of

---

19 Fiey, *Jalons pour une histoire de l'église en Iraq*; S. Gero, *Barsauma of Nisibis*.
20 On Mar Aba I, see *Synodicon orientale*, ed. and trans. Chabot; Labourt, *Le christianisme dans l'empire perse*; Arthur Vööbus, *History of the school of Nisibis*; J.-M. Fiey, *Jalons pour une histoire de l'église en Iraq*; Fiey, *Nisibe*.

John Chrysostom. More radically, he accepted the creed of Chalcedon, which was anathema to the East Syrian church. However, his interpretation of that creed remained independent: he argued that there were two natures in Jesus Christ, but one person and one hypostasis in Jesus Christ. The opposition of faculty, administrators and students led to his firing by Bishop Paul of Nisibis.

Despite the controversy, in 572 he was named director of the theological school at Nisibis and survived the efforts of two synods called (585, 596) in attempts to remove him. His most severe critic, Babai the Great, wrote a volume entitled *The union in the incarnation* to counteract the ideas of Henana. His appointment eventually led to a split in the school of Nisibis. More than 300 students left the institution, which never recovered its status.[21]

The religious geography of Persia became more complicated because of the sixth-century Byzantine imperial pogroms against the West Syrian (Miaphysite) church. Monasteries were founded in the northern mountains and some villages and cities became primarily Miaphysite.[22]

The experiences of many nations

The resources documenting the history of Christian communities in other areas of Asia and East Africa vary significantly. Here, because of space limitations, the discussion is restricted to major geographical, political or ethnic units that can be reasonably defended as definable areas during the period being discussed. Attention is given to Adiabene, Armenia, Georgia, India, Egypt (Coptic Christians), Nubia, Ethiopia, South Arabia, Soqotra, Central Asia and China.

Adiabene[23]

Adiabene was sometimes an independent buffer state between the Persian and Roman empires. It was south and east of the kingdom of Osrohoene. Its capital was Irbil (= Arbela). Adiabene had a large Jewish population and at times Jewish monarchs. The Jewish monarchs were removed by the emperor Trajan, who took the area in 115–16. Adiabene was an early centre of Christian activity. Tradition ascribes the evangelisation of the area to Addai. It was

---

21 On the theological academy at Nisibis, see Arthur Vööbus, *The statutes of the school of Nisibis*; Vööbus, *History of the school of Nisibis*; Fiey, *Nisibe*.

22 For more detail on this period, see *Synodicon Orientale*, ed. and trans. Chabot; Labourt, *Le christianisme dans l'empire perse*; Vööbus, *History of the school of Nisibis*; Fiey, *Jalons pour une histoire de l'église en Iraq*; Fiey, *Nisibe*.

23 N. Pigulevskaia, *Les villes de l'état iranien*; J.-M. Fiey, 'Vers la réhabilitation de l'histoire de Karka Bét Slöh'.

eventually (second Christian century) incorporated into the Parthian empire. The major source for Adiabene, the *Chronicle of Arbela*, recounts the lives of the early bishops of Arbela, beginning about 100. The second bishop, Samson, was martyred by the Parthian king Xosroes during a period of Parthian occupation. By the time that the Persian empire was supplanted by the Sassanid empire (226), Christianity was well established. Two fourth-century bishops became martyrs: John of Arbela (343) and Abraham (344). The Sassanid persecution of Christians had a major impact on the region. From the end of the fourth century, Christianity flourished in the area. Later Syriac chronicles describe Christian churches and monasteries built in the area, but the area functioned merely as a region of the Sassanid Persian empire.

Armenia[24]

Some of the traditions of Christian evangelism in Armenia attribute the first efforts to Addai who was supposed to have worked in the early first century; others suggest Bartholomew or Thaddaeus. It is uncertain when Christian communities in Armenia first developed, but even Tertullian (*Adversus Judaeos* 7.4) wrote of Christian villages in the area of Armenia, which then comprised not only the present republic, but also much of what is now Eastern Turkey. Certainly the early biblical versions and the liturgy suggest that the country was first evangelised from Syria. As otherwise in the development of early Christianity in Asia, the impetus seems to have been the contact between traders and their companions; in this case the contact appears to have been with representatives of the Greek and Syriac churches.

Essential to the history of Armenia during our period was its role as a buffer state between the Roman and Persian empires. During the mid-third century, Tiridates III and members of his party were forced by the Parthians to flee to Roman protection. Gregory, son of an anti-Parthian prince, spent the exile in Caesarea of Cappadocia where he studied Christianity and married. After Tiridates III was returned to power with Roman assistance (278–87), Gregory returned to Armenia. His refusal to support the traditional religious celebration of the restoration led to his punishment and a general persecution of Christians. The tradition says that after a series of miracles wrought by Gregory, Tiridates III was converted; Gregory then returned to Caesarea to be consecrated bishop. The tradition is quite uniform that the definitive conversion of the nation took place through the efforts of Gregory the Illuminator

---

24 S. Lyonnet, *Les origines de la version arménienne et le Diatessaron*; S. Der Nersessian, *The Armenians*; R. W. Thomson, *Agathangelos*; R. W. Thomson, *Moses Khorenats'i*; R. W. Thomson, *Studies in Armenian literature and Christianity*.

(*c.* 240–332), who converted King Tiridates III in the late third or early fourth century. At that point Christianity became the state-supported religion; many of the sons of earlier Armenian religious leaders became clergy and resources were made available for the support of the clergy. Schools were established to teach Greek and Syriac. This transition took place in the face of a resurgent Zoroastrianism in the Sassanid Persian empire and at a time when the Parthian influence in Persia had been largely eradicated.

The first successor to Gregory the Illuminator was his son, Aristakes, a monk, who represented the Armenian church at the Council of Nicaea (325), Gregory being too old to make the trip. It was, however, the Athanasian Creed that was first promulgated as normative for the Armenian church.[25] Aristakes and other church leaders were killed by Armenian princes who attempted to suppress Christianity. Aristakes was succeeded by his brother Vartan, who according to the Armenian historians made dying in battle against the Persians the equivalent of martyrdom. Houssik, the grandson of Gregory, was also consecrated at Caesarea of Cappadocia, but his efforts to achieve social justice in Armenia angered King Tiran who sought to replace him before he himself was captured, blinded and replaced by Sapor II of Persia. The new king, Arshak, named the great-grandson of Gregory, Narses, as leader of the Armenian church. However, the turmoil in the leadership of the church continued during the fourth century because of pressures from the Persian and Roman empires, and the conflict between the church and Armenian leaders over what the bishops considered moral lapses.

When Armenia was divided into spheres of influence between Theodosius and Sapor III (*regn.* 384–9), two-thirds of Armenia was given to the Persians. Christians in Armenia were persecuted and partly because of this the Armenians revolted, appealed to Theodosius, and eventually won from the Persians (between about 420 and 439) the title of king for their leader, freedom of religion and some economic benefits. Despite the turmoil, the Armenian church was represented at the Councils of Constantinople (381) and Ephesus (431). Within Armenia, synods were held to condemn both the Messalians, also known as the Paulicians, and the resurgence of Zoroastrianism under the influence of the Persian Mazdaean clergy.

It is in this context that the development of the Armenian alphabet and the restoration of the ecclesial hierarchy need to be understood. In an effort to limit the foreign influence and resultant political implications, the decision was made to develop the Armenian infrastructure of the church and

25 P. Gatherdjian, *De fidei symbolo*, 51–62.

Armenian culture. The Armenian alphabet was developed, at royal instruction, by Mashtots and Sahak during the early fifth century. An ambitious translation project from Syriac was undertaken. Many early Syriac texts were translated into Armenian, followed by significant Greek and later Arabic works. Thus Armenian language texts preserve Christian and Jewish texts that were otherwise lost, including works by Philo, Irenaeus, Ephrem, Severian of Gabala and Nonnus of Nisibis, among others. Original literature was also produced. Early Armenian Christian writers include Agathangelos, Korium, Eznik of Kołb, Lazar P'araec'i, Moses of Khorene and Gregory the Illuminator.

It is also as part of this struggle for national identity over against its neighbours that the sixth-century decisions about the theological identity of the Armenian church need to be understood. In 506, the Armenian patriarch John I Mandakuni hosted at the Armenian political capital of Dvin a synod to evaluate the theological decisions of the Council of Chalcedon (451).[26] The council included representatives of the Georgian and other ethnic Caucasus churches in addition to the Armenians. They rejected the Chalcedonian creed, being troubled by the language of the 'two natures'. The Armenian church remained a Miaphysite church although the others would, under pressure, return to the Byzantine fold. This theological independence was encouraged by political concerns. Byzantium had designs on Armenia. Byzantium was, however, unable to protect Armenia from military incursions from the south or southeast. Therefore the theological animosity was politically useful as it freed Armenia from the opprobrium of perceived identity with the Byzantine empire. Since the fourth century, the Armenian church has served to unite Armenians against foreign pressures and influences.

Georgia[27]

The conversion of Georgia is ascribed, by the historian Rufinus who claims to have heard it from a Georgian priest in about 395, to the efforts of a Christian Cappadocian slave woman, Nino, whose healing gifts were brought to the attention of Queen Nana. She healed the queen through prayer and investiture with her cloak and was also instrumental in saving the king, Mirian, when he was on a hunting expedition. Both were converted. At Nino's instruction a church was built at Mcxeta about 330. Byzantine priests were solicited as teachers, who brought the Georgian church and state into a more constructive

---

26 See K. Sarkissian, *The Council of Chalcedon and the Armenian church*.
27 P. Peeters, 'Le début du christianisme en Georgie'; D. M. Lang, *The Georgians*; on the development of theological literature, see R. P. Blake, 'Georgian theological literature' and M. Tarchnisvili, *Geschichte der kirchlichen georgischen Literatur*.

relationship, helping to offset the emerging interest of Byzantium in the region and the emerging religious and political importunities of the Zoroastrian Persian empire. For the first century of its existence, the Georgian church remained firmly in the orbit of the Byzantine church.

Georgian ecclesial (and national) independence was asserted by King Vaghtan Gorgaslan (446–510) through participation in the Armenian-led Council of Dvin in 506, which rejected Chalcedon along with Byzantine imperial intentions. However, near the end of the sixth century, under the leadership of the Georgian catholicos Kyrion (*sed.* 585–610), and under pressure from the Byzantine empire, the Georgian church accepted Chalcedon and the current Byzantine orthodoxy. As a result, they were excommunicated, meaninglessly, by the Armenian church.

Indian Christianity[28]

The sources for the history of Christianity in both North and South India are few and problematic for the period during our discussion. Any written texts that may have existed were destroyed by either European Catholic and Protestant forces or Indian religious partisans. Efforts continue to rediscover this history, and a more complete narrative may eventually be possible. The sources that do exist are tantalising but problematic. There are the early traditions preserved in the Greek and Syriac writers referring to the missions of Thomas (and/or Thaddaeus and/or Bartholomew) and his colleagues during the first Christian century. However, the traditions are fraught with internal inconsistencies and none can be proved or disproved on the basis of the details included. Some lists of bishops in attendance at Nicaea include a certain John of Persia representing the Persian and Indian churches. Certainly that is possible; there were demonstrably Christian communities in both North and South India by the end of the first Christian century. Alexandrian Christian theologians studied in India during the second and third centuries, and probably longer.

From the fourth century onward there are references in Persian Syriac documents to what appear to have been regular contacts between the churches in Persia and those in India. This would be expected from the importance of the trade between India and Mesopotamia during the Persian period. A certain David, bishop of Bassarah (*c.* 300), was said to have resigned from the episcopacy and travelled to India where he worked effectively as an evangelist.

---

28 On early Indian Christianity, see S. G. Pohan, *Syrian Christians of Kerala*; A. M. Mundadan, *From the beginning up to the middle of the sixteenth century*; J. England, 'The earliest Christian communities in Southeast and Northeast Asia'.

A community of Christians in South India, the 'Canaites', claim to be descended from a group of Syrians (perhaps 400 families) who arrived in South India, possibly as refugees, in 345. Indian scholars also made their way to Edessa, the most famous of whom was David the Syrian who prepared a new translation of the *Epistle to the Romans* from Greek into Syriac (*c.* 425). It is recorded that about 470 Bishop Mana of Riwardashir, Persia, sent to India a collection of the books he had translated into Syriac. There may also have been a Christian community (of even more uncertain ethnicity) in Sri Lanka by the late fifth century. However, at present there are no traditional historical sources that can supply a narrative to the disparate and diverse fragments of material culture and the occasional comments of Christian historians and theologians in Europe, Byzantium and Asia.

Coptic Christianity[29]

Coptic Christianity refers to the traditions of the Copts, the indigenous, generally non-Greek, inhabitants of Egypt, a linguistic distinction that traces its way back to the Greek *Aigyptioi*. From early in the Christian period there were Christians among the Copts, and their traditions were generally not different in languages and culture from the Greek population that was consolidated by Alexander the Great. The decisions of the Council of Chalcedon (451) led to the deposition of Bishop Dioscorus I. The local populace remained loyal to him and to the memory of Cyril of Alexandria (*c.* 375–444). These persons and their churches were configured into a new non-Chalcedonian Miaphysite organisation. Coptic and Greek were used for the liturgy. Within a century, the non-Chalcedonian churches dominated Egyptian religious and cultural life. Extensive numbers of loose translations were made of Greek texts. The Coptic Orthodox church had connections to the Syriac churches, Nubia, Ethiopia and probably the southern parts of the Arabian peninsula as well as India, following the trade routes.

Nubian Christianity[30]

Data about the Nubian church is still fragmentary despite the large number of texts and material cultural items unearthed and preserved in the second half of the twentieth century. Without doubt there were Christians along the Nile

---

29 M. Roncaglia, *Histoire de l'église copte*; B. Pearson and J. Goehring, eds. *The roots of Egyptian Christianity*; L. S. B. MacCoull, *Coptic perspectives on late antiquity*; and especially A. S. Atiya et al., *Coptic encyclopedia*.

30 E. R. Dinkler, ed., *Kunst und Geschichte Nubiens in christlicher Zeit*; P. L. Shinnie, 'Christian Nubia'.

trade routes from an early period. However, the adoption of Christianity as the official government-sponsored religion of the Nubians took place in the mid-sixth century. John of Ephesus describes the conversion of the kingdom of Norbaria through a mission project sponsored by the Miaphysite supporter, the Byzantine empress Theodora. The other two Nubian kingdoms soon followed into the Christian community.

Ethiopian Christianity[31]

The traditions of the Ethiopian church usually begin with the arrival of two Palestinian Syriac (?) brothers, Frumentius and Aedesius, from Tyre who were shipwrecked on the Ethiopian coast. Perhaps they were enslaved, but they became important officials in the Ethiopian government at Axum. Desiring ordination commensurate with his responsibilities, Frumentius made his way to Alexandria where tradition has it that he was ordained bishop of Ethiopia by Athanasius. Later the Arian Byzantine emperor Constantius II attempted to replace Frumentius with an Arian bishop, but to no avail. Minted coins with Ethiopian kings and crosses prove that the royal family of Ethiopia became Christian during the fourth century.

After the Council of Chalcedon (451), the Ethiopian church joined the Copts in rejecting the decisions of the council. The subsequent persecution of Miaphysite clergy in northern Mesopotamia and Palestine resulted in a large number of refugee monks making the trek to Ethiopia where they supported mission efforts among the people. By the early sixth century, observers could affirm (probably an exaggerated claim) that Ethiopia was a Christian nation. The earliest translation work from Greek to Ethiopic (Ge'ez) probably took place during the fifth century.

Arabia, South Arabia, Soqotra and the Persian Gulf[32]

From the second century, there is record of Christians among the Arabic-speaking populations of the lands bordering the Roman empire. Once again, there is evidence of Christianity following the commercial connections between the Arabic population and the Syriac and Coptic merchants. By the fifth century, numerous Arabic Christian centres had developed at the edges of the desert and along the coastlines of the Arab peninsula, especially on the

---

31 E. Ullendorff, *Ethiopia and the Bible*; R. Cowley, *Ethiopian biblical interpretation*; E. Haberland, *Altes Christentum in Süd-Äthiopien*; Michael A. Knibb, *Translating the Bible*.

32 *History of the martyrs of Nagrân*, ed. Esteves Pereira as *Historia dos martyres do Nagran* and Shahid as *The martyrs of Nagrân*; *The book of the Himyarites*, ed. Moberg; J. Ryckmans, *La persecution des chrétiens himyarites*.

Persian Gulf and along the Red Sea where they often encountered Buddhist merchants, sometimes in merchant villages, a presence still marked by local place names.

In South Arabia, and on the island of Soqotra, there was a Christian presence from early Christian times. The kingdom of Himyar was the focus of mission work by Theophilus the Indian who built churches in Nagran and Zafar during the fourth century. In 378, the Himyarites achieved political freedom from Ethiopia. At this point persecution of the Christians began at the hands of the king Dhu Nuwwas, a convert to Judaism and an ally of Persia, which was seeking to establish control of South Arabia. The persecution was certainly because of the Ethiopian connections of the Christians. At the beginning of the sixth century the Christian communities were decimated by the persecution. From 523 to 525 the Ethiopian military, at the suggestion of the Byzantine emperor Justin I, mounted an expedition to rescue the Christians. Despite some initial success (described in numerous accounts extant in Syriac, Greek, Armenian, Georgian, Arabic and Ethiopic), the influence of both Byzantium and Ethiopia declined. Southern Arabia fell under the sway of the Persian empire in 575 and remained thus until the Islamic conquests. Archaeological sites, place names and textual evidence attest the strong presence of Christianity throughout the Arabic-speaking regions during our period. However, there is insufficient material to provide a narrative account of the three centuries of organised Christian community development before the seventh century.

Central Asia[33]

Trade routes between China and Tibet in the east and the Persian, Kushan and Roman empires and India ran through what is now northern Iran and through Central Asia around the area now known as Afghanistan. Many of the cities had long supported Jewish communities. For example, one of these, Ecbatana (today's Hamadan), was the burial site of biblical Queen Esther. It had a large Jewish population and Esther's tomb served as a pilgrimage site. It was also home to the parents of Mani, who were apparently involved in a baptistic sect that may have had Christian connections in the second Christian century. At about this same time, Bardaisan notes the presence and influence of Christians

---

33 Bardaisan, *The book of the laws of the countries*, trans. Drijvers; Gregory Barhebraeus, *Gregorii Barhebraei Chronicon ecclesiasticum*, ed. Abbeloos and Lamy; A. Mingana, 'Early spread of Christianity'; *Histoire nestorienne*, ed. Scher; Hsing Ta, *Xi'an and Western culture*; Menahem ben Shemuel Halevi, *Matsevet Mordekhai ve-Ester*; P. Pelliot, *Recherches sur les Chrétiens d'Asie centrale et d'Extrême Orient*.

in various Central Asian areas, including Kushan. By the end of the fifth century, missionaries including John of Resaina had established churches among the White Huns in Bactria. During this same period there were East Syrian bishoprics established in cities along the Oxus river, in Naishapur, Herat, Gilan and Merv. Other bishoprics were established in Kaskar, Samarkand and Turkmenistan. There were certainly Christians there to support these bishoprics when they were established. In 591, Turkic soldiers with crosses tattooed on their heads, who asserted that they were Christians, were captured by Byzantine mercenaries in northern Persia. The Syriac texts note when these areas were absorbed into the ecclesial structures of the East Syrian church or the arrival of other traditions: Armenian, Melchite, and West Syrian. However, they do not provide data about the earlier developments. It is hoped that scholarly archaeological research in the area might provide more clues to this history.

China[34]

Early evidence about China is suggestive, but at this time the data still remains fragmentary. Bardaisan suggested, about 180, that there were Christians in China, a not unreasonable possibility given the activity on the trade routes. Certainly there were political/economic embassies between the Chinese and Roman empires during this period. By the late sixth century (c. 578), there was an East Syrian missionary, Mar Sergius, residing in Lint'ao. By 635, another East Syrian missionary, A-lo-pen (Abraham? Rabban? Aba?) arrived in China with a mandate to organise the Christians and to represent them before the emperor. At this point there is no indication of the nature of the communities he found there, although permission was given to establish (and populate!) a monastery during the reign of the Emperor T'ai-Tsung (627–49). The most important source for the period 635–781 is the so-called 'Nestorian stele' at Xi'an, which includes names of Syriac and Chinese Christian leaders in China, as well as a list of Chinese Christian texts. Other early Chinese Christian documents excavated in western China were edited with photographic reproductions by Y. Saeki.

---

34 Mingana, 'Early spread of Christianity'; P. Yoshiro Saeki, *The Nestorian documents*; Pelliot, *Recherches sur les chrétiens d'Asie centrale et d'Extrême Orient*; S. H. Moffett, *A history of Christianity in Asia*, vol. I; England, 'The earliest Christian communities in Southeast and Northeast Asia'; D. Bundy, 'Missiological reflections on Nestorian Christianity during the Tang dynasty'.

Conclusion

There are similarities in the fragmentary stories of the development of Christianity in Asia and Eastern Africa during the fourth to sixth centuries. As it had from the beginning, it followed the trade routes as merchants and missionaries took with them their faith. Because of this people to people transmission, there was a high degree of comfort with cultural and theological diversity that was not found to the same degree in Byzantium or in the remnants of the Latin West. There was also an interconnectedness of historical experience and influences along the trade routes and in the intellectual centres. On the other hand, international politics and religious strife separated communities along primarily national and cultural lines. Creeds intended to unify thought and practice within the Byzantine empire had the opposite effect. There was also, in much of Asia, a common alienation from political and social power. In both the Asian Christian heartlands of Mesopotamia and Persia, there was no pretence to real cultural power or influence. When church and state merged, it was as part of an effort to ensure the political survival and cultural identity of the ethnic group. There were apparently few dreams of empire among Christians in Asia. Survival, the opportunity to follow one's religious practices, and the opportunity to confess one's faith to one's neighbours, were central values. The fragmentary nature of the textual and material culture evidence for the stories of the lives of these communities is due to these larger cultural realities.

Select Bibliography

PRIMARY SOURCES

Assemani, S. E. *Acta sanctorum martyrum orientalium et occidentalium* (Rome, 1748; reprint: Westmead, 1970)

Bardaisan. *The book of the laws of the countries*, trans. H. J. W. Drijvers (Assen, 1964)

The book of the Himyarites, ed. A. Moberg (Lund, 1924)

Ephrem. *Carmina Nisibena* (CSCO 218–19, 240–1)

　Hymni de Abraham Qidunaya et Juliano Saba (CSCO 322–3)

　Hymni de azymis, de crucifixione et de resurrectione Christi (CSCO 248–9)

　Hymni de ecclesia (CSCO 198–9)

　Hymni de fide (CSCO 154–5)

　Hymni contra haereses (CSCO 169–70)

　Hymni de ieiunio (CSCO 246–7)

　Hymni de natiuitate (CSCO 186–7)

　Hymni de paradiso et contra Julianum (CSCO 174–5)

　Hymni de uirginitate (CSCO 223–4)

Sermo de Domino Nostro (CSCO 270–1)

Sermones (CSCO 305–6, 311–12, 320–1, 334–5)

Sermones de fide (CSCO 212–13)

Sermones in Hebdomadam Sanctam (CSCO 412–13)

The eucharistic prayer of Addai and Mari, ed. and trans. A. Gelston (Oxford, 1992)

Expositio totius mundi et gentium (SC 124)

Gregory Barhebraeus. *Gregorii Barhebraei Chronicon ecclesiasticum*, ed. J. B. Abbeloos and T. J. Lamy (Louvain, 1872–7)

Histoire nestorienne (Chronique de Séert), ed. A. Scher (PO 7.2)

History of the martyrs of Nagrân. Ed. F. M. Esteves Pereira, *Historia dos martyres do Nagran: Versão ethiopica* (Lisbon, 1899); I. Shahid, *The martyrs of Nagrân: New documents* (Brussels, 1971)

Hymn of the pearl. Ed. and trans. Johan Ferreira, *The hymn of the pearl. The Syriac and Greek texts with introduction, translation and notes* (Sydney, 2002)

Julius Africanus. *Kestoi*. Ed. Jean Pierre Vieillefond. *Les 'Cestes' de Julius Africanus. Étude sur l'ensemble des fragments avec édition, traduction et commentaires* (Florence / Paris, 1970)

Philoxenus. *Commentary on John's prologue* (CSCO 380, 381)

Commentary on Matthew and Luke (CSCO 292, 293)

Discourses, ed. and trans. E. A. Wallis Budge (London, 1893–4)

Letter to the monks of Senoun (CSCO 231, 232)

Three letters of Philoxenos of Mabbogh (sc., to Emperor Zeno, to the monks of Beth Gaugal, and to unknown monks), ed. and trans. A. Vaschalde (Rome, 1902)

De Trinitate et incarnatione (CSCO 9, 10)

Synodicon orientale ou recueil des synodes nestoriens, ed. and trans. J. B. Chabot (Paris, 1902)

SECONDARY SOURCES

Adam, A. *Die Psalmen des Thomas und das Perlenlied als Zeugnisse vorchristliche Gnosis*, BZAW 24 (Berlin, 1959)

Atiya, A. S. et al. *Coptic encyclopedia* (New York, 1989)

Baarda, T. *The Gospel quotations of Aphrahat the Persian sage* (Meppel, 1975)

Black, M. 'Rabbula of Edessa and the Peshitta', *Bulletin of the John Rylands Library* 33 (1951): 203–10

Blake, R. P. 'Georgian theological literature', *JTS* 26 (1924): 50–64

Blum, G. G. *Rabbula von Edessa*, CSCO 300 Sub. 34 (Louvain, 1969)

Brock, S. *The harp of the Spirit* (London, 1983²)

The luminous eye: The spiritual world vision of St. Ephrem the Syrian (Kalamazoo, 1992²)

St. Ephrem the Syrian: Hymns on paradise (Crestwood, NY, 1990)

The Syriac fathers on prayer and the spiritual life (Kalamazoo, 1987)

Brun, O. *Das Buch der Synhados* (Stuttgart, 1990)

Bundy, D. 'The Anti-Marcionite commentary on the Lucan parables (pseudo-Ephrem A): Images in tension', *Le Muséon* 103 (1990): 111–23

'Bishop Vologese and the Persian siege of Nisibis in 359 C.E.: A study of Ephrem's *Memre on Nicomedia*', *Encounter* 63 (2002): 55–63

'Jacob Baradaeus: State of research, a review of sources and a new approach', *Le Muséon* 91 (1978): 45–86

'Jacob of Nisibis as a model for the episcopacy', *Le muséon* 104 (1991): 235–49

'The life of Abercius: Its significance for early Syriac Christianity', *Second century* 7 (1989–90): 163–76

'Missiological reflections on Nestorian Christianity during the Tang dynasty', in F. Flinn and T. Henricks, eds., *Religion in the Pacific era* (New York, 1985), 14–30

'Vision for the city: Nisibis in Ephrem's *Hymns on Nicomedia*', in Richard Valantasis, ed., *Religions of late antiquity in practice* (Princeton, 2000), 189–206

Cowley, R. *Ethiopian biblical interpretation: A study in exegetical traditions and hermeneutics* (Cambridge, 1989)

Cureton, W. *Ancient Syriac documents* (London, 1864; reprint: Amsterdam, 1967)

Dillemann, L. *Haute Mésopotamie orientale et pays adjacents* (Paris, 1962)

Dinkler, E. R., ed. *Kunst und Geschichte Nubiens in christlicher Zeit* (Recklinghausen, 1970)

Drijvers, H. J. W. *Bardaisan of Edessa* (Assen, 1966)

Cults and beliefs at Edessa, Études préliminaires aux religions orientales dans l'empire romain 82 (Leiden, 1980)

East of Antioch (London, 1984)

History and religion in late antique Syria, Collected Studies Series 464 (Aldershot, 1994)

'Marcionism in Syria: Principles, problems, polemics', *Second century* 6 (1987–8): 153–72

England, J. 'The earliest Christian communities in Southeast and Northeast Asia: An outline of the evidence', *Missiology* 19 (1991): 203–15

Farquhar, J. N. 'The apostle Thomas in North India', *Bulletin of the John Rylands Library* 10 (1926): 80–111

'The apostle Thomas in South India', *Bulletin of the John Rylands Library* 11 (1927): 20–50

Fiey, J.-M. *Jalons pour une histoire de l'église en Iraq* (Louvain, 1970)

Nisibe: Métropole syriaque orientale et ses suffragants des origines à nos jours (Louvain, 1977)

'Vers la réhabilitation de l'histoire de Karka Bét Slôh', *Analecta Bollandiana* 82 (1964): 189–223

Gatherdjian, P. *De fidei symbolo quo Armeni utunter observationes* (Vienna, 1893)

Gero, S. *Barsauma of Nisibis and Persian Christianity in the fifth century* (Louvain, 1981)

Gribomont, J. 'La symbole de foi de Séleucie-Ctésiphon (410)', in Robert Fisher, ed., *A tribute to Arthur Vööbus* (Chicago, 1977)

Griffith, S. 'Ephraem, the deacon of Edessa, and the church of the empire', in T. Halton and J. P. Williams, eds., *Diakonia: Studies in honor of Robert T. Meyer* (Washington, D.C., 1986)

Haberland, E. *Altes Christentum in Süd-Äthiopien* (Wiesbaden, 1976)

Halevi, Menahem ben Shemuel. *Matsevet Mordekhai ve-Ester asher ba-'ir (Shushan) Hamadan (Paras): Ha-minhagim ha-shayakhim lah veha-agadot ha-nishma'ot 'aleha 'im he'arot u-veurim mi-tsad ha-mehaber* (Jerusalem, 1931)

de Halleux, André. *Philoxène de Mabbog: Sa vie, ses écrits, sa théologie* (Louvain, 1963)

'La symbole des évêques perses au synode de Séleucie-Ctésiphon', in G. Wiessner, ed., *Erkenntnis und Meinungen* (Wiesbaden, 1978), 161–90

Hidal, S. *Interpretatio Syriaca* (Lund, 1974)

Honigmann, E. *Évêques et évêchés monophysites d'Asie antérieure au VIe siècle* (Louvain, 1951)

Hsing Ta. *Xi'an and Western culture during the Tang dynasty* (in Chinese) (Beijing, 1957)

Jansma, T. *Natuur, lot en vrijheid: Bardesanes, de filosoof der Arameërs en zijn images* (Wageningen, 1969)

Kleyn, H. G. *Jacob Baradaeus: Founder of the Syrian church* (Cambridge, 1990; translation from the original Dutch: Leiden, 1882)

Klijn, A. F. J. *The Acts of Thomas*, Supplements to Novum Testamentum 5 (Leiden, 1962)

Knibb, Michael A. *Translating the Bible: The Ethiopic version of the Old Testament* (Oxford, 1999)

Labourt, J. *Le christianisme dans l'empire perse sous la dynastie Sassanide (224–632)* (Paris, 1904)

Lang, D. M. *The Georgians* (London, 1966)

Lyonnet, S. *Les origines de la version arménienne et le Diatessaron* (Rome, 1950)

McCarthy, C. *St. Ephrem's commentary on Tatian's Diatessaron: A translation of the Chester Beatty Syriac MS 709* (Oxford, 1993)

MacCoull, L. S. B. *Coptic perspectives on late antiquity* (Aldershot, 1993)

McVey, K., trans. *Ephrem the Syrian: Hymns* (New York, 1989)

Mansour, T. B. *La pensée symbolique de Saint Ephrem le Syrien* (Kaslik, 1988)

Mathews, E. G., Jr. and Joe Amar, trans. *St. Ephrem the Syrian: Prose works*, FOTC 91 (Washington, D.C., 1995)

Mingana, A. 'Early spread of Christianity in Central Asia and the Far East', *Bulletin of the John Rylands Library* 9 (1925): 297–371

Mitchell, C. W., E. A. Bevan and F. C. Burkitt, eds. and trans. *Prose Refutations* (London, 1912, 1921)

'The early spread of the gospel in India', *Bulletin of the John Rylands Library* 10 (1926): 435–510

Moffett, S. H. *A history of Christianity in Asia, vol. I: Beginnings to 1500* (San Francisco, 1992)

Mundadan, A. M. *From the beginning up to the middle of the sixteenth century*, History of Christianity in India 1 (Bangalore, 1984)

Murray, Robert. *Symbols of church and kingdom: A study in the early Syriac tradition* (Cambridge, 1975; Piscataway, NJ / Edinburgh, 2004²)

Der Nersessian, S. *The Armenians* (London, 1969)

Neusner, Jacob. *Aphrahat and Judaism* (Leiden, 1971)

'The Jewish–Christian argument in fourth century Iran: Aphrahat on circumcision, the Sabbath, and the dietary law', *Journal of ecumenical studies* 7 (1970): 282–90

Pearson, B. and J. Goehring, eds. *The roots of Egyptian Christianity* (Philadelphia, 1986)

Peeters, P. 'Le début du christianisme en Georgie d'après les sources hagiographiques', *Analecta Bollandiana* 50 (1932): 5–58

'La légende de Saint Jacques de Nisibe', *Analecta Bollandiana* 38 (1920): 289–91

'La Vie de Rabbula, évêque d'Edesse', *Recherches d'histoire et de philologie orientale* (Brussels, 1951), 139–70

Pelliot, P. *Recherches sur les chrétiens d'Asie centrale et d'Extrême Orient*, Œuvres posthumes de P. Pelliot 1, ed. J. Dauvillier et L. Hambye (Paris, 1973)

Petersen, W. L. *The Diatessaron and Ephrem Syrus as sources of Romanos the Melodist* (Louvain, 1986)

Phillips, G. *The doctrine of Addai* (London, 1876)

Pigulevskaia, N. *Les villes de l'état iranien aux époques parthe et sassanide* (Paris, 1963)

Pohan, S. G. *Syrian Christians of Kerala* (Madras, 1963)

Poirier, P.-H. *L'Hymne de la perle des Actes de Thomas*, Homo Religiosus 8 (Louvain, 1981)

Quispel, G. *Makarius: Das Thomasevangelium und das Lied von der Perle*, Supplements to Novum Testamentum 15 (Leiden, 1967)

Roncaglia, M. *Histoire de l'église copte* (Beirut, 1985)

Ryckmans, J. *La persecution des chrétiens himyarites au VIe siècle* (Louvain, 1956)

Saeki, P. Yoshiro. *The Nestorian documents and relics in China* (Tokyo, 1951²)

Sarkissian, K. *The Council of Chalcedon and the Armenian church* (London, 1965)

Segal, J. B. *Edessa the blessed city* (Oxford, 1970)

Shinnie, P. L. 'Christian Nubia', in J. D. Farge, ed., *The Cambridge history of Africa* (Cambridge, 1978)

Tarchnisvili, M. *Geschichte der kirchlichen georgischen Literatur* (Vatican, 1955)

Teixidor, J. *Bardesane d'Édesse: La première philosophie syriaque* (Paris, 1992)

Thee, Francis C. R. *Julius Africanus and the early Christian view of magic*, Hermeneutische Untersuchungen zur Theologie 19 (Tübingen, 1984)

Thomson, R. W. *Agathangelos: History of the Armenians* (Albany, 1976)

  Moses Khorenats'i: History of the Armenians (Cambridge, MA, 1978)

  Studies in Armenian literature and Christianity (Brookfield, 1994)

Ullendorff, E. *Ethiopia and the Bible* (London, 1968)

Vööbus, Arthur. *History of the school of Nisibis* (Louvain, 1965)

  The statutes of the school of Nisibis (Stockholm, 1962)

Wiessner, G. *Zur Märtyrerüberlieferung aus der Christenfolgung Schapurs II*, Untersuchungen zur syrischen Literaturgeschichte 1; Abhandlungen der Akademie der Wissenschaften in Göttingen. Philologisch-historische Klasse, 67 (Göttingen, 1967)

PART II

★

CHRISTIANITY CONTESTED

5

Religious dynamics between Christians and Jews in late antiquity (312–640)

GUY G. STROUMSA

Introduction

Augustine called the Jews *librarii nostri*.[1] Beyond the reference to God's revelation of the scriptures to Israel, this expression emphasises the fact that the deep, essential and intimate relationship between Christians and Jews remained a concrete and permanent one at the turn of the fifth century. In the mid-sixth century, John of Ephesus, the leading Miaphysite church historian and hagiographer, reports a monk visiting a mountainous village east of the Euphrates and asking the people he meets: 'Are you Christians or Jews?'[2] As this vignette shows, it was sometimes difficult to distinguish a Christian from a Jew in the late ancient Near East. Both could speak the same language and look the same way. This was probably also the case all around the Mediterranean: there was usually no clear-cut or visible differentiation between the two estranged communities. Both Augustine of Hippo and John of Ephesus testify to the state of affairs after the watershed of the fourth century, which had seen a radical reversal of the relationship between Judaism and Christianity.

Indeed, the conversion of Constantine was only the prelude to other deep transformations of the relationship between Christians and Jews, up to the Muslim conquests. Before Constantine, while Judaism was a *religio licita*, the Christians had remained beyond the fringes of legality. Moreover, the last two generations of scholarship have radically shaken the old perception (nurtured by theological prejudice) according to which the Jews had begun a drastic process of social and intellectual seclusion after 70, accelerated by the bloody revolts in Alexandria and then in Palestine during the early second century. Soon after Constantine, who reportedly described the Jews as 'slayers of the

---

1 Augustine, *Enn. Ps.* 56.9, cf. 40.14 and *id. Hom.* 5.5, cited by J. Cohen, *Living letters of the law*, ch. 1, n. 35.
2 John of Ephesus, *Lives of Eastern saints* 16 (PO 17: 234).

prophets and killers of the Lord',[3] things began to change. Throughout the fourth century, while Christianity moved fast from prohibition to toleration to preferred status to state religion, the Jews saw a series of grave infringements upon their rights and social status, limiting in drastic ways their integration into society. Judaism was now tolerated, at best, only because the Jews cherished the Old Testament (which, Christians said, they misread in some important ways). After 380, when Theodosius I published in Thessalonica his edict *Cunctos populos*, making Christianity into the state religion, the Jews became for all practical purposes second-class citizens, although they were not demoted from the status of *cives romani*. In a sense, they had become *'dhimmis' avant la lettre*. (In 388, Theodosius prohibited marriage between Christians and Jews).[4] Such a modicum of toleration, it should be noted, was offered neither to pagans nor to heretics. This process of segregation, to be sure, was not a straight line. John Chrysostom's eight 'sermons against the Jews' of 386 were actually written not against the Jews, but as a direct rebuke of the Judaising tendencies amid Antiochene Christians.[5] To follow Harnack, the Jew appears here as a rhetorical device: it is the Jew as the Christian feared him. Indeed, the violence of these sermons shows the extent to which Judaism had retained its power of attraction at the end of the fourth century. It also echoes the fear this attraction could generate, twenty years after the failure of Julian's attempt at rebuilding the Jerusalem Temple. Chrysostom's invectives are usually perceived as reflecting the last stage, as it were, of Judaism's attractive powers. One should perhaps also question this view, and wonder whether the clear legal and social worsening of the Jews' status necessarily meant the disappearance of the cultural interaction between Jews and Christians. The following pages will seek to review some of the ways in which Jews and Christians interacted under the Christianised Roman empire, as well as under the Sassanid empire, where both were religious minorities.

While the two communities were of course incommensurable in their numbers and legal status in the early Byzantine empire, their common biblical heritage entailed a religious *koinè* of sorts and continuous exchanges that went well beyond religious polemics.[6] The period under study saw the formation and crystallisation of both Byzantine and rabbinic theology, and would prove crucial for the future of both religions. Yet studying primarily theology overlooks a number of historical complexities. Many of the cultural dialectics of

---

3 Eusebius, *Life of Constantine* 4.27.
4 On the laws pertaining to the Jews, see A. Linder, *The Jews in Roman imperial legislation*.
5 See R. L. Wilken, *John Chrysostom and the Jews*, chs. 3 and 4.
6 See G. G. Stroumsa, 'Religious contacts in Byzantine Palestine'.

these contacts are not specifically religious. Most Jews, like most Christians, were no theologians, and the study of religious dynamics must deal with the various ways in which they interacted, for instance in language, folklore or magic.

The Islamic conquest must also be taken seriously. It would again change in drastic ways the terms of the relationship throughout the Near East and North Africa. From then on, both Jews and Christians partook, more or less, of the same status as *ahl al-kitab*, a religious community tolerated because it had a scripture. More precisely, one can perhaps claim that the emergence of Islam represents one result of the cultural dynamics between Christianity and Judaism. Mohammed knew both and both rejected and used parts of each. In a sense, the very concept of *ahl al-kitab* represents a broadening to Christians (and to Zoroastrians) of the Christian theological attitude toward Jews since the fourth century, while the imperial legislative limitations would be echoed in the Islamic concept of the *ahl al-dhimma*.[7] Even the Byzantine empire's definition of itself developed religiously and politically in relationship to the emerging competitor to Christianity, Islam, yet the immediate counterpoint of Byzantine identity, at least from a religious viewpoint, remained the Jews, both in their present gloomy obstinacy and in the past glory of their sacral kingship.[8]

A few caveats are in order. First, the two communities (or, rather, webs of communities) are far from being comparable by almost any criterion. While we remain ignorant about Jewish demography in late antiquity, the Jews were much less numerous in the fourth century than they had been under the early Roman empire (although they probably never represented a significant part of the overall population, as estimated by some).[9]

The relations between Christians and Jews in antiquity are usually compared to those between Christians and pagans, and the natural tendency is to focus upon the Roman empire, forgetting that some important Christian communities (both Miaphysites and Nestorians) were present in the Sassanid empire, and had some cultural visibility, as doctors (Nestorians in Gundishapur, for instance) and translators of Greek literature. They must have developed at least some contact with the Jewish communities there, sharing Aramaic as

---

7 See A. Fattal, *Le statut légal des non-musulmans en pays d'Islam.*
8 For Byzantine anti-Jewish polemics, see A. Külzer, *Disputationes Graecae contra Judaeos.* For the relationship of the Byzantine emperors to Israelite kingship, see G. Dagron, *Emperor and priest.*
9 See B. McGing, 'Population and proselytism: How many Jews were there in the ancient world?'

their common language. The chief significance involves the leading role of late ancient Jewish Babylonian communities in defining the religious identity of and a cultural agenda for the Jews in Palestine as well as in the various diasporas through their interpretation of normative rabbinic Judaism, which came to dominate Jewish life after the Islamic conquests.

The fact that Jews and Christians were competing in a direct and sometimes violent clash, both communities claiming the same inheritance, often draws attention to their polemics and obscures the fact that many aspects of their lives were common to both. By definition, polemical literature insists on what divides, ignoring the many points of agreement between two groups.[10] The *koinos bios* of both in late antiquity is highly significant for a richer understanding of the cultural dynamics between them. Folklore provides an example. Galit Hasan-Rokem has recently shown how one can closely read Midrashic literature as 'tales of the neighbourhood', reflecting the common daily life and attitudes of Jews and Christians (and not only of them) in the Galilee of late antiquity.[11]

Localities of Jewish populations in late antiquity

In our period, significant Jewish communities existed throughout the Christian Roman empire, whether East or West. Christian attitudes toward Jews, both public and private, apparently varied in different areas. If there was cultural exclusivity in Byzantium, for instance, the fact that there were fewer Jews in the West does not seem to have promoted more lenient attitudes towards them. On the contrary, anti-Jewish legislation evidently was harsher in the West. But the most important Jewish communities of later antiquity were located outside the Roman empire. We find significant Jewish communities in Arabia, for instance, where the Jewish king Dhu Nuwwas (*regn.* 517–25) persecuted the Negus Christians in Najran. Jews also lived particularly in the Sassanid empire.

Palestine represents a special case, as both the country of the Jews, who call it 'the land of Israel', and the Christians, who name it 'the Holy Land' (a term which appears for the first time in sixth-century hagiographical literature from Palestine). We know little of Jewish communities in Alexandria – and in the rest of Egypt – after the mid-second century. In North Africa, where the existence of notable communities is attested from the time of Tertullian to that of Augustine, we remain in the dark as to their size and their activities, including

---

10 See P. Fredriksen and O. Ir Shai, 'Christian anti-Judaism, polemics and policies: From the second to the seventh century'.

11 G. Hasan-Rokem, *Tales of the neighborhood*.

their cultural life – though there is nothing to suggest much consequence to either. Some similarities between Tertullian's patterns of thought and Jewish law are not enough to permit extrapolations. Jews who thought they had been wronged in a real-estate deal could ask for justice and protection from Bishop Augustine, but he does not seem to have known very much about (or to have retained an interest in) Jewish practices.

There were Jewish communities in Visigothic Spain, but here too the scanty evidence is enough to suggest that they were dwindling at the time of the Islamic invasion. Isidore of Seville, in the seventh century, does not seem to have met Jews. Everywhere in the Roman empire, Jews formed minority communities, while the Christians asserted themselves as belonging to the majority. This imbalance was shattered only in the Sassanid empire, where both Jews and Christians represented minorities, rather similar in various ways. This important situation is interesting in the relations between Christians and Jews within the Euphrates valley during late antiquity.

After the fourth century, the evidence about Jews in general, and about Jewish–Christian relationships in particular, is twofold: archaeological and literary. The former can sometimes be used to sharpen the insights provided by the literary sources.[12] While the archaeological data from Byzantine Palestine is remarkable, the remains of Jewish synagogues or funerary monuments in the diaspora are meagre. As for Jewish documents, we have nothing except the literature produced in both Palestine and Mesopotamia, to which should be added the various magical inscriptions, on bowls or papyri. On the other hand, the evidence provided by Christian texts is mainly of a theological nature, and includes biblical exegesis, spiritual exhortation, homiletics and polemical as well as theological tractates. To these sources should be added imperial legislation, in particular as it appears in the codices of Theodosius and of Justinian, which tells us a lot about daily practices and conceptions.

Civic religions or scriptural religions?

When we speak of communities, we tend to assume that this was the natural mould of religious expression for both Jews and Christians.[13] But one should avoid isolating these two special groups from the broader context. In the ancient world, religion was above all a matter of state, of public life. The

---

12 See e.g. H. Kennedy, 'Syria, Palestine and Mesopotamia'; Sh. Cohen, 'Jews and Judaism in the Greco-Roman world'.
13 See G. Fowden, 'Religious communities'.

heart of religious cult was public, from Egypt and Babylonia to Rome. The Jerusalem Temple reflected the Israelite version of ancient civic religion (as best expressed in Varro's conception of *religio civilis*). After its destruction, Judaism underwent a deep transformation, and religion became to a great extent internalised, while religious life was centred upon the synagogue cult and learning the Torah in the community. The early Christians, of course, lived their religious life within communities, as any form of public expression of their faith was prohibited. In adopting Christianity, Constantine thought that the new faith could advantageously replace the old cult of the gods and provide a new civic religion for the empire. This was a gross miscalculation, of course, as Machiavelli saw so well: Christianity was not really fitted as a civil religion, as it preached another, heavenly, kingdom.

Like Judaism, Christianity was essentially a religion of communities, based upon books.[14] Christian scriptures were translated into various languages, in and outside the empire. Such a web of communities went against the grain of a civic religion that could provide a unification principle for the empire. Actually, between the fourth and the seventh centuries, there was a significant and at points dramatic decline in economic activity and long-distance communications throughout the Mediterranean. Indices such as naval commerce are directly relevant here. The growth of religious communities in late antiquity, fostered by Judaism and Christianity, is one of the significant but still rather understudied marks of this global decline.

Another characteristic of the Christianised empire was the new central importance of religion (as distinguished from other aspects of culture) in the perception of identity. Since Hellenistic times, identity had been usually phrased in terms of culture (including religion). Traditional ethnic frameworks of identity had been replaced, to a great extent, by broader horizons. Identity was no longer necessarily given with birth, but could be chosen. One only needed to speak Greek (or Latin) in order to identify oneself as a member of a society with ecumenical dimensions. Just as one could adopt a culture, one also could move into a new religion. Conversion had been a recognised possibility since Alexander.[15] With the victory of Christianity, however, the nature of conversion changed in very significant ways. Unlike other religions in the Roman empire (including the mystery cults) with the exception of Judaism, Christianity insisted upon truth as a central aspect of religion. Choice was now endowed with a consequence unknown elsewhere.

---

14 See G. G. Stroumsa, 'Early Christianity, a religion of the book?'
15 See A. D. Nock's classic *Conversion*.

The new insistence on religious identity permitted the development of an identity based essentially on community. This new communitarian identity, which remains too often unrecognised, is of crucial importance for the correct understanding of the religious dynamics between Christians and Jews in late antiquity. Indeed, despite the deep differences between minority (the Jews) and majority (the Christians), the relationships between the two groups were based upon their common self-understanding as religious communities. While the religious elites worked on building and maintaining the boundaries of the communities, autonomous and self-enclosed, these boundaries were constantly eroded by daily intercourse.

The radically new status of Christianity in the fourth century was not quite unparalleled in Judaism, in the sense that only then did the rabbinic movement succeed in imposing its view of things on the great majority of Jews. Until then, it seems that the Jewish public was much more amorphous in its beliefs and attitudes than would eventually become the case, often harbouring syncretistic beliefs that did not square well with the theology of the rabbis.[16]

Some scholars, in particular Jacob Neusner, following Rosemary Radford Ruether and himself followed by Daniel Boyarin, have noticed that only in the fourth century did Jews and Christians come into possession, for the first time, of clear-cut identities; hence, for Neusner, the historical meeting between Judaism and Christianity occurred in the fourth century.[17] To Neusner's analysis, one should add the contemporary emergence of both Jewish and Christian intellectual culture, the former bilingual in nature (Hebrew and Aramaic, both in Palestine and in Mesopotamia), the latter expressed in a plurality of languages (at least Greek, Latin, Syriac, Coptic, Armenian and Persian). It is the combination of these two factors that explains the power of the new dynamics between Jews and Christians.

Structural comparison of Judaism and Christianity

Fourth-century Judaism and Christianity were religions that had undergone some deep transformations. They were in their essence sacrificial religions, but of a special kind, since no sacrifice actually took place. Structurally, these religions were of course vastly different, due to the absence of priests and monks among the Jews. As a consequence of this state of affairs, the synagogue, or *beit ha-midrash*, became a centre of polyvalent ('interdisciplinary') cultural

---

16 See S. Schwartz, 'Rabbinisation in the sixth century'.
17 See J. Neusner, *Judaism and Christianity in the age of Constantine* and D. Boyarin, *Dying for God*.

activity unequalled in Christianity, where cult and culture usually remained clearly distinguished, the first in church, the second in the monastery.

Both were originally eschatological religions, but in both the eschatological drive had been more or less neutralised, and was now limited to episodes of flaring messianism or to marginalised groups. Both were establishing themselves as 'religions of the book', in a cultural environment that remained largely based upon orality. Among the Jews, in particular, as among other cultures of the Near East, such as the Iranians, the idea of the book itself remained to a great extent oral. Among the rabbis, books were redacted but not committed to writing. Last but not least, both Judaism and Christianity had succeeded, in the preceding centuries, in establishing orthodoxies. In various ways, dissenting tendencies had been declared heretical and marginalised. Among the Christians, these groups were now in the process of being simply outlawed, like pagans. That left the Jews as the only officially authorised dissenting religious group in the Christian empire. From one strong perspective, Christianity could be seen as a Jewish heresy – but it had now turned the tables on *vetus Israel*, and had transformed Judaism, as it were, into a Christian heresy.

Jewish–Christian interaction in a Christian empire

Both the legal and the social situation of the Jews seriously deteriorated from the end of the fourth century. As intercommunal violence between Jews and Christians became more and more common, the authorities hesitated between legal protection of the Jews and passive or even active support of the Christian mobs, who often moved with the blessing of the bishops. In a famous (or rather infamous) letter to Theodosius I, written in 388, Bishop Ambrose of Milan opposes the emperor's decision to punish those responsible for burning down a synagogue in Callinicum, a town on the Euphrates. To strengthen his case, Ambrose lists cities where Jews had burned churches: Gaza, Ascalon, Beirut, Alexandria. The outcome of the Callinicum affair seems to have brought the emperors to reaffirm in legal documents the right of the Jews to meet unhindered in their synagogues, as did, for instance, Theodosius himself in 393.

Two examples of ecclesiastical policy discouraging social interaction between Jews and Christians may be mentioned. The Council of Elvira, held in early fourth-century Spain, had forbidden intermarriage between Christians and Jews. The Council of Vannes, in Gaul, meeting between 461 and 491, stated that it was 'shameful and sacrilegious for Christians to eat [the Jews'] food'. In doing so, the council was applying against the Jews, in reverse, as it were, the strong Jewish limitations on social contact with Christians.

A particularly striking document on the wave of violence against the Jews, up to forced conversion, is the remarkable letter written by Severus, the bishop of Minorca. In his *Letter concerning the Jews*, Severus recounts how the Jewish community on the island was converted to Christianity in 418. A polemic between Christians and Jews soon turned into a street battle, ending in the burning of the synagogue. Severus notes, however, that the Christian arsonists took great care to save the holy books from the fire. He concludes his account by reporting that in the days following the burning of their synagogue, 540 Jews converted to Christianity out of fear for their lives, eventually building a church on the ruins of the synagogue. Even if this text cannot be taken at face value in all its details, it remains emblematic of the new state of affairs, and reflects the deep worsening of the Jews' status. From the same year, 418, an imperial edict forbids the Jews ('those living according to the Jewish superstition') to join the armed forces. The same edict, however, reaffirms their right to be legal advocates and town councillors.

Developments in Palestine

Palestine, as we have seen above, constituted a special case. From the beginning Christianisation on the emperor's direct orders had been quite intensive there. In particular, geography had been modified through a series of churches that punctuated the landscape, defining it as a 'holy land'. Places hallowed by the earthly presence of Jesus, of his mother, but also of the patriarchs, became landmarks which underlined that the *terra repromissionis* of the Jews, to use Jerome's term, had now become the Land of *verus Israel*. This transformation of the land was visible in places like Galilee or Hebron, but it was nowhere more obvious than in Jerusalem, a city from which the Jews, who had been expelled by the pagan Roman emperors, remained officially excluded. One would have therefore thought that Byzantine Palestine would not be a place where Jewish culture could thrive. And yet, the evidence points to the opposite. Literary creativity produced an impressive series of works. The Palestinian Talmud was redacted in Tiberias during the fourth century. Some of the major works of Midrashic literature, such as *Genesis Rabbah* and *Leviticus Rabbah*, stem from the fifth century in Palestine. The origins of synagogal poetry, the *piyyut*, are to be found there also. Yose ben Yose, the first *paytan* (composer of liturgical poems, from Greek *poietès*) whose name is known to us, for instance, lived in Palestine during the early fifth century.

Jerome, who lived in Jerusalem and Bethlehem from the 380s until his death in 419, carried on in Palestine a dialogue that he had begun in Rome with rabbis and Jewish converts. His major interest in pursuing his contacts with Jews was intellectual in nature. First, he needed them as teachers of Hebrew, a language he never succeeded in quite mastering, despite his constant efforts. Second, he wanted to learn from them about various hermeneutical and exegetical traditions of the biblical text. *Hebraica veritas*: Jerome's motto singled him out as a philologist in a world that did not particularly appreciate, or even understand, such an urge.[18] Indeed, his correspondence with Augustine reveals how the latter remained unable to understand Jerome's efforts to read the Bible in the original Hebrew. (Jerome appears here to be a lonely figure, also in his dealings with Jews, but he is following Origen, an earlier biblical exegete.) Jerome's contacts with Jews do not seem to have helped him develop any sympathy for them. Regular contacts, indeed, have never represented a panacea against ethnic, religious or community tensions.

Archaeological remains, which often reflect a more positive image of the interaction between communities than polemics, also reflect a blossoming of Jewish communities, groups that did not shun cultural influences from the surrounding world. Jews and Christians lived both in towns (except Jerusalem on principle) and villages. In Tiberias, the seat of the Jewish patriarchs until 420, the spread of Christianity seems to have been inhibited for some time. The villages were often mixed, but there seems to have been a tendency toward separation between the communities in these villages. Synagogue mosaics from Byzantine Palestine, in particular, show an impressive ability to play with non-Jewish themes. While such themes are not directly Christian, it is highly plausible that they sometimes reflect use among Christians, hence echoing the polemical dialogue between the two communities. One instance may be the depiction of the *Akedah* on the floor of the Beit Alpha synagogue. The importance of Abraham's sacrifice of Isaac among late ancient Jews might well reflect its centrality among Christians, for whom Isaac (as well as the ram) was a *typos*, or *sacramentum futuri*, of Jesus Christ.[19]

Midrashim *and* catenae

Midrashic Hebrew literature is a literary genre *sui generis*, which was born in late antiquity and continued to develop throughout the middle ages. The fact that it was composed and redacted orally, and only later committed to writing, makes the exact dating of the texts quite difficult. Yet it is possible to establish

---

18 On Jerome and *hebraica veritas*, see A. Fürst, *Hieronymus: Askese und Wissenschaft in der Spätantike*, 102–6 and bibl. 316–17, as well as R. Gonzalez Salinero, *Biblia y polemica antijuida en Jeronimo*, 53–91.

19 G. Stroumsa, 'Christ's laughter: Docetic origins reconsidered'.

that some of the earliest and most important collections of *midrashim* date from Byzantine Palestine. It has been suggested, again recently by Nicholas de Lange, that the genre *midrash* offers striking similarities to the series, or *catenae* ('chains'), of patristic interpretations of biblical texts.[20] It so happens that the first *catenae* were also composed in late fifth-century or early sixth-century Palestine. Procopius of Gaza (*c.* 465–*c.* 530) apparently created this genre, in which he worked the different exegeses into a sort of continuous interpretation, in which the wordings of all of them appeared.[21] Some kind of contact between the two phenomena is plausible, but we must not forget their common ground: 'secular' rather than 'pagan' culture, as can be seen in Gaza. Only a comparative study, however, might be able to seek an answer to the link between them.

We are still far from understanding the mythopoietic process involved in the formation of Midrashic literature. We do not even know their original purpose: were the collections of *midrashim* meant to be used as 'raw material' for the preparation of homilies? Obviously, they were taught (and learned by heart) in the rabbinical *paideia*, as they would not otherwise have been preserved before they were committed to writing. Various *midrashim* show at least a blurred consciousness of Christian doctrines. Does this indicate that they were redacted as offering a Jewish answer to Christian biblical interpretation? Similarly, we still do not know the original function of the *catenae*, although they may well have been used for homiletic purposes.

Hermeneutic practices and the *koinos bios*

In any case, both genres show the extent to which Jews and Christians, in Byzantine Palestine, partook of a very similar hermeneutical tradition of the same texts, even though they were reading them and commenting upon them in different languages. Indeed, the idea of a *koinos bios* should refer not only to the material aspects of life, but also to intellectual and spiritual life, to patterns of mind and of religious life. The case for such an intellectual and spiritual *koinos bios* might be made, of course, for all the various groups living in Byzantine Palestine, including Samaritans and polytheists, both Hellenised and Bedouins. But it is all the more true about Jews and Christians.

The comparative study of synagogal *piyyut* and Byzantine liturgical poetry (*kontakia*), which has barely begun, might also shed light on the dynamics

20 N. de Lange, 'Midrach et Byzance. Une traduction française du Midrash Rabba'. See further N. de Lange, 'Jews and Christians in the Byzantine empire: Problems and prospects'.
21 See *The Palestinian catena on Psalm 118* (SC 189: 7).

between minority and majority culture in Byzantine Palestine. We have here, in both cases, a highly sophisticated literary genre, whose origins remain unclear. The audience of the *piyyut* must have been educated Jews, who would have memorised the Bible. Note that the word itself testifies to the acculturation process to which the phenomenon belongs. The *piyyut* offers unambiguous evidence for the rabbinisation of liturgical practice in sixth-century Palestine, as Seth Schwartz reminds us (he also points out that we do not know how widespread the practice was).[22]

Following Pirkoi ben Baboi (ninth–tenth century Babylonia), Steven Bowman has speculated that *piyyutim* offered a legitimate way (since it was done within the legally permitted synagogal cult) to study the law through a poetical summary; this argument takes into account Justinian's laws forbidding the study of the *deuterosis* (a term that does not refer exclusively to the Mishnah, but generically to commentaries).[23] In 553, Justinian's *Novella* 146 prohibited the study of the *deuterosis*. This law also interfered with Jewish cult (something unheard of until then) by demanding the use of specific biblical translations and threatening those who denied resurrection, the last judgment and the angels. Justinian also enforced baptism upon the Jews. The *Novella* may have been meant as the emperor's retaliation for the Jews' support of the Donatists and the Arian Visigoths. Procopius tells us that it was then that the treasures of the Temple were brought from Rome to Constantinople.

One should also analyse the *piyyut* together with other kinds of Christian poetry, such as Ephrem's hymns. We know from Chrysostom, after all, that at least in late fourth-century Antioch Christians could participate in synagogal services more than was acceptable to the clergy. Similar attitudes may have appeared in Byzantine Palestine or elsewhere. In 407, Theodosius, Arcadius and Honorius issued a law against 'the new crime of superstition' of 'the unheard name of heaven worshippers (*caelicolae*).' The name of this group active in the early fifth century might point to their identity as later followers of the Judaisers of old, the *theosebeis*, or *yir'ei shamaim* (*phoboumenoi, metuentes*).

The linguistic milieus

For both Christians and Jews, the political borders of the Roman empire were far from coinciding with linguistic boundaries. The Jews of North Africa, Italy, Gaul or Spain, who left so few written traces of their thought or literary creativity, spoke Latin. In the great cities of the Eastern part of the empire,

22 S. Schwartz, *Imperialism and Jewish society*, 263.
23 S. Bowman, 'The Jews in Byzantium'.

for instance in Asia Minor, Jews spoke Greek. In the Near East, however, including Palestine, they usually spoke Aramaic, like the native Christians, who cultivated their own version of Aramaic, Syriac. In that sense, Palestine may be misleading, since there the Christian elites often spoke Greek, which the Jewish elites understood (the dealings of Origen with the rabbis in Caesarea Maritima were obviously carried on in Greek), but which was not their language of written expression. In the Syrian Orient, however, Jews and Christians shared more or less the same language, Aramaic, which had been the *lingua franca* of the area for a long time. This was the case on both sides of the political border between the Romans and the Sassanids.

The essential difference in the linguistic scene between Jews and Christians is of course a matter of weight. It is in Greek, and sometimes in Latin, that the leading Christian thinkers expressed their theologies. (Other Christian literatures – Syriac in particular, but also Coptic and Armenian – although very rich, remain marginal to the centres of political power in the empire.) For the Jews of the East, in contradistinction, literary creativity took place in Aramaic and Hebrew. There are no literary remains whatsoever of the powerful Jewish communities who spoke either Greek or Latin. The striking disappearance of Hellenistic Jewish literary culture, already noted by Joseph Justus Scaliger, remains to this day a historical puzzle. On the face of it, the Jewish communities in the Byzantine empire would appear to be the direct heirs of Hellenistic Judaism.

This sharing a language is clearly meaningful for the Jewish and Christian northern Syrian and Mesopotamian communities (in both cases, minorities, sometimes persecuted), where the geographical proximity adds to the probability of some degree of mutual cultural influence and of interdependence of literary works. Scholars have long searched the Syriac literature for evidence of rabbinic influences. In the fourth century, one of the early and major Syriac authors, Aphrahat, surnamed 'the Persian sage', retains in his *Demonstrations* various traces of rabbinic exegetical traditions.[24]

Scripture, exegesis, identity

What Jews and Christians had in common was of course, first and foremost, the Jewish scripture (albeit the Christians read it only in translation). But the Bible was also what divided them. To a great extent, the history of the cultural

---

24 See already J. Parkes, *The conflict of the church and the synagogue*, 276–8. Jacob Neusner, who claims that Aphrahat and the rabbis had nothing in common, remains a lonely voice.

relationship between them is the history of Jewish–Christian polemics in their biblical exegesis. Much has been said about Jewish influences on Christian exegesis in late antiquity. Günter Stemberger has duly noted the 'highly excessive claims' made in the early days of scholarship regarding the dependence of the church fathers on the rabbis. On the other hand, he adds, possible Christian influences on Jewish exegesis in late antiquity have never been explored in a systematic way. To be sure, it must not be assumed that the relationship was symmetrical.[25] Altogether, it is probable that more information flowed from Jews to Christians than vice versa, either directly (both Origen and Jerome, to name two obvious cases, tell us of their use of Jewish 'native informants') or indirectly (echoes of *midrashim* in Aphrahat or of Philo in Ambrose, for instance).

While concern with Judaism was central to Christian theology, the reverse is not true. Yet the Jews surely were painfully conscious of the obvious success of Christianity, which had first claimed their scripture, then conquered the empire and finally begun to humiliate them in some very concrete ways. Similarly, they must have been aware of the way in which Christian theologians interpreted at least some crucial biblical texts. Hence, in some cases, Jewish biblical interpretation reflects – and is meant to refute – Christian perceptions.

Seth Schwartz has recently argued that if Jewish life seems to have been so flourishing in Byzantine Palestine, this is because the Christianisation of the empire was one of the main causes for what he calls 'the re-judaization of the Jews'.[26] At the same time that the emperors marginalised the Jews, they empowered them. In other words, in the pagan Roman empire, the Jews were much less limited in the spectrum of possible cultural and religious postures. For them, eclecticism meant acculturation. In the Christian empire, the very religious rigidity and uniformity promoted by the emperor among Christians, through the definition as heretical of any deviant teaching or behaviour (with its radical legal consequences), also had an effect on the Jews, now defined, more than ever before, as a community. In this community, too, the process of 'orthodoxisation' forced aside and sought to erase every attempt at deviance. It is only in the fourth century, then, that we may speak of the emergence of a single Jewish culture. Similarly, Martin Goodman has spoken of the end of the fourth century as representing, for the Jews, 'the end of uncertainty'. Until

---

25 See G. Stemberger, 'Exegetical contacts between Christians and Jews in the Roman empire'.
26 Schwartz, *Imperialism and Jewish society*, esp. part 3, ch. 1.

then, he argues, one should retain serious scepticism about the applicability of rabbinic evidence outside the immediate circles of the rabbis.[27]

Schwartz's powerful argument sees in the Jewish cultural explosion of late antiquity a response, in some complex ways, to the gradual Christianisation of the Roman empire. Yet his study does not account for the significance of the Talmudic movement, at the same time, in Babylonia. While we have no archaeological remains of the Babylonian Jewish communities, we may assume that the cultural blossoming reflected by the Babylonian Talmud was not singularly literary. We must also look for cultural interaction between Jews and Christians in the Sassanid empire. There, such interaction can perhaps be studied more easily (although only in a rather speculative way, alas, as the sources are terribly scarce), since we are dealing with two fairly comparable minorities. In this context, it may be worth referring to the name for Christians in Pahlevi: *tarsak*, lit. 'fearer'. Shlomo Pines has proposed that we see in this name a trace of the origins of Christianity in Iran, which would have developed through the Jewish communities there.[28] Mesopotamian Jews and Christians partook of the same language, Aramaic, a major fact which goes a long way to explain their cultural relationship in the East.

Indeed, as J. B. Segal noted long ago, 'The early advance of Christianity in Mesopotamia was upon ground already prepared by the Jews. It was in a great degree the intellectual and cultural resources of Mesopotamian Jewry that enabled the Aramean strain in the Church of Edessa to stand aloof from the violent theological controversies that took place before the fifth century.' Segal adds that 'in the course of time, the Jewish and the Christian communities had moved far apart'.[29] We should look for cultural interaction between Jews and Christians in Babylonia not only in explicit theology and hermeneutics, but also in mystical theology and praxis.

Similarities in mysticism

Another example of the religious dynamics between Jews and Christians in late antiquity emerges in some striking similarities between early Christian and Jewish mystical texts and traditions. 'Blessed are the pure in heart, for they will see God' (Matthew 5:8). The sixth beatitude of the Sermon on the

---

27 M. Goodman, 'Jews and Judaism in the Mediterranean diaspora of the late-Roman period'.
28 Sh. Pines, *The Iranian name for Christians and the 'God-fearers'*.
29 J. B. Segal, 'Mesopotamian communities from Julian to the rise of Islam'.

Mount set the agenda for two millennia of Christian mysticism. In Christian territory, the vision of God is possible, but under certain conditions, having to do with both purity and interiority. The beatitude also points to the origin of the Christian ideal of seeing God: the Jewish background of the Sermon on the Mount. Like Christianity, rabbinic Judaism was born in the first century. Therefore, studying the early development of mysticism in the two religions from a comparative perspective should help.

In the first stages of Jewish mysticism, which Gershom Scholem mistakenly referred to as 'Jewish Gnosticism',[30] one can identify three main visual trajectories:

1 The vision of God's Body, usually referred to as *Shi'ur Qoma*
2 The vision of God's Palace (or palaces: *Hekhalot* literature)
3 The vision of God's Chariot, or *Merkavah* (referring to Ezekiel, chapter 1).

The exact dating of the late ancient Hebrew texts developing these themes is notoriously difficult. We are condemned to remain in the *longue durée*, where the most one can do is call attention to shared trajectories and to structural similarities of the main themes in early Jewish mysticism with various patristic texts. Nevertheless, it seems that such similarities developed mainly during our period, in particular within Christian milieus less touched by Platonist patterns of thought – which permitted a completely spiritual perception of the *visio mystica*. What counts in our perspective is to insist that mystical traditions, even if they start earlier, continue during our period.

A preliminary investigation of structural and thematic similarities between Jewish and Christian mystical traditions in late antiquity brings enough circumstantial evidence to show the plausibility of contacts between them.[31] Only a systematic study of sources could detect the extent to which patristic references reflect knowledge of rabbinic sources or traditions. A final caveat: similarities and parallels do not necessarily point to influences, as we deal with two traditions both rooted in biblical exegesis. Moreover, the sustained research that is needed will have to deal with the *Sitz im Leben* of mystical traditions among Jews and Christians in late antiquity. Texts outside of context remain meaningless. The significant questions relate to the function of these texts in religious praxis. What we should seek to understand better, ultimately, is a puzzling chapter in the history of religious dynamics between Jews and Christians.

30 G. Scholem, *Jewish Gnosticism, Merkabah mysticism and Talmudic tradition*.
31 See G. G. Stroumsa, 'To see or not to see'.

Education and theological culture

One can perhaps extrapolate, *mutatis mutandis*, from the few examples of contacts between mystical stances among Christians and Jews to other fields of cultural contact. Mystical experience, at least what we can know from our sources, was a matter for intellectuals, or at least religious *virtuosi*. Education, religious law and theology are fields in which it is plausible to expect some kind of cultural dynamics between the elites of the two communities. Despite the deep lack of symmetry between them, stemming from the fact that the Christians represented (in the Roman empire) the religion in power, and from the lack among the Jews of both priests and monks or nuns, there are still likenesses.

Polemics is perhaps even more difficult to use because we do not possess a single autonomous Jewish voice, and what we hear from the Christians is usually what they liked to say when they wrote against the Jews. In Babylonia, at least, the Jews had over the years established some kind of educational system (the *yeshivot*, or Talmudic academies), but this system was organised on principles greatly different from those of the Christian academies in the East, like the one in Nisibis. The variance is due essentially to the lack of Greek philosophy in the literary canon of the Jews, and to the huge contrast in the expression of theological thought that ensued. The two systems of theological education must have remained quite impermeable to one another – except for Jewish converts to Christianity (we do not hear of any Christian convert to Judaism in our period). In the West as well as in the East, the monasteries began to offer a parallel educational system, which gave up the grounding in classical *paideia*. Without Greek philosophy, Jewish theology remained, to a great extent, implicit, and focused upon religious law. Christians, on the other side, focused upon theological discussions, usually linked to the fight with heresies of all sorts, leaving law, mainly, to imperial legislation.

Popular piety and magic

The whole fields of popular piety, magic, and holy men must be considered. The evidence for relationships between the two groups is here much less ambiguous than in theological or mystical thought, although the lack of sources here remains even more dreadful than elsewhere. Jewish holy men played in their community, *mutatis mutandis*, a role similar to that played by Christian holy men in their own community. Popular religion is in many ways a problematic concept, postulating a dubious two-tiered hierarchy. But there is certainly a 'middle ground', a 'religious *koinē*' where Jews and Christians (and not only they) meet, both in urban context and in the villages. The clearest example of such a religious 'commonwealth' is probably the role of magical beliefs and practices. The magical papyri from Egypt, both in Greek and in Coptic, show a considerable amount of religious syncretism and interest in showing off Jewish (or 'Hebrew-sounding') theophoric words and names. New discoveries of Aramaic magic bowls coming from late ancient Mesopotamia highlight such common practices of Christians, Jews, Zoroastrians, and others, such as Mandeans or Manichaeans.[32]

The real common ground of Christians and Jews in late antiquity was not so much the Old Testament – that offered the major cause for the permanent clashes between them. It was, rather, the ground they shared with the other communities throughout the Mediterranean and the Near East, a *tertium quid* that did not reflect any specific religious identity. The innumerable and invisible demons which magic practices were meant to tame did not really belong to either the realm of God or that of Satan. They were, simply, part of the structure of the universe, as objective as the sun, the moon, rain and drought.

Underlying the different theological and ethnic conflicting identities, there existed in the late ancient Mediterranean and Near East a 'religious *koinē*'. On this religious 'commonwealth' Jews and Christians (as well as others) would meet without conflict, as they shared its implicit assumptions. This common-wealth was primarily magical beliefs and practices. It is almost impossible to disentangle religion from magic, at least in the ancient world, yet too often scholars have assumed magic to belong to the sphere of 'popular religion', leaving the higher spheres of theology 'intact'. The role of the *Chaldaean oracles* and the place of theurgy in later Neo-Platonism would be sufficient to cast serious doubts on such a view. In late antiquity, magic apparently moved up, and became more readily acceptable to the higher classes, including the intellectuals. Certainly both the church fathers and the rabbis strongly condemn magic, which they usually consider as the alien, doubtful and dangerous religiosity of the other. But a closer view shows that their own attitudes also accept the principles of magical thought and practice. Recent scholarship has shown a broad diffusion of magic among both Palestinian and Babylonian Jews, also among the rabbis. Magical power is part of the holy man's charisma, also among the desert monks. From Egypt through Palestine to Babylonia, spells, formulae, bowls and papyri provide a glimpse of a wide

---

32 See J. Naveh and Sh. Shaked, *Magic spells and formulae: Aramaic incantations of late antiquity*.

spectrum of magic themes and practices. In this respect, there are some obvious links between magic and mysticism, reflected both in Jewish and in Christian texts.

A final point should be mentioned in the search for the proximate channels permitting the transmission of knowledge between Jews and Christians. It appears more and more probable that Jewish Christian communities remained extant much after the fourth century, when they were usually thought to have become extinct. As late as the first half of the eighth century, for instance, John of Damascus knew of a Jewish Christian community on the shores of the Dead Sea.[33] Even if the size of these communities and their geographical location makes them quite marginal, the very fact of their existence cannot be ignored, and cannot have remained without consequences upon the perceived boundaries between Christians and Jews.

The impact of Islam

In conclusion, we may ask whether, at the end of our period, the relationship between Jews and Christians was more or less significant than it had been at its start. There is no doubt that it was different. The Jews in the Christianised Roman empire were now clearly lowered to the more or less stable nadir, a state of total weakness and humiliation to which they would be confined for more than a millennium, until at least the Emancipation. Both in the Latin West and in the Greek East, they seem to have generated much less interest for theologians than in an earlier period. Christians no longer expected conversion as when Theodoret had noted, in the fifth century, that the Jews struck a disturbing note in an ecumene that saw the conversion of various exotic peoples to Christianity. Christian writers certainly seem to have known much less about Judaism and about Jewish exegetical traditions than in previous generations. To a great extent, later Byzantine and Latin polemical literature reflect this state of affairs.

In the Near East, however, the situation was different, as the Christians had in their turn been reduced in the new Islamic empire to a situation comparable to that of the Jews. For Eastern Christians, the nemesis was now Ismael, not Israel. For John of Damascus, the worst heresy was the most recent one, that of the Ismaelites.[34] The Jews do not seem to have overly concerned him. But such an attitude was also shared by Christians in the Byzantine

---

33 See G. G. Stroumsa, 'Gnostics and Manichaeans in Byzantine Palestine'.
34 See D. J. Sahas, *John of Damascus on Islam*.

empire, who would now seek to redefine themselves religiously and politically in relationship to the emerging competition with Islam. The contenders without (the Muslims) had replaced, to a great extent, the contenders within (the Jews).

The trophies of Damascus, a Greek work of anti-Jewish polemics redacted in 681, exemplifies the new locus of the relationship between Jews and Christians. The scene of the disputatio takes place in an urban context, within a public space, and is attended not only by Christians and Jews (different kinds of them), but also by Saracens, heretics and Samaritans. We have here a whole spectrum of communities, united by their common self-definition as 'religions of the book', and fighting, as it were, a hermeneutical joute courtoise. Soon, Arabic would replace Greek and Aramaic as the sole lingua franca of the East, permitting, after many centuries, the return of the Jews to a shared intellectual life and hence a renewal of Jewish dialectical theology, putting it on a par with Christian thought. Jews and Christians, now both dhimmi communities, would soon become engaged in redefining the parameters of cultural and religious life through an intensive movement of translations. A new intellectual relationship between them would then become possible. But that is another story.

Bibliography

PRIMARY SOURCES

Eusebius. Life of Constantine (GCS Eusebius Werke, I)
John of Ephesus. Lives of Eastern saints (PO 17–19)
The Palestinian catena on Psalm 118 (SC 189–90)
Severus of Minorca. Letter on the conversion of the Jews, ed. S. Bradbury, OECT (Oxford, 1996)
Trophies of Damascus (PO 15)

SECONDARY SOURCES

Bowersock, G. W., P. Brown and O. Grabar, eds. Late antiquity: A guide to the classical world (Cambridge, MA, 1999)
Bowman, S. 'The Jews in Byzantium', in Steven Katz ed., The Cambridge history of Judaism (Cambridge, 2006), IV: 1035–52
Boyarin, D. Dying for God: Martyrdom and the making of Christianity and Judaism (Stanford, CA, 1999)
Cohen, J. Living letters of the law: Ideas of the Jew in medieval Christianity (Berkeley, 1999)
Cohen, Sh. 'Jews and Judaism in the Greco-Roman world', in Robert Kraft and George Nickelsburg, eds., Early Judaism and its modern interpreters (Atlanta, 1986), 33–56.

Dagron, G. *Emperor and priest: The imperial office in Byzantium*, trans. Jean Birrell (Cambridge, 2003)

Fattal, A. *Le statut légal des non-musulmans en pays d'Islam* (Beirut, 1955)

Fowden, G. 'Religious communities', in G. W. Bowersock, Peter Brown and Oleg Grabar, eds., *Late antiquity: A guide to the post-classical world* (Cambridge, MA, 1999), 82–106

Fredriksen, P. and O. Ir Shai. 'Christian anti-Judaism, polemics and policies: From the second to the seventh century', in S. Katz, ed., *The Cambridge history of Judaism* (Cambridge, 2006), IV: 977–1035

Fürst, A. *Hieronymus: Askese und Wissenschaft in der Spätantike* (Freiburg, 2003)

Gonzalez Salinero, R. *Biblia y polemica antijuida en Jeronimo* (Madrid, 2003)

Goodman, M. 'Jews and Judaism in the Mediterranean diaspora of the late-Roman Period: The limitations of evidence', *Journal of Mediterranean studies* 4 (1994), 205–24

Hasan-Rokem, G. *Tales of the neighborhood: Jewish narrative dialogues in late antiquity* (Berkeley, 2003)

Kennedy, H. 'Syria, Palestine and Mesopotamia', in A. Cameron, B. Ward-Perkins and M. Whitby, eds., *The Cambridge ancient history* (Cambridge, 2000), XIV: 588–611

Külzer, A. *Disputationes Graecae contra Judaeos: Untersuchungen zur byzantinischen antijüdischen Dialogliteratur und ihrem Judenbild* (Stuttgart, 1999)

de Lange, N. 'Jews and Christians in the Byzantine empire: Problems and prospects', in D. Wood, ed., *Christianity and Judaism* (Oxford, 1992), 15–32
  'Midrach et Byzance. Une traduction française du Midrash Rabba', *Revue de l'histoire des religions* 206 (1989): 171–81

Linder, A. *The Jews in Roman imperial legislation* (Detroit, 1987)

McGing, B. 'Population and proselytism: How many Jews were there in the ancient world?', in J. R. Bartlett, ed., *Jews in the Hellenistic and Roman cities* (London, 2002), 88–106

Naveh, J., and Sh. Shaked. *Magic spells and formulae: Aramaic incantations of late antiquity* (Jerusalem, 1993)

Neusner, J. *Judaism and Christianity in the age of Constantine: History, Messiah, Israel, and the initial confrontation* (Chicago, 1987)

Nock, A. D. *Conversion: The old and the new in religion from Alexander the Great to Augustine of Hippo* (Oxford, 1933)

Parkes, J. *The conflict of the church and the synagogue: A study in the origins of antisemitism* (London, 1934; reprint: New York, 1981)

Pines, Sh. *The Iranian name for Christians and the 'God-fearers'* (Jerusalem, 1967)

Sahas, D. J. *John of Damascus on Islam: The "heresy of the Ishmaelites"* (Leiden, 1972)

Scholem, G. *Jewish Gnosticism, Merkabah mysticism and Talmudic tradition* (New York, 1960)

Schwartz, S. *Imperialism and Jewish society, 200 BCE to 640 CE* (Princeton, 2001)
  'Rabbinisation in the sixth century', in P. Schaefer, ed., *The Talmud Yerushalmi and Greco-Roman culture*, Texte und Studien zum antiken Judentum 71, 79, 93 (Tübingen, 1998–2002), III: 55–69

Segal, J. B. 'Mesopotamian communities from Julian to the rise of Islam', *Proceedings of the British Academy* 41 (1955), 109–39

Stemberger, G. 'Exegetical contacts between Christians and Jews in the Roman empire', in M. Sæbø, ed., *Hebrew Bible/Old Testament: The history of its interpretation* (Göttingen, 1996), I: 569–687

Stroumsa, G. G. 'Christ's laughter: Docetic origins reconsidered', *JECS* 12 (2004): 267–88

'Early Christianity, a religion of the book?', in M. Finkelberg and G. G. Stroumsa, eds., *Homer, the Bible and beyond: Literary and religious canons in the ancient world*, Jerusalem Studies in Religion and Culture 2 (Leiden, 2003), 153–73

'Gnostics and Manichaeans in Byzantine Palestine', *SP* 18 (1985): 73–8

'Religious contacts in Byzantine Palestine', *Numen* 36 (1989): 16–42

'To see or not to see: On the early history of the *visio beatifica*', in P. Schäfer, ed., *Wege mystischer Gotteserfahrung/Mystical approaches to God* (Oldenburg, 2006), 67–80

'Vetus Israel: Les juifs dans la littérature hiérosolomitaine d'époque Byzantine', *Revue de l'histoire des religions* 205 (1989): 115–31

Wilken, R. L. *John Chrysostom and the Jews: Rhetoric and reality in the late fourth century* (Berkeley, 1983)

6

Christianity and paganism, I: Egypt

DAVID FRANKFURTER

One notices it first in the early documents of Coptic art: crosses in the shape of the ancient hieroglyph for 'life', symbols of Christian triumph juxtaposed to archaic desert beasts, tombs awash with classical nymphs and heroes, saints posed in armour, on horseback, wielding weapons against demonic chaos just like the god Horus several centuries earlier.[1] Clearly the assimilation of Christianity in Egypt took place in creative ways that challenge older notions of 'conversion'. Christianisation certainly served as more than just a way for peasants to keep their heathen ways, as many nineteenth-century historians judged it. Yet it was also more complex a process than the arrival of spiritual truth to a culture bereft of its gods and temples. In essence we may say that, over the third to sixth centuries, a distinctive Christianity came about in the land of Egypt *both* through conversation with active local traditions of religious expression *and* simply in 'being there' – taking root in a landscape where people pursued the same work and demanded of any religious system the same attention to needs as in earlier ages.

Christianisation and syncretism in the local sphere

To understand the Christianisation of Egypt as well as the conflicts with native religion that this process entailed, we need to make some tentative distinction between the Christianity of texts, literate creedal formulations and central authority, on the one hand, and, on the other, the Christianities assembled locally in villages, the products of quotidian needs, local church or monastic personalities, and regional lore. These two spheres of Christianity would in no way have been divorced from each other, for local expressions – stories of monks and saints, ritual traditions – influenced the literate central culture, while the texts, liturgy and notions of orthodoxy that developed in urban

---

1 See, e.g., J. Doresse, *Des hiéroglyphes à la croix.*

centres (and that were themselves often in competition) exerted much influence on village culture. But Christianisation involves not so much 'influence on' as 'appropriation by' – even 'synthesis of': local religious leaders actively assemble a coherent religious world from those central ideas and religious forms *and* from surrounding traditions of sacred sites, efficacious ritual, and holy people. It is a dialectic not unlike what anthropologists like Robert Redfield and McKim Marriott have observed in India, Mexico and the Andes as 'great' and 'little traditions'.[2]

Each of these cultural modes, moreover, the local and the central/literate, will also construct a discrete 'heathenism': that is, a notion of the old, repudiated, and potentially insidious religious ways that lie on the periphery of proper or acceptable religious practice. This was a particularly complex cultural endeavour in late Roman Egypt, for 'religion' everywhere had for centuries comprised a locally coherent conglomerate of familiar images, divine names, shrines, and ritual experts from Egyptian as well as from Greek and Roman traditions. Even if the basic frame of reference was most often Egyptian, the gods might be hailed in inscriptions and papyri as Kronos or Aion, Nemesis or Aphrodite or Demeter. For many intellectuals in Egypt – whether traditional or Christian in religious orientation – the gods, their cults and mythologies, were most cogently discussed in their Hellenistic guises. Thus, in the process of constructing a non-Christian sphere of religious practice recognisable from the centre, leaders typically pointed to the use of statuary, devotion to old gods by their Egyptian or (most often) Greek names, the perpetuation of official cults (but with Greek caricatures of sacrifice), or practically anything different from official practice. Even heterodox notions of Christ might fall under the label 'heathen'. In the local world, 'heathenism' may comprise the ancient temple precincts and their priestly rites, or sometimes religious practices perceived as Hellenic, but usually not devotions at minor shrines or the gestures, lore and festival times that pervaded late antique social experience. Across late antique Egyptian culture, heathenism emerged as an artificial and perpetually shifting construction only occasionally corresponding to real native religion as it persisted through the fourth and fifth centuries. For this reason, lest readers imagine a real constituency behind the term, we will use the archaic term 'heathen' (rather than the more typical 'pagan') to designate the *image* of native religion cultivated among Christian writers.

2 Robert Redfield, *The folk culture of the Yucatan* and *Peasant society and culture*; McKim Marriott, 'Little communities in an indigenous civilization'; Michael J. Sallnow, *Pilgrims of the Andes*.

In the course of defining a Christianity of all-powerful blessings, images and saints, bishops and monks inevitably signified some local traditions as reprehensibly heathen while preserving others as indispensable to the construction of a Christian culture. If the ancient gods and their shrines were often demonised, the new Christian worldview also depended upon familiar notions of harmful and beneficial power, ritual efficacy, and communication with divine beings. We may call this inevitable process of mediating new ideologies within traditional schemes of ritual power 'syncretism', but only to the extent that it involves indigenous local agency and a genuine engagement with the authority of the new worldview, and *not* in the older sense of 'pagan survival' or 'native misunderstanding'. Syncretism is essential to Christianisation, not its by-product. Indeed, syncretism may be said even to underlie the starkest efforts of Christian holy men to demonise, exorcise and demolish the old gods and their habitats, for in this process they preserve the old gods in repudiated form, even drawing on older schemes of apotropaic ritual in their efforts to repel those gods.[3]

Religious identity in names and places

Our first significant signs of people assuming some kind of Christian identity appear in naming (onomastic) practices. By the latter half of the fourth century, papyrus documents from Karanis, Hermopolis, Dionysias, Arsinoë and several other Egyptian cities show that a high proportion of children were being named *not* after Egyptian gods but rather after biblical and gospel heroes (Elias, Maria, Paul) and an ostensibly monotheistic 'God' (Coptic: *noute*). What does this mean about the 'conversion' of the populace: an exclusive Christian allegiance and repudiation of old gods, or people's mere hope that Christian names might carry some protective power for infants *alongside* that gained at local shrines and festivals? The increasing influence of biblical texts and ecclesiastical sermonising in Upper Egypt, or the efflorescence of an eclectic folklore of Christian heroes and holy names, such as we find in ritual spells of subsequent centuries – not so much replacing as augmenting stories of ancestors and gods? The onomastic evidence challenges the historian with multiple explanations beyond older Protestant notions of families' emotional 'conversion'.

Even more importantly, this evidence for *certain* cities' Christian naming practices must be balanced with the equally significant evidence, from other

---

3 See David Frankfurter, 'Syncretism and the holy man'.

places in Egypt, for the continuation of local temple cults and the various traditional rites these cults performed: festival processions and celebrations, oracles of various sorts, the opening and closing of images' portable shrines, the maintenance of Nile devotions, and the issuing of amulets and gods' blessings. Even on the diminished scale in which many cults had come to operate after the economic collapses of the third century, Egyptian traditional religion continued to draw an enthusiastic popular piety, as we see in the *proskynêmata*, 'devotions', inscribed on key parts of temple walls: usually in Greek, sometimes in florid and metrical strophes, though more often just a simple name: 'Sansnos', 'Panouchem, son of Tabolbolou'. As late as the mid-fourth century in Abydos the cult of Bes, an ancient fertility god, was attracting pilgrims and *proskynêmata* from all over the Mediterranean world (and local Egyptians as well). As late as 489, the cult of Isis the Healer at Menouthis, just outside Alexandria, was promising divine favours and dream revelations. Public devotions to Isis continued at the temple of Philae, at the far southern border of Egypt, well into the sixth century – and for several centuries in the same precinct as a small Christian cult. These are the best-known centres of continuing Egyptian religion; and they suggest not simply the existence of other, more localised, cults, but also the fundamentally *non-uniform* nature of religious transformation in Egypt.[4]

Christianity envisioned in the Egyptian landscape

Yet even when temple cults had clearly dwindled and their buildings had begun to collapse, we see many ways in which people still regarded the temples as potent points in the landscape. The Memnonion of Abydos, where the Bes-oracle operated, was still feared (or respected) as the abode of the *demon* Bes a century after the emperor Constantius II had closed it down, for the monk Moses of Abydos pits himself against the spirit in a dramatic exorcism recalled by his hagiographer. Temples were marked structures in villagers' minds, and we can infer this lingering power not only from the exorcisms recalled in hagiography but also from the countless gouges still visible in the corners and across traditionally powerful external points of Egyptian temples. Deriving especially from the era after the temples' decline, these gouges show the self-determination and perspicacity of people in search of blessings from the landscape – the tactile residues of ancient structures or places imaginatively

---

4 Onomastic evidence: R. S. Bagnall, 'Religious conversion'; cf. G. H. R. Horsley, 'Name change'; Ewa Wipszycka, 'La valeur de l'onomastique'. Effects of economic collapse: R. S. Bagnall, 'Combat ou vide'. Continuing cults: D. Frankfurter, *Religion in Roman Egypt*.

associated with strength and protection. In the words of one anonymous but censorious ecclesiastical observer of the fifth or sixth century, 'some of [the people] practise abominations in city and village. For it is said that some of them ablute their children in polluted water and water from the arena, from the theatre . . .'[5] Even the sites of civic spectacle might be thus appropriated, using water as a medium for preserving a place's potency.

Christianity neither repels nor supplants this aspect of indigenous religion. Christianisation requires the assimilation of Christian ideas *to* the landscape, and then the development of a Christian sacred landscape. In Egypt, this process did not involve simply the re-consecrating of older shrines. Although one occasionally finds evidence of such re-consecrations – Egyptian temples reoriented to Christian saints – more often the Christian shrines built within Egyptian temples seem simply to have taken over useful, attractively situated buildings with no sense that the ancient buildings might still carry some numinous power.[6] Instead, the new Christian landscape was oriented to the places of the saints: martyrs like Colluthus, culture heroes like Menas, local holy men like Abraham of Farshut, relic-imports like the 'doctors' John and Cyrus. Already in the third century (under the imperial religious edicts) an anonymous Christian author had envisioned a landscape of tortured bodies, fonts of healing blood, whose very presence would fructify the earth, raise the sun, and bring dew (*Apocalypse of Elijah*). In the fourth century Bishop Athanasius depicted (caustically) the reverence Egyptian Christians held for corpses even if their saintly identities were unclear. The urgency to find ever more saints to sanctify towns inspired, he felt, preposterous relic inventions. Still in the fifth century, the severe abbot Shenoute railed against the continuing popular enthusiasm for finding relics and visiting martyr-shrines. Yet it is at this time that the church embraced the cult of saints in all its fullness: promoting relic inventions and translations; developing stational liturgies through which people might comprehend their landscape as a veritable network of heavenly patrons; and sponsoring the composition of martyrologies to be read aloud at saints' festivals. Thus communities that had accepted Christian authority and moral schemes might now understand how (for example) the saint-protector of their village had once been a soldier in heathen times; how he had asserted his faith and thus lost skin, blood and eyes along his slow route up the Nile; and how he promised ever more to be present in his shrine as healer and revealer to all pilgrims. Through liturgical procession, martyr-shrines, and

---

5 pseudo-Athanasius, *Homily on the Virgin* 92, 95 (ed. Lefort, 35–6).
6 J. Heil, ed., *Vom Tempel zur Kirche*.

martyrological literature Egyptians came to understand Christianity through the landscape – in trees and villages and buildings.[7] We may add another medium through which Egyptian Christians gathered a sense of Christianity as an Egyptian thing – part of landscape and legend: to wit, Coptic literature. From historiography (the *Cambyses legend*, the *Alexander-romance*, the *Chronicle of John of Nikiu*) to biblical apocrypha (*Testaments of Isaac and Jacob*, *Testament of Job*; apocryphal acts like *The preaching of Bartholomew in the city of the oasis*), the Coptic literature flourishing by the time of the Muslim conquest reasserted important Egyptian traditions of key historical events, like the beginning of Persian and Greek rules, while weaving that history with sacred events and heroes of early Christianity. Sometimes they would even bring the gospels' heroes into Egypt itself. Stories of the evangelist Mark and the foundation of Christianity in Alexandria, of the Holy Family's tour of Egypt (after Matthew 2.13–29), and even John the Baptist's and Elijah's persistent epiphanies to desert hermits, all lent the landscape a central position in the epic of Christianity. Coptic language and church tradition thus served to create a quasi-national ideology, if only for monastic writers. Egypt became the place of saints, orthodoxy and foreign depredations.[8]

Christianisation of ritual traditions

Religion for many in the late antique Mediterranean world provided a layout, a rationale, for identifying and wielding supernatural power for practical purposes, like health, safety, success and social tension. Local cults and ritual experts in Egypt, no less than elsewhere in antiquity, had long addressed these needs with amulets, decrees from gods, special iconography and ritual performances. As with popular attention to sacred landscape, interest in the sources of effective 'blessing' constituted a part of Egyptian religion with which monks, bishops and ecclesiastical writers had particularly to contend. Christian writers often constructed an insidious Egyptian 'magic' as the counterpoint to Christian ritual power, a caricature they based on classical notions of Egypt as a land of wizards. Such Christian polemics against Egyptian ritual were overt, yet distanced, conjuring a fictional world of stock romantic characters.

---

7 *Apocalypse of Elijah* 4–5; Athanasius, *Festal letters* 41–2; *Life of Anthony* 90–1; Shenoute, 'Those who work evil' (ed. Lefort, 225–30). See in general T. Baumeister, *Martyr invictus*; Arietta Papaconstantinou, *Le culte des saints en Égypte*; David Frankfurter, 'Introduction'.
8 On Egyptian traditions and 'nationalising' tendencies in Coptic literature see H. Behlmer, 'Ancient Egyptian survivals'; Terry G. Wilfong, 'The non-Muslim communities'; and Ewa Wipszycka, 'Le nationalisme'.

Jerome's *Life of Hilarion* and the pseudo-Clementine *Clement romance* depict youthful Christians (or spiritual seekers not yet converted) seduced into the demonic sorceries of Egyptian priests. Another response to the great diversity of popular Egyptian ritual practices might be found in Athanasius' *Life of Anthony*. Anthony expels demons, heals and delivers blessings solely through the sign of the cross, in contrast to the more complex *bricolages* of ritual substances and spells associated with 'magic': 'I, Abrasax, shall deliver. Abrasax am I! ABRASAX ABRASICHOU, help little Sophia-Priskilla. Get hold of and do away with what comes to little Sophia-Priskilla, whether it is a shivering fit – get hold of it! Whether a phantom – get hold of it! Whether a daimon – get hold of it! . . .'[9]

Egyptian religion might thus be repudiated in its *ritual forms*, cast as sorcery, as inferior piety, as demon-worship. Yet, as we know from the numerous Christian amulets prepared in late antiquity on papyrus and leather, the techniques of signifying Christian power as something concrete and efficacious quite often involved just such expert *bricolages* as temple priests had constructed in earlier times:

> At the moment that N. child of N. will be anointed with this oil, you must take away from him all sicknesses and all illnesses and all magic and all potions and all mishaps and all pains and all male spirits and all female spirits . . . Let them all be dispelled through the power of Eloie Elemas Sabaoth Abaktani Abanael Naflo AKRAMACHAMARI, and the power of the one who has come down upon the altar on the 29th of Choiak, and the one who has come down upon the waters of the Jordan as a dove. He must come upon N. to protect him from all evil. Rule over N., who seals it. Apa Anoup has sealed this oil. Michael is the one who intercedes. Jesus Christ is the one who gives healing to N., that he may be renewed in his whole body, like the tree of life that is in the middle of paradise, all the days of his life, yea yea, at once, at once!'[10]

Thus Shenoute, also an opponent of 'magic', could complain quite explicitly in the fifth century about a 'great monk' who was fashioning amulets out of fox claws, crocodile teeth and snakes' heads, and about church elders dispensing sacred oil and water.[11] Here we begin to see how religious competition with Egyptian religion often came down to the ritual ingenuity of monks, shrine attendants, priests and scribes – those representing Christian authority in the landscape – with their maverick power-bundles. Through these experts' everyday efforts the Egyptian gods of ritual power Horus, Isis, Thoth and

---

9 *P. Lund. Univ. Bibl.* IV.12, inv. 32; trans. in H. Betz, ed., *Greek magical papyri*, 302.
10 *Berlin kopt.* 11347; trans. in M. Meyer and R. Smith, eds., *Ancient Christian magic*, 117–19.
11 Shenoute, 'Acephalous work' A14 (ed. Orlandi, 18–21).

Bes were gradually replaced with Saints Victor and Colluthus, Mary, Christ, Gabriel and Michael. (Some Coptic spell manuals from the fifth or sixth centuries actually include both pantheons: Christ and Michael in one section, Horus and Isis in the other.)[12] By the fifth century, indeed, a prominent leader like Shenoute did not know where to turn in combating unorthodox practices. One moment he might see 'magic' in the lingering heathenism of his region; the next, he would decry unsavoury ritual practices among the very ranks of Christians.

Christianity and the need for divination

Among the most basic functions served by temple cults in Egyptian society was divination: understanding the main temple god's judgments on social dilemmas through some ritual scenario. The god might be seen to move on his processional barque, or speak from an image in an incubation chamber, or issue written responses. Divination was the ritual means by which gods were involved in political and social life. Divination defined the gods' powers in society and, as in other traditional societies, articulated the traditional cosmology in the context of everyday life. Thus, in Athanasius' *Life of Anthony* 23 and 31–3, the chief powers of the 'demons', to which the saint's own powers are juxtaposed, consist of indicating future events, confirming arrivals, and reporting on the Nile's annual surge. Athanasius does not ridicule these services – indeed, he attributes the demons' mantic abilities to their quick flight – but rather reflects the diversity of ways that Egyptians, if not people throughout the Mediterranean world, sought larger, divine frameworks for their actions and experiences.

Much of the evidence for Egyptian religion in the second to fifth centuries comes, indeed, from the world of divination and exhibits the variety of media through which contact with a divine world was maintained. A large portion of the spells in the Greek and Demotic 'magical' papyri from this period seek access to divine insight, answers or epiphanies, usually according to ritual frameworks based in Egyptian temple practices. Two major fourth- and fifth-century cults – Bes of Abydos and Isis of Menouthis – were famed specifically for their oracles; and a wealth of papyri, archaeological and literary evidence through the third century testify to the centrality of divination as a basic feature of Egyptian temple practice. Even Athanasius, it was said, interpreted

12 E.g., Meyer and Smith, *Ancient Christian magic*, 95–7.

the squawks of crows in the courtyard of the Sarapeum in Alexandria, but ironically: as heralding the death of the emperor Julian.[13]

Athanasius' subtle insertion of the hermit Anthony into the field of Egyptian divination was therefore hardly peripheral to his overall promotion of the saint as an exemplary friend of God. Divination was the primary field in which desert saints seem to have made their marks on society – as interpreters of Christian authority in the framework of civic arbitration.[14] The fourth-century John of Lycopolis is hailed in the *Historia monachorum in Aegypto* as a prophet for pilgrims from all over, informing them on matters identical to those once brought to temple oracles, and even on the kinds of political issues that had brought the wrath of Rome down on temples and diviners in earlier times: the fate of political conspiracies, the success of military campaigns, the safety of travellers, the culprits in village crimes, the timing of the Nile surge and the resulting crop-yield. Another fourth-century monk, in the village of Boushêm, is recalled with somewhat less favour for

> telling people events that had not yet taken place and they would take place. In a word, he controlled them through these predictions. Indeed, if all the people's possessions were lost, he would say to them, 'Go to a certain place and you will find them,' and they would go and find them. He would also tell them when war was going to take place and how many people were going to die and it happened just as he had said.[15]

This monk's chief sin in ecclesiastical memory actually lay in teaching an extreme sexual renunciation for layfolk. His prophetic claims were not rejected outright but merely lampooned as overreaching. Holy men, indeed, were expected to provide such services. Through mediating otherworldly knowledge they demonstrated affiliations with God.

Egyptian Christian leaders worked within a religious worldview in which gods were assumed and expected to speak to their devotees, whether in dreams and visions, the prophetic utterances of holy men, or holy texts. The Bible should serve as the main source of divination, Athanasius argued against those tempted by arcane visionary texts purveyed by apocalyptic sects.[16] But from about the fifth century on, pilgrims bringing their demands for clairvoyance

---

13 *Apophthegmata patrum* Epiphanius; Sozomen, *H.E.* 4.10.
14 Cf. Peter Brown, 'The rise and function of the holy man'; Frankfurter, *Religion in Roman Egypt*, 145–97, esp. 184–93.
15 Palladius, *H.L.* 17, Coptic recension (ed. Chaîne, 246); trans. in Tim Vivian, *Four desert fathers*, 110.
16 Athanasius, *Festal letter* 39; see David Brakke, 'Canon formation and social conflict'.

and mediation to the holy martyrs at their shrines enjoyed a new means of communication with holy beings: the issuing of oracle 'tickets'. This was a millennia-old Egyptian ritual technique by which one would deliver a question to the god in two alternative written answers. The god, or now saint, would return the correct ticket, which would thereby assume the form of a protective amulet for the recipient. The procedure was aided by scribes and shrine attendants. Ticket oracles arose and thrived around saints like Colluthus, Philoxenus and Leontius. The requests would be formulated as appeals to God himself, suggesting an ecclesiastical hand insinuating a Christian orthodoxy into this altogether Egyptian ritual practice: 'O God of our patron St. Philoxenus, if you command us to bring Anoup to your hospital, show [your] power, and let the message come forth.'[17] But if an earlier age of historians saw this kind of syncretism as tantamount to the smothering of Christianity under heathen ritual, we can now regard such practices as giving sanction and definition to Christianity in the landscape. As in Latin America, local ritual traditions offered Christianity a voice textured to the cultural landscape, not separate and imposed.[18]

The Christian construction of Egyptian religion: Sorcery and atrocity

The fluidity of local religion – its foundations in sacred landscape and practical ritual – made it a slippery (if actually identifiable) opponent for church leaders, as well as a malleable element for the popular recognition and assimilation of Christian schemes of power. Local religion did not, therefore, provide an effective counterpoint to Christian self-definition. Rarely do we find attacks on real cult practices like Shenoute's polemic against popular devotion to the cult of Shai, a deity of civic fortune, which he reports as taking place around lamps in homes in Panopolis.[19] Heteropraxy here is a function of folk piety, not priestly sacrifice. By the fifth century Christian ideology needed to define itself against an identifiable enemy, a heathenism, an organised religion with full-scale temple cults. However, these cults had to be largely constructed from memory and caricature. One example of this caricatured invention of heathen cult is the depiction of the cult of the god 'Kothos' in the *Panegyric on Macarius of Tkow* (fifth/sixth century), where a temple and its popular

---

17 *P. Oxy* 1150; trans. Meyer and Smith, *Ancient Christian magic*, 52–3.
18 Papaconstantinou, *Le culte des saints en Égypte*, 336–9; David Frankfurter, 'Voices, books, and dreams'.
19 Shenoute, 'The Lord thundered' (ed. Amélineau, I: 379).

devotions, maintained alongside Christian neighbours, allegedly provide cover for bloody sacrifices. The priests lure Christian children, slaughter them on the altar, then extract their organs to make magical harps for treasure-hunting. There may well have been a cult of the god Agathos Daimon (Egyptian Shai) co-existing with Christians in this area in the fifth century, but it would hardly have engaged in atrocities. The atrocity-story, however, legitimates the cult's demolition by the holy man Macarius. A growing intolerance among Christian leaders for Egyptian temple cults from the late fourth century probably arose with a revival of martyrological lore, especially lore about the sacrifices that the martyrs had eschewed, brought on by Julian's attempt (361) to reinvigorate a rarefied temple paganism. Sacrifice came to be seen as evil and predatory, its temples dangerous to Christian society. Christian demolition of temples would save society and inaugurate a perfect Christendom.[20] And the secret corridors and austere priestly rites once romanticised in Hellenistic literature now – in Theodosian codes and local legends – became the loci of sorcery, 'magic' in its most subversive, bloodthirsty sense. Stories revelled in the penetration of secret rooms, divulging blood-spattered altars and horrible statues, the very image of danger to civic stability.[21]

Violence in the expression of religious difference; the fate of the Hellenic intelligentsia

The diverse legends of monks' spiritually motivated attacks on temple cults over the course of the fourth century have little verifiable historicity, but they allow that such acts took place idiosyncratically. In one legend, for example, Apollo halts an image-procession in Hermopolis by force of incantation, while in another Macedonius destroys the sacred falcon of Philae.[22] The watershed of violence occurred in the late fourth century in Alexandria, after a maverick temple-destruction campaign instigated by the praetorian prefect Cynegius Maternus (384–8). There followed in short order the installation of Theophilus as patriarch of Alexandria (385) and then the emperor Theodosius' draconian new edicts against temples (391ff.), all in a period of increasing, and easily fanned, tensions between Christian and non-Christian mobs in the city.

20 Shai: Shenoute, 'The Lord thundered' (ed. Amélineau, I: 379); child-sacrifice cult: pseudo-Dioscorus, *Panegyric of Macarius of Tkow* 5; sacrifice fears and intolerance of traditional cults: H. A. Drake, 'Lambs into lions'.
21 Cf. *CTh* 16.10.12. See in general Marie Theres Fögen, *Die Enteignung der Wahrsager*, 40–5, 222–53, and Hans G. Kippenberg, 'Magic in Roman civil discourse'.
22 Apollo: *Historia monachorum* 8; Macedonius: Paphnutius, *History of the monks of Upper Egypt* 29–36.

For Theophilus, a Christian city required a Christian infrastructure, a new sacred topography of churches; and it was in preparing the foundation of one basilica that – so rumours alleged – workmen discovered a secret grotto with the remains of human sacrifices. Theophilus exploited the discovery by launching a mock-parade of some old shrine-images through the streets of Alexandria, an act of symbolic assault sufficiently powerful to incite the non-Christians in the city to form violent mobs. When imperial soldiers pushed them back, the mobs retreated to the halls of the great Serapeum, and the soldiers were ordered to take the building. At some point during this invasion of the Serapeum some soldier's individual act of defacement sparked an orgy of iconoclasm and demolition that spread throughout the city, culminating in the dismemberment and public exposure of the temple's great chryselephantine image of Serapis.

Christians hailed these events as Christ's victory over Egyptian heathenism, while the Hellenic intelligentsia lamented it as a cosmic catastrophe. This intelligentsia, consisting of figures like Sosipatra, Antoninus and Hypatia, who led schools in Alexandria and Panopolis, belonged more to the urban culture of Julian's 'pagan revival' than to Egyptian religion in its traditional forms. Yet they often claimed the traditional temples as their sacred spaces in a sort of staged nostalgia. Thus the fall of such a monument to Mediterranean religious heritage as the Serapeum, symbolic not of parochial devotions but of the best and most transcendent of ancestral piety, took on eschatological overtones: as the philosopher Eunapius put it, that 'some mythic and formless darkness would reign over the most beautiful things on earth'.[23]

If only for about a decade, the events of 391 seem to have affected Egypt up and down the Nile, and certainly well beyond the cities. Alexandrian religion and religious politics had, of course, long swirled apart from the various traditional temple complexes of Upper Egypt, even if Hellenistic literature and iconography had become inextricable parts of religious life in Egyptian cities. Moreover, the evidence for Christian iconoclastic acts before the late fourth century had reflected quite localised rural expressions – a holy man's exorcistic demonstration, a village mob's mutilation of 'demonic' images. But the shock waves of the Serapeum's fall extended into the countryside with the potential to force a divide between Christian and non-Christian. Abbot Shenoute, for example, seems over the later 390s to have launched crusades against temples

---

23 Eunapius, *Lives of the philosophers* 471; cf. Rufinus, *H.E.* 2.22–30; Socrates, *H.E.* 5.16; and, in general, Françoise Thelamon, *Païens et chrétiens*, 247–59. On the Hellenic intelligentsia, see Polymnia Athanassiadi, *Damascius*, and David Frankfurter, 'The consequences of Hellenism'.

in Atripe and its environs, trying to provoke allegiance one way or the other –
to Christ or to the devil – among people of his region.[24] His disciples and
protégés Moses of Abydos and Macarius of Tkow were said to have taken up
his anti-heathen militancy, although their legends portray their violent acts
as meant more to protect Christians than to provoke heathens. Alexandria
itself continued as the site of violent demonstrations and clashes throughout
the early fifth century. Much of this violence had religious overtones, stoked
particularly by Bishop Cyril (*sed.* 412–44). In 415 alone we find: the expulsion of
Jews and burning of synagogues; the invasion of Nitrian monks to attack Cyril's
nemesis the Roman prefect; and the public murder and dismemberment of
the philosopher Hypatia.[25]

When the healing cult of Isis in Menouthis was destroyed in 489, after
co-existing for half a century with a small Christian healing shrine, the ini-
tiators of violence were not monks but *philoponoi*, a fanatic Christian con-
fraternity, who secured both the bishop's approval for the raid and the
company of monks. These last, from the Enaton monastery, proved themselves
experts in overcoming the demons in Egyptian divine images, chanting psalms
against the statues' potency. Yet as the historian and eyewitness Zachariah of
Mitylene reports this episode, the tensions expressed in iconoclasm and
demolition were not so much Christian-versus-Egyptian cult as Christian-
versus-Hellenic intelligentsia, with undercurrents of intra-Christian theological hostilities. The suburban temple, unthreatening and unnoticed for a century since the Serapeum's downfall, exhibited the deceptive heathen tricks
with which the heathen intellectuals had (it was accused) associated themselves and thus provided a convenient focus for inciting Christian solidarity in
a time of theological and monastic schism. The traditional temple became the
'fall-guy' amid much more complex tensions.

Indeed, if the destruction of temples did not obliterate the fundamental
sentiments of Egyptian religion, neither did such dramatic attacks deflate the
Hellenic intelligentsia. Their schools continued, albeit in diminished form
and progressively disconnected from Egyptian temple religion. Over the fifth
and sixth centuries we see figures like Asclepiades and Horapollon trying
to attach themselves to existing shrines and reinventing priestly traditions for
themselves; while others, like Hypatia's student Synesios and the poet Nonnos,
assumed Christian idioms for their writing.[26]

24 Stephen L. Emmel, 'From the other side of the Nile'.
25 Socrates, *H.E.* 7.13–15; in general, see C. Haas, *Alexandria in late antiquity*, 295–316.
26 Cf. Johannes Geffcken, *The last days of Greco-Roman paganism*; Alan Cameron, 'Wandering
poets'.

Conclusion: Constructing and reifying the heathen other

Egyptian religion by the middle of the fourth century was largely indefinable for Christian opponents. Beyond those cults that continued in diminished splendour, offering festival processions, oracles, and ritual attention to the Nile surge (and hardly objecting to Christian practices in their locales), the traditional religious attitudes of ordinary people focused on landscape, time and festival, rituals of health and protection, and any potent means for discerning divine guidance. The evidence from late antique religion in Egypt suggests that Christian leaders did not oppose this sphere of traditional Egyptian religion but, rather, articulated Christianity in its terms: new landscapes of martyrs' shrines, healing and protective spells in Christian idiom, Christian divination centres. Yet hagiographies suggest that ecclesiastical caricatures of heathen cult as a horrific theatre of blood-sacrifice contributed to perceptions of Egyptian cults as well; and such caricatures sanctioned acts of iconoclastic violence in the decades following the destruction of the Serapeum. For the monks and *philoponoi* who committed these deeds, demolition of heathen cults extirpated the memory of Julian and the legendary horrors of Diocletian. Demolition purified the landscape while forcing those who might imagine themselves participants in both religions – certainly a plausible and typical scenario – to choose sides. Finally, demolition and iconoclasm of traditional temples offered violently schismatic groups the possibility of a common focus.

Bibliography

PRIMARY SOURCES

Apocalypse of Elijah, eds. A. Pietersma et al. (Missoula, MT, 1981)
Apophthegmata patrum, alphabetical collection (PG 65)
Athanasius. *Festal letters* (CSCO 150–1)
 Life of Anthony (SC 400)
(pseudo-)Athanasius. *Homily on the Virgin*. Ed. L.-Th. Lefort, 'L'homélie de S. Athanase des papyrus de Turin', *Le muséon* 71 (1958): 5–50
pseudo-Dioscorus. *Panegyric of Macarius of Tkow* (CSCO 415–16)
Eunapius. *Lives of the philosophers*. In W. C. Wright, *The lives of the Sophists. Philostratus and Eunapius*, LCL (London, 1922)
Historia monachorum in Aegypto. Ed. A.-J. Festugière, *Historia Monachorum in Aegypto: Édition critique du texte grec* (Brussels, 1961)
Palladius. *Historia Lausiaca*, Coptic recension. Ed. M. Chaîne, 'La double recension de l'Histoire Lausiaque dans la version copte', *Revue de l'Orient chrétien* 25 (1925/6), 232–75

Paphnutius. *History of the monks of Upper Egypt*. In E. A. Wallis Budge, ed., *Miscellaneous Coptic texts. Coptic texts, vol.* v, *parts 1 & 2* (London, 1915; reprint, New York, 1977), I: 432–95; also trans. Tim Vivian. Cistercian Studies 140 (Kalamazoo, 2000)

Rufinus. *Historia ecclesiastica* (GCS *Eusebius Werke*, II)

Shenoute. 'Acephalous work', in Tito Orlandi, ed., *Shenute: Contra Origenistas* (Rome, 1985)
  'The Lord thundered', in Émile Amélineau, ed., *Œuvres de Schenoudi* (Paris, 1909)
  'Those who work evil', in Émile Amélineau, ed., *Œuvres de Schenoudi* (Paris, 1909); L.-Th. Lefort, 'La chasse aux reliques des martyrs en Égypte au IVᵉ siècle', *La nouvelle Clio* 6 (1954): 225–30

Socrates. *Historia ecclesiastica* (PG 67)

Sozomen. *Historia ecclesiastica* (GCS, N.F. 4: *Sozomenus Kirchengeschichte*)

Zachariah of Mitylene. *Life of Severus* (PO 2)

SECONDARY SOURCES

Athanassiadi, Polymnia. *Damascius: The Philosophical history* (Athens, 1999)

Bagnall, R. S. 'Combat ou vide: Christianisme et paganisme dans l'Égypte romaine tardive', *Ktema* 13 (1988): 285–96
  'Religious conversion and onomastic change', *BASP* 19 (1982), 105–24

Baumeister, Theofried. *Martyr invictus: Der Martyrer als Sinnbild der Erlösung in der Legende und im Kult der frühen koptischen Kirche* (Münster, 1972)

Behlmer, Heike. 'Ancient Egyptian survivals in Coptic literature: An overview', in A. Loprieno, ed., *Ancient Egyptian literature: History and forms* (Leiden, 1996), 567–90

Betz, H., ed. *Greek magical papyri in translation* (Chicago, 1986)

Brakke, David. *Athanasius and the politics of asceticism* (Oxford, 1995)
  'Canon formation and social conflict in fourth-century Egypt: Athanasius of Alexandria's thirty-ninth *Festal letter*', *HTR* 87 (1994): 395–419

Brown, Peter. 'The rise and function of the holy man in late antiquity', *JRS* 61 (1971): 80–101; reprinted in Peter Brown, *Society and the holy in late antiquity* (London, 1982)

Cameron, Alan. 'Wandering poets: A literary movement in Byzantine Egypt', *Historia* 14 (1965): 470–509

Doresse, Jean. *Des hiéroglyphes à la croix: Ce que le passé pharaonique a légué au christianisme* (Istanbul, 1960)

Drake, H. A. 'Lambs into lions: Explaining early Christian intolerance', *Past and present* 153 (1996): 3–36

Dunand, Françoise. 'Miracles et guérisons en Égypte tardive', in Nicole Fick and Jean-Claude Carrière, eds., *Mélanges Étienne Bernand* (Paris, 1991), 235–50
  Religion populaire en Égypte romaine (Leiden, 1979)

Emmel, Stephen L. 'From the other side of the Nile: Shenute and Panopolis', in A. Egberts, B. P. Muhs and J. van der Vliet, eds., *Perspectives on Panopolis: An Egyptian town from Alexander the Great to the Arab conquest* (Leiden, 2002), 95–113

Fögen, Marie Theres. *Die Enteignung der Wahrsager* (Frankfurt, 1993)

Fowden, Garth. 'Bishops and temples in the Eastern Roman empire, A. D. 320–435', *JTS* 29 (1978): 53–78

Frankfurter, David. 'The consequences of Hellenism in late antique Egypt: Religious worlds and actors', *Archiv für Religionsgeschichte* 2 (2000): 162–94

'Introduction: Approaches to Coptic pilgrimage', in *Pilgrimage and holy space in late antique Egypt* (Leiden, 1998), 3–48

Religion in Roman Egypt: Assimilation and resistance (Princeton, 1998)

'Syncretism and the holy man in late antique Egypt', *JECS* 11 (2003): 339–85

'Voices, books, and dreams: The diversification of divination media in late antique Egypt', in Sarah Iles Johnston and Peter Struck, eds., *Mantikê. Studies in ancient divination* (Leiden, 2005), 233–54

Geffcken, Johannes. *The last days of Greco-Roman paganism*, trans. Sabine MacCormack (Amsterdam, 1978)

Haas, Christopher. *Alexandria in late antiquity: Topography and social conflict* (Baltimore, 1997)

Heil, Johannes, ed. *Vom Tempel zur Kirche* (Leiden, forthcoming)

Horsley, G. H. R. 'Name change as an indication of religious conversion in antiquity', *Numen* 34 (1987): 1–18

Kippenberg, Hans G. 'Magic in Roman civil discourse: Why rituals could be illegal', in Peter Schäfer and Hans G. Kippenberg, eds., *Envisioning magic: A Princeton seminar and symposium* (Leiden, 1997), 137–63

Marriott, McKim. 'Little communities in an indigenous civilization', in *Village India: Studies in the little community* (Chicago, 1955), 171–222

Meyer, Marvin, and Richard Smith, eds. *Ancient Christian magic: Coptic texts of ritual power* (San Francisco, 1994)

Papaconstantinou, Arietta. *Le culte des saints en Égypte des Byzantins aux Abbassides. L'apport des sources papyrologiques et épigraphiques grecques et coptes* (Paris, 2001)

Redfield, Robert. *The folk culture of the Yucatan* (Chicago, 1941)

Peasant society and culture: An anthropological approach to civilization (Chicago, 1956)

Richter, Siegfried G. *Studien zur Christianisierung Nubiens* (Wiesbaden, 2002)

Sallnow, Michael J. *Pilgrims of the Andes: Regional cults in Cusco* (Washington, DC, 1987)

Thelamon, Françoise. *Païens et chrétiens au IVe siècle: L'apport de l'"Histoire ecclésiastique" de Rufin d'Aquilée* (Paris, 1981)

Vivian, Tim. *Four desert fathers: Pambo, Evagrius, Macrius of Egypt & Macarius of Alexandria* (Crestwood, NY, 2004)

Wilfong, Terry G. 'The non-Muslim communities: Christian communities', in C. Petry, ed., *The Cambridge history of Egypt* (Cambridge, 1998), I: 175–97

Wipszycka, Ewa. 'La christianisation de l'Égypte aux IVe–VIe siècles. Aspects sociaux et ethniques', *Aegyptus* 68 (1988): 117–65

'Le nationalisme a-t-il existé dans l'Égypte byzantine?', *Journal of juristic papyrology* 22 (1992): 83–128

'La valeur de l'onomastique pour l'histoire de la christianisation de l'Égypte', *ZPE* 62 (1986): 173–81

7

Christianity and paganism, II: Asia Minor

FRANK R. TROMBLEY

Asia Minor was a region of broad religious diversity in the time of the Tetrarchy and afterwards, under the successor regimes established by Licinius, Constantine and his sons (284–361). Significant communities of Jews and Christians populated its cities and their territories amid the great pagan Greek majority. Christians were a tiny minority c. 300, perhaps 5 to 10 per cent in most cities except in some places like Nicomedia and Eumeneia, and in villages throughout Phrygia, where large numbers lived.[1] Its institutional expansion is reflected in the fact that, in 325, the representatives of some 150 episcopal sees in Asia Minor attended the Council of Nicaea. This posed a serious ideological challenge to the pagan temple cults of Asia Minor. Their priesthoods were filled by city councillors who had accrued great wealth from their agricultural estates. The ancestral cults of the agricultural cycle were considered the basis for preserving the 'peace of the gods', whose chief manifestation lay in the regularity of the forces of nature; their neglect was thought to cause the meteorological catastrophes that periodically damaged agricultural production. A decree of the emperor Maximinus Daia in 312 sums up this theological argument in some detail.[2]

Education in grammar, rhetoric and the Greek *paideia* provided an ideological basis for the city councillors' religious opinions; it was a key factor in their resistance to Christian ideas, particularly where the conflicting theologies gave rival interpretations of particular questions, such as the divine nature, cosmogony and ethics. The importance of the Greek *paideia* is particularly evident in the writings of Themistius, who taught rhetoric in Ancyra in the mid-fourth century, but also in many Christian inscriptions.[3]

The fourth century marked a critical transition in relations between pagans and Christians in Asia Minor. The eastern emperors of the second Tetrarchy,

---

1 T. Drew-Bear, ed., *Nouvelles inscriptions*, no. 48, etc.
2 A. D. Lee, *Pagans and Christians*, 77f.
3 SEG 6, no. 17; SEG 27, no. 847; W. Jaeger, *Early Christianity and Greek paideia*.

Galerius and Maximinus Daia, were the architects of a policy of using state power to strengthen adherence to the traditional cults; the Great Persecution sought to destroy the institutional fabric of the local churches by forcing Christian clergy to sacrifice. The local pagan cults were reorganised, with a high priest in each provincial capital overseeing the priests of the urban and rural temples. This policy is visible in the continuing performance of sacrifice by the priesthood of Stratonicea as late as 312. It was a response to an imperial rescript published at Sardis on 6 April 312, inviting the Greek cities to expel Christians living in their midst to ensure the peace of the gods.[4] Inscriptions also indicate late third- or early fourth-century priesthoods at Dorylaeum, and the high priest and prophet Epitynchanos in the Upper Tembris valley in Phrygia c. 313–14.[5] An inscription from 311 or 312 records a petition of the Lycian and Pamphylian cities, asking for the expulsion of the Christians, and calling them a people demented (*manikoi*) by the disease of a novel religion which contravened the ancestral cult of the gods. The Tetrarchs personally inspired the political spin and timing of the complaint.[6]

> . . . O most divine emperors, since the gods of our race have given recompense to humankind in their every act of goodwill, for which their worship is practised on behalf of the perpetual safety of our emperors, who are most victorious in all things, we think it good to have recourse to [your] immortal *imperium* and petition that the Christians who have for a long time been demented in adhering to this sickness be stopped, and that they no longer be allowed to transgress [the worship] that is owed to the gods by means of their dubious and novel cult. It would be conducive to this, if it were decreed to everyone by your divine and perpetual assent . . . that all people should devote themselves to the cult of the gods of our race, in the interest of our eternal and incorruptible empire . . .

The co-operation between the Tetrarchs and city councillors provoked Christian attacks on Greek temples. This was a response to the destruction of churches, beginning with the Christian basilica lying opposite the imperial palace in Nicomedia. For example, the life of St Theodotus of Ancyra reports that a group of Christians demolished a *temenos* of Artemis in the city's territory.[7] Eusebius mentions the destruction of an unnamed Phrygian town in 303 whose population was mostly Christian. It has been identified as Eumeneia

---

4 Lee, *Pagans and Christians*, 78f.
5 SEG 38, nos. 1303, 1307; SEG 43, no. 943.
6 *CIL* 3, nos. 12132 and 13625b; *ILCV*, no. 1a–b.
7 S. Mitchell, 'The life of Saint Theodotus of Ancyra', 96.

because of the unusually large number of third-century Christian inscriptions found there.[8] At Nicomedia, the residence of Diocletian where the edicts of persecution were first published, the large number of martyrdom narratives suggests the existence of a significant Christian population and many executions in the capital.[9] Rural inscriptions in Bithynia mention the presence of Christians in the environs of Nicomedia as well.[10] The historically reliable account of the Forty Martyrs of Sebaste in Armenia belongs somewhat later, in the time of Licinius (308–24).[11] A certain M. Iulius Eugenius, a city councillor of Kouessa and civil servant for the governor of Pisidia, refused to sacrifice and was tortured during Maximinus Daia's persecution. He survived, and went on to serve as bishop for twenty-five years, commemorating his career in a great funerary inscription that he erected around 340.[12] After the Great Persecution ended in 313, the sarcophagi of some third-century martyrs were newly inscribed, like that of St Tribimis of Sillyon in Pamphylia, as a gesture of victory.[13]

The geographical extent of the early and mid fourth-century Christian communities can be gauged from funerary inscriptions at urban sites like Cotyaeum, Eumeneia, Nicaea, Nova Isaura and Prusias.[14] Early fourth-century Christian inscriptions appear at rural sites as well, like present-day Çeşmeli Zebir and Güllüköy in Phrygia, Dinek Serai in the territory of Nova Isaura in Isauria, Kalos Agros in Bithynia, and Kindiraz in Lycaonia.[15] A particularly important series of inscriptions discovered at the village of Kurdköy in Phrygia expresses the religious divisions in a family that accepted Christianity in the first half of the fourth century.[16]

The growth of the Christian communities is reflected in numerous provincial councils that met in the cities of Asia Minor between *c.* 343 and 381.[17] The canons of the Councils of Laodicea and Gangra address liturgical and disciplinary questions involving the intrusion of pagan religious customs into Christian practice. The celebration of local pagan festivals was a serious

---

8 Drew-Bear, *Nouvelles inscriptions*, no. 48, etc.; Leclercq, 'Euménie', *DACL* 5.1: 734–44.
9 Eusebius, *HE* 9. 9a. 1. 5. *BHG*, 27, 39, 134, 135, 198, 296, 462, 548, 549, 572, 616, 1219, 1273, 1325y, 1412z, 1544, 1781, 2053, 2058, 2139, 2173, 2464. *BHO*, 63, 129, 163, 173, 254, 286, 370, 551, 835, 1182.
10 SEG 20, no. 35; SEG 28, no. 1037; SEG 29, no. 1321; SEG 37, no. 1072.
11 H. Musurillo, *Acts of the Christian martyrs*, 354–61.
12 W. Wischmeyer, 'M. Iulius Eugenius'.
13 SEG 38, no. 1440B.
14 SEG 6, no. 466; SEG 15, no. 796; SEG 20, no. 35; SEG 28, no. 1129; SEG 29, nos. 1321, 1324.
15 SEG 6, nos. 480, 488, 491; SEG 13, no. 544; SEG 19, no. 719; SEG 20, no. 35; SEG 37, no. 1072.
16 SEG 6, nos. 137–40.
17 P.-P. Joannou, ed., *Discipline générale antique.*

distraction to the numerous catechumens.[18] These seasonal events saw processions of images, ritual dancing and fire-walking – the practice of priestesses walking on hot coals with no sensation of pain.[19] One of the more important festivals was the Basket of Artemis, which was still being celebrated even in the mid-fifth century.[20] The habitual sacrifices to pagan divinities put Christians at risk of apostasy. A canon of the Council of Gangra mentions the availability of meats from sacrifices at pagan temples.[21] An important remedy for contact with pagan cult was exorcism by anointing with oil.[22] It was the recognised ritual in baptism and afterward, but was also seen as a weapon against the daemons thought to cause disease and socially disordered behaviour.[23] In addition, clerics were forbidden to participate in agapes, which resembled pagan sacrifices celebrated in Christianised form, as they involved the laying of couches in churches.[24]

The synod of Laodicea forbade participation in the Anatolian cult of angels, beings that were considered to be quasi-divine in Syrian, Phrygian and Greek religion, in local Judaism, and in Christianity:

> Christians must not abandon the church of God, and go out, and call the names of angels, and make assemblies, which are forbidden. If anyone is caught practising this secret idolatry, let him be anathema, because he has abandoned our lord Jesus Christ the son of God, and has gone over to idolatry.[25]

The Christian cult of angels was an indirect outgrowth of this. A good example is found in St Michael, whose iconography was borrowed from Attis-Men, consort of the Great Mother Cybele, and whose assemblies became common in Phrygia and Pisidia by the early fifth century.[26] Pre-Christian angels were often worshipped at *hagiasmata*, numinous springs that were thought to be sacred to chthonic gods like Attis, whose domains included the celestial and the subterranean spheres. At Chonae near Colossae, Christians established competing shrines next to those of pagan Phrygians and worshipped their own angels in synoikism with the pre-Christian cult.[27] In the fifth century, places

---

18 Trombley, *Hellenic religion and Christianization*, II: 129–31; catechumens: Council of Laodicea, canons 19, 31.
19 Strabo, *Geography* 12.2.7; C. Laodicea, canon 39; R. Lane Fox, *Pagans and Christians*, 102–67.
20 Strabo, *Geography* 13.4.5; Callinicus, *De vita S. Hypatii* 45.
21 Council of Gangra, canon 2.
22 Exorcists: C. Laodicea, canon 24, 26.
23 Ibid., canons 26, 48.
24 Ibid., canons 27, 28.
25 Ibid., canon 35; *ILS*, no. 8882.
26 Theodoret of Cyrrhus, *In Coloss.* 2.18 (PG 82: 613); C. Mango, 'St. Michael and Attis'.
27 Trombley, *Hellenic religion and Christianization*, I: 153–6; II: 82f.

like Germia went over to the Christian cult of angels, but small numbers of pagans continued nevertheless to worship their angels there.[28] Cults for the intercession of quasi-divine friends of Christ, including martyrs, Christian angels and the Old Testament patriarchs, came later. In the sixth century, non-Christian angels were still being invoked in amulets, and on boundary stones demarcating tilled fields, where the daemons thought to animate clouds full of hailstones were adjured to turn back from the sacred perimeter.[29] There were some elements in pre-Christian culture that pagans and Christians alike rejected, among them magic practices condemned in the canons of Basil of Caesarea.[30] The synod of Laodicea forbade bishops and ordinary clerics to be magicians, sorcerers or astrologers, and clergy were also forbidden to concoct amulets – metal apotropaic objects on which syncretistic formulae and the names of unknown angels were often inscribed.[31] Their manufacture was tolerated only at recognised sites of Christian pilgrimage.

There were too few rural churches and ecclesiastical personnel to ensure that catechumens fully absorbed the teaching of uncompromising monotheism. Yet catechumens wishing to receive baptism were supposed to show a higher level of commitment by submitting to weekly instruction in the scriptures and canons. The synod of Laodicea established a system of sending out rural priests called *periodeutai* to assist these congregations.[32] This replaced the earlier practice of installing bishops wherever there was a sizeable Christian community, whether in a city, village or rural estate. This was a product of the unsupervised movement of Christianity into the countryside. Orkistos in the territory of Nacolea in Phrygia was such a place. A rescript of the emperor Constantine the Great allowed it to secede from pagan Nacolea and granted it semi-independent, quasi-urban status.[33]

The framers of the canons of Laodicea were aware of convivial social relations between Christians and pagans. They forbade bishops, clerics, monks and laypersons from attending the baths, alluding to a law of Hadrian (*regn.* 117–36) that showed they were a source of reproach even among the pagans.[34] Conventionally minded Christians naturally participated in civic, religious and family events with their pagan neighbours. Christians were required to eat their food

---

28 SEG 6, no. 73; C. Mango, 'Germia'.
29 *Recueil des inscriptions grecques-chrétiennes d'Asie Mineure*, ed. Grégoire, no. 341 *ter* and commentary.
30 See below.
31 Council of Laodicea, canon 36.
32 Ibid., canon 57.
33 *CIL* 3, no. 352; cf. SEG 43, no. 941.
34 Council of Laodicea, canon 30.

circumspectly at weddings, many of which would have been celebrated in the houses of pagan families, and to avoid wild leaping and dancing.[35] This was perhaps an overreaction to liturgical dance in pagan cult, particularly the frenzied enthusiasm that accompanied the rites of Dionysus and Cybele.[36]

The pagan city councillors of Asia Minor greeted Julian's rise to sole power in November 361 with great enthusiasm, as a dedicatory inscription of the imperial cult at Pergamum reveals.[37] Although the institutional fabric of pagan temples was weakened, it had not been extinguished. One of Julian's letters c. 354 praises Pegasius, Christian bishop of Alexandria Troas, who guided him through the shrines of the heroes from the Trojan War. Julian found the temples intact and sacrifices still being performed, with Pegasius' tacit approval. The bishop spoke partly out of local patriotism, partly out of enthusiasm for Homer and the Greek *paideia*. He may have accepted baptism and joined the clergy in the reign of Constantius II to avoid the financial burdens that fell on city councillors, all the while retaining a sense of Hellenic piety.[38] The story that Pegasius performed sacrifice may be put down to the slander of his enemies. Another letter of Julian to Arsacius, high priest of the *temenos* of Cybele at Pessinus, sets forth the criteria for priestly behaviour and the management of the goddess's finances, with a view to increasing the appeal of the 'church' of Cybele to pagans and Christians alike. Sacrifices had recently begun again, after the traditional first-fruit offerings had lapsed with the demise of the emperor Licinius in 324. Julian now commanded priests and temple wardens to extend hospitality to travellers and to look after their cemeteries, just as the Christians did. Priests were also supposed to observe the same high standards of morality as Christian presbyters and bishops. Julian offered the income of the imperial estates to pay the salaries of the priests of Cybele who worked at other trades, in order to give the temples a full-time 'clergy'. He even promised additional monies 'if the entire people should once again become suppliants of the Mother of the Gods'.[39] His aim was to roll back adherence to Christianity by the pagan priesthood setting a good example. His concern for the pagan villages of Galatia reflects the slow progress of Christianity in some rural districts.

The temple of Hadrian at Ephesus was repaired after an earthquake, possibly that of 358, and a new frieze was incorporated into its interior, making use of

---

35 Ibid., canon 53.
36 Trombley, 'Christianisation of rite', 63f.
37 *ILS* 751 = *CIL* 3.7088.
38 Julian, *Ep.* 19.
39 Ibid., 22.

pre-existing material. Probably dating from the time of Julian, Section D of the frieze may represent the emperor himself (a man of average height in military garb), his father (a somewhat taller man wearing a mantle that resembles a toga) and his grandfather the deified Constantius I.[40] It is one of the latest examples of pre-Christian religious art to have survived in Asia Minor.

The correspondence of Basil, archbishop of Caesarea in Cappadocia (370–9), reflects relations between pagan and Christian communities in a late fourth-century urban setting. As a Christian Hellenist Basil authored the protreptic essay 'Advice to young men on how to derive profit from Hellenic literature', a work designed to protect students from the subversive content of pagan Greek literature. His remarks dealt particularly with Homer, whose poetry had become the scripture of pagan Greek theology, and who with Plato is the most frequently cited author in Basil's correspondence.[41] Basil's letters contain many classical allusions. He refers to the *Odyssey* in a letter to Antipater, governor of Cappadocia, in 374 and uses the adjective *kourotrophos* ('fostering mother') – an epithet of Artemis and Hekate, divinities still worshipped in late fourth-century Asia Minor.[42] Other writers and works likely referred to include the poet Simonides, Aesop, Aristophanes, Aristotle, Euripides, Herodotus, Theophrastus, Diogenes Laertius' lives of the philosophers, and late Hellenistic moralists like Plutarch.[43] Most of the letters containing allusions to the *paideia* were addressed to pagan and Christian public officials, not clergy.[44]

Basil's theological correspondence gives the impression of Christian cultural and demographic dominance in Cappadocia, but this is deceptive. *Chôrepiskopoi*, or rural presbyters, are often mentioned, suggesting that there were not enough Christian village congregations to justify building churches and installing presbyters and deacons.[45] Basil complains that the *chôrepiskopoi* were not effective in enforcing 'the canons of the Fathers'.[46] He once visited

---

40 R. Fleischer, 'Der Fries des Hadrianstempels in Ephesos', 23–71. The author of this study does not commit himself to these identifications. The figures in question are D8, D9 and D12, pp. 31–4 and plate 17. I take the deified figure to be *divus* Constantius I. He stands next to a figure that seems to be Hercules, the tutelary divinity of Constantius I's branch of the Tetrarchy. I take the figure in military garb to be Julian (D12) – who distinguished himself as a military commander in Gaul. He is surrounded by the female divinities Athena, Aphrodite and Hekate. Julian doubtless held Athena in special reverence as the philosopher goddess, and Hekate through the influence of the theurgist Maximus of Ephesus. These opinions are provisional. For fuller discussion, see F. R. Trombley, 'The imperial cult' (forthcoming).

41 Basil, *Epp.* 14, 74, 135, 147.

42 Ibid., 186.

43 Ibid., 3–5, 8, 9, 14, 63, 135, 140, 189, 291, 334.

44 Ibid., 3–5, 9, 14, 63, 74, 147, 186, 189, 334.

45 Inscriptions: Harper, 'Tituli Comanorum Cappadociae', no. 8.06.

46 Basil, *Ep.* 54.

an assembly of presbyters in a mountainous district, but the expansion of rural Christianity in Cappadocia remains difficult to quantify. Many applications seeking admission to the subdiaconate that he received in the early 370s came principally from men seeking to avoid military conscription.[47] Basil later formulated strict ordinances for admission to the clergy in his canonical letters to Amphilochius of Iconium. The church of Caesarea still seems to have had many catechumens in the 370s. When Basil mentions Christian baptism, it is often to urge adults who had not yet accepted it, at other times to explain the fate of the soul in the divine milieu.[48] He used the term 'regeneration' (*palingenesis*) for it when an acquaintance of his, the general and consul Arinthaeus, received the sacrament just before his death.[49]

Basil was concerned about Christians lapsing into pagan cult. This can be measured from the list of prohibitions found in his three canonical letters to Amphilochius of Iconium in AD 374–5.[50] The eighty-four canons were intended for baptised Christians and not catechumens. Some of the rules refer to sacrifice, others to magic and poisoning, whose practitioners are broadly classified as 'idol-worshipers'.[51] Basil remarked to Amphilochius: 'If the mind has been injured by daemons, it will worship idols or will be turned aside to some other form of impiety.'[52] Sacrifice as a retrospective denial of baptism seems to lie behind the offence of 'insulting Christ after receiving the name of Christianity', as also that of 'despising Christ and transgressing the mystery of salvation'.[53] In the latter instance, the offenders could be re-admitted to the sacrament only at the point of death. Such a severe penalty suggests that recently baptised Christians still participated in sacrifice as members of communities when pagan festivals, public and private, were celebrated. Another canon recommends leniency for those who perform their penance diligently, citing the Christian God's love of mankind (*philanthrôpia*).[54] The barbarian enemies who raided the empire were often not Christian, and they seem to have forced their captives to sacrifice. Basil saw this as a mitigating factor. His rule on this was partly based on the canonical letter of Gregory Thaumatourgos, a work that had been published in response to the mid third-century raids of seafaring Goths and the Sassanid king Shapur I:[55]

47 Ibid.
48 Ibid., 10, 175, 269.
49 Ibid., 269.
50 Ibid., 188, 199, 217.
51 On 'sacrilege' (*hierosylia*): Basil, *Ep.* 199, canon 44; on 'idolatry': Basil, *Ep.* 233.
52 Basil, *Ep.* 233.
53 Basil, *Ep.* 199, canon 45; *Ep.* 217, canon 73.
54 Basil, *Ep.* 217, canon 74.
55 Ibid., canon 81.

Since many persons have transgressed their faith in God at the time of barbarian invasion and have fulfilled barbarian oaths, tasting certain illicit things, which were offered to them in the presence of magic idols, they shall be disciplined in accordance with the canons already published by the Fathers . . . Those who, without great necessity, have betrayed their faith in God, and have touched the table of daemons and have sworn pagan oaths, [shall suffer a longer penance].

Gregory and Basil both specify 'magic idols', hinting that some of the forbidden sacrifices took place in Cappadocia and the Armenian borderlands, where Zoroastrians are reported to have lived in large numbers in the fourth and fifth centuries.[56] Basil's report about them to Epiphanius of Salamis fails to mention the existence of fire temples, but the temple undoubtedly still existed in Cappadocia at this time.[57] The theophoric names of dedicants at Comana in Cappadocia suggest that Mithra and other Iranian divinities were gods in the local pantheon,[58] but they were worshipped using conventionalised names of cognate Greek divinities.[59]

Anatolian liturgical practices influenced Christian folk religion in certain respects. The story of Glycerius may be an example of this. As deacon of a rural commune called Venesa, he wore unusual robes and acquired a retinue of the local youths and unmarried women who were criticised for dancing and otherwise boisterous conduct at a local festival (*synodos*). Basil does not tell us whether this event lay in the Christian or pagan liturgical calendar. Basil condemns Glycerius for leading his congregation into the abyss (*barathron*, akin to *bathos* and *bothron*).[60] The term may well allude to the gaseous subterranean water channels and caverns that had a numinous significance in Anatolian religion, and whose tutelary divinities were sometimes Attis or Cybele.[61]

Families in Basil's congregation were at times divided on questions of religious allegiance. He cites two instances where the sons of aristocratic families accepted baptism. One was a certain Dionysius whose mother remained pagan, the other the son of pagan Harmatius, whom Basil counselled to forget his bitterness: 'Since [your son] has preferred the God of us Christians, that is true God, before the gods of your people, which are numerous and are worshipped

56 Basil, *Ep.* 258; Lee, *Pagans and Christians*, 169–73.
57 Procopius, *De bellis* 1.17.18; F. W. Deichmann, 'Frühchristliche Kirchen in antiken Heiligtümern', 129, no. 62.
58 Harper, 'Tituli Comanorum Cappadociae,' nos. 1.01, 2.02, 2.04, 2.05, 2.11, 3.01, 5.24, 5.25, 6.10.
59 Ibid., nos. 2.05, 3.02 (3rd century AD).
60 Basil, *Epp.* 169, 170.
61 Damascius, *Epit. Phot.* 131 (ed. Zintzen, 176; trans. Asmus, 78 and 174); cf. Basil, *Ep.* 74.

through material symbols, do not be angry with him but admire instead his nobility of soul . . .'[62] Wives who apparently accepted Christianity after marriage were forbidden to divorce their husbands on the ground of unbelief, but there was no analogous rule for men.[63] Pagan and Christian extra-marital miscegenation was noticeable to judge from the prohibition of sexual liaisons between pagans and deaconesses.[64]

Basil knew that magical practices existed within and outside the Christian community. He condemns magic and poisoning, both of which entailed sacrificing rare species of plants, insects and the organs taken from recently deceased corpses.[65] This probably explains Basil's prohibition of grave robbery, but there were also sacrifices designed to get the help of subterranean divinities to discover buried wealth in tombs.[66] Sorcerers caused anxiety when they deliberately left traces of magical substances to terrify their intended victims. The recognised remedy for this was Christian exorcism, but baptised persons nevertheless sometimes consulted mantics, bringing them into their houses to discover magic substances and perform purification rituals.[67] The most common type of spell found in the Greek magical papyri is the erotic charm, in which the malefactor bound a daemon to obsess the person of his or her desire until carnal union was achieved. Basil draws a connection between this and such disparate acts as poisoning and even abortion:[68]

Even if someone mixes a questionable drug for another reason and causes death, we recognise such an act as voluntary. Women often act in this way when, by certain incantations and magic bindings, they strive to bring men under their spell, and offer them drugs that cause the darkening of their intelligence. Such women, then, when they kill, although they did one thing while intending another, because of the questionable and forbidden nature of their pursuit, are nevertheless counted among those who commit murder voluntarily. And so women who give drugs that induce abortion are themselves also murderers, and also those who consume foetus-killing poisons.

Basil decried consultation with oracle-givers, diviners and rustic shamans, but himself practised Christian dream interpretation. He once explained the dream of a woman of senatorial or curial rank, and advised her to cultivate

---

62 Basil, *Epp.* 10, 276.
63 Basil, *Epp.* 188, canon 9.
64 Basil, *Epp.* 199, canon 44.
65 Basil, *Epp.* 217, canon 65.
66 Basil, *Ep.* 199, canon 49.
67 Basil, *Ep.* 217, canon 83.
68 Basil, *Ep.* 188, canon 8; on poisoners, see also canons 2, 7.

the type of vision where God could 'really' be seen.[69] This may have been a gentle warning not to let Hellenic dream interpretation displace reading the Christian scriptures. Basil was sharply critical of hired dream interpreters, whose pronouncements, he feared, might stir up criticism against himself.[70] Basil nowhere condemns Christian dream divination in his canons. On another occasion, Basil counselled a man to be cautious about a folk superstition perhaps fuelled by 'daemonic prompting' that numinous powers (*ta automata*) existed in the nature of water.[71] He may have been referring to a sacred spring whose healing waters lay in the tutelary domain of an underworld deity.

The movement of Christianity into the countryside as late as *c.* 443–6 is indicated in the life of Hypatius of Rufinianae (*ob.* 446), who on 3 April 400 established the monastery of Sts Peter and Paul on an estate in the territory of Chalcedon.[72] Hypatius' life provides abundant examples of how monastic colonisation led to the demise of pre-Christian religion. In the 430s, Hypatius summoned local archimandrites with the ringing phrase 'fight with me' and marched on Chalcedon, intending to disrupt the celebration of the Olympia in the theatre. The festival would have involved athletic, literary and musical competitions, but it was also the occasion of sacrifices performed in private houses. In a heated interview with the archbishop Eulalius, Hypatius threatened to disrupt the festival by physically attacking the urban prefect of Constantinople, who was scheduled to be in attendance, and suffering martyrdom at the hands of Christian officials. In consequence, the festival was cancelled.[73] Hypatius' démarche points to disagreements between hard-line ascetics and the ecclesiastical hierarchy about tolerating sacrifice, for the archbishop is reputed to have said: 'Do you simply wish to die if no one compels you to sacrifice? You are a monk. Sit down and let the matter rest. This is my affair.'[74] One of Hypatius' associates is said to have put it differently: 'The Olympia, an outrageous festival of Satan, was full of idol madness and at the same time a slippery and destructive thing for Christians.'[75]

The monks of Rufinianae took strident measures in the countryside. Whenever Hypatius heard of a sacred tree being worshipped, he had it cut down and burned. In this way the rustics became Christian 'in part'.[76] Rumours about

---

69 Basil, *Ep.* 283.
70 Basil, *Epp.* 210, 211.
71 Basil, *Ep.* 298.
72 Callinicus, *De vita S. Hypatii* 8.7.
73 Ibid., 33.
74 Ibid., 33.5–8.
75 Ibid., 33.16.
76 Ibid., 30.1.

the activity of Artemis prevailed in some districts. Hypatius was reputed once to have seen an epiphany of the goddess, who was thought to hold court in groves surrounded by lesser daemons at the hour of noon, and to attack travellers who disturbed the places sacred to her:

> [Hypatius] went to inner Bithynia where the Rebas River is. There was at that time . . . the Basket of the defiled Artemis, [a festival] which the countryside keeps every year, and people do not go out onto the main road for fifty days. When he wanted to travel, the locals said to him: 'Where are you going, man? The daemon will meet you on the road. Do not travel, for many are caught.' When he heard this, he smiled and said: 'You fear these things, but I have Christ as my travelling companion.' . . . [He] met a very aged woman with the height of ten men. She went around spinning and grazed pigs. When he saw [the apparition], he sealed himself [with the sign of the cross] and stood there praying to God. At once she became invisible and the pigs fled with a great rush and Hypatius came through unharmed.[77]

Hypatius once denounced a man who came to the monastery wearing a 'three-tailed belt' of Artemis.[78] Pagans in the countryside continued to sacrifice, like a group of forty men living in a building – possibly a temple – near the monastery.[79] Negating the effects of magic was one of Hypatius' regular activities. He once lured a diviner to his monastery, conversed with him for a while and then interned him in one of the monks' cells. The man admitted making sacrifices to angels: 'If someone speaks to me about some matter, it is revealed to me at once during the night, and I tell them each to go and sacrifice a cow, a sheep or a bird at the idol-temple, and furthermore, if an angel reveals something to me, I tell.'[80]

Hypatius cared for many civil servants from Constantinople, some pagan, others Christian, whose political enemies had made them ill by subjecting them to magic spells and poisoning. Among them were the *illustris* Antiochus, and the subordinates and friends of the imperial chamberlain Urbicius.[81] Hypatius made the sign of the cross on them with oil, sheltered them at the monastery and sometimes brought them to the martyr-shrines to bring about their cure. Hypatius welcomed pagans and performed many baptisms.[82] For example, a pagan civil servant named Egersius had misplaced some official documents; after the monk accurately prophesied their recovery, the man

77 Ibid., 45.
78 Ibid., 43.3–8.
79 Ibid., 43.16–23.
80 Ibid., 43.12.
81 Ibid., 12.4–9; 22.20.
82 Ibid., 36.1–2.

accepted baptism.[83] Hypatius summed up all his activities tersely, remarking, 'Christianity is not a chance thing,' and 'The battle is not against flesh and blood, but against evil daemons.'[84]

Aphrodisias, the 'city of Aphrodite' and provincial capital of Caria, was the place of a century-long ideological conflict between pagans and Christians. Its city councillors remained devoutly pagan until early in the reign of Justinian the Great. The provincial governors alluded to pagan priestly titles in their inscriptions and seldom, if ever, used a cross. The first identifiably Christian governor took up residence in Aphrodisias only c. 450.[85] The grandson of Tatian, one of the last pagan praetorian prefects of Oriens (388–92), honoured his famous ancestor by re-installing his statue in the early fifth century.[86] The archbishops and civil authorities in Constantinople were suspicious of this, but could do little about it apart from spitefully renaming the city Stauropolis ('City of the cross') in official communiqués and ecclesiastical documents.[87] It is thought that the city councillors sympathised or co-operated in the rebellion of Leontius and Illus against the emperor Zeno in 484.[88] This may have been the occasion of converting the temple of Aphrodite into a church, the archaeological and architectural data suggesting a date after 450.[89] The building was marked with crosses to signify the new state of affairs, and much of the pagan statuary was defaced, with the noses of the gods and priests being cleanly chiselled off.[90] The Christian victory was a matter of political fact by the early sixth century. An acclamation inscription from the reign of the emperor Anastasius asserts: 'The faith of the Christians conquers!'[91]

The last phase of Christianising the empire began in the reign of Justinian the Great, whose law of 529 required every citizen of the empire to accept baptism.[92] The codification of 534 repeated the ban on sacrifice found in previous legislation.[93] Persons living on the fringes of the catechumenate

---

83 Ibid., 40.27–36.
84 Ibid., 48.
85 Roueché, *Aphrodisias*, no. 42.
86 Ibid., no. 37.
87 Ibid., no. 42.
88 Trombley, *Hellenic religion and Christianization*, II: 20–9, 60f.
89 Cormack, 'The temple as cathedral'; for a list of temple conversions in Anatolia, see Bayliss, *Provincial Cilicia*, 124–9.
90 Personal observation, 21 September 2004; for the statuary, see K. T. Erim, 'Portrait sculpture at Aphrodisias'; K. T. Erim and R. R. R. Smith, 'Sculpture from the theatre: A preliminary report'; R. R. R. Smith, 'Late Roman philosophers'; R. R. R. Smith, 'Archaeological research at Aphrodisias 1989–1992'.
91 Roueché, *Aphrodisias*, no. 61.
92 The law in question was *CJ* 1.11.9 and 1.11.10; Honoré, *Tribonian*, 46f.; cf. Coleman-Norton, *Roman state & Christian church*, 1048–50.
93 *CJ* 1.10.

sometimes joined the churches unwillingly and without much instruction. Specially appointed imperial officials investigated recalcitrant pagans, and pronounced sentences of exile and capital punishment on some, as one sees in the inscription of Hyperechius the *referendarius* and imperial judge at Sardis.[94] The numerous crosses marked on the pagan statuary and public monuments of Ephesus may well date from this time. Hagiographic texts mention sacrifice less often, and report the adoption of pre-Christian rituals in the countryside, a process sometimes called 'Christianisation of pagan ritual' (*Ritenchristianisierung*).[95] Justinian offered funding to John of Ephesus, to complete the Christianisation of Asia, Caria, Lydia and Phrygia. He was nicknamed 'the idol-breaker' and 'over the pagans' for baptising as many as 80,000 persons between *c.* 536 and 566, and for constructing some ninety-eight churches and twelve monasteries.[96] He destroyed many sacred trees, and any surviving temples where sacrifice was still practised. Among them was the *temenos* of the Isodromian Mother at Dareira in the rugged mountains of Caria above Tralles.[97]

Little is known of the institutional life of the church in Lycia until the time of St Nicholas of Hagia Sion (*ob.* 565).[98] Nicholas' older relatives built a number of rural monasteries in the territory of Myra, the provincial capital. Nicholas became a monk at one of these places, Hagia Sion (probably present-day Karabel). The rural population had officially accepted Christianity by this time, but their acculturation in the canons and scriptures had not kept pace with the requirements of the law. Few of the rural church buildings in the territory of Myra appear to predate the early sixth century. In consequence, the rural population was still in great awe of numinous trees and springs, which were still widely believed to be the dwelling places of chthonic gods like Artemis.

Nicholas of Hagia Sion's life identifies some exemplary cases of the rural religious psychology. The most significant is that of a large and ancient cypress tree in the village of Plakoma, which may have been situated on former temple lands near a *temenos*. It was said to contain 'a spirit of an unclean idol', and to interfere with the agricultural work of the villagers, 'destroying men and the land'. The 'spirit' was probably the local Artemis, one of the least hospitable divinities of the Greek pantheon, who was thought to attack anyone who

---

94 *Sardis VII. Greek and Latin inscriptions*, no. 19; cf. F. R. Trombley, 'Religious transition in sixth-century Syria', 180–2.
95 Kirsten, 'Artemis von Ephesus', 465.
96 John of Ephesus, *HE* 2.45 and *Lives of the Eastern Saints* (PO 18: 681); Trombley, 'Paganism,' 329–34.
97 John of Ephesus, *HE* 3.36; F. R. Trombley, 'Paganism', 329.
98 SEG 17, no. 714; SEG 40, no. 1278.

passed near her rural shrines.[99] At Plakoma pagan sacrifices had probably lapsed after the villagers accepted Christianity, but the perception persisted that the divinity, whose rites had been long observed, was punishing the villagers, possibly by ruining their harvests. Nicholas had the tree cut down, exorcised the spirit, and then used the lumber to put a roof on the new church at Hagia Sion. There is a similar story about an 'ancient spring' (*archaia pêgê*) probably situated in a *temenos* that was inhabited by a chthonic or underworld divinity at the village of Arnabandeon:

> We have an ancient spring. A woman went out to draw water, and the unclean spirit cast her into the spring, and she died. We are imperilled along with our quadruped beasts, for since that time the water has been disturbed and become muddy. Fear grips us. No one goes near that spring and we are perishing with our quadrupeds.[100]

The villagers felt compunction at the rage of the unnamed god for their failure to perform sacrifice, and saw it as the cause of the woman's drowning and the pollution of their spring with silt. Nicholas' rituals did not reassure the villagers, for in the end they asked him to divine for hidden subterranean water elsewhere. A central task of Nicholas' mission was to convince the rustics that he controlled these geological phenomena in the name of Christ.

Nicholas felt compelled to introduce Christianised sacrifices into the village chapels of Lycia. The author of his life provides a catalogue of names of the numerous sites that Nicholas visited to perform these liturgies, protesting that the sacrifices imitated those of King David. The pre-Christian ritual consisted of laying couches, sacrificing animals, and distributing bread and wine. The Christian side of the ritual was signified by the clergy's use of large processional crosses.[101] By transferring the traditional sacrifices to the Christian church, the monks put the peasantry into compliance with Justinian's laws against sacrifice.

The epigraphic evidence suggests that the villages of Galatia were being Christianised in the fourth century.[102] Their situation in the late sixth century is known from the life of St Theodore (*ob.* 613), proprietor and head of the monastery of St George at Sykeon, a village near the Roman bridge on the Sargarius river and lying in the territory of Anastasiopolis. Traditional conceptions about the chthonic divinities persisted until the time of Theodore's

---

99 *Vita S. Nicolai* 13–14; Trombley, *Hellenic religion and Christianization*, II: 78f.
100 *Vita S. Nicolai* 16.
101 Ibid., 54–7; Robert, 'Villes et monnaies', 197–200; Trombley, 'Paganism', 339.
102 SEG 6, no. 75.

youth. He once visited a sacred grove to see if the epiphanies of Artemis bruited about in 'wild rumours' still occurred:

> He heard about a certain place which was about eight miles away called Arkea, where it was impossible to approach, because there was a clamour that Artemis lived there with many daemons and harmed people unto death. Astonished at this rumour, he went to that place at a run . . . and spent the entire afternoon in the place believed to belong to Artemis. When no evil activity was manifested, through the activity of Christ, he returned to the *martyrium* [of St George].[103]

As a mature monk, Theodore took an interest in ridding the villages of magicians and sorcerers. He is reported to have induced a fellow named Theodotus Kourappus to burn his magic books and accept baptism.[104] On other occasions, Theodore visited villages to perform exorcism. One consequence of the ruralisation of the sixth-century economy was much building activity in villages. Rural builders frequently cannibalised pagan tombs in the Anatolian countryside for limestone blocks. Most villagers were aware of the taboos connected with tombs, where inscriptions called upon the spirits of the underworld to torment the grave-breaker.[105] When this occurred, villagers sometimes lapsed into a type of 'possessed' behaviour that involved wrecking houses, killing farm animals and engaging in seemingly senseless laughter after being set upon by the guardian spirits. Theodore was frequently summoned to calm the villagers by performing group and individual exorcisms. He did this by summoning St George, the tutelary saint of his monastery, the Theotokos, and Christ.[106]

A formal orthopraxy in Anatolian Christianity existed in the late sixth century, but its origin was hybrid. The earlier pagan rituals and aetiologies persisted, but Christian cult formulae displaced the older pagan invocations. So, for example, the use of apotropaic circles to protect tilled fields from hail-bearing clouds and overflowing rivers was adopted, and the gods who controlled these phenomena were degraded to the status of daemons. Eradicating the names of the pagan gods from folk culture nevertheless proved difficult. A canon of the Council in Trullo of 691–2 forbade the practice of invoking the name of Dionysus at the time of the Brumalia, a calendar event associated with the pouring of fermented wine into bottles.[107] The sources refer to other pagan

103 George the Monk, *Vita S. Theodori Sykeon* 16.
104 Ibid., 37–8.
105 *IGRR* 4, no. 1281; SEG 32, nos. 1288–9.
106 George the Monk, *Vita S. Theodori Sykeon* 114.
107 Council of Trullanum, canon 62 (ed. Joannou, *Discipline générale*, 198–200).

divinities as well. Photius, patriarch of Constantinople (ninth century), mentions a divinatory sacrifice to the goddess Ge made to discover buried treasure, and the worship of *baityloi* or meteorite stones in central Greece.[108] Further, Cosmas of Jerusalem mentions the continued practice of ritual castration in honour of Cybele in eighth-century Caria.[109] The formalities of Christianisation, in terms of baptising the population of Asia Minor, were completed by the late sixth century, but the full acculturation of villages to the standards of the Mediterranean cities was a longer process that was still incomplete in some villages even in the early twentieth century.[110]

Bibliography

PRIMARY TEXTS

Basil. *Letters*. Ed. Yves Courtonne, *Saint Basile. Lettres* (Paris, 1957, 1961, 1966)
Bidez, J., and F. Cumont, eds. *Imperatoris Caesaris Flavii Claudii Iuliani epistulae, leges, poemata, fragmenta varia* (Paris, 1922)
Callinicus of Rufinianae. *De vita S. Hypatii liber* (Leipzig, 1895); *SC* 177
Codex Justinianus (CJ). Ed. P. Krüger, *Corpus iuris civilis* (Berlin, 1929)
Cosmas of Jerusalem. *Scholia in Gregorii Nazianzeni carmina* (PG 38: 341–680)
Damascius. *Das Leben des Philosophen Isidors von Damaskios aus Damaskos*, trans. R. Asmus (Leipzig, 1911)
　Vitae Isidori reliquiae, ed. C. Zintzen (Hildesheim, 1967)
Eusebius. *Historia ecclesiastica* (SC 31, 41, 55, 73)
George the Monk. *Vie de Théodore de Sykéôn*, ed. A.-J. Festugière, *SH* 48 (Brussels, 1970)
Hagios Nikolaos. Der heilige Nikolaos in der griechischen Kirche, ed. G. Anrich (Leipzig, 1913–17)
Hefele, C. J. *Histoire des conciles d'après les documents originaux*, trans. H. Leclercq (Paris, 1907–49)
John of Ephesus. *Historia ecclesiastica, pars tertia.* (*CSCO* 105, 106)
Julian. *The works of the emperor Julian*, trans. W. C. Wright, LCL (London, 1913)
The life of St. Nicholas of Sion, eds. I. Ševčenko and N. Ševčenko (Brookline, MA, 1984)
Photius. *The Letters of Photius*, ed. J. N. Baletta (London, 1864)
Procopius. *De bellis*. Ed. J. Haury and G. Wirth, *Procopius. Opera omnia* (Leipzig, 1962–4), I–II
Strabo. *The Geography of Strabo*, trans. H. L. Jones, 3 vols., LCL (London, 1917–32)

EPIGRAPHIC AND PAPYROLOGICAL COLLECTIONS

Drew-Bear, T., ed. *Nouvelles inscriptions de Phrygie* (Zutphen, 1978)
Monumenta Asiae Minoris antiqua, eds. W. M. Calder et al. (Manchester, 1928–56)

---

108 Photius, *Epistula* I. 20 (PG 102: 788); Damascius, *Epitome Photiana 203* (ed. Zintzen, 276).
109 Cosmas of Jerusalem, *Scholia in Gregorii Nazianzeni carmina* (PG 38: 502).
110 Lawson, *Modern Greek folklore*.

Papyri Graecae magicae: Die griechischen Zauberpapyri, eds. K. Preisendanz et al. (Stuttgart, 1973–4)
Recueil des inscriptions grecques-chrétiennes d'Asie Mineure, ed. H. Grégoire (Paris, 1922; reprint: Chicago, 1980)
Roueché, C. *Aphrodisias in late antiquity* (London, 1989); available on-line: http://insaph. kcl.ac.uk/ala2004/refer/concord.html
Sardis VII. Greek and Latin inscriptions. Part 1, eds. W. H. Buckler and D. M. Robinson (Leiden, 1932)

SECONDARY SOURCES

Anderson, J. G. C. 'Exploration in Galatia cis Halym', *Journal of Hellenic studies* 19 (1899): 52–134, 280–318
    'Paganism and Christianity in the Upper Tembris valley', in W. M. Ramsey, ed., *Studies in the art and archaeology of the Eastern Roman provinces* (Aberdeen, 1906), 183–227
Barnes, T. D. *Constantine and Eusebius* (Cambridge, MA, 1981)
Bayliss, R. *Provincial Cilicia and the archaeology of temple conversion*, BAR International Series 1281 (Oxford, 2004)
Brixhe, C. 'Interactions between Greek and Phrygian under the Roman empire', in J. N. Adams, M. Janse and S. Swain, eds., *Bilingualism in ancient society. Language contact and written text* (Oxford, 2002), 246–66
Buckler, W. H., W. M. Calder and C. W. M. Cox. 'Asia Minor, 1924. I. – Monuments from Iconium, Lycaonia and Isauria', *JRS* 14 (1924): 24–84
    'Asia Minor, 1924. V. – Monuments from the Upper Tembris valley', *JRS* 18 (1928): 21–40
Buresch, K. *Klaros. Untersuchungen zum Orakelwesen des späteren Altertums* (Leipzig, 1889; reprint: Aal, 1973)
Cabrol, F., and H. Leclercq, eds. *Dictionnaire d'archéologie chrétienne et de liturgie* (Paris, 1903–50)
Calder, W. M. 'Colonia Caesareia Antiocheia', *JRS* 2 (1912): 78–109
    'Corpus inscriptionum neo-Phrygianum', *Journal of Hellenic studies* 31 (1911): 161–215
    'Corpus inscriptionum neo-Phrygianum. – II', *Journal of Hellenic studies* 33 (1913): 97–104
    'Early Christian epitaphs from Phrygia', *Anatolian studies* 5 (1955): 25–38
    'The Eumenian formula', in W. M. Calder and J. Keil, eds., *Anatolian studies presented to William Hepburn Buckler* (Manchester, 1939), 15–26
    'A journey through the Proseilemmene', *Klio* 10 (1901): 323–42
    'Julia-Ipsus and Augustopolis', *JRS* 2 (1912): 233–66
    'Philadelphia and Montanism', *Bulletin of the John Rylands Library* 7 (1922–3): 336–54
    'Studies in early Christian epigraphy', *JRS* 10 (1920): 42–59
    'Studies in early Christian epigraphy: II', *JRS* 14 (1924): 85–92
Chaniotis, A. 'Zwischen Konfrontation und Interaktion: Christen, Juden und Heiden im spätantiken Aphrodisias', in A. Ackermann and K. E. Müller, eds., *Patchwork* (Bielefeld, 2002), 83–127
Chuvin, P. *Chronique des derniers païens: La disparition du paganisme dans l'empire romaine, du règne de Constantine à celui de Justinien* (Paris, 1991)

Coleman-Norton, P. R. *Roman state & Christian church* (London, 1966)

Cormack, R. 'The temple as cathedral', in C. Roueché and K. T. Erim, eds., *Aphrodisias papers: Recent work on the architecture and sculpture* (Ann Arbor, 1990), 75–88

Cox, C. W. M. 'Bishop Heortasius of Appia', in W. M. Calder and J. Keil, eds., *Anatolian studies presented to William Hepburn Buckler* (Manchester, 1939), 63–6

Cumont, F. 'Les anges du paganisme', *Revue d'histoire des religions* 72 (1915): 159–82

Deichmann, F. W. 'Frühchristliche Kirchen in antiken Heiligtümern', *Jahrbuch des Deutschen Archäologischen Instituts* 54 (1939): 105–36

Dodds, E. R. *Pagan and Christian in an age of anxiety* (Cambridge, 1965)

'Theurgy', in *The Greeks and the irrational* (Berkeley, 1951), 283–311

Drew-Bear, Th. and Ch. Naour. 'Divinités de Phrygie', in W. Haase, ed., *Aufstieg und Niedergang der antiken Welt* 2.18.3 (Berlin, 1990), 1907–2044

Erdmann, K. 'Feuerheiligtum-Kreuzkuppelkirche', in A. Alföldy et al., eds., *Neue Beiträge zur Kunstgeschichte des 1. Jahrtausends*, (Baden-Baden, 1952), I: 52–70

Erim, K. T. 'Portrait sculpture at Aphrodisias', in C. Roueché and K. T. Erim, eds., *Aphrodisias papers: Recent work on the architecture and sculpture* (Ann Arbor, 1990), 152–60.

Erim, K. T. and R. R. R. Smith. 'Sculpture from the theatre: A preliminary report', in K. T. Erim and R. R. R. Smith, eds., *Aphrodisias papers 2* (Ann Arbor, 1991), 67–98

Feld, O., and H. Weber. 'Tempel und Kirche über der korykischen Grotte (Cennet Cehennem) in Kilikien', *Istanbuler Mitteilungen* 17 (1967): 254–78

Fleischer, R. 'Der Fries des Hadrianstempels in Ephesos', in *Festschrift für Fritz Eichler zum achtzigsten Geburtstag* (Vienna, 1967), 23–71

Frend, W. H. C. *The archaeology of early Christianity. A history* (London, 1996)

Geffcken, J. *The last days of Greco-Roman paganism*, trans. S. MacCormack (Amsterdam, 1978)

Gough, M. 'The Church of the Evangelists at Alahan', *Anatolian studies* 12 (1962): 173–84

'A temple and church at Ayas (Cilicia)', *Anatolian studies* 4 (1954): 49–64

Hahn, J. *Gewalt und religiöser Konflikt* (Berlin, 2004)

Halkin, F. *Actuarium Bibliothecae Hagiographicae Graecae*, SH 47 (Brussels, 1969)

Bibliotheca Hagiographica Graeca 1–2, SH 8a (Brussels, 1957)

Hanson, R. P. C. 'The transformation of pagan temples into churches in the early Christian centuries', *Journal of Semitic studies* 23 (1978): 257–67

Harl, K. W. 'From pagan to Christian in cities of Roman Anatolia during the fourth and fifth centuries', in T. S. Burns and J. W. Eadie, eds., *Urban centers and rural contexts in late antiquity* (East Lansing, 2001), 301–22

Harnack, A. von. *Die Mission und Ausbreitung des Christentums in den ersten drei Jahrhunderten* (Leipzig, 1924)

Harper, R. P. 'Tituli Comanorum Cappadociae', *Anatolian studies* 18 (1968): 93–147

Hasluck, F. W. *Christianity and Islam under the sultans* (Oxford, 1929)

Hellenkemper, H. 'Die Kirche im Tempel: Zeustempel und Paulus basilica am Kalykadnos', in *Orbis Romanus Christianusque ab Diocletiani aetate usque ad Heraclium: Travaux sur l'antiquité tardive rassemblés autour des recherches de Noël Duval* (Paris, 1995), 191–203

Honoré, Tony, *Tribonian* (London, 1978)

Hunt, D. 'Julian', in Averil Cameron and P. Garnsey, eds., *The Cambridge ancient history* (Cambridge, 1998), XIII: 44–77

Jaeger, W. *Early Christianity and Greek paideia* (Cambridge, MA, 1961)

Joannou, P.-P. *La législation impériale et la christianisation de l'empire romaine (311–476)*, OCA 192 (Rome, 1972)

Joannou, P.-P., ed. *Discipline générale antique (IVe–IXe s.)* (Rome, 1962–3)

Jones, A. H. M. *The later Roman empire 284–602: A social, economic and administrative survey* (Oxford, 1964)

Jones, C. P. 'A family of Pisidian Antioch', *Phoenix* 36 (1982): 264–71

Kirsten, E. 'Artemis von Ephesus und Eleuthera von Myra mit Seitblick auf St. Nicolaus und auf Commagene', in S. Sahin et al., eds., *Studien zur Religion und Kultur Kleinasiens: Festschrift für Karl Dörner* (Leiden, 1978), II: 457–88

Kitzinger, E. 'The cult of images in the age before iconoclasm', *DOP* 8 (1954): 83–150

Lane Fox, R. *Pagans and Christians* (London, 1986)

Lawson, J. C. *Modern Greek folklore and ancient Greek religion* (Cambridge, 1910)

Lee, A. D. *Pagans and Christians in late antiquity. A sourcebook* (London, 2000)

Lemerle, P. 'L'histoire des Pauliciens d'Asia mineur d'après les sources grecques', *Travaux et mémoires* 5 (1973): 1–144

Mango, C. 'Germia: A postscript', *Jahrbuch der Österreichischen Byzantinistik* 41 (1991): 297–300

'St. Michael and Attis', *Deltion tês Christianikês Etaireias* 12 (1984): 39–62

Mitchell, S. 'The life of Saint Theodotus of Ancyra', *Anatolian studies* 32 (1982): 93–113

'Maximinus and the Christians in A. D. 312: A new Latin inscription', *JRS* 78 (1988): 105–24

Momigliano, A., ed. *The conflict between paganism and Christianity in the fourth century* (Oxford, 1963)

Mullen, R. L. *The expansion of Christianity. A gazetteer of its first three centuries* (Leiden, 2004)

Musurillo, H., ed. *Acts of the Christian martyrs* (Oxford, 1972)

Ramsay, W. M. *Cities and bishoprics of Phrygia* (Oxford, 1895)

'The Tekmorian guest-friends: An anti-Christian society on the imperial estates at Pisidian Antioch', in *Studies in the history and art of the Eastern Roman provinces* (Aberdeen, 1906): 305–77

Robert, L. 'Didymes à l'époque byzantine', *Hellenica* 11–12 (1960): 495–502

'Villes et monnaies de Lycie', *Hellenica* 10 (1955): 188–222

Rochow, I. 'Die Heidenprozesse unter Kaisern Tiberios II. Konstantinos und Maurikios', in F. Winkelmann et al., eds., *Studien zum 7. Jahrhundert in Byzanz* (Berlin, 1976), 120–30

'Zu einigen oppositionellen religiösen Strömungen I: Zur Rolle der Anhänger antiker Kulte und Bräuche', in F. Winkelmann, ed., *Byzanz im 7. Jahrhundert* (Berlin, 1978), 227–55

Saradi-Mendelovici, H. 'Christian attitudes to pagan monuments in late antiquity and their legacy in later Byzantine centuries', *DOP* 44 (1990): 47–61

Schneider, C. M. 'Leibestätigkeit als Strafe: Bemerkungen zu einer Inschrift an Sardis', in P. Wirth, ed., *Polychordia: Festschrift Franz Dölger zum 75 Geburtstag* (Amsterdam, 1966), I: 284–9

Sheppard, A. R. R. 'Pagan cult of angels in Roman Asia Minor', *Talanta* 12–13 (1980–1): 77–101

Smith, R. R. R. 'Archaeological research at Aphrodisias 1989–1992', in C. Roueché and R. R. R. Smith, eds., *Aphrodisias papers 3* (Ann Arbor, 1996), 9–72

'Late Roman philosophers', in K. T. Erim and R. R. R. Smith, eds., *Aphrodisias papers 2* (Ann Arbor, 1991), 144–58

Snyder, G. *Ante pacem. Archaeological evidence of church life before Constantine* (Macon, 1985)

De Ste. Croix, G. E. M. *The class struggle in the ancient Greek world from the archaic age to the Arab conquest* (London, 1981)

Tabbernee, W. *Montanist inscriptions and testimonia. Epigraphic sources illustrating the history of Montanism* (Macon, 1997)

Trombley, F. R. 'Christianisation of rite in Byzantine Anatolia: F. W. Hasluck and continuity', in D. Shankland, ed., *Anthropology, archaeology and heritage in the Balkans and Anatolia: The life and times of F. W. Hasluck 1878–1920* (Istanbul, 2004), II: 55–75

'The destruction of pagan statuary and Christianization (4th–6th c. C.E.)', in S. Herbert, E. Friedland and Y. Eliav, eds., *The sculptural environment of the Roman Near East: Reflections on culture, ideology and power* (Louvain, forthcoming)

Hellenic religion and Christianization c. 370–529 (Leiden, 1993–4; reprint: 1995, 2001)

'The imperial cult in late Roman religion (c. A.D. 244–395): observations on the epigraphy', in J. Hahn, ed., *From temple to church* (Berlin, forthcoming)

'Monastic foundations in sixth-century Anatolia and the role in the social and economic life of the countryside', *Greek Orthodox theological review* 30 (1985): 45–59; reprinted with corrections in N. M. Vaporis, ed., *Byzantine saints and monasteries* (Brookline, MA, 1985), 45–59

'Paganism in the Greek world at the end of antiquity: The case of rural Anatolia and Greece', *HTR* 78 (1985): 327–52

'Religious experience in late antiquity: Theological ambivalence and Christianization', *Byzantine and modern Greek studies* 24 (2000): 2–60

'Religious transition in sixth-century Syria', *Byzantinische Forschungen* 20 (1994): 153–95

Whitby, M. 'John of Ephesus and the pagans: Pagan survivals in the sixth century', in M. Salomon, ed., *Paganism in the later Roman empire and in Byzantium* (Cracow, 1991), 111–31

Wischmeyer, W. 'M. Iulius Eugenius. Eine Fallstudie zum Thema "Christen und Gesellschaft im 3. und 4. Jahrhunderte"', *ZNTW* 81 (1990): 225–46

8

Christianity and paganism, III: Italy

MICHELE RENEE SALZMAN

The spread of Christianity in Italy – as elsewhere throughout the empire – was greatly aided by the imperial support it received from the time of the emperor Constantine's conversion. It was, after all, in Italy (near the Milvian Bridge just north of Rome, to be precise) that Constantine in later life claimed to have experienced his vision that he came to see as a sign of his victory from the god of the Christians.[1] Beginning with this emperor and continuing largely without interruption for the next centuries, imperial support, monies and privileges flowed into the Christian community and its institutions in Italy. In particular, the episcopate benefited from imperial largesse and attention. All throughout Italy's cities, bishops came to take on increasingly prominent social and political roles over the course of the fourth and fifth centuries.

It would be misleading, however, to see the spread of Christianity and the concomitant demise of polytheism in Italy in the years 300–600 as predicated solely on imperial or episcopal influence. Indeed, the notion that religious change can be explained as the result of a simple top-down model of influences ignores the realities of social and religious life in late antiquity. Religion and politics were intimately connected, it is true, but no emperor could rule in the fourth and fifth centuries as an autocrat, nor could any bishop control his flock without the legitimising support of the senatorial, civic and military elites who peopled the late Roman civic government and imperial bureaucracies. These persons of high status played leading roles in Italy's political and social life for centuries after the last western emperor in 476. Indeed, it was the municipal and senatorial elites who, more than emperors, provided constancy in Italy's civic life. Hence, the Christianisation of Italy's upper classes

---

1 Eusebius, *Life of Constantine* 3.47; variant accounts appear in Eusebius' *Ecclesiastical history* and Lactantius, *On the deaths of the persecutors* 44.5. The bibliography on Constantine's conversion is vast. For a good modern discussion of the vision and its historiography, see H. Drake, *Constantine and the bishops*, 9–19.

is of importance for understanding how Christianity spread, took hold and developed in this region. The conversion of Italy's elites is one significant marker of religious change; once the 'elite' – in Rome especially, as we will see, but also throughout Italy – had converted, the empire could be proclaimed Christian.

The importance of understanding the conversion of Italy's elites is high-lighted by what we know in general about the status of Christianity in Italy prior to Constantine's vision at the Milvian Bridge. The Christian population in the empire before 312 was a minority, estimated at no more than 10 per cent of the population at large, with smaller numbers in the Western than in the Eastern empire.[2] All the evidence indicates that Christianity spread first in Italy's cities. Yet in Rome, which is well attested as having had a Christian community and a bishop who could claim the seat of St Peter, there is no good evidence for large, public meeting places before 312. There are very few securely attested Christians among the senatorial aristocracy prior to Constan-tine, and although Christians do appear among the municipal elites in Italy before 312,[3] the majority of Italy's upper classes, like the population at large, converted in the century and a half after Constantine's reign.

This chapter will focus on three separate social elites in three different but important cities in Italy: the senatorial aristocracy in Rome; the municipal provincial elite in Aquileia; and the imperial bureaucratic upper class in Milan. The elite of each city adopted Christianity over the course of the fourth and fifth centuries, but the paths they took and the Christianity they embraced differed. Rome's senatorial elite, men and women who held the rank of *claris-simus*, appear as the most resistant of all three groups of high-status people to religious change; with resources and traditions deeply embedded in civic poly-theism, they were among the last of Italy's elites to convert. The Christianity that they came to accept was one that spoke in Virgilianising verses, as Pope Damasus' inscriptions on the tombs of martyrs in Rome did; it was a Chris-tianity that incorporated traditional values. In contrast to Rome, Aquileia's municipal elite appears from early on in the fourth century to have been open to Christianity. Lacking a senatorial tradition of independence and with lim-ited resources, Aquileia's municipal elite appear to have been much influenced

---

2 R. MacMullen, *Christianising the Roman empire*, 5, 25–42; Robin Lane Fox, *Pagans and Christians*, 268–9, 272.

3 For Christian senatorial elites before Constantine, see M. R. Salzman, *The making of a Christian aristocracy*, 3 n. 9. For Christianity among the municipal elites, as in Aquileia, see below.

by Greek-speaking Easterners and Jewish immigrants to the city and by the example set for them by some notable Christian senatorial families who were active in the region. Milan's people of high status emerge as the most willing of the three urban Italian elites to embrace Christianity; by the end of the fourth century, there is little evidence of paganism there. The conversion of Milan's upper class reveals the influence of a resident Christian imperial court that was deeply involved in the conflicts between Nicene and anti-Nicene factions in the city. Imperial involvement and factional strife hastened the Christianisation of Milan's elite by intensifying allegiance. Indeed, the late fourth-century bishop of Milan, Ambrose, used this intra-city conflict to further the conversion of Milan's elite to Nicene Christianity, the dominant version of Christianity in the West.

Although the Christianisation of the elites of Rome, Aquileia and Milan differed, there is one issue that goes to the heart of the role that all would play in the religious transformation of Italy – patronage; written and epigraphic sources are explicit about the importance of the elites as patrons and donors in cities and countryside. For centuries, those of high status had been the primary patrons within Roman society and had taken on leadership roles, as priests or donors, in public pagan cult sites and rites. As patron and priest, the upper class expressed and augmented their status and honour in Roman society. In Italy, aristocrats passed on patronage ties with cities and cults within families from one generation to the next. Once the emperor had declared his support for Christianity, what role would Italy's elites play in this new cult? The role of patron was an especially controversial one in some cities, like Milan and Rome, where eminent citizens faced strong competition for prestige from powerful bishops. How each city's aristocrats responded to the possibilities of patronage had a lasting effect on the Christianity that developed locally and in Italy as a whole.

The conversion of Italy's elites was a gradual process of change within which the encouragements of emperors and bishops were mediated by specific elite institutions, ideas and behaviours. The first step was a gradual turning away of pagans from pagan institutions. Simultaneously, emperors and church leaders strove to assure those of high status that changing religion would neither deny them social esteem nor undermine the institutions upon which their social position rested. In essence, they made Christianity conform in certain key ways to the status concerns of the elite with whom they interacted. Charity, for example, was interpreted in ways consonant with upper-class notions of patronage. In looking at the Christianisation of Italy's upper classes, we see how the message of Christianity was shaped to address elite concerns. In essence,

Christianity became aristocratised, even as its elites were Christianised. At the same time, the Christianity that emerged in these three separate cities in Italy also partook of certain empire-wide trends observable throughout the Christianity of late antiquity.

The senatorial elite of Rome

At the beginning of the fourth century, the senatorial elite in Rome devoted its religious energies to the pagan gods. This continued even after Constantine's public support for Christianity; the mid fourth-century anonymous author of the *Expositio totius mundi et gentium* observed of the Romans, 'They are devoted to the gods, but above all to Jupiter and Sol.'[4] On statues in honour of aristocrats like Valerius Proculus, consul in 340, pagan priesthoods were prominently and proudly noted alongside public offices.[5] The civic traditions of polytheism provided strong justification for the continuity of the public cults; the games, festivals and building projects that were for the good of the state's gods were also for the good of the state. In 384, the pagan senator Symmachus urged that the Christian emperors continue support for the public cult because it had 'for so long benefited the state'.[6]

For the senatorial aristocracy of Rome, adherence to the pagan cults was an element of social identity; they and their families had strong and public ties as patron and priest to specific cults. So for example, Mithras was embraced in Rome by an upper-class father, Aurelius Victor Augentius, and his sons, one of whom also proudly proclaimed that he had built a cult site (a cave) for and funded the worship of the god.[7] Some families saw it as a point of honour that one of their own would hold a priesthood of Sol.[8] These ties of families to pagan cults extended beyond the confines of the city of Rome, to cities

---

4 *Expositio totius mundi et gentium* (ed. Valentini and Zucchetti, 1: 265): 'colunt autem et deos ex parte Iovem et Solem'.
5 *CIL* 6.1690 = D.1240, *CIL* 6.1691 and 1693 = D. 1241.
6 Symm. *Rel.* 3.3: 'repetimus igitur religionum statum, qui reip. Diu profuit'.
7 Aur. Victor Augentius 2, in *PLRE* 1: 125, and his sons, Tamesius Olympius Augentius 1, *PLRE* 1: 124–5, and Aemilianus Corfo Olympius 14, *PLRE* 1: 646. See too the Roman aristocratic woman, Paulina, who honoured her recently deceased husband, Vettius Agorius Praetextatus, with a funerary monument that listed his many priesthoods and their shared rituals of initiation, *CIL* 6.1779 = D. 1259.
8 Salzman, *The making of a Christian aristocracy*, 64; Aurelian wanted to appeal to the family pride of the senatorial elites when he instituted his cult of Sol in 274 and chose families to serve as his *pontifices Solis*; this group continued in this role into the late fourth century.

all throughout Italy and beyond, and they could be passed down from one generation to the next.[9] The senatorial aristocrats of Rome who were deeply attached to their polytheistic traditions had the material as well as social resources to maintain their religious activities in the face of growing pressures from Christian emperors and bishops to convert. The senate's distance from the court (now in Milan) favoured autonomy, and the senate at Rome prided itself on its independence from imperial influence. Indeed, if Rome was no longer the capital of the empire, it was still a great cultural and economic urban centre, whose senate was now increasingly in control of its own economic and political needs. Fourth-century emperors tended to accept the autonomy of Rome's senate because, among other things, the emperors relied on the senatorial aristocracy to maintain control over the urban plebs. Moreover, since the senatorial aristocracy had little real access to the military, they were not seen as potential usurpers of imperial power.

These social and institutional factors help to explain why Rome through the first half of the fourth century appears to have enjoyed a relatively peaceful period of accommodation between pagan elites and Christianising emperors and bishops, even as Christianity was gradually being assimilated into Roman society. One of the most eloquent indicators of these trends is the fourth-century Codex-Calendar of 354, a deluxe calendar compiled for use in the city of Rome; like its accommodating urban environment, the Codex-Calendar of 354 incorporated illustrations of pagan holidays and astrological signs along with lists of the depositions of saints and martyrs which were included in a book produced for a member of Rome's Christian elite.[10] Similarly, the inclusion of pagan imagery in Christian burial contexts, as at S. Costanza or in the Via Latina catacomb, indicates the fluidity of ideas and the reality of co-habitation within Roman upper-class society.

The social and political pressure on the Roman senatorial elite to convert to Christianity intensified in the second half of the fourth century. Christian emperors, beginning with Constantine, showed their support for Christianity through their building projects, laws and pronouncements even as they denigrated pagan cult. The intensity of these Christianising efforts varied over the course of the fourth century, depending on the individual emperor's inclination

---

9 So, for example, at the end of the fourth century, Nicomachus Flavianus the Younger was hailed as *patronus originalis* of Naples, a title that gave him honorary citizenship and hence made him a leading patron in that city's social and religious life, a distinction that he had most likely inherited: see D. 8985 and Jens-Uwe Krause, *Spätantike Patronatsformen*, 27ff.
10 M. R. Salzman, *On Roman time*, 23–60.

and position, but by and large, imperial policy attempted to use law to restrict certain pagan practices deemed offensive to Christians, notably animal sacrifice. The language of the earliest surviving law restricting pagan sacrifice preserved by the Theodosian Code and dated to 341 exemplifies the public stance taken by the fervent pro-Christian emperor Constantius II, Constantine's son:

> Let superstition cease. Let the madness of sacrifices be exterminated; for if anyone should dare to celebrate sacrifices in violation of the law of our father, the deified Emperor, and of this decree of our Clemency, let an appropriate punishment and sentence immediately be inflicted on him.[11]

The stridency of such imperial pronouncements supporting Christianity and attacking paganism went hand in hand with the honours and offices granted to Christian members of the elite and to bishops. Indeed, imperial privileges made the bishop of Rome, and bishops throughout Italy, among the most prestigious figures in the urban landscape. One indicator of their new social prestige was the privilege of tax exemption granted to bishops, and their freedom from public service. And in a striking innovation, bishops were even granted the unusual privileges of manumitting slaves in church and of adjudicating disputes between Christians and non-Christians.[12] Such honours, initially bestowed by Constantine and extended by subsequent emperors, likened bishops to state officials. No wonder, then, that the pagan senator Vettius Agorius Praetextatus quipped with Damasus, the bishop in Rome: 'Make me the Bishop of Rome and I will immediately be a Christian.'[13] By the late fourth century, the holder of the Roman bishopric was so prestigious that the historian Ammianus Marcellinus (27.4.3) remarked, concerning the winner of this post, that he 'is sure to become rich through the gifts of aristocratic ladies, to ride in comfortable carriages, to dress splendidly, and to serve feasts on a scale fit to rival the tables of kings'.

The growing prestige of Christianity and the willingness of emperors to honour and advance Christians and Christian leaders had an impact on Rome's pagan elite. In the year 383 the pagan senator Symmachus complained of men

---

11 CTh 16.10.2, from the emperor Constantius II Augustus to Madalianus; trans. from B. Croke and J. Harries, *Religious conflict in fourth-century Rome*, 19. Constantius' law refers to a law of Constantine that does not survive.

12 For emperors beginning with Constantine granting exemptions to clerics, see CTh 16.2; for bishops' judicial authority deemed 'sacred' and final, see CTh 1.27.1 (dated to 318).

13 Jerome cites Damasus' remark in his *Against John of Jerusalem* 8: 'Facite me Romanae urbis episcopum et ero protinus Christianus.'

who stayed away from the pagan altars out of ambition.[14] This comment reflects a wider social and religious change, evidenced also by what we know about the conversion of elite families in Rome. The conversion of the Turcii from Rome provides a good example. The family can be traced to one L. Turcius Secundus, suffect consul in 300. Its members were prominent civic officials, pagans like L. Turcius Apronianus signo Asterius, urban prefect of Rome in 362/3. Yet in the second half of the fourth century, we find some members of the family embracing Christianity; a pagan, Turcius Apronianus, married the Christian woman Avita and converted to Christianity around the year 400.[15] Thus, although pagan rituals and celebrations continued in Rome, there was a gradual turning away from pagan cults by urban elite aware of the mounting social and political liabilities in maintaining these traditions.[16]

One of the most striking aspects of the conversion of Rome's elite in the post-Constantinian period is the lack of attestation for overt physical conflict between pagans and Christians. There had been physical conflict between pagans and Christians in other cities, such as Alexandria, and among Christians in Rome as well. Although we do not hear of such outbursts in Rome, we should not think that there was no religious conflict between pagans and Christians in the city. There survives, from the Rome of the 380s, one of our best-attested verbal dialogues between these two groups. In the year 382, the emperor Gratian broke decisively with the pre-existing imperial policy of toleration for pagan cults. He confiscated the revenues for maintaining pagan cults, diverted property willed to priesthoods and Vestals for the upkeep of pagan rituals and ceremonies to the imperial treasury and abolished the exemption of pagan religious officials from compulsory public duties. In this same year, he ordered the removal of the Altar of Victory from the Roman senate house.[17] When, in the next year, Gratian was overthrown and his thirteen-year-old brother, Valentinian II, a weak successor, ascended to the throne, the pagan senatorial aristocrats saw the opportunity of making a public stand in defence of the state religion. Symmachus, then urban prefect of Rome, sent a State Paper in July 384 on the senate's behalf to the ruling emperors requesting the return of the imperial policy of tolerance for pagan cult as well as the replacement of the Altar of Victory. The bishop of Milan, Ambrose, heard of this request and

---

14 Symmachus, *Letter* 51, 'Fuerit haec olim simplex divinae rei delegatio: nunc aris desse Romanos genus est ambienti.'
15 Salzman, *The making of a Christian aristocracy*, 80–1.
16 Salzman, *On Roman time*, 205–9.
17 The edict is referred to in a law of 415, *CTh* 16.10.20. The removal of the Altar is the subject of Symmachus' *Third Relatio* and Ambrose's *Letters* 17 and 18.

wrote letters in opposition to it. In the end, the pagan request was denied by the emperor resident in Milan.

No violence erupted after this change in imperial policy, although some of Rome's pagan elite no doubt were angered and concerned. Resentment over religion allegedly led one leading Roman aristocrat, Niocomachus Flavianus, to support the usurper Eugenius in his attempt to gain control over the Western empire. During the decisive battle between the forces of Eugenius and those of Theodosius I in 394 at the river Frigid, the pagan gods were invoked to aid Eugenius, but it is clear that the key issue in the conflict was domination of the Western empire, not the defence of paganism. After Theodosius' victory, no pagans are said to have died for their religion, nor was there a bloody backlash against pagans as such.[18] The defeat of Eugenius gave Theodosius sole authority over the Western empire, and in the ensuing decade this aggressive emperor passed the harshest and most stringent laws against the pagan cult. With the success of Theodosius, orthodox Christianity was embraced as the state religion.

It is under Theodosius, in the last decade of the fourth century, that the senatorial elite of Rome converted in large numbers. According to our literary sources, conversion required the active intervention of the emperor: the sixth-century pagan historian Zosimus and the fourth-century Christian poet Prudentius claim that the emperor Theodosius came to Rome after his victory at the Frigid river in the year 394 to convince Rome's upper class to 'cast off their previous error', paganism. According to Prudentius, the senate, of its own free will and without coercion, voted for Christianity; Zosimus claimed that the opposite was true, that no one obeyed the emperor's summons.[19] Modern historians argue over this imperial visit, its date and intent, but these narratives offer evidence of the issues at stake as well as the importance of the conversion of Rome's senatorial elite to contemporaries. Epigraphic and prosopographic evidence significantly supports the textual indications for dating the conversion of the Roman senatorial aristocracy; by the first quarter of the fifth century, Christianity was the dominant religion among the senatorial elite of Rome.[20] Not even the sack of Rome by the Goths in 410, which was attributed by some critics to the failure of the leading citizens to maintain pagan traditions, reversed this trend.

18 For discussion of this battle and its interpretation see Salzman, *On Roman time*, 233–5; and C. Hedrick, Jr., *History and silence*, 39–57.
19 Prudentius, *Against Symmachus* 1.506–23. Zosimus, *New History* 4.59.
20 Salzman, *The making of a Christian aristocracy*, 73–81.

If we accept the late fourth-early fifth-century date for the conversion of Rome's senatorial upper class, it had taken almost a century to convince the majority of Rome's elite to give up their pagan ways. Key to this process was the rising status of Christianity and the willingness of bishops and emperors to reassure Rome's aristocracy that conversion would neither involve a loss of social status nor undermine the institutions upon which their social position rested. But would conversion to Christianity allow Rome's senatorial elite to exercise their traditional social role as patron?

Rome's elite as patrons and religious leaders

Only with Constantine did Rome receive its first grand-scale, public Christian buildings.[21] The emperor demonstrated support for his new cult by building large, lavishly decorated, public places of worship. Basilicas like that of S. Giovanni in Laterno – erected in a largely residential but high-status area of the city, in the upper-class green belt of the city of Rome – became emblematic of the favoured status of Christianity. In the century after Constantine, virtually every bishop built a church or a *martyrium* in Rome. On each main road into Rome where, for centuries, the aristocrats had built elaborate tombs for their dead, emperors and bishops commemorated with fittingly ornate funerary basilicas the martyrs of the church as heroes.[22]

This building activity elevated the prestige of Christianity in the city in ways that appealed to its status-conscious senatorial elite. It also allowed the upper classes of Rome to take on the role of donor. Indeed, emperors (by their example) and bishops (by direct appeal) encouraged the senatorial aristocracy of Rome to take on their traditionally honoured place of patron, but now within a Christian context. So the Roman matron Anastasia and her husband were honoured and allowed to decorate a building attached to St Peter's, probably in the episcopate of Damasus (366–84).[23] The aristocratic holder of the illustrious office of urban prefect, Longinianus, built a baptistery, perhaps by S. Anastasia.[24] The Roman senator Pammachius (d. 410) built a *xenodochium* at Rome's port, Ostia, and he and his wife donated the monies for the building of the church of SS. Giovanni e Paolo on the Caelian Hill in Rome during the second half of the fourth century; in the mid-fifth century, the wealthy woman Demetrias, a member of the powerful

---

21 L. M. White, *The social origins of Christian architecture*, 5–30.
22 Zosimus, *New history* 4.59.
23 *ILCV*. N.S. 2. no. 4097 = *Epigrammata Damasiana* 94–6.
24 *ILCV* 92, and Flavius Macrobius Longinianus, urban prefect 400–2, *PLRE* II: 686–7.

Anician family, built a church to St Stephen on the Via Latina three miles from Rome.[25]

In addition to such traditional building activities, the senatorial elite of Rome were encouraged to give charity. The senator Pammachius' feast for the poor at St Peter's represents the channelling of a traditional act of patronage before a new audience, an act that will win him (in Paulinus of Nola's striking phrase) recognition among those who are truly 'noble', the prophets, apostles and martyrs who compose the 'heavenly senate'.[26] It was with an awareness of their audiences that bishops frequently emphasised the rewards of such acts. In fourth-century sermons advocating charity, the arguments are directed toward the spiritual well-being of the donor; the poor are faceless and there is little attention to them.[27] This notion of charity was very apt for Rome's aristocratic audiences, and we hear of the wealthy responding to these arguments with record acts of generosity; the wealthy Melania the Younger is said to have distributed funds to 'Mesopotamia, Syria, all of Palestine and Egypt', in short, to 'all the West and the East': she gave whole islands to the church.[28] Although bishops emphasised that Christian patronage was different from that practised by pagans because it was done with a humble attitude, neither with pride nor out of self-pity, there were a good number of Rome's elite who saw it as a continuation of their traditional role.[29]

The acquisition of social status by Christianity in Rome was gradual, and it had to rise in the face of deeply imbedded pagan aristocrats, wedded to their traditions. These factors help to explain why it took approximately a century after Constantine for Rome's senatorial elite to adopt Christianity. It is only in the fifth century that a clerical career had become a viable option for Rome's upper-class families; none of the fourth-century bishops of Rome come from socially privileged backgrounds, and the first election of a pope from one of the noble families occurred in 496 with the elevation of Anastasius, a member of the Symmachan family.[30] By the late fifth century, the identification of elite status with civic polytheism had been completely transferred to Christianity. The senatorial aristocracy of Rome, however, was among the last of Italy's

---

25 *Liber pontificalis* 47.1 (ed. Duchesne, I: 238); see too Demetrias in *PLRE* II: 351–2; on Pammachius, see *PLRE* I: 663.
26 Paulinus of Nola, *Carm.* 21.202–24 (CSEL 30.164–5).
27 B. Ramsey, 'Almsgiving in the Latin church'.
28 Melania was a model of Christian generosity: see *Life of Melania the Younger* 19 (SC 90: 162–9).
29 Ambrose, *De officiis* 1.30, Jerome, *Tract. in ps.* 133.164–74, and other texts noted by Salzman, *The making of a Christian aristocracy*, 206 n. 36.
30 C. Piétri, 'Aristocratie et société clericale'.

upper class to convert. The municipal people of high status in Aquileia have a markedly different trajectory.

The municipal elite of Aquileia

The city of Aquileia, in the northeastern region of Italy, Venetia, was one of the great cities of Italy; Ausonius praised its walls and harbours, ranking the city fourth in Italy and ninth in the empire when he wrote his *Ordo urbium* (*c*. 388). Aquileia had grown, benefiting from being a transit point in trade between the transalpine regions and the Mediterranean; goods produced in the northern regions passed through Aquileia on to the Eastern empire and on to Rome, Africa or Illyria.[31] Aquileia, like its surrounding cities, attracted a good number of immigrants, especially Jews and Greek-speaking Easterners, among whom Syrians are most widely attested. Some 10–20 per cent of the population of Aquileia and of this region is estimated to have been Greek-speaking Eastern-ers and Diaspora Jews in the early fourth century.[32] This influx of immigrants, attested by inscriptions with Greek, Syrian and Jewish names, helps to explain the religious fabric of the region. In addition to Jews and Christians, a wide variety of mystery cult devotees appear here in the third and fourth centuries.[33]

The Christian community in the late third century and continuing into the fourth century included a number of these Eastern immigrants. Some of these were fairly wealthy, or at least that is what the late third-century Bishop Victorinus of nearby Poetovium (modern-day Ptuj) indicates.[34] With wealth comes respectability, and some of these Christians were likely members of the local elite. However, wealthy Christian notables, whoever and how many, are not recorded for Aquileia, and as in Rome there are no major public places of worship or titular churches attested for the Christian community there until the time of Constantine. Only with the Edict of Milan did the Christian community in Aquileia and its bishop set about building large-scale public places of worship. The growing numbers of Christians and rising basilicas contributed to Aquileia's reputation, in our ancient sources, as the first centre of westward expansion for Italian Christianity.[35] By the second decade of the fourth century, we can identify wealthy Christian laypeople acting as patrons; some of these were presumably members of the municipal elite since they are not attested as holders of senatorial status.

---

31 Lellia Cracco Ruggini, 'Religiosità e chiese nelle Venezie', 31.
32 R. Bratož, *Il cristianesimo Aquileiese*, 471–6.
33 M. C. Budischovsky, 'Dieux et cultes d'origine égyptienne'.
34 See Victorinus of Poetovium, *On the apocalypse* 3.3 (SC 423: 62.1–7).
35 R. Lizzi, 'Ambrose's contemporaries', 164.

Aquileia's elite as patrons

Unlike the written accounts that exist for the conversion of Rome's elite, the evidence for Aquileia's municipal upper classes comes largely from archaeological sources. We are fortunate to possess a telling record of how Aquileia's municipal aristocrats came to act as patrons of the basilicas that were built in the city; the mosaic floors in three key basilicas in Aquileia, dating from the fourth to the late fifth centuries, explicitly record local patronage activities. It is worth looking at these in some detail.

The earliest of the three monumental, public Christian buildings to have survived in Aquileia is the episcopal or Theodorian complex, whose first level of mosaic flooring dates to the years right after Constantine's conversion (313–19).[36] The uniformity and organization of the mosaic flooring have led scholars to see a centralised control of the design, presumably under the supervision of the clergy or even of the bishop, whose identification and designation as *'felix'* provide a *terminus post quem* for the mosaic; Theodore died in 319. What is of particular interest here is that Theodore did not pay for the mosaic floor; an inscription in the south room indicates that 'Theodore with the help of God and of his flock' made this mosaic possible. The names and portraits of some fourteen donors are represented on the basilica floor. Some of these donors were quite wealthy, judging from the extent of mosaic they donated. So, several laypersons donated mosaic work roughly matching the 880 Roman feet noted for a certain donor named Januarius, also presumably a layman. The wealth of these lay donors is displayed also by the attire of the men and women depicted in the south room's mosaics.[37] These donors were, in all likelihood, Christianised municipal elites.

A second basilica at Aquileia, associated with a funerary monument, just 2 km south of the ancient urban centre, sheds further insight into the Christianisation of Aquileia's municipal upper classes in the second half of the fourth and early fifth centuries. Here, at the Basilica del fondo Tullio, some twelve names of donors survive. Three who have clearly Greek or Syriac names – Anatolius, Malchos and Euticius – paid for relatively modest amounts of flooring, only 33 Roman feet (approx. 2.9 m²) each. This floor suggests, as one sees elsewhere, that the Christian community of Aquileia contained a number

---

36 I follow the dating of these mosaics provided by J. P. Caillet, *L'évergétisme monumental*, 123–33.

37 Caillet, *L'évergétisme monumental*, 131–7. The dedicatory inscription has multiple interpretations for the key phrase, but I follow the *communis opinio* and read *poemnio* as denoting the lay flock with whose aid Theodore made this floor and building. C. Sotinel, *Identité civique et christianisme*, 86–7, has challenged the early dating for the Januarius inscription, but there is no doubt about the Constantian dating for the other, unnamed donors.

of Easterners, possibly recent immigrants, of modest wealth. But this community also included some very wealthy, local Christian lay donors, such as the couple Primenius and Leontia who paid for some 300 Roman feet (approx. 27 m²) of mosaic here, as well as for some 200 Roman feet (approx. 18 m²) of flooring for the nearby Christian basilica at Monastero in Aquileia. This couple were probably members of the municipal elite, for, although wealthy, neither Primenius nor Leontia is attested as having senatorial status or high office that would have conferred the rank of *clarissimus*. Nor were they alone in their patronage; Splendonius and Hilara, and Nonnosus and Severiana, both lay couples and, again, probably members of the municipal aristocracy, gave 200 Roman feet (approx. 18 m²) of mosaic each.[38]

Judging from the mosaic pavements, Christianity was deeply entrenched in Aquileia's local upper class by the early fifth century. The third extant Christian basilica at Aquileia, the Basilica del Monastero, just a little beyond the ancient city walls, has mosaic flooring dated to two phases, the early and second half of the fifth century respectively. Among the thirty-nine donors are some extremely wealthy patrons. In particular, Victor and Theosebes, presumably two heads of households and of Greek extraction, donated 2000 Roman feet (approx. 180 m²) of flooring, while one couple, Probus and Severa, donated 1000 Roman feet (approx. 90 m²).[39] The amounts attested suggest that we are seeing some of the wealthiest members of the local municipal elite. In keeping with notions of status, the wealthiest donors wished to demonstrate their position within the community through their monetary contributions.

The willingness of the notables in Aquileia and the surrounding areas to support such acts of patronage beginning as early as 313 suggests not only an earlier but also a more widespread adoption of Christianity than was the case among Rome's senatorial class. The influx of Eastern and Jewish immigrants into Aquileia may have contributed to Aquileia's openness; it certainly lent a distinctive Greek and Eastern identity to Aquileia's Christian community. Indeed, some of Aquileia's Christian donors, Greek-speaking Easterners or Christianised Jews, judging from their names, may have been Christian prior to migrating.

Although Aquileia's Christian upper class could boast of many fine basilicas and mosaic floors, they did not have the resources or wealth that was available to Rome's senatorial elite. Interestingly, too, unlike in Rome or Milan, we do not find in Aquileia's patron list wealthy Christian women acting as sole donors.

38 Ibid., 146–57.
39 Ibid., 184–7.

Rather, at Aquileia donors are recorded only within the family unit, either as a couple or as the heads of households. This, more conservative, familial pattern of Christian patronage may reflect the relatively limited means of this city's provincial, municipal upper class; it may also reflect the more conservative society of the provinces.

Aquileia's municipal elite did not have the autonomy and tradition of independence of Rome's senatorial elite. Rather, Aquileia's notables relied on wealthier, more powerful persons of senatorial rank for patronage and favours. A number of these powerful senatorial aristocracies active in this area were Christian. We know, for instance, that the Anicii, one of the most influential, Christian senatorial families of Rome, played a prominent role in Aquileia, acting as patrons for this city and holding property there; one member of this family, the fifth-century Anicia Ulfina, was likely honoured by being buried in this city.[40] The fourth-century governor of Venetia, Parecorius Apollinaris, built what has been identified as a Basilica of the Apostles in Aquileia.[41] The Petronii, another influential Christian senatorial family of Rome, were also active in Aquileia and its environs as office holders and patrons,[42] as were the Christian Eusebii; a tomb of a child from this family with a cache of inscribed silver spoons and jewellery was uncovered on what has been identified as family property. This funerary monument suggests one way in which urban Christian elites spread their religion in the area around Aquileia.[43] Indeed, it was widely assumed that the wealthy landowner was responsible for the religiosity of the rural population living on his estates.[44] In rural areas, as in cities like Aquileia, the Christian senatorial class modelled behaviour and represented Christianity as a high-status option, factors which likely contributed to making the municipal elite of Aquileia more open to Christianity.

By the fifth and sixth centuries senators who held the rank of *clarissimus* are attested as patrons of Christianity in the region of Aquileia. So, at Vicenza a church was dedicated to SS. Felix and Fortunatus with the support of a senatorial *clarissimus* by the name of Felix, along with the support of two

---

40 Sotinel, *Identité civique*, discusses the base of the statue dedicated to this family as their patrons and the likely authenticity of the fifth-century inscription.
41 Parecorius Apollinaris' monument is attested epigraphically; *CIL* 5.1582; Caillet, *L'évergétisme monumental*, 144–6.
42 Salzman, *The making of a Christian aristocracy*, 258; Piétri, 'Aristocratie et société clericale', 89–137.
43 L. Villa, 'Aspetti e tendenze della prima diffusione del cristianesimo', 391–4.
44 In Theodosius' law of 392, *CTh* 16.10.12.2–3, for example, landholders in rural areas were held responsible for enforcing prohibitions of pagan cult on their property. Cf. Augustine's praise for Pammachius for having convinced his tenant farmers to adopt the 'correct' Christianity: Augustine, *Letter* 48.1 (written in 401).

senatorial women, Toribus and Immola; a *vir laudabilis* (probably a senator) named Salonius Mauricus paid for a section of the mosaic floor there as well.[45] The presence of *clarissimi* as fifth-century donors suggests some significant changes both in the elite and in the Christian community in the area. Clearly, the prestige of the Christian community was rising, for it now numbered *clarissimi* among its members. Some of these *clarissimi* rose from the local municipal aristocracy. Thus, the Christian community in Aquileia now enjoyed a more elevated roster of members who patronised their local Christian communities. Aquileia's clergy also appears to be drawn from the upper class by this date, for we find some clerics making substantial gifts to the church, an indicator that here, as in fifth-century Rome, the leadership of the church is being recruited from their city's wealthy notables.[46]

Like the senatorial elite of Rome, the municipal elite of Aquileia were led to act as patrons by the urging of their bishop. The preaching of Aquileia's late fourth-century bishop, Chromatius, is in many ways typical of the kinds of arguments directed at the leading classes in Italy in general:

> If anyone is burdened by the evil desire of avarice, which is more oppressive than any other disease of the soul (for the love of money is the root of all evils, as the Apostle says), the precept concerning good works is necessary for him, so that he might know that he cannot be healed unless from avariciousness he turn to mercy and from greediness to generosity.[47]

Chromatius is modifying the traditional Roman criticism of avarice as morally destructive into a Christian framework that justifies wealth as a means of charity. By emphasising the benefits of such actions to the donor, he encouraged the patronage of Aquileia's municipal upper classes. In this regard, his arguments were indeed typical, focusing on charity as a means to self-improvement and salvation. If we can judge from the mosaic pavement floors at Aquileia, Chromatius' views were convincing. But the elite most open to such persuasion was that of Milan.

The imperial, bureaucratic elite of Milan

The choice of Milan as a tetrarchic capital by Maximian, Diocletian's co-emperor (*regn.* 293–305), is understandable within the political and military

---

45 Piétri, 'Aristocratie et société cléricale', 119 n. 115, and see *CIL* 5.1952 = Diehl 121.
46 Maximus, notarius and defensor for the church of Aquileia, contributed with his brother, *clarissimus* Agnellus, and with his parents, to pay for the remaking of the suburban basilica of Trieste; Piétri, 'Aristocratie et société cléricale', 132 n. 175.
47 Chromatius, *Sermon* 12.7 (CCSL 9a.56).

landscape of the later Roman empire. Situated close to the frontiers, Milan lay on the crossroads of the east–west and north–south highways from the Balkans to Gaul and from Africa and Rome to the Alpine passes and the Rhineland. With Milan as his base, the emperor could respond in person to threats from across the Rhine as well as maintaining communication between the Eastern and Western empire. It was in this tetrarchic capital that the victorious emperor Constantine met with his eastern co-emperor Licinius soon after his victory over Maxentius, and where the victors crafted, among other laws, a post-persecution policy of toleration toward Christians, issued later by Licinius but traditionally known as the Edict of Milan.[48]

The imperial court continued to make Milan its seat of power; emperors returned there after military campaigns and intermittently resided there to administer the Western empire from the time of Constans and Constantius II continuing down to Theodosius II (between 340 and 402). The presence of the emperor and his court opened up new possibilities for Milan's provincials as the city grew in prominence and size. The best estimates indicate that the city increased from a pre-fourth-century population of 30–50,000 to 130–150,000.[49] By the end of the fourth century, Milan had earned a reputation as a wealthy and important city, with 'numberless elegant mansions' and – as was required for an imperial capital and the seat of the governor of Liguria, the praetorian prefect of Italy and the *vicarius* of Italy – possessing an elite class that was 'able, eloquent and cheerfully disposed'.[50]

The fourth-century imperial presence in Milan helps to explain how the city and its aristocracy came to adopt Christianity so easily, so early, and in such large numbers. Christian emperors encouraged and supported co-religionists as courtiers and bureaucrats. It was advantageous, if one were an upwardly mobile provincial from Milan, to be able to attend church services in the presence of the emperor. How much and how quickly Milan's Christian community grew is hard to say with certainty, for the origin and extent of the Christian community in Milan prior to Constantine's Edict of 313 is not well attested; Paul the Deacon's claim that Milan's episcopate was founded by Anatolius, the envoy of the apostle Peter, lacks historical veracity.[51] Yet, by the second half of the fourth century, the Christian community in the city was large

---

48 Drake, *Constantine and the bishops*, 193–8.
49 F. Monfrin, 'À propos de Milan chrétien', 19; although certainty about the scale of Milan's increase is impossible, the vast granaries in Milan lend credence to this notion of a booming city: see M. Mirabella Roberti, *Milano Romana*, 75–7.
50 Ausonius, *Ordo urbium nobilium* (trans. White, I: 272).
51 Monfrin, 'À propos de Milan chrétien', 9–12 n. 12.

enough to support two competing factions. Indeed, the imperial court fuelled divisions within Milan's Christian community and contributed greatly toward making this city play a leading role in the political and theological controversies of the day. These controversies also contributed to the conversion of Milan's upper classes for they intensified allegiance to strong Christian leaders, perhaps the most successful of whom was the late fourth-century bishop Ambrose.

The Christian community in Milan was divided between two competing Christianities. One group, traditionally designated the 'orthodox' position, supported the idea of Christ's consubstantiality with the Father, as laid down by the Nicene Creed and advocated by Athanasius of Alexandria. Opposed to this view were Christians who held that Christ was merely similar to the Father. This position, denigrated as 'Arian' in antiquity and often associated with Easterners, is sometimes termed, in modern scholarly parlance, anti-Nicene. Both groups appealed to the emperor resident in Milan for support and many rulers, following Constantine's example, did intervene in favour of one or the other faction. A central figure in this conflict was the emperor Constantius II. Once firmly established in office by 353, he supported the anti-Nicenes and elevated the anti-Nicene Auxentius to the bishopric of Milan. Despite the opposition of the largely pro-Nicene bishops in Italy, this man held support from enough of Milan's Christian community and from the tolerant court of Valentinian I to remain in office down to his death in 374.

With Auxentius' demise, the pro-Nicene faction in Milan saw an opportunity for advancing their candidate. Conflict between these two factions soon led to outright fighting in the streets. A governor, the *consularis* of Aemilia, was sent to quell the rioting. This bureaucrat, himself an aristocrat, was only a catechumen, but he became the compromise candidate; Ambrose was baptised and consecrated bishop on 8 December 374. He soon disappointed the anti-Nicene faction, for he quickly revealed himself to be a strong pro-Nicene proponent, and one of the most actively Christianising bishops in all fourth-century Italy.

Ambrose's influence over the young co-emperor in the West, Gratian (359–83, *regn.* 375–83), who was early in his rule tolerant of the anti-Nicenes, was such that Gratian changed his opinion and adopted Ambrose's strong pro-Nicene position by the end of 378. Perhaps the most dramatic demonstration of Ambrose's position and the elite community that supported him occurred in defence of Nicene orthodoxy and episcopal authority during Holy Week of 386; Ambrose refused to hand over a basilica, the Portiana, to the anti-Nicene Christian community for the celebration of Easter. Ambrose's refusal flew in the face of a recent 386 law (*CTh* 16.1.4) of the young emperor, Valentinian

II, which had guaranteed the right of public worship to the anti-Nicenes. In retaliation, imperial troops surrounded the Episcopal Basilica of Milan where Ambrose continued to conduct services and lead his congregation in a night of non-stop hymns. The emperor and his anti-Nicene mother, Justina, backed down.[52]

Ambrose's defence of Nicene Christianity and episcopal autonomy was successful in part due to the weakness of the Western rulers and the disarray in the imperial court, but it was also due in no small part to his ability to unite behind him the strong, elite, pro-Nicene Christian community of Milan. This community included a number of powerful men and women, many of whom were deeply imbedded within the imperial bureaucracy and court. Indeed, 'many faces from the consistory must have appeared each Sunday in the bishop's basilica'.[53] Ambrose's congregation included men like Benivolus, an affluent and pious former civil servant who had stepped down from his office as *magister memoriae* rather than take any part in the drafting of a law favourable to Arians. Many were men who, once active in state service, settled in Milan after retirement, like the former *tribunus et notarius*, Nicentius. These were politically adept congregants, like the upwardly mobile Africans Ponticianus, an *agens in rebus* in imperial service, and the brilliant professor of rhetoric, the future saint Augustine, who had come to Milan to take up a teaching position. The court and the bishop attracted to Milan men with intellectual leanings, like the former praetorian prefect of Gaul, Mallius Theodorus, a leading proponent of Neoplatonism who assumed the consulate in Milan in 399. Such wealthy, influential men lent credibility and support, intellectual as well as political, to Ambrose's attempts to spread Nicene Christianity. Their numbers swelled the growing Christian community of Milan's upper class, now increasingly united in support of their actively pro-Nicene bishop.

Patronage in Milan

For such a prestigious and growing community, Ambrose, following the example of the bishops of Rome, was eager to build imposing places of worship. Milan already possessed a large, centrally located church, the Basilica Nova, whose expensive decoration suggests that it was an emperor who first financed this, probably in the 350s. However, Ambrose is responsible for the dedicatory inscription on the basilica's baptistery, if not for the baptistery itself. And he

---

52 M. Colish, 'Why the Portiana?', 363–4. The emperor and his mother may have held out
   for several more months, until Ambrose's discovery of the relics of SS. Gervasius and
   Protasius on 17 June of that year.
53 N. McLynn, *Ambrose of Milan*, 220.

is responsible for three large basilicas built outside the city walls: the Basilica Ambrosiana (S. Ambrogio) and the Basilica Apostolorum (S. Nazaro) were completed by 386, and the Basilica Virginum (S. Simpliciano) was planned shortly before his death in 397.[54] All three are located on major roads leading into Milan, a building pattern that seems to intentionally echo the extra-urban martyr-basilicas in Rome, as well as serving to house the growing number of converts and pilgrims. The hasty construction and the use of less expensive materials to erect these extra-urban basilicas may indicate that the funding came largely from Ambrose's family.[55] But additional support and gifts from Milan's elite adorned these basilicas, as is attested by the elaborate sarcophagus of the unidentified high dignitary in the Basilica Ambrosiana.[56]

Milan's wealthy, pious men and women, in response to injunctions from their bishop for charity, willingly took on the role of donor and patron in the city. Indeed, Ambrose instructed the bishops under his authority to preach in such a way as to encourage acts of charity: 'Let them [your congregations] learn to search for the riches of good works . . . The beauty of riches is not in the purses of the rich, but in their support for the poor.'[57] The upper-class Christian patrons of Milan were encouraged to feel comfortable in continuing their traditional patterns of expenditure on their cities within an approved, Christian context. Even women in Milan, as in Rome, became patrons. So, the wealthy Daedalia, 'distinguished in birth and richly endowed in worldly goods', is praised on her tombstone not only for being a consecrated virgin, but also for her charity toward the poor, for which she earned the title of 'mother of the needy'.[58] Her conspicuous burial place in the Basilica Ambrosiana is one further indication of how this city's elite came to play a key role in making Nicene Christianity the dominant source of social prestige for women as well as men.

Conclusion

The spread of Christianity in Italy in the century after Constantine was a largely urban phenomenon. Examining the reaction of three important urban elites in Italy highlights the ways in which Nicene Christianity became normative within Italy's cities. And once Italy's urban elites had converted, they became

54 R. Krautheimer, *Three Christian Capitals*, 69–71.
55 McLynn, *Ambrose of Milan*, 69.
56 Matthews, *Western aristocracies*, 198–200.
57 Ambrose, *Letter* 36[2].26 (CSEL 82².17), and see Lizzi, 'Ambrose's contemporaries', 156–73.
58 See *ILCV* 1700 for her epitaph and McLynn, *Ambrose of Milan*, 221–2.

instrumental in bringing about religious change. The upper classes of Italy took the lead, at the urging of bishops and emperors, in converting the rural pagans living on their estates as tenant farmers and in villages under their control.[59] So Christianity spread and came to dominate in Italy in the century after Constantine.

Bibliography

PRIMARY SOURCES

Ambrose. *Letters* (CSEL 82)
  De officiis, ed. Ivor J. Davidson (Oxford, 2001)
Ammianus Marcellinus. Ed. W. Seyfarth. *Ammiani Marcellini rerum gestarum libri qui supersunt* (Leipzig, 1999)
Augustine. *Letters* (CSEL 34, 44, 57, 58)
Ausonius. *Ordo urbium nobilium*. In H. G. E. White, trans., *Ausonius*, LCL (London: 1919–21)
Chromatius. *Sermons* (CCSL 9a)
Codex Theodosianus 16 (SC 497)
Eusebius. *Ecclesiastical History* (GCS *Eusebius Werke*, II)
  Life of Constantine (GCS 7 *Eusebius Werke*, I)
Expositio totius mundi et gentium. In R. Valentini and G. Zucchetti, eds., *Codice topografico della città di Roma* (Rome, 1940–53)
Ferrua, A. *Epigrammata Damasiana* (Rome, 1942)
Inscriptiones christianae urbis Romae septimo saeculo antiquiores: nova series, ed. I. B. de Rossi and A. Silvagni (Rome, 1922–)
Jerome. *Against John of Jerusalem* (PL 23)
  Tractatus in psalmos (CCSL 78)
Lactantius. *On the deaths of the persecutors* (SC 39)
Liber pontificalis, ed. L. Duchesne (Paris, 1886, 1892); supplementary volume, ed. C. Vogel (Paris, 1957)
Life of Melania the Younger (SC 90)
Paulinus of Nola. *Carmina* (CSEL 30)
Prudentius. *Psychomachie; Contre Symmaque, Œuvres* t. III, ed. M. Lavarenne (Paris, 1948)
Symmachus. *Letters*, ed. J. P. Callu (Paris, 1972–2002)
  Relationes, ed. R. H. Barrow, *Prefect and emperor: The Relationes of Symmachus, A.D. 384* (Oxford, 1973)
Victorinus of Poetovium. *On the apocalypse* (SC 423)
Zosimus. *New history*, ed. F. Paschoud (Paris, 1971–89)

SECONDARY SOURCES

Bratož, R. *Il cristianesimo Aquileiese prima di Costantino: fra Aquileia e Poetovio*, trans. M. Rener, ed. S. Tavano and L. Pani (Udine, 1999)

---

59 Lizzi, 'Ambrose's contemporaries', 156–73; G. Cantino Wataghin, 'Christianisation et organisation ecclésiastique des champagnes'.

Budischovsky, M.-C. 'Dieux et cultes d'origine égyptienne dans l'espace adriatique', in C. Delplace and F. Tassaux, eds., *Les cultes polythéistes dans l'Adriatique romaine* (Bordeaux, 2000), 239–61

Caillet, J. P. *L'évergétisme monumental chrétien en Italie et à ses marges d'après l'épigraphie des pavements de mosaïque (IVe–VIIe siècle)* MEFRA Suppl. 75 (Rome, 1993)

Cantino Wataghin, G. 'Christianisation et organisation ecclésiastique des champagnes: L'Italie du nord aux IVe–VIIIe siècles', in G. P. Brogiolo, N. Gauthier and N. Christie, eds., *Towns and their territories between late antiquity and the early middle ages* (Leiden, 2000), 209–34

Colish, M. 'Why the Portiana? Reflections on the Milanese basilica crisis of 386', *JECS* 10 (2002): 361–72

Cracco Ruggini, Lellia. 'Religiosità e chiese nelle Venezie (II–V secolo)', *Antichità Altoadriatiche* 47 (2000): 17–42

Croke, B. and J. Harries. *Religious conflict in fourth-century Rome: A documentary study* (Sydney, 1982)

Drake, H. A. *Constantine and the bishops. The politics of intolerance* (Baltimore, 2002)

Hedrick, Charles W., Jr. *History and silence. Purge and rehabilitation of memory in late antiquity* (Austin, 2000)

Jones, A. H. M., R. Martindale and J. Morris. *The Prosopography of the later Roman empire* (Cambridge, 1971–92)

Krause, Jens-Uwe. *Spätantike Patronatsformen im Westen des römischen Reiches* (Munich, 1987)

Krautheimer, Richard. *Three Christian capitals: Topography and politics* (Berkeley, 1983)

Lane Fox, Robin. *Pagans and Christians* (New York, 1986)

Lizzi, R. 'Ambrose's contemporaries and the Christianization of Northern Italy', *JRS* 80 (1990): 156–73

McLynn, N. *Ambrose of Milan* (Berkeley, 1994)

MacMullen, R. *Christianising the Roman empire: A.D. 100–400* (New Haven, 1981)

Matthews, J. *Western aristocracies and imperial court AD 324–425* (Oxford, 1975)

Mirabella Roberti, M. *Milano Romana* (Milan, 1984)

Monfrin, F. 'À propos de Milan chrétien. Siège épiscopal et topographie chrétienne IVe–VIe siècles', *Cahiers archéologiques* 39 (1991): 7–46

Piétri, C. 'Aristocratie et société clericale dans l'Italie chrétienne au temps d'Odoacre et de Théodoric', *MEFRA* 93 (1981): 417–67

Ramsey, B. 'Almsgiving in the Latin church: The late fourth and early fifth centuries', *Theological Studies* 43 (1982): 226–59

Salzman, M. R. *The making of a Christian aristocracy: Social and religious change in the Western Roman empire* (Cambridge, MA, 2002)

   On Roman time: The Codex-Calendar of 354 and the rhythms of urban life in late antiquity (Berkeley, 1990)

Sotinel, C. *Identité civique et christianisme: Aquilée IIIe–VIe siècles, BEFAR 324* (Rome, 2005)

Villa, L. 'Aspetti e tendenze della prima diffusione del cristianesimo nel territorio Aquileiese alla luce dei dati archeologici', *Antichità Altoadriatiche* 47 (2000): 391–437

White, L. M. *The social origins of Christian architecture* (Valley Forge, PA, 1990)

9

Christianity and paganism, IV: North Africa

ANNA LEONE

The diffusion of Christianity in North Africa was marked by complex inter-action on several fronts, initially between pagans and Christians, and later within the church itself as schisms occurred. The Christianisation of North Africa resulted in a progressive acquisition of power (both religious and secu-lar/economic) by the clergy. This chapter will synthesise the main phases of this process, paying particular attention to the role of the clergy, its transfor-mation over the centuries and the impact of Christianisation on society and economy. Our evidence will be taken from both written and archaeological sources.

Pagan and Christian communities

The earliest Christian communities of North Africa frequently interacted with, and reacted to, local pagan traditions. Some episodes in Augustine's life described this interaction. In general, fourth-century pagan tradition was still very lively; it provided one of Augustine's main opponents. For instance, he mentions a strong pagan community at *Liber de promissionibus et predi-cationibus Dei* 3.38. There, Augustine writes that pagans revolted against the decision by Christian clergy to build a basilica above the temple of Caelestis in Carthage.[1] This insurrection prompted the tribune Ursus to destroy the tem-ple completely and build a new church on the site. On-going pagan practice is also confirmed by several mosaics of distinctly pagan iconography found in both private and public buildings. A Dionysiac scene discovered in the so-called 'schola' at Carthage (built probably at the beginning of the fifth century)

---

1 The exact location of this building has not been identified. On the problem of the identi-fication of religious buildings in Carthage, see L. Ennabli, *Carthage* and N. Duval, 'L'état actuel des recherches archéologiques sur Carthage chrétienne'.

indicates active devotees to this god.[2] In some North African cities, theatres and amphitheatres were still pulling in big audiences, as in the Bulla Regia mentioned by Augustine.[3]

Some pagan traditions developed into Christian ones. The pagan practice of holding banquets and celebrations on tombs, to keep the anniversary of the death, continued in the Christian tradition. This observance consisted of bread mixed with water and wine, which was first consumed by the visitors (*epulis praegustandi*) and then given to the deceased (*largiendis*). Tertullian considered the funerary banquets a rite of unity with the dead.[4] Augustine totally rejected this practice, emphasising instead its connection with the pagan tradition. In several of his sermons, Augustine mentions that these rites – the *parentalia* – were celebrated on several occasions, i.e., *memoriae sanctorum*, *memoriae defunctorum* and *memoriae martyrum*. This custom was widely practised in North Africa during the fourth century, even though it was already forbidden in Milan and other parts of the empire.[5] For example, we know that episodes of dancing and singing preceded the 'celebration' of Cyprian's death in Carthage.[6] In 392, Augustine suggested in a letter to Aurelius, the bishop of Carthage, that he should forbid this practice; in 397, a council legislated against it.[7] About fifteen years later, Augustine alludes to the fact that a small number of these banquets survived and they were more likely to be considered as vigils.[8] And yet it would seem that, around 411, the tradition survived only in the Donatist church (see below) and had disappeared among the Catholics. This is witnessed by the fact that this problem (among others) was discussed that year in the Council of Carthage, with the participation of a large number of bishops from both groups (Catholic and Donatist), including Augustine.[9]

---

2 The function of this building has been discussed at length; see, e.g., Picard, 'Une schola de collège à Carthage' and *La Carthage de St. Augustin*, 180.

3 Augustine, *Sermo* 301.1: 'O fratres Bullenses, circumaquaque prope in omnibus civitatibus vicinis vestris lascivia impietatis obmutuit. Non erubescitis, quia apud vos solos remansit turpitudo venalis? An delectat vos, inter frumentum, vinum, oleum, animalia, pecora et quaecumque in romanis, vel nundinis venundantur, etiam turpitudinem emere et vendere? Et fortassis ad talia commercia huc veniant peregrini, et dicitur: Quid quaeris? Mimos, meretrices? Bulla habes.'

4 Tertullian, *Spect.* 13.2–5. On this aspect, see V. Saxer, *Morts, martyrs, reliques en Afrique chrétienne*, 134–5.

5 Augustine, *Conf.* 6.2. We know in fact the famous episode of Augustine's mother wanting to celebrate a banquet in Milan in 385, but this practice was forbidden by Ambrose; see Saxer, *Morts, martyrs, reliques en Afrique chrétienne*, 134–5.

6 On the problem of the churches dedicated to Cyprian in Carthage, see N. Duval, 'Les monuments chrétiens de Carthage'; N. Duval *Les églises africaines à deux absides*; and Ennabli, *Carthage*.

7 Augustine, *Letters* 22.3 and 16.57–8.

8 Augustine, *City of God* 8.27.

9 For a complete analysis of the council see the edition of the Acts by Lancel: *SC* 194.

Promoting Catholic Christianity in Roman North Africa

The various cultural negotiations that characterised early Christian interaction with local pagan traditions were frequently complicated by problems internal to the church. 'You must know, my friends,' said Augustine 'how the mutterings [of the pagans] join with those of the heretics and the Jews. Heretics, Jews and pagans: they have formed a unity over against our unity.'[10] The combative posture of the Catholic Church against pagans – but also Jews and, perhaps especially, other Christians – is striking. Even as pagans become decreasingly visible in the history of Roman North Africa, Christians who are self-consciously *not* in communion with Rome come to fill their place as the 'other'. The historical context of Augustine's remarks, for example, was a major crisis that had raged for nearly a century and that saw the African church divided by schisms, only to be redressed ultimately by the council of 411.

In Peter Brown's summary, 'the rise of the schismatic church – which had begun in Carthage in 311 and by the time of Augustine had won over the majority of African Christians – created the situation that posed the problem of coercion in its classic form: that is, this church was not only prohibited but, during the episcopate of Augustine, its congregations were subjected to official pressure to join the Catholic Church'.[11] By 400, the Catholic Church had attained privileges and was able to have its rivals repressed to various degrees. The Theodosian Code contains several laws that favour the supremacy of the Catholic Church.[12] These laws specified acts contrary to Catholic morality for which people could be punished through the loss of civic rights, exclusion from public employment and so on. Some actions were subjected to increasing penalties: heretics were fined, and later a harsher punishment (namely, proscription and exile) was extended to the Donatist clergy, who 'polluted' the Catholic sacraments by re-baptism.[13] Pagan temples were confiscated and access to them restricted; statues were to be destroyed (although archaeological evidence apparently does not confirm that these measures were taken). Heretical churches were given to the Catholics and illicit meeting places were confiscated.[14]

---

10 Augustine, *Sermo* 62.18, trans. from P. Brown, *Religion and society*, 303; see also P. Brown, *Augustine of Hippo*.
11 Brown, *Religion and society*, 303.
12 Ibid. 438. On *CTh*, see J. Harries and I. Wood, *The Theodosian Code*.
13 *CTh* 16.5.21; see further Brown, *Religion and society*, 303ff.
14 *CTh* 16.10.18, 16.10.19 (dated to 407/8); 16.5.43, 16.6.2, 1.

Official repression of Christianity gave rise to the Donatist controversy. It took hold of North Africa, which had only been partially Christianised by the beginning of the fourth century. This movement originated during the Diocletian persecution that ended in March 305, just before Diocletian and Maximian abdicated. During that oppression, Christians were requested to hand over the holy books to the municipal authority (the Latin word for handing over, *traditio*, is widely used in this context). Many Christians refused to obey, but several clerics and bishops, to keep from being persecuted, turned over religious texts and liturgical items such as vestments and chalices. After the persecution ended, a controversy arose about whether priests who had co-operated with the state during the persecution could be re-admitted into the church. The supporters of Donatus regarded these people as *traditores* (literally, 'those who hand over', but here with the specific sense of 'traitors') and insisted that they had to be re-baptised to be accepted again.[15] In 311, Caecilian was chosen as the new bishop of Carthage, but the Donatists considered him a *traditor*.[16] The Numidian clerics therefore opposed his election and later chose in his place Donatus of Casae Nigrae (on the Saharan border of Numidia), who quickly won the support of both Carthaginian and Numidian elements in opposition to Caecilian. However, Miltiades, the bishop of Rome, supported Caecilian (313) and Donatus was condemned. Despite this decision, public opinion in North Africa was strongly in favour of Donatus.

After the 'Peace of Constantine', several successive emperors attempted to resolve this problem, first by exiling Donatist bishops and confiscating Donatist property,[17] then by promoting reunification; such was the goal of the afore-mentioned council of 411 in Carthage. Government support for Caecilianus' party was ultimately determinative. In 347, the emperor Constans proclaimed the reconciliation of the Donatists and Catholics under the authority of Bishop Gratus.[18] This event led to a sudden collapse of Donatism in Carthage and in Africa Proconsularis.[19] From 348, Catholicism was on the rise. We have, however, documentation of Donatists surviving into the early sixth century.[20] In particular, the Donatist community continued to be active in Numidia during

---

15 This was based on Cyprian's idea that there is no *salus* (salvation, or health) outside of the church, and consequently these people needed to be re-admitted into the community.
16 Caecilianus was also supported by Constantine, after he defeated Maxentius at the Milvian Bridge in 312.
17 See Augustine, *Letter* 105.9: 'Legem contra partem Donati dedit severissimam.'
18 *Passio Maximiani et Isaaci* 1 (*PL* 8: 768).
19 Optatus, *De scismate Donatistorum*, 3.1; *Passio Maximiani et Isaaci* (*PL* 8: 768); W. H. C. Frend, *The Donatist church*, 177–82.
20 Frend, *The rise of the Monophysite movement*, 2.

the Vandal and Byzantine periods. In Ain Zirara, where the dedication to the apostles Sts Peter and Paul in the Vandal period is followed by the formula '{semper De}o laus et g{loria}'[21] – which is probably a conventional Donatist exhortation – they still existed.[22] The same evidence has been found in a fifth-century inscription from Ain Ghorab.[23]

Even though there were some reversals (such as probable Donatist involvement in two major political revolts, dated approximately 372 or 375 and 397/8,[24] and the triumphant return of the Donatist leaders recalled from exile by the emperor Julian, 361–3), the movement as a whole fell into a decline from the mid-fourth century. That weakening became irrevocable after the revolt in 398.

This decline was hastened by the dangerous situation in Italy and the invasions of the Western provinces of the Empire by various Germanic tribes. Schismatic groups came under increasing pressure as civil authorities tried to make the society more unified and to eliminate conflicts. Many of the Germanic invaders were Arian Christians and consequently both Catholics and Donatists were persecuted during the Vandal domination in Africa. Another important role in the re-affirmation of the Catholic Church was Augustine's intervention. By 399, he had already been actively working against Donatists for six years: in 393 he wrote the *Psalmus contra partem Donati*,[25] and around three years later he composed the *Contra epistolam Donati*.[26]

The clergy and the power of the church

The society that sustained the rising power of the Catholic Church was already different from the classical society of the imperial period. Transformations occurred within the society itself and its system of managing the lands.[27] The creation of a patrimony that could guarantee the economic independence of the clergy assisted the progressive acquisition of power by

---

21 *CIL* 8, no. 17746.

22 Frend, *The Donatist church*, 2nd edn.

23 On this church, see Leschi, 'Basilique et cimitière donatistes de Numidie'. For further analysis of the continuity of Donatism during Vandal and Byzantine time see Frend, *The Donatist church*, 308.

24 See Frend, *The Donatist church*, 197–9, 220–6; for the suggestion that Donatist leaders may have been allied to the leadership of the rebellion, see S. Mazzarino, *Antico, tardoantico ed era costantiniana*, 438, with reference to *CTh* 16.5.52.

25 *PL* 43: 25–52.

26 This work is mentioned in the historical sources but it has not survived.

27 For an overview of the transformations of the relationship between state and aristocracy see F. Millar, 'Italy and the Roman empire: Augustus to Constantine'; and for land-management, see A. Leone and D. J. Mattingly, 'Vandal, Byzantine and Arab rural landscapes in North Africa'.

the Church. The stages of development that resulted in the rise of clerical properties and estates are not easily identifiable; sources are only partial. Archaeologically the impact of this phenomenon on both urban and rural landscapes can hardly be detected. However, Buenacasa Perez has recently confirmed that this process probably did not take place before the fourth century in North Africa.[28] Even though the data are sometimes difficult to interpret, it is nonetheless possible to identify some phases of these actions. First of all, after the *pax Constantiniana* (313), the *Liber pontificalis* speaks of the donation by Constantine of some territories in North Africa, Greece and Sicily to the Lateran baptistery.[29] These lands offered by Constantine in these provinces were all *massae* (i.e., large estates resulting from the unification of several *fundi*),[30] located in fertile areas near road networks and sources of water.[31]

Private donations certainly increased the patrimony of the clergy in North Africa. Augustine provides precise information about some gifts, but for other parts of North Africa unfortunately the paucity of documentation prevents us from offering a detailed account of the whole process. As regards Hippo, Augustine refers to donations by the deacons Severus and Eraclius and the priest Leporius, and also mentions some *fundi* belonging to the church.[32] The *fundus Victorianensis* given by Barnabas is clear chronologically. Barnabas, a priest at Hippo, tried unsuccessfully to rent out the land annually for 40 *solidi*, before donating it to the church.[33] In the same context, Augustine also refers to some houses given to his church. On the other hand, some properties were

---

28 C. Buenacasa Perez, 'La creación del patrimonio ecclesiástico de las iglesias norte-africanas en época romana'; a similar trend is also recorded in other provinces, as for instance in Egypt: see R. S. Bagnall, *Egypt in late antiquity*.

29 Ed. Duschesne, I: 175: (*Intra partes Africae*): *Massa Iuncis, territorio Mucario, praest. Sol. DCCC; Massa Capsis, territorio captitano, praest. Sol. DC; Massa Varia Sardana, territorio Mimnense, praest. Sol. D Massa Camaras, territorio Cryptalupi, praest. Sol. CCCCV; Massa Numas, territorio Numidiae, praest. Sol. DCCXX; Massa Sulphorata, territorio Numidiae, praest. Sol. DCCXX; Massa Walzari olearia, territorio Numidiae, praest. Sol. DCCCCX.* For donations in Italy and their principal characteristics, see D. De Francesco, 'Le donazioni costantiniane nell'Agro Romano', 69.

30 On the definition of *massae*, see D. Vera, '*Massa fundorum*'.

31 D. De Francesco, 'Chiesa Romana e proprietà fondiaria nel suburbio'; for an overview of the properties held by the Church of Rome in Italy, see Pietri, *Roma Christiana*. In North Africa a *massa Candida* is mentioned by Augustine (*En. in Ps. 49.9; Sermo 306.2* and 311) and Prudentius (*Peristephanon, 13.76–87*): According to their narrative, 300 Christians were martyred there in AD 258 (also mentioned by Paulinus of Nola, *Carm. 19.44*, and found in an inscription found at Calama – *V 2070*). In this case there is no precise evidence attesting that this land belonged to the church.

32 Augustine, *Sermo 356*.

33 See Augustine, *Sermo 356.15*.

also purchased, like the villa bought by the deacon Heraclius on behalf of the church of Hippo.[34] Aurelius, the Catholic bishop of Carthage, provides comparable evidence for donations to the church in Africa Proconsularis by a private individual.[35]

Some properties are mentioned without any information about how and when the church acquired them. That is true about the territory of Vaga in North Africa. It was already a part of the holdings of the church in the fourth century, but we do not know exactly how and when it became church property.[36] In other cases, anecdotes are useful for understanding the attitude of the church and the Catholics towards these donations, but they shed very little light on the progressive acquisition of properties by the church. The case of Melania the Younger is significant in this respect.[37] Melania and her husband Pinianus wanted to donate their inheritance to the church so at one point they came to Africa to disperse it. Their holdings were huge – larger than the territory of Thagaste – and included 'a villa, numerous artisans working gold and silver and two bishops, one a Catholic and one a heretic'.[38] Augustine, Alypius and Aurelius recommended that the couple should give the church houses and revenues, which would survive for ever. This illustrates the principle that the clergy generally preferred donations of money, revenues or buildings, rather than lands.[39]

Another factor may have attracted some rich landowners directly into the clergy: the immunities from various financial responsibilities that were awarded to the church.[40] It is, however, difficult to gauge the extent of these advantages. Furthermore, when such landowners managed their lands it is

---

34 Augustine, *Sermo* 356.5, 7 and 10. See on this also H. Jaïdi, 'Remarques sur la constitution des biens des églises africaines', 174 and n. 29.

35 In this case, the donation was originally made because the donor thought he could not have children. Later, when Aurelius found out that that man had a son, he returned the donation; Augustine, *Sermo* 355.5; see also Jaïdi, 'Remarques sur la constitution des biens des églises africaines', 188.

36 Symmachus, *Letter* 1.68 (ed. Callu, 1: 380): 'Symmachus Celsino Titiano Fratri: Rufus Pontificalis arcarius prosequitur apud te mandata collegii, cui prae ceteris retinendi, Vaganensis saltus cura legata est.'

37 See the detailed study by A. Giardina, 'Carità eversiva'.

38 Gerontius, *Life of Melania* 21.16 ss.: 'dedit autem et possessionem multum prestantem reditum, quae possessio maior etiam erat civitatis ipsius, habens balneum, artifices multos, aurifices, argentarios et aerarios; et duos episcopos, unum nostra fidei et alium haereticorum'.

39 Jaïdi, 'Remarques sur la constitution des biens des églises africaines', 181.

40 On the exemptions of the clergy from the *munera municipalia*, see F. Marazzi, I 'patrimonia Sanctae Romanae Ecclesiae', 23 n. 9. On the senatorial clergy, see also F. D. Gilliard, 'Senatorial bishops in the 4th century'.

often impossible to determine whether they were acting as clergymen or as landowners. This happened far in advance of the *patrimonium Petri*. The first attempt to create it was made much later by Pope Gelasius at the end of the fifth century.[41] As Lepelley has observed, a bishop was still a 'private person' in the fourth century: probably churches and their properties were controlled independently.[42]

The status of the church in Roman North Africa becomes clearer by considering the evidence of economic activity involving the clergy. In the acts of some councils,[43] members of the clergy are asked to stay away from *administratio vel procuratio domorum* (indeed, from *saecularia negotia* in general), to avoid acting as *conductores* or *procuratores* (terms we will encounter again, below) and not to attend the *nundinae* excessively.[44] The sources also refer to the activity of *procuratores*. Kolendo has argued that, in North Africa, the *procuratores* controlled large areas (*regiones*), rather than a single *latifundium* (*saltus*).[45] In this case it is possible that they were managing extensive and large territories, as owners or as tenants. Fourth-century bishops were very influential people and their economic power must have been significant. This could also explain the reproaches to the clergy (found in both the councils and in the *Codex Theodosianus*) for being too involved in commercial activities and land management. These reproaches apparently attempted to reduce their power by instructing them to focus principally on their religious duties. That clergy were acting as *conductores* is related to another aspect of land management and its organisation in late antique North Africa. As demonstrated principally by Vera, in this part of the empire the primary form of land possession in late antiquity was an *enphyteusis*.[46] (In such an agreement, the *conductor* – who was therefore called an *enphyteuticarius* – had indefinite possession of the land and the terms of the agreement could never be altered.) Bishops, deacons and priests often acted as administrators in both senses, that is, first as a *conductor* and later as an *enphyteuticarius*. Augustine names such a clergyman, a Donatist

---

41 On the creation of the patrimony of the Church of Rome, see Marazzi, *I 'patrimonia Sanctae Romanae Ecclesiae'*.
42 Lepelley, 'Le patronat épiscopal aux IVᵉ et Vᵉ siècles', 17.
43 See, e.g., Council of Carthage (345–8), 6 (CSEL 149: 6); Breviarium Hipponiense 15 (CSEL 149: 38); Canones in causa Apiarii 150 (CSEL 149: 122).
44 Mansi, III: 948, XLIII: *de clericis, qui extra necessitatem ad nundinas vadunt.*
45 T. Kolendo, 'La hiérarchie des procurateurs dans l'inscription d'Ain-el-Djemala' and D. Vera, 'Enfiteusi', 288.
46 Vera 'Enfiteusi', 273; for an overview of the problem, see Leone and Mattingly, 'Vandal, Byzantine and Arab rural landscapes in North Africa', 153–4.

bishop called Crispinus, and laments that the emperor was renting his lands to a Donatist.[47] Leaving aside the religious problem, the information confirms that bishops – and indeed other clergy – were renting lands directly from the emperor. The land rented by Crispinus (which was located in the large area of saltus Imperiales in the Medjerda valley in Africa Proconsularis) must have been very big, and it probably included around twenty families of *coloni* (or, as Augustine puts it, *octoginta ferme animas*). The case of Crispinus is also instructive in that, as a Donatist bishop, he imposed the re-baptism of all the people working in the *massa*.[48] This suggests that managing land brought a double advantage to the clergy: an increase of their patrimony and of the number of believers. This brings us to a further element in the practicalities of land management in Roman North Africa: the *enphiteuticarius* was able to act as the *dominus* (lord). In some cases bishops, also acting as *conductores*, abused their power within the lands under their control, like Bishop Antoninus of Fussala.[49]

The presence of monasteries in Roman North Africa also requires consideration. Monasteries were particularly important in Egypt, but not much is known about such buildings in Africa Proconsularis. The lack of distinct archaeological evidence for Catholic monasteries could be owed to the practice of bishops' houses doubling as monasteries. Possidius, for example, describes Augustine's house as having been a monastery and broadly indicates that other bishops emulated that practice.[50] 'Clerical monasteries' like Augustine's would not necessarily have distinctive architectural features that would set them apart. In any case, the existence of monastic communities is attested by other sources. We know that Aurelius of Carthage offered some lands to monks in Thagaste near the end of the fourth century.[51] Furthermore, we read in the *Life of Fulgentius* 2–3 that monasteries were proliferating in North Africa at the beginning of the sixth century.

---

47 Augustine, *C. litt. Petiliani* 2.83.184 (CSEL 52: 114) and *Letter 66*; *CTh* 5.15.15; on this topic, see also Lepelley, 'Deux témoignages de Saint Augustin'.

48 The episode was mentioned by Augustine as a scandal, although Crispinus was acting exactly as Augustine himself was suggesting to his friends: *En. in Ps.* 54.13; *Letters* 58 (Pammachius), 89 (Festus), 112 (Donatus), 251 (Pancarius). See also D. Vera, 'Conductores domus nostrae, conductores privatorum', 475.

49 S. Lancel, 'L'affaire d'Antoninus de Fussala' and Vera, 'Conductores domus nostrae, conductores privatorum', 483–4; Antoninus was managing land belonging to a Roman woman of senatorial rank.

50 Possidius, *Life of Augustine* 22.1–7.

51 See Jaïdi, 'Remarques sur la constitution des biens des églises africaines', 176 n. 46; on the monasteries in North Africa, see also Gavigan, *De vita monastica*.

The Vandal invasion and the Arian persecution

In 439, the Vandals, who were Germanic Arians, entered Carthage. The Vandal kings showed varying attitudes towards the Catholic Church in North Africa; persecution and tolerance followed one another, sometimes within the same reign. The persecution of Catholics was probably harsher in Africa Proconsularis than elsewhere; in Byzacena and Tripolitana it was almost non-existent.[52] Modéran identifies two main phases during the Vandal period: the first started in 439 and culminated in the great persecution of 483–4; the second was characterised by a more benevolent attitude towards Catholics.[53]

Sources tell us that only three churches survived the sack of Geiseric's army: Hippo, Cirta and Carthage.[54] Geiseric initiated a long persecution of Catholics and the remaining Donatists.[55] In Carthage, the churches of Restituta and two of Cyprianus became Arian churches; Geiseric also seized other religious buildings, i.e., churches and basilicas of saints, cemeteries of martyrs and monasteries.[56] The Catholic see of Carthage was vacant from 440 to 454. Then Deogratius was nominated, but after three years he was exiled. Only after Zeno's treaty with the Vandals (481) was that see occupied again.[57] Huneric (477–84) summoned all bishops, Catholic and Arian, to a conference in May 483. Some 466 bishops are named as participants in the Notitia provinciarum et civitatum Africae.[58] Huneric turned the laws made to restrict Donatists against many Catholic bishops: they could choose conversion or exile. Under Guthamund (regn. 484–96), some Catholic bishops were deported in 492, while churches were taken over by Arians.[59] Catholics, however, remained intellectually superior and no defender of Arianism appeared after Thrasamund (regn. 496–523).[60] Hilderic allowed exiled bishops to return, Catholic churches to re-emerge,

---

52 Ch. Courtois's Les Vandales et l'Afrique used a new approach and claimed that the Vandal conquest was not destructive. But Y. Modéran, 'L'Afrique et la persécution vandale,' 254 and 'L'établissement territorial des vandales en Afrique', 107 refuted that view for North Africa as a whole.

53 Modéran, 'L'Afrique et la persécution vandale', 254.

54 Possidius, Life of Augustine 23.

55 The persecution has been interpreted by Modéran, 'L'Afrique et la persécution vandale', 252 as part of the Vandal government's aim to impose its power especially in Zeugitania.

56 Victor of Vita, 1.4.

57 Valentinian II demanded this election: Victor of Vita, 1.25–6.

58 Forty-five Catholic bishops were from Zeugitania, but with a disproportionate number of 120 from Mauretania Caesariensis, also under Vandal dominion. The persecutions were extreme in Zeugitania, while rulers in other regions were more tolerant.

59 Victor of Vita, 3.2; later, Guthamund forced Catholics to convert: ibid., 3.14.

60 Modéran, 'L'Afrique et la persécution vandale', 254 suggests that persecutions under Guthamund and Thrasamund continued but were less violent.

and church councils to meet at Junca and Sufes, in Byzacena, during 525.[61] Gelimer (*regn.* 530–4) followed the same practice. General Belisarius defeated the Vandals in 533 and re-established the Catholic Church.

The fortunes of the Catholic Church in this period are difficult to track archaeologically. Shifts of buildings from Catholic to Arian control leave no trace. Properties confiscated, whether those of senators, of the Catholic Church or lands in Proconsularis, are nearly impossible to detail.[62] From 439 and 477 until 523 (with the probable exception of 484) Vandals only took over churches and prohibited Catholics from worshipping in Proconsularis.

Defining the presence and power of Catholic or Arian communities is challenging. Pagan communities were still active in fourth-century North Africa and lasted into the Vandal period. Yet the decay, already present before the Vandals, was completed during their dominance. Temples were abandoned or put to other use. By contrast, despite the extensive confiscation of Catholic properties and the frequent exile of bishops, Catholic churches and monasteries were built or restored. Vandals also needed churches, too. New churches appeared at Thibiuca, Thala, and two at Sufetula while the church of Bishop Bellator there was enlarged. A basilica at Belalis Maior was also restored.[63] The church erected over the civil basilica in the forum of Sabratha (probably during the Vandal period) may have been either Catholic or Arian.[64] The church constructed over the temple of Caereis in Thuburbo Majus and the Basilica of Hildenguns are dated to the fifth century because of German names in the graves near them.[65] Other buildings cannot be dated except as late fourth or early fifth century.

The Byzantine period

Even though Catholic Christianity in North Africa suffered many reversals due to the rise of schisms and heresies, it became very powerful during the Byzantine period as part of Justinian's Christian empire. This new status represents the high point of the Christianisation of North Africa. It is

---

61 Mansi, VIII: 636.
62 Modéran, 'L'établissement territorial des vandales en Afrique', 102 n. 111 (Victor of Vita, 1.12–14); Modéran, 'L'Afrique et la persécution vandale' and 'L'établissement territorial des vandales en Afrique', 107 tried to identify them.
63 F. Bejaoui, 'Nouvelles données archéologiques à Sbeitla', 40; Duval, *Les églises africaines à deux absides*, 163–7; Mahjoubi, *Recherches d'histoire et d'archéologie*, 228–33.
64 Duval, 'Études d'archéologie chrétienne nord-africaine: XVI', 288.
65 M. A. Alexander et al., *Thuburbo Majus*, 159; F. Prévot, *Recherches archéologiques*, 45–58.

characterised, first of all, by the large number of monumental churches that were built in towns and in the countryside. Religious building became the symbol of the church's power in much the same way that temples and fora had represented the Roman empire. They were the meeting places and, when fortified, also defensive buildings in which the population could take refuge in danger.[66] At the same time, the wealth of the Catholic Church would be conspicuously advertised by the rich mosaics and decoration.

To that end, Justinian initiated a building programme with the aim of re-organizing and re-decorating numerous North African cities with rich and monumental churches. The scale of this activity was such that Procopius ded-icated the whole of his De aedificiis 6 to Africa.[67] Procopius wrote that book to celebrate Justinian's accomplishments as a 'restorer of the state through victory; builder of cities, supporter of the true faith, codifier of the laws, bringer of internal harmony and external peace, strengthener of frontiers'.[68] The African material record gives credence to that description. Procopius offers detailed information of the building activity carried on in Carthage.[69] In par-ticular, he refers to a church dedicated to the Virgin Theotokos constructed in the proconsular palace and a fortified monastery called the Mandracium. In both cases the identification of the buildings is dubious.[70] In addition to details about those churches, Procopius gives information about the build-ing of baths named after the empress Theodora, the restoration of the city wall and the building of a ditch. The city of Carthage was, in other words, deeply re-organised during the Byzantine restoration and it is reasonable to think that more activities were carried out in the Justinian period. Procopius' description of Carthage can be contrasted to what he wrote about Justinian's building programme in Lepcis Magna, in Tripolitania.[71] In the case of Lepcis, he specifically emphasises churches because his aim is to highlight Justinian's divine inspiration. The construction of religious buildings can be seen as an attempt to promote orthodoxy.[72]

66 D. Pringle, The defence of Byzantine North Africa.
67 The book is probably unfinished and the sources used are of different qualities and reliability (Averil Cameron, 'Byzantine Africa – The literary evidence', 33).
68 Procopius, Aed. 1.1.6–11, trans. from Averil Cameron, Procopius and the sixth century, 86–7. The building activity resulted not only in religious complexes, but also in forts (see further Pringle, The defence of Byzantine North Africa).
69 Procopius, Aed. 6.5.8–11.
70 See Ennabli, Carthage and Duval, 'L'état actuel des recherches archéologiques sur Carthage chrétienne'; on the Mandracium, see H. Hurst, The sanctuary of Tanit at Carthage in the Roman period.
71 Procopius, Aed. 6.4.1–11.
72 See Cameron, 'Byzantine Africa – The literary evidence', 34.

Studies of the evidence from the Byzantine economy[73] show that bishops had important secular responsibilities.[74] The emperor was personally involved in the election of new bishops.[75] In Africa, as elsewhere, the bishops in effect became the chief secular officers in Byzantine towns.[76] The archaeological record suggests a stricter connection between churches and production from the end of the sixth century. Some churches were evidently enlarged to incorporate an olive press or to provide a place for craft activities. For example, at Sufetula (Sbeitla), in the basilica of Sts Gervasius, Protasius and Tryphon (Basilica V) an olive press was built across the principal street crossing the city.[77] There was apparently a connection between religious monuments and olive presses. In other parts of the Roman empire, a relation between production centres (especially for pottery, glass and bricks) and churches has been recorded.[78] In some cases at least, these shops were intentionally set up to produce material to decorate the church; in other cases, these centres were evidently used by the church itself for producing goods.

Another index of the importance of bishops is the sum total of them in North Africa, which reports the highest number of bishops within the empire. Compared with other Roman provinces, Africa already had a large group of bishops in the third century.[79] The organisation of the province favoured this trend. In Zeugitania the large number of urban settlements called for the creation of many bishoprics. Independent cities were not very far from each other in northeastern Tunisia: there were about 160 towns in 1200 km². Bishops were also placed in many rural agglomerations and even in the tribal territories.[80] This multiplication of bishoprics was exacerbated by the number

---

73 J. Durliat, 'Evêques et administration municipale au VIIe siècle'.
74 The case of Carthage is peculiar in this respect. As testified by epigraphy, it was subdivided into ecclesiastical regions (following the examples of Rome), perhaps by Aurelius between the end of the fourth century and the beginning of the fifth. Sources mentioned these regions in AD 403, 404, 407, 409, 410 (CCSL 149: 203, 208, 211, 214, 220), referring to the councils. Two of Augustine's *sermones*, moreover, refer to the *regio* III (PL 38: 116). All the other information we have that speaks of the *regiones* belongs to the Byzantine period.
75 J. Durliat, 'Les attributions civiles des évêques byzantins'; see also J. Durliat, 'Les grandes propriétaires africains et l'état byzantin'.
76 Durliat, 'Évêques et administration municipale au VIIe siècle'.
77 For some comments on this aspect see A. Leone, 'Topographies of production in North African cities', 264–5; for the urbanism of Byzantine Sufetula, see N. Duval, 'L'urbanisme de Sufetula-Sbeïtla en Tunisie'.
78 For a synthesis see A. Martorelli 'Riflessioni sulle attività produttive nell'età tardoantica e altomedievale'.
79 N. Duval, 'L'Évêque et la cathédrale en Afrique du nord', 345.
80 Y. Duval, 'Densité et répartition des évêchés'; sources attest to the Christianisation of local tribes starting from the fourth century, some of them being mentioned by Augustine (see Modéran, *Les Maures et l'Afrique romaine*, 512–31).

of schisms in the African church. At their peak, the trends resulted in about 700 bishops in North Africa at a single time.

During Heraclius' reign (610–41), the church faced the monothelite controversy concerning one or two wills in Jesus Christ. The implications of the crisis were felt very widely. Archaeological evidence shows the progressive abandonment of churches at the end of the seventh century. As a result, when the Arabs conquered Carthage in 698, the Catholic community was already seriously weakened. Archaeological data connected with churches are particularly difficult to interpret, because these structures were mainly excavated between the end of the nineteenth and the beginning of the twentieth centuries when stratigraphic information was seldom collected. Thus it is still impossible to clarify what the situation of the Catholic Church was when the Arabs arrived. Therefore we cannot state with certainty whether the churches were decaying before the Arab invasion or if they survived here (as they did in other regions, such as Jordan) into the first century of Arab domination.

Bibliography

PRIMARY SOURCES

Augustine C. litt. Petiliani (CSEL 52)
> City of God (CCSL 47, 48)
> Confessions, ed. J. J. O'Donnell (Oxford, 1992)
> Enarrationes in Psalmos (CCSL 38, 39, 40)
> Letters (CSEL 34$^{1-2}$, 44, 57, 58, 88)
> Psalmus contra partem Donati (CSEL 51)
> Sermons (PL 38, 39)
Concilia Africae a.345–a.525 (CCSL 149); for the Council of Carthage, 411, in particular, see
> S. Lancel's edition, SC 194, 195, 224, 373
(ps.–?) Ferrandus. Life of Fulgentius (PL 65: 117–50)
Gerontius. Life of Melania. Ed. P. Laurence, Gérontius. La vie latine de saint Mélanie (Jerusalem, 2002)
Liber pontificalis, ed. L. Duchesne (Paris, 1886, 1892); supplementary volume ed. C. Vogel (Paris, 1957)
Optatus. De scismate Donatistorum (SC 412, 413)
Passio Maximiani et Isaaci (PL 8: 767–74)
Paulinus of Nola. Carm. (PL 61: 437–710).
Possidius. Life of Augustine. Ed. A. A. R. Bastiaensen, Vite dei Santi: Vita di Cipriano, Vita di Ambrogio, Vita di Agostino (Milan, 1975)
Procopius. De aedeficiis. Ed. J. Haury and G. Wirth. Procopius. Opera omnia (Leipzig, 1962–4), IV
Prudentius. Peristephanon (PL 60: 275–590)
Symmachus. Letters, ed. J.-P. Callu (Paris, 1972–)
Tertullian. De spectaculiis (SC 332)

Victor of Vita, ed. S. Lancel. *Victor de Vita. Histoire de la persecution vandale en Afrique. La passion des sept martyrs. Registre des provinces et des cités afriques* (Paris, 2002)

SECONDARY SOURCES

Alexander, M. A., A. Ben Abed Khader, D. Soren and M. Spiro. *Thuburbo Majus. Les mosaïques de la region et mise à jour du catalogue de Thuburbo Maius et les environs. 2.4. Les mosaïques de Ain Mziger, Bir Chana, Draa Ben Jouder et Zaghouan* (Tunis, 1994)

Bagnall, R. S. *Egypt in late antiquity* (Princeton, 1993)

Bejaoui, F. 'Nouvelles données archéologiques à Sbeitla', *Africa* 14 (1996): 37–63

Brown, P. *Augustine of Hippo. A biography*, rev. edn. (London, 2000)

Religion and society in the age of Saint Augustine (London, 1972)

Buenacasa Pérez, C. 'La creación del patrimonio ecclesiástico de las iglesias norteafricanas en época romana (siglos ii–v): Renovación de la visión tradicional', *Sacralidad y arqueologia: homenaje al Prof. Thilo Ulbert*, Antigüedad y cristianismo 21, eds. J. Ma. Blázquez Martínez and A. González Blanco (Murcia, 2004)

Cameron, Averil. 1982. 'Byzantine Africa – the literary evidence', in J. H. Humphrey, ed., *Excavations at Carthage 1978 conducted by the University of Michigan. Carthage VII* (Ann Arbor, 1982), 29–62

Procopius and the sixth century (London, 1985)

'Vandal and Byzantine Africa', in Averil Cameron, Bryan Ward-Perkins and Michael Whitby, eds., *The Cambridge ancient history* (Cambridge, 2000), xiv: 552–69

Carton, L. 'Les lignes d'auges des églises et d'autres monuments de l'Afrique ancienne', in *Recueil des notices et memoires de la société archéologique de Constantine* (1915): 81–91

Courtois, Ch. *Les Vandales et l'Afrique* (Aalen, 1964)

Durliat, J. 'Les attributions civiles des évêques byzantins: L'exemple du diocèse d'Afrique (533–709)', in *Akten XVI Internationalen Byzantinistenkongress* (Vienna, 1982): 73–84

'Évêques et administration municipale au VIIe siècle', in C. Lepelley, ed., *La fin de la cité antique et le début de la cité médiévale de la fin du IIIe siècle à l'avènement de Charlemagne* (Bari, 1993), 273–86

'Les grandes propriétaires africains et l'état byzantin', *Les cahiers de Tunisie* 29 (1981): 517–22

Duval, N. 'Afrique', *Antiquité tardive* 8 (2000): 386–91

Les églises africaines à deux absides (Paris, 1973)

'Encore sur les monuments à auges d'Afrique: Tébessa Khalia, Hr. Faraoun', *MEFRA* 88 (1976): 929–59

'L'état actuel des recherches archéologiques sur Carthage chrétienne', *Antiquité tardive* 5 (1997): 309–47

'Études d'archéologie chrétienne nord-africaine: xvi. Une basilique chrétienne à deux absides à Sabratha (Tripolitaine)? La Basilique I: Une révision récente', *Revue des études augustiniennes* 33 (1987): 269–301

'L'évêque et la cathédrale en Afrique du nord', *Actes du XI congrès international d'archéologie chrétienne* (Lyon, 1989), ii: 345–403

'Les monuments chrétiens de Carthage', *Corsi di cultura sull'arte Ravennate e Bizantina* 19 (1972): 95–104

'L'urbanisme de Sufetula-Sbeïtla en Tunisie', *ANRW* ii, 10.2 (1982): 596–632

Duval, N. and J. C. Golvin. 'Haidra à l'époque chrétienne. Le monument à auges et les bâtiments similaires', *CRAI* (1972): 133–73

Duval, Y. 'Densité et répartition des évêchés dans les provinces africaines au temps de Cyprien', *MEFRA* 96 (1984): 493–521

Ennabli, L. *La Basilique de Carthagenna et le locus de sept moines de Gafsa* (Paris, 2000)

Carthage. Une métropole chrétienne du IV à la fin du VII siècle (Paris, 1997)

Les inscriptions funéraires chrétiennes de Carthage, II: La basilique de Mcidfa, CollÉFR 62 (Rome, 1982)

De Francesco, D. 'Chiesa Romana e proprietà fondiaria nel suburbio tra il IV secolo e l'età gregoriana. Riflessioni e problemi', in P. Pergola, R. Santangeli Valenzani and R. Volpe, eds., *Il suburbio di Roma dalla crisi del sistema delle ville a Gregorio Magno*, CollÉFR 311 (Rome, 2003), 515–43

'Le donazioni costantiniane nell'Agro Romano', *Vetera Christianorum* 27 (1990): 47–75

Frend, W. H. C. *The Donatist church* (Oxford, 1952, 1971²)

The rise of the Monophysite movement (Cambridge, 1972)

Gavigan, I. I. *De vita monastica in Africa septentrionali inde a temporibus S. Augustini usque ad invasiones Arabum*, Biblioteca Augustiniana Medii Aevi – Series II (Rome, 1962)

Giardina, A. 'Carità eversiva: Le donazioni di Melania la Giovane e gli equilibri della società tardoromana', *Studi storici* 29 (1988): 127–42

Gilliard, F. D. 'Senatorial bishops in the 4th century', *HTR* 77 (1984): 153–75

Harries, J. and I. Wood. *The Theodosian Code. Studies in the imperial law of late antiquity* (London, 1993)

Hugoniot, Chr. *Rome en Afrique. De la chute de Carthage aux débuts de la conquête arabe* (Paris, 2000)

Hurst, H. *The sanctuary of Tanit at Carthage in the Roman period* (Ann Arbor, 1999)

Jaïdi, H. 'Remarques sur la constitution des biens des églises africaines à l'époque romaine tardive', in A. Chastagnol, S. Demougin and C. Lepelley, eds., *Splendidissima civitas. Études d'histoire romaine en hommage à François Jacques* (Paris, 1996), 169–91

Kolendo, T. 'La hiérarchie des procurateurs dans l'inscription d'Ain-el-Djemala (CIL VIII, 25943)', *REL* 46 (1968): 319–29

Lancel, S. 'L'affaire d'Antoninus de Fussala: Pays, choses et gens de la Numidie d'Hippone, saisis dans la durée d'une procédure d'enquête épiscopale', in *Les lettres de Saint Augustine découvertes par J. Divjak* (Paris, 1982), 267–85

Leone, A. 'Topographies of production in North African cities during the Vandal and Byzantine periods', in L. Lavan and W. Bowden, eds., *Theory and practice in late antique archaeology* (Leiden, 2003), 255–87

Leone, A. and D. J. Mattingly. 'Vandal, Byzantine and Arab rural landscapes in North Africa', in N. Christie, ed., *Landscapes of change. Rural evolutions in late antiquity and early middle ages* (Aldershot, 2004), 135–63

Lepelley, C. 'Deux témoignages de Saint Augustin sur l'acquisition d'un domaine impérial à bail emphytéotique', *BCTH* 17B (1984): 273–83

'Le patronat épiscopal aux IVᵉ et Vᵉ siècles: Continuités et ruptures avec le patronat classique', in É. Rebillard and C. Sotinel, eds., *L'évêque dans la cité du IVᵉ au VIᵉ siècle. Image et autorité*, CollÉFR 248 (Rome, 1998), 17–33

Leschi, L. 'Basilique et cimitière donatistes de Numidie', *Revue africaine* 68 (1936): 35–47

Mahjoubi, A. *Recherches d'histoire et d'archéologie à Henchir el-Faouar, Tunisie: La cité des Belalitani Maiores* (Tunis, 1978)

Marazzi, F. *I 'patrimonia Sanctae Romanae Ecclesiae' nel Lazio (secoli IV–X): Struttura amministrativa e prassi gestionali* (Rome, 1998)

Martorelli, A. 'Riflessioni sulle attività produttive nell'età tardoantica e altomedievale: Esiste un artigianato ecclesiastico?', *Rivista di archeologia cristiana* 75 (1999): 571–96

Mazzarino, S. *Antico, tardoantico ed era costantiniana* (Rome, 1974)

Millar, F. 'Italy and the Roman empire: Augustus to Constantine', *Phoenix* (1986): 295–318

Modéran, Y. 'L'Afrique et la persécution vandale', *Histoire du christianisme* (Paris, 1998), III: 247–78

'L'établissement territorial des vandales en Afrique', *Antiquité tardive* 10 (2002): 87–122

Les Maures et l'Afrique romaine (IVᵉ–VIIᵉ siècle), Bibliothèque des Écoles françaises d'Athènes et de Rome 314 (Rome, 2003)

Monceaux, P. *Histoire littéraire de l'Afrique chrétienne depuis les origines jusqu'à l'invasion arabe* (Paris, 1920)

Séance du 8 Juillet, *BSNAF* (1903): 283–5

Nestori, A. 'Una ipotesi sugli edifici "à auges" africani', *RendPontAcc* 53–4 (1980–2): 313–23

Picard, G.-Ch. *La Carthage de St. Augustin* (Paris, 1967)

Pietri, C. *Roma Christiana. Recherches sur l'église de Rome, son organisation, sa politique, son idéologie de Miltiade à Sixte III (311–440)* (Rome, 1976)

'Une schola de collège à Carthage', *CRAI* (1952): 215–18

Prévot, F. *Recherches archéologiques franco-tunisienne à Mactar. V. Les inscriptions chrétiennes*, CollÉFR 34 (Rome, 1984)

Pringle, D. *The defence of Byzantine North Africa* (Oxford, 1981)

Saxer, V. *Morts, martyrs, reliques en Afrique chrétienne aux premiers siècles. Les témoignages de Tertullien, Cyprien et Augustin à la lumière de l'archéologie africaine* (Paris, 1980)

Vera, D. 'Conductores domus nostrae, conductores privatorum. Concentrazione fondiaria e redistribuzione della ricchezza nell'Africa tardoantica', in M. Christol, S. Demougin, Y. Duval, C. Lepelley and L. Pietri, eds., *Institutions, société et vie politique dans l'empire romain au IV siècle ap. J.C.*, CollÉFR 159 (Rome, 1992), 465–90

'Enfiteusi, colonato e trasformazioni agrarie nell'Africa Proconsolare del tardo impero', *Africa Romana* 4 (1988): 267–93

'*Massa fundorum*. Forme della grande proprietà e poteri della città in Italia fra Costantino e Gregorio Magno', *MEFRA* 11.2 (1999): 931–1025

'Terra e lavoro nell'Africa romana', *Studi storici* 4 (1988): 967–92

10

The intellectual debate between Christians and pagans

ALAN BROWN

The character of Christian–pagan debate

Intellectual debate between 'Christians' and 'pagans'

To juxtapose 'paganism' and 'Christianity' in late antiquity is not to compare like with like. 'Christianity' designates a specific religious tradition, anchored materially and semantically in the recognition of the crucified and risen Jesus of Nazareth as Christ and Lord.[1] 'Paganism', on the other hand, demarcates indiscriminately the whole stretch of Greco-Roman religious belief, myth, rite and ritual,[2] whose phenomena originate variously in Greece, Rome, Asia Minor, Egypt, Mesopotamia and Persia.[3]

Such lack of specificity is due to the term 'pagan' itself. The very demarcation of Greco-Roman religion generally by means of the term *paganus* – a word that previously designated 'that which is inferior' – was an innovation of fourth- and fifth-century Latin Christian Orthodoxy. It constituted part of Christianity's successful attempt to achieve lexicographical self-differentiation from the religious world of the pre-Christian Roman empire that had surrounded it from its earliest days.[4]

Consequently, when we speak of 'Christian–pagan intellectual debate', we are not concerned with a debate between the articulate representatives of two confessional groupings. Rather, 'intellectual debate between pagans and Christians' designates all the intellectual arguments on religious matters that late antique Christians had with anyone and everyone who was neither Christian nor Jewish.

---

1 Michael J. Wilkins, 'Christian'; Wolfhart Pannenberg, *Jesus – God and Man*, 53–88.
2 Cf. R. MacMullen, *Paganism*; A. H. Armstrong, ed., *Classical Mediterranean spirituality*.
3 Cf. e.g. the lists of gods in Lucian, *Jup. trag.* 8f., 12; Athenagoras, *Leg.* 14; Eusebius, *De laud. Const.* 13.4f.; Minucius Felix, *Octavius* 6.1.
4 See Peter Brown, 'Pagan'.

The form of debate

Despite this internal heterogeneity of paganism, late antique Christian–pagan intellectual debate possessed considerable uniformity. For it was always conducted with reference to the framework of the Platonic philosophical thought of the day. This framework formally unified the discussions and arguments between pagans and Christians. The pagans expressed themselves within this framework, while the Christians correlated Christianity – whose primary conceptual framework is that of late-Jewish apocalyptic – critically with this framework which pagan intellectuals took for granted.

True *Logos*, appearance and allegory

At the heart of this Platonic framework was the opposition of the true *logos* (meaning) of being to the literally understood μύθοι of the poets, a distinction stretching back to pre-Socratic philosophy.[5] This determined a basic stance of critical opposition to all religion insofar as it was tied to a literal reading of the poetic myths.

Within this framework, such myth – and the pagan religion articulated in terms of it – was salvaged through modes of allegorical interpretation, modes that originated in Hellenistic Stoicism.[6] These were premised upon the belief that the ancients had possessed a wisdom containing the true *logos* of being now generally forgotten.[7] They expressed this ontology symbolically; later, the poets, not understanding these symbols, incorporated them within their fabulous stories.[8] Thus while the myths were literally nonsense, hidden within them was the true ontology of the ancients, and this could be recovered through techniques of allegorical interpretation of the appropriate sections of the poetic myths.[9] *A fortiori*, pagan religious practices that were articulated in terms of mythical discourse need not be understood as enactments of specious nonsense, but could be recognised rather as symbolic modes of action in which one conformed to true being.

---

5 Cf. e.g. Xenophanes, DK 21b 11–16; Heraclitus, DK 22b 1, 2; Parmenides, DK 28b 1.29–30, 2.3–5, 6.1–2, 7.3.

6 Cf. Charles Kannengeisser, *Handbook of patristic exegesis*, 1: 248–55; G. R. Boys-Stones, *Post-Hellenic philosophy*.

7 Thus, Cornutus, *De natura deorum* 35.75.18–76.5: 'the ancients were no ordinary men, but capable of understanding the cosmos and inclined to use symbols and riddles in their philosophical discussions of it'. Cf. Aristotle, *Meta.* Λ.8, 1074b1–14 and, for the general background to this way of thought, Hesiod, *Op. et dies* 106–201.

8 Cf. Cicero, *Nat. deor.* 11.63, 70.

9 For examples of such exegesis see Plutarch, *Is. et Os.*; Porphyry, *Ant. nymph.* Cf. Sallustius, *Deis et mundo*, 3–4.

The morphology of mythological interpretation

I. Being and becoming, soul and body

In practice, the allegorical interpretation of pagan myth and ritual consisted in the interpretation of paganism in terms of late antique Platonic philosophical thought. Fundamental to the conceptual morphology of such Platonism was the opposition of eternal being (*ousia*) to temporal becoming (*genesis*), an opposition delineated principally by Plato.[10] For the Plato of the middle dialogues, what one knows when one knows the meaning (*logos*) of an abstract term (e.g. 'justice', 'goodness', 'beauty') is a 'Form' or 'Idea'. The Form is the timeless immaterial being (*ousia*) by which particular changeable material beings were beings (*onta*). Such beings exist by 'participation' (*methexis, koinônia*) in the Form.[11]

Since the Form-as-*ousia* was what one understood of the material being-in-*genesis*, *ousia* was equated with the intelligible, and γένεσις with the material and sensible. This in turn grounded the Platonic division of soul from body. The soul belonged to the intelligible realm, the body to the sensory. Whereas the body *qua* corporeal was mortal, the soul, *qua* self-moved, was eternal; as such, it existed before the body and would continue to exist after the body's demise.[12] Personal identity was located in the soul, not the body. The soul and not the body was taken to have a 'kinship' to the divine,[13] and was understood to be in the body either as a punishment,[14] or as a result of natural necessity (*ananke*).[15] Either way, its connection to the body was an unhappy affair, and fulfilment of the person required the soul's liberation from the body.

II. Divine Intellect

For Plato himself, the Forms were conceived as independent beings. Later Platonists, however, rejected such a notion and, from the first century BC, combined the doctrine of the Forms with the Aristotelian notion of a Supreme and Divine Intellectual Principle (*archê*). For Aristotle this Principle was an individual immaterial being (*ousia*), understood as pure self-reflexive Intellect, 'thought thinking itself' (νόησις νοήσεως).[16] The Platonists now identified the

---

10 Plato, *Tim.* 27e–28a.
11 Plato, *Phaedo* 65d–e, 100c.
12 Plato, *Phaedr.* 245b–e.
13 Plato, *Phaedo* 80a.
14 Plato, *Crat.* 400c; *Phaedo* 62b.
15 Plato, *Resp.* 617d.
16 Aristotle, *Meta.* Λ.9, 1074b34–6; Λ.7, 1072b14–31.

Forms with the thoughts of this Supreme Intellect.[17] And as the Forms were identified with true being (*ousia*) – not becoming – this Intellect was equated with being (*ousia*) itself and was opposed to the realm of becoming.

III. Creation

The relation of this Intellect to the creation of the cosmos was, however, controversial among Platonists. In the *Timaeus*, Plato had depicted the cosmos mythologically as created at some past moment of time by a demiurge who, using the Forms as ideal models,[18] forged the world from pre-existent matter as an ensouled being,[19] forming in the process *chronos* – i.e., regular cyclical time measured by the rotation of the heavenly spheres.[20] While later Platonists all sought to correlate their account of creation to this account, how they did so differed from Platonist to Platonist. Some identified the demiurge with the Intellectual Principle (so that the Divine Intellect was understood as creator), while others took the demiurge to be subordinate to the Divine Intellect (since the demiurge looked to the Forms which are the intellections of the Divine Intellect). Moreover, it was controversial among Platonists whether the creation of the ensouled world was to be conceived of as taking place in time (as per the Timaeus-myth),[21] or whether 'creation' had to be seen as eternal – on the grounds that the Intellectual Principle, being equated with the eternal Forms, had itself to be eternal, and so could not act in time.[22]

IV. The One and Good beyond Intellect

Similarly, there was divergence over whether the Divine Intellect (however understood) was to be understood as the Supreme Principle. In the Republic, Plato had taken the 'Form of the Good' – which he later equated with 'the One'[23] – to be beyond all other Forms. In that these other Forms were identified with the level of being (*ousia*), the Form of the Good was asserted to be 'beyond being' (ἐπέκεινα τῆς οὐσίας).[24] And since *ousia* was what was understood when one understood something, the Form of the Good, as beyond *ousia*, was

---

17 Albinus, *Intr.* 4; Atticus ap. Eusebius *Praep. ev.* 15.13.4–5; Alcinous, *Epit.* 9–10; Seneca *Ep.* 65.7; Plotinus, *Enn.* v.5; Syrianus, *In meta.* 106.26–107.1.

18 Plato, *Tim.* 29a.

19 Ibid., 34b–37a.

20 Cf. W. K. C. Guthrie, *History*, v: 299.

21 Thus Plutarch, *De an. proc. in Tim.*; Atticus, ap. Eusebius, *Praep. Ev.* xv.6. Cf. also the review of earlier writers holding this position in Proclus, *In Tim.* 1.276–7, 381–2.

22 So Calvisius Taurus (ap. Philoponus, *De aet. m.* vi.21; ed. Rabe, p. 186.17); Albinus, *Intro.* 10, 14; Proclus, *Aet. mund.*

23 Cf. Aristotle, *Meta.* A.6, 987b14–35.

24 Plato, *Resp.* 509c.

thereby beyond definition, *logos* and intelligibility. Thus Plato postulated the One / Good as a Supreme Principle beyond the reach of intellect.

Later Platonists who identified the Forms with the Divine Intellect oscillated on how to follow Plato here. Plato's identification of the Supreme Principle with the Good entailed that value was to be equated with ontological proximity to the Supreme Principle; in this all subsequent Platonists concurred. But they differed among themselves on how to correlate Plato's One / Good with the Divine Intellect. For some, the two were to be identified;[25] while for others, the One / Good was to be posited as a subsistence (*hypostasis*) above and beyond that of the Divine Intellect,[26] thereby asserting the Supreme Principle to be incomprehensibly beyond the reach of intellectuality.[27] As late antiquity progressed, the latter position became dominant.

V. Providence, daemons and divinity

For those forms of Platonism which exalted the One as Supreme Principle beyond Intellect, it was taken for granted that this One did not exercise providence: the One was too exalted to be related directly to the ordering of the material world.[28] It was controversial, however, whether the transcendent Intellect could be understood as provident.[29] Those who denied direct providence understood the governance of the world to be carried out by divine and daemonic intermediaries. These were imagined as standing midway in the ontological hierarchy between the transcendent Principles and the changeable world, the gods standing hierarchically above the daemons.[30] Belief in the daemonic, however, was presumed by Platonists generally (after all, Plato spoke of Socrates himself as having a *daemon*).[31] Despite this distinction between daemons, gods and the uppermost Principles, all were taken to be 'divine' (*theios*), on the grounds that in Greek to be *theios* meant simply to be immortal and to have a power beyond that possessed naturally by humans.[32]

VI. Religion and human fulfilment

The understanding of the connection of pagan religion to human fulfilment followed from this. Fulfilment was identified with the attainment to that which

---

25 E.g., Plutarch, *Is. et Os.* 77, 382c; Numenius of Apamea, ap. Proclus, *In Tim.* 3.103.28–32.

26 Cf. Plotinus, *Enn.* v.i.

27 So Alcinous, *Epit.* 4, 10.

28 Cf. Apuleius, *Deo Socr.* 3.

29 For Platonists vehemently supportive of the notion that the divine Intellect *does* exercise providence, cf. Plutarch, *De def. or.* 30, 426c; Atticus, ap. Eusebius, *Praep. Ev.* xv.5.

30 Cf. Maximus of Tyre, *Dial.* 57.8.

31 Plato, *Apol.* 31d; cf. Apuleius, *Deo Socr.*

32 Cf. E. R. Dodds, *Pagan and Christian*, 74.

was most valuable – i.e. the uppermost divine principles. Such attainment consisted of both the realisation of likeness (*homoiôsis*) and of union (*henôsis*) with divinity.[33]

What connected this with commitment to pagan ritual was the notion of the transcendent remoteness of the divine principles. Because these principles were unreachable by humanity unaided, it followed that they could not be attained by man directly, but only through daemonic mediation. As such, pagan ritual was justified in that it was through participation in such ritual that human beings sought and attained the daemonic intermediation that was necessary for their own fulfilment.[34]

The pagan rejection of Christianity

Polemical pagan rejections of Christianity

This Platonic framework of thought provided the conceptual ground upon which Christians and pagans debated and argued. Historically, this debate began in the first Christian centuries when intellectual pagans objected that specific fundamental aspects of Christianity could not be coherently understood in terms of this Platonic framework, and that Christianity therefore had to be rejected as *alogon* (irrationally meaningless).[35] This tradition is represented paradigmatically by Celsus' second-century *Alêthês logos*, by Porphyry's third-century *Contra Christianos* and by Julian the Apostate's fourth-century *Contra Galileos*, all of which were still being read and refuted through to at least the middle of the fifth century (when, in 448, the burning of *Contra Christianos* was ordered).

Aside from politically motivated accusations that Christians were disloyal to the empire, the basis of such intellectual pagan attacks on Christianity was the denial of any legitimate allegorical interpretation of the Christian scriptures.[36] From here, intellectual pagans mocked the narratives of the Christian scriptures as metaphysically absurd,[37] and raised a number of exegetical *aporiai* for biblical interpretation.[38] They rejected the call of the gospel to the ungodly on

---

33 E.g. Plato, *Tim.* 176b; Iamblichus, *Myst.* 1.12.
34 For such reasoning, see esp. Maximus of Tyre, *Dial.* 8.8c–d. Cf. 8.8a–f; 11.12a–e.
35 Cf. P. de Labriolle, *La réaction païenne*; J. Geffcken, *The last days of Greco-Roman paganism*; R. L. Wilken, *The Christians as the Romans saw them*; P. Chauvin, *A chronicle of the last pagans*; S. Benko, 'Pagan criticisms of Christianity during the first two centuries AD'.
36 E.g. Celsus, ap. Origen, *Contr. Cels.* 4.48–51; Porphyry ap. Eusebius, *Hist. Eccl.* 6.19.
37 Origen, *Contr. Cels.* 1.28.
38 This is evident throughout the pagan works. Cf., e.g., Porphyry ap. Jerome, *Ep.* 57.8–9; Julian, *Contr. Gal.* 1.214–15 for discussions of Isaiah 7.14.

the grounds that the gods were well disposed to the righteous, not to sinners.[39] Beyond this, and most fundamentally, intellectual pagans rejected Christian faith in the incarnation and resurrection upon the basis of their incompatibility with late antique Platonism. For, according to the morphology of Platonic thought, value was to be equated with ontological proximity to the Supreme Principle. Therefore matter, as that which was understood as being furthest removed in existence from the Supreme Principle, was the least valuable mode of being. As a result, it made no sense within this frame of thought for the supreme divinity – already possessed of all that is valuable – to join itself to worthless matter in incarnation,[40] nor for the immaterial souls of the blessed, when freed from the body by death, to be re-united with those bodies for eternity in corporeal resurrection.[41]

Ontological conservatism

In general, however, the political triumph of Christianity meant that – excepting the brief rule of Julian the Apostate – the period of the fourth to seventh centuries was not one in which pagans were free to compose polemical refutations of Christianity. Rather, during this period, pagan intellectual interaction with Christianity was primarily indirect, taking place through the conservative maintenance and articulation of pagan Platonic ontological interpretations of religion. The visible upholding of such understandings in a Christian empire, understandings which were fundamentally incompatible with Christianity, constituted a quiet but firm intellectual rejection of Christianity. This was the principal means by which pagan intellectuals during this period engaged Christianity intellectually.

Anti-ritualism in third-century philosophy

But the primary form which this anti-Christian philosophy took was determined not by specifically anti-Christian argumentation, but by the rejection of particular monistic and anti-ritualistic trends in the third-century Platonic philosophies of Plotinus and his disciple Porphyry. These trends did not deny the existence of pagan gods and daemons, but considered their invocation and supplication irrelevant for the attainment of human fulfilment,[42] this being attainable only through the philosophical life.

---

39 Origen, *Contr. Cels.* 3.59; Cf. Julian, *Caes.* 336B.
40 Cf. Origen, *Contr. Cels.* 4.14; Porphyry, *Contr. Chr.* fr. 77.
41 Cf. Origen, *Contr. Cels.* 5.14.
42 Cf. Porphyry, *Vit. Plot.* 10.

I. Plotinus

For Plotinus, the highest ontological principles were immediately present to the core of the self,[43] so that the self can attain to them – and hence attain to the fulfilment of his being – by a solitary turn inwards and upwards (μόνου πρὸς μόνον).[44] One turns inwards to one's soul, and, since the highest point of the soul remains in the intellectual realm, one discovers at the metaphysical height of oneself the presence of the hypostasis of Intellect.[45] Beyond this, one goes beyond oneself, laying aside all otherness – even the otherness of Intellect – and attains union with the supreme hypostasis of the One.[46] Such ascent to union required no tertiary intermediaries,[47] so supplication of gods and daemons – and hence pagan ritual in general – is unnecessary.

At the root of this position was Plotinus' view that the notions of 'distance' and 'remoteness' were spatial categories belonging to the ontological domain of bodies, and that these categories had no application to higher (supracorporeal) levels of being.[48] The uppermost Principles of Intellect and One, being beyond the domain of the bodily, were themselves everywhere present, and as such were neither ontologically remote nor distant from human beings.[49] Rather, the human being, at his highest point, was united ontologically to the hypostasis of Intellect,[50] and thereby to the One which was directly constitutive of such Intellect.[51]

II. Porphyry

This rejection of hierarchical remoteness was radicalised by Porphyry, who 'telescoped' the principal hypostases of One, Intellect and Soul – hypostases that Plotinus had insisted were distinct, although not separate[52] – to the point of fusion. First the distinction between soul and intellect was denied outright.[53] Second, the One was fused with Intellect by means of a triadic analysis of Intellect. The One was understood as pure existence (*hyparxis, einai*)[54] whose *energeia* proceeded as life[55] and which reverted back to the One as

---

43 Cf. Plotinus, *Enn.* VI.4.14.17ff.
44 Plotinus, *Enn.* VI.9.9.51.
45 Plotinus, *Enn.* V.1.10.
46 Plotinus, *Enn.* VI.9.7–11.
47 Cf. e.g. the accounts of ascent in Plotinus, *Enn.* V.1; VI.9.
48 Cf., ibid., VI.1.1–4, 14, VI.2.15–16.
49 E.g., ibid., VI.4.3 (for Intellect) and III.9.4 (for the One).
50 Cf. ibid., VI.4.14.
51 Cf. ibid., V.1.11.
52 Cf. ibid., II.9.1.
53 Cf. Iamblichus, ap. Stobaeus, *Ecl.* 365.16–1.
54 Porphyry, *In Parm.* 12.23–7.
55 Ibid., 14.7–8.

intellection,[56] thus constituting the hypostasis of Intellect as a triad of *hyparxis–zoê–noêsis*.[57] Thus the One was the first triadic moment of Intellect, not remotely transcendent of it. The combination of such telescoping with Porphyry's firm location of human identity in the soul (and not in the body or the soul–body compound)[58] meant that there was no ontological hierarchy separating the human being (as soul/intellect) from the supreme principle (Intellect with the One as its first triadic term). The supreme principle could be attained entirely through intellectual introversion and ascent, and required no participation in pagan ritual. (Thus, although Porphyry attempted to provide positive interpretations of pagan religious phenomena,[59] he never succeeded in finding a universal justification of paganism consonant with his own ontology.)[60]

The Iamblichean tradition of philosophical paganism

The philosophical tradition which rejected this Plotinian–Porphyrian indifference to ritual and whose views became the conservative norm for intellectual pagans in the fourth to seventh centuries was the tradition founded by the Syrian philosopher Iamblichus of Chalcis, a former pupil of Porphyry. It was founded by Iamblichus' polemical *De mysteriis*, a text written in response to a variety of criticisms mounted by Porphyry to pagan ritual practices. Iamblichus presented his response as an exposition of the combined *mystagogia* of the Egyptians and that of the Chaldaeans, which he took to be the basis of Greek wisdom,[61] and which he considered to provide the true *logos* in terms of which pagan religion was to be understood.[62] The account which Iamblichus and his successors provided sought to demonstrate the necessity of pagan ritual through the articulation of an ontological hierarchy which required the ritually invoked mediation of intermediate beings were humans to reach the highest principles whose attainment constituted humans' fulfilment.

I. The re-interpretation of participation

The basic metaphysical commitment which justified and underlay Iamblichean anti-Porphyrian hierarchicalism was that of the denial of the presence of one

---

56 Ibid., 14.19–20.
57 Ibid., 14.15–16.
58 Cf. Porphyry, *Ad Marcellam* 280.22.
59 Cf. esp. Porphyry, *De philosophia ex oraculis*; *De regressu animae* and the *Epistula ad Anebonem*.
60 Cf. Augustine, *Civ. Dei.* 10.32.
61 Iamblichus, *Myst.* 1.1.2–3.
62 Ibid., 1.1.4.

level of the ontological hierarchy in another level. This was affected through a re-interpretation of the traditional Platonic language of 'participation'.

For Plato, the participation of many entities in one Form signified the undivided and ontologically constitutive presence of the one Form in the many entities. On such a scheme, that which is participated-in (to metechomenon), in virtue of the fact that it belongs to the realm of οὐσία not γένεσις, has existence in itself (kath' auto). Yet, because it is immediately present undividedly in its participant (metechon), it is also present in another (eis allo) which subsists on the level of genesis not ousia. Thus, in a participatory relationship, to metechon has directly present to it, in ontologically constitutive fashion, a being of higher ontological level.

In opposition to such an understanding, the Iamblichean tradition understood participation as a threefold relationship between the participant (to metechon), the participated (to metechomenon) and the unparticipated (to amethekton).[63] Now, what exists kath' auto is to amethekton, which now causes to metechomenon, which in its turn exists only eis allo, in to metechon. In concrete situations of participation, there is one amethekton that causes several metechomena each of which exists with a metechon.[64] The unparticipated cause is a 'monad' that causes a 'series' (seira, taxis) of metechomena, in which metechonta participate.[65]

A fortiori, within the series of metechomena, there are distinguished two sorts of causal effects of to amethekton, one consisting of internally complete metechomena (αὐτοτελῶν ὑποστάσεων), and the other consisting of irradiations which have their substantiality in something other than themselves (ἐλλάμψεων ἐν ἑτέροις τὴν ὑπόστασιν κεκτημένων).[66] This distinction pertains to the level of subsistence (hypostasis) rather than of content. All metechomena belong in content to the ontological level that is the ontological level of the monad from which they proceed. But metechomena which are irradiations do not subsist at that ontological level. Rather, they subsist at the ontological level of ta metechonta of which they are ta metechomena. Conversely, internally complete metechomena cause ta metechonta that participate in them to subsist at their own level. This in turn means that it is possible for a being to subsist at a higher level than that of its content.

Two consequences follow from this. On the one hand, no being of a higher level of subsistence than that of a particular being is directly present within that

---

63 On what follows cf. Proclus, El. theol. 23–4. Cf. also El. theol. 67–9; Proclus, In Tim. 1.426.3ff.
64 Cf. Proclus, In Tim. 11.252.21ff.; 312.30ff.; Proclus, In Alc. 65.16ff.
65 Proclus, El. theol. 21.
66 Ibid., 64.

being (only irradiations of higher levels are thus present, but subsisting at that being's own subsistential level). On the other hand, a being may participate in another (subsistent) being such that it subsists at the higher level of that in which it participates. From these follow (a) the Iamblichean tradition's denial of the possibility of the Plotinian understanding of the attainment of human fulfilment through an individual turn to one's interiority; (b) its re-affirmation (essentially against Porphyry) of a multi-layered and gradiated ontological hierarchy; and (c) its own view that fulfilment – which it equates with the divine level, topped by the One – can be attained only through pagan theurgical ritual.

II. The rejection of the attainment of fulfilment through a turn to interiority
Upon this basis follows the Iamblichean tradition's rejection of the Plotinian understanding of the attainment of human fulfilment through a turn to inte-riority. For no hypostasis of a higher level of subsistence is present within a being. Since human beings subsist at the level of embodied soul, neither the One, nor the Intellect, nor any other divine principle is present within them. (Only their irradiations are thus present.) As such no such principle may be attained through an unaided turn to one's interiority.

III. The re-affirmation of the ontological hierarchy
Upon the basis of this general understanding of participatory hierarchy, philosophers in the Iamblichean tradition then stressed there to be several different levels to this hierarchy. Not only did they reject the Porphyrian col-lapse of the ontological hierarchy; they discriminated several new levels beyond those that had previously been discriminated by Platonists.

a. Soul First, against Porphyry, Iamblichus and his successors insisted strongly on the distinction of soul and intellect.[67] The motivation for this was the belief that pure intellect, being eternal, required an intermediary to link it to the temporal world of sensible reality.[68] This intermediary was soul, which was understood to be in essence eternal, but in activity temporal.[69]
The distinction thus postulated between the orders of intellect and soul meant that, on the principles of the Iamblichean tradition's metaphysics, there had to be both an intellectual series and a psychical series. The unparticipated Intellect caused the existence of participable intellects, and the unparticipated Soul caused the existence of participable souls. Each intellectual soul (including

67 Iamblichus, ap. Stobaeus, Ecl. 1.36.5–21.
68 Cf. Proclus, El. theol. 29, 55.
69 Cf. ibid., 191.

pre-eminently the unparticipated Soul) participated in a self-complete intellect, so that such souls had their subsistence on the level at which the intellect in which they participated subsisted. Other souls possessed only an irradiation of intellect, and accordingly subsisted either at the level of soul (were they self-complete souls), or at the lower level of that which participated in them (were they incomplete souls).

Moreover, since souls which participated in self-complete intellects subsisted at a suprapsychical level, they actualised the highest form of intellectual activity possible for them – namely temporally ceaseless intellection (in contrast to intermittent or periodic intellection).[70] Conversely, however, this meant that souls which did not possess ceaseless intellection did not participate in the self-complete intellects, but possessed (at best) irradiations of intellect which subsisted at the level of soul.[71] And as this is the case with human beings, it follows that the subsistential level of intellect is in no way directly present to the human soul; rather, all that is directly present to human beings is the irradiation of intellect existing psychically.[72] As such, no human soul can turn within itself and discover the highest principles of being (whether – now unparticipated – Intellect, the One or any other of the highest principles which the Iamblichean tradition would add). Rather, it can only find within itself irradiated effects that subsisted at its own ontological level.

b. Intellect At the intellectual level, the Iamblichean tradition combined the Porphyrian triadic analysis of Intellect into Being (ὄν), Life and Intellect with the Plotinian denial that Intellect could constitute the Supreme Principle. But they radicalised this distinction, discriminating Being, Life and Intellect respectively as three separate Hypostases, with Being ontologically prior to Life, and Life ontologically prior to Intellect.[73] The primary motive for this was the rejection of the Plotinian equation of the act of intellection with the intelligible, on the grounds that the object of intellection had to proceed its intellect. Hence Being (ὄν) was identified as 'the Intelligible' (*to noêton*);[74] and Intellect as 'the Intellectual' (*to noeron*).[75] Life, which came midway between these, was accorded the median appellation of 'the Intelligible and Intellectual' (*to noêton kai noeron*).[76]

70 Ibid., 175, 184, 211.
71 Ibid., 211.
72 Proclus, *In Tim.* 3.333.28ff.; *El. theol.* 211; Simplicius, *De an.* 6.12–17.
73 Proclus, *El. theol.* 101.
74 Ibid., 161.
75 Proclus, *Th. Plat.* 5.1.5.
76 Ibid., 4.1.5.

As a result, being, life and intellect each constituted separate series. Each had an unparticipated monad at its head (Unparticipated Being, Unparticipated Life, Unparticipated Intellect), which caused the existence of participable terms of the series (participable beings, participable lives, participable intellects), some of which subsisted on the same ontological level as the monad, others of which subsisted at lower ontological levels. Thus for example, a participable being could be self-complete and subsist at the level of being; or it could be an irradiation that only subsisted in the lower level of soul, so that it only subsisted at the ontological level of soul.

c. Henads and the One For the Iamblichean tradition, the fact that each being was one being meant that each being participated in unity, which is to say, that each being participated in the ὑπόστασις of the One. Therefore, according to the Iamblichean tradition's understanding of participation, one had to distinguish here between *to amethekton, ta metechomena* and *ta metechonta*. Each being, insofar as it is one being, is a *metechon* that participates in a *metechomenon* that is caused to exist by *to amethekton*. This *amethekton* stands as the monad at the head of the series of *metechomena*. The One is then identified as the unparticipated cause of the participable 'ones' (*henades*),[77] each of which is participated in by one being, making it to be one being. Furthermore, in line with the Iamblichean tradition's understanding of a series, there must be distinguished self-complete henads from henads that have subsistence only as irradiations in lower levels of being. Thus, for example, the henad by which a subsistent human soul is one soul is an irradiation which subsists only in the human soul, and so subsists at the ontological level of soul – a far lower subsistential level than that of a self-complete henad subsisting above the level of being.

d. The One and the Ineffable The only significant divergence of opinion within the Iamblichean tradition concerned whether the One was in fact the Supreme Principle. Iamblichus himself, and later Damascius, held that it was not, that beyond the One lay a higher principle, which could be identified only as πάντῃ ἄρρητος ('entirely unlimited').[78] This was on the grounds that unity has meaning only relative to plurality, and therefore cannot be an absolute principle beyond relativity, so that there must be an absolute principle beyond the One from which the One comes forth as One.[79] For Syrianus and Proclus, however, the postulation of a principle beyond the One was unnecessary, since

---

77 Cf. Proclus, *El. theol.* 113–16.
78 Iamblichus, ap. Damascius, *De princ.* 1.86.
79 Cf. Damascius, *De princ.* 1.4–6.

it was only the henads which were caused by the One that were one-relative-to-many, so that the One itself was entirely beyond such relativity.[80]

IV. The theurgical attainment of fulfilment

Having denied the possibility of attainment of fulfilment through introversion, and having so multiplied the ontological hierarchy that human beings were removed from the uppermost principles by several ontological stages, the Iamblichean tradition proceeded to affirm that human fulfilment was still to be identified with attainment of the uppermost principles, and that such attainment was effected through pagan ritual, understood as theurgy (θεουργία).[81]

a. The triadic analysis of reality The principle which grounded this understanding of fulfilment through theurgy was the principle that being was fundamentally triadic. For the Iamblichean tradition, reality was a triadic circuit stretching from the remaining (*monê*) of a monad (*monas*) through procession (*proödos*) to a multiplicity (*plêthos*) to the reversion (*epistrophê*) of that multiplicity back to its monadic source.[82]

Thus, according to the Iamblichean tradition, beings which come from a cause (i.e., *metechonta* which participate in the *metechomena* of an *amethekton*) do not merely proceed from the cause; they also revert back to that cause, by which reversion they attain to their good.[83] In an absolute sense, this meant that all being proceeded from the One which remained, and then reverted back to the One.[84] But it held in general for each and every series. It was true for each and every series in that the multiplicity of members of the series proceeded from the monad from which they came, and then reverted back to that monad.[85] It held also for each and every being: any particular being participated in the effects of a monad, and was said to 'remain' (*menein*) in that monad insofar as it was identical in character to the monad; it was said to 'proceed' (*proeinai*) from the monad insofar as it differed from the monad; and it was said to 'revert' (*epistrephein*) back to the monad insofar as it turned back to it as its source.[86] Thus both series of beings and individual beings in

---

80 Cf. Proclus, *El. theol.* 20, 123.
81 On the term θεουργία, see Hans Lewy, *Chaldaean oracles and theurgy*, 461–6; E. R. Dodds, *The Greeks and the irrational*, 283–311.
82 Proclus, *El. theol.* 35.
83 Ibid., 31.32–4.
84 Ibid., 13.
85 Ibid., 21, 23.
86 Ibid., 30, 31.

themselves were constituted ontologically by this triadic circuit of remaining, procession and reversion.

In terms of this triadic analysis of being, the Iamblicheans were able to further multiply the ontological hierarchy. This triad of *monê–proödos–epistrophê* was applied not only to the three hypostases of Being, Life and Intellect collectively (so that Being was equated to *monê*, Life to *proödos* and Intellect to *epistrophê*), but also to each hypostasis individually. Thus the hypostases of Being, Life and Intellect were each said to be constituted internally by their own triadic circuit of μονή-πρόοδος-ἐπιστροφή. And, beyond this, within these internal triads there was further multiplicity. Each of the three triads internal to Being was itself deemed to be triadic; as was each of the three triads internal to Life; while the first two triads of Intellect were further subdivided triadically. As a result the hypostases of Being and Life were each ennadic composites of nine terms, while Intellect was a seven-membered hebdomad.

b. The identification of the uppermost principles with pagan gods With the ontological hierarchy thus further multiplied, the Iamblichean tradition was able to identify the pagan gods with the different entities in this hierarchy.[87] Thus the One was identified with Chronus. The sub-triad of the first member of the triad of Being was then identified as consisting of the gods Aether, Chaos and the Orphic cosmic egg. The sub-triad of the second member of Being was identified with the Orphic entities of the golden dog, the egg-membrane and the cloud. Being's third member's sub-triad was then equated with the gods Phanes, Ericapaeus and Metis. Similar identifications follow for the subdivided hypostasis of Life. The sub-triad of the first member of the triad of Life is said to comprise the three Orphic Nights. The second member of the triad of Life is the god Ouranos, and the third member the Orphic Centimani. In like manner, the triadic subdivision of the first member of the triad of Intellect is identified with the three 'Fathers', Kronos, Rhea and Zeus. Zeus is identified with the Platonic demiurge. (But he is not held to create in time – the world, for the Iamblichean tradition, is eternal.)[88] The triadic subdivision of the second member of Intellect is then equated with the three Kouretes; while the third member of the triad of Intellect (which is not internally triadic) is identified with the Titans. Here we may observe that all these gods from Aether to the Titans occupy the ontological space which Plotinus and certain earlier Platonists had identified simply with the hypostasis of the divine Intellect.

87 Here I will follow Proclus' account. Cf. Lewy, *Chaldaean oracles and theurgy*, 483–4; H.-D. Saffrey and L. G. Westerink, 'Introduction', lxv–lxix. Cf. also the interpretation of Egyptian deities in Iamblichus, *Myst.* 8.
88 Cf. Proclus, *Aet. mundi*.

Beneath this level are found the hypercosmic and encosmic levels of gods, levels into which Zeus extends, and which also includes Poseidon, Pluto, Artemis, Persephone, Athena, Apollo, the Corybantes, Hephaistos, Demeter, Hera, Hermes, Aphrodite, Hestia and Ares. These gods are grouped functionally and hierarchically into demiurgic gods (who fashion the cosmos), vivificatory gods (who infuse it with life), elevating gods (who help the produced being to revert to its principles), and *achrantoi* gods (who ensure a proper degree of ontological separation between the demiurgic gods and what they fashion). Underneath these gods in the ontological hierarchy are found the daemonic levels of beings (angels, daemons, heroes), which function as intermediaries between the gods and humans and natural reality.[89] Each daemon mediates some specific aspect of the divine activities of the hypercosmic and encosmic levels of divinity. Daemons thus function as the lowest rung of an ontological and theological hierarchy so bloated as to eliminate any notion of Plotinian–Porphyrian attainment of the One through noetic introversion.

What distinguished gods from daemons primarily was the level of subsistence of each. Gods subsisted at the henadic level – that is to say, each god was a henad (a participable unity whose monad was the imparticipable One), in which various lower levels of being participated and had their subsistence.[90] Daemons, however, subsisted at the intellectual level – their henad was an irradiation of unity, not a self-complete unity.[91]

c. Human fulfilment as theurgical attainment of the gods The fulfilment of all beings is the One. For the fulfilment of a being is the fulfilment of the triad which constitutes it (*monê–proödos–epistrophê*). And that which it reverts to are the monads of the series which constitute it. Since beings of the lower ontological levels belong to many series, they have many revertive fulfilments. But since the monads of all series other than the series whose monad is the One themselves belong to this series, this series is the ultimate series, so that the ultimate fulfilment of each being lies in its reversion to the head of this series, namely the One.[92] As such the attainment of the primal unity that is the One is the ultimate fulfilment of each being – hence the One is the Good itself.[93] But since the gods are self-complete henads they subsist precisely in this unity of the One which is the fulfilment of all beings. As such they have unity with each other in their unity with the One. Consequently, the fulfilment

89 Proclus, *In Tim.* 3.152–67.
90 Proclus, *El. theol.* 114.
91 Iamblichus, *Myst.* 1.15.45.
92 Proclus, *El. theol.* 33.11–19; 100.
93 Cf. ibid., 31–4, 13.

of all creatures – lying in unity with the One – also entails coming into unity with the gods who are already united in this unity.[94] As such, the fulfilment of human beings lies in their achievement of union with the One and the other gods.[95]

However, since human beings do not subsist on the henadic level they do not possess within themselves the ontological resources to ascend to the henadic level on their own. Instead, they can only achieve such an ascent by the aid of superior powers. That the gods give such aid follows directly, for the Iamblicheans, from their being gods. For every god – in virtue of its proximity to the One which is the Good itself – is superessentially good,[96] and as good exercises providence (*pronoia*) and love (*philia*) over the members of the series of which it is head.[97] That is to say, as the heads of different series, the gods act 'to unify what participates in [them]'.[98] Similarly, the daemonic order, in that it is overall subordinate to the divine, mediates this to the sub-daemonic levels of being. This providence, however, is nothing less than the very overflowing of power (*dynamis*) that constitutes the being of the sub-divine creature in the first place (since this being is a triadic circuit consisting not merely of remaining but also of proceeding and reverting).[99]

However, since (a) no effect is equal in power to its cause;[100] (b) the later terms of a series are less perfect than the earlier terms;[101] and (c) *dynamis* is automatically diminished as it is divided between a plurality of beings,[102] it follows that the *dynamis* present in the lower levels of a series is less powerful than that present in the higher levels. As such, the *dynamis* enabling reversion to the highest levels of reality is, in the lowest levels of reality, diminished and diffused among a multitude of beings. At such levels, where it is present most strongly is in the 'characters' (*idiotai*) of the composite members of the series by which such members are members of the series of which they are members.[103] Since these beings only possess revertive *dynamis* to the extent that they possess the character by which they are members of the series of which they are members, the *dynamis* is pre-eminently identified with such 'characters'.[104]

---

94 Ibid., 113.
95 Iamblichus, *Myst.* 10.1.
96 Proclus, *El. theol.* 119.
97 Ibid., 120; Iamblichus, *Myst.* 1.12.42.
98 Proclus, *El. theol.* 13.
99 Ibid., 27, 81.
100 Ibid., 7.
101 Ibid., 36.
102 Ibid., 61.
103 Ibid., 145.
104 Cf. Iamblichus, *Myst.* 3.17.

This provides the basis for theurgical elevation. The theurgist unites different characters and thereby unites the *dynameis* of each. Thereby, in the act of uniting these, he himself becomes what we might call a 'synthetic' and 'enacted' character, and comes to contain in himself a revertive *dynamis* composed of the *dynameis* of the individual characters which he unites.[105] If this *dynamis* is sufficiently strong, it effects the reversion of the theurgist to the subsistential level of the goal of the revertive *dynamis*. Proclus gives the following analogy: '. . . if a wick which has been heated beforehand is placed under a lamp, not far from the flame, you will see it light up even though it has not touched the flame, for the transmission of the flame takes place downwards.'[106] By this reversion the theurgist acquires a divine *energeia* by which he comes to subsist on the higher ontological level of the reversion.[107]

The possibility of reversion is dependent upon the reverting being possessing something in common with the monad of the subsistential towards which the reverting being reverts. But, since human beings contain within themselves illuminations of all the higher ontological levels (i.e., they have as irradiations a henad (the 'flower of the intellect'),[108] a being, a life and an intellect), it is therefore possible on the Iamblicheans' account for a human soul to revert all the way to henadic divinity.[109] For, in that the levels of intellect, life, being and henad all exist already within the human soul, it is possible for the human soul to be energised by divine *energeia* such that he comes to subsist on the levels of intellect, life, being or henad.

Such theurgical elevation, however, must take place stage by stage. For, according to the Iamblicheans, a lower circuit of remaining–procession–reversion must be completed before a higher circuit from which the lower circuit proceeded can be completed.[110] As such, there are different levels of theurgy, with each level being appropriate for human souls who subsist on the ontological level beneath that to which the theurgy would revert them.

And it is here that the Iamblichean tradition justifies pagan rituals. For they hold that such rituals are the theurgical manipulation of embodied characters with the aim of reverting the soul of the participant (now theurgist) to the level of intellect (i.e., to the level of subsistence of the daemons).[111] Such rituals

---

105 Cf. ibid., 1.15.
106 Proclus, *De sacr. et mag.* 149.
107 Iamblichus, *Myst.* 1.12, 2.9.
108 E.g. Proclus, *Th. Plat.* 1.3.
109 Cf. Iamblichus, *Myst.* 5.22.230.
110 Proclus, *El. theol.* 38.
111 Iamblichus, *Myst.* 5.15.219.

constitute the first level of theurgy.[112] Beyond this level, however, theurgy becomes the reversion of the immaterial soul to divine levels beyond the intellectual (i.e., to the levels of life, being and finally one); as such it is an entirely 'intellectual and incorporeal' matter, involving no sacrifices.[113] In that such theurgy moves beyond the intellectual, it also moves beyond the reach of philosophy, which is a noetic and discursive activity, to a level of supra-intellective faith (*pistis*) that unites with the gods in a silence beyond *logos*.[114] (That such ascent transcended ritual was of course no problem for the Iamblichean tradition's affirmation of pagan myth, rite and ritual – since it was only through pagan ritual that one could move onto the higher levels of theurgy.)

This hierarchical and theurgical metaphysic was characteristic of late antique paganism in the fourth to seventh centuries. It is at once philosophical (providing a *logos* of the myths) and faithful to the pagan Platonic grammar of the philosophical interpretation of religion (indeed, making space for everything within it). It is thoroughly pagan (endorsing not only myth but ritual practice), and in its presuppositions is trenchantly anti-Christian. It continues to postulate a hierarchy of value rendering matter valueless to such a degree as to make incarnation and bodily resurrection nonsensical. Beyond this, in maintaining that an effect must be inferior to its cause, it denies the possibility of the Son's co-essentiality to the Father, and, in upholding the traditional view that the world is eternal, it rejects the notion of *creatio ex nihilo*.

The Christian rejection of paganism

Christian Apologia

In the early centuries of the church, Christians responded to polemical pagan objections to Christianity through the composition of *apologiae*, in which they defended themselves from the pagan criticisms of Christianity and mounted anti-pagan counter-objections of their own.[115] This apologetical tradition, including in the second and third centuries the works of Justin Martyr, Tatian, Athenagoras, Clement, Tertullian and Origen, reached its climax with Eusebius of Caesarea's mammoth *Praeparatio* and *Demonstratio evangelica* in the first half of the fourth century, and with Augustine's *De civitate Dei* in the

112 Ibid., 5.14–15.
113 Ibid., 5.18.
114 Ibid., 2.11.96–7. Cf. Proclus, *In Alc.* 357.
115 On these cf. Pelikan, *Christian tradition*, I: 27–41; Dulles, *Apologetics*, 22–71. Cf. also J. Daniélou, *Gospel message and Hellenistic culture*; R. M. Grant, *Greek apologists*.

first half of the fifth.[116] From the middle of the fifth century the triumph of Christianity meant that there was no live need for Christians to write new anti-pagan apologetical treatises.

The earlier apologetic, by highlighting the fundamental intellectual points at issue between Christians and pagans, set the conceptual parameters within which Christian intellectual engagement with paganism would take place during this era. Pagan critiques of Christian narratives as absurd were to be rejected.[117] The Hellenic myths were dismissed as untenable.[118] The ontology of the ancients that the ancients sought was said to be in reality the wisdom of the Hebrews.[119] Against mythological polytheism, the divine monarchy of the one God the Father was to be upheld.[120] In opposition to Platonic ontology, the soul was not to be considered immortal.[121] Creation was not to be understood as the formation of pre-existing matter, but was to be recognised rather as occurring ex nihilo by the will of God.[122] Time was not to be thought of as cyclical but linear.[123] The cosmos was to be seen as ordered providentially by God himself.[124] And the triumph of the Roman empire was to be supported by Christians as according to the divine *oikonomia*.[125]

While such points continued to be made in Christian controversial literature of the fourth and fifth centuries, they were not new to the period of imperial Christianity. Rather, they were principally re-statements of points made in earlier apologetic. Accordingly, they do not characterise what is distinctive about Christian intellectual engagement with paganism in the period of the fourth to seventh centuries. This distinctiveness lies not in apologetical confrontation, but rather in the formation by Christians of ontologies which showed, against the pagan detractors, that Christianity was not *alogon* but in fact could be expressed coherently as manifesting the true *logos* of being.

---

116 Additionally, for the centuries with which we are concerned, we may note Arnobius, *Adversus nationes*; Lactantius, *Divinae institutiones*, Prudentius, *Contra Symmachum*; Eusebius, *Theophania*; Athanasius, *Contra gentes*; John Chrysostom, *Demonstration to Jews and Greeks that Christ is God*; Gregory of Nazianzus, *Orationes contra Julianum Imperatorem*; Macarius Magnes, *Apocriticus*; Cyril of Alexandria, *Contra Julianum Imperatorem*; Theodoret of Cyrrhus, *Graecarum affectionem curatio*.

117 Cf. e.g. Theophilus, *Autol.* 2.22; Lactantius, *Inst.* 4.8.3.

118 E.g. Athenagoras, *Leg.* 21.3; Theophilus, *Autol.* 1.9; Clement, *Prot.* 2.39.1; Tertullian, *Nat.* 2.12.17; Cyprian, *Donat.* 8.

119 E.g. Justin, *1 Apol.* 59–60; Origen, *Contr. Cels.* 6.19; Theophilus, *Autol.* 1.14; Augustine, *Doct. Chr.* 2.28.43; Clement, *Prot.* 6.70.1.

120 Irenaeus, *Adv. haer.* 2.30.9.

121 Tatian, *Orat.* 13.

122 Theophilus, *Autol.* 2.4; 2.10; Tertullian, *Hermog.* 21.2; Clement, *Prot.* 4.63.3.

123 Origen, *Contr. Cels.* 4.67.

124 Tertullian, *Jejun.* 4.1; Origen, *Orat.* 6.3.

125 Tertullian, *Nat.* 2.17.19; Eusebius, *De laud. Const.*, *passim*.

Christian ontological formation

The fourth to seventh centuries constitute precisely the time at which Ortho-dox Christianity, in the theology expressed in the Seven Ecumenical Councils, responded definitively to the pagan charge that Christianity was incapable of coherent ontological articulation. Christianity did so, however, mediately and indirectly, through its correction of various aspects of earlier Logos-theology and its rejection of the Arianism and Origenism which developed from such theology. That this amounted to a response to paganism was due to the fact that Logos-theology was itself an attempt (indeed, the first significant Christian attempt) to respond to the pagan charge of Christian ontological incoherence by providing what the pagan objection alleged impossible – namely a coher-ent ontological articulation of Christianity. In correcting Logos-theology and in rejecting its misconceived progeny, the Orthodox Christianity of this era essentially adopted its project, so that its own ontological articulations were, mediately, responses to the pagan objection that Christianity could not be coherently articulated ontologically.

Divinity

I. The divinity of Father, Son and Holy Spirit

This Orthodox ontological self-articulation of the fourth to seventh centuries began at the beginning of the fourth century with Arius' rejection of the notion of different ontological grades of divinity as found in the Platonic framework for interpreting religion. In line with the Christian scriptures – and in contrast to earlier Logos-theology[126] – Arius insisted that there could be only one Divinity, which must be understood as subsisting at the highest ontological level.[127]

Arius drew from this the conclusion that the Logos who proceeds from the Father and who became incarnate in Jesus Christ was a mere creature and not God.[128] But such a conclusion was unacceptable for Orthodox Christianity. For, according to Orthodoxy, this Christ saves us from sin, death and corruption, restores us to communion with God and deifies us through incorporating us into himself.[129] But only God – and not any creature – can thus restore and unite us to God, on the grounds that a being cannot effect union with what is ontologically transcendent of it and hence beyond its power to unite

---

126 Athenagoras, *Leg.* 10.5; Justin, *1 Apol.* 13; Origen, *Contr. Cels.* 5.39; 6.61.
127 Arius, ap. Athanasius, *De synod.* 16.4.3–6; Arius, ap. Epiphanius, *Panarion* 3.157.15–16.
128 Cf. n. 127.
129 E.g. Athanasius, *Inc.* 54; *Adelph.* 4; *Contr. Ar.* 1.38.

something to.[130] Since the incarnate Logos does effect such a union, the Logos that became incarnate in Jesus Christ must therefore be divine. *A fortiori*, as there is only one Divinity, this Logos must share the same Divinity as God the Father, subsisting thereby on the same ontological level as the Father. That is to say, the Logos must share the same being (*ousia*) as the Father – Father and Son must be of one being (*homoousios*).[131]

Similarly, as it is by the Holy Spirit – who pours forth from the Father through the Son – that we are incorporated into Christ and deified, it follows that the Holy Spirit too must be divine as the Son is divine. For were it otherwise, the Holy Spirit could not possess any role in our deification, since only God can deify.[132] As such, the Holy Spirit must be ὁμοούσιος with the Father and the Son.[133]

Negatively, these affirmations, articulated decisively in the fourth century by Athanasius and the Cappadocian fathers, constituted a fundamental rejection of the Platonic conception of a graded ontological hierarchy of divine hypostases. On the one hand, it was now stated clearly that there could be no grades of divinity – all hypostases which subsisted at an ontological level lower than that of the First Principle were not to be understood as divine. But on the other hand, whereas the Platonists had insisted that there was one and only one hypostasis that occupied the highest ontological level of divinity, Orthodox Christianity affirmed there to be three such hypostases, all possessing the one divine *ousia*.

Such affirmations did not resolve, but sharpened, the pagan questions regarding the possibility of a coherent ontological articulation of Christianity. It remained for Orthodox Christianity to clarify ontologically how there could be three causally related hypostases of Father, Son and Holy Spirit having one divine *ousia*, and how it could be that human fulfilment consists in the union with the divinity thus understood, effected by Jesus Christ.

II. The Holy Trinity

Intellectual Christians agreed with intellectual pagans that the supreme ontological level of divinity (which for Christians was, of course, the only divine ontological level) was to be equated with the Good and was to be acknowledged as transcendent of human knowledge and language. To be knowable or conceptualisable presupposed boundedness (πέρας, ὅριον, περιγραπτόν) in

---

130 Athanasius, *Inc.* 20; Athanasius, *Syn. Arim. et Sel.* 51.
131 Athanasius, *Syn. Arim. et Sel.* 50.
132 Athanasius, *Ad Serap.* 1.24.
133 Gregory of Nazianzus, *Or.* 31.10.

order that it be thematised for knowledge or language.[134] But something can be bounded only by its opposite, so that divinity, being wholly good, could be bounded only by evil.[135] But evil cannot have ontological priority over goodness, since evil is parasitic of goodness.[136] Therefore, divinity, as good, cannot be ontologically bounded. Hence divinity must be infinite, beyond boundary and therefore beyond knowledge and concept.[137]

But this, the Orthodox argued, entailed that there was no incoherence in affirming the hypostases of Father, Son and Holy Spirit each to be divine.

First, it did not follow from the derivation of the Son and Spirit from the Father that the hypostases of Son and Spirit were sub-divine in subsistence. For 'begetting' and 'outpouring' are linguistic concepts. As such, neither they nor the terms 'unbegotten', 'begotten' and 'outpoured' could pertain to the divinity per se, since the divinity is beyond language and thought.[138] Consequently, divinity cannot be equated with 'unbegottenness' (any more than with 'begottenness' or 'outpouredness') such that only what is 'unbegotten' is divine (or such that only what is 'begotten' or 'outpoured' is divine). Thus the fact that Father, Son and Spirit are related ontologically as 'unbegotten', 'begotten' and 'outpoured' does not prevent each from being divine.

Second, this was not inconsistent with the affirmation that there was one Divinity, not three divinities. For, on the one hand, properly speaking, the Divinity which Father, Son and Holy Spirit share is the *ousia* that is common (*koinon*) to them.[139] This *ousia*, precisely as common, is one and undivided, so that there is one Divinity rather than three divinities.[140] On the other hand, the reason why, in the case of human beings, we do not speak of, say, Peter, James and John as being one human, but rather as three humans, is that the activities (*energeiai*) of human beings do not simply express human *ousia* in its fullness and undividedly, but rather express it incompletely, dividedly and in opposition to one another in the conflictual situation of fallen existence. Consequently, human beings do not subsist according to the unity of their humanity, but rather do so separately according to their individual division, and it is in virtue of this individual dividedness that three human beings are said to be three human beings, not one human being.[141] But this is not the case with

---

134 Ibid., 28.10.
135 Gregory of Nyssa, *Vit. Mos.* 2.236–7.
136 Dionysius the Areopagite, *Div. nom.* 4.18–35.
137 Gregory of Nyssa, *Vit. Mos.* 2.235–8; cf. Gregory of Nazianzus, *Or.* 28.4, 17.
138 Basil of Caesarea, *Contr. Eun.* 1.5–17; Gregory of Nyssa, *Ad Ablab.* (GNO 3/1.56–7).
139 Basil, *Ep.* 214.4.
140 Gregory of Nyssa, *Ad Ablab.* (GNO 3/1.40).
141 Gregory of Nyssa, *Ad Ablab.* (GNO 3/1.47); *De hom. op.* 16–18; Maximus the Confessor, *Amb.* 41 (PG 91:1309A), 42 (1340Cff.); Maximus the Confessor, *Ad Thal.* 61 (PG 90: 636B).

Father, Son and Holy Spirit, who subsist divinely, entirely in and according to the communion of the divine nature (κοινωνία τῆς φύσεως).[142] As such, in the Holy Trinity, the divinity and the *energeia* of the hypostases is absolutely common and 'undivided with regard to the number' of hypostases.[143] Hence the unity of the nature is not disfigured by a fallen mode of existence and Father, Son and Holy Spirit constitute, in accordance with their nature, one God and not three gods.

Deification

I. Incorporation into Christ

The Orthodox ontological articulation of the Christian understanding of human fulfilment as consisting in deification effected in Jesus Christ was expressed in terms of the eschatological unification of all things in Jesus Christ. Jesus Christ, as the Logos of God, was the one by whom and for whom all created being was created.[144] All creation finds its fulfilment by eucharistic incorporation into his body, through which 'recapitulation' God becomes 'all in all'.[145]

II. The ontological fulfilment of created being in Christ

For Orthodox Christianity, this account (*logos*) of the fulfilment of creation was to be strictly equated with true fulfilment of the meaning (*logos*) of created being in general and of the meaning (λόγος) of every created being in particular. On the one hand, beings are created freely by the divine will,[146] so that they are ontologically constituted precisely as expressions of this will.[147] On the other hand, the will of God is itself meaningful (*logikos*), so that each expression of the divine will is the expression of a meaning (*logos*). Consequently, the true ontological meaning (*logos*) of each being – the meaning that is intrinsic to the being itself – is precisely the divine meaningful volition that constitutes each being.[148] ('The definition of all nature is the *logos* of its essential *energeia*.')[149] And as the fulfilment of the divine will for each and every created being is incorporation into Jesus Christ, it follows that such incorporation is the

---

142 Basil, *Spir. Sanct.* 18.47.
143 Gregory of Nyssa, *Ad Ablab.* (GNO 3 / 1.47–8).
144 Colossians 1.15–17; Cf. Maximus, *Amb.* 7 (PG 91: 1080B).
145 1 Cor. 15.28; Eph. 1.10, 23; Cf. Maximus the Confessor, *Amb.* 7 (PG 91: 1092C, 1096C, 1097A) and see also N. Loudovikos, Ἡ εὐχαριστιακὴ ὀντολογία, 33–84.
146 Cf., e.g., Athanasius, *Contr. Ar.* 1.33; 2.2.
147 Dionysius, *Div. nom.* 5.8 (PG 3: 824C).
148 Cf. Maximus the Confessor, *Amb.* 7 (PG 91: 1085A–B).
149 Ibid., 5 (PG 91: 1057B).

ontological fulfilment of the intrinsic meaning (logos) of each and every created being. Jesus Christ is thus the divine Logos (meaning), constituting at once the ultimate content of the divine will for creation and the ultimate ontological meaning of created being. The logoi of created beings are thus constituted and fulfilled by the Logos, in which each of the logoi are participations, so that 'the one Logos is many λόγοι and the many logoi are one Logos'.[150]

This understanding of the ontological fulfilment of being in Christ entailed for Orthodox Christianity a particular ontology of created being. All created being has for its telos incorporation into Christ. As such, every being possesses within itself movement (kinêsis), in that it tends towards the goal that is the body of Christ, which is its fulfilment and so the rest (stasis) of its movement.[151] Time, being movement measured,[152] is then understood ontologically as the measurement of the meaningful and teleologically ordered κίνησις according to which created being moves towards attainment of enchristic incorporation. Consequently the attainment of union with Christ is the transcendence of time, so that being which is united with Christ, by virtue of its participation in Christ, becomes, like Melchisedec, 'without beginning and without end, . . . possessing . . . the divine life imparted by the indwelling Word of God that is everlasting and not limited by any form of death'.[153] As a result, and in contrast to pagan philosophical understandings of time, time is not to be understood as cyclical nor as a wholly negative ontological situation: time is the measured path by which temporal created being moves to its ontological fulfilment in Christ.

The ontological unification of all things in Christ is achieved in his incarnate dispensation through his overcoming of the divisions of the created order and of the division of created from Uncreated. Such unification consists in the overcoming of the fundamental dualities (diaireseis) of male / female, paradise / oikoumenê (inhabited world), heaven / earth, intelligible / sensible and created / uncreated.[154] The ontological locus for such unification is the human being, who contains within himself and is capable of uniting the elements of the first four dualities, and who, by love, is capable of uniting these to uncreated divinity.[155] In that such ontological unification, being what is realised in

150 Ibid., 7 (PG 91: 1081C).
151 Ibid., 7 (PG 91: 1069B, 1073B).
152 Maximus, Schol. in Div. Nom. 5.8 (PG 4: 336A–B).
153 Maximus the Confessor, Amb. 10 (PG 91: 1144C).
154 Gregory of Nyssa, Contr. Eun. 1.270–2; 3.6.62–7; Maximus the Confessor, Amb. 41 (PG 91: 1304D–1305A).
155 Maximus the Confessor, Amb. 41 (PG 91: 1305A).

Christ, is the fulfilment of human being, it is natural to humans to constitute such a *syndesmos* (bond) of being. That fallen human beings do not do so is due to their turning away from the natural *kinêsis* that leads their being to fulfilment. This leads to a mode of existence in which the sexes are divided and opposed by lust; to an unholiness through which the inhabited world is cut off from paradise; to the vice which separates heaven from earth; to the ignorance which severs the realm of sensible beings from that of angelic intelligence; and to the self-love (*philautia*) which cuts it off from the God who is love (*agapê*).[156]

In the dispensation of his incarnation, Christ ontologically re-unites in his own person the divisions of being. In his assumption of human nature, the Logos unites himself immediately to elements of the four created dualities. And in his life, death, resurrection and ascension he unites these elements so that, although they remain different, they are no longer divided. By his virgin birth he overcomes the opposition of the sexes; by his death and resurrection he destroys the division of paradise and *oikoumenê*; by his ascension he unites heaven and earth; by passage through the ranks of angels to the Father, he restores the unity of the sensible and the angelic; and by his return to the Father, he unites the creation (wholly united within himself) to Divinity.[157]

III. Deification in Christ

It is in terms of this ontology that human deification is understood. Man is adopted and incorporated into Christ by the grace of baptism.[158] This incorporation contains the fullness of deification, but potentially. Through baptism he receives the gift of the Holy Spirit, by which he is enabled to move in accordance with his nature – i.e., to live according to the unificatory mode of existence which is natural to human being, and which has been actualised perfectly and fully in Christ.[159] Concretely, for a once-fallen human being to move in such a way is for their mode of existence to be transformed from its previous lustful, unholy, vice-ridden, ignorant and self-loving mode to the mode of being manifested in Christ, which is non-sexual, holy, virtuous, knowing the true *logoi* of beings and possessed above all by a selfless love for God. To the extent to which the baptised person, by the power of the Holy Spirit, actively achieves this in his own freedom, his potential deification is actualised,

---

156 Cf. ibid., 41 (PG 91: 1305C–1308C).
157 Ibid., 41 (PG 91: 1308D–1309D).
158 Maximus the Confessor, *Cap. car.* 4.73; *Myst.* 24 (PG 91: 712B).
159 Maximus the Confessor, *Myst.* 24 (PG 91: 712B).

as Christ becomes incarnate in him.[160] Insofar as this is indeed so, 'the whole man participates in the whole God',[161] as he realises in act his participated unity with Christ *kata logon*.

IV. The rejection of pagan philosophical ontology

All this entails the comprehensive Christian rejection of pagan philosophical ontology. First, the Iamblichean tradition's tripartite understanding of participation is repudiated. For, on the one hand, the *logos* of each being is a direct participation in the *Logos*; it is not the case that the Logos is remote from the *logoi* of mundane beings. On the other hand, all created being is taken up directly in the incarnation of the hypostasis of the *Logos*, in which it has its participated fulfilment. Thus Divinity is immediately present to all beings, and does not stand at the high-point of an ontological hierarchy, touching the lower levels of being only indirectly through causal intermediaries. (It is not that there is no hierarchical ontological gradation; it is just that this hierarchy has no role to play in determining the union of divinity with humanity in the incarnate Logos.)

Consequently, it follows, second, that for Christians the one triadic divinity exercises direct providence over the material world.[162] Providence is not the work of a subordinate entity. Nor is providence merely the work of the Logos – for the unity of *ousia* in the Trinity means that the providential act of the Trinity is common to Father, Son and Holy Spirit.

Moreover, third, there is a rejection of the pagan understanding of theurgical ascent up a metaphysical hierarchy. Certainly, for Christians, one's unification to Christ takes place over time and gradually, but this is a gradation of the level of participation in Christ, not an ascent of levels of gradiation which lead to Christ.

Fourth, the pagan deprecation of the body and identification of true personhood with the disembodied soul is rejected. For body too is incorporated directly into divinity in Jesus Christ. And if the fulfilment of human being consists in functioning as a *syndesmos* linking all aspects of creation to the divinity, then human being is intrinsically bodily. Therefore, human personhood cannot be identified with a disembodied soul, which can only be seen as an unnatural – and hence deficient – state.[163]

---

160 Maximus the Confessor, *Ep.* 2 (PG 91: 401B); *Amb.* 10 (PG 91: 1113B–C).
161 Maximus the Confessor, *Amb.* 7 (PG 91: 1088C).
162 Cf. Gregory of Nazianzus, *De prov.* (PG 37); Theodoret of Cyrrhus, *De prov.* (PG 83: 556–773).
163 Maximus the Confessor, *Amb.* 7 (PG 91: 1100A–1101C).

Fifth, the rejection of pagan commitment to hierarchical hypostases of, e.g., being, life, intellect does not entail the abandonment of the language of 'being', 'life' and 'intellect'. For all the meanings (*logoi*) of all the ontological features of all the beings in creation subsist beforehand in the undivided Trinity as their cause. As such, the being of the Holy Trinity may be called itself 'being', 'life' and 'intellect'. But equally, since the divine nature transcends language, it must also transcend these terms. In this manner, God is generally both 'nameless and yet possessed of the names of everything that is'.[164] He is nameless with regards to his *ousia* that transcends language, but named from his *energeiai*, his active presence to us, through which we participate in him.[165]

Such, then, was the nature of the (mainly indirect) Christian response to intellectual paganism in the fourth to seventh centuries.

Bibliography

PRIMARY SOURCES

Albinus. *Introductio in Platonem (Intr.)*. Ed. K. F. Hermann, *Platonis dialogi secundum Thrasylli tetralogias dispositi* (Leipzig, 1853), VI: 147–51

Alcinous. *Epitome*. Ed. P. Louis, *Albinos. Épitom* (Paris, 1945)

Apuleius. *De Deo Socratis*. Ed. J. Beaujeu, *Apulée. Opuscules philosophiques (Du dieu de Socrate, Platon et sa doctrine, Du monde) et fragments* (Paris, 1963)

Aristotle. *Metaphysics (Meta.)*. Ed. W. D. Ross (Oxford, 1953²)

Athanasius. *Contra Arianos (Contr. Ar.)*. Ed. H. G. Opitz, *Athanasius Werke* (Berlin, 1940), II.1: 87–168

    De decretiis Nicaenae synodi (De synod.). Ed. H. G. Opitz, *Athanasius Werke* (Berlin, 1940), II.1: 1–45

    Epistula ad Adelphium (Adelph.) (PG 26: 1072–84)

    Epistulae quattuor ad Serapionem (Ad Serap.) (PG 26)

    De incarnatione (Inc.) (SC 199)

    De synodis Arimini in Italia et Seleuciae in Isauria (Syn. Arim. et Sel.). Ed. H. G. Opitz, *Athanasius Werke* (Berlin, 1940), II.1: 231–78

Athenagoras. *Legatio*. Ed. W. R. Schoedel (Oxford, 1972)

Augustine. *De civitate Dei* (CCSL 47, 48)

    De doctrina Christiana. Ed. R. P. H. Green (Oxford, 1996)

Basil of Caesarea. *Contra Eunomium* (PG 29: 497–669, 672–768)

    Epistulae (Ep.). Ed. Y. Courtonne, *Saint Basile. Lettres* (Paris, 1957–66)

    De Spiritu Sancto (SC 17bis)

Cicero. *De natura deorum*. Eds. O. Plasberg and W. Ax (Stuttgart, 1961)

Clement. *Protrepticus (Prot.)* (SC 2²)

---

164 Dionysius, *Div. nom.* 1.7 (PG 3: 596C).
165 E.g., Basil, *Ep.* 234.1.

Cornutus. *De natura deorum*. Ed. C. Lang, *Cornuti theologiae Graecae compendium* (Leipzig, 1881): 1–76

Cyprian. *Ad Donatum* (SC 291)

Damascius. *De principiis*. Ed. C. É. Ruelle, *Damascii successoris dubitationes et solutiones* (Paris, 1889–99), I: 1–324; II: 1–4

Diels, H. and W. Kranz, eds. *Die Fragmente der Vorsokratiker* (DK) (Berlin, 1951⁶)

Dionysius the Areopagite. *De divinis nominibus* (PG 3: 585–984)

Epiphanius. *Panarion* (GCS Epiphanius, Bände 1–3)

Eusebius. *De laudibus Constantini* (GCS Eusebius Werke, Band 1: 195–259)

    Praeparatio evangelica (GCS Eusebius Werke, Band 8)

Gregory of Nazianzus. *De providentia* (PG 37)

    De Spiritu Sancto (*Or. 31*). Ed. J. Barbel, *Gregor von Nazianz. Die fünf theologischen Reden* (Düsseldorf, 1963), 218–76

    De theologia (*Or. 28*). Ed. Barbel, *Gregor von Nazianz*, 62–126

Gregory of Nyssa, *Ad Ablablium* (GNO 3/1)

    Contra Eunomium (GNO 1/2)

    De hominis opificio (*De hom. op.*) (PG 44: 124–256)

    De vita Mosis (*Vit. Mos.*) (SC 1ᵗᵉʳ)

Hesiod. *Opera et dies*. Ed. F. Solmsen, *Hesiodi opera* (Oxford, 1970): 49–85

Iamblichus. *De mysteriis* (*Myst.*). Ed. É. des Places, *Jamblique. Les mystères d'Égypte* (Paris, 1966)

Irenaeus. *Adversus haereses* (SC 34, 100, 152–3, 210–11, 263–4, 293–4)

Jerome. *Letters* (CSEL 54, 55, 56)

Julian. *Caesares*. Ed. C. Lacombrade, *L'empereur Julien. Oeuvres complètes* (Paris, 1964), II.2: 32–71

    Contra Galilaeos. Ed. C. J. Neumann, *Juliani imperatoris librorum contra Christianos quae supersunt* (Leipzig, 1880)

Justin. *Apologia*. Ed. E. J. Goodspeed, *Die ältesten Apologeten* (Göttingen, 1915), 26–77

Lactantius. *Divine institutes*. Eds. E. Heck and Antoine Wlosok (Saur, 2005)

Lucian. *Jupiter tragoedus*. Ed. A. M. Harmon, *Lucian* (Cambridge, MA, 1915; reprint: 1960), II: 90–168

Maximus the Confessor. *Ambigua* (PG 91: 1032–1417)

    Capita de caritate (PG 90: 960–1080)

    Epistulae (PG 91: 364–649)

    Mystagogia (PG 91: 657–717)

    Quaestiones ad Thalassium (PG 90: 244–785)

    Scholia in corpus Areopagiticum (PG 4: 15–432, 527–76)

Maximus of Tyre. *Dialexis*. Ed. H. Hobein, *Maximi Tyrii philosophumena* (Leipzig, 1910)

Minucius Felix. *Octavius*. Ed. B. Kytzler (Stuttgart, 1992²)

Origen. *Contra Celsum* (SC 132, 136, 147, 150)

    De oratione (GCS Origenes Werke II: 297–403)

Philoponus. *De aeternitate mundi*. Ed. H. Rabe (Leipzig, 1899)

Plato. *Apologia Socratis*. Ed. J. Burnet, *Platonis opera* (Oxford, 1900), I

    Cratylus. Ed. Burnet, *Platonis opera* I

    Phaedo. Ed. Burnet, *Platonis opera* I

Phaedrus. Ed. J. Burnet, *Platonis opera* (Oxford, 1901), II

Respublica. Ed. J. Burnet, *Platonis opera* (Oxford, 1902), IV

Timaeus. Ed. Burnet, *Platonis opera*, IV

Plotinus. *Enneades*. Eds. P. Henry and H.-R. Schwyzer, *Plotini opera* (Leiden, 1951–73)

Plutarch. *De animae procreatione in Timaeo*. Ed. C. Hubert, *Plutarchi moralia* (Leipzig, 1954), VI.1: 143–88

De defectu oculorum. Ed. W. Sieveking, *Plutarchi moralia* (Leipzig, 1929), III: 59–122

De Iside et Osiride. Ed. W. Sieveking, *Plutarchi moralia* (Leipzig, 1935), II.3: 1–80

Porphyry. *De antro nympharum*, Arethusa Monographs I (Buffalo, NY, 1969)

Contra Christianos. Ed. A. von Harnack, *Porphyrius. Gegen die Christen*, Abhandlungen der preussischen Akademie der Wissenschaften, Philosoph.-hist. Kl. I (Berlin, 1916)

Epistula ad Anebonem. Ed. A. R. Sodano, *Porfirio. Lettera ad Anebo* (Naples, 1958)

Ad Marcellam. Ed. W. Pötscher (Leiden, 1969)

De philosophia ex oraculis. Ed. G. Wolff, *Porphyrii de philosophia ex oraculis haurienda* (Berlin, 1856; reprint: Hildesheim, 1962)

In Platonis Parmenidem commentaria. Ed. P. Hadot, *Porphyre et Victorinus* (Paris, 1968) II: 64–112

De regressu animae. Ed. J. Bidez, *Vie de Porphyre, le philosophe néo-platonicien: Avec les fragments des traités Peri agalmátôn et De regressu animae* (Leipzig, 1913)

De vita Plotini. Eds. P. Henry and H.-R. Schwyzer, *Plotini opera* (Leiden, 1951), I: 1–41

Proclus. *De aeternitate mundi*, ap. Philoponus (q.v.); see now the Greek text, with trans. and commentary, and the Arabic version of Argument I, prepared by Helen S. Lang, A. D. Macro and J. McGinnis (Berkeley, 2001)

Elements of theology. Ed. E. R. Dodds (Oxford, 1963²)

In Platonis Alcibiadem I. Ed. L. G. Westerink, *Proclus Diadochus. Commentary on the first Alcibiades of Plato* (Amsterdam, 1954)

In Platonis Timaeum commentaria. Ed. E. Diehl (Leipzig, 1903–6; reprint: Amsterdam, 1965)

De sacrificio et magia. Ed. J. Bidez, *Catalogue des manuscrits alchimiques grecs* (Brussels, 1928), VI: 148–51

Theologia Platonica. Eds. H. D. Saffrey and L. G. Westerink, *Proclus. Théologie platonicienne* (Paris, 1968–97)

Sallustius. *De deis et mundo*. Ed. G. Rochefort, *Saloustios. Des dieux et du monde* (Paris, 1960)

Seneca. *Epistulae*. Ed. L. D. Reynolds (Oxford, 1965)

Simplicius. *In libros Aristotelis de anima commentaria (De an.)*. Ed. M. Hayduck (Berlin, 1882)

Stobaeus. *Ecloge*. Eds. O. Hense and C. Wachsmuth, *Ioannis Stobaei anthologium* (Berlin, 1884–1912)

Syrianus. *In metaphysica commentaria*. Ed. W. Kroll (Berlin, 1902)

Tatian. *Oratio ad Graecos*. Ed. E. J. Goodspeed, *Die ältesten Apologeten* (Göttingen, 1915): 268–305

Tertullian. *Adversus Hermogenem*. Ed. J. H. Waszink (Utrecht, 1956)

De jejunio (CCSL 2: 1257–77)

Ad nationes (CCSL 1: 9–75)

Theodoret of Cyrrhus, *De providentia* (PG 83.556–773)

Theophilus. *Ad Autolycum*. Ed. R. M. Grant (Oxford, 1970)

SECONDARY SOURCES

Armstrong, A. H., ed. *Classical Mediterranean spirituality: Egyptian, Greek, Roman* (New York, 1986)

Benko, S. 'Pagan criticisms of Christianity during the first two centuries AD', in H. Temporini and W. Haase, eds., *Aufstieg und Niedergang der römischen Welt* (Berlin, 1980), XXIII.2: 1055–1118

Boys-Stones, G. R. *Post-Hellenic philosophy: A study of its development from the Stoics to Origen* (Oxford, 2001)

Brown, Peter. 'Pagan', in G. W. Bowersock, P. Brown and O. Grabar, eds., *Late antiquity: A guide to the postclassical world* (Cambridge, MA, 1999), 625

Chauvin, P. *A chronicle of the last pagans: Revealing antiquity* (Cambridge, MA, 1990)

Daniélou, J. *Gospel message and Hellenistic culture* (Philadelphia, 1973)

Dodds, E. R. *The Greeks and the irrational* (Berkeley, 1951)

  Pagan and Christian in an age of anxiety: Some aspects of religious experience from Marcus Aurelius to Constantine (Cambridge, 1965)

Dulles, Avery. *A history of apologetics* (London, 1971)

Geffcken, J. *The last days of Greco-Roman paganism* (Amsterdam, 1978)

Grant, R. M. *Greek apologists of the second century* (Philadelphia, 1988)

Guthrie, W. K. C. *A history of Greek philosophy* (Cambridge, 1962–81)

Kannengeisser, Charles. *Handbook of patristic exegesis: The Bible in ancient Christianity* (Leiden, 2004)

de Labriolle, P. *La réaction païenne: Étude sur le polémique antichrétienne du Ier au VIe siècle* (Paris, 1934)

Lewy, Hans. *Chaldaean oracles and theurgy: Mysticism, magic and Platonism in the later Roman empire*, ed. Michel Tardieu (Paris, 1978²)

Loudovikos, N. Ἡ εὐχαριστιακὴ ἀντολογία. Τὰ εὐχαριστικὰ θεμέλια τοῦ εἶναι, ὡς ἐν κοινωνίᾳ γίγνεσθαι, στὴν ἐσχατολογικὴ ὀντολογία τοῦ ἁγίου Μαξίμου τοῦ Ὁμολογητῆ (Athens, 1992)

MacMullen, R. *Paganism in the Roman empire* (New Haven, 1981)

Pannenberg, Wolfhart. *Jesus – God and Man*, trans. L. L. Wilkins and D. A. Priebe (London, 1968)

Pelikan, J. *The Christian tradition: A history of Christian doctrine* (Chicago, 1971–89)

Saffrey, H.-D. and L. G. Westerink, 'Introduction', in H.-D. Saffrey and L. G. Westerink, eds., *Proclus, théologie platonicienne* (Paris, 1968), ix–clxv

Wilken, R. L. *The Christians as the Romans saw them* (New Haven, 1984)

Wilkins, Michael J. 'Christian', in D. N. Freedman et al., eds., *Anchor Bible dictionary* (New York, 1992), I: 925–6

Christianity and Manichaeism

SAMUEL N. C. LIEU

The religion of Mani arose from a Judaeo-Christian milieu in southern Mesopotamia in the third century – a time of both cultural and religious syncretism. When it was first proclaimed in the Roman empire by missionaries from the Syriac-speaking parts of the Persian empire it was attacked by pagan emperors as a Persian religion bent on destroying the moral fabric of the empire and by Christian leaders as a Gnostic-type heresy embodying a strong element of Marcionism as well as numerous pagan and foreign (mainly Iranian) features. The discovery of genuine Manichaean sources, from Turfan in Central Asia and from Medinet Madi and Kellis (Ismant el-Kharab in the Dakhleh oasis) in Egypt, has shown that Manichaeism was a universalist religion founded not to imitate but to surpass other major religions of late antiquity in order to absorb their followers into its fold. In an important mission statement preserved in a Coptic text from Medinet Madi, Mani declares:

The church that I have chosen is superior in ten aspects over the first churches. So, one: [. . . the apostles] that were sent to them chose a church with much toil. Some of them came in . . . only; others among them have come in . . . alone; and each of them came in, [they chose the] churches that they chose in the places and the cities where they were disclosed. The one who chose his church in the west, his church did not reach to the east; the one who chose his church in the east, his election did not come to the west. Thus, there are some of them: their name did not display in other cities.

However, my hope, mine: It is provided for it to go to the west and also for it to go to the east; and in every language they hear the voice of its proclamation, and it is proclaimed in all cities. In this first matter my church surpasses the first churches: Because the first churches were chosen according to place, according to city. My church, mine: It is provided for it to go out from all cities, and its good news attains every country.

[The second]: My church surpasses in the wisdom and . . . which I have unveiled for you in it. This [immeasurable] wisdom I have written in the holy books, in the great *Gospel* and the other writings; so that it will not be changed after me. Also, the way that I have written it in the books: [This] also is how I have commanded it to be depicted. Indeed, all the [apostles], my brethren who came prior to me: [They did not write] their wisdom in books the way that I, I have written it. [Nor] did they depict their wisdom in the *Picture (-Book)* the way [that I, I have] depicted it. My church surpasses [in this other matter also], for its primacy to the first churches.

[The third: My] church will remain henceforth and be unveiled through the world; because [. . . the first] churches, after they were revealed according to . . . they were stretched, they remained in the world for [a short time] only. Afterwards, they [. . . the apostles went] out from the world; but their churches . . . remained behind them, after them, in their likeness. However, my church, mine: It has attained (its) disclosure and can [not] be hidden from this time on; it has attained its fastness and cannot be shaken, continuing on till the end of the world.

The fourth: The writings and the wisdom and the revelations and the parables and the psalms of all the first churches have been collected in every place. They have come down to my church. They have added to the wisdom that I have revealed, the way water might add to water and become many waters. Again, this also is the way that the ancient books have added to my writings, and have become great wisdom; its like was not uttered in all the ancient generations. They did not write nor did they unveil the books the way that I, I have written it.

The fifth: The persecutions and the temptations and the afflictions that the first apostles proclaimed; they themselves prophesy that they are provided to happen to this church. Look: They have happened to it just as is written! [However, it], it has been strong. It has persisted against [all] the temptations; it was not overcome, nor was it thrown back. Happen you know that the crucifixions and the afflictions, which are different to each; the slaughters that are not like one another; these did not occur in all the churches. They have happened in my church for its primacy to all the other churches.[1]

The remaining five reasons are poorly preserved, but central to Mani's self-identity as the leader of a universal religion was his self-declared title of 'Apostle of Jesus Christ' and in Western Manichaean sources he was sometimes identified as the personification of the Paraclete. Although Mani rapidly became a Buddha as the religion spread eastwards across Central Asia, his most important title in Manichaean sources found in Turfan remains the 'Envoy of Light'

---

1 Mani, *Kephalaia* 154 (ed. Polotsky et al., 370–1); trans. Gardner, in I. M. F. Gardner and S. N. C. Lieu, eds., *Manichaean texts from the Roman empire*, 265–6. The following editorial signs are used in this chapter: round brackets ( ) indicate explanatory material added by the author; square brackets [ ] indicate lacunae in the text.

and in this respect he foreshadows Mohammed as no other religious leader in the Judaeo-Christian milieu in late antiquity made such claims to apostolic and divine lineage. This putative apostolic link also meant that the religion was able to expand as a form of Christianity during the post-Constantinian era in the Roman empire.

Mani and the 'baptists'

Mani's parents originally hailed from Hamadan in Parthia but they moved to Assuristan (southern Mesopotamia) and settled at first in the Parthian (winter) capital of Ctesiphon where his father Patik was converted to the strict ascetic teaching of a baptising sect known in a tenth-century Arabic source as the Mughtasilah (i.e., 'those who baptise themselves'). His wife Maryam was pregnant with Mani at the time of Patik's conversion (c. 216) and he later brought the child into the sect. Our information on the first two decades of Mani's life is heavily dependent on the Greek *Cologne-Mani Codex* (CMC). Measuring only 38 × 45mm but with up to twenty-seven lines of text per page, this tiny vellum codex might have come originally from a tomb in the region of Lycopolis. It contains a semi-autobiographical account of Mani in Greek in the form of an anthology of witness accounts given by his earliest disciples that was intended as a prelude to a history of the growth and expansion of the Manichaean church. The fragmentary opening pages of the codex describe the young Mani as the recipient of a special *gnosis* from his divine twin or companion (Gr. *syzygos*). Later, the young Mani was challenged on this self-imposed withdrawal from the rules of the sect that required its followers to gather vegetables and to purify them by ritual washing. He defended himself through appealing to a number of incidents associated with a certain Alchasaios (*sic*) whom he and his fellow baptists regarded as the founder of the sect:

'If you now make accusations against me concerning baptism, carry on then, and I will show you by your own Rule and the revelations which were granted to your leaders, that you must not baptise yourelf.'

For Alchasaios (*sic*), the founder of your Rule, expounds this. You see, when he (once) went to wash in some water, he saw a man appear in the spring of waters. This apparition said to him: 'Is it not enough that your animals abuse me? Even you yourself mistreat [my place] and offend against my water!' So Alchasaios [was amazed] and spoke to the apparition: 'The fornication, the filth and the impurity of the world are thrown at you, and you make no objection. But on account of me you are grieved!' It answered him: 'It may be that all these have not recognised who I am. But why have you not held

me in honour, you, who claim to be a servant of God and a just man?' Then
Alchasaios was taken aback and did not wash himself in the water.

Again, a long time after, he wanted to wash in a stretch of water and told
his disciples to look for a place [with little] water, so that he could wash there.
His disciples [found the] place for him. As he [was preparing] himself to wash,
again he saw in that spring also the apparition of a man. It spoke to him: 'We
and those other waters in the lake (literally: "sea" i.e. lake or river) are one.
Now you have come here to offend against us and to abuse us.' Alchasaios, in
great alarm and agitation allowed the dirt to dry on his head and then [shook]
it off.

[Again] (Mani) expounded how Alchasaios kept ploughs [lying ready] and
went [to] them. [The earth] however made its voice heard and said to him:
'[Why] do you make your profit from me?' Then Alchasaios took clods of the
earth which had spoken to him, wept, kissed them, took them to his bosom
and began to speak: 'This is the flesh and blood of my lord' (Matth. 26, 26–27).

Again (Mani) said, that Alchasaios came upon his disciples as they were
baking bread and the bread therefore spoke to him. He then ordered that
there should be no more baking of bread.[2]

Mani's Judaeo-Christian upbringing might explain his familiarity with certain
Jewish and Christian scriptures. He and his followers made extensive use of
both the Gospel texts (possibly through a harmony like Tatian's *Diatessaron*)
and the Pauline corpus, which he acquired probably through reading the
writings of Marcion as part of his reaction against the Jewish element in the
teaching of the sect.

The *gnosis* of Mani

While there is little doubt that Mani had come under Judaeo-Christian influence from an early stage of his life, the core of his teaching consists of a myth
which finds few echoes in mainstream Judaeo-Christian teaching even though
some of its main themes have parallels in esoteric Jewish and Gnostic writings.
The dualism of Manichaeism is primarily a dualism of body (which is entirely
evil) and spirit (which is a part of divinity). To explain how the intermingling
of good and evil took place before the creation of mankind, Mani developed
an elaborate and polytheistic cosmogonic myth of a primeval invasion of the
Kingdom of Light by the forces of Darkness. The former is ruled over by
the Father of Greatness who is the epitome of all that is good, beautiful
and honourable and his realm is completely insulated from the horrors of

---

2 *Cologne Manichaean Codex* 94.1–97.10 (eds. Koenen and Römer, 66–8); trans. Lieu et al., in
Gardner and Lieu, *Manichaean texts from the Roman empire*, 63.

war and suffering. It is composed of five Light Elements: Air, Wind, Light, Water and Fire; and it also consists of five dwellings: Intelligence, Knowledge, Reason, Thought and Deliberation. The latter is the dominion of the Prince of Darkness, who is depicted as a multiform monster and whose infernal kingdom is characterised by concupiscence and strife. As the Kingdom of Light is not equipped for war, not even for its own self-defence, its ruler has to evoke other deities to fulfil this unaccustomed role. He calls forth from within himself the Mother of Life (also called the Great Spirit) and she in turn calls forth the Primal Man whom she arms with the five Light Elements. In the initial encounter, the Primal Man is overwhelmed by the powers of Darkness and is lulled into a death-like sleep and his armour of Light Elements is partly devoured by the Archons of Darkness. The Father then evokes a new series of divinities for the rescue of the Primal Man. Of these the Living Spirit with his five Sons who were his evocations – the Custodian of Splendour, the Great King of Honour, Adamas of Light, the King of Glory and Atlas – come down and call out to him in a piercing voice, whereupon the Primal Man responds and is awakened. This leads to a reunion of the Primal Man with the Father and heralds a complex process for the redemption of the Light Elements held captive as Light-Particles in the bodies of the Archons of Darkness. Ten heavens and eight earths are created and in their lower sections are imprisoned the Archons of Darkness. A new evocation, the hermaphroditic (Third) Envoy, then seduces the male and female Archons with his/her good looks and induces them to ejaculate or abort the Light-Particles held captive in them. These fall on the earth and bring forth plant and animal life. A complex system involving a set of Three Wheels of wind, of water and of fire is constructed and empowered by them; the main planetary and stellar bodies are then set in motion to return the Light-Particles to their original abode. The redeemed Light-Particles are transported via the Column of Glory whose visible appearance is the Milky Way. The Light-Particles are drawn up, refined and sublimated and at the same time conveyed along the Milky Way from the moon to the sun. The two stellar bodies are both receiving stations for the Light-Particles as well as vessels for their conveyance. The periodic waxing and waning of the moon is therefore caused by the migration of these Light-Particles. From the sun the Light-Particles eventually go to a New Earth, which is created by the Great Builder. This New Earth or Paradise ruled by the Primal Man is not the same as the Kingdom of Light but is made of the same substance. Its main function is to be a home for the deities that have been evoked and the Light that they have redeemed so that the Kingdom of Light may remain aloof from the turmoil.

Smarted by this apparent defeat, the Prince of Darkness creates a pair of male and female demons. The former devours the offspring of the abortions and thereby ingests their Light-Particles within them and copulates with his partner who gives birth to the First Man (Adam) and the First Woman (Eve), who are microcosms – exact miniatures of the universe (macrocosm) – since both possess a mixture of Light and Matter.

Made blind and deaf by Matter, Adam is unaware and forgetful of his distant divine origin. His soul, firmly bound to the accursed body, has literally 'lost consciousness'. It is at that moment that the transcendent Jesus – whom the Manichaeans termed (in Syriac) *Yishô' Zîwâ*, that is, 'Jesus-the-Splendour' or 'Jesus of Light' – comes to his aid. In this way, Jesus, whose role for the Manichaeans as also for Gnosticism is significantly cosmic in scope, fulfils his more usual function of teacher and as exorciser of demons. He shows Adam the Father in the heights and his own self which is cast down before the teeth of wild beasts, devoured by dogs, mingled with and imprisoned in everything that exists, shackled in the corruption of darkness. Jesus also raises him and makes him eat of the Tree of Life through which he comes to full realisation of the imprisonment of his divine soul by his sinful body. To achieve the separation of these elements, the Third Envoy evokes the 'Column of Glory', up which the particles of Light can climb. First they take their place in the moon, and when the moon wanes they are transported to the sun and, from there, on to Paradise. Eventually a new Paradise is constructed for the light-gods. When the Light-Particles in the world have been purified enough for them to come together into the last 'statue', the end of the world starts. A Universal Fire of 1,468 years takes place and finally the darkness is compressed into a lump (Gr. *bolos*), in which certain sinful souls remain.

The long-term imprisonment of Light by Matter in the physical universe, which the Manichaeans see as a form of crucifixion and personified by the 'suffering Jesus' (*Jesus patibilis*), has important practical consequences for those who have been illumined by Mani's *gnosis*. Their duty is to be instruments for the liberation of this Light. To do this requires both a conscious effort for virtue by the individual and the avoidance of any action that might harm the Light or prolong its captivity. The Manichaeans are therefore enjoined to observe the 'Five Commandments' (fasting, alms-giving, no killing, no flesh-eating and poverty) and the 'Three Seals', i.e., those of 'mouth, hands and breast'. Strict observance of these rules is of course only possible for a select few and the sect therefore consists of a dyarchy of Elect (who endeavour to keep all the laws) and the Hearers (who are allowed to marry and to procreate and generate wealth as long as they serve the daily needs of the Elect).

The Manichaean canon

Mani was a prodigious author who was anxious that his teaching should survive him, and the sect came to revere a canon of his writings:

1 the *Living gospel*
2 the *Treasure of life*
3 the *Pragmateia*
4 the *Book of mysteries*
5 the *Book of the giants*
6 the *Epistles*
7 *Psalms and prayers.*

In addition to these the Manichaeans possessed a picture-book illustrating the cosmogonic teaching of Mani, which is known as the *Ardahang* in Middle Iranian sources. Of the seven canonical works, only the *Epistles* were found among the Coptic Manichaean codices discovered at Medinet Madi in 1930, but, sadly, before the codex was conserved and photographed, it was lost at the end of the Second World War. Even so, about two dozen letters survived on a few leaves and a similar number of other letters have also been found at Kellis, which are now being edited and published separately.[3]

The titles of most of the canonical works were known to the fathers, with the result that citations from them have survived in polemical as well as Manichaean texts. The *Living gospel* is twice cited in the *Cologne Mani-Codex* (65.23–68.5 and 68.5–69.8), but the first citation from the prologue is more fully preserved in two Middle Iranian fragments from Turfan:

(a) *Middle Persian version*[4]
Header He teaches the Gospel Aleph.[5]
(She was praised and be praised), the Maiden of Light head of all wisdoms. It was praised and is praised, the holy church, by the power of the Father, by the praise of the Mother, and [by the wisdom of the Son], and on the speakers and hearers of the true word. (*8 lines left blank*) Let there be praise and honour to the Father and to the Son and to the Holy Ghost and [to the holy book.]

[. . . *ca. 15 lines lost* . . . which instructs eye and] ear, and teaches the fruit of truth. (*8 lines left blank*)

---

3 The letters from the surviving leaves of the now lost Epistle-Codex are currently being edited by W.-P. Funk. The letters from Kellis are being edited by I. M. F. Gardner for the publications of the Dakhleh Oasis Project.
4 M17 (ed. and trans. D. N. MacKenzie, 'I, Mani . . .', 184 and 186–90).
5 Middle Persian: 'rb. According to Arabic sources, the Gospel of Mani was composed of twenty-two chapters, each after a letter of the Semitic alphabet.

I Mani, apostle of Jesus the friend, by the will of the Father, the true God, he from whom I came to be, . . . is after all (things), and everything which has been and will be stands by his power. The fortunate receive this (good) news, the wise recognise (it), the strong don (it, *sc.* as their armour), the learned [consider (?)](it to be) better . . .

The polytheistic nature of the work is established by the praise given in the first extract to two female deities unknown to Christianity; there can be no doubt that the Manichaean version of the life of Jesus contained in the *Living gospel* was dissimilar to the accounts found in the Christian Gospels.

Manichaeism in a Christian milieu in the Roman empire

Mani won the support of the Sassanid King of Kings Shapur I, who allowed him to disseminate his religion in the now considerably enlarged Persian empire. It was missionary success in frontier cities like Edessa, Nisibis and Palmyra that brought the religion into the Roman empire. Mani continued to enjoy the patronage of the Persian court until the accession of Vahram I who had Mani thrown into jail, where he died of torture (*c.* 276). The martyrdom of Mani was commemorated annually at the Feast of the Bema, the most important event in the Manichaean calendar in which an image of Mani was placed on a special platform (*bema*). The event falls near the Christian celebration of Easter. According to Augustine, this meant that Manichaean converts from Christianity celebrated the Feast of the Bema with the same fervour as the Paschal Feast which they once held dear.[6]

One of the earliest notices of the missionary endeavours of Manichaeism in the Roman East is a pastoral letter from a Christian leader warning the faithful against followers of the 'madness' (a pun on Mani's name in Greek) of Mani:

Again the Manichaeans speak [falsely against marriage saying that] he does well [who does not] marry. [Paul] says that the man who does not marry [does better;] but that adulterer and forni[cator are evil is manifest from the] Holy Scriptures, from which we learn [that marriage is honoured by God, but that He abominates forni]cators and adulterers. Whereby it is manifest [that He condemns] them also that worship the creation who [. . . have committed adultery] with sticks and stones. Not but what God commandeth us [to chastise the man that doeth] evil: in these words [If there be found man or woman] in one of the cities which the Lord thy God giveth thee that has

6 Augustine, *Contra epistolam fundamenti* 8 (CSEL 25¹: 202–3)

wrought wickedness in the sight of the Lord thy God and hath worshipped [the sun or any of the host of heaven,] it is an abomination unto the Lord thy God. Every one that doth [these things is an abomination unto the Lord] thy God.

And the Manichees manifestly wor[ship the creation (? and that which they say)] in their psalms is an abomination to the Lord [. . . (saying) 'Neither] have I cast it (*sc.* the bread) into the oven: another hath brought me this and I have eaten it without guilt.' Whence we can easily conclude that the Manichaeans are filled with such madness; especially since this 'Apology to the Bread' is the work of a man filled with much madness.

As I said before, I have cited this in brief from the document of the madness of the Manichaeans that fell into my hands, that we may be on our guard against these who with deceitful and lying words steal into our houses, and particularly against those women whom they call 'elect' and whom they hold in honour, manifestly because they require their menstrual blood for the abominations of their madness . . .[7]

Despite the efforts of the early missionaries to promote Manichaeism as a superior form of Christianity, they were limited in their ability to claim that their teaching was biblical because they could not compromise Mani's teaching which they were obliged to copy and disseminate as laid down in his canonical writings. A literal acceptance of the historical and scientific truth of Mani's cosmogonic myth is essential for the believer as it alone gives the rationale for the cult's two-tiered structure and asceticism. This 'totalitarian *gnosis*' allows for no allegorical interpretation of Manichaean myth. As one of the earliest critics of Mani's teaching, the Neoplatonist Alexander of Lycopolis, observes:

Besides, the Manichaeans went far beyond the creators of myth, those who emasculate Uranus, dream up the plots hatched against Kronos by his son, desirous of seizing power, or who, still with this same Kronos, have his children eaten, then say how he was deceived by the appearance of the stone. Are not their utterances of the same order when they introduce, quite frankly, a combat fought by the matter against God? And they do not even mean it in a figurative sense, like the way in which Homer, in the Iliad, shows Zeus taking pleasure in the spectacle of the gods in confrontation with one another, in order to indicate thereby that the world is made up of dissimilar elements adjusted one to another which sometimes dominate and are sometimes dominated.[8]

This literalism raises the important question as to whether Manichaeans saw themselves as polytheists despite their close affinity to monotheistic

---

7 *P. Rylands Greek* 469, ll. 12–34; trans. C. H. Roberts, *Catalogue of the Greek and Latin papyri*, 43.
8 Alexander of Lycopolis, *Contra Manichaei opiniones disputatio* 10 (ed. Brinkmann, 16.9–20); trans. Lieu in Gardner and Lieu, *Manichaean texts from the Roman empire*.

Christianity. The 'Prayer of the Emanations' from Kellis, which was composed in Greek, throws fascinating new light on this important aspect of Manichaean self-definition. The text was found inscribed on both sides of a single wooden board; the style of the Greek is too good for it to be a translation and it is therefore likely to have been an original composition in that language.[9] The text begins with praise for the Great Father of Lights (i.e. Father of Greatness), the principal deity of the Manichaean pantheon:

> I worship and glorify the Great Father of Lights from pure thought. With a guileless word have been glorified and honoured you and your majesty and the wholly blessed aeons. For you in glory have perfected their foundation. Your power and glory and your light and word and your majesty and the aeons of affirmation and all your counsel have been glorified. For you are God the foundation of every grace and life and truth.[10]

But then the author of the prayer gives praise to other Manichaean deities and does not hesitate to call them gods (theoi):

> I worship and glorify all gods, all angels, all splendours, all luminaries, all powers, those which are from the great and glorious f(ath)er, those which subsist in his holiness and in his light are nourished, purified from all darkness and malignance.[11]

Despite this polytheistic teaching, the Manichaean community in Kellis (an isolated location in the late third and early fourth centuries) saw themselves as true Christians. The lack of pressure for religious conformity and of administrative coercion in the Dakhleh oasis enabled the Manichaean community there to develop its doctrines without having to reconfigure the inherent polytheism of its cosmogony in line with the general trend towards monotheism. The fact that a normative text from Paul's letter to the Romans (2.6–29) in the Sub-Achmimic dialect was found in House 3 at Kellis[12] indicates that New Testament texts were read by the sect and probably used as a stylistic model for presenting Manichaean literature in Coptic. They also identified themselves as 'members of the holy church, the sons and/or daughters of the Light Mind (Nous).'[13] The Light-Nous, a divine messenger and enlightener, is often met in

---

9 Cf. 'The Prayer of the Emanations in Greek from Kellis', ed. Jenkins.
10 Prayer of the Emanations, ll. 2–14; trans. Jenkins, 255.
11 Prayer of the Emanations, ll. 15–22; trans. Jenkins, 255.
12 P. Kell. Copt. 6 (ed. I. M. F. Gardner, Kellis literary texts, I: 82–4).
13 P. Kell. Copt. 31.1–4 (eds. I. M. F. Gardner et al., Coptic documentary texts from Kellis, I: 209–11).

genuine Manichaean sources in Coptic from Medinet Madi and also in texts in Middle Iranian, Old Turkish and Chinese in Central Asia – yet it was never mentioned by the fathers, not even by Augustine, in their voluminous works against the sect. Clearly the fathers' polemic, including Augustine's, possibly did not know and certainly did not understand the significance of 'Light Mind (*Nous*)'.

The church fathers and Manichaeism

The end of the Great Persecution against the Christians heralded a period of religious peace in the Roman empire from which the Manichaeans were able to benefit. The sect gained followers in almost all parts of the Roman empire, especially in Syria, Mesopotamia, Egypt, North Africa and Italy. Christian leaders soon directed polemics against the sect, especially to counter the claim by the sect that its martyred founder was stamped with the 'seal of the prophet'. One of the most popular works against the sect – the *Acta Archelai* – depicts Mani as a failed prophet who was jailed by the Persian king for failing to cure his son. He escaped from jail and crossed over to the Roman empire but was worsted in a public debate by a Christian bishop called Archelaus at Carchar (= Carrhae?). He was later recaptured by the Persians and was tortured and flayed alive for having bribed the guards to facilitate his earlier escape.[14] This version of Mani's life, which is accompanied by a summary of his teaching, enjoyed wide circulation.[15] Polemicists like Epiphanius based their attack on the founder of the sect almost entirely on the information provided by the *Acta*.[16]

Manichaean missionaries were noted for the reverence they paid to their scriptures, but the secretive nature of the sect coupled with the destruction of confiscated Manichaean books by officials meant that the fathers often did not have direct access to genuine literature of the sect. Two of the earliest polemics against the sect in Greek, by Titus of Bostra[17] and Serapion of Thmuis,[18] both display only secondary knowledge of the sect's writings and they both appear to have used a similar florilegium of Manichaean citations, which was probably

---

14 *Acta Archelai* 62–7 (GCS 16: 82–97); trans. M. Vermes, *Hegemonius*, 140–51.
15 See further Lieu, *Manichaeism in Mesopotamia and the Roman East*, 132–52.
16 Epiphanius, *Panarion* 66.1–31 (GCS edn, III: 13–31).
17 Titus of Bostra, *Adversus Manichaeos*; on Titus as a source see esp. P. Nagel, 'Neues griechisches Material zu Titus von Bostra'.
18 Serapion of Thmuis, *Contra Manichaeos*; on Serapion, see esp. K. Fitschen, *Serapion von Thmuis*, 19–57 and 164–204 (trans.).

compiled by the Christian church for the purpose of refutation. Serapion, Titus and Epiphanius alike attack the dualistic implications of Mani's teaching, especially as evident in the first act of the Manichaean cosmic drama. However it is very hard to work out whether a genuine Manichaean tenet was being attacked or whether it was a suppositious one, invented for the purpose of refutation by inference from the general premises of dualism.[19] Epiphanius, who had made use of a summary of Manichaean cosmogony derived from the *Acta Archelai*,[20] simply derided the details of Manichaean cosmogonic myth as a clear indication of the impotence of the Father of Greatness to exert his influence over forces of Darkness and as proof that the other deities of the Manichaean pantheon were on a par with the gods of the pagan theogony and mythology.[21]

The notable exception among the Christian polemicists in their knowledge of Manichaeism was of course Augustine of Hippo, who spent nine years as a Manichaean Hearer while he was a student and teacher at Carthage. He was the only church father (with the possible exception of Severus of Antioch)[22] to have preserved for us a substantial number of extracts from the genuine writings of Mani. Particularly notable are a long passage from the *Thesaurus* and a considerable number of fragments from a work known as the *Epistula fundamenti*, which was probably one of Mani's canonical epistles. His friendship with Faustus of Mileu, the most erudite of Manichaean debaters, enabled him to witness a Manichaean missionary at work and his lengthy refutation of the 'Apologia' of Faustus is an invaluable source of Manichaean and anti-Manichaean positions on the authority of the Christian scriptures.

One area of contention between the polemicists and the Manichaeans is the figure of Jesus who features prominently in Manichaean texts both East and West. He fulfilled both the role of the Gnostic saviour (or enlightener) and of the historical Messiah who was a prefiguration of Mani. However, because of their abhorrence for human conception and birth, the Manichaeans believed that if Christ was born of a woman, even if she were a virgin, he could not have been divine. For a Son of God to take human nature would be to contaminate

---

19 For an excellent survey of all known anti-Manichaean writings in Greek, see W. Klein, *Die Argumentation in den griechisch-christlichen Antimanichaica.*
20 *Acta Archelai* 7–13 (GCS 16: 9–22) = Epiphanius, *Panarion* 66.25–31 (GCS edn, III: 53–72).
21 Epiphanius, *Panarion* 66.46–9 (GCS edn, III: 83–7).
22 See Severus, *Cathedral homily* 123 (PO 29: 124–88); the homily was originally composed in Greek although it has only survived in Syriac recensions. Severus cites from an unnamed work of Mani and the citations he gives appear much fuller and more genuine than those normally found in Greek anti-Manichaean writings.

himself with evil. As a divine figure, he never truly suffered death on the cross; the Manichaeans believed instead that he feigned death. His suffering was a similitude, an *exemplum* for the deliverance of our souls; it was the Evil One (and not the real Christ, as other Gnostic teachers alleged) who at a distance stood and laughed at the crucified Christ. As the 'Jesus of Light', he is also a redeemer of the enslaved Light and alongside the Mother of Life and the Living Spirit helps to ferry the freed Light-Particles from the moon to the sun. Finally, as Jesus *patibilis*, he personifies the suffering of Light-Particles 'crucified' in Matter.[23] A Manichaean preacher like Faustus, therefore, could speak in a similar but not identical theological language on such basic doctrinal issues as the Trinity:

> We worship one deity, under the threefold title of the Almighty God the Father, and His Son Christ, and of the Holy Spirit. While these are one and the same, we believe also that the Father properly dwells in the highest or principal light, which Paul calls light inaccessible, and the Son is His second or visible light. And as the Son is Himself twofold, according to the Apostle, who speaks of Christ **as** the power of God and the wisdom of God, we believe that His power dwells in the sun, and His wisdom in the moon. We also believe that the Holy Spirit, the third Majesty, has set His seat and His home in the whole circle of the atmosphere. By His influence and spiritual infusion, the earth conceives and brings forth the suffering Jesus, who, as hanging from every tree, is the life and salvation of men. Though you oppose these doctrines so violently, your religion resembles ours in attaching the same sacredness to the bread and wine that we do to everything, this is our belief, which you will have an opportunity of hearing more of, if you wish to do so.[24]

The sect's rejection of substantial parts of the Old Testament as essential for salvation would have given it an obvious edge in debates given the ambivalent attitude of most Christians towards the Old Covenant in late antiquity. Moreover, the Manichaeans claimed to be true Christians who did not rely on a revision of basic Christian tenets, but who instead maintained that the essence of Christianity was conduct rather than doctrine. Faustus claimed that he accepted the gospel, but by gospel he meant the preaching of Christ – and by the preaching of Christ, he meant exclusively the moral commands. The essence of Christianity therefore was morality, not theology, and Faustus was not slow to insist that professing a doctrine is incomparably easier than submitting to a set of strict moral commands:

23 Augustine, *c. Faust.* 20.11 (CSEL 25[1]: 550).
24 Augustine, *c. Faust.* 20.2 (CSEL 25[1]: 536).

Do you accept the Gospel? – You ask me whether I accept it when it is clear to me that I accept it because I observe what it commands. Or shall I ask you whether you accept it even though there seems to be no indication of acceptance of the Gospel? I have left father and mother, wife, children and whatever else that is commanded by the Gospel (Matt. 19:29) and you ask whether I accept the Gospel? Unless you are still ignorant of what it is that is called the Gospel. For it is nothing other than the commandments of Christ. I have rejected silver and gold and have ceased to keep even copper in my waistband. I am content with my daily food, caring nothing for that of tomorrow, not anxious as to how my stomach is to be filled or my body covered (Matt. 10:9 ff and 6:25 ff.) and you ask me if I accept the Gospel? You see in me those Beatitudes of Christ (Matt. 5:3 ff.) which make up the Gospel; and you ask whether I accept it? You see me poor, you see me meek, you see me peace-loving, one pure in heart, mourning, accepting hunger, thirst, and suffering persecutions and hatred for righteousness' sake and you doubt if I accept the Gospel?[25]

Since Manichaean asceticism bore so many practical resemblances to its Christian counterpart, the Manichaeans were not unjustified in thinking that their version was superior in that it was demanded of all the Elect and was the *sine qua non* of full salvation. The strict moral commands of the sect do not stem from a desire for personal holiness but from a strictly negative view of the human body – especially its sexual functions. Moreover, because the Manichaeans saw the cosmos as we know it as the product of concupiscence on the part of the Archons of Darkness, their theory of the subsequent imprisonment of the soul in matter was an attempt to explain the mixture of good and evil in men. This explanation, which absolves both the Godhead and mankind from being the source of evil, was a great attraction to the young Augustine – and, no doubt, to many others – and it therefore had to be countered intellectually with full force. Manichaean dualism appeared to Christian theologians in late antiquity to eliminate or weaken moral responsibility by assuming that evil (like goodness) has a real substantial existence and that its appearance in human life is due to the mixture of two dissimilar substances in the constitution of man. Unlike theologians who followed Paul's pessimistic view of an enfeebled and corrupt human nature that suffers from the fall of Adam, Christian opponents of Manichaean dualism had to begin their defence with the insistence that man is by nature good and that evil is the result of behaviour guided by an unhealthy will. Against Manichaeans who would argue that natural disasters (such as earthquakes and volcanic eruptions) and human

25 Augustine, *c. Faust.* 5.1 (CSEL 25[1]: 271).

catastrophes (such as wars and massacres) stem from an evil first principle, a Christian father like Titus would defend the Christian position of a benevolent Creator-God by arguing that human greed and propensity to live sinfully lay at the heart of many such human miseries and that many of these problems could be alleviated by ascetic living and a peaceful outlook. Moreover, death brings to the Christians not only the end of their struggle against sin but also the enjoyment of the fruits of their labour of virtue that accrue to the pious after death.[26]

Manichaean asceticism and cultic practice featured strongly in the anti-Manichaean writings of Leo the Great (sed. 440–61), who was the only pope to take to the offensive against the sect. Shortly after he had ascended the throne of St Peter, he received a report which informed him of certain obscene rites which were celebrated by the Manichaeans and he immediately ordered a full inquiry. A number of Manichaean Elect of both sexes were summoned before a commission and they confessed under interrogation to hideous crimes involving ceremonial intercourse between a youth and girl of ten arranged by a Manichaean bishop. In his sermons, Leo pointed out that Mani's claim to be the Paraclete was bogus because the Holy Spirit had already been given to the apostles at Pentecost. Leo also pointed out that the excessive fasting of the Manichaeans was due to their denial of the humanity of Christ rather than to any genuine ascetical principles. He also attacked the interest shown by Manichaeans in astrology as a form of fatalism. Above all, the Manichaeans relied not only on canonical Christian scriptures but also on apocryphal Christian writings for their canon of scriptures.[27] The findings of Leo's investigative committee duly prompted the reigning emperors to issue orders for the arrest of Manichaeans and severe penalties for those who had committed sacrilege; they also declared adherence to the sect to be a public crime.[28]

Within the context of a Christian empire, some of the sect's membership might have developed into either a philosophical school or an extreme ascetic movement that relied more on the continuing re-interpretation of the essence of Mani's teaching than on a strict adherence to the canonical writings of the original founder. An increasingly tenuous connection to the original texts by the Manichaeans themselves, coupled with the aforementioned ignorance of Manichaean sources among their Christian opponents, made the liberal use of

---

26 Titus of Bostra, *Adv. Manich.* 2.24 (ed. de Lagarde, 41.4–42.30).
27 Leo the Great, *Tractatus* 16.4 (CCSL 138: 64) and *Tractatus* 9.4 (138: 37); see esp. all the relevant material by Leo on Manichaeism collected in H. G. Schipper and J. van Oort, *Leo Magnus, sermones et epistulae*, 11–16 and 39–51.
28 CTh, *Leges Novellae Valentiniani* 18 (eds. Mommsen and Meyer, II: 103–5).

the term 'Manichaean' for abuse increasingly easy during the major theological debates of the fourth and fifth centuries. Even as staunch an opponent of Manichaeism as Severus of Antioch was anathematised as a Manichaean.[29] The severe persecution of the sect instigated by Justinian marked the end of the use of Manichaean scriptures both by the sect and by its opponents.[30] It was this demythologised and sanitised version of Manichaeism that would later be used by the orthodox-minded churchmen in Byzantium and the medieval West as a heretical prototype against neo-Gnostic sects such as the Paulicians of Asia Minor, the Bogomils of the Balkans, the Paterenes of Italy and above all the Cathars of Languedoc.

Bibliography

PRIMARY SOURCES

Note: M + number denotes one of the manuscript signatures of Manichaean Text fragments, in the Manichaean script, housed in several institutions and museums in Berlin.

Acta Archelai (GCS 16)

Alexander of Lycopolis. *Contra Manichaei opiniones disputatio*, ed. A. Brinkmann (Leipzig, 1895)

Augustine. *Contra epistulam fundamenti* (CSEL 25¹)
   Contra Faustum (CSEL 25¹)

Codex Theodosianus (CTh). Eds. T. Mommsen and P. Meyer, *Theodosiani libri XVI cum Constitutionibus Sirmondianis et leges novellae ad Theodosianum pertinentes* (Berlin, 1954²)

Cologne Manichaean Codex. Eds. L. Koenen and C. Römer, *Der Kölner Mani-Kodex (Über das Werden seines Leibes), Kritische Edition aufgrund der von A. Henrichs und L. Koenen besorgten Erstedition* (Opladen, 1988)

Epiphanius. *Panarion* (GCS: *Ancoratus und Panarion*)

Eustathius the Monk. *Epistula de duabus naturis adversus Severum* (CCSG 19)

Leo the Great. *Tractatus septem et nonaginta* (CCSL 138, 138a)

Mani, *Kephalaia*, eds. H.-J. Polotsky, A. Böhlig and W.-P. Funk (Stuttgart, 1940–)

Prayer of the Emanations. Ed. R. G. Jenkins, 'The Prayer of the Emanations in Greek from Kellis', *Le muséon* 108 (1995): 243–63

Serapion of Thmuis. *Contra Manichaeos.* Ed. P. P. Casey, *Serapion of Thmuis against the Manichees*, Harvard Theological Studies 15 (Cambridge, MA, 1931)

Severus of Antioch. *Cathedral homily 123* (PO 29)

Titus of Bostra. *Adversus Manichaeos.* Ed. P. A. de Lagarde, *Titi Bostreni quae ex opere contra Manichaeos edito in codice Hamburgensi servata sunt* (Berlin, 1859)

Zachariah of Mitylene. *Life of Severus* (PO 2: 1–115)

---

29 Zachariah of Mitylene, *Life of Severus* (PO 2: 349); see also Eustathius the Monk, *Epistula de duabus naturis adversus Severum* 3 (CCSG 19: 413).

30 Cf. S. N. C. Lieu, 'An early Byzantine formula for the renunciation of Manichaeism'.

SECONDARY SOURCES

Fitschen, K. *Serapion von Thmuis, Echte und Unechte Schriften sowie die Zeugnisse des Athanasius und Anderer*, PTS 37 (Berlin, 1992)

Gardner, I. M. F., ed. *Kellis literary texts*, I, Dakhleh Oasis Project: monograph 4 (Oxford, 1996)

Gardner, I. M. F., Anthony Alcock and Wolf-Peter Funk, eds. *Coptic documentary texts from Kellis*, I, Dakhleh Oasis Project: monograph 9 (Oxford, 1999)

Gardner, I. M. F. and S. N. C. Lieu, eds. *Manichaean texts from the Roman empire* (Cambridge, 2004)

Klein, W. *Die Argumentation in den griechisch-christlichen Antimanichaica* (Wiesbaden, 1991)

Lieu, S. N. C. 'An early Byzantine formula for the renunciation of Manichaeism', *JbAC* 26 (1983): 152–218

Manichaeism in Mesopotamia and the Roman East (Leiden, 1994)

Manichaeism in the later Roman empire and medieval China (Tübingen, 1992²)

MacKenzie, D. N. 'I, Mani . . .', in H. Preißler and H. Seiwert, eds., *Gnosisforschung und Religionsgeschichte, Festschrift für Prof. Kurt Rudolph* (Marburg, 1994), 183–98

Nagel, P. 'Neues griechisches Material zu Titus von Bostra', in H. Ibscher, ed., *Studia Byzantina* (Berlin, 1973), II: 285–350

Roberts, C. H., ed. and trans. *Catalogue of the Greek and Latin papyri in the John Rylands Library Manchester, Vol. III: Theological and literary texts* (Manchester, 1938)

Schipper, H. G. and J. van Oort. *Leo Magnus, sermones et epistulae*, Corpus Fontium Manichaeorum, Series Latina 1 (Turnhout, 2000)

Vermes, M. *Hegemonius, Acta Archelai*, Manichaean Studies 4 (Turnhout, 2001)

12

Heresiology: The invention of 'heresy' and 'schism'

J. REBECCA LYMAN

Heresiology was the combative theological genre for asserting true Christian doctrine through hostile definition and ecclesiastical exclusion. In the fourth to sixth centuries the union of Christian orthodoxy with Roman political power can easily seem to modern eyes to be a bad match. Emperors peeved by the inability of religious practitioners to come to an enforceable consensus for the protection of the state worked with bishops increasingly polarised by local traditions and civic unrest in a high stakes game of imperial orthodoxy. The unprecedented Roman imperial legislation on religious dissent was entwined with the general expansion of bureaucracy and law in the later empire. In this political context heresy was increasingly no longer only an ecclesiastical matter or a serious theological challenge, but a problem of public safety since correct belief and worship ensured the unity and stability of society. Heresiological categories were often a means to establish or maintain common boundaries. The development of creeds and imperial law, however, was matched by an increasing theological and political complexity so that conflicts in at least North Africa, Syria and Egypt persisted due to regional concerns and local theological traditions.

The literary genre of heresiology shifted in this era as older Christian sectarian structures gave way to ecumenical councils and increasingly sophisticated theological definitions. Heresiology can be read as the political claim of an exclusive ideology made through the demonisation, exclusion and silencing of 'the other'. Ironically, this can simply be the negative reading of the apologetic historical narrative that presented an evolutionary orthodox core that was defended from incursions.[1] Actual historical practice did not match the analytical clarity of this binary category. Rather than merely a defensive

---

1 Compare R. Lim's largely political analysis of a dogmatic Christianity in *Public disputation, power, and social order in late antiquity* to J. Pelikan's apologetic in *The emergence of the catholic tradition*. A. Cameron discusses these problems in 'How to read heresiology'.

declaration of established belief or power, heresiology reveals the creative theological definitions and social anxieties involved in a continual construction of ancient Christian identity. Rhetorical techniques such as labelling or genealogies and literary genres such as cultural histories or intellectual catalogues can be examined in historical context to reveal not only social or religious attempts at expulsion, but also theological negotiation with contemporary cultural problems of multiplicity and difference in Roman society. Ecclesiastical unity and doctrinal clarity were to be achieved as much as defended. The increasing classification of error therefore reflected the dynamism of the theological tradition as well as the general codification of Roman life and thought during the later empire.

Genres of disputation and identity in late antiquity

Heresiology developed in the first three centuries as a Christian literary discourse to define and refute theological error as a means of ensuring correct belief and exclusive identity. Like many products of late antiquity it was a hybrid of various local cultural and religious traditions that had been placed in dialogue by the unified Roman empire; the authors of the Second Sophistic, for example, argued for Hellenism as the ancient universal tradition.[2] Linking the biblical images of demonically inspired false prophets to the succession of teachers which underlay the integrity of the philosophical schools, Justin Martyr in second-century Rome began to use the neutral term for sect or choice (*hairesis*) as a demonic label for Christian error: 'heresy'. The labelling of opponents as erroneous or innovative and the construction of genealogies to show their illegitimate successions were acknowledged means of debate in Hellenic culture. However, the uniting of demonic inspiration with doctrinal error created the sharp spiritual and apocalyptic boundary between truth and 'heresy' by Justin in his *Apology* and continued by Irenaeus of Lyon in *Against all heresies*; this theological category mirrored of course the high religious and sociological boundaries of their early sectarian communities. Saving belief could not be a neutral choice. Those whose choices or communities were different were literally demonised. The image of the 'heretic' was further cast rhetorically in a combination of immoral charges (deceptive, unfaithful, duplicitous and promiscuous) as well as social violations

---

2 See G. Bowersock, *Hellenism in late antiquity*; Tim Whitmarsh, *Greek literature and the Roman empire*.

(superstitious, elitist, social climbing, plagiarist, rebellious). These literary strategies of pejorative and excluding labels, immoral charges, and demonic and therefore external genealogies became the foundation in Christian thought and life for categorising theological opponents.[3] These negative images highlighted starkly the saving authenticity of apostolic succession, true doctrine as unchanging, and the community as essentially unified. The later development of handbooks of heresies or the diptychs of holy ancestors were the expansion and public codification of these early individual polemical techniques. As we will discuss below, problems developed in these later comprehensive handbooks since they now included, or the diptychs now excluded, ancestors who in earlier genealogies or local contexts had been considered orthodox.

The development of central institutions of theological and imperial authority in the fourth to sixth centuries transformed the sectarian practices of Christian unity and diversity. No central institution or political process had existed to regulate belief before the fourth century, but rather communication among local communities created webs of theological and ecclesiastical consensus. Given the geographical diversity of Christianity, doctrinal variations were inherent, if gradually regulated by literature that established common beliefs and emerging boundaries; Irenaeus noted over an argument on the dating of Easter, 'Our diversity in the fast confirms our agreement in the faith.'[4] Local tradition was rooted in genealogies and practices from earliest missionaries, and often defensively defined in controversy with others such as the conflict on baptism between Cyprian of Carthage and Stephen of Rome. From the fourth century on, theological controversies were public and often lengthy, punctuated by new representative councils called and enforced by emperors. They also involved powerful urban bishops, sometimes several to a city, as representatives of local traditions rather than individual house church leaders or teachers engaged in mainly literary battles. Not surprisingly, lasting theological consensus was slow to be achieved, politically as well as theologically, due both to the complexity of questions concerning God and salvation, and the difficulty of fully reconciling different theological traditions. Bishops on the defensive appealed to their own inherited local faith, refusing to be placed in a hostile doctrinal genealogy: 'We have neither been followers of Arius (because how should we who are bishops follow a presbyter?) nor have we accepted any other form of faith than that which was set out at the

---

3 A. Le Boulluec, *La notion d'hérésie*.
4 Eusebius, *H.E.* 5.24.13; see also Caroline Bammel, 'Peacemaking and religious tolerance in the early church' and R. Williams, 'Does it make sense to speak of pre-Nicene orthodoxy?'

beginning . . .'[5] Heresiology as an aggressive language of conflict was used deliberately for calculated effect, and for constructing borders to give meaning to compromised and often still volatile centres of definition.

Rhetorically, this unified diversity of apostolic teaching inside the tradition was also made through the boundaries against 'outside' religious traditions as Christian debates over legitimate succession and authentic teaching were consciously positioned within the cultural debates concerning antiquity and universality in ancient religion and society. Thus, the condemnations of Judaism as 'outmoded' and philosophy as 'multiple' or 'human' were means to define Christianity as the only legitimate representative of the sole transcendent truth, even if it obviously contained aspects of these traditions. Associating a heresy with traits of Judaism or Hellenism, if at times appropriate in exegetical debate, rhetorically marginalised opponents within the community, and increasingly reinforced a singular and universal truth revealed only in Christianity. Thus Christianity, in essence, according to Eusebius, was neither Jewish nor Hellenist, but the primary origin of both, so that one could see pre-figurements of Christianity in traditional Mediterranean literature; in contrast Epiphanius argued that Judaism and Hellenism were not incomplete traditions, but heresies opposed to the one truth of Christianity. John of Damascus added Islam to the list of heresies as a result of the later invasions.[6] In spite of the eloquent defence of Hellenism by Celsus, Porphyry and Julian, Christianity defined itself as the only legitimate religious tradition by its antiquity and universality. This transcendence and antiquity therefore enabled some legitimate use and synthesis with these traditions; imbalance, however, would result in heresy. Heresiology was an argument about religious assimilation and authority in the larger Roman context as well as an internal argument concerning theological formulae.[7]

The Nicene controversy

The Nicene controversy lasted over sixty years and resulted in the fundamental re-structuring of Christian theology and ecclesiastical authority through creeds and councils. Historians would no longer contrast an implicit orthodoxy

---

5 For the letter that accompanied the Creed of Antioch (341), see R. Hanson, *The search for the Christian doctrine of God*, 285. See also the protests of Western bishops at being associated with Arius, ibid., 123–5.

6 On Eusebius and Epiphanius, see A. Jacobs, *Remains of the Jews*, 44–8; D. Boyarin, *Border crossings*, 205–6; D. Sahas, *John of Damascus on Islam*.

7 On apologetics and heresiology, see H. Inglebert, *Les romains chrétiens* and R. Lyman, 'The politics of passing'.

to heresy in the complex debates of this century, but rather trace the gradual emergence of a new articulation of incarnation and Trinity over several
generations of theological debate. The origins of the controversy were a local
theological conflict in Alexandria in 318–20 between a presbyter, Arius, and
his bishop, Alexander of Alexandria. Both claimed to be authentic representatives of tradition in their description of the origin of the Son from the Father:
Arius objected to the bishop's apparent carelessness in blurring the distinction of natures between the Father and the Son by his emphasis on eternal
generation, whereas Alexander accused Arius of denying the divinity of the
Son. Both used heresiological categories to give a negative boundary to the
theological formula they were trying to define, rejecting Gnostic, Manichaean
or Sabellian formulae; all these labels had currency in the history of Christian
controversy in Egypt.[8] Positive theological teaching was therefore shaped and
assembled by the array of negative labels. These labels were also applied to each
other as Alexander accused Arius of being 'Jewish' and 'Greek' in his thought,
and denied that his own theology was 'Sabellian'.[9] Although Constantine
responded to the conflict as a minor philosophical dispute among teachers
who should compromise for the sake of imperial peace, the opponents went
on to build alliances based on teaching genealogies and apostolic truth. Not
surprisingly, the Council of Nicaea also worked largely in negative terms. The
short formula defending the eternal unity of the Father and Son included
homoousios, a suspect and little-known term, largely to exclude Arius who had
already repudiated it; the creed also for the first time included anathemas in
order to define and to legislate unacceptable theological formulae.[10]

As the controversy continued Arius as a historical person was rapidly dis-
carded, but as a polemical category he became the eternal archetype for any
teaching which denied the essential divinity of the Son. After Arius' sudden
death in 336, Athanasius attached the theology, and therefore the genealogy,
of Arius to opponents of Nicaea as a means of discrediting them. 'Arians' as
a coherent heretical group were created for future historiography, though
their only commonality was non-acceptance of Nicaea.[11] The construction
of the heretical system followed the older rules of accusing a doctrine of
demonic origin, philosophical speculation, and the association with outsiders

---

8 See Arius' letter to Alexander (ed. Opitz, *Urkunde* 6). On Gnostic Christianity in Egypt
   and the controversy with Dionysius over charges of 'Sabellianism', see Hanson, *The
   Search for the Christian doctrine of God*, 190–3; R. Lyman, 'Arians and Manichees on Christ'.
9 Letter of Arius to Alexander 4 and 46 (ed. Opitz, *Urkunde* 14).
10 O. Skarsaune, 'A neglected detail in the Creed of Nicaea (325)'.
11 M. Wiles, 'Attitudes to Arius in the Arian controversy'.

to the tradition. The motivations and styles of orthodox heresiologists range from the adamant demonisation of any dissent from Alexander's Nicene Creed by Athanasius to Cyril of Jerusalem, who defined orthodoxy as the middle ground between theological extremes of adoptionism and Sabellianism.[12] Equally important, the arguments with 'Arius' opened new theological debates with Marcellus of Ancyra or Apollinarius whose attack on 'Arianism' was viewed to be inadequate from other sides; Sabellianism continued to be a potent label in the East for those defending the essential unity of Father and Son.[13] Polemically, the claims of 'simplicity' and 'scripture' emerged to distance oneself from the image of contentious philosophical disputes, except that all sides claimed to follow ancient apostolic tradition, correct interpretation of scripture and asceticism; indeed more was held in common than disputed, which ironically lent added virulence to the discussion of differences.[14] Basil of Caesarea attempted to distinguish the divisions with an increased vocabulary of schism and heresy, noting that many factions were separated by issues of discipline or leadership rather than doctrine; one needed to proceed cautiously at such a complex time.[15] Finally, the control of popular or public participation became a new concern as urban factions supported various sides of the debate; charges of disorder or violence became important weapons to gain imperial favour.[16]

Nicene orthodoxy gradually arrived through the theological compromises of Athanasius at Alexandria in 362 and the enforcement of the Nicene formula by Theodosius at Constantinople in 381. Enjoying widespread authority as the definitive Christian statement, Nicaea was no longer received as a short defensive statement of faith, but was accepted as a universal confession setting forth positive definitions of divine nature and activity. The condemnation of theological teachings or persons now fixed by legislation and enforced by emperors gave increasing social potency to these literary images of 'heresy'. The boundaries of religion in earlier Roman law had been marked by categories of magic and superstition.[17] Although some heresies followed this classification – the Eunomians for example were linked with magic – the development reflected a scale of harm with, therefore, appropriate penalties. The Eunomians lost social status and property, but they were neither executed nor exiled as in later

12 R. Lyman 'A topography of heresy'.
13 J. Lienhard, 'Basil of Caesarea, Marcellus of Ancyra and "Sabellius"'.
14 R. Vaggione, *Eunomius of Cyzicus and the Nicene revolution*, 100f.
15 W. Löhr, 'Schisma'.
16 T. Gregory, *Vox populi*.
17 The legislation on heresy is collected in *CTh* 16; see further K-L. Noethlichs, *Die gesetzgeberischen Massnahmen der christlichen Kaiser* and Caroline Humfress, 'Roman law'.

Christian history. However, 'Christian' was a name reserved for the orthodox only, and contemporary heretics were externalised by being linked by name and succession to the traditional genealogies of error.

The final enduring legacy of the Nicene crisis was the evocation of the Nicaeno-Constantinopolitan creed at Chalcedon in 451, and its continuing use on all sides of the Christological controversies as a sign of traditional orthodoxy. Although the Nicene Creed had been sufficient, new heresies of the fourth century had called for the expansion of the creed during the contemporary controversies; those who rejected Chalcedon showed their orthodoxy by placing the Nicene Creed within worship for the first time.[18] By the sixth century, the Nicene Creed was used for school exercises by children.[19]

Problematic ancestors and catalogues of error

If councils were setting new universal parameters for the local churches through the actions of bishops, the establishment of doctrinal norms inevitably revealed 'heresy' past and present. Epiphanius, writing during the bitter divisions of Christians in Antioch over the Christological errors of Apollinarius, once a defender of Nicaea, and reflecting the doctrinal multiplicity he had encountered in the desert, insisted that only the orthodox faith of the church was the antidote to the varied poisons of heresy in his encyclopaedic heresiology, *Panarion* or 'The medicine box': 'I shall be telling you the names of the sects and exposing their unlawful deeds like poisons and toxic substances, matching the antidotes with them at the same time – cures for those who are already bitten and preventatives for those who will have this experience.'[20] As Martha Nussbaum notes, medical arguments are concerned with health and restoration: truth is already known, and then applied to the patient by the professional.[21] As mentioned above, Epiphanius' encyclopaedia offered a classification of all traditions outside Christianity as 'heresies', as well as genealogies and theological refutations. Significantly, he included contemporary figures that were known by contemporary standards to have shifted from orthodoxy to error, such as Apollinarius or Origen. In the totalising view of Epiphanius, external and internal error had been collapsed into one opposition to saving

---

18 H. Chadwick, 'Orthodoxy and heresy from the death of Constantine'; A. de Halleux, 'La réception du symbole œcuménique'; P. Gray, *The Defence of Chalcedon in the East*.
19 Papyrus *O.Heid.Inv.* 419, in P. Garnsey and C. Humfress, *The evolution of the late antique world*, 134.
20 Epiphanius, *Panarion, proem* 1; A. Pourkier, *L'hérésiologie chez Épiphane*.
21 M. Nussbaum, *The therapy of desire*, 494–6. On medical images in Epiphanius, see R. Lyman, 'Origen as ascetic theologian'.

truth, i.e., heresy. Heresy was both external opposition and a lurking internal poison within the tradition in seemingly holy men.[22]

Epiphanius signalled a new level of encyclopaedic classification of heresiology.[23] Handbooks of error would be created and copied in order to summarise and control theological diversity, echoing the emerging canon law. Thus, Epiphanius was shortened to *Anakephalaios* at the end of the fourth century; later Latin handbooks included Filastrius of Brescia, Augustine's *De haeresibus* in 428, and the anonymous *Praedestinatus* (432). Gennadius of Marseille wrote *Adversus omnes haereses* at the end of the fifth century. In the East such works also expanded Epiphanius to address new divisions in the church over Chalcedon as well as the emergence of Manichees and Islam. John of Damascus therefore expanded the *Anakephalaios* to one hundred heresies. New cultural movements were placed within the genealogies of the original truth and error.

Needless to say, this stark literary umbrella of classification did not regulate all conflicts that proceeded with theological synthesis and astute negotiation. As shown by Elizabeth Clark, the controversy over Origen of Alexandria blended ecclesiastical ambition, ascetic practices, social networks and theological issues.[24] If speculative, Origen's spiritual and theological writings were widely circulated; no less a figure than Athanasius had quoted him in favour of Nicene orthodoxy, and Anthony and the Cappadocians had drawn on his teachings for ascetic practice. The attack on Origen as an allegoriser included fears that his spiritual exegesis undercut the transformation of the body so essential to practising ascetics as well as signalling a new control of exegesis in line with church practice. Focusing on Nicene orthodoxy as well as scriptural translation and ascetic practice, the controversy in the fourth century engaged Jerome, the influential biblical scholar and one-time admirer of Origen, Theophilus of Alexandria, and Epiphanius. Socrates, the later church historian, portrayed Epiphanius as a simple-minded, if pious, meddler; he was criticised for his lack of understanding of local conditions as well as his harsh judgment of theological ancestors.[25] Basil of Caesarea likewise warned him about the breadth of understanding within orthodoxy itself.[26] Epiphanius presented orthodoxy as a matter of public safety with the necessity of policing both the internal conscience as well as the external boundaries. In practice, not everyone agreed;

22 R. Lyman, 'The making of a heretic'.
23 W. Löhr, 'Catalogues of heretics'.
24 Elizabeth A. Clark, *The Origenist controversy*.
25 Socrates, *H.E.* 6.10. The events in Constantinople are discussed by Jon Dechow in *Dogma and mysticism in early Christianity*, 408–13.
26 Basil, *Letter* 258.3; see Philip Rousseau's comments in his *Basil of Caesarea*.

with escalating consequences polemics could be a delicate tool as well as a potent weapon.[27] However, the practice of condemning theological ancestors to ensure contemporary definitions would be an important practice in the continuing construction of imperial orthodoxy.

Local traditions and imperial consensus

The conflicts of the fourth century bequeathed a system of imperial enforcement of ecclesiastical councils to a religious community geographically and culturally divided. For the first time in Roman law, religious dissent was classified and ordered. Appeals to antiquity and the apostolic succession of the episcopacy, as well as pilgrimage, shrines and liturgical traditions, strengthened not only the larger religion of Christianity, but the local incarnation of it. In the fifth century in particular, the Donatist controversy and the Miaphysites in the East reflected the strength of local practices and traditions that were not easily dislodged by councils or imperial edicts. Ironically, the councils and edicts in fact could work to further define and cement local practice in opposition to its being perceived as 'heresy' by the larger church.

The Donatist controversy had ebbed and flowed from the early fourth century in North Africa to the fifth century. Rooted in particular African traditions as well as clerical scandals surrounding the community of Carthage during the last imperial persecution of 303, the conflict between a 'true' church and a 'contaminated' church resounded in earlier writings of Tertullian and Cyprian and the unresolved conflict with Stephen of Rome. Within the geographical diversity of ancient Christianity, the indigenous tradition of a church whose sacraments and identity were inviolate and singular had never been challenged. Labelled as 'Donatists' (after their leader Donatus) and portrayed as 'purists' and 'rigorists', these North Africans in fact represented the biblical and apocalyptic legacy of Cyprian and Tertullian. They believed the identity of the church itself as the place of the Holy Spirit was compromised by the apostasy of the believers.[28]

The violence of the Donatist controversy was an ironic echo of the fervency of the church of the age of persecution. Like Athanasius, they accepted imperial power when the ruling was in their favour, otherwise in their eyes the state simply continued the persecution of the earlier pagan rulers. The broad support in the countryside and the criticism of wealth also reveal significant

27 R. Lyman, 'Ascetics and bishops'; S. Elm, 'The dog that did not bark'.
28 M. Tilley, *The Bible in North Africa*.

differences between the new imperial, universal church and local sectarian traditions; the work of Tyconius and Augustine on the mixed nature of the saving community reveals sociological as well as theological strains in North Africa.[29] As seen in the arguments about theological ancestors, distinctions had to be made about new divisions within the imperial church. The continuity, strength and intimacy of the conflict led Augustine to revise inherited categories of 'heretic' to conclude that the Donatists were not heretics, but rather 'schismatics' since they were divided from the church not by doctrinal error, but by lack of charity or discipline; Jerome argued that schismatic divisions eventually led into error and heresy.[30] For some Donatists fear of assimilation to a corrupted church and loyalty to their own tradition prevented lasting compromise. The imperial coercion of the movement after the Council of Carthage in 411 made it a minority, but did not erase the movement itself.

Local traditions and violence also haunted the continuing Christological controversies of the Eastern church. The ecclesiastical rivalries of Alexandria and Constantinople that had earlier involved a skirmish between Theophilus and John Chrysostom broke out in open doctrinal war between Cyril and Nestorius. Cyril's passionate defence of the Alexandrian piety of the one enfleshed Logos could unfortunately seem to embrace the problems of the mixture of divine and human natures earlier condemned in Apollinarius; the one nature formula was in fact drawn from an Apollinarian forgery, attributed to Athanasius. Schooled in the 'two natures' Christology of the Antiochene tradition, Nestorius became bishop at Constantinople with a passion to defend the true faith from heresy, suppressing an Arian church and attempting to correct the popular devotional term 'theotokos' for fear of its association with paganism. If impatient with theological error, Nestorius distinguished between those simply confused, and those belonging to certain heretical labels such as Arian or Manichaean.[31] In the ensuing conflict opponents of Nestorius such as Eusebius and Cyril contrasted his teachings to Paul of Samosata to show their similarity; Cyril even advised the people not to obey a heretical bishop.[32]

The attempted resolution of these two great traditions resulted in a compromise, but only after the deposition and exile of Nestorius following the

---

29 W. H. C. Frend, *The Donatist Church*; R. Markus, *Saeculum*, 105–26.
30 Löhr, 'Schisma'; W. Löhr, 'Pelagius' Schrift *De natura*'.
31 On Nestorius' zeal see Socrates, *H.E.* 7.21 and P. Allen, 'The use of heretics and heresies'. The tactics of the dispute are described in Gregory, *Vox populi*, 81–127.
32 H. M. Sillett outlines the progressive labelling of Nestorius as a 'heretic' with a 'school' in *Culture of controversy*, 5–56.

Council of Ephesus in 431. The theology of conciliation at Chalcedon in 451 that attempted to combine the Christological insights of both Alexandria and Antioch, however, was not universally received in the Eastern church, even with appeal to the revered Nicene Creed. Orthodox interpretation of Chalcedon was therefore defended by genealogies of saintly or demonic theologians. Cyril had compiled a florilegium to show how incarnation should be understood as well as a means of validation for a particular understanding of the past.[33] In response Theodoret defended the Antiochene ancestors Diodore and Theodore in his *Haereticarum fabularum compendium*. Significantly, he shifted away from the polemical model of genealogy, and argued that conflict as well as give and take were necessary processes for the discernment of truth.[34]

These opposing collections of florilegia were exercises in local genealogy as well as showing the continuing strength of orthodoxy resting on geographical and chronological breadth. However, in the East Christianity remained divided by region and theology with the Miaphysite churches of Egypt, Armenia and Syria rejecting the Chalcedonian formula of imperial orthodoxy. In 543–4, the emperor Justinian anathematised Theodore of Mopsuestia and his writings, certain writings of Theodoret of Cyrus, and the letter of Ibas to Maris in the 'Three Chapters' controversy.[35] This edict was an attempt to reassure Miaphysites of Chalcedon's orthodoxy by condemning Antiochene theologians who were associated with Nestorius. This was not successful in the East – particularly among the East Syrians[36] as well as the Egyptians – and provoked a crisis with the pope, who rejected this move as critical of Rome's defence of two natures. Ironically, this was partly to distract attention from Justinian's condemnation of Origen as interpreted through a later ascetic theologian, Evagrius. However, Origen was also condemned *post mortem* in 553 by the Fifth Ecumenical Council. Lists of saints and heresiarchs therefore shored up the boundaries of theological discourse as well as defining ecclesiastical community. Equally importantly, heresiological labels were also attached to both sides of the dispute on Chalcedon, including 'Nestorian' for the defenders and 'Manichaean' for the opponents, in hopes of showing their errors.[37] Genealogies and labels were used therefore as a means of enclosing the interpretation of the definition.

---

33 H. Chadwick, 'Florilegium'; L. Abramowski, 'Die Streit um Diodor und Theodor zwischen den beiden ephesinischen Konzilien'.
34 Helen Sillett, 'Orthodoxy and heresy in Theodoret of Cyrus' *Compendium of heresies*'.
35 C. J. Hefele, *A history of the councils of the church*, IV: 29–365.
36 See chapter 4, above.
37 On charges against the emperor Anastasius I as 'Manichaean', see Garnsey and Humfress, *The evolution of the late antique world*, 163.

Rhetorical and political demonisation: Pelagius and Priscillian

As often noted in recent scholarship, the construction of a heretical theological system, 'Pelagianism', for the purposes of orthodox refutation reveals an intense level of literary combat in later orthodoxy.[38] The international escalation of an ascetic controversy concerning the role of the human will in Christian living reflected not only the vigilant creativity of Augustine's thought, but also shifts in the understanding of Christian life and institutions. Pelagius' traditional teaching of a co-operative grace that necessarily included individual effort was largely commonplace in earlier Christianity and contemporary asceticism. In response to what he saw as a passive fatalism in Augustine's *Confessions*, Pelagius defended the power of human nature to be sinless in his work *On nature*. Later, reading this optimistic work together with the condemnations of the more extreme theology of Pelagius' pupil Caelestius, Augustine responded with *Nature and grace*, in which he refuted the implications of Pelagius' theology. After defending himself successfully at a synod in Diospolis in Palestine, Pelagius disappeared from historical view, but his 'system' of theology continued to be attacked by Jerome and Augustine. Two North African synods condemned theological propositions, and sent an annotated copy of *On nature* to Pope Innocent seeking his condemnation as well. Only when the theology was described as a 'secret movement' was Pelagius condemned by the emperor Honorius, and his followers expelled from Rome. Many Italian bishops objected both theologically and also politically to the power of North Africa to define orthodoxy in Rome: they declared themselves to be 'orthodox persecuted by orthodox'.[39] Augustine's theological response to Julian of Eclanum, who portrayed him as an unreformed Manichaean, was to turn from construction or speculation to the defence of the core of the tradition.[40] The demonisation and exaggeration of the teaching of Pelagius was part of a means of excluding not only actual teaching, but theological possibilities, from 'orthodoxy'.

The Western dispute over the life and teachings of Priscillian also reflected important shifts in episcopal and ascetic understanding of scriptural study and practice as well as the deadly charge of 'Manichaeism' in Christian life.[41] Since the condemnation of Manichaeans in 295 by Diocletian, the Manichaeans

---

38 For what follows, see Peter Brown, *Augustine of Hippo*, 343–6; Robert Markus, 'The legacy of Pelagius'; Löhr, 'Pelagius' Schrift *De natura*'.
39 Markus, 'The legacy of Pelagius', 215.
40 Brown, *Augustine of Hippo*, 396–7.
41 For what follows, see V. Burrus, *The making of a heretic*.

had been consistently persecuted and also continually successful as ascetic missionaries. Manichaeans offered a dualistic interpretation of Christianity which ultimately offended others by its docetic Christology and cosmology. Those overly interested in ascetic practice or cosmology could therefore easily acquire this polemical tag in the complex controversies of the century. Thus, the Priscillian controversy, as embracing episcopal discomfort with strict ascetic practices, association with women, and the use of apocryphal literature, lent itself to labels of 'Manichaean' or 'sorcerer'. Originating as a local dispute in Spain with his bishop Hydatius, Priscillian was rapidly demonised from an independent and private ascetic to a Manichaean and sorcerer. Convicted of these charges, he sought rehabilitation in Rome and Milan, but was refused audience by local bishops. Unfortunately, the new emperor Maximus used the controversy around Priscillian to showcase his intolerance of heresy; two trials resulted in conviction and finally execution for sorcery. Although his execution was condemned by Ambrose and Martin of Tours, the heresiological label 'Priscillianism' began to be used to represent the dangerous insider, associated with the Gnostic seducer of women. Repudiating his life and teaching became a means for ascetics such as Jerome to defend their own socially marginal lifestyles; Priscillian represented one whose speculations, perceived as magic or Manichaean, placed him beyond acceptable boundaries. The heresiarch here could be cited as a representative of dangerous or rebellious individualism that was a threat not only to public episcopal orthodoxy, but also to the structures of patriachical society itself.[42] The interpretation of contemporary institutional and theological problems by demonisation was now a literally deadly means of defeating an opponent.

Conclusion

In religious history the links between literary images and social realities are always complex, but the negative force of heresiology in Western history compounds the problem of historical interpretation. Ancient heresiology was both the literary reflection of diverse Christian communities and a dynamic force in shaping theological identity, though we must remain cautious about assuming a steady congruence or development between certain communities and definitions. The development of Christian heresiology in catalogues of errors and diptychs of saints and heretics mirrored the public expansion of the church and the legal centralisation of the empire in the fourth to sixth centuries.

42 V. Burrus, 'The heretical woman as symbol'; H. Maier, 'The topography of heresy and dissent'.

Polemical literary categories and labels were codified by imperial legislation and classified historiographically within heresiological handbooks. The growing complexity of theological error reflected both the authoritarian society of a centralised empire and the increasing sophistication and disorder of theological debate. Ironically, the sectarian origins of Christianity created fierce local traditions that could only be negotiated into fragile unities through agreement on boundaries as much as theological centres. This tension between universality and multiplicity in Christianity made the establishment of theological and cultural boundaries through the demonic opposition of heresy all the more important. Contemporary dissent was often associated with ancient heretics in order to reinforce the sharp and eternal distinction between truth and error. Other religious traditions were given a conceptual history that placed them in a negative relation to the original and universal Christian truth. The history of these labels and classifications, however, provides important clues as to the negotiation with surrounding culture, and the resulting theological creativity, if not innovation, which is sometimes hidden by the polarising rhetoric of the polemic. Even as he prepared to write his own handbook of heresies, Augustine admitted the pastoral danger of identifying any suspect position as 'heresy'.[43] Amid the diversity of ascetic life, the varied traditions of the great Christian capitals, and individual intellectual creativity, stability was achieved through the regulation of theological thought in line with ancient revelation and the shifting of boundaries to define it. The category of 'schism' developed as a middle ground for marking significant disagreements, yet not excluding as a 'heretic'. The continuing controversies are therefore a testimony to the lasting vitality of Christian life as well as politics of power. Heresiology was not a matter of unchanging literary traditions, but rather a dynamic means of cultural assimilation, historiography and social stability.

Bibliography

PRIMARY SOURCES

Athanasius. *Athanasius Werke*, Band III.1: *Urkunden zu Geschichte des Arianischen Streites*, ed. H.-G. Opitz (Berlin, 1934–5), 318–28
Augustine, *Letters* (CSEL 34, 44, 57, 58)
Basil, *Letters*. Ed. Yves Courtonne, *Saint Basile. Letters* (Paris, 1957, 1961, 1966)
Epiphanius of Salamis. *Panarion* (GCS 25, 31, 37)
Eusebius. *Historia ecclesiastica* (GCS *Eusebius Werke*, II)
Socrates. *Historia ecclesiastica* (GCS, N.F. 1: Sokrates Kirchengeschichte; SC 477, 493–)

43 Augustine, *Ep.* 222.

SECONDARY SOURCES

Abramowski, L. 'Die Streit um Diodor und Theodor zwischen den beiden ephesinischen Konzilien', *ZKG* 67 (1955–6): 252–87

Allen, P. 'Monophysiten', *TRE* 23: 219–33

'The use of heretics and heresies in the Greek church historians: Studies in Socrates and Theodoret', in G. Clarke, ed., *Reading the past in late antiquity* (Rushcutters Bay, 1990), 265–89

Bammel, Caroline. 'Peacemaking and religious tolerance in the early church,' in *Tradition and exegesis in the early Christian writers* (London, 1995), 1–13

Barnard, L. 'The criminalization of heresy in the later Roman empire: A sociopolitical device?', *Journal of legal history* 16 (1995): 121–46

Becker, Adam H. and Annette Yoshiko Reed, eds. *The ways that never parted. Jews and Christians in late antiquity and the early middle ages* (Tübingen, 2003)

Benoit, J. J. *Saint Jérôme et l'hérésie* (Paris, 1999)

Bowersock, G. *Hellenism in late antiquity* (Ann Arbor, 1996)

Boyarin, D. *Border crossings. The partition of Judaeo-Christianity* (Philadelphia, 2004)

Brisson, J.-P. *Autonomisme et christianisme dans l'Afrique romaine de Septime Sévère à l'invasion vandale* (Paris, 1958)

Brown, P. 'Pelagius and his supporters: Aims and environment', *JTS* n.s. 19 (1968): 93–114; reprinted in P. Brown, *Religion and society in the age of Saint Augustine* (London, 1972)

Power and persuasion in late antiquity: Towards a Christian empire (Madison, WI, 1992)

Augustine of Hippo. A biography, rev. edn. (London, 2000)

Brox, N. 'Häresie', *RAC* 13: 248–97

Bunge, G. 'Origenismus-Gnostizismus: Zum geistesgeschichtlichen Standort des Evagrios Pontikos', *VChr* 40 (1986): 24–54

Burns, J. P. *Cyprian the bishop* (London, 2001)

Burrus, V. 'The heretical woman as symbol in Alexander, Athanasius, Epiphanius, and Jerome', *HTR* 84 (1991): 229–48

The making of a heretic. Gender, authority, and the Priscillianist controversy (Berkeley, 1995)

Cameron, A. *Christianity and the rhetoric of empire: The development of Christian discourse* (Berkeley, 1991)

'Heresiology', in G. Bowersock, Peter Brown and Oleg Grabar, eds., *Late antiquity. A guide to the postclassical world* (Cambridge, MA, 1999), 488–90

'How to read heresiology', *Journal of medieval and modern studies* 33 (2003): 471–92

'Texts as weapons: Polemic in the Byzantine Dark Ages', in A. Bowman and G. Woolf, eds., *Literacy and power in the ancient world* (Cambridge, 1994), 198–215

Chadwick, H. 'Florilegium', *RAC* 7 (1969): 1131–60

'Orthodoxy and heresy from the death of Constantine to the eve of the first Council of Ephesus', *The Cambridge ancient history* (Cambridge, 1998), XIII: 562–80

Clark, Elizabeth A. *The Origenist controversy. The cultural construction of an early Christian debate* (Princeton, 1992)

Constantelos, D. J. 'Justinian and the Three Chapters controversy', *Greek Orthodox theological review* 8 (1962): 71–94

Crouzel, Henri. 'Origenism', *Encyclopedia of the early church*, ed. Everett Ferguson (New York, 1997), 623–4

Dechow, J. *Dogma and mysticism in early Christianity* (Macon, 1988)

Elm, Susanna. 'The dog that did not bark: Doctrine and patriarchical authority in the conflict between Theophilus of Alexandria and John Chrysostom of Constantinople', in L. Ayres and G. Jones, eds., *Christian origins. Theology, rhetoric and community* (London, 1998), 68–93

'The polemical use of genealogies: Jerome's classification of Pelagius and Evagrius Ponticus', *SP* 33 (1997): 311–18

Evans, R. *Pelagius: Inquiries and reappraisals* (London, 1968)

Frend, W. H. C. *The Donatist Church* (Oxford, 1952, 1971²)

Garnsey, P. and C. Humfress, *The evolution of the late antique world* (Cambridge, 2001)

Goehring, J. *Ascetics, society, and the desert. Studies in early Egyptian monasticism* (Harrisburg, PA, 1999)

Gray, P. *The defence of Chalcedon in the East (451–553)* (Leiden, 1979)

Gregory, T. *Vox populi. Violence and popular involvement in the religious controversies of the fifth century* A.D. (Columbus, 1979)

Grillmeier, Aloys. *Christ in the Christian tradition. From Chalcedon to Justinian I* (Atlanta, 1987)

Guillaumont, A. *Les 'Kephalaia gnostica' d'Évagre le Pontique et l'histoire de l'origénisme chez les grecs et chez les syriens* (Paris, 1962)

Halleux, A. de. 'La réception du symbole œcuménique, de Nicée à Chalcédoine', *Ephemerides theologicae Lovanienses* 61 (1985): 1–47; reprinted in A. de Halleux, *Patrologie et œcuménisme: Recueil d'études*, BETL 93 (Louvain, 1990), 25–67

Hanson, R. *The search for the Christian doctrine of God* (Edinburgh, 1988)

Harvey, S. Ashbrook, 'Nestorianism', *Encyclopedia of early Christianity²*, 806–9

Hass, C. *Alexandria in late antiquity* (Baltimore, 1997)

Hefele, C. J. *A history of the councils of the church*, trans. H. N. Oxenham and W. R. Clark (Edinburgh, 1871–96)

Humfress, C. 'Heretics, laws on', in Bowersock et al., *Late antiquity*, 490–1

'Roman law, forensic argument and the formation of Christian orthodoxy (III–VI centuries)', in S. Elm, E. Rébillard and Antonella Romano, eds., *Orthodoxie christianisme histoire. Orthodoxy Christianity history* (Rome, 2000), 125–47

Inglebert, H. 'L'histoire des hérésies chez les hérésiologues', in B. Pouderon and Y.-M. Duval, eds., *L'historiographie de l'église des premiers siècles* (Paris, 2001), 105–25

Les romains chrétiens face à l'histoire de Rome (Paris, 1996)

Jacobs, A. *Remains of the Jews. The Holy Land and Christian empire in late antiquity* (Stanford, 2004)

Le Boulluec, Alain. *La notion d'hérésie dans la littérature grecque IIe–IIIe siècles* (Paris, 1985)

Lienhard, J. 'Basil of Caesarea, Marcellus of Ancyra and "Sabellius"', *Church history* 58 (1989): 157–67

Lieu, S. N. C. *Manichaeism in the later Roman empire and medieval China: A historical survey* (Tübingen, 1992²)

Lim, R. 'Christian triumph and controversy', in Bowersock et al., *Late antiquity*, 196–218

Public disputation, power, and social order in late antiquity (Berkeley, 1995)

Löhr, W. 'Catalogues of heretics', in Siegmar Döpp and Wilhelm Geerlings, eds., *Dictionary of early Christian literature*, trans. M. O'Connell (New York, 2000), 276–7

'Pelagius' Schrift *De natura*: Rekonstruktion und Analyse', *Recherches augustiniennes* 31 (1999): 235–94

'Schisma', *TRE* 30: 129–30

Louth, A. *St. John Damascene: Tradition and originality in Byzantine theology* (Oxford, 2002)

Lyman, R. 'Arians and Manichees on Christ', *JTS* N.S. 40 (1989): 493–503

'Ascetics and bishops: Epiphanius on orthodoxy', in S. Elm, E. Rébillard and Antonella Romano, eds., *Orthodoxie christianisme histoire. Orthodoxy Christianity history* (Rome, 2000), 149–61

'The making of a heretic: The Life of Origen in Epiphanius *Panarion* 64', *SP* 31 (1997): 445–51

'Origen as ascetic theologian: Orthodoxy and authority in the fourth century church', in W. Bienert and U. Kuhneweg, eds., *Origeniana septima* (Louvain, 1999), 187–94

'The politics of passing: Justin Martyr's conversion as a problem of "Hellenization"', in K. Mills and A. Grafton, eds., *Conversion in late antiquity and the early middle ages* (Rochester, NY, 2003), 36–60

'A topography of heresy: Mapping the rhetorical creation of Arianism', in M. R. Barnes and D. H. Williams, eds., *Arianism after Arius* (Edinburgh, 1993), 45–62

McClure, J. 'Handbooks against heresy in the West from the late fourth to the late sixth centuries', *JTS* N.S. 30 (1979): 186–97

McLynn, N. 'Christian controversy and violence in the fourth century', *Kodai³* (1992): 15–44

Maier, H. 'Private space as the social context of Arianism in Ambrose's fourth century Milan', *JTS* N.S. 45 (1994): 72–93

'The topography of heresy and dissent in late fourth century Rome', *Historia* 44 (1995): 232–49

Maier, J. L. *Le dossier du donatisme*, TU 134–5 (Berlin, 1987)

Markus, R. 'Christianity and dissent in Roman North Africa: Changing perspectives in recent work', in D. Baker, ed., *Schism, heresy and religious protest* (Cambridge, 1972), 21–36

The end of ancient Christianity (Cambridge, 1990)

'The legacy of Pelagius: Orthodoxy, heresy and conciliation', in R. Williams, ed., *The making of orthodoxy. Essays in honour of Henry Chadwick* (Cambridge, 1989), 214–34

Saeculum: History and society in the theology of Saint Augustine (Cambridge, 1970/1989)

Meredith, T. 'Orthodoxy, heresy and philosophy in the latter half of the fourth century', *Heythrop journal* 16 (1975): 5–21

Noethlichs, K-L. *Die gesetzgeberischen Massnahmen der christlichen Kaiser des vierten Jahrhunderts gegen Häretiker, Heiden und Juden*, Dr. Theol. dissertation (Cologne, 1971)

Norris, F. 'Three Chapters', *Encyclopedia of Early Christianity²*, 1129–30

Nussbaum, M. *The therapy of desire. Theory and practice in Hellenistic ethics* (Princeton, 1994)

Paschoud, F. 'L'intolérance chrétienne vue et jugée par les païens', *Cristianesimo nella storia* 11 (1990): 545–77

Pelikan, J. *The Christian tradition: A history of the development of doctrine. Vol. I: The emergence of the catholic tradition (100–600)* (Chicago, 1971)

Pourkier, A. *L'hérésiologie chez Épiphane de Salamine* (Paris, 1992)

Rees, R. *Pelagius. A reluctant heretic* (Woodbridge, Suffolk, 1988)

Richard, M. 'Notes sur les florilèges dogmatiques du Vᵉ et du VIᵉ siècle', *Actes du VIᵉ Congrès Internationale d'Études Byzantines* (Brussels, 1950), 1: 307–18

Rousseau, P. *Basil of Caesarea* (Berkeley, 1998)

Sahas, D. *John of Damascus on Islam* (Leiden, 1972)

Shaw, B. 'African Christianity: Disputes, definitions and "Donatists"', in *Orthodoxy and heresy in religious movements: Discipline and dissent* (Lewiston, NY, 1992), 5–34

Sillett, H. M. *Culture of controversy: The Christological disputes of the early fifth century*, PhD dissertation, University of California, Berkeley, 1999

'Orthodoxy and heresy in Theodoret of Cyrus' *Compendium of heresies*', in S. Elm, E. Rébillard and Antonella Romano, eds., *Orthodoxie christianisme histoire. Orthodoxy Christianity history* (Rome, 2000), 261–73

Simon, M. 'From Greek *hairesis* to Christian heresy', in W. Schoedel and R. Wilken, eds., *Early Christian literature and the classical intellectual tradition* (Paris, 1979), 101–16

Skarsaune, Oskar. 'A neglected detail in the Creed of Nicaea (325)', *VChr* 41 (1987): 34–54

Speyer, W. *Büchervernichtung und Zensur des Geistes bei Heiden, Juden und Christen* (Stuttgart, 1981)

Tengström, E. *Donatisten und Katholiken: Soziale, wirtschaftliche und politische Aspekte einer nordafrikanischen Kirchenspaltung* (Göteborg, 1964)

Tilley, M. *The Bible in North Africa. The Donatist world* (Minneapolis, 1997)

Turner, H. 'Nestorius reconsidered', *SP* 13 (1975): 306–21

Vaggione, R. *Eunomius of Cyzicus and the Nicene revolution* (Oxford, 2000)

Vanderspoel, J. 'The background to Augustine's denial of religious plurality', in H. A. Meynell, ed., *Grace, politics and desire* (Calgary, 1990), 179–93

Wermelinger, O. *Rom und Pelagius: Die theologische Position der römischen Bischöfe im pelagianischen Streit in den Jahren 411–432* (Stuttgart, 1975)

Whitmarsh, Tim. *Greek literature and the Roman empire. The politics of imitation* (Oxford, 2001)

Wiles, M. 'Attitudes to Arius in the Arian controversy', in M. R. Barnes and D. H. Williams, eds., *Arianism after Arius* (Edinburgh, 1993), 31–44

Wilken, R. 'Monophysitism', *Encyclopedia of Early Christianity²*, 776–8

Williams, Rowan. 'Defining heresy', in A. Kreider, eds., *The origins of Christendom in the West* (Edinburgh, 2001), 313–35

'Does it make sense to speak of pre-Nicene orthodoxy?', in Rowan Williams, ed., *The making of orthodoxy. Essays in honour of Henry Chadwick* (Cambridge, 1989), 1–23

Winkler, D. *Koptische Kirche und Reichskirche: Altes Schisma und neuer Dialog* (Innsbruck, 1997)

PART III

⋆

CHRISTIAN CULTURE
AND SOCIETY

13

Towards defining a Christian culture: The Christian transformation of classical literature

BRONWEN NEIL

The culture of late antiquity was a curious blend of classical pagan forms and newly developed Christian ones. This chapter deals solely with aspects of late antique literary culture, and investigates the degree to which the rise of Christianity impacted traditional Greco-Roman literary forms. Christian writers took various attitudes towards their Hellenistic literary and philosophical inheritance. The literary production of the mid-fourth to sixth centuries will be considered according to genre. I will examine the individual approaches to each genre by six church fathers, who wrote in Greek or Latin. Finally I will briefly consider the effect of the eastern expansion of Christian culture on the Syriac, Armenian and Coptic communities, which were somewhat freer from the constraints of the Hellenistic heritage.[1]

Introduction

The Christian authors of the fourth to sixth centuries whose work survives achieved a remarkable synthesis of Greco-Roman rhetoric and philosophy, which had its origins in Athens in its golden age, the fourth and fifth centuries BC, the age of Plato and Aristotle. It is indisputable that late ancient literary culture was shaped by these early Hellenic influences. The reception of the philosophical thought of Plato and Aristotle in Neo- and Middle Platonism and Stoicism was profoundly influential on all the Christian writers whose work is examined below. Not only was the philosophical tradition inherited by the teachers and writers of the newly created fourth-century Christian Roman empire of profound consequence, but the forms of literary expression first adopted by the Greeks, and developed by their Roman imitators, lived on

---

1 I am very grateful to Prof. Pauline Allen for comments on the drafts of this chapter.

in various forms within almost all the genres of late antique Christian literature. The genres common to both cultures included commentaries, letters, treatises, public orations, biography, historiography and poetry. The advent of Christianity gave rise to some new, hybrid forms such as homilies and florilegia. The only distinctively Christian genres that the new dominant culture produced were popular forms, such as liturgical hymns, the pilgrim's journal, and monastic literature.

A common thread in all these literary forms was the fundamental importance of the Christian scriptures. These were made up of the Septuagint – a Greek translation of the Hebrew scriptures, with its inclusion of Judaeo-Hellenistic apocryphal books – together with the Greek version of the New Testament. The fact that the New Testament was passed down in Greek rather than the spoken language of Jesus and the Jewish people (Aramaic) or the official language of the Roman empire (Latin) was of great import for the future shape of Christian culture and its literature.[2] The twenty-seven-book canon of the New Testament was set down by Athanasius, patriarch of Alexandria, in his *Paschal letter* of 367.[3] It took longer for the various Christian communities to agree upon the status of the Judaeo-Hellenistic apocrypha, with the West being initially more favourable to them than the East. Christian culture, and especially in its literary aspects, was grounded in the scriptures. They provided the richest source of allusions and quotations in Byzantine literature. This is self-evident in the case of biblical exegesis, in the form of commentaries and homilies, but the Christian scriptures also influenced other literary genres in less obvious ways, as we shall see.

Different exegetical techniques came to characterise particular schools, including the school of Alexandria – a school of Hellenic philosophy that adopted the speculative and allegorical methods of Stoic interpretation of classical and philosophical texts, and applied them to scripture[4] – and its rival at Antioch, a school of rhetoric. The Antiochene approach, represented by little more than a loose group of theologically disparate figures who included Arius, Paul of Samosata, Diodore of Tarsus, Nestorius and Theodore of Mopsuestia, was associated with what became known as the literal or 'historical' method of exegesis, and was more interested in the text itself than the ideas

---

2 Jaroslav Pelikan, *Christianity and classical culture*, 3; Pelikan draws a great deal from W. Jaeger's classic *Paideia*.

3 Athanasius, *Letter* 39.18 (trans. Campani, 511); for the complicated history of the New Testament canon, see Bruce Metzger, *The canon of the New Testament*.

4 See Frances M. Young, 'The Rhetorical Schools'. Before the Alexandrian school was taken over by Christian thinkers – notably Clement and Origen – the Jewish philosopher Philo had already applied these methods to the biblical text.

expressed.[5] The typological approach of Theodore of Mopsuestia was taken up in the Syriac tradition by the school of Edessa, and out of this the school of Nisibis emerged in the late fifth century. Under the leadership of the Syriac theologian Narsai, the school of Nisibis flourished until the early seventh century, becoming known even today as 'one of the great institutions of learning of the Middle Ages'.[6] In the sixth century it produced Junillus Africanus, who studied the Nisibean style of interpretation at Constantinople under Paul the Persian, a lecturer at Nisibis.[7] Junillus wrote the influential pamphlet *Instituta regularia divinae legis*, a primer for students of exegesis based on Antiochene approaches. The text was introduced to the Latin West during the 'Three Chapters' controversy in the 540s. Cassiodorus (*c.* 485–580) was responsible for its great popularity in Western monasteries in the early medieval period.[8]

The Roman senator Cassiodorus, after a successful career in the Ostrogothic court at Ravenna, was inspired by the school of Nisibis to set up his own centre of Christian scholarship and teaching at the monastery at Vivarium, on the coast of the Ionian Sea. In Constantinople Cassiodorus had made contact with Junillus, Justinian's *quaestor*, and there learned of the experiment at Nisibis. His major works after his conversion (*Institutiones, Auctores historiae ecclesiasticae* – an abbreviation of previous Christian histories – and *Expositio Psalmorum*) were a deliberate contribution to building Roman Christian culture at a time when the secular schools were being replaced by monastic centres of learning. Indeed, his early attempt to establish, with the help of Pope Agapetus, a Christian school in Rome in the 530s came to fruition only with the founding of the Vivarium monastery some twenty years later.[9]

The importance of schools in the transmission of the new Christian culture cannot be overestimated, although the practical details remain elusive.[10] Theological education seems to have been in the hand of clerics or monks,

---

5 Edward G. Mathews, 'Excursus on the schools of Antioch and Nisibis', 97.
6 Ibid., 102.
7 Junillus, *Instituta regularia divinae legis, praef.* 1 in Michael Maas, ed., *Exegesis and empire.*
8 Mathews, 'Excursus on the schools of Antioch and Nisibis', 102 and 111.
9 James J. O'Donnell, *Cassiodorus,* 179 writes: 'Indeed, the strongest direct evidence for the survival of rhetorical schools in the ancient tradition is Cassiodorus' own opening remark in the *Institutiones* . . .: "When I saw secular studies being pursued with great fervor, so much so that a great mass of men believed such studies would bring them the wisdom of this world, I confess I was seriously perturbed that there should be no public professors of Holy Scripture, when worldly texts were the beneficiaries of a distinguished educational tradition" (*Inst.,* praef. 1). The clear import of this passage seems to be that there really were secular schools flourishing into Cassiodorus' own middle age.' On the attempt to found a Christian school at Rome, see further O'Donnell, *Cassiodorus,* 108 and 182.
10 P. Lemerle, *Le premier humanisme byzantin,* and its revised English edition, *Byzantine humanism,* 43–79, are a valuable source on education in the early Byzantine period.

who taught alongside pagans in the schools to which young men of means were sent. From around six years of age all boys and some girls were educated in grammar, i.e. reading and writing and syntax, with an emphasis on the literary classics of Virgil in the Latin West and Homer in the Greek East. Even more significant than these literary classics was the Bible, and particularly the Psalms, which were memorised in the same way as Virgil and Homer.[11] From about the age of fourteen, boys were educated in rhetoric. Basil of Caesarea's treatise to his nephews on their education in pagan literature, *Ad adolescentes de legendis libris gentilium*, remains our most valuable source of information on this subject from a Christian perspective.[12] Young men could continue their studies with philosophy and the four arts: arithmetic, music, geometry and astronomy.[13]

Two significant events in relation to schools delimit the chronological boundaries of our investigation: the education edict of the emperor Julian in 362, which gave the emperor the authority to make teaching appointments,[14] and the closing of the secular schools by the emperor Justinian (*regn.* 527–65) in 529. In that same year, Benedict of Nursia founded the monastery at Monte Cassino, an indication that the mantle of learning had passed from secular philosophers to Christian monks.

The emperor Julian, known as 'the Apostate' because he renounced the Christianity in which he was brought up, studied with Gregory of Nazianzus at the Athens school in the summer of 355. During his reign of less than two years, from 361 to 363, he sought to revive the Hellenic religions. His reforms included restoring pagan temples to their former usage, cancelling clerical privileges, discriminating against Christians in public offices, and transferring church wealth back to the state.[15] Julian's education edict was followed by a rescript banning Christians from teaching classical literature because they did not believe what they taught.[16] Julian attempted to break the bond Christians had been forging with classical culture, and to re-forge the bond between that culture and traditional religion.[17] In his critique of Christianity, *Against the*

---

11 Synesius of Cyrene, bishop of Ptolemais (*c.* 410–14) boasted that his nephew had learnt fifty lines of Homer a day.
12 *Saint Basil on the value of Greek literature*, ed. Wilson.
13 To these basic studies, specialisations in law, medicine or physics could be added. See Steven Runciman, *Byzantine civilization*, 178–9, and more broadly H. I. Marrou, *A history of education in antiquity*.
14 The text of the rescript is found in *CTh* 13.3.5.
15 'Julian "the Apostate". *Against the Galileans*', trans. Burr, 144.
16 Such sentiments are expressed in Julian's *Letter* 36.
17 R. L. Wilken, *The Christians as the Romans saw them*, 175–6.

Galileans, Julian criticised Christians for taking up the worst features of both Hellenic religion and Judaism.[18] He declared Hebrew culture inferior to the Greek in respect to the study of logic, medicine and philosophy.[19] He attacked Christian scriptures as being insufficient to teach courage, prudence and justice.[20] If Christians were serious about the superiority of their sacred writings, they would not allow anyone to read classical literature.[21] The successful re-appropriation of classical culture by Christians after Julian depended precisely upon disconnecting it from classical religion.

After Julian's brief attempt to restore pagan religion and culture to their former glory, there were no more non-Christian emperors. Christianisation of the majority of imperial institutions continued to the point that in 438 Theodosius I claimed – no doubt erroneously – that there were no pagans left in the empire.[22] The apogee of imperial Christianity could be seen in Justinian's move to close the famous philosophy school at Athens during 529 by confiscating its endowment.[23] He forbade the teaching of law except at Rome, Beirut and Constantinople, and stipulated that all teachers must be Christian. This was the antithesis of Julian's attempts at reform.

Six key figures in early Christian literary production

Before embarking on a brief analysis of the literary genres identified above, some introduction to their most outstanding proponents is required. Six outstanding authors have been chosen: Jerome, Ambrose of Milan, Augustine of Hippo, John Chrysostom, Gregory of Nazianzus, and Theodoret of Cyrrhus. The first three wrote in Latin, the latter three in Greek. Together they constitute the flower of the patristic golden age, the mid-fourth and fifth centuries. Although they came from a variety of religious backgrounds, both pagan and Christian, all were educated in classical oratory. As Christians, their attitude towards the Hellenistic tradition was profoundly ambivalent, reflecting their desire to take the best and leave behind what was unprofitable for the spiritual life.

18 Julian, *Against the Galileans* 42E; trans. Burr, 146.
19 Julian, *Against the Galileans* 221E; trans. Burr, 152.
20 Julian, *Against the Galileans* 229E; trans. Burr, 153.
21 Julian, *Against the Galileans* 229C (trans. Burr, 152): 'If it is enough for you to read your own Scriptures, why do you sample the learning of the Hellenes?'
22 Runciman, *Byzantine civilization,* 29.
23 Alan Cameron, 'The last days of the academy of Athens'; John Glucker, *Antiochus and the late academy.*

Jerome of Stridon (347–419)

Jerome's early life exemplifies what good use a Christian convert could make of his pagan rhetorical training.[24] Born in Stridon, on the border of Dalmatia and Pannonia, he was educated in rhetoric at Rome, where he converted to Christianity. He undertook theological studies at Trier. The giant of Latin rhetoric, and the main model for his secular education, was Cicero. For Cicero, eloquence was synonymous with wisdom,[25] and the practice of rhetoric for any end was itself a kind of philosophy. How important should such a pagan exemplar be for the new Christian rhetoric? The story of Jerome's dream reveals his dilemma.[26] He dreamt that he was brought before a tribunal where a judge (God) asked him his status. He replied that he was a Christian. 'And He who sat upon the judgment seat said: "Thou liest. Thou art a Ciceronian, not a Christian. *Where thy treasure is, there is thy heart also*" (Matthew 6.21).'

Thereupon Jerome (in his dream) renounced his attachment to Cicero and all pagan literature, swearing an oath: 'O Lord, if ever I possess or read secular writings, I have denied thee.'[27] The opposition is an interesting one, indicating just how far from the usual patterns of education and rhetorical practice a Christian had to deviate if he were to be clear of any charge of secularism. After his relations with clergy in Rome soured, he withdrew to Bethlehem in 386. There he became one of the most prolific writers and translators of Christian literature in the West, undertaking a revision of the Old Latin version of the Old Testament, based on the Greek Septuagint, and a second Latin version based directly upon the Hebrew scriptures. In this task he was greatly helped by access to Origen's *Hexapla*. Together with his earlier revision of the Gospels, this new Latin version of the Old Testament from Hebrew became the standard, or 'Vulgate'.[28] In addition, he produced numerous letters, treatises, homilies and biblical commentaries. He was the translator and continuator of Eusebius of Caesarea's *Chronicle*. He wrote three lives of ascetic saints, and a catalogue of outstanding Christian authors and their works, *De viris illustribus*.

Ambrose of Milan (c. 339–97)

Ambrose, bishop of Milan (c. 374–97), seems to have been a member of a Neoplatonic reading circle in that city. He had enjoyed a successful career

24 J. N. D. Kelly, *Jerome* offers an excellent general and literary biography.
25 Cicero, *De inventione* 1.1, cited by J. Pelikan, *Divine rhetoric*, 17.
26 Jerome describes his dream in *Letter* 22.30.
27 This account of his dream should not be taken as Jerome's last word on the subject, as T. C. Lawler warns (ACW 33.1: 243–4).
28 Kelly, *Jerome*, 162.

as governor of the north Italian province of Aemilia and Liguria before he was nominated (unwillingly, by his own account) bishop at Milan in 374.[29] Although only enrolled as a catechumen, he undertook baptism and rapidly rose through the clerical orders, being consecrated as bishop eight days later. As governor, Ambrose had enjoyed a great amount of worldly status, and he maintained this as bishop in his relations with other leaders of church and state, famously in forcing the emperor Theodosius to do public penance for the massacre of citizens in Thessalonika. His clash with the pagan senator Symmachus over the re-establishment of the Altar of Victory in the senate, and his eventual victory, bear witness to an irreversible shift in the governing bodies of Rome with respect to their pagan past. Ambrose's homilies, ninety-one letters, treatises, biblical commentaries and funeral orations display a most effective use of rhetoric in public contexts.[30] As a product of his conflict with the Arian community in Milan, and the 'basilicas controversy' of the mid-380s, in which both parties were vying for the use of major church buildings,[31] Ambrose penned the first Latin hymns. His eloquence and mastery of the three styles of rhetoric received the highest praise from Augustine.[32]

Augustine of Hippo (354–430)

Augustine could also have been open to the charge of being a Ciceronian, given that his embracing of Christianity depended upon his prior reading of Cicero's Hortensius. Although brought up as a Christian by his mother Monica, he chose to pursue Manichaeism as a young adult.[33] In his nineteenth year, while studying rhetoric in Carthage, he turned to the Hortensius, in pursuit of eloquence. This work kindled within him a love for wisdom, which, as he notes in the Confessiones, the Greeks call 'philosophy'.[34] He followed this by investigating the school of Academics. More years passed before he took up the call of Christ, but in the meantime he taught rhetoric in Africa and then Rome from 383, before accepting a professorship of rhetoric in Milan. There he met Bishop Ambrose, under whose instruction he enrolled as a catechumen and was baptised in 386. Ordained priest in 391 and bishop of Hippo in 396,

29 On Ambrose's secular and ecclesiastical careers, see Neil B. McLynn, *Ambrose of Milan*.
30 Boniface Ramsey, *Ambrose*, 55–68, provides a useful summary of Ambrose's works. He notes (55) that only four or five sermons have survived as such, although reworked sermons formed the basis of many of his treatises and exegetical writings.
31 See ibid., 25–9 on the 'basilicas controversy'.
32 Augustine, *De doctrina christiana* 4.21.50 (trans. Hill, 233, mod.): '. . . that is [speaking], as the matter requires, plainly and clearly, or in rather more ornate and flowery language, or with fiery vigour . . .'
33 The definitive biography of Augustine is Peter Brown's *Augustine of Hippo*.
34 Augustine, *Confessiones* 3.4.7–8.

Augustine produced his spiritual autobiography, *Confessiones*, and a vast history of God's working throughout history, *De civitate Dei*. He left a record of his biblical commentaries and treatises in the *Retractationes*, composed towards the end of his life. Only a fraction of his letters and homilies survives. His many works reveal his capacity to adapt rhetorical style to suit the audience. For instance, the early philosophical works such as *De quantitate animae* and *De bona vita* are reminiscent of Latin classics on similar themes. *De magistro* takes the form of a Socratic dialogue with his son Adeodatus.

Gregory of Nazianzus (c. 330–c. 390)

Gregory of Nazianzus, known as 'the Theologian', was a master of rhetoric as well as a composer of poetry.[35] The son of Gregory the Elder, bishop of Nazianzus in Cappadocia, he learnt well how to appropriate classical rhetoric to the Christian cause. He described the Christian rhetor's purpose as follows: 'to be of good words in treating of the Word, and in neither direction to overstep the mean'.[36] He delivered many brilliant sermons during his brief time as patriarch of Constantinople (379–81), including the *Five theological orations*.[37] As a young man, Gregory studied rhetoric and philosophy in Athens, in the company of Julian and Basil of Caesarea. The Trinitarian writings of all three Cappadocians – Gregory of Nazianzus, Basil and his brother Gregory of Nyssa – were grounded in the Neoplatonic tradition, and much influenced by their study of Origen and Athanasius of Alexandria. Gregory of Nazianzus and Basil sought to preserve Origen's attempts to Christianise Platonism through a selective compendium of his writings, the *Philokalia*. Together they sought 'to transform and incorporate the Greek philosophical and literary heritage into the emerging Christian culture'.[38] Their challenge was to adapt the principles of the polytheistic, fatalistic philosophy of the Hellenists to the new Christ-centred theology. Gregory later wrote a bitter apology against Julian (*Or.* 4), in which he defended the cultivation of the Greek language as 'the supreme expression of authentic Hellenism'.[39] As well as his homilies, orations and poems, he was responsible for a voluminous epistolary correspondence.

35 An excellent account of Gregory's life and theological contribution is given by John A. McGuckin, *St. Gregory of Nazianzus*.
36 Gregory of Nazianzus, *Oration* 42.13 (trans. NPNF II, 7: 390); cited by Pelikan, *Divine rhetoric*, 22 n. 24.
37 Gregory, *Orations* 27–31; these are translated by F. Williams and L. Wickham with commentary by F. Norris, in *Faith gives fullness to reasoning*.
38 Thus Nonna Verna Harrison, in her translation of Gregory of Nazianzus' *Homily on the nativity of Christ*, 443; that homily is Gregory's *Oration* 38.
39 Gregory, *Oration* 4.103 (SC 309: 252–4); cited by Pelikan, *Christianity and classical culture*, 176.

John Chrysostom (c. 349–407)

John Chrysostom, priest of Antioch and bishop of Constantinople (398–404), is perhaps best known for his homilies and treatises, which earned him the sobriquet of 'the Golden Mouth (Gk *Chrysostomos*)'. His training as a rhetorician occurred in his birthplace, Antioch, under a pagan orator, who has been identified with some certainty as Libanius.[40] Following his graduation from these studies at the age of eighteen, he was baptised and attached himself to the pro-Nicene Bishop Meletius as an aide. He undertook ascetic instruction at an *asketerion*, and then spent six years in the mountains following rigorous ascetic practice. He was ordained in 386, and spent the next eleven years as presbyter to the then-dominant Nicene faction. During 397 he was removed from this see to take up the patriarchate in Constantinople. His pastoral and political agenda in Constantinople antagonised members of various powerful cliques in addition to the bishop of Alexandria, Theophilus. John was deposed from his see in 403 through the intrigues of Theophilus, and exiled but recalled at once by the emperor Arcadius. Less than a year later he was banished to Armenia. He died in 407, while being transported further afield to Iberia. All of his surviving letters date from the period of his exile, to which we return below.[41]

Theodoret of Cyrrhus (c. 383–c. 460)

Theodoret of Cyrrhus, 'the last apologist', was born at Antioch, and received his education in a monastic school there under John Chrysostom and Theodore of Mopsuestia.[42] He entered a monastery at Nicerte upon the death of his parents, and seven years later became bishop of Cyrrhus, a Syrian town. Thus it was that Theodoret left the solitude of the monastery to undertake the busy life of a diocese. He was active in self-funding public works in the pagan tradition of *philanthropia*,[43] and in the persecution of heretics, who were flourishing in his diocese.[44] Theodoret is best known for his involvement in the Christological controversies that engulfed him in his later years. At the 'Robber' Synod of Ephesus (449), he was deposed and forced into exile by the Miaphysite party led by Dioscorus of Alexandria. Recalled by the emperor Marcian, he was finally re-instated by the Council of Chalcedon (451), upon his condemnation of Nestorius. During this time he composed a Christological dialogue in the

---

40 This brief account of John's life is based on Wendy Mayer and Pauline Allen, *John Chrysostom*, 5–11.
41 Ibid., 196.
42 Sr M. Monica Wagner, 'A chapter in Byzantine epistolography', 125.
43 P. Allen, 'The Syrian church through bishop's eyes'.
44 See for example Theodoret, *Letter* 81 (SC 98: 196–8).

Socratic tradition, the *Eranistes*. As with our other five authors, his commentaries on scripture and homilies testify to his teaching role as bishop. His corpus of extant letters (now around 250, but twice that number were known in the fourteenth century) was addressed to many recipients within a limited social and geographical range – mostly from the Near East and usually elite secular or ecclesiastical officials.[45] He compiled a *Historia ecclesiastica* for the period 323 to 428, a *Historia religiosa* about the monks of Syria, and a treatise against paganism, to which we return below.

Late antique Christian literary genres

The most interesting aspect of the Christian appropriation of pagan genres involves how they adapted these forms to suit new audiences and new themes. In this section I will examine the continuities with existing genres, and the innovations and subversions introduced by Christian authors. To illustrate each category, I will consider the writings of one or two authors from the six identified above.

Commentaries on scripture

Biblical commentary was inspired by both Jewish and Hellenistic traditions. The Jewish Midrash traditions, first written down *c.* 200, could be divided into two kinds of exegesis of the Tanakh (Hebrew Bible): legal, pertaining to the Torah, and non-legal. As in the later Christian commentaries, various modes of interpretation were accepted, ranging from the literal or direct meaning to the mystical meaning. Neoplatonist commentators treated the writings of Plato in much the same way as Jews and Christians treated scripture.[46] The *Enneads* of the philosopher Plotinus (205–70), for instance, sought to present the tensions and inconsistencies in Plato's thought as 'perfectly reasonable and consistent'.[47] Augustine is a good example of the educated Christian's struggle to come to terms with the vagaries of the Hebrew and Greek scriptures, as he read them in translation in the *Vetus Latina*, the old Latin version superseded by Jerome's *Vulgate*.

Augustine's attempts to write a commentary on Genesis extended over thirty-eight years, beginning with *De Genesi contra Manichaeos* (*GnM*) and the

---

45 Wagner, 'A chapter in Byzantine epistolography', 126–7; see also Ian G. Tompkins, *The relations between Theodoret of Cyrrhus and his city and its territory*, 26–30.
46 See further Robert Lamberton, *Homer the theologian*.
47 Thus, A. H. Armstrong in his preface to the Loeb volume, *Plotinus. Enneads*, I: xiii.

incomplete *De Genesi ad litteram* (*GnI*), later replaced by *De Genesi ad litteram libri duodecim* (*GnL*), and culminating in *De doctrina christiana* (*DCC*).[48] His understanding of the limits of literal exegesis underwent significant change over the course of these writings, as his skill in figurative exegesis matured. His terms for the distinction ranged from the 'carnal' *vs.* 'spiritual' interpretation (*GnM* 1.19.30) to the proper sense *vs.* the allegorical (*GnL* 8.2.5); the literal *vs.* metaphorical meaning (*DDC* 2.32) to the literal *vs.* the allegorical (*Retr.* 1.18). In *GnM* 2.2.3 Augustine speaks of understanding the text literally, 'just as the letter sounds', but in *GnL* the literal sense 'seems to involve a highly sophisticated interpretation that is quite metaphysical and not what we would ordinarily call the literal sense'.[49] For Augustine, 'the literal sense goes beyond the letter of the text'.[50]

In book 1.1 of *GnL*, Augustine outlines his approach to the fourfold meaning of the text: the allegorical, the historical, the prophetic and the moral. A narrative can be legitimately taken in a historical or figurative sense. As Augustine puts it: 'No Christian will dare say that the narrative must not be taken in a figurative sense.'[51] In his earliest commentary on Genesis, *GnM*, he ascribed this level of understanding to 'spiritual believers'. In *GnL*, however, he presents the spiritual interpretation as the only one possible, thereby demanding more of all readers of scripture, and taking a less elitist approach than in *GnM*.

In Augustine's manual on biblical exegesis, *De doctrina christiana* (396–426), we find the mature bishop reiterating his insistence on the reader's responsibility to make the correct distinction between the literal and metaphorical senses of scripture, a distinction which he had already emphasised in the *Literal commentary on Genesis*. Each verse must be treated *sui generis*, and he put the onus on the reader to determine if its meaning should be taken as literal 'in its plain sense', or as figurative, or both. The reader's interpretation should be based on careful study, keeping in mind the hermeneutical principles he presented in book 2, and his version of Tyconius' rules in book 3. As a young convert, he had been repulsed by the lowly style of the scriptures, when he compared them with Cicero's dignified prose.[52] As a mature bishop, he distinguished between wisdom and eloquence, at least in relation to scripture.[53]

---

48 This discussion is based upon my 'Exploring the limits of literal exegesis: Augustine's reading of Gen. 1:26'.
49 Thus, Roland J. Teske in FOTC 84: 17–18 n. 39.
50 *La Genèse au sens littéral en douze livres*, eds. Agaësse and Solignac, 40.
51 Augustine, *The literal meaning of Genesis* 1 (ACW 41: 19).
52 Augustine, *Confessiones* 3.5.9.
53 Augustine, *De doctrina christiana* 4.7.21.

Letters

Letter-writing among Christian elites served many of the same purposes as in the classical period. Epistles were used to establish or reinforce networks of influence and patronage: for instance, a letter might accompany a gift, or offer a personal recommendation for an individual. For bishops, letter-writing served a number of additional functions in the realm of pastoral care: an epistle could deliver judgments on disciplinary or doctrinal matters; or offer spiritual advice to a member of the flock.

The classical *consolatio* genre originated as a letter of consolation to someone who had suffered a loss or tragedy, the *consolatio ad exulem* being an epistle of consolation to an exile, drawing on Stoic philosophy to advocate patient endurance in adverse circumstances. Such letters also functioned as self-consolation, through the exile's application of the lessons of Stoic philosophy to his own situation. Christian authors adapted these elements by incorporating the themes of Jewish exilic literature and a distinctively Christian notion of divine providence. The self-righteous tone of the Christian *consolatio* also characterised the exilic writings of pagans such as Ovid, Cicero and Seneca the Younger.[54]

In John Chrysostom's exilic letters,[55] we find the concerns of pastoral care struggling against a tendency towards introspection and self-pity. John's major concern, in his pastoral epistles to individual friends, clergy and others who could influence his congregation's direction in his absence, was that his addressees respond in kind with a letter indicating that his correspondence has been appreciated and obeyed.[56] This is the consolation that John seeks in exile: the knowledge that he may still intervene effectively in parish affairs *in absentia*.

John Chrysostom's letter of consolation to the bereaved urban prefect Studius (*ep.* 197) may usefully be compared with the classical paradigm. John falls back on philosophy as a source of comfort in a similar situation. He asks his friend Studius, who is 'intelligent and experienced in philosophy', to bear the death of his brother with equanimity. The virtue of the departed man should bring considerable consolation. Both this attitude towards virtue

---

54 J.-M. Claassen, *Displaced persons*, 26, notes the difference between the pagan *consolationes* and the self-denigrating stance of Augustine in his *Confessions*.

55 Some 240 of these survive: see J. N. D. Kelly, *Golden Mouth*, 260. R. Delmaire gives a comprehensive summary of the letters, their recipients and their dates, in 'Les lettres d'exil de Jean Chrysostome'.

56 See for example *Letters* 117 (trans. Mayer and Allen, 199), 197 (ibid., 200), 203 (ibid.), 212 (ibid., 200–1), 217 (ibid., 202), 34 (ibid., 203–4); see also *Letter* 185 to Pentadia (PG 52: 716) and *Letter* 190 to Brison (PG 52: 718).

and his scorn of the present life are equally Stoic and Christian.[57] A noticeable departure from Stoic tradition, however, is his standard interpretation of death as not the end of life, but the beginning of eternal life. He advises Studius to rejoice instead of grieving:[58] virtuous and godly living will ensure immortality. The epistles of consolation by John's student, Theodoret of Cyrrhus, also demonstrate the new Christian approach to grief within the Stoic and Cynic philosophical framework.[59] Even in such a letter of consolation to the bishop Irenaeus, however, 'the tyranny of rhetorical tradition' rules, producing a false note as Theodoret emphasises the Christian viewpoint, while at the same time insisting on philosophical reasoning as the correct antidote to sorrow in bereavement.[60] Here too the tension between the new Christian attitude and its pagan forebears is evident.

Homilies

Homilies were identified in our introduction as a 'hybrid' genre, because they incorporate elements of panegyric, exegesis, moral treatise and other rhetorical techniques common to classical public declamations. A homily (ὁμιλία in Greek, sermo in Latin) was a speech, either prepared or impromptu, that was delivered in a liturgical context. The so-called 'desk homily' was 'written in homiletic form but was intended for private reading or study'.[61] The origins of the homily are thus far-flung: from pagan diatribe to Jewish exegesis. The pagan diatribe can be traced to the preaching of better morals by itinerant Cynic-Stoic preachers. School dialogues from teachers of ethics, and addresses of travelling philosophers such as Maximus of Tyre (125–85), were also written in the form of the diatribe.[62] While scholars have not yet established a historical relationship with either Jewish-Hellenistic diatribes or the homiletic midrash of the third and fourth centuries, there appear in both earlier traditions several characteristics of the dialogue, such as imitation of characters and changing of voice, that point to such a relationship.[63] Rabbinic exegesis of the non-legal

---

57 John Chrysostom, Letter 197 (trans. Mayer and Allen, 199): 'For you know the perishable nature of human affairs, and that events mimic the flowing waters of a river, and how one should consider blessed only those who with firm hope dismiss the present life.'
58 John Chrysostom, Letter 197 (trans. Mayer and Allen, 200).
59 See Wagner, 'A chapter in Byzantine epistolography', 157–60.
60 Ibid., 160.
61 Mary B. Cunningham and Pauline Allen, Preacher and audience, 1.
62 K.-H. Uthemann, 'Forms of communication in the homilies of Severian of Gabala', 139.
63 Ibid., 150–1; Alastair Stewart-Sykes, 'Hermas the prophet and Hippolytus the preacher', has pointed to the importance of parainetic prophecy, that is, prophecy that offered guidance to the prophet's congregation, in very early Christian preaching such as Hermas' The shepherd.

portions of the Hebrew Bible was delivered in a chiefly homiletic context. These *midrashim* presented philosophical or mystical expositions of biblical cosmology, legends and parables, as well as the liturgical occasions for feasts and fasts.

Christian homilies covered a similar variety of content, ranging from exegetical material to moral or ethical treatises, or celebrations of a particular person or saint. Festal and panegyrical homilies predominate among the homily collections that survive.[64] It is important to note that these homilies were presented to the uninitiated as well as the baptised in the Liturgy of the Word, before the catechumens were dismissed from the church for the duration of the eucharistic liturgy. Series of catechetical homilies were delivered to catechumens in the weeks leading up to their baptism. After the sixth century there was a decline in catechetical homilies, and homiletic evidence in general becomes sparse. Preaching was usually reserved for bishops, although it is clear that a gifted preacher like John Chrysostom was allowed to preach in Antioch while still a presbyter. Homilies, which could last for up to three hours, were occasions for rhetorical display, and thus attracted a degree of public interest, even though the audience had to stand during the delivery unless they were very wealthy. Sometimes several homilists preached in succession. John Chrysostom complains that in Constantinople he had to compete with horse races at the hippodrome and plays at the theatres for an audience.[65]

Chrysostom's homilies and treatises deal with subjects relevant to the daily life of Christians, such as the priesthood, marriage and virginity, and martyrs, as well as explicit warnings against pagan culture, as in his homily *Against the games and theatres*. In the case of Ambrose, the sermon's cross-over with exegesis and treatises is very clear: only four or five sermons have survived as such, although many of his works were based on sermonic material.[66]

Moral and dogmatic treatises

A treatise was a tract designed to give moral or ethical instruction, or to illustrate a dogmatic position. The moral treatise was often based on a classical theme with a distinctively Christian thrust: for instance, Ambrose's *De officiis ministrorum* (377–91?) was modelled on Cicero's *De officiis*, also in three books, but dealing with ecclesiastical rather than secular office. It offered moral instruction to the Milanese clergy in the virtues appropriate to their office.[67]

64 Cunningham and Allen, *Preacher and audience*, 6.
65 John Chrysostom, *Against the games and theatres* (trans. Mayer and Allen, 119–25).
66 Ramsey, *Ambrose*, 55.
67 See the commentary on the text by Ivor J. Davidson in his *Ambrose. De officiis*.

These included the four Stoic cardinal virtues of justice, temperance, fortitude and prudence. Other treatises dealt with particularly Christian themes such as virginity, the subject of four treatises by Ambrose.[68] Often based on sermonic material, these were usually addressed to Christian audiences.

Dogmatic treatises, on the other hand, were directed at pagans, Jews or heretical Christians. Theodoret's treatise against paganism, *Graecarum affectionum curatio*, is a good example of the first. In this work, Theodoret sought to discredit the writings of Greek philosophers, borrowing heavily from florilegia (on which, see below), by comparing them with scripture passages on the same subject. By this means he offered a caricature of Greek learning's inconsistencies as opposed to the 'quiet certainty of revelation'.[69] His position was 'faith before knowledge'.[70] By the year 448, Theodoret could claim that there were no heretics left in his diocese.[71]

Historiography

Christian historiography shows strong continuities with earlier histories, such as Livy's *Natural history*, but with a decisive difference: a Christian history had its roots in apologetic, in that it meant to reveal the economy of God working out his salvation plan for humankind.[72] For our period, Augustine's *De civitate Dei* (412–26) represents perhaps the clearest example of this Christian redeployment of historiographic techniques. In his preface, Augustine writes that he was inspired by a need to explain to pagan critics how God could have allowed such a catastrophe as the sack of Rome by Alaric in 410. Augustine creates a negative Christian re-write of Roman history, in his attempt to demonstrate that the pagan gods of the Romans had never afforded them any protection. Beginning with the sacred text of pagan Rome's triumphalism, Virgil's *Aeneid*, Augustine suggests that the Roman gods were more protected than

---

68 Those treatises are *De virginibus, De virginitate, De institutione virginis* and *Exhortatio virginis*.

69 Lemerle, *Byzantine humanism*, 46.

70 Theodoret, *Thérapeutique des maladies helleniques* 93 (SC 57¹: 128), cited by Lemerle, *Byzantine humanism*, 46 n. 5. Philip Rousseau, '*Historia religiosa*', 324, asserts that Theodoret forges a very strong link in this work between a correct interpretation of history (*historia*) and belief or faith (*pistis*).

71 Theodoret, *Letter* 81 (SC 98: 196.21–4).

72 See Pauline Allen, 'Some aspects of Hellenism', for a summary of the ways that apologetic – 'that is, arguments against and reactions to Hellenism' – shaped the histories of Eusebius, Socrates and Theodoret. In reference to their attitude to *paideia*, Allen comments: 'The fact that the *Church Histories* of both Eusebius and Theodoret exhibit fewer classical citations and allusions than some of their other works seems to indicate they were of the opinion that this manifestation of *paideia* had to be played down in a *Church History*.'

protectors.[73] He proceeds with illustrations from Horace, Sallust, Livy and Lucian, among others, to deconstruct the pagan story of Rome's elite triumphing over their enemies, guided by destiny and protected by the gods.

Augustine's overtly Christian re-telling of history is a departure from the precedent set by the first Christian chronicler, Eusebius of Caesarea, whose *Historia ecclesiastica* sought to establish the antiquity of the Judaeo-Christian tradition from the birth of Abraham. There is, however, room to compare the two in that both Augustine and Eusebius incorporated Christian apologetic into their accounts of history. More strictly in line with Eusebius' approach is Jerome, whose *Chronicle* was a Latin adaptation of Eusebius up to 325, supplemented by the history of events to 378. Theodoret's *Historia ecclesiastica*, covering the period 324 to 428/9, concentrates mainly on ecclesiastical affairs.

Pagan authors continued to contest these interpretations of historical events as manifesting the providential hand of God. Ammianus Marcellinus produced a pagan history that was critical of leading Christian figures of the third to fifth centuries, and full of praise for Julian. In the early sixth century the pagan Zosimus, in response to Christian historical revisionism, wrote a *New history* which covered the first four centuries of the Roman empire, ending just before the sack of Rome in August 410. Zosimus did his own revision of the facts of history, by changing the dates of key events, such as the conversion of Constantine, to suit his narrative, which attributed the collapse of Rome to its neglect of pagan sacrifices.[74]

Public orations

Libanius reports somewhat smugly that with the accession of Julian, 'the art of prophecy came again into its own, that of oratory came again to be admired',[75] reflecting a common feeling that Christianity had led to the degradation of one of classical culture's jewels, public oratory. Certain categories of the classical *oratio*, such as epideictic rhetoric (speeches of praise or blame), were well used by Christian authors to make a case for their religion publicly, or to criticise an opponent (as for instance Gregory of Nazianzus' *Or.* 4, an apology against Julian). A convincing case has recently been made for the relevance of two other branches of ancient Greek oratory to a full understanding of

---

73 Augustine, *De civitate Dei* 1.3.
74 E.g., Constantine's conversion was moved to 326 so that his military successes appeared to belong to the pagan era, and no mention was made of Arianism or the Council of Nicaea in 325; see *Zosimus: New history*, trans. Ridley, xiii–xiv and 157 n. 64.
75 Libanius, *Autobiography* 119 (trans. Norman, 185).

the forty-five speeches of Gregory of Nazianzus in particular. These are the judicial (or forensic), which was intended to sway the mind of the listener, and the deliberative, which aimed to teach.[76] A sub-category of epideictic was the panegyric, a speech in praise of someone recently deceased. Gregory of Nazianzus' *Or.* 43, a panegyric for his friend Basil of Caesarea,[77] is of particular interest for the information it gives concerning Basil's education in Caesarea, Constantinople and then at Athens, where he met his fellow student Gregory. Gregory cannot hide his reverence for Athens ('a city truly of gold and the provider of all that is fine'). However, his ambivalence is revealed when he then immediately turns to criticise the futility of the education they received there.[78] In Constantinople, on the other hand, 'classical elitism had been overcome by the Christian faith'.[79] It was in Constantinople that John Chrysostom delivered a series of orations against the Jews, ones that typify the anti-Semitic stance of Christians in this period.

Florilegia

This genre, which was original to Christian authors, will be dealt with only briefly. Florilegia were collections of proof texts from patristic authorities to demonstrate the orthodoxy of one side or the other in a theological controversy. While classical florilegia of philosophical texts were known in earlier centuries, and proved an important resource for writers like Clement of Alexandria whose access to the original full texts was limited,[80] the use of such collections to demonstrate a theological point began with Theodoret. In his *Eranistes* (*c.* 447), written in the form of a dialogue between an Orthodox speaker and the heretic Eranistes, he provides a 'bouquet' of quotations disproving the doctrine of one nature in Christ (called 'Miaphysitism,' or, polemically, 'Monophysitism') that was imputed to his opponents at the 'Robber' Council at Ephesus and at Chalcedon. After the Council of Chalcedon, Theodoret also compiled the *Haereticarum fabularum compendium*, to combat the major heresies

---

76 Celia Milovanović, 'Sailing to *Sophistopolis*'; Milovanović argues (232) that 'many of Gregory's orations are semi-fictitious speeches of a forensic and deliberative kind. As such, they follow the well-established tradition of Greek declamation and are closely related to the procedures of Aelius Aristides, who in turn was looking back toward Plato as a literary model.'

77 In *Discours funèbres en l'honneur de son frère Césaire et de Basile de Césarée*, ed. Boulenger.

78 Lemerle, *Byzantine humanism*, 48 n. 11.

79 *Or.* 42.11; cited by Pelikan, *Christianity and classical culture*, 172.

80 In his introduction to the edition of Clement of Alexandria's *Paedagogus* (SC 70: 66–73), Henri-Irénée Marrou concluded that the only authors whom we can be sure that Clement had studied in the original text were Homer and Plato.

of his day – Arianism, Eunomianism, Encratism and Marcionite Gnosticism – from the perspective of the fifth-century Christological disputes.[81]

Florilegia were also often attached to the acts of church councils. They might include forgeries, or texts spuriously attributed to more reputable sources than the original author. Their aim was to illustrate that the 'orthodox' position followed predecessors, and was therefore safe from innovation, which was tantamount to heterodoxy. Such collections of excerpts were distinct from *catenae*, a method of textual commentary that originated with the pagan Procopius of Gaza. Christian *catenae* were collections of interpretations for particular verses of scripture, strung together as if in a chain.

Biography/autobiography

Perhaps the best example of early Christian biography is Jerome's *De viris illustribus*, written in 392/3. This was loosely modelled on the silver age Latin author Suetonius' biographies of Roman poets (*De poetis*) and his *De grammaticis et rhetoribus*. Jerome states in his preface to the work that he wished to 'do for our writers what he [Suetonius] did in chronicling eminent secular authors'.[82] He was careful to identify the pedigree for this sort of enterprise among Greek and Roman authors. Jerome focused strictly on famous Christian writers 'who have published anything memorable on the Holy Scriptures',[83] with entries starting from Simon Peter the apostle and ending with himself. Other significant authors, such as the anonymous scholar known as Ambrosiaster, did not rate a mention.

Jerome also availed himself of the opportunity to make certain snide remarks about his enemies, who were not few. For instance, of Ambrose he wrote: 'Ambrose, Bishop of Milan, continues to write. Since he is still alive I shall withhold my judgment lest, should I express any opinion, I be blamed for either flattery or truthfulness' (*De vir. ill.* 124).[84] Jerome had already accused Ambrose of plagiarising Greek sources in *De Spiritu Sancto*, of which work Jerome, adapting a Terentian tag, claims, 'I saw bad things in Latin taken from good things in Greek.' For Jerome to accuse anyone of plagiarism is ironic, considering his own great debt to Origen.[85]

Jerome was unusual in applying such a modern standard of literary criticism to his contemporaries. Most Christian writers, in keeping with the

---

81 Tompkins, *The relations between Theodoret of Cyrrhus and his city and its territory*, 238.
82 Jerome, *On illustrious men*, preface (FOTC 100: 1).
83 Ibid.
84 Cited by Ramsey, *Ambrose*, 53.
85 See for example Heine, *The commentaries of Origen and Jerome*.

Greco-Roman tradition, sought not originality but continuity with their Christian forebears, as mentioned above in relation to florilegia. For all its shortcomings, *De viris illustribus* represents the first attempt to make a more or less complete catalogue of Christian authors, and as such testifies to a growing awareness that Christian literary production was developing its own traditions. It was explicitly aimed against those 'rabid dogs barking against Christ', the pagans Celsus, Porphyry and Julian and their followers, who 'think that the church has had no philosophers, no orators, no men of learning'.[86]

Christian prose autobiography began with Augustine's *Confessiones* (397–401); its first nine books are a record of his gradual conversion to Christianity, the religion of his mother Monica, culminating in his baptism in 386. The *Confessiones* reveal an intimacy and a willingness to share the writer's inner world with the reader that was quite new for its fifth-century Latin readers. Augustine applies the lens of sin leading toward salvation to even the most trivial events of his early life, such as his infantile rivalry at the breast of his nurse. The Greek world had an early model of pagan autobiography in the *Bios* of the rhetor Libanius. It is unlikely that this had a direct influence upon Augustine, however. Gregory of Nazianzus was the author of several autobiographical poems before 390. The longest of these has been compared with Augustine's *Confessiones*, but it stands alone due to its poetic form.

Hagiography

A special category of Christian biography is hagiography, or the *vitae* of saints. Christian hagiography developed to meet a devotional need in the monastic movement of the third and fourth centuries. The antecedents of saints' *Lives* were the martyr acts of the second and third centuries, as well as pagan *Lives* such as Suetonius' *Vitae Caesarum*. The *Lives* of holy men and women, portraying the bishop or ascetic as an imitator of Christ, were read privately and in monastic communities. The earliest Christian *vita* was that of Anthony of Egypt, composed in the mid-fourth century by Athanasius of Alexandria. Anthony's solitary struggle to overcome the desires of the flesh in the desert was depicted as battles with demons, both real and imagined. It had wide appeal, and quickly became the pattern for his many imitators.

Most *vitae* presented a stylised account of key moments in the saint's life according to the following formula: early youth, characterised by love of philosophy and scorn for earthly pursuits; the decision to embrace the ascetic life, either as a solitary or in a *coenobium*, accompanied by the renunciation of

---

86 Jerome, *On illustrious men*, Preface (FOTC 100: 2).

worldly goods; the reluctant assumption of the role of spiritual leadership; the saint's spiritual teachings; the battle against demons; persecution by secular authorities; his/her welcome death (often foretold by the saint), followed by miracles attesting to his/her holiness. A rare example of a female saint's *Life* is the *Vita Macrinae*, written by Gregory of Nyssa, Macrina's younger brother.

Some of these stock themes are also found in Porphyry's *Vita Plotini*,[87] the *Life* of the third-century Neoplatonist philosopher Plotinus. Although Porphyry (232–305) was hostile to Christianity, and although his *vita* was directed at an elite pagan audience, his account of his teacher's life and teaching prefigures many of the characteristics of fourth-century Christian *vitae*, such as Plotinus' scorn of the body (1–2); his love of wisdom (philosophy) (3); his withdrawal to country estates to practise philosophy (5 and 12); and his attracting of disciples (7), including women (9). Even an element of the miraculous is found in Plotinus' demonstration of supernatural powers of clairvoyance (11). These similarities are testimony to the continuity of Neoplatonic and Stoic ideals within Christian asceticism.

Other popular literature included pilgrim journals, such as the account of the fourth-century nun Egeria's travels to the Holy Land, which remains a valuable source for Eastern liturgical practices.[88] Jerome's *Liber locorum* and *Liber nominum*, based on Eusebius' *Onomasticon*, and describing the Hebrew names and sites of places of spiritual interest in the Holy Land, could also be included in this category. From the fourth century, monastic literature enjoyed a huge florescence. It included rules (*regulae*) and collections of holy sayings, as well as monastic histories such as Theodoret's *Historia religiosa*, consisting of the biographies of about thirty monks and three nuns of Syria,[89] and the anonymous *Historia monachorum in Aegypto*. These were also used in devotional contexts.

Poetry and hymns

Hymns could also be described as a form of popular literature. While the poetry of Gregory of Nazianzus was extremely polished and usually directed towards some dogmatic purpose (e.g., his poem on marriage is one of the most moving tributes to this institution in the whole Christian canon, all the more striking for its rarity), hymns were usually directed at a less learned audience, and were written for use in the liturgy. Ancient Greek and Roman influences on

---

87 An English translation is available in M. Edwards, *Neo-Platonic saints*; a partial translation by Richard Valantasis can be found in his *Religions of late antiquity in practice*, 50–61.
88 Egeria, *Travels* (SC 296).
89 On the place of ascetics in the life of the Syrian church, see Rousseau, '*Historia religiosa*'.

both the Eastern and Western traditions of hymnography can be traced.[90] In the West, the Christian hymnographic tradition is thought to have begun with Ambrose, whose first hymns were originally published in 386, at the height of his struggle to contain the Arian faction in Milan. These hymns were meant to maintain morale among the Nicene congregation as they held all-night vigils against their opponents.[91] Only four of the many hymns attributed to him are unanimously ascribed to Ambrose.[92] Their influence spread quickly throughout the West.

In a similar period in the East, Ephrem of Syria was writing liturgical hymns to convey complex theological truths in a simple form that everyone could grasp. In this he was immensely successful. Syriac hymns were in regular use in Theodoret's churches in Cyrrhus.[93] This takes us to the development of other, more distinctive, literary productions of the East.

Diverse Christian literatures in the East

Most of the distinctively Christian genres originated not in Latin or Greek, but other languages, or emerged independently there, as did the Syriac tradition of liturgical hymns. This originality could be put down to the geographical and cultural distance from centres of Roman and Greek culture. At the same time, the bilingualism of Syriac culture (Syriac and Greek) must be recognised as an important facilitator of cultural exchange. For instance, there is evidence that the Greek *kontakia* associated with the Syrian Romanos the Melodist, and popular in Constantinople from the late fifth to the seventh centuries, were influenced by Ephrem's hymnography.[94] As the example of the *Odes of Solomon* shows, 'Syriac poetry not only formed models for Greek composition, but was also translated directly into Greek.'[95]

Some of the earliest surviving translations of scripture are the Syriac and Armenian versions of the Gospels. The late fifth-century Armenian history, *Patmut'iwn Hayoc'* (*History of the Armenians*) is peppered with hagiographic passages that contain classical *topoi* appearing for the first time in a Christian milieu, some of which later became *topoi* of hagiographic literature

---

90 See the magisterial study by Michael Lattke, *Hymnus*.
91 Paulinus of Milan, *The life of Saint Ambrose* 13 (trans. Ramsey, *Ambrose*, 201).
92 Ramsey, *Ambrose*, 65; these four are *Aeterne rerum conditor, Iam surgit hora tertia, Deus creator omnium* and *Intende qui regis Israel* (trans. Ramsey, 167–73). Among the most well-known of uncertain attribution are the *Exultet* and *Te Deum*.
93 Tompkins, *The relations between Theodoret of Cyrrhus and his city and its territory*, 134.
94 Tompkins, ibid., 132–3, summarises the evidence for this connection.
95 Ibid., 134.

generally.[96] Early monastic literature, such as the Coptic and Syriac traditions of *Apophthegmata patrum* (*Sayings of the desert fathers*), also found a wide readership in Egypt, Syria, and beyond. Seven *Letters* of St Anthony survive in Coptic, Greek, Georgian, Latin, Syriac and later Arabic versions.[97] These letters reflect a subtly but importantly different image of Anthony from that found in the *Vita Antonii*, the first Christian saint's life, which had an enormous impact on East and West, playing a crucial role, for instance, in the conversion of Augustine.[98] The earliest monastic rule, the *Rule of Pachomius*, composed in Coptic in the third century, spawned many imitations in both Eastern and Western coenobitic communities, including the *Small asketikon* and *Great asketikon* of Basil of Caesarea,[99] and the *Rule* of Augustine of Hippo.

Conclusion

Christian writers did not hesitate to build upon the rhetorical and philosophical foundations of Greco-Roman culture, but adapted these to suit their own theological purposes, which included apologetic, pastoral, polemical and exegetical concerns. Some literary genres were taken over in form but not in content, such as letters, and particularly letters of consolation. From the classical forms of treatises, panegyrics and textual commentaries emerged Christian hybrids.

The literary genres discussed here were also used to address a broader range of audience than their classical paradigms, which had been usually directed to the elite. The hearers and readers of Christian texts ranged from Christian congregations of all classes to pagan and Jewish elites, elite converts, imperial leaders, heterodox Christians, and adherents of asceticism. An important characteristic of Christian literature of the mid-fourth to fifth centuries is the element of conflict that was generated by the clash of the new *paideia* with the old. Gregory of Nazianzus valued his education in the pagan classics, the subject of high praise in his *Oration* 43, but criticised it on other occasions. Jerome, Augustine, Theodoret and Basil of Caesarea manifested a higher level of ambivalence towards the pagan texts that were the foundation of their

---

96 Marco Bais, 'Presenza di *topoi* classici in pagine agiografiche armene'; one example given by Bais is that of the Eastern Roman emperor Valens, who is characterised as adopting the pose of a meditating philosopher while listening to a homily of the patriarch Nersēs. This image also turns up in a late fifth-century Greek *Life of Arsenius* (as yet unedited).
97 Samuel Rubenson, *The letters of St. Antony*, 15–34, examines the relationships between these versions.
98 Augustine, *Confessiones* 8.12.29; cf. 8.6.15 on its influence in the conversion of two court officials at Trier.
99 See the recent translation and study by Anna Silvas, *The Asketikon of Basil the Great*.

education. They took up what suited them, and left the rest behind. Following Basil's admonition to his nephews, they preferred to use pagan literature selectively, taking only what was of spiritual benefit, just as bees plucked honey from flowers:[100] 'For these [bees] neither approach all flowers equally, nor indeed do they attempt to carry off whole those upon which they alight, but take only so much of them as is suitable for their work, leaving the rest untouched.' The hive of Christian culture preserved and was nourished by the honey of its pagan forebears, the overtly despised but often secretly admired masters of classical rhetoric. Through an inventive appropriation of classical genres – textual commentaries, epistolary forms, orations, treatises, biographies and histories – the patristic writers developed new and hybrid forms in the realm of homiletics, hagiography, florilegia and hymnography, and monastic literature. As the emerging Christian culture gained support and confidence during the fourth and fifth centuries, its increasing literary output revealed a triumphant transformation of its Hellenistic inheritance. With the decline in secular education in the sixth century, symbolised by the closing of the school of philosophy at Athens, the role of Christian authors in maintaining Greco-Roman literary traditions became even more crucial. Away from literary and urban centres, however, and particularly in monastic communities, original expressions of the Christian culture, now established as dominant, flourished and evolved to meet the needs of a far-flung and ever-increasing audience.

Bibliography

PRIMARY SOURCES

Ambrose. *De officiis*, ed. Ivor J. Davidson (Oxford, 2001)
Athanasius of Alexandria. *Festal letters*. Trans. A. Campani, *Lettere festali. Atanasio di Alessandria* (Milan, 2003)
Augustine. *De civitate Dei* (CCSL 47, 48)
    Confessions, ed. J. J. O'Donnell (Oxford, 1992)
    De doctrina christiana, ed. and trans. R. P. H. Green (Oxford, 1995); trans. E. Hill, *Teaching Christianity* (New York, 1996)
    De Genesi ad litteram libri duodecim. Eds. P. Agaësse and A. Solignac, *La Genèse au sens littéral en douze livres*, Œuvres de S. Augustin 48 (Bruges, 1972); trans. ACW 41, 42
    On the literal interpretation of Genesis, trans. FOTC 84
    Two books on Genesis against the Manicheans, trans. FOTC 84

---

100 Basil, *Ad adolescentes de legendis libris gentilium* 4 (ed. Wilson, 23, 42–6; trans. Deferrari and McGuire, *St Basil. The letters*, IV: 391, modified). A similar image is provided by Theodoret, *Thérapeutique des maladies helléniques* 1.126 (SC 57: 136).

Basil of Caesarea. *Ad adolescentes de legendis libris gentilium*. Ed. Nigel Wilson, *Saint Basil on the value of Greek literature* (London, 1975); trans. Roy J. Deferrari and Martin McGuire, *St Basil. The letters*, IV: *Address to young men on reading Greek literature*, LCL (London, 1934; reprint, 1970)

Cicero. *De inventione libri duo*. Ed. Guy Achard, *Ciceron. De l'invention* (Paris, 1994)

Clement of Alexandria. *Paedagogus* (SC 70, 108, 158)

Egeria. *Travels* (SC 296)

Gregory of Nazianzus. *Faith gives fullness to reasoning: The five theological orations of Gregory Nazianzen*, trans. and ed. Frederick W. Norris et al. (Leiden, 1991)

    Homily on the nativity of Christ, trans. Nonna Verna Harrison, in Valantasis, *Religions of late antiquity in practice*, 443–53

    Oration 43. Ed. F. Boulenger, *Discours funèbres en l'honneur de son frère Césaire et de Basile de Césarée* (Paris, 1908)

    Orations 4–5, 'Against Julian' (SC 309)

Jerome. *On illustrious men*, trans. FOTC 100

    The letters of St Jerome; ACW 33

John Chrysostom. *Against the games and theatres*. Trans. W. Mayer and P. Allen, *John Chrysostom*, The Early Church Fathers (London, 2000)

Julian 'the Apostate'. *Against the Galileans*. Trans. Elizabeth Geraldine Burr, in Valantasis, *Religions of late antiquity in practice*, 143–55

Libanius. *Autobiography and selected letters*, trans. A. F. Norman, LCL (Cambridge MA, 1992)

Paulinus of Milan. *The life of Saint Ambrose*. Trans. B. Ramsey, *Ambrose* (London, 1997)

Plotinus. *Enneads*, trans. A. H. Armstrong, LCL (London, 1966)

Porphyry. *On the life of Plotinus and the order of his books*, trans. Valantasis, in *Religions of late antiquity in practice*, 50–61; also in M. Edwards, trans., *Neo-Platonic saints: The lives of Plotinus and Proclus by their students* (Liverpool, 2000)

Synesius of Cyrene. *Correspondence*, ed. Antonio Garzya (Paris, 2000)

Theodoret of Cyrrhus. *Correspondence* (SC 40, 98, 111, 429)

    Eranistes; trans. FOTC 106

    A History of the monks of Syria, trans. R. M. Price (Kalamazoo, MI, 1985)

    Thérapeutique des maladies helleniques (SC 57)

Zosimus. *New history*, trans. Ronald T. Ridley (Sydney, 1982; reprint, 2004)

SECONDARY SOURCES

Allen, Pauline. 'Some aspects of Hellenism in the early Greek church historians', *Traditio* 43 (1987): 368–81

    'The Syrian church through a bishop's eyes: The letters of Theodoret of Cyrrhus and Severus of Antioch', *SP* 42 (2006): 3–22

Bais, Marco. 'Presenza di *topoi* classici in pagine agiografiche armene', in Alfredo Valvo, ed., *La diffusione dell'eredità classica nell'età tardoantica e medievale. Forme e modi di trasmissione* (Alessandria, 1997), 19–30

Bielawski, M. and D. Hombergen, eds. *Il monachesimo tra eredità e aperture*, SA 140 (Rome, 2004)

Brown, Peter. *Augustine of Hippo. A biography* (Berkeley, CA, 2000[2])

Cameron, Alan. 'The last days of the academy of Athens', *Proceedings of the Cambridge philological society* 195 (N.S. 15) (1969): 7–29

Claassen, Jo-Marie. *Displaced persons. The literature of exile from Cicero to Boethius* (Madison, WI, 1999)

Cochrane, Charles Norris. *Christianity and classical culture: A study of thought and action from Augustus to Augustine* (London, 1944; reprint, 1957)

Cunningham, Mary B. and Pauline Allen, eds. *Preacher and audience. Studies in early Christian and Byzantine homiletics* (Leiden, 1998)

Delmaire, R. 'Les lettres d'exil de Jean Chrysostome. Études de chronologie et de prosopographie', *Recherches augustiniennes* 25 (1991): 71–180

Glucker, John. *Antiochus and the late academy* (Göttingen, 1978)

Hägg, Tomas and Philip Rousseau, eds. *Greek biography and panegyric in late antiquity* (Berkeley, 2000)

Harrison, Carol. *Augustine: Christian truth and fractured humanity* (Oxford, 2000)

Heine, Ronald E. *The commentaries of Origen and Jerome on St Paul's epistle to the Ephesians* (Oxford, 2002)

Jaeger, Werner. *Paideia: The ideals of Greek culture*, trans. Gilbert Highet (New York, 1939–44)

Kelly, J. N. D. *Golden Mouth: The story of John Chrysostom – ascetic, preacher, bishop* (Ithaca, NY, 1995)

Jerome: His life, writings and controversies (London, 1975)

Lamberton, Robert. *Homer the theologian* (Berkeley, 1986)

Lattke, Michael. *Hymnus. Materialien zu einer Geschichte der antiken Hymnologie* (Freiburg, 1991)

Lemerle, P. *Le premier humanisme byzantin. Notes et remarques sur enseignement et culture à Byzance des origines au Xe siècle* (Paris, 1971); *Byzantine humanism*, trans. H. Lindsay and A. Moffatt, Byzantina Australiensia 3, rev. edn. (Canberra, 1986)

Maas, Michael, ed. *Exegesis and empire in the early Byzantine Mediterranean: Junillus Africanus and the Instituta regularia divinae legis* (Tübingen, 2003)

McGuckin, John A. *St. Gregory of Nazianzus: An intellectual biography* (Crestwood, NY, 2001)

McLynn, Neil. *Ambrose of Milan* (Berkeley, 1994)

Marrou, Henri-Irénée. *A history of education in antiquity*, trans. G. Lamb (London, 1956[3])

Mathews, Edward G. 'Excursus on the schools of Antioch and Nisibis', in Michael Maas, ed., *Exegesis and empire in the early Byzantine Mediterranean: Junillus Africanus and the Instituta regularia divinae legis* (Tübingen, 2003), 94–111

Metzger, Bruce. *The canon of the New Testament: Its origins, development, and significance*, repr. with corr. (Oxford, 1988)

Milovanović, C. 'Sailing to *Sophistopolis*: Gregory of Nazianzus and Greek declamation', *JECS* 13 (2005): 187–232

Neil, B. 'Exploring the limits of literal exegesis: Augustine's reading of Gen. 1:26' *Pacifica* 19 (2006): 144–55

Norris, F. 'Your honor, my reputation: St. Gregory of Nazianzus's funeral oration on St. Basil the Great', in Thomas Hägg and Philip Rousseau, eds., *Greek biography and panegyric in late antiquity* (Berkeley, 2000), 140–59

O'Donnell, James J. *Cassiodorus* (Berkeley, 1979)

Pelikan, Jaroslav. *Christianity and classical culture: The metamorphosis of natural theology in the Christian encounter with Hellenism* (New Haven, 1993)

Divine rhetoric: The Sermon on the Mount as message and as model in Augustine, Chrysostom and Luther (Crestwood, NY, 2001)

Pollman, Karla and Mark Vessey, eds. *Augustine and the disciplines: From Cassiciacum to Confessions* (Oxford, 2005)

Ramsey, Boniface. *Ambrose* (London, 1997)

Rousseau, Philip. *The early Christian centuries* (London, 2002)

'Moses, monks, and mountains in Theodoret's *Historia religiosa*', in M. Bielawski and D. Hombergen, eds., *Il monachesimo tra eredità e aperture*, SA 140 (Rome, 2004), 323–46

Rubenson, Samuel. *The letters of St. Antony. Monasticism and the making of a saint* (Minneapolis, 1995)

Runciman, Steven. *Byzantine civilization* (Cleveland, 1956; reprint, 1970)

Schucan, L. *Das Nachleben von Basilius Magnus ad adolescentes: Ein Beitrag zur Geschichte des christlichen Humanismus* (Geneva, 1973)

Silvas, Anna. *The Asketikon of Basil the Great* (Oxford, 2005)

Stewart-Sykes, Alastair. 'Hermas the prophet and Hippolytus the preacher: The Roman homily in its social context', in Mary B. Cunningham and Pauline Allen, eds., *Preacher and audience, Studies in early Christian and Byzantine homiletics*, 33–63

Tompkins, Ian G. *The relations between Theodoret of Cyrrhus and his city and its territory, with particular reference to the letters and* Historia religiosa, DPhil dissertation, University of Oxford, 1993

Uthemann, Karl-Heinz. 'Forms of communication in the homilies of Severian of Gabala: A contribution to the reception of the diatribe as a method of exposition', in Mary B. Cunningham and Pauline Allen, *Preacher and audience. Studies in early Christian and Byzantine homiletics*, 139–77

Valantasis, Richard, ed. *Religions of late antiquity in practice* (Princeton, 2000)

Valvo, Alfredo, ed. *La diffusione dell'eredità classica nell'età tardoantica e medievale. Forme e modi di trasmissione* (Alessandria, 1997)

Wagner, Sr M. Monica. 'A chapter in Byzantine epistolography. The letters of Theodoret of Cyrus', *DOP* 4 (1948): 119–81

Wilken, Robert Louis. *The Christians as the Romans saw them* (New Haven, 1984)

The spirit of early Christian thought – seeking the face of God (New Haven, 2003)

Young, Frances M. 'The rhetorical schools and their influence on patristic exegesis', in R. Williams, ed., *The making of orthodoxy: Essays in honour of Henry Chadwick* (Cambridge, 1989), 182–99

14

Bishops and society

RAYMOND VAN DAM

'I too am a bishop, appointed by God.' Constantine's portrayal of himself was presumably meant to amuse the bishops at his court. His knowledge of Greek was competent enough to realise that *episkopos* could be a good pun: they were 'bishops' for internal ecclesiastical affairs, and he was 'overseer' of everything else. This quip suggests that the first Christian emperor respected bishops and churchmen. It was also rather pointedly hollow humour. In the early fourth century Christianity was not widespread or influential in Roman society, and most likely there were comparatively few bishops and clerics. At the famous Council of Nicaea in 325 over 200 bishops attended. These bishops were mostly from the Eastern provinces, with only a handful from the West. Constantine had made an advantageous choice, because in the early fourth century most people were still outside the church.[1]

The patronage of Constantine and subsequent emperors during late antiquity transformed bishops and their roles in totally unforeseen ways. In earlier centuries the number of bishops had been limited; now almost every city in the empire had a bishop, and classical cities survived as episcopal sees. Since these bishops and many of their lesser clerics were recruited primarily from the class of local notables, increasingly the ecclesiastical hierarchy attracted men away from service as municipal magistrates. In earlier centuries bishops had been loosely connected through letters, visits and occasional councils; now they developed a more extensive organisation that was modelled on the imperial administration. The consolidation of this new hierarchy led to a heightened emphasis on new attitudes about clerical service, such as ambition and competition, that seemed at odds with Christian ideals. In earlier centuries bishops and their congregations had been marginalised in Roman society; now Christian emperors were ready to use churchmen as judges and envoys. As their financial resources increased, bishops founded charitable institutions, constructed

---

1 Constantine's quip: Eusebius, *Vita Constantini* 4.24.

churches and shrines, and presided at festivals. Eventually bishops became the peers of the emperors at Constantinople and rivals to the barbarian kings in the West. During late antiquity Christianity became not just the leading religion in the old Roman world. As its bishops appropriated or sanctioned more and more nominally secular activities, Christian spirituality also became the dominant worldview.

From cities to sees

The administrative and cultural bedrock of Roman society was its cities. At the beginning of the fourth century there were perhaps about 900 cities in the Eastern empire and more than 1,000 in the Western empire, with the densest concentrations in core Mediterranean regions like central Italy, southern Gaul, North Africa, central and southern Greece, western Asia Minor, and parts of Syria, Palestine and Egypt. A few of these cities were very large in both population and area, such as Rome, Constantinople, Alexandria, Antioch and Carthage. Some were medium sized, famous as ports, residences of imperial officials or centres of education. The vast majority were quite modest, each consisting of a small built-up urban centre that administered a surrounding rural territory and dependent villages. After Constantine a bishop would have been consecrated for almost every city, and for some of the villages too. Since controversies over doctrines often led to the consecration of rivals, some cities had two or even more bishops. The controversy between the Catholic and the Donatist churches essentially doubled the number of bishops in North Africa; the rise of churches opposed to the Council of Chalcedon in 451 led to the appearance of rival bishops throughout the Eastern Mediterranean. In the Roman empire at the height of the doctrinal disputes between the later fourth and the later fifth centuries there were, at any given moment, well over 2,000 bishops.

Most of these bishops were as humble and ordinary as the cities and villages they served. Each had his own distinctive foibles and obsessions. In the remote outback of Pontus a bishop of Amaseia carefully studied the exemplary orations of the great Demosthenes for hours on end, while in the classical heartland of southern Gaul a bishop of Cahors tediously memorised the endless genealogies of the Old Testament. Bishops had many official duties, including the selection and supervision of clerics, the administration of finances, and the management of charitable foundations. As local patrons they represented their cities and individual citizens before imperial magistrates. Their primary task, however, was their spiritual ministry, in particular the celebration of the liturgy and preaching. Every week throughout the Roman empire bishops and their priests preached thousands of sermons and celebrated the liturgy with millions of parishioners. To accept an episcopacy was to commit to a lifetime of service and devotion. During the ceremony of consecration new bishops could literally feel the heavy spiritual weight of the office settling on their shoulders. A young, and very hungry, ascetic knew exactly how demanding this episcopal burden might be, since he was driven by a similar commitment to 'oversight':

> I am a bishop for the kitchens, the taverns, the tables, and the crockery. If the wine is bitter, I excommunicate it; but I drink the fine wine. I am a bishop for the cooking pot too. If salt or some other spices are missing, I sprinkle them in, season [the food], and eat it. This is my episcopacy, and I have received my consecration from the craving of my appetite.[2]

This network of cities had been responsible for many of the important administrative functions in the Roman empire, above all the maintenance of order and the collection of imperial taxes. But from the later third century, changes in the imperial administration had challenged the viability of these cities. By sanctioning the existence of multiple legitimate emperors Diocletian increased the number of imperial courts. He and his fellow emperors in the Tetrarchy more than doubled the size of the imperial administration by dividing provinces and adding more layers of administrators. They then recruited more secretaries and bureaucrats to serve in the ministries attached to courts, prefects, vicars and provincial governors. In addition to this expansion of the imperial administration they considerably enlarged the army. Since these reforms certainly stressed the resources available to the state, cities had to pay the price. To finance this larger administration and larger army emperors confiscated more of the municipal revenues raised from rents on landed endowments and from local taxes and tolls.

For centuries local notables had proudly served as civic magistrates and decurions ('councillors') on their municipal councils. As magistrates and decurions they had assumed responsibility both for the administration of their cities and for the fulfilment of imperial obligations, such as the collection of taxes and the levying of recruits for the army. As private patrons they had furthermore used their own wealth to fund buildings, games, and other amenities in their cities. In return their grateful fellow citizens hailed them as benefactors and commemorated them in public dedications. After these administrative reforms, however, the expenses and responsibilities of civic service increasingly became

---

2 Demosthenes: Asterius of Amaseia, *Homiliae* 11.1. Old Testament: Gregory of Tours, *Historiae* 5.42. Oversight: Palladius, *Historia Lausiaca* 35.10.

an obligation and an onerous financial burden. Now many local notables tried to avoid service as decurions.

Even as the imperial administration wanted local notables to serve as decurions, it also multiplied the means for them to avoid this obligation. Wealthier provincial elites had more opportunities to hold offices and acquire higher ranks by making a career in the imperial administration; lesser notables could find jobs as secretaries and functionaries in the palatine ministries, official staffs and provincial bureaus, or serve as soldiers and officers in the army. Once Constantine inaugurated Constantinople as a new capital, it needed new senators to match the venerable senate at Rome. Local elites from the Eastern provinces left their hometowns and migrated to New Rome. By the late 350s the senate at Constantinople had about 300 members, by the 380s 2,000 members. The acquisition of senatorial rank, through membership in the senate at the capital, holding a high office, or long service in the imperial civil service, conferred immunity against service as decurions.

By extending a similar immunity to bishops and clerics Constantine effectively made clerical service as attractive and as important as service in the imperial administration and the army. According to his son Constantius, the reward for the 'singular virtue' of clerics was 'perpetual immunity'. Julian, the last pagan emperor, of course tried to cancel this privilege; subsequent Christian emperors modified and restricted it; but they did not withdraw this grant of immunity. This sign of respect for Christianity had significant, and perhaps unintended, political and social consequences. From the fourth century most of the known bishops with known origins were from the class of local notables who would otherwise have been expected to serve as municipal magistrates and decurions.[3]

Some of the most prominent bishops were also some of the best examples. In the early fourth century, the father of Gregory of Nazianzus was most likely a decurion at Nazianzus in Cappadocia. But after he witnessed Constantine's patronage for the bishops travelling to the Council of Nicaea, he converted to Christianity and soon became bishop of his hometown. His sons then used contrasting strategies to avoid municipal obligations. One was offered membership in the senate at Constantinople and started a career in the imperial administration. The other, Gregory himself, served as a priest and then, off and on, as a bishop, including a stint at Constantinople. The family of Basil

---

3 Singular virtue: *CTh* 16.2.16. Julian: *CTh* 12.1.50 = 13.1.4. A. H. M. Jones, *The later Roman empire*, 923–4: 'The great majority of the higher clergy, the urban deacons and priests and the bishops, were drawn from the middle classes, professional men, officials, and above all *curiales*.'

of Caesarea owned estates throughout central Asia Minor and in the past had paid taxes in three different provinces. Yet none of this family's sons served as a decurion. Basil became a priest and then metropolitan bishop of Caesarea, Gregory served as bishop of Nyssa, and Peter became bishop of Sebasteia. John Chrysostom's ancestors, including his father, had been civil servants. In North Africa Augustine's father was a humble municipal decurion. Augustine himself tried to make a career as a teacher of rhetoric in Milan, before returning to Africa to become a priest and then bishop of Hippo. The father of Severus, bishop of Antioch in the early sixth century, was a decurion, although his father in turn had already been a bishop. Service as a bishop in fact became such an attractive alternative for decurions that some men even paid fees to ensure their consecrations. In the early fifth century, bishops in western Asia Minor were forced to confess their bribery: 'We thought this was a suitable strategy so that we might expect to be liberated from service on the town council.' But these bishops were not embarrassed by their corrupt behaviour. Instead, even though they were on the verge of being deposed, they were more worried about the wrath they might face at home. 'We would like to recover the gold we paid. Some of us had to sell our wives' clothing.' By taking advantage of this immunity, in one or two generations men could transform their curial families into ecclesiastical families.[4]

Some municipal notables started careers in the imperial administration before switching. Bishop Eleusius of Cyzicus had previously served at the imperial court; Gregory of Nazianzus claimed that his brother had decided to abandon his office as a treasurer responsible for imperial revenues in Bithynia in order to serve at another 'court' in heaven. For these lesser magistrates the heightened status of bishops and clerics had made clerical service an acceptable alternative to service in the imperial administration. Other secular backgrounds were apparently more difficult to assimilate to episcopal service. Only a few former soldiers became bishops. The most famous was Martin of Tours, who surpassed his lengthy hitch of almost twenty-five years in the army with an even longer tenure as bishop of Tours during the later fourth century. The clergy of Gaul seem to have been open to enlisting veterans. Another was Victricius, Martin's younger contemporary, who became bishop of Rouen. Likewise very few senators or men who had held high offices in the imperial administration became clerics during the fourth century. Those who did

---

4 Careers of Cappadocian bishops: R. Van Dam, *Families and friends.* John Chrysostom's father: Palladius, *Dialogus de vita Iohannis Chrysostomi* 5. Augustine's father: Augustine, *Confessiones* 2.3.5; Possidius, *Vita Augustini* 1. Severus' father: Zachariah Scholasticus, *Vita Severi* (PO 2: 11). Bribery: Palladius, *Dialogus de vita Iohannis Chrysostomi* 15.

typically became bishops immediately. The most notable was Ambrose, whose father had served as a powerful prefect in Gaul. He himself was governor of a province in northern Italy when he was acclaimed as bishop of Milan in 374. Another was Nectarius, a senator at Constantinople when the emperor Theodosius promoted him as bishop of the capital in 381.[5]

As service as a bishop became more prestigious, however, and as more local notables acquired senatorial rank, more senators became bishops. In the early 440s Cyrus reached the height of the imperial administration by serving simultaneously as prefect of the East and prefect of Constantinople. After his downfall he became bishop of Cotyaeum in Phrygia. For him episcopal service was a suitable, even if temporary, sinecure. This transition was perhaps most apparent in fifth-century Gaul, where the shrinking of Roman rule meant that local aristocrats who managed to acquire senatorial rank had fewer opportunities to hold additional high offices in the imperial administration. In the early fifth century Germanus served as a provincial governor before becoming bishop of Auxerre. After serving as prefect of the city of Rome in the mid-fifth century, Sidonius returned to Gaul to become bishop of Clermont. At Tours in the second half of the fifth century, three consecutive bishops were all descendants of a senatorial family. Eventually some great families became episcopal dynasties and produced bishops over several generations, sometimes at the same city. 'I am pregnant with a bishop,' one expectant wife announced to her surprised husband; their son was Nicetius, bishop of Lyon in the mid-sixth century. When Gregory became bishop of Tours in the later sixth century, he claimed that all but five of his episcopal predecessors had been relatives.[6]

As these senators became bishops, they transferred some of the language and ideals of aristocratic ideology. Paulinus was a Gallic notable who served as a provincial governor in Italy before adopting an ascetic life. He considered his subsequent episcopacy at Nola as a promotion. 'What did I have when I was called a senator that is similar to what I have here and now when I am called a pauper?' Bishop Hilary of Arles once disparaged the family connections of an episcopal predecessor in order to praise his new ecclesiastical pedigree instead: 'the peak of nobility is to be reckoned among the sons of God'. Just as local notables might enter the clergy in order to preserve their municipal influence while sidestepping service as decurions, so by becoming bishops great senators could now preserve and even enhance their nobility. Service as

---

5 Eleusius of Cyzicus: Sozomen, *H. E.* 4.20.2. Gregory of Nazianzus' brother: Gregory of Nazianzus, *Orationes* 7.15.
6 Pregnant: Gregory of Tours, *Vita patrum* 8.1.

a bishop conferred the same honour and dignity as holding a high office in the imperial administration.[7]

The transformation of the classical city is one of the great themes of the later Roman empire. Most cities survived, and so did their local notables. In the East, although municipal councils largely disappeared after the fifth century, decurions continued to perform municipal and imperial duties. In the West decurions still collected taxes in some of the barbarian kingdoms. Despite these outward indications of continuity, the political utility and the ideological significance of cities were quite different. Their political affairs were increasingly dominated by provincial governors in the Eastern empire, by royal magistrates in the Western barbarian kingdoms, and, everywhere, by the most prominent of the local landowners. Once cities became dependent on the public resources of state officials and the private generosity of wealthy local patrons, they had lost much of the autonomy that had made them so useful to the administration of the Roman empire.

The rise of bishops hence cannot be separated from this fundamental transformation of classical cities, even if the exact nature of this interaction is difficult to determine. If this decline was due to the political decisions that siphoned resources from cities and provided local notables with alternative careers in the imperial administration, then bishops benefited from the failure of cities. In that case Diocletian and his fellow pagan emperors who instigated these administrative reforms deserve some (unwitting) credit for assisting in the rise of episcopal leadership. But if imperial patronage had made Christianity so attractive that increasingly more citizens, especially notables, were prepared to abandon their municipal responsibilities in favour of ecclesiastical service, then the rise of Christianity was a stimulus for the erosion of cities. In that case Constantine and subsequent Christian emperors deserve some (equally unwitting) blame for undermining the cities that were so important to successful imperial administration. Whichever was the catalyst or the consequence, the rise of bishops and the transformation of classical cities during late antiquity were complementary processes.[8]

Bishops and clerics were, above all, motivated by their spiritual commitment. Even Augustine, perhaps the greatest thinker of the era, was sensitive enough to wear a tunic a woman had woven for her deceased brother simply because he knew it would be a comfort to her. But in the course of living out their devotion clerics were also able to enhance their own local prestige and authority. For

---

7 Paulinus of Nola, *Carmina* 21.458–9. Hilary of Arles, *Sermo de vita Honorati* 4.
8 J. H. W. G. Liebeschuetz, *Decline and fall*, 138: 'The "rise of the bishop" was . . . the obverse of the decline of civic political institutions, and classical political culture.'

men of slender means clerical service offered the possibility of upward social mobility. For more distinguished local notables episcopal or clerical service offered the possibility of lateral social mobility. They might see service as a bishop or a cleric as an opportunity to avoid the onerous responsibilities of municipal service while still retaining their capacity to benefit their cities. The appropriation of aristocratic ideology meant that even senators and their descendants might be attracted to episcopal service. The rise of bishops was as much a social and political process as a religious transformation.[9]

Hierarchy and rivalries

Just as the roles of bishops developed within the context of traditional classical cities, so the church's organisation corresponded to the structure of the imperial administration. This imitation of the civil hierarchy reinforced and clarified a hierarchy among bishops and their sees. By the early fourth century the empire had been divided into over one hundred provinces, each administered by a provincial governor. Ecclesiastical provinces corresponded to these civil provinces, and the bishop of the capital city in each province became the metropolitan bishop. These metropolitan bishops were charged with convening provincial councils to resolve disputes between bishops, or between a bishop and his clergy or his congregation. Metropolitan bishops also had some jurisdiction over the other bishops in their province, and their consent was required for the appointment of new bishops. The acknowledgment of particular bishops as metropolitans was a consequence of the civil prominence of their sees as provincial capitals.

This correspondence between secular and religious hierarchies was not always smooth. Old rivalries kept reappearing. In a civil war at the end of the second century, the people of Nicomedia had supported the emperor Septimius Severus, and the people of Nicaea one of his rivals. A century later the emperor Diocletian had resided in Nicomedia as his Eastern capital. The bishop of Nicomedia was the metropolitan of the province that included Nicaea. But the great ecumenical council of 325 had met at Nicaea, and at the Council of Chalcedon the bishop of Nicaea tried to claim metropolitan rank. New rivalries popped up. In the civil administration Caesarea was a provincial capital in Palestine. One of the cities in its province was Jerusalem, which benefited from the patronage of Constantine and subsequent pious emperors to become the prime destination of pilgrims to the Holy Land. Yet the Council

---

9 Augustine, *Epistulae* 263.

of Nicaea had already insisted that, despite 'ancient tradition', Jerusalem was to be subordinate to Caesarea. By trying to maintain a correspondence with the secular administration the ecclesiastical hierarchy was out of synch with the new geography of sacred pilgrimage. The Council of Chalcedon finally associated the bishop of Jerusalem with the bishops of Rome, Constantinople, Antioch and Alexandria by classifying him too as a patriarch.[10]

The bishops of some cities were so consistently at odds that their rivalry had clearly generated its own momentum. Basil of Caesarea was upset that the bishop of Tyana had acquired the rank of a metropolitan when his city became a new provincial capital upon the division of Cappadocia. This new metropolitan bishop retaliated by holding up Basil on the road with his 'gang of bandits'. Their successors continued the feud by bickering over prerogatives so minor that observers dismissed them as 'some contemptible claim of right'. Not surprisingly, on every important issue these bishops were on opposite sides. During the dispute over the suitability of John Chrysostom as bishop of Constantinople, the bishop of Tyana supported John, while the bishop of Caesarea corresponded with John's opponents. At the Council of Ephesus in 431 the bishop of Caesarea supported Cyril, bishop of Alexandria, while the bishop of Tyana supported Nestorius, bishop of Constantinople. After the council the triumphant bishop of Caesarea tried to oust his rival from Tyana. Once cities and their leading notables had competed over rank and status in a Roman context; now they competed just as fiercely in an ecclesiastical context. Rather than resolving differences, this hierarchy of cities and their bishops often reinforced old rivalries and created new feuds.[11]

The ecclesiastical organisation may have imitated the imperial administration, but it also differed in several important respects. Most noticeably, it was even larger. Since the reign of Diocletian emperors had considerably expanded the size of the imperial administration by creating more provinces and governors, by adding more layers of high-level officials such as vicars and prefects, and by increasing the size of the staffs supporting those officials and the imperial courts. Up to one hundred lesser bureaucrats served on the staff of each provincial governor, and up to 1,000 on the staff of each prefect. By the end of the fourth century there were about 125 high-level prefects, vicars and governors,

---

10 Claim of Nicaea: ACO II.1.3: 57–62 (416–21). Jerusalem and Caesarea: Council of Nicaea, canon 7. Jerusalem as patriarchate: ACO II.1.3: 5–7 (364–6).

11 Bandits: Gregory of Nazianzus, *Orationes* 43.58. Contemptible claim: Severus of Antioch, *Epistulae* 2.2. Dispute over John Chrysostom: Palladius, *Dialogus de vita Iohannis Chrysostomi* 9. Ouster of rival: Theodoret of Cyrrhus, *Commonitorium ad Alexandrum Hierapolitanum* (ACO I.4.2: 87; SC 429: 157–8).

with over 17,000 men serving on their staffs, another 5,500 or so holding very good jobs in the palatine ministries, and thousands more holding lesser positions. Many of these bureaucratic jobs were new during the fourth century.

Each of the over 2,000 bishops had his own clergy. The number of clerics varied considerably city by city. Most cities were small, and their bishops supervised a small clerical staff of priests, deacons, subdeacons, readers and gravediggers. Metropolitan bishops had larger staffs for their episcopal churches, as many as sixty or more. The clergy of cities that administered large surrounding territories included still more priests and deacons who served in parish churches and shrines. Basil of Caesarea's subordinate clergy included fifty 'rural bishops', who presumably ministered to the labourers on the vast imperial estates and ranches in Cappadocia. The bishops at the largest cities had enormous clerical staffs that kept expanding. At the end of the fifth century there were more than 500 clerics at Carthage. By the middle of the sixth century, the emperor Justinian decreed that the staff at Constantinople should be set at 'the ancient number' of 485 clerics, including 60 priests, 100 deacons, 90 subdeacons, 110 readers, 25 singers and 100 doorkeepers, as well as 40 deaconesses. The true astonishment is that this new total was a *reduction* in size, and that it represented only the primary clergy. Justinian also sanctioned a corps of 800 men to provide proper funerals.[12]

A century after Constantine the total of bishops and clerics in the empire was approximately one-third, perhaps even one-half, the size of the Roman army, and it certainly surpassed the number of magistrates and bureaucrats in the imperial administration. Many of these episcopal and clerical offices were also new during the fourth century. Increases in the size of the imperial administration and the army had already strained the resources of the empire and its cities. Now this large brotherhood of bishops and clerics was added to the financial burden.

A second important distinction from the imperial administration was a difference in tenure and attitudes. The imperial administration went down from the imperial courts to the level of provinces and cities. Even at its lower levels men used offices in the imperial ministries to improve their rank, prestige and wealth. Ambition fuelled office-holding, and men hoped for promotions by moving upward from office to office. At its upper levels men held offices for comparatively short tenures, governorships typically for a year or two, vicarates and prefectures for longer periods, and they would often return to

---

12 Rural bishops in Cappadocia: Gregory of Nazianzus, *Carmina* 2.1.11.447. Clerics at Carthage: Victor of Vita, *Historia persecutionis Africanae provinciae* 3.34. Constantinople: Justinian, *Novellae* 3.1, 43.1.

private life for long interludes before assuming another, hopefully more prestigious, office. The hierarchy of the imperial administration hence acknowledged ambition and competition. But by guaranteeing regular promotion at
the lower levels and fairly rapid turnover among upper-level office holders,
the emperors ensured wide participation, and hence relative harmony, among
both great senators and provincial notables.

In contrast, the ecclesiastical hierarchy went up only to the level of cities.
These cities may then have been organised into ecclesiastical provinces, some
bishops became metropolitans, and all bishops attended councils, but they
focused their activities on their cities. The horizons of episcopal service were
local. Bishops and clerics furthermore held their offices for life, with no possibility of occasional retirement and subsequent return. Clerics were supposed
to stay attached to the city at which they had been first ordained. Some of them
might move sideways to become bishops at other cities. But bishops were then
supposed to remain faithful to their sees for life. A see was a bishop's wife.

The absence of ambition and competition was supposed to make these limited expectations and severe restrictions acceptable. In fact, these restrictions
readily led to confusion and even resentments. Long-serving bishops at small
sees would have more seniority, and more prestige, than their metropolitan
bishops. When Gregory became metropolitan bishop of Tours in his mid-
thirties, he found one senior suffragan bishop diligently turning his own
see into 'new Rome' by dedicating a new cathedral with relics of St Peter
and St Paul. Distinguished bishops at small sees could not be moved up to
become metropolitan bishops. If bishops lived too long, their sees would
not become vacant at the right moments and qualified lesser clerics might
never become bishops. Although lesser clerics could move up in the clerical
ranks, during the late fourth and early fifth centuries the bishops of Rome
tried to rationalise these promotions by insisting upon minimum terms in
a standard sequence of clerical offices. The models for these proposals were
'secular offices' and the hierarchy of the army, in which even a general first
had to serve as a recruit. As a result, although the sheer size of the ecclesiastical organisation may have accommodated many men in the huge puddle of
lesser clerical offices at its base, lifetime tenure and restrictions about moving
severely limited the possibility of upward promotion, for both promising clerics and bishops at small sees. Rather than readily promoting men up through
more prestigious offices, the ecclesiastical hierarchy was relatively stagnant.[13]

---

13 Felix of Nantes: Fortunatus, *Carmina* 3.8.20. Secular model: Zosimus, *Epistulae* 9.2 (PL
20: 671a).

Serving in a large city clearly offered huge advantages in terms of prestige and rank, and the bishops of large cities quickly floated to the top of the ecclesiastical hierarchy. In the Eastern empire Antioch was a very important city during the fourth century. Not only was it the actual birthplace of Christianity, distinguished in Christian traditions as the city where the followers of Jesus were first called Christians. Not only had the Council of Nicaea already acknowledged that its bishops had a regional jurisdiction of some sort. Antioch furthermore was often the residence of emperors such as Constantius, Julian and Valens who were campaigning against the Persians. But all the neighbouring provinces already had their own metropolitan bishops, and rather than conceding primacy to the see of Antioch, these neighbouring bishops often schemed over its episcopacy. The episcopacy of Antioch was so important that during the fourth century it was contested by two, three, even four rival bishops who represented different factions.

Alexandria became an even more influential see. Its bishops claimed metropolitan rights over the whole of Egypt, even after it had been subdivided into smaller provinces, as well as over the neighbouring region of Cyrenaica. They then reinforced their jurisdiction with their enormous wealth. Bishop Theophilus was notorious for disguising the 'stench' of his ambition with the 'fragrance' of his bribes. To ensure support for the decisions of the Council of Ephesus in 431, Cyril of Alexandria distributed over a thousand pounds of gold to members of the court at Constantinople, as well as numerous carpets, rugs, tapestries, curtains, cushions and ivory thrones. These new pharaohs of Egypt hence exercised a vast influence that could readily lead them to meddle in ecclesiastical affairs throughout the Eastern empire.[14]

The foundation of Constantinople posed a particularly direct challenge to the bishops of Alexandria. At least initially, its significance in the ecclesiastical hierarchy was solely a consequence of its importance for emperors in the imperial administration. At the Council of Nicaea there was no bishop from Byzantium in attendance. Once Byzantium was inaugurated as the new capital of Constantinople, however, it became the most important residence for Eastern emperors and other magistrates. The ecumenical council that met at Constantinople in 381 finally acknowledged the city's eminence as 'New Rome', and it defined a 'seniority of honour' for the bishop of the capital 'second only to the bishop of Rome'. This council furthermore limited the authority of the bishops of both Antioch and Alexandria to the civil dioceses

---

14 Theophilus' stench: Palladius, *Dialogus de vita Iohannis Chrysostomi* 8. Cyril's gifts: Cyril of Alexandria, *Breve directorum ad mandatarios Constantinopolim missos* (ACO 1.4.2: 224–5).

of Oriens (from the Taurus Mountains to Egypt) and Egypt respectively. By implication, the bishop of Constantinople had priority in the other Eastern dioceses that included Greece and almost all of Asia Minor. By taking the structure of the imperial administration as its guide, this council had promoted the prestige of the upstart bishops of Constantinople and limited the authority of the bishops of Alexandria and Antioch.[15]

The bishops of Alexandria were sore losers. In fact, shortly before the Council of Constantinople Bishop Peter of Alexandria had tried to install his own candidate as bishop at the capital. In the early fifth century, Theophilus of Alexandria would mobilise opposition to John Chrysostom of Constantinople both at the imperial court and among bishops in western Asia Minor. John was soon sent into exile. At the Council of Ephesus in 431, Cyril of Alexandria opposed Nestorius of Constantinople and his theology. Nestorius was soon sent into exile. At the Council of Ephesus in 449, Dioscorus of Alexandria connived at the deposition of Flavianus of Constantinople. The Council of Chalcedon finally deposed Dioscorus. Many sighed with relief at this demotion of Alexandria and its bishop. One wag suggested that a huge boulder be placed on Cyril's grave to prevent him and his meddling spawn from ever returning.[16]

Looming over all these cities was Rome. As a political centre Rome was in decline already by the reigns of Diocletian and Constantine. Its population was shrinking, its monuments were often in need of repair, and emperors rarely resided there, or even visited. Although the old capital had celebrated the millennium anniversary of its founding in 248 with vast games and shows, it hardly celebrated its next centennial in 348: 'to such an extent has concern for the city of Rome dwindled day by day', sighed one historian. If, as with Constantinople, its importance in the civil administration was to determine its ecclesiastical reputation, then Rome seemingly had a limited future.[17]

Instead, its significance in the ecclesiastical hierarchy was on the rise. The Council of Nicaea had in fact cited Rome as the model for the primacy of Alexandria in Egypt. Constantine set an example for subsequent emperors by founding churches and bestowing lavish gifts and endowments. With these extensive resources at their disposal the bishops of Rome had customarily asserted metropolitan rights over the provinces in southern Italy. In addition, they usurped a more universal primacy by presenting themselves as successors

15 New Rome: Council of Constantinople, canon 3.
16 Boulder: [Theodoret of Cyrrhus,] *Epistula ad Iohannem Antiochenum cum mortuus esset Cyrillus* (ACO IV.I: 135–6).
17 Dwindling concern: Aurelius Victor, *De Caesaribus* 28.2.

to the apostle Peter. A year after the Council of Constantinople had defined the respective authority of the bishops of Constantinople, Alexandria and Antioch, Damasus, the bishop of Rome, based his claim for priority upon the authority of St Peter. This precedence simply transcended any deliberations in mere councils. 'The holy church of Rome has priority over the other churches not because of the decisions in canons; it has obtained primacy through the saying of our Lord and Saviour recorded in the gospel.' In the mid-fifth century, Leo of Rome in particular emphasised the primacy of Rome's bishops in ecclesiastical affairs by stressing their standing as the full heirs of St Peter. As its population declined and its political role was diminished, Rome became a ghost town; but it still had historical memory and apostolic legend on its side.[18]

In the Western empire Rome certainly had no rivals as an apostolic see. Bishops from other cities hence appealed to its bishops for support in local disputes. Bishops of Arles, for instance, repeatedly appealed to Rome. With the collapse of the Roman administration in northern Gaul Arles had become the residence of the prefect of Gaul. Its bishops parlayed this enhancement of the city's civil standing into acknowledgment of their standing as metropolitans; they also began to promote the cult of St Trophimus, the legendary first bishop of Arles who had supposedly been sent to Gaul by the bishop of Rome. In the early fifth century, Zosimus of Rome extended the jurisdiction of Arles over some neighbouring provinces, at the expense of the metropolitan rights of Narbonne, Marseille and Vienne. Subsequent bishops of Rome were more circumspect, however, and soon withdrew these prerogatives. In the mid-fifth century even the emperor Valentinian III rebuked Hilary, bishop of Arles, for his presumption and 'illicit audacity'. Not only had Hilary not recognised the 'reverence of the apostolic see', that is, of Rome, he was also trying to impose new bishops forcibly through his 'band of armed thugs'.[19]

In the Roman world provincial notables had competed relentlessly for prestige and influence. Their home cities had been the arenas for those competitions, as local worthies manoeuvred for offices and honours. Cities had also been the recipients of the generosity through which these notables solicited support and demonstrated their excellence. At the same time the cities were competing among themselves for prestige and authority. With the extension of Roman rule the emperor or his administrators were often the final arbiters, as they conferred new names and titles, distributed cults and priesthoods, or simply honoured cities with their visits. In the later Roman empire, the

18 Priority of Rome: Damasus, *Explanatio fidei* (ed. Turner, 1.1.2: 156).
19 Rebuke of Hilary: Valentinian III, *Novellae* 17 (PL 54: 637).

rise of Christianity offered both provincial notables and cities a new medium for extending those traditional rivalries. Men now competed to become clerics, to become bishops, even to move to a more prestigious see. Cities now schemed to become metropolitan sees or to extend their ecclesiastical authority. Hierarchy, in the form of a sequence of clerical offices and the ranking of sees, was profoundly disruptive to creating a harmonious and ecumenical Christian community. As in the early empire, 'under the guise of religion cities disintegrated into rivalries'.[20]

In these rivalries some cities even changed their names as evidence of their enhanced status. In Cappadocia Caesarea had seemed to clinch its standing as provincial capital and metropolitan see through its imperial name, derived from Augustus Caesar. But once Tyana became another provincial capital and hence another metropolitan see in Cappadocia, it hoped to surpass its rival's imperial name by adopting the more impressive Christian name of Christoupolis. In a Christian empire 'Christ's city' could trump 'Caesar's city'.[21]

Spirituality and secular society

Personal devotion certainly motivated Christian emperors to demonstrate their patronage for bishops and clerics. But these emperors might well have additional political reasons for promoting the status and influence of bishops. From the beginning emperors had had to worry about challengers, such as the great senators who represented the traditions of the old Roman republic and who held offices in the imperial administration. To undermine the collective prestige of senators, emperors had promoted equestrians and provincial notables to high offices, and they had sometimes even relied upon the advice of freedmen, slaves, or, occasionally, their own mothers, wives and mistresses. During late antiquity some emperors were promoting eunuchs at court and barbarians to serve as military officers. The primary reason for the attractiveness of eunuchs and barbarians could also be applied to bishops and clerics: even though they were close advisers, they could not replace emperors. The ecclesiastical hierarchy became more prominent and influential from the early fourth century in part because emperors wanted to promote another counterweight to the influence of other prominent groups in Roman society, such as senators and military commanders. In the perspective of emperors, bishops

20 Rivalries: Tacitus, *Annales* 3.63.
21 Tyana as Christoupolis: *Notitiae graecae episcopatuum* 1.21, 250.

and clerics were attractive as advisers and agents because, like equestrians, freedmen and slaves in the early empire and eunuchs and barbarians in the later empire, they did not become emperors. In theory, at least, they had no political ambitions.

Constantine and subsequent Christian emperors were quick to endorse the involvement of bishops in secular affairs. One obvious example is the appropriation of episcopal hearings. Bishops had long settled disputes within their own congregations; now emperors designated their mediation as a formal court hearing, open to all types of civil conflicts. Constantine allowed bishops to hear cases at the request of only one party, although by the early fifth century both parties had to agree to the venue. No appeal was possible, and civil magistrates were expected to enforce bishops' decisions. Although Augustine preferred to hear cases involving clerics or ecclesiastical disputes, occasionally he considered strictly civil issues. In one of his letters he posed a series of questions about the hiring and sale of child labour, presumably in anticipation of deciding a case. Such legal technicalities only made him sigh about the excessive time he had to spend on legal arbitration. 'We are obliged to endure these disputes of the quarrelsome.'[22]

With his extensive education Augustine seems to have had some familiarity with Roman law. Other bishops sat with professional lawyers as advisers. But most bishops were profoundly ignorant of the niceties of Roman law, and in the Eastern provinces they did not understand Latin either. Even though Abraham was a native Syriac speaker who understood neither Greek nor Latin, as bishop of Carrhae in the early fifth century he nevertheless decided many judicial cases. 'He persuaded some disputants to reconcile, and compelled those who were not persuaded by his gentle instructions.' Bishops who knew some Roman law might nevertheless reject it. Gregory of Nazianzus noted that, even though the possibility of divorce was conceded in Roman law, 'divorce is completely disagreeable to our laws'. 'Roman laws are excessive and harsh, while our laws are useful and generous.' Because bishops so often based their decisions on biblical precedents and ecclesiastical concerns, at the local level the acquisition of justice was increasingly an aspect of pastoral duty and Christian spirituality rather than of the strict application of Roman law codes.[23]

Christian emperors were also ready to enhance the financial standing of churches and their bishops. Since churches were now allowed to own property

---

22 Child labour: Augustine, *Epistulae* 24*. On episcopal courts, see R. W. Mathisen, ed., *Law, society, and authority*.
23 Opinions about Roman law: Gregory of Nazianzus, *Epistulae* 78.6, 144.4. Abraham of Carrhae: Theodoret of Cyrrhus, *Historia religiosa* 17.8.

legally, the income from their estates supplemented the revenues from individual offerings and the government subsidies that sometimes included grain. Not surprisingly, Constantine was very generous to various churches. At Rome he endowed the churches with estates located throughout the empire that produced over 400 pounds of gold annually in rents, and he brightened their interiors with silverware, gold chandeliers and porphyry columns. Some private benefactors, including bishops themselves, were almost as bountiful. Gregory of Nazianzus left most of his possessions to his family's hometown church in Cappadocia; the heiress Melania the Younger donated an enormous estate to Thagaste in North Africa. This accumulation of property was of course a gradual process, and during the fourth century most sees still had limited resources. Bishop Gregory of Nyssa once apologised for having to haggle over the wages of workmen hired to construct a new shrine by pleading poverty. But unlike wealthy families, whose assets were dispersed over a few generations, churches kept on acquiring more property through legacies and gifts. At the large sees the annual revenues were considerable, and much of this income went to bishops to be spent at their discretion. Even at Anastasiopolis, a small city in Galatia, the bishop received an annual income of five pounds of gold during the late sixth century. His income surpassed the salaries of grammarians, rhetoricians and doctors, and matched those of provincial governors.[24]

Bishops used their resources for the good of their cities. One conspicuous benefit was care for the poor. Many bishops acquired reputations as nourishers of the poor who founded or supervised almshouses and hospitals and distributed subsidies of cash and food. On his deathbed Paulinus, bishop of Nola, still remembered to pay for clothing to be donated to the poor. This relief work was so successful that even non-Christians were impressed. In the mid-fourth century the emperor Julian once suggested that pagan priests should imitate Christians by establishing hostels for strangers, and he offered to contribute grain and wine. But his justification of such open-handed generosity by citing a proof text from his pagan scriptures, the epic poems of Homer, could no longer compete with biblical injunctions to charity and mercy for the helpless. Christian charity expanded as ecclesiastical resources increased. In the early fifth century Porphyry, bishop of Gaza, offered daily maintenance to all poor people, whether citizens or strangers. In Gaul churchmen kept

---

24 Constantine's gifts to churches at Rome: *Liber pontificalis* 34. Gregory of Nazianzus' will: ed. Beaucamp. Melania's gift: *Vita Melaniae iunioris* (Latin) 21. Poverty at Nyssa: Gregory of Nyssa, *Epistulae* 25.16. Salary at Anastasiopolis: Georgius of Sykeon, *Vita Theodori Syceotae* 78.

registers of the poor people who received support from churches and shrines. By the early seventh century the register of the church at Alexandria included 7,500 recipients of charity.[25]

Another benefit for cities was the construction of new churches and shrines. In the early Roman empire, Christians had had difficulties assimilating into the urban society of the Roman world. As one telling indication of their earlier marginality, Christians had often constructed their churches and shrines on the outskirts of cities. When Gregory of Nazianzus' father became bishop of Nazianzus in 329, he inherited a 'wild and rustic' church. His response was to fund the construction of a 'beautiful and celestial' church in the shape of an octagon, surrounded by two perambulatories and topped by a dome. This dazzling new church was a conspicuous symbol of the triumph of Christianity, and incidentally of the prominence of his family, in his hometown. At Gaza the 'old church' was outside the city's walls. When Porphyry arrived as the new bishop in the late fourth century, the locals covered the road with thistles and filth; when he led his congregation out to the church, they returned to find the city's gate had been locked. Eventually, with the support of the imperial court at Constantinople, the Christians demolished the city's pagan shrines and constructed an enormous new church 'in the centre of Gaza'. The most visible indication of the increasing prominence of bishops in these ancient cities was the new skyline of churches and shrines.[26]

Sometimes, rather than the bishops and their congregations moving inside to take over cities, cities followed them to the suburbs. In Cappadocia Basil founded a large complex outside Caesarea that included a church, a residence for the bishop and clerics, a hostel for travellers, a hospital for the ill, and a poorhouse. Not so surprisingly, this 'new city' was named Basilias, after Basil himself. During the fifth and sixth centuries, the bishops of Tours repeatedly refurbished the large church that held the tomb of St Martin. As a result, most pilgrims ignored the cathedral inside the city and instead visited this shrine in a suburb outside the city's walls. Even at Rome many of the prominent churches were on the edges, close to or outside the walls. In the early fifth century, Jerome would hint at these new priorities when he recalled his earlier residence at Rome. 'The golden sheen of the Capitol is filthy. The people rush

---

25 Paulinus of Nola: Uranius, *De obitu Paulini* 3. Pagan hostels: Julian, *Epistulae* 22. Gaza: Mark the Deacon, *Vita Porphyrii* 94. Alexandria: Leontius of Neapolis, *Vita Iohannis Eleemosynarii* 1 (ed. Festugière, 348).

26 Churches at Nazianzus: Gregory of Nazianzus, *Orationes* 1.6, 18.16. Churches at Gaza: Mark the Deacon, *Vita Porphyrii* 17, 20, 53.

past the ruins of the pagan shrines and hurry to the martyrs' tombs.' In terms of civic topography Christian cities were often inverted images of classical cities.[27]

Accompanying this new ecclesiastical topography was a new re-configuration of ritual time. Christian festivals and processions now replaced municipal ceremonies and pagan celebrations. As the bishops of Tours built new churches and shrines, they also revamped the schedule of liturgical festivals and annual processions to include the universal Christian festivals such as Easter and Christmas, the festivals of local Gallic saints, and the festivals of foreign saints. All around the Roman world Christian communities venerated new saints, including their legendary apostolic founders, local martyrs and former bishops. Eventually there were so many festivals that they seemed to disrupt ordinary life. A man at Evaux in central Gaul decided to skip the festival of an eccentric hermit. 'Do you think that a man who slipped from a tree while satisfying his appetite has been included in the company of angels, so that he ought to be venerated as a saint?' This man stayed home to brew some beer – and paid the price for his disrespect when his house burned down. Since bishops of course presided in these churches during these festivals, the construction of a new sacred topography and the imposition of a new sacred time were powerful reinforcements of episcopal authority in cities.[28]

During late antiquity bishops gradually came to dominate more and more activities of the old classical cities and of Roman society in general. Their direct involvement slowly transformed the application of justice, the extension of charity, the funding of construction projects and the celebration of municipal ceremonies into manifestations of Christian spirituality and devotion. All aspects of ordinary life, from the courts of emperors and kings to the sufferings of paupers, were now measured against the expectations of Christian teachings. The dominance of Christianity even defined the essence of non-belief, since pagans (or polytheists) can be properly defined, simply, as 'non-Christians'. The increasing prominence of bishops led to an effective desecularisation of everyday affairs in Roman and, after the fifth century, post-Roman society. Now rulers and intellectuals would have to struggle to re-invent the notion of a profane, secular society that was independent of a Christian worldview.

27 Capitol at Rome: Jerome, *Epistulae* 107.1.
28 Festival: Gregory of Tours, *In gloria confessorum* 80.

Even warfare became a concern of bishops. For centuries warfare and the use of violent coercion had been reserved for emperors and their armies. But with the increase in pressure from the barbarians on the long northern frontier and the Persians on the eastern frontier troops were withdrawn, and occasionally local notables tried to provide regional protection with private armies. Sometimes bishops took the lead in defending their cities. In the early fifth century when the bishop of Syene in Upper Egypt faced the raids of nomads, he asked the emperor Theodosius II to place the local garrison under his command. Other bishops drew upon their own resources. In northern Gaul Bishop Nicetius of Trier repeatedly feuded with Frankish kings during the mid-sixth century. These kings were helplessly intimidated. Not only had Nicetius fortified his huge castle with thirty towers, his weapons included holy relics and his own catapult. Across the Mediterranean in the early fifth century, another bishop likewise demonstrated his military valour. In a battle against Persians east of the Euphrates Bishop Eunomius commanded a catapult on the wall of his see of Theodosiopolis. According to the historian Theodoret, himself a bishop in Syria, God now protected the Roman emperor not through the might of his troops, but through the prowess of this bishop. Even his devastating weapon was yet another reminder of how a Christian worldview had come to supersede a Roman perspective. The true defenders of a Christian realm were now a bishop and his patron saint: Eunomius' fearsome catapult was known as 'the Apostle Thomas'.[29]

In the mid-fifth century an emperor became a bishop. Avitus had been elevated as emperor in 455 with the support of the Gallic aristocracy and the Visigoths who had settled in southwestern Gaul. A year later he was overthrown and became bishop of Piacenza in north Italy.[30]

Avitus was unique in moving from emperorship to bishopric. But increasingly other rulers might adopt episcopal leadership as an exemplar for civil government. Gregory the Great became bishop of Rome in 590. Previously he had served as prefect of Rome, the highest civil magistrate in the old capital. Afterwards he became a monk and a deacon and lived for several years in Constantinople. Gregory was the first monk to become bishop of Rome, and soon after his consecration he wrote a treatise in which he attempted to reconcile his preferred life of contemplation with his new responsibility as

29 Appion of Syene: D. Feissel and K. A. Worp, 'La requête d'Appion'. Nicetius' castle: Fortunatus, *Carmina* 3.12. Eunomius' catapult: Theodoret of Cyrrhus, *H. E.* 5.37.5–10.
30 Gregory of Tours, *Historiae* 2.11.

a pastor. His solution was a merger, in which private contemplation readied a pastor for his public ministry. This formulation was a comfort to bishops engaged in active ministries, since contemplation was not only their past, but also their future goal. It furthermore precluded men from becoming bishops out of private ambition and pride. The essence of leadership was service: 'all who govern should be happy not when they command people but when they help them'. Gregory's insistence on the need for humility in episcopal service had a powerful influence in the medieval West, for kings and civil magistrates as well as for bishops and clerics. In the early seventh century, Bishop Honorius of Rome recommended that the king of Northumbria read the works of Gregory, 'your preacher'. With this interest in Gregory's 'Shepherd book' as a handbook for civil rulers it is not surprising that the first English translation was by a Christian monarch, King Alfred of Wessex.[31]

Another model for rulers was, of course, the first Christian emperor, Constantine himself. In his representation of his own authority he had probably chuckled when he identified himself as a bishop. But it was precisely that sort of patronising pun, with its unstated implication that bishops were in fact the peers of an emperor, that had allowed episcopal leadership gradually to become a model for kings and emperors throughout Christendom. The emperor Theodosius started his reign as a new Constantine. At his inauguration he wore Constantine's imperial robe, and his imperious behaviour during his reign sometimes recalled his predecessor's meddling in ecclesiastical affairs. Upon his death in 395 Theodosius was buried with Constantine at Constantinople. Soon, however, these emperors were sharing their mausoleum with the patriarchs of the Eastern capital. In death, as in life, emperors now had to acknowledge the authority and prestige of bishops. Theodosius may have had his confrontations with Ambrose at Milan, but in the end he seems to have acknowledged the bishop's supremacy. As Ambrose remembered the emperor's deathbed, 'with his last breath, he asked for me'. Augustine too, long before he became a bishop himself, had immediately recognised Ambrose's authority. 'That man of God welcomed me like a father, and he cherished my arrival *satis episcopaliter.*' For subsequent Christian leaders, whether ecclesiastical, imperial, or royal, the great bishops of late antiquity had set the standards for governing 'like a proper bishop'.[32]

---

31 All who govern: Gregory the Great, *Regula pastoralis* 2.6. Your preacher: Bede, *H. E.* 2.17.
32 Constantine's robe: George the Monk, *Chronicon* 9.8. Mausoleum: Sozomen, *H. E.* 2.34. Last breath: Ambrose, *De obitu Theodosii* 35. Ambrose's authority: Augustine, *Confessiones* 5.13.23.

Bibliography

PRIMARY SOURCES

Ambrose. *De obitu Theodosii* (CSEL 73)
Asterius of Amaseia. *Homiliae*, ed. C. Datema. *Asterius of Amasea. Homilies I–XIV* (Leiden, 1970)
Augustine. *Confessiones*, ed. J. J. O'Donnell (Oxford, 1992)
  Epistulae (CSEL 34$^{1-2}$, 44, 57, 58)
  Epistulae* (CSEL 88)
Aurelius Victor. *De Caesaribus*, ed. F. Pichlmayr and R. Gruendel (Leipzig, 1970)
Bede. *Historia ecclesiastica.* Eds. Bertram Colgrave and R. A. B. Mynors, *Bede's Ecclesiastical history of the English people* (Oxford, 1969)
Codex Theodosianus. Eds. T. Mommsen and P. Meyer, *Theodosiani libri XVI cum Constitutionibus Sirmondianis: Et leges novellae ad Theodosianum pertinentes* (Berlin, 1954^2); for *CTh* 16, see now SC 497
Cyril of Alexandria. *Breve directorum ad mandatarios Constantinopolim missos* (ACO 1.4.2)
Damasus. *Explanatio fidei*, in C. H. Turner, ed., *Ecclesiae occidentalis monumenta iuris antiquissima: Canonum et conciliorum graecorum interpretationes latinae* (Oxford, 1904), 1.1.2
Eusebius. *Vita Constantini* (GCS 7 *Eusebius Werke*, 1)
Fortunatus. *Carmina* (MGH aa IV.1)
George the Monk. *Chronicon*, eds. C. de Boor and P. Wirth (Stuttgart, 1978^2)
Georgius of Sykeon. *Vita Theodori Syceotae.* Ed. A. J. Festugière, *Vie de Théodore de Sykeôn*, SH 48 (Brussels, 1970)
Gregory the Great. *Regula pastoralis* (SC 381, 382)
Gregory of Nazianzus. *Carmina* (PG 37)
  Epistulae. Ed. P. Gallay, *Saint Grégoire de Nazianze. Lettres* (Paris, 1964–7) and SC 208
  Orationes (PG 35, 36; also SC 247, 250, 270, 284, 309, 318, 358, 374, 405)
  Will, in ed. J. Beaucamp, 'Le testament de Grégoire de Nazianze', in L. Burgmann, ed., *Fontes minores* x, Forschungen zur Byzantinischen Rechtsgeschichte 22 (Frankfurt, 1998), 1–100
Gregory of Nyssa. *Epistulae* (SC 363)
Gregory of Tours. *Historiae* (MGH scr.mer. 1.1)
  In gloria confessorum = *Miracula* VIII (MGH scr.mer. 1)
  Vita patrum = *Miracula* VII (MGH scr.mer. 1)
Hilary of Arles. *Sermo de vita Honorati* (SC 235)
Jerome. *Epistulae* (CSEL 54, 55, 56)
Julian. *Epistulae.* Ed. W. C. Wright, *The works of the emperor Julian*, LCL (London, 1923), III
Justinian. *Novellae.* Eds. R. Schöll and G. Kroll, *Corpus iuris civilis* 3 (Berlin, 1928^6)
Leontius of Neapolis. *Vita Iohannis Eleemosynarii.* Ed. A. J. Festugère, *Léontios de Néapolis. Vie de Syméon le Fou et Vie de Jean de Chypre*, Bibliothèque archéologique et historique 95 (Paris, 1974), 343–409
Liber pontificalis, ed. L. Duchesne (Paris, 1886, 1892); supplementary volume, ed. C. Vogel (Paris, 1957)

Mark the Deacon. *Vita Porphyrii.* Eds. H. Grégoire and M.-A. Kugener, *Marc le Diacre. Vie de Porphyre, évêque de Gaza* (Paris, 1930)

Notitiae graecae episcopatuum. Ed. G. Parthey, *Hieroclis Synecdemus et Notitiae graecae episcopatuum* (Berlin, 1866; reprint, Amsterdam, 1967), 55–261

Palladius. *Dialogus de vita Iohannis Chrysostomi* (SC 341, 342)

Historia Lausiaca. Ed. C. Butler, *The Lausiac history of Palladius, II. The Greek text edited with introduction and notes,* Texts and Studies 6.2 (Cambridge, 1904); see also G. J. M. Bartelink, ed., *Palladio. La storia lausiaca* (Milan, 1974)

Paulinus of Nola. *Carmina* (CSEL 30)

Possidius. *Vita Augustini.* Ed. A. A. R. Bastiaensen, *Vite dei santi: Vita di Cipriano, Vita di Ambrogio, Vita di Agostino* (Milan, 1975)

Severus of Antioch. *Epistulae.* Ed. and trans. E. W. Brooks, *The sixth book of select letters of Severus, patriarch of Antioch, in the Syriac version of Athanasius of Nisibis* (London, 1902–4)

Sozomen. *Historia ecclesiastica* (GCS, N.F. 4: *Sozomenus Kirchengeschichte*)

Tacitus. *Annales,* ed. H. Goelzer (Paris, 1938)

Theodoret of Cyrrhus. *Commonitorium ad Alexandrum Hierapolitanum,* Collectio Casinensis 134 (ACO I.4.2, reprinted with French translation in SC 429)

Epistula ad Iohannem Antiochenum cum mortuus esset Cyrillus (ACO IV.1)

Historia ecclesiastica (GCS, N.F. 5: *Theodoret Kirchengeschichte*)

Historia religiosa (SC 234, 257)

Uranius. *De obitu Paulini* (PL 53)

Valentinian III *Novellae* 17 (= Leo the Great, *Letter* 11; PL 54: 636–40)

Victor of Vita. *Historia persecutionis Africanae provinciae.* Ed. S. Lancel, *Victor de Vita. Histoire de la persecution vandale en Afrique. La passion des Sept Martyrs. Registre des provinces et des cités afriques* (Paris, 2002)

Vita Melaniae iunioris. Ed. P. Laurence, *Gérontius. La Vie latine de Sainte Mélanie* (Jerusalem, 2002)

Zachariah Scholasticus. *Vita Severi* (PO 2)

Zosimus. *Epistulae* (PL 20)

SECONDARY SOURCES

Brown, P. *Augustine of Hippo: A biography* (London, 1967)

Poverty and leadership in the later Roman empire (Hanover, NH, 2002)

Dagron, G. *Naissance d'une capitale: Constantinople et ses institutions de 330 à 451* (Paris, 1974)

Feissel, D. and K. A. Worp. 'La requête d'Appion, évêque de Syène, à Théodose II: P. Leid. Z revisé', *Oudheidkundige Mededelingen uit het Rijksmuseum van Oudheden te Leiden* 68 (1988): 97–111

Frend, W. H. C. *The rise of the Monophysite movement* (Cambridge, 1972)

Haas, C. *Alexandria in late antiquity: Topography and social conflict* (Baltimore, 1997)

Jones, A. H. M. *The later Roman empire 284–602: A social, economic and administrative survey* (Norman, OK, 1964)

Klingshirn, W. E. *Caesarius of Arles: The making of a Christian community in late antique Gaul* (Cambridge, 1994)

Liebeschuetz, J. H. W. G. *Decline and fall of the Roman city* (Oxford, 2001)

McLynn, N. B. *Ambrose of Milan: Church and court in a Christian capital* (Berkeley, 1994)

Markus, R. A. *The end of ancient Christianity* (Cambridge, 1990)

    Gregory the Great and his world (Cambridge, 1997)

Mathisen, R. W., ed. *Law, society, and authority in late antiquity* (Oxford, 2001)

Pietri, C. *Roma christiana: Recherches sur l'église de Rome, son organisation, sa politique, son idéologie de Miltiade à Sixte III (311–440)*, CollÉFR 224 (Rome, 1976)

Rapp, C. *Holy bishops in late antiquity* (Berkeley, CA, 2005)

Rebillard, E. and C. Sotinel, eds. *L'évêque dans la cité du IVᵉ au Vᵉ siècle*, CollÉFR 248 (Rome, 1998)

Sterk, A. *Renouncing the world yet leading the church* (Cambridge, MA, 2004)

Trout, D. E. *Paulinus of Nola: Life, letters, and poems* (Berkeley, 1999)

Van Dam, R. *Becoming Christian: The conversion of Roman Cappadocia* (Philadelphia, 2003)

    Families and friends in late Roman Cappadocia (Philadelphia, 2003)

    Leadership and community in late antique Gaul (Berkeley, 1985)

15

Synods and councils

MARK EDWARDS

'Throughout the provinces of the Greek world', writes Tertullian, 'councils are gathered out of every church' (*On fasting* 3.6). The Latin *ab universis ecclesiis* must refer only to churches within the same district,[1] for in the 1,950 years that have now elapsed since the 'Apostolic Council' in Jerusalem, there has not been one occasion on which the leaders of all the churches have assembled in the same locality. In Tertullian's day such a gathering might have been conceivable, but could hardly have been convened without the mandate, or sustained without the resources, of an emperor. The synods of which we hear are generally local ones – the commonest, and consequently the least often reported, being no doubt a small conclave between a bishop and his presbyters to rule on a single matter within the diocese. The bishop might then communicate the judgment to other bishops, as Serapion did when he confiscated the *Gospel of Peter* in Antioch (Eusebius, *Church history* 6.12); and where a decision touched the interests of other congregations, the defence of it might be addressed not to the major sees alone but to the clergy of a whole province. Even then, the purpose of such a document as Victor's letter announcing his suppression of the Asiatic date for Easter in Rome was to enjoin compliance, not to arouse debate (ibid. 5.24.9). Victor had already obtained the signature of the bishops outside Asia to a protocol approving the imposition of a uniform date for Easter in the capital; their colloquy might almost be called ecumenical, but no minutes have survived.[2] More numerous, but less diverse in origin, were the Africans who mustered almost annually to endorse the resolutions of their metropolitan bishop, Cyprian of Carthage. The proceedings of these councils

---

1 See H. Hess, *The early development of canon law*, 10. General works on the history of the ecumenical councils include: C. Hefele, *Histoire des conciles*; H. R. Percival, *The seven ecumenical councils of the undivided church*; E. Schwartz (ed.), *ACO* 1; H. J. Sieben, *Die Konzilsidee in der alten Kirche*.
2 Eusebius, *Church history* 5.22–24.1, records that Polycrates attended the council, but not that he signed the agreement.

show that they followed the pattern of the Roman senate: a roll of names was taken, a motion put, and every delegate required in turn to say *placet* or *non placet*.[3] No *non placet*, however, is recorded, even when the number of bishops rose to ninety or more; these parliaments, like local synods, functioned as a megaphone for the bishop, and were, if anything, less hospitable to dissent than the political institutions of this age.

More controversial in form, though no less certain in their outcome, were the courts held for the examination of heretics, of which Origen's *Dialogue with Heraclides* is the longest extant specimen. Origen, as the most learned of the presbyters, was co-opted to elicit a recantation from the accused, or by refuting him to justify the sentence that the bishops had come to pronounce. Origen was employed in the same capacity against Beryllus of Bostra (Eusebius, *Church history* 6.33.1–2), but the greatest affair of this kind took place some years after his death when a certain Malchion, a teacher of rhetoric, on behalf of eighty bishops from neighbouring provinces, exposed the false Christology of the Antiochene bishop Paul of Samosata. Such a combination against an episcopal colleague was unprecedented – and so was the aftermath, for the judges, being unable to enforce the deposition, turned successfully to Aurelian, the pagan emperor (ibid. 7.30.19). An account of his intervention and the cause of it was sent to the bishops of Rome and Alexandria, while he himself entrusted to Rome the choice of Paul's successor. Thus it became apparent that contumacy was not to be overcome without the goodwill of the sovereign, while the sovereign would not act without involving the rest of Christendom.[4] In the half-century after Aurelian, civil war, the division of the realm and persecution stood in the way of a general council; when the troubles ceased and the bishops met again, it was not to try a single malefactor or agree on a single custom, but to find a balm for all the abuses, grievances and schisms that survived to augment the sufferings of the church.

From the persecution to Constantinople

The first council, in the East or the West, that is known to have issued canons was held at Elvira in Spain on 15 May of a year between 295 and 314. (It is commonly dated to 305 or 306.) Of the eighty-one canons attributed to it, perhaps only the first twenty-one are to be considered as a product of this council. They include a canon fixing a period of penance for a mistress who

---

3 Hess, *The early development of canon law*, 17–29.
4 On the proceedings, see H. de Riedmatten, *Les actes du procès de Paul de Samosate*; G. C. Stead, 'Marcel Richard on Malchion and Paul of Samosata'.

has whipped her slave to death (c. 5) and another one decreeing the lifelong excommunication of those that use black magic (c. 6).[5] Nineteen bishops and twenty-four priests had assembled, among them Bishop Ossius of Cordova, who was to be involved in such important councils as the synods of Nicaea (325), Serdica (343) and Sirmium (357) before his death some fifty years later. How its decisions were to be enforced we cannot say, as no lay sovereign had yet become a Christian.

The first council that could boast an imperial mandate was convened at Arles in 314, after Constantine had been asked to review the acquittal of Caecilian by a synod of Italian and Gallic bishops under Miltiades of Rome.[6] Constantine, disclaiming any power to reverse the verdict of an ecclesiastical gathering, had sent letters to bishops in all the Western provinces, and the names of those who obeyed the summons are listed in the Acts. Whether or not the emperor took a seat at it,[7] the council nursed his interests by condoning military service and enjoining uniformity in the celebration of Easter. Caecilian's tenure in Carthage was endorsed first by his colleagues, then by Constantine, who satisfied his own doubts by a private interrogation. Sylvester of Rome, however, did not attend – a fact lamented by the bishops, half ironically, when they wrote to acquaint their 'brother' with the rulings that they had none the less disseminated without his *imprimatur*.

In the East neither papal nor imperial authority was needed to underwrite the councils that took place in the aftermath of Licinius' victory over Maximinus Daia in 313. At Ancyra penalties commensurate with the fault were enjoined on those who had lapsed under persecution; the chief concern of a council held in Neocaesarea was to provide for the expulsion and restoration of those who committed heinous sins in a time of peace.[8] A few years later, doctrine claimed the attention of a council once again when Alexander of Alexandria persuaded the clergy of Egypt to condemn his presbyter Arius as a heretic.[9] Arius' following numbered only half a dozen presbyters and two bishops, but he found an ally in Bishop Eusebius of Nicomedia, who convened a

---

5 E. J. Jonkers, *Acta et symbola*, 5–23; on the scholarly debate see P. Badet and D. DeDecker, 'Historicité et actualité'.
6 See Optatus, *Against the Donatists* 1.25, appendix 4; perhaps also 1.22. In the longer version, edited by C. Munier (CCSL 148: 9–22), supplementary canons and a copious list of signatures are appended, but there is no allusion to a presiding magistrate and no criticism of the absent pontiff.
7 The name of the president has fallen out of the closing sentence to Optatus, appendix 4.
8 Jonkers, *Acta et symbola*, 28–38.
9 On Arius' refusal to admit that the Son is God see Alexander's letters at Theodoret, *Church history* 1.3 and Socrates, *Church history* 1.6, together with Arius' letters of defence (Theodoret, *Church history* 1.5 and Sozomen, *Church history* 1.15).

provincial synod to reverse the Egyptian judgment. The controversy between
the two great bishoprics was silenced, but not healed, by Licinius' prohibition
of synods (Eusebius, *Life of Constantine* 1.51.1). Constantine took the affair in
hand in 324. His conduct, like his treatment of the Donatists, exemplified his
belief that a strong king ought to make strong bishops: at a preliminary session,
held in Antioch, it was not a co-opted presbyter, like Origen or Malchion, but
Ossius of Cordova who interrogated a number of his colleagues and discovered
that they had gone so far with Arius as to deny a common nature to God the
Father and his Son.[10]

Ossius was present again for the gathering at Nicaea in June and July of
325. Over 200 prelates attended, only six of whom held Western bishoprics;
nevertheless, historians ever since have joined Eusebius in styling this the First
Ecumenical Council (*Life of Constantine* 3.6.1). It met, as Socrates tells us, with
three objects: to determine the date of Easter, to arrive at a common mind on
the nature of Christ and to resolve the Melitian schism in Alexandria (*Church
History* 1.8). In two of these tasks the throne collaborated with the altar, for
it was Constantine, according to Eusebius, who inserted the word *homoousios*
into the creed, and who insisted after the council that the death of Christ was
not to be celebrated at the time of the Jewish Passover, but according to the
lunisolar calendar of Rome (Eusebius, *Life of Constantine* 3.17–19). The principle
that the unity of the church should be exhibited in its liturgy was reinforced
by canons that ordained that penitent followers of Paul of Samosata could be
reconciled only by a second baptism, without imposing the same condition on
the rigorist followers of the Roman presbyter Novatian. At the same time, by
requiring the Melitians to submit to Alexander (Athanasius, *De decretis Nicaenae
synodi* 36), by confirming the authority of every metropolitan within his own
province (c. 6), and even by prohibiting the translation of bishops from see to
see in the hope of restraining clerical ambition (c. 15), they proclaimed that
only a Catholic magisterium, observing strict degrees of power and deference,
could sustain this common obedience in Christ.[11]

There now ensued, according to Athanasius, a decade of cabals disguised as
synods, all contrived by the Arian party to procure the deposition of certain
bishops who had opposed it at or after the Nicene council. The defendants were
charged, like Paul of Samosata in 268, with faults in conduct and in doctrine;
like him, Eustathius of Antioch and Paul of Constantinople were degraded in
their own cities (Athanasius, *History of the Arians* 4; 7). The emperor, though

---

10 H. Chadwick, 'Ossius of Cordova'.
11 For the canons, see Jonkers, *Acta et symbola*, 39–47.

consenting, was not present, but his legate superintended the proceedings against Athanasius, the Alexandrian bishop, in 335. The case at Tyre followed due forensic process, the accusers being routed in open court (as he claims) by the friends of Athanasius; nevertheless his judges were determined to find him guilty, notwithstanding the protests of the Egyptians and the reluctance of the legate. Sentenced to deposition, he showed that he had grasped the new constitution of affairs by fleeing directly to the capital. Less fortunate than Caecilian in 314, he was banished by Constantine, and, after a brief remission, this decree was ratified by Constantine's heir, Constantius II.[12]

Athanasius professed to be scandalised by the persistent intervention of Constantius in ecclesiastical quarrels (*Historia Arianorum* 52). Constantius might have answered that in all constitutional matters the stronger party creates its own law, that Nicaea itself had been the *fait accompli* of his father – that history, in short, is what prevails, and that the language of Athanasius savoured too much of Donatus' insolence to the emperor Constans. We have already seen that the church had turned to the senate and the courts of law to furnish itself with principles of governance; it would not be surprising if a Christian monarch felt empowered to countermand or enforce the customary practices by extraordinary sanctions. And again, of course, it was only to be expected that the notion of clerical sovereignty would be cherished whenever the clergy found their own voices. As though it were not the crown that had relieved them of Athanasius, the bishops who met at Antioch in 341 to refute Marcellus of Ancyra forcefully declared their episcopal authority. 'How could we, being bishops, follow a presbyter?' they retorted against the imputation of Arianism. They issued a creed which omitted the watchword *homoousios* (Athanasius, *Synods* 22) Their letter was answered and refuted by Julius, bishop of Rome, who spoke, with the full consent of everyone but the Donatists, as metropolitan of the Latin West (Athanasius, *Apologia* 21–35). He heightened the pretensions of his see by calling the Easterners to explain their case in Rome; when they abstained, the imperial colleagues Constans and Constantius intervened, appointing Serdica, the bridge between their dominions, as the site for a general council. The Easterners, some eighty in all, seceded on the grounds that the deposition of Athanasius had been wilfully set aside by the Western party.[13] Reiterating a creed that had already been unsuccessfully presented by an Eastern delegation at the court of Constantius in Trier, they published an encyclical excommunicating Julius and his satellites, while paying so little

---

12 See Athanasius, *Apologia* 71–86, with D. W. H. Arnold, *The early episcopal career of Athanasius* and T. D. Barnes, *Athanasius and Constantius*.
13 See Hess, *The early development of canon law*, 105–11.

heed to royal policy that it recognised Donatus as bishop of Carthage.[14] The Westerners, though they brandished the authority of the imperial summons, found occasion to magnify the prerogatives of Rome (c. 3 and 4 of the Council of Serdica) and to extend the Nicene canon (c. 15) against episcopal migration (c. 1), which was thought to have been aimed at the late Eusebius of Nicomedia.[15] Both halves of the council struck at the hegemony of the lay sovereign – though when the Donatists set about recovering their liberties in Africa, the deployment of imperial troops was justified by a council under the Catholic bishop Gratus, c. 345–8.

Little offence was given in 351 by the Council of Sirmium, which ousted Photinus, disciple of Marcellus of Ancyra, from his bishopric in that city (Athanasius, *Synods* 27). Yet controversy prospered, and factions multiplied. Constantius II, now ruler of East and West, suspected Athanasius of involvement with the usurper Magnentius. Preparing a sentence of exile against the Alexandrian bishop, Constantius made a council in Milan condemn Athanasius. In 357 Constantius orchestrated the 'Blasphemy of Sirmium', which prohibited the term *ousia* (and therefore *homoousios*) under the signatures of Ossius of Cordova and Liberius of Rome, along with a host of Eastern bishops (Athanasius, *Synods* 28). In 359 this interdict was confirmed under his direction by two councils, though at Rimini the Catholics of the West sent out a remonstrance, while at Seleucia a majority of bishops rejected the Homoian creed proposed by the emperor and reiterated the creed of the Council of Antioch in 341 (Athanasius, *Synods* 7–13, 29–30). Even this proviso was withdrawn at Constantinople in 360, where bishops who persisted in maintaining anything more than that the Son was 'like' the Father were dispossessed (Athanasius, *Synods* 30). Small wonder that Athanasius, restored to his see by Julian when Constantius died in 361, at once convened a synod of his own to defend the edicts of Nicaea and the Western Council of Serdica (*Tome to the Antiochenes* 3). It also attempted to mediate in Antioch, where Paulinus was regarded by most Westerners as the successor to Eustathius, while Meletius, a protégé of Constantius but now a Homoousian, was the favourite of the East.

Other affairs were handled by provincial or local moots without the assistance of the monarch. Thus the canons of Gangra (c. 343) restrained the conduct of ascetics, while the first synodical inventory of the scriptures (omitting the

---

14 Hilary of Poitiers, *Against Valens and Ursacius* 1.2.1. As the letter was directed to Carthage it may be that they meant to foster a schism; they were subjects of Constantius II at this time, while the West was ruled by his brother Constans.

15 Jonkers, *Acta et symbola*, 61–73.

Apocalypse) was issued at about the same date by the Council of Laodicea.[16] Other decrees forbid priests to lend at interest and the laity to marry their kin or share a meal with heretics. Our knowledge of these events comes from the digests of conciliar legislation that the church of the late fourth century compiled in imitation of the jurists. Not every local canon became an ecumenical law, for to endorse the canons was to endorse the president, while conversely any weakness in his position marred the authority of the council. Thus Flavian of Antioch (381–404) may have hoped to confirm his title as a bishop by condemning the 'Messalians', a name given to contemplatives whose pursuit of God through imageless prayer was thought to bespeak a low esteem for the sacraments and other ministrations of the clergy. Yet Photius attaches less weight to his synod than to the trial of the Messalians in 388 at Side, where they were outflanked by Amphilochius of Iconium;[17] perhaps it was only in 431 at Ephesus that they sustained an irreversible defeat.[18]

When the Homoousian party triumphed in 379 and 381 it was no doubt partly because the world was weary, partly because emperors Theodosius and Gratian were of one mind, but above all because the policies of these emperors had been shaped by a vigilant coalition of bishops who had made a talisman of the Nicene Creed. Gratian was content to let the bishop of Rome dictate both law and truth to the Western provinces, but he himself took the chair in 379 at a contest of orthodoxy that ended in 381, at the Council of Aquileia, with the defeat of the Homoians by the champion of the Homousians, Ambrose of Milan.[19] The principles of Roman litigation were observed, though loosely enough to enable Ambrose to arrive at Aquileia as the defendant and emerge as the prosecutor.[20] His eloquence, supported by royal favour, tamed the West, but in the East it passed to the strength of Theodosius the Great to appease the bickering of the 150 bishops whom he brought to Constantinople in 381.[21] The choice of venue, flattering as it was to the new metropolitanate, was offensive to the older ones.[22] The emperor was present and confirmed the

---

16 Jonkers, ibid., 81–96 assigns a date of 343 to the Council of Gangra, but allows that Laodicea may have convened at any date between 341 and 381.
17 Photius, *Bibliotheca* 52; cf. C. Stewart, *Working the earth of the heart*, 24–42. As the date of his assault on the Messalians is unknown, we cannot be sure that Flavian was universally recognised as bishop.
18 N. Tanner and J. Alberigo, *Decrees of the ecumenical councils*, I: 66–7.
19 See 'Atti del colloquio internazionale sul concilio di Aquileia'.
20 Thus, N. B. McLynn, *Ambrose of Milan*, 124–37.
21 On the caliginous history of this council see Socrates, *Church history* 5.8; Sozomen, *Church history* 7.7 and above all Theodoret, *Church history* 5.9–13. For the decrees, including the creed, see Tanner and Alberigo, *Decrees of the ecumenical councils*, I: 21–35.
22 See canon 3 (Tanner and Alberigo, *Decrees of the ecumenical councils*, I: 32) on the privileges accorded to Constantinople and ratified at Chalcedon.

decrees of the council by an imperial edict (*CTh* 16.1.3). The Roman bishop, however, withheld his assent. The first president, Gregory of Nazianzus, was an ardent Nicene, but resigned after he was found to be in breach of the Nicene canon against episcopal translation. He revenged himself by writing against the futility of councils,[23] and it was seventy years before the church reclaimed the most enduring legacy of Constantinople – the addition to the Nicene Creed of clauses on the Spirit, and an assurance that Christ's reign would have no end. In the following year the Eastern bishops assembled again in Constantinople and confirmed their theological teaching in a letter to a Roman synod that had been convened by Pope Damasus at the same time.

Popes and councils in the late Western empire

Records of the Latin-speaking councils were preserved with more minuteness and tenacity. Africa was singularly rich in this as in other forms of literature, even if it did not succeed in holding a council every year as Aurelius, primate of Carthage, had urged at Hippo in 393. In fact the next session of which any acts survive was the Second Council of Carthage in 397, which confirmed the decrees of Hippo and established the African canon of the scriptures.[24] Catholicity – more pragmatically, opposition to the Donatists – was the sieve that determined membership of the councils whose proceedings have come down to us; and catholic they were, to judge by the frequency with which they are commended in the Decree of Gratian, and the fact that its rulings were cited among the canons of the Byzantine Council in Trullo in 692.[25] Yet the Donatists too held regular conventicles, which anathematised not only the Catholic party but the malcontents within their own communion. Both sides agreed in one thing, that the question should be tried within the province, and on 1 May 418 a Catholic session at Carthage put into words the long-standing principle that no appeals should be made outside of Africa.[26] This maxim was put to the test as early as the council of 419, which was convened after Apiarius, a presbyter convicted of numerous felonies, appealed to Rome and Bishop Zosimus overruled the verdict of the province. When the Africans claimed their rights, he adduced a 'Nicene' canon that empowered the bishop

23 Gregory of Nazianzus, *Carmen* 2.1.7–9 (PG 37: 1024–9).
24 C. Munier, 'La tradition littéraire', 9.
25 Munier, 'La tradition littéraire', 1 and C. Munier, 'Canones Conciliorum Africae', 3–10.
26 Council of Carthage (525), citing the council of 418 (CCSL 149: 227); cf. the citation from the council of 424: 'Ut nullus ad Romanam ecclesiam audeat appellare' (ibid.), on which see also C. Munier, 'Un canon inédit'.

of Rome to review the judgments of his colleagues. The Africans were aware of no such ruling, and it was found in no Greek record; at length it was ascertained that the Nicene canons had been augmented by those of Serdica in the copies held at Rome.[27]

Opponents of the Donatists could adduce an empirical test of catholicity, for it was they who were in communion with Rome and hence with the Eastern congregations which were not at odds with Rome. In their dealings with the Pelagians, on the other hand, the Africans first determined what was catholic, then challenged the rest of Christendom to concur. In 415 the Council of Diospolis in Palestine declared Pelagius innocent. Augustine, the mouthpiece of Africa, excused the Greeks on the plea that they were ignorant of his most pernicious writings; but when Zosimus (himself a Greek) repeated the acquittal in Rome, the Africans were incensed. No match for Augustine in theology, he was forced to concede, and on 1 May 418 Pelagius and Caelestius were condemned at a council in Carthage for having taught that humankind was created mortal, and that the first man's sin ruined no one but himself.[28] The exclusion of the Donatists may have prejudiced the outcome, for the puritan who undertook to bleach the robe of Christ by his own lustrations would have been the natural patron of the lay heretic who believed that we can escape the toils of Adam by our own zeal. Finally, in 411 the Donatists came to a conference in Carthage at the summons of its Catholic bishop Aurelius.[29] For all the candid scrutiny of Constantinian records, the outcome was already assured by numbers, for when the roll was taken a number of Catholics were able to declare, 'I have no rival.' The Donatists ignored the ecumenical endorsement of the conference, and within the Catholic fold new ruptures prompted decrees from Carthaginian synods against the contumacy of excommunicated clergy and the introduction of strange prayers at the altar. Schism was eliminated only when Christianity was smothered in Northern Africa by the triumph of Islam.

A long succession of Spanish councils opens with the attainder of Priscillian in 380 at Saragossa.[30] The colourful (and perhaps misjudged) heresiarch escaped immediate punishment, but was denounced in 381 to the Western

---

27 See *Concilia Africae* (CCSL 149: 91–4). The code of 419 ratified the canon of scripture laid down in 397 (ibid., 142), which ignored the distinction made elsewhere between the Hebrew and the Greek books of the Old Testament.
28 *Concilia Africae* (CCSL 149: 74–7).
29 The *Gesta Conlationis Carthaginis* contains the proceedings and Augustine's *Brevis collatio*.
30 See PL 84: 315–18 and H. Chadwick, *Priscillian of Avila*, 12–15. On the first Council of Toledo (400), see ibid. 171–219, and on the putative second council of Saragossa in 395, ibid., 27–30.

tyrant Maximus Magnus, and was beheaded in 385 after a council in Bordeaux upheld the charges (Sulpicius Severus, *Chronicle* 2.49.5–6). His sect flourished none the less, and among the errors imputed to it by the first Council of Toledo in 400 were astrology, the confusion of Son and Father and the deification of the human soul.[31]

The principal aim of other Western councils was the preservation of unity through order. Pope Innocent, in his own codicil to a synod which appeased a Gallic schism, urged that Rome should be the sole arbiter of disputes that could not be resolved within one province,[32] but the exercise of this principle in Gaul was impeded both by competition between the bishoprics and by the obstinacy of 'semi-Pelagian' teachers who affirmed that faith is voluntary, though works depend on God. The mandates of Turin (post-397), of Riez in Provence (439), of Orange (441) and of Vaison (442) were concerned above all with the reconciliation of heinous sinners and the restraint of lawless or ambitious clerics.[33] Another body of canons, rich in penalties for heretics and malefactors, passes under the name of the Second Council of Arles: the last awards to this city alone the metropolitan status that it had been required to share with Vienne by a temporising judgment at Turin.[34] Doctrine was at this time left to private controversy, but a council of uncertain date appointed Germanus and Lupus as Catholic emissaries to Britain. Here they convoked the first synod known to have taken place on the island, and after a candid disputation (as Bede assures us), the heresy of Pelagius was condemned on his native soil (Bede, *H. E.* 1.17).

The road to Chalcedon

In the East a series of momentous gatherings was set in train by the feud between two great cities. In 402, at the 'Synod of the Oak' held near Chalcedon in Asia Minor, John Chrysostom, bishop of Constantinople, was arraigned by Theophilus of Alexandria and thirty-six of his confederates. As no defence was admitted, John was easily convicted of irregular ordination, the illegal protection of fugitives and habitual insolence to his fellow bishops.[35] Innocent of Rome demurred (Palladius, *Dialogue* 12–15), and the emperor Arcadius also

---

31 G. Martínez Díez and F. Rodriguez, eds., *La colección canónica*, IV: 340–4.
32 Innocent, *Letter* 2 (PL 20: 269–81).
33 *Concilia Galliae 314–506* (CCSL 148: 52–104).
34 CCSL 148: 111–25; see further C. J. Turner, 'Arles and Rome'. On the number of councils in Turin, the date of this ruling and the innovations in provincial government that gave rise to it, see M. E. Kulikowski, 'Two councils of Turin'.
35 See the table of charges in SC 342: 100–14; trans. J. N. D. Kelly, *Golden Mouth*, 299–301.

wavered, until the defendant courted exile by inveighing against the empress. Theophilus had his way though at no small cost, for it was the universal judgment of posterity that Chrysostom, if not innocent, was much the better Christian of the two.

Ancient witnesses formed a different estimate of Nestorius, who was appointed bishop of Constantinople in 428. Almost at once he found himself playing host to two groups of refugees – Pelagians under the ban of Rome and malcontents expelled from Alexandria, whose appeal had been entrusted to him by the emperor Theodosius II. Celestine of Rome held that Nestorius had no duty but to accept the judgment of his ecclesiastical superior;[36] Cyril of Alexandria declined the arbitration of a man whom he regarded as a heretic. The error of Nestorius, as Cyril explained to Celestine, was to dissociate Christ the Logos from the human Jesus, alleging that the Word alone was born of God, the man alone from Mary.[37] If one drew the corollary that Jesus the man was saved by co-operation with the Logos, this was a new variety of Pelagianism; since the recent trial of a certain Leporius in Carthage seemed to betoken a recrudescence of this heresy,[38] Celestine made Cyril his lieutenant at the council which Theodosius (in answer to a petition from Nestorius) now proposed to hold at Ephesus.

Though this was in intention a general council, the emperor governed only through his legate. Cyril arrived on time with his Egyptians, but a smaller party, favourable to Nestorius and led by John of Antioch, was delayed. When they arrived, the Antiochenes found that Cyril had initiated proceedings against the wishes of the legate. Nestorius, having refused to face a jury composed entirely of his accusers, had been sentenced to deposition in his absence. Two of Cyril's letters to him were canonised, while Celestius the Pelagian was condemned. John of Antioch held his own tribunal and deposed Cyril, but the majority, accusing him of wilful procrastination, declared that their acts had satisfied both justice and the behest of Celestine.[39] Theodosius adjourned the council to Chalcedon, restoring Cyril and exculpating John when they signed a formula of reunion in 433.[40] Nestorius, however, remained in exile, and it was Cyril and Celestine, not their royal patron, who were remembered as the presidents of this 'Third Ecumenical Council'.

36 Schwartz, ACO 1.1.5; Nestoriana, ed. Loofs, 170.
37 Schwartz, ACO 1.1.6.
38 Hefele, Histoire des Conciles, 11.1, 215–17.
39 For the proceedings, see Schwartz, ACO 1; Tanner and Alberigo, Decrees of the ecumenical councils, 1: 37–74.
40 Tanner and Alberigo Decrees of the ecumenical councils, 1: 69–70.

The cardinal phrase in the formula of reunion – 'consubstantial with us in humanity, and with the Father in divinity' – was contested by the monk Eutyches in 448 at a synod held under Bishop Flavian of Constantinople. Flavian condemned him, informing Rome of his decision, while Eutyches appealed to Theodosius. A letter from Leo of Rome[41] – underwriting and thereby overruling Flavian's verdict – was dispatched in 449, but his legates found themselves in the middle of a second council at Ephesus, convened by Theodosius under the presidency of Dioscorus of Alexandria. Notwithstanding the veto of the Romans, the meeting ended with the vindication of Eutyches and the deposition of Flavian; the latter, severely beaten by supporters of the Egyptian patriarch, died a short while after. Leo, whose letter had not been read, dubbed this a 'robbers' council' (*Latrocinium*); the remedy, which he accepted but did not propose, was the Fourth Ecumenical Council at Chalcedon in 451, under the auspices of Marcian and Pulcheria, Theodosius having died in the previous year.

But for their insistence on a new formula, the proceedings would have ended when Leo had ratified the trial and deposition of Dioscorus.[42] The theological issue was debated at a new session, which commenced with the recitation of the Nicene Creed of 325, together with its successor of 381. Cyril's letters, together with the reunion formula of 433, were approved again and, after a sharp debate, all those attending were required on pain of anathema to agree that Leo's letter to Flavian was consistent with these touchstones. The resultant 'definition' (as we call it) was rather a gloss, in which a Cyrilline affirmation that the man and the Word are one was juxtaposed with clauses indicating the presence of two natures, one drawn from the formula of reunion and one from Leo's Tome.[43]

The principle that the emperor may give authority to the council was established in a preamble, which ascribed the First Ecumenical Council to Constantine and the Fourth to Marcian and Valentinian. At the same time, by joining Celestine's name to that of Cyril in its reference to the Third Council, while omitting all mention of Theodosius II, the Chalcedonian fathers also hinted that, in the absence of the lay sovereign, the power of sanctioning might devolve on the apostolic see.

---

41 *Letter* 128, better known as 'the Tome of Leo': Tanner and Alberigo, *Decrees of the ecumenical councils*, 1: 77–82.
42 For the full proceedings see ACO ii, with Tanner and Alberigo, *Decrees of the ecumenical councils*, 1: 77–103.
43 Tanner and Alberigo, *Decrees of the ecumenical councils*, 1: 86.

Among those who had been appointed to judge Dioscorus was Theodoret of Cyrrhus, an apologist for Nestorius deposed at the *Latrocinium*; Ibas of Edessa reaped the benefit of a subsequent decree that countermanded almost all the decisions reached on that occasion.[44] Juvenal of Jerusalem retained his see, though not the sympathy of his congregation, by transferring his support from Dioscorus to the council (Zacharias Rhetor, *Church history* 3.3). The Egyptians appointed Timothy Aelurus as successor to Dioscorus in 454, but, even when he had frankly abandoned Eutyches, his fellow bishops urged that his appointment was invalid. He was exiled in 458, but restored by the usurper Basiliscus after a third council in Ephesus in 475.[45] Soon after, Basiliscus was deposed, the Asiatic bishops repented of their presence at this council, and Alexandria was once again marooned (Evagrius, *Church history* 3.9). The Christology of Nestorius could be banished but not suppressed, and a council held in Persia by his sympathisers (one of the first to take place outside the empire) established the independence of a new and long-lived church.[46] Pope Leo accepted and defended the dogmatic position of the Council of Chalcedon; he objected, however, to canon 28, which, by according second place to Constantinople at future councils, seemed to hint that Rome held primacy only so long as she was the capital of the empire, and not through her inalienable status as the apostolic see.[47]

The Western kingdoms after the fall of Rome

Rome was no longer mistress of the world, though Leo hardly seemed to know it and the papacy grew tall by the amputation of its rivals. The Vandal kings of Africa set out to repress the Catholics who kept up a dangerous intercourse with other remnants of the dissolving empire. In 484, King Huneric, having brokered a debate between the Catholics and the 'Arians' at Carthage, put the force of law behind the Homoian creed which had been framed, he said, by a thousand saints at Rimini and Seleucia (Victor of Vita, *Vandal persecution* 3.5). The hostility of the government could be propitious to theological reflection, as in 523, when a group of exiled prelates in Sardinia, with Fulgentius of

---

44 See H.-M. Diepen, *Les Trois Chapitres*, 75–98.
45 W. H. C. Frend, *Monophysite movement*, 154–5, 159–61, 170–2.
46 On the Council of Seleucia, see the Armenian historian Sebeus, *Histoire d'Heraclius*, trans. and ed. Macler (Paris 1904), 113. For a general introduction to this church, see now Wilhelm Baum and Dietmar Winkler, *The apostolic church of the East*.
47 A. Grillmeier, *Christ in Christian tradition*, II.2: 120–49.

Ruspe at their head, composed a treatise upholding the Augustinian theory of election against the 'semi-Pelagians' of Gaul.[48] It was in the same year at Junca in Byzacena that Liberatus, the primate of this region, induced his suffragans to award him rights that encroached on the prerogatives of Carthage. A new king eased the burdens of the Catholics, and bishops from the other African provinces met at Carthage in 525 to assist their primate Boniface in suppressing the usurpation.[49] In 536, when the province had been re-conquered for Byzantium, the Catholic bishops addressed a letter from Carthage to Justinian, requesting that their property be restored and that their clergy be prevented from migrating to Italy, now that there was no tribulation to warrant such a flight.[50]

Synods in Gaul continued to deplore – and thereby prove that they were unable to curb – the rapacity and incontinence of the clergy. The sanctions of the Council of Agde (506)[51] were reinforced at Orléans in 511 and at Epaon in 517.[52] At the same time, the monasteries were urged not to contemn their dissolute bishops. Cloth and cowl could not afford to bicker under Arian, pagan or even Catholic despots, and the Council of Lyon (between 518 and 523) recommended the cloister as an asylum for priests who had failed to convert a hostile suzerain.[53] The theology of Gaul was reconciled with that of Africa in 529, when a council at Orange,[54] tacitly contradicting the decrees that Faustus of Riez had persuaded his colleagues to endorse at Arles (c. 470), denied that human beings can collude in their own salvation.

In Spain the Visigoths oppressed the Catholics, and a mere ten bishops met at Tarragona in 516 to prohibit the marriage of ecclesiastics above the order of subdeacon.[55] The eight delegates who gathered at Toledo in the fifth year of King Amalaric (527) believed none the less that they spoke for the church at large in forbidding any delegation of clerical duties to the laity.[56] It was a local council in Braga in 561 that pronounced the final condemnation of the Priscillianists, and another in 572 that dealt with problems of church

48 Hefele, *Histoire des conciles*, II.2: 1058.
49 CCSL 149: 255–81.
50 Hefele, *Histoire des conciles*, II.2: 1136–9.
51 For the canon enumerating degrees of kinship which precluded marriage, see CCSL 148: 227.
52 *Concilia Galliae 511– 695* (CCSL 148a: 1–37).
53 CCSL 148a: 39.
54 CCSL 148A: 59 and 63. On Faustus, see T. A. Smith, *De gratia*, 57–60, citing Faustus' *Letters* 1 and 2.
55 Martínez Díez and Rodriguez, *La colección canónica*, IV: 268–81; but for the date (later than that fixed by the putative editor, Isidore of Seville), see E. A. Thompson, *The Goths in Spain*, 33.
56 Letter of Montanus, in Martínez Díez and Rodriguez, *La colección canónica*, IV: 359.

order and discipline.[57] A synod under royal auspices and in imitation of the ecumenical councils assembled by the Roman emperors became possible when King Reccared embraced the Catholic faith. In 589 both Catholic and Arian bishops, forced by civil officers, were summoned to Toledo and required to celebrate the conversion of the Visigothic nation to Nicene orthodoxy.[58] The legislation of the council was confirmed by royal decree.

Byzantium and the papacy

The papacy acknowledged only the emperor in Constantinople as monarch, and put itself at the head of Eastern affairs at a time when the Western empire was overwhelmed by German invaders. In 482, the emperor Zeno undertook to reconcile the Miaphysites by promulgating his infamous *Henotikon*, or 'formula of union' (Evagrius, *Church history* 3.16). This edict was received with jubilation in Alexandria, but when the bishop, Peter, took occasion to disparage the Chalcedonian definition, Acacius of Constantinople and Felix of Rome were both asked to consider his offence. The Roman sentence of excommunication and anathema was accompanied by a reprimand to Acacius, who, as one of the principal authors of the *Henotikon*, was unwilling to break communion with Peter.[59] Acacius, still defiant, was condemned by a tribunal under Felix.[60] It was at about this time that a Roman synod, having first refused to sit until the summons of Theoderic had been ratified by the presence of Pope Symmachus, decreed that causes touching the clergy can be tried only by ministers of God.[61]

The rupture between the two capitals was healed in 519 when the Eastern patriarch, at the behest of the emperor Justin, denounced Acacius and was reconciled to Pope Hormisdas (*Avellana collectio* 115, 160, 167). Throughout these years, however, the local synods of Antioch, Alexandria and Constantinople belaboured one another with anathemas and polemics. The Miaphysites (or proponents of a single nature in Christ after the incarnation) prevailed in Antioch, but suffered when the the irenic policy of Zeno was revoked by Justin. Justinian, his successor, summoned spokesmen of the two parties to

---

57 PL 84: 561–77. The second council ordained that, in accordance with the fifth canon of Nicaea, every province should hold a synod twice a year for the chastisement of offending clergy.
58 Martínez Díez and Rodriguez, *La colección canónica*, v: 54–73; but for the date (which Isidore gives as 627) see again Thompson, *The Goths in Spain*, 33.
59 Zacharias Rhetor, *Church history* 5.10–6.7; Evagrius, *Church history* 3.16–22; *Life of Daniel the Stylite* 70–85; Frend, *Monophysite movement*, 174–83.
60 See *Letter* 70 in the *Avellana collectio*.
61 See MGH AA XII: 416–32.

the capital in 531. The conference ended much as it had begun, and he resolved henceforth to be his own theologian. In 533 he endorsed, and persuaded Rome to approve, the theopaschite dictum 'One of the Trinity has suffered'; but, having gone so far with the Miaphysites, he allowed his own protégé Menas, patriarch of Constantinople, to denounce their leaders as heretics.[62] In 543, having been convinced that nothing less than an ecumenical council would unite the church, he nonetheless sought to guide its deliberations in advance by addressing to Menas a condemnation of three notorious Dyophysites, all long dead. Theodore of Mopsuestia – mentor if not tutor to Nestorius – had never been the defendant at a council; Ibas and Theodoret had been rehabilitated at Chalcedon only because their depositions were illegal, not because their works were sound. Justinian demanded that the works of all three should suffer public censure, together with those of Origen, whose ill fame had been purposely aggravated by Theophilus in his assault on Chrysostom.[63] In 553, the Second Council of Constantinople pronounced a posthumous anathema on all four men, appending a denunciation of fifteen propositions, which were not attached to any name but coincided largely with the eleven ascribed to Origen by Justinian in his letter of 543.

Vigilius of Rome had made it clear before the council that he would not acquiesce in a libel on the dead. Captivity in Byzantium had failed to break his spirit, but when the council threatened to add his name to the condemnation, he subscribed to its resolutions.[64] The Fifth Ecumenical Council – as it was to be called – had not attempted to pacify the Nestorians, and did not prevent the installation in 576 of a new Miaphysite patriarch in Egypt by a 'Sanhedrin' of seventy bishops.[65] Its sentence on Origen was, however, upheld in 592 by a synod at Antioch: in his judgment, the patriarch Ephrem alludes to earlier conferences at Antioch and Gaza, which appear to have inspired Justinian's letter of 543.[66] Yet no more than any other see would Antioch consent to be taught by fiat, and in 565 it led the protest of the Eastern church against Justinian's espousal of the 'aphthartodocetic' heresy, which held that the flesh assumed by Christ was not like that of ordinary men (Evagrius, *Church history* 4.39–40).

---

62 See Frend, *Monophysite movement*, 267–75.
63 On Origen, see Evagrius, *Church history* 4.38, with Whitby's notes (*The Ecclesiastical history of Evagrius Scholasticus*, 242–9). On the 'Three Chapters', see Grillmeier, *Christ in Christian tradition*, II.2: 419–29. For Justinian's letter, see Schwartz, ACO 3, 189–91.
64 Hefele, *Histoire des conciles*, III.1: 1–40 and 133–50.
65 Frend, *Monophysite movement*, 327, citing John of Ephesus, *Church history* 4.12.
66 Hefele, *Histoire des conciles*, II.2: 1174–81, citing Cyril's *Life of Sabas* 85.

Justinian died in 565. His long and vigilant reign had proved on the one hand that a council in the East had no more power than the throne was ready to put behind it, and on the other that the emperor himself could not enforce his will in the teeth of a resolute clergy. Rome had learned in the meantime that she must either become a satellite of Byzantium or seek another patron. The matter was decided in the last quarter of the sixth century, when Byzantium once again relinquished Italy to the barbarians, who attached themselves to Rome at her own behest because they saw in her the one unfallen pillar of the empire.

Bibliography

PRIMARY SOURCES

Athanasius. *Apologia de sua fuga*. Ed. H. G. Opitz, *Athanasius Werke* (Berlin, 1935–41), II.1; SC 56
  De decretis Nicaenae synodi, ed. Opitz, II.1
  Historia Arianorum, ed. Opitz, II.1
  Synods, ed. Opitz, II.1
  Tome to the Antiochenes (PG 26)
Avellana collectio. Epistulae imperatorum, pontificum, aliorum (CSEL 35)
Bede. *Historia ecclesiastica*. Eds. Bertram Colgrave and R. A. B. Mynors, *Bede's Ecclesiastical history of the English people* (Oxford, 1969)
Concilia Africae, a.345–a.525 (CCSL 149)
Concilia Galliae, a.314–a.506 (CCSL 148)
Concilia Galliae, a.511–a.695 (CCSL 148a)
Cyril of Scythopolis. *Life of Sabas* (TU 49)
Eusebius. *Church history* (GCS Eusebius Werke, II)
  Life of Constantine (GCS Eusebius Werke, I)
Evagrius Scholasticus. *Church history*. Eds. J. Bidez and L. Parmentier, *Euagrius. The Ecclesiastical history* (London, 1898; reprint, Amsterdam, 1964); trans. M. L. Whitby, *The Ecclesiastical history of Evagrius Scholasticus* (Liverpool, 2000)
Faustus of Riez. *Letters* (CSEL 21)
Gesta Conlationis Carthaginis (CCSL 149a)
Gregory of Nazianzus. *Carmina* (PG 37)
Hilary of Poitiers. *Against Valens and Ursacius*, fragments (CSEL 65)
Innocent. *Letters* (PL 20)
Life of Daniel the Stylite. Ed. H. Delehaye, *Les saints stylites*, SH 14 (Brussels, 1923)
Nestoriana: Die Fragmente des Nestorius, ed. F. Loofs (Halle, 1905)
Optatus. *Against the Donatists* (SC 412, 413)
Origen. *Dialogue with Heraclides* (SC 67)
Palladius. *Dialogue on the life of John Chrysostom* (SC 341, 342)
Photius. *Bibliotheca*, ed. and trans. R. Henry (Paris, 1959–91)

Sebeus of Bagratunik'. *Histoire d'Heraclius*, trans. and ed. F. Macler (Paris, 1904)
Socrates. *Church history* (GCS, N.F. 1: *Sokrates Kirchengeschichte*; SC 477, 493–)
Sozomen. *Church history* (GCS, N.F. 4: *Sozomenus Kirchengeschichte*)
Sulpicius Severus. *Chronicle* (CSEL 1)
Tertullian. *On fasting* (CCSL 2)
Theodoret. *Church history* (GCS N.F. 5)
Victor of Vita. *Vandal persecution*. Ed. S. Lancel, *Victor de Vita. Histoire de la persecution vandale en Afrique. La passion des Sept Martyrs. Registre des provinces et des cités afriques* (Paris, 2002)
Zacharias Rhetor. *Church history* (CSCO 83–4, 87–8)

SECONDARY SOURCES

Arnold, D. W. H. *The early episcopal career of Athanasius* (Notre Dame, 1991)
'Atti del colloquio internazionale sul concilio di Aquileia', *Antichità Altoadriatiche* 21 (1981)
Badet, P. and D. DeDecker. 'Historicité et actualité des canons disciplinaires du concile d'Antioche', *Augustinianum* 37 (1997): 315–25
Barnes, T. D. *Athanasius and Constantius: Theology and politics in the Constantinian empire* (Cambridge, MA, 1993)
Baum, Wilhelm and Dietmar Winkler. *The apostolic church of the East: A concise history* (London, 2003)
Chadwick, H. 'Ossius of Cordova and the presidency of the Council of Antioch', *JTS* N.S. 9 (1958): 292–304
Priscillian of Avila. The occult and the charismatic in the early church (Oxford, 1976)
Diepen, H.-M. *Les Trois Chapitres au Concile de Chalcedoine* (Oosterhuit, 1953)
Flemming, J., ed. *Akten der ephesischen Synode vom Jahre 449* (Göttingen, 1917)
Frend, W. H. C. *The rise of the Monophysite movement* (Cambridge, 1972)
Grillmeier, A. *Christ in Christian tradition, part II: Church of Constantinople in the sixth century, Vol. II. From the Council of Chalcedon (451) to Gregory the Great (590–604)*, trans. J. Cawte and P. Allen (Oxford, 1995)
Hefele, C. *Histoire des conciles d'après les documents originaux*, trans. H. Leclercq (Paris, 1907–49)
Hess, H. *The early development of canon law and the Council of Serdica* (Oxford, 2002)
Jonkers, E. J. *Acta et symbola conciliorum quae saeculo quarto habita sunt* (Leiden, 1954)
Kelly, J. N. D. *Golden Mouth: The story of John Chrysostom, ascetic, preacher, bishop* (London, 1995)
Kulikowski, M. E. 'Two councils of Turin', *JTS* 47 (1996): 159–68
McLynn, N. B. *Ambrose of Milan* (Berkeley, 1994)
Martínez Díez, G. and F. Rodriguez, eds. *La colección canónica Hispana* (Madrid, 1966–92)
Munier, C. 'Un canon inédit du XXe concile de Carthage', *Revue des sciences religieuses* 40 (1966): 113–26
'Canones conciliorum Africae qui in Gratiani Decreto citantur, cum indicatione fontium', *Monumenta iuris canonici*, series C, subsidia 5 (Vatican, 1976), 3–10
'La tradition littéraire des dossiers africains (345–525)', *Recherches augustiniennes* 10 (1975): 3–22

Percival, H. R. *The seven ecumenical councils of the undivided church* (London, 1900)

de Riedmatten, H. *Les actes du procès de Paul de Samosate: Étude sur la christologie du IIIe au IVe siècle* (Fribourg, 1952)

Sieben, H. J. *Die Konzilsidee in der alten Kirche* (Paderborn, 1979)

Smith, Thomas A. *De gratia. Faustus of Riez's treatise on grace and its place in the history of theology* (Notre Dame, 1990)

Stead, G. C. 'Marcel Richard on Malchion and Paul of Samosata', in H. C. Brennecke, E. L. Grasmück and C. Markschies, eds., *Logos. Festschrift für Luise Abramowski* (Berlin, 1993), 140–50

Stewart, Columba. *'Working the earth of the heart': The Messalian controversy in history, texts, and language to A.D. 431* (Oxford, 1991)

Tanner, N. and J. Alberigo. *Decrees of the ecumenical councils* (London, 1990)

Thompson, E. A. *The Goths in Spain* (Oxford, 1969)

Turner, C. J. 'Arles and Rome', *JTS* 17 (1916): 236–47

16

The growth of church law

KENNETH PENNINGTON

Canon law was born in communities that felt great ambivalence about the relationship of law and faith. Custom governed early Christian communities, not a body of written law. It was custom informed by oral traditions and sacred scripture. Christians did not arrange their lives according to a Christian law but according to the spiritual goals of the community and of individual Christians. St Paul wrote to Roman Christians who knew and lived under the law created by the Roman state and reminded them that faith in Christ replaces Jewish law with a quest for salvation (Romans 7.1–12, 10.1–11). Law, he sharply reminded the Galatians, cannot make a man worthy before God; only faith can bring life to the just man (Galatians 3.11–12). After the apostolic age, Paul's words were interpreted much more broadly. Later canonists applied them to secular law and even to canon law itself. They created a tension between the faith and conscience of the individual and the rigour of law that never has been and never will be completely resolved in religious law.

Christian communities lived without a comprehensive body of written law for more than five centuries. Consequently, in the early church, 'canon law' as a system of norms that governed the church or even a large number of Christian communities did not exist. To some extent the Roman state already regulated religious practice and so it quite naturally legislated for the church as the empire began to become Christian from the beginning of the fourth century. From the time of Constantine, Roman emperors issued decrees that regulated the affairs of the Christian church. Only gradually did the church in the West begin to conceive of itself as a corporate body that had the authority to produce rules to govern itself and exercise a separate judicial role in society. In the East the Roman emperor who ruled over Greek Constantinople continued to legislate and regulate ecclesiastical institutions until its collapse in 1453, but from the sixth century Byzantine canon law had already begun to merge with civil law. The first legal collections contained only ecclesiastical norms ('canons') or secular norms ('laws'). In the late sixth and early seventh centuries Byzantine canonists combined these two sources: these collections were named *nomokanons*, although the name did not become common until the eleventh century.

The apostolic and conciliar age

In the first three centuries Christians drew their rules and norms from the Gospels and sacred scripture. Some communities produced 'handbooks' that provided guidance for various aspects of Christian life. Only a few of these have survived.[1] One of the earliest was the *Didache*, which established rules governing the liturgy, the sacraments and lay practices such as fasting.[2] The *Didache* was probably written in Greek for a Syrian community. The book purported to contain the teachings of the twelve apostles and dealt with matters of liturgy and discipline. During the third century, the *Traditio apostolica*, attributed to Hippolytus but possibly written by someone else, detailed the rites and practices of the Roman Christian community.[3] It contains instructions for the consecration of bishops, priests, and deacons and for administering baptism. Again during the third century an unknown author wrote *Didascalia apostolorum* for Christian communities in Syria.[4] It was written in Syriac and was incorporated into later compilations, especially a work of the late fourth century, the *Apostolic constitutions*.[5] The *Apostolic constitutions* 8.47 contains a collection of 85 canons, the *Canons of the apostles*, which later were also transmitted separately and found their way into canonical collections.

These very early Christian texts share several characteristics. Their authority derived from their apostolic origins, not from ecclesiastical institutions. They drew upon scripture and practice for their norms. Their focus is Christian discipline, worship and doctrine. They were intended to serve as manuals of guidance for the clergy and, to some extent, for the laity. These texts were not, however, compilations of legal enactments. Although Christians had the model and example of Roman law, early Christian communities did not yet have institutional structures or a sense of corporate identity that would have encouraged them to produce legal norms governing themselves.

The most important window into the structures and customs of Christian communities are the so-called Pastoral Epistles: 1 Timothy and Titus. Their

---

1 For an overview, see B. E. Ferme, *Introduzione*, 45–56.
2 See W. Rordorf and A. Tuilier's edition: SC 248.
3 G. Dix and H. Chadwick, eds., *The Treatise on the apostolic tradition*.
4 R. H. Connolly, ed., *Didascalia apostolorum*.
5 SC 320, 329, 336.

unknown author used these letters to establish rules for early Christian communities, and when he wrote he claimed Paul's authority. At Titus 1.5, the author reminded Titus that he had left him behind in Crete in order to correct those things that needed correcting. He was to appoint elders (Greek: *presbyteroi*) in each city to govern the community. The elders should be married only once, their children should be Christians, and they should not live in luxury or moral turpitude. The author of Titus listed the qualifications of an *episkopos* (Greek for 'steward') as being humble, kind, abstemious, peaceful, prudent and hospitable (Titus 1.7–8). This list of virtues was for the stewardship of small Christian communities who met in households and who received missionaries from other communities from time to time. The *episkopoi* were married to their churches and should not move from place to place. The author of 1 Timothy gives details about the governance of early Christian communities. He calls the church, strikingly, the 'house of God' (*oikos theou*) that is 'the church of the living God' (1 Timothy 3.15). The implication of these metaphors is that the church is organised like a Greek or Roman household.

The author of 1 Timothy established norms for procedure in cases when accusations were levelled against the clergy. These rules would remain a part of the canonical tradition for centuries. Christians could accuse elders (*presbyteroi*) only when two or three witnesses could substantiate the charges (1 Timothy 5.19). This passage also illustrates how Christians drew upon the Old Testament for procedural norms. Deuteronomy 19.15 had established that two or three witnesses were necessary for convicting a person of a crime. In addition 1 Timothy 5.20 used public humiliation to chastise sinners: wrongdoers should be publicly rebuked. Their public humiliation would serve as a deterrent for others.

The New Testament epistles were a primary source for the earliest norms of canon law, but they were thoroughly inadequate as guides for Christian communities as they began to evolve into larger, more complicated and integrated organisational structures throughout the Mediterranean world. If the Greco-Roman *domus* was a model for the organisation of early Christian churches, Greco-Roman public assemblies most likely provided procedural and institutional models for early Christian assemblies. These ecclesiastical assemblies offered a forum for making doctrinal and disciplinary decisions, for garnering the consent of the community and for establishing norms for local communities. These assemblies became a part of ecclesiastical governance very early. Although later church fathers, particularly John Chrysostom, did justify conciliar assemblies on the basis of Acts 15, modern scholars have concluded that the assembly described in Acts 15 at Jerusalem cannot be described as a 'council' or 'synod'.[6] There is no evidence that Christians of different communities gathered together to decide matters of discipline or doctrine until the late second century. Nonetheless they undoubtedly resolved questions inside their local communities with congregational assemblies regularly.

The emergence of ecclesiastical assemblies that established canonical norms took place almost simultaneously in the East and West. In the early third century, Tertullian reported that councils (*concilia*) were held to decide questions and to represent the 'whole Christian name' (*repraesentatio totius nominis Christiani*). The exact nature of these assemblies has been debated, but there can be no doubt that they promulgated norms and made decisions for Christian communities.[7] We know of assemblies in Asia Minor at Iconium, Synnada, Bostra and other localities in the early third century. In the second half of the century these assemblies became more common. The Council of Carthage under Bishop Agrippinus that can be dated between 220 and 230 was the first Western assembly about which we are well informed. Cyprian provides information that the participants confronted the issues surrounding the legal rules of baptism. He also mentions another council that condemned Privatus, the bishop of Lambaesis, for his crimes. Cyprian presided over a number of councils while bishop of Carthage and used councils as a means to govern the churches of North Africa.[8] In 251, he summoned a synod to establish rules for reconciling those Christians who had abandoned their faith because of persecution. During the next year, he gathered sixty-seven bishops to treat questions of reconciliation (again) and of infant baptism. Cyprian wrote a letter to a certain Fidus in which he informed him of the actions that the council had taken. This is the oldest conciliar letter that has survived.[9] Subsequently councils were held in Carthage almost every year during Cyprian's reign as bishop (248/9–58).

Councils challenged the developing authority of the monarchical bishop because they limited his freedom to govern his church. There was an evolving conviction in Christian communities that there were norms and procedures that should be followed in all the local churches. Nevertheless, Cyprian believed that a bishop should have great freedom of action and forcefully stated that he was answerable only to God. When he quarrelled with Pope Stephen

---

6 H. J. Sieben, *Die Konzilsidee*, 415–23, discusses the assembly at Jerusalem and its use as a model for conciliar action in the fourth century.

7 Tertullian, *De jejunio* 13.6; see Hamilton Hess, *Early development*, 10–15 at 10–11 with references.

8 See Hess, *Early development*, 17–20.

9 Cyprian, *Letter* 64.

over the question of the validity of schismatic and heretical baptisms, the inherent conflict between local episcopal control and general norms, whether established by a centralised authority or councils, raised an issue of ecclesiology and obedience that would bedevil the church for centuries. Cyprian's response to Pope Stephen in 256, after his council had rejected the validity of heretical baptisms, reveals his ambivalence towards any conception of canonical rules or norms that would govern the entire church:

> We are not forcing anyone in this matter; we are laying down no law (*legem*). For every appointed leader has in his government of the Church the freedom to exercise his own will and judgment, while having one day to render an account of his conduct to the Lord.[10]

Cyprian recognised no system of canon law and, if he had been asked the question (anachronistically), he would probably have opposed the idea that the church should have a uniform system of law to which the clergy and laity would be subject.

By the fourth century bishops had established themselves as administrators of local churches. They also recognised their role in governing the affairs of nearby churches in councils as well as their responsibility to confront questions that touched upon the interests of the universal church. In the East and the West councils became the main vehicles for promulgating norms that regulated the lives of clergy and the organisation of the churches.

It is during the fourth century that the enactments that these assemblies produced became called 'canons', from the Greek word 'κανών', which became 'canon' in Latin. In Greek 'canon' did not mean 'law' but simply a 'straight rod' or a 'rule'.[11] As we shall see, the primary focus of conciliar legislation in the fourth century was the structure of church and clerical discipline. The earliest council for which we have a set of legislative decrees is one that was held *c.* 306 in Elvira (Iliberri), a small town that once existed near Granada, Spain. This council issued rulings that dealt with a wide range of matters, from clerical celibacy to apostasy. Although the eighty-one canons commonly attributed to the council may be the product of several subsequent fourth-century councils in Iberia, it is clear that the focus of the canons was on the sexual mores of the clergy and laity.[12] Elvira was the first Western council to stipulate that priests should be celibate. Its canons, however, did not circulate widely.

---

10 Cyprian, *Letter* 72.3, 2 (trans. ACW 47: 54); see Hess, *Early development*, 19, 32–3.
11 See H. Ohme, *Kanon ekklesiastikos*.
12 Hess, *Early development*, 40–2, discusses the textual problems of the legislation at Elvira.

In 314, the emperor Constantine convened a council in the West at the city of Arles in order to settle the Donatist controversy in North Africa. It was a comparatively large assembly with thirty-three bishops and many lower clergy. Twenty-two canons were issued and sent to Pope Sylvester. They dealt with various matters. For example, the date of Easter should be determined according to Roman custom (c. 1). Canon 9 corrected the African view that baptism by heretics is invalid. Bishops from abroad travelling to Rome should be given a church where they can celebrate the eucharist (c. 19).[13] Arles was the first Western council that did not report that laymen had participated in its proceedings. The Councils of Elvira and Arles can be seen as milestones on the road that led to the councils becoming assemblies in which the will of clergy constituted the only legitimate source of canonical norms.[14]

In this early period, councils met more frequently in the East. In 314, bishops from cities that were under the influence of the church in Antioch gathered in the Galatian city of Ancyra. The council issued twenty-five canons that concerned themselves with a variety of recent problems, such as the discipline of the clergy, the alienation of ecclesiastical property, chastity, bestiality, adultery, murder and magic.[15] As can be seen from this list, the bishops tried to resolve disparate problems that must have been of immediate concern in various Eastern churches. Later councils continued this practice of unsystematic legislation, never attempting to produce a comprehensive set of norms for Christian communities. Between 315 and 319, another council was held at Neocaesarea, a Christian community to the east of Ancyra near the Black Sea. Again no systematic set of norms was produced. The canons covered random subjects. Thus, priests are not allowed to marry after ordination (c. 1), penance is prescribed for bigamy (c. 3), pregnant women are not to be excluded from baptism (c. 6), a minimum age for priests of thirty years is stipulated (c. 11) and the number of deacons in one community is restricted to seven (c. 15).[16] Although these two early Eastern councils were never considered ecumenical, their canons were accepted as normative and were later placed in many canonical collections of the East and West.

After his victory over Licinius in 324, Constantine decided to hold an imperial council in the East to settle the doctrinal controversies raised by the teaching of Arius, a presbyter from Alexandria. Shortly afterwards, in June

13 CCSL 148: 9–13.
14 Hess, *Early development*, 44.
15 P.-P. Joannou, *Discipline générale antique*, 1.2: 56–73.
16 Ibid. 1.2: 75–82.

325, about 250 bishops assembled for Constantine's council in Nicaea, a town in Bithynia. Few Western clergy were present. The council issued not only a creed, but also a synodical letter to the Church of Alexandria and twenty canons.

The twenty canons of the Council of Nicaea eventually became universal norms in the Christian church. Again they seem to treat random subjects, but the focus is on ecclesiastical discipline and the structure and organisation of the church. Eunuchs who voluntarily castrated themselves are excluded from the clergy (c. 1). Rapid promotion of converts in the hierarchy is forbidden, so that catechumens would have a time of testing before being made priests and bishops (c. 2). This rule was later modified to permit newly baptised Christians to be elevated into the clergy in cases of urgent necessity. Bishops, priests and deacons were not permitted to live with women unless they were relatives (c. 3). Clergy could not practise usury (c. 17). Other canons deal with relapsed soldiers (c. 12), the administration of the eucharist to the dying (c. 13), apostasy among the clergy (c. 10) and the laity (c. 11). Canons 4 to 6 envisage a structure for the church that parallels the provincial organisation of the Roman empire. Canon 6 confirms the authority of the bishop of Alexandria over the bishops of Egypt, Libya and Pentapolis and compares Alexandria's prerogatives to Rome's. The bishops and clergy were required to remain in the churches in which they had been ordained (c. 15 and 16). This prohibition against the translation of bishops enforced a norm that permeated the ancient church and became one of the few general canonical rules that was generally respected in the late antique period. Bishops were translated in the early church only rarely. A bishop could never be made pope in the early middle ages because his translation to Rome would have violated the conciliar canon. Of all the norms established by the early church the prohibition against translating bishops is one of the few that the later church completely rejected.

The hierarchical structure of the church characterised by a 'monarchical episcopate' clearly emerges in the canons of Nicaea. A metropolitan bishop was to head each province. He and the bishops of his province would hold synods twice a year to decide matters of ecclesiastical discipline. The synod would be the highest ecclesiastical court of the province (c. 5). Canon 18 established the ranks within the clergy. Bishops and priests were ranked higher than deacons, and this order could not be compromised, especially during liturgical ceremonies like the eucharist.[17]

---

17 Joannou, *Discipline générale antique*, 1.1: 23–41.

During the second half of the fourth century collections of Greek conciliar decrees began to circulate in the East and West.[18] None of the original collections are preserved, but we can know of their contents with some certainty from later collections (even though some of the latter survive only in translation). The oldest collection of conciliar decrees, called the *Corpus canonum Oriente* (*Syntagma Antiochenae* or *Syntagma canonum*), was probably put together in its earliest version *c.* 342–81 in Antioch. It was a chronological collection and the canons of the synods of Ancyra (314), Neocaesarea (314/25), Gangra, Antioch and Laodicea (343–80) were added to it in the early stages of its development. Later the canons of the general Councils of Nicaea (325), Constantinople (381) and Chalcedon (451) were also joined to it.[19] The *Corpus canonum* provided the foundation of all the later Byzantine canonical collections. In the sixth century the collection was supplemented with canons of the Councils of Ephesus (431), Carthage (418) and Serdica (343).

In the West, the oldest collection of conciliar decrees dates to the early fifth century. This collection has not survived but has been reconstructed with the texts of later collections. The *Corpus canonum Africano-Romanum* probably results from a controversy between the African churches and see of Rome that arose when in 417/18 a certain Apiarius, a priest from Proconsular Africa, appealed against his excommunication to Pope Zosimus. The pope decided in his favour and justified his intervention by citing canons of the Council of Nicaea that made Rome the arbiter of appellate cases. The African churches reacted by sharply contesting this right. They requested copies of the authentic Nicene canons from the East. These texts proved that Zosimus cited canons from Serdica (343), not Nicaea.[20] It may have been at this time that the Africans produced a collection of authentic conciliar canons that was sent to Rome where it was revised and expanded a few years later. The *Corpus canonum Africano-Romanum* contained a Latin translation of the Greek *Corpus canonum*, and several texts that put an uncompromising emphasis on the primacy of the Roman see.[21] The Latin and the Greek collections provided later compilers of canonical collections with authoritative texts. As Hamiltion Hess has observed, these collections may have prepared 'the way towards the gradual acceptance of the concept of an ecclesiastical code'.[22]

---

18 Hess, *Early development*, 69–75, discusses the drafting and publication of conciliar decrees.
19 See Schwartz, 'Die Kanonessammlungen der alten Reichskirche'; for the influence of the Antiochene collection among the Oriental churches, see W. Selb, 'Die Kanonessammlungen der orientalischen Kirchen'.
20 Hess, *Early development*, 55–6.
21 Mordek, 'Karthago oder Rom?'
22 Hess, *Early development*, 82.

The first collections of canon law
within Christendom

Until the fourth century the Old and New Testaments, apostolic traditions, real and apocryphal, custom, and synodal and conciliar canons constituted the four main sources of ecclesiastical norms. These sources did not, together or individually, constitute a 'canon law'. Conciliar legislation, for example, was too narrow in its focus and topics to provide the basis for a general body of canon law. During the course of the fourth century, two other sources of authoritative norms emerged in the Christian church: the writings of the fathers of the church and the letters of bishops, particularly the bishops of Rome. In the Eastern church, the 'Canons of the fathers' were recognised as norms some time between 381 and 451 and later were included in canonical collections. They consisted of letters (rescripts) or other writings directed to specific persons by the Eastern fathers. In canon 2 of the Quinisext Council (692), twelve bishops and patriarchs were named as having authoritative force, among them Dionysius of Alexandria (d. 264/5), Peter (d. 311), Athanasius (d. 373) and Cyril (d. 444), archbishops of Alexandria; Basil of Caesarea (d. 379), archbishop of Caesarea in Cappadocia; and Gregory (d. 394), bishop of Nyssa.[23] Basil's 'canonical' *Letters* that he wrote to Amphilochius, bishop of Iconium, were the most important. They were divided up into eighty-five canons and extracted according to topic and then placed into canonical collections.[24] These episcopal letters took their place alongside synodal canons in Eastern canonical collections of the sixth century.

In the Latin West, a parallel development during the fourth and fifth centuries put papal decretal letters on an equal footing with conciliar canons. These letters were the pope's responses to requests for answers to problems of ecclesiastical doctrine, discipline and governance. The form of the requests was based on similar letters (*rescripta*) sent to the Roman emperors on specific questions of law. In the fourth century, bishops in the Western church had begun to turn to Rome for answers to questions about discipline and doctrine. A letter of Pope Siricius (*sed.* 384–99) to Bishop Himerius of Tarragona (modern Saragossa, Spain) is the earliest surviving example of a papal response to a series of questions that originated far from Rome.[25] Himerius had written to Siricius' predecessor, Pope Damasus (*sed.* 366–84). He had posed questions

---

23 Joannou, *Discipline générale antique*, I.1: 120–5.
24 Ibid. II: 92–195; Basil's letters are 188, 199 and 217 in modern editions.
25 For the latest analysis of the complex problem of the 'first' papal decretal with full bibliographical details see D. Jasper and H. Fuhrmann, *Papal letters*, 28–32.

about the validity of baptisms performed by heretics, the rules for bestowing baptism, the treatment of Christians who lapse into paganism and the punishment of monks and nuns who have fornicated. Damasus died before answering Himerius' letter, but Siricius responded soon after he became pope. Clerical celibacy and continence were issues in the Iberian church, and Siricius devoted a long passage to the problem of married priests and deacons who had children with their wives after their ordination. The pope mandated that, whereas priests who would live continently from then on could keep their ecclesiastical offices, those who did not were to be stripped of all their authority and offices.

There are several elements of the letter that would remain characteristic of papal decretals for centuries. Siricius noted that the letter was read aloud before him and other clergy (*in conventu fratrum sollicitius legeremus*) and implied that he discussed the problems posed by Himerius openly with his clergy. Papal consultation with his curia would become a standard practice in the papal curia. By the twelfth century, popes began to render decisions regularly with the phrase, 'with the advice of our brothers [the cardinals] we ought to ordain' (*de consilio fratrum nostrorum debemus statuere* – Pope Alexander III [*sed.* 1159–81]) or, as Pope Innocent III (*sed.* 1198–1216) established the formula for future papal decretals, 'with the advice of our brothers we are led to respond' (*de consilio fratrum nostrorum taliter in hujusmodi duximus respondendum*). The validity and authority of a papal decretal were based on the prestige and primacy of the bishop of Rome and the support of the Roman Christian community. In Siricius' time the community was represented by the *conventus fratrum*; by the time of Innocent III, the community was represented by the College of Cardinals.

At the end of the decretal Pope Siricius asked Himerius to forward the decretal letter to all his fellow bishops on the Iberian peninsula. Even at this early date, the pope conceived of his letter as establishing authoritative norms for regions far beyond Rome. Almost immediately collections of papal letters began to circulate in the Western church. Eight papal decretals formed the core of these early collections.[26] Siricius' letter was followed by letters from Popes Innocent I, Zosimus and Celestine. Although we have no manuscript that contains only this small collection, Pope Leo I quite likely referred to such a collection in one of his letters.[27] Consequently, papal decretal letters took their place among conciliar canons as sources of norms for the Christian church.

---

26 Jasper and Fuhrmann, *Papal Letters*, 22–6.
27 P. Jaffé, ed., *Regesta pontificum romanorum*, JK 402.

The fifth century was marked by the gradual acceptance of the Eastern conciliar canons in Rome. Latin translations were made of the canons of the Greek councils, and they began to circulate widely as authoritative texts. By the pontificate of Pope Gelasius I (492–96), the sources of canonical norms in the West were widely scattered in different languages and codices. For the first time, attempts were made to compile a collection of canonical texts. The most famous of these was made by a learned Greek, Dionysius Exiguus, who arrived in Rome at the end of the century. Since he was fluent in both Latin and Greek, his first task was to provide fresh and accurate translations for the texts of the Greek councils. He produced at least two translations of the conciliar canons of the Greek churches and published them in three versions, the third version known only indirectly from one manuscript. Taking as his basis the old Greek *Corpus canonum* (as mentioned above) and adding the Canons of the apostles and canons and correspondence relating to the Council of Carthage (419), Dionysius arranged the text chronologically and supplied an index ordered according to subject matter that facilitated consultation.[28] In the third and final version of his collection of canons, commissioned by Pope Hormisdas (*sed.* 514–23), Dionysius placed Greek and Latin versions of the texts in the book so that readers could compare them. This collection is no longer extant. He also compiled a collection of forty-one papal decretals that presented decretal letters from Pope Siricius (*sed.* 384–99) to Pope Anastasius II (*sed.* 496–8) in chronological order.

Both the early versions of the collections of conciliar canons and his collection of decretals were probably composed during the so-called 'Laurentian schism' that deeply divided the Roman church. Dionysius ultimately combined these two works in a *corpus canonum* that scholars have given the name *Collectio Dionysiana*. It was not an official collection of canonical norms – private collections would remain the only vehicles for preserving and disseminating canonical texts until the thirteenth century – but it circulated widely. Thirty-four manuscripts of the collection (a remarkably high number) still exist in European libraries. Later canonists supplemented the *Collectio Dionysiana*. Even more importantly, Pope Hadrian I (*sed.* 772–95) sent an augmented copy of the *Collectio Dionysiana* to Charlemagne that is known as the *Collectio Dionysiana-Hadriana*. Although other collections of canonical texts were also used in the Carolingian period, the *Dionysiana-Hadriana* enjoyed enormous popularity in Northern Europe from the ninth to the eleventh

---

28 Dionysius' first collection is edited by A. Strewe, *Die Canonessammlung*. The second is only available in G. Voellus and H. Justellus, *Biblioteca iuris canonice veteris*, I: 101–74 (councils) and 183–248 (decretals).

centuries. More than one hundred manuscripts of the work have been found to date. Dionysius Exiguus established the canons of the fourth-century Eastern Greek councils and papal decretals as the foundation of Western Latin canon law.

An Italian cleric named Cresconius built on the work of Dionysius by composing a canonical collection probably in the sixth century – the date is not quite certain. In contrast to Dionysius' chronological organisation, Cresconius produced one of the first collections that adopted a systematic arrangement. In this case, the collection was arranged according to 300 topics.[29] As he tells us in his preface addressed to a certain Bishop Liberinus (who had commissioned the collection), the aim of his work was practical. His systematic arrangement aimed to make ecclesiastical law accessible, not only for the ignorant and for pupils, but also for those judges (probably bishops) who sat in judgment. He began and ended with the sacrament of ordination, but in between he covered marriage, clerical discipline and other subjects. To facilitate access to the material, he prefaced his collection with an index that listed the topics and the sources. Cresconius called his collection a 'Concord of conciliar canons' (Concordia canonum conciliorum). He brought concord to his collection by arranging and indexing them. However, Cresconius was only moderately successful in reducing the complex norms found in the canons of councils and papal letters to a few fundamental topics.[30] Five centuries later another canonist, Gratian of Bologna, would attempt to bring concord to canon law systematically. In Cresconius' time the law was too young and the sources were too limited to require him to reconcile conflicting opinions and texts. There were not yet significant conflicts with which he must struggle.

Canonical collections originated in various Western Christianities. The Iberian peninsula and the Roman province of Gaul were particularly productive in this respect. These regions were important centres of late antique Roman learning and culture. We have information about church councils in the Iberian peninsula during the fifth, sixth and seventh centuries. The canons issued by these councils were collected and added to the received texts of the Eastern councils. The most important collection of this extensive and frequent legislative activity was the Collectio Hispana.[31] Although sometimes attributed to

---

29 K. Zechiel-Eckes, Die Concordia canonum; on the preface of Cresconius, see the translation and interpretation of Robert Somerville and Bruce C. Brasington, Prefaces to canon law books.

30 Zechiel-Eckes, Die Concordia canonum, 50–65.

31 Eds. G. Martínez Díez and F. Rodríguez, La colección canónica Hispana.

Isidore of Seville, the earliest version was compiled by an anonymous canonist in the first half of the seventh century (mostly likely between 633 and 636). It circulated widely in Europe but especially in France and northern Italy. After the Arab invasion of 711 the collection was even translated into Arabic and remained important for the Iberian church in various recensions. It remained a significant collection until the twelfth century, surviving in many manuscript copies. The *Collectio Hispana* influenced canonical collections in the Carolingian realm. It was based on the scholarship of earlier authors, such as the small collection prepared by Archbishop Martin of Braga (d. 580). He compiled a collection of canons that drew on the canons of Eastern councils and was divided into two subject areas: canons that dealt with the clergy and those that covered the laity.[32]

In Gaul, the bishops of Arles and others in southern Gaul also held many church councils. Arles became the most important Roman city in southern Gaul: during 395, the emperors moved the seat of the praetorian prefect from Trier to Arles and, in the first quarter of the fifth century, Arles developed into the administrative capital of Gaul.[33] A series of able bishops transformed the city into a powerful ecclesiastical centre.[34] The canons of these Gallic councils were collected and augmented by other councils and decretals. The most important of the Gallican collections was the *Collectio vetus Gallica*.[35] It was compiled in the early seventh century, probably in the vicinity of Lyon. Although the authorship is uncertain, the collection may be the work of Etherius, bishop of Lyon. Like Cresconius' *Concordia canonum conciliorum*, this collection was topically arranged, but, even though it was copied and used in lands north of the Alps, it circulated far less widely than the *Dionysiana* or Cresconius' *Concordia canonum conciliorum*. Etherius' chief concerns were the holding of synods, clerical discipline, the rights of metropolitan bishops, and the protection of ecclesiastical property.

After the sixth century the compilers of canonical collections began to include local synods in their collections. The significance of this development was that the canons of obscure synods eventually found their way into Gratian's *Decretum* and other standard collections of the high middle ages. The canonists became accustomed to using a wide range of sources when dealing with canonical problems.

---

32 See Ferme, *Introduzione*, 96 and C. W. Barlow, ed., *Martini episcopi Bracarensis opera omnia*.
33 W. E. Klingshirn, *Caesarius of Arles*, 53–4.
34 The evidence for Arles's importance as a centre for canon law is discussed by Jasper and Furhmann, *Papal letters* 32–3.
35 Hubert Mordek, *Kirchenrecht und Reform*.

Greek canonical collections

About fifty years after Dionysius worked in Rome, a priest from Antioch, John Scholasticus, gathered canonical texts into a new collection called the *Collectio L titulorum.*[36] John drew upon an earlier collection that is now lost, the *Collectio LX titulorum.* His principal sources were the established tradition of Greek conciliar canons from the early Councils of Nicaea, Ancyra and Gangra, to the later Councils of Constantinople I and Chalcedon. This part of the collection was very similar to Dionysius'. John added texts, however, to his collection from the writings of an Eastern church father, Basil of Caesarea, that were not yet accepted as canonical in the West. John divided two of the so-called 'canonical letters' of Basil (*Letters* 199 and 217) into sixty-eight chapters and arranged them systematically according to subject matter. All of this material John placed under fifty titles that began with the honour due to the patriarch (title one) and ended with a title that dealt with the canon of prayers and the date of Easter (title fifty). John Scholasticus' *Synagoge of 50 titles* occupies a position in the Eastern church similar to that of Dionysius Exiguus' collection in the West. It is the oldest and first important collection of canon law in the East. It was a private collection, but all later Greek canonical collections were based on it or used it as a source. Dionysius introduced papal letters as a source of canonical norms equal to conciliar canons; John established the writings of the church fathers (primarily the Eastern church fathers) as authoritative sources in canonical collections. Later the Third Council of Constantinople (*in Trullo*) of 692 decreed that the writings of Eastern church fathers had juridical authority equal to conciliar canons. John also drew from imperial legislation. When Justinian had compiled his great codification (533–4), he included legislation governing church government and clerical discipline at the beginning of his Codex. Further, after promulgating his *Corpus iuris civilis*, he produced extensive legislation that dealt with ecclesiastical matters in his *Novellae*. John Scholasticus 'canonised' this material by producing a collection of eighty-seven excerpts from Justinian's *Novellae*, the so-called *Collectio LXXXVII titulorum*. Since John Scholasticus was patriarch of Constantinople (565–77), his office gave his collection prestige and authority in the Greek church. Three hundred years later, St Methodios translated John's *Synagoge* into Slavonic. It then became the text upon which the Slavonic and Russian churches based their legal systems.

---

36 V. N. Benesevic, ed., *Ioannis Scolastici Synagoga*; see also E. Schwartz, *Die Kanonessammlung des Johannes Scholastikos*.

Western canonists also began to include patristic writings into canonical collections during the sixth century. It is only in the course of the ninth century that Western collections began to include fragments of Roman law, but these texts mainly dealt with procedural law. Consequently, by *c.* 900 all the sources for Eastern and Western canon law were the same to a greater or lesser extent – with the significant exception that papal letters were not recognised as authoritative in the East. The contentious issue of papal primacy can be clearly detected in the canonists' choices of sources in the Latin and Greek canonical collections of the early middle ages. This tension would be resolved only with the Schism of the Latin and Greek churches in 1054.

Bibliography

OLDER HISTORIES OF CANON LAW AND REFERENCE WORKS

Dictionnaire de droit canonique, 7 vols. (Paris, 1924–65)

García y García, Antonio. *Historia del derecho canónico, 1: El primer milenio* (Salamanca, 1967)

Gaudemet, Jean and Gabriel Le Bras, eds. *Histoire du droit et des institutions de l'église en occident:*

Vol. I: Gabriel Le Bras. *Prolégomènes* (Paris, 1955)

Vol. II: Jean Dauvillier. *Les temps apostoliques: Ier siècle* (Paris, 1970)

Vol. III: Jean Gaudemet. *L'église dans l'empire romain: IVᵉ–Vᵉ siècles* (Paris, 1958)

Jaffé, P., ed. *Regesta pontificum romanorum* (Leipzig, 1885–8 reprint Graz, 1956)

Maassen, Frederick. *Geschichte der Quellen und Literatur des canonischen Rechts im Abendland, 1; Die Rechtssammlungen bis zur Mitte des 9. Jahrhunderts* (Graz, 1870; reprinted, 1965)

Stickler, A. M. *Historia iuris canonici latini, 1: Historia fontium* (Turin, 1950)

Van Hove, A. *Prolegomena. Commentarium Lovaniense in Codicem iuris canonici* (Malines/Rome, 1945²)

RECENT GENERAL HISTORIES OF EARLY CANON LAW

Brundage, James A. *Medieval canon law. The medieval world* (London, 1995)

Erdö, Péter. *Storia della scienza del diritto canonico: Una introduzione* (Rome, 2000)

Ferme, Brian Edwin. *Introduzione alla storia del diritto canonico: 1: Il diritto antico fino al decretum di Graziano*, Quaderni di Apollinaris 1 (Mursia, 1998)

Gallagher, Clarence. *Church law and church order in Rome and Byzantium: A comparative study*, Birmingham Byzantine and Ottoman Monographs 8 (Aldershot, 2002)

Gaudemet, Jean, *Sources du droit de l'église en occident du IIᵉ au VIIᵉ siècle* (Paris, 1985) *Sources du droit de l'église en occident du VIIIᵉ au XXᵉ siècle: Repères canoniques, sources occidentales* (Paris, 1993)

Kéry, Lotte. *Canonical collections of the early middle ages (ca. 400–1140): A bibliographical guide to the manuscripts and literature*, History of Medieval Canon Law (Washington, DC, 1999)

The growth of church law

Larrainzar, Carlos. *Introducción al derecho canónico*, Instituto de Derecho Europeo Clásico, serie B: monografías (Santa Cruz de Tenerife, 1991)

Reynolds, Roger. 'Law, canon: To Gratian', *Dictionary of the middle ages* (New York, 1986), VII: 395–413

Van de Wiel, Constant. *History of canon law*, Louvain Theological and Pastoral Monographs 5 (Louvain, 1991)

SELECTED SPECIALISED STUDIES AND SOURCES

Aimone, P. V. 'Le falsificazioni simmachiane', *Apollinaris* 68 (1995): 205–20

Apostolic constitutions (SC 320, 329, 336)

Barlow, C. W., ed. *Martini episcopi Bracarensis opera omnia* (New Haven, 1950)

Benesevic, V. N., ed. *Ioannis Scolastici Synagoga L titulorum* (Munich, 1937)

Collins, Raymond F. 'The origins of church law', *The jurist* 61 (2001): 134–56

Concilia Africae a.345–a.525 (CCSL 149)

Concilia Galliae a.314–a.506 (CCSL 148)

Concilia Galliae a.511–a.695 (CCSL 148a)

Connolly, R. H., ed. *Didascalia apostolorum. The Syriac version translated and accompanied by the Latin Verona fragments* (Oxford, 1929; reprint, 1969)

Cyprian. *Letters* (CSEL 3²)

Didache (SC 248)

Dix, G. and H. Chadwick, eds. *The Treatise on the apostolic tradition of St. Hippolytus of Rome* (London, 1992³)

Gauthier, A., O.P. *Roman law and its contribution to the development of canon law* (Ottawa, 1996)

Hess, Hamilton. *The early development of canon law and the Council of Serdica* (Oxford, 2002)

Humfress, Caroline. 'Advocates', 'Defensor ecclesiae', 'Heretics, laws on', 'Law courts' and 'Law schools', in G. W. Bowersock, P. Brown and O. Grabar, eds., *Late antiquity: A guide to the postclassical world* (Cambridge, MA, 1999): 277–8; 405–6; 490–1; 540–1

'A new legal cosmos: Late Roman lawyers and the early medieval church', in P. Linehan, and J. Nelson, eds., *The medieval world* (London, 2001), 557–73

Jasper, Detlev and Horst Fuhrmann. *Papal letters in the early middle ages. History of medieval canon law* (Washington, DC, 2001)

Joannou, P. P., ed. *Discipline générale antique (IVᵉ–IXᵉ s.)* (Rome, 1962–3)

Klingshirn, W. E. *Caesarius of Arles. The making of a Christian community in late antique Gaul* (Cambridge, 2004)

Martínez Díez, G. and F. Rodríguez, eds. *La colección canónica Hispana* (Madrid, 1966–92)

Mordek, Hubert. 'Karthago oder Rom? Zu den Anfängen der kirchlichen Rechtsquellen im Abendland', in R. J. Cardinal Castillo Lara. *Studia in honorem Eminentissimi Cardinalis Alfonsi M. Stickler*, Studia et Textus Historiae Iuris Canonici 7 (Rome, 1992), 359–74

Kirchenrecht und Reform im Frankenreich: Die Collectio Vetus Vallica, die älteste systematische Kanonessammlung des fränkischen Gallien: Studien und Edition, Beiträge zur Geschichte und Quellen des Mittelalters 1 (Berlin, 1975)

Ohme, H. *Kanon ekklesiastikos*, Arbeiten zur Kirchengeschichte 67 (Berlin, 1998)

Schwartz, E. 'Die Kanonessammlungen der alten Reichskirche', in *Gesammelte Schriften* (Berlin, 1960), IV: 177–205

Die Kanonessammlung des Johannes Scholastikos, Sitzungsberichte der Bayerischen Akademie der Wissenschaften (Munich, 1933)

Selb, W. 'Die Kanonessammlungen der orientalischen Kirchen und das griechische Corpus canonum der Reichskirche', in H. Lentze and I. Gampl, eds., *Speculum iuris et ecclesiarum: Festschrift für Willibald M. Plöchl zum 60. Geburtstag* (Vienna, 1967), 371–83

Sieben, H. J. *Die Konzilsidee in der alten Kirche*, Konziliengeschichte, Reihe B (Paderborn, 1979)

Siricius. *Letter to Himerius of Tarragona* (PL 13: 1131–47)

Somerville, Robert and Bruce C. Brasington. *Prefaces to canon law books in Latin Christianity: Selected translations, 500–1245* (New Haven, 1998)

Strewe, A., ed. *Die Canonessammlung des Dionysius Exiguus in der ersten Redaktion*, Arbeiten zur Kirchengeschichte 16 (Berlin 1931)

Tertullian. *De jejunio* (CCSL 2)

Voellus, G. and H. Justellus. *Biblioteca iuris canonice veteris* (Paris, 1661)

Zechiel-Eckes, Klaus. *Die Concordia canonum des Cresconius*, Freiburger Beiträge zur mittelalterlichen Geschichte 5 (Frankfurt am Main, 1992)

17

The church, society and political power

H. A. DRAKE

Near the beginning of the period covered by this volume, Bishop Eusebius of Caesarea, the celebrated 'father of church history', composed two addresses in which he praised the accomplishments of Constantine's reign. Toward its end, another Christian clergyman, the deacon Agapetus, addressed a series of aphorisms on kingship to the emperor Justinian.[1] The two works serve as a convenient means to bracket the monumental changes that the church underwent during these centuries as it moved from the periphery to the centre of Roman social and political, as well as religious, thought. This is a story traditionally told in terms of Christianity's 'innate intolerance' and imperial 'Caesaropapism', explaining at once the ruthless suppression of traditional religions that accompanied this movement and the intrusion of the state into the domain of the church. But these are concepts that (to borrow words coined for a vastly different situation) have by now outlived their uselessness. The writings of Eusebius and Agapetus open the way to a more complex, but also far more interesting, story, one that involves questions of imperial ideology, Christian identity, and demographic disruptions whose impact we have only recently come to appreciate.

The heavenly icon

The first of Eusebius' two writings was a speech, 'On the Holy Sepulchre', composed for the eight-day Encaenia ceremony celebrating the dedication of Constantine's magnificent Church of the Holy Sepulchre in Jerusalem in September 335.[2] Ostensibly a reply to critics who thought the structure a waste

---

1 *Agapetos Diakonos*, ed. and trans. Riedinger; about half of the text is translated in E. Barker, *Social and political thought in Byzantium*, 54–61.
2 The speech, which I have labelled *De sepulchro Christi*, comes down mingled with the text of Eusebius' *Laus Constantini* (hereafter, *LC*), where it appears as chs. 11–18. (To avoid confusion, I have retained the traditional numbering.) In the form we have it, the speech may include modifications Eusebius made when he repeated it for Constantine two

of imperial resources and 'frankly demeaning', the speech is primarily a lengthy justification of the incarnation. In ch. 11, Eusebius sets out to demonstrate the many benefits that Christianity had produced. Previously, he declaims, the human race had been beset by war, conflict and disunity, but now the whole world is united in peace under a single ruler and a single god. This was no accident, so far as Eusebius was concerned. As part of God's plan, 'two great powers – the Roman Empire, which became a monarchy at that time, and the teaching of Christ – proceeding as if from a single starting point, at once tamed and reconciled all to friendship. Thus each blossomed at the same time and place as the other' (ch. 16.5–6).

The seeds planted by this idea of a joint mission of Rome and Christianity took fruit in the second of Eusebius' orations, which he delivered in the summer of 336 as part of the closing ceremonies of Constantine's Thirtieth Jubilee year. Here Eusebius put forward the idea that the empire was not merely a part of God's plan but indeed an earthly reflection of that heavenly kingdom over which the emperor ruled in imitation of the divine King: 'Thus outfitted in the likeness of the kingdom of heaven, he pilots affairs below with an upward gaze, to steer by the archetypal form' (ch. 3.5). After a long series of comparisons (ch. 2), in which he equates the actions of the Logos in the heavenly sphere with those of Constantine in the earthly sphere, Eusebius proclaims that the emperor – to whom he refers repeatedly as 'God's friend' – 'has modelled the kingdom on earth into a likeness of the one in heaven'.[3]

Two centuries later, little seemingly had changed. Agapetus testified to the continued significance of this theme by using it to begin his advice to Justinian, written some time between Justinian's accession in 527 and the death of Theodora in 548. From his opening words, in which he compares 'the sceptre of earthly power' to 'the likeness of the heavenly kingdom', the theme of a close relationship between emperor and deity is woven through the seventy-two headings under which Agapetus catalogued his advice, which echoed through the centuries of Byzantine rule.[4] The emperor is a 'divinely

---

months later in Constantinople. The text of both speeches is GCS 7 (= Eusebius Werke, 1), 195–259. Translations are from H. A. Drake, In praise of Constantine. On the date and circumstances, see Drake, In praise of Constantine, 40–3; T. D. Barnes, 'Two speeches by Eusebius'; P. Maraval, Eusèbe de Césarée, la théologie politique de l'empire chrétien, 29–36.

3 Eusebius, LC 4.4. For the emperor as God's φιλός see, e.g., LC 1.6, 2.1, 2.2, 2.3, 2.4, 5.1, 5.4. In the Praeparatio evangelica, written about twenty years earlier, Eusebius uses the phrase φιλός τῷ θεῷ to describe the earliest Hebrews. See, e.g., PE 7.4, 8. These men had no need of religious legislation because their souls were naturally pure: PE 7.5–6.

4 Agapetus, Ekthesis, cap. 1. On the date, see Patrick Henry III, 'A mirror for Justinian', 283. On Agapetus' influence, see I. Ševčenko, 'Agapetus East and West'.

made image (ἄγαλμα) of piety' (5) who, 'in the authority attached to his dignity', is 'like God' (21). He is the eye of the world (46), a luminary like the sun (51), who has 'received the sceptre of kingship from God' (61). Such phrases seem amply to confirm the subservient role that Western scholars once assumed was the lot of Eastern Christians, a condition summed up by the label of 'Caesaropapism'. But this is a conclusion that can only be reached by ignoring the religious nature of the ancient state, and even more the late antique world's particular understanding of that state.

In 'Caesaropapism' there are two distinct entities, a secular state and a spiritual church, each with its own defined sphere of authority. The problem arises when the secular ruler, Caesar, asserts authority over the church, acting thus like a pope. But just as the term 'Caesaropapism' is modern, so too is the distinction between church and state. The ancient state was always itself a religious institution, and a chief duty of all ancient rulers in whatever kind of polity was to maintain the goodwill of divinity.[5] If there was one thing on which pagans and Christians agreed, it was that such goodwill was the single most important factor in determining the successful outcome of an event. Never was this more so than in the late empire, when for a variety of reasons imperial legitimacy came increasingly to be associated with the favour of a divine ally, or *comes*.[6]

The significance of this easily overlooked difference between ancient and modern states is that divisions that come so readily to the modern mind – between 'religious' and 'political' office, for instance, or between 'church' and 'state' – would have been meaningless to an ancient one. The same officials who discharged what today we would call secular duties were also responsible for maintaining the goodwill of the gods. These were (it goes without saying) the gods of the state – deities conceived as having a special relationship with one's particular polity.[7] When Augustus, the first of the Roman emperors, assumed the title of *pontifex maximus*, he – and his successors – also assumed primary responsibility for maintaining this relationship with the divine. There was, thus, a sanctity attached to the office of emperor that cannot be lightly discounted when considering the relationship Christians had with the empire – after Constantine as well as before him.

5 The earliest citation recorded in the *Oxford English Dictionary* is to an article in the *Edinburgh review* for April 1890, in which the author uses the term in reference to the rule of Justinian. See further G. Dagron, *Emperor and priest*, ch. 9.
6 A. D. Nock, 'The emperor's divine *comes*'; see further H. A. Drake, *Constantine and the bishops*, ch. 3.
7 S. R. F. Price, 'Between man and God'; R. Gordon, 'Religion in the Roman empire'.

This sanctity was, if anything, only enhanced by the consensus in political theory that had developed in late antiquity. Whereas classical political analysis divided government into three basic types (democracy, aristocracy, monarchy) and their corrupt counterparts (ochlocracy, oligarchy, tyranny), by late antiquity a sole ruler had prevailed for hundreds of years in the West, and even longer in the East. Monarchy, accordingly, was considered the only viable form of government.[8] Alternatives, if they were considered at all, were used only in negative contrast to the benefits of monarchy. Eusebius, for instance, confidently asserts in his oration that 'Monarchy excels all other kinds of constitution and government,' deriding 'a polyarchy based on equality' as the cause of anarchy and civil war (LC 3.6). In a bit of vintage Constantinian reasoning, the first Christian emperor echoed these sentiments when he defended his choice of monotheism by pointing to the lack of a clear chain of command in polytheism: 'To which one should prayers and entreaties be made first, and which last?' he asks.

> How could I cultivate one especially without dishonouring the others? If I gave thanks to one for granting some earthly favour, I would cast aspersions on the one who opposed it. From which one should I expect to learn the cause of a crisis and how to resolve it? Or suppose that a response had been given us through revelations or oracles but it was not within their power and belonged to a different god . . . Wrath and strife and recriminations would ensue, and through greed no one would be content with his own lot or station until there was complete and utter confusion.[9]

Polytheism brought discord. Only monotheism could create unity and concord on earth to mirror the unity and concord of the heavenly realm.

Because of this consensus, late antique thinkers focused not on the variety of constitutions, but on the variety of rulers. The virtue of the monarch was all-important, for it was by means of this virtue that he maintained that bond with the divine that was so essential to successful rule. One strand of political thought that Rome inherited from the monarchies of the Hellenistic world held that the ruler's duty was to appear to his subjects as a likeness, or εἰκών, of the heavenly kingdom; indeed, true rulers could be distinguished from false by the degree to which they inspired virtue in their subjects. As one such tract put it, 'merely to look upon a good king ought to affect the souls of

---

8 Discussed from various aspects in Emma Gannagé et al., eds., *The Greek strand in Islamic political thought*. See further G. Fowden, *Empire to commonwealth*; A. Al-Azmeh, *Muslim kingship*.

9 From the speech known as 'The oration to the saints' (*Oratio ad sanctorum coetum*), 3.3–4 (GCS – Eusebius Werke, I: 156–7).

those who watch him no less than a flute or harmony could do'.[10] These iconic
qualities made the virtues of the emperor the most significant factor in political
analysis, and speeches in praise of emperors a means of engaging in political
dialogue.[11] The content of these virtues varied little over the centuries: just as
a golden shield was dedicated by the senate to the first emperor, Augustus,
virtutis clementiaeque iustitiae et pietatis causa, so orators three centuries later
continued to praise imperial bravery, clemency, justice and piety, as well as
such other desirable virtues as benevolence, magnanimity and foresight. But
while a bland similarity prevailed on the surface of these orations, a skilful
orator could juggle the virtues or flesh them out in ways that sent important
signals about a given ruler's abilities and policies.[12]

Thus, although the emperor might have been in heaven, the devil (as is often
so) lay in the details.

The Christian emperor

One key to a proper understanding of the rhetoric of Eusebius and Agapetus
is to realise that the ancient state was always a religious institution. Another is
to learn how to give advice and warning in an autocracy. Though the modern
ear is inclined to hear no more than vain adulation in their speeches, those
wise in the ways of autocracy know that such praise can be as much a means
of control as can criticism, and is frequently more effective. Being reminded
of the standard criteria for a good king just might lead an erring monarch
to mend his ways; even if not, the ceremonial act of listening to such advice
had the effect of publicly committing him to acknowledge those criteria. That
is one reason for reading these speeches, despite their jejune appearance, as
records of power being negotiated. Another is because of the way Christian

10 From a tract attributed to the Hellenistic thinker Diotogenes, quoted in Stobaeus,
Anthologium 4.7.62 (eds. Wachsmuth and Hense, IV: 265–70); trans. E. Barker, *From Alexander to Constantine*, 366. See also G. F. Chesnut, *The first Christian histories*, ch. 7. Dated,
but still useful, is E. R. Goodenough, 'The political philosophy of Hellenistic kingship'.
On authenticity, see H. Thesleff, 'On the problem of the Doric Pseudopythagorica'; L.
Delatte, *Les traités de la royauté*.
11 Averil Cameron, *Christianity and the rhetoric of empire*, 129.
12 For a handbook from late antiquity, see D. A. Russell and N. G. Wilson, eds. and
trans., *Menander Rhetor*. For recent studies, see R. M. Errington, 'Themistius and his
emperors'; M. Whitby, ed., *The propaganda of power*; D. Felton, 'Advice to tyrants'. Still
useful are Lester K. Born, 'The perfect prince according to the Latin panegyrists' and
M. P. Charlesworth, 'The virtues of a Roman emperor'. On the questionable existence
of a 'canon' of virtues, see A. Wallace-Hadrill, 'The emperor and his virtues'. For the
wording on Augustus's shield, see Robert S. Rogers et al., eds., *Caesaris Augusti Res gestae
et Fragmenta*, cap. 34.

speakers like Eusebius and Agapetus redeployed and redefined the standard virtues.

When Eusebius proclaimed, for instance, at *LC* 5.4 that Constantine had been 'furnished by God with natural virtues' that made him 'perfectly wise, good, just, courageous, pious and god-loving' (ἀποτελεσθεὶς σώφρων, ἀγαθός, δίκαιος, ἀνδρεῖος, εὐσεβής, φιλόθεος) – that made him, in fact, 'a philosopher-king' (φιλόσοφος βασιλεὺς) – he was clearly drawing on standard watchwords of Hellenistic kingship, in this case throwing in as well a reference to Plato's by now proverbial definition of an ideal ruler. But as Eusebius develops these standard themes a new emphasis emerges: *pietas* (εὐσέβεια) is now the central virtue.[13] Constantine, Eusebius says, is a 'high-minded sovereign, learned in divine matters', who 'pursues things higher than his present life' and does 'all things with piety' (πάντα τε σὺν εὐσεβείᾳ πράττων).[14] In classical times, *pietas* meant doing one's duty to men and gods; here, it has a more restricted sense, one more familiar to modern ears. Constantine's piety leads him to offer 'his subjects, just as if they were students of a good teacher, the holy knowledge of the Supreme Sovereign' (*LC* 5.8). Piety is the basis for the special relationship between the emperor and the divine: it is because of his piety, Eusebius says, that Constantine has been permitted the thirty years of rule now being celebrated (*LC* 2.5). Piety is what makes the emperor a 'friend of God'.

In their emphasis on piety, both speeches represent a subtle transaction between speaker and listener. For with his words of praise, Eusebius also delineates a code of behaviour that the emperor is expected to live up to: 'For he who would bear the title of sovereign with true reason has patterned regal virtues in his soul after the model of that distant kingdom' (*LC* 5.2). The emperor is expected not only to lead his subjects to God, but also to proclaim 'laws of genuine piety' (*LC* 5.8). To bring home the message, Eusebius contrasts such genuine sovereignty with its opposite, bluntly warning that

> one who has alienated himself from these virtues and who has denied the Universal Sovereign, who has neither acknowledged the Heavenly Father of souls nor adopted a decorum proper to a sovereign, but who has instead taken into his soul the chaotic and shameful and traded for regal kindness the spirit of a wild beast; . . . one who has surrendered himself to these, even if on occasion he be considered to rule by despotic power, at no time will he hold the title of sovereign with true reason. (*LC* 5.2)

---

13 Chesnut, *The first Christian histories*, ch. 10.
14 *LC* 5.8; see also his 'abundance of piety' (εὐσεβείας ὑπερβολῇ, *LC* 7.12).

Two centuries later, Agapetus had similar words for Justinian:

> Know, O divinely wrought image of piety, that by however much you are deemed worthy by God of great gifts, by that much more are you obligated to make a fitting return to Him. (cap. 5)

> Since you have received the sceptre of kingship from God, take thought how you may repay the one who has given you this gift; just as you have been preferred by Him before all men, so you should be eager to honour Him above all. (cap. 61)

The sting in these admonitions lies in the unspoken issue of who will judge whether or not laws are 'pious', and what the reaction will be to laws deemed 'impious'. Even more than the new emphasis on piety itself, this implicit threat is what makes Eusebius and Agapetus stand apart from classical works in this genre. By the fourth century, pagan emperors needed to demonstrate these divine ties as much as a Christian like Constantine would.[15] Even if the emperor were, in fact, a brute, the genre – which came to be known as *speculum principis* – permitted speakers to praise his sense of honour and love of learning, in the hope that by their holding such a mirror up to him the ruler would learn to perceive his own features there. Pagan orators could also warn about the evils that accompanied misrule. The difference in this case was one of enforcement. The artists and intellectuals who delivered such speeches to pagan emperors represented an extremely important community – the elites on whose support emperors depended to keep order established and taxes flowing – but one that had little recourse if the intended recipient chose not to follow their advice. Pliny the Younger, author of a paradigmatic speech delivered to one of the traditional 'good emperors', boasted at length of the liberty of the senate under Trajan and that emperor's deference to their opinions, but when it came to saying what would happen to emperors who were less well behaved, the most Pliny could muster was a warning that they would be sorry after they died.[16]

Such toothless sanctions were worse than no sanctions at all, and that is undoubtedly why so many such orators chose instead to dwell on the positive results that would follow from obeying their advice. But Eusebius was a bishop and Agapetus a deacon. Both represented an institution, the Christian church, with an identity akin to that of the Roman senate. It only takes a moment's reflection to see that the judgment of emperors – the decision as to whether

---

15 Nock, 'The emperor's divine *comes*', 114; G. F. Chesnut, 'The ruler and the Logos'.
16 Pliny the Younger, *Panegyricus* 53.5 (trans. Radice): 'there will be neither time nor place for the shades of disastrous rulers to rest in peace from the execrations of posterity'.

they were to be remembered as heavenly icons or wild beasts – now lay with the clergy. Moreover, Christianity's unique development in the first centuries of its existence had left this institution with a capacity for acting and behaving independently such as senators had not known since the closing days of the republic, and Constantine's settlement had endowed the clergy with both the legitimating authority that had made the senate an important partner in the principate and patronage resources that rivalled, and eventually supplanted, those of the traditional elites.[17] Increasingly during this period, bishops also assumed civic duties that neither local elites nor (especially in the West) imperial administrators were able to discharge. Implicit in Eusebius and Agapetus' exhortations, therefore, was the warning that an emperor who did not live up to them ran the risk of alienating a constituency that could, and would, withdraw its support. In effect, as T. D. Barnes has put it, 'By the end of the fourth century Christian orthodoxy had been added to the traditional list of virtues required in a legitimate emperor.'[18]

This dissonance in imperial and episcopal thinking about their relationship is the common denominator beneath two explosive confrontations that occurred within twenty years of each other at the turn of the fifth century. The first followed in the wake of a disastrous conflict between the army of Theodosius the Great and the citizens of Thessalonica in 390 that resulted in a wholesale slaughter of innocent civilians.[19] As the story came to be told, Ambrose placed himself between Theodosius and the entry to the church in Milan, refusing the emperor admittance until he humbled himself through a very public act of penance. Fourteen years later, Constantinople's bishop, the fiery John Chrysostom, engaged in a similar test of will with the empress Eudokia, but in this case the result was his exile and eventual death. Because of their different outcomes, the two incidents came to be used as exemplars for the independence of Western Christianity and the subservience of its Eastern counterpart. But this is a very selective reading, one that ignores significant contingencies. In the Western conflict, for instance, Ambrose could rely on a unified clergy and a congregation whose loyalty had been forged in decades of significant encounters, whereas Theodosius, hundreds of miles from his permanent court at Constantinople, was definitely the outsider, and

---

17 See P. Brown, *Poverty and leadership*; C. Lepelley, 'Le patronat épiscopal'; R. Lizzi, 'The bishop, *vir venerabilis*'.
18 T. D. Barnes, *Athanasius and Constantius*, 174.
19 The numbers vary, and even the most commonly accepted figure of 5,000 should be viewed with suspicion. See N. McLynn, *Ambrose of Milan*, 315–23; Daniel Washburn, 'The Thessalonian affair'.

accordingly more vulnerable to the type of challenge that Ambrose posed. Even so, modern scholars are inclined to see mutual advantage as the reason for the success of Ambrose's bold move, which actually provided Theodosius with an opportunity to put behind him a particularly damaging incident in a way that restored confidence in his rule.[20] Conversely, in Constantinople Chrysostom faced precisely the imperial establishment that Ambrose could ignore, as well as a divided clergy whose opposition was led by the formidable bishop of Alexandria. In spite of these obstacles, he was able to score brilliant successes in asserting ecclesiastical precedence against some of the most powerful individuals in Constantinople before giving in to precisely the sort of hot-blooded rhetoric he had condemned as a young priest in Antioch.[21] Ironically, if this reading is correct, the short-term beneficiary of Ambrose's *beau geste* was the state, not the church, whereas the opposite could be said of Chrysostom's confrontation, which was only resolved when the court yielded to popular pressure and gave its blessing to his sanctification.

Yet even when these untidy particulars are left aside, the real significance of these two encounters for present purposes lies not in the different outcomes, but in the common premise on which both bishops acted. For both were addressing a question left unanswered by the Constantinian settlement. Put bluntly, in a Christian empire, was the church to be part of the empire, or the empire part of the church? Ambrose and Chrysostom both argued that the latter was the case. While still a priest in Antioch, Chrysostom had insisted that even the royal head lay in priestly hands, while Ambrose chided the young Valentinian II with the explicit proposition that 'the emperor is within the Church, not above the Church'.[22] With Theodosius I, Ambrose was even more assertive. In a confrontation with a far less edifying basis that preceded the Thessalonica episode, the bishop of Milan bullied Theodosius into overlooking the destruction of a synagogue in the Eastern frontier town of Callinicum. Casting himself as Nathan to Theodosius' David, Ambrose showed himself particularly adept at exploiting the subversive message of the Hebrew Bible

---

20 McLynn, *Ambrose of Milan*, 323; P. Brown, *Power and persuasion*, 112.
21 Chrysostom won significant victories in confrontations with Gainas and the emperor Arcadius without needing to mobilise his congregation, as had Ambrose: see J. Stephens, 'Ecclesiastical and imperial authority', ch. 4. In his discourse on Antioch's martyr-bishop Babylas, Chrysostom contrasted the licence (γλώσσης ἀκολασίαν) of Shimei's censure of David in 2 Samuel 16.7 with true freedom of speech (παρρησία): *Pro Babylas* 38 (SC 362: 138).
22 Ambrose, *Ser. c. Aux.* (PL 15: 1018): 'Imperator enim intra Ecclesiam, non supra Ecclesiam est.' For Chrysostom, see *Ad populum Antiochenum homiliae* 3.2 (PG 49: 50).

that kings should be obeyed only so long as they themselves were obedient to priests and prophets.[23]

In each case, the bishop was testing the limits of the novel situation created when Constantine moved into the public sphere a religion that had previously been restricted – and then only grudgingly – to the private domain of personal choice. Due to this change the state became in some way responsible for the maintenance of the church, and vice versa. This is precisely what made the distribution of power such a delicate issue, since emperor and bishop now shared responsibility for maintaining relations with the divine.[24] The novelty of this situation proved fertile soil for a theory always implicit in Christian thought to blossom and begin to bear fruit.

The long-run impact of this change far outweighs the immediate results of the two confrontations.

Auctoritas and potestas

Eusebius and Agapetus have opened a door into the thought world of late antiquity. Both in their flattery and their stipulations, these Christian authors were drawing on a long tradition that helps show how anachronistic terms like 'Caesaropapism' actually are. They have also shown how in this new Christian empire examples of good rule, when put forward by clerical speakers, amounted to enforceable standards. But on one issue they are immutably silent: who speaks for God? In a world that believed as firmly as did that of late antiquity in the regular intervention of deity in the day-to-day affairs of humans, the question was not merely theoretical; although no one in that world would have put it this way, it is clear to our age that whoever was recognised as having that authority was in a position to wield enormous power.

It is in this context that the conflicts involving Ambrose and Chrysostom need to be read, for concentrating on the different outcomes of these events obscures the most revolutionary part of their narrative. Neither bishop was arguing for a separation of 'church' and 'state'; this is a later concept, read back too hastily into these confrontations. Instead, both asserted a priority for their authority in a sphere that they still envisioned as encompassing both church and state. The difference comes out most clearly when their positions are

---

23 Deuteronomy 17.18 enjoins kings to obey the laws of the priests. See further Edmund Leach, 'Melchisedech and the emperor'.
24 On the distribution of authority in late antiquity, see now C. Rapp, *Holy bishops in late antiquity*.

compared with that of two other well-known advocates for the independence of the church from imperial oversight.

Even before John Chrysostom's audacious assertion of the primacy of episcopal authority and Ambrose of Milan's dramatic demonstration of that potential, the case for a sphere of religious authority that existed apart from the boundaries of the traditional state was being made, gingerly, but with increasing confidence, by those who found themselves out of step with the plans of the imperial court. Athanasius' criticisms of Constantine's son, Constantius II, are well known, but they are of diminished significance here because they were intended solely for a limited body of the faithful; when addressing the emperor himself, Athanasius carefully stayed within the bounds of traditional thought.[25] Two other documents are more significant, because they were addressed directly to the emperor. These are a letter sent by Ossius of Cordoba to Constantius II in 343, and another that Pope Gelasius I addressed to Anastasius about a century and a half later.

In the first of these, Ossius, an early adviser of Constantine's, urged the emperor's son to remember that

> God put the empire in your hands, to us he entrusted the affairs of the Church. Just as he who usurps your rule contradicts God's established order, so you must beware lest, by taking upon yourself the affairs of the Church, you be held accountable to a greater charge. 'Render,' it is written, 'unto Caesar the things that are Caesar's, and unto God the things that are God's.' So it is not given unto us to exercise earthly power, nor, emperor, that you have spiritual authority. I write these things out of concern for your salvation.[26]

Gelasius' letter to Anastasius took this point further, asserting the principle that 'two forces rule this world – the sacred authority (*auctoritas*) of the bishops and the royal power (*potestas*)' of the emperors.[27]

Although Gelasius' distinction of the 'two powers' is far better known, Ossius' letter was, for its time, by far the more audacious. Jesus' words at Matthew 22.21 were at most a declaration of indifference to worldly concerns; they had previously been applied only to the narrow issue of obligations such as taxation (the situation that prompted the remark) or, as in the case

---

25 As Kenneth Setton put it, 'It was one thing to think ill of the Emperor; it was quite another to stand in the Sacred Presence and speak ill of the Emperor': *Christian attitude towards the emperor in the fourth century*, 103. For a comparison of Athanasius' depiction of Constantius II in his *History of the Arians* and his *Apology to Constantius*, see pp. 78–9.

26 Ossius ap. Athanasius, *Historia Arianorum* 44.7–8 (ed. Opitz, II.1: 208); for a Latin translation, PL 8: 1328–32.

27 Gelasius, *Ep.* VIII *Ad Anastasium imperatorem* (PL 59: 41–7).

of 1 Peter, to obligations in general. In using them to identify two separate spheres of authority, those we now know so clearly as 'church' and 'state', Ossius gave the text a more sweeping political meaning, using it to assert the first clearly articulated limitation on the scope of a ruler's power.[28] But the significance of this breach lay in the future; at the time he wrote, Ossius' claim for a separate and independent sphere of religious authority pales against the efforts of Ambrose and Chrysostom.

Like Ossius, both Ambrose and Chrysostom were indeed asserting a place for the phenomenon of an independent clergy in the ancient state. But far from advocating a *separation* of the two spheres they were both rather thinking within the context of a state that was both religious and secular. The difference emerges when Chrysostom's reading of 'Render unto Caesar the things that are Caesar's' is compared with Ossius'. Certainly, Chrysostom reasoned, Jesus never intended by such a statement to suggest that his followers should obey laws that were inconsistent with 'piety' (εὐσέβεια). Therefore, a good Christian will hold everything the emperor orders to the standard of God's laws.[29] In this way, Chrysostom turned Ossius' distinction on its head, arguing not for the separation of the two forms of obligation but for the priority of one obligation over the other.

A similarly profound implication underlies Ambrose's position, although it is best seen not in the Thessalonica incident but in the earlier conflict that he provoked over the destruction of Callinicum's synagogue. Chrysostom's theory carried the implicit threat that in cases where imperial and divine law came into conflict Christians would have to disobey even the emperor; Ambrose made the threat explicit: when the claims of religion and public order conflict, he told Theodosius, 'judgment should yield to faith'. He drove the point home by raising the spectre of any Christian emperor's two worst nightmares: being labelled a persecutor and losing control of volatile urban populations. Warning Theodosius that he was about to make a martyr of the bishop of Callinicum, Ambrose hinted broadly that in such an event clergy could not be expected to play their traditional role as moderators of public passions.[30] In each case, the bishop was testing the limits of the novel proposition posed by Christianity's new role in the state by arguing for the primacy of his own spiritual authority over that traditionally wielded by the emperor.

There is a more important difference. Ossius' and Gelasius' letters were prompted by imperial intrusions into what they regarded as matters internal

---

28 Dagron, *Emperor and priest*, 158.
29 Chrysostom, *In Matthaeum homiliae* 70/71 (PG 58: 656).
30 Ambrose, *Ep.* 40.11 (PL 16: 1105): 'Cedat oportet censurem devotioni.'

to the church. Ossius wrote in response to Constantius II's heavy-handed efforts to achieve theological unity by banishing Athanasius; Gelasius, in turn, was reacting to efforts to make Rome share its primacy among Christian patriarchates with the bishop of Constantinople. Both were, in other words, defensive measures, undertaken to protect the decision-making process of the church from what was regarded as overly aggressive intervention by the state. Such a motive highlights the daring displayed by Ambrose and Chrysostom, for in both of these cases the effect was to project the authority of the church into the sphere that both Ossius and Gelasius readily conceded belonged to the state. In contrast to the Thessalonica affair, which he cast as a matter of pastoral care, Ambrose had little call to exert pressure on Theodosius for ordering the restoration of the synagogue of Callinicum, which was simply a matter of maintaining public order. Chrysostom betrays the same attitude in the vigorous sermons he preached in Antioch subsequent to the famous 'Riot of the Statues' in 387. In response to the event, Antioch's aged bishop, Flavian, undertook an embassy to the emperor to plead for mercy, and John's sermons to a frightened city anxiously awaiting word of Theodosius' reaction encouraged them to take heart from the moral sway that bishops hold over emperors – a position fully in keeping with his own theories. So fervent are Chrysostom's arguments that their most surprising feature frequently goes unnoticed: it is not his constant assertion of the moral superiority of bishops; rather, it is the fact that Flavian had undertaken this mission in a cause – rioting over taxes – that had nothing directly or indirectly to do with the church. Rather, it fell squarely in the domain of the traditional civic authorities.[31]

Read in the light of this distinction, Gelasius' letter to Anastasius takes a giant step back from the ground staked out by Ambrose and Chrysostom. The episcopal jurisdiction that he claims for the church is restricted to liturgy, 'discharging the venerable mysteries' (*pro erogandis venerabilibus . . . mysteriis*), and to claim even this relatively narrow sphere he must concede that bishops in their turn recognise and submit to imperial rule over the public sphere, as is also divinely ordained.[32] But the retreat is not a rout. For the terms that Gelasius used to distinguish the power of the church from that of the empire – *auctoritas* (roughly, 'prestige', or moral authority) and *potestas* (coercive force) – carried a potent charge in Roman political thought. They are precisely the terms used by the first emperor, Augustus, to distinguish the type of power he wielded after his famous *beau geste* of 27 BC, when he laid down

31 As observed by Stephens, '*Ecclesiastical and imperial authority*', 62.
32 PL 59: 42C.

dictatorial powers and accepted a commission from the senate to rule at its behest.[33] The story was on bronze tablets that Augustus ordered placed at the site of his mausoleum and replicated throughout the empire.

The tablets may not have survived to Gelasius' day, but the distinction clearly did. Augustus was referring to what he wanted to be perceived as a distinct change, resulting from his act of refusal, in the nature of the power by which he ruled. No longer was he obeyed because he was the most powerful man in Rome, but because he was the most just. This is what gives an edge to Gelasius' use of the same distinction. Gelasius' application of this difference to the nature of the power wielded by emperor and priest effectively appropriates to that body the moral authority that the first emperor arrogated to himself (and, implicitly, to his successors). Now, Gelasius was saying, government must rely on the church for its moral legitimacy. Thus, in words virtually indistinguishable from Chrysostom's, Gelasius claims that, of the two powers, 'the priestly burden is by far the heavier, because on Judgment Day they must give account to the Lord even for the actions of rulers'. For this reason, he continues, Anastasius must recognise 'that you are given precedence in rank over all men, but Your Piety must yield on religious matters to the leadership of those upon whose actions your own salvation depends'.[34] Ultimately, Gelasius' distinction of the 'two powers' owes less to the thinking of Chrysostom and Ambrose than it does to that of Augustine, whose *City of God*, rejecting the bond between the heavenly and earthly realms, decisively re-oriented Western Christian thought.[35] With the waning of imperial influence in the West, Gelasius' letter illustrates the deliberate way in which church officials began to assume imperial status as well as functions during this period.

East or West, it was dangerous for an emperor to interfere too often or too overtly in the priestly sphere. Ironically, given the view Western scholars have taken of Eastern independence, for many centuries the Eastern church actually demonstrated far more ability to manoeuvre than did their counterparts in the West. Ambrose's confrontation with Theodosius became an enduring myth, but still it was only a myth; in the East, bishops of Constantinople actually did bar emperors from entering the church, on more than one occasion.[36]

---

33 Rogers et al., eds., *Caesaris Augusti Res gestae et Fragmenta*, cap. 34: *Post id tem[pus a]uctoritate [omnibus praestiti, potest]atis au[tem n]ihilo ampliu[s habu]i quam cet[eri qui m]ihi quoque in ma[gis]tra[t]u conlegae f[uerunt*. See further M. Grant, *From imperium to auctoritas*.
34 PL 59: 42AB.
35 G. Chesnut, 'The pattern of the past'.
36 Dagron, *Emperor and priest*, 104–10.

The more important question that needs to be asked is, in this new alignment where the church wielded such authority, would as many safeguards be available for emperors when bishops like Ambrose intruded in civil affairs?

Heaven and earth

The suppression of traditional religions in the new Christian empire is the point at which all of the topics of this chapter – the church, society and power – intersect. The law codes preserve increasingly severe penalties placed on the practice of traditional religion from the time of Constantine, and literary sources are widely quoted for their graphic protests against the assaults of rampaging monks – 'men in appearance [who] led the lives of swine', as one hostile account characterises them.[37] These are less delicate records of Christianity's insertion into the public sphere, and the traditional reason for them – Christianity's innate 'intolerance' – one that is most urgently in need of re-thinking. Yet on this most important of topics, Eusebius and Agapetus prove to be less certain guides. The problem lies in a significant difference in the way the two chose to illustrate the use of imperial power. To Eusebius, the emperor is engaged in a cosmic battle against polytheism and idolatry. Armed with standards provided from above, he 'subdues and chastises the visible opponents of truth by the law of combat', while his divine counterpart wages similar battle against all the invisible powers that 'used to fly through the earth's air and infect men's souls' (LC 2.3; cf. 7.1, 12). He confiscates temple treasures and suppresses the debauchery of the polytheists (LC 8). Such activity is absent from Agapetus, who has an entirely different message to deliver. To him, nothing justifies an emperor's rule more than charity and concern for the poor. To earn the crown of 'invincible kingship', he cautions Justinian, 'you must also acquire the garland of well-doing (εὐποιΐα) to the poor' (53). In a radical call for re-distribution of wealth, Agapetus argues that a society divided between the rich, who are 'afflicted by satiety', and the poor, who are 'destroyed by hunger', is an unhealthy society that will only be restored to health through taxation – 'the remedy of subtraction and addition' – by which means equality replaces inequality (16). Just as the suppression of Eusebius' 'opponents of truth' is absent from Agapetus, so his radical social agenda can be found nowhere in Eusebius' speeches. And this is the problem.

---

37 Eunapius, Vitae philosophorum 472 (trans. Wright); equally famous is the rhetor Libanius's characterisation of monks as 'this black-robed tribe, who eat more than elephants': Or. 30.8 (trans. Norman, II: 107). On imperial efforts to control monks, see now D. F. Caner, Wandering, begging monks.

Eusebius' combative words reinforce the view that Christians seized the opportunity afforded by Constantine's conversion to carry out a long-cherished agenda to be the sole religion of the empire, aided and abetted by a compliant emperor whose one consistent aim was, in Norman Baynes' famous phrase, 'the triumph of Christianity and the union of the Roman state with the Christian Church'.[38] Conversely, the absence of such an agenda from Agapetus' strictures would mean that by Justinian's time the continued existence of those religions was no longer an issue. Such a conclusion, unfortunately, does not correspond to what is known of the policies of those two emperors.

Shortly after the victory in 312 that traditionally prompted his change of faith, Constantine met in Milan with his Eastern colleague, Licinius, whose report to the governor of the province of Bithynia on the decisions reached at that conference has come to be known as the 'Edict of Milan'.[39] In their meeting, the imperial colleagues sought to lay to rest a crisis that had been provoked by their predecessor Diocletian's decision to force Christians to conform to the practices of the traditional state religion. Christian resistance to this 'Great Persecution' had put the empire in turmoil for a good ten years, and Constantine and Licinius wished to make it clear that they would adhere to a different policy. Henceforward, Christians had a 'free and absolute permission' to worship their own deity, and immediate restitution would be made of property seized during the persecution, with the cost to be borne by the imperial fisc.

Because of such provisions, the document has usually been depicted as a charter of Christian liberty, which it certainly was. But its other provisions were much more sweeping. Repeatedly, the emperors assert that their intent was for all their subjects to be free 'to follow whatever religion each one wished'. With scrupulous neutrality, the emperors confine themselves to the most general terminology for deity, speaking only of a 'supreme Divinity' (*summa divinitas*) and exhibiting openness to diversity in such phrases as 'whatever divinity there is in the seat of heaven' (*quicquid [est] divinitatis in sede caelesti*) that stand in refreshing contrast to the dogmatism of their predecessors. Scholars are not in agreement on this point, but a case can be made that – with one exception to

---

38 N. H. Baynes, *Constantine the Great and the Christian church*, 83 n. 57.
39 Lactantius, *De mort. pers.* 48.2–12 reproduces the edict. It also survives in a Greek translation included by Eusebius, *H.E.* 8.17. Translations are from J. L. Creed, *Lactantius. De mortibus persecutorum.* Creed compares the two versions on p. 123. On the significance of this document, see H. Dörries, *Constantine and religious liberty*; F. Kolb, 'Der Bussakt von Mailand: Zum Verhältnis von Staat und Kirche in der Spätantike'.

be discussed below – Constantine adhered to this pluralist policy throughout his reign.[40]

Justinian, on the other hand, is associated with two of the most shocking developments in the long, sad story of Christian coercion: the decision to close Plato's Academy and an order to deny privileges of citizenship to non-Christians.[41] Both of these acts occurred at the beginning of his tenure, right around the time Agapetus is most likely to have been writing, and they were followed by purges and pogroms throughout his reign. Neither Eusebius' zeal for the suppression of paganism nor Agapetus' lack of interest in such activity, therefore, accurately reflects the priorities of their respective imperial auditors.

Scholars have no trouble understanding Justinian's sweeping measures. According to the standard explanation of Christian success, his behaviour was easily predictable. It was, in fact, inevitable, due to the intolerance of other ways of worshipping the divine that came with Christianity's monotheistic creed. The sentiment is as old as Gibbon, who identified intolerance as one of his five reasons for the triumph of the Christian religion.[42] Intolerance is certainly a part of the explanation, but its *prima facie* reasonableness (Christians do only recognise one god and reject all others, don't they?) masks profound contradictions. It depends, for instance, on the equally plausible notion that polytheists, since they worship many gods, must be inherently tolerant. Constantine's pluralistic policy, on the other hand, fits rather badly with such notions, and scholars have had to exercise extraordinary ingenuity in order to salvage the thesis, even going so far as to claim that the First Christian Emperor never really was a Christian after all. But that is not the only contradiction. In the paragraphs above, for instance, it is a pagan (Diocletian) who uses coercion as a tool of religious policy. This contradiction would have been more easily detected, were it not for the popularity of the idea that, by the time of Diocletian, pagans had realised that they were locked in a 'life-and-death' struggle with Christians, from which there could emerge only one victor. Desperate times require desperate measures.[43]

On an entirely theoretical level the argument has some force, though even on that level it fails to account for the sporadic but real persecutions that Christians endured at the hands of pagans in the centuries prior to Diocletian.

---

40 For opposing views, see H. A. Drake, 'Constantine and consensus'; T. D. Barnes, 'Constantine's prohibition of pagan sacrifice'.
41 Citizenship: *CJ* 1.11.10; Alan Cameron, 'The last days of the Academy at Athens'.
42 E. Gibbon, *Decline and fall*, ch. 15 (ed. Bury, II: 3).
43 Outstanding examples are in A. Momigliano, ed., *The conflict between paganism and Christianity in the fourth century*.

Gibbon, to his credit, at least attempted to address this contradiction, but his solution – that zealous Christians provoked tolerant authorities – amounts to little more than 'blame the victim'.[44] There is an even more serious lacuna. While intellectuals on both sides might well have perceived irreconcilable differences in the two religious systems, there is abundant evidence for others who thought a *via media* could be found: Christians who were more than ready to make their peace with pagan neighbours, as well as pagans who were shocked and repelled by the coercive measures taken against Christians.[45] One important point was lost in the haze of preconceived notions: pagan eloquence only starts to devote itself to the subject of toleration in the aftermath of the establishment of Christianity, and when it is put to this service it draws largely on Christian argument to do so.[46]

It is not so much that intolerance is wrong as an explanation as that it is insufficient. It rests on theological arguments, and even as a theological argument it is incomplete, for it does not attempt to explain how a religion whose most revolutionary commandment is to return hatred with love, and which fostered a strong tradition that true belief could not be coerced, was unable to find a more pluralistic path to success. The canons of the fourth-century Council of Elvira are suggestive in two ways: first, because bans the bishops place on sharing fine clothing with pagan neighbours and attending public sacrifices show that Christians of a certain status were interacting quite comfortably with pagan neighbours – more comfortably, indeed, than the bishops found acceptable. Second, and most significant, the bishops also refused to sanction militancy, denying the title of martyr to those who die in attacks on pagan temples 'because we find it written nowhere in the Gospels nor ever done by the Apostles' (*in Evangelio scriptum non est neque invenietur sub apostolis unquam factum*, c. 60). Traditionally, the council has been dated to the first decade of the century, but a plausible argument has been made that the canons in their present form are a compilation of the decisions of a series of councils held throughout the fourth century.[47] The later such principles guided episcopal decision-making, the less sufficient the intolerance argument becomes, because its effect has been to anoint the militant group as the normative Christians, and correspondingly to dismiss others as 'semi-Christians', those

---

44 Gibbon, *Decline and fall*, ch. 16 (ed. Bury, ii: 87).
45 Drake, *Constantine and the bishops*, 245–50.
46 P. Garnsey, 'Religious toleration in classical antiquity' is fundamental. On the language of toleration, see C. Ando, 'Pagan apologetics and Christian intolerance in the ages of Themistius and Augustine'.
47 J. Suberbiola Martinez, *Nuevos concilios Hispano-Romanos*; for the canons, see G. Martínez Díez and F. Rodriguez, eds., *La colección canónica Hispana, IV*, 233–68.

in whom conversion did not completely take, thereby obscuring the intensity of a debate that lasted for most of the fourth century. The question that needs to be addressed is why Christian zeal came to manifest itself in acts of resistance, rather than in acts of love. The answer to this question will be found not in theological tendencies but in the broader realm of the political process.

As the preceding discussion of the nature of the late antique state showed, that state knew no bounds between the worlds we now so easily classify as 'religious' and 'secular'. It was one in which the emperor had always been the highest religious authority, responsible above all else for ensuring that divinity received its proper due. As Diocletian's lieutenant Galerius explained in his own attempt to lay the Great Persecution to rest, this was precisely what motivated that disastrous policy: 'we had earlier sought to set everything right in accordance with the ancient laws and public discipline of the Romans and to ensure that the Christians too, who had abandoned the way of life of their ancestors, should return to a sound frame of mind'.[48]

Constantine transferred his allegiance to the Christian god, but he did not change his understanding of his duties. As path-breaking as the Edict of Milan was in other ways, it remained bound to this ancient concept of the state. So the emperors explain in the penultimate sentence of that document: they have determined on freedom of religious choice because, 'In this way it will come about, as we have explained above, that the divine favour towards us, which we have experienced in such important matters, will continue for all time to prosper our achievements along with the public well being.'[49] The tie between earthly prosperity and heavenly favour, negotiated by the charismatic power of the emperor, remained intact.

Ironically, this failure to break with ancient political thought, rather than Christian intolerance, is what opened the door to coercion. For once Constantine recognised the Christian god as one of those responsible for the well-being of the empire, he was duty bound to use his powers to ensure that this god received his proper due, in the proper way. Hence the one form of coercion to which Constantine acceded: not suppression of pagans, but of deviant Christians, heretics, the notorious 'wolf in sheep's clothing' (or, in more modern terminology, the 'enemy within'). Subsequent to the epochal Council of Nicaea, Constantine exiled Arius and the few bishops who supported him – a decision that pleased Athanasius no end, until he was sent into exile in his turn ten years later. Able for the first time to put the coercive powers of the

48 Lactantius, *De mort. pers.* 34.1 (trans. Creed, 53).
49 Ibid., 48.11.

state into their struggle against doctrinal error, the bishops failed to discern the potential for this power to be used against themselves, should a shifting consensus come to deem their own beliefs heretical. Instead, it took only a small step, one well within the bounds of reason, to turn the logic of the ancient state against their former tormentors, and sanctify the use of force not only to suppress traditional religions but even to compel worship of Christ. Augustine is a well-known example, initially opposed to coercion on the traditional Christian grounds that God can only be accepted by a willing heart, then changing his mind because, well, it worked.[50]

The unique nature of the Christian community also plays an important role. In contrast to virtually any other ancient religion, Christians defined themselves according to a set of beliefs, rather than by ancestral association or practice. Western thought is now so imbued with the Judaeo-Christian perspective that it is difficult to imagine how radically Christianity differed in this way from the traditional religions of the ancient world. The difference lies less in the theology of the message (although there was plenty there to give non-Christians pause) as in the way Jesus defined and constituted his community. Traditional religions were city- or kin-based: you worshipped the gods you did because they were the ones honoured by your city or your family. Jesus built his movement out of strangers. Repeatedly, he is quoted in the Gospels as emphasising that his followers are to relate to each other by a different standard. Told, for instance, in the Gospel of Mark (3.33–35), that his mother and brothers were calling for him outside, he responded, 'Who are my mother and my brothers? Whoever does the will of my Father in heaven is mother and brother, sister and father to me.' Followers of Jesus shared an ideology rather than a family; in modern terminology, they were, in the words of Benedict Anderson, an 'imagined community',[51] identifying with each other on the basis of a shared historical narrative and, even more, commitment to a common set of beliefs.

The effect of this difference on religious thought has long been understood: Christianity introduced a need for 'conversion' that was largely absent from traditional religion.[52] But the social implications of this change have rarely been spelled out. Much can be gained by thinking of Christianity in more neutral terms as a social movement.

Certain advantages accrue to a community based on ideology rather than birth. For one thing, it is not limited to a particular geographical location; for

---

50 Augustine, *Retractationes* 31.
51 B. Anderson, *Imagined communities* – a watershed work.
52 The classic study is A. D. Nock, *Conversion*.

another, demographic restrictions on growth imposed by childbearing do not apply: growth is only restricted by the extent to which non-members are motivated to join the movement. Indeed, the only potential bar to growth would be the rigour of requirements for membership. While the lengthy process of learning and examination that preceded baptism, as well as the rigorous code to which members were held under pain of expulsion, was indeed daunting, it was one that – unlike a kinship requirement that could only be met at the moment of birth, or the wealth required for induction into the several mystery cults of the empire – could be met by anyone sufficiently motivated to do so. A movement with a highly attractive message can experience periods of spectacular growth. In order to achieve even the seemingly modest size it had in the early fourth century, Christianity would need to have grown by an average of 3.4 per cent per year, or something like 40 per cent every decade, over the previous three centuries.[53]

Such growth brings disadvantages as well: no amount of preparation or training can make up for the type of acculturation that occurs when members are brought up in the community from birth. This is a fact acknowledged by Christians themselves. In the *Life* of Porphyry of Gaza, a bishop of the early fifth century, his flock gives voice to grave reservations about the numbers of converts his controversial methods have coerced into becoming Christians. Porphyry does not dispute their fear that the neophytes may 'come doubting', but quickly adds that their children will be saved by virtue of being raised in the right company.[54]

The robust growth necessary for Christians to have comprised even 10 per cent of the Roman population by the early fourth century makes it likely that in any given generation prior to Constantine a plurality, if not a majority, of Christians would have been made up of those who had joined the community as adults. This would have been even more the case in the period after Constantine, when imperial favour not only removed those liabilities that had previously served as a brake on membership, particularly for the empire's elite, but also made it both fashionable and advantageous to become Christian. Large numbers of newcomers are potentially destabilising to any group; for an ideological group like Christianity, for which correct adherence to a belief system is paramount, adult converts posed even more of a threat. A fresco in

---

53 R. Stark, *The rise of Christianity*, 7; cf. K. Hopkins, 'Christian number and its implications', 193.
54 Mark the Deacon, *Life of Porphyry* 72–3; the *Life* is a problematic work, at least parts of which were written significantly later than it purports, but in this instance a later date would make the qualms reflected in this exchange even more telling.

the Constantinian-era necropolis uncovered by excavations under the Vatican in the 1950s shows why: it depicts the four-horse chariot of the sun (two of the horses obliterated by subsequent construction) driven by a Jesus whose image is superimposed over a sun that has beams radiating from it in the form of a cross.[55] The context is undeniably Christian, but this is evidently the tomb of a Christian who found his way to the faith via the popular cult of sun worship. The fresco is thus a reminder that, however sincerely attached to and trained in the new faith, adult converts would inevitably have brought with them a range of beliefs and assumptions that, while not necessarily incompatible with their new faith, potentially threatened to take it in directions that, at least in the eyes of the host community, were unwelcome. This inherent tendency to destabilise, compounded by the heresy wars of the fourth century, greatly enhanced the role of the bishop as judge and protector of his flock. It is the place to look in order to understand how a message of love and forbearance came to be replaced by one of resistance and suppression.

Like all successful mass movements, Christianity has a multi-faceted message that can be adapted to changing circumstances. As important to Christians as the central commandment to love one's enemies is the duty to resist Satan and all his acts. Theoretically the two duties are not mutually exclusive; in practice, however, they may loosely be seen as prompting two different responses to the external world of non-Christians. To resist Satan is to look with suspicion at the world of non-believers, since this is the world where Satan lives. It is a practice that encourages exclusivity and isolation. Engagement with Satan's world, if it is to occur at all, will be confrontational, consisting in acts of resistance or even aggression. The commandment to love even enemies encourages a different dynamic: to reach out to non-believers and bring them God's message of love and salvation. To these Christians, the outside community is thought of as misled rather than evil. Broadly speaking, both messages were necessary for the triumph of Christianity: without the impulse to accommodate and convert, Christians would likely have remained a small, exclusive and isolated group, similar to that which authored the Dead Sea scrolls; without the well-established boundaries and limits set by rejecting Satan and his domain, they might instead have been absorbed into one or another of the syncretistic, monotheistic beliefs with which Christianity was in competition.

---

55 Mausoleum M (tomb of the Julii); see M. Wallraff, *Christus Verus Sol*, 158–65. On recent restorations: A. Sperandio and P. Zander, *La tomba di San Pietro*. Earlier: J. Toynbee and J. Ward Perkins, *The shrine of St. Peter and the Vatican excavations*, 72f.; A. Grabar, *Early Christian art*, 80.

At moments of crisis, moments of internal and external threat, the fears of militants attain greater credibility. The half-century between Constantine and Theodosius I constitutes one of these flash points, and it should not be surprising that, in this very period, Christian militants – those members of the community who had always adopted an aggressive and hostile attitude toward other beliefs – should have gained the upper hand. In polarised situations such as this, moderates are vulnerable. The real surprise is that the alternative tradition that true belief cannot be compelled persisted as long as it did. The effect of the aggressive marketing of the examples of Ambrose and Chrysostom was that even emperors were taught to yield in order to keep the peace. The process begun in 300 by the persecution of Diocletian ends in the sixth century with persecution by Christian emperors. Both owe their policies to a concept of the ancient state, and even more to the role of the ruler in that state. In subsequent centuries, the idea of a state that is responsible for the moral and spiritual well-being of its citizens became more and more attenuated, but it continues to provide the intellectual underpinnings for disputes over the appropriate role of the modern state in the formation of its citizens.

Bibliography

PRIMARY SOURCES

Agapetus the Deacon, ed. and trans. R. Riedinger. *Agapetos Diakonos, Der Fürstenspiegel für Kaiser Iustinianos* (Athens, 1995)
Ambrose. *Epistulae* (PL 16)
  Sermo Contra Auxentium (= *Letter* 75a; PL 15)
  Ekthesis (P6 86: 1164–85)
Athanasius. *Historia Arianorum*. Ed. H. G. Opitz, *Athanasius Werke*, II. i, 183–230.
Augustine. *Retractationes* (CCSL 57)
  In Matthaeum homiliae 1–90 (PG 57)
Chrysostom. *Ad Populum Antiochenum homiliae* 1–21 (PG 49: 15–222)
  Pro Babylas (SC 362)
Codex Justinianus, ed. P. Krüger. *Corpus iuris civilis* (Berlin, 1929[11])
Constantine. *Oratio ad sanctorum coetum* (GCS Eusebius Werke, I: 154–82)
Eunapius. *Vitae philosophorum*, trans. W. C. Wright, LCL (London, 1922)
Eusebius. *Historia ecclesiastica* (GCS Eusebius Werke, II)
  De laudibus Constantini (GCS Eusebius Werke, I)
  Praeparatio euangelica (GCS Eusebius Werke, VIII)
Gelasius. *Epistulae* (PL 49)
Lactantius. *De mortibus persecutorum*, ed. and trans. J. L. Creed (Oxford, 1984)
Libanius, *Oratio* 30 'Pro templis', in *Libanius. Selected works*, trans. A. F. Norman, LCL (London, 1977), II

Mark the Deacon, *Life of Porphyry, bishop of Gaza*. Eds. H. Grégoire and M.-A. Kugener, *Marc le Diacre. Vie de Porphyre, évêque de Gaza* (Paris, 1930)

Martínez Díez, G. and F. Rodriguez, eds. *La colección canónica Hispana, IV: Concilios Galos, concilios hispanos: primera parte* (Madrid, 1987)

Pliny the Younger, *Letters and Panegyricus*, trans. B. Radice, LCL (London, 1969)

Rogers, R. S. et al., eds. *Caesaris Augusti Res gestae et Fragmenta* (Detroit, 1990²)

Russell, D. A. and N. G. Wilson, eds. and trans. *Menander Rhetor* (Oxford, 1981)

Stobaeus. *Anthologium*, eds. C. Wachsmuth and O. Hense (Leipzig, 1884–1912; reprint: Berlin, 1958)

SECONDARY SOURCES

Al-Azmeh, A. *Muslim kingship: Power and the sacred in Muslim, Christian and pagan polities* (London, 1999)

Anderson, B. *Imagined communities*, rev. edn. (London, 1991)

Ando, C. 'Pagan apologetics and Christian intolerance in the ages of Themistius and Augustine', *JECS* 4 (1996): 171–207

Barker, E. *From Alexander to Constantine: Passages and documents illustrating the history of social and political ideas, 336 B.C.–A.D. 337* (Oxford, 1956)

 Social and political thought in Byzantium: From Justinian I to the last Palaeologus (Oxford, 1957)

Barnes, T. D. *Athanasius and Constantius: Theology and politics in the Constantinian empire* (Cambridge, MA, 1993)

 'Constantine's prohibition of pagan sacrifice', *AJP* 105 (1984): 69–72

 'Two speeches by Eusebius', *GRBS* 18 (1977): 341–5

Baynes, N. H. *Constantine the Great and the Christian church* (London, 1972²)

Born, Lester K. 'The perfect prince according to the Latin panegyrists', *AJP* 55 (1934): 20–35

Brown, P. *Poverty and leadership in the later Roman empire* (Hanover, NH, 2002)

 Power and persuasion in late antiquity: Towards a Christian empire (Madison, WI, 1992)

Cameron, Alan. 'The last days of the Academy at Athens', *Proc. Cambr. Phil. Soc.* 195 (1969): 7–29

Cameron, Averil. *Christianity and the rhetoric of empire* (Berkeley, 1991)

Caner, D. F. *Wandering, begging monks: Spiritual authority and the promotion of monasticism in late antiquity* (Berkeley, 2002)

Charlesworth, M. P. 'The virtues of a Roman emperor: Propaganda and the creation of belief', *Proc. Brit. Acad.* 23 (1937): 105–33

Chesnut, G. F. *The first Christian histories: Eusebius, Socrates, Sozomen, Theodoret and Evagrius* (Macon, GA, 1986²)

 'The pattern of the past: Augustine's debate with Eusebius and Sallust', in J. Deschner et al., eds., *Our common history as Christians: Essays in honor of Albert C. Outler* (New York, 1975), 69–95

 'The ruler and the Logos in Neopythagorean, Middle Platonic and Late Stoic political philosophy', *ANRW* II, 16:2 (Berlin, 1978), 1310–32

Dagron, G. *Emperor and priest: The imperial office in Byzantium*, trans. J. Birrell (Cambridge, 2003)

Delatte, L. *Les traités de la royauté d'Ecphante, Diotogène et Sthénidas* (Liège, 1942)

Dörries, H. *Constantine and religious liberty*, trans. Roland Bainton (New Haven, 1960)

Drake, H. A. 'Constantine and consensus', *Church history* 64 (1995): 1–15

    Constantine and the bishops: The politics of intolerance (Baltimore, 2000)

    In praise of Constantine: A historical study and new translation of Eusebius' tricennial orations (Berkeley, 1976)

Errington, R. M. 'Themistius and his emperors', *Chiron* 30 (2000): 863–904

Felton, D. 'Advice to tyrants: The motif of "enigmatic counsel" in Greek and Roman texts', *Phoenix* 52 (1998): 42–54

Fowden, G. *Empire to commonwealth: Consequences of monotheism in late antiquity* (Princeton, 1993)

Gannagé, Emma et al., eds. *The Greek strand in Islamic political thought*, published as *Mélanges de l'Université Saint-Joseph* 57 (2004)

Garnsey, P. 'Religious toleration in classical antiquity', in W. J. Shiels, ed., *Persecution and toleration* (Oxford, 1984), 1–27

Gibbon, E. *The decline and fall of the Roman empire*, ed. J. Bury (London, 1909–14)

Goodenough, E. R. 'The political philosophy of Hellenistic kingship', *Yale classical studies* 1 (1928): 55–102

Gordon, R. 'Religion in the Roman empire: The civic compromise and its limits', in M. Beard and J. North, eds., *Pagan priests: Religion and power in the ancient world* (Ithaca, NY, 1990), 235–55

Grabar, A. *Early Christian art (AD 200–395)*, trans. S. Gilbert and J. Emmons (New York, 1968)

Grant, M. *From imperium to auctoritas: A historical study of the Aes coinage in the Roman empire, 49 B.C.–A.D. 14* (Cambridge, 1946)

Henry, Patrick, III. 'A mirror for Justinian. The Ekthesis of Agapetus Diaconus', *GRBS* 8 (1967): 281–308

Hopkins, K. 'Christian number and its implications', *JECS* 6 (1998): 184–226

Kolb, F. 'Der Bussakt von Mailand: Zum Verhältnis von Staat und Kirche in der Spätantike', in H. Boockmann et al., eds., *Geschichte und Gegenwart: Festschrift für Karl Dietrich Erdmann* (Neumunster, 1980), 41–74

Leach, E. 'Melchisedech and the emperor: Icons of subversion and orthodoxy', *Proc. Royal Anthro. Instit.* 1972 (London, 1973): 5–14.

Lepelley, C. 'Le patronat épiscopal aux IVᵉ et Vᵉ siècle: Continuités et ruptures avec le patronat classique', in É. Rebillard and C. Sotinel, eds., *L'évêque dans la cité du IVᵉ au VIᵉ siècle. Image et autorité*, CollÉFR 248 (Rome, 1998), 17–33

Lizzi, R. 'The bishop, *vir venerabilis*: Fiscal privilege and status definition in late antiquity', *SP* 34 (2001): 125–44

McLynn, N. *Ambrose of Milan* (Berkeley, 1994)

Maraval, P. *Eusèbe de Césarée, la théologie politique de l'empire chrétien: Louanges de Constantin* (Paris, 2001)

Momigliano, A., ed. *The conflict between paganism and Christianity in the fourth century* (Oxford, 1963)

Nock, A. D. *Conversion* (Oxford, 1933)

'The emperor's divine *comes*', *JRS* 37 (1947): 102–16

Price, S. R. F. 'Between man and God: Sacrifice in the Roman imperial cult', *JRS* 70 (1980): 28–43

Rapp, C. *Holy bishops in late antiquity* (Berkeley, 2005)

Setton, K. *Christian attitude towards the emperor in the fourth century* (New York, 1941; reprint: 1967)

Ševčenko, I. 'Agapetus East and West: The fate of a Byzantine mirror of princes', *Revue des études sud-est européennes* 16 (1978): 3–44

Sperandio, A. and P. Zander. *La tomba di San Pietro. Restauro e illuminazione della Necropoli Vaticana* (Milan, 1999)

Stark, R. *The rise of Christianity: A sociologist reconsiders history* (Princeton, 1997)

Stephens, J. 'Ecclesiastical and imperial authority in the writings of John Chrysostom: A reinterpretation of his political philosophy', PhD dissertation, University of California, Santa Barbara, 2001

Suberbiola Martinez, J. *Nuevos concilios Hispano-Romanos de los siglos III y IV: La colección de Elvira* (Málaga, 1987)

Thesleff, H. 'On the problem of the Doric Pseudopythagorica: An alternate theory of date and purpose', in K. von Fritz, ed., *Pseudepigrapha I: Huit exposés suivis de discussion* (Geneva, 1972), 57–102

Toynbee, J. and J. Ward Perkins, *The shrine of St. Peter and the Vatican excavations* (New York, 1956)

Wallace-Hadrill, A. 'The emperor and his virtues', *Historia* 30 (1981): 298–323

Wallraff, M. *Christus Verus Sol: Sonnenverehrung und Christentum in der Spätantike*, Jahrbuch für Antike und Christentum, Ergänsungsband 32 (Münster, 2001)

Washburn, D. 'The Thessalonian affair in the fifth-century histories', in H. Drake, ed., *Violence in late antiquity: Perceptions and practices* (London, 2006), 215–24

Whitby, M., ed. *The propaganda of power: The role of panegyric in late antiquity*, Mnemosyne Supp. 183 (Leiden, 1998)

PART IV

CHRISTIAN BELIEFS
AND PRACTICES

18

Discourse on the Trinity

KHALED ANATOLIOS

The background to fourth-century Trinitarian debates

The church of the fourth century inherited a tradition of Trinitarian discourse that was pervasively embedded in its worship and proclamation, even if it was lacking in conceptual definition. No less than their Jewish counterparts, the early Christians were strict monotheists who gave unqualified adherence to the *Shema* of Deuteronomy 6.4: 'Hear, O Israel, the Lord is our God, the Lord alone.' Yet their belief in Jesus Christ as Saviour was expressed in terms which referred to Jesus as the Son, Word, and Wisdom of God and as the one who grants to his disciples the grace of adoption through the bestowal of God's Spirit (cf. Galatians 4.4–7). The first centuries of Christian theological reflection assimilated the confessions of both the oneness of God and the triadic form of Christian discipleship with varying degrees of concern for conceptual clarity and logical synthesis. The first major instance of a debate concerned with conceptualising the Christian experience of God as Trinity and bringing into coherence the emphases on divine unity and triadic distinction occurred in the third century. Tertullian (*fl.* 200), Hippolytus (*c.* 170–*c.* 236) and Novatian (mid-third century) all opposed doctrines that insisted on the radical singularity of God and attenuated the distinctions between Father, Son and Spirit to the level of modes of appearance. Tertullian insisted that the unity of God must itself be interpreted through the Trinitarian 'economy' and attempted terminological differentiations that made it possible to speak of God in terms of a monotheistic Trinitariansim: Father, Son and Spirit are one in 'substance', 'condition' and 'power' (*substantia, status, potestas*) while three in 'degree', 'form' and 'aspect' (*gradus, forma, species*).[1] After the work of Tertullian, Hippolytus and Novatian, the conceptions of God as a radically

---

[1] Tertullian, *Adv. Prax.* 2.

singular being and of Son and Spirit as merely modes of divine operation came to be associated with a certain 'Sabellius' and Paul of Samosata, third-century figures whose writings are no longer extant and who are known to us only through the hearsay of their opponents. Nevertheless, their impact was such that it became *de rigueur* for the articulation of a Christian doctrine of God to claim rejection of an interpretation of divine unity that was 'Sabellian' and conformable to that of 'the Samosatene'.

This lesson was well learned by Origen, arguably the greatest and most influential theologian of the third century, whose teaching cast a large shadow on the Trinitarian controversies of the fourth century. With Origen, there is a pronounced emphasis on Father, Son and Spirit as distinct subsistences (*hypostases*) and on the eternal generation of the Son from the Father. Origen spoke of varying degrees of transcendence among the three hypostases, though he strictly differentiated the divine Trinity from creation. More fatefully, he conjectured that God's eternal sovereignty, mediated by the pre-existent Word and Wisdom, necessitated that there was always a creation over which God was sovereign. This line of reasoning seemed to indicate an intrinsic link between the eternal generation of the Word from the Father and the everlasting existence of creation over which the Father exercised sovereignty through the Word.[2] As Origen's teaching on the everlasting existence of creation came under severe criticism, most notably in the later part of the third century by Methodius of Olympus, the doctrine of creation from nothing was brought to the foreground of theological reflection. This development set the stage for raising the question as to whether the affirmation of the uniquely unoriginated (*agennêtos*) status of the one God necessitated asserting that the derivation of the Son from the Father also involved a kind of 'creation from nothing'. Thus, by the time of the inauguration of Constantine's reign in the early fourth century, Christian discourse had access to a Trinitarian grammar but it was also vexed by conceptual ambiguities regarding the proper way to conceive the relations of Father, Son and Spirit vis-à-vis the created realm.

The Trinitarian controversies of the fourth century

The Trinitarian controversies of the fourth century constitute the most crucially formative period in the development of the Christian doctrine of God. A plausible rendering of the outbreak of the debate is given by the fourth-century historian, Socrates. He tells us that an Egyptian priest, Arius, took issue with

---

2 Origen, *De princ.* 1.2.9, 10.

the preaching of Alexander, the bishop of Alexandria, on the mystery of 'the unity of the holy Trinity'.[3] Alexander's doctrine prominently stressed Origen's teaching on the eternal generation of the Son from the Father. By contrast, the doctrine of Arius combined Origen's emphasis on the real distinctions within the Trinity with an unflagging insistence on the utter singularity of the one unoriginated and unbegotten God. Thus, while we can speak of a divine Trinity, only the first is truly and fully God. The unity of this Trinity, composed of unequal entities (*hypostases*) is one of will, rather than substance. This doctrine does not amount to a denial of the Son's divinity; rather, it endorses the framework of a graded hierarchy of transcendence in which it is possible to speak of variations in degree within the divine realm. Such a framework is operative in the thought of the Christian apologists of the second century and commonplace in Platonic metaphysics, which in the movement from Middle Platonism to Neoplatonism placed an increasingly emphatic stress on the remote transcendence of the first principle from lower levels of divinity.[4] The fluidity of this model of divinity allowed Arius to balance scriptural attributions of divine honour to the Son with a strict interpretation of biblical monotheism. Given the demarcation between the unoriginate God and the creation that comes to be from nothing by divine will, the Son must be placed in the latter category. His generation from the Father is thus the first and highest instance of creaturehood. Following Origen's insistence that all creatures are changeable by nature and equipped with the freedom of moral self-determination, Arius contended that the Son also is changeable by nature. Yet, because of his foreseen merits, the Son was granted an unparalleled share of divine glory such that his divine status is a consequence of grace, rather than nature.

The controversy between Arius and Alexander was conditioned and exacerbated by factions within the Egyptian church dating back to the Diocletianic persecution, as well as by different styles of theological discourse within the Egyptian Christian tradition. But both the political unification under Constantine and the centrality to Christian teaching of the issues under discussion ensured that the controversy would quickly cross Egyptian boundaries and spread throughout the Roman empire. Constantine became sole emperor in 324 after defeating his Eastern rival, Licinus, and he quickly set about the task of redressing the threat to unity created by this ecclesial debate. A church council was held in Nicaea, in 325, attended by Arius and Alexander, as well

---

3 Socrates, *H.E.* 1.5.
4 See R. Williams, *Arius*, 192–7.

as other bishops and theologians predominantly from the Eastern part of the empire. This council rejected Arius' slogan that 'there was once when the Son was not', asserting that the Son's generation from the Father was of a different order than that of creation: 'God of God, Light of Light, true God of true God, begotten not made'. It used the term *homoousios* ('of one substance') to describe the relation between the Son and the Father, less as a positive attempt to represent a description of divine being than as an apophatic pronouncement that sought to rule out any suggestion that the Son was created from nothing.

The Christian imagination has tended to portray the Nicene council as ushering in the victory of Athanasian 'orthodoxy' over 'the Arian heresy' with the inspired confession of the *homoousios*. However, the reception of Nicaea was a far more convoluted process than that account suggests. In point of fact, the Council of Nicaea resulted in more confusion than resolution, at least in the short term, and neither Arius nor Athanasius was a primary figure in the immediate aftermath of the council. Arius' slogan that 'there was once when the Son was not' was a cause of embarrassment even to those who were uncomfortable with the teaching of Nicaea. The project of articulating an alternative theology to that propounded by Nicaea passed to the leadership of Eusebius of Nicomedia, Eusebius of Caesarea, and Asterius.

Eusebius of Nicomedia was an early supporter of Arius but shunned references to the Son's origination from nothing. His own theology emphasised that the divine title of 'unbegotten' (*agennēton*) is applicable only to one. Eusebius is wary of any language of communication of substance as suggesting 'two unbegottens' or a materialistic fragmentation of the divine substance. The Son who is produced by the Father's will differs from the Father in substance and power but is united to him through a 'likeness of disposition'.[5] Eusebius of Caesarea, the illustrious church historian and theological disciple of Origen, also disowned Arius' doctrine of the Son's origination from nothing. But he also rejected Origen's teaching on the eternal generation of the Son. Whereas Origen used the framework of 'participation' to articulate the unity of the Trinity, Eusebius follows a Middle Platonic emphasis on the inaccessible transcendence of the first principle by identifying it as 'unparticipated'.[6] Eusebius of Caesarea had reluctantly agreed to the Nicene *homoousios* but his own doctrine, often articulated in terms of the Son's being the 'image of the Father's substance', is centrally concerned with maintaining the clear priority of the Father over the Son.

---

5 Eusebius of Nicomedia, *Letter to Paulinus* 3.
6 Eusebius of Caesarea, *Prep. ev.* 7.12.2.

Asterius' doctrine is also distinct from Arius' in several important respects. Not only does he avoid speaking of the Son's origination from nothing, but he identifies the Son as 'the unchanging image of the substance and will and glory and power' of the Father'.[7] This is a decisive modification of Arius' stress on the incomparability of the Father. Moreover, Arius' doctrine that God was not always Father is replaced with the notion that fatherhood can be eternally predicated of God as a generative capacity that precedes the generation of the Son. Yet, Asterius did share significant common ground with Arius in his affirmation that the Son is not integral to the divine essence but a creature, produced by the Father's will.

Even though Asterius and the two Eusebii all supported Arius at some point, their theologies cannot be simply reduced to that of Arius. The notion of 'Arianism' thus has no objective referent in the form of a unified and coherent theology. In the fourth century, it was above all Marcellus of Ancyra and Athanasius of Alexandria who devised the label to counter all theologies that admitted a plurality of strictly subordinated hypostases and construed the relation between the Son and the Father as a unity of will, rather than substance.

In the decades following Nicaea, we find diverging tendencies in the Eastern and Western parts of the empire with regard to ecclesial politics, doctrinal emphases, and terminology. This line of demarcation, however, is serviceable only in a rough and general sense and with the notable exception that the church of Alexandria belonged doctrinally rather on the Western side. Moreover, the Western bishops came to be dominated by the two Easterners, Marcellus of Ancyra and the Egyptian Athanasius.

Marcellus, bishop of Ancyra, was present at the Council of Nicaea and interpreted its teaching in a distinctly unitarian direction. God is a single being, one *prosopon*, of whom no plurality can be predicated. Marcellus' theology of divine oneness dealt with the plethora of scriptural titles applied to Jesus by insisting that they all apply only after the incarnation, with the exception of the title of 'Logos'. The Logos is not distinct from God, just as a human word is not distinct from its speaker. It is enunciated in the act of creation and is differentiated from God only in the incarnation. This differentiation will cease once the redemptive work of Christ is accomplished and the Son becomes subject to the Father (cf. 1 Corinthians 15.28).

Marcellus propounded his theology by way of a denunciation of Asterius' doctrine of the Son as a subordinate hypostasis produced by the Father's will. His own theology and his attempts to present this teaching as the true

---

7 Asterius, frag. 10.

interpretation of Nicaea made Nicene doctrine at least as problematic, in the eyes of many, as the teaching of Arius. Branded as a 'new Sabellius' by the authoritative figure of Eusebius of Caesarea, Marcellus was deposed by a synod in Constantinople in 336. While exiled in Rome, he joined forces with his fellow exile, Athanasius, in a polemical campaign against those whom they called 'Arians'.

Athanasius had been present at the Council of Nicaea as a young deacon accompanying his bishop, Alexander. He succeeded Alexander as bishop of Alexandria, in 328, embarking on a forty-six-year reign over the Church of Egypt, punctuated by seventeen years of exile. But we do not have any sustained public refutation of 'Arianism' from Athanasius until the early 340s, some fifteen years after the Council of Nicaea, when he penned his *Orations against the Arians*. Though Athanasius adopted Marcellus' polemical strategy of identifying all subordinationist theologies as 'Arian' and approved of the terminology of 'one hypostasis' to refer to the relation of Father and Word, his understanding of this relation is markedly different. A central, though generally overlooked, indication of this difference is manifest in Athanasius' treatment of the scriptural titles (*epinoiai*) of the Son in his *Orations against the Arians*. While Marcellus accepts only Logos as applicable to the pre-existence of Christ, Athanasius makes much of a whole series of other scriptural titles – such as Son, Image, Wisdom and Radiance – in order to designate the eternal correlativity of Father and Son.[8] Differentiation within the Godhead is thus an essential feature of Athanasius' doctrine of God in a way that is precluded in the doctrine of Marcellus.

Together, Marcellus and Athanasius were at the centre of East / West tensions in the 340s. These differences are well illustrated by two councils from this period: the Council of Antioch (341) and the Council of Serdica (343). The former followed upon failed negotiations between Pope Julius and the Eastern bishops to convoke a synod in Rome. Meeting separately, the bishops of Antioch indignantly disavowed being followers of Arius. But their main theological opponent was Marcellus, whose doctrine they countered by insisting that Father, Son and Spirit are three hypostases. They shunned the language of unity of substance, employing the biblical terminology of 'image' to designate the relation between Father and Son (cf. Colossians 1.15). The unity of the Trinity was expressed in moral, rather than ontological, terms: 'one in concord'. The Council of Serdica, convoked by the Western emperor Constans, was also originally intended to bring together East and West. But the Western insistence

---

8 See K. Anatolios, '"When was God without Wisdom?"'.

that Athanasius and Marcellus be in attendance proved unacceptable to the Eastern bishops and the two sides met separately. At Serdica, the Western bishops defended Athanasius and Marcellus, the latter having persuaded the council attendees that his views had been misrepresented by 'Arians'.

The profession of faith promulgated at Serdica is designed primarily to rule out any form of subordinationism as 'Arian'. Any notion of an attenuated divinity of the Son is proscribed and the unity of Father, Son and Spirit is expressed as 'one hypostasis'. As these two councils indicate, we do not have an obvious line of demarcation at this time between an 'orthodox' Trinitarianism and a heretical 'Arian' subordinationism. Rather, there is a dialectical tension between an emphasis on divine unity and an emphasis on the irreducible distinctions within the Trinity. This tension is further complicated, however, by the fact that there are modalistic overtones to the emphasis on divine unity (as in Marcellus) and subordinationist interpretations within the emphasis on Trinitarian distinctions (as in Asterius).

With the 350s, there emerge several more starkly defined theological positions that were to have the cumulative effect of bringing the debate to clearer resolution. Acacius of Caesarea, the successor of Eusebius, and Eudoxius of Antioch were at the vanguard of a movement that accented the subordinationism of Arius' doctrine, even while rejecting the label of 'Arian' and the doctrine that the Son was created 'from nothing'. This type of theology, having its roots in the teaching of Eusebius of Caesarea rather than Arius himself, clearly insisted that the Son was a creature and a product of the will of the Father. With arguments that were often based on scriptural accounts of the human limitations of the incarnate Word, it did not shy from reiterating the incomparable superiority of the Father to the Son and clarified, further, that the Spirit in turn was inferior to the Son. Its preferred designation for the relation of the Son to the Father was *homoios* – the Son was 'like' the Father – though this likeness was understood very much in a subordinationist vein. This 'homoian' theology found expression in a series of councils in the 350s, in both East and West, under the patronage of the emperor Constantius. It reached a climactic point at the Council of Sirmium in 357, which combines an outright rejection of the *homoousios*-language of Nicaea with an undisguised subordinationism: 'And nobody is unaware that this is Catholic doctrine, that there are two Persons of the Father and the Son, and that the Father is greater, and the Son is subjected in common with all the things which the Father subjected to him.'[9]

---

9 Second Creed of Sirmium (357); trans. R. P. C. Hanson, *The search for the Christian doctrine of God*, 345.

An even starker subordinationism is found in the theology propounded by Aetius and Eunomius, sometimes referred to as 'Neo-Arianism'. In fact, this theology differed in key ways from the theology of Arius, most notably in replacing Arius' doctrine that the Son does not know the Father with the teaching that the knowledge of God's substance is available to all rational creatures and is manifest in the divine names. Most centrally, for both Aetius and Eunomius, the primary name revelatory of the divine nature is that of *'agennêtos'*, unoriginate and unbegotten. Therefore, the Son, as begotten, is of a different nature than the true God. The unbegotten nature of God precludes any communication of being in either the act of an (intra-divine) generation or an incarnation. Unlike the Homoians, Aetius and especially Eunomius were not shy of applying *ousia*-language to God in order to declare unflinchingly the incomparable difference in ontological status between Father and Son.

The emergence of radical expressions of anti-Nicene subordinationism in the 350s spawned significant countervailing theological currents. The successor of Marcellus, Basil of Ancyra, still shy of the Nicene *homoousios*, nevertheless insisted that the relation of the Son to the Father must be articulated as 'like according to essence *(homoios kat' ousian)*' in order to preclude attributing creaturehood to the Son. This position came to be identified with the slogan of *homoiousios* ('like in essence'), though that term itself was not used by Basil. Athanasius went farther, emerging in the 350s as a leading promoter of Nicaea. In his *On the Council of Nicaea (De decretis)*, Athanasius defends Nicaea against those who disapproved of its terminology as non-scriptural. He explains that the Nicene bishops were forced to resort to this term in order to safeguard the intent of scriptural language. This intent is manifest in the scriptural titles of the Son – such as Word, Wisdom, Radiance – which represent him as correlative to the Father's being. The Nicene *homoousios* was the only way to rule out interpretations of scriptural language that imputed creaturehood to the Son. Even the terminology of likeness of essence, which in the theology of Basil of Ancyra lacked subordinationist overtones, was inadequate as leaving the way open to a homoian interpretation.[10]

As the decade wore on, developments in ecclesial politics under the influence of the Eastern emperor Constantius served to undermine the position of 'the Homoiousians' and to further polarise pro-Nicene and anti-Nicene forces. In 359, Constantius convoked a twin council, the Western contingent of which met at Ariminum in Italy and the Eastern at Seleucia, near Antioch. The councils were presented with a creed (known as the 'Dated' creed of 22 May

10 Athanasius, *De synodis* 53.

359) that endeavoured to effect a compromise between a 'Homoian' theology that rejected language of community of substance between Father and Son and the 'Homoiousian' theology of Basil of Ancyra. But the Western synod simply reasserted its fidelity to Nicaea, while the Eastern attendees, divided between 'Homoians' and followers of Basil of Ancrya, failed to reach a consensus. Constantius then forced both synods to sign a version of the Dated Creed that settled matters in a Homoian direction, describing the Son as 'like' the Father and omitting the original qualification of 'in all respects'. In 360, the Homoian Acacius presided over another council in Constantinople, at which Basil of Ancrya and his followers were deposed.

As anti-Nicene positions became more explicit in the 350s, the supporters of Nicaea rallied to negotiate a consensus among those who believed in the full divinity of the Son and Spirit. Such a consensus required a clearer articulation of a non-modalist interpretation of the Nicene *homoousios*, as well as a rapprochement among those who wished to confess the complete divinity of both Son and Spirit but advocated different terminologies, i.e, *homoousios* as opposed to *homoios kat' ousian* ('like in substance') and 'one hypostasis' as opposed to 'three hypostases'. We find significant traces of such theological diplomacy in the writings of Athanasius from that period. Though a leading advocate of the Nicene confession of the unity of Father and Son, he clarifies that God is a Trinity 'not only in name and linguistic expression but Trinity in reality and truth. Just as the Father is the "One who is" (Ex. 3.14), so likewise is his Word the "One who is, God over all" (Rom. 9.5). Nor is the Holy Spirit non-existent but truly exists and subsists.'[11] He also concedes that those who follow the 'likeness of essence' terminology of Basil of Ancyra are substantially in accord with his own, Nicene, teaching,[12] though he continues to prefer the language of *homoousios*. We find a similar conciliatory overture in Hilary of Poitier's *On the Trinity*, written in the early years of the 360s. Hilary was careful to interpret the *homoousios* in a way that clarified the real distinction between Father and Son, thus avoiding the spectre of modalism, and he was even more explicit than Athanasius in his allowance of the legitimacy of *homoiousios*.[13]

A significant development in the movement toward a pro-Nicene consensus was a council headed by Athanasius in Alexandria, in 362. This council met in order to deal with a schism that had arisen between two pro-Nicene bishops: Paulinus, who confessed the 'one hypostasis', and Melitius, who confessed 'three hypostases'. The decision of this council was to allow for both usages,

11 Athanasius, *Ad Serap.* 1.28.
12 Athanasius, *De synodis* 41.
13 Ibid., 71.

as long as both the unity and distinction were safeguarded and neither an 'Arian' subordinationism nor a 'Sabellian' modalism was intended. The Alexandrian council thus based its terminological tolerance on an admission from both sides of the validity of the other's emphasis, whether that be the unity of the substance or the irreducible reality of the three divine subsistents. However, the lack of terminological consensus continued to undermine the commitment to tolerance, which was further tested by attempts to integrate hypostasis-language with that of *prosopon* (or, in Latin, *persona*).

Indications of the tense history that followed upon the seeming resolution of the Alexandrian council are found in the epistles of Basil of Caesarea and Jerome.[14] Basil had originally exhibited some discomfort with the Nicene *homoousios*, as vulnerable to modalistic interpretations. His acceptance of this term was conditioned by his construction of an accompanying set of terminology to designate the threeness of God: Father, Son and Spirit are each a distinct hypostasis, with a unique manner of subsistence (*tropos hyparxeôs*). Basil, a supporter of Melitius, pressed the followers of Paulinus to adopt the language of 'three hypostases' in order to safeguard Nicene theology from a Sabellian interpretation. The 'Paulinians' were not insensible to that concern but considered that it was sufficiently addressed by acknowledging that each of the Trinity is a distinct person, or *prosopon*. But this stratagem was deemed inadequate by Basil, since the term *prosopon* could mean simply 'role' or 'manifestation', and thus even a Sabellian could subscribe to such a confession:

> It is not enough to count differences in the Persons (*prosopa*). It is necessary also to confess that each Person (*prosopon*) exists in a true *hypostasis*. The mirage of persons (*prosopa*) without *hypostases* is not denied even by Sabellius, who said that the same God, though he is one subject, is transformed according to the need of each occasion and is thus spoken of now as Father, now as Son, and now as Holy Spirit.[15]

Meanwhile, Jerome became embroiled in the controversy, expressing his shocked disapproval of the language of 'three hypostases' to Pope Damasus, and articulating the triunity as 'one substance, three persons (*una substantia, tres personae*)'. Jerome's discomfort with the 'three hypostases' language of Basil and Meletius is readily explicable inasmuch as the Greek term, hypostasis, can be literally calqued in Latin as *substantia*. It was under such pressures that Basil came to insist on a distinction between the significations of the terms

14 On the following, see André de Halleux, '"Hypostase" et "personne"'.
15 Basil, *Ep.* 210.5.

ousia and *hypostasis*. As Jerome protested, such a distinction was somewhat novel inasmuch as the two terms were regularly employed as synonyms. Nevertheless, the construction of such a distinction became invaluable inasmuch as the affirmation of being underlying both terms ensured that both the unity and the distinction within the Trinity were confessed as having equally radical ontological status. At the same time, the two terms were distinguished by Basil as having the same relation as that of the common to the particular. Thus, *ousia* signified the unity of being, while *hypostasis* referred to the particular mode of being which is irreducibly distinct in each of the three. In this way, the Nicene *homoousios* came to be supplemented by an equal emphasis on the distinctions within the triune God.

Another important development beginning in the late 350s, which led to a clearer definition of a pro-Nicene Trinitarianism, was the foregrounding of the question of the status of the Holy Spirit. In the aftermath of the dispute between Arius and Alexander on the relation between Father and Son, the Council of Nicaea adverted to the Holy Spirit in what might seem like a mere afterthought: 'And we believe in the Holy Spirit'. Arius himself largely bypassed the subject of the Spirit, though he certainly considered the Spirit to be a creature. In the course of giving clear expression to the subordinate status of the Son relative to the Father, the 'Homoians' as well as Eunomius also maintained that the Spirit in turn was subordinate to the Son and not an object of worship. But the subordinationism of the Spirit was not always conceived in tandem with that of the Son. In some circles, in the late 350s and 360s, it was combined with an acknowledgment of the equality of the Son to the Father. This was the case with two movements, whose adherents have been called the 'Tropici' and the 'Macedonians'.

The former was a group of Egyptian Christians who based their subordination of the Spirit to the Father and Son chiefly on scriptural grounds, most notably Amos 4.13 (in which the prophet communicates God's saying, 'I, who establish thunder and create spirit . . .'), Zechariah 1.9 ('These things says the angel that speaks within me . . .') and 1 Timothy 5.21 ('I adjure you in the sight of God and Christ Jesus and the elect angels . . .'). Their opponents branded them 'Tropici' as a pejorative allusion to their use of scriptural figures or 'tropes' in their argumentation. On the basis of the aforementioned biblical texts, the Tropici concluded that the Spirit was created as an angel, the chief of God's 'ministering spirits' (cf. Hebrews 1.14). Their reasoning was also based on the premise that the equality of the Son to the Father is constituted by the relation of generation; since the Spirit lacks such a relation to the Father, it is external to the divine nature. This point was given a rhetorical cast by saying that if the Spirit were integral to the divine nature, it would have to be another Son, as a brother of the Son, or even a son of the Son, and thus grandson of the Father.

The 'Macedonians' were named after Macedonius, the bishop of Constantinople, though his connection with this doctrine is tenuous, the most prominent exponent of this view being rather Eustathius of Sebaste. The Macedonians also believed in the full divinity of the Son, under the rubric of 'likeness of essence', but withheld both worship and confession of divinity from the Spirit, on the bases of scriptural and logical arguments that were largely similar to those of the 'Tropici'.

The development of these subordinationist views of the Spirit was countered chiefly by Athanasius and Basil of Caesarea. Athanasius dismisses the exegetical arguments of those who deny the divinity of the Holy Spirit as specious: the reference to the created spirit in Amos pertains not to the divine Spirit, but to the spirit of creatures. Since the scriptures attribute to the Spirit the creative and sanctifying work of God, the Spirit must be God. Moreover, this work is brought to consummation in the individual Christian through the sacramental event of baptism, of which the Spirit is an agent. If the Spirit were not God, baptism could not be an initiation into divine life. Athanasius analyses the patterns of scriptural language to come to the conclusion that 'the Spirit has the same relation of nature and order with respect to the Son as the Son has with respect to the Father'.[16] As to the precise distinction between the Son's generation, and the relation by which the Spirit is derived from the Father, he maintains an apophatic silence.

In his treatise *On the Holy Spirit*, Basil follows Athanasius' line of reasoning, that the scriptural account of the names and activities of the Spirit indicate his divinity, and also dwells on the Spirit's agency in Christian baptism. He deals with Aetius' argument that the differences in liturgical prepositions ('from the Father, through the Son, in the Spirit') are indicative of differences of essence by showing that each of these prepositions is variously applied in the scriptures to all three. Ultimately, however, Basil refrains from directly calling the Spirit 'God' or *homoousios*, choosing to make the point in the more experiential language of worship: the Spirit is of 'equal honour (*isotêmos*)' to the Father and the Son.[17] Many of the arguments of Athanasius and Basil are reproduced in the writings of Western defenders of Nicene doctrine, though already the Greek apophaticism regarding the procession of the Spirit is attenuated in

16 Athanasius, *Ad Serap.* 1.21.
17 Basil, *De Spiritu Sancto* 6.13.

the West by references to the double procession of the Spirit from Father and Son.[18]

After the Macedonian controversy, the clear confession of the full divinity of the Holy Spirit became another significant ingredient in the formation of a pro-Nicene consensus that was now spreading in both East and West. But the polarisation between East and West continued on the political front. Constantius, who had lent forceful support to the Homoian position, died in 360. He was succeeded briefly by his cousin Julian, who had renounced Christianity and sought to purify the empire from Christian influences, and by Jovian, who showed signs of favouring pro-Nicenes during his brief reign. In 364, imperial authority was again divided, now between Valens in the East (*regn*. 364–78) and Valentinian in the West (*regn*. 364–75). Valens was an active promoter of the Homoian cause, while Valentinian followed a non-interventionist policy that was nevertheless sympathetic to the Nicene position. Upon his death in 375, Valentinian was succeeded by his son Gratian, who adopted a policy of general tolerance. The more fateful succession followed upon the death of Valens, who died at the hands of the Goths in the battle of Adrianople in 378. He was succeeded in 379 by Theodosius, who quickly showed himself to be a strong supporter of the emerging pro-Nicene consensus. He issued an edict in 380 (*Cunctos populos*) that announced the single divinity of Father, Son and Spirit to be the official doctrine of the empire, and another in January 381 (*Nullius haereticis*) that expressly forbade anti-Nicene factions from congregating in churches. The stage was thus set for a pro-Nicene council, which was called to meet in Constantinople, in 381.

The Council of Constantinople was attended by approximately 150 Eastern bishops. The large majority of these were already sympathetic to pro-Nicene theology, with the exception of about thirty 'Macedonian' bishops. Negotiations with the Macedonian party were attempted but proved to be unfruitful and they walked out of the council proceedings. The first canon of the Constantinopolitan council re-confirmed the Council of Nicaea and anathematised all those who rejected the full and equal divinity of either Son or Spirit, making reference to 'Eunomians' and 'Arians', as well as 'Semi-Arians', i.e., those who accepted the full divinity of the Son but did not accord the same status to the Spirit. It equally rejected the modalist doctrine of Marcellus and his Western disciple, Photinus, as well as the teaching of Apollinarius, which asserted that the incarnate Word did not assume a fully human soul. At the Council of Chalcedon of 451, the archdeacon of that city read out a

---

18 Cf. Epiphanius, *Panarion*, 62.4.1; Ambrose, *De Spir.* 1.11.120.

creed announced to be the confession of faith of the Council of Constantinople. The acts of Chalcedon thus present us with the first official record of a
Constantinopolitan creed, which runs as follows:

> We believe in one God the Father Almighty, maker of heaven and earth and
> of all things visible and invisible; and in one Lord Jesus Christ the Son of God,
> the Only-begotten, begotten by his Father before all ages, Light from Light,
> true God from true God, begotten not made, consubstantial with the Father,
> through whom all things came into existence, who for us men and for our
> salvation came down from the heavens and became incarnate by the Holy
> Spirit and the Virgin Mary and became a man, and was crucified for us under
> Pontius Pilate and suffered and was buried and rose again on the third day in
> accordance with the Scriptures and ascended into the heavens and is seated at
> the right hand of the Father and will come again with glory to judge the living
> and the dead, and there will be no end to his kingdom; and in the Holy Spirit,
> the Lord and Life-giver, who proceeds from the Father, who is worshipped and
> glorified together with the Father and the Son, who spoke by the prophets;
> and in one holy, catholic and apostolic Church. We confess one baptism for
> the forgiveness of sins; we wait for the resurrection of the dead and the life of
> the coming age. Amen.[19]

The paucity of clear reference prior to Chalcedon of a creed produced by
the Council of Constantinople has led some modern scholars to question
whether this creed was in fact promulgated on that occasion. But the consensus
of modern scholarship is that the witness of the Chalcedonian council was
correct, and the lack of reference to a 'Constantinopolitan creed' prior to
Chalcedon is explicable in light of the understanding that this council did not
consider its confession of faith to be a new creed but rather a restatement of
Nicene faith.[20] It is also likely that the Council of Constantinople drew on an
earlier Western creed that was a pro-Nicene re-statement of the Old Roman
creed, supplemented by an enlargement of the confession of the divinity of
the Holy Spirit.[21]

The Constantinopolitan redaction of the earlier Western creed amounts
to a highly condensed summary of both the content and form of Basil of
Caesarea's approach to the subject. It declares the Spirit's divinity not by the
application of ontological terminology but by ascribing to the Spirit divine
titles and activities – 'the Lord, the Life-Giver' – and by affirming the equality

---

19 Trans. Hanson, *The search for the Christian doctrine of God*, 816.
20 For a full treatment, see J. N. D. Kelly, *Early Christian creeds*, 296–331.
21 This is the thesis of L. Abramowski, 'Was hat das Nicaeno-Constantinopolitanum (C)
   mit dem Konzil von Konstantinopel 381 zu tun?'

of the Spirit to Father and Son as an object of honour and worship. Apart from the development of the confession of the Spirit, there are various discrepancies between the creeds of Nicaea and Constantinople that tend to support the theory of an intermediary creedal formula redacted by Constantinople. Among these discrepancies, we can note two of some significance: the omission of the Nicene anathema against those who speak of the Son as another 'hypostasis' from the Father, reflecting the terminological rapprochement achieved by the Council of Alexandria of 362, and the addition of the statement that Christ's kingdom will not end. The latter addition was inserted as a rebuttal of what was considered to be the doctrine of Marcellus, that the expansion of the divine activity from monad to triad would be eschatologically retracted into the monad, and thus the kingdom of Christ would be re-enfolded into the kingdom of the Father.

The Cappadocian and Augustinian syntheses

The creed of Constantinople constituted the decisive moment in the reception of the Council of Nicaea. But this reception involved certain clarifications and re-interpretations that amounted to a much more conceptually developed account of the church's Trinitarian faith than had been possible at Nicaea. In the East, such an account is given expression by the Cappadocian theologians: Basil of Caesarea, his brother Gregory of Nyssa, and their friend Gregory of Nazianzus. Although the theological visions of these three are not homogenous, there are enough overlapping emphases to warrant speaking of a Cappadocian 'synthesis'. In the West, Augustine incorporated the results of the debates surrounding the Council of Nicaea into an original synthesis that was to be hugely influential in the Western tradition.

The Cappadocian synthesis is best seen as a response to the anti-Nicene developments that began in the 350s, spearheaded by Aetius and Eunomius. As we have seen, the fundamental principle of this theology was that the name of 'unbegotten' or 'ingenerate' (*agennêtos*) is disclosive of the divine essence. Much of Cappadocian Trinitarian thought is intelligible as an attempt to deal with this premise on two fronts: first, by asserting that knowledge of the divine essence is attainable only indirectly, by experience of the divine operations rather than by a direct intellectual circumspection of the divine nature; and, second, by clarifying that the term *agennêtos* is indicative of the order of relations within God and not of the divine essence.

The first issue broaches the question of theological epistemology, the Cappadocian version of which contains a strong emphasis on divine incomprehensibility. In the teaching of Gregory of Nyssa on the infinity of the divine essence, this emphasis amounts to an original contribution to the Platonist philosophical tradition, which for the most part had shunned applying the attribute of infinity to the divine. Over against the Eunomian assertion that the divine substance can be encompassed by the human mind's comprehension of the divine names, the Cappadocians insisted that the essence of God can be no more circumscribed by the mind than it can by matter. But Cappadocian apophaticism was also complemented by an insistence on the necessity for knowledge of God and the assurance that God is known through positive relation, or worship, the outgoing human response to the manifested glory of divine revelation.[22] From an anthropological perspective, such knowledge is co-extensive with the process of deification. Theologically, such an epistemology dictated that the divine essence is revealed through the divine operations manifest in the works of creation and salvation. Thus, much of the exegetical labours of Cappadocian Trinitarian theology are concerned to show that the work of Son and Spirit is divine work and therefore indicative of their belonging to the divine essence. The crucial and primary principle is that unity of operation indicates unity of essence.[23]

Once this principle is implemented to assert the equality of Father, Son and Spirit as co-agents of the divine operations, the question of the significance of the divine title of 'unbegotten' can be properly situated. It cannot be understood as an exhaustive representation of the divine essence in a way that excludes Son and Spirit, whose divine operations testify to their sharing in the divine essence. But, insofar as these same divine operations (and the scriptural titles that name them) indicate an order of relations within the divine agency, the title of 'unbegotten' must be placed within that order of relations. In that framework, it denotes the primacy of the Father as source of Son and Spirit within the divine being and thus the originating principle of the 'movement' of God in relation to creation: 'There is one motion and disposition of the good will which proceeds from the Father, through the Son, to the Spirit . . . we cannot enumerate as three gods those who jointly, inseparably, and mutually exercise their divine power and activity of overseeing us and the whole creation.'[24]

Divine names, therefore, must be distinguished between those that pertain to the divine essence as a whole, which are uncircumscribable but manifest

---

22 Gregory of Nazianzus, *Or.* 28.9, 17; Basil, *De Spiritu Sancto* 1.2.
23 On the importance of this principle for pro-Nicene theology, see M. R. Barnes, 'Rereading Augustine's theology of the Trinity'.
24 Gregory of Nyssa, *Ad Abl.* (GNO 3¹: 48–9); trans. E. R. Hardy, *Christology of the later fathers*, 262.

as a unified active agency, and those that pertain to the divine relations that constitute the divine essence, which are equally incomprehensible but also manifest in the ordered relations which constitute the unified active agency. Thus, the principle that the divine essence is manifest in divine operations allows for the assertion that Father, Son and Spirit equally belong to the divine essence, without any claim to an exhaustive comprehension or definition of that essence: 'Whatever your judgement suggests and however it suggests as to the essence of the Father (for it is impossible to superimpose any definite concept upon the immaterial because of our persuasion that it is above every concept), this you will hold for the Son and likewise for the Spirit.'[25]

This quotation from Gregory of Nyssa helps us to contextualise the much-vaunted contribution of the Cappadocians in providing a terminological resolution of the Trinitarian controversies in the formula of 'one nature, three persons (*mia ousia, treis hypostases*)'. In fact, the formula thus stated occurs infrequently in Cappadocian theology and is only one of various versions of an attempt to state the simultaneity of unity and distinction within the Godhead.[26] Nevertheless, it remains true that the construction of a linguistic framework to denote respectively the unity of divine being and the real distinctions between Father, Son and Spirit was a crucial step toward resolving the Trinitarian debates of the fourth century.

As we have seen, Basil, who was most responsible for regulating a distinction between *hypostasis* and *ousia*, related the two as the common to the particular.[27] Such language can imply that Basil's understanding of the oneness of the Trinity amounts to merely 'a generic unity', but such an account fails to do justice to his rejection of the application of number to the Trinity and his emphasis on the single *ousia* of God as a concrete reality.[28] Moreover, the other Cappadocians pointedly dismiss the appropriateness of a 'social analogy' of the Trinity.[29] It is better to understand the Cappadocians on their own terms, in which the terminological distinction between *ousia* and *hypostasis* designates the unfathomable mystery of God as manifest through a single divine activity composed of the correlated agency of Father, Son and Spirit.

The formula of 'one nature, three persons' was not incorporated into the creed of Constantinople but the conceptual framework behind the formula,

---

25 (ps.-)Basil, *Ep.* 38.3; FOTC 13: 86–7.
26 See J. T. Lienhard, 'Ousia and hypostasis'.
27 Basil, *Ep.* 214.4.
28 Basil, *De Spiritu Sancto* 17.41; see the discussion in Hanson, *The search for the Christian doctrine of God*, 696–9.
29 Gregory of Nazianzus, *Or.* 31.15, Gregory of Nyssa, *Ad Abl.* (GNO 3[1]: 47–8).

as constructed by Cappadocian theology, was a significant ingredient in that council's reception of Nicaea. The official conciliar reception of this terminology occurs in the first canon of the Second Council of Constantinople of 553, which closely echoes the synodal letter of 382 that was issued by the first Council of Constantinople.

Until fairly recently, it was customary in modern scholarship to draw a stark contrast between the Cappadocians and Augustine with reference to the doctrine of God.[30] It is said that the Cappadocians begin with the three persons while Augustine begins with the one nature. But this is inaccurate on both counts. In terms of the sheer literary sequence of a given text, it is not uncustomary for the Cappadocians to begin with the mystery of the divine nature.[31] On the other hand, there are Augustinian texts where he begins his exposition of the Christian doctrine of God by adverting to the missions of the Son and the Spirit, as these are narrated in the scriptures. That is how he begins his classic treatise, *On the Trinity*, composed over a period of two decades (*c.* 400–*c.* 420), and representing his mature teaching on the subject.

In this text, Augustine elaborates his Trinitarian theology over against both the anti-Nicene subordination of Son and Spirit and the Platonist rejection of the incarnation. He analyses the theophanies of the Old Testament as symbols (*similitudines*) of divine self-revelation. This 'regime of symbols' culminates in the supreme symbol of the incarnation of the Word, whose human nature provides a symbolic disclosure of his own divine nature shared with the Father and the Spirit. The mission of the Son in the incarnation is accompanied by the mission of the Spirit, who testifies to the Son and makes him known. Augustine subscribes to the same foundational principle as do the Cappadocians, that inseparability of activity is indicative of unity of essence.[32] In books I–IV of *De trinitate*, he shows that Father, Son and Spirit are equally, though distinctly, co-agents of the divine activity of creation and salvation and thus belong to the one divine essence.

Having reflected, in books I–IV, on the missions of the Son and Spirit as revelatory of the triunity of God, Augustine turns in book V to the question of the appropriate conceptual framework to articulate this triunity. He comes to the subject in a polemical stance, in response to the 'Arian' argument that the titles of 'unbegotten' and 'begotten' are revelatory of the difference in natures

---

30 For a critique of this assumption, see M. R. Barnes, 'Augustine in contemporary Trinitarian theology'.
31 See Gregory of Nazianzus, *Or.* 27; Gregory of Nyssa, *Cat. or.*, prol.
32 See Barnes, 'Rereading Augustine's theology of the Trinity'; L. Ayres, '"Remember that you are Catholic"'.

between Father and Son. Both the position presented as 'Arian' and Augustine's own response are couched in the Aristotelian categories of 'substance' and 'accident', and both depend on an account of divine simplicity that precludes the attribution of accidents to the divine essence.

Augustine presents the 'Arian' argument that if everything that is truly predicated of God is predicated with reference to substance (*secundum substantiam*) and not to accidents, then the titles of 'unbegotten' and 'begotten' must be taken as referring to different substances. Like Gregory of Nazianzus before him, Augustine maintains that the titles of 'unbegotten' and 'begotten' signify neither the divine substance nor accidents, but rather relation. But Augustine seems more aware of the logical difficulty of this position, inasmuch as 'relation' belongs to the category of accidents in the Aristotelian schema. Without explicitly stating this objection, Augustine articulates a rationale that overcomes it. He explains that 'accidents' pertain to the changeable properties of substances. Among creatures, whatever is not predicated of a substance must be attributed to it as an accident. In reference to God, however, nothing can be predicated by way of accident, since there is nothing changeable in God. Relation is not predicated of God accidentally because the divine relations are eternal and unchangeable.

In this way, Augustine adjusts the logic of the Aristotelian categories and subordinates it to biblical language. This language speaks of God as Father and Son, which are relational terms, and also indicates the eternality and immutability of both Father and Son such that they cannot be understood as accidents:

> But since the Father is only called so because he has a Son, and the Son is only called so because he has a Father, these things are not said with reference to substance, as neither is said with reference to itself but only with reference to the other. Nor are they said with reference to accidents, because what is signified by calling them Father and Son belongs to them eternally and unchangeably. Therefore, although being Father is different from being Son, there is no difference of substance, because they are not called these things by way of substance but by way of relation, and yet this relation is not an accident, because it is not changeable.[33]

Augustine is also aware of the terminological distinctions drawn by the Cappadocians between language that refers to what is common and that which refers to the distinctions among Father, Son and Spirit. In his own terminology, he speaks of what is shared among the persons as applicable to each 'of itself

---

33 Augustine, *Trin.* 5.6.7; trans. Hill, 192 (modified).

(*ad se*)', while what is distinct is applicable to each as related to the others (*ad invicem*).[34] Thus, the attributes of the divine nature, such as wisdom and power, are applicable to each of the persons 'of itself (*ad se*)' but the names of the persons refer to relations within the Godhead.

In his inference from unity of activity to unity of essence, as well as in his attempts to articulate terminological boundaries between what is common in the divine nature and what is distinguished through the mutual relations, Augustine is simply exemplifying the prevailing pro-Nicene theology of both East and West that developed in the second half of the fourth century. Augustine's individual genius is more apparent in two other doctrines that have had a powerful impact in the Western tradition, his characterisation of the Holy Spirit and of the Trinitarian image in the human being. In both cases, Augustine adapted elements already found in the Western tradition but gave them a much more forceful presentation.

With regard to the doctrine of the Holy Spirit, Augustine's biblical exegesis, prompted by earlier interpretations by Hilary of Poitiers, led him to characterise the Spirit as 'gift (*donum*)' (cf. John 4.10, Acts 8.20) and as divine 'love' (cf. Romans 5.5). It is these two characterisations that condition Augustine's teaching on the double procession of the Spirit: the Spirit's procession is the mutual love of Father and Son poured out as Divine Gift. Yet, Augustine is also clear that the Father is the 'first principle' of this procession; the Son derives his being a co-principle from the Father and so is *principium de principio*.[35]

Like his teaching on the double procession of the Spirit, Augustine's doctrine of the Trinitarian image in humanity has become one of the more prominent markers that distinguish the Western tradition of Trinitarian reflection from that of the East. Yet, the starting point for Augustine's reflection on the Trinitarian image in humanity has some affinities with the theological posture of the Cappadocians. Augustine too placed great emphasis on the incomprehensibility and incomparability of God, and on knowledge of God as attainable only through relationship and participation in the divine life. The challenge for Trinitarian faith is to believe in the triune God even while we have no conception of anything else that is triune in the same way.

Augustine's project is not so much to construct an objective analogical representation of divine triunity as to find a way to enter into relationship with the triune God, a way that extends from our immanent experience into the unfathomable mystery of God: 'What we are asking, though, is from what

---

34 Augustine, *Trin.* 5.11.12.
35 Augustine, *c. Max.* 2.17.4; *Trin.* 15.17.29.

likeness or comparison of things known to us are we able to believe, so that we may love the as yet unknown God.'[36] On the basis of the biblical teaching that humanity is made in the image of God, and with some influence from the Platonic teaching that the authentic self resides in the intelligible, rather than physical, aspects of the human being, Augustine seeks to find the way to the Triune God in the very structure of human consciousness. Through an ascent of self-reflection that is guided by Nicene doctrine, Augustine finds such a way into the mystery of the divine Trinity in the mind's mutually indwelling differentiations of memory, intellect and will. This Trinitarian image, however, becomes fulfilled only when the mind's orientation is properly ordered toward remembering, understanding and loving God.[37] Moreover, such an ordered orientation cannot be accomplished by mere exertion and discipline but rather through faith in the salvific work of Christ. It is by attending in faith to the work of Christ in history that the mind is initiated into the truth of the eternal reality of the triune God.[38]

Augustine's influence on the subsequent Western tradition of Trinitarian reflection is difficult to overestimate. His characterisations of the Trinitarian image in humanity in terms of a procession of the intellect and a procession of love are taken over by Aquinas, where they are much more directly applied to divine being than is the case with Augustine.[39] Within the time period with which we are presently concerned, the dominance of Augustine's influence can already be seen in the work of Boethius (*c*. 480–*c*. 524). Boethius, a statesman and theologian who came to be considered as an authoritative source by the Western medieval tradition, presented his own Trinitarian theology as the fruit of the seeds of Augustinian thought.

In particular, the Augustinian seeds that fructified in Boethius' own reflections were the earlier bishop's analysis of Trinitarian predications in book v of *De trinitate*. Boethius was principally preoccupied with post-Chalcedonian debates on the proper way to articulate the union of humanity and divinity in Christ. Efforts to dramatise the salvific import of this union, especially as evident in such slogans as 'One of the Trinity suffered in the flesh,' reopened concerns about articulating unity and distinction in the Trinity. In addressing these concerns, Boethius' approach is to clarify the church's Trinitarian doctrine through the use of the Aristotelian categories. He argues that the distinctions among the persons do not amount to a numerical difference inasmuch as

---

36 Augustine, *Trin.* 8.5.8; trans. Hill, 248.
37 Augustine, *Trin.* 14.11.15.
38 Ibid., 13.
39 Cf. Aquinas, *Summa theologiae* I-I, qu. 27, ar. 1–5.

difference in number among those in the same species is caused by difference in accidents. But there are no accidents in God, since God is pure form without admixture of matter and it is matter that is the substrate of accidents. Like Augustine, Boethius locates the Trinitarian distinctions within the category of relation.

His central argument for why the order of relations within the Trinity does not constitute difference depends on a distinction between intrinsic and extrinsic predication. Relation is considered as an extrinsic predication that applies to a comparison between two things without affecting the substance of what is compared: 'It cannot therefore be affirmed that predication of relationship by itself adds or takes away or changes anything in the thing of which it is said.'[40] Moreover, he observes, predications of relations apply not only to things that are unlike, such as master–slave, but also to things that are like each other.

At the end of such technical rational manoeuvring, Boethius is nevertheless compelled to conclude on an apophatic note. The likeness between the Trinitarian persons is altogether unique 'because of the otherness natural to all perishable, transitory objects'.[41] The human effort to come to some understanding of this transcendent reality involves abstracting from all material images. Boethius' approach is one that focuses on the logical apparatus by which the substance of Trinitarian doctrine can be formulated. His contribution lies in his analysis of key terms that had developed to express this doctrine, such as substance, relation and person, the last famously defined by him as an 'individual substance of a rational nature'.[42] Boethius' reflections on Trinitarian relations, which by later standards seem to involve a lack of integration between the categories of 'relation' and 'substance', came to be completed and complemented by Aquinas' understanding of the divine persons as 'subsistent relations'.[43]

The Trinity and the 'Christological' controversies

The distinction between 'Trinitarian theology' and 'Christology' is a relatively modern phenomenon. Within the framework of this distinction, it is customary to speak of the 'Trinitarian controversies' of the fourth century and the 'Christological controversies' of the fifth and sixth centuries. This distinction

---

40 Boethius, *De Trin.* 5.17–9; trans. Stewart et al., 27.
41 Boethius, *De Trin.* 6.22–4; trans. Stewart et al., 31.
42 Boethius, *Contra Eutychen* 3; trans. Stewart et al., *Boethius*, 85.
43 Aquinas, *Summa Theologiae* I-I, qu. 29, ar. 4.

is serviceable enough insofar as it is undoubtedly true that the main stream of Christian thought after the Council of Constantinople moved from a presumption of the equality and unity of the Trinity to a more focused consideration of the inter-relation of Christ's humanity and divinity in the fifth and sixth centuries. It would be very misleading, however, to see these as two separable sets of debates. The Trinitarian controversies were always most essentially about the identity of Jesus Christ, and they emerged precisely because the scriptural identification of Jesus Christ, as Son and Word of the Father and sender of the Spirit, was embedded in Trinitarian language. The Christological question, even narrowly defined as that of the relation between Christ's humanity and divinity, was also consistently integral to that debate.

Aside from a zealous concern for scriptural monotheism, the logic of anti-Nicene theology drew heavily on the assumption that the one who became human and suffered could not be a fully transcendent God. On the other hand, Nicene theology was compelled to insist that humanity did not compromise the full transcendence of the Word. It also typically included the soteriological argument, made forcefully by Athanasius, that only if the ultimate identity of Jesus resided fully in the Godhead could he truly work the salvation and deification of humanity. Throughout the Trinitarian debates of the fourth century, theologians grappled with the task of balancing the soteriological requirement of God's solidarity with humanity and the theological requirement of divine transcendence. This task necessarily involved different configurations of Trinitarian and Christological doctrine that tended to yield different results over a wide spectrum of doctrine, ranging from varying ways of construing the God–world relationship to the affirmation or denial of Christ's human soul.

A significant case in point is the figure of Apollinaris, bishop of Laodicea, who represents something of a bridge between the 'Trinitarian' and 'Christological' debates.[44] A friend, dedicated student and younger contemporary of Athanasius, Apollinaris was a defender of Nicaea who vigorously attacked 'Arian' doctrine. At the same time, he rejected the modalist doctrine of Marcellus and affirmed the irreducibility of three distinct hypostases or *prosopa*. His doctrine that the Logos takes the place of the human soul in the incarnate Word is designed to counter both Arian and Marcellian doctrine.[45] Arius' teaching that the Son, as creature, is changeable by nature was decisively refuted by asserting that the mutability of the human soul was

---

44 On the important role played by Apollinaris in the Christological debates, see ch. 19 in this volume.
45 The following is indebted to Kelley McCarthy Spoerl, 'Apollinarian Christology and the anti-Marcellan tradition'.

replaced by the immutability of the Word in Jesus Christ. At the same time, Apollinaris' Christology is directed against Marcellus' insistence on locating all differentiation between the incarnate Word and the Father strictly in the humanity of Jesus, so as to avoid imputing differentiation to the Godhead. This prompted Marcellus to emphasise the full humanity of Jesus in all the tension of its difference from divinity, a move that led his opponents to accuse him of teaching 'two sons'. Apollinaris' Christology is designed to counteract this 'dyoprosopic' Christology with a strongly unitive Christology in which the immutable Word is the single subject of the man Jesus. Thus, the immutability of divine transcendence is safeguarded while the soteriological principle of solidarity is asserted: God remains unchangeable and assumes human flesh, granting it his own immutability.

Of course, Apollinaris' opponents objected that such solidarity was phantasmal, since it was not the full structure of humanity that was united to the Word according to this model. In the Cappadocian polemic against Apollinaris' Christology, we find a soteriological model of solidarity that incorporates both Trinitarian and Christological claims. Human salvation is accomplished when the one who is fully God, enjoying unqualified possession of the divine nature, joins himself to our integral humanity: 'Let them not deny us our complete salvation . . . Keep the whole human being and mingle it with the divinity that you may benefit the whole of me.'[46]

The same dialectic of safeguarding both divine transcendence and God's saving solidarity with humanity was at the heart of the Christological controversies of the fifth and sixth centuries. All the significant parties involved in these Christological debates accepted Nicene doctrine on the Trinity and therefore were in agreement that Jesus Christ is ultimately to be identified with the Son, Word and Wisdom who is equal to the Father. Differences arose over just how this identification was to be conceived, and it is significant that in the controversy between Cyril and Nestorius, which broke out in 428, both cast the issue as a matter of the correct interpretation of the creed of Nicaea. Nestorius' discomfort with the title of 'theotokos' and with Cyril's manner of identifying the divine Word as the subject of Jesus' humanity stemmed from a concern that this compromised divine immutability and transcendence. Referring back to the Nicene Creed, Nestorius chides Cyril: 'the divine chorus of the Fathers did not say that the coessential Godhead is passible or that the Godhead which is coeternal with the Father has only just been born'.[47]

46 Gregory of Nazianzus, *Ep.* 101.33–6.
47 *Second Letter to Cyril*; trans. Richard A. Norris, *The Christological controversy*, 136.

While also adhering to the doctrine of divine impassibility, Cyril's essential response is that the heart of the Christian message goes beyond a mere reiteration of divine transcendence with the affirmation that the transcendent God is now directly identified with humanity such that he becomes the subject of the human condition. For Cyril, the meaning of Nicaea had to do with inserting the scriptural account of Jesus' life, death and resurrection into the very identification of God the Word: 'Now the great and holy synod stated that the unique Son himself . . . descended, was enfleshed, became human, rose on the third day, and ascended into the heavens.'[48] The Council of Ephesus of 431 sided with Cyril's interpretation. The Council of Chalcedon of 451 transferred the terminological distinctions formulated in the Trinitarian controversies to the double identification of Jesus Christ as both human and divine. The Nicene *homoousios* was used to identify not only the eternal Word's relation to the Father, but also the incarnate Word's relation to humanity. The humanity and divinity of Jesus Christ are distinguished as two 'natures' (*physes*), and united as concurring in a single concrete subject or 'person' (*hypostasis, prosopon*). Yet this did not resolve the ambiguity of just where this unity of subject is to be located. In 553, the Second Council of Constantinople sought to resolve this ambiguity in a Cyrillian direction, identifying the Chalcedonian 'one person' with the eternal hypostasis of the Son.

Underlying the complexity of Trinitarian and Christological debates throughout the crucial period of the fourth to sixth centuries is a soteriological vision which proved decisive: that humanity attains salvation and participation in divine life – deification – when the fully transcendent God identifies himself with the human condition in Jesus Christ. The logic of this vision necessitated confessing the full and unqualified divinity of Christ in the Nicene *homoousios*, the authenticity of both Christ's humanity and divinity at Chalcedon, and the attribution of the human condition to the very subject of God's person in Ephesus and Constantinople II. The central proclamation at the heart of the doctrinal tumult of this period is rendered in simple poetic cadence by the Syrian deacon and theologian, Ephrem:

> It is He who was begotten of Divinity
> according to His nature,
> and of humanity,
> which was not according to His nature,
> and of baptism,
> which was not His habit;

---

48 *Second Letter to Nestorius*; trans. Norris, *The Christological controversy*, 133.

So that we might be begotten of humanity,
according to our nature,
and of divinity,
which is not according to our nature,
and of the Spirit,
which is not our habit.[49]

Bibliography

PRIMARY SOURCES

Alexander of Alexandria. *Letter to Alexander of Byzantium (he philarchos).* Ed. H. G. Opitz, *Athanasius Werke,* III/1, *Urkunde* 14; trans. W. Rusch, *Trinitarian controversy*
Letter to all bishops (henos somatos). Ed. H. G. Opitz, *Athanasius Werke* III/1, *Urkunde* 4b; trans. W. Rusch, *Trinitarian controversy*
Ambrose. *On the Holy Spirit (De Spir.)* (CSEL 79); NPNF 2, x
Apollinaris. *Detailed confession of the faith (Kata meros pistis).* Trans. Hans Lietzmann, *Apollinaris von Laodicea und seine Schule* (Tübingen, 1904)
Asterius of Cappadocia. *Syntagmation.* Trans. M. Vinzent, *Asterius von Kappadokien. Die theologischen Fragmente* (Leiden, 1993)
Athanasius. *Letters to Serapion concerning the Holy Spirit (Ad Serap.).* (PG 26: 529–676); trans. C. R. B. Shapland, *The letters of Saint Athanasius regarding the Holy Spirit* (London, 1951)
On the Council of Nicaea (De decretis), ed. H. G. Opitz, *Athanasius Werke,* II.1; trans. K. Anatolios, *Athanasius* (2004)
On the Councils of Ariminum and Seleucia (De synodis), ed. H. G. Opitz, *Athanasius Werke,* II.1; NPNF 2, IV
Orations against the Arians (c. Ar.). Eds. K. Metzler et al., *Athanasius Werke,* I.1. (Berlin, 1998); NPNF 2, IV
Augustine. *Against Maximinus (c. Max.).* (PL 42); WSA I.18 (1995)
On the Trinity. (CCSL 50, 50a); trans. Edmund Hill, *The Trinity,* WSA (New York, 1990)
Basil of Caesarea. *Against Eunomius.* (SC 299, 305)
Letters. Ed. Yves Courtonne, *Saint Basile. Lettres* (Paris, 1957, 1961, 1966); FOTC 13, 28
On the Holy Spirit (De Spiritu Sancto) (SC 17); trans. David Anderson, *St. Basil the Great. On the Holy Spirit.* (Crestwood, NY, 1980)
Boethius. *The theological tractates,* trans. H. F. Stewart, E. K. Rand and S. J. Tester. LCL (Cambridge, MA, 1973)
Cyril of Alexandria. *Letters.* Ed. L. Wickham, *Cyril of Alexandria. Selected letters* (Oxford, 1983)
Ephrem the Syrian. *Homily on our Lord* (CSCO 270, 271); FOTC 91
Epiphanius of Salamis. *Panarion* (GCS 25, 31, 37); trans. F. Williams, *The Panarion of Epiphanius of Salamis* (Leiden, 1987)
Eunomius of Cyzicus. *Apology.* Ed. and trans. Richard P. Vaggione, *Eunomius. The extant works* (Oxford, 1987)

49 Ephrem, *Homily on our Lord* 2.1; trans. FOTC 91: 276.

Eusebius of Caesarea. *Against Marcellus* (GCS 4)

Preparation for the gospel (Prep. ev.) (PG 21); ed. E. H. Gifford, *Eusebii Pamphili evangelicae praeparationes*, libri IV, 4 vols. (Oxford, 1903)

Eusebius of Nicomedia. *Letter to Paulinus of Tyre* (Opitz, *Werke* III / I, Urkunde 8)

Gregory of Nazianzus. *Letters (Ep.)*. Ed. P. Gallay, *Saint Grégoire de Nazianze. Lettres*. (Paris, 1964, 1967)

Orations (Or.). (SC 250); trans. Frederick W. Norris, Lionel Wickham and Frederick Williams, *Faith gives fullness to reasoning: The five theological orations of Gregory Nazianzen* (Leiden, 1991)

Gregory of Nyssa. *Against Eunomius*. GNO 1, 2; NPNF II.5

Catechetical oration (Cat. or.) SC 453; tr. Cyril Richardson in Edward R. Hardy, ed., *Christology of the later fathers*, Library of Christian classics (Philadelphia, 1954), 268–325

To Ablabius on not three Gods (Ad Abl.). GNO 3¹; trans. Cyril Richardson in Edward R. Hardy, ed., *Christology of the later fathers*, Library of Christian Classics (Philadelphia, 1954), 256–67

Hilary of Poitiers. *On the synods (De syn.)* (PL 10); NPNF II.9

On the Trinity (SC 443, 448); FOTC 25

Marcellus of Ancyra. *Fragments*. Trans. M. Vinzent, *Markell von Ankyra. Die Fragmente. Der Brief an Julius von Rom*, Supp. *VigChr* 39 (Leiden, 1997)

Origen. *On first principles (De princ.)* (SC 252, 253, 268, 269, 312); trans. Henry Butterworth, *Origen: On first principles* (Gloucester, MA, 1973)

Socrates. *Ecclesiastical history* (H. E.) (PG 67); NPNF II.2

Tertullian. *Against Praxeas (Adv. Prax.)*. Trans. Ernest Evans, *Tertullian's treatise against Praxeas* (London: SPCK, 1948)

Thomas Aquinas. *Summa theologiae*, ed. P. Caramello (Taurini, 1948)

SECONDARY SOURCES

Abramowski, L. 'Was hat das Nicaeno-Constantinopolitanum (C) mit dem Konzil von Konstantinopel 381 zu tun?', *ThPh* 67 (1992): 481–513

Anatolios, K. *Athanasius*, Early Church Fathers (London, 2004)

Athanasius. The coherence of his thought (London, 1998)

'"When was God without Wisdom?" Trinitarian hermeneutics and rhetorical strategy in Athanasius' *SP* (forthcoming)

Arnold, Johannes. 'Begriff und heilsökonomische Bedeutung der göttlichen Sendungen in Augustinus *De trinitate*', *Recherches augustiniennes* 25 (1991): 3–69

Ayres, L. *Nicaea and its legacy. An approach to fourth-century Trinitarian theology* (Oxford, 2004)

'"Remember that you are Catholic" (*serm.* 52, 2): Augustine on the unity of the triune God', *JECS* 8 (2000): 39–82

Barnes, Michel René. 'Augustine in contemporary Trinitarian theology,' *Theological studies* 56 (1995): 237–50

'The fourth century as Trinitarian canon', in L. Ayres and G. Jones, eds., *Christian origins: Theology, rhetoric, and community* (London, 1998), 47–67

The power of God: Dynamis in Gregory of Nyssa's Trinitarian theology (Washington, DC, 2000)

'Re-reading Augustine's theology of the Trinity', in S. T. Davis, D. Kendall and G. O'Collins, eds., *The Trinity: An interdisciplinary symposium on the doctrine of the Trinity* (Oxford, 1999), 145–76

Barnes, M. R. and D. H. Williams, eds. *Arianism after Arius* (Edinburgh, 1993)

Barnes, T. D. *Athanasius and Constantius* (Cambridge, MA, 1993)

Beck, E. *Ephräms Trinitätslehre: Im bild von Sonne/Feuer, Licht und Wärme*, CSCO Subsidia 62 (Louvain, 1981)

Behr, J. *The Nicene faith* (Crestwood, NY, 2004)

Brachtendorf, J. *Die Struktur des menschlichen Geistes nach Augustinus: Selbstreflexion und Erkenntnis Gottes in 'De trinitate'* (Hamburg, 2000)

Brennecke, H. C. *Hilarius von Poitiers und die Bischofsopposition gegen Konstantius II. Untersuchungen zur dritten Phase des arianischen Streites (337–361)*, PTS 26 (Berlin, 1984)

Studien zur Geschichte der Homöer: Der Osten bis zum Ende der homöischen Reichskirche (Tübingen, 1988)

Chevalier, I. *Saint Augustin et la pensée grecque. Les relations trinitaires* (Fribourg, 1940)

Daley, Brian E. 'Divine transcendence and human transformation: Gregory of Nyssa's anti-Apollinarian Christology', *SP* 32 (1997): 87–95

'Revisiting the "Filioque": Roots and branches of an old debate', *Pro ecclesia* 10 (2001): 31–62

Drecoll, Volker Henning. *Die Entwicklung der Trinitätslehre des Basilius von Cäsarea: Sein Weg vom Homöusianer zum Neonizäner* (Göttingen, 1996)

Halleux, André de. '"Hypostase" et "personne" dans la formation du dogme trinitaire', (c. 375–381) *RHE* 79 (1984): 313–69, 625–70; reprinted in André de Halleux, *Patrologie et œcuménisme: Recueil d'études*, BETL 93 (Louvain, 1990), 215–68

'Personnalisme ou essentialisme trinitaire chez les pères cappadociens?', *Revue théologique de Louvain* 17 (1986): 129–55, 265–92; reprinted in André de Halleux, *Patrologie et œcuménisme: Recueil d'études*, BETL 93 (Louvain, 1990), 113–214

Hanson, R. P. C. *The search for the Christian doctrine of God. The Arian controversy 318–381 AD* (Edinburgh, 1988)

Kannengiesser, C. *Athanase d'Alexandrie, évêque et écrivain: Une lecture des traités contre les Ariens* (Paris, 1983)

Kelly, J. N. D. *Early Christian creeds* (London, 1972)

Kopecek, T. A. *A history of Neo-Arianism* (Philadelphia, 1979)

Lienhard, Joseph T. 'The Arian controversy: Some categories reconsidered', *Theological studies* 48 (1987): 415–36

Contra Marcellum: Marcellus of Ancyra and fourth century theology (Washington, DC, 1999)

'Ousia and hypostasis: The Cappadocian settlement and the theology of "one hypostasis"', in S. T. Davis, D. Kendall and G. O'Collins, eds., *The Trinity: An interdisciplinary symposium on the doctrine of the Trinity* (Oxford, 2000), 99–121

Löhr, Winrich. *Die Entstehung der homöischen und homöousianischen Kirchenparteien: Studien zur Synodalgeschichte des 4. Jahrhunderts* (Bonn, 1986)

'A sense of tradition: The Homoiousian church party', in M. R. Barnes and D. H. Williams, eds., *Arianism after Arius* (Edinburgh, 1993), 81–100

Lorenz, R. *Arius judaizans? Untersuchungen zur dogmengeschichte Einordnung des Arius* (Göttingen, 1979)

Louth, Andrew. 'The use of the term *idios* in Alexandrian theology from Alexander to Cyril', *SP* 19 (1987): 198–202

Lyman, Rebecca J. *Christology and cosmology: Models of divine activity in Origen, Eusebius, and Athanasius* (Oxford, 1993)

McGuckin, J. A. *Saint Gregory of Nazianzus: An intellectual biography* (Crestwood, NY, 2001)

St. Cyril of Alexandria. The Christological controversy. Its history, theology, and texts (Crestwood, NY, 2004)

Markschies, Christoph. 'Was ist lateinischer "Neunizanismus"?' *ZAC* 1 (1997): 73–95

Martin, Annick. *Athanase d'Alexandrie et l'église d'Égypte au IVᵉ siècle (328–373)*, CollÉFR 216 (Rome, 1996)

Meredith, Anthony. *The Cappadocians* (Crestwood, NY, 1996)

Meslin, Michel. *Les Ariens d'Occident* (Paris, 1967)

Mühlenberg, E. *Die Unendlichkeit Gottes bei Gregor von Nyssa* (Göttingen, 1966)

Norris, Richard A., ed. *The Christological controversy* (Philadelphia, 1980)

Opitz, H. G., ed. *Athanasius Werke* (Berlin, 1934–41)

Otis, Brooks. 'Cappadocian thought as a coherent system', *DOP* 12 (1955): 95–124

Patterson, Lloyd G. *Methodius of Olympus: Divine sovereignty, human freedom, and life in Christ* (Washington, DC, 1997)

Prestige, G. L. *God in patristic thought* (London, 1952)

Ricken, Friedo. 'Zur Rezeption der platonischen Ontologie bei Eusebios von Kaisareia, Areios und Athanasios', *ThPh* 53: 321–52

Ritter, Adolf-Martin. *Das Konzil von Konstantinopel und sein Symbol* (Göttingen, 1965)

Rousseau, Philip. *Basil of Caesarea* (Berkeley, 1994)

Rusch, William G. *The Trinitarian controversy* (Philadelphia, 1980)

Sesboüé, Bernard and Joseph Wolinski. *Le Dieu du salut*. Histoire des dogmes, tome 1 (Paris, 1994)

Simonetti, Manilo. *La crisi ariana nel IV secolo*, SEA 11 (Rome, 1975)

Spoerl, Kelley McCarthy. 'Apollinarian Christology and the anti-Marcellan tradition', *JTS* N.S. 45 (1994): 545–68

Studer, Basil. *The grace of Christ and the grace of God in Augustine of Hippo: Christocentrism or Theocentrism*, trans. M. J. O'Donnell (Collegeville, MN, 1997)

Trinity and incarnation: The faith of the early church (Edinburgh, 1993)

Tetz, Martin. *Athanasiana: Zu Leben und Lehre des Athanasius* (Berlin, 1995)

'Zur Theologie des Markell von Ancyra', *ZKG* 75 (1964): 217–70

'Zur Theologie des Markell von Ancyra II', *ZKG* 79 (1968): 3–42

Torrance, Thomas F. *The Trinitarian faith* (Edinburgh, 1988)

Turcescu, Lucian. 'Prosopon and hypostasis in Basil of Caesarea's *Against Eunomius* and the Epistles', *VigChr* 51 (1997): 374–95

Vaggione, Richard P. *Eunomius of Cyzicus and the Nicene revolution* (Oxford, 2000)

Widdicombe, Peter. *The fatherhood of God from Origen to Athanasius* (Oxford, 1994)

Williams, Rowan. *Arius: Heresy and tradition* (London, 2001²)

'*Sapientia* and the Trinity: Reflections on the *De trinitate*', in B. Bruning, M. Lamberigts and J. van Houten, eds., *Collectanea Augustiniana: Mélanges T. J. Van Bavel* (Louvain, 1990), 317–32

19

History of Christology to the
seventh century

KARL-HEINZ UTHEMANN

The earliest biblical confessions of Jesus were varied, yet linked. He was the Messiah, the fulfilment of Israel's hopes and the eschatological accomplishment of God's reign, even as he was also a prophet promised by Moses and a teacher in the wisdom tradition. His death demonstrated God's salvation; his resurrection proclaimed him alive. Therefore, as the Christian community moved from the Old Testament, the word of God, to the Christian Bible, these different Christologies were connected. Nevertheless, in constantly changing contexts, diverse Christological confessions emerged within a broader understanding of the apostolic kerygma.

The faith of Christians quickly came to be determined by their hope of being redeemed by God himself. From the Old Testament prophets, the community learned that the one God of salvation (Isaiah 43.11, 45.21, 63.9) brought this salvation in Jesus Christ. This Jesus was the presence of God on earth (see *Epistle of Barnabas* 3.35–37). 'Brothers, we must think about Jesus Christ, as *we do about God*, the judge of the living and the dead. We ought not to think lowly things about our salvation,' says 2 *Clement*, the oldest extant Greek homily. These words correspond with Barnabas: God is the saviour (Isaiah 49.7); he is the Lord (Kyrios) whose suffering for our sake made Christians the true heirs of Moses' Testament.[1]

Such juxtaposed but reconciled claims – Old Testament monotheism and belief in Jesus Christ as the redeemer – led to the first Christian theology. Although modern scholarship has sometimes depicted it as heretical modalistic monarchianism, in fact it reproduced the Great Church's doctrine. When Hippolytus of Rome (d. 235) and Tertullian (d. after 220) contested it, it was the majority formula of faith: Jesus Christ is God. His divinity is not different from the Father's; this monotheism preserved 'the one dominion' (*monarchia*)

---

1 Cf. Barnabas 14.4–9, where there are citations from Isaiah 42.6–7; 49.6–7; 61.1–2.

of God. 'I know only one God, Jesus Christ, and apart from him no other conceived and passable', taught, for example, Pope Zephyrinus (*sed.* 198/9–217).

The origin of the confession of the unity of God and human being: Apollinarius and his historical presuppositions

In confessing the one God and the Logos Jesus Christ as God and saviour,
the first verses of John's prologue provide the point of departure for a Logos-
theology. But a 'monarchian' formulation of this Logos-theology does not
correspond with either the original meaning of the prologue of the Gospel
of John, or the Logos-theology of Justin Martyr, Origen or Tertullian, who
considered the Logos a second subordinate divinity or mode of existence of
the one God (which is called subordinationism, or a 'two-level theory'). By
contrast, the monarchianists presented the Logos as God's wisdom, proper to
the sole God or Father, as a power immanent in him that is manifested in creation and incarnation. The monarchianists offered no ontological distinction
in God himself. Their opponents labelled them patripassionists, implying that
they believed it was the transcendental God and not the saviour, Jesus Christ,
who had been crucified. Their opponents also objected that monarchian theology would confess Father, Son and Holy Spirit as mere appearances of the
one God the Father. Although this doctrine had already been attacked by Hippolytus and Tertullian, it was only at the beginning of the fourth century that
this position was generally rejected. The heresiologists of the early church
attributed it to a certain Sabellius (third century), a Noetian teacher in Rome,
about whom we know hardly anything.

The treatise *De Trinitate* by Novatian attests to the continuation of the
original monarchianist tradition. Novatian distances himself from Sabellius,
responds to the 'two-level theory' of this 'new theology' and establishes with
respect to God's immanence that there is an ontological difference between
Father and Son. From 251, Novatian was Rome's anti-pope. Although he considered the Son as 'second person after the Father' and as subordinate to him,
his guiding rule of faith (*regula*) depended on John 17.3: 'Eternal life is this: to
know you, the only true God, *and* him whom you have sent, Jesus Christ.'
According to John 1.14, Christ is God and also a human being. He is the 'Word
of God', he is the only-begotten Son of the 'one and only God' and – according
to the monarchianists' interpretation of John 1.1c – he is God. Through him
the Father redeemed humanity. Before him, 'nothing existed but the Father',

in whom 'he was timelessly before all time and from whom he emerged when the Father wanted it'.

Novatian professes both one God and Jesus Christ as God. His Logos-theology ascribes to the Son eternal existence in the Father. This pre-temporal conception and birth can only be reconciled with the one and only God, because the Son received everything which he is – *viz.*, word, wisdom, power, light – 'from the Father' and is thus only called a 'divinity that has been handed down' (*divinitas tradita*). For this divinity is a 'power, transmitted by the Father and communicated to the Son', and returned again by the Son to the Father, the one true God (1 Corinthians 15.28). But Novatian does not say how this concept of the Son's divinity (which is predicated on the history of salvation) can be consistent with the eternal procession of the Son from the Father, nor does he articulate how the concept of a 'second person after the Father' can establish that difference between Father and Son that is emphasised by anti-monarchian theology.

Forms of monarchianist theology continued to exist well into the fourth century. It is precisely in opposition to this theology – which viewed the Logos immanent in the one God with no ontological difference and interpreted the confession of Nicaea (325) accordingly – that the real theme of the Christolog-ical debate arose: how does the unity of God and human being occur in the one Jesus Christ? How can confessing one Lord Jesus Christ indicate that the union of God and human being is real and that both divinity and humanity are actual? This debate questions the understanding of the Logos' incarna-tion and hence Nicaea's confession of God's only-begotten Son, who is of one nature (*homoousios*) with the Father, the one God and creator, and who, for our salvation, became 'flesh and man' (John 1.14).

The critique of Apollinarius and its antecedents: Athanasius, Marcellus and Noetus

Apollinarius of Laodicea (*c*. 310–90) became the focal point of such question-ing. He was only partly aware of the theological assumptions underlying the position he was developing. Professing the incarnate Logos as a union of the human reality of Jesus (i.e., the flesh) with the Logos of the one God on the level of being, he engaged with two theological positions.

First, he rejected the Arian claim that everything human that the Bible reported about Christ was proper to the Logos, *as such*. This applied not only to statements of his lowliness, which characterise his *kenosis* (Philippians 2.7), but also to claims about the 'assumed glory' (Philippians 2.9) in the resurrection and ascension.

Second, he objected to a Christology that separated the human reality of Christ, 'the flesh', from the divinity, as if the body, 'the flesh', born of the Virgin, was independent of the Logos. With this position, contemporary theologians, such as Marcellus of Ancyra, defended Nicaea's confession against the Arians and supported a monarchianist Logos-theology.

Apollinarius was not conscious of the historical background of these positions when he distinguished them from the church's doctrinal tradition he saw defined in Nicaea. Moreover, he did not fully recognise the tradition of theological questions that determined both these positions and his own standpoint. He confessed, namely, that the incarnate Logos is the subject of all Christological statements, and therefore also of all the antitheses that separate God and creatures: 'one and the same is visible and invisible, created and uncreated, mutable and immutable'. For him and his contemporaries, claiming one subject of these antitheses only reiterated the traditional teaching of the church. They were not aware that this form of confessing Christ as both God and redeemer went back to the early church's dispute with Gnosticism. Above all they knew nothing about the anti-Gnostic rule of faith of Noetus of Smyrna that had a powerful if largely invisible impact on the subsequent Christological debate.

With Athanasius against Arianism

Apollinarius emphasises the antithetical nature of the Christological predicates precisely in order to stress the divinity in the statements of lowliness. 'The one incarnate Logos is visible in his body, although as God he is invisible.' 'He emptied himself in the form of a slave (Philippians 2.7), although in his divine essence he is not emptied and is unchangeable.' Apollinarius' picture of Christ is determined by this view of the incarnate Logos' divinity.

In all this, Apollinarius only follows 'the common teacher' of all Nicene Christians, Athanasius of Alexandria (c. 293–373), and presupposes his biblical exegesis against Arianism. In his exegesis, Athanasius relates everything human, changeable and transient that is said about Jesus Christ in the Bible to 'the flesh of Christ' and not, as the Arians did, to the Logos. It distinguishes sentences about divine and human as statements about two different subjects, the Logos and the human being, Jesus ('the flesh'), even if in the incarnation they are inseparably united. Yet it remains firmly in the framework of a 'Christology from above': the Logos is the active subject in salvation, ultimately the one concrete subject of all biblical statements about Christ. Everything purely human is said of him 'according to the flesh', while the glorification and exaltation of 'the flesh' is understood as a consequence of the 'appropriation of everything human by the Logos'.

Athanasius establishes his exegesis by saying that 'the divinity took up its abode in the flesh' and hence assumed a body as an appropriate instrument in order to operate in the world (this is how he understood Colossians 2.9). Because the Logos 'through his body, which is proper to him, carries out the works proper to him', i.e., the miracles attested in the New Testament, therefore everything 'which is proper to the flesh is said of the Logos' (*Contra Arianos* 3.31). For if, according to John 1.14, 'the Logos became flesh and dwelt among us', then 'the Logos became a human being and did not come into a human being' (3.30). First, Jesus is not an inspired human; he is something other than a prophet. Second, the Logos made 'the flesh' his own (*idiopoieisthai*), and with it everything that his body suffers (3.33). Hence the believer recognises that 'both', which operated in a divine way and in a human way, proceed from 'only one' (3.35).

Everything in the Bible about the Logos and 'the flesh' ultimately speaks of this one, the incarnate Logos and Son of God. This view determines Athanasius' picture of Christ. He always sees the human in the Logos. That which is human is not said of him – as the Arians would say it – 'according to the divinity', but 'according to the flesh'. To this extent Athanasius distinguished in *Contra Arianos* an ultimate subject of Christological predicates, the incarnate Logos, and two subjects for each class of the biblical predicates, namely, the purely divine and the purely human.

In his 'Letter to Epictetus', who was bishop of Corinth, Athanasius articulates the same position. For the *fides Nicaena* the paradox was that 'the one who suffered and the one who did not suffer is the same', namely, the Logos, who as God is impassible, but yet suffered, insofar as the body proper to him suffered. In spite of this appropriation by the Logos, the incarnate One's body is not changed to become 'one (or the same) nature with the godhead' (*homoousios*). Some Christians, who remain anonymous, held that view. Their position is refuted in the 'Letter to Epictetus'.

Apollinarius knew this letter, which was to play a decisive role in the debate about the orthodoxy or otherwise of the Christological traditions of Alexandria and Antioch, in the fifth century (at the height of the Christological controversy). Both supporters and opponents of Apollinarius could conceive of his teaching in a way that assimilated it to the Christological position that Athanasius had challenged in this letter. Yet Apollinarius thought that there was no difference between Athanasius' and his confession of the incarnate Logos.

Against Marcellus of Ancyra

In distancing himself from Marcellus, however, Apollinarius went beyond Athanasius. Athanasius never considered in detail the divine and the human union in the incarnate One; for him this was not an issue in the Arian controversy. In this respect he agreed with Eustathius of Antioch (he probably died before 337, though other dates have been suggested: 343/5, or 370), who established the anti-Arian exegesis that led to the Antiochene confession of Christ's two natures. Apollinarius' situation was different. For him Nicaea's confession and Athanasius' viewpoint regarding the appropriation 'of the flesh' by the Logos were irreconcilable with Marcellus' teaching. For the Alexandrian, the one Son of God was 'God and human being, both as one', 'both at the same time'. Athanasius' anti-Arian exegesis excludes any Christology that confesses two separate subjects (i.e., the God Logos and the human being Jesus) and, instead of stressing the one unique person (*prosopon*), nature (*physis*) and hypostasis, confesses a duality of them. For Apollinarius, such a Christology cannot claim to remain faithful to the creed of Nicaea; it is a 'Christology from below'. Instead of confessing the incarnate God, it understands the human being Jesus as one inspired by God (*entheos*), in whom the Logos acts, without being ontologically present, and thus incarnate. Like pagans and Jews, these Christians do not acknowledge the divinity of him 'who was born of a woman' (Galatians 4.4).

Early on, perhaps before 341, Apollinarius attacked Marcellus and his disciple, Photinus, the bishop of Sirmium. Following a line of argument first developed by Eusebius of Caesarea (d. 339) Apollinaris identifies the third-century bishop of Antioch, Paul of Samosata (finally excommunicated as a heretic by a synod in 268) as the father of this Christology. Eusebius' critique, in turn, had its precursor in the polemic against a monarchianism, or Sabellianism, that formulated a Logos-theology in terms of an ontological difference in the one God. Tertullian, Hippolytus and, it would seem, Novatian articulated this position, even if in the latter's case the older conception remains.

For Marcellus, the Logos, eternally present in the one God as his power (*dynamis*), proceeded from God first in creation and then in the incarnation. He is in both cases the active force (*energeia*). The one God expanded and extended his monad to a duality, a dyad, of Father and Son. The difference exists in the extension of the monad, and thus God is a dyad 'only in activity (*energeia*)'. According to 1 Corinthians 15.28 ('When he has done this, then the Son himself will be made subject to him who put everything under him, so that God may be all in all'), the dyad will be nullified at the end of the history of salvation. This, however, does not affect the one God, for he remains 'inseparably' only a monad. Marcellus rejected an ontological distinction (i.e., on the level of being) in the unique hypostasis of the one God, in order to undermine the radical subordinationism of Arian Logos-theology. Because he did not concede that the Logos, in the activity of creation and incarnation, has his own separate existence alongside the Father, he cannot establish for the incarnation an ontological relation between the Logos and Jesus, the assumed human being.

Apollinarius accepted Eusebius' polemical conclusion: like Paul of Samosata, Marcellus cannot confess Jesus Christ as God, but only as a being 'from below', 'from the earth', i.e., apparently a mere man inspired by God.

Because Marcellus stands in the monarchianist tradition, he does not recognise this defect of his *apologia* for the Nicene faith. For him Christ is God because he is the saviour. According to Christians, the passage at Baruch 3.35–37 about God 'being seen on the earth' refers to Christ, who is anointed as saviour and whose work is the Father's. From his standpoint Marcellus clearly rejected the concept of Christ as a mere inspired man.

'The paradoxical one': Noetus against the Gnostic separation of Christ and Jesus

As has been stressed above, Athanasius and Apollinarius, as well as their contemporaries, did not recognise that their confession of the one incarnate Logos as the single subject of all Christological statements followed the tradition of anti-Gnostic monarchianism. Noetus of Smyrna (mid-second century) had created, by means of his rule of faith, a formula of antitheses, which would have a powerful impact on the history of the Great Church, the *catholica*.[2]

Noetus' antitheses

Noetus' *regula fidei* knows no pre-temporal birth of the Son, but only his virgin birth (Luke 1.35). Although this may seem strange to later readers, virgin birth is what Noetus attributes to the sole God, the Father. The *regula* defines this God as 'the paradoxical one'; he is the single subject to whom both the philosophical divine predicates and, as antitheses to these, the biblical statements about Jesus Christ apply. Noetus' *regula* – the text of which is transmitted in Hippolytus of Rome's *Refutatio omnium haeresium* – contains some excerpts from a homily:

2 See R. M. Hübner, *Der Paradox Eine*. Hübner recognises that his thesis has already been put forward by previous scholars: see, e.g,. A. Harnack, 'Monarchianismus'.

One and only is the Father and God of the universe,
invisible, yet visible, when he appeared (on earth),
incomprehensible, yet comprehensible in the Son,
unconceived, yet conceived, as soon as he was born of the virgin,
impassible, yet he suffered for us,
immortal, yet he died for us (in the flesh).

These antitheses characterise God's coming and suffering as redeemer. Noetus' *regula* established for theology a tradition of theopaschite language – language, that is, about God suffering. This language can only be misunderstood as a denial of divine transcendence if we forget its origin in the aforementioned paradox of antithetical claims that are attributed to the one divine subject. In the second century, for example, it was taken up by Melito of Sardes (in his Easter homily), by the author of the letters of Ignatius of Antioch, and by Irenaeus of Lyon.

The one God is visible, comprehensible, passible and mortal 'in the flesh', that is, in the saviour Jesus Christ. As saviour, he is 'in the spirit', *pneuma*, invisible, incomprehensible, without suffering and immortal. It is 'one and the same God . . . who was attested to those who saw him as Son, because he was born (of a virgin) and is still the Father and has not hidden anything from those who can comprehend it'.

With this formula, Noetus wanted to demarcate the *catholic* confession of the one God and of the saviour Jesus Christ's divinity from the Christology of the school of the Gnostic Valentinus and its myth of the saviour's descent and ascent. For Valentinus' disciples, as is generally true for Christian Gnostics, the saviour descended from the *pleroma* – the region of divine transcendence – into a completely different cosmos, only to re-ascend later through the spheres of the planets, unbeknown to the masters of these planets, who are themselves the angels of the demiurge. This saviour is 'invisible, untouchable, impassible', and hence 'someone different' from Jesus, 'who was born and suffered' (Irenaeus). In various expressions and turns of phrase,[3] the Gnostics effectively split the one saviour into two figures, separating the Christ from above and the Jesus from below. Some of the Gnostics (e.g., Theodotus, a Valentinian) also divided him into two elements or components, which could be called natures, i.e., into the pneumatic Christ on the one hand, and the suffering body of the physical Christ, 'the flesh', on the other hand. For the Gnostics, everything stemming from the *pleroma* does not participate in the passion. Some Gnostics even went as far as saying that it was not Jesus who was nailed to the cross. According to

3 For a good account, see K. Rudolph, *Die Gnosis*, 162–78.

them Jesus assumed Simon of Cyrene's appearance, looked on, and ridiculed the lords of the cosmos, the demiurge's angels. A Gnostic, then, would see two figures on the cross: 'one, glad and laughing on the tree – another, whose hands and feet they are striking'. The first figure is 'the living Jesus', the second 'his fleshly part, which is the substitute being put to shame'. A third figure, who approaches the scene and reveals the meaning of what is happening, is 'the saviour woven in a Holy Spirit' (NHC VII: 3).[4]

By maintaining the identity of the one suffering with the only true God and thus confessing the one suffering as God and saviour, Noetus firmly opposed this tearing apart of that saviour into two figures or 'natures', into unchangeable substance and changeable appearance (NHC VII: 4).

Two conceptions of Christ as the one subject

The impact of Noetus' confession of the one God and redeemer as the one subject of the antitheses can be observed in the 'new Logos-theology' advanced by Hippolytus of Rome and Tertullian of Carthage. Detached from the name of Noetus and from its original anti-Gnostic context, this confession became common property and thus the basis of the Christology in the *fides Nicaena*. Because of its paradoxical character, it excludes naïve theopaschite language from Christology.

However, the confession of the antitheses' one subject allowed two conceptions of Christ, the one incarnate Logos, to emerge:

1. One conception could stress that *at the same time* he is God *and* human being, invisible and visible, so that statements of divine majesty apply to him as God, and *simultaneously* the biblical statements of lowliness refer to him as a human being. The symmetrical picture of Christ formulated by Hippolytus and Tertullian exemplifies this point of view. As Tertullian expressed it so tersely, paving the way for the Christologies of Augustine and Pope Leo the Great, Christ revealed himself as 'God *and* human being in one person, preserving the identity of both substances, so that the spirit (i.e., God) in him carried out the works proper to him – and the flesh endured the sufferings proper to it'.

2. The second conception arises when the divinity of Christ is emphasised and simultaneously the biblical statements of lowliness are accentuated as antitheses. Apollinarius did this when, following the lead of Athanasius, he said: 'The one incarnate Logos is visible in his body, although as God

---

4 Cf. H. W. Havelaar, *The Coptic Apocalypse of Peter*, 177–80; D. Voorgang, *Die Passion Jesu* offers a comprehensive collection of materials.

he is invisible ... although he is the true God ... although according to his divine essence he ... is immutable.' Apollinarius always drew attention to the incarnate Logos, to God in whom 'the new human being' exists. To this extent his picture of Christ is asymmetrical and open to the charge of employing naïve theopaschite language. Here the one subject of all Christological statements is the incarnate Logos. According to Apollinarius, the conception that distinguishes both God *and* human being in Christ has the effect of abolishing the unity of the one subject, i.e., it divides Christ into two subjects (*dihairesis*). For him, this therefore implies a 'Christology from below', like Paul of Samosata's.

The difference between the two Christological conceptions was intimated by Apollinarius and disputed by Alexandrian and Antiochene Christologies. It led to the introduction of mutually exclusive Christological confessions that ultimately resulted in mutual misunderstandings and reciprocal claims of heresy. This happened although both traditions, the Alexandrian and the Antiochene, favoured a 'Christology from above', had recourse to Nicaea and laid claim to Nicene orthodoxy. They both agreed to defend the one Christ as the one subject, to distance the suffering of Christ from the divinity and to preserve the *apatheia* of God. As God, Christ the redeemer could not suffer.

The Christological confession of Apollinarius of Laodicea – with, and beyond, Athanasius

Like Marcellus of Ancyra, Apollinarius of Laodicea could also write impressively about the divinity of Christ as saviour, for example in his *Anakephelaiosis*. Yet in contrast to Marcellus he stresses the ontological unity of the God-man and confesses that 'it was God who was crucified by the Jews', that on the cross 'God himself died', even if God, as God, cannot suffer. As God the incarnate One is unchangeable; he took on the condition of the *kenosis*, or self-emptying, by assuming the form of a slave (Philippians 2.7). What was assumed is 'no *other beside* God', who suffers and is prayed to, but God's flesh, God's body, because 'he is inseparable from that which is his body'. To this extent Christ's body is uncreated and of 'one (or the same) substance' (*homoousios*) with God. This is true even if, in the union, neither the nature of the body nor that of the divinity is changed.

Apollinarius refuses to speak of the human being Jesus. He concedes only a similarity with *the* human being (!), which the pre-existing one had added in his incarnation. Insofar as it is 'a question of what characterises Jesus Christ in the real sense', he is not 'of the same nature as us' (*homoousios*). The salvation of humanity is only guaranteed when the incarnate One possesses an 'immutable intellect', which does not conflict with 'the flesh'. The incarnate One accomplishes 'pure virtue' – without any asceticism! – and achieves that freedom from every sin to which human beings owe their salvation. This intellect can only be the Logos himself as the intellect of God; no human intellect was assumed in the incarnation. This is why Apollinarius disputed that Christ – in 'God's incarnate intellect' – had a rational human soul. He excluded therefore a 'Christology from below' that understood Christ as an inspired human being. He found the biblical foundation for this, for example, in the events in Gethsemane (Matthew 26.36–39). Here the anti-Arian exegesis of Athanasius affirmed God's one will and understood the resistance, the fear of death and the obedience of Christ as a drama of divine pedagogy for the faithful (*oikonomia*). Apollinarius accepted this interpretation, but maintained as a consequence of this that there was no human intellect in Christ. The incarnate One suffered 'as God'. Only he can redeem mankind.

This confessional language, particularly its theopaschism, could sound provocative, especially if the qualifications arising from Athanasius' anti-Arian exegesis were ignored. It must be said, however, that Apollinarius constantly emphasised these qualifications. Moreover, had he confined himself to remaining silent about the soul of Christ instead of explicitly denying its existence, he would not have shocked so many of his contemporaries. Although Athanasius, adapting the language of the Bible, could talk of the soul of Christ, for him it was 'not a theological factor'.[5] On this point he agreed on the one hand with Eusebius of Caesarea, who abandoned not only Origen's concept of the pre-existence of souls, but also his teaching on Christ's soul (unlike the so-called Origenists, such as Evagrius Ponticus (*c.* 345–99)).[6] On the other hand, Athanasius even agreed with his Arian opponents on this point. For they ascribed all the mental experiences of Christ related in the Bible reports to the Logos 'become flesh', as Logos. As we see from statements by Asterius that Athanasius quotes, this conception is also presupposed by Arian soteriology,

---

5 In this way A. Grillmeier summarises the discussion triggered by M. Richard, 'Saint Athanase'. Still worth reading, however, are J. B. Liébaert, *Christologie*, 73 n. 68 and P. Galtier, 'Saint Athanase et l'âme du Christ'.

6 Evagrius saw in Christ that intellect (*nous*) which always remained united to the God Logos, in contradistinction to all other spiritual beings, and for that reason did not, like the latter in their revolt against God, enter as soul into a body. This Christ or *nous*, not the Logos, became incarnate in Jesus, in order to save the fallen souls. There are more details in A. Guillaumont, *Les 'Kephalaia Gnostica'*, 117–18, 151–6.

which, basing salvation on the immutable obedience of the Logos to the will of the Father, implies the denial of Christ's soul.[7]

The express denial of a rational soul in Christ, however, is clearly encountered only in Arians of the second generation. They deny the Nicene confession of the Logos becoming a human being, and speak only of his incarnation. They argue that the human soul in the one Christ introduces a second intelligence beside that of the Logos and therefore destroys the unity of Christ's 'one composite nature'. However, it seems that this conception of a 'soulless Christ' had already been maintained by the first generation of Arians: Eustathius of Antioch contested it shortly after the Council of Nicaea. First, he distinguishes two natures, the God Logos and the 'human being of Christ', in order to ward off psilanthropism (i.e., the idea that Christ is a mere man). Second, he stresses the rational soul of this human being. A 'soulless Christ' cannot be the 'cause of salvation' (Hebrews 5.8–9).[8]

Apollinarius' Christology encompasses all those questions and concepts that would be at issue during the debates between conflicting Alexandrian and Antiochene Christologies at the Council of Ephesus (431). Everything that comes after him in the East in effect debates with him and the tradition of Christological questions he inherited. Therefore he deserves detailed study. His denial of Christ having a human understanding, and thus a human soul, encountered resistance in East and West alike and was condemned as heresy. Yet after the death of Athanasius (373), Apollinarius' perspective of the Christological union (i.e., that the Logos is the one and only subject of all Christological statements – a concept that is itself initially derived from Athanasius) became decisive for Cyril of Alexandria (d. 444) and his asymmetrical picture of Christ. Cyril was particularly influenced by Apollinarian forgeries, i.e., writings of Apollinarius and his disciples that were promulgated under the names of Athanasius of Alexandria, Pope Felix (d. 273/4) and Pope Julius (337–52).

Apollinarius confesses the incarnate One 'as one sole God, one sole hypostasis and one sole person', as 'the one incarnate nature of the God Logos'. Thus he creates precisely that formula that Cyril of Alexandria would later favour.

---

7 R. C. Gregg and D. E. Groh, *Early Arianism*; but note that the authors' thesis that soteriology, not radical monotheism, was Arius' principal concern has been rejected by subsequent research.

8 The textual basis for the Christology of Eustathius has been considerably expanded by the edition of previously unknown excerpts of that treatise from which Theodoret of Cyrus took the only quotation that claims that the Arians would deny the human soul of Christ. Cf. J. H. Declerck in his edition of Eustathius, CCSG 51: 63–126; K.-H. Uthemann, Review of Declerck; K.-H. Uthemann, 'Eustathios von Antiochien'.

The 'Miaphysites', who were inaccurately labelled 'Monophysites' in their opponents' polemics, summarised their confession with the same formula after the Council of Chalcedon (451). With the formula 'the one and only nature of the incarnate One', Apollinarius intends to emphasise that 'one and the same', as the single subject of the incarnation, is God and human being, 'both at the same time', 'both as one'. Apollinarius excludes a confession of two sons, one the Son of God and the other a human son 'from Mary'. Therefore he refuses to speak of 'two natures' or 'two prosopa', or to accept an independent human intellect in Christ, the incarnate intellect of God. For this reason, with respect to the logic of Christological statements, he stresses against Marcellus of Ancyra that there is one subject *as such* of 'both everything corporeal as well as everything divine'. For him this corresponds to biblical language, which shows that the Logos has appropriated 'the flesh' to himself.

Apollinarius founded his 'logic of Christological statements' on the ontological unity (*henotes*), or union (*henosis*), of the divine and the human. For him the unity of the 'one sole life', attested in the New Testament, shows that 'God' and 'human being' 'communicated' with each other, and that both were still united, even while preserving the characteristic differences that distinguish each of them: 'each in its own name'. Thus the 'flesh of Christ' possesses two characteristics. On the one hand – as born from the Virgin – it is a human being; on the other hand it transcends human nature by virtue of its union with the Logos. This elevation, proclaimed at Philippians 2.9 and John 17.5, is called 'glory'. Thus 'the flesh' possesses properties (*idiomata*) held in common with the Logos.

In his dispute with the Arians, Athanasius had not suppressed Christ's elevation, but understandably he had not cared to emphasise it. Apollinarius is a different matter. Regarding the community or *koinonia* of the properties, he distinguishes three classes of biblical sayings. Apart from those that apply exclusively to either the divinity or the flesh, there is a third class of combined statements. These are predicated mutually (*koinôs*)[9] of the Logos and 'the flesh': they are predicated, that is, of the whole as one sole subject. These joined sentences include Christ's miracles and his elevation and glorification, which are the statements that Apollinarius stresses in his Christological confession.

To ensure the difference in the inseparable unity of Logos and flesh, Apollinarius employs the concept of mixture (*krasis* (blending), *mixis* (combination))

9 Apollinarius' term is *epikoinonein.*

that Tertullian had already used in the West and that was present in previous philosophy.[10] The divinity remained unchangeable in the incarnation. For the power of God (Luke. 1.35) 'performed the work of incarnation' and remained nevertheless the power of God. 'In the same way the Logos of God, during his human life on earth, preserved his divine omnipresence, because he accomplished everything and at the same time in a special way was mixed with the flesh.' In the incarnate One 'the uncreated being exists in a mixture with the created'. This mixture is compared to the mixture in the human being of body and soul, in which both preserve their own qualities or properties. He maintains that the preservation of the differences *a fortiori* applies in the incarnation, in which the divinity in its immutability remains unmixed. To this extent the category of mixture serves the purpose of enabling the confession of the incarnate One as 'the paradoxical One'.

Apollinarius repeatedly uses this anthropological paradigm[11] to rule out in Christ any mixture in which what is proper to God or the flesh is changed into something inappropriate to them according to their nature. In line with philosophical tradition, he calls this type of mixture a *synchysis*.[12] He also uses the comparison, already proposed by Origen, of iron glowing in the fire; for Apollinarius, it is Christ's body, which in the union with the Logos (here, the fire) remains body, 'although he grants the divine energies to those who are able to touch him'.

His concept of mixture implies an ontology of 'the part and the whole' which, however, he qualifies for Christological statements. This has not always been recognised by his contemporaries, or indeed by modern scholars. In the constitution of the individual human being, body and soul are incomplete parts, because in their very natures they complement each other. Such a 'connaturality' (*symphyia*) does not exist in the incarnate One; *a fortiori*, the properties of the parts remain preserved in Christ. Thus Apollinarius can use the concepts of *synthesis* and of the one as a whole, without conceiving the Logos and 'the flesh' as incomplete parts. He nevertheless excludes a union 'of two complete beings', that is, of two sons, the Son of God and a son of man. For such a human being does not owe her/his existence to the union with the Logos, whereas the one born of the Virgin does.

---

10 A brief depiction is offered by H. A. Wolfson, *The philosophy of the church fathers*, 374–85.
11 On the history of the paradigm as Christological argument, cf. U. M. Lang, *John Philoponus*, 101–34 (with bibliography).
12 Cf. n. 10.

Critique of Apollinarius: On the way
to the Nestorian crisis

After Apollinarius, the history of Eastern Christology is essentially a history of setting boundaries with regard to him. From this dispute two confessions emerge, one from Alexandria and one from Antioch. These two confessions clashed in a controversy that arose in Constantinople in 428 about the Marian title of 'mother of God' ('theotokos'). At that time, Nestorius, a monk and priest from Antioch whom the emperor had appointed bishop of Constantinople, entered the fray with a series of homilies. He did not contest the use of the title *theotokos* by 'the simple believer', but he insisted, for homiletic purposes and in the liturgy, on designating and venerating Mary only as the mother of Christ. 'Mary did not give birth to a god. I cannot worship a god who was born, died and was buried.' Cyril, the patriarch of Alexandria, found this 'a scandal for the churches', attacked Nestorius, notified Rome and thus initiated a process that led to the confrontation of two Christologies. Despite his confession of a rational soul in Christ, Cyril perpetuated Apollinarius' distinction between a 'Christology from above' (which satisfied the Council of Nicaea) and a 'Christology from below' (which conceives 'the flesh' as something independent vis-à-vis the God Logos and hence 'only as a human being', i.e., psilanthropism). Thus God *and* human being are divided and two sons introduced. With this polemical distinction, Cyril endorsed both the concepts and the arguments of Apollinarius.

Different voices: An overview

In 376/77, a debate about Apollinarius was triggered in Antioch, where three Christian communities, each following Nicaea, competed with each other: (1) the old-Nicenes under the leadership of Paulinus, who cherished the memory of Eustathius' fight against Arianism and who had long lived in ecclesial fellowship with Marcellus of Ancyra; (2) the neo-Nicene community of Meletius; and (3) the Apollinarian community, closely associated with the latter, under Vitalis their bishop. At about that time Epiphanius of Salamis came to Antioch. Although Paulinus carried no weight with Epiphanius, the heresy-hunter maintained that Paulinus' complaint against the Apollinarians was justified. Then, in a conversation with Vitalis, Epiphanius discovered that the Apollinarians denied that Christ had a rational soul. He immediately incorporated their heresy into his voluminous heresiological encyclopaedia, the *Medicine chest against all heresies* (*Panarion adversus haereses*), which shortly afterwards he published (*Pan. haer.* 77). The incident at Antioch may have been preceded by a critique of the Christology of Apollinarius, written by two anonymous authors in Alexandria and preserved under the name of Athanasius. One of these works was to influence the Nestorian crisis.[13]

In Cappadocia as well, Apollinarius' Christology encountered fierce opposition. In 381 Gregory of Nazianzus cautioned his congregation against the Apollinarian machinations. In 382 Gregory of Nyssa (c. 335–95) attacked Apollinarius' teaching, on the basis of his Christology of the two natures, which emphasised the paradox of the incarnation and concepts such as 'unmingled mixing' and the appropriation of the human by the Logos. Gregory of Nyssa broke new ground with his statement that 'the new human being' in Christ is the first and only one who possesses 'in his soul and body' a 'mode of hypostasis' produced by the divine power (dynamis) creating this human being and 'permeating' the entire nature of the mixed. Gregory's proposal was to influence theologians of the sixth and seventh centuries, like Leontius of Byzantium and Maximus the Confessor. On the other hand, in his Antirrhetikos, Gregory did not dare speak of Christ's single prosopon. Yet he had introduced this concept, solely on biblical grounds, two years before against the neo-Arian, Eunomius of Cyzicus. In the context of his arguments against Apollinarius, he cites the 'anthropological paradigm', speaking of individual human beings as 'one sole prosopon' from two natures.

Another type of critique from the Antiochene neo-Nicenes had the most historical impact. Diodore of Tarsus (d. before 394) and Theodore of Mopsuestia (c. 352–428) presented in treatises about the incarnation their own detailed image of Christ. This Christology had arisen out of the confrontation with Arianism emphasising the human being of Christ as 'God and man' and was for this reason already different from the exegesis of both Athanasius and Apollinarius.

Diodore, the bishop of Tarsus from 378, certainly wrote at least one work against Apollinarius; the Laodicean at least twice took up the pen against Diodore. All but one of Diodore's extant fragments stem from two dossiers. They were used by all the sources known to us and presumably derive from a single dossier compiled by the followers of Apollinarius. It is therefore difficult to establish an adequate picture of Diodore's Christology. One thing, however, is clear: Diodore rejected Apollinarius' presentation of the mixing that interpreted the unity of the Logos with the flesh. For Diodore that mixing cannot preserve the properties of the divine and human in Christ. However,

---

13 Cf. the two writings named in CPG 2231. In their critique, both writings, like Gregory of Nyssa (discussed below), objected to the theologoumenon of the descent of the Logos into Hades, held by Apollinarius, but also by Athanasius and the Arians; like Eustathius of Antioch (n. 8) they ascribed this descent to the soul of Christ.

it should be noted that Apollinarius did not accept Diodore's critique on this point, because it is precisely his concept of 'mixing' that is meant to preserve the divine and human properties in Christ. Gregory of Nazianzus and Gregory of Nyssa claimed the same for their Christological concept of 'mixing'.

In order to ward off Apollinarian theopaschitism, Diodore proceeded dialectically. He takes up the Apollinarians' arguments against a theology of the two sons, but, in contrast to them, he refuses to express the antitheses of the divine and the human predicates in terms of 'one and the same'. He refuses to do this, even when it is expressly added – as by both Athanasius and Apollinarius – that the divine predicates are ascribed to the one subject 'according to the divinity', and the human predicates to the same 'according to the humanity'. The decisive idea of Athanasius and – following him – of the Apollinarians, that in the incarnation the God Logos appropriated everything human, is totally foreign to Diodore. In this way he follows the tradition of Antiochene anti-Arian exegesis deriving from Eustathius.

Diodore distinguishes between 'the God Logos as the Son of God according to nature' and 'the son of David', who 'is the son from Mary' (Eustathius' 'man of Christ'). 'According to his nature [this human being] is son of David, yet according to grace Son of God.' Both, however, 'are one son'. The worship of God for 'the human being from Mary' is an honour bestowed upon him as the 'temple of the Logos', because of God's indwelling or presence in him. These phrases correspond to the picture that the Apollinarians had of the doctrine of 'two sons' as held by the supporters of Nicene orthodoxy, who by contrast conceived of the incarnation as a real becoming human and as the receiving of a human soul. It is presumably in order to confirm their heresiological prejudice that the Apollinarians incorporated these phrases into their dossier of Diodore's teaching.

However, some phrases in Diodore's fragments occasionally indicate a more differentiated position. He accepts that, in biblical statements about Christ, God is called man and man is called God. This scriptural usage should not confuse anyone: 'know that the God-Logos is called man, because he indwells in the son of man'. This indwelling does not mean that God *becomes* man or man *becomes* God. It is a matter of statements about the two natures as such, or, as Apollinarius renders Diodore's position in his own reply, of clauses without a common meaning – *koine eponymia*. Diodore contests Apollinarius' view of the so-called communication of *idiomata*.[14] Yet he did not claim that the two natures are two subjects that remain divided in a higher unity, 'in one

---

14 See above, n. 7.

Son'. Instead, biblical terminology suggests to him 'common designations' of God *and* human being, which he sees as based on the Logos indwelling in the 'human being from Mary'.

Cyril of Alexandria, however, reads this as though Diodore, speaking of two natures and two sons – one born in time from Mary, and one begotten by the Father before time –, juxtaposes them, as though God and human being 'each exists for itself' (*kat' idian*). According to Cyril, Diodore talks about 'the one Christ', but reserves the name Christ uniquely for the God Logos. For, as he says, the son of man is Christ through the grace of God; he is this only because of honour given him by God. Thus, Cyril argues, Diodore advocates a union, 'not, however, one which we profess'.

In the only fragment not stemming from the Apollinarian dossier, Diodore says that Mary indeed gave birth to a human being; however, as the virginal conception shows, 'one bound with the Logos'. Because of the union with the Logos, she is called mother of God ('theotokos').

Theodore of Mopsuestia

Antiochene Christology can be misinterpreted as confessing two sons and two persons (*prosopa*) if the context and characteristics of the Christological language of the Antiochene tradition are ignored. When in 438 Cyril of Alexandria discovered the work of Theodore of Mopsuestia, following in the footsteps of the Apollinarians he foisted precisely this misinterpretation on it. Even modern scholars like R. A. Sullivan and others interpreted Theodore's Christology from Cyril's standpoint. Theodore could be seen as only paving the way for the Nestorianism attacked by Cyril.

On the basis of the twofold transmission of Theodore's *De incarnatione*, a writing composed *c.* 382 against Arius and Eunomius as well as against Apollinarius, and especially on the basis of that text of *De incarnatione* which L. Abramowski has called 'the crux for interpreting Theodore', it is difficult to obtain an adequate picture of Theodore's Christology that is not superimposed by other dogmatic interests. As in the case of Diodore's fragments, here again Apollinarians were busy interpolating phrases into *De incarnatione*, as Theodore reports thirty years after its publication. Therefore, particularly Theodore's commentary on John's Gospel and his baptismal catecheses must be taken into account for a critical exposition, even if the latter were delivered for catechumens and not for theologians and are extant only in a Syriac translation whose only manuscript seems to display a particular dogmatic interest.

Theodore's Christology continued the tradition of Antiochene exegesis and hermeneutics by adopting the concept of *prosopon*. He used this concept specifically in the context of his polemic against the Arians in order to stress the fundamental unity of the Christological subject to which both the divine and human predicates are attributed. In this way, Theodore advocated the fundamental Antiochene formula of Christology: 'two natures and one person (*prosopon*)'. He affirms that scripture speaks about the natures of Christ and their distinction, 'by their being related to one single person'. What scripture says about the eternal Son and about the son born of Mary, it attributes to 'one single Son and thus the glory of the only-begotten Son of God in his pre-existence and the dignity of the human being assumed in the incarnation and elevated in the resurrection.' According to Philippians 2.10, the latter is entitled to be worshipped. In this way the elevated human being has a share in the divine prerogative: it is worshipped in the one person. For Theodore the Bible's one *prosopon* of the two natures is 'one on account of worship', inseparable, because of the 'one single Son', and hence the one liturgical *prosopon*.[15]

This agrees with a fragment from Theodore's writing against Eunomius, which states: 'The *prosopon* of our Lord Christ signifies honour and greatness and worship.' Here Theodore intends to exclude a second concept of the *prosopon*, which 'characterises the hypostasis and that which each one of us is'. Thus the names 'Peter' and 'Paul' denote their '*prosopon* and hypostasis', while the name 'Christ' denotes that *prosopon*, which the God Logos created through his revelation 'in the humanity': 'he combined the honour of his [divine] hypostasis with the visible'. Hence, in the commentary on John 5.23, the human being, the son of Mary, 'is honoured with the same honour, with which the Father together with the [eternal] Son is honoured'. This, Theodore says, occurs because he 'in the worship of the God Logos is united [with the latter]'. The indwelling of God in Christ takes place 'as it were[16] in his Son'. Theodore justifies this with 'the work of the Godhead, which accomplished

---

15 L. Abramowski, 'Zur Theologie Theodors'.

16 This 'as it were' (Greek: *hôs*) is the standard terminology of the Antiochenes in the Nestorian crisis. It has its origin in the exegesis that, with the customary hermeneutical technical '*prosopon*', denotes the subject of a statement. If a predicate denotes 'the flesh', then this is the *prosopon* of the statement. The same applies to the predicates that denote the Logos as such. But if it is a matter of a predicate, which denotes 'God and human being', then it is possible, as the Antiochenes did, to retain the terminology, just referred to, of two *prosopa* ('God Logos' and 'assumed human being'), and to say that the combined statements denote 'as it were one *prosopon*'. 'In this both natures are known.' If Gregory of Nyssa (see above), Augustine (see below) and the formula of union of 433 (see below) reserve the concept of *prosopon* for the one Christ, and for the two first-named *prosopa* use the concept of 'nature', 'which are known in the one *prosopon*', then the term 'nature' acquires a twofold meaning. On the one hand, it denotes as the subject of the predication concrete individuals ('God Logos' and 'the flesh'), and, on the other hand, that which characterises God and human being according to their essence or concept, that is, all divine or human predicates.

everything in the humanity' of Christ. The work of the Godhead here has a similar function as Athanasius' and Apollinarius' notion of 'appropriation' (*oikeiosis, idiopoiesis*).

The phrase 'the one *prosopon* of the worship' is meant to contrast Theodore's concept of 'the one *prosopon* of the two natures' with Apollinarius' worship 'of the one nature of the hypostasis of the incarnate Logos'.

In many places Theodore speaks as an exegete with technical terminology. For example, he says that there are biblical statements to be read as *ex persona hominis assumpti*, in which 'the human being from Mary' appears as *prosopon*.[17] These are distinguished from the 'combined' statements in which at the same time something is predicated which can only apply to God himself. Because 'both' cannot be predicated 'at the same time of one nature', both must refer 'on account of the connection (*synapheia*)' to a single *prosopon* common to both – *prosopon koinon*. In this *prosopon*, 'God *and* human being are united in the one Christ'.

The result before the crisis: Two Christological perspectives – two concepts: Appropriation versus indwelling in the son

Reference to 'the one common *prosopon* of God *and* human being', and not to the incarnate Logos, determines Antiochene Christology. Symmetry dominates the Antiochene picture of Christ. There are the two natures, that of God, who 'as in his Son indwells in a human being', *and* that of the 'human being from Mary', whom they encounter in the Gospels. Those who do not recognise Christ in his true reality take the latter for simply a human being inspired by God. Only the believer realises that in this human being God 'indwells as in his Son'. In this sense the Antiochenes, too, exclude a 'Christology from below'. Their symmetry of the *koinon prosopon* is described by R. A. Norris, and others, as 'dualism'. Like the asymmetrical Christology of the Alexandrians and of Apollinarius, Antiochene Christology is rooted in a biblical exegesis with an anti-Arian orientation. The Antiochenes do not know the dynamic notion of the appropriation of everything human by the God Logos. Therefore they do not view the incarnation from the side of the Logos, but consider the result (*apotelesma*) of God's free work and intention in the assumption of a human being as son in the indwelling 'as it were in his Son'.

What differentiates the two major Christologies is primarily the perspective of their exegesis and their attitude towards worship, and only then the concepts with which they both justify their religious point of view and rule out a different

---

17 Cf. n. 16.

hermeneutics. The presentation of Antiochene Christology by Diodore and Theodore, even if it is connected to Eustathius, cannot be understood without their opposition to Apollinarius. That Apollinarius gained anything from his debate with Diodore is improbable.

Will the representatives of both Christologies in the Nestorian crisis remain each trapped in their own perspective? Are they only intent on enforcing their own confession? Will they seek a compromise formula only because they are forced by political circumstances? Or can each of them recognise in dialogue the relativity of their confession from the perspective of the other?

The confrontation between Alexandria and Antioch

When Nestorius (c. 381–451), after his appointment as patriarch of Constantinople in 428, triggered the dispute about the Marian title 'mother of God', he entered the fray with homilies in which he called upon the Antiochene Christology familiar to him. Cyril of Alexandria intervened with the journalistic means available at that time. For reasons of ecclesiastical politics, Cyril was anything but a fair arbiter; his attitude was heavily biased against Nestorius. Cyril wrote three official letters to Nestorius, adding to the third an 'ultimatum' of twelve anathemas.

The Nestorian crisis as a confrontation of arguments

Nestorius saw in the title 'mother of God' a hidden danger of Apollinarianism. This salutation of Mary defeats 'the distinction of the natures'[18] and involves their connection (synapheia) not as one of dignity and worship, but one of nature and hence as a mixing (krasis, mixis).

Nestorius' teaching at the beginning of the crisis and in Cyril's ultimatum

In the tradition of anti-Arian exegesis, Nestorius – like Apollinarius of Laodicea – distinguishes three classes of statements about Jesus. In contrast to Apollinarius, however, he sees in this the justification for a Christology of two natures. The Bible has statements (1) about the Godhead, (2) about the humanity, and (3) about both at the same time. Nestorius maintains that the Bible can speak either about the eternal Son of God or about the human being

---

18 In the terminology of the Antiochenes, the term dihairesis originally meant distinction, insofar as it is a question of the two natures, yet it means division if it is a question of the union of the two natures. On the way to Chalcedon the terminology introduced by Cyril prevailed, namely, to use in the first case only the term diaphora.

born of Mary. These are the first of two classes. Further, as Nestorius says, the Bible connects the suffering and death of Christ not with the Godhead, but rather with 'Christ or the Son or the Kyrios'. Christ, as subject of a statement (*onoma prokeimenon*), signifies both, 'God *and* human being', and thus the two natures. The same is true for the titles 'Son' and 'Kyrios'. These can serve as the subject of all three classes of statements, for, as Nestorius writes to Cyril, they denote 'something common' (*koina tina*).

Christ is 'the invisible and the visible', as Nestorius often says in his sermons. Christ is 'the hidden (God) *and* he who appears visibly' for all human beings; yet in his invisible reality, as Theodore of Mopsuestia also stresses, he is only recognised by believers, not by Jews, the devil, etc. Because of the hidden, Nestorius worships the visible. For the latter is inseparably connected with God and reveals God. Cyril was to cite these propositions in his third letter because for him they showed that Nestorius taught in fact two Christs. For, according to Cyril, Nestorius denied a union that justifies that 'the one Christ Jesus, the only-begotten Son' (John 1.14, 18) – that is, for Cyril, the Logos – 'is adored together with his flesh'.

Cyril says this without acknowledging, or perhaps even considering, that Nestorius stated in the immediate context: 'I distinguish the natures; however, I worship the One.' By this Nestorius meant 'the one *prosopon* of worship', of which Theodore of Mopsuestia spoke, even if Nestorius did not use the term *prosopon* in this sense in his homilies. Nestorius uses *prosopon* only as a characterisation of the concrete nature, as when he says that Christ has 'assumed the *prosopon* of the nature'.

Cyril's 'union according to the hypostasis'
versus *prosopon*

In Nestorius' terminology, the concept of nature as *prosopon* is no longer clearly associated with its original exegetical context.[19] Cyril, in his second letter to Nestorius, goes on the attack by employing the expression 'union according to the hypostasis', which he had already introduced in his aggressive tract *Contra Nestorium*. He uses it now in this letter for the first and last time consistently in order to interpret the incarnation as appropriation of the flesh. On the basis of this union, it is the Logos who is worshipped, but not Christ 'as human being together with the Logos'. For him appropriation means that 'the Logos *became* flesh' (John 1.14) and 'did not unite the *prosopon* of a human being with him'. Therefore he states that a 'union of *prosopa*' in Christ is ruled out by 'the union

19 See n. 16, above.

according to the hypostasis' that excludes the union of natures, understood as *prosopa*, and thus justifies calling Mary 'the mother of God'.

Nestorius opposes Cyril's subject of the *kenosis* and the concept of appropriation

In his response, Nestorius drops the concept '*prosopon* of the nature' and limits himself to showing that the title Christ 'as it were characterises the impassible and passible *ousiai* in the one single *prosopon*' (see n. 16, above). According to the confession of Nicaea and Paul in Philippians 2.5–8, the subject of the *kenosis* is Christ, 'the name common to both natures', and not the Logos. For the latter, Paul could not have stated that he died on the cross (Philippians 2.8). Through this predication, the difference of both natures 'in the one single *prosopon*' is preserved unmingled; the one sonship is not divided. This *prosopon* or 'the combining (*synapheia*) of the one *prosopon*' is Nestorius' counter-expression to Cyril's 'union according to the hypostasis'. He says so with reference to Cyril's polemical *Contra Nestorium*. In that treatise Cyril had employed this very same expression, thereby imputing that Nestorius 'divides' the one Christ 'into two *prosopa* and hypostases'. Cyril justifies this there with Nestorius' teaching (see above), or, respectively, with that of the Antiochenes, that the titles 'Christ, 'Son', and 'Kyrios' are *onomata koina* – titles that are common to God and human being. He understands Nestorius as if he and the Antiochene tradition used these titles as common to independent hypostases or persons, as signifying something like a community. When Nestorius argues with the three classes of biblical statements, Cyril suspects a separation of hypostases or *prosopa* because Nestorius ascribes some biblical statements only to the Logos as such, others only 'to him born of a woman' (Galatians 4.4) as such and thus seems ultimately to admit of only two classes.

It is important to recognise that Nestorius introduces something new in the Antiochene tradition. In the conclusion of his reply he takes up the concept of appropriation from Cyril's critique and accepts it, insofar as the term describes the notion of an indwelling God as the connection (*synapheia*) of God and human being. However, at the same time he excludes a particular understanding of the appropriation's result. He characterises this appropriation with the term *oikeiotes*, which in the Latin dossiers on the Nestorian crisis is mostly rendered as *familiaritas*, a term also used in a translation of Cyril's *Scholia de incarnatione*,[20] which Cyril himself had commissioned for Rome. Thus for Nestorius the result cannot be a type of kinship between the

---

20 CPG 5225.

transcendental Logos and the assumed human being. For 'properties of the flesh', such as birth, suffering and dying, are to be excluded in a natural or an ontological sense from an appropriation carried out by the Logos. A natural or ontological appropriation would be a pagan notion, proposed by heretics like Apollinarius and Arius. Nestorius can accept Cyril's concept insofar as the latter says that the Godhead indwells in Christ and the assumed human being is its temple and as such the property of God. Later, in a letter to Alexander of Mabbug, Nestorius defines more precisely which concept of appropriation seems correct to him. This letter reflects the discussion of Cyril's concept of appropriation, which began in Antioch after 431, and of Athanasius' letter to Epictetus.

Cyril's fourth anathema

Cyril's third letter (the 'ultimatum') with the attached twelve anathemas arrived in Constantinople on 30 November 430. It offered nothing new and took no account of Nestorius' reply to the second letter. It is striking that Cyril here calls 'union according to the hypostasis' also 'union according to the nature', or 'natural union'. That for him the concepts 'nature' and 'hypostasis' are interchangeable is shown with complete clarity by the third anathema. For here he does not – as one would expect – charge Nestorius with 'the separation of the natures', but rather with the separation 'of the hypostases'.

Decisive for the history of the confrontation of Alexandria and Antioch is Cyril's fourth anathema. As in the polemical writing *Contra Nestorium*, Nestorius is also condemned because he divided the biblical statements about Christ between 'two *prosopa* or hypostases'. On Cyril's reading he allows the statements of divinity or sovereignty to apply only to the Logos, while the statements of lowliness refer 'as it were to a human being, who *beside* the . . . Logos is considered *for himself*'. Here Cyril does not mention the third class of biblical statements. He is convinced that all biblical statements are expressed of the Logos as the one subject of the *kenosis* and *for that very reason* of the one single *prosopon*, the one incarnate hypostasis of the God Logos. Hence for him there are as such only two classes, statements of sovereignty and statements of lowliness.

Nestorius' reaction to the ultimatum: A strange formula

Nestorius' reaction to Cyril's provocative third letter can be gauged from the sermon he preached on 25 March 431 (CPG 5716). The sermon responds at the same time to a homily of Proclus of Constantinople (CPG 5800). In this homily – a showpiece of ecclesiastical rhetoric – Proclus, who succeeded

Nestorius as patriarch of Constantinople (434–46), had confessed the incarnate God and the mother of God ('theotokos'). Nestorius, by contrast, affected a consciously simple style in his homily; he examined a sentence of Proclus, in which the latter maintained that Christ as the incarnate Logos was appointed high priest for the sake of the salvation of human beings. With this statement Proclus had advertised his agreement with Cyril's tenth anathema (in the third letter) that was directed against a particular homily of Nestorius.

Discussing this sentence of Proclus' homily, Nestorius now attempted to explain his Christology: Christ has two natures; however, as Son he is one. For this reason, Nestorius says, he confesses 'two hypostases of the natures'. In Nestorius' mouth this is surprising and is best understood as a testy or derisive reaction to the third anathema (in the third letter), with which Cyril condemns anyone 'who divides the hypostases after the union'.

The condemnation of Nestorius and its consequences

The Third Ecumenical Council of Ephesus (431), under the presidency of Cyril and in the absence of the Antiochenes, deposed Nestorius and approved Cyril's second letter to Nestorius, but not the third letter, Cyril's ultimatum, with the attached twelve anathemas. The third letter was only read out and subsequently recorded in the *Acta*. In opposition to Cyril's council, the Eastern Antiochenes concentrated specifically on refuting the twelve anathemas of Cyril's third letter. This possibly contributed to the emperor Justinian's (*regn.* 527–65) and some of his contemporaries' impression that Cyril's third letter had also been approved by the Council of Ephesus.

Cyril's attack on Nestorius and thus on the Antiochene tradition resulted in the *oikoumenê* being divided into two camps, one comprising the followers of Cyril, who was also supported by Rome and thus by Western Christianity, and the other the adherents of the Antiochenes. In the difficult correspondence between the two, there was always talk of discord, difference and two irreconcilable viewpoints (*dichonoia*). Both sides sought to establish a basis for peace. The Antiochenes wanted Cyril to retract his anathemas and called upon Athanasius' letter to Epictetus as a way to reach an appropriate understanding of the Nicene confession. Cyril made a concession when he explained that the twelve anathemas of his third letter were directed solely against Nestorius, not against the Antiochene tradition. In this sense Cyril always held fast to his third letter to Nestorius in the subsequent course of events. However, he himself also sought for a way out of the impasse, a formula that demonstrated that the Antiochenes did not think the same as Nestorius.

After the Antiochenes had assented to Nestorius' deposition and had condemned his teaching, without saying exactly what they meant, the way was
open for peace. That occurred in 433 through the mediation of Paul of Emesa.
What concerns us here are the ideas that led Cyril and the Antiochenes
to a formula of union, not the political machinations that undergirded the
decisions.

The union of 433

The extent to which the Antiochenes were prepared to meet Cyril halfway with
their formula of union, without surrendering, is shown in two homilies that
Paul of Emesa preached publicly in Alexandria (CPG 6365–6). Paul pointed out
that Antiochene Christology was in fundamental agreement with Athanasius'
letter to Epictetus. For his part, Cyril was also prepared for a compromise;
the extent to which he was prepared to meet the theological concerns of his
opponents is shown in his homily that replied to Paul's second homily and
placed it in his own perspective (CPG 5247).

In their formula of union,[21] the Antiochenes accept the title 'mother of God'
and compromise with Cyril on the question about the subject of Nicaea's symbol. By confessing the 'union of two natures', in which both remain unmingled,
they maintain their standpoint, but abandon their traditional term (*synapheia*).
To justify their view of the unmingled union of the natures,[22] they return to
the traditional classification of biblical statements about Christ. Thus they
distinguish (1) that class of statements which the tradition, namely 'the theologians', so interpret that 'something common' is expressed, insofar as these
statements are related 'as it were [*hôs*: see n. 16, above] to one single *prosopon*',
and (2) those two classes which in the tradition were so understood that they
'separate' (n. 18), by applying 'as it were (*hôs*) to the natures'. For the one
relates 'divine statements to the divinity of Christ', the other 'statements of
his lowliness to his humanity'.

Cyril accepts and interprets this formula in his *Laetentur* letter, the so-called
'Letter of peace' (CPG 5339), by introducing the Logos as the subject of the
incarnation or *kenosis*. In doing this, however, he takes up the words of the
Antiochenes and says that the Logos in his incarnation 'is known as it were in
one single *prosopon*'. In order to rebut the Antiochene objection still raised after
the union that he was dependent on Apollinarius, he excludes the notion of

---

21 Text: ACO I.I.4: 8.19–9.8; repeated by Cyril in the *Letter of peace* 4–5 (ACO I.I.4: 17–20).
22 Excluded here and in all places in the rest of this chapter, where there is talk of exclusion
   of a mingling, is a particular type of mingling, the *synchysis*, which Apollinarius already
   would not accept.

a mixing. With the Antiochenes he confesses the 'unmingled union' (*asynchytos henôsis*), but at the same time introduces the argument of appropriation, which – although missing in the formula of union – was, however, covered by Athanasius' letter to Epictetus.

The Antiochenes had attached to their formula of union a copy of Athanasius' letter to Epictetus, their original having come from the old library of the Eustathians. Cyril also now appends to his Letter of peace his copy of this letter that was the copy of an exemplar in the ancient Alexandrian archives. He does this, he says, in order to place at the disposal of the Antiochenes an incorrupt exemplar. Later he is clearer and claims that Paul of Emesa's text had deliberate omissions and additions and was created to prove the agreement between Athanasius and Nestorius. He insists that the original letter in fact refuted Nestorius. Although J. Lebon believed he could distinguish an Antiochene and an Alexandrian recension on the basis of the extant twofold transmission of this letter,[23] this question needs further investigation.

After the union Cyril saw himself forced to justify the formula of union and hence to make clear what the difference between the teaching of Nestorius and that of the Antiochenes was. From a historian's standpoint, he failed to verify those three points on which he wanted to clarify the difference (CPG 5340). Principally his effort revolved around the concept of appropriation. As Cyril's *Scholia de incarnatione* clearly shows, he was still convinced in the winter of 432/3 that the Antiochenes and not just Nestorius maintained 'the separation of God and human being' in Christ even when they spoke of the appropriation of everything human by God. For 'they think God and human being each for itself (*kat' idian*)[24] and separate the natures from each other'. For this reason they could understand the appropriation 'only in the mode of relation', but not as a union on the level of being, which justifies confessing the Logos himself as the subject of the *kenosis* and ascribing to him all the statements of lowliness.

After the union Cyril still avoided using the concept of the common *prosopon* and in general the notion of community (*koinonia*) that for the Antiochenes characterised the third class of biblical statements. However, in his *Scholia de incarnatione* he employed the terms *koinopoieisthai* and *koinon* and thus dealt with 'something common to God and human being'. In those places he describes not the conception of the Antiochenes, but his own. And he wrote the *Scholia* with a view to the negotiations with the Antiochenes and sent them in a Latin translation to Rome in 433.

---

23 Lebon, 'Altération doctrinale'.
24 In the text of the *Scholia de incarnatione*, this is translated as *in parte*.

It is interesting to observe that the translated text, unlike the Greek original, in some places favours a Dyophysite understanding. This is especially the case for those passages in which the translation speaks of *operationes communes* and *communis passio*. Pope Leo integrated these phrases into his own Christology, which otherwise followed the lead of Augustine.[25] It was precisely on account of these phrases, included in his *Tomus ad Flavianum*, that Leo would encounter criticism at the Council of Chalcedon (451).

Cyril writes: 'the Logos appropriates to himself, on the one hand everything that belongs to the flesh . . . , but on the other hand communicates to his flesh the work of that divine power, which is in him'. In this manner the Logos could bring about his miracles in the flesh. In the Latin translation sent to Leo, the communicating – *koinopoieisthai* – of divine power is transmitted as a realising of 'common operations' and as what 'the divine majesty together with the flesh effects'. Moreover, in these *Scholia*, Cyril continued justifying that 'the flesh' and therefore the passions are proper to the Logos by employing the conception of the 'appropriation' of everything human. In the translation, however, it is said that the passion is something common to the Logos and his flesh, namely *communis passio*. This has little to contribute to the theme of 'what is common to God and the human being', but is rich in consequences.

The Fourth Ecumenical Council of Chalcedon

The events leading up to the Council of Chalcedon here interest us only insofar as they contribute directly to an understanding of the council's *Definitio fidei*.

On the way to Chalcedon

The confessional formulae of the Constantinopolitan patriarchs Proclus (*sed.* 434–46) and Flavian (*sed.* 446–9) need to be mentioned first. In a homily (CPG 5822), Proclus made a distinction between the concepts of nature and hypostasis.[26] In the one Son he sees two natures united in one single hypostasis.[27] Flavian added the concept of the one *prosopon* to that of the one *hypostasis*. In order to distance themselves from Nestorius, both combined two Christologies and in this way they both interpreted the concept approved at Ephesus as 'union according to the hypostasis'.

Opposition from both camps to the union of 433 triggered the dispute about Diodore of Tarsus and Theodore of Mopsuestia and consequently about the

---

25 On Augustine's Christology, see H. R. Drobner, *Person-Exegesis und Christologie*.
26 Proclus, *Homily* 23.11 (ed. Martin, 46.10–13).
27 ACO II.I.I: 114.9–10.

orthodoxy of the Antiochene tradition and, more specifically, its proximity or otherwise to the teaching of Nestorius.

After Cyril's death (444), his successor, Dioscorus, pursued a tough political agenda by pushing for the acceptance of 'the whole Cyril', which means in particular his third letter with the twelve anathemas that advocated a Miaphysite Christology. This agenda was successful at the so-called 'Robber Council' of Ephesus (August 449), which rehabilitated the archimandrite Eutyches, a radical Monophysite, who had been anathematised by Flavian in 448. Like the extreme Apollinarians and under the influence of their forgeries already mentioned, Eutyches disputed that 'the flesh' of Christ is of human nature, i.e., 'consubstantial with ours'. This apparent victory, however, led to the breakdown of the anti-Nestorian alliance between Alexandria and Rome; Pope Leo in his *Tomus* (June 449) had confirmed the condemnation of Eutyches' position pronounced by Flavian of Constantinople.

In this state of affairs, in order to restore religious peace within the empire, three conditions had to be met. (i) The interpretation of Cyril at the Third Ecumenical Council of Ephesus had to be accepted. (ii) Just as Cyril's authority had to be upheld, the condemnation of Nestorius needed to be retained. (iii) Rome, as the new and, in fact, natural theological ally of Antioch (inasmuch as both Rome and Antioch agreed on a 'symmetrical' Christology implying a concept of person that was derived from biblical exegesis), had to agree to a possible compromise. These three conditions outline the task given to the synod of Chalcedon by the emperor.

Chalcedon's definition of faith

After an initial formula foundered because of opposition from the Roman legates as well as from the Antiochenes, the emperor threatened to transfer the council to Rome. Under this pressure a commission in the chapel of St Euphemia worked out the doctrinal decision of the council; the plenum of the council accepted it without further discussion. In its introduction, the document said that the creed of Nicaea (325) was sufficient in order to satisfy the Council of Ephesus (431). In order to justify this, the commission begins with Cyril's second letter to Nestorius and his 'Letter of peace', insofar as these, as the commission says, are in agreement. It designates both as 'the synodal letters of Cyril', i.e., those letters on the basis of which, on the one hand, the condemnation of Nestorius in Ephesus (431), and on the other hand, the creed of Nicaea are to be interpreted, if one is to understand the statement (*ennoia*) intended in them. In this way, the council avoided taking a stance with regard to Cyril's anathemas. With this approach the synod interpreted the decision of the Council of Ephesus in 431 not as final, but rather as inaugurating a process of clarification, for which Cyril's understanding of the 433 formula of union is important. This opened a way for the synod to interpret Cyril himself and, at the same time, on the basis of Cyril to formulate its own *Definitio fidei*.[28] It also gave the synod the possibility, as it itself says, 'rightly' to combine Pope Leo's *Tomus ad Flavianum* with Cyril's two synodal letters 'in a certain accommodation'. Therefore, at the same time it could condemn as heresies the teaching of both Eutyches and Nestorius.

For this reason, the council juxtaposed phrases from Cyril and Leo in its *Definitio fidei*, which is formulated in a highly differentiated manner, consisting of a single sentence whose linguistic unevenness indicates a hasty redaction. The *Definitio* reads – with some abbreviations – as follows:

1   So following the saintly fathers, we all with one voice teach
    the confession of one and the same Son, our Lord Jesus Christ,
    the one and the same . . . truly God . . . and truly human being
    consubstantial (*homoousios*) with the Father as regards his divinity
5   and the same consubstantial (*homoousios*) with us as regards his humanity;
    like us in all respects except for sin [Hebrews 4.15]
    . . . one and the same Christ, Son, Lord, Only-begotten
    acknowledged in two natures, unconfused (*asygchytôs*), unchanged,
    undivided (*adihairetôs*), unseparated;
10 at no point was the difference (*diaphora*) taken away through the union,
    but rather the property of both natures is preserved
    and come together into a single person, that is[29] *hypostasis*;
    he is not parted or divided into two persons,
    but is one and the same only-begotten Son, God, Lord Jesus Christ,
15 just as the prophets taught from the beginning,
    . . . and as the Lord Jesus Christ himself instructed us
    and as the creed of the fathers [Nicaea] handed it down to us.

The *Definitio* combines Leo's confession preserving the particularity of the two natures (ll. 11–12), directed against Eutyches, with the words of Cyril. The Cyrillian phrases defend his own view of the union, emphasised against Nestorius, against the misunderstanding that 'the difference of the natures is removed on account of the union' (l. 10). The words inserted justify the statement in the *Definitio* about Christ's two natures. Thus Cyril was the primary source and Leo's statements were understood through Cyril. At the

---

28 In this sense the Christology of Chalcedon is Cyrillian. Cf. the fundamental work of A. de Halleux, 'La définition christologique à Chalcédoine'.
29 The *kai* employed by the council is a *kai* explicative, which interprets Leo's concept of person by Cyril's terminology of *hypostasis*.

same time Chalcedon rejects two misunderstandings: first, the interpretation of Cyril through Dioscorus' Monophysite Christology, and second, the assertion that the two natures, according to Leo, were Nestorius' teaching of two sons or persons.

In adding to Leo's formula the concept of the one hypostasis, the synod endorsed the interpretation of 'union according to the hypostasis' of both Proclus and Flavian of Constantinople. In this way it signalled that it was possible to reconcile Alexandrian and Antiochene Christologies. Did Leo's formula mediate between the two by articulating a point of view transcending the two positions or did it ultimately amount to the formulation of a compromise, like the 433 formula of union, and thus in effect support the Christology of the Antiochenes? The question remained open.

The *Definitio* introduces the more comprehensive title 'one and the same Son, our Lord Jesus Christ' as the subject of the confession. Then on a par he is called both 'Christ' and also 'the God Logos', while he is – following the Nicene confession – at the same time designated as the 'only-begotten Son' (John 1.14, 18). Thus Chalcedon combines the perspectives of both Cyrillian and Antiochene / Western Christology. 'The one Son of God', who, as Nicaea confesses, 'descended from heaven, became incarnate and assumed a human being' is, as 'God *and* human being' both 'Christ' and also 'the incarnate Logos'. As Christ he is 'known in two natures'. With this phrase the council has recourse to Basil of Seleucia's formula, which earlier at the council he had justified on the basis of Cyril's second letter to Nestorius. Like Basil of Seleucia, the council wanted to exclude any mixture (*synchysis, krasis*) and thus a Miaphysite Christology. But Basil also assumes, just as Chalcedon does, that the Council of Ephesus in 431 rejected the 'separation of the natures' attributed to Nestorius, namely the teaching of two sons or two independent subjects of Christological predication. This explains why the commission redacted into Basil's formula the famous adverbs 'unconfused, unchanged, undivided, unseparated'.

On the reception of the 'Tome of Leo' at Chalcedon

Basil of Seleucia's confession of 'one Christ who is known in two natures' raises a question about the three classes of biblical statements in the 433 formula of union. The synod of Chalcedon takes up this query and with its *Definitio* attempts to protect the concerns of both Alexandrian and Antiochene Christologies. However, it omits in its definition the concepts 'appropriation' and 'community (*koinonia*) of the natures in the *prosopon*' or 'common *prosopon*' and any justification for them. In this way it avoids recalling the failed attempts to find a compromise by adapting and re-interpreting the terminology of the other side.

Why it did so cannot be answered on the basis of the *Acta* of the council. Did the council expect the parties in the future to seek a combination of the two Christologies without these loaded ideas? Certainly they are excluded because they seem unnecessary for the combination of both Christologies, which the council intends by introducing the Tome of Leo into the *Definitio* and in this way interpreting it. For it introduces the Tome only to the extent that it is compatible with both the synodal letters of Cyril and thus is to be interpreted on the basis of Cyril.

This is in accordance with the declaration introducing the *Definitio fidei* that 'combines' the Tome with both letters of Cyril 'in a certain accommodation'. In its *Definitio* the council wants to 'harmonise' Leo and Cyril with Cyril as the base and it wants to preserve what has been combined without explaining what makes the combination possible. Did the commission believe that it was sufficient to pass over in silence any justifications for the concepts of 'appropriation' and 'community'?

How deeply problematical the project of simply combining both Christologies was emerged already during the council itself, when the bishops of Illyria and Palestine raised three doubts about the Tome of Leo, and, from the perspective of Cyrillian Christology, accused Leo of a latent Nestorianism.[30]

In reaction the leaders of the council attempted to avoid criticism of the Tome of Leo and to show Leo's agreement with Cyril. Quite apart from the different soteriologies (a topic that had been mooted at the council), the debate concerned Cyril's reception of the 433 formula of union, which the Illyrians and Palestinians could not reconcile in particular with two statements of the pope. On the one hand, it was a question of Leo's view of Christ's operations as an acting in which each of the natures effected what was proper to it 'in community with the other'. On the other hand, the issue was his statement that in Christ, despite 'the one person of God *and* human being', a duality is to be distinguished which establishes 'something common to God and human being' (*commune in utroque*). Leo cites as examples the ignominy (*contumelia*) common to both and the glory (*gloria*) common to both.

It is important to observe that, when the leaders of the council did not know how to proceed further, Theodoret of Cyrus, a renowned Antiochene theologian, referred to Cyril's *Scholia de incarnatione*, in order to point out the agreement between Leo and Cyril. With this move Theodoret named

---

30 For more detail on the following, see K.-H. Uthemann, 'Zur Rezeption', 582–93.

the very source from which Leo had drawn his concept of the community of operations and of suffering of the divine and human natures in Jesus Christ. If Leo speaks of something common in God and human being, then he means, in the terminology of the Antiochenes, their common *prosopon*, and, in the words of Augustine, which he takes up in his Tome, that unity (*unitas*) 'which is known in each of the two natures'. The council could assent to that through the words of Basil of Seleucia. Even Nestorius would have no objection, as particularly his second *apologia* (CPG 5751) shows. This 'unity of person', as the 433 formula of union portrays it, can be recognised when reading in the Bible statements which were here called 'combined'. Because, as Leo says, 'by God's majesty the lowliness was assumed', the ignominy of the cross and the glory of the resurrection are something common to the divine and the human nature. In what is common (which, one has to add, always remains a paradox) is 'the unity of the person in both natures to be recognised'.

To sum up, what separates Alexandria from Rome and Antioch is a difference in terminology, which derives from the two divergent traditions of anti-Arian exegesis and is based on their different Christological perspectives. What separates them still remained, even if Chalcedon's *Definitio fidei* tried to combine both interpretations. This combining is achieved because the council added to Leo's formula (which stresses the preservation of the characteristics of each of the two natures and the coming together of these characteristics in a single person): 'and indeed[31] in one single hypostasis'.

The reception of Chalcedon

The *Definitio fidei* of Chalcedon is open to two interpretations, one Cyrillian and one Leonine. According to the Leonine interpretation, the Antiochene legacy remains intact. Therefore it is not apropos, when narrating the history of Chalcedon's reception, to distinguish a 'strict Chalcedonianism' from other modes of reception. For if there had been a 'strict Chalcedonianism', then it could not have been anything but either a mere repetition of the *Definitio* or an attempt to nullify what separates the two Christologies the *Definitio* combines by stressing what unites them. Each time the latter approach was undertaken, one side won. Scholars like M. Richard, Ch. Moeller or A. Grillmeier (to name but the most prominent), who supported the idea of a 'strict Chalcedonianism' and wanted to find it in the sources, in fact equated Chalcedon with the Leonine interpretation. It was their intention, among other concerns, to introduce the

---

31 See n. 29.

concept of 'neo-Chalcedonianism' for the sixth century, or more precisely for Justinian's Christology,[32] which was accepted by the Fifth Ecumenical Council as church teaching. 'Neo-Chalcedonianism', they argued, in contrast to 'strict Chalcedonianism', failed to safeguard the letter and the spirit of the *Definitio fidei* of Chalcedon.

From a historical perspective, 'neo-Chalcedonianism' was, however, a victory for the Cyrillian interpretation of Chalcedon.[33]

The difference between Alexandrian and Roman-Antiochene perspectives remained. Cyrillian interpretation emphasises the Logos as the subject of the incarnation. It characterises the work of salvation as the act of the Logos, who from and in the Virgin (Luke 1.35; Matthew 1.20) created 'the new being' as the reality proper to him, by appropriating everything human 'apart from sin' (Hebrews 4.15).[34] Theologians in this tradition sought a deeper understanding of the incarnation's subject, of the one hypostasis. For them the task was filling out with concrete religious detail the 'union according to the hypostasis' that Cyril had introduced as if from nowhere. They wanted to recognise, from and in the union, the upholding of the two natures in their characteristics and to make this accessible to the faithful, when they heard or read biblical narratives or apostolic preaching. The one hypostasis determined the Christological thought of 'neo-Chalcedonianism', 'Dyophysite monenergism' and 'monothelitism': From the viewpoint of religious intuition, the hypostatic union of both natures was real, if it were seen as the basis for the one operation and will, which was manifested in Christ's miracles and suffering. For 'erudite theology' the one hypostasis was real, if it justified with it or derived from it such concepts as 'the one hypostatic energy (*energeia*)' and 'the one hypostatic will (*thelêsis*) of the Incarnate'.[35]

The Leonine interpretation is principally concerned with preserving the two natures, that is, God's transcendence and what 'the human being Jesus Christ as mediator between God and humankind' (1 Timothy 2.5) contributes to the work of salvation. It is a question of both and hence of 'Christ, God *and* human being'. Salvation involves both God and the mediator, the sole innocent (as Leo and Theodore of Mopsuestia say) who through his unlawful death broke the claim of death of the devil and opened to human beings a

---

32 Cf. K.-H. Uthemann, 'Kaiser Justinian'.

33 On the problems of terminology in the history of dogma, cf. K.-H. Uthemann, 'Neuchalkedonismus', 373–9.

34 This interpretation is mostly connected with the so-called physical or mystical theory of salvation. Cf. R. M. Hübner, *Die Einheit des Leibes Christi*.

35 Cf. Uthemann, 'Neuchalkedonismus'; F. Winkelmann, *Der monenergetisch-monotheletische Streit*.

new future with God. Instead of this law-oriented conception, other reasons can be introduced in order to emphasise the significance of the human act of Christ. For instance, this significance can be discerned in Christ's obedience with regard to God's salvific will, in the symmetry of God *and* human being. In this tradition, the one hypostasis of Chalcedon's *Definitio fidei* remains – to a certain extent – empty, even if the concept is received as self-evident and is equated with 'the one (common) person of God and human being'. However, the way in which believers are here affected religiously is not connected with the concept of the incarnate hypostasis of the Logos, but with the picture 'of the one person of God *and* human being'. They see this person when they read the Bible and when they encounter him in the liturgy of his word.

For this reason the advocates of the Leonine interpretation opposed the emperor Justinian's condemnation in his Three Chapters: Theodore of Mopsuestia, the works against Cyril by Theodoret of Cyrus, and a letter of Ibas of Edessa to Maris: all Antiochenes who had opposed in some way or other the theology of Cyril of Alexandria. They agreed with the Christology of Theodore of Mopsuestia, established in the context of anti-Arian exegesis. They did not see in it that Nestorianism which was defined as a construct of heresiology on the basis of Cyril's polemic. They did not understand how their symmetrical Christology could be suspected of advocating the confession of two sons. For them as well, the human being, Jesus, was not simply a prophet or inspired human being, but the redeemer sent by God and thus 'God *and* human being', the one Son of God. On this account, a theologian of the seventh century like Anastasius of Sinai could put into the mouth of Cyril the distinction of the three classes of biblical statements. Since they are present in the 433 formula of union, on the basis of this short formula he could with some justification call upon 'the whole Cyril' for his symmetrical picture of Christ. Obviously, this did not exclude for him calling Jesus 'our God'.[36]

Just as little as the Leonine interpretation of Chalcedon could disregard Cyril, so the Cyrillian interpretation could not drop the Tome of Leo. In due time this had the consequence that the Cyrillian tradition, precisely in the light of the different soteriologies, corrected Cyril: it discovered 'the human being Jesus' and integrated it into the conception of the appropriation by the Logos. In this manner it tried to preserve the human individuality in its subsistence and to define it in contradistinction to the personal independent subsistence of the hypostasis of the incarnate Logos.

36 See further K.-H. Uthemann, 'Anastasius Sinaites'.

Shortly before 518, John the Grammarian composed a writing in which he established the basis of this correction.[37] He understands the *Definitio* of Chalcedon as a condemnation of two positions at the same time. By rejecting Eutyches as well as Nestorius, he argues, the *Definitio* dialectically maintains only that there is in Christ a twofold *homoousion*, perfect in every way, the divine and the human *ousiai*. They are 'unconfused', which excludes Eutyches, but nevertheless 'undivided', which introduces Cyril's critique of Nestorius. Both *ousiai* exist as something common (*koinon*) to all their hypostases 'unconfused in Christ', yet they are 'in Christ undivided', for there is only one single subject of the incarnation, the Logos, who from the first moment of the incarnation had united to himself Christ's human existence, his 'flesh'. Therefore this 'flesh' is undivided from the hypostasis of the Logos and – insofar as it is unique – no mere human being, but an individual *ousia* which is distinguished from all other human individuals.

Unlike all other human individuals, this 'flesh' possesses everything that characterises it in its individuality *in the Logos*. To him 'belong on the basis of his nature [as God] everything divine and on account of the enhypostatic union everything human' which the Bible says about Christ. For his 'flesh' possessed *in him* its hypostasis. 'In two *ousiai*, which are united and individual, I acknowledge the one Christ,' namely Christ, 'God *and* human being'. The union of both is 'the one person, the one hypostasis of Christ'. Thus the Grammarian distinguishes between individuality and being a person. The latter means in the real sense an independent subsistence, a 'subsisting in and for itself'.[38] On account of this difference the author sees in anthropology *the* paradigm for Christology. For him, then, the human being is an unconfused and yet undivided unity of two individual natures, body and soul 'in a single hypostasis'.

In John the Grammarian all statements about the two natures of Christ are tied to Cyril's dynamic salvation-historical view of 'the one incarnate Logos', who appropriates to himself everything that befits the human being Jesus Christ, i.e., his 'flesh'. Just as the *Florilegium Cyrillianum* (which was published in Alexandria *c.* 482)[39] had already maintained, John to this extent understood the *definitio* of Chalcedon as the reception of Cyrillian Christology. From the viewpoint of the most important Miaphysite theologian, Severus of Antioch (*sed.* 512–38, after 518 in exile), an outstanding expert on the history

---

37 On the following, see K.-H. Uthemann, 'Definitionen'.
38 On the starting point and constant relationship to the Aristotelian theory of predication, see ibid., 83–7.
39 R. Hespel, *Le florilège cyrillien*.

of Christology, both works, the *Florilegium* and John's *apologia*, missed their target. He articulated his critique first in the *Philalethes*, dedicated to Cyril 'the lover of truth', and then in exile in the *Liber contra Grammaticum*.

The works of Leontius of Byzantium and of Leontius of Jerusalem are to be placed in the perspective characteristic of Cyril. For Leontius of Jerusalem, the great theme of Christology is the divinisation of the human nature in Christ, which remains preserved in its individuality in the hypostatic union. Only this type of union can exclude the mingling, propounded by the Mono-physites, which results in a single God-human nature. Leontius of Byzantium attempted to interpret Chalcedon in a systematic fashion and consequently asks about 'the first principles' or axioms. Only their plausibility can demonstrate the single dogma of Chalcedon that corresponds to them. To carry this out, he concentrates on the anthropological paradigm of Christology, to which we have already referred. The attempt of some scholars to identify him with that Leontius who between 531 and 543 is attested as one of the monks from Palestine, who propagated the Origenism condemned in 553 and who for that reason had as a central theme the *nous*-Christology of Evagrius Ponticus, has failed to convince.[40] If Leontius of Byzantium in an early writing emphasised the preservation of the natures and to this extent elaborated a symmetrical picture of Christ, he nevertheless started from a Cyrillian perspective. As he later stressed against critics, the Cyrillian perspective of the union in the Logos is richer than any other and at the same time the highest possible union.

With this position Leontius of Byzantium is close to the remarkable idea of Maximus the Confessor (*c.* 580–662), that the human nature in what is proper to it is all the more realised the more it is united with God. For Maximus this insight arose with regard to the human existence of Christ.

Apologists for Chalcedon during the Justinian era, particularly Anastasius I of Antioch (*sed.* 559–70, 593–98/9), emphasised that the divinisation of the human nature of Christ, the divine-human activity of Christ, is grounded in the unity of the natures in the one hypostasis. It is against the background of this theology and its reception that the theological development of Maximus the Confessor can be understood as a process leading to a position which, while preserving Cyril's dynamic view focused on salvation history, tried to differentiate and to stress, in particular, the salvific significance of 'the human being Jesus Christ' (1 Timothy 2.5).

---

40 The recent attempt of D. B. Evans (*Leontius of Byzantium*) to demonstrate the Origenism of Leontius has been almost unanimously rejected by other scholars.

On the one hand, at about 640, Maximus came to conceive of Christ's fear of death and obedience in Gethsemane as an existential predicament and the free act of the human being, Jesus. He recognised in them the decisive human contribution to redemption.[41] With this important insight he does justice – without indicating it – to the intent of the Antiochenes, such as Theodoret of Cyrus. On the other hand, the fact that the Tome of Leo insisted on the common operation of the two natures led Maximus to a revision of the conception of Christ's operation and will; this revision was carried out within the framework of the sixth-century Cyrillian tradition.[42] By emphasising what combined the two interpretations of Chalcedon, Maximus, in order to save the Cyrillian interpretation in which he remained embedded, arrived after 640 at a definition of the one hypostasis which fundamentally refrained from fitting it out with religious, intuitive contents. For these, Maximus maintained, were always related to the natures, while the hypostasis as the principle of the ultimate independent subsistence – in contradistinction to individuality – can only be conceived as 'empty' or 'metaphysical', that is, as a self or centre that is principally not defined by categories of nature.[43] With this highpoint of human endeavour to think through, in an appropriate way, the confession of Christ as 'the new human being', who is God, and to safeguard the paradox of God's incarnation, the Christology of the early church comes to a fitting conclusion.

Bibliography

PRIMARY SOURCES

Apollinarius of Laodicea, *Opera*, in H. Leitzmann, ed., *Apollinaris von Laodicea und seine Schule* (Tübingen, 1904)

Athanasius. *Contra Arianos*. Ed. H. G. Opitz, *Athanasius Werke* (Berlin, 1935–41), II.I.

'Letter to Epictetus'. Ed. G. Ludwig. *Athanasii Epistula ad Epictetum* (Jena, 1911)

ps.-Athanasius. *De incarnatione contra Apollinarium libri II* (PG 26: 1093–1165)

Cyril of Alexandria. *Contra Nestorium*

---

41 Cf. F.-M. Léthel, *Théologie de l'agonie du Christ*.
42 Cf. Uthemann, 'Neuchalkedonismus', 404–11.
43 Cf. K.-H. Uthemann 'Das anthropologische Modell der hypostatischen Union bei Maximus Confessor'; 'Das anthropologische Modell der hypostatischen Union'. In order to understand this, one has to heed the distinction between what defines a nature (*logos*) and the modality (*tropos*), which Maximus derived from the Cappadocians and developed further: modality here means that each nature always exists individually. In Christ modality characterises a renewal of human nature, and is therefore grounded in the fact that the Logos as a hypostasis of the one God is also its hypostasis. With regard to this, see F. Heinzer, *Gottes Sohn als Mensch* and I. H. Dalmais, 'L'innovation des natures'.

Homily 3: 'De Paulo Emeseno' (ACO I.I.4)
Letter of peace ('Laetentur') (ACO I.I.4)
Letter to Acacius ('ep. 40') (ACO I.I.4)
Letters to Nestorius ('epp. 2, 4, 17') (ACO I.I.1)
Scholia de incarnatione (ACO I.5.1)
Epiphanius. *Panarion adversus haereses* (GCS 25, 31, 37)
Epistle of Barnabas (SC 172)
Eustathius of Antioch. *Works* (CCSG 51)
Formula of union (433) (ACO I.I.4)
Havelaar, H. W. *The Coptic Apocalypse of Peter,* TU 144 (Berlin, 1999) (= NHC VII)
Hippolytus of Rome. *Refutatio omnium haeresium* (PTS 25)
Leo. *Tomus* (ACO II.2, IV.1)
Nestorius. *Apologia* ('Liber Heraclidis'). Ed. P. Bedjan, *Nestorius, Le livre d'Héraclide de Damas* (Paris, 1910)
  Sermon 27: 'In commemoratione sanctae Mariae' (ACO I.5)
Novatian. *De Trinitate* (CCSL 4)
Paul of Emesa. *Homiliae II de nativitate Alexandriae habitae* (ACO I.I.4)
Proclus. *Homily 1:* 'De laudibus s. Mariae' (ACO I.I.1)
  Homily 23: 'De dogmate incarnationis'. Ed. C. Martin, 'Un florilège grec d'homélies christologiques des IVᵉ et Vᵉ siècles sur la Nativité', *Le muséon* 4 (1941): 44–8
Severus of Antioch. *Philalethes* (CSCO 133–4)
  Liber contra Grammaticum (CSCO 93–4, 101–2, 111–12)
Theodore of Mopsuestia. *De incarnatione.* Ed. H. B. Swete, *Theodori episcopi Mopsuesteni in epistolas B. Pauli commentarii* (Cambridge, 1882), II.

SECONDARY SOURCES

Abramowski, L. 'Zur Theologie Theodors von Mopsuestia', *ZKG* 72 (1961): 263–93
Dalmais, I. H. 'L'innovation des natures d'après S. Maxime le Confesseur', *SP* 15 (1984): 285–90
Drobner, H. R. *Person-Exegesis und Christologie bei Augustinus* (Leiden, 1986)
Evans, D. B. *Leontius of Byzantium. An Origenist Christology* (Washington, DC, 1970)
Galtier, P. 'Saint Athanase et l'âme du Christ', *Gregorianum* 36 (1955): 555–89
Gray, P. T. R. *The defense of Chalcedon in the East (451–553)* (Leiden, 1979)
Gregg, R. C. and D. E. Groh. *Early Arianism: A view of salvation* (London, 1981)
Grillmeier, A. *Christ in Christian Tradition,* I; II.1; II.2; II.4 (London, 1975–96); *Jesus der Christus im Glauben der Kirche* II.3 (Freiburg, 2002)
Guillaumont, A. *Les 'Kephalaia Gnostica' d'Évagre de Pontique et l'histoire de l'origénisme* (Paris, 1962)
Halleux, A. de. 'La définition christologique à Chalcédoine', *Revue théologique de Louvain* 7 (1976): 3–23, 155–70; reprinted in A. de Halleux, *Patrologie et œcuménisme: Recueil d'études,* BETL 93 (Louvain, 1990), 445–80
Harnack, A. 'Monarchianismus', *RE* 13 (1903), 303–36
Heinzer, F. *Gottes Sohn als Mensch* (Fribourg, 1980)
Hespel, R. *Le florilège cyrillien réfuté par Sévère d'Antioche* (Louvain, 1955)

Hübner, R. M. *Die Einheit des Leibes Christi bei Gregor von Nyssa. Untersuchungen zum Ursprung der 'physischen' Erlösungslehre* (Leiden, 1974)

Der Paradox Eine. Antignostischer Monarchianismus im zweiten Jahrhundert (Leiden, 1999)

Die Schrift des Apolinarius von Laodicea gegen Photin (Pseudo-Athanasius, Contra) und Basilius von Caesarea, PTS 30 (Berlin, 1989)

Lang, U. M. *John Philoponus and the controversies over Chalcedon in the sixth century* (Louvain, 2001)

Lebon, J. 'Altération doctrinale de la "Lettre à Épictète" de saint Athanase', *RHE* 31 (1935): 713–61

Léthel, F.-M. *Théologie de l'agonie du Christ. La liberté humaine du Fils de Dieu et son importance sotériologique mises en lumière par saint Maxime le Confesseur* (Paris, 1979)

Liébaert, J. *Christologie. Von der Apostolischen Zeit bis zum Konzil von Chalkedon (451)* (Freiburg, 1965)

Lorenz, R. 'Die Christusseele im Arianischen Streit', *ZKG* 94 (1983): 1–51

Mühlenberg, E. *Apollinaris von Laodicea* (Göttingen, 1969)

Norris, R. A. *Manhood and Christ. A study in the Christology of Theodore of Mopsuestia* (Oxford, 1963)

Otto, S. *Person und Subsistenz. Die Philosophische Anthropologie des Leontius von Byzanz* (Munich, 1968)

Richard, M. 'Saint Athanase et la psychologie du Christ selon les Ariens', *Mélanges de science religieuse* 4 (1947): 5–54

Rose, E. *Die manichäische Christologie* (Wiesbaden, 1979)

Rudolph, K. *Die Gnosis* (Göttingen, 1978)

Seibt, K. *Die Theologie des Markell von Ankyra* (Berlin/New York, 1994)

Sullivan, R. A. *The Christology of Theodore of Mopsuestia* (Rome, 1956)

Torrance, I. R. *Christology after Chalcedon: Severus of Antioch and Sergius the Monophysite* (Norwich, 1988)

Uthemann, K.-H. 'Anastasius Sinaites', in G. Conticello and V. Conticello, eds., *La théologie byzantine et sa tradition*, 1 (Turnhout, forthcoming)

'Das anthropologische Modell der hypostatischen Union', *Kleronomia* 14 (1982): 283–312

'Das anthropologische Modell der hypostatischen Union bei Maximus Confessor: Zur innerchalkedonischen Transformation eines Paradigmas', in F. Heinzer and C. Schönborn, eds., *Maximus Confessor, Actes du Symposium sur Maxime le Confesseur* (Fribourg, 1982), 223–33

Christus, Kosmos, Diatribe. Themen der frühen Kirche als Beiträge zu einer historischen Theologie (Berlin/New York, 2005)

'Definitionen und Paradigmen in der Rezeption des Dogmas von Chalkedon bis in die Zeit Kaiser Justinians', in J. van Oort and J. Roldanus, eds., *Chalkedon: Geschichte und Aktualität*, SPA 5 (Louvain, 1997), 5–122

'Eustathios von Antiochien wider den seelenlosen Christus der Arianer', *ZAC* (forthcoming)

'Kaiser Justinian als Kirchenpolitiker und Theologe', *Augustiniamum* 39 (1999): 5–83

'Der Neuchalkedonismus als Vorbereitung des Monotheletismus. Ein Beitrag zum eigentlichen Anliegen des Neuchalkedonismus', *SP* 29 (1997): 373–413

'Zur Rezeption des *Tome of Leo* in und nach Chalkedon. Wider den dogmenhistorischen Begriff "strenger Chalkedonismus"', *SP* 34 (2001): 572–604

Review of J. H. Declerck, ed., *Eustathii Antiocheni* (CCSG 51), *Jahrbuch der Österreichischen Byzantinistik* 54 (2004): 279–82

Voorgang, D. *Die Passion Jesu und Christi in der Gnosis* (Frankfurt-am-Main, 1991)

Winkelmann, F. *Der monenergetisch–monotheletische Streit* (Frankfurt-am-Main, 2001)

Wolfson, H. A. *The philosophy of the church fathers. Faith, Trinity, incarnation* (Cambridge, MA, 1970³)

20

Sin and salvation: Experiences and reflections

AUGUSTINE CASIDAY

'The Son of Man is come to seek and save that which is lost' (Luke 19.19): with this description of their Lord's mission, Christians understandably came to regard salvation and sin as master themes for their lives. In fact, these themes are so pervasive that discussions of them take on as many forms as Christianity itself does. This near ubiquity makes it exceedingly difficult to appreciate the subject in a way that does justice to evidence from across the Mediterranean basin and Near East; in attempting to navigate through the wealth of information, it is very easy to adopt the categories of regional controversies and subsequently to ascribe universal significance to localised preoccupations. One way forward is to think about how Christians considered baptism (itself a practice that was comparably widespread), which was regarded as a vital step in the process of salvation and indeed as the font of Christian identity. In explaining, preparing for and celebrating this sacrament, Christians of all types were confronted in a powerful way with the dynamics of sin and salvation – and these experiences in turn shaped their habits of reflecting upon salvation.[1] Baptism and the events surrounding it provide important evidence for how Christians during our period understood sin and the measures they took to deal with it, as well as how they conceived of salvation.

Records about early Christian views on baptism survive in a variety of forms, such as catechetical lectures, rites (and commentaries on them), pilgrims' journals, hymns and letters. As for the former, the justly famous homilies of Cyril of Jerusalem and Theodore of Mopsuestia are but two series of such lectures. Similar instruction survives from Augustine of Hippo, Gregory of Nazianzus, John Chrysostom (from his younger days in Antioch), Quodvultdeus of Carthage, Severus of Antioch and Zeno of Verona. Our other sources similarly come from numerous authors and represent an impressive geographic and chronological

---

1 This is particularly evident in Augustine of Hippo's theological analysis of the baptism of infants, as we shall see below.

range. This abundance of information reduces the likelihood of distortions that might emerge by taking local debates (for example, those in fifth-century Gaul about ancestral sin, from which the terms of medieval Augustinianism derive) as good indicators for the primary concerns and interests of contemporary Christians at large. If instead we look to the range of sources, we encounter patristic views about human separation from, and reconciliation to, God that represent general trends.

Background

Christians were far from innovative in attributing religious significance to ritual washing. Already in biblical purity laws, bathing is established for purification (e.g., at Leviticus 15.5, 15). Ritual ablution for cleansing was practised at Qumran (see 'The community rule' (1QS) 3.5; cf. Josephus, *Jewish War* 2.8.7.137–42) and the practice is already explicitly linked in the records of that community to initiation, purification and understanding ('Community rule' 4.21–2) – all elements that are retained and enlarged upon by Christians of our period. Other groups similarly valued ritual cleansing. Though we know rather less than one might like about the background of Mani, it is clear that he was reared in a baptising sect that claimed as one of its founders a certain Elchasai and that used baptism widely and frequently: according to the *Cologne Mani-Codex*, Mani took exception to their practice of baptising their vegetables![2] Devotees of Eastern deities like Magna Mater, Cybele or Mithras also observed a cleansing ritual, already established in Rome during the Antonine period, that was called the *taurobolium* or *criobolium* (depending upon whether the sacrificial animal in whose blood the rite was performed was a bull or a goat). The initiate returned from the ceremony *taurobolio crioboliog[ue] in aeternum renatus*[3] – but even so, for the scrupulous, the effects of the rite could be renewed after twenty years.[4] In short, baptism was a custom observed by a variety of late ancient religious communities; it was therefore manifestly *not* a distinctively Christian rite.

Christians give baptism a distinctive character by presenting and interpreting it in terms of participating in the death of Christ. This connection is clearly

---

2 CMC 80.1–3, 80.23–82.23, 88.13–5; see further S. N. C. Lieu, *Manichaeism in the later Roman empire and medieval China*, 35–50, but also the note of caution sounded by G. P. Luttikhuizen, *The revelation of Elchasai*, 220–2.
3 'reborn for eternity by the *taurobolium* and the *criobolium*'.
4 For epigraphic evidence, see *CIL*, VL.i: 97, 98 (items 510, 512); for a description of the Mithraic rite, see F. Cumont, *Textes et monuments*, I: 334–5. See also the various contributions in Ugo Bianchi and Maarten J. Vermaseren, eds., *La soteriologia dei culti orientali*.

drawn by Paul, whose teaching on life, death, renewal and participation in the death of Christ is held together by his claims about baptism (see especially Romans 6). Later generations would further enrich this network of associations by interpreting Christ's own baptism – a 'going down into the deep' – as an anticipation of his descent into Hades.[5] This connection of themes is but the beginning of what will ultimately appear as an intricate tapestry of symbols and events. At a more practical level, early Christian literature indicates that procedures for, and interpretations of, baptism were developing among Christians from a very early stage.[6] Already in the post-apostolic generations, we find baptism linked to ecclesiastical hierarchy, to a remission of sins that enables one to live purely, and to the eucharist.[7] If Bishop Bernard's persuasive arguments regarding the provenance of the *Odes of Solomon* are accepted, one may find in 'the continual stress laid by the Odist upon the privileges of Divine grace which have lately been placed within his reach' some stirring evidence of a late second-century response to the effects of baptism.[8]

By the time of the Constantinian settlement, abundant resources were already available to Christians for the purposes of discussing sin and salvation in terms of baptism.

Drawing near the waters of regeneration

Baptism is the culmination of the rites associated with full membership in the church, and as such is preceded by several important observances. A generalised outline based on evidence from around the Mediterranean can be advanced as follows: enrolment as a learner and subsequent instruction, scrutiny, several exorcisms, the renunciation of Satan and swearing of allegiance to God, the baptism proper, vesting in white clothes, unction and communion. Throughout much of this period, baptisms took place as an integral part of the Easter festivities as a matter of course (though, as we shall

---

5 E.g., Origen, *Homilies on Exodus* 5.2 (SC 321: 154–6); see further J. H. Bernard, *The Odes of Solomon*, 32–9.

6 E.g., *Didache* 9.5 and *Letter of Barnabas*, especially 16.8.

7 The examples are taken from Ignatius, *To the Smyrnians* 8.2; Hermas, *Precepts* 4.3; Justin, *Apology* 1.66.1. Although the authors mentioned so far are part of the developing tradition of Christian orthodoxy, reflecting upon baptism in this way was not the preserve of the orthodox. Some of Clement of Alexandria's writings contain fragmentary evidence of robust interpretations of Christ's death and baptism as elements in a complex Gnostic Christian synthesis: see Clement, *Excerpta e Theodoto* 76–86 (SC 23: 198–212). For further treatment of baptism among the Sethian Gnostics, see J.-M. Severin, *Le dossier baptismale séthien*.

8 Bernard, *The Odes of Solomon*, 3; cf. J. H. Charlesworth, *The Odes of Solomon*, vii. For further discussion, see especially M. Lattke, *Die Oden Salomos*, bd. 3.

see, there were exceptions to this general practice). Enrolment would often take place many months – perhaps even a year or more – before baptism to allow adequate time for instruction and training. The learner (or 'catechumen') was sometimes regarded as already belonging to the church, albeit in an incomplete or defective sense. There are two aspects to such incomplete membership: on one hand, the catechumens could be seen as enjoying a specific situation within the community that set them apart from unbelievers; on the other, the catechumens' situation was by definition inferior to that of fully initiated believers. Even so, some believers maintained their affiliation to the church as catechumens for years. But since such instances come increasingly to constitute special cases, we will want to turn our attention first to the developing norm of following a limited period of intense instruction with full incorporation into the community.

Catechesis and orthodoxy

Instruction for catechumens ('catechesis') provided them with the intellectual, moral and spiritual resources that they would need after renouncing the devil and embracing life in Christ. The major vehicle for instruction was the catechetical homily, which during Lent senior clergy would deliver to those who had expressed a serious interest in becoming Christian. Often the bishop would deliver these homilies (as with Cyril of Jerusalem; Egeria also mentions this practice in her *Travels*), though in some cases they were given by a priest (such as John Chrysostom was, when giving his catechetical homilies in Antioch). Standard fare for these homilies included the literal and spiritual exposition of Scripture.[9] The learners were often accompanied by their sponsors, who in some cases seem to have also undertaken to offer the learners additional instruction.[10] Other Christians might well attend the homilies, too. When several monks from the Syrian countryside chanced into Antioch during a series of his lectures (*c.* 390), Chrysostom availed himself of the opportunity to illustrate the manner of living that he was urging the catechumens to lead by referring them to the renunciations that the ascetics had undertaken. Circumstance thus provided an excellent opportunity for Chrysostom to exhort his catechumens to moral living. But the arrival of the Syriac monks also demonstrates something unexpected that could transpire during the catechetical lectures. In the Christian Near East especially, it sometimes happened that

---

9 E.g., Egeria, *Travels* 46.2 (SC 296: 308).
10 E.g., Dionysius, *Eccl. hier.* 2.2.2 (PTS 36: 70); Egeria, *Travels* 45.2, 46.1 (SC 296: 306, 308); for a warm description of baptism and catechism in Augustine's Hippo, see F. van der Meer, *Augustine the bishop*, 347–82.

these lectures were attended by mixed audiences of Greek-, Syriac- and Latin-speakers. With a characteristically brilliant rhetorical flourish, Chrysostom took this as proof that, even when language and culture separated Christians, their faith transcended these differences.[11]

Something rather more prosaic than the charisma of Pentecost may have been at work in overcoming language barriers, however: Egeria indicates that a priestly translator was on hand for those who spoke Syriac, while others present – perhaps monks and nuns – assumed responsibility for translation into Latin as needed.[12] The international composition of the audience neatly mirrors the catholic aim of the instruction. Through instruction in morals, basic articles of the faith and the exposition of sacred texts, the catechumens were being introduced into a community of cross-cultural dimensions. This cosmopolitanism was reinforced by references to collectively formulated creeds that sought to establish unity across the Mediterranean.[13]

Creeds played a significant part in the formation of Christians. The catechist would summarily exposit the creed; the catechumens 'inscribed it on the fleshly tables of their hearts' and were expected to recite it at a later stage in their conversion.[14] This emphasis on a correct profession of faith naturally implied an emphasis on correct understanding and correct procedure, though there would come to be characteristic differences between Eastern and Western Christians in the matter of how much importance to attach to an orthodox baptism.

In the Christian East, the conventional practice was to disregard any previous baptism as being null and void. Heretical or schismatic Christians were therefore received by baptism (not, be it noted, by *re-baptism*). Chrysostom, for example, preached vigorously against Arian baptism.[15] Several early Western churchmen subscribed to quite a similar view: Novatian, Tertullian and Cyprian considered right belief an indispensable element for effective

---

11 Chrysostom, *Baptismal homilies* 8.1–6 (SC 50: 247–51).
12 Egeria, *Travels* 47.3–4 (SC 296: 314); that her *alii fratres et sorores grecolatini, qui latine exponunt eis* were probably monks and nuns, see L. Th. A. Lorié, *Spiritual terminology*, 39. Despite this mention of Latin, it is not particularly likely that the Westerners in attendance had come to the East in order to be baptised. Probably they were pilgrims for whom attending the lectures held the promise of further edification; see Juliette Day, *Baptism in early Byzantine Palestine*, 38–9.
13 See, e.g., Chrysostom, *Baptismal homilies* 1.19–24 (SC 50: 118–21).
14 The quotation is taken from the anonymous Carolingian florilegium in which John the Deacon's *Epistula ad Senarium* is preserved (see Wilmart's edition of the *Epistula*, at p. 159). According to Egeria, *Travels* 46.3 (SC 296: 308–10), the explanation of the Creed took place after the fifth week of Lent.
15 Chrysostom, *Baptismal homilies* 1.22, 2.26 (SC 50: 119–20, 147–8).

baptism.[16] In their view, a baptism that is performed without right belief in God does not confer the saving presence of the Holy Spirit; such a baptism, in effect, is done in the name of an unreal divinity. (Such thinking sheds light on why Gregory of Nazianzus based his argument for the Holy Spirit's divinity, as against the Pneumatochians, on the fact that the Spirit is invoked in the rite of baptism: because God is at work in baptism, the invocation of the Holy Spirit implies that the Spirit is God; here, practice gives rise to theory.)[17] Athanasius the Great made the case against Arian baptism with alacrity: 'For by intending to receive baptism into what is not, they have received nothing at all; and being aligned with a creature they will have no help from the creation.'[18] It was perhaps in response to such sharp criticism that Eunomius, a later figure who was sympathetic to Arius' position, altered the terms of the service. For his followers, baptism was pronounced into the death of Christ, rather than in the name of the Trinity.[19] This modification allowed Eunomius to underscore the mediating function of Christ's death and thus secure a meaningful and consistent interpretation of baptism, while defending his position against his opponents (albeit at the cost of using the Matthean formula for baptism).

As late as *c.* 500, it was possible for a Roman figure to reject Arian baptisms using comparable arguments,[20] but this was atypical and, on the whole, the Western perspective on heretical or schismatic baptisms developed along a different trajectory. In the Christian West, broadly speaking, heretical or schismatic Christians tended to be accepted into the Catholic communion by having the hands of the bishop placed on their heads rather than by being

---

16 Tertullian, *On baptism* 15 (ed. and trans. Evans, 32–4); Cyprian, *Letters* 69–75 (CSEL 3²: 749–827); for Novatian, see Cyprian, *Letter* 73.2 (CSEL 3²: 779–80).

17 Gregory of Nazianzus, *Or.* 31.28 and 33.17 (SC 250: 330–2 and SC 318: 194–6); see further the commentary on *Or.* 31.28 by Norris, *Faith gives fullness to reason*, 207–9.

18 Athanasius, *Orations against the Arians* 2.43 (trans. Anatolios, 138); see also Athanasius' *Letters to Serapion on the Holy Spirit* 1.30 (trans. Anatolios, 229): 'The faith in the Trinity, which has been handed down to us, is one, and it is this faith which unites us to God, whereas anyone who takes anything away from the Trinity and is baptized in the name of the Father only, or in the name of the Son only, or in the name of the Father and the Son apart from the Spirit, receives nothing but remains empty and unsanctified – both he and the one who appears to be administering the consecration. After all, it is a consecration in the Trinity!'

19 See Socrates, *H.E.* 5.24 (GCS, N.F. I, 306–7); this passage is discussed by Kopecek (*A history of Neo-Arianism*, II: 397–400), who also notes (I: 160–1) that a generation earlier other Arian baptismal liturgies were apparently modified so as to avoid the triple immersion or the invocations of the Son and the Spirit. On Eunomius, see now R. P. Vaggione, *Eunomius of Cyzicus and the Nicene revolution.*

20 John the Deacon, *Epistola ad Senarium* §9 (ed. Wilmart, 176).

baptised.[21] This practice was enshrined in the decision of the first Council of Arles (314/15) that neither schism nor heresy invalidates a properly executed baptism, by which is understood a baptism with the Trinitarian formula in keeping with Matthew 28.19.[22] That council itself, and indeed the conventional Latin approach generally, may be attributed to a distinctively Roman response to imperial persecution, wherein ritual purity and contamination figured very prominently. Confronted with the claims that a compromised church infects its adherents through the very rituals that are meant to save them,[23] Augustine came to affirm that any Trinitarian baptism is in itself holy because Christ is at work in it, irrespective of the sins of the ministering clergy.[24] (Here, as often, Augustine's view is not idiosyncratic: a similar perspective on Christ himself performing the baptism is attested in Greek and Syriac sources.)[25] This claim does not imply that any baptism whatever will lead to salvation, for schismatic or heretical coteries cannot effectively promote and sustain the Christian life. Nevertheless, Augustine's insistence that baptisms in such communities are to be respected was widely accepted by Western Christians. Fulgentius of Ruspe carried forward this line of thinking when he called 'repeated baptism' a 'great crime' worthy of tears, even while rejecting the possibility that a schismatic or heretical baptism can ultimately lead to salvation.[26]

Alongside this emphasis on right belief came an equally strong emphasis on right behaviour. John Chrysostom tirelessly preached the need (even

---

21 Thus, Pope Stephen (as cited by Cyprian, *Letter* 73.1 (CSEL 3²: 778–9)) maintained that the traditional discipline in such cases was the laying on of hands and pointedly *not* a baptism.

22 Canon 8 (in P. Labbé and N. Coleti, eds., *Sacrosancta concilia*, I: 1451–2).

23 Thus, the Donatist perspective (see Augustine, *Against the letter of Parminian* 2.5.10–13.27 (CSEL 51: 55–79)) – which can profitably be compared to the letters of Cyprian, as cited above; see further J. P. Burns, *Cyprian the bishop*.

24 Augustine, *Against the letter of Petilian* 2.37.88 (CSEL 52: 73–4); *On baptism* 4.12.18, 5.4.4 (CSEL 51: 244, 265–6); cf. *Tractates on John* 5.18, 6.7 (CCSL 36: 51, 57): 'those whom Judas baptises, Christ baptises'; 'if Peter should baptise, it is [Christ] who baptises; if Paul should baptise, it is he who baptises; if Judas should baptise, it is he who baptises'. See also Optatus' *Against the Donatists* 5.6.1–7.13 (SC 413: 140–50). Augustine's perspective on baptism is well presented in terms of his understanding of Christian society by Carol Harrison, *Augustine*, 144–57.

25 E.g., Chrysostom, *Hom. in Matt* 50.3 (PG 58: 507): 'when you are baptised, it is not he [sc., the clergyman] who baptises you, but God who holds your head with invisible power'; *Baptismal homilies* 2.10 (SC 50: 138–9, trans. ACW 31: 46–7): 'For it is not a man who does what is done, but it is the grace of the Spirit which sanctifies the nature of the water and touches your head together with the hand of the priest.' Cf. too Theodore of Mopsuestia, *Cat. hom.* 14.15 (ST 145: 432) and three West Syriac commentaries studied by Brock ('Some early Syriac baptismal commentaries', §XIV, at 42–3).

26 Fulgentius, *On the forgiveness of sins* 1.22.1 and *On the faith* 43–4 (CCSL 91a: 671, 740–2).

before baptism) for leading a sober and morally upright life that would befit a Christian. Dionysius, in his highly condensed description of the 'mystery of illumination', strongly suggests that the sponsor ought to convince himself of the suitability of the would-be Christian's manner of living; he does not, however, mention the *scrutiny* – a more formal process whereby the candidate for baptism is examined and questioned by clergy.[27] Even so, the strong presumption is evident that the candidates would not only learn theological formulae and moral precepts, but would also make progress in virtuous living, even before baptism. The necessity of integrated belief and practice is a standard implication of the catechist's message, as indeed it is of Christian thought during this period in general.

Mystical transformation, moral reformation

The assumptions of moral rectitude and increased understanding do not imply an optimistic view (or anything else, for that matter) about unaided human ability: it will be recalled that the catechumens already occupy a designated place within the church, albeit one more removed than that of, say, the communicating faithful. In other words, catechumens already enjoy a certain relationship to Christ inasmuch as they are catechumens. And yet, even though catechumens already have a part in the Christian community, their baptism brings about a radical change in their status. As Chrysostom puts it, 'Instead of the man who descended into the water, a different man comes forth, one who has wiped away all the filth of his sins, who has put off the old garment of skin [cf. Genesis 3.21] and has put on the royal robe.'[28] Descriptions of baptism as a cleansing, or change, of the surface are common enough; it is a ritual washing, after all.[29] But this must not mislead us into thinking that the change

---

27 Dionysius, *Eccl. Hier.* 2.2.2 (PTS 36: 70). For the 'scrutinies', see Egeria, *Travels* 45.3–4 (SC 296: 306); John the Deacon, *Epistola ad Senarium* §4 (ed. Wilmart, 173); A. Dondeyne, 'La discipline des scrutins dans l'église latine avant Charlemagne'. Perhaps Dionysius discreetly omitted the scrutiny because of his belief that the clergy, like God, ought to bestow their gifts liberally: *Eccl. hier.* 2.2.3 (PTS 36: 71).

28 Chrysostom, *Baptismal homilies* 2.25 (SC 50: 147; trans. ACW 31: 52).

29 For instance, one recurring image is baptism making an Ethiopian white – an image presumably inspired by Philip baptising Queen Candace's eunuch, which cleverly subverts an old dictum about Ethiopians changing their skin colour (cf. Acts 8.26–39; Jeremiah 13.23), even though it retains the racist overtones. See Gregory of Nyssa, *On Song of Songs* 7 (GNO 6: 205); cf. Ephrem, *Hymns on the faith* 83.4–5, 'On the pearl' (CSCO 154: 255): 'Eunuchum ex Aethiopia in curru sedentem/ vidit Philippus. Occurrit nigro/ agnus lucis ex lineis/ cum legeret/ Baptizatus est Aethiops/ et induit lucem et splenduit et abiit.// Instruxit et docuit. Ex nigris/ fecit albos et Aethiopes/ nigrae margaritae/ factae sunt Filio. Obtulit Patri suo/ coronam splendentem margaritis.' For a general overview of St Ephrem's teaching, see E. Beck, 'Le baptême chez Saint Éphrem'.

is regarded as superficial. When Chrysostom returned to this theme, he was even more explicit:

> The grace of God has entered these souls and moulded them anew, reformed them, and made them different from the way they were. It did not change the substance, but made over their will (*tên proairesin metaseuasasa*), no longer permitting the tribunal of the mind to entertain an erroneous notion, but by dissipating the mist which has blinded their eyes, God's grace made them see the ugly deformity of evil and virtue's shining beauty as they are.[30]

Serapion of Thmuis similarly describes the change as creating a fellowship with the angels and changing one's status from fleshly to spiritual.[31]

Considering how deep this change was thought to be, post-baptismal sin posed an acute problem for most of our authors. Gregory the Illuminator, the 'Apostle to the Armenians', spoke to the point: the one who has been baptised 'will not be renewed a second time'.[32] Zeno of Verona, whose baptismal statements are surely the pithiest to survive from antiquity, urged his flock to 'drink with confidence while you may ... Fill your vessels with all urgency and with much devotion, so that you will always have enough water, remembering this before all else that you can never spill a drop or come to fetch it again.'[33] John Chrysostom was equally forthright in his message, though he did provide a clear option for remitting sins: repentance.[34] In this, he was followed by the remarkable Coptic bishop and theologian, Rufus of Shotep (*fl. c.* 575–600), who exhorted his audience in the following terms:

> Let the catechumen give thought to his rebirth through the washing of baptism, and the believer take care to wash away his sins through the tears of repentance and give thought to testing his soul through the spirit of mercy and if you reform yourself in this way and set your soul in order through repentance ... and adorn your mind through the practice of good deeds, your soul will be nourished from the storehouses of righteousness and then the holy spotless bridegroom will desire it.[35]

What is surely important here is the Pauline principle, 'One Lord, one faith, one baptism ...' (Ephesians 4.5): sins are forgiven by baptism only once.

---

30 Chrysostom, *Baptismal homilies* 4.14 (SC 50: 190; trans. ACW 31: 71–2).
31 Serapion of Thmuis, *Euchologium* 2.11 (TU 17: 3b).
32 Gregory the Illuminator, *Teaching* 454 (trans. Thomson, 102).
33 Zeno, *Invitation* 7 (CCSL 22); on Zeno, see Gordon Jeanes, *The day has come!*
34 Chrysostom, *Baptismal homilies* 3.23 (SC 50: 164; trans. ACW 31: 63 (modified)): 'There is remission, but not a second remission by the laver [of baptism].' But repentance restores baptismal radiance to those 'who received this gift in the past' (Ibid., 5.24 (SC 50: 212; trans. ACW 31: 90)).
35 Rufus of Shotep, *On Matthew* 67 (trans. Sheridan, 162–3).

Now plucky souls like Jerome could try to entice a young protégé with confident predictions of accomplishment, and the truly daring might insist that actual sinlessness was within reach.[36] But the majority of our sources are more ambivalent; they encourage virtue even as they acknowledge the likelihood of lapses. Cyprian put the matter down to a lack of faith that enabled the devil to return.[37] Serapion of Thmuis recognised that, even after one had renounced Satan, mutability in one's character and manner of life was a serious problem that only God's intervention could rectify.[38] When Fulgentius of Ruspe addressed himself to the problem, he put a salutary emphasis on the humility needed in these circumstances. This kind of humility is at work when one is willing to acknowledge one's sins and seeks to be healed by the 'physician of souls'.[39] For Fulgentius' near contemporary, Mark the Monk, sins result from a failure to keep the commandments in a manner worthy of one who has been liberated for precisely that purpose: 'Holy baptism *does* represent perfection – but it does not perfect someone who does not keep the commandments . . . Thus holy baptism is perfect with respect to us, but we are imperfect with respect to it.'[40] Mark stands in continuity with Macarius' claim that Christians enjoy (and are responsible for cultivating) a baptismal deposit of grace.[41] The apex of Greek sophistication in these matters is found in Maximus the Confessor's response when basically the same question about post-baptismal sin is put to him by Thalassius.

The manner of birth from God within us is two-fold: the one bestows the grace of adoption, which is entirely present in potency (*dynamei*) in those who are born of God; the other introduces, wholly by active exertion (*kat' energeian*), that grace which deliberately (*gnômikôs*) reorients the entire free choice of the one being born of God toward the God who gives birth.

36 Jerome, *Letter* 130.9 (CSEL 56: 189): 'But let us ignore penitence, lest we should sin easily. It is a second plank for the misfortunate after a shipwreck; but the ship is saved by a chaste virgin.' This sentiment was well known (and frequently attacked by Reformers) in the Angelic Doctor's paraphrase (*Summa Theologiae* III, qu. 84, art. 6, *Sed contra*): 'Jerome says that penance is a second plank after shipwreck.' For a call to sinlessness pure and simple, see the Pelagian homily 'On the possibility of not sinning' (in C. P. Caspari, ed., *Briefe*, 114–22).
37 (ps.-?)Cyprian, *On rebaptism* 16 (PL 3: 1199): 'Manifestum est diabolum in baptismo fide credentis excludi, si fides postmodum defecerit, regredi.'
38 Serapion, *Euchologium* 2.9: 'continually keep his character and manner [of life] unchangeable'.
39 See Fulgentius, *Letter* 7.5–6, 'To Venantia' (SC 487: 264–6).
40 Mark the Monk, *On holy baptism* 2.7–8 and 5.208–9 (SC 445: 298, 342); a comparable discussion can be found in Diadochus, *Gnostic chapters* 76–9 (SC 5: 134–7).
41 Macarius, *Great letter* 2 (ed. Jaeger, 233–4).

Because the second 'birth' does not follow automatically, but only after active engagement in the pursuit of Christian virtue and knowledge, it is the case that some who have experienced the first 'birth' will nevertheless have a will (*gnômê*) that is inclined toward sin. Unless and until the will is 'wholly endowed with the Spirit by participation in divine mysteries that are made known through active endeavour',[42] it will continue to issue forth in sin. The quotidian experience of Christians is thus characterised by a deep and abiding tension between the renewal that comes from baptism and the temptations which they face daily.

Regeneration and renewal

This abiding tension that characterises Christian life after baptism may help-fully be thought of as a sign of the kingdom of God being at hand. In the treatments of baptism and salvation that we have considered – and especially in the discussions of post-baptismal sin – most of our authors take for granted that, in a very real (albeit incomplete) sense, the Christian has already returned to paradise. Baptismal rites reinforce the point that to enter the church is itself to enter God's presence, or, even more boldly, to enter heaven. The eschato-logical and the social dimensions alike of this ecclesiological claim deserve our attention.

Entering paradise

It was a widespread custom during the patristic era for the recently baptised to receive communion immediately thereafter.[43] This practice is tellingly glossed in the seventh-century baptismal *Ordo* of Severus of Antioch as follows: 'The fruit which Adam did not taste in Paradise has been put in your mouths.'[44] This comment marks the confluence of mystical interpretations of the sacraments with much earlier ideas about the heavenly status of the newly baptised. Origen had long since remarked that 'those who have been regenerated through divine baptism are established in paradise, that is, in the church, to do the spiritual deeds that are within'.[45] Basil indicates that it is impossible for those 'who have not been sealed with baptism' to ascend into heaven – and this view bears

---

42 Maximus, *Ad Thalassium* 6 (CCSG 7.69–70; trans. Wilken and Blowers, 103, slightly modified).
43 Thus, e.g., Chrysostom (*Baptismal homilies* 2.27 (SC 50: 148–9)) and Denys (*Eccl. hier.* 2.3.8 (PTS 36: 78)).
44 Cited from Bernard, *The Odes of Solomon*, 21; the *ordo* echoes Ephrem's *Hymn of the Baptized* 17 (trans. NPNF 2, XIII: 283): 'The fruit which Adam, tasted not in paradise: – this day in your mouths, has been placed with joy.'
45 Origen, *Sel. in Genesim* (PG 12: 100.28).

comparison with Cyril of Jerusalem's repeated insistence that baptism opens the gates to paradise.[46] The idea that one enters paradise through baptism is maintained into the ninth century, as we find it implicitly stated in Moses bar Kepha's *On the mysteries of baptism* 24: 'The entrance to the Holy of Holies signifies the entering in to the tree of life from which Adam was prohibited.'[47]

It is not communion alone that provides commentators with an opportunity to compare baptism to the gate of paradise. Theodore of Mopsuestia remarks upon the white, linen garments worn by the bishop who celebrates the baptism in the same way: 'Instead of his usual clothes, he is wearing a delicate, shining linen vestment. He is wearing new garments which denote the new world you are entering; their dazzling appearance signifies that you will shine in the next life; its light texture symbolizes the delicacy and grace of that world.'[48] The neophytes, too, were clad in garments of white linen. Indeed, Frederic van der Meer plausibly explains the choice of linen ('the cool vegetable product') by pointing to its popularity from the time of the Pythagoreans as a symbol for ritual purity: 'It is the symbol of their own inward purity and of the stainless life to which they are now committed.'[49] But, taking Theodore's remark for guidance, we may wish to go further, for it is easy to envisage his interpretation extended to the neophytes as well. The garment does not simply outwardly denote an inward state; rather, it manifests in the present the brilliance of the future.

The solidarity of the saved

To enter into baptismal newness of life was to enter simultaneously into a community.[50] The required feats of memorisation and recitation that neophytes were obliged to perform were a means of ensuring that they subscribed to the community's standards. And, as we have already had occasion to note in passing, the candidates were supported in their efforts by sponsors. Not only did the sponsors vouch for the candidates, they also joined them in attending

---

46 Cyril, *Procatechesis* 15, *Catechesis* 19.9.
47 Trans. Aytoun, 357; on bar Kepha (*c.* 819–903), see further Baby Varghese, *Les onctions baptismales*, 230–44.
48 Theodore of Mopsuestia, *Cat. hom.* 13.17.
49 Van der Meer, *Augustine the Bishop*, 369; his claim is strengthened by the observation that, in the Carthiginian rite of baptism at least, the catechumens had divested (and then trodden upon) woollen clothes before the baptism proper – which, according to van der Meer, indicates a total rejection of the worldly and an acceptance of the heavenly.
50 By the seventh century, this principle would be invoked in Visigothic Spain with a crude political gesture, whereby the baptism of all Jews was mandated within those kingdoms: see *Laws of Receswinth* 12.2.3 (MGH leg II.1: 413–14).

catechetical lectures.[51] They were presumably more readily approachable by the candidates than were the catechists. Dionysius for his part envisages the sponsors answering questions put to them by the candidates, and Moses bar Kepha goes so far as to describe the sponsor as '"Teacher" because he has to teach him [sc., the candidate] how to conduct himself in the Church precincts and in the pious practices of asceticism'.[52] It is in this way that they are best able to act as guarantors for the 'contract' (synthêkê) that is baptism.[53]

The sponsor's role as a 'guarantor' is even more in evidence in the case of an infant's baptism. There is evidence for resistance to paedobaptism in the patristic era, for example from Tertullian. But his objection is limited in scope: he would have baptism come as a deliberate choice, which is manifestly impossible for children. His final word on the matter was 'let them be made Christians when they have become competent to know Christ'.[54] By contrast, Origen sounds the note that reverberates through the early Christian centuries when he commends the practice, even attributing to it an apostolic origin. With an eye to Psalm 50[51].5 ('in sin did my mother conceive me'), Origen states, 'It is on this account as well that the Church has received the tradition from the apostles to give baptism even to little children. For they to whom the secrets of the divine mysteries were committed were aware that in everyone was sin's innate defilement, which needed to be washed away through water and the Spirit.'[55] Children as humans were seen as being implicated in the fallen condition of the human race.[56] This unhappy solidarity in separation from God is therefore answered by the joyful reconciliation that comes through belonging to the community that aspires to godliness.

It should be noted that even Christians who rejected the idea of inherited sin would not scruple to use a different baptismal formula for (putatively sinless) children.[57] These claims were made in the context of a debate about the consequences of Adam's sin that has been repeatedly taken up by Western

---

51 Chrysostom, Baptismal homilies 2.15–16 (SC 50: 141–3); Theodore of Mopsuestia, Cat. hom. 12.16 (ST 145: 347–9); Egeria, Travels 45.2, 46.1 (SC 296: 306, 308).
52 Moses bar Kepha, Mysteries of baptism 3d (trans. Aytoun, 346–7).
53 Chrysostom, Baptismal homilies 2.17–21 (SC 50: 143–5); cf. Moses bar Kepha, The mysteries of baptism 3b (trans. Aytoun, 346).
54 Tertullian, On baptism 18 (ed. and trans. Evans, 38–9).
55 Origen, Commentary on Romans 5.9, 11 (PG 14: 1017).
56 Cf. Cyprian, Letter 64.5 (CSEL 3²: 720), in which Cyprian reports the positive recommendation of infant baptism by the bishops who met at the Council of Carthage in 252: '. . . infans qui recens natus nihil peccauit, nisi quod secundum Adam carnaliter natus contagium mortis antiquae prima natiuitate contraxit'.
57 E.g., Pelagius, On the faith 7 (PL 15: 1718): 'Baptisma unum tenemus, quod iisdem sacramenti uerbis in infantibus, quibus etiam in maioribus, asserimus esse celebrandum.' Cf. Caelestius, ap. Augustine, On the grace of Christ and original sin 2.5.5 (CSEL 42: 169–70).

Christians. In this period, the most prominent figures involved in the debate were Jerome, Augustine, Pelagius and Caelestius; others contributed to the discussion as well – one thinks of Rufinus the Syrian, Ambrose of Chalcedon, John Cassian, Vincent of Lérins, Prosper of Aquitaine and Julian of Eclanum – and it is important not to reduce the complexities of this debate into a bipolar contrast between Augustine and Pelagius, because such a reduction can only be at the expense of the rich variety of perspectives that emerged (and often clashed) for several decades.[58] And yet it is possible to see the lineaments of the discussion as a whole within the topical debate between Augustine on the one hand and Pelagius and Caelestius on the other with regard to infant baptism.

The baptism of infants features prominently in Augustine's position on the inherited sin of Adam. He takes the very form of the rite – including the exorcism that precedes the immersion – as meaningful and as straightforwardly true. Thus, he asks, 'How would it be possible then for [the sponsor] to declare that he renounces the devil, who is not at all in [the infant]? How that he is converted to God, from whom he had never been turned away? How that he believes (among other things) in the forgiveness of sins, when none have been attributed to him?'[59] We have no evidence that the Pelagians ever rose to the challenge of these hard questions. Their own claims about the effects of baptism upon infants lack the cogency of Augustine's incisive theological interpretation of the sacrament.

In the main, they rejected the idea that sin can be imputed where under-standing and will are lacking: for Pelagius, the so-called 'Sicilian Anonymous' and Caelestius, there can be no sin that is not willed.[60] Their aetiology of sin accounts for their refusal to ascribe sin to infants, whose lack of an operative will is axiomatic. In this way, Pelagius and like-minded fellows privilege the

---

58 The polarised schema from which I am dissenting underlies much scholarship on the *Rezeptionsgeschichte* of Augustine's writings, from his lifetime to the Second Council of Orange (529), and has traditionally resulted in the use of 'Semi-Pelagianism' as a category for historical interpretation. Scholars have increasingly disavowed that category, but in many instances the underlying polarity remains unchallenged. For a thoroughgoing critique of 'Semi-Pelagianism' as an anachronistic misrepresentation of events that is rooted in dubious assumptions about the normativity of Augustinian theology, and an extended analysis of a major figure in this period that challenges the traditional polarisation, see A. M. C. Casiday, *Tradition and theology in St John Cassian*.

59 Augustine, *On the merit and remission of sins and on infant baptism* 1.34.63 (CSEL 60: 64).

60 Pelagius, *On nature* ap. Augustine, *On nature and grace* 30.34 (CSEL 60: 258); Sicilian Anonymous, *'Hon tuae'* 1 (in C. P. Caspari, ed., *Briefe*, 6); Caelestius, ap. Augustine, *On human perfection in righteousness* 2.1 (CSEL 42: 4): 'Ante omnia interrogandus est qui negat hominem sine peccato esse posse, qui sit quodcumque peccatum: quod uitari potest an quod uitari non potest. Si quod uitari non potest, peccatum non est; si quod uitari potest, potest homo sine peccato esse, quod uitari potest. Nulla enim ratio uel iustitia patitur saltem dici peccatum, quod uitari nullo modo potest.'

reason and volition of consenting adults. This is nowhere clearer than in Julian of Eclanum's claim that free will 'emancipates' one from God.[61] Here, he follows in Pelagius' footsteps, who maintained that the ability to choose makes us 'sui iuris'.[62] Moral analysis for the Pelagians begins with adulthood and rational agency. Their ideal is an autonomous person functioning in a godly manner.

Augustine's ideal is otherwise; for him, the very idea of autonomy leading to godliness is hopeless. He sees human nature as profoundly wounded because of ancestral sin. His bleak view on the condemnation of unbaptised babies (who are punished eternally, albeit 'most lightly')[63] is well known – but what is not as widely appreciated is the extent to which the Christian baby is symbolic of an important Augustinian insight into Christianity. Augustine sees in the babe at the mother's breast an image of the utter dependence of the creature upon the Creator.[64] This warm and loving image is applicable to fully mature Christians no less than Christian babies, who are all alike reliant on the sustaining love of God. This perception of the basic parity of the community helps us understand why Augustine sees the sacrament of baptism (even understood as the 'sacrament of the faith') applying in the same way to all persons: every good thing – including will and faith – must ultimately come from God the Spirit.[65] Because salvation is first and foremost a divine action, infants are not distinct in principle from adults simply because they cannot speak, act or believe for themselves; it is not because of their speaking, acting or believing that adults are saved through baptism, but because God is at work in baptism.

Augustine has no more difficulty in acknowledging the efficacy of a baptism where the sponsors and indeed the church as a whole are able to act on behalf of infants than he does in acknowledging the efficacy of an adult's

---

61 Julian, ap. Augustine, *Incomplete work against Julian* 1.78 (CSEL 85: 93): 'Libertas arbitrii, qua a deo emancipatus homo est, in ammittendi peccati et abstinendi a peccato possibilitate consistit.'

62 Pelagius, *To Demetrias* 4 (PL 33: 1101). Because of this claim by Pelagius, one may reject Gisbert Greshake's assertion that emancipation from God does not follow human freedom according to *pelagisch* thought: see Greshake, *Gnade als konkrete Freiheit*, 65–6, and, for the difference between something that is *pelagisch* and something that is *pelagianisch* (an admirable distinction not available in English), 27 n. 3.

63 Augustine, *On the merit and remission of sins and on infant baptism* 1.16.21 (CSEL 60: 20).

64 Cf. Augustine, *Confessions* 4.1.1 (ed. O'Donnell, 1: 33): 'For what am I to myself without you, but a guide to my own downfall? Or what am I, even at my best, but one sucking your milk and feeding upon you, the food that does not perish? But what is any man at all, when he is merely a man?'.

65 Thus, Augustine, *Free will* 3.23.67.227–8 (CCSL 29: 314–15), *On baptism* 4.24.31 (CSEL 51: 259–60), and esp. *Letter* 98.2 (CSEL 34²: 521–3); cf. Camelot, 'Sacramentum fidei'.

baptism. For the adult no less than for the infant, the 'whole society of the saints and the faithful' is integrally involved in the process of salvation – which is precisely why a heretical or schismatic community can perform a proper baptism, without being able to sustain the one thus baptised along the arduous pilgrimage of the Christian life.[66] These supporting links within the community are indispensable. Consequently, the claims made on behalf of the infant by the sponsors are taken very seriously indeed. In fact, there is evidence for a strong presumption that the vows of the sponsor are binding upon the newly baptised Christian, even when that Christian matures to adulthood – and that, well before any form of ritual confirmation is attested.[67] In all these cases, what emerges is the possibility of the community in general (and the sponsors and celebrants in particular) acting on behalf of children who could not act for themselves.

One of the factors that led to increased prominence for baptising infants during this time was surely that it neatly complemented another favoured cause: the struggle *against* postponing baptism. Noteworthy men had often delayed seeking baptism. Perhaps the most conspicuous was the emperor Constantine, whose decision Eusebius characterised as a way of taking very seriously the ritual purity conferred by the event.[68] He may have been right. But there is no reason to doubt that many other Roman men were likely motivated by pragmatic concerns; they postponed baptism in order to manage competing loyalties.[69] And yet, at the same time, there is no reason to doubt that people could sincerely hold to such a belief, which in itself is a perfectly comprehensible and indeed pious attitude toward the life-changing event. It seems entirely probable that numerous catechumens shared in this belief. For similar reasons, the scions of pious Christian families (or at least devout Christian mothers!) were sometimes not baptised until the heat of youth had abated; one thinks of

---

66 See Augustine, *Letter* 98.5 (CSEL 34²: 526–7).
67 See Cassian, *Incarnation* 6.3–23 (CSEL 17: 327–51), where he exposits the baptismal creed of Antioch and challenges Nestorius to remain true to it – even if it were recited by sponsors on his behalf as a child: for this rhetoric to have any effect at all, Cassian must have supposed most people would think the sponsors' vows obliged the child even into adulthood. A comparable argument against an unnamed opponent is found in Mark the Monk, *On the incarnation* 40 (SC 455: 298).
68 Eusebius, *Life of Constantine* 4.61–4; see further the discussion by Averil Cameron and Stuart G. Hall in *Eusebius. Life of Constantine*, 340–1. Jacob of Sarug's 'On the baptism of Constantine' (ed. Frothingham) indirectly emphasises the (ritual) purification of baptism by drawing on a legend about Constantine being leprous.
69 Thus, Peter Brown, *The body and society*, 342 – with references to the Council of Elvira, canon 45 (in F. Lauchert, ed., *Die Kanones der wichtigsten altkirchlien Concilien*, 20) and to Augustine, *Divjak letters* 2.4.1–7 and 7.4 (CSEL 88: 11–12, 14): 'O Firmus, so infirm in purpose . . .'

Ambrose and of Augustine as examples.[70] Against this background, Chrysostom – not to mention Ambrose and Augustine themselves – railed against the perceived indigence of delays.[71] Anyone who deliberately delayed baptism was made to appear, at best, unsure where his loyalties lay or, at worst, positively opportunistic. Dwelling on the margins of the community as a catechumen came to seem a way of evading the responsibilities that came with the baptismal 'contract'. This surge in calling for full commitment to Christ and his church naturally buttressed the pious habit of bringing infants to the font.

Another circumstance in which the community is conspicuously involved in baptism occurs when a seriously ill, perhaps even unconscious, person is baptised. Several such examples are known to have occurred in North Africa. Augustine, for example, famously relates that in his youth this once happened to a friend. (The young man recovered, but when Augustine teased him about having undergone the rite, his friend was deeply offended; looking back on the event, Augustine was suitably mortified by his own callow behaviour.)[72] Later, Augustine would liken the custom to baptising an infant: '. . . it will be profitable for them because their will is already known from their Christian faith; consequently, they are baptised in the same way that infants are baptised whose will has not yet matured'.[73] This practice – including the requirement for some evidence of the will or intention of the stricken catechumen – was established in African Catholicism by canon 34 of the Third Council of Carthage (397) and was re-affirmed in canon 45 of the council of 418.[74] The question arose again some decades later when Ferrandus, a deacon in Carthage, addressed a question to Fulgentius of Ruspe: Ferrandus queried whether the baptism was legitimate in a case in which a man had followed through the entire course of catechism, only to succumb to a debilitating (and ultimately lethal) disease, and was carried to the font and baptised 'as though an infant'. Fulgentius responded in the affirmative.[75]

In all these cases, then, we find a willingness to act on behalf of others. Although this is clearest in cases where infants or invalids are baptised, in that

---

70 Paulinus, *Life of Ambrose* 7 (ed. Bastiaensen, 60–2); Augustine, *Confessions* 1.11.17 (ed. O'Donnell, 1: 9–10). It will be recalled that Ambrose was not yet baptised when he was popularly acclaimed bishop of Milan; in this, he may be compared to Nectarius, another unbaptised man of rank who was elevated to the prominent see of Constantinople in 381 (see Sozomen, *H.E.* 7.8 (GCS – *Sozomenus*, 310–11)).

71 Chrysostom, *Hom. P.-K.* 1.4–11; see also Ambrose, *De sacramentiis* 3.13 and *De Elia* 22.83–5 (CSEL 32²: 463–5); for Augustine, see n. 68, above.

72 Augustine, *Confessions* 4.4.8 (ed. O'Donnell, 1.35–6).

73 Augustine, *De adulterinis coniugiis* 1.26.33 (CSEL 41: 380).

74 For the council of 397, see CCSL 149: 335; for the council of 418, see PL 67: 195.

75 See Fulgentius, *Letters* 11, 12 (PL 65: 378–87).

they cannot act for themselves, it also applies to the support offered more generally by a sponsor. Helping others – like helping those who cannot help themselves – is thus fundamental to the building up of the Christian community, from the very point of entering the community. In this way, baptism joins those baptised to the fellowship of Christians and so has a horizontal dimension. But it also joins them to God, creating vertical connections as well. Together, these connections are for all practical purposes indispensable for the salvation of the Christian. We have noted that Augustine, Fulgentius and others placed great emphasis on belonging to the Catholic church, even though they were prepared to acknowledge that Christ was at work in non-Catholic baptisms. The network of relations, to other Christians and especially to God, that is established in baptism makes sense of Augustine's and Fulgentius' counter-intuitive position: it is the abiding presence of God within the church that makes it possible for the Christian who abides in the church to be saved. But precisely how are Christians joined to God? The answer to this question emerges most clearly when our authors contemplated Christ's baptism at the hands of John and, in the process, allowed their interpretation of Christ's own baptism to inform their understanding of Christian baptism in general.

Celebrating salvation

Meditations on Christ's baptism attain fullest form in the sacred poetry for the feast commemorating that event: Theophany (also called Epiphany in the Byzantine tradition). In reflecting upon what Christ accomplished – not least through his humble submission to baptism – for the human race and how he thus gave rise to a society of believers, Eastern Christians in particular would dwell on the anointment that follows baptism. They considered this anointment (or 'chrismation') an integral part of the rite of baptism, for being anointed with the holy chrism is how mere mortals can participate in the anointing that makes Christ, Christ. We will therefore consider, in turn, two aspects of the liturgical celebration of baptism: the feast of Christ's baptism, and baptismal chrismation.

The feast of Epiphany

As Christians thought about the meaning of baptism, they frequently returned to the liturgical celebration of Christ's baptism as a source of inspiration. Christ's baptism was not only a point of departure in the tradition for explaining the significance of the baptism of his followers; in time it also provided an opportunity for making very precise claims about how Christ is both like, and unlike, his followers. In this way, exegesis and hymnography of Christ's baptism became significant sources for Christians to articulate their understanding of salvation. At a practical level, too, the link between Christ's baptism and Christians' baptism was compelling – so much so that some effort was required to maintain the norm of baptism at Easter. It seems that, by the mid-fifth century, more baptisms were taking place on Epiphany than during Eastertide in Sicily.[76] Why was this date so appealing?

St Paul influentially claimed that baptism was a way of participating in Christ's death (see Romans 6.1–11 – verses often met in ancient baptismal rites). During the age of martyrs, this connection could be realised in a shockingly direct way: a martyred catechumen is to be buried as a Christian, for example, on grounds that 'he is baptised in his own blood'.[77] Such a baptism quite simply is a perfect witness to Christ and an actual participation in Christ's death. Near the beginning of our period, in the aftermath of episodic official persecutions, Christians continued to link Christ's baptism to his followers' baptisms. Already in Gregory the Illuminator's catechesis, we encounter the straightforward claim:

> The Son of God, therefore, came and was baptized, to establish the baptism of all who would be baptized, that handing on this tradition he might reveal salvation to all, and be understood and known, and that by this he might open his life-giving teaching of truth to be revealed to the world.[78]

Gregory's assertion that Christ's baptism 'established the baptism of all' is elegant in its simplicity. But eventually the precise relation of Christ's baptism to the baptisms that he 'established' became the subject of refined discussion. For example, by the sixth century some theologians were prepared to advance the more sophisticated claim that Christ's very death was actually

---

76 In 447, Leo the Great, who wished to eradicate the practice, was struggling mightily to make a sharp distinction between the commemoration of Christ's baptism at Epiphany and the commemoration at Easter of Christ's death – when from his pierced side there flowed 'the blood of ransom and the water of baptism' – and resurrection; see his *Letter* 16 (PL 54: 695–704). Leo's case, however, is not entirely persuasive and there are a number of puzzling silences. For example, his evaluation of the Sicilian custom remains at the level of asserting traditional practice and Roman precedents. He conspicuously fails to engage with anything like a rationale for the Sicilian custom. His attempts at re-interpreting Epiphany as the commemoration of the adoration of the Magi, without a mention of Christ's baptism for several lines, seem diversionary. Leo appears to be working against a reasonably powerful current of assuming that Christ's baptism is deeply significant and its commemoration is therefore an appropriate time to perform baptisms.

77 *Canons of Hippolytus* 101 (TU 6[4]: 91).

78 Gregory the Illuminator, *Teaching* 420 (trans. Thomson, 91).

the fulfilment of his own baptism, and to stipulate that Christ's baptism was a *Christian* baptism. Theodore of Mopsuestia argued that, as Christ was sinless, he was not baptised into John's baptism (which was 'for remission of sins' – Mark 1.4); instead, he was baptised into 'our baptism, and presented an anticipation of it' by being baptised 'with the Holy Spirit and fire' (see John 1.26 / Matthew 3.11).[79] Shortly thereafter, in Spain, an anonymous homily on Epiphany combined elements from (pseudo-)Ambrose's *Hymn* 7 with the Christological principles of the Councils of Ephesus (431) and Chalcedon (451) into a remarkable statement of how Christ's own baptism sanctified the waters so that, through them, the world might be saved.[80] Philoxenus of Mabbug also described how Christ's baptism relates to Christian baptism generally. Like Theodore of Mopsuestia, his near-contemporary, Philoxenus maintains that Christ was baptised with 'our baptism' (despite the fact that he had no need of baptism).[81] In fact, Philoxenus connects 'our baptism' and Christ's baptism so closely that he can be taken as suggesting that it is Christ's baptism itself that makes his sacrificial death available to Christians through the sacrament of their baptism.[82]

It is interesting that Philoxenus regularly specifies in creedal statements that Jesus was baptised *in the Jordan*. In making this claim, he is followed by Armenian sources.[83] Among the Greek and Latin authors, Eusebius seems to show a similar concern for where Christ was baptised, when he notes that Constantine was moved to be baptised in the Jordan.[84] Chiefly on the basis of his testimony, it has become something of a commonplace to state that pilgrims made their way to Palestine not least for baptism. Could it be that the motivation to anchor Christian baptism in Christ's baptism may have inspired Christians to seek baptism in the river Jordan?

79 Thus, Theodore of Mopsuestia, *Baptismal homily* 3.23–5 (quoting 3.23).
80 The homily is preserved in the *Liber ordinum*, and its conclusion is typical of the tone and sophistication of the whole (ed. Férotin, 526): 'Sed neque hic dies lucifluo tantum fulgore sideris Magorum uultibus claruit; sed etiam multis Christi signorum uirtutibus coruscauit. Hoc die namque Christus, fluenta Iordanis ingrediens, fluminis undas corporis sui tinctione sacrauit: non ut ip[s]e [per] lauacrum carnis purificationem indigeret, sed potius ut sanctificaret diuino spiramine aquas, in quibus pollutum uitiis mundum babtismate sacro ablueret.'
81 Philoxenus, *Commentary on John's Prologue* (CSCO 381: 158–9).
82 Philoxenus' *On Matthew, frag.* 13 (CSCO 392: 19; trans. 393: 16–17): 'He was baptised (of) our baptism, because he was going to give it to us, because it is a type of his death and of his resurrection. And just as he died and rose and became for us the first-fruits from the dead [cf. 1 Corinthians 15.20], so he was baptised sacredly for our baptism, and immediately he gave it to us.' See further A. Grillmeier, 'Die Taufe Christi und die Taufe der Christen'.
83 See Grillmeier, 'Die Taufe Christi und die Taufe der Christen', 140–1 n. 7.
84 For Eusebius' account of Constantine's baptism, see n. 68, above.

There is in fact only episodic evidence for such a practice, and it can be doubted whether pilgrim baptism ever was a common undertaking.[85] We can be reasonably certain that, for most Christians, the sacramental link between Christ's baptism and their own baptisms did not need to be reinforced by reference to the place of Christ's baptism. Instead, the evidence suggests that they were far more concerned to find in their own baptisms the power at work that Christ brought to restore the devastated human condition. Perhaps, in keeping with the idea that, through the incarnation, Christ had assumed all that being a human entails in order to heal it,[86] some Christians may have held that this power was activated by Christ's baptism as a man (though I am unaware of any source that makes such a claim). What is clear is that, during this period, Christians generally demonstrated a preference for certain symbolic connections. On the whole, Christians preferred to associate their baptisms with Christ's resurrection by holding them during the feast of Easter (rather than with his baptism, at Epiphany); the symbolic and sacramental connection that is implicit in that choice may help to explain why we have no real evidence that Christians during this period were bothered to secure their baptisms to Christ's by seeking to be baptised in the Jordan. But even so, the liturgical celebration of Jesus' own baptism clearly enriched Christian reflection upon salvation, not least through reinforcing the belief that effects of baptism are the work of God. What occurs at baptism is thus a theophany – a manifestation of God, who works salvation for his people.

Becoming christs

What results for the people for whom God works salvation? The available evidence in answer to that question takes us from the domains of moral performance and spiritual understanding to what might broadly be called mystical experience. Through actualising the grace of baptism in their lives (as described by Mark the Monk, Macarius and others), Christians believed they would enjoy an intimate relationship to God. That baptism is a decisive event in the process is clear from Dionysius the Areopagite's gloss on baptism as 'the most divine mystery of God being born' in the Christian.[87] Philoxenus similarly says that, by baptism, 'God [becomes] in all and all in God.'[88] In view of such claims, it was perhaps inevitable that controversy should arise.

85 See Day, *Baptism in early Byzantine Palestine*, 38–9.
86 Thus, Origen, *Dialogue with Heracleides* 7 (SC 67: 71–2) and Gregory of Nazianzus, *Or.* 29.19 (SC 250: 216–18) and *Letter* 101 (SC 208: 36–68).
87 Dionysius, *Eccl. hier.* 4.2.11 (PTS 36: 102).
88 Philoxenus, *On Matthew, frag.* 12 (CSCO 392: 19; 393: 16).

Philoxenus himself took an active role in establishing the limits for legitimate usage of mystical language when he denounced the teachings of Stephen bar Sudaili, an Edessan monk who settled in Palestine (c. 512–15). Philoxenus wrote to two priests in Edessa, Abraham and Orestes, warning them against the universalist and pantheistic tendencies of Stephen's teaching about the end times. The initial cause for concern was that Stephen had allegedly written on the wall of his cell, 'All nature is consubstantial with the Divine Essence.'[89] In expressing his views, he made use of ideas that were current at the time and that looked for inspiration to the writings of Evagrius Ponticus.[90] But Philoxenus resisted the implications that St Peter and Judas would enjoy the same glory, that the baptism of pagans was superfluous and that the saved would have the same nature as God.[91] At approximately the same time and in the same region, fierce controversies were raging and (though the primary material does not provide a satisfactory overview of the situation) it seems that one major problem was the question of whether Christians could in a very real sense become 'equals to Christ'. Whether or not any given person ever held to these views, it is more than clear that orthodox leaders felt a response was called for.

One of the aims in denouncing this pantheistic, universalist eschatology was to establish parameters within which Christians could continue to appropriate the theological legacy about salvation that we have been considering. By precluding any direct identification of human and divine natures, by decisively asserting that equality to Christ is not a possible outcome, in short, by rejecting a potential interpretation of Origen's thinking as mediated through Evagrius (and probably re-worked by subsequent enthusiasts), the orthodox fathers were providing a frame of reference in which certain traditional claims could be preserved and understood in terms of highly articulate standards of Christological and Trinitarian orthodoxy. The debates of the mid-sixth century were at least in part concerned to reconcile an important theological insight drawn from liturgy with standard principles of doctrinal theology. It would be a mistake to think of this process as a tidying-up necessitated by cultural conservatism or theological inertia; rather, it represents the creative appropriation

---

89 Philoxenus, *To Abraham and Orestes* (ed. Frothingham, 42–3).
90 See A. Guillaumont, *Évagre le Pontique*, 302–32; it is open to question, however, how much of Stephen's teaching should be ascribed to Evagrius. One can dissent from Guillaumont's attribution of certain ideas and systems to Evagrius himself even as one gratefully acknowledges the scope and profundity of Guillaumont's work. For more on Stephen, Frothingham's seminal *Stephen bar Sudaili, the Syrian mystic* retains its value.
91 Philoxenus, *To Abraham and Orestes* (ed. Frothingham, 30, 32).

of an intellectual heritage. Some specific examples from that heritage should be considered.

Cyril of Jerusalem insouciantly stated that baptised Christians, who have thus become partakers in Christ, 'are properly called Christs'.[92] This bold affirmation is not eccentric. In a baptismal address dated to the late fifth or early sixth century and attributed to Athanasius, the catechist explains the effects of the holy chrism to his audience in this way: 'It is to make you a sharer with him [sc., Christ], to show you to be anointed[93] in same way; it is an anointing that is in truth most scented of all.'[94] The resonance of the claim is somewhat lessened in English; in the Syriac version, as, no doubt, in the Greek original, the recurring term 'anointment' is part of the semantic domain that includes the word 'Christ' (lit., 'the anointed one'). Baptismal unction thus makes the Christian 'another Christ'.

It would be a mistake to think that the claims about 'another Christ' were made simply because of linguistic pressure and semantic resonances. Tertullian, who was able to write treatises (now lost) in Greek, knew perfectly well what the Greek term *christos* meant, but even so he did not claim that the anointment of baptism makes 'christs'.[95] Augustine, although he insists that chrismation unites the Christian to Christ, is likewise far more circumspect than any of the Greek fathers here surveyed.[96] It is not self-evident why the Western fathers did not pursue this theme further; but the difference in emphases might help explain why the Greek tradition did not develop (as the Latin tradition did) a separate rite for anointment. In the West, anointment from a relatively early date became the preserve of bishops, as Pope Innocent states in his letter to Decentius.[97] For Eastern Christians, the close connection

---

92 Cyril of Jerusalem, *Cat* 21.1 (= *Cat. myst.* 3.1; PG 33: 1088).

93 *mšiha*; Brock's note: 'I.e. *christos*'.

94 (ps.-)Athanasius, 'Baptismal address' §11 (ed. Brock, 101–2). For an excellent study of chrismation in Greek and Syriac Christian sources, see Varghese, *Les onctions baptismales*.

95 That he could use the term is clear from Tertullian, *On baptism* 7 (ed. and trans. Evans, 16–17): 'That is why [the high priest] is called a christ, from "chrism" which is [the Greek for] "anointing": and from this also our Lord obtained his title.' He does not, however, apply the principle to Christians.

96 Augustine, *City of God* 20.10.

97 Innocent, *Letter* 25 'To Decentius' (PL 20: 551–61); there is an interesting parallel in canon 38 of the Council of Elvira (306), which allows even a lay Christian to baptise a catechumen *in necessitate*, but stipulates that if the newly baptised Christian survives he should be taken to the bishop 'ut per manus impositionem perfici possit' (ed. Lauchert, 19). By the time John the Deacon responded to a certain Senarius (c. 500), the possibility of a baptised Christian dying before chrismation had become a cause for concern: see his *Epistola ad Senarium* §14 (ed. Wilmart, 178–9). On the development of chrismation as a distinct sacrament, see J. D. C. Fisher and E. J. Yarnold, 'The West from about AD 500 to the Reformation'.

between baptismal chrismation and becoming partakers in Christ would have precluded this development.

But we must be wary of making facile contrasts along cultural and political lines that often shifted and were in any case never impermeable. Far more important than a superficial difference in terminology is the striking agreement about the spiritual dynamic of 'becoming christs'. In this matter, we find a profound similarity, especially as regards the need for humble acknowledgment of one's sinfulness. As Ambrose says, 'One who takes refuge in the baptism of Christ acknowledges himself to be a human.'[98] Baptism is predicated on an awareness of one's fallen condition – or, in other words, on humility. Chrysostom proclaimed the same message, in consequence of his meditations upon Matthew 11.29.[99] These two quotations set up a neat contrast to the earlier claims about partaking of Christ, and that contrast tells us a great deal about how salvation could be viewed during this period. These insights centre on St Paul's exhortation: 'Humble yourselves in the sight of the Lord, and he will lift you up.' In confessing oneself a human – that is, in sorrowfully acknowledging one's sins, but also and especially in joyfully acknowledging oneself as the handiwork of God – the Christian is re-created by God through the sacrament of baptism. Being thus incorporated into the 'body of Christ' and anointed with chrism, the sinful person lives according to Christ and becomes another 'christ'.[100]

In the adroit hands of Maximus the Confessor, this teaching is stated in such a way as to obviate the Christological problems that were attributed to Stephen bar Sudaili and that could in any case emerge from a different interpretation of earlier patristic writings. According to Maximus' teaching, there is no sense in which the Christian becomes 'equal to Christ'; instead, he speaks of the Christian having by the grace of God the experience of God's own life.[101] This clarion teaching can be applied back to our Christological exposition of baptism: whatever the Christian has of Christ, it is always properly Christ's

---

98 Ambrose, *De sacramentiis* 3.2.14 (ed. Chadwick, 27): 'Ergo agnoscit se hominem qui confugit ad baptismum Christi.'

99 See Chrysostom, *Baptismal homilies* 1.28–31 (SC 50: 122–4).

100 For a contemporary evaluation of *theôsis* that lays appropriate emphasis on its communal dimensions, see F. Norris, 'Deification: Consensual and cogent'.

101 See Maximus, *Ad Thalassium* 6 (CCSG 7: 70–1; trans. Wilken and Blowers, 104): 'With those undergoing the (second mode of) birth, the Holy Spirit takes the whole of their free choice and translates it completely from earth to heaven, and, through the true knowledge acquired by exertion, transfigures the mind with the blessed light-rays of our God and Father, such that the mind is deemed another "god," insofar as in its habitude it experiences, by grace, that which God himself does not experience but "is" in his very essence.'

own and the Christian's only by grace. This general claim is perhaps so basic for the Christian life as a whole that it typically goes unnoticed, but for Eastern and Oriental Christians it is made dramatically clear by the emphasis placed on chrismation. Based on what we have seen, it is no exaggeration to claim that, through chrismation, the Christian receives from God an identity that derives from Christ. From the fourth to the sixth centuries, the numerous themes enfolded into baptism enriched it conceptually, so it is hardly surprising that consideration of sin and salvation in the literature of our period regularly has a baptismal character. But it may be hasty to suppose that, exotic as such a view might seem, it is the distinctive patrimony of Eastern Christianity, or perhaps of the early middle ages. On 15 May 1881, in the course of a sermon preached at Liverpool, Gerard Manley Hopkins advanced a similar claim: 'Christ was himself but one and lived and died but once; but the Holy Ghost makes of every Christian another Christ, an AfterChrist . . .'[102] Or, as he put it even more strikingly in his 'As kingfishers catch fire, dragonflies draw flame':

> I say more: the just man justices;
> keeps grace; that keeps all his goings graces;
> Acts in God's eye what in God's eye he is –
> Christ. For Christ plays in ten thousand places,
> Lovely in limbs, and lovely in eyes not his,
> To the Father, through the features of men's faces.[103]

Conclusion

In the foregoing pages, we have noted characteristic features of discourse about baptism during the 'golden age' of patristic Christianity, insofar as they illuminate patristic ideas about sin and salvation. In this way, our attention has been drawn to catecheses, letters, treatises and liturgical rubrics. What has emerged from these sources is a regular effort to understand Christian life with reference to Christ's life. Indeed, as we have just observed, many Eastern Christians (and, thanks to Hopkins, not a few Liverpudlian Christians) were positively encouraged to think that baptism made them into 'other Christs'. But here, as elsewhere, this encouragement was framed with articulate principles of Christian orthodoxy.

One major function of the creed – as indeed of the catechetical lectures during which Christians would have had their first exposure to the creed – was precisely to ensure that the deeply personal encounter with God through

---

102 G. M. Hopkins, *Sermons and devotional writings*, 100.
103 G. M. Hopkins, *Poetical works*, 141.

baptism became more than deeply personal, became in fact the point at which the Christian entered a new, sacramental, community. Thanks to the renewal brought about by baptism, this new community was characterised as a return to paradise in that the waters of baptism washed away all sins, collective and private, that had previously separated God's creatures from God.

Bibliography

PRIMARY SOURCES

Ambrose. *De Elia* (CSEL 32²)
    Hymns. Ed. J. Fontaine, *Ambroise de Milan. Hymnes* (Paris, 1992)
    De sacramentiis. Ed. H. Chadwick, *St Ambrose on the sacraments* (London, 1960)
Athanasius. *Letters to Serapion on the Holy Spirit* (PG 26). Trans. K. Anatolios, *Athanasius* (London, 2004)
    Orations against the Arians. Eds. K. Metzler et al., *Athanasius Werke* I.I (Berlin, 1998); trans. K. Anatolios, *Athanasius* (London, 2004)
ps.-Athanasius. 'Baptismal address'. Ed. Sebastian Brock, 'A baptismal address attributed to Athanasius,' *Oriens Christianus* 61 (1977): 92–102
Augustine. *De adulterinis coniugiis* (CSEL 41)
    Against the letter of Parminian (CSEL 51)
    Against the letter of Petilian (CSEL 52)
    On baptism (CSEL 51)
    City of God (CCSL 47, 48)
    Confessions, ed. J. J. O'Donnell (Oxford, 1992)
    Divjak letters (CSEL 88)
    Free will (CCSL 29)
    On the grace of Christ and original sin (CSEL 42)
    On human perfection in righteousness (CSEL 42)
    Incomplete work against Julian (CSEL 85, PL 45)
    Letter 98 (CSEL 34²)
    On the merit and remission of sins and on infant baptism (CSEL 60)
    On nature and grace (CSEL 60)
    Tractates on John (CCSL 36)
Bernard, J. H. *The Odes of Solomon*, Texts and Studies 8, 3 (Cambridge, 1912)
Brock, Sebastian. 'Some early Syriac baptismal commentaries', *OCP* 46 (1980): 20–61
Canons of Hippolytus (TU 6⁴)
Caspari, C. P., ed. *Briefe, Abhandlungen und Predigten aus den zwei letzten Jahrhunderten des kirchlichen Alterthums und dem Anfang des Mittelalters* (Christiania, 1890; reprint: Brussels, 1964)
Clement. *Excerpta e Theodoto* (SC 23)
Cologne Mani-Codex. Eds. L. Koenen and C. Römer, *Der Kölner Mani-Kodex (Über das Werden seines Leibes), kritische Edition aufgrund der von A. Henrichs und L. Koenen besorgten Erstedition* (Opladen, 1988)

'The community rule (1QS)'. Trans. G. Vermes, *The Dead Sea Scrolls in English* (London, 1995⁴), 69–89
Concilia Africae a.345–a.525 (CCSL 149)
Cyprian. *Letters* (CSEL 3²)
(ps.-?)Cyprian. *On rebaptism* (PL 3)
Cyril of Jerusalem. *Catecheses* (PG 33)
Diadochus. *Gnostic chapters* (SC 5)
Didache (SC 248)
Dionysius. *Ecclesiastical hierarchies* (PTS 36). Trans. C. Luibheid, *Pseudo-Dionysius: The complete works* (New York, 1987)
Egeria. *Travels* (SC 296)
Ephrem. *Hymn of the baptized*; trans. NPNF 2, XIII
   Hymns on the faith (CSCO 154–5)
Eusebius. *Life of Constantine* (*GCS Eusebius Werke* 1). Trans. Averil Cameron and Stuart G. Hall, *Eusebius. Life of Constantine* (Oxford, 1999)
Férotin, Marius, ed. *Liber ordinum: Le liber ordinum en usage dans l'église wisigothique et mozarabe d'Espagne du cinquième au onzième siècle* (Paris, 1904)
Fulgentius. *On the faith* (CCSL 91a)
   On the forgiveness of sins (CCSL 91a)
   Letters (SC 487 and PL 65)
Gregory the Illuminator. *Teaching*. Trans. Robert W. Thomson. *The teaching of St Gregory. An early Armenian catechism* (Cambridge, MA, 1970)
Gregory of Nazianzus. *Letter* 101 (SC 208: 36–68)
   Orations (PG 35, 36; SC 250, 318)
Gregory of Nyssa. *On Song of Songs* (GNO 6)
Hermas. *Precepts* (SC 53)
Ignatius. *To the Smyrnians* (SC 10)
Innocent. *Letters* (PL 20)
Jacob of Sarug. 'On the baptism of Constantine'. Ed. A. L. Frothingham, 'L'omelia di Giacomo di Sarug sul battesimo di Costantino imperatore', *Atti della Reale Accademia dei Lincei*, anno. CXLXXX, ser. 3, Memorie della Classe di Scienza Morale, Storiche e Filologiche, vol. 8 (Rome, 1883): 167–242
Jerome. *Letters* (CSEL 54, 55, 56)
John Cassian. *Incarnation* (CSEL 17)
John Chrysostom. *Baptismal homilies* (SC 50); trans. ACW 31
   Homiliae in Matthaeum (PG 58)
   Homilies P.-K. Ed. A. Papadopoulos-Kerameus, *Varia Graeca sacra* (St Petersburg, 1909; reprint: Leipzig, 1975)
John the Deacon, *Epistola ad Senarium*. Ed. André Wilmart, *Analecta reginensia*, ST 59 (Rome, 1933): 170–9
Josephus. *Jewish War*, LCL (*Josephus*, II–III) (London, 1927–8)
Justin. *Apology* (PTS 38)
Labbé, P. and N. Coleti, eds. *Sacrosancta concilia ad regiam editionem exacta* (Venice, 1728–33)
Lauchert, F., ed. *Die Kanones der wichtigsten altkirchlien Concilien: nebst den apostolischen Kanones* (Freiburg, 1896)

Laws of Receswinth (MGH leg II.I)
Leo the Great. *Letters* (PL 54)
Letter of Barnabas (SC 172)
Macarius. *Great letter.* Ed. W. Jaeger, *Two rediscovered works of ancient Christian literature* (Leiden, 1954)
Mark the Monk. *On holy baptism* (SC 445: 296–396)
  On the incarnation (SC 455: 252–314)
Maximus. *Ad Thalassium* (CCSG 7). Trans. Robert Louis Wilken and Paul Blowers, *Saint Maximus the Confessor: On the cosmic mystery of Jesus Christ* (Crestwood, NY, 2003)
Moses bar Kepha. *The mysteries of baptism.* Trans. R. A. Aytoun, 'The mysteries of baptism by Moses bar Kepha compared with the odes of Solomon', *The expositor* ser. 8.2 (October 1911): 338–58
Optatus. *Against the Donatists* (SC 413)
Origen. *Commentary on Romans* (PG 14)
  Dialogue with Heracleides (SC 67)
  Homilies on Exodus (SC 321)
  Selecta in Genesim (PG 12)
Paulinus. *Life of Ambrose.* Ed. A. A. R. Bastiaensen, *Vite dei santi: Vita di Cipriano, Vita di Ambrogio, Vita di Agostino* (Milan, 1975)
Pelagius. *On the faith* (PL 15)
  To Demetrias (PL 33)
Philoxenus of Mabbug. *Commentary on John's Prologue* (CSCO 380, 381)
  Fragments of the commentary on Matthew and Luke (CSCO 392–3)
  To Abraham and Orestes. Ed. A. L. Frothingham, Jr., *Stephen bar Sudaili, the Syrian mystic and the book of Hierotheos* (Leiden, 1886), 28–48
Rufus of Shotep. *Homilies on the Gospels of Matthew and Luke*, ed. and trans. J. Mark Sheridan, OSB (Rome, 1998)
Serapion of Thmuis. *Euchologium* (TU 17)
Socrates. *Historia ecclesiastica* (GCS, N.F. I: *Sokrates Kirchengeschichte*; SC 477, 493–)
Sozomen. *Historia ecclesiastica* (GCS: *Sozomenus Kirchengeschichte*)
Tertullian. *On baptism.* Ed. and trans. E. Evans, *Tertullian's homily on baptism* (London, 1964)
Theodore of Mopsuestia. *Catechetical homilies.* Eds. Raymond Tonneau and Robert Devreesse, *Les homélies catéchétiques de Théodore de Mopsueste*, ST 145 (Vatican, 1949)
Thomas Aquinas. *Summa theologiae*, ed. P. Caramello (Taurini, 1948)
Zeno. *Invitations* (CCSL 22)

SECONDARY SOURCES

Beck, Edmund, OSB. 'Le baptême chez Saint Éphrem', *L'Orient syrien* I (1956): 111–37
Bianchi, Ugo and Maarten J. Vermaseren, eds. *La soteriologia dei culti orientali nell'impero Romano* (Leiden, 1982)
Bonner, Gerald. 'Baptismus paruulorum', in Cornelius Mayer et al., eds., *Augustinus-Lexikon* (Basel, 1986–), I: 592–602
Brock, Sebastian. 'Baptismal themes in the writings of Jacob of Serugh', *Symposium Syriacum 1976*, OCA 205 (Rome, 1978): 325–47

Brown, Peter. *The body and society* (New York, 1988)

Burns, J. Patout. *Cyprian the bishop* (London, 2001)

Camelot, T. 'Sacramentum fidei', in *Augustinus magister* (Paris, 1954), ii: 891–6.

Casiday, A. M. C. *Tradition and theology in St John Cassian* (Oxford, 2006)

Charlesworth, J. H. *The Odes of Solomon* (Oxford, 1973)

Cumont, Franz. *Textes et monuments figurés relatifs aux mystères de Mithra* (Brussels, 1896–9)

Day, Juliette. *Baptism in early Byzantine Palestine, 324–451*, Joint Liturgical Studies (Cambridge, 1999)

Dondeyne, A. 'La discipline des scrutins dans l'église latine avant Charlemagne', *Revue d'histoire ecclésiastique* 28 (1932): 5–33, 751–87

Finn, Thomas M. *Early Christian baptism and the catechumenate: Italy, North Africa, and Egypt* (Collegeville, MN, 1992)

Early Christian baptism and the catechumenate: West and East Syria (Collegeville, MN, 1992)

Fisher, J. D. C. and E. J. Yarnold, 'The West from about AD 500 to the Reformation', in C. Jones et al., eds., *The study of the liturgy* (London: 1992²), 144–52

Graffin, François, SJ. 'La catéchèse de Sévère d'Antioche', *L'Orient syrien* 5 (1960): 47–54

Green, Matthew. 'Initium omnis peccati superbia: Augustine on pride as the first sin', *University of California publications in classical philology* 13, no. 13 (1949): 407–32

Greshake, Gisbert. *Gnade als konkrete Freiheit: Eine Untersuchung zur Gnadenlehre des Pelagius* (Mainz, 1972)

Gribomont, Jean. 'La catéchèse de Sévère d'Antioche et le Credo', *Parole d'Orient* 6–7 (1975–6): 125–58

Grillmeier, Aloys. 'Die Taufe Christi und die Taufe der Christen. Zur Tauftheologie des Philoxenos von Mabbug und ihrer Bedeutung für die christliche Spiritualität', in Hans auf der Maur Jorg, ed., *Fides sacramenti – sacramentum fidei* (Assen, 1981), 137–75

Guillaumont, Antoine. *Les Képhalaia Gnostica d'Évagre le Pontique et l'histoire de l'Origenisme chez les grecs et chez les syriens* (Paris, 1962)

Harrison, Carol. *Augustine: Christian truth and fractured humanity* (Oxford, 2000)

Hopkins, Gerard Manley. *The poetical works of Gerard Manley Hopkins*, ed. N. Mackenzie (Oxford, 1990)

The sermons and devotional writings of Gerard Manley Hopkins, ed. C. Devlin (London, 1959)

Jeanes, Gordon. *The day has come! Easter and baptism in Zeno of Verona* (Collegeville, MN, 1995)

Kopecek, Thomas. *A history of Neo-Arianism* (Cambridge, MA, 1979)

Lattke, M. *Die Oden Salomos in ihrer Bedeutung für Neues Testament und Gnosis* (Göttingen, 1986)

Lieu, S. N. C. *Manichaeism in the later Roman empire and medieval China* (Tübingen, 1992²)

Lorié, L. Th. A. *Spiritual terminology in the Latin translations of the Vita Antonii* (Nijmegen, 1955)

Luttikhuizen, Gerard P. *The revelation of Elchasai* (Tübingen, 1985)

Norris, Frederick et al. *Faith gives fullness to reason: The five theological orations of Gregory of Nazianzen*, Supp. VChr 13 (Leiden, 1991)

'Deification: Consensual and cogent', *Scottish journal of theology* 49 (1996): 411–28

Roten, P. de. *Baptême et mystagogie. Enquête sur l'initiation chrétienne selon s. Jean Chrysostome* (Münster, 2005)

Russell, Norman. *The doctrine of deification in the Greek patristic tradition* (Oxford, 2004)

Sevrin, J.-M. *Le dossier baptismale séthien: Études sur la sacramentaire gnostique* (Quebec, 1986)

Slenczka, Wenrich. *Heilsgeschichte und Liturgie: Studien zum Verhältnis und Heilsteilhabe anhand liturgischer und katechetischer Quellen des dritten und vierten Jahrhunderts* (Berlin, 2000)

Vaggione, R. P. *Eunomius of Cyzicus and the Nicene revolution* (Oxford, 2000)

van der Meer, F. *Augustine the bishop. Church and society at the dawn of the middle ages* (New York, 1965)

Varghese, Baby. *Les onctions baptismales dans la tradition syrienne*, CSCO 512 (subs. 82) (Louvain, 1989)

Whitaker, E. C. *Documents of the baptismal liturgy* (London, 1970²)

Yarnold, Edward, SJ. *The awe-inspiring rites of initiation: The origins of the R. C. I. A.* (Edinburgh, 1994²)

21

From Antioch to Arles: Lay devotion in context

GEORGIA FRANK

The legalisation of Christianity by the emperor Constantine launched a new era for Christian devotion, as urban processions, sumptuous churches and monastic settlements lent greater visibility to this religious minority. In the aftermath of imperial toleration, theologians reflected ever more profoundly on the incarnation, the belief that God sanctified the human body in the person of Christ. The proliferation of pilgrimage centres, relics, and eventually sacred images lent even richer expression to the notion that God entered matter – not just one body, but several, not just one place, but the created world and all it contained. In this revelatory drama, Christians explored how the body might know God through each of its physical senses and its movements in space. The ascetic movement, in its intense scrutiny and discipline of the body, reflects this incarnational impulse. Yet, so too can the lives of ordinary Christians, who never imagined for themselves any withdrawal or flight from the thick web of this world.

Despite the religion's greater visibility in that day, the 'voices' of ordinary Christians remain difficult to recover. Prominent bishops and church leaders wrote extensively to lay Christian elites. With rare exception, however, letters by lay Christians to these leaders have not survived. Details about daily life and devotions of ordinary Christians emerge on the margins of sacred biography. Sermons preached to lay Christian audiences may also yield insight into urban realities, but inevitably through the homilist's eyes.[1] Despite such biases, sermons are one of the few Christian genres delivered in settings where laypersons gathered in significant numbers. Recent research on such homilies has revealed valuable information on the diversity of the audience and its interactions with the preacher. Even when preachers betrayed their tendency

---

[1] See the useful case studies in Mary B. Cunningham and Pauline Allen, eds., *Preacher and audience*. Unless otherwise noted, quotations are taken from FOTC.

to dictate behaviours, their prescriptions often conceded local realities that render sermons as much goldmine as landmine to the historian.

Linked to the paucity of written sources by lay Christians, there remains the challenge of locating lay Christians in an age better known for its ascetics. To Christians who did not forsake food, family, sex or money, the phrase 'lay devotion' might have seemed an oxymoron. As the preacher John Chrysostom (349–407) once imagined a congregant saying, 'I cannot live in the world and in the midst of so many concerns and be saved.'[2] Such despair is not difficult to imagine for a laity whom pastors often cast in the shadows of ascetic heroes. Even if shaped by ascetic ideals, the lay men and women could aspire to know God by other means than the austerities of monastic regimens.

This fraught relation between location and salvation provides a useful framework for investigating lay devotion. Like the ascetic movement, for which the desert provided a potent symbol, the laity also defined itself through places and transformed them during the fourth to sixth centuries. Just as asceticism made 'the desert a city', as Athanasius of Alexandria (c. 293–373) famously said, lay devotion re-made home, tomb and church. This essay, then, approaches lay devotion as situated in space rather than defined primarily by actions. Some church leaders expressed reservations about practices that bound Christian identity too closely to place, as in Gregory of Nyssa's (c. 335–95) famous critique of pilgrimage: 'change of place does not effect any drawing nearer unto God' (Ep. 2). Such criticism did not slow the laity's attempts to 'draw nearer' within their own homes, churches and cities. These attempts to downplay holy places remind us how deeply locative Christian piety had become in the centuries after legalisation.

Place – particularly home, church and tomb – can serve as a framework for examining lay devotion. With reference to these places, we may investigate what practices and dispositions constituted lay devotion. We may also consider how places were more than a backdrop for practices, but even moulded those practices. Built space can reveal many features of piety, such as the typical size of a gathering, how bodies moved through space, and what perceptions shaped devotions in that space. Also worth asking is how devotions transformed existing spaces. For instance, how did devotions in the home transform that space or evoke others? Or, how did church architecture adapt to accommodate new devotional realities? To describe lay devotion, then, is to situate it.

2 Chrysostom, *On repentance*, Hom. 9.2 (FOTC 96: 127).

Domestic piety

'Busy yourself in your home in such a way that you do not neglect your soul,' Caesarius of Arles (c. 470–542; *Serm.* 196.2) advised his congregants during Lent. Busying oneself in piety extended to many aspects of domestic life. From the naming of newborns to the decoration on walls, the home was where Christians were born and formed. Well into the fifth century, while baptism remained a ritual reserved for mature adults, Christian devotions introduced many to the faith. No surprise, then, that church leaders took it upon themselves to advise parents on raising a Christian child. John Chrysostom, for instance, warned parents to choose baby names wisely. In some homes, he remarked, it was the custom to light several lamps and assign a name to each lamp and choose the name of the lamp that burned longest, in the hopes that the child would likewise live a long life (*Hom. in 1 Cor.* 12.13). Instead, martyrs, bishops or apostles would provide better models for childrearing and parenting.

During Lent, Christians sought advice on appropriate devotions. Church leaders like Athanasius of Alexandria and Caesarius of Arles recommended that Christians dedicate the forty days prior to Easter to adopting an ascetic regime of prayers, vigils, sexual abstinence, fasting, devotional reading, charity and hospitality.[3] For some, those devotions were not confined to Lent. In his eulogy for Gorgonia, the Cappadocian theologian Gregory of Nazianzus (c. 329–89/90) recalled his sister's 'intelligent chanting of the psalms . . . her reading, explanation, and timely recollection of the divine oracles'. The intensity of her genuflections, he notes, left her knees 'callous and, as it were, attached to the ground, in her tears to cleanse her stains with contrite heart and humility of spirit'.[4]

Beyond prayer, hymnody and vigils, Christians were also advised to cultivate other devotions within the home. For educated elites, John Chrysostom promoted private reading and writing as a form of devotion. 'Tell me,' he challenged his congregants, 'who of you, when at home, ever takes the Christian Book in his hands and goes through what is contained therein and studies Scriptures?' (*Hom. in Ioh.* 32) Still, he often advised his congregants to set aside one day of the week to study the Gospel selection to be read at the next *synaxis*. 'Seek a time and place of quiet,' Chrysostom advised on another occasion,

---

3 David Brakke, *Athanasius and the politics of asceticism*, 182–99; Caesarius of Arles, *Serm.* 196.2–3 (FOTC 66: 42–3).
4 Gregory of Nazianzus, *Gorg.* 13 (FOTC 22: 110); cf. *On his Father* 8 (FOTC 22: 125–6).

so that like a judge deliberating in chambers, the Christian might meditate within the confines of the bed curtains (*Hom. in Matt.* 42). Miniature codices and amulets that have survived from this period also point to the devotional use of small books, carried in a pocket or worn around the neck as a pendant.[5] Some amulets consisted of the opening words of a Gospel or psalm inscribed on a small piece of papyrus, leather or wood. That the wearing of scriptures should be condemned in 360 by the Council of Laodicaea (canon 36) indicates the practice was sufficiently widespread to merit ecclesiastical attention.

Night time in the home provided an ideal occasion for vigils. In an extended praise of night-time prayer, Chrysostom exhorted 'both men and women' to become the seeing eye that gazes upon all but is seen by none. Those who awoke at night could contemplate the Creator and last things in the stillness of the night (*Hom. in Act.* 26). By the light of day, men and women were preoccupied by household order. But at night, according to Chrysostom, the beauty of the divine 'household' came into sharper focus. The still darkness draws the soul to compunction, but also toward transcendence. He maps the contemplative eye's path. Initially plunged into darkness it eventually beholds the stars above, such that each star in the firmament is like 'ten thousand eyes'. It then peers outside a window to witness a silent street, then returns indoors to contemplate how the slumbering bodies appear as if in a tomb. With these sights fresh in the mind, the sleepless one can 'bend . . . knees, send forth groans' and plead for mercy from God who 'is more moved by prayers in the night'. Prayer at night, he concludes, can re-make a dormant house into a vigilant church. If husband and wife engage in these prayers, and even children (so far as they are able to remain awake), the house will 'become a church through the night'.

Christians found other ways to simulate the church in their homes. An Alexandrian house recently excavated at Kom el-Dikka offers a striking example of the integration of church and domestic spaces in a late sixth-century home.[6] Located along a main thoroughfare, House D, as excavators named it, consisted of two or more storeys with a workshop and showroom facing the street and a balustrade above it. On entering the house, one encountered a long (16 m.) open-air courtyard, with five rooms flanking it on each side. Most interesting for our purposes are the common spaces. The presence of no less

---

5 Home reading: Chrysostom, *Hom. in Ioh.* 11 (FOTC 33: 104); cf. *Hom. in Matt.* 72. Additional examples in Harry Y. Gamble, *Books and readers*, 231–41. On formal distinctions between amulets and miniature codices, see M. Kruger, 'P. Oxy. 840'; S. Davis, *The cult of Saint Thecla*, 145.

6 The following description is based on C. Haas, *Alexandria in late antiquity*, 189–206.

than nine ornate crosses on the ground-floor walls leave no doubt that this was a Christian house. Moreover, that some 150 flasks bearing images of St Menas turned up in the vicinity suggests that the neighbourhood was heavily frequented by Christian residents and pilgrims. The courtyard also boasted a highly crafted fresco of an enthroned Virgin and child flanked by what appears to be an archangel and a saint or patron. The image's strong resemblance to Egyptian church and monastery decoration reveals the influence of public spaces on private iconography. Nearby stone benches and the presence of two iron brackets for hanging lamps by the fresco suggest to archaeologists that the courtyard also doubled as an oratory, a space dedicated to communal prayers.

Church breached the confines of home in other ways. John Chrysostom advised wealthier members of his congregation to 'make a little chest for the poor at home . . . near the place at which you stand praying . . . as often as you enter in to pray, first deposit your alms, and then send up your prayer' *(Hom. in I Cor.* 48.7). Accustomed to encountering the needy at the doors of the church, the wealthy were encouraged to re-imagine almsgiving. A perfunctory rite prior to entering the church precincts, when shifted to the home, might become as frequent as hand washing before prayer.[7] The domestic alms box symbolised the encroachment of urban poverty on domestic interiors of Antioch's wealthy Christians. Images also reflected this mingling of devotional spaces, as in the portrait of a beloved bishop that adorned bowls and jewellery, as well as the walls of Antiochene Christians' rooms.[8] More than decoration, Christian symbols provided occasions for protection and remembrance. Lamps displayed crosses and holy letters (as in the *chi-rho*, the Greek monogram using the first two letters in Christ's name). A sixth-century silver spoon bearing the name PETROS on the stem of its handle probably belonged to a set of twelve, each bearing the name of a different apostle.[9] Images from distant shrines also reappeared in the home. These *eulogiae*, typically tokens or miniature flasks containing water, oil or earth that had come in contact with a holy person or place, were famous for healing the sick at great distances from the saint's shrine or holy place from which they originated.

In addition to physical objects originating from other devotional settings, it is worth noting the range of symbols that often adorned common household areas and objects. Lamps, utensils, wall decorations and garments often bore crosses, monograms and portraits of saints, as a way to avert misfortune.

---

7 A. van den Hoek and J. Herrmann, Jr., 'Paulinus of Nola, courtyards, and canthari', 185–6.
8 John Chrysostom, *Hom. encom. in Meletium*, (PG 50: 516), trans. in C. Mango, ed., *The art of the Byzantine empire*, 39–40.
9 E. Maguire et al., eds., *Art and holy powers*, 1–33, esp. 25, 132 (= § 65).

In time, such motifs found their way onto the walls and doorways of churches, suggesting that the power of these symbols extended beyond the home. Such iconographic evidence lends new insights into sermons that call upon Christians to import church practices into the home. From childrearing to night vigils, the home had the potential to assume – or even replace – devotions typically associated with churches. Efforts to *substitute* home for church (as in restrictions on women's attendance at vigils or on gatherings in domestic oratories) were doomed, if the repeated efforts to legislate these practices are any indication.

To many Christians, however, neither home nor church was interchangeable. Home was as much a training ground for the church as church was a model for the home. Caesarius of Arles, for instance, instructed his congregants to prepare for mass in the home and city by giving alms, settling disputes, confessing sins, and abstaining from sex before they could approach to take communion (*Serm.* 14.2; 16.2; 188.6; 229.4). The home, then, was not simply a satellite to church life, but a node where a complex network of churches and shrines intersected. Before we turn to this wider network, it is worth considering the church as a space for Christian self-formation.

Church

In the decades following legalisation, the skyline of many cities changed rapidly, as Constantine launched a vigorous programme of church construction that his successors would continue into the sixth century.[10] Modelled on Roman assembly halls of the times, many Christian churches began as longitudinal buildings with a narthex, a nave, and an apse at the opposite end. Within a generation, the plan would assume an even grander scale to include several aisles with colonnades. With some regional variations, that longitudinal plan remained in place during the fourth century. The basilica served as a prime space for showing Christians to one another but also for forming Christian identities through the routines of daily services, semi-weekly homilies, vigils, hymn-singing, memorials and the celebration of feast days. Such habituation rendered the church, in the words of Chrysostom, a veritable 'dyer's vat' for individual transformation (*Hom. in Act.* 29).

To appreciate the relation between the shape of space and the liturgy within it, I shall focus on the Byzantine Divine Liturgy. The linear design of the basilica

10 R. Krautheimer, *Early Christian and Byzantine architecture*, 39–67, esp. 43.

served this ritual's aims effectively. Already in the fourth century, the liturgy comprised a series of processions, or Entrances, and showings.[11] In the First Entrance, the people joined the celebrant, the deacon carrying the Gospel, and the clergy carrying candles as they entered the church. They proceeded from the narthex through the nave. The laity occupied the nave and aisles, while the clergy proceeded to the apse. After greeting the crowd, the celebrant ascended the throne in the apse, then began the Liturgy of the Word, a series of scriptural readings interspersed with the chanting of psalms and sermons. Although assigned to different spaces in the church, the laity had a remarkable degree of access to the rites. Readers processed along the *solea*, a reserved passageway that jutted out into the nave. As the deacon processed with Gospel in hand, throngs of laypeople reached across the *solea* to touch it, eliciting for one observer the image of waves lapping on a peninsula. The Liturgy of the Word concluded when the unbaptised Christians were dismissed, and the doors of the church closed. Until this moment, however, all congregants witnessed the clergy and celebrants' actions in full view. Whatever barriers demarcated reserved spaces, they were never high enough to obstruct any sight-lines among the laity.

For the baptised, that openness extended to the second part of the liturgy, known as the Great Entrance or Entrance of the Mysteries. In this procession, the faithful prostrated themselves as deacons led the procession with candles and incense, followed by a deacon carrying an elaborate fan, with which to keep flies away from the sacrament. More deacons followed holding the veils to cover the ceremonial chalices and patens. Next came the full chalices and patens, and the great veil to be spread over all the gifts, once transferred from the place of preparation to the altar.[12] Throughout this part of the liturgy, the altar remained visible.

The laity's power to behold the eucharist and be transformed by that gaze was not lost on preachers at this time. Sermons delivered to new converts not only instructed the neophytes on *how* to take communion, but also on what to see as the eucharistic preparations unfolded before their eyes. Only by gazing more intently on the preparations might new converts confront how alien, or even plain, the bread and wine appeared at first. Neophytes were advised to superimpose a different set of mental images to situate both

---

11 My summary is based on T. F. Mathews, *The early churches of Constantinople*, esp. 127, 138–75, a magisterial discussion of the movements and processions that characterised the early rites at Constantinople.

12 On liturgical vessels, see M. M. Mango, *Silver from early Byzantium*; fan at 147–53.

bread and wine in the drama of Christ's death. The deacons and celebrants were thereby enlisted in this mental drama to fill out the various roles. In Syria, Theodore of Mopsuestia (c. 350–428/9) called on catechumens to find the 'complete representation' of Jesus' death in the eucharist (*Hom. cat.* 5). The deacons arranging the linens signify the preparation of the burial shroud, as their fanning recalls funerary rites for dignitaries. Each gesture at the altar reminds the laity of their role as silent onlookers and stunned mourners at Jesus' funeral. Such re-imaging of the eucharist would not have been possible without having the eucharistic rites in plain sight.

To hold that spectacle before the laity's eyes required an architectural design with clear sight-lines. Thus, the linear design of the basilica kept the laity's gaze fixed on the altar and the processions that led to it. By this sensory engagement in the eucharistic drama, lay Christians learned to see the altar as grave. That association became even more explicit in the time of Gregory the Great, when the Roman *ordo* for consecrating an altar required the bishop to seal three grains of incense into the altar as a symbol of the spices used in burial.[13] Through preaching and the repeated gestures of ritual, then, such associations and perception became naturalised. As with the home, then, the church setting also functioned as repository for other devotional spaces.

In addition to the tomb, saints' shrines figured in liturgical celebration. By the fifth century, a majority of saints' *Lives* were composed for use in liturgical settings. In addition to the public reading of saints' *Lives* at the saint's shrine on the appropriate feast day, the stories found their ways into mass, prayers for the dying, blessings for pregnancy and childbirth, and funeral services. As Thomas Heffernan observes, lay men and women were exposed to 'virtually incessant liturgical celebration' of the saints.[14]

In the East, architectural and liturgical transformations during the sixth century eventually transformed lay men and women's perceptions of these biblical dramas. As liturgical historians observe, the laity's visual and tactile contact with the events in the apse were curtailed by greater sacralisation of the apse. Changes in the layout of church interiors reveal that separation, as the processions, readings and showings withdrew from the nave and became concentrated in the apse. Communion practices also reflected that distancing. The use of spoons in the eucharist curtailed the physical contact between clergy and the communicants' hands. As one architectural historian described the transition, 'The liturgy was gradually made ever more remote, untouchable,

13 John Crook, *The architectural setting of the cult of saints*, 13.
14 T. J. Heffernan, 'The liturgy and the literature of saints' Lives', in T. J. Heffernan and E. A. Matter, eds., *The Liturgy of the medieval church*, 73–105, esp. 79.

inaccessible, invisible.'[15] The period from Constantine to Justinian, then, marks a transition in the ways Christians encountered church interiors. Whereas the timber-roofed basilica put attention ahead, the advent of the decorated dome summoned the gaze upward. Thus, fourth-century processions toward a tomb-like apse gave way to stationary contemplation of the cosmos in the Divine Liturgy, a transition that was fully realised in the middle Byzantine period with the introduction of the icon screen.

Not far from the altar, some Christians experienced another dramatic space: the baptistery. A privileged space, reserved for the final stages of initiation, the font belonged to a series of rooms connected to the basilica or in a separate structure adjacent to it. During the fourth and into the fifth century, baptism was mainly for adults, although the baptism of children was not unknown.[16] Lent, the forty days prior to Easter, was normally the time of preparation for baptism. For eight weeks, the baptisands were expected to fast and undergo repeated exorcisms and instruction on matters of scripture, creeds and morality. Fasting, prayers and instruction intensified during Holy Week, until the night of Holy Saturday, when catechumens were led into the baptistery for final initiations. In the West, the bishop touched the candidate's nostrils and ears to 'open' them to the ceremonies ahead. In the East, candidates for baptism stripped naked, then olive oil was applied to the entire body, 'from the topmost hairs of [the] head to the soles of [the] feet', as Cyril of Jerusalem put it. With male deacons on hand to prepare male baptisands and female deacons tending to the women, the oily touch marked the entire body and not just the mouth to renounce Satan. Candidates faced west to rebuke Satan, then they turned east, toward the light, to pledge loyalty to Christ. Once in the waist-high scented waters of the bath, the baptisand was immersed three times. With some baptisteries elevated yet partially concealed by curtains or veils, baptisands were the central spectacle in a performance of new identity. In the West, *myron* was poured over the neophyte's head, or in some cases applied serially to the forehead, ears, nose, mouth and breast to mark the awakening of each sense to divine mysteries.[17] Following the signing by the bishop, neophytes dressed in white robes, processed into the church with candles in their hands and took first communion on Easter morning.

15 Mathews, *The early churches of Constantinople*, 127. Robert F. Taft, 'Byzantine communion spoons', esp. 213–19, 238.

16 On catechetical instruction, see the introduction and homilies in Yarnold, *The awe-inspiring rites of initiation*. On the performative dimensions, see A. J. Wharton, *Refiguring the post classical city*, 75–85, 114–31; T. Finn, 'It happened one Saturday night'.

17 Cyril of Jerusalem, *Cat. myst.* 3.3–4 (FOTC 64: 171–2); Wharton (*Refiguring the post classical city*, 121) finds no evidence for nudity or full-body anointment in Ambrose's descriptions.

Although the font signified the paradoxes of death and resurrection, burial and birth,[18] the *place* baptisands heard most often evoked was the tomb. That 'grave of water', as the fifth-century Syrian Narsai called it, allowed the baptisand approaching it to imitate the transfer of Christ's body from the cross to the sepulchre, as Cyril of Jerusalem claimed (*Cat. myst.* 2.4). Even the triple immersion was likened to Christ's three days in the tomb. With each plunge downward, the initiate experienced a sightless moment in Hades. Not just the rites, but also Lent itself, the time of preparations for baptism, was the season of the grave, as the renunciations and sleeplessness reduced the baptisands to the walking dead anticipating the death of another. Thus, baptism mapped a piecemeal symbolic death on the initiand's body. The simulated death, through the extinction of each sense, created the conditions for a stimulation and re-creation of the new person after the font.

Nocturnal transformations were not limited to baptism, however. Night vigils at churches often drew large crowds, many of them women.[19] Despite clergy and husbands' efforts to curtail or even ban women's attendance, few women were convinced that prayer in the home could replace the proximity to the saint's presence in the church or shrine. The sixth-century *Life of Matrona of Perge* captures the obstacles women faced. Her husband's misgivings echoed those of preachers, who blamed vigils for sexual promiscuity. When she finally convinced him to let her go, she spent the entire night engaged in psalmody and prayer at the Church of the Holy Apostles. She would have stayed longer, had not an exhausted attendant asked her to vacate the premises in the morning.[20] The night vigil was also an occasion for engagement with the biblical past. The sung sermons of Romanos the Melodist (d. after 555) comprised dialogues, which re-told the major events of Christ's life as well as stories about his mother, various disciples, and even a host of silent characters from the Gospels. These vivid dialogues enlisted the audience to identify with various biblical characters. The raw emotions evoked carried into the streets, where all-night processions took the faithful through the city then out to suburban shrines.[21]

Prayer, preaching and the eucharist, then, evoked other devotional spaces within the church's walls. To grasp this interpenetration of devotional spaces,

18 Sebastian P. Brock, 'Some important baptismal themes'.
19 John Chrysostom, *De sacerdotio* 13.69 (SC 272: 217); on legislation prohibiting women from attending all-night vigils, see R. Taft, 'Women at church in Byzantium', 72–4.
20 *Life of Matrona of Perge* 3, *Acta Sanctorum Novembris* (Brussels, 1910), III: 790–813; trans. Jeffrey Featherstone in A.-M. Talbot, ed., *Holy women of Byzantium*, 18–64, see esp. 20.
21 Socrates, *H.E.* 6.8, discussed in R. Taft, *The liturgy of the hours*, 170–4.

we turn to the tomb, the site of divine power evoked already in the home and church rituals.

Tomb

To the consternation of many church leaders, lay men and women focused their attentions on the tomb. Christians continued the Roman custom of dining at the gravesite of relatives.[22] Typically held on the day of the funeral, at the end of the nine-day mourning period, and on anniversaries of the death, the *refrigerium*, as this funerary banquet was called in the West, took place close to the tomb in an enclosed dining area. These rooms were furnished with stone benches and cisterns for water, and in some cases small tables and stone chairs. If the wall paintings and decorations in these rooms are any indication, the simple meals consisted of the customary bread, cakes, wine, water and a porridge Romans typically associated with the dead. A special seat was reserved for the departed to join in the meal, where food was set out for them and wine poured either on the sarcophagus or in a tube through it. Despite church leaders' protests, *refrigeria* continued through the sixth century in North Africa, Milan, Nola, Verona and Syria. In extending the intimacy of the home to the tomb, the *refrigerium* bound the living to the dead, but also the home to the beyond. In a manner of speaking, the *refrigerium* can be understood as the inversion of domestic vigils. If, according to Chrysostom (discussed above), the sight of one's loved ones sleeping should prompt contemplation of death, then dining with the dead evoked the waking activities of the home.

That intimacy extended to the veneration of saints and especially martyrs. Beyond the city walls, shrines at the martyrs' graves drew large crowds. Christians gathered in cemeteries to hear tales of the martyrs' sufferings, deaths and miraculous powers, as well as to feast. A variety of wine, meat, lentils and special breads were served on festival days, as payment records attest from Egyptian papyri.[23] At the festival, men and women conducted all-night vigils and listened to homilies, scriptural readings and stories about the saint. The saint's relics, however fragmentary, bore inexhaustible power, so much

---

22 For a helpful synthesis of the literary and archaeological evidence, see C. Vogel, 'Le banquet funéraire paléochrétien'. Beyond Rome: M. S. Venit, *Monumental tombs of ancient Alexandria*, 181–6, cf. 126–33.

23 Festivals: P. Maraval, *Lieux saints et pèlerinages d'Orient*, 213–43. Asia Minor: J. Leemans et al., 'Let us die that we may live', esp. 3–22. North Africa: Augustine, *City of God* 8.27 and cf. *Confessions* 6.2. Papyrological evidence: A. Papaconstantinou, *Le culte des saints en Égypte*, 317–22.

so that visitors collected oil, earth, water, dust or a rock from the place. Chrysostom catalogues these devotions in one sermon delivered at a martyr's festival:

> Stay beside the tomb of the martyr; there pour out fountains of tears. Have a contrite mind; raise a blessing from the tomb. Take her as an advocate in your prayers and immerse yourself perpetually in the stories of his struggles. Embrace the coffin, nail yourself to the chest. Not just the martyrs' bones, but even their tombs and chests brim with a great deal of blessing. Take holy oil and anoint your whole body – your tongue, your lips, your neck, your eyes.[24]

Visitors had many ways to 'raise a blessing' from a saint's tomb. A spoon from Egypt with the words *phage mana* (eat manna) bears strong connections to the tomb of John the Evangelist in Ephesus, which emitted a miraculous dust. As the sixth-century bishop Gregory of Tours describes the end of John's life, the evangelist 'descended into a tomb while he was still alive and ordered that he be covered in the ground. Still today his tomb produces manna with the appearance of flour; blessed relics of this manna are sent throughout the entire world and perform cures for ill people.' According to Gregory, the tomb of the apostle Andrew also overflows with a similar manna and fragrant oil every year on the saint's feast day. The quantity of the oil was thought to predict the fate of that year's crops. Beyond its agricultural worth, the oil was converted to 'salves and potions' providing 'great relief to ill people'.[25] *Eulogiae*, as these contact relics were called, took many forms. Dirt or rocks from the holy place were carried home such that the saint's power emanated from the shrine back to the home. At the church of St Stephen outside Jerusalem, oil or water could be poured into reliquaries equipped with funnels. After the liquid came in contact with the relics, it was collected in a basin beneath the reliquary and then distributed to pilgrims.[26] The power of relics to infuse other matter, whether cloth, stone, liquid or even skin, is evident in the cult of martyrs in Tours, where the relics' unlimited division and portability showed no weakening of their powers to cure and instruct the laity or sanctify distant places.

In addition to the *eulogiae* carried home from the shrine, pilgrims sought access to the saint's powers by other means. They requested the saint's protection and assistance in graffiti they left on walls and various portable objects,

---

24 Chrysostom, 'A homily on martyrs' (PG 550: 661–6, esp. 664); trans. Mayer and Allen, 96.
25 Gregory of Tours, *Glory of the martyrs* 29–30 (trans. van Dam, 47–9); the spoon is discussed in Papaconstantinou, *Le culte des saints en Égypte*, 351.
26 P. Donceel-Voûte, 'Le rôle des reliquaires dans les pèlerinages', 191–2.

such as pieces of bone or pottery (*ostraca*), on terracotta medallions or small lamps bearing the saint's name. Requests were sometimes submitted in writing in both positive and negative form, as in one ticket that asked St Philoxenus at Oxyrhynchus, 'if it is your will and you are helping me to take the banking business, I beseech you to bid me learn this, and speak'. Another slip, written in the same hand, states the same request but in negative terms (i.e., 'if it is NOT your will').[27] The supplicant would submit both questions to the shrine attendant, with one ticket returned as the saint's response. Oracle tickets from several shrines in Egypt typically requested advice on business affairs, marital questions, pregnancies, future travel, fugitive slaves, various ailments, and real estate transactions.

For more extensive dialogue with the saint, pilgrims looked to dreams. Not far from Alexandria, the shrines of Sts Cyrus and John at Menouthis and that of Abu Mena at Mareotis allowed pilgrims to sleep close to the saint's tomb in order to have a vision of the saint.[28] Incubation, as this Greco-Roman practice is called, allowed the devotee to see and hear the very saints whose remains they touched by day. That desire to sleep close to the saints, even in the sleep of death, gave rise to competition among elite Christians to be buried near the tombs of saints. Families who could afford the privilege of *depositio ad sanctos*, as it was called, expected unfettered access to the saint's intercessory powers not just in death, but also at the resurrection.

Visitors' prayers, however, did not end at their departure. In return for the saint's attentions, many visitors continued to supplicate or thank the saint by leaving various objects at the shrine. A sixth-century pilgrim to Jerusalem, known as the Piacenza pilgrim, describes the bracelets, rings, tiaras, plaited girdles, belts, emperors' crowns of gold and precious stones deposited at the Holy Sepulchre. At the Thecla shrine at Meriamlik in Asia Minor, birds from exotic lands delighted (and on one occasion even cured) children. Specific prayers and thanks were often recorded on small objects purchased at the shrine. Small crosses or decorated plaques made of wood or metal typically depicted the saint or simply the body part healed, such as eyes, feet or hands. Some bore messages, such as 'in thanksgiving', 'in fulfilment of a vow', 'Lord, help', or simply the word, *euprosdekta* ('may they be acceptable').[29] These objects allow us to track the widespread renown of some shrines. At Kom

---

27 *P. Rendel Harris* 54, cf. *P. Oxy.* 16 (1926); see Papaconstantinou, *Le culte des saints*, 336–7. Further examples in Lucia Papini, 'Fragments of the *Sortes Sanctorum*'.
28 Dominic Montserrat, 'Pilgrimage to the shrine of SS Cyrus and John'.
29 Theodoret of Cyrrus, *Graecorum affectionum curatio* 8.64; Mango, *Silver from early Byzantium*, 240–5.

el-Dikka (discussed above), the 150 objects depicting St Menas testify to the shrine's importance for the life of the home and church.

Already in the late fourth century, that vast and intertwined network of homes, churches and tombs spanned the Mediterranean, as pilgrims flocked to Palestine, Egypt and Syria. With imperial and aristocratic patronage, new churches, hospices, monasteries and shrines intensified pilgrims' access to sacred power and linked them to the biblical past. The late fourth-century pilgrim Egeria spent three years travelling to pray at biblical holy places in the environs of Jerusalem as well as to seek out ascetics at monasteries in Egypt, Syria and Asia Minor. Paula and Eustochium, a widowed mother and her daughter, travelled with Jerome from Rome to Palestine and eventually Egypt. Given the celebrity of wonderworking ascetics at this time, it is easy to overlook the role of rank-and-file monastics in guiding and lodging Christian pilgrims, as well as promoting the holy places. Whereas pilgrims tell us little about the devotions back home, the archaeological evidence completes their story. By the sixth century, the diary of the Piacenza pilgrim recounts the various images, relics and markers he kissed, touched and embraced. Not much later, those very sites reverberated in the stories connected to local holy places. The traffic in relics included not only fragments of apostles' bodily remains or pieces of Jesus' cross, but even the wonders effected by the packing material in which they were shipped, or water that had washed the relic. Sensory access to the biblical past was hardly confined to the 'land of the Bible', as distant local shrines extended this growing network of holy places and people.

To conclude, the story of lay devotion in the fourth to sixth centuries can be told as a tale of encroachments. Church encroached on home, as preachers put steady pressures on lay men and women to integrate practices normally associated with the church (almsgiving and Bible study) into the home. Within the church, the tomb encroached on the altar and baptistery, thereby connecting local churches with outlying cemeteries and shrines. The tomb proper preserved the intimacy of the home through graveside meals and other sensory engagement with the relics they contained. Pilgrims to the Holy Land encountered the centripetal power of a vast network of shrines. Practices typically associated with local tombs and wonderworkers converged on the holy places to articulate a sensory engagement with the biblical past. Those rituals, however, also had a centrifugal force, as relics from the Holy Land (or at least with stories that connected them to the Holy Land) attracted regional pilgrimages. This fluidity of space was also shifting, as the fourth to sixth centuries anticipated other imagined spaces. Sepulchral associations would give way in the late sixth century, as the emerging cult of icons, domed churches, and liturgical reforms prompted the laity to re-imagine the church as a window on the heavens rather than on the grave. As much as the lay men and women demonstrated the power to resist some encroachments, even to reject them, they also exercised the religious imagination to recombine these spaces. Contrary to what the preachers said, location *did* grant salvation.

Bibliography

PRIMARY WORKS

Cyril of Jerusalem. *Catecheses mystagogicae* (SC 126); trans. FOTC 61, 64
Egeria. *Travels. Égérie, Journal de voyage* (SC 296); trans. John Wilkinson, *Egeria's travels to the Holy Land* (Warminster, 1999³)
Gregory of Tours. *Glory of the martyrs*, trans. Raymond Van Dam. (Liverpool, 1988)
John Chrysostom. Selected works. Trans. Wendy Mayer and Pauline Allen, *John Chrysostom* (London, 2000)
Romanos the Melodist. *Hymns. Sancti Romani Melodi cantica: Cantica genuina*, eds. Paul Maas and C. A. Trypanis (Oxford, 1963); trans. Ephrem Lash, *St. Romanos the Melodist, Kontakia: On the life of Christ* (San Francisco, 1995)
Vie et miracles de Sainte Thècle, ed. and trans. Gilbert Dagron, SH 62 (Brussels, 1978)

ANTHOLOGIES OF PRIMARY TEXTUAL SOURCES

Festugière, André-Jean, trans. *Sainte Thècle, Saints Côme et Damien, Saints Cyr et Jean (extraits), et Saint Georges* (Paris, 1971)
Itineraria et alia geographica. CCSL 175; translated selections in John Wilkinson, *Jerusalem pilgrims before the crusades* (Warminster, 2002²)
Leemans, Johan et al., trans. *'Let us die that we may live': Greek homilies on Christian martyrs from Asia Minor, Palestine and Syria (c. AD 350–AD 450)* (London, 2003)
Mango, Cyril. *The art of the Byzantine empire 312–1453* (Toronto, 1986)
Talbot, Alice-Mary, ed. *Holy women of Byzantium* (Washington, DC, 1996)

SECONDARY WORKS

Allen, Pauline. 'The homilist and the congregation: A case-study of Chrysostom's Homilies on Hebrews', *Augustinianum* 36 (1996): 397–421
Baldovin, John F. *The urban character of Christian worship: The origins, development, and meaning of stational liturgy*, OCA 228 (Rome, 1987)
Brakke, David. *Athanasius and the politics of asceticism* (Oxford, 1995)
Brock, Sebastian P. 'Some important baptismal themes in the Syriac tradition', *The harp* 4 (1991) 189–214
Brown, Peter. *The cult of the saints: Its rise and function in Latin Christianity* (Chicago, 1981)
Brubaker, Leslie. 'Icons before iconoclasm?' In *Morfologie sociali e culturali in Europa fra tarda antichità e alto medioevo* (Spoleto, 1998), II: 1215–54
Cameron, Averil. 'The language of images: The rise of icons and Christian representation', in Diana Wood, ed., *The church and the arts* (Oxford, 1992), 1–42

Caseau, Béatrice. 'Christian bodies: The senses and early Byzantine Christianity', in Liz James, ed., *Desire and denial in Byzantium* (Aldershot, 1999), 101–9

Chadwick, Henry. 'Prayer at midnight', in Jacques Fontaine and Charles Kannengiesser, eds., *EPEKTASIS: Mélanges patristiques offerts au Cardinal Jean Daniélou* (Paris, 1972), 47–9

Clark, Gillian. 'Victricius of Rouen: Praising the saints', *JECS* 7 (1999): 365–99

Crook, John. *The architectural setting of the cult of saints in the early Christian West, c. 300– c. 1200* (Oxford, 2000)

Cunningham, Mary B. and Pauline Allen, eds. *Preacher and audience: Studies in early Christian and Byzantine homiletics* (Leiden, 1998)

Davis, Stephen J. *The cult of Saint Thecla: A tradition of women's piety in late antiquity* (Oxford, 2001)

Donceel-Voûte, Pauline. 'Le rôle des reliquaires dans les pèlerinages', in *Akten des XII. Internationalen Kongresses für Christliche Archäologie, Jahrbuch für Antike und Christentum*, Ergänzungsbände, 20: 1–2 (Münster, 1995), I: 184–205

Duval, Yvette. *Auprès des saints corps et âme: L'inhumation 'ad sanctos' dans la chrétienté d'Orient et d'Occident du IIIe au VIIe siècle* (Paris, 1988)

Finn, Thomas M. 'It happened one Saturday night: Ritual and conversion in Augustine's North Africa', *JAAR* 58 (1990): 589–616

Frank, Georgia. *The memory of the eyes: Pilgrims to living saints in Christian late antiquity* (Berkeley, 2000)

'"Taste and see": The eucharist and the eyes of faith in the fourth century', *Church history* 70 (2001): 619–43

Frankfurter, David, ed. *Pilgrimage and holy space in late antique Egypt* (Leiden, 1998)

Gamble, Harry Y. *Books and readers in the early church: A history of early Christian texts* (New Haven, 1995)

Haas, Christopher. *Alexandria in late antiquity: Topography and social conflict* (Baltimore, 1997)

Harvey, Susan Ashbrook. 'Embodiment in time and eternity: A Syriac perspective', *St. Vladimir's theological quarterly* 43 (1999): 105–30

Heffernan, Thomas J. and E. Ann Matter, eds. *The liturgy of the medieval church* (Kalamazoo, 2001)

Hoek, Annewies van den and John J. Herrmann, Jr., 'Paulinus of Nola, courtyards, and canthari', *HTR* 93 (2000): 173–219

Jacobs, Andrew S. and Rebecca Krawiec. 'Fathers know best? Christian families in the age of asceticism', *JECS* 11 (2003): 257–63

Jensen, Robin Margaret. *Understanding early Christian art* (London, 2000)

Kitzinger, Ernst. 'The cult of images in the age before iconoclasm', *DOP* 8 (1954): 83–150

Krautheimer, Richard. *Early Christian and Byzantine architecture* (New Haven, 1986⁴)

Kruger, Michael J. 'P. Oxy. 840: Amulet or miniature codex?', *JTS* N.S. 53 (2002): 81–94

Leyerle, Blake. 'Appealing to children', *JECS* 5 (1997): 243–70

Linders, Tulia and Güllog Nordquist, eds. *Gifts to the gods* (Stockholm, 1987)

Maguire, Eunice Dauterman, Henry P. Maguire and Maggie J. Duncan-Flowers. *Art and holy powers in the early Christian house* (Urbana, 1989)

Mango, Marlia Mundell. *Silver from early Byzantium: The Kaper Koraon and related treasures* (Baltimore, 1986)

Maraval, Pierre. *Lieux saints et pèlerinages d'Orient: Histoire et géographie des origines à la conquête arabe* (Paris, 1985)

Markus, Robert. 'How on earth could places become holy? Origins of the Christian idea of holy places', *JECS* 2 (1994): 257–71

Mathews, Thomas F. *The early churches of Constantinople: Architecture and liturgy* (University Park, PA, 1971)

'"Private" Liturgy in Byzantine architecture: Toward a re-appraisal', *Cahiers archéologiques* 30 (1982): 125–38; reprinted in Thomas F. Mathews, *Art and architecture in Byzantium and Armenia: Liturgical and exegetical approaches* (Aldershot, 1995)

Maxwell, Jaclyn LaRae. 'Preaching to the converted: John Chrysostom and his audience in Antioch', Ph.D. dissertation, Princeton, 2000

Miller, Patricia Cox. *The poetry of thought in late antiquity: Essays in imagination and religion* (Aldershot, 2001)

Montserrat, Dominic. 'Pilgrimage to the shrine of SS Cyrus and John at Menouthis in late antiquity', in David Frankfurter, ed., *Pilgrimage and holy space in late antique Egypt* (Leiden, 1998), 257–79

Ousterhout, Robert, ed. *The blessings of pilgrimage* (Urbana, 1990)

Papaconstantinou, Arietta. *Le culte des saints en Égypte des byzantins aux abbassides: L'apport des inscriptions et des papyrus grecs et coptes* (Paris, 2001)

Papini, Lucia. 'Fragments of the *Sortes Sanctorum* from the Shrine of St. Colluthus', in David Frankfurter, ed., *Pilgrimage and holy space in late antique Egypt* (Leiden, 1998), 393–401

Ramsey, Boniface, O.P. 'Almsgiving in the Latin church: The late fourth and early fifth centuries', *Theological studies* 43 (1982): 226–59

Taft, Robert F. 'Byzantine communion spoons: A review of the evidence', *DOP* 50 (1996): 209–38

The liturgy of the hours in East and West: The origins of the divine office and its meaning for today (Collegeville, MN, 1986)

'Women at church in Byzantium', *DOP* 52 (1998): 27–87

Venit, Marjorie Susan. *Monumental tombs of ancient Alexandria: The theater of the dead* (Cambridge, 2002)

Vikan, Gary. *Byzantine pilgrimage art* (Washington, DC, 1982)

Vogel, Cyrille. 'Le banquet funéraire paléochrétien: Une fête du défunt et des survivants', in B. Plongeron and R. Pannet, eds., *Le christianisme populaire: Les dossiers de l'histoire* (Paris, 1976), 61–78

Wharton, Annabel Jane. *Refiguring the post classical city: Dura Europos, Jerash, Jerusalem and Ravenna* (Cambridge, 1995)

Yarnold, E. J. *The awe-inspiring rites of initiation* (Collegeville, MN, 1994²)

'The fourth and fifth centuries', in Cheslyn Jones et al., eds., *The study of liturgy* (London, 1992²), 91–5

22

Saints and holy men

CLAUDIA RAPP

The period beginning around the year 300 was a time of experimentation with expressions of faith, piety and belief. The legitimating of Christianity at the end of the Persecutions in 312 and the prospect of lasting imperial support for Christianity and its practitioners opened up new opportunities for social acceptance and public expression of the faith. By around the year 600, experimentation had turned to solidification and a firm groundwork was established that future generations would evoke as binding precedent. One of the great novelties of the period was the cult of saints.

The focus of studies on saints has commonly been on 'the very special dead', as Peter Brown has called them, centred on the cult at their tomb.[1] Yet, other influential publications of the same scholar have drawn attention to the importance of living 'holy men' within the socio-economic landscape of late antiquity. There is no clear dividing line between them in terms of the veneration they received. Dead saints and living holy men alike were believed to hold a special connection to the divine that they were able to share with those who approached them. As will emerge from the following, many acts of veneration shown to saints after their death had their origin in the connections of the faithful to living holy men.

The cultural context

The Christian notion of personal sanctity cannot be understood divorced from its cultural context. The idea that certain individuals held an elevated status among humans because of their connection to the divine was common in ancient culture. In ancient Greece, heroes like Heracles, the son of Zeus, for example, were the descendants of gods and goddesses. They held superhuman powers and received divine honours at their tombs. There are even some

---

1 P. Brown, *The cult of the saints*.

instances where the bones of heroes were dug up and transferred to another location by a city community in order to claim an association with the hero for political purposes.[2] The cult of heroes in the Greco-Roman world provided fertile ground for the belief in the possibility of a direct physical connection between the burial spot of certain humans and the divine. Other cults, such as that of Asklepios, the son of Apollo, enjoyed more extensive dissemination with at least 500 sites, many of which attracted visitors in search of a cure for illness. German scholars of the *religionsgeschichtliche Schule* at the end of the nineteenth and in the early twentieth centuries uncovered the hero cult as one of the pagan antecedents for popular religious practices of Christianity,[3] but scholars now tend to reject this idea. While the hero cult was a relatively rare occurrence generally centred on one particular location, the cult of the saints became ubiquitous in the middle ages, with every Christian church or foundation in Latin West and Greek East claiming an association with at least one saint who was present in his or her relics.

The Christian cult of saints shares some features with late antique Judaism, such as pilgrimage to a specific site and the performance of certain rituals to honour the particularly prominent dead. In Palestine, the tomb of the prophet Jeremiah, for example, became a prominent pilgrimage site.[4] The Oak at Mamre, where the angels had visited Abraham, was the location of a popular annual festival that attracted Jews, pagans and Christians alike until the emperor Constantine claimed the site by the construction of a Christian church.[5]

In the early centuries, two new developments took place that provided fertile ground for Christianity's evolving appreciation for holy men and saints. First, the Roman empire increasingly embraced the ruler cult that celebrated the sacrality of emperors. Julius Caesar was declared *divus* ('divine') after his death. His successor Augustus was deified through apotheosis, also after his death. Later emperors received divine honours already during their lifetime, a practice that became common under Diocletian. The ritual expressions of recognition of the divinity of the emperor included the offering of incense and the celebration of the *adventus* ceremony at his arrival in a city. Both were later used to celebrate saints and relics. The specific adjectives designating holy men and saints (*hagios, sanctus*) also had their antecedents in the imperial cult.

---

2 Orestes' bones were moved from Tegea to Sparta (Herodotus, *Histories*, 1: 65–8).
3 E. Lucius, *Die Anfänge des Heiligenkults*; H. Usener, *Legenden der heiligen Pelagia*.
4 J. Jeremias, *Heiligengräber in Jesu Umwelt*.
5 Sozomen, *H.E.* 2.4.

Second, pagan holy men became popular within the context of Greco-Roman religion. The best known among them was Apollonius of Tyana, an itinerant preacher during the first century who lived a life of ascetic renunciation in imitation of the ancient philosopher Pythagoras. Apollonius was held in such high regard that even the emperor Constantine, who was famous for his support of Christianity, had a statue of him in his palace. Apollonius' direct connection to the gods was evident in his miraculous abilities: he made rain, healed people from illness, exorcised demons, and even resurrected a dead boy. His biography by the sophist Philostratos, published around 217, was a great literary success.[6] Later, in the competitive religious marketplace of the fourth century, the philosophical school of Neoplatonism brought forth a number of pagan holy men who engaged in philosophical contemplation and adopted a strict ascetic regimen.[7]

Greek heroes, Roman emperors and pagan philosophers thus provide the cultural background for the rise of the cult of saints. But the avowed and explicit models for Christian holy men, the exemplars whom they themselves profess to emulate, have to be sought within the religious context of Christianity. These were the protagonists of the Old and New Testaments – Elijah, Elisha, John the Baptist and Paul – and the martyrs as the heroes of the Persecutions, a time that dominated Christian historical memory and shaped Christian identity.[8] The imitation of Christ is surprisingly rare in late antique representations of saints in literature and art.

The Christian context

In pre-Constantinian times, individual Christians proved their faith through martyrdom and Christian communities derived their group identity from witnessing the death of their martyrs and observing the traditional Roman funerary rites and subsequent commemorations at their tombs. The cult of martyrs developed on the basis of the traditional Roman care of the dead, especially the annual commemoration at the tomb, including a shared meal, which the Christians adopted for their own purposes. It is particularly well documented, in written and archaeological sources, for Roman North Africa, beginning with the second century.[9] From there, it spread to Italy during the third century. It is also attested, although on a smaller scale, for the Greek East.

---

6 Philostratus, *Life of Apollonios of Tyana.*
7 G. Fowden, 'The pagan holy man in late antique society'; for biographical sketches of these pagan holy men, see Eunapius' *Lives of the sophists.*
8 H. Delehaye, *Sanctus*; E. E. Malone, *The monk and the martyr.*
9 Y. Duval, *Auprès des saints, corps et âme.*

After the end of the Persecutions, it was the Christian ascetics who proved their faith through a daily martyrdom of the body. In contrast to the martyrs, these men and women attracted admirers, disciples and miracle-seekers already during their lifetime. The hallmarks of a holy man or woman were an exceptional life of devotion and asceticism and the ability of intercessory prayer on behalf of others that could sometimes result in miracles. After his or her death, a holy person became a saint through the establishment of a cult at the tomb or other relevant site, laudatory documentation in hagiographical writing, and the annual commemoration in the liturgy. The origins of the cult of the saints must be sought at the intersection between the Christian cult of martyrs, on the one hand, and the veneration of living holy men, on the other.

There were many paths to gain recognition as a holy man in the third to sixth centuries: ascetics who either lived in solitude, like Anthony of Egypt, the pioneer of eremitic monasticism, or in communal monasteries, like Pachomius, the founder of coenobiticism, were the first and provided the baseline, as it were, for others to aspire to and imitate. These men had severed their ties to the world, seeking a position of liminality that allowed them eventually to re-enter society in an altered, elevated status, no longer subject to its hierarchies and conventions.[10] The miraculous powers that could result from such exertions marked the ascetic as a holy man. He had also achieved the ability to act as a mediator in conflict and patron to those in need.[11] Holy men embodied the monastic ideals of detachment from the world, concentration on heavenly things, and physical and emotional *apatheia*. But not all monks were considered holy men or, after their death, saints. The recognition of that status depended on their interaction with others and the acknowledgement of its beneficial, even miraculous effect on visitors, distant followers and disciples.

In addition to the holy man from the monastic milieu, a new type of sanctity emerged in the last decades of the fourth century, the holy bishop. Martin of Tours, Ambrose of Milan, Augustine of Hippo, Epiphanius of Cyprus and Porphyry of Gaza represent the first generation of this phenomenon. Rather than in the seclusion of the desert, holy bishops lived in cities in close interaction with their population as they fulfilled their liturgical function as priests and their administrative duties.[12]

---

10 A. Goddart Elliott, *Roads to paradise*.
11 P. Brown, 'The rise and function of the holy man in late antiquity'; see also the reflections on the Brown thesis in the special issue of *JECS* 6 (1998; guest editors S. Elm and N. Janowitz), and in J. Howard-Johnston and P. A. Hayward, eds., *The cult of saints in late antiquity and the early middle ages*.
12 C. Rapp, *Holy bishops in late antiquity*.

In the intense but blurry religious atmosphere of late antiquity, when Christianity was beginning to explore the possibilities of engagement with the empire and vice versa, personal sanctity could also be sought or achieved by emperors. Theodosius II was particularly noted for his exceptional piety,[13] Marcian was hailed as a 'new Paul' and 'new David', and Constantine and Justinian received liturgical commemoration as saints after their death.[14]

Sanctity was equal opportunity, regardless of status and gender. Theodore of Sykeon, for example, a popular holy man in late sixth- to early seventh-century Galatia, was the son of an unmarried working woman and an absentee father who was an imperial messenger. Women, too, could achieve sanctity in various ways. Like men, they could be ascetics, living either as hermits in the desert or in monastic communities. Family connections played an important role. Macrina, the sister of Basil of Caesarea, was recognised as a saint, along with their mother Emmelia, because these two women had turned their household into a monastic community. Monica, the mother of Augustine, and Marta, the mother of Symeon the Stylite, were considered saints because of their sons. Particularly popular types of female saints in late antiquity were the beautiful prostitute who repented and the runaway housewife who became a transvestite monk.[15]

Three examples for the cult of saints

The cult of a saint was prepared long before that person's death, in the admiration and adulation of disciples and visitors to the holy man or woman and in the reports that circulated about their miraculous interventions. The impresarios who set in scene the holy man's popularity during his lifetime and orchestrated his cult immediately after his death were usually close associates or disciples. Over time, saints' cults developed into important rallying points for the people and the powerful of their locality and region. Especially in the Latin West, bishops and aristocrats vied for the opportunity to patronise a cult through building activity, donations to the saint at his resting place, and literary displays of devotion from their own pen. A case in point is Damasus (304–84), bishop of Rome, who boosted the local cult of martyrs by identifying their tombs in the catacombs and adorning them with large marble plaques that carried short poems he had composed in their honour. These inscriptions

---

13 J. Harries, 'Pius princeps'.
14 G. Dagron, Emperor and priest, esp. 127–57.
15 Holy women of Byzantium, ed. A.-M. Talbot; E. Patlagean, 'L'histoire de la femme déguisée en moine'.

were incised by Philocalus, the finest stonecutter of the day, in letter shapes that were especially created for this purpose. By the end of our period, saints had become legal persons, who could receive financial and other donations and were able rightfully to own church buildings and landed property. In this way, the growth of the cult of a saint contributed to the greater wealth and power not only of its location, but especially of those clerics who administered it.

The interplay between discipleship, the production and dissemination of texts, and patronage in creating a cult can be illustrated in three examples from different regions of the later Roman empire: Martin of Tours in Gaul, Felix of Nola in Italy and Symeon the Stylite in Syria.

Martin, a native of Pannonia, was the typical ascetic *parvenu* who attracted a local following of disciples and eventually generated sufficient interest on a regional scale to suggest himself as a suitable candidate for the episcopal see at Tours (*c.* 372). He was renowned for his ability to work miracles of exorcism and healing, which often resulted in the conversion of pagans in the countryside. His miraculous powers were in such demand that people removed threads from his clothing, which were reported to heal from illness.[16] Among Martin's followers was Sulpicius Severus, who celebrated him as the Western counterpart to Anthony of Egypt in a *Life*, which he composed while the saint was still alive, and in a *Dialogue* on the life of Martin, written after his death. Martin died in Candes in 397, and the return of his body to Tours three days later, accompanied by huge crowds, resembled the triumphant *adventus* of an emperor. His monastic cell at Marmoutier became a site of local pilgrimage immediately after his death. Visitors would lie on his bed or seek to position themselves in his customary place of prayer.[17] The cult at his monastic site was eventually eclipsed by that at his episcopal see in Tours. This was not an immediate development, but rather depended on active promotion by later bishops. Two generations after Martin's death, Bishop Perpetuus built a new basilica over his tomb. The date of the inauguration of that church, 4 July (which was chosen to coincide with the anniversary of Martin's accession to the episcopate), was added to the liturgical calendar which already celebrated his death on 11 November, so that the city of Tours was now able twice a year to attract visitors, pilgrims and a thriving and profitable market. Perpetuus also commissioned an updated written account of Martin's miracles. Over time, Martin's cult, encouraged by later bishops including Gregory of Tours in the sixth century, who composed a treatise on the miracles of Martin (*De virtutibus*

16 Sulpicius Severus, *Life of Martin* 18.4–5.
17 Gregory of Tours, *Libri de virtutibus sancti Martini episcopi* 2.39.

Martini), attracted the patronage of the Merovingian aristocracy. By the late seventh century, the cloak (*capella*) that Martin had shared with a beggar in his most famous miracle – an act of charity that was rewarded with a vision of Christ – became the most important protective relic for the Merovingian kings. It was tended by special clergy (*capellani*, the origin of English 'chaplain') and carried onto the battlefield, a custom that the Carolingian kings continued. At the last count, there were at least 3,602 parishes dedicated to Martin in France alone.[18] Neither the location of Martin's cult nor its later success could have been anticipated at the time of his death. His popularity was the result of the intermittent initiatives of later bishops of Tours, which was one of the three places that could lay claim to him.

The cult of Felix at Nola, near Naples, illustrates the close interconnection between a saint and his patron and the role that literary production can play in this context. The original promoter of the cult of St Felix was Paulinus. The offspring of a noble family from Spain, Paulinus shocked his extensive network of learned friends when he decided to abandon status, marriage and wealth in order to lead an ascetic life. He was eventually called to the priesthood in Nola, and soon became bishop of that city, a position he retained for many years until his death in 431.

In Nola, Paulinus developed a special affinity for Felix, a local martyr in the Great Persecution. He applied his literary skill to the composition of fifteen 'Birthday poems' (*carmina natalicia*) which celebrated the anniversary of Felix' death. And he applied his significant financial resources to the promotion of Felix' cult by constructing a splendid basilica complex over the martyr's tomb, complete with structures for visitors and pilgrims. When Paulinus died, he was buried next to his beloved Felix, and his deacon and successor delivered a funerary oration that had the potential of developing into hagiographical celebration. In his death and burial, Paulinus was thus even more closely linked to his saint Felix than in life.

Paulinus pressed his network of Christian literati into service to promote Felix' cult. Sulpicius Severus in Gaul, the biographer of Martin of Tours, contributed poems to be inscribed along the walls of the new basilica at Nola. Paulinus reciprocated by composing poems celebrating St Martin for a similar purpose at Tours. And a question he addressed to Augustine in North Africa prompted the latter to compose a treatise on how to look after the dead, including the 'very special dead' (*De cura pro mortuis gerenda*), which is dedicated to Paulinus and makes favourable mention of Felix' cult. In short, the

18 *Bibliotheca Sanctorum*, col. 1274.

cult of St Felix would not have flourished without Paulinus whose education and wealth enabled him to promote, in word and in stone, the cult of a local martyr, dead for at least a century, for whom he felt great personal affinity.

The popularity of Symeon the Stylite's (c. 389–459) cult in Syria, by contrast, depended less on its posthumous promotion by enterprising individuals than on the large number of grateful admirers from all over the world during his lifetime. After he had gained some experience as a monk, Symeon became the sole resident of a hillside 75 km northeast of Antioch where he positioned himself on a succession of three ever-taller pillars. He spent the last decades of his life on a small platform, at a maximum height of 16.5 m, without shelter and exposed to the elements. Scholars in search of continuities with pagan practices have noted that it was not uncommon in this region for religiously motivated men to live a life of isolation on top of pillars or tall pillar-shaped phalloi.[19] One of Symeon's biographers has his own explanation for this novel form of ascetic bravado and his elevated position: 'he longs to soar to heaven and leave this earthly sojourn'.[20]

In spite of his remote location, Symeon's interaction with people secured his popularity: for several hours every day, he settled disputes and dispensed advice to those who came to see him. His prayers brought healings and exorcisms, but his miraculous abilities could also have a dark side when he punished wrongdoers. He even intervened, by letter, with the emperor Theodosius II to make him rescind an order to the Christians to pay retribution to the Jews. Several monks and priests lived in a community on the hilltop and tended to the needs of Symeon and the crowds of visitors, and there was a thriving town with at least one monastery at the base of the mountain.

Symeon's cult was seemingly spontaneous and almost immediate. Already during his lifetime, the people who visited his column came from all over the world and included non-Christians.[21] Although women benefited from his miracles at a distance and took part in his funeral, Symeon did not permit them to enter his enclosure. Even his mother was turned away with the promise of a reunion in the hereafter. She died that same night and was then buried at the foot of his column.[22]

Symeon's protective ability knew no bounds. The dust from the base of his pillar was collected and pressed into moulds, to generate small pilgrim tokens that carried the image of the holy man atop his column. These could serve as

19 D. Frankfurter, 'Stylites and Phallobates'.
20 Theodoret, *History of the monks in Syria* 26.12.
21 Ibid., 26.11.
22 *Life of Symeon the Stylite* 14.

mementos and, when dissolved in water and ingested or otherwise applied to the body, as miraculous healing agents. The image of Symeon was so popular that it was even affixed above the entrance to shops in Rome. Symeon's death was kept secret for four days for fear of a riot, until 600 soldiers arrived from Antioch. Under their protection and in the presence of seven bishops, along with Arabs on horseback and huge crowds carrying candles, Symeon's body was taken down from the pillar and brought to Antioch for burial. Although his tomb in Antioch is said to have produced many miracles, the largest centre of Symeon's cult remained his column. It became the focal point of a unique form of pilgrimage church, with four naves of equal length extending from an octagon centred on the column. The complex, which was completed about thirty years after his death, also included a hostel, a baptistery and a number of other buildings to accommodate the flow of pilgrims.

Symeon was equally renowned in literature: fifteen years prior to his death, Theodoret of Cyrrhus included a chapter on him in his *History of the monks in Syria*, written in Greek. At an unknown date, a monk by the name of Antonius composed a separate biography in Greek, and a Syriac *Life* was written before 473. In the late sixth century, Evagrius Scholasticus devoted a chapter of his *Church history* to Symeon and the efficaciousness of his relics, reporting on the exhumation of his head at the behest of a general who wished to take it with him on a military campaign.[23] Symeon had many admirers, followers and imitators far and wide. Daniel, who later became a stylite on the outskirts of Constantinople, spent several months as his disciple, and after Symeon's death received his leather tunic.[24] The knowledge about Symeon's spectacular asceticism spread at a rapid pace. In the sixth century, Gregory of Tours included a chapter on Symeon in his *Glory of the confessors*.[25]

By this time, the cult of saints was so well established that it formed part of the religious formation of children and provided ample inspiration for adults, a case in point being the deacon Vulfolaic. From earliest youth, Gregory of Tours reports, he had a great fondness for St Martin and even obtained dust from his tomb that he carried around his neck. But as his model of asceticism Vulfolaic chose Symeon, whose immobile stance on top of a pillar he imitated near Trier until a delegation of bishops chastised him: 'It is not right, what you are trying to do! Such an obscure person as you can never be compared with Symeon the Stylite of Antioch! The climate of the region makes it impossible for you to keep tormenting yourself in this way. Come down off your column,

23 Evagrius, *H.E.* 1.13.
24 *Life of Daniel the Stylite* 22.
25 Gregory of Tours, *Glory of the confessors* 26.

and live with the brethren whom you have gathered around you.'[26] These reproachful bishops were not merely concerned about the adverse effects of the local climate, but also motivated by the desire to rein in any spontaneous and extreme expressions of ascetic piety instead of the organised monasticism that it was in their power to regulate and control.

The examples of Martin, a monk turned bishop, Felix, a long-dead martyr, and Symeon, a champion ascetic, show the great variety of developments that led to the establishment of a saint's cult. The expressions of that cult, once established, are much more uniform and ubiquitous: pilgrimage to the saint's tomb or other meaningful site, the wish to touch or to possess relics, and the desire to be buried next to the saint. At the root of the cult of saints is thus the desire to establish a tangible connection with the holy man's body, as it had now become an instrument of his salvation and a potential source of divine assistance for others.

The cult of relics and its origins in living discipleship

These cultic practices are usually associated with the cult of dead saints. But – as I would like to argue – all these phenomena are also present in the interaction between living holy men, including martyrs before their execution, and their followers and disciples.

Comparable to pilgrimage to a saint's tomb are the frequent visits to a holy man by admirers – some, but by far not all of them, miracle-seekers – and the presence of disciples around him. Anthony of Egypt was compelled by the continuous throngs of visitors to retreat to increasingly remote locations where he lived the last years of his life assisted by two disciples. To chart more fully the ordinary and daily interactions of holy men and their followers than the sensationalist tendency of hagiography permits, it is helpful to turn to other kinds of sources. The most immediate documentation are letters exchanged between a holy man and his correspondents. Such letter collections survive from fourth- and sixth-century Egypt, and from sixth-century Palestine, where the correspondence of Barsanuphius and John contains no less than 848 items.[27] These documents show the holy man at the centre of a community of followers, which was bound by mutual prayer. Not only was the holy man asked for his prayers, his correspondents always reciprocated by offering their prayers on his behalf. In some cases, the holy man was informed that his prayers

26 Gregory of Tours, *History of the Franks* 8.15.
27 Eds. F. Neyt and P. de Angelis-Noah, trans. L. Regnault, SC 426, 427, 450, 451, 468.

resulted in a miracle, such as healing from an illness, but these are rare.[28] The actual messages in these letters are rather mundane: the exchange of news, confirmation of the receipt of certain materials, or requests for spiritual counsel and concrete advice. These documentary sources thus provide a valuable counterpoint to the hagiographers who constitute the bulk of our literary evidence and who tend to focus on the miraculous. In reality, miracles must have been an integral but minor part of a holy man's activities.

Central to the cult of saints are their relics.[29] The saint's body, which had become the instrument of his personal perfection in the faith, was believed to carry the same powers of intercession with God after death as the living holy man had during his lifetime. Hence the cult at the burial site, where the body exuded sanctity in tangible form. The connection between the cult of the dead, the special veneration of martyrs and the inspirational effect of such practices is highlighted for the first time in the *Martyrdom of Polycarp*, bishop of Smyrna, who died in 167. After he had been executed in the arena and his body cremated, the Christians were allowed access:

> Thus at last, collecting the remains that were dearer to us than precious stones and finer than gold, we buried them in a fitting spot. Gathering here, so far as we can, in joy and gladness, we will be allowed by the Lord to celebrate the anniversary day of his martyrdom, both as a memorial for those who have already fought the contest [of martyrdom] and for the training and preparation of those who will do so one day.[30]

In subsequent centuries, the physical remains of martyrs and saints were eagerly sought after by bishops, monks and lay men and women alike, generating a lively activity of finding a saint's relics that were hitherto unknown (*inventio*), and an intense traffic in moving relics from one place to another (*translatio*).[31] The first *translatio* is that of Babylas, a martyr of the Decian persecution, in c. 351 from its burial place in the cemetery outside Antioch to a new church in the suburb of Daphne which had been constructed over a temple of Apollo. The first *inventio* similarly served to claim symbolic territory. It was performed by Ambrose, bishop of Milan, who 'uncovered' the over-sized, bleeding skeletons of the local martyrs Gervasius and Protasius in 386, just in time to have them transported to his newly constructed basilica in a show of strength against the local Arian opposition. In his sermon to

28 C. Rapp, '"For next to God, you are my salvation"'.
29 A. Angenendt, *Heilige und Reliquien*.
30 *Martyrdom of Polycarp* 18.
31 M. Heinzelmann, *Translationsberichte und andere Quellen des Reliquienkultes*.

celebrate the occasion, Ambrose called the martyrs 'leaders of the people, defenders, soldiers (*principes populi, defensores, milites*)' and 'patrons (*patroni*)'.[32] The patronage over the city of Milan that these dead martyrs were believed to exercise through the presence of their relics is evocative of the function of the holy man as *patronus* which Peter Brown identified as the salient characteristic in the religious landscape of fifth-century northern Syria.

The precious relics of martyrs and later of saints in their tombs signalled their continued efficacy in providing a tangible connection to the divine, hence their designation as a 'pledge (*pignoria*)'. The faithful created contact relics by collecting the dust around the tomb, placing pieces of cloth (*brandea*) on top of it, or bringing oil or water in contact with the relics through openings in the coffin. The beneficial effect of the physical remains themselves could be multiplied by subdividing them, because each smallest hair, tooth or other particle encompassed the full extent of the saint's powers. The subdivision of saint's bodies was a widespread practice in the East by the fourth century, and became commonly accepted in the West by the seventh century.

The creation of contact relics may well have its precedent in holy men and martyrs prior to their death. In Carthage in 203, the badly wounded Saturus, about to end his life in the arena shortly after Perpetua's martyrdom, took a ring from the finger of Pudens, one of the soldiers in attendance: '. . . and dipping it in his wound gave it back again for an heirloom, leaving him a pledge and memorial of his blood'.[33] We are not told what the soldier did with this ring, but it is safe to assume that he treasured this object as a memento and perhaps even more, as a potentially miraculous object. Such motivation is clearly imputed to a Roman officer, a lapsed Christian, who offered his own clothes in exchange for the sweat-soaked garments of Bishop Cyprian of Carthage shortly before the latter's martyrdom in 258, perhaps in the desire to gain a token of the martyr's intercession for having fallen into apostasy.[34]

A particularly important form of contact relics were textiles placed on the saint's tomb. Again, their use is also attested by living holy men who offered clothing they had worn to their followers and disciples as a token of reassurance. James of Cyrrhestica, a hermit in northern Syria, gave a cloak he had worn to Theodoret (*c.* 383–460), bishop of Cyrrhus. This cloak provided Theodoret with protection 'stronger than any defences of steel'.[35] Receiving the worn cloak of one's spiritual father was a strong affirmation and encouragement of

32 Ambrose, *ep.* 22.
33 *Martyrdom of Perpetua* 21.
34 Pontius, *Life of Cyprian* 16.
35 Theodoret, *History of the monks in Syria* 21.16.

discipleship: Barsanuphius of Gaza offered spiritual reassurance to an unnamed 'brother' by wearing the latter's monastic cloak for two days and then sending it back with his prayers.[36] After a holy man's death, clothing that he had worn was often passed on to a favoured disciple. Of the two cloaks of Anthony of Egypt, one was passed on to his disciple Serapion, the other to Athanasius, the patriarch of Alexandria, who reports this proudly in his *Life of Anthony* in order to prove his credentials as a member of Anthony's inner circle.[37]

The centrality of a saint's tomb for his cult has already been highlighted. It also became a sought-after location for the burial of the faithful, who wished by this physical proximity to benefit from the saint's intercession on the day of the last judgment, as Paulinus had intended for his own burial next to Felix (burial *ad sanctos*).[38] But just as the gift of textiles signalled a confirmation and strengthening of discipleship, the promise of a joint burial is equally found in the context of a shared ascetic or monastic life. Holy men would arrange to be buried either with their close associates, or with their disciples. Barsanuphius made this promise to his disciple: 'I expect that we will be placed in the same tomb, as I have told you before, the two of us together; God has brought us together so that we may receive assistance from one another.'[39] The *Sayings of the desert fathers* relates the case of a young man who wished to form a lifelong attachment to his spiritual guide 'and to die with him'.[40] As these examples show, the physical connection to relics sought by the faithful as part of the cult of dead saints had its parallel in the interaction between living holy men and their followers.

The cult of the saints and its expression in literature

There is no clear correlation between the immediate existence of a cult and the popularity of a saint in literature. The *Life of Anthony*, for example, became an instant literary success, although his burial place remained unknown to his contemporaries, in accordance with his wishes.[41] Other holy men and their activities are mentioned in texts that are not primarily intended to advertise their popularity. The fifth-century church historian Sozomen, for example,

---

36 Barsanuphius, *Letter* 210.
37 Athanasius, *Life of Anthony* 91.8–9.
38 B. Kötting, *Der frühchristliche Reliquienkult*.
39 Barsanuphius, *Letter* 69; see also *Letter* 60, with the promise of joint resurrection.
40 *Sayings of the desert fathers. Systematic collection* 10.174.
41 Athanasius, *Life of Anthony* 91.6–7. Anthony wanted to avoid the ancient Egyptian practice of embalming dead bodies.

remarks on a number of holy men of his own time, but not all of them became the focus of a later cult.[42]

There is a vast and diverse body of literature – hagiography in the proper sense – specifically devoted to promoting the memory of a saint and his cult.[43] The most basic form of commemoration of a deceased martyr or holy man is the liturgical calendar, a simple list of 'birthdays' in heaven (*dies natalis*), which records the date and month of his death. The earliest such calendar of saints' days to survive is the *Martyrology of Edessa*, written in Syriac, which was copied in 411. It was one of the sources of the so-called *Martyrology of Jerome*, which was compiled in around 450 in northern Italy and revised in Gaul more than a century later. This became the common basis for all later Latin martyrologies.[44]

Just as the cult of saints developed and expanded in the fourth to sixth centuries, so did its reflection in writing, leading to a new, Christian form of rhetoric.[45] Authors adapted ancient literary genres to new use. Biographies were now written not only of famous statesmen and generals, but also of pagan holy men and of Christian saints. Athanasius' *Life of Anthony*, composed shortly after the latter's death in 356, served as the blueprint for all later saints' *Lives*. Jerome, the first Latin author to try his hand at the new genre, wrote his *Life of Paul*, a hermit near Thebes, and his *Life of Hilarion*, a monastic leader near Gaza in Palestine, as a marked counterpoint to Athanasius' emphasis on Anthony as the prototype of a holy man and on Egypt as the cradle of monasticism.[46] Panegyrics were delivered not only to celebrate the arrival of the emperor in a city, but also to mark the *adventus* of a saint's relics. Victricius of Rouen, for example, in 396 hailed the arrival of a gift of relics from Ambrose in a speech and in the process formulated a detailed theology of relics that, even though they may be subdivided, are consubstantial with God. Tomb inscriptions in the form of short poems commemorating the life and career of the deceased now also served the purpose of honouring the saintly conduct and miraculous abilities of holy men and women.

Christian authors not only adapted pagan literary forms, but also developed entirely novel ways of writing about the saints. Sermons, which had been developed to explicate Scripture and provide moral exhortation, could on

---

42 Sozomen, *H.E.* 3.14.
43 A. de Vogüé, *Histoire littéraire*; H. Delehaye, *The legends of the saints*; R. Aigrain, *L'hagiographie.*
44 J. Dubois, *Les martyrologes du moyen âge latin*; G. Philippart, *Les legendiers latins et autres manuscrits hagiographiques.*
45 Averil Cameron, *Christianity and the rhetoric of empire.*
46 A. A. R. Bastiaensen, 'Jérôme hagiographe'.

special feast days be devoted to a particular saint, setting up his or her life as an inspiration and a model for the audience. A new Christian genre of writing exclusively devoted to the cult of saints was that of miracle stories that recorded remarkable occurrences at the cult site. The keepers of a shrine maintained a written log of miracles, selections of which would be recited when pilgrims assembled to celebrate a saint's feast day. Later redactors assembled these miracle stories, added a preface and then circulated them as edifying literature. An early example is found in the *Miracles of St Thecla*.

For the modern reader of these texts, it is vital to remember that they were not written with posterity in mind. Their aim was not to provide later generations with historical information about the life and times of their protagonists, nor to offer insights into the religious mentality of their followers. Rather, the hagiographers pursued the goal of generating instant discipleship on two levels: they assumed for themselves the stance of the prototypical follower and eyewitness to the holy man's accomplishments, while instilling in their audience the desire to imitate, admire and venerate the saint.[47]

Criticisms and doubts among contemporaries

The cult of saints attained enormous popularity, both in East and West. Not surprisingly, this opened the door to abuses. The greatest concerns were exploitation for personal gain and the authenticity of relics.

Pachomius, for example, demanded for himself an unmarked burial site, for fear that a *martyrium* would be erected over his tomb. Such practices he labelled outright as 'commercializing the bodies of the saints'.[48] Personal greed could also lead to the creation of false relics: Gregory the Great reported that 'certain Greek monks' had dug up bones of dead men in the vicinity of the Church of St Paul in Rome in order to pass them off as relics back home.[49]

Scattered remarks in hagiographical texts show that even those who themselves had every expectation of being considered holy were weary of false relics: James of Cyrrhestica explained that he had stayed away from the *adventus* celebrations for the relics of St John the Baptist because he was worried that they belonged to another man by that name.[50] And Martin of Tours unmasked the tomb of a supposed martyr as the burial site of a robber.[51]

---

47 C. Rapp, 'Storytelling as spiritual communication'; D. Krueger, *Writing and holiness*.
48 *Bohairic Life of Pachomius* 122.
49 Gregory the Great, *Registrum epistularum* 4.30.
50 Theodoret, *History of the monks in Syria* 21.20.
51 Sulpicius Severus, *Life of Martin* 11.

One of the great critics of the validity of the cult of relics was Vigilantius, a priest in Gaul (c. 406). 'Why do you adore and kiss a bit of powder wrapped up in cloth?' he asked, insinuating that this kind of veneration reeked of pagan idolatry. Jerome rebuked him in no uncertain terms: 'If apostles and martyrs while they are still in the body can pray for others, when they should to be concerned for themselves, how much more [can they do this] when they have achieved their crowns [of victory], victories and triumphs?'[52] Jerome here points to the power of intercessory prayer as the distinctive feature of future martyrs and living holy men, a power that was multiplied after their death. To Jerome and many others after him, the cult of the saints really was an extension of their interaction with 'the very special living'.

Bibliography

INTERNET RESOURCES

http://mendota.english.wisc.edu/~hagio
Hagiography society website, with links
www.the-orb.net/encyclop/religion/hagiography/btrans1.htm
Entry site on Hagiography of the Online reference book for medieval studies (ORB) by Thomas Head
www.fordham.edu/halsall/sbook3.html
Internet medieval sourcebook. Saints' Lives
www.kbr.be/~socboll/
Societé des Bollandistes
www.doaks.org/translives.html
Survey of translations of Saints' Lives from Greek into English, French, German, Italian, organised according to the century in which the saint lived

PRIMARY SOURCES

Ambrose. Letters (CSEL 82[1-4])
Athanasius. Life of Anthony (SC 400); trans. R. C. Gregg (New York, 1980)
Barsanuphius and John of Gaza. Correspondance (SC 426–7, 450–1, 468)
Bohairic Life of Pachomius. Trans. A. Veilleux, Pachomian koinonia (Kalamazoo, MI, 1980), I
Burkitt, F. C., ed. Euphemia and the Goth with the Acts of the martyrdom of the confessors of Edessa (London, 1913)
Eunapius. Lives of the sophists. Trans. W. C. Wright, Philostratus and Eunapius. The Lives of the sophists, LCL (Cambridge, MA, 1968)
Evagrius Scholasticus. Church history, eds. J. Bidez and L. Parmentier (London, 1898; reprint: Amsterdam, 1964); trans. M. L. Whitby (Liverpool, 2000)

52 Jerome, Against Vigilantius 4.4, 6 (PL 23: 342, 344).

Gregory the Great. *Registrum epistolarum* (CCL 140–140a)

Gregory of Tours. *Glory of the confessors* (MGH scr.mer. 1); trans. R. van Dam (Liverpool, 1988, rev. edn. 2004)

History of the Franks (MGH, SRM 1.1); trans. L. Thorpe (Harmondsworth, 1974)

Libri de virtutibus sancti Martini episcopi (MGH scr.mer. 1). Trans. R. van Dam, *Saints and their miracles in late antique Gaul* (Princeton, 1993)

Holy women of Byzantium: Ten saints' Lives in English translation, ed. A.-M. Talbot (Washington, DC, 1996)

Jerome. *Against Vigilantius* (PL 23)

Life of Daniel the Stylite. Ed. H. Delehaye, *Les saints stylites*, SH 14 (Brussels, 1914); trans. E. Dawes and N. H. Baynes, *Three Byzantine saints* (London/Oxford, 1948; reprint: 1977)

Life of Plotinus and Life of Proclus. Trans. M. J. Edwards, *Neoplatonic Saints. The Lives of Plotinus and Proclus by their students* (Liverpool, 2000)

Life of Symeon the Stylite (TU 32.4). Trans. R. Doran, *The Lives of Symeon Stylites* (Kalamazoo, MI, 1992)

Martydom of Perpetua. Ed. and trans. H. Musurillo, *The Acts of the Christian martyrs* (Oxford, 1972)

Martyrdom of Polycarp. Ed. and trans. H. Musurillo, *The Acts of the Christian martyrs* (Oxford, 1972)

Paulinus of Milan. *Life of Ambrose*. Ed. and trans. Sister M. S. Kaniecka, *Vita sancti Ambrosii, mediolanensis episcopi, a Paulino eius notario ad beatum Augustinum conscripta* (Washington, DC, 1928)

Paulinus of Nola. *Carmina natalicia* (CSEL 29–30). Trans. P. G. Walsh, *The poems of St. Paulinus of Nola* (New York, 1975)

Philostratus. *Life of Apollonius of Tyana*; trans. C. P. Jones (Harmondsworth, 1970)

Pontius. *Life of Cyprian* (CSEL 3.3); FOTC 15

Sayings of the desert fathers. Systematic collection (SC 387, 474)

Sozomen. *Church history*. (GCS, N.F. 4: *Sozomenus Kirchengeschichte*)

Sulpicius Severus. *Life of Martin of Tours* (SC 133–5)

Theodoret of Cyrrhus. *History of the monks in Syria* (SC 234, 257); trans. R. M. Price (Kalamazoo, 1985)

Victricius of Rouen. *In praise of the saints* (CCL 64: 53–93). Trans. G. Clark, 'Victricius of Rouen: Praising the saints', *JECS* 7 (1999): 365–99

SECONDARY SOURCES

Aigrain, R. *L'hagiographie. Ses sources, ses méthodes, son histoire*, SH 80 (Brussels, 1953; reprint: 2000)

Angenendt, A. *Heilige und Reliquien: Die Geschichte ihres Kultes vom frühen Christentum bis zur Gegenwart* (Munich, 1997)

Barone, G., M. Caffiero and F. Scorza Barcellona, eds. *Modelli di santità e modelli di comportamento* (Turin, 1994)

Bastiaensen, A. A. R. 'Jérôme hagiographe', in G. Philippart, ed., *Hagiographies: Histoire internationale de la littérature hagiographique latine et vernaculaire en Occident des origines à 1550* (Turnhout, 1994–2001), I: 97–123

Bibliotheca sanctorum, 12 vols. (Rome, 1961–9)

Boesch Gajano, S., ed. *Agiografia altomedievale* (Bologna, 1976)

Brown, P. 'Arbiters of the holy: The Christian holy man in late antiquity', in *Authority and the sacred. Aspects of the Christianization of the Roman world* (Cambridge, 1995), 55–78

The cult of the saints: Its rise and function in Latin Christianity (Chicago, 1981)

'The rise and function of the holy man in late antiquity', *JRS* 61 (1971): 80–101; reprinted in *Society and the holy in late antiquity* (London, 1982)

'The saint as exemplar in late antiquity', *Representations* 1 (1983): 1–25; a slightly different (shorter) version appears in J. Hawley, ed., *Saints and virtues* (Berkeley, 1987), 3–14

Cameron, Averil. *Christianity and the rhetoric of empire: The development of Christian discourse* (Berkeley, 1991)

Dagron, G. *Emperor and priest. The imperial office in Byzantium*, trans. Jean Birrell (Cambridge, 2003)

Delehaye, H. *The legends of the saints*, ed. and trans. T. O'Loughlin (Dublin, 1998)

Sanctus. Essai sur le culte des saints dans l'antiquité (Brussels, 1927)

Drijvers, H. J. W. 'Spätantike Parallelen zur altchristlichen Heiligenverehrung unter besonderer Berücksichtigung des syrischen Stylitenkultes', in Fairy von Lilienfeld, ed., *Aspekte frühchristlicher Heiligenverehrung*, Oikonomia: Quellen und Studien zur orthodoxen Theologie 6 (Erlangen, 1977), 54–76

Dubois, J. *Les martyrologes du moyen âge latin* (Turnhout, 1978)

Duval, Y. *Auprès des saints, corps et âme: L'inhumation 'ad sanctos' dans la chrétienté d'Orient et d'Occident du IIIe au VIIe siècle* (Paris, 1988)

Edwards, M. J. and S. Swain, eds., *Portraits. Biographical representation in the Greek and Latin literature of the Roman empire* (Oxford, 1997)

Farmer, S. *Communities of St. Martin. Legend and ritual in medieval Tours* (Ithaca, NY, 1991)

Fontaine, J. 'Le culte des saints et ses implications sociologiques, réflexions sur un récent essai de P. Brown', *AB* 100 (1982): 17–42

Fowden, G. 'The pagan holy man in late antique society', *Journal of Hellenic studies* 102 (1982): 33–59

Frankfurter, D. 'Stylites and Phallobates: Pillar religion in late antique Syria', *V Chr* 44 (1990): 168–98

Goddart Elliott, A. *Roads to paradise. Reading the Lives of the early saints* (Hanover, NH, 1987)

Grabar, A. *Martyrium. Recherches sur le culte des reliques et l'art chrétien antique* (Paris, 1946)

Hackel, S., ed. *The Byzantine saint. University of Birmingham fourteenth spring symposium of Byzantine studies* (London, 1981)

Harries, J. 'Pius princeps: Theodosius II and fifth-century Constantinople', in P. Magdalino, ed., *New Constantines: The rhythm of imperial renewal in Byzantium, 4th–13th centuries* (Aldershot, 1984), 33–44

Heinzelmann, M. *Translationsberichte und andere Quellen des Reliquienkultes* (Turnhout, 1979)

Jeremias, J. *Heiligengräber in Jesu Umwelt: Eine Untersuchung zur Volksreligion der Zeit Jesu* (Göttingen, 1958)

Kötting, B. *Der frühchristliche Reliquienkult und die Bestattung im Kirchengebäude* (Cologne, 1965)

Krueger, D. *Writing and holiness. The practice of authorship in the early Christian East* (Philadelphia, 2004)

Leclerq, H. 'Reliques et reliquaries', *DACL* xiv.2: 2294–359

Lucius, E. *Die Anfänge des Heiligenkults in der christlichen Kirche*, ed. G. Anrich (Tübingen, 1904)

Malone, E. E. *The monk and the martyr: The monk as the successor of the martyr* (Washington, DC, 1950)

Patlagean, E. 'L'histoire de la femme déguisée en moine et l'évolution de la sainteté feminine à Byzance', *Studi medievali* ser. 3, 17 (1976): 597–623

Philippart, G. *Les legendiers latins et autres manuscrits hagiographiques* (Turnhout, 1977)

Pietri, Ch., 'Les origines du culte des martyrs (d'après un ouvrage récent)', *Rivista di archeologia cristiana* 60 (1984): 293–319

Rapp, C., '"For next to God, you are my salvation": Reflections on the rise of the holy man in late antiquity', in J. Howard-Johnston and P. A. Hayward, eds., *The cult of saints in late antiquity and the middle ages* (Oxford, 1999)

    Holy bishops in late antiquity: The nature of Christian leadership in a time of transition (Berkeley, 2005)

    'Storytelling as spiritual communication in early Greek hagiography: The use of *diegesis*', *JECS* 6 (1998): 431–48

Trout, D. *Paulinus of Nola. Life, letters and poems* (Berkeley, 1999)

Usener, H. *Legenden der heiligen Pelagia* (Bonn, 1879)

van Dam, R. *Saints and miracles in late antique Gaul* (Princeton, 1994)

van Uytfange, M. 'L'hagiographie: Un "genre" chrétien ou antique tardif?', *AB* iii (1993): 135–88

Vogüé, Adalbert de. *Histoire littéraire du mouvement monastique dans l'antiquité* (Paris, 1991–2005)

23

Pastoral care and discipline

ROWAN A. GREER

Any attempt to imagine and describe pastoral care in the early church encounters a great many obstacles. The evidence we possess is almost entirely literary, and it is not only fragmentary but also ambiguous. Moreover, we cannot speak of any uniform practice. It is obvious that there are differences both because of conditions that changed over time and because even in a single period pastoral care and discipline varied from place to place. Finally, to speak of pastoral care we ought to understand what it looked like to those who received it. But most of what we can know is told by the pastors themselves. We have pieces of the puzzle, but most of them are lost. Nevertheless, there are some general conclusions that are persuasive. One of them is that pastoral care did not confine itself to Christian morality. The cure of souls involved guiding Christians towards their final destiny in the age to come as well as helping them live the kind of life that would fit them for that destiny. Moreover, pastoral care also involved practical ways of dealing with the basic necessities of this life. Widows and orphans, the poor and the sick, prisoners and captives – all received pastoral care. The care of the body may even have been more obvious to the ordinary Christian than the cure of souls. The pastors who had these responsibilities were, in the first instance, the bishops and their priests and deacons in the cities and their environs. But there were others who also functioned as pastors – monks, holy women, teachers. And we should not forget the care given by ordinary Christians to one another and to those outside the faith. Let us turn first to three paradigms of the pastoral ideal as it was articulated in the fourth century.

Fourth-century paradigms: Gregory Nazianzen, John Chrysostom and Ambrose

While each of these three figures wrote for a particular purpose, they supply us with an understanding of pastors and their work that in broad terms remains an ideal throughout the period we are examining. All agree that the character of the pastor is a crucial prerequisite for his work and must involve both the spiritual and the moral dimensions of the Christian life. The example of vision and virtue, as well as the pastor's words, supplies the people with a challenge and with a power enabling them to respond to it. Gregory Nazianzen, writing in 362, argues that the pastor 'must himself be cleansed, before cleansing others . . . draw near to God, and so bring others near' (2.71).[1] This assessment of the priest's character coincides with the pastoral task (2.22):

> But the scope of our art is to provide the soul with wings, to rescue it from the world and give it to God, and to watch over that which is in His image, if it abides; to take it by the hand, if it is in danger; or restore it, if ruined; to make Christ to dwell in the heart by the Spirit: and, in short, to deify, and bestow heavenly bliss upon, one who belongs to the heavenly host.

The pastor's chief task, then, is to be a spiritual guide towards the contemplative goal, understood in Christian Platonist terms as the perfection of the image of God and of the soul's likeness to him.

John Chrysostom expresses a similar idea, but articulates it quite differently. 'The soul of the Priest should shine like a light beaming over the whole world' (6.4).[2] He thinks of this primarily in the context of the eucharist. The priest's office, though exercised on earth, is heavenly and requires him to be pure and so 'enabled to draw nigh to that blessed and pure nature' (3.4–5). While Chrysostom still thinks of salvation and of a heavenly destiny, his emphasis is upon bringing a heavenly life to earth (3.5): 'For they who inhabit the earth and make their abode there are entrusted with the administration of things which are in Heaven, and have received an authority which God has not given to angels or archangels.' Chrysostom, like Gregory, embraces the monastic ideal; but he thinks of it not so much in contemplative terms as in its liturgical dimension and its relation to the implementation of a common life of fellowship and of a victory over the passions. Understood this way, the monastic ideal can be brought to the city; and the priest who 'is able to guide his ship safely in the midst of the sea' of urban life is better than the monk 'who sits at the helm in harbour' (6.6). To be sure, Chrysostom's emphasis upon the heavenly life of Christians has a strong moral dimension; but he also thinks of it as enabled by the sacraments of the church and as a present participation in a heavenly destiny.

---

1 Gregory of Nazianzus, *Oration* 2; trans. NPNF ii, 7.
2 Chrysostom, *On the priesthood*; trans. NPNF i, 9. NB: the section numbers differ from SC 272.

In his *De officiis*, written like Chrysostom's dialogue in the late 380s, Ambrose articulates the ideal shared by pastors and their flocks by transforming Cicero's dialogue, which has the same title and finds its model in a treatise by the Stoic philosopher Panaetius of Rhodes. Ambrose follows Cicero in arguing that duties derive both from what is honourable or virtuous (*honestum*) and from what is beneficial or expedient (*utile*). The interaction of these two sources proves problematic, but Ambrose is clear that 'we [Christians] have no interest in anything unless it is seemly and honourable, and we measure that by the standard of the future, not the present' (1.27–8).[3] Like Cicero Ambrose equates the honourable primarily with the four cardinal virtues – prudence (or wisdom), justice, courage and temperance. But while Cicero gives pride of place to justice and its relation to the Stoic cosmopolitan ideal, Ambrose treats prudence as the 'first source of duty' because it involves showing 'devotion and reverence for our creator' and because it is 'also the source from which all the other virtues derive' (1.126). He corrects Cicero on the grounds that it is essential that wisdom should be the foundation of justice, since justice cannot stand 'unless it has a foundation. And the foundation is Christ. It is faith, then, that comes first' (1.252–3). The pastor and teacher must observe this priority, and doing so involves prayer and attending to scripture (1.70, 88; 2.5). In principle, the teacher must learn before teaching (1.3). We find at least hints of the spiritual ideal Ambrose elsewhere embraces in Platonising rather than Ciceronian terms.

No matter whether we think of the spiritual life as contemplation, participation in the sacraments, or meditation upon scripture, it cannot be severed from the moral life. Here, too, the ideal is one pastors must exemplify so as to persuade their people to aspire to it. Gregory treats the moral life primarily as a healing of the passions, a task that must first be undertaken by the physicians themselves (2.26). Shifting the metaphor he can speak of this as a warfare and of victory as the repudiation of vice and the acquisition of virtue. Such a healing and victory is enabled by contemplation, but it is also a prerequisite for the spiritual life. 'For it is not everyone who may draw near to God, but only one who, like Moses, can bear the glory of God' (2.92). Chrysostom can agree with Gregory that the ideal pastor must acquire virtue in order to draw himself and others to spiritual fellowship with God through Christ. Despite the dignity given to priests danger remains. Priests must sail through a stormy sea where they are apt to founder upon 'that most terrible rock of vainglory' and the wild beasts that dwell upon it. These are 'wrath, despondency, envy,

---

3 Ambrose, *De officiis*; trans. Davidson.

strife, slanders, accusations, falsehood, hypocrisy, intrigues . . . love of praise, desire of honour . . . contempt of the poor, paying court to the rich' (3.9). The virtuous life of priests, who are pastors and teachers, is in principle no different from the ideal held before all Christians. 'For this is the perfection of teaching when the teachers both by what they do, and by what they say as well, bring their disciples to that blessed state of life which Christ appointed for them' (4.8).

Ambrose, like Chrysostom, seems more concerned with the moral than with the spiritual life. The pastor must exemplify the life of virtue (2.60):

> . . . when it comes to obtaining good advice, it is uprightness of life, an obvious preference for all the best virtues, a steady practice of goodwill, and a pleasant and courteous manner that are the qualities which matter most. After all, who would look for a spring in a patch of mud? If all we find in an individual is decadence, a lack of temperance, and a medley of every imaginable vice, who would suppose there should be a single good draught to be drawn from such a source?

Prudence or wisdom, as we have seen, is the spiritual source of moral virtue. And it is the second cardinal virtue, justice, that Ambrose treats most fully (1.130–74). Justice primarily refers to 'promoting the fellowship of the human race' and 'furthering community' (1.130). This has a direct bearing upon how we should understand property. God's plan was that 'the earth would be . . . the common possession of us all. Nature produced common rights, then; it is greed that has established private rights' (1.132). Private property is the consequence of the fallen state in which humans find themselves. While it cannot be abolished, its right use for the common good is necessary for justice. Chrysostom agrees that almsgiving is a central feature of the virtuous life. Ambrose most clearly Christianises his account of justice by insisting upon non-retaliation (1.131). Here we find a tension with his treatment of courage, where he recognises the possibility of a just war (1.175–209). His discussion of temperance leads him to discuss chastity and the ideal of clerical celibacy (1.68–9, 76–80, 248–9; 2.27).

All three writers attack pastors who fall short of the ideal and who use their office to gain power or wealth for themselves. Nevertheless, repudiating these instances of vainglory does not mean that they fail to argue that the pastor must be set over his flock. To be sure, pastoral authority must be largely persuasive and must involve the paradox of patronage. That is, the pastor as patron must be both above his clients and at the same time fully identified with their interests. One of the things this means is that the cure of souls must always be adapted to the particular needs of those receiving pastoral care. Gregory, who had refused ordination partly because he did not think himself competent to 'ascend to rule from being ruled' (2.5), employs the analogy of the physician and sees ruling over the body of Christ as a persuasive 'art of arts and science of sciences' (2.15–16). For this reason the pastor must take account of the great diversity of those whom he seeks to guide (2.15, 28–34). Chrysostom also makes the point by using the same metaphor of the pastor as physician (2.3). Ambrose recognises the requirement in a similar way (1.148, 174, 213–14). The pastor rules and guides the people not only as a physician of souls but also as a teacher; and both metaphors imply the persuasive character of pastoral care. More than anything else rhetoric is the means whereby the pastor draws the people into the Christian spiritual and moral ideal. The pastor is the preacher. This conclusion suggests that the public character of pastoral care is central in the early church and finds its focus in the corporate and liturgical life of the church.

Pastoral care also includes the care of the body, and so we must turn to what we can know of the way that care was exercised. It is somewhat surprising that Gregory makes no mention of this dimension of the pastor's work in his oration. Chrysostom, however, among his other reasons for refusing ordination, speaks of 'the question of superintending widows . . . or of the care of virgins' (3.16). Widows are a problem because their financial needs must be met, presumably by giving them money from the church's funds or by helping them manage their property. A second problem has to do with enrolling them in the order of widows with the provisions of 1 Timothy 5.9–16 in mind. The priest must also administer money to care for strangers, the poor and the sick. With respect to virgins the issue is guardianship more than money (3.17). We have no more than glimpses of the financial and institutional arrangements implied, but can be sure that many of those who needed assistance were somehow placed on the church's rolls. Chrysostom constantly insists upon the duty of almsgiving in his homilies, and in several places argues that the church's administration of financial help ought not to be used to excuse individual Christians from their responsibility to care for the needy.[4] The financial resources administered by the churches derived not only from voluntary contributions, but also from imperial munificence. Theodoret tells us that after the Council of Nicaea Constantine instructed the provincial governors, 'directing that provision-money should be given in every city to virgins and widows, and to those who were consecrated to the divine services' (*H.E.* 1.10).

---

4 See, for example, *Homily* 14.3 on 1 Timothy.

Ambrose tells us far more than Gregory or Chrysostom about pastoral care designed to meet physical needs. His advice is usually fairly general in character, and he illustrates it by scriptural examples. Giving advice is one aspect of the pastor's task, and Ambrose thinks of Solomon's judgment regarding the two women who claimed the same child (2.44–47: 1 Kings 3.16–28). Unlike money, 'advice can never be exhausted' (2.75). Hospitality is another pastoral duty, and Abraham supplies an example (2.103–8). Pastors should invite the poor (2.126), and they should be wary of attending banquets given by outsiders (1.86). They should attach great importance to distributing alms to the poor, the elderly and the infirm, and should use prudence and justice in their work (1.38–9, 143–59; 2.76). Those who benefit by the distribution of food and money must include 'those who are ashamed to show their needs openly'. It is the responsibility of officers 'such as a priest or an almoner' to find such people and inform the bishop (2.69). Though Ambrose does not say enough to enable us to understand the details, it is clear that his advice has an institutional background. We can make the same judgment regarding deposits given the church to manage (1.168, 253–4; 2.144–51). Ambrose gives the specific example of a widow in Pavia whose deposit was protected by the church against a civil attempt to deprive her of it (2.150–1). Care for prisoners (1.148; 2.77) and the ransoming of captives (2.70–1) are also pastoral duties. Ambrose defends himself against those who disapproved of him 'because we had broken up sacred vessels in order to ransom prisoners' (2.136–43). Finally, pastoral work includes dealing with the recurring problem of famine (3.37–52).

The institutional dimension of the church's charitable work includes the Christian hospice. Gregory Nazianzen in his panegyric on Basil the Great speaks of the hospice Basil built on the outskirts of Caesarea in Cappadocia (*Or.* 43.63). This 'new city, the storehouse of piety', where the rich have stored their wealth safe from thieves and moths, is a place 'where disease is regarded in a religious light'. It is no longer possible to see 'that terrible and piteous spectacle of men who are living corpses . . . driven away from their cities and homes . . . Basil's care was for the sick, and the relief of their wounds, and the imitation of Christ, by cleansing leprosy, not by a word, but in deed.' The evidence is scanty, but we do know of hospices founded by Constantine and by Paulinus of Nola. In the early fifth century there were more than 500 hospital attendants in Alexandria.[5] It seems likely that every city and monastery had a hospice of some kind. Perhaps the most important evidence is a letter (*Ep.* 84) Julian the Apostate wrote to the high priest of Galatia in the summer

---

5 Jones, *The later Roman empire*, II: 911.

of 362. The letter belongs in the context of Julian's attempt as emperor to restore and organise paganism. Julian orders the high priest to establish 'numerous hospices in each city', and he specifies that they must be open to 'the impious Galileans', since their hospices have been open to pagans.

If it is difficult to understand the institutional aspects of pastoral care, it is equally hard to grasp its scale. But it is at least clear that the bishop as chief pastor relies upon priests, deacons and others for discharging his responsibilities. Ambrose gives specific instructions for deacons (1.246–59), and he refers to readers, exorcists and sacristans (1.216). We must understand the financial and institutional aspects of pastoral care in the light of late antique conventions regarding patronage. The bishop and his assistants are patrons, conferring benefits on the church's members. The ideal may have been egalitarian in its implications, and we can speak of a Christian transformation of patronage. Christians should have all things in common, and Chrysostom in his homilies clearly strives for this ideal, arguing that in Christ rich and poor have equal value. But the reality is a hierarchically ordered society in which the many found themselves primarily the recipients of pastoral care in its social and economic forms. A tension begins to emerge between the cure of souls and the care of necessary physical needs. The pastor as preacher, teacher, priest and healer of souls employs rhetoric and persuasion to enable Christians in their growth towards a moral and spiritual destiny. The pastor as patron confers benefits upon the flock, providing them with a secure place in an ordered Christian society. Freedom to pursue a Christian version of the late antique quest for virtue contrasts with freedom from want and from alienation in this world.

Holy people and holy places

So far we have confined attention to pastoral care as administered by the episcopal structures of the church. We must now say something briefly of the way people experienced such care from holy people and monastics, both male and female, and from resorting to the shrines of martyrs and the holy places in Jerusalem and elsewhere. Neither asceticism nor the cult of saints was a novel phenomenon. Nevertheless, in the century and a half following the Constantinian revolution they became central to Christianity in a way they had not been before. Households of virgins and the order of widows served an ascetical and pastoral purpose well before the fourth century, and we can also remember Origen's school and its spiritual ideal. Both the church and private Christians also preserved the martyrs' relics at least from the time of

Polycarp in the second century. Nevertheless, as a movement monasticism and its wider ascetical aims were a post-Constantinian development that may have in part originated as a protest against a church gone public. It was the wisdom of people like Athanasius, Basil the Great, Chrysostom and John Cassian that bound monasticism to the bishops and the church – an alliance that, of course, was not without its tensions. With regard to the cult of the saints the same pattern obtains. Not only did the martyrs' relics and their shrines grow in importance, the church increasingly took control of them. Both holy people and holy places tended to function more as sources of patronage and power than as persuasive means of encouraging Christians to pursue the spiritual life.

It is important to qualify this last conclusion, particularly with respect to holy people. The school that Diodore established in Antioch in the 360s was called the *asketerion* and must have resembled a monastery. Yet its chief purpose was to train people like Theodore of Mopsuestia and Chrysostom in their understanding of scripture and for leadership in the cure of souls. Similarly, Didymus the Blind was a teacher in and near Alexandria about the same time. While he must have been in touch with the monasteries, his concern was not merely ascetical but also theological. The Origenist spirituality he derived from scripture correlates with Gregory Nazianzen's understanding of the spiritual and moral dimensions of the cure of souls. Our sources can also present the anchorites and monks of whom they speak as examples and teachers of spiritual and moral virtue, in other words as pastors. In the preface to his *Life of Anthony* Athanasius tells the story 'so that you also might lead yourself in imitation of him'. More obviously, John Cassian's *Conferences*, written early in the fifth century, presents the wisdom of the desert fathers – and almost certainly of Evagrius – in the form of their lectures, designed to instruct people and to draw them to a spiritual life that is ascetical and, in principle, contemplative. In his introduction to the *Institutes*, Cassian turns the reader's attention away from miracles, which provide 'astonishment' but 'no instruction in the perfect life' (NPNF 2, xi: 200).

Nevertheless, it is difficult to escape the conclusion that holy people functioned more often as sources of power that helped others with the common problems of life, whether or not that power was displayed miraculously. In his *History of the monks in Syria*, written towards the middle of the fifth century, Theodoret does speak of his saints as exemplifying 'the goad of divine love' that perfects our yearning and desire for God, a desire 'that does not admit the laws of satiety' (*Epilogue* 4). And yet this love, which is true virtue, has a power that time cannot remove (*Epilogue* 14–15). For this reason the main body of his history focuses upon deeds of power. Peter the Galatian healed his mother's eye, and Macedonius cured her barrenness so that Theodoret was himself a miraculous child. Symeon Stylites not only healed the sick but gave people sound advice. Abraham by protecting villagers from the tax collectors became their patron. The close connection between monks and village life may also have obtained in the earlier days of the Pachomian monasteries in Upper Egypt. Other illustrations abound to show that Theodoret's holy people are primarily sources of benefaction. Holy women, particularly wealthy ones like Rufinus' friend Melania the Elder and her granddaughter by the same name, and like Chrysostom's friend Olympias, served the same function.

Particularly in the West in the fourth and early fifth centuries holy people posed a problem for the church. Priscillian of Avila, a highly charismatic figure, got into trouble ostensibly for his supposedly Manichaean views and was finally executed on a civil charge of sorcery, probably in January 385. Martin, a holy man and the bishop of Tours, parted company with the bishops who helped engineer Priscillian's fate. Sulpicius Severus' biography of Martin looks like a last-ditch attempt to defend the role of the holy man. Martin's power preceded his ordination and 'was by no means granted him while he was bishop' (*Dialogues* 2.4; NPNF 2, XI: 39–40). Much more could be said, and it would be necessary to examine the controversies with Vigilantius and Jovinian as they are reflected in the writings of Jerome and Augustine. Suffice it to say that one central dimension of the problem revolved around the inability of the church to control holy people, while another had to do with an elitist understanding of ascetical Christians. Augustine rejected Pelagius and his followers by insisting upon the sovereignty of God's grace, but the other issues are not far beneath the surface.

Turning from holy people to holy places, the emphasis upon pastoral care as benefaction is still more obvious. To be sure, the martyrs whose relics the church preserved exemplified the ideals of the Christian life, but they were more important as powerful patrons. Gregory of Nyssa was deeply committed to teaching a spirituality that emphasised the role of human freedom in progress towards God and the good. But in his homily on Theodore the Martyr he shifts attention to Theodore's power as 'our invisible friend' and an ambassador 'on behalf of our fatherland to the universal King'. The martyr's relics have already revealed their power by repelling an invasion of the Scythians (GNO 10.1.2: 70). Damasus, who was bishop of Rome from 366 till his death in 385, organised the relics of the saints in Rome, placing inscriptions on many of the tombs and procuring better access to them. Early in the next century the Spanish poet Prudentius wrote his *Crowns of martyrdom*. The stories of the saints he tells are associated with their cult places and portray them as guardians of the community by their gifts of healing and forgiveness. Paulinus of Nola in his poems and letters gives us vivid evidence for the pastoral function of the shrine of St Felix. The martyr through his relics finds lost oxen, provides meat for the poor, exorcises demons, protects his servants, and heals the sick (*Poems* 18, 20, 23, 26). The shrine of St Felix included a hospice, and we can certainly understand the pastoral function of this and other such places as caring for the sick and disadvantaged. The miracles effected by the relics of the saints that Augustine describes in the last book of the *City of God* fit the same picture. Pilgrimages to holy places included those in Jerusalem. As early as the middle of the fourth century Cyril of Jerusalem in his catechetical homilies refers to them and to the true cross set up in the Golgotha in the basilica built by Constantine's mother, Helena, to honour the empty tomb of Christ. Pieces of the true cross travelled west to Paulinus of Nola, who sent one to his friend Sulpicius Severus. Much later Gregory of Tours tells of the piece of the true cross that arrived at Radegund's convent near Poitiers and for which Fortunatus wrote the *Vexilla regis*. In sum, what we find are sources of pastoral care slightly to one side of the episcopal structures of the church, and sources that focus more upon that care as benefaction than upon its understanding as the cure of souls.

The end of late antiquity

Defining historical periods is always interpretive and in some degree arbitrary. But it is reasonable to treat the beginning of the seventh century as the end of late antiquity, largely because it was then that the three heirs of ancient Rome began to emerge – Byzantium, Western Christendom and Islam. To oversimplify, three factors in the fifth and sixth centuries contributed to this development and determined the contexts for pastoral care. Perhaps most obvious is the gradual process by which the West became a set of barbarian kingdoms and suffered still greater devastation by the Byzantine recovery of North Africa and Italy in the sixth century – a recovery that was short-lived in Italy. Even in the East the expansion of the Persian empire and barbarian raids threatened, if they did not overcome, Constantinople. A second and related factor was the diminishment and in some cases the collapse of civic life and the increasing importance of the countryside. The weakening of imperial control allowed regional and local differences to take on new importance. Finally, the church itself broke apart because of the Miaphysite schism after the Council of Chalcedon in 451 and because of the consequent tensions between Constantinople and Rome. Pastoral care continued to involve the cure of souls and the care of the body, and it is arguable that the general lines of the fourth-century paradigms did not disappear. At the same time, preachers and teachers tended to see the spiritual life primarily as participation in the liturgy and the hearing of scripture; and they were often content with a more modest understanding of the moral demands upon Christians. The monasteries became more important as centres of pastoral care than they had been at the end of the fourth century. Attending to the sick and the poor fell more and more to the lot of the monasteries, which provided sanctuary both literally and figuratively to people caught up in the chaos of war and of social and economic disruption.

For much of the period there are few sources; consequently, we may restrict discussion to a few of them. It may seem odd to speak first of the pseudo-Dionysian writings, but they supply what can be understood as a liturgical understanding of the Christian life and may well have been designed to implement the cure of souls. No one knows who Dionysius really was, and the first mention of the corpus is found in the writings of Severus, the Miaphysite patriarch of Antioch, early in the sixth century. By the middle of the century John Philoponus promoted Dionysius in miaphysite Alexandria, while John of Scythopolis, a Chalcedonian, edited and commented on the corpus. We can be sure that Dionysius had an impact on understandings of the spiritual life in Constantinople. Another example of liturgical change in the capital city is the work of Romanus the Singer, who in the sixth century wrote and introduced numerous *kontakia* for the Constantinopolitan liturgy. Somewhat earlier Diadochus of Photice wrote his *Centuries on Christian perfection*. We have some evidence, then, for liturgical and spiritual developments in Byzantium. And it is reasonable to say that these developments demand consideration in speaking of the cure of souls.

After 451, Syria presents us with a more complicated picture. Syriac-speaking Christians appear to have ignored the boundaries between the Roman and the Persian empires, and we are obliged to speak of the church in Persia. The West Syrians tended to be Miaphysites, as was Philoxenus, who was bishop of Mabbug from 485 till 519, when he was driven out by the Chalcedonians only to die a few years later. We possess thirteen of his homilies, which though addressed primarily to monks envisage a wider audience. They reflect earlier conventions regarding the spiritual life and do make mention of pure prayer and the contemplation of God. But Philoxenus' emphasis is upon the moral life – renunciation of the world and the ascetic struggle against fornication and gluttony. John of Ephesus, who died a Miaphysite martyr in 586, wrote fifty-eight *Lives* of the Eastern saints, making it clear that holy men and women functioned as pastors outside the usual institutional structures of the church. One of the most interesting of the Syrian pastors was Narsai, born in Persia at the very end of the fourth century. He crossed the border to attend the school of the Persians in Roman Edessa, a school possibly founded by Ephrem or his disciples after they left Nisibis when it was ceded to the Persians in 361. By 437 Narsai was head of the school in Edessa and a supporter of Ibas, the Nestorianising bishop from 435 till his death in 457. A Miaphysite bishop succeeded Ibas, and over a period of time the Nestorian teachers in the school fled. Narsai probably went to Nisibis in 471, where he took charge of a small school that became the chief centre of the Nestorian church in Persia. The school of Nisibis developed systematic training for ministry, educating clergy, monks and teachers, as well as missionaries who ultimately founded churches in India and China. The school of Nisibis helped inspire Cassiodorus' plan to establish a school in Rome in the middle of the sixth century, and may well have been an influence on the monastery he established in southeastern Italy.

In Egypt Miaphysitism dominated after Chalcedon, even though the Miaphysite church throughout the Near East did not become fully organised till 531. Outside Alexandria the monasteries tended to dominate church life, as seems also to have been the case in the Nestorian church and was certainly true of Celtic Christianity in Ireland and the north of Britain. The gradual emergence of Coptic Christianity remains obscure. But Shenoute was the first Coptic writer we know. As a young man he entered the White Monastery about 370, becoming its superior about 388 and dying at an advanced age. His writings, which require further study, supply evidence for pastoral care not only within but outside the monasteries. The further we move from the centre of the old Roman empire, the dimmer our knowledge.

We do, however, know a good deal more about the Western development. The letters of Apollinaris Sidonius give us a vivid picture of the church in Gaul in the latter part of the fifth century. Sidonius was the son-in-law of the Gallic emperor Avitus and urban prefect of Rome in 468, and he became shortly after that date the bishop of Clermont-Ferrand. His letters not only tell us of the cession of the Auvergne to the Visigoths in 475 but also help us understand the way an aristocratic bishop exercised pastoral care as well as the complications involved in electing bishops. Should they be those who had grown up in the ranks of the clergy? Should they be, so to speak, local squires? Should they be holy people and monks? Probably about ten years after Sidonius' death, Pomerius (a refugee from North Africa) settled in Arles as a priest and a teacher of rhetoric. In the first years of the sixth century he wrote a dialogue entitled *On the contemplative life*, which is really a treatise on how an ascetic who became a bishop should conduct his life and work. The contemplative life seems more ascetical than mystical, and Pomerius underlines the importance of meditating upon scripture. The active life involves not only a high standard of morality but also communal living and the duties of charity. Pomerius' pupil, Caesarius, who left the monastery at Lérins to live in Arles, became bishop of the city in 502, a position he occupied throughout the years when Arles was subject to Theodoric's Ostrogothic kingdom before being ceded to the Franks in 542. Caesarius' homilies give the impression that the focus of pastoral care was upon persuading Christians to avoid the obvious sins of fornication, gluttony and drunkenness. Nevertheless, Caesarius also founded a monastery and a convent; and he sought to provide for the poor and to ransom captives. Other evidence for pastoral care, especially in the northern parts of Gaul, may be sought in the writings of Gregory of Tours, who died in 594.

While Pomerius' *On the contemplative life* and Caesarius' homilies are important sources for understanding pastoral work, Gregory the Great's *Pastoral rule* is the best known and most influential writing of the sixth century. Gregory belonged to a Roman senatorial family, and when he was about thirty years old in 572 became urban prefect. Two years later he left civil office to lead a monastic life. In 579 Pope Pelagius II, having made him one of the seven deacons of Rome, sent him as papal legate to Constantinople. Gregory returned to his monastery in Rome some six or seven years later, and was elected Pelagius' successor as pope in 590. The *Pastoral rule*, written at this time, represents Gregory's attempt to come to terms with an honour and obligation he would have preferred to avoid. The *Pastoral rule*, however, insists upon the necessity of contemplation as a necessary aspect of the pastor's duties. The pastor must balance the external functions of preaching, teaching and administrating the church and its charitable work with constant attention to the inner life of the spirit. Gregory's word for pastor is *rector*, but he does not think of the term in an authoritarian way. The ruler is also a guide, teacher and preacher. Gregory's title for himself is 'servant of the servants of God'. The hierarchical structure of the church, divided into the 'rulers', the 'continent', and the 'married', is in principle a functional one. The three parts of Gregory's treatise concern the pastor's qualifications and character, his life, and the way he must adapt that work to the great diversity to be found in his flock. In broad terms there is continuity with the paradigms of pastoral care articulated by

Nazianzen, Chrysostom and Ambrose. At the same time, Gregory no longer draws explicitly upon Platonism or Stoicism, and late antiquity has begun to fade. His ideal is more oriented towards the monastic spirituality found in Augustine and Cassian and to the contemplation of scripture and its spiritual meaning. Of course, Benedict is one of his heroes. Gregory's death in 604 is as good a date as any for marking the beginning of the medieval period in the West.

Discipline and penance

An aspect of pastoral care that deserves separate treatment has to do with disciplinary measures employed by the church to secure the moral demand of the gospel. We may leave to one side the civil and judicial powers given bishops after Constantine, as well as the temporal functions they often acquired as Roman authority faltered. From a pastoral perspective the implementation of moral discipline attached first of all to catechetical preparation for baptism. As a consequence of the Constantinian revolution the church tended to tighten discipline at this level. Catechumens could not participate in the kiss of peace or in the liturgy of the faithful. Catechists carefully examined, as well as instructing, those who presented themselves for baptism. Discipline also extended to sins after baptism, and this must be our focus. The penitential system that developed in the third century had as its aim reconciling the demand of the gospel with its promise of forgiveness. It attached only to those who had committed what would much later be called mortal sins – apostasy, adultery and murder. Confession, the period of penance and probation, and reconciliation were usually public rather than private. Moreover, penance could not be repeated; and this helps explain the common practice in the fourth century of delaying baptism.

The canons of the Council of Elvira, which must have taken place towards the end of the Diocletianic persecution, perhaps in 306, appear to be an attempt to maintain the customs of the third century and established long and rigorous periods of penance, even though some of the Spanish bishops who endorsed them later subscribed to the more lenient canons of the Council of Arles in 314. The few pieces of evidence we possess suggest that there was a good deal of difficulty involved in adapting the earlier customs of the church to the changed situation after Constantine's recognition of Christianity. It seems that it was no longer possible to maintain a rigorous implementation of penance, partly because of the confusion following the Great Persecution and partly because of the new influx of converts. In general terms penance gradually became largely voluntary in character, and in some respects was often no longer entirely public. Moreover, side by side with public penance for major sins there had always been pastoral direction and forms of penance for sins that did not require excommunication. In sum, there were aspects of penance, both public and private, that paved the way for the introduction of the Celtic system towards the end of our period. We may consider two pieces of evidence – the three canonical letters of Basil the Great and the accounts given by Socrates and Sozomen of the abolition of the office of priest penitentiary by Nectarius, bishop of Constantinople.

Basil's three letters (188, 199, 217 in vol. 3 of LCL) were written to Amphilochius of Iconium in 374–5. In the first letter Basil admits he has never studied the questions Amphilochius has raised, and he sees his task as 'both to recall whatever we have heard from our elders, and independently to draw conclusions akin to what we have been taught'. The customary discipline he seeks to adapt is the system of graded penance found in the canonical letter of Gregory Thaumaturgus, the bishop of Neocaesarea, a letter to be dated about 260. The various grades of penitents, apparently related to the distinction between ordinary catechumens and those signifying their readiness for baptism, have the following order. The 'mourners' must remain outside the doors of the church, imploring the prayers of those entering. The 'hearers' enter the narthex of the church and leave with the catechumens before the kiss of peace. The 'prostrates' have admittance to the nave of the church, but must kneel; they, too, must leave with the catechumens. The 'standers' may stand with the faithful in the nave throughout the liturgy, but may not receive communion. This system spread from Neocaesarea throughout Asia Minor but never obtained elsewhere even though it is reflected in the canons of Nicaea (325). At first Basil's detailed rules implementing this system appear quite rigorous. But he does allow flexibility in the times allotted to the different grades of penance (canons 74, 84), and he recognises a difference between those who volunteer for penance and those who are denounced by others (canon 61). Moreover, canon 71 imposes a penalty on those who fail to denounce a serious sin they have witnessed. *Letter* 288 is Basil's frustrated attempt to deal with someone who has refused to accept penance. It looks as though the system increasingly depends upon volunteers, and that volunteers are the exception rather than the rule.

The story of Nectarius' abolition of the office of priest penitentiary shortly after Theodosius the Great's return to Constantinople in 391 is told somewhat differently by Socrates (*H.E.* 5.19) and Sozomen (*H.E.* 7.16). Both historians understand the office as a means for allowing the private confession of sin to a priest, who then assigns the period of penance. It is not impossible that Basil assumes the same procedure. The private confession, however, was followed by public penance and reconciliation. And this penance for serious sins could not be repeated. Socrates traces the origin of the priest penitentiary to the aftermath of the Decian persecution in 250 and the necessity of dealing with large-scale apostasy. Sozomen notes that public penance continued in Rome at this time, and it does seem the case that some form of public penance persisted in the West after it began to disappear in the East. In the West what little evidence we possess suggests that penance was almost always voluntary, and that, since it could not be repeated, it tended to become the last rites for a dying person. This, of course, meant that penance, which was in principle public, now became private not only in confession but also in reconciliation. At the same time the Gelasian sacramentary includes directions for a ceremony of public reconciliation to be held on Maundy Thursday. Caesarius of Arles allowed a second public penance, a provision condemned in Spain at the Third Council of Toledo in 589. These details and others are quite confusing, but they point in the direction of a double conclusion. The system of public penance gradually broke down, but there were also certain private provisions that were added to try to make it work. The ground was ready for the introduction of the Celtic system. In Wales, Ireland and the north of Britain spiritual direction, as practised in the monasteries, spread to the laity and became a private and repeatable form of penance. By adding priestly absolution we have what became the usual form of penance in the West. At the end of the sixth century, Columbanus established monasteries in Gaul and Lombardy, and his penitential, which reflects the Celtic system, helps explain its gradual spread throughout the West.

Bibliography

PRIMARY SOURCES

Ambrose. De officiis, ed. and trans. Ivor Davidson (Oxford, 2001)
Athanasius. Life of Anthony (SC 400)
Augustine. City of God (CCSL 47, 48)
Basil, The Letters, LCL (London, 1926–34)
Caesarius of Arles. Homilies (CCSL 103, 104)
Diadochus. Centuries (SC 5)
Dionysius. Works (PTS 33, 36)
Gregory the Great. Pastoral rule (SC 381–2); trans. NPNF II, 12
Gregory of Nazianzen. Oration 2: Apology for his flight to Pontus (SC 247); trans. NPNF II, 7
John Cassian. Conferences (CSEL 13)

John Chrysostom. *On the priesthood* (SC 272); trans. NPNF 1, 9
    Institutes (CSEL 17)
John of Ephesus. *Lives of Eastern saints* (PO 17–19)
Julian. *The works of the emperor Julian*, trans. W. C. Wright, LCL (London, 1913)
Paulinus of Nola. *Poems* (PL 61)
Philoxenus. *The discourses of Philoxenus, bishop of Mabbogh*, A.D. 485–519, ed. and trans. E. A.
    Wallis Budge (London, 1893–4)
Prudentius. *Crowns of martyrdom* (PL 60)
? Romanus. *Kontakia*. Ed. Paul Maas and C. A. Trypanis, *Hymns. Sancti Romani Melodi*
    Cantica: Cantica genuina (Oxford, 1963)
Sidonius Apollinaris. *Letters*. Ed. A. Loyen, *Sidoine Apollinaire, Correspondance* (Paris, 1970;
    reprint, 2003)
Socrates. *Historia ecclesiastica* (GCS, N.F. 1: *Sokrates Kirchengeschichte*; SC 477, 493–)
Sozomen. *Historia ecclesiastica* (GCS, N.F. 4: *Sozomenus Kirchengeschichte*
Sulpicius Severus. *Dialogues* (CSEL 1)
    Life of Martin (SC 133, 134, 135)
Theodoret of Cyrrhus. *Historia ecclesiastica* (GCS, N.F. 5: *Theodoret. Kirchengeschichte*)
    History of the monks in Syria (SC 234, 257)

SECONDARY SOURCES

Brakke, David. *Athanasius and the politics of asceticism* (Oxford, 1995)
Brock, Sebastian P. and Harvey, Susan A. *Holy women of the Syrian Orient* (Berkeley,
    1987)
Brown, Peter. *The body and society: Men, women, and sexual renunciation in early Christianity*
    (New York, 1988)
    The cult of the saints: Its rise and function in Latin Christianity (Chicago, 1981)
    The rise of Western Christendom (Oxford, 2003[2])
    Society and the holy in late antiquity (London, 1982)
Cameron, Averil. *Christianity and the rhetoric of empire: The development of Christian discourse*
    (Berkeley, 1991)
Chadwick, Henry. *Priscillian of Avila: The occult and the charismatic in the early church* (Oxford,
    1976)
Clark, Elizabeth A. *Jerome, Chrysostom, and friends: Essays and translations* (Toronto, 1983)
    The life of Melania the younger: Introduction, translation, commentary (Toronto, 1985)
Ferguson, Everett, ed. *Studies in early Christianity, vol. 16: Christian life: Ethics, morality, and*
    discipline in the early church (New York, 1993)
Grant, Robert M. *Early Christianity and society* (San Francisco, 1977)
Gryson, R. *The ministry of women in the early church*, trans. Jean Laporte and Mary Louise
    Hall (Collegeville, MN, 1976)
Jones, A. H. M. *The later Roman empire, 284–602* (Oxford, 1964)
Klingshirn, W. *Caesarius of Arles: The making of a Christian community in late antique Gaul*
    (Cambridge, 1984)
Leyser, Conrad. *Authority and asceticism from Augustine to Gregory the Great* (Oxford, 2000)
Markus, Robert A. *The end of ancient Christianity* (Cambridge, 1990)
    Gregory the great and his world (Cambridge, 1997)

Rousseau, Philip. *Ascetics, authority, and the church in the age of Jerome and Cassian* (Oxford, 1978)

Pachomius: The making of a community in fourth century Egypt (Berkeley, 1985)

Thurston, Bonnie D. *The widows: A women's ministry in the early church* (Minneapolis, 1989)

Volz, Carl A. *Pastoral life and practice in the early church* (Minneapolis, 1990)

Vööbus, Arthur. *History of asceticism in the Syrian Orient*, CSCO Subsidia 14, 17 (Louvain, 1958 and 1960)

History of the school of Nisibis, CSCO Subsidia 26 (Louvain, 1965)

Watkins, Oscar D. *A history of penance* (New York, 1961)

24

Sexuality, marriage and the family

DAVID G. HUNTER

The years under consideration in this volume witnessed the remarkable trans-formation of Christianity from a persecuted minority sect into the dominant political and cultural force in the Mediterranean world. One aspect of this development was the formation of a set of discourses and practices regarding sexual, marital and familial life. The extension of ecclesiastical (and, to a lesser extent, imperial) authority into areas of human life previously regarded as pri-vate produced what has been called a 'totalising discourse', one that assisted Christianity in establishing its influence in early medieval and Byzantine soci-ety.[1] This new cultural activity manifested itself in many ways, most notably in the laws of emperors, bishops and church councils, in liturgical practice, and, above all, in preaching and theological discourse.

Civil and ecclesiastical legislation

Christianity arose at a time when the Roman empire itself had begun to stress the importance of legitimate marriage and childbearing for the maintenance of social and political life. The emperor Augustus issued several laws that imposed inheritance restrictions on men and women who remained unmar-ried or who failed to produce children in marriage; conversely, those who married and had children were accorded certain social and economic privi-leges (*Lex Julia de maritandis ordinibus*, 18 BC; *Lex Papia-Poppaea*, 9 AD). While such legislation affected only a small percentage of the population, it reflected the emperor's desire to reinforce the institution of marriage and legitimate childbirth. The Augustan legislation also made adultery (defined as sexual relations by a married woman with a man other than her husband) a public crime, rather than a private, family matter. Husbands were now required to

---

1 On the origin of the term 'totalising discourse' in the writings of Michel Foucault and its application to early Christian studies, see Averil Cameron, *Christianity and the rhetoric of empire* and 'Redrawing the map: Early Christian territory after Foucault'.

divorce their adulterous wives, or risk prosecution for pandering (*Lex Julia de adulteriis*).[2]

Stoic philosophers in the early empire likewise stressed the importance of marital morality and its relevance to the maintenance of social order. Musonius Rufus, for example, held that sex should occur only within marriage and only for procreation (frag. 12). Like most Stoics, Musonius regarded marriage and family as essential to the maintenance of civic life, for 'whoever destroys human marriage destroys the household, the city, and the entire human race' (frag. 14).[3] In practice, of course, a double standard prevailed. Prostitution was legal, and young men were expected to acquire sexual experience before marriage. Married men, likewise, were not held to the same standards as their wives; sexual activity with slaves (male or female) or with prostitutes was widely regarded as morally unproblematic. Christian preachers later tried to remedy this situation, apparently with minimal success.

In the fourth century the rise of Christianity to greater prominence in Roman society led to some incremental changes in Roman legal practice relating to marriage and family. In 320, probably as a concession to the ascetic ideals of the Christians, the emperor Constantine repealed Augustus' marriage laws, thereby revoking the penalties imposed on those who chose celibacy or remained childless (*CTh* 8.16.1; *CJ* 8.57.1). In 331, Constantine also severely limited the reasons why either a man or a woman might initiate a unilateral divorce or *repudium* (*CTh* 3.16.1). It is unclear, however, whether or to what extent this legislation was influenced by specifically Christian values. In any case, these laws applied only to unilateral divorce. Divorce by mutual consent remained unpenalised until 542 when the emperor Justinian tried unsuccessfully to prohibit it (*Novel* 117).[4]

Justinian attempted in other ways to conform imperial legislation more closely to Christian teaching. He issued several laws to protect women from forced prostitution, closed brothels in Constantinople, and strongly encouraged prostitutes to reform their lives (*CJ* 6.6.1.4; *Novel* 14). Justinian also acted more vigorously than previous emperors to suppress homosexual activity.

---

2 For a summary and discussion of the Augustan legislation, see Judith Evans Grubbs, *Women and the law in the Roman empire*, 83–7.

3 Both philosophical and medical writers supported the ideal of sexual moderation for men as well as for women. See the discussions in M. Foucault, *The history of sexuality*, III and A. Rousselle, *Porneia*.

4 Justinian's successor, Justin II, reinstated the procedure of divorce by mutual consent (*Novel* 140). In his decision Justin noted that he had received many complaints from couples who suffered terrible domestic discord (*proelia discordiasque*), but who were unable to provide legal grounds for divorce under Justinian's regulations. See the discussion in James A. Brundage, *Law, Sex, and Christian Society*, 114–17.

Recalling the provisions of the *Lex Julia de adulteriis*, Justinian subjected homosexual relations to the same penalty as adultery (*Inst.* 4.18.4). In later legislation Justinian declared that homosexual relations were not only contrary to nature, but also responsible for famines, earthquakes, and pestilence (*Novel 77* and 141). As James A. Brundage has observed, 'Justinian's antihomosexual legislation is perhaps the area of his legislative activity where the influence of Christian authorities is most clearly evident.'[5]

If imperial legislation showed only modest influence from Christian teaching, the efforts of ecclesiastical authorities were more ambitious. Through preaching and the imposition of penitential discipline, the bishops of the fourth, fifth and sixth centuries scrutinised and attempted to regulate the sexual lives of their congregations with rigorous precision. By the middle of the sixth century, Dionysius Exiguus had compiled many of these regulations into his *Codex canonum ecclesiasticorum*, which was to serve as the basis of canon law in the West until the twelfth-century *Decretum* of Gratian. In 692 the Council in Trullo (Quinisext Council) provided the Eastern church with a similar corpus of canons drawn from earlier councils (c. 2). This large body of canonical literature functioned in a manner analogous to the Christological discussions and heresiological treatises of this period. It was part of a virtual explosion of Christian discourse that aimed to classify, analyse and define the acceptable contours of Christian thought and practice.

The ecclesiastical canons treated a broad range of sexual behaviours, from bestiality and incest to adultery and re-marriage. Around the year 375, Basil of Caesarea composed three letters to Bishop Amphilochius of Iconium in which he discussed a series of rulings that he had inherited from his predecessors. Men who engaged in homosexual relations or bestiality were given the same penance as those who committed adultery, that is, fifteen years of exclusion from communion spent in the successive classes of penitents: 'mourners', 'hearers', 'prostrates' and 'standers' (c. 62–3). Church officials tended to treat sodomy and bestiality as analogous offences, since both were regarded as 'unnatural'. According to the *Apostolic constitutions*, a handbook of church regulations compiled at the end of the fourth century, 'the sin of the Sodomites is contrary to nature, as is also that with irrational animals' (6.5.28). The Council of Ancyra, which met early in the fourth century, prescribed penalties for bestiality based on a sliding scale, depending on the age and marital status of the offender (c. 16).

---

5 Brundage, *Law, Sex, and Christian Society*, 123; but see John Boswell, *Christianity, social tolerance, and homosexuality*, 169–74, who has argued that Justinian and Theodora used the law primarily to prosecute personal enemies.

Divorce, adultery and re-marriage were issues frequently addressed by church officials. The Spanish Council of Elvira, which produced one of the earliest sets of canons (c. 305/6), proposed lifelong excommunication for a woman who left her husband without cause and married another man (c. 8). If a woman abandoned her husband because of his adultery and married another man, she was allowed communion only on her deathbed (c. 9). Stringent penalties were imposed on men and women who committed adultery: if the offence occurred only once, five years of penance were imposed on both sexes (c. 69); if the man was a multiple offender, he was excluded from communion until the hour of death (c. 47). Although Basil of Caesarea prescribed a penance of fifteen years for a man or woman convicted of adultery, the Council in Trullo modified this to seven years (c. 87).

One of the difficulties church officials encountered was the double standard that existed on the issue of male and female extra-marital activity. Roman law, which defined adultery as a crime committed by a married woman (or by a man with a married woman), required husbands to divorce their adulterous wives, but did not allow women to divorce their husbands on the grounds of infidelity. Basil of Caesarea pointed out the inconsistency of this practice but did not challenge it: 'Therefore the wife will receive her husband when he returns from fornication, but the husband will dismiss the polluted woman from his house. Even though the logic in these matters is not easy, this is the custom' (c. 21).[6] Other Christians, however, strongly opposed this 'custom', among them Basil's friend, Gregory of Nazianzus: 'I do not accept this legislation; I do not approve this custom. They who made the law were men, and therefore their legislation is hard on women' (Or. 37.6).

Re-marriage after the death of a spouse was also a practice which church officials sought to restrict. Although the apostle Paul had allowed the widowed to remarry (1 Corinthians 7.9), many Christians in the first three centuries disapproved of the practice. The second-century apologist Athenagoras, for example, regarded a second marriage as merely 'well veiled adultery' (euprepês . . . moicheia; Leg. 33); his sentiments were echoed by later rigorists, such as Tertullian. By the fourth century re-marriage was permitted under church law, although it was not highly regarded. Early in the fourth century, the Council of Neocaesarea forbade presbyters to be present at the weddings of digamists (c. 7). In his canonical letters Basil imposed varying periods of penance on

6 According to Basil (c. 58), the penalty for adultery by a man or woman was fifteen years of penance, whereas the penance for fornication was seven. If a married man had sexual relations with an unmarried woman, he was guilty of fornication, but not adultery (c. 21).

those who married a second or third time (c. 4); he regarded third marriages as merely 'restricted fornication' (*porneian kekolasmenên*) and 'the filth of the church' (*rhypasmata tês Ekklêsias*; c. 50). According to the *Apostolic constitutions*, a fourth marriage is 'fornication and unquestionable uncleanness' (*porneia kai aselgeia anamphibolos*; 3.1.2). Digamists were universally excluded from the clergy in accordance with the regulations of the Pastoral Epistles (1 Timothy 3.2, 12; Titus 1.6).

Irregular marriages and extra-marital sexual activity were not the only matters that church officials attempted to regulate. Even sexual activity within a legitimate marriage was treated with caution and, occasionally, contempt by some church authorities. In the West Augustine articulated the view that marital intercourse carried with it a 'venial fault' (*culpa venialis*), if sought purely for the sake of pleasure and not with the aim of procreation (*The good of marriage* 6.6). Married couples were expected to wash away the stain of such 'daily sins' (*quotidiana peccata*) by the daily practice of almsgiving or the recitation of the Lord's Prayer (*ser.* 9.18; *ser.* 354a.12). In the late sixth century, Pope Gregory the Great re-affirmed Augustine's view that married persons exceeded the rights of marriage if they engaged in sex without intending to procreate: 'That is why they must apply frequent prayers to wipe away the corruption they cause by mixing pleasure into the beautiful form of intercourse' (*Regula pastoralis* 3.27.28).

Over time, the sexual lives of married Christians were circumscribed by numerous prescriptions. Some legal materials imply that marital intercourse, even if sinless, was considered the source of ritual pollution. The *Statuta ecclesiae antiqua*, a collection of canons from fifth-century Gaul, ruled that a couple should remain celibate on their wedding night out of respect for the nuptial blessing they had just received (c. 13). Caesarius of Arles in the early sixth century proposed that a married couple should not enter a church for thirty days after marrying (*Sermon* 44.5) and should abstain from sex for several days prior to receiving communion (*Sermon* 1.12). The Irish penitential books, which began to appear in the sixth century, added further prohibitions: married persons were to practise sexual continence during Advent, Lent and the forty days after Pentecost, according to the *Penitential of Finnian* (c. 46). Failure to observe these restrictions could have drastic consequences: Caesarius claimed that children conceived during a woman's menstrual cycle were liable to be born as lepers, epileptics or demoniacs, if conception occurred on a Sunday or church feast day (*Sermon* 44.7).

The Irish penitentials introduced another note into the discussion of sex in Western Christianity. Topics formerly treated within the context of private spiritual direction by monastic authors such as John Cassian (e.g., masturbation, nocturnal emissions and sexual fantasies) now became subjects of ecclesiastical penance. The synod of North Britain, convened in Wales in the early sixth century, provided penalties for those who had 'defiled themselves' that varied according to the age and ecclesiastical status of the offenders (c. 2). The *Penitential of Finnian* imposed penances for sinful thoughts and intentions, as well as deeds (c. 1–3). The extension of monastic practices of self-examination into the manuals of penance laid the foundation of the later Catholic confessional and opened a new chapter in the history of the 'technologies of the self'. As Foucault has observed, confession now became a primary locus of 'the transformation of sex into discourse', that is, a ritual for the production of truth about sex.[7]

Finally, the impact of ecclesiastical restrictions on sex also fell upon members of the clergy, monks and consecrated virgins. In the West attempts to impose celibacy on married bishops, presbyters and deacons appeared as early as the Council of Elvira (c. 33) and were repeated regularly thereafter. The Eastern church, by contrast, while it forbade higher clerics to marry after ordination, allowed presbyters and deacons to remain sexually active after ordination; only bishops were required to be celibate (Council in Trullo, c. 6, 12–13, 48). Both in the East and the West, consecrated virgins who subsequently married were subjected to harsh penalties: in 385 Pope Siricius recommended lifelong penance for broken vows (*Letter* 1.6.7); Basil specified that professed virgins who married should be treated as adulterers (c. 60). Later the Council of Chalcedon imposed excommunication for this offence, although it acknowledged that the local bishop might exercise compassion in the matter (c. 16).

Marriage and liturgical practice

Another way in which the sexual and marital lives of Christians were drawn into the ambit of ecclesiastical control was by their gradual absorption into the liturgical traditions of the church. Since the making of marriage in antiquity was primarily a family affair, the process was slow and piecemeal. The early second-century Bishop Ignatius of Antioch had recommended that Christians should contract their marriages 'with the permission of the bishop' (*meta*

---

7 Cf. M. Foucault, *The history of sexuality*, 1: 61: 'From the Christian penance to the present day, sex was a privileged theme of confession.' As Elizabeth A. Clark has noted, the unpublished fourth volume of Foucault's history of sexuality was to be titled *The confessions of the flesh*: 'Foucault, the fathers, and sex', 621.

gnômês tou episkopou; To Polycarp 5.2), but this did not lead immediately to the development of a Christian marriage liturgy. In the first three centuries it was usual for Christians to marry using the same rituals that non-Christians did, although rigorists like Tertullian insisted that pagan religious symbols and practices should be avoided (*De idololatria* 16.3; *De corona* 13.4).

Only in the fourth century do we see the beginnings of specifically Christian liturgical practices for marriage, initially within the context of ceremonies in the family home. Because marriage rituals in antiquity were notably boisterous affairs, clergy were hesitant at first to participate. Erotic songs, dances and plays were a regular feature of wedding feasts. The leading of the bride to the home of her new husband (*domumductio*) was accompanied by a raucous street parade that included clowns and prostitutes. While church fathers, such as John Chrysostom, denounced these 'satanic orgies', they remained a prominent aspect of civic life during late antiquity. In the mid-fourth century the Council of Laodicea decreed that clergy should not witness the plays at weddings and must depart before the players appeared (c. 54; repeated in c. 24 of the Council in Trullo). The same council forbade the celebration of marriages during Lent (c. 52).

Despite the inherent difficulty of 'Christianising' an institution such as marriage, the clergy gradually acquired a role in the celebration of Christian marriages. Gregory of Nazianzus said that priests were sometimes asked to bless the couple at the moment when they received their nuptial crowns, although he disapproved of the practice. Gregory thought that the bride's father should perform this customary ritual (*Letter* 231). Somewhat later, John Chrysostom recommended that priests should be summoned to the nuptials in order to pronounce 'prayers' (*euchai*) and 'blessings' (*eulogiai*) upon the bride (*Hom.* 48 on Genesis). Chrysostom was also the first to provide a Christian interpretation of the nuptial crowns: they signified the victory of those who arrived at marriage without succumbing to fornication (*Hom.* 9 on 1 Timothy). In some regions of the East, such as Armenia, the blessing of the nuptial crowns by a priest had become a well-established practice by the middle of the fourth century and was carefully regulated by the fifth century.[8]

In the Western church the movement towards a Christianised ritual of marriage seems to have begun earlier than in the East. The bestowal of a nuptial blessing by a bishop or presbyter had become common by the end of the fourth century, at least in Rome. The Roman presbyter Ambrosiaster was

---

8 See the detailed discussion in K. Ritzer, *Le mariage dans les églises chrétiennes*, 145–9.

the first to mention this blessing (*c.* 380), which he says was bestowed only on first marriages (*Comm. on 1 Cor.* 7.40). Several years later Pope Siricius decreed that married candidates for ordination must have entered their marriages under the blessing of a priest (*Letter* 1.9.13); Siricius linked the blessing to the bestowal of the nuptial veil (*Letter* 1.4.5). Early in the fifth century, Paulinus of Nola described the nuptials of the future bishop Julian of Eclanum and his bride Titia, apparently the earliest instance of a wedding ceremony in a church (*Carmen* 25). Such elaborate ceremonies, however, were probably rare; both Julian and his bride were the children of bishops.[9]

In the middle of the fifth century the anonymous Roman author of the *Praedestinatus* spoke of 'priests who bless the beginnings of marriage, consecrating and uniting them in the mysteries of God' (3.31). This is probably an allusion to a nuptial eucharist. By the early sixth century there existed a set formula for the nuptial mass, whose rubrics are preserved in the Verona sacramentary. Following Roman tradition, the liturgical blessings were addressed only to the bride. Prayers were offered to enhance her fertility and fidelity, and the biblical figures of Rachel, Rebecca and Sarah were proposed for her emulation. The nuptial blessing of the Verona sacramentary stressed the original goodness of God's creation and the perpetual value of procreation: 'Thus you have decreed that the marriage bed should be shared for the increase of the human race, so that these unions may link the whole world together and establish ties among the whole human race.'

While the strictures of canonical legislation and the blessings of the Verona sacramentary presented contrasting viewpoints on sex, marriage and family life, they performed a common function. The former focused on prohibited behaviours and the violation of norms; the latter emphasised the positive aims and intentions of marriage. But both sets of practices facilitated the incorporation of sex and marriage into a 'totalising' Christian discourse that defined and regulated all acceptable and unacceptable expressions of sexual activity. Moreover, the gradual development of Christian marriage rites, like the emergence of penitential discipline, brought the marital relationship under the closer scrutiny and control of the clergy. Although it would take centuries for marriage to be effectively absorbed into the sacramental system, the foundations for this development were laid in the period under review.

---

9 Evidence from North Africa in Augustine's day indicates that the most common practice was to invite a priest or bishop to bestow a blessing in the family home, although there is no indication that such a blessing was required for the legitimacy of the marriage itself, either for the clergy or laity. See David G. Hunter, 'Augustine and the making of marriage in Roman North Africa'.

Theological perspectives on marriage

From the beginning, Christian tradition was notably fractured on the question of the theological value of marriage and family. Jewish tradition, by and large, affirmed the goodness of procreation, viewing Genesis 1.28 ('Be fruitful and multiply') as the first commandment (Mishnah, *Yebamoth* 6.6). The eschatological sayings of Jesus recorded in the Synoptic Gospels, however, raised a question mark over marital and familial relationships (Luke 14.26, Mark 12.25, Matthew 19.12), even though Jesus himself affirmed the permanence of marriage (Mark 10.5–9). Similarly, the apostle Paul bequeathed an ambiguous legacy to posterity when he advised unmarried Christians, 'in view of the impending crisis, it is well for you to remain as you are' (1 Corinthians 7.26) and 'even those who have wives should be as though they had none' (1 Corinthians 7.29), although Paul acknowledged that sexual relations between married Christians were permissible (1 Corinthians 7.5). Later New Testament writings, however, stressed the compatibility between the Christian life and the traditional Greco-Roman household. The author of the Pastoral Epistles, for example, insisted that church leaders should be distinguished by their conventional achievements in the time-honoured art of household management: 'For if someone does not know how to manage his own household, how can he take care of God's church?' (1 Timothy 3.5).

In the second century these diverse traditions developed into open divisions within the Christian community. Marcion, who believed that an inferior and immoral Creator-God produced the world, forbade Christians to marry or procreate children, lest they perpetuate a corrupt creation (Tertullian, *Adversus Marcionem* 1.29.1–9; Clement, *Stromateis* 3.3.12; 3.4.25). A less radical perspective was presented by Tatian, alleged founder of the 'Encratite' heresy. According to Tatian, human beings were originally created as a harmonious union of body, soul and spirit. Only after rejecting union with the divine Spirit did they become susceptible to sex, birth and death (*Oratio ad Graecos* 13.1–2). Tatian acknowledged that sexual relations were necessary in the old dispensation, but he insisted they were no longer to be tolerated in the new era inaugurated by Christ.[10] Labelled as 'heresy' by Irenaeus, Hippolytus and Clement of Alexandria, Tatian's views remained congenial to many second-century Christians, especially in Syria. In the second and third centuries, a variety of 'apocryphal'

---

10 The most extensive source of Tatian's 'Encratite' teaching is the fragments of his treatise *On perfection according to the Saviour*, preserved in the third book of Clement of Alexandria's *Stromateis*. See also Irenaeus, *Haer.* 1.28.1. For a recent account of Tatian's theology, see Emily Hunt, *Christianity in the second century*.

gospels and acts appeared that espoused the central tenets of Encratism, such as the *Acts of Judas Thomas* and *The Protoevangelium of James*. The widespread circulation of these writings in the fourth century and beyond is evidence of the continued attraction of radical renunciation among Christians.

In the third century two writers appeared who would exercise a profound influence on the subsequent shape of Christian thought. The North African Tertullian (*fl. c.* 197–220) vigorously defended marriage against Marcionite attack (*Adversus Marcionem* 1.29.6–7). But under the influence of the 'New Prophecy', which proclaimed the imminent end of this age, Tertullian also spoke of marriage as a 'sin' and barely preferable to fornication. Commenting on Paul's famous dictum in 1 Corinthians 7.9 ('It is better to marry than to burn'), Tertullian argued that marriage is 'good' merely by comparison with something evil and, therefore, 'it is not so much a good as it is a kind of lesser evil' (*De exhortatione ad castitatem* 3). In the fourth century Tertullian's rigour was to find new expression (sometimes verbatim) in the ascetical writings of Jerome.

Another influential third-century author, Origen of Alexandria, likewise bequeathed to posterity a view of sex, marriage and family life that closely resembled the rigorist stances of Tatian and Tertullian. Because Origen believed that God had created the material world as a response to the fall of pre-existent rational spirits, he viewed the body, and sexuality in particular, as fraught with ambiguity. Since the goal of rational creatures was to return to their pre-lapsarian state of spiritual contemplation, sexual activity was regarded as a dangerous distraction from the spiritual life. As Origen put it in his *Fragments of commentary on First Corinthians*:

> Do not think that the body is meant for sexual intercourse, just because 'the stomach is meant for food and food for the stomach' [cf. 1 Corinthians 6.13]. If you want to know the chief reason for the existence of the body, take note: It is meant to be a temple for the Lord, and the soul is meant to be holy and blameless, to serve as a handmaid to the Holy Spirit and to become a priest to the Holy Spirit that is within you. For Adam had a body in paradise, and yet it was not in paradise that 'Adam knew his wife Eve' [Genesis 4.1], but when he had been expelled after the disobedience.[11]

In the fourth and fifth centuries, enthusiasm for monasticism and other forms of ascetic practice reinforced the anti-sexual sentiments inherited from the

---

11 Origen, *On 1 Cor.*, frag. 29; text in Jenkins, 'Origen on I Corinthians', *JTS* 9 (1908): 370. Origen's teaching on marriage and celibacy has been thoroughly studied by Henri Crouzel, *Virginité et mariage selon Origène*; see also P. Brown, *Body and society*, 160–77.

earlier tradition. Many continued to follow the Origenist (and Encratite) paradigm by regarding sex and procreation as strictly post-lapsarian developments. In this view it was the 'original sin' of Adam and Eve – and their consequent mortality – that made sexual reproduction necessary to sustain the human race. This position is found in a number of the Greek fathers, among them Gregory of Nyssa (De opificio hominis 17) and John Chrysostom. In one of his early ascetical treatises Chrysostom argued that in paradise the first human beings lived in a wholly non-sexual state: 'Desire for sexual intercourse, conception, labour, childbirth and every form of corruption had been banished from their souls. As a clear river shooting forth from a pure source, so were they in that place adorned by virginity' (De virginitate 14.3). Marriage, by contrast, 'springs from disobedience, from a curse, from death' (14.6).[12]

These negative tendencies in some of the Greek fathers were occasionally balanced by a serious concern with the moral formation of children. The writings of John Chrysostom are instructive on this matter. In his early treatise Against the opponents of the monastic life, Chrysostom argued that monasteries provided the ideal context for the education of young men. The city was filled with too many temptations to allow for proper moral formation. But as his thought matured, Chrysostom came to see the Christian household as the primary place for education in Christian values. His essay On vainglory and the right way to educate children is virtually unique in patristic literature for its detailed advice to parents on how to shape the character of their children and help them to avoid the vices of urban life. Abandoning his earlier enthusiasm for monastic education, Chrysostom placed responsibility for the moral formation of children squarely on the shoulders of Christian parents (De inani gloria 22). Outside of the writings of Chrysostom, however, the moral and religious education of children remained an underdeveloped topic in early Christian discourse.[13]

The question of the original condition of Adam and Eve and the place of procreation in God's plan also exercised the minds of Christians in the West. Following the Greek fathers, Jerome observed that Adam and Eve had fulfilled the command to 'increase and multiply' only after the fall: 'Eve was a

---

12 Trans. Shore, 21–2; Chrysostom's thinking on this topic, however, may have evolved. In Hom. 20.1 on Ephesians (PG 62: 135), he describes sexual desire (erôs) as a power implanted in human nature 'from the beginning' (ex archês).

13 Exceptions are rare. Basil of Caesarea, for example, accepted children of both sexes into his monasteries and provided for their education (Regulae fusius tractatae 15). The Apostolic constitutions urged Christians to adopt orphaned children and to arrange suitable marriages for them. Bishops were encouraged to assist young men in learning a trade so that they could become self-sufficient (4.1.1–2).

virgin in paradise. After the garments of skins her married life began' (Letter 22.19.3). The close association between sex and original sin led Jerome, among others, to relegate Christian marriage to the lowest rank in a hierarchy of ascetic merit: the hundred-fold, sixty-fold and thirty-fold fruit in the parable of the Sower belonged respectively to virgins, widows and chaste married persons. This articulation of a 'states of life' hierarchy determined by degrees in sexual renunciation was yet another form of Christian discourse that served to 'naturalise' and institutionalise power relations based on sex. Not surprisingly, the Western requirement of sexual continence for clerics in higher orders (bishop, presbyter, deacon) emerged at precisely the time when the 'states of life' hierarchy was establishing itself.

This rhetoric of ascetic hierarchy, however, did not go unchallenged by Christians in the West. In the late fourth and early fifth centuries, a series of writers questioned the prevailing orthodoxy that ascribed superior value to sexual renunciation. Helvidius, Jovinian and Vigilantius argued that the elevation of celibacy over marriage degraded sex and implicitly impugned the Creator's work. Each received a stinging rebuttal from Jerome, and Jovinian was even condemned as a heretic by Pope Siricius and Ambrose of Milan in 393. Early in the fifth century, the bitter conflict between Jerome and Jovinian led many Christians to wonder whether it was possible to uphold the superiority of celibacy without actually condemning marriage. In order to answer this pressing question, Augustine of Hippo entered the debate and provided the most extensive theological discussion of marriage in the early church.

Augustine's thinking on sexuality and marriage is subtle, complex and often misunderstood. Although he supported the notion of the ascetic hierarchy, Augustine skilfully subverted it. In his treatises The good of marriage and On holy virginity, Augustine sought to mediate between Jerome and Jovinian, although he did not mention either of them by name (Retractationes 2.2). He accepted the idea that celibacy was superior to marriage. But Augustine also argued that there were virtues in the Christian life of greater importance than celibacy; obedience, humility and readiness for martyrdom are the ones that he names. As a result, Augustine concluded, a married person might actually be superior to a celibate, if the married person possessed the higher virtue. And since virtues often lie hidden until tested, no one really knows for certain whether he or she is superior (On holy virginity 46.47). Moreover, Augustine believed, God's gifts are too numerous to be limited to the thirty-fold, sixty-fold and hundred-fold fruit enumerated in the Gospel parable (ibid. 45.46). Hence, while the ascetic hierarchy remained in theory, its application in practice became extremely problematic.

Augustine also devoted significant attention to the crucial question about the nature of the original creation and, specifically, of sexuality. Early in his career, while still under the influence of the allegorical interpretation of scripture he had learned from Ambrose of Milan, Augustine tended to interpret the opening chapters of Genesis symbolically. In *Confessions*, for example, Augustine suggested that the 'increase and multiply' of Genesis 1.28 might refer to the ability of the human mind to generate a multitude of thoughts to express a single concept or to give an obscure text a plurality of meanings (*Conf.* 13.24.37). Similarly, in his early treatise *On Genesis against the Manichaeans* (*c.* 388), Augustine had preferred to give the creation stories in Genesis a spiritual, rather than a physical, interpretation.[14]

But early in the fifth century, as he composed *The good of marriage* in response to the debate between Jerome and Jovinian, Augustine acknowledged that the Genesis text might be taken literally; perhaps God had intended Adam and Eve to reproduce sexually, even if there had been no sin (*The good of marriage* 2.2). Within a decade the new direction in Augustine's thought had solidified. By the year 410, in the ninth book of his *Literal commentary on Genesis*, Augustine expressly rejected the view that sexual union and procreation were devised only in response to human sin and mortality. Now Augustine argued that sexual reproduction was God's original intention for humanity from the very beginning of creation (*De Gen. ad litt.* 9.9.14–15).

This shift in Augustine's interpretation of Genesis was to have a notable influence on his views of sex and marriage. By acknowledging that sex was essential to God's original creation, Augustine had grounded marital life firmly within the positive will of the Creator. Augustine now had solid grounds on which to argue that procreation was one of the genuine goods of marriage and the object of God's original blessing. However, once he had rooted the body and human sexuality in the pre-lapsarian world, Augustine began to envision original sin as damaging human nature precisely in its procreative urges. Now Augustine concluded that the primary effect of the sin of Adam and Eve was the emergence of the 'concupiscence of the flesh', a disorder of the human heart that was manifested most patently in the disordered desires of the human body (*De Gen. ad litt.* 11.31.41). For Augustine, the Pauline 'law of sin' that caused the apostle to do what he did not wish to do (cf. Romans 7.15–16) was evident especially in the tendency for sexual desires to run contrary to the rational control of mind or will.

---

14 Excellent accounts of the development of Augustine's teaching can be found in Elizabeth A. Clark's '"Adam's only companion"' and 'Heresy, asceticism, Adam, and Eve' and in P. Brown's *Body and society*, 387–427.

Despite these pessimistic tendencies in his thought, Augustine remained relatively positive about the basic goodness of human marriage itself. As he noted in the *Literal commentary on Genesis*, the evil of concupiscence did not negate the essential goodness of marriage: 'For what is good in marriage and that by which marriages are good can never be sin' (*De Gen. ad litt.* 9.8.12). For Augustine the good in marriage was threefold:

> *Fidelity* means that there must be no relations with any other person outside the marriage bond. *Offspring* means that children are to be lovingly received, brought up with tender care, and given a religious education. *Sacrament* means that the marriage bond is not to be broken, and that if one partner in a marriage should be abandoned by the other, neither may enter into a new marriage even for the sake of having children.[15]

Although he added some novel elements, Augustine's reflections on conjugal life reinforced the basic tendencies of the previous Christian tradition and provided a coherent theological foundation on which Western sexual ethics developed.

Bibliography

PRIMARY SOURCES

Acts of Judas Thomas, in R. A. Lipsius and M. Bonnet, eds., *Acta apostolorum apocrypha* (Leipzig, 1891–1903; reprint: Hildesheim, 1959), I, 1
Ambrosiaster. *Commentary on 1 Cor.* (CSEL 81)
Apostolic constitutions (SC 320, 329, 336)
Athenagoras. *Legatio*, ed. W. R. Schoedel (Oxford, 1972)
Augustine. *Confessiones*, ed. J. J. O'Donnell (Oxford, 1992)
　　De Genesi ad litteram (PL 34); trans. ACW 41, 42
　　On Genesis against the Manichaeans (PL 34)
　　The good of marriage (CSEL 41)
　　On holy virginity (CSEL 41)
　　Retractationes (CSEL 36)
　　Sermons (PL 38)
Basil of Caesarea. *Canons*, in P. P. Joannou, ed., *Discipline générale antique (IIe–IXe s.)*, II (Rome, 1962)
　　Letters to Bishop Amphilochius of Iconium (188, 199 and 217, in modern editions). Ed. Y. Courtonne, *Saint Basile. Lettres* (Paris, 1957, 1961, 1966); also in P. P. Ioannou, ed., *Discipline générale antique (IIe–IXe s.)*, I, 1 (Rome, 1962)
　　Regulae fusius tractatae (PG 31)
Caesarius of Arles. *Sermons* (CCSL 103, 104)

---

15 Augustine, *De Gen. ad litt.* 9.7.12; trans. ACW 42.2: 78.

Clement. *Stromateis* (SC 30, 38, 278, 279)

Codex Justinianus (CJ). Ed. P. Krüger, *Corpus iuris civilis* II (Berlin, 1929[11])

Codex Theodosianus (CTh). Eds. T. Mommsen and P. Meyer, *Theodosiani libri XVI cum Constitutionibus Sirmondianis et leges novellae ad Theodosianum pertinentes* (Berlin, 1954[2])

Council of Ancyra, in P. P. Joannou, ed., *Discipline générale antique (IIe–IXe s.)*, I, 2 (Rome, 1962)

Council of Chalcedon (ACO II.1–6)

Council of Elvira, in J. Vives, ed., *Concilios Visigóticos e Hispano-Romanos* (Barcelona, 1963)

Council of Laodicea, in P. P. Joannou, ed., *Discipline générale antique (IIe–IXe s.)*, I, 2 (Rome, 1962)

Council of Neocaesarea, in P. P. Joannou, ed., *Discipline générale antique (IIe–IXe s.)*, I, 2 (Rome, 1962)

Council in Trullo ('Quinisext' Council), in P. P. Joannou, ed., *Discipline générale antique (IIe–IXe s.)*, I, I (Rome, 1962)

Dionysius Exiguus. *Codex canonum ecclesiasticorum*. Ed. A. Strewe, *Die Canonessammlung des Dionysius Exiguus in der ersten Redaktion* (Berlin, 1931); G. Voellus and H. Justellus, *Biblioteca iuris canonice veteris* (Paris, 1661), I

Gregory the Great. *Regula pastoralis* (SC 381, 382)

Gregory of Nazianzus. *Letters*. Ed. P. Gallay, *Saint Grégoire de Nazianze. Correspondance* (Paris, 1964–7) and SC 208

 Orations (PG 35, 36)

Gregory of Nyssa. *De opificio hominis* (PG 44)

Ignatius of Antioch. *To Polycarp* (SC 10)

Irenaeus. *Aduersus haereses* (SC 100, 152, 153, 210, 211, 263, 264, 293, 294)

Jerome. *Letters* (CSEL 54, 55, 56)

John Chrysostom. *Against the opponents of the monastic life* (PG 47)

 Homilies on Ephesians (PG 62); ed. F. Field, *Ioannis Chrysostomi interpretation omnium epistularum Paulinarum* (Oxford, 1845–62), IV

 Homilies on Genesis (PG 53)

 Homilies on 1 Timothy. Ed. F. Field, *Ioannis Chrysostomi interpretation omnium epistularum Paulinarum* (Oxford, 1845–62), VI

 On vainglory and the right way to educate children (De inani gloria) (SC 188)

 De virginitate (SC 125). Trans. Sally Rieger Shore, *John Chrysostom: On virginity. Against remarriage* (New York/Toronto, 1983)

Justinian. *Institutes*. Eds. P. Krüger and T. Mommsen, *Corpus iuris civilis* I (Berlin, 1928[16])

 Novels. Eds. R. Schöll and G. Kroll, *Corpus iuris civilis* 3 (Berlin, 1928[6])

Mishnah, *Yebamoth*, in I. Epstein, ed., *The Babylonian Talmud. Seder Nashim* (London, 1936), I–II

Musonius Rufus. *Works*, ed. O. Hense (Leipzig, 1990)

Origen, *Fragments of the commentary on 1 Corinthians*. Ed. Claude Jenkins, 'Origen on I Corinthians', *JTS* 9 (1908): 231–47, 353–72, 500–14; 10 (1909): 29–51

Paulinus of Nola. *Carmina* (PL 61)

Penitential of Finnian, in L. Bieler, ed., *The Irish Penitentials* (Dublin, 1963)

Praedestinatus (PL 53)

Protevangelium of James. Ed. Michel Testuz, *Nativité de Marie: Papyrus Bodmer V* (Cologne, 1958)

Siricius. *Letters* (PL 13)

Statuta ecclesiae antiqua (CCSL 148)

Synod of North Britain (Brevi), in L. Bieler, ed., *The Irish Penitentials* (Dublin, 1963)

Tatian. *Oratio ad Graecos*, ed. M. Whittaker (Oxford, 1982)

Tertullian. *Adversus Marcionem* (SC 365, 368, 399; CCSL 2)

    De corona (CCSL 2)

    De exhortatione ad castitatem (CCSL 2)

    De idololatria (CCSL 2)

Verona sacramentary. Eds. L. C. Mohlberg, L. Eizenhöfer and P. Siffrin, *Sacramentarium Veronense* (Rome, 1978³)

SECONDARY SOURCES

Boswell, John. *Christianity, social tolerance, and homosexuality* (Chicago, 1980)

Brown, P. *The body and society* (New York, 1989)

Brundage, James A. *Law, sex, and Christian society in medieval Europe* (Chicago, 1987)

Cameron, Averil. *Christianity and the rhetoric of empire* (Berkeley, 1991)

    'Redrawing the map: Early Christian territory after Foucault', *JRS* 76 (1986): 266–71

Clark, Elizabeth A. '"Adam's only companion": Augustine and the early Christian debate on marriage', *Recherches augustiniennes* 21 (1986): 139–62

    'Foucault, the fathers, and sex', *JAAR* 56 (1988): 619–41

    'Heresy, asceticism, Adam, and Eve: Interpretations of Genesis 1–3 in the later Latin fathers', in *Ascetic piety and women's faith: Essays on late ancient Christianity* (Lewiston, 1986), 353–85

Crouzel, Henri. *Virginité et mariage selon Origène* (Paris, 1963)

Evans Grubbs, Judith. *Women and the law in the Roman empire: A sourcebook on marriage, divorce, and widowhood* (London/New York, 2002)

Foucault, M. *The history of sexuality, I: An introduction*, trans. Robert Hurley (New York, 1978)

    The history of sexuality, III: The care of the self, trans. Robert Hurley (New York, 1986)

Hunt, Emily. *Christianity in the second century: The case of Tatian* (London, 2003)

Hunter, David G. 'Augustine and the making of marriage in Roman North Africa', *JECS* 11 (2003): 63–85

    Marriage, celibacy, and heresy in ancient Christianity (Oxford, 2007)

Nathan, G. *The family in late antiquity* (London and New York, 2000)

Ritzer, K. *Le mariage dans les églises chrétiennes du Iᵉʳ au XIᵉ siècle* (Paris, 1970)

Rouselle, Aline. *Porneia: On desire and the body in antiquity*, trans. F. Pheasont (Oxford, 1988)

25

The growth of liturgy and the church year

BRYAN D. SPINKS

The fourth to the seventh centuries represent a period of considerable change as well as continuity for the Christian churches, and this was true of their worship. The Constantinian peace afforded the opportunity for new spacious church buildings, and a more public celebration of liturgy with more elaborate forms. The doctrinal battles of the fourth and fifth centuries – Arianism, Eunomianism, the Nicaeno-Constantinopolitan Trinity, and the later struggle between Cyril and Nestorius – left their marks on worship forms and texts.[1] The development of the monastic movement, with its concern for constant prayer, also influenced worship patterns. A Spanish nun named Egeria visited the Holy Land *c.* 382, and kept a travelogue for her sisters back in Spain. Of worship in Jerusalem during Lent, Egeria wrote:

> On Sundays the bishop reads the Gospel of the Lord's resurrection at first cockcrow, as he does on every Sunday throughout the year. Then till daybreak, they do everything as they would on an ordinary Sunday at the Anastasis and the Cross. In the morning they assemble (as they do every Sunday) in the Great Church called the Mysterium on Golgotha behind the Cross, and do what is usual to do on Sunday. After the dismissal in this church they go singing, as they do every Sunday, to the Anastasis, and it is after eleven o'clock by the time they have finished. Lucernare [service of lighting candles] is at the normal time when it always takes place in the Anastasis and At the Cross and in all other holy places; for on Sundays there is no service at three o'clock.[2]

Egeria reveals a well-established liturgical calendar, and she describes the various weekday services in the holy city. Some are attended by monks and nuns, the *'monazontes* and *parthenae'*; others are for the laity and clergy, too, witnessing to a vibrant worshipping community. What is more, worship was not

---

1 For example, doxologies which seem to subordinate the Son or the Spirit were replaced, references to Christ as 'your servant' become more rare; phraseology from the Christological disputes finds its way into the prayers.
2 *Egeria's Travels* 27.2–5; trans. Wilkinson, 148–9.

confined to church buildings, but was 'stational' – moving from one place to another, and in a sense, sacralising the whole city and its environs.

Egeria's account is an exceptional document, coming as it does from a woman religious on pilgrimage. On the whole, however, the surviving evidence comes from clergy, in catechetical homilies and a few collections of prayers, and thus is written from the point of view of the ordained. Furthermore, our sources are not extensive.

An attempt to conserve links with earlier worship patterns can be seen in two pseudonymous church orders – the so-called *Apostolic tradition* and the *Apostolic constitutions*.

Until recently, liturgical scholars accepted the contention of E. Schwartz and R. H. Connolly that, from a variety of Egyptian and Syrian church orders, it was possible to re-constitute a work called *Apostolic tradition*, alluded to on the plinth of a headless statue discovered during 1551 in Rome. The plinth contained names of some books that antiquity had attributed to Hippolytus, a rival Roman bishop during the early third century. This liturgical material was dated *c*. 215, and came to be regarded as typical of the church in Rome and elsewhere at that time. More recent studies show that this was a composite document, having layers of material from different periods (and possibly places) which were brought together by a dissident group in Rome, during either the late third century or, more probably, the early fourth century.[3] This community looked back to house churches when each had its own presbyter-bishop. Its liturgical material probably represents an idealised view of worship that they imagined had been used in the early third century by their presbyter-bishop, Hippolytus. Though parts of the text may well represent third-century usages of that particular community, it has been overlaid, updated, and then projected back in time. At least one reason for its composition was that it attempted to conserve, even if in idealised form, worship of an earlier era. According to this church order, the church had special prayers for the ordination of bishops, presbyters and deacons; forms for appointment of other ministries, such as readers and subdeacons; a ritual of baptism with prayers, and one for the eucharist; it also assumes times each day for communal or individual prayer.

The *Apostolic constitutions*, consisting of eight books, is dated *c*. 360–80, and was arranged in the vicinity of Antioch. The compiler seems to have had Eunomian or Eusebian Christological convictions that Jesus was subordinate to God the Father, and claimed that the work was by Clement of Rome in the

---

3 Paul F. Bradshaw et al., *The apostolic tradition*.

second century. The collector used earlier material. Since the amalgamation of sources results in contradictory usages, it is unlikely that it all represented contemporary liturgical practice.[4] In part the piece seems to show how earlier traditions vindicated the present usage, and Christology, of his community; perhaps there is also a nostalgic element. As with the editor(s) of the *Apostolic tradition*, this and other church orders (e.g., the *Testamentum Domini* in Syria) reveal compilers who looked back to what they perceived as continuity with an earlier era.

Although the liturgical rites of this period have a great deal in common, there are important regional differences.

Jerusalem and Antioch

In addition to the travelogue of Egeria, some idea of worship in Jerusalem is given in the homilies of Cyril, bishop of Jerusalem (*sed.* 349–87). We have a protocatechesis and eighteen pre-baptismal catechetical lectures by him, together with five mystagogical, or post-baptismal, homilies (these latter are sometimes attributed to his successor, John).

By the time Cyril served, the city had been re-built in splendid style by Constantine, who constructed buildings over the traditional places of Jesus' passion, death and resurrection. This meant that ceremonies could be given a dramatic celebration, linking them with their appropriate historical location. Worship thus took on a 'rememorative' dimension. Pilgrims coming to Jerusalem took news of these ceremonies back home where their communities adapted them.

Baptism was a staged rite. According to Egeria, those catechumens wishing to be baptised had to submit their names before Lent. They assembled in the Martyrium with their sponsors for examination and enrolment. Throughout Lent the candidates received exorcisms and catechesis – though the length and number of these is uncertain.[5] At the Paschal Vigil they were baptised – probably in the baths behind the Anastasis – and then brought to the Martyrium. After Easter they received further instruction. We can thus see the pattern that anthropologists explain as separation, liminality ('in between') and then aggregation (baptised as members of the church).

---

4 The *Didache* (*c.* 80) and the *Didascalia* (*c.* 230); he drew on what appears to be Greek versions of synagogue prayers; and he selected from the material found in some of the *Apostolic tradition* documents. He also authored themes himself, or borrowed from sources that have not survived outside the collection.
5 Alexis James Doval, *Cyril of Jerusalem, mystagogue.*

The baptismal rite described by Cyril included the renunciation of Satan and commitment to Christ, stripping, anointing, and baptism with a threefold dipping. In the mystagogical catechesis, Cyril stresses the image of dying and rising (Romans 6). As we shall see, this was not the typical image emphasised. After the baptism came an anointing with chrism (olive oil and balsam), which Cyril links with the giving of the Holy Spirit. Finally a white garment was put on the neophytes.

The mystagogical catechesis also gives a sketch of the eucharistic rite. The structure mentioned in c. 150 by Justin Martyr, the Christian philosopher who taught in Rome, is still discernible: readings, intercessions, homily, giving of the kiss of peace, prayer over the bread and wine, and reception of communion. Cyril mentions the washing of the hands by the priest (bishop) and presbyters, citing Psalm 26.6, and the deacon's announcement of the kiss of peace. However, he is mainly concerned to trace the contours of the eucharistic prayer said over the bread and wine. His outline has some echoes of the later eucharistic prayer named the Anaphora of St James. In Jerusalem, after the opening dialogue between celebrant and people (*sursum corda*, 'lift up your hearts'), the first thanksgiving took the form of listing the created elements – sun, moon, stars, rivers, seas, and the angelic host that hymn the Creator. He mentions the *sanctus* (hymn of adoration), the *epiklesis* or calling on the Spirit to make the bread and wine the body and blood of Christ, and intercessions for the living and then the departed. He attaches considerable significance to the petition for the Spirit, the *epiklesis*. There is no reference to the recitation of the institution narrative, though he discusses it in an earlier lecture. Some scholars think that he assumed it, and because already discussed it was not repeated. Others, noting that Cyril moves carefully from one section to another using the word *eita* (next), believe that the narrative was not yet a universal feature of eucharistic prayers. After that prayer, the Lord's Prayer was recited, and the *Hagia hagiois* – 'Holy things for holy people'. He also gives advice on how to receive the consecrated elements.

From Egeria we learn something of the daily prayers in Jerusalem. Hymns, psalms and antiphons (sung alternately between two choirs) are mentioned, as well as prayers between the hymns. At dawn there are morning hymns. At midday they again assemble for psalms and antiphons. At three there is a similar celebration, but at four, Lychnicon or Lucernare takes place, and lamps and candles are lit. In addition to psalms, hymns and antiphons, reference is made to intercessions in litany form. Jerusalem Vespers at this time probably comprised the lighting of lamps, vesperal psalms including Psalm 140, and antiphons, during which the bishop entered. Then came more hymns or antiphons, intercessions and blessing, and dismissal, followed by stations before and behind the cross, with prayers and blessings.[6]

For baptism at Antioch we have the witness of the *Apostolic constitutions* and homilies of John Chrysostom. The lectures of Theodore of Mopsuestia, who was a presbyter at Antioch, probably reflect something of Antiochian use. Instruction is given, apparently ritualised by prayer and the laying on of hands. There is a renunciation of Satan, with formula, a turning from the west to the east and the recitation of a creed, then an anointing 'for the remission of sins', and a blessing of the water with a prayer. Baptism is in the name of the Trinity, followed by an anointing with *myron* (chrism) and prayer. For these writers, the dominant theme of baptism is new birth from the womb.

The *Apostolic constitutions* describes the eucharist in several places, but the fullest, and probably most contemporary, description is in book 8. It refers to the following elements:

- Readings from the law and prophets, the epistles, Acts and the Gospels.
- Dismissal of the catechumens, energumens (demoniacs, insane and physically handicapped) and penitents from the assembly prior to the intercessions.
- Intercessions.
- The kiss of peace.
- The washing of hands, and bringing of the gifts to the altar.
- A lengthy eucharistic prayer, giving thanks for salvation history from creation through to Joshua, and then after the recitation of the *sanctus* continuing with Jesus the new Joshua. Then thanksgiving for salvation in Christ, the recitation of the institution narrative, and an *epiklesis* and intercessions.
- Instructions for the sequence of receiving communion.
- Post-communion prayers, dismissal and blessing.

Theodore of Mopsuestia gives a similar picture. His writings open with an allegorical interpretation of the rites. For example, when the deacons bring the bread and wine to the altar, they are bringing the dead body of Christ to the tomb. This trend, further developed by Dionysius the Areopagite, led to a Neoplatonic understanding of the Eastern rites, each movement and ritual signifying a heavenly counterpart. The writers inherited a ritual pattern and some fixed prayers, but they developed a tradition of interpretation of the ritual, akin to the Platonising allegory found in pagan cult practices.

6 Robert Taft, *The liturgy of the hours*, 51.

Though impossible to date precisely, the great 'classical' eucharistic prayers recited over the bread and wine apparently reached their more or less final structure and form in the fourth century. The main three in use in the Greek-speaking West Syrian areas and Palestine were St Basil, St John Chrysostom and St James. Each has its own peculiarities; it is probable that some of the recensions of St Basil were re-worked by the bishop himself. That of St James, associated with Jerusalem, has parallels with the description given by Cyril, but represents a later synthesis and consolidation. For example, it has no thanksgiving for redemption, and contains the institution narrative. All three have what is termed the 'Syro-Byzantine' structure: thanksgiving for creation, or praise of the Trinity, sanctus and benedictus, thanksgiving for redemption, institution narrative, anamnesis, epiklesis and then intercessions for living and departed.

We mainly learn something of the daily prayers of this area from the Apostolic constitutions. It describes two daily services, morning and evening, with Psalms 62 and 140 as the nucleus. It also details a Vigil for Sundays. Book 7.47 gives a version of the Gloria in excelsis and chapter 48 an evening hymn compiled from Psalm 121.1 and the Nunc dimittis (The Song of Simeon: Luke 2.29–32). Book 8.34 lists prayers in the morning, at the third, sixth and ninth hours, in the evening and at cockcrow. The primitive core of the office here was psalmody (Psalm 62 or 140), litanies, a collect, and a prayer of blessing and dismissal.[7] We have no idea who attended these services, but if Egeria's Jerusalem experience is typical, only the monks and nuns were present at all services. We also detect a difference between daily prayer with the bishop, secular clergy and devout laity (the 'cathedral' office), with an emphasis on praise and intercession; and those for the monks and nuns (the 'monastic' office), with an emphasis on the recitation of the psalter and reading scripture.

East Syria

East Syria, being on the edge of the Roman empire, and later within the Persian empire, is generally thought to preserve traditions of a more Semitic and less Hellenised nature. The Church of the East (the modern descendant) still uses the eucharistic prayer attributed to Addai and Mari (perhaps late second century), which has no institution narrative. The two early theologians of the Syrian tradition, Aphrahat and Ephrem, offer some indirect information, particularly about baptism. Aphrahat gives allusions perhaps to the renunciation of Satan at baptism, and the anointing, blessing of water and baptism. Ephrem's

7 Ibid., 46

Hymns allude to stripping off the old Adam and putting on the new Adam.[8] There are references to anointing, and baptism in the name of the Trinity. The *History of John the son of Zebedee* invokes the Trinity, makes the sign of the cross over oil, and mentions the seraphim singing *sanctus*.[9] The candidate is stripped, anointed and baptised. Afterwards a white garment is placed on the person. All three in this tradition do not include post-baptismal anointing. Thus there were different ritual patterns in various localities. This East Syrian pattern is confirmed in the *Liturgical homilies* of Narsai, a teacher in Nisibis (d. c. 502). Narsai outlines the baptismal process that included the renunciation of Satan, anointing with oil, and the baptism. The overriding theme in Narsai is baptism as new birth from the womb of the font.

The eucharist follows, and here Narsai mentions the preparation of the elements, the eucharistic prayer (Narsai spends much time discussing the importance of the *epiklesis*) and the details of the fraction. Narsai's allusions to eucharistic prayers are unclear. The East Syrian tradition came to have two more in addition to *Addai and Mari*, called after *Nestorius* and *Theodore*.[10] That of Nestorius is an expansion and Syriac adaptation of *St Basil* and *St John Chrysostom*; *Theodore* seems to have drawn on *Addai and Mari*, *Nestorius* and Theodore of Mopsuestia's catechetical homilies. Both prayers of *Nestorius* and *Theodore* contain the institution narrative and have a structure slightly different from the Syro-Byzantine pattern, placing the intercession prior to the *epiklesis*.

Little is known of daily prayer in this tradition before the early seventh century, when some elements are mentioned in the commentary of Gabriel Qatraya (c. 615). The nave of the churches was divided by a north–south barrier, with men and women separated, and a large *bema* (throne) in the middle from which most of the office was recited and sung. The form for a vigil seemingly includes the raising of the sanctuary curtain, and a clergy procession to the *bema*. Three *marmyata* (canticles inspired by the Old Testament) were sung, followed by prayers. There was also a procession to the sanctuary during a chanted *'onita Subbaha* (psalm with refrain), a *Tesbohta* (poetic doxology), litany and prayer. Lauds featured Psalms 148–50, the *Benedicite* ('Bless ye the Lord'), *Gloria in excelsis* and *Trisagion*. Vespers included Psalms 140, 141 and 118.105–12.

When the sources from Jerusalem, Antioch and East Syria are compared, the regional differences both in the ritual patterns and to a certain degree in

---

8 *Ephrem the Syrian. Hymns*, trans. McVey.
9 Texts in E. C. Whitaker and Maxwell E. Johnson, *Documents of the baptismal liturgy*, 15–22.
10 The East Syrian church refused to condemn Nestorius, and drew freely on the writings of his teacher, Theodore of Mopsuestia; texts in *The liturgy of the holy apostles Adai and Mari*.

the theological understanding – for example, whether baptism is primarily death/resurrection, or rebirth from the womb of the font – are quite clear.

Egypt

The liturgical evidence suggests that within Egypt, as in Syro-Palestine, usage differed from diocese to diocese. *Strasbourg Papyrus Gr.254* appears to preserve a eucharistic prayer which may be pre-Nicene. Like *Addai and Mari*, it has no institution narrative, but anchors the rationale of the eucharist in Malachi 1.11 ("'My name will be great among the nations, from the rising to the setting of the sun. In every place incense and pure offerings will be brought to my name, because my name will be great among the nations," says the LORD Almighty'). The main liturgy of Egypt is from Alexandria, called *St Mark*. The eucharistic prayer has a unique structure, being mainly intercessory. After an initial praise for creation the prayer mentions the sacrifice that is offered, and switches to petition, with intercessions. The intercessions provide also the context for the *sanctus* which becomes a springboard for petition for consecration, leading into the institution narrative, an *anamnesis*, an *epiklesis* and final doxology.

From the fourth century we have the so-called 'euchology' (liturgical service book) of Serapion, and the *Canons* of Hippolytus. The latter is a recension of the so-called *Apostolic tradition*, with clear adaptations to what was Egyptian usage. The former is a collection of prayers purported to have been made by Serapion, bishop of Thmuis (*sed.* 330–62), a friend of Anthony and Athanasius.[11] The collection represents the needs of a rural bishop. The prayers are blessings of oil, a burial prayer, the eucharist, baptism and ordination, though the copyist of the manuscript has muddled the sequence. The anointing prayers provide for a pre-baptismal anointing and a post-baptismal anointing, but there are also prayers after reception as a baptisand (one being baptised), and after coming up from the baptismal waters. The burial prayer, which asks for the repose and rest of the person, is one of the first liturgical witnesses we have for a burial liturgy. The prayers of the eucharist include one for the Lord's Day, and after the sermon. There are also prayers of intercession for various groups of people such as catechumens and the sick, as well as for the harvest. A eucharistic prayer has some characteristics in common with West Syrian eucharistic prayers, but also with the Egyptian tradition. Its opening thanksgiving centres on the Logos,

---

11 Bernard Botte, finding Christological subordination in some of the prayers, wanted to call the author 'pseudo-Serapion', but most scholars accept that Serapion was the compiler; see further Maxwell E. Johnson, *The prayers of Sarapion of Thmuis*.

followed by a lengthy lead in to the *sanctus*, an institution narrative with echoes from the *Didache* (counted as canonical scripture in the Egyptian church), and an *epiklesis* of the Logos rather than the Spirit. It suggests a time when Logos and Spirit were interchangeable. There are also intercessions at the end of the eucharistic prayer. Another prayer has a heading that indicates the fraction, and there is also one for the laying on of hands after the communion, and one post-communion. Provision is made for prayers to be said at the laying on of hands for the ordination of deacons, presbyters and bishops. That for a deacon includes the petition:

> Appoint also this person a deacon of your catholic Church and give to him a spirit of knowledge and discernment in order that he may be able to serve in this ministry in the midst of your holy people in purity and blamelessly, through your only-begotten Jesus Christ through whom be to you the glory and the power in holy Spirit both now and to all the ages of ages.[12]

Egypt was a great centre for monasticism. John Cassian, who lived in Scetis from 380 to 399, offers some details of monastic daily worship in his *Institutes*, even though the description was written some twenty years later in Gaul. There were two daily offices, one at cockcrow and one in the evening. Cassian mentions lessons, and the use of the *Gloria patri* at the end of the psalms.

Another monastic tradition was derived from the monk Pachomius, the Pachomian office. The regulations attributed to Horsiesos (*c.* 346) attest that the monks began by making the sign of the cross. The office probably contained scriptural passages heard seated, a sign of the cross with all standing and the Lord's Prayer, penitential prayer said prostrated, and then standing to pray in silence. It also included chanted psalmody. What we see here is the distinction between what has become called the 'cathedral' or daily service in secular churches, and the 'monastic' office, the daily services said by monks. Whereas the former consisted of selected psalms for the time of the day, intercessions and hymns, the latter centred on the reading of scripture and the recitation of large chunks of psalmody.

Eastern worship at this time had an increasing emphasis on 'awe' and holiness, and at times some actions during the eucharist were carried out behind drawn curtains, hidden from the eyes of the laity. A variety of reasons have been suggested for this: a growing division between ordained and lay; the influx of pagans into the church and concern over worthiness and impurity; imitation of imperial court ritual, with the altar becoming as guarded as the

---

12 Text in ibid.

emperor's throne. The result was that fewer from the congregation received communion.[13]

Rome and the West

Our evidence for worship in the Western churches is rather sparser than that for the East. We have the writings of Ambrose of Milan, which are comparable to the works of Cyril, John Chrysostom and Theodore in the East; we have catechetical homilies from Zeno of Verona, and Augustine for North Africa; we have the letter of Innocent I (*sed.* 402–17) to Decentius of Gubbio, and the writings of Leo I. The *Verona sacramentary* (worship service book), formerly called the *Leonine sacramentary*, preserves some liturgical materials dated from 440–560. The *Later Gelasian sacramentary* may include elements from the latter part of the seventh century. Hardly anything survives as witness to the North African tradition – even though liturgical Latin apparently had its origin there. The Gallican and Visigothic churches also had their own usage, but it is extremely difficult, if not impossible, to differentiate earlier material from that of the eighth and ninth centuries.

Ambrose wrote towards the end of the fourth century, and claimed to follow Roman custom in most, but not all, traditions. In *De sacramentis* and *De mysteriis*, he outlined and explained both the baptismal and something of the eucharistic worship in Milan.

According to him, on Saturday night the candidates for baptism assembled, and the bishop touched their ears and nostrils, ritualising the *effeta* ('bringing forth') miracle of the Gospel (Mark 7.31ff.). He explains that the nostrils are substituted for the mouth because women are present among the candidates. In the baptistery the candidates were anointed as athletes, to give them protection for the forthcoming spiritual struggle. There was a renunciation, and then the bishop exorcised the water. He then 'utters invocation and prayer that the water may be sanctified and that the eternal Trinity may dwell there'. It seems that during the blessing a wooden cross was thrown or placed in the water. Ambrose attests a threefold immersion, and a post-baptismal anointing with chrism. At Milan there was also a ceremony of foot washing, as Ambrose says, a difference from Roman practice.[14] He also mentions a 'sealing', but it

---

13 Edmund Bishop, 'Fear and awe attaching to the eucharistic elements', in R. H. Connolly, ed., *The liturgical homilies of Narsai*.
14 Ambrose, *De sacramentis* 3.4; trans. in Edward Yarnold, *The awe-inspiring rites of initiation*, 122

is unclear whether this act that he associated with the gift of the Spirit also included a laying on of hands.

Ambrose gives some information about the eucharist, in particular the eucharistic prayer. Requests for kings and other people may allude to the intercessions, the first part of the Romano-Milanese eucharistic prayer, or the canon of the mass. It has a petition for consecration, the institution narrative and some post-narrative prayers – all of which have parallels with the Roman canon of the mass. Though our first texts of the latter are seventh century, Ambrose seems to confirm that its substance was well established by the fourth century. The Milanese bishop also witnesses to daily prayer, and indicates that there the usual psalmody (118, 119; 140) was employed at morning and evening.

The letter of Innocent to Decentius was written in March 416 to the bishop of Gubbio (Umbria), and shows a pope seeking to maintain liturgical uniformity in the bishoprics under his authority. It discusses various practices different from those at the town of Gubbio. Innocent I attempts to persuade Decentius to follow the liturgical customs as observed in Rome. From this letter we learn that at Rome there were two post-baptismal anointings, the first administered by the presbyter, but a second by the bishop (who also laid hands on the candidates with prayer). In the eucharist, whereas most churches seemed to exchange the Peace immediately prior to the preparation of the eucharistic elements and the recitation of the eucharistic prayer, at Rome it came immediately before the communion. Innocent also discusses the recitation of the names of offerers at the eucharist. He describes the practice of the *fermentum* – i.e., the sending of a particle of consecrated bread from the papal mass to the titular churches in Rome, so that the particle could be added to the host. It is not clear whether this was to effect consecration at rites presided over by presbyters or to symbolise the unity of the Roman church. Innocent further mentions fasting on Saturday, penance, and the ministry to the sick.[15] As in Jerusalem, so in Rome there were stational liturgies – assembling at one church and processing through the city to the church chosen for the particular Sunday service. Not only does this letter reveal something of the liturgical ceremonies and customs of Rome; it also witnesses to the considerable local differences that persisted.

The *Verona sacramentary* is a collection of *libelli missarum* – a variety of formulae for one or more masses – prayers, preface, introduction to the *hanc igitur* ('Accept therefore this [offering]'). It does not contain the canon of the mass, though it presupposes it, or the readings of chants. Part is missing; we

---

15 Martin F. Connell, *Church and worship in fifth-century Rome.*

have only the material gathered from the middle of April until December. What it attests is a set of texts for Sundays and certain observances of martyrs and saints.

The canon of the mass – already echoing Ambrose – is first found in the older *Gelasian sacramentary*. In contrast to the Eastern prayers with their fixed texts, the Roman eucharistic prayer had a variable opening – a proper preface – according to the day or season. It led into the *sanctus* and *benedictus*. After the *sanctus* and *benedictus* are sung or recited, the prayer resumes with petition for the offerers, and clearly conceives of the eucharist as something which is being offered. This leads to the *quam oblationem* that is a petition for consecration, and then the recitation of the institution narrative. After an *anamnesis*, there follows another offering, mention of Abel and Melchizedek, and finally the naming of saints and other departed persons. It seems to reflect a theology articulated by Cyprian of Carthage (in his *ep. 63*) in the third century, and found in Ambrose: consecration is effected by petition followed by recitation of the institution narrative. The Roman canon used the language of pagan votive offerings, thus suggesting that Christ fulfilled the older religions.

Taking the various documents together, it would seem that in Rome the eucharist consisted of the following elements:

- Introit psalm.
- Greeting.
- Collect.
- Epistle.
- Psalmody.
- Gospel.
- Intercessions. These latter seem to have been a series of bidding prayers, each followed by silence, and then a collect, the latter becoming eventually a set text. This form was preserved in the Good Friday solemn prayers, but in the Sunday liturgy was later to be replaced by a litany after the Eastern pattern. Some time later this disappeared. The *kyrie eleison* ('Lord have mercy') at the beginning of the rite was once thought to be a remnant of the litany, but more recently scholars have concluded that the *kyrie eleison* was a deliberate composition placed at the beginning of the rite because it was popular and allowed congregational participation.
- The gifts of bread and wine placed on the altar with the prayer the *super oblata* or 'secret'.
- The canon of the mass.
- Lord's Prayer.

- The Peace, and, in Rome, the *fermentum* at this point in the Titula Stational churches.
- Communion.
- Brief prayer and dismissal.

Little is known about Roman daily prayers used in cathedrals. Much more is known of monastic prayers, their form derived from the 'cathedral' form, especially in the sixth-century Rule of St Benedict. Some suggest that the 'cathedral' form for Morning Prayer consisted of Psalms 50, 62 and 66, with a Gospel canticle, prayers, Lord's Prayer and collect. According to the *Rule of Benedict* 13, it consisted of Psalm 66, Psalm 50, two variable psalms, a canticle, a Bible reading, responsory (a chant usually of scripture verses), hymn, Gospel canticle, litany and Lord's Prayer. In Vespers the older cathedral form seems to have had six psalms that were later reduced to five and then four in Benedict's Rule. In the latter we find a service for the monks consisting of four psalms, a lesson, a responsory, a hymn, versicle (a short sentence, often from the Psalms, spoken or sung antiphonally), Gospel canticle, litany, Lord's Prayer and dismissal (*Rule* 17, 18).

In Spain and Gaul the baptismal rites varied, and in some places echoed Milan with a foot washing and a single post-baptismal anointing by the presbyter with laying on of hands. In other places rite and practice were rather like those of Rome. The eucharistic rite seems to have had three lections – one from the Old Testament, as well as an epistle or a reading from Acts (called 'The Apostle') and Gospel. It seems that the *Benedicite* was commonly sung between the epistle and Gospel. Prayers for the people followed, with dismissal of the catechumens. The eucharistic prayers in both Spain and Gaul are notable for the fact that apart from the *sursum corda*, *sanctus* and *benedictus*, and institution narrative they are entirely variable according to the day or feast day.

The forms of daily prayer in Spain can be gleaned from Isidore of Seville (made bishop c. 600) and the canons of various councils. The content of Vespers resembles that described by Egeria in fourth-century Jerusalem. Information for the monastic office in Gaul is provided by Cassian, and for Spain by Isidore in his *Rule for monks*, written between 590 and 600. As elsewhere, the monastic office adds scripture reading, and sometimes additional psalms.

The liturgical year

Christians assembled on the Lord's Day, which seemingly established itself quickly as the weekly worship day. In addition the *Didache* mentioned fasting on Wednesdays and Fridays. During the fourth century we see the development of particular feasts and seasons. Egeria mentions Lent, Easter, Pentecost and Epiphany, and indicates that her community in Spain was well aware of these feasts and seasons.

Lent and Holy Week

In the second century we know that Easter was observed by some communities on the Sunday nearest Nisan 14, and at least by some in Asia Minor on Nisan 14 itself, giving rise to the Quartodeciman dispute. By the third century it seems that most churches were observing it on the Sunday nearest Nisan 14, though there is evidence that some communities adopted 25 March as the date. In the fourth century we witness the further development of a pre-Easter season period of fasting, evidence of which is already found in the second century in the controversy with Victor of Rome. Perhaps a number of factors coalesced to form Lent. The Syrian tradition apparently kept two vigils on the two nights before Pascha, thus extending the 'Easter' event over three days; some see here the beginning of the Triduum – Maundy Thursday and Good Friday. Since Easter was a time for baptism, apparently a three-week period of instruction and fasting for the baptismal candidates developed near it. Evidence has been adduced for Alexandria having a forty-day fast period following on from Epiphany, commemorating the temptations in the wilderness.[16] At Jerusalem, with the building of churches on historical sites, the events there – witnessed by the countless pilgrims who wished to emulate them – commemorated the events from Palm Sunday and Maundy Thursday through to the resurrection of Easter Sunday. Egeria noted that on Palm Sunday the bishop and the people descended from the Mount of Olives, carrying palms and singing antiphons, moving down the hill to the Church of the Anastasis. These factors seem to have resulted in the season of Lent that combined fasting, instruction of catechumens and the development of the Triduum. Egeria attests to an eight-week Lent in Jerusalem, though elsewhere in the East it was seven weeks, depending on whether the Saturdays and Sundays were counted. In the West Gregory the Great moved the beginning of Lent to a Wednesday. By excluding Sundays but adding Good Friday and Holy Saturday, he preserved the number forty.

Pentecost and Ascension

The observance of Pentecost and Pascha was evidently the Christian transformation of their Jewish counterparts, both rooted in the resurrection and

16 Thomas J. Talley, *The origins of the liturgical year*.

giving of the Spirit. Pentecost was fifty days after Easter and brought the Easter season to an end. Originally Pentecost commemorated both the ascension and the giving of the Spirit, but in the fourth century Ascension became a separate feast in its own right.

Christmas and Epiphany

The earliest mention of Christmas, 25 December, is at Rome by the Chronographer of 354, itself based on a calendar going back to 336. It combines Christian and Roman civil days of note. That day is recorded as both the birth of Christ in Bethlehem, and also a Roman civil holiday as 'N(atalis) Invicti'. This relatively late attestation has suggested to some that Christmas was a post-Nicene festival, instituted in opposition and reaction to the emperor Aurelian's *dies natalis solis invicti*, the birthday of the invincible sun, established in 274. The winter solstice in the East was observed on 6 January, which was the counterpart. Others have argued that the Donatists were already celebrating Christmas, that is, it pre-dates the fourth century (perhaps being observed as early as 243), and that it was computed.[17] The annunciation was established on 25 March, in the East 6 April. Nine months forward gave 25 December and 6 January in West and East. Thus these dates may pre-date 274, and were not necessarily a counterpart to a pagan feast. However, in the fourth century East and West adopted each other's days, though with some changes. In the West, 25 December seemingly was a unitive feast – simply the nativity. In a Christmas sermon *c.* 386–8, St John Chrysostom observed that the feast was popular, and had spread because it was regarded as appropriate.[18]

In the East, 6 January apparently commemorated the nativity, the baptism of Jesus, and the miracle of water into wine, with an emphasis on the baptism. It appears that 25 December was adopted in Constantinople *c.* 380, and in Antioch by 386, but not at Jerusalem (where it was the feast of David and James) until the sixth century. The Armenian church never embraced 25 December. In Rome and Gaul, 6 January became popular only in the fourth century, but as a commemoration of the visit of the magi.

Advent

The precise origins of Advent are shrouded in mystery. The Council of Saragossa (380) prescribed that the faithful be zealous in attending church from 17 December until Epiphany, but there is no hint of treating this as a fast. Filastrius of Brescia (*c.* 385) speaks of a fast before Christmas, but as one of four

17 Ibid.
18 PG 49: 351–62.

fasts.[19] At Rome, 15–23 December seems to have been regarded as the end of the agricultural year, perhaps suggesting the theme of the end of history. In the East the themes of this season were concerned with Annunciations. The number of Sundays has also varied considerably. The only conclusion is that the season had its origins in the fourth century in pre-Christmas themes that differed from place to place.

Saints' days

Already in the second century, we have evidence from a letter of the church of Smyrna regarding the martyrdom of its bishop Polycarp that the remains of martyrs were regarded as precious relics. Commemorations were kept at the tomb of martyrs, their death day being celebrated as their heavenly birthday. At Rome the tombs associated with Peter and Paul were venerated, though their observance in the calendar cannot be attested prior to the fourth century. The claim to have relics of a founding apostle became increasingly important, and a life of sanctity and the working of miracles came to be as good as martyrdom to warrant commemoration and a place in a developing calendar. Many saints were recognised and commemorated only locally, but biblical personages such as the apostles gradually became universally commemorated. The feasts of Mary as Theotokos gained in popularity after the Council of Ephesus (431). The Koimysis or Dormition ('falling asleep') of Mary was being observed in Jerusalem by the fifth century. The faithful departed, and those known for their holiness, were regarded as eschatological beings, already with God, encouragers of the church militant here on earth. The observance of the day of their 'birth into heaven' served to underline the belief that, in all Christian worship, the voice of the temporal church joined with the heavenly choirs to sing unending praise to the glory of the triune God.

Bibliography

PRIMARY SOURCES

Ambrose. *De sacramentiis.* Ed. H. Chadwick, *St Ambrose on the sacraments* (London, 1960)
Apostolic constitutions (SC 320, 329, 336)
Benedict. *Rule* (SC 181–3)
Bradshaw, Paul F., Maxwell E. Johnson and L. Edward Phillips. *The apostolic tradition* (Minneapolis, 2002)

19 Council of Saragossa, canon 4 (ed. J. Vives, *Concilios Visigóticos e Hispano-Romanos* (Barcelona/Madrid, 1963), 17); Filastrius of Brescia, *Diversorum hereseson liber* 149.2 (CSEL 38: 120–1)

Canons of Hippolytus (TU 6⁴)
Connell, Martin F. *Church and worship in fifth-century Rome* (Cambridge, 2002)
Cyril of Jerusalem. *Catacheses* (PG 33)
Egeria's Travels (SC 296), trans. John Wilkinson (Warminster, 1999³)
Ephrem the Syrian. *Hymns*. Trans. Kathleen E. McVey, *Ephrem the Syrian. Hymns* (New York, 1989)
Innocent. *Letter 25* 'To Decentius' (PL 20: 551–61)
Jeanes, Gordon P. *The origins of the Roman rite*, 2 vols. (Bramcote, 1991; Cambridge, 1998)
John Cassian. *Institutes* (CSEL 17)
Johnson, Maxwell E. *The prayers of Sarapion of Thmuis*, OCA 249 (Rome, 1995)
The liturgy of the holy apostles Adai and Mari (London, 1893; reprint: Piscataway, NJ, 2002)
Narsai. *The liturgical homilies of Narsai*, trans. R. H. Connolly with E. Bishop (Cambridge, 1909)
Sacramentarium Leonianum, ed. F. Sauer (Graz, 1960)
Theodore of Mopsuestia. *Catechetical homilies*. Eds. Raymond Tonneau and Robert Devreesse, *Les homélies catéchétiques de Théodore de Mopsueste*, ST 145 (Vatican, 1949)
Zeno. *Invitations* (CCSL, 22)

SECONDARY SOURCES

Bradshaw, Paul F. *The search for the origins of Christian worship* (New York, 2002)
Connolly, R. H. *The so-called Egyptian church order and derived documents* (Cambridge, 1916)
Doval, Alexis James. *Cyril of Jerusalem, mystagogue* (Washington, DC, 2001)
Riley, Hugh M. *Christian initiation* (Washington, DC, 1974)
Roll, Susan K. *Towards the origins of Christmas* (Kampen, 1995)
Schwartz, Eduard. *Über die pseudoapostolischen Kirchenordnungen* (Strasbourg, 1910)
Shoemaker, Stephen. *Ancient tradition of the Virgin Mary's Dormition and Assumption* (Oxford, 2003)
Smyth, Matthieu. *La liturgie oubliée. Le prière eucharistique en Gaule antique et dans l'Occident non romain* (Paris, 2003)
Spinks, Bryan D. *The Sanctus in the eucharistic prayer* (Cambridge, 1991)
Worship: Prayers from the East (Washington, DC, 1993)
Taft, Robert F. *The liturgy of the hours in East and West: The origins of the divine office and its meaning for today* (Collegeville, MN, 1986)
Talley, Thomas J. *The origins of the liturgical year* (New York, 1986)
Vives, J., ed. *Concilios Visigóticos e Hispano-Romanos* (Madrid, 1963)
Wegman, Herman. *Christian worship in East and West* (New York, 1985)
Whitaker, E. C. and Maxwell Johnson. *Documents of the baptismal liturgy* (London, 2003³)
Wybrew, Hugh. *The Orthodox liturgy* (London, 1989)
Yarnold, Edward. *The awe-inspiring rites of initiation* (Collegeville, MN, 1994)

26

Interpreting scripture

PAUL M. BLOWERS

Well into the fourth century, the Christian biblical canon was still being finalised, as betrayed by Cyril of Jerusalem's admonition that believers were never privately to read sacred texts that were not being read publicly in the liturgy.[1] For many Christians, moreover, a fully composite Bible was late in coming. Even Augustine knew only acquired clusters of scriptural texts (Psalms, Gospels, Pauline epistles, etc.) on which to comment and preach. Churches were nevertheless confident that the sacred texts authenticating the apostolic rule of faith had already been identified and universally appropriated. Already scriptural narratives, prophecies, psalmody, doxology, confessional formulae and sapiential instruction infused the theological discourse, liturgical rituals, spiritual experience and moral conscience of churches from Mesopotamia to Britain. In an age when Christianity was transitioning from persecuted *superstitio* to imperial religion, it was also supplanting the hegemony of the Greco-Roman classics with its own 'alternative literary culture' based on the Bible.[2]

From 300 to 600, as before, virtually every function of the life of Christian communities intersected with biblical interpretation. The developing science, techniques and 'schools' of patristic exegesis in this period, the subject of abundant studies, are only part of a much bigger picture. Interpretation arose in diverse contexts and literary genres – baptismal catechesis, liturgy, scholarly commentary, preaching, apologetics, theological dialectics, conciliar decrees, martyrology, hagiography and monastic spiritual pedagogy. The hermeneutical overlap among them, however, was substantial.[3] Whether their audience was catechumens, laypersons of variable religious maturity, clergy or ascetics,

1 Cyril, *Catecheses* 4.35 (PG 33: 497–500).
2 Frances Young, *Biblical interpretation*, 49–75, 257–64; Averil Cameron, *Christianity and the rhetoric of empire*.
3 See Young, *Biblical interpretation*, 218–20.

biblical commentators of the fourth to sixth centuries looked to deepen commitment to the Christian worldview and way of life.

'Interpretation' in this period was a project at once 'contemplative', aspiring to a comprehensive vision (*theôria*) of God's revelation to and in the world, and 'performative', embodying itself in ritual actions and in moral *praxis*. The Bible was not just a treasury of 'senses' (literal, allegorical, moral, anagogical, etc.) awaiting exposition by erudite commentators. It was prophecy still being fulfilled. Beneath its textual veil lay a glorious mystery bursting the bounds of human writ, a redemptive drama that had climaxed in Jesus Christ and now had its denouement in the foreground of the church's life and mission. As Augustine suggested in a symbolic reading of the miracle at Cana, Jesus turned the 'water' in clay jars (i.e., the ages of prophecy) into a new wine 'intoxicating' for the church's consumption – a wine previously only latent in that prophetic water.[4]

Scriptural prophecy and Christian discernment

Christians in the fourth century and beyond inherited two major strategies of biblical interpretation from their pre-Constantinian forebears. One was the model of expounding the harmony of Old and New Testaments through prophetic proof-texts (*testimonia*) and the enhancements of sophisticated typological exegesis. Integrally related to it, the legacy of the Alexandrian tradition was a cultivated non-literal interpretation that grasped for moral instruction and mysterious allegorical or anagogical insights transcending the material letter (*gramma*) of scripture.

Mapping the correspondences between prophetic events or figures (*typoi*) in the Old Testament and their fulfilments or antitypes under the Christian dispensation had long served to confute Jewish and pagan criticism of the novelty of Christianity, establishing a sacred past and credible identity for the Christian movement. Eusebius of Caesarea continued this discipline in the early fourth century, interpreting numerous prophecies as 'literally' Christocentric and in various works employing typology to demonstrate the Gentile church's displacement of Judaism in the incipient Constantinian regime. Constantine himself, for Eusebius, became an antitype of Moses the liberator: like Moses raised under the regime of 'tyrants' and polytheists whom he would defeat; like Moses destroying his nemesis Maxentius in a watery deluge (the Tiber

4 Augustine, *Johannis evangelium tractatus* 9.3–6 (CCSL 36: 91–4).

river); like Moses guiding his people from persecution to new security.[5] Countering hopeful Jewish interpretations of prophecies of the Promised Land and the restoration of Jerusalem, Eusebius, though once considering these purely eschatological promises for the church (as did Origen before him and Jerome after), subsequently applied Ezekiel's vision of the New Jerusalem to the earthly city now emerging as a Christian centre under imperial patronage.[6] By contrast, contemplating the decadence of Roman culture in the West at the turn of the fifth century, Paulinus of Nola rendered the lament in Psalm 136(137), with its graphic image of the victors bashing the heads of the enemy's infants on the rocks, as a prophecy of Christianity itself as the New Jerusalem at last usurping the 'Babylon' of the old empire.[7]

These exegetes well knew that faithful interpretation of scriptural prophecy meant retaining the suspense of fulfilment or outcome (*ekbasis*). Indeed, in God's good time, the prophecies might have more than one fulfilment: in the Jews' own latter history, in the church here and now, and in the eschatological consummation. The church-in-the-world was the grand theatre in which this drama was still unfolding.

To explore a single example in detail, patristic exegetes, honouring the Psalms as prophecy, were especially intrigued by those psalms that in the Septuagint bore the title *To the end (telos), for those who will be changed*. One such is Psalm 59(60), a song of David's praise for victory over his enemies. Few are the commentators, like Theodoret of Cyrrus,[8] who saw this psalm as merely presaging events in later Jewish history. Eusebius comments that David was looking beyond his own victories to a 'change' when Israel would wither from her former glory; but he was also pointing toward the *telos* at *the end of the ages* (cf. Hebrews 9.26), the glorious transformation being inaugurated in the calling of the Gentiles.[9] According to the pseudo-Athanasian *Expositions of the Psalms*, David is speaking in Psalm 59 in the persona of Christ himself, projecting his grand conquest of the Gentiles and a time when penitent Jews will see Gentiles as kinsmen.[10] The Cappadocian bishop Basil of Caesarea echoes Eusebius' sense that the victory of the converted Gentiles would itself

---

5 Eusebius, *Life of Constantine* 1.12 (GCS 7 = *Eusebius Werke*, I: 13–14); H.E. 9.9.5–8 (GCS 9 = *Eusebius Werke*, II.2: 828–30).
6 On Eusebius' shifting interpretation, see Robert Wilken, *The land called holy*, 78–81, 93–100.
7 Paulinus of Nola, *Carmen* 9 (PL 61: 451–2).
8 Theodoret, *Comm. in Ps.* 59 (PG 80: 316–17).
9 Eusebius, *Comm. in Ps.* 59 (PG 23: 556).
10 ps.-Athanasius, *Expositiones in Ps.* 59 (PG 27: 268–9).

be the beginning of an eschatological transformation, signalled in the church's mission to bring all peoples to true piety.[11]

Basil's younger brother Gregory of Nyssa, however, moves from the ecclesiological dimension of this change to its properly moral and spiritual implications, still within an eschatological framework. The 'end' in Psalm 59 is still Christ's victory, but the domain of the struggle is the larger frontier between mutable creatures and the immutable God, the divide across which all souls must upwardly advance by imitating the biblical saints in prayer and in virtue.[12] Later, in the early seventh century, Maximus the Confessor was to describe this eschatological change in Psalm 59 as the dramatic transformation of free will among all the faithful, already breaking forth in this, *the end of the ages* (cf. 1 Corinthians 10.11).[13]

In the Latin tradition as well, Augustine, like Hilary of Poitiers before him and Cassiodorus after, interpreted psalms entitled *To the end* – including Psalm 59 – in reference precisely to Christ as *the end of the law* (*finis legis*, Romans 10.9).[14] For Augustine such psalms signalled the Saviour's solidarity with his church in its pilgrimage toward ultimate perfection.

Biblical prophecy, so understood, bridged history and eternity, with the church, as interpreting community, poised between the 'already' and the 'not yet'. Salvation history was not a 'flat' or transparent linear pattern of sacred events, it was *dimensional*, training the church forward and upward to a transformed order, the new creation. Underlying typology, like the more purely symbolic forms of allegory and anagogy, was a view of biblical revelation as a dense web of signification and evocation, its multiple senses hanging together at various levels, their connections needing patiently to be sifted according to the discernible 'plot' (*hypothesis*) and 'intention' (*skopos*) of the Bible as a whole. We are helped by the rich patristic notion of 'economy' (*oikonomia*; *dispensatio*), which envisioned the forward progress of sacred history, from creation to consummation, as shot through with the 'vertical' dynamics of divine condescension and human ascent, or as Maximus would eventually call them, the 'ages' of 'incarnation' and 'deification' defying purely chronological delimitations.[15]

---

11 Basil the Great, *Hom. super Ps.* 59 (PG 29: 460–4).
12 Gregory of Nyssa, *Inscriptiones in Ps.* 11.4 (GNO 5: 72–4).
13 Maximus the Confessor, *Expositio in Ps.* 59 (CCSG 23: 3–4).
14 Augustine, *Enarrationes in Ps.* 59 (CCSL 39: 753–65); cf. Hilary, *Tract. in Ps.* 53, 2 (CSEL 22: 136); Cassiodorus, *Exp. in Ps.* 59 (CCSL 97: 529–37).
15 Maximus, *Ad Thalassium* 22 (CCSG 22: 137–43).

Even the pre-eminent exegetes associated with the school of Antiochene hermeneutics – Diodore of Tarsus, Theodore of Mopsuestia, John Chrysostom and Theodoret of Cyrrus – all of whom disparaged unwarranted allegory and privileged the 'plain reading' (*lexis*) of scriptural texts, conceded that sacred *historia* provided the groundwork of a higher vision (*theôria*) of the economy of salvation. Allegory having been properly restricted, 'we are not hindered', writes Diodore, 'from reverently envisioning (*epitheôrein*) things and elevating the spiritual substance [of scripture] into higher anagogy'.[16]

Scripture and *mimêsis*: The formation of faith and virtue

Theôria, even *allegoria*, were nurtured on sophisticated forms of figural interpretation that fused the biblical narratives 'intertextually' with the narratives or testimonies of the church's contemporary experience.[17] Much of catechesis and preaching in the period 300–600, and not least the liturgical and sacramental rituals with which they were connected, looked to construct a common semantic 'world' or horizon inhabited at once by the biblical witnesses, the Christian faithful in the present, and most importantly Christ himself, the Logos who indwells both scripture and the church. One important goal of this interpretive enterprise was to distil patterns of imitation (*mimêsis*), to engrain models of faith and virtue in Christians as the latest *dramatis personae* in the unfolding economy of salvation.

Some interpretation isolated individual profiles of virtue or vice from the biblical narratives and straightforwardly presented them for imitation or eschewal. When Christians in Antioch panicked over Theodosius' wrath against political insurgents, John Chrysostom recommended the patience and fortitude of Job and the three young Jews who faced Nebuchadnezzar's fiery furnace.[18] Elsewhere he emboldened Christian slaves by pointing to Joseph in Egypt, who found true spiritual freedom precisely in captivity.[19] This mimetic pattern naturally pervaded moral preaching but appeared in other genres too. Ambrose of Milan's treatise *De officiis*, emulating Cicero's classic of the same title, holds up the four cardinal virtues as exemplified by biblical rather than pagan heroes – Abraham embodying prudence, Moses and Elisha justice, Job

---

16 Diodore, *Comm. in Ps.*, Prol. (CCSG 6: 7).
17 The notion of 'intertextuality' in postmodern literary theory has proved useful in assessing the dynamics of patristic exegesis; see Young, *Biblical interpretation*, II, 97–9, 103.
18 John Chrysostom, *Hom. on the Statues* 4 (PG 49: 59–68).
19 John Chrysostom, *Hom. in 1 Cor.* 19 (PG 61: 156–8).

fortitude and David temperance – and commends these to Christian clerics charged with setting their own souls in order.[20] Elsewhere, Patrick, in his autobiographical *Confession* in the fifth century, depicts his own calling and mission as a fairly direct *mimêsis* of the ministry of Paul. Like the apostle, Patrick has risen above a troubled past and received his commission directly from God. He has overcome doubters and scoffers and anticipates persecution in his ministry. He is a virtual slave to his calling. His mission is to *all* Gentiles. He experiences a vision and a voice drawing him to Ireland (cf. Acts 16.6–10). Patrick even mimics Paul's phrasing: 'I have God as my witness that I do not lie in what I tell you' (cf. Galatians 1.20).[21]

With greater intertextual complexity, the expanding hagiographical literature of late antiquity similarly looked to read the life and passion of Jesus and the biblical saints into the *vitae* of holy men and women who shared in Christ's mediation between the divine and human realms. The saint became a proxy of Christ, whose training of the body and mastery of its deeds re-enacted the condescension of divine incarnation and provided an icon for veneration and emulation. Though there are abundant examples in Syriac, Greek and Latin alike, a particularly adventurous one, rich in the interweaving of scriptural images and overtones, is Leontius of Neapolis' *Life* of the sixth-century ascetic Symeon the Holy Fool. What appears an outrageous lampooning of sanctity, Symeon's asceticism-in-reverse is actually a trenchant commentary on the scandal of the gospel embodied in the ministry of Jesus. Refusing the haven of the desert, Symeon dramatically enters the Syrian city of Emesa dragging a dead dog (a parody of Jesus' triumphal entry into Jerusalem on a donkey) and thereupon assails the cultic centre of the city by overturning tables. He performs lewd acts in public that are nonetheless intertwined with miraculous feats of exorcism, healing and benevolence. The ostensible charade disguises the saint's secret holiness and, when appropriately interpreted as an inversion, betrays the true prophetic witness of Symeon who, like Jesus, heaps scorn upon himself while casting judgment on the complacent earthly city.[22]

The more sophisticated the 'intertextual' interpretation, the richer the patterns of *mimêsis*. The church's initiatory rituals, for example, constituted an intensive saturation in biblical typology, collapsing themes and interweaving images from Old and New Testaments so as to frame the Christian's baptism as an epitome of the whole antecedent drama of sacred history. The Gospels'

---

20 Ambrose, *De officiis* 1.25.117–1.29.142; 1.36.179–1.39.204; 1.43.219–1.45.230 (ed. Davidson, 184–200, 220–36, 242–50).
21 *Saint Patrick: Confession et Lettre à Coroticus*, eds. Hanson and Blanc, SC 249: 70–132.
22 Analysis and full translation in Derek Krueger, *Symeon the Holy Fool*.

account of Christ's baptism in the Jordan was itself the hermeneutical axis, the intersection of the biblical themes of creation, incarnation, redemptive death and eschatological paradise.[23] An individual believer's baptism was to be an imitation of, and sacramental participation in, Christ's own immersion and anointment.

Such is conspicuous in the symbolically fertile liturgical and homiletical poetry of the Syriac tradition. Ephrem the Syrian links the Jordan, long identified by patristic authors with the 'cosmic waters' of creation and redemption, to the 'watery womb' of the Virgin, whence the New Adam, the one also acknowledged as eternal Son at his baptism, took the garment of the first Adam ('swaddling clothes') in order to bestow on him, not a garment of leaves but, with the cloak of sanctified water, an unprecedented garment of glory.[24] 'The nature of Adam's clay,' writes Narsai in the early fifth century, 'the Creator took and fashioned in water and heated in the Spirit; and it acquired beauty.'[25] Baptismal and incarnational images from scripture are thus intimately connected in conveying the mystery of deification. Some writers connected Jesus' baptismal descent into the Jordan with his cross, burial, and descent to the dead to rescue Adam from the abyss, thereby aligning the individual Christian's baptism with the Lord's death (Romans 6.3–4).[26] All of these were added to the well-established typologies of baptism as a saving Deluge (1 Peter 3.20–21) and a new Exodus (1 Corinthians 10.1–11).

Beyond the baptismal context, preaching in liturgical and festal settings reached out to draw the Christian faithful into the biblical drama. Gregory of Nazianzus in his *Oration 38* (*On the theophany of Christ*), after waxing eloquent on the mystery of the incarnation, invokes his hearers to assume their role in Jesus' nativity:

> Now then I pray you accept his conception [in the womb], and leap before him; if not like John from the womb, yet like David, because of the resting of the ark. Revere the enrolment on account of which you were written in heaven, and adore the birth by which you were loosed from the chains of your birth, and honour little Bethlehem, which has led you back to Paradise; and worship the manger through which you, being without sense, were fed by the Word . . .[27]

---

23 See Kilian McDonnell, *The baptism of Jesus in the Jordan*.
24 Ephrem, *Hymns on the church* 36.1, 3–6 (CSCO 198: 90–2); *Hymns on Epiphany* 12.1 (CSCO 187: 173).
25 Narsai, *Homily on the Epiphany of Our Lord* 370ff., trans. F. McLeod in T. Finn, *Early Christian baptism and the catechumenate: West and East Syria*, 182.
26 Narsai, *Homily on the Epiphany of Our Lord*, 250–69 (Finn, 179–80); Jacob of Serugh, *Memra* 7, 185–94 (Finn, 194); also Ephrem, *Hymns on Epiphany* 10.9 (CSCO 187: 167).
27 Gregory of Nazianzus, *Or.* 38.17 (PG 36: 329–32); trans. NPNF 7: 351 (modified).

Gregory's *Oration* climaxes by exhorting the audience to participate mimetically in the ministry and passion of Christ. 'Travel without fault through every stage and faculty of the life of Christ. Be purified; be circumcised ... After this teach in the Temple, and drive out the sacrilegious traders ... Taste gall for taste's sake, drink vinegar; seek for spittings; accept blows, be crowned with thorns ...'[28]

In extraordinary lyrical displays, Romanos the Melodist, the sixth-century Byzantine hymnist inspired by Ephrem and doubtless familiar with the preaching of Gregory of Nazianzus, composed *kontakia*, or sermonic hymns, that often imaginatively re-shaped the scriptural narratives in order to engage their audiences' existential response. Romanos' *kontakion On Judas*, used during Holy Week, for example, re-told the story of betrayal by addressing Christ, Judas and the creation itself in a simulated dialogue.

[To Christ] When he plotted his trickery, when he planned your
  murder –
the one who had been loved and rejected you,
called and abandoned you, crowned and insulted you,
then you, compassionate, long suffering,
wanting to show the murderer your ineffable love for mankind,
filled the basin, bowed your neck, became slave of slaves.
And Judas presented you his feet for you to wash them, Redeemer ...

[Narrator] Lifting his feet, the deceiver went brazenly to the devil,
and when he reached the murderous gang,
betraying Christ like a stranger, he fawned,
'What are you willing to give?'
he says to those willing to buy the blood of the One who lives and
  abides.

[To Creation] Listen, earth, and shudder. Sea, flee in haste, for a
  murder is being agreed. The price of the One without price is being
  discussed, and the slaughter of the Giver of life.

[To Judas] Now your insatiable greed has appeared; now your
  voracious appetite has been revealed,
you ravenous, profligate, implacable,
shameless, and gluttonous, conscienceless lover of money!
'What are you willing to give?'
you say to those willing to buy the blood of the One who lives and
  abides.

28 Gregory of Nazianzus, *Or.* 38.18 (PG 36: 332).

What fair thing did you not possess? What did you not share?
What were you ever refused?
With the things below you possessed those on high, and do you now
sell your God?[29]

The choral refrain of Romanos' *kontakion* in turn bespeaks the collective disposition of repentance warranted by the story of betrayal: *Be merciful, merciful, merciful to us, you who are patient with all, and wait for all.*

Neither allegory nor typology accurately describes Romanos' interpretive model, which enhances the dramatic effect of the scriptural narratives in the form of amplified paraphrase. He upholds the 'literal' sense provided we understand it as something more than transparent history. Rowan Williams, identifying the literal sense with the church's ongoing interaction with scripture, urges that 'Christian interpretation is unavoidably engaged in "dramatic" modes of reading: we are invited to identify ourselves in the story being contemplated, to reappropriate who we are now, and who we shall or can be, in terms of the story. *Its* movements, transactions, transformations, become *ours*; we take responsibility for this or that position within the narrative.'[30] Such ably describes Romanos' approach. For him, the story of Judas leaped from the pages of scripture to implicate the church in the betrayal of Jesus. Penitence – as an enduring ecclesial practice, not just a momentary liturgical response – would constitute the church's interpretive 'performance' of the story's anticipated effect, roused and shaped by the utter tragedy of the betrayal of the Son of God and by a healthy fear of complicity in Judas' sin.

In the monastic context, where the monks' sense of living in the last days in advance of divine judgment was profound, 'performative' interpretation thrived. The *Apophthegmata patrum* (*Sayings of the desert fathers*), recording the conferences of ascetic sages with their disciples, reflect an oral culture where scripture was primarily spoken and heard, not read, and where a strict economy of words was, like silence itself, highly valued.[31] The Bible was seen as a vast collection of hard sayings having the power to bring all of life into redemptive focus. Often its commandments, especially those of compunction and charity, were straightforward, as in the many cases where monks, likened to the rich young man querying Jesus (Matthew 19.16), asked elders to give them a 'word' of salvation. 'A brother questioned Abba Poemen saying, "What ought I to

---

29 Romanos, *Kontakion* 17 ('On Judas') 2, 14–15 (eds. Maas and Tyrpanis, 123, 127–8); trans. Lash, 115–16, 120–1.
30 R. Williams, 'The literal sense of scripture', 125.
31 See Douglas Burton-Christie, *The word in the desert*.

do?" He said, "it is written, I confess my iniquity, I am sorry for my sin" [Psalm 38.18].'[32]

Other commandments, however, especially those embedded in biblical narratives, demanded unpacking, which the sages offered not by theological explanation but by object lessons that enjoined specific actions on the monks to help them toward deeper insight into the scriptural word. In one story, a Messalian ascetic, reputed to have spurned manual labour in favour of prayer and quietude, reproaches Abba Silvanus and some industrious brothers on Mt Sinai by quoting two Gospel texts: 'Do not labour for the food which perishes' (John 6.27) and 'Mary has chosen the good portion' (Luke 10.42). The Abba instructs that the ascetic be left alone in a cell with only a book to read. When he emerges, enquiring why he has not been called to dinner, the wise Silvanus answers, 'Because you are a spiritual man and do not need that kind of food. We, being carnal, want to eat, and that is why we work. But you have chosen the *good portion* and read the whole day long and you do not want to eat carnal food.' When the ascetic begs the Abba's forgiveness, he responds, 'Mary needs Martha. It is really thanks to Martha that Mary is praised [by the Lord].'[33] The demonstration clearly served to frame the true meaning of the Mary and Martha narrative and to elicit from it not a repudiation of manual labour but the mutual relation of physical work and 'spiritual' servanthood.

Scripture as the love language of the church

A significant aspect of biblical interpretation from 300 to 600 was the continuing development of 'spiritual' exegesis, the search for the sublime, the alluring mystery behind and beyond the letter. A major part of that story, ably reconstructed by Henri de Lubac,[34] is the perpetuation of Origen's legacy East and West, the doctrine of the three- or fourfold senses of scripture, which thrived especially (though not exclusively) in monastic exegesis.[35] In addition there is the deepening exploration of scriptural language itself as a medium of God's

---

32 *Apophthegmata patrum* Poemen 153 (PG 65: 360); trans. Ward, 188.
33 *Apophthegmata patrum* Silvanus 5 (PG 65: 409); trans. Ward, 223.
34 H. de Lubac, *Medieval exegesis*.
35 Origen's hermeneutical legacy in the East was perpetuated, in part, by exegetical devotees like Eusebius, Didymus the Blind, Gregory of Nyssa and Evagrius Ponticus, and by the publication of the *Philocalia* of Origen by Basil of Caesarea and Gregory of Nazianzus. This anthology included Origen's treatise on interpretation, *On first principles*, book 4 (SC 312: 179–203). In the West, Origen's legacy was borne by prolific imitators like Hilary, Ambrose and Gregory the Great, and by the Latin translations of Origen's exegetical works by Jerome and Rufinus of Aquileia.

condescending grace. Here we will highlight the extraordinary achievements of Gregory of Nyssa, Augustine and Dionysius the Areopagite.

Gregory's analysis of scriptural language evolved in the ongoing struggle with Neo-Arianism in the fourth century. The church, he insisted, had already learned from scripture itself that no human terminology, not even scripture's own, could directly signify the divine nature but could only facilitate conceptual constructions about the mystery of the Trinity.[36] 'Apophatic' language (negations like 'ineffable', 'invisible', 'infinite') was meanwhile appropriate to honour the strict hiatus (*diastêma*) separating Creator and creation and thereby to facilitate the mystical quest. And yet Gregory also recognised that much biblical language directly flamed the soul's deep-seated desire for God. The seemingly egregious erotic language of the Song of Songs, the subject of *Homilies* late in Gregory's career, bespoke an intricate, beautiful and theologically enriching allegory of the God who eternally trains pious desire precisely by eluding it. The Song, for example, graphically imagines Christ the Bridegroom's nuptial bedding of the bride (soul) in the *darkness* of night, whereupon the bride actually finds herself alone, calling him in vain and searching the *city* for him (Song 3.1). Gregory finds here a magnificent testimony to the soul's sublime frustration precisely at the moment of her intimate union with Christ. Her true satisfaction comes in the discovery of the Bridegroom's utter transcendence, to which the whole *city* of intelligible creation adds its witness.[37] Only erotic language like this could for Gregory express the paradox at the heart of the Bible's mystical theology, the simultaneity of the soul's utter satisfaction in God and perpetual frustration to experience God more deeply. Only erotic language, as Denys Turner notes, could do justice to the dialectics of differentiation and sublime union, compulsion and freedom, which Christian mystical theologians struggled to articulate.[38]

Likewise in his *Life of Moses* Gregory often finds scripture's most anthropomorphic language the most potent in conveying divine mysteries. The work climaxes in the Sinai theophany and the ritual wherein Moses stood in a cleft in the rock while the divine glory passed by and the prophet was able to behold God's *back side* (Exodus 33.17–23). The *historia* begging for spiritual exposition, Gregory envisions Christ himself as the 'rock' on whom the virtuous one securely 'stands' and yet is paradoxically 'moved' by the God who in 'passing'

---

36 Gregory of Nyssa, *Ad Ablabium* (GNO 3.1: 42–3).
37 Gregory of Nyssa, *Hom. in Canticum* 6 (PG 44: 892–3).
38 D. Turner, *Eros and allegory*, 56–68.

graciously leads the way forward, upward, and thereby shows the desiring soul his 'back side' but never his 'face', his essence.[39]

While Gregory dwelt upon provocative individual words and images in the sacred text, his larger purpose was to identify and follow out the higher 'sequence' (*akolouthia*) of spiritual instruction and elevation that bridged history and eternity. As with the Song of Songs, assiduous interpreters were to be rapt, as it were, into that sublime sequence such that the scriptural narrative and its language became, sacramentally and vicariously, their own narrative and language of devotion.

A comparable pattern emerged in spiritual engagement with the Psalms, each of which could be a potent narrative sequence, a 'history of the soul'.[40] Athanasius extolled the rich language of the psalter as capable of virtually incarnating itself in the soul so as to illuminate or transform it in its varied conditions and passions.[41] John Cassian similarly advised monks to weave the Psalms so intimately with their own experience that they would become their virtual authors.[42] The unrivalled classic, however, is the *Confessions*, where from the very outset the psalmist's language articulates Augustine's experience of the dramatic re-making of his self through the *amor Dei*. 'Even at this very moment,' Augustine writes in a typical appropriation, 'you are delivering from this terrifying abyss the soul who seeks for you and thirsts for your delights [Psalm 41.3], whose heart tells you *I have sought your face; your face, Lord, I will seek* [Psalm 26.8].'[43]

In his *De doctrina christiana*, Augustine forced the issue by outlining in theory how all of scriptural language ultimately functions as the church's love language. Scripture is an infrastructure comprising *res* ('things'), its divinely intended substance, and the broad array of *signa* – both lucid and ambiguous 'signs' – that point to those 'things' being taught. Astute exegesis, observing Augustine's meticulous rules, can see even the most ambiguous or opaque signs as tributary to the *res*, the worthy objects of creaturely 'enjoyment' (*delectatio*) at the core of biblical revelation: the mystery of the Trinity and the subsidiary truths of the church's rule of faith. But pursuing that enjoyment through scripture, a process that Augustine compared to a journey homeward to the bosom of God's wisdom, is impossible save for those who, along the

---

39 Gregory of Nyssa, *De vita Moysis* II (GNO 7.1: 117–21).
40 See Rowan Williams, 'Augustine and the Psalms', 17.
41 See Athanasius, *Epistola ad Marcellinum in interpretationem psalmorum* (PG 27: 11–46).
42 Cassian, *Collatio* 10.11 (CSEL 13: 305).
43 Augustine, *Confessiones* 1.18.28; trans. Chadwick, 20.

hermeneutical way, are learning the love of God and of neighbour embedded throughout the scriptures.[44]

Beyond Augustine, Dionysius the Areopagite (c. 500), whose identity remains mysterious but whose literary corpus commanded attention East and West, re-located the analysis of scriptural *signa* within a panoramic vision of divine revelation in 'procession' down through the celestial and terrestrial hierarchies to uplift all creatures toward perfect unity with God and with one another. Gregory of Nyssa's apophaticism appears with new force in the Areopagite, as does the notion of divine accommodation through even the most unseemly scriptural language. Along with the lofty titles of 'Good', 'Beauty', and 'Light', Dionysius re-visits language eliciting God's love for humanity, and vice versa, in terms of desire or 'yearning' (*erôs*).[45] The result is a trenchant analysis of the mutually 'ecstatic' love of God and of creation evoked in scripture. '[God] is, as it were, beguiled by goodness, by love, and by yearning and is enticed away from his transcendent dwelling place and comes to abide within all things, and he does so by virtue of his supernatural and ecstatic capacity to remain, nevertheless, within himself.'[46] *Erôs* for the Areopagite is equivalent to *agapê* as communicating God's incarnational love and human beings' reciprocal passion for God and for unity in God. 'It is left to the divine Wisdom [in scripture] to lift them and to raise them up to a knowledge of what yearning (*erôs*) really is, after which they take no offense.'[47]

The literal sense and theological interpretation

By now it is clear that, unlike their counterparts in modern higher criticism, patristic interpreters were scarcely preoccupied with reconstructing the original meaning of biblical texts as frozen in a particular historical or cultural location. Their Bible divulged a new world, a new horizon, and even its 'literal' sense had more to do with its *divine* authorship and ultimate intention (*skopos*) for the church than with the human authors' constrained, albeit inspired, frame of reference.

The 'literal' sense, historically speaking, has hardly been monolithic. Sometimes it has denoted the allegedly transparent meaning, as with Augustine's simple non-metaphorical *signa*, scriptural words having unambiguous

---

44 Augustine, *De doctrina christiana* 1.2.2–1.40.44 (ed. Green, 12–54).
45 Dionysius, *De divinis nominibus* 4.11–12 (PTS 33: 156–8; evidencing the appropriateness of divine *erôs* in scriptural discourse, Dionysius cites Proverbs 4.6, 8 (LXX) and Wisdom 8.2.
46 Dionysius, *Div. nom.* 4.13 (PTS 33: 159), trans. Luibheid, 82.
47 Dionysius, *Div. nom.* 4.12 (PTS 33: 158), trans. Luibheid, 81.

referents. Their lucidity, Augustine notes in a crucial caveat, presupposes an accurate translation.[48] Differing versions, nevertheless, already occasionally triggered significant differences of theological interpretation. A monumental case in point is Romans 5.12, where the Old Latin seemed to suggest that death spread to humanity in the one *in whom all sinned* (*in quo omnes peccaverunt*). For Augustine and other Latin writers the words *in quo* referenced Adam and the human race's implication in his guilt, exegetically funding the doctrine of original sin.[49] Eastern Christian exegetes instead saw the Greek *eph hô* ('inasmuch as' or 'since'), implying that death spread to humanity *because* all human beings sinned for themselves – not inheriting Adam's guilt but imitating his example and incurring the same punishment.[50] This difference of 'plain meanings' of a prepositional phrase engendered a virtual exegetical schism between East and West on a decisive issue of theological anthropology.

The 'literal' sense, however, could also indicate the coherence of biblical narratives, a major concern of exegetes like Jerome and Theodoret. For Theodoret, the literal sense often appears simply as grammatical, literary or historical elucidation, yet its purpose is to ground the church's interpretations – including its 'spiritual' ones – in salvation-historical reality. Such was a decidedly different project, as Hans Frei has observed, from the modern historical-critical judgment of 'literal' meaning in terms of the credibility and accuracy of texts in relating historical facts. Narrative coherence, for early Christian interpreters, ultimately concerned the 'realism' of the whole biblical drama, according to which individual stories could be judged 'literally' true in their 'figural' relation to the larger narrative, just as what was 'literally' true *now* in the church's experience was what made sense in the light of that commanding story.[51]

More controversial by modern standards was the 'literal' sense arising from those instances where patristic interpreters understood scriptural texts to be overtly instructing the church in mysteries of the faith. In the Latin tradition, the finest specimen is Augustine's commentary *On the literal meaning of Genesis*, the last in his series of attempts to explain the creation account against errant (especially Manichaean) interpretations. The 'literal meaning' here is actually

---

48 Augustine, *De doctrina christiana* 2.11.16–2.15.22 (ed. Green, 72–82).
49 Following Ambrosiaster, *Comm. in Rom.* 5.12, cf. Augustine, *Contra duas epistulas Pelagianorum* 4.4.7 (CSEL 60: 527–8); *De nuptiis et concupiscentia* 2.42, 45 (CSEL 42: 296, 298–9); *Contra Julianum* 1.3.8; 1.7.33 (PL 44: 645, 663–4). Erasmus later identified the weakness of the Old Latin reading, and of Augustine's consequent interpretation, in his *Annotationes in Rom.* 5.12, first published in 1516.
50 E.g., John Chrysostom, *Hom. in Rom.* 10 (PG 60: 473–84); Theodoret, *Comm. in Rom.* (PG 82: 100); Cyril of Alexandria, *Comm. in Rom.* (PG 74: 784).
51 Hans Frei, *The eclipse of biblical narrative*, 1–3.

patient of a variety of approaches to the text, including typology and allegory. Since figures, metaphors and anthropomorphisms are thoroughly interwoven with straightforward historical description, sophisticated navigation is necessary to do justice to the 'thickness' of the narrative. Beginning with Genesis 1.1, Augustine suggests that *heaven* may well indicate spiritual beings in a state of perfection when they are created, and *earth* bodily matter awaiting completion and perfection.

> *The earth*, says Holy Scripture, *was invisible and formless, and darkness was over the abyss* [Genesis 1.2]. These words seem to indicate the formless state of bodily substance. Or does the second statement imply the formless state of both substances, so that bodily substance is referred to in the words, *The earth was invisible and formless*, but spiritual substance in the words, *Darkness was over the abyss?* In this interpretation we should understand 'dark abyss' as a metaphor meaning that life which is formless unless it is turned toward its creator.[52]

When the text says that *God created*, it demonstrably signifies the whole Trinity, for the Father inaugurates the work, speaking creation into being through his co-eternal Son (Logos), with the Spirit *stirring above the water*.[53] *Let there be light* (Genesis 1.3) comes not from a corporeal voice, but indicates an intelligible utterance through the Logos in which light is conceived, while the subsequent phrase *and there was light* signals the actual conversion and illumination of the formless intellectual creation in relation to the Logos, its exemplar.[54] In this manner Augustine expounds the Genesis cosmogony as a complex event embracing both the pre-temporal divine causation (*conditio*) and the spatio-temporal production and administration (*administratio*) of the world.

In the Greek tradition too, this theological-literal sense, or 'deductive' reading as Frances Young calls it,[55] dominated the Trinitarian and Christological controversies. Athanasius and Gregory of Nyssa both confuted the ostensibly naïve literalism of Arian hermeneutics by pointing to the true theological objective (*skopos*) of sensitive scriptural texts, intuited through the church's insight (*theôria*). One such text was Proverbs 8.22 – *The Lord created me the beginning of his works* – which Arians understood to be the Son of God, *qua* Wisdom, confessing that he was a created being. Athanasius and Gregory pointed to the intrinsically enigmatic nature of proverbial language and to the evidence of other scriptures declaring the Son *begotten* of the Father, in which

---

52 Augustine, *De Genesi ad litteram* 1.1.2–3 (CSEL 28¹: 4–5); trans. ACW 41: 20.
53 Ibid., 1.2.6; 1.5.10–1.7.13; cf. 3.19.29 (CSEL 28¹: 6–7; 9–11; 84–6).
54 Ibid., 1.9.15–17 (CSEL 28¹: 11–13).
55 Young, *Biblical interpretation*, 40.

case any 'plain sense' of the term *created* could apply only to the Lord's flesh in the *oikonomia* of his incarnation.[56]

The integrative character of the theological-literal sense stands out especially in Cyril of Alexandria, who, like Athanasius and the Cappadocian fathers, envisions the mystery of Christ and the Trinity as the ultimate *skopos* of all scripture. In his extensive *Commentary on John*, as elsewhere, Cyril frequently juxtaposes the 'literal' (historical) and 'spiritual' senses, but both clearly work in the same direction. Christ's miracle at the wedding in Cana (John 2.7–10) historically exhibited his power to bless human marriage and remove the curse on women associated with childbirth; spiritually it intimated the deeper mystery of Christ as the true Bridegroom and his incarnational 'marriage' to human nature.[57] In the healing of the blind man (John 9.1–41), Christ not only overturned the Jews' errant doctrines of ancestral sin (and by extension the Origenists' theory that pre-existent souls sinned and were punitively embodied), he also claimed to be the true Light, making the healing a *typos* for his calling of the Gentiles. On a deeper mystical level, moreover, this miracle, happening on the Sabbath at week's end, symbolised the advent of the Son in this, the last age. The Saviour's salve of 'clay and spittle' bespoke the grace of the incarnation, while his enjoining the blind man to bathe in the pool of Siloam signalled the grace of baptism, now afforded the once-blind Gentiles.[58] For Cyril, such complex exegesis of individual pericopae, each one a montage of the mystery of the incarnation, suited the Gospel of John, interpreted in a theologically literal way as a manifesto of Christology.

Conclusion

The Bible provided the narrative framework in which Christians of late antiquity interpreted their world, and was the 'script' by which they carried forward their own performance, or continuation, of the salvation story.[59] As noted previously, a history of early scholarly commentary on scripture simply cannot give a full account, since this interpretive performance played out in diverse contexts in which Christians enacted their faith.[60] In teaching, preaching, liturgical celebration and sacramental participation, in literary and

---

56 Cf. Athanasius, *Orationes contra Arianos* 2.44–82 (PG 26.240–321); Gregory of Nyssa, *Contra Eunomium* II (GNO 2: 10–23).

57 Cyril, *Comm. in Johannem* II (PG 73: 225–39).

58 Cyril, *Comm. in Johannem* VI (PG 73: 940–65).

59 See Frances Young, *The art of performance.*

60 For these broad contexts, see Paul M. Blowers, ed., *The Bible in Greek Christian antiquity*; Jacques Fontaine and Charles Pietri, eds., *Le monde latin antique et la Bible.*

iconographic expression, in pastoral care offered and received, in ethical and ascetical commitments made, Christians were taking up their roles in the company of the biblical saints in a collective drama steadily moving toward that culmination in which Christ would truly be *all in all* (1 Corinthians 15.28).

Liturgy, in particular, modulated Christians' appropriation of scripture. As Gérard Nauroy notes, 'Scripture itself was first experienced by the faithful of the early church through a *lectio*,' a reading framed within liturgy.[61] By the fourth century a lectionary was in place in Jerusalem and other churches were following suit, so that the liturgical reading of the Bible was co-ordinated with the developing Christian festal calendar. Theological interpretation, meanwhile, serviced worship and other Christian practices by explicating the Trinitarian and Christocentric *oikonomia* underlying the biblical narrative, an economy embracing Christians here and now as those created, baptised, redeemed and prospectively deified by the God of Abraham, Isaac and Jacob.

In the final analysis we must return to *theôria* – 'contemplation', an embracing spiritual vision of divine revelation – as the principal key to understanding scriptural interpretation in late antiquity. *Theôria* was the cultivated intuition of the church, at once shaping and shaped by exegesis, developing in constant tandem with the lived 'performance' of the scriptures. Fed by varying approaches to the biblical text yet transcending any particular one as exhaustive, and thriving on the diverse media through which scripture infused Christian faith and thought, *theôria* represented the early church's aspiration to discern the fullness of the power (*dynamis*) and purpose (*skopos*) of the ever-contemporary word of God.

Bibliography

PRIMARY SOURCES

Ambrose. *De officiis*, ed. I. Davidson (Oxford, 2002)
Apophthegmata patrum, alphabetical collection (PG 65). Trans. Benedicta Ward, *The sayings of the desert fathers* (Kalamazoo, MI, 1975)
Athanasius. *Epistola ad Marcellinum in interpretationem psalmorum* (PG 27)
    Orationes contra Arianos (PG 26)
ps.-Athanasius. *Expositiones in Ps.* (PG 27)
Augustine. *Confessiones*, ed. J. J. O'Donnell (Oxford, 1992). Trans. H. Chadwick. *Saint Augustine. Confessions* (Oxford, 1998)
    Contra duas epistulas Pelagianorum (CSEL 60)
    Contra Julianum (PL 44)

---

61 G. Nauroy, 'L'écriture dans la pastorale d'Ambroise de Milan', in Fontaine and Pietri, *Le monde latin antique et la Bible*, 382–3.

De doctrina christiana, ed. R. P. H. Green (Oxford, 1996)

Enarrationes in Pss. (CCSL 38, 39, 40)

De Genesi ad litteram (CSEL 28^1); trans. ACW 41, 42

Johannis evangelium tractatus (CCSL 36)

De nuptiis et concupiscentia (CSEL 42)

Basil the Great. *Hom. super Pss.* (PG 29)

Cassiodorus. *Exp. in Pss.* (CCSL 97, 98)

Cyril of Alexandria. *Comm. in Johannem* (PG 73)

Comm. in Rom. (PG 74)

Cyril of Jerusalem. *Catacheses* (PG 33)

Diodore. *Comm. in Ps.*, Prol. (CCSG 6)

Dionysius. *De divinis nominibus* (PTS 33). Trans. Colm Luibheid, *Pseudo-Dionysius: The complete works* (New York, 1987)

Ephrem. *Hymns on the church* (CSCO 198)

Hymns on Epiphany (CSCO 187)

Eusebius. *Comm. in Ps.* 59 (PG 23)

Historia ecclesiastica (GCS Eusebius Werke, II)

Life of Constantine (GCS Eusebius Werke, I)

Gregory of Nazianzus. *Orationes* (PG 36)

Gregory of Nyssa. *Contra Eunomium* (GNO 2)

Ad Ablabium (GNO 3.1)

Hom. in Canticum (PG 44)

Inscriptiones in Pss. (GNO 5)

De vita Moysis (GNO 7.1)

Hilary. *Tract. in Pss.* (CSEL 22)

John Cassian. *Collationes* (CSEL 13)

John Chrysostom. *Homiliae in 1 Cor.* (PG 61)

Homiliae in Rom. (PG 60)

Homilies on the Statues (PG 49)

Maximus the Confessor. *Expositio in Ps.* 59 (CCSG 23)

Ad Thalassium (CCSG 22)

Origen. *On first principles* (SC 252, 253, 268, 269, 312)

Patrick. *Confession* and *Letter to Coroticus*. Eds. R. P. C. Hanson and Cécile Blanc, *Saint Patrick: Confession et Lettre à Coroticus* (SC 249)

Paulinus of Nola. *Carmina* (PL 61)

Romanos. *Kontakia*. Eds. Paul Maas and C. A. Tyrpanis, *Sancti Romani Melodi Cantica* (Oxford, 1963); trans. Ephrem Lash, *On the life of Christ: Kontakia* (San Francisco, 1995)

Theodoret. *Comm. in Pss.* (PG 80)

Comm. in Rom. (PG 82)

SECONDARY SOURCES

Blowers, Paul M., ed. and trans. *The Bible in Greek Christian antiquity* (Notre Dame, 1997)

Brock, Sebastian. *The Bible in the Syriac tradition* (Kerala, 1988)

Burton-Christie, Douglas. *The word in the desert: Scripture and the quest for holiness in early Christian monasticism* (New York, 1993)

Cameron, Averil. *Christianity and the rhetoric of empire* (Berkeley, 1996)

Canévet, Mariette. *Grégoire de Nysse et l'herméneutique biblique* (Paris, 1983)

Daniélou, Jean. *The Bible and the liturgy* (Notre Dame, 1956)

Finn, T. *Early Christian baptism and the catechumenate: West and East Syria* (Collegeville, MN, 1992)

Fontaine, Jacques and Charles Pietri, eds. *Le monde latin antique et la Bible* (Paris, 1985)

Frei, Hans. *The eclipse of biblical narrative* (New Haven, 1974)

Guinot, Jean-Noël. *L'exégèse de Théodoret de Cyr* (Paris, 1995)

Hollerich, Michael. *Eusebius of Caesarea's Commentary on Isaiah: Christian exegesis in the age of Constantine* (Oxford, 1999)

Kannengiesser, Charles, ed. *Handbook of patristic exegesis* (Leiden, 2004)

Kerrigan, Alexander. *St. Cyril of Alexandria: Interpreter of the Old Testament* (Rome, 1952)

Krueger, Derek. *Symeon the Holy Fool: Leontius's "Life" and the late ancient city* (Berkeley, 1996)

La Bonnardière, Anne-Marie, ed. *Saint Augustin et la Bible* (Paris, 1986)

Lubac, Henri de. *Medieval exegesis: The four senses of scripture*, trans. Mark Sebanc (Edinburgh, 1998, 2000).

McDonnell, Kilian. *The baptism of Jesus in the Jordan: The Trinitarian and cosmic order of salvation* (Collegeville, MN, 1996)

Margerie, Bertrand de. *An introduction to the history of exegesis*, I: *The Greek fathers* (Petersham, MA, 1993)

An introduction to the history of exegesis, II: *The Latin fathers* (Petersham, MA, 1995)

An introduction to the history of exegesis, III: *St. Augustine* (Petersham, MA, 1993)

Pizzolato, Luigi. *La dottrina esegetica di sant' Ambrogio* (Milan, 1978)

Rondeau, Marie-Josèphe. *Les commentaires patristiques du psautier (IIIᵉ-Vᵉ siècles)* (Rome, 1982)

Simonetti, Manlio. *Biblical interpretation in the early church: An historical introduction to patristic exegesis*, trans. John Hughes (Edinburgh, 2001)

Turner, Denys. *Eros and allegory: Medieval exegesis of the Song of Songs* (Kalamazoo, MI, 1995)

Wilken, Robert L. *The land called holy: Palestine in Christian history and thought* (New Haven, 1992)

Williams, Rowan. 'Augustine and the Psalms', *Interpretation* 58 (2004): 17–27

'The literal sense of scripture', *Modern theology* 7 (1991): 121–43

Young, Frances. *The art of performance: Toward a theology of Holy Scripture* (London, 1990)

Biblical interpretation and the formation of Christian culture (Cambridge, 1997)

27

Asceticism and monasticism, I: Eastern

SAMUEL RUBENSON

The emergence of monasticism in the East, its rapid development in the fourth and fifth centuries and its establishment as a major institution in Christianity are among the most significant phenomena in the history of Christianity. Although asceticism as such has deep roots in ancient society, both in the various religious traditions of the Eastern Mediterranean and in the Greek philosophical tradition, the emergence of monasticism constitutes a strikingly rapid and radical change of social, political and religious culture. Almost totally absent in our sources up to the mid-fourth century, monasticism becomes a major concern in Christian literature by the end of the century. What was a new phenomenon in the early fourth century was by the early fifth century already a major force (as well as a major problem!) for the church. From the late fourth century onwards, issues related to monasticism are on the agenda at almost every council in the East, and monks can be seen as playing a pivotal role within all the important conflicts of the church in the East during this period.

Previous scholarly attempts to identify a single source for, and to trace a unified development of, Eastern monasticism have met with a conspicuous lack of success. In its early formation, monasticism took inspiration from a number of traditions – particularly from scripture,[1] but from other sources as well, Christian and non-Christian – and throughout the period under consideration the monastic impulse found expression in numerous varieties ranging from hermits to large-scale monasteries, from itinerant groups of preachers to recluses strictly enclosed in cells, from unwashed stylites to aristocratic households. The development of the monastic tradition was, moreover, regionally distinct, depending on geographical, social, political and religious factors. In

---

1 The account of the first Christian community in Jerusalem (Acts 4) is taken as programmatic for monastic life by many authors and may account for the spontaneous development of broadly similar forms of behaviour in different areas. See, e.g., A. Vööbus, *History of asceticism in the Syrian Orient*, I: 147; L. Verheijen, *Saint Augustine's monasticism*.

this chapter, a discussion of some general characteristic features will precede a typological description of the main varieties and a sketch of the tradition's emergence in the five major areas, Egypt, Palestine, Syria, Asia Minor and Constantinople.

Characteristics

The first question to be asked is, what is meant by monasticism? The word *monachos* as a social designation turns up for the first time in Egyptian documentary papyri during 323 AD.[2] Although absent from the Septuagint, the word occurs in other Greek translations of the Hebrew Bible for *yehidim* in Psalm 68.7, as well as in second-century texts such as the *Gospel of Thomas* and the *Dialogue of the Saviour* from the Nag Hammadi Library. The word designates a person who is single-minded, that is, someone who is celibate and devoted to a spiritual life. The first specific depictions of Christian ascetics as monks are found in Eusebius (*c.* 260–340) and Athanasius (*c.* 296–373).[3] The use of *monachos* in the papyri, where it is often combined with other more specialised terms such as *parthenos, apotaktikos, monazontos* and *anachoretes*, indicates that it gradually became the standard general term for a variety of ascetic lifestyles. The emergence and rapid spread of a more unified terminology was most probably prompted by a need in the Constantinian period for a stricter differentiation between the 'ordinary' Christian on one hand and all ascetics on the other; another index of this differentiation is the contemporary emphasis on physical separation, as we shall see. In this way, the term *monachos* first came to embrace many approaches to Christian spiritual life and then its meaning was restricted to specific accepted forms of ascetic life. This process is evident in the use of the common expression 'pseudo-monks'. Occurring regularly from the late fourth century, it shows not only that 'monk' was universally considered a positive term, but also that the term could be used even to characterise individuals who varied from the norm.

Earlier scholarly attempts to define monasticism with reference to a complete detachment from society and the creation of a *Sonderwelt* are problematic. These attempts drew heavily on later literary descriptions of early Egyptian monks (not least by Latin authors such as Jerome and Cassian, whose works will be discussed below), which are highly idealised and not well supported by the historical sources. For example, in the earliest documents, we find monks

---

2 Malcolm Choat, 'The development and the usage of terms for "monks"'.
3 On the history of the terminology see Françoise-E. Morard, 'Monachos, moine', and Choat, 'The development and usage of terms for "monk"'.

living in the cities and towns; there is also evidence for strong economic and social interaction between rural monks and the towns.[4] The great recorded variety of monastic lifestyles makes it difficult to specify formal criteria for monasticism other than a celibate life, an emphasis on ascetic practice and a strong sense of independence in relation to society – and often in relation to church institutions as well.

All the varieties of monastic life exhibit an emphasis on renunciation of traditional forms of social life (including marriage, private wealth and secular responsibilities), deprivation of bodily needs and concentration on spiritual goals. In one way or another, all of them also link this to a zeal for communion with God through Christ and interpret this communion in eschatological terms. The basic ideal is therefore freedom, that is, liberation from social as well as bodily concerns in the pursuit of a new status characterised by detachment, peace and invulnerability. These basic ascetic ideas can be found already in the earliest strata of Christian tradition as a practical expression of eschatological ideas, as well as in several of the philosophical traditions of antiquity in which they are linked to a quest for unity and simplicity in the face of diversity and disorder. In Manichaean as well as in the heterodox Jewish and Christian literature that is usually labelled Gnostic, the same ideals are combined with strongly dualistic views about the necessity of liberating the spirit from the body. The ascetic framework and the ascetic reading of the scriptures is thus not an invention of emerging monasticism; rather, it is deeply rooted and universally attested in the church from the apostolic age, as indeed in late ancient society generally.

In addition to Christian ascetic practices, early monasticism drew heavily upon the Greek philosophical tradition. Philosophy was primarily understood as the pursuit and teaching of the perfect way of life, the precondition for pure knowledge and illumination by the divine. A philosophical life was thus a life characterised not only by intellectual activity but also by detachment from social and political affairs and freedom from concern for wealth or bodily pleasure.[5] The first Christian writers to present a philosophical and theological setting for the ascetic ideals were Clement of Alexandria and Origen, who were both to have a great impact on the ideas of the earliest monastic leaders, especially in Egypt. Clement's basically Stoic understanding of ethics (with its emphasis on virtues and passions), as well as his emphasis on esoteric

---

4 The evidence for Egypt is collected in Ewa Wipszycka, 'Le monachisme égyptien et les villes', and for Syria and Asia Minor in Daniel Caner, *Wandering, begging monks*.
5 For ancient philosophy as a main influence on the development of monasticism see Pierre Hadot, *Exercises spirituels*.

knowledge or *gnosis*, is fundamental for both Anthony the Great and Evagrius. The influence of Origen, who was widely read in the early Egyptian monastic tradition, is a matter of debate among scholars, but it is clearly visible in basic cosmological ideas about man, angels and demons, as well as in the understanding of prayer, church and scripture.[6] A number of other texts coming out of the Alexandrian theological tradition, such as the 'Sentences of Sextus' or 'Teachings of Silvanus' in the Nag Hammadi corpus, have close parallels in early monastic literature. They show that we must look at the intellectual climate of early monasticism as part of a more general Greek educational and philosophical context. Even in the earliest literary sources, monks are already regarded as persons pursuing a philosophical life, and there are numerous descriptions of monks as the successors to (no less than competitors of) the philosophers. Parallels and interaction between Christian monastic literature and pagan philosophical literature are also found and many early monastic texts are based on the models used in classical rhetorical education. For example, the *Apophthegmata patrum*, or 'Sayings of the desert fathers', as well as the writings of Evagrius, have parallels in collections of aphorisms, as well as in the exercises of rhetorical education. The *Life of Anthony* is partly modelled upon a *Life of Pythagoras*,[7] and the so-called 'Paraenesis of Anthony' is a lightly Christianised Stoic tractate circulating under the name of Anthony the Great.

Although deeply formed by Greek cultural traditions, early monasticism also drew upon non-Greek religious traditions. For the emergence of Syrian monasticism, the apocalyptic and Gnostic literature of Jewish background is quite significant. Here the most important image is not the school with its teacher, but the apostle and missionary, the travelling preacher bringing the message to ever new audiences. As a monk the messenger not only preaches about the world to come, but is a living sign of it, and the monastic communities are the visible results of the preaching. The religious traditions of Egypt and Syria have also left their marks on emerging monasticism. Not only do we find in Egyptian monastic material a clear link to Egyptian wisdom traditions, but it is also likely that the emphasis upon seclusion and retreat to tombs in

---

6 For the debate see Samuel Rubenson, 'Origen in the Egyptian monastic tradition'. Origen's influence on the main theoretician of early monasticism, Evagrius of Pontus (c. 345–99), is well documented in all works on Evagrius.

7 Except for the *Life of Anthony* little has hitherto been done in the way of rhetorical studies of early Greek and Syriac monastic literature. The Latin tradition, including works of translation, is treated in Adalbert de Vogüé, *Histoire littéraire*. For the *Life of Anthony* see also the works discussed in G. J. M. Bartelink, 'Die literarische Gattung der *Vita Antonii*'.

Egyptian monasticism is related to older models for spiritual life.[8] Likewise the strong emphasis on homelessness and on a life in the wilderness in the texts from Syria probably have ancient roots. It has also been argued that the differences between Egyptian and Syriac monastic tradition are partly due to differences between an Egyptian agrarian and a Syriac mercantile tradition.[9] Although the interpretation of ascetic behaviour and the social organisation of it are new in Christian monasticism, there is no reason to think that the monks did not avail themselves of existing social models. Even so, instead of seeing this as non-Christian influence, we ought to think of it as Christian re-interpretation and transformation of older forms and ideas.

In trying to understand how these various traditions combined into a gradually cohesive and ideologically united monastic movement, we have to focus on its two basic characteristics: the absolute emphasis on permanent celibacy and the renunciation of responsibility for the preservation of secular society. Here there is a radical break with ancient traditions. The concern is now almost entirely for the individual or the community to which one belongs, rather than for the family, the city or the empire. The liberation sought is not the liberation of the soul from the body, but of the entire self from the passing world. The transformation to be achieved is not a transformation of the world, but of the entire self. The universality of this idea, the invitation to anyone to join and the promises of real and visible results had a tremendous impact in a society where unrest, poverty and social insecurity were widespread. That such a strongly individualistic ideology could sustain an enduring social institution, which has made an immense contribution to the development of the society, is by and large due to the establishment of a new social organisation, the coenobitic monastery. Although monastic life in the East never became totally identified with life in a monastery, it was the creation of monasteries that saved the radical revival movement of the fourth and early fifth centuries.

It has been suggested that, on the social level, the rise of monasticism is linked to a demand for holy men as arbitrators in late ancient society.[10] As independent persons with direct access to heavenly powers, the monks could intervene on behalf of the poor, the sick and the displaced. From an early text like the *Life of Anthony* to the biographers of later monastic saints such as the stylites on the

---

8 For Egyptian traditions see Miriam Lichtheim, *Late Egyptian wisdom in the international context* and Wolf-Peter Funk, 'Ein doppelt überliefertes Stück spätägyptischer Weisheit'.
9 A. Guillaumont, 'Le dépaysement comme forme d'ascèse', 50; R. Murray, *Symbols of the church and kingdom*, 28.
10 The discussion on the social role was initiated by the article by Peter Brown, 'The rise and function of the holy man'. A more recent addition is his 'Holy men'.

outskirts of Constantinople, we constantly see the monks interacting between rulers and citizens, as arbitrators in conflicts and as sources of consolation and inspiration in periods of distress. More problematic is the issue of the relation between monks and the ecclesiastical offices. In several of the earliest sources the monks are depicted as keeping a distance between themselves and the hierarchy. Later in the fourth century the bishops seem to have actively sought to make use of monks in various services, including ordaining them as bishops. During the fifth century, a tradition rapidly developed in the East that all bishops ought to be monks. There is, however, no evidence for any attempts to integrate all monks into the ordained ministry. Instead we find an interpretation of monastic life as a special ministry belonging to those who were not ordained (for example, in the late fifth-century writings of Dionysius the Areopagite: see his *Ecclesiastical hierarchy* 6). There is growing evidence that, in the late fourth century, there were conflicts between monks and bishops and attempts by the bishops to define proper monastic conduct. In the fifth century, we see a more active role of monastic communities in various ecclesiastical affairs, especially in the large cities, as well as attempts by different parties to enrol monks in their support. This practice is particularly pronounced in the wake of the Council of Chalcedon.

Sources for female monasticism are, unfortunately, less abundant. There seems, however, not to have been anything gender-specific about becoming or being a monk in the earliest period. The specific condition for female monks was only a reflection of the general position of women in late antiquity. Thus female ascetics were supposed to be weaker and in need of protection, and thus not suited for life in the wilderness. Female monks in the desert did in fact pretend to be men and, when their identity was revealed, were often hailed as having become male.[11] Women were on the one hand not expected to appear and to speak in public, but on the other they were famous for their role as founders, supporters and organisers of monastic communities. Hagiographical accounts of female monks, as well as their correspondence, show that they were expected to be as educated, as well-versed in the Bible and as competent in theological discourse as the men. It is striking that, from the beginning, women from the highest social classes took an active part in the emerging monastic tradition. This practice reached as high as the imperial family: fifth- and sixth-century empresses were among the most significant and politically important promoters of monasteries. The support given to various

---

11 For female monks in early Egyptian tradition see Palladius, *H.L.* 3, 6, 28, 33, 34, 41, 46, 54-7, 59-61, 63-4, 69.

monastic communities from secular and ecclesiastical authorities was very often channelled through the hands of influential women.[12]

Varieties

Debates about proper monastic conduct and necessary conditions for being regarded as a monk seem to have been part of the developments from the beginning. Various terms were used to signify particular monks, and attempts were made to define the main varieties and to set standards for proper monastic lifestyles. The best known of these were made by the Latin authors Jerome and John Cassian, who both claimed that there were three basic sorts of monks: anchorites, coenobites and a third group called by Jerome *sarabaites* and by Cassian *remnuoth*. The first two groups were easily identified with the already famous examples of Anthony and Pachomius, respectively, and the third characterised people who pretended to be monks and who were recognised by their instable life and wandering lifestyle. Since Jerome and Cassian were tremendously influential in reporting to the West on Eastern monasticism, this threefold scheme has been predominant in descriptions of monasticism and indeed continues to inform modern discussions of the history of monasticism. It is, however, evident that these categorisations are part of a broad-based polemic against contemporary monks and cannot be taken as a proper depiction of monastic varieties at that time. Jerome admits this by stating that the third group includes most of the monks of his era.[13] It is actually not possible to draw a sharp line between anchoritic and coenobitic monks; as for the monks who were on the move, some were actually living a rather strict coenobitic life, whereas others were hermits.

Ultimately, the combined efforts of secular and ecclesiastical authority succeeded in getting rid of the wandering monks, thus gradually reducing the kinds of monasticism to the two preferred groups. But there is no doubt that Jerome and Cassian's politically motivated conceptualisation fails to capture the complex richness of late ancient monasticism.

---

12 Early biographies of prominent female monks include Gregory of Nyssa's *Life of Macrina*, Jerome's *Letter to Marcella* and the *Life of Melania the Younger*. The role of rich women for the monastic establishments is well documented in the correspondence of both Jerome and John Chrysostom. The female part of early monastic tradition is analysed in Susanna Elm, 'Virgins of God'.

13 See Jerome, *Letter* 22.34 and John Cassian, *Conlationes* 18.4, whose claims are enshrined in the *Rule of St Benedict* 1. The letter by Jerome is discussed in de Vogüé, *Histoire littéraire*, I: 288–325. The entire idea of *genera monachorum* as presented by Jerome and Cassian is critically analysed in Caner, *Wandering, begging monks*, 4–18. See also Choat, 'The development and usage of terms for "monks"'.

A less biased and more comprehensive view of the landscape of early monasticism makes it clear that there were in fact many varieties of monasticism in the first centuries. It seems possible to distinguish, at least theoretically, between six different kinds of monks on the basis of how and where they lived:

- *Monks attached to a church, or a shrine*; in our early sources these are primarily either female ascetics (known as virgins and widows) who lived attached, more or less closely, to a church and had certain rights and duties in the congregation, or else ascetic teachers and preachers who sometimes travelled from one congregation to another but did not adopt a permanent itinerant lifestyle. Celibate ascetics of this kind are known from all over the early church. They are acknowledged in the church orders from the *Apostolic tradition* onwards and are mentioned in apocryphal texts as well as *Acts* of martyrs.[14] They were most probably a significant element in the Montanist movement as well as in congregations sharing the radically dualist views of Marcion or other teachers of *gnosis*, though they are also prominent in the major centres of the early church. In most texts, the urban male celibate ascetics are soon designated 'monks' under the influence of the rapid growth of monasticism outside the cities and the spread of monastic literature, whereas the female celibate ascetics continue to be called 'virgins'. In general, the urban monks and virgins attached to churches and shrines were responsible for prayer and charitable work, ideally under the supervision of the bishop.
- *Members of an ascetic household*; here, the head of the household turns the family estate into a kind of monastery. This practice is first visible in the mid-fourth century, the best-known example being the household of the widowed mother of the Cappadocian fathers Basil of Caesarea and Gregory of Nyssa.[15] There is, however, no reason to suppose that these were the first Christian households where a celibate ascetic life was a rule, at least after the birth of one or two children. These monastic households were, as far as our sources reveal, mainly established on the initiative of women, but could also include their husbands if they committed to continence. In some cases these household monasteries were made up of the family and their servants; in other cases non-relatives were invited to join, but the monastery remained the sole property of the founding family on whose wealth the establishment still depended. Due to continuous criticism and even complete rejection of

---

14 See Hippolytus, *The Apostolic tradition*, 10, 12, 30.
15 See Gregory of Nyssa, *Life of Macrina*.

any cohabitation of female and male ascetics,[16] and the increased control of monastic practice by the bishops, the monastic households disappear in the fifth century. Many of them were undoubtedly transformed into separate monasteries for men and for women and opened up to non-members of the original family and its dependants.

- *Itinerant monks without any habitation of their own*; this group corresponds to the *remnuoth* or *sarabaites*, mentioned above. Quite probably the first use of the term *monachos* in the *Gospel of Thomas* refers to ascetics of this kind and it is not impossible that Jerome is correct when stating that, outside Egypt, this kind of monk is the most common. The evidence we have for itinerant monks in the fourth and fifth centuries mainly comes from Syria and Asia Minor. In the fourth century these celibate itinerant ascetics seem to have increasingly come in conflict with the established local churches and the bishops, over the questions of who had the right to preach and who had the right to material support from the Christian community. The independence of these monks from local clergy and liturgical life and from social ties, combined with their preaching of radical asceticism, made them the target of denunciations by local councils in the fourth and fifth centuries. Despite the attempts to eliminate this form of monasticism, it survived into the seventh century.[17]
- *Recluses or hermits, physically isolated in cells within or outside a monastery*; examples are found in both urban and rural settings. In some cases there seems to be a direct relation to the tradition of itinerant preaching, where the life as recluse follows upon a life of wandering; in other cases the background seems to be more in the tradition of the perfect philosophical life. However, many of the sources on recluses, especially on female recluses, depict the life of a recluse as a life of penitence. A major theme in the description of recluses is the emphasis on the need to flee from popularity earned either by preaching or by miracles. This does not mean that the hermit does not continue to teach, as we see from the examples of John of Lycopolis in the fourth century and Varsanuphios the Elder in the sixth. The latter, like several other recluses, lived in the middle of a monastery, but refused to speak with anyone except a trusted disciple. A different type of hermit, not

---

16 Canons against cohabitation of male and female ascetics begin with the canons of Elvira (306), Ancyra (315) and Nicaea (325) and the theme is a prominent feature in fourth-century literature on asceticism; for further references and discussion, see Elm, '*Virgins of God*', 47–51.

17 The sources are gathered and discussed in Caner, *Wandering, begging monks*, 50–82 and 104–16.

hidden from sight but still untouchable, is primarily found in Syrian sources that relate the lives of monks fixed to a tree, a certain stone or a pillar. The most famous of these was the older Symeon the Stylite, who stood on his pillar on a hilltop in northern Syria for forty-seven years until his death in 458.[18] Such a monk is both immovable and out of reach, but still visible and often also to be contacted through a trusted disciple.

- *Anchorites living in cells, usually a master and one or two disciples often clustered in larger groups*; this form of monasticism is characterised by its interaction with society and the wider monastic community and by its stress on the teaching of disciples. The emergence of organised anchoretic monasticism seems to be largely an Egyptian matter, represented early in the fourth century by St Anthony and later by the desert fathers of Nitria and Scetis, among them Evagrius. With a strong emphasis on authority based in experience, on the teaching of disciples and on obedience, the anchoretic tradition gives an impression of having its roots partly in the tradition of philosophical teaching. The emphasis on the complete isolation and remoteness of the cell of the single monk, stressed in the sources, is in many cases probably a literary ideal, rather than a physical reality.

- *Coenobites, monks living in a centrally organised monastery, often enclosed by a wall*; this completely new model is first visible in the foundations by Pachomius in Egypt. The rapid growth and diffusion of this type of monastic life throughout the empire and its successful history is yet to be explained. Undoubtedly rooted both in the urban establishment of ascetic households and the anchoretic tradition of a master and his disciple, the communal monasteries create new models of ascetic life and establish new tensions in Christianity by providing strong alternative institutions within the church. In the sources for the earliest monasteries of this kind, three traits stand out as characteristic. The first is the emphasis on learning and teaching. The members of the community are not only taught the rules necessary for an organised community but also the motives behind them and the biblical support given to them, and are supposed not only to listen to exhortations, but to undertake study through reading. Second, the monasteries are organised for common work, primarily either agricultural or social, and in their relations to other sections of society they function as economic entities. Third, the

18 On Symeon there are three different *Lives*: one by Theodoret in his *Historia religiosa* 28, one by a disciple called Antonius, and an anonymous Syriac *Life*. All three are conveniently gathered in English translation with references to editions and explanatory notes in Robert Doran, *The Lives of Simeon Stylites*.

monasteries are governed by a defined leadership responsible for all relations to the authorities, civic as well as ecclesiastical.

Even with this classification scheme in place, it should be noted that not all monks were defined by these categories, that not all monks remained within a given category all their life, and that communities occasionally changed over time. Especially during the fourth and the earlier part of the fifth century, before the increase of episcopal power as an outcome of the Council of Chalcedon, the monastic scene was characterised by experiments and a high degree of mobility. It is only later that a clear tendency towards coenobitism appears, with the result that ascetics in the cities form single-sex communities and recluses as well as itinerant monks attach themselves to, or create, stable communities.

Local developments

Since there is no single origin and no unified development of monasticism, and since there were significant differences in the monastic developments between various regions of the Eastern Mediterranean due to different historical backgrounds as well as different social and political circumstances, the history of early monasticism will here be treated separately for five main regions: Egypt, Palestine, Syria, Asia Minor and Constantinople. However, this should not blind us to the great mobility within monasticism between the various regions and the rapid diffusion of ideas, models and texts. A certain bias towards Egypt is caused first by the uneven distribution of the sources, and second by the fact that the developments in Egypt to a great extent both pre-dated and (through the literary portrait of Egyptian monasticism) deeply influenced developments in the other regions.

Egypt

Earliest evidence from Egyptian papyri shows that 'monk' was a current designation for persons who were clearly engaged in business and were property owners; most probably, it denoted someone who was celibate for religious reasons. This kind of social involvement is borne out by further evidence from two larger archives for communities of monks in fourth-century Egypt, which contain letters dealing with pastoral and business matters: the archives of Paphnutius attest to a monk (addressed as a spiritual father) who was apparently a well-known representative of Bishop Athanasius' opponents, and the

Nephoros archives describe the business activities of a larger monastery.[19] In the absence of any archaeological evidence for fourth-century monasticism in Egypt, these documents are invaluable sources to complement the literary sources. They prove that Anthony, Pachomius and their successors were not the only monks in Egypt in the first half of the fourth century, and that the early monastic tradition was both literate and socially integrated in the economic and cultural environment. The latter fact is also substantiated by the report of Epiphanius about a certain monk, Hieracas, who was writing in the 320s and by the literary papyri from monastic libraries of the fourth century.[20]

The first monk about whom we have more extensive knowledge is Anthony the Great. His international reputation was secured through the biography written by Athanasius soon after his death in AD 356, which appeared in two Latin versions shortly thereafter. The Latin version, as is well known, figures prominently in the eighth book of Augustine's *Confessions*, thus indicating the tremendous impact the *Life* had within thirty years of its initial appearance. Yet it is clear from other sources that it was not the biography that made Anthony famous, but rather that the bishop wrote his version of Anthony's life both to claim Anthony for the church and to promote his own view of monastic ideals. In addition to the *Vita*, our main sources for information about Anthony are his letters, the *Apophthegmata patrum* and the references to him in several other early monastic texts. However, these other sources are silent regarding many biographical details and it is only the *Vita* that tells us that he was born to wealthy parents in 251, that at the age of eighteen he gave up all his belongings after their death, and that he then lived as a recluse for more than twenty years. Similarly, the *Vita* is our only source for the history of his withdrawal into the interior desert and his visit to Alexandria to strengthen the martyrs under Licinius. A reference to him in the index to the festal letters of Athanasius makes it clear that he was a well-known monastic figure in 337, and a passage in the *Life of Pachomius* shows him to be an old man revered as a pioneer for monasticism at the death of Pachomius in AD 346. His letters, which seem to be a kind of testament of his teaching, most probably appeared around 340. His death in 356 is attested by Jerome. The letters show that Anthony was a teacher acquainted with contemporary Alexandrian traditions represented

---

19 Editions by H. I. Bell, *Jews and Christians in Egypt*; B. Kramer and J. C. Shelton, *Das Archiv des Nephoros*.
20 For a broad discussion of these matters see Samuel Rubenson, *The letters of St. Antony*, 116–25.

by Clement and Origen, and the subsequent tradition in Egypt and Palestine makes it clear that his influence was far-reaching.[21]

At the time of Anthony's death, monasticism in Lower Egypt – especially in the area known as Nitria and Scetis (the modern Wadi 'n-Natrûn) – experienced an immense growth and the circulation of the *Life of Anthony* drew the attention of the wider Christian tradition to the Egyptian desert.[22] In the last quarter of the century, a kind of 'ascetic tourism' developed with numerous visitors from abroad coming to see, admire and emulate the fathers of the desert, some even staying in Egypt for years. Among these were prominent Christian intellectuals like Rufinus, Melania the Elder, Jerome, Evagrius of Pontus, Palladius, John Cassian and the anonymous author of the *History of the monks in Egypt*. Through their writings and their own establishments the forms of life and the teachings of the monks had a deep impact throughout the Christian empire during the first decades of the fifth century. Of particular importance is Evagrius, who had served under Gregory of Nazianzus in Cappadocia and Constantinople and after a short stay in Jerusalem settled in Nitria. He was condemned in the sixth century on account of some esoteric speculations, but his ascetic writings have remained basic for Eastern monasticism to this very day. The most important and widely diffused source for the transmission of the ideals of the early Egyptian tradition, the *Apophthegmata patrum*, was collected and edited anonymously in Palestine in the second half of the fifth century and later enlarged, re-organised and re-edited in all the languages of early Christianity.[23]

The first-known monk to have organised and supervised larger monastic communities was Pachomius, who in the 320s established a series of monasteries for both men and women that were linked to each other at Tabennesi in Upper Egypt. Under his leadership and that of his successors, a series of rules developed which through translations came to influence the entire monastic tradition. Sharing many of the basic ascetic ideals and their biblical and theological foundations with Lower Egyptian monasticism, the Pachomian tradition is marked by a much stronger emphasis on communal responsibilities and

---

21 The various sources on Anthony are discussed in ibid., 163–84.

22 Rufinus gives the figure 3,000 for the monks in the area of Nitria, outside Alexandria, in 373 (*H.E.* 2.3), and fifteen years later Palladius counted 5,000 monks (*H.L.* 7.2); of course, these figures need not be taken as precise demographic calculations to appreciate the point: the desert had become a city.

23 The first to record sayings of the desert fathers in writing was Evagrius in the 390s, but there is no evidence for larger collections before the mid-fifth century. For a Palestinian original redaction see L. Regnault, *Les pères du désert*, 65–83 and the discussion and references in Graham Gould, *The desert fathers on monastic community*, 9–17.

on establishing a new alternative society in opposition to the surrounding pagan culture. While the ascetic goal (that is, purity of heart and seeing God) remained the same, the monks were also expected to help each other and work for the common good of the monastery.[24] The Pachomian monasteries, as well as other similar institutions, rapidly became important economic enterprises and no doubt contributed to the growth of a Coptic literate society and thus to the rapid decline of the Greek tradition, which was identified as pagan. The most famous monastery coming out of this tradition was the White Monastery near Sohag. Under the leadership of Shenoute (c. 360–466), it became the most significant centre for monasticism in Upper Egypt.[25] Shenoute was himself a prolific writer in Coptic and, judging from the preserved Coptic papyri, his monastery became a centre for Coptic literature and learning. Shenoute is primarily known for his rules and the strict organisation of monastic life in his establishments as well as his attacks on pagan tradition and heretics.[26]

In addition to these well-known early centres of Egyptian monasticism, evidence from the papyri and from several accounts given by visitors and historians indicates that there were numerous other monasteries with thousands of monks already in the fourth century. Many of these are likely to have belonged to the Melitian party, condemned by the Council of Nicaea, and others, no doubt, held theological opinions not acceptable to the church. Not only the Nag Hammadi codices, but also other apocryphal writings, were read and presumably copied in monastic circles, and there is ample evidence for debate and uneasiness about differences in belief.[27] Although there is no clear evidence for non-Christian monasteries, it is likely that there were centres for both Manichaeism and non-Christian Gnosticism that were similar to the early monastic centres.[28] Indeed, it is possible that some of the persons called monks in our texts were not only heterodox in belief but were perhaps even non-Christians.

---

24 On Pachomius, see Philip Rousseau, *Pachomius*. The primary material about Pachomius and his monasteries is available in English translation: Armand Veilleux, trans., *The Pachomian Koinonia*.
25 On the early career of Shenoute, see now Stephen Emmel, 'Shenoute the monk'.
26 For Shenoute and the White Monastery, see Rebecca Krawiec, *Shenoute and the women of the White Monastery*; Stephen Emmel, *Shenoute's literary corpus*; Johannes Hahn, *Gewalt und religiöser Konflikt*, 223–69.
27 The relationship between the Nag Hammadi Codices and Pachomian monasticism has created a long-standing debate. For a summary and new reflections, see James Goehring, 'The provenance of the Nag Hammadi Codices once more'.
28 On Manichaeism in Egypt see G. Stroumsa, 'The Manichaean challenge to Egyptian Christianity'.

During the fourth century there seems to have been increasing tensions between parts of the monastic tradition and the ecclesiastical leadership in Alexandria. Bishop Athanasius (*sed.* 328–73) struggled to promote not only an ascetic tradition within the Church of Alexandria but also to connect the various forms of monastic experiments in Egypt to the orthodox tradition and to the Alexandrian patriarchate.[29] He inaugurated a policy of ordaining leading monastic figures as bishops, which, although successful in the long run, was strongly resisted by many of the monks who regarded the bishop's office as in itself incompatible with a true monastic life. There are also signs of a growing conflict between a more powerful established church and monastic groups. In the last decade of the fourth century the tension erupted into a violent conflict, originating with monastic critique of Theophilus, the bishop of Alexandria (*sed.* 385–412), but manifested in a clash over the legacy of Origen as part of the so-called 'First Origenist Controversy'.[30] The result was that, in 399, the intellectual leaders of Lower Egyptian monasticism were expelled from Egypt on the accusation of being Origenists. One of these monks, Evagrius of Pontus, whose writings afford us a privileged glimpse into the appropriation of Origen by these monks, had died a few months before.

During the fifth century, a rapid decrease in the anchoretic tradition in Egypt was caused by series of nomadic attacks on the often wealthy monastic establishments (especially on the unprotected communities in the deserts near Alexandria) and by the tightening of ecclesiastical control. In response to the nomads, monks gathered in larger monasteries with protecting walls and, in response to the patriarch, they began cultivating good relations with civic and ecclesiastical authorities. Close relations between the patriarchate of Alexandria and the monasteries was strengthened by the establishment of important monasteries near the city, which directly contributed to the almost universal monastic support for the patriarchs in the Christological conflicts and the strong monastic opposition to the Council of Chalcedon in 451. (A direct link between the ascetic ideals of the Egyptian monastic tradition and the rejection of any 'two natures' formula in Christology has also been suggested).[31] During the persecutions of the non-Chalcedonians in Egypt in the sixth and especially the early seventh centuries, the monasteries became the centres of the Coptic church and its refusal to accept the policy of the emperors. According to the Coptic sources the monasteries became the refuge of

---

29 See David Brakke, *Athanasius and the politics of asceticism.*
30 See Elizabeth Clark, *The Origenist Controversy*, with references to previous literature. Still useful is H. G. Evelyn-White, *The monasteries of the Wâdi 'n Natrûn*, II: 125–44.
31 See Jan-Eric Steppa, *John Rufus.*

the non-Chalcedonian patriarchs in time of persecution, especially under the turbulent years of the emperor Heraclius (*regn.* 610–41). The Muslim conquest of Egypt in 641 confirmed the monastic imprint on the entire Church of Egypt.

Palestine

Due to the very special ecclesiastical position of Palestine after the building activities of Helena and Constantine and the rapid growth of pilgrimage to the holy sites in the fourth century, monastic developments followed very different lines here than in Egypt. From its beginnings, monasticism in Palestine was international and multicultural. Pilgrims from all over the Christian world settled in and around the holy places and established monasteries functioning as hostels and houses of prayer adjacent to the churches. These were naturally dependent on the support of wealthy families and the ecclesiastical hierarchy. Also the strong desert tradition, especially of Judaea, was largely controlled by the hierarchy and dependent on imperial support.[32] Due to the various backgrounds of the monks there were linguistic barriers and soon Latins, Syrians, Armenians and Georgians established their own monasteries with prayers in their own languages. Monastic leaders were thus often foreigners and the monasteries by and large did not have much relation to each other. The major exceptions were the monasteries founded by or closely related to John Saba (439–532),[33] the greatest figure in early Palestinian monasticism.

No documentary or archaeological evidence has yet appeared that can convincingly demonstrate any monastic settlements or institutions before the middle of the fourth century. The tradition that Chariton was the first monk in Palestine and settled in the Judaean desert before the time of Constantine depends solely on the hagiographical account of his life written in the sixth century.[34] His name is, however, preserved in the place names of some of the earliest monastic sites in Judaea (e.g., Wadi Khureitun, Khirbet Khureitun and Mu'allak Khureitun) and this fact tends to corroborate the view that he was a historical figure who lived a monastic life in the desert in the middle of that century.[35] The sources are also meagre for Hilarion, who is claimed by Jerome to have been the first monk in Palestine, establishing himself near Gaza around 310; we are mainly dependent on Jerome's story of his life written in the

---

32 On monasticism in Palestine see Derwas Chitty, *The desert a city* and John Binns, *Ascetics and ambassadors of Christ.*
33 See Joseph Patrich, *Sabas, Leader of Palestinian monasticism.*
34 See *Life of Chariton,* ed. Garitte. For a survey of archaeological evidence on the monastic settlement of this region, see O. Sion, 'The monasteries of the "Desert of the Jordan"'.
35 For references to the *Life of Chariton* and the sites, see Chitty, *The desert a city,* 14–15.

380s – a story which in fact appears to have been written in order to show that monasticism in Palestine emerged simultaneously with the Egyptian tradition and that Hilarion was an associate of Anthony.[36] It is only with the famous heresiologist Epiphanius, who according to Jerome had been a close associate of Hilarion, and who must have been a monk of some repute in 367 when he was elected bishop of Salamis on Cyprus, that we encounter a Palestinian monk about whom we have several independent sources, and from whom we also have writings.

The first mention of monks to be found in Palestine are the monks of Jerusalem referred to in the catecheses of Cyril of Jerusalem, a text dated to the 350s.[37] It is also in Jerusalem that the first monasteries we have any details about are found. These are the Latin establishments of Innocent the Italian and Melania the Elder, later joined by Rufinus, which were erected in Jerusalem in the 370s. Soon numerous other monasteries were also found in and around Jerusalem, and in the 380s Jerome settled in Bethlehem where he was joined by a group of ascetic women from Rome. In the early fifth century, further Latin establishments (among others) grew up in Jerusalem, primarily catering to pilgrims. These monasteries were naturally closely related to the bishops – later, patriarchs – of Jerusalem, and thus also to imperial ecclesiastical policy. Recent research on the development of liturgical life in Jerusalem indicates that these monastic establishments played a significant role, especially in the development of the canonical hours.[38]

Although the first steps towards monastic life in Palestine were probably taken by ascetic Christians settling in the desert independently of events in Egypt, and in spite of the fact that many of the leading figures came from Rome or Asia Minor, there is no doubt that the emergence of monasticism in Palestine was deeply influenced by the Egyptian tradition. Several of the prominent pioneers had either visited Egypt or referred to the stories about the Egyptian scene that quickly spread in the last decades of the fourth century. But the main vehicle for Egyptian influence was most probably the influx of monks from Egypt in the first half of the fifth century. Already in 399/400, a large group of monks from Nitria and Scetis came to Palestine as the result of the so-called Origenist crisis. Later others emigrated due to the attacks on the monastic settlements by the nomads of the desert. Some settled in Sinai, but

---

36 See Jerome, *Life of Hilarion*. For critical comments on the historicity of the text see Rubenson, *The letters of St. Antony*, 176–7.

37 Cyril of Jerusalem, *Catecheses* 4.24, 13.33.

38 See Stig Fröyshov, 'L'horloge "georgien" du Sinaiticus Ibericus 34'; the publication of Dr Fröyshov's thesis is forthcoming.

others went to the plains around Gaza, the Judaean desert, or the Jordan valley. The tradition they brought with them, codified in the stories and sayings of the *Apophthegmata patrum*, made a strong impact and several of the monks from Egypt became leading figures in Palestine, like Abba Isaiah and Abba Zeno, who were to have a prominent role in the growth of the important monastic establishments in the Gaza region.[39]

In the Judaean desert, monasticism grew rapidly in the first decades of the fifth century. A major figure was Euthymius, a young monk from Armenia, who settled as a hermit in the desert close to Jerusalem in 404. Soon other monks (among them, Theoctistus) joined him and groups of cells soon became more or less coenobitic monasteries. Here a tradition emerged, which was later followed by John Saba,[40] according to which young novices were first schooled into monasticism in strictly coenobitic houses and later allowed to move to the semi-anchoritic monasteries, which were called *laura* in Palestine. The origin of the word is unknown, but it probably signifies a lane or kind of market, since it is used of clusters of cells along a ridge centred on a common church. Here contact with other monks was less frequent than in the coenobium during the daily routine of individual life. The proximity to the holy places and the international character of these desert establishments resulted in very lively communications and strong bonds to the ecclesiastical and political centres in Palestine and abroad. This can be seen not least in the deep involvement of several monks in the conflicts around the Councils of Ephesus in 431 and 449 and Chalcedon in 451.

For monasticism in Palestine, the Council of Chalcedon in 451 was a watershed. The rich Egyptian connections (especially in the region of Gaza), as well as opposition to developments in theology and cult, which were regarded as threats to the original and pure tradition, resulted in a vigorous hostility to the very idea of a council, supported by imperial force, deposing the patriarch of Alexandria and introducing new rules and new definitions of faith. The patriarch of Jerusalem, Juvenalis, who had promised to defend the tradition, was seen as a traitor and prevented from returning to his see. Instead a monk named Theodosius was elected as new patriarch. When imperial power was restored a year later the monasteries in and around Jerusalem gradually decided to accept Chalcedon and Juvenalis. A significant role was played in this by the empress Eudokia, the estranged wife of Theodosius II, who had settled in a tower in the wilderness east of Jerusalem in the 440s. But monasteries further away and in

---

39 See Samuel Rubenson, 'The Egyptian relations of early Palestinian monasticism'.
40 Cyril of Scythopolis, *Life of Sabas* 7.

the plains remained anti-Chalcedonian. Threatened by imperial force, several leading monastic figures among the anti-Chalcedonians fled to Egypt. After the conflicts over Chalcedon, the close relation between the patriarchate and the monastic leaders in and around Jerusalem evolved into a system whereby one or more heads of monasteries were appointed in charge of all monastic communities with the title 'archimandrite'.[41]

Due to increasing imperial interest in Palestine as well as a steadily growing flow of pilgrims, the monasteries in Palestine and especially in the Judaean desert were flourishing in the sixth century. An important centre was established in 483 in the desert east of Bethlehem by John Saba, who like many of the prominent Palestinian monks came from Asia Minor. His *laura* soon attracted numerous educated monks from various backgrounds. Conflicts about leadership and theology led to a schism, and the establishment of the New *Laura*, which became a centre for the defence of the Evagrian-Origenist tradition.[42] Several factors combined to produce enmity towards Sabas and his leadership, part of them probably referring to his lack of education, others to the strictness of his rule, to his monastic organisation and perhaps also to financial matters. Sabas, however, gained and retained the support of the patriarch and later the emperor. As part of the Second Origenist Controversy he, like his 'Origenist' adversaries, travelled to Constantinople. After the death of Sabas in 532, the 'Origenists' gained in influence, but the decisions of the council in Constantinople in 543 and the ecumenical council of 553 settled the issue. It seems that the close contacts between the monasteries and the patriarchate of Jerusalem, as well as the importance of Jerusalem to the imperial family, made it impossible for any opposition to retain control of Palestinian monasteries.

Syria

Although many of our early sources indicate an Egyptian background for Syrian monastic tradition, there is no doubt that the origins of monasticism in Syria are independent of developments in Egypt. The earliest references to independent Christian ascetics point to a tradition of itinerant preachers claiming a kind of apostolic authority.[43] A first description of communities

---

41 See Binns, *Ascetics and ambassadors of Christ* and Steppa, *John Rufus*.
42 See especially Cyril of Scythopolis, *Life of Cyriacus*; but note, too, the prudent call for caution with regard to the use of Cyril's work sounded by D. Hombergen in his *The Second Origenist Controversy*.
43 The most important sources that combine itinerant preaching and ascetic life in Syria are *The Acts of Thomas*, probably written in the first half of the third century, and the two letters to the virgins, attributed to Clement of Rome but most probably written in Syria in the third century.

of ascetics is found in the early fourth-century Syriac writer Aphrahat. The ascetics are here called *bnay qyama*, a term which most probably refers to some kind of vow or covenant. The *bnay qyama* lived in ascetic and celibate households in the towns, in some cases men and women together, something Aphrahat disliked. Another Syriac term that is used to describe monks, *ihidaya* (meaning 'only-begotten', but also 'single-minded'), indicates that the monk was in some sense identified with Christ the 'Only-Begotten'. Like the use of the expression *bnay qyama*, this term points to a Jewish background. This background is also visible in the references to monks in the writings of Ephrem the Syrian.[44]

Although both Aphrahat and Ephrem indicate that there were settled monastic communities in Syria in the mid-fourth century, it is evident that the more common form of monastic life in Syria in the fourth century was the itinerant monk, with or without a group of followers. These itinerant monks are known mostly from hostile sources, especially the denouncement of some of them as heretics. They are often referred to as Messalians or Euchites, meaning those who pray constantly, and under this name condemned by councils in Syria and Asia Minor in the 390s, in Constantinople in 426 and in the Ecumenical Council of Ephesus in 431.[45] Their spiritual tradition is represented by the so-called Macarian homilies, which were probably written in Syria in the later fourth century. There are several indications that, in the early fifth century, some with their followers went from Syria through Asia Minor to Constantinople. In addition to being accused of doctrinal error, they are often denounced as lazy beggars and accused of both immoral behaviour and neglect of sacraments and church order. An important community of this background was the so-called *akoimetoi*, that is, the 'Sleepless Ones', a group founded by a certain Alexander. According to his biographer, he was a well-educated scribe in Constantinople who had renounced his possessions and become a monk in a Mesopotamian monastery during the 370s.[46] He soon left the monastery and lived as an itinerant preacher with a large following of ever-praying disciples who begged for their livelihood. They were active mainly in the countryside, but were sometimes also found in cities, including Antioch. In the 420s

---

44 See Caner, *Wandering, begging monks*, 55–7; Sidney Griffith, 'Asceticism in the Church of Syria'; Philippe Escolan, *Monachisme et église*; Sebastian Brock, *The luminous eye*, 131–41.
45 For recent studies on the 'Messalians' see Columba Stewart, *"Working the earth of the heart"*; Klaus Fitschen, *Messalianismus und Antimessalianismus*; Marcus Plested, *The Macarian legacy*.
46 *Life of Alexander the Sleepless* (PO 6); see further J. Pargoire, 'Un mot sur les acémètes'.

Alexander settled in Constantinople; in due course, we will need to say more about the monastery that he established there.

These forms of Syrian monasticism often attracted condemnations, which had an impact on the literary evidence: even in the *Life of Alexander the Sleepless* one detects an unmistakable defensiveness. But not all contemporary writings on early Syriac monks reflect these controversies. For example, Theodoret of Cyrrhus (*c.* 393–*c.* 460), whose *History of the monks of Syria* provides the first detailed description of Syrian monasticism, is much more positive in his account of the early monks. According to him, the first monks were James of Nisibis, who lived as an ascetic hermit before he became bishop of the town before 325, and Julian Saba, who founded a community in the 320s. From his writings, it appears that the earliest tradition is to be found in Osroene and Mesopotamia, and that it was only towards the end of the fourth century that numerous monastic establishments began to appear around Antioch, Apamea and Beroe as well. But Theodoret's account focuses on the radical practices of hermits in northeastern Syria, and should not be taken as a trustworthy image of the entire monastic tradition in Syria.

The most famous monk depicted by Theodoret was Symeon the Elder, the first stylite.[47] As a young man, Symeon became a monk at the monastery of Teleda in 403. But he was forced to leave the monastery after some ten years, on account of his severe ascetic practice. He established himself as an open-air solitary on a small hill. To manifest his persistence and immovable standing in prayer, he attached himself to a rock and later stood on a pillar. The height of his pillar was gradually increased until it reached approximately eighteen metres. Symeon's standing on a pillar attracted people not only from northern Syria but from all over the empire – even in his own lifetime, small statues of him were found in Rome! This does not mean, however, that Symeon lacked critics. Several sources reveal that his lifestyle was called into question. These criticisms were so significant that Theodoret devoted a section of his description to defending Symeon's actions. (It should be noted that Theodoret was writing while Symeon was still alive.) The emphasis here on the role of Symeon as a missionary to the pagans of the area and especially to the nomads is important. It places Symeon in the tradition of the apostolic preacher, albeit now not an itinerant ascetic, but someone who instead attracts the world to himself. The sources on Symeon also reveal a probably widespread tension in

47 Hans Lietzmann, *Das Leben des heiligen Symeon Stylites*, is still the only major analysis of the various *Lives* of Symeon. Also useful is Hartmut Gustav Blersch, *Die Säule im Weltgeviert*. For a more recent contribution, see Susan Ashbrook Harvey, 'The Stylite's liturgy'.

Syrian monasticism between the celebrated solitary ascetics and the communities. Several other sources also show a strong emphasis on the individual and describe the role of the monastery as largely consisting in being a preparatory arena and a source of support for the most celebrated ascetics.

In Syria (as in Palestine), the monastic tradition generally sided with the opposition against the Council of Chalcedon in 451; further east, monks were already aligning themselves against the Council of Ephesus in 431. Even taking into consideration the theological issues involved, it is clear that the monks were largely concerned to express dissatisfaction with the close collaboration between the bishops, who were often well-educated men from the wealthy classes, and government officials. The Syrian monks described in our sources were usually at home in the rural areas or among the poorer strata of society. Those who were settled in monasteries or as hermits at the outskirts of the towns were deeply attached to the local population and acted on their behalf in the time of crisis. Our best source for monasticism in Syria after 451 is the account by John of Ephesus (c. 507–86).[48] By his time, the coenobitic tradition seems to have overshadowed the earlier forms of monastic life. The monasteries were well-developed and autonomous centres. Within them, both ecclesiastical leaders and recluses found their place and support. The monasteries functioned as both schools and hospitals and a refuge in time of crisis – an important consideration for inhabitants of eastern Syria, which was after all border country between the Roman and the Persian empires during a period often at daggers drawn. Although persecuted by the authorities for their opposition to the Council of Chalcedon, the monasteries remained strongholds in the conflicts with the Persians.

Asia Minor

The rise of monasticism in Asia Minor is linked to Eustathius of Sebaste, an ascetic leader who became bishop of Sebaste in the 360s. By that time, he was already a famous figure and highly regarded as a monastic pioneer in Constantinople as well as in Caesarea.[49] The canons of the synod of Gangra, most probably held in 340, give us a glimpse of the practices and views of his followers.[50] In addition to wearing special clothes, not cutting their hair and allowing male and female ascetics to live together, there is a radicalisation of

48 See Susan Ashbrook Harvey, *Asceticism and society in crisis*.
49 Sozomen, *H.E.* 4.27, 4.20.
50 Our source for Gangra is the *epistula synodica*, which is found in P.-P. Joannou, ed. *Discipline générale antique*. For the date, see J. Gribomont, 'Saint Basile et le monachisme enthousiaste', 126. T. D. Barnes, 'The date of the Council of Gangra', argues for 355.

the gospel by way of condemning marriage, wealth and manual work, and there is also a certain contempt for the clergy of the church. Even though care is needed in making use of the condemnations from Gangra, it is not implausible that they are a substantially accurate description of contemporary monastic practices; after all, its description is broadly corroborated by evidence from Syrian sources about the radical itinerant celibate ascetics who were later repeatedly rejected as Messalians. But there is no need to posit Syrian influence to explain the phenomenon. After all, Asia Minor had since the second and third centuries been home to such groups as the Montanists and other radical Christians; the synod at Gangra could well have been responding to an occurrence that had simply arisen locally. When Eustathius became a bishop, his more radical followers refused to settle in the city and serve the poor; instead, according to Epiphanius, they continued their itinerant open-air monastic life.[51] References to begging as well as itinerant monks in Asia Minor are subsequently found in numerous other sources, although only occasionally equated with Messalians.[52] Even if designating Eustathius' followers as Messalians is questionable, the simple fact that the monks constantly moved no doubt facilitated the exchange of ideas and literature between groups and individuals in Syria, Asia Minor and Constantinople.

More settled forms of monastic life are first attested in the description of the turning of the household of Emmelia, the mother of Basil and Gregory, into a monastery after the death of her husband, around 345.[53] According to Gregory, Macrina (325–80), the oldest sister, who had decided for a celibate ascetic life already in her youth, was instrumental in the change and was the real head of the monastery even before Emmelia's death. The monastery was located on the family estate and included both a section for men and a section for women. The monks were family members as well as servants and former slaves. Situated in a rural area, the life of the monastery was divided between manual work, including agriculture and hunting, and prayer. The monastery of Macrina stands out as the first ascetic household turned monastery that we know of, as well as the first independent female institution of its kind. To what extent there were other similar family monastic estates in Asia Minor then and later we do not know.

A major impulse for settled monastic life in Asia Minor came from the activities of Basil of Caesarea. When returning from his studies in Athens in 351, Basil, under the influence of Eustathius, decided to live a celibate ascetic

---

51 Epiphanius, *Panarion*, 75.2.3 and 75.3.2.
52 Caner, *Wandering, begging monks*, 104–77, 158–205.
53 Gregory of Nyssa, *Life of Macrina*; for an analysis see Elm, *'Virgins of God'*, 78–105.

life and made attempts to settle as an anchorite in the countryside near the monastery of Macrina.[54] His ideal was closer to the philosophical tradition of a solitary life in accordance with nature and devoted to contemplation. For unknown reasons, Basil gave up his life in the country and settled in the city, where he was soon ordained presbyter and later bishop. In Caesarea, Basil established a monastery under his supervision, and most importantly wrote down guidelines for the monastic life, subsequently known, rather imprecisely, as his monastic 'rules'.[55] The monastery was to serve the poor and the sick. The most significant difference was that it should be under strict control of the bishop and that obedience was made a fundamental rule. Due to the influence of Basil and the spread of his writings, this new type of urban monastery came to have a great influence in the following centuries.

One of our best sources for urban monasticism in Asia Minor is, however, the writings of Nilus of Ancyra.[56] Unfortunately we know very little about him, his biography having been conflated with another Nilus, a monk of Sinai. He is not mentioned by any contemporary source. Another problem is that, after Evagrius was condemned, some of Evagrius' writings circulated under Nilus' name. His first writing seems to be a letter dated 390, written at a time when he was already a monastic leader, and his last text must have been written c. 430.[57] Palladius reports that, in Nilus' time, Ancyra had at least 2,000 virgins as well as a number of patrons willing to support virgins and monks alike.[58] In Nilus' writings, we find a vivid depiction and forceful condemnation of unsettled and uneducated monks menacing urban residents, begging for food in exchange for prayer and hymns, as well as of more wealthy citizens fleeing their social duties and trying to survive as monastic farmers on their country estates, but compromising themselves in the markets. According to Nilus, monasticism is incompatible with the necessity of begging no less than with manual work in order to subsist. His ideal is the silent monastery of contemplation where regular manual work is for the control of passions, rather than for subsistence. The proper economic basis should thus be either the wealth of the founder or the patronage of affluent benefactors. Monks are to stay in their monastery and be properly educated in monastic philosophy and monastic virtues, not

---

54 For the monastic experiences and experiments of Basil see Philip Rousseau, *Basil of Caesarea*, 61–82, 136–44, 190–232.
55 See now A. Silvas, *The Asketikon of St Basil the Great*.
56 There is no major study of Nilus. For an analysis of his writings, see Karl Heussi, *Untersuchungen zu Nilus dedem Asketen* and Marie-Gabrielle Guérard, 'Nil d'Ancyre'.
57 In 1668, Allatius published over a thousand letters attributed to Nilus; his collection is reprinted in PG 79: 81–581.
58 Palladius, *H.L.* 66–7.

walk around trying to please benefactors by sweet preaching, beautiful prayers or useless blessings. Nilus' letters reveal a strong emphasis on education and spiritual guidance.[59]

Constantinople

The beginnings of monasticism in Constantinople are linked to one of the earliest bishops of the city, Macedonius, and to his deacon Marathonius. The latter is said to have been encouraged by Eustathius of Sebaste. According to Sozomen, he founded not only urban monasteries, but also hospitals and poorhouses served by the monks, thus initiating a close link between monastic life and care for the poor and sick in the capital.[60] The monastic houses in Constantinople seem to have been primarily located in the outskirts and often attached to important shrines where relics of martyrs or saints were protected and honoured by the monks. In the fifth century, there seems to have been an almost endless row of shrines and monastic settlements in the suburbs of Constantinople leading off along the Bosporus. These monastic houses and their welfare programmes were financed by the patronage of rich officials and families, including the emperor himself. This is made clear in the history of the first famous monk of Constantinople, Isaac, who arrived in the city in the 370s to combat Arianism and who, after the rise of Theodosius, became the central figure of Constantinopolitan monasticism until his death around 416.[61] In this period, monastic presence in Constantinople grew rapidly as the capital had great appeal for anyone who was in search of better income, a larger audience or a higher reputation. Attempts by the emperors to ban monks from the city proved futile and eventually had to be retracted. Thus the emperor Theodosius I in 392 cancelled a law promulgated only two years earlier ordering all monks to stay in deserted places.[62] These bans were impractical because the monks had made themselves indispensable for civic administration by becoming providers of welfare for a growing poor and potentially disruptive layer of society (not to mention serving as spiritual advisers in times of crisis). The growth of monasticism, its imperial and aristocratic patronage and its service to the people made the city's monastic leaders (archimandrites) into

---

59 On the problem of the letters attributed to Nilus, see Averil Cameron, 'The authenticity of the letters of St. Nilus of Ancyra'.

60 Sozomen, *H.E.* 4.27.4.

61 For early monasticism in Constantinople see Caner, *Wandering, begging monks*, 191–9 and Gilbert Dagron, 'Les moines et la ville'.

62 *CTh* 16.3.1; see Caner, *Wandering, begging monks*, 199 for further references.

alternative centres of power competing with the bishops, something that John Chrysostom, Nestorius and Flavian all had to experience.

This competition for power, both in relation to the imperial family and other prominent patrons and in relation to the public at large, was no doubt an essential factor behind the four major conflicts between the bishops of Constantinople and monastic groups in the city in the period 400–51. A second unmistakable factor was the city's attraction for vagabonds and beggars, many of whom pretended to be monks – at least according to the official sources. Conflicts over interpretation of the gospel and its commands probably constituted a third factor, for the preaching of a radical exactitude (*akribeia*) among some monks was considered extremely dangerous to the church and its position in society. In the first conflict during the period, John Chrysostom's attempts to get control over the life of the monks of the city greatly contributed to his fall, in which the extremely powerful archimandrite Isaac took a leading role. In this, Isaac was joined by his imperial patrons, large sections of the public whose patron he was, and Theophilus the bishop of Alexandria, who provided ecclesiastical backing.[63]

The second clash came with the decision to expel from the city Alexander the Sleepless, whose earlier careers in Syria we have already described. In the early 420s, he had settled in an abandoned temple in the centre of the city. There he attracted monks both from outside the capital and from other monastic groups in the city. In his candid preaching, Alexander criticised all who did not live according to apostolic standards. His banishment from Constantinople in the mid 420s came as a joint action of the urban magistrates and the bishops.[64] Given that a council in Constantinople in 426 condemned Messalians, it is possible (though not self-evident) that he was denounced explicitly as a Messalian. But, as we have already seen, the relationship between Alexander's *akoimetoi* monks and the Euchites is unclear.

A third clash came in 428 when the archimandrites of the city turned against the new bishop, Nestorius. From his arrival in the city, Nestorius (himself a Syrian monk) set out to reform the church. He was especially keen to confine the monks to their monasteries, accusing them of unseemly behaviour in the streets and secret visits to the houses of the rich, and their abbots of not taking care of their flocks.[65] Nestorius' support for an academic Antiochene

---

63 Our main source is Palladius, *Dialogue on the life of St John Chrysostom*.
64 On this conflict see Caner, *Wandering, begging monks*, 126–57.
65 The main sources for Nestorius' dealings with the monks are his own *Liber Heraclides* and the later 'Nestorian' *History* of Barhadbeshabba; see Cane, *Wandering, begging monks*, 212–23.

theological rejection of traditional piety – especially in regard to its under-standing of Jesus Christ as God born by Mary – made his position even more difficult. Finally the emperor had to give in to the combined forces of the monks of the city and the bishop of Alexandria, supported by Rome. A final clash between Eutyches, a venerated old archimandrite, and Bishop Flavian (as well as his successor) in 450–1 finally led to a formal solution of the struggle for power by the promulgation of the fourth canon at the Council of Chalcedon. At that council, the new emperor decided to back the demand of the bishops to put all monks and monastic houses under their authority, with the explicit demand on the bishops to provide for their needs.

These conflicts between the bishops and the monks should not, however, give the impression that monasticism in Constantinople was very different from other places or less orthodox. Instead, they indicate the much more difficult position the bishop had in a city where there were many other sources of power and patronage, especially if he did not belong to the city itself (as, for example, John Chrysostom and Nestorius did not).

Conclusions

In spite of the great differences between the various regions, due to social, political and ecclesiastical factors, there are some common features in the early development of monasticism in the East. First, there is a clear tendency towards communal life and coenobitic structures. The reasons for this are both internal and external. Internally, there was a need for an educational setting and common support. The *Sayings of the desert fathers* as well as the writings of Evagrius clearly describe the need for training (and the dangers of total solitude); they also emphasise the necessity of routines, which pre-supposes an overarching scheme of organisation to co-ordinate the lives of individual monks. Externally, there was the danger of violent attacks on scat-tered and isolated monastic houses, but there was also considerable pressure from bishops and secular authorities for monks to remain settled and orderly. By denouncing unwanted monastic groups as heretics and by legislating about ecclesiastical control, itinerant monastic groups were forced either to settle down or to accept exile. In various ways the ascetic groups in the cities, as well as the ascetic households, were transformed into monasteries. The ideas of total solitude as well as homelessness were given a coenobitic context, as in the examples of recluses inside monasteries and rules stressing total renunciation of ancestry and family. In monastic communities, the spiritual direction of the disciple by his master or the answers of the solitary monks to those seeking advice were gathered and transmitted in growing collections of spiritual wisdom. In spite of the Pachomian rules' detailed character, the regulations by Shenoute and the different sets of rules by Basil, Eastern monasticism never became governed by rules in the way Western monasticism did, nor indeed did it become characterised by orders. Instead these collections, varying from one monastery to another, and including stories about the founders of the monastic communities, became decisive for the formation of the monks.

Second, the impact the monastic tradition made on society at large is clearly visible in imperial as well as ecclesiastical legislation. Beginning in the 370s, several imperial edicts attempt to circumscribe the monastic movement. Some edicts are directed against monks who are accused of serving rich people in order to lay hold of their fortunes,[66] others are directed against those who have left their homes and civil duties (in these cases, some of the people concerned are likely to have belonged to or joined the emerging monastic tradition).[67] Again, other edicts explicitly forbid monks from entering into and staying in the cities.[68] Monastic involvement in imperial affairs is, however, already visible in the conflicts between Constantine and Athanasius and in the various synods during the Arian Controversy. At the end of the fourth century Patriarch Theophilus of Alexandria enlisted imperial force to expel a large section of the leading monks in Egypt when they were becoming too powerful, and in the fifth and sixth centuries clashes between groups of monks and imperial force were numerous, as seen especially in the context of imperial persecution of non-Chalcedonians. Although overshadowed by the Christological conflict, a major issue at the Council of Chalcedon was the authority of the bishops over all monastic institutions.[69] On the other hand, imperial and aristocratic funding was an essential part of the success of many monastic establishments, not only in Palestine, but also in Constantinople, Asia Minor and Syria, where monasteries were part of the fortification of the border of the empire. In the sixth century, the funding of monasteries (such as St Catherine and Mar Saba by Justinian and Syrian monasteries by Theodora) contributed not only to the wealth of the monasteries but also to the preservation of early monastic literature and the development of monastic liturgical tradition.

---

66 *CTh* 16.2.20 (issued 370).
67 *CJ* 11.51.1 (issued 386) and *CJ* 11.52.1 (issued 393), both on *stabilitas loci*, *CTh* 14.18.1 (issued 382) and 14.14.1 (issued 397), both against beggars.
68 *CTh* 16.3.1 (issued 390).
69 Canons 4, 8, 23 and 24 all deal with problems concerning monks who act on their own. The most important decision is in canon 4, according to which no monastery might be established without the consent of the local bishop.

The impact of the monastic tradition on the life and theology of the Eastern church in these centuries can hardly be overestimated. Beginning already in the mid-fourth century monks were increasingly drawn into church administration and ordained bishops or made responsible for various affairs of the dioceses. Within fifty years, the episcopacy was well on its way to becoming the exclusive preserve of monks and, after 400, the majority of Eastern Christian authors, and almost all theologians, were monks. Early Greek monastic literature was quickly translated either from Coptic or Syriac into Greek or from Greek into Syriac, Coptic and Latin and added to ever growing collections. With the development of an elaborate structure for the prayer life of the monastic communities, the influence of monastic prayer upon the liturgical life of the cathedrals grew, and in places like Jerusalem the monks were more or less responsible for the entire liturgical life. Pilgrims who came to Egypt, Palestine and Syria did not only come to see holy places, but perhaps primarily to see the famous monks and their monastic communities. The strong emphasis on hospitality and care for the poor and sick resulted in making the monasteries of the fifth and sixth centuries into centres visited by all levels of society.

At a deeper level, the theological developments in the East also betray a strong impact of the monastic tradition. There are good reasons to view even the Christological interpretations of Cyril of Alexandria against a monastic background (especially in view of their emphasis on transformation), and the subsequent development of a neo-Cyrillian or neo-Chalcedonian theology is clearly rooted in monastic tradition. Furthermore, the theological views of the *Corpus Dionysiacum* and their immediate success in the early sixth century is to be understood against the backdrop of a monastic culture and a monastic theological tradition. Both Maximus the Confessor and John of Damascus were not only monks, but were deeply indebted to monastic theology and early monastic authors such as Evagrius of Pontus and the anonymous author of the Macarian homilies.

Bibliography

PRIMARY SOURCES

Barhadbeshabba. *History* (PO 9, 23)
Benedict. *Rule* (SC 181–6)
Codex Justinianus (CJ). Ed. P. Krüger, *Corpus iuris civilis* 2 (Berlin, 1929[11])
Codex Theodosianus 16 *(CTh)* (SC 497)
Cyril of Jerusalem. *Catecheses* (PG 33)
Cyril of Scythopolis. *Life of Cyriacus* (TU 49.2)
    Life of Sabas (TU 49.2)

Dionysius the Areopagite. *Ecclesiastical hierarchy* (PTS 36)

Epiphanius. *Panarion* (GCS: *Ancoratus und Panarion*)

Gregory of Nyssa. *Life of Macrina* (SC 178)

Hippolytus. *The apostolic tradition*. Eds. Gregory Dix, OSB and Henry Chadwick, *The Treatise on the apostolic tradition of St Hippolytus of Rome, bishop and martyr* (London, 1992)

Jerome. *Letters* (CSEL 54, 55, 56)

    Life of Hilarion. Ed. A Bastiaensen, *Vita di Martino. Vita di Ilarione. In memoria di Paola* (Milan, 1983²)

Joannou, P.-P., ed. *Discipline générale antique (IVᵉ–IXᵉ s.)*, I.ii: *Les canons des synodes particuliers* (Rome, 1962)

John Cassian. *Conlationes* (CSEL 13)

Life of Alexander the Sleepless (PO 6)

Life of Chariton. Ed. G. Garitte, 'La vie prémétaphrastique de S. Chariton', *Bulletin de l'Institut historique belge de Rome* 21 (1941) 16–46

Life of Melania the Younger. Latin: ed. P. Laurence, *Gérontius. La vie latine de saint Mélanie* (Jerusalem, 2002); Greek: SC 90

Nestorius. *Liber Heraclides*. Ed. P. Bedjan, *Nestorius. Le livre d'Héraclide de Damas* (Paris/Leipzig, 1910)

Palladius. *Dialogue on the life of St John Chrysostom* (SC 341, 342)

    Historia Lausiaca. Ed. C. Butler, *The Lausiac History of Palladius, II. The Greek text edited with introduction and notes*, Texts and Studies 6.2 (Cambridge, 1904); see also ed. G. J. M. Bartelink, *Palladio. La Storia Lausiaca* (Milan, 1974)

Sozomen. *Historia ecclesiastica* (GCS, N.F. 4: *Sozomenus Kirchengeschichte*)

Theodoret of Cyrrhus. *History of the monks of Syria* (SC 234, 257)

SECONDARY SOURCES

Barnes, T. D. 'The date of the Council of Gangra', *JTS* 40 (1989): 121–4

Bartelink, G. J. M. 'Die literarische Gattung der *Vita Antonii*: Struktur und Motive', *VChr* 36 (1982): 38–62

Bell, H. I. *Jews and Christians in Egypt* (London, 1924)

Binns, John. *Ascetics and ambassadors of Christ: The monasteries of Palestine, 314–631* (Oxford, 1994)

Blersch, Hartmut Gustav. *Die Säule im Weltgeviert. Der Aufstieg Simeons, des ersten Säulenheiligen* (Trier, 1978)

Brakke, David. *Athanasius and the politics of asceticism* (Oxford, 1995)

Brock, Sebastian. *The luminous eye. The spiritual world vision of Saint Ephrem the Syrian* (Kalamazoo, MI, 1992)

Brown, Peter. 'Holy men', in Averil Cameron, Bryan Ward-Perkins and Michael Whitby, eds., *The Cambridge ancient history* (Cambridge, 1998), XIV: 601–31

    'The rise and function of the holy man in late antiquity', *JRS* 61 (1971): 80–101; reprinted in *Society and the holy in late antiquity* (London, 1982)

Cameron, Averil. 'The authenticity of the Letters of St. Nilus of Ancyra', *GRBS* 17 (1976): 181–96

Caner, Daniel. *Wandering, begging monks. Spiritual authority and the promotion of monasticism in late antiquity* (Berkeley, 2002)

Chitty, Derwas. *The desert a city* (Oxford, 1966)

Choat, Malcolm. 'The development and the usage of terms for "monks" in late antique Egypt', *JbAC* 45 (2002): 5–23

Clark, Elizabeth A. *The Origenist Controversy. The cultural construction of an early Christian debate* (Princeton, 1992)

Dagron, Gilbert. 'Les moines et la ville: Le monachisme à Constantinople jusqu'au concile de Chalcédoine (451)', *Travaux et mémoires* 4 (1970): 229–76

Doran, Robert, trans. *The Lives of Simeon Stylites* (Kalamazoo, MI, 1992)

Elm, Susanna. '*Virgins of God'. The making of asceticism in late antiquity* (Oxford, 1994)

Emmel, Stephen. 'Shenoute the monk: The early monastic career of Shenoute the archimandrite', in M. Bielawski and D. Hombergen, eds., *Il monachesimo tra eredità e aperture*, SA 140 (Rome, 2004), 151–74

Shenoute's literary corpus, CSCO 599–600 (Louvain, 2004)

Escolan, Philippe. *Monachisme et église. Le monachisme syrien du IV*ᵉ *au VII*ᵉ *siècle: Un ministère charismatique* (Paris, 1999)

Evelyn-White, H. G. *The monasteries of the Wâdi 'n Natrûn* (New York, 1926–33)

Fitschen, Klaus. *Messalianismus und Antimessalianismus. Ein Beispiel altkirchlicher Ketzergeschichte* (Göttingen, 1998)

Fröyshov, Stig. 'L'horloge "georgien" du Sinaiticus Ibericus 34. Tome I: Edition et traduction. Tome II: Commentaire', thèse de doctorat (Université Paris Sorbonne–Paris IV, 2003)

Funk, Wolf-Peter. 'Ein doppelt überliefertes Stück spätägyptischer Weisheit', *ZÄS* 103 (1976): 8–21

Goehring, James. 'The provenance of the Nag Hammadi Codices once more', *SP* 35 (2001): 234–53

Gould, Graham. *The desert fathers on monastic community* (Oxford, 1993)

Gribomont, J. 'Saint Basile et le monachisme enthousiaste', *Irénikon* 53 (1980): 123–44

Griffith, Sidney. 'Asceticism in the Church of Syria: The hermeneutics of early Syrian monasticism', in Vincent L. Wimbush and Richard Valantasis, eds., *Asceticism* (Oxford, 1995), 220–45

Guérard, Marie-Gabrielle. 'Nil d'Ancyre', *DSp* XI: 345–56

Guillaumont, A. 'Le dépaysement comme forme d'ascèse dans le monachisme ancien', *Annuaire de l'École Pratique des Hautes Études, Sect. Sc. Rel.* 76 (1968–9): 31–58

Hadot, Pierre. *Exercises spirituels et philosophie antique* (Paris, 1993³)

Hahn, Johannes. *Gewalt und religiöser Konflikt: Studien zu den Auseinandersetzungen zwischen Christen, Heiden und Juden im Osten des Römischen Reiches (von Konstantin bis Theodosius II)* (Berlin, 2004)

Harvey, Susan Ashbrook. *Asceticism and society in crisis. John of Ephesus and The Lives of the Eastern saints* (Berkeley, 1990)

'The Stylite's liturgy: Ritual and religious identity in late antiquity', *JECS* 6 (1998): 523–39

Heussi, Karl. *Untersuchungen zu Nilus dedem Asketen*, TU 42.2 (Leipzig, 1917)

Hombergen, Daniël, OSCO. *The Second Origenist Controversy: A new perspective on Cyril of Scythopolis' monastic biographies as historical sources for sixth-century Origenism*, SA 132 (Rome, 2001)

Kramer, B. and J. C. Shelton. *Das Archiv des Nephoros und verwandte Texte* (Mainz, 1987)

Krawiec, Rebecca. *Shenoute and the women of the White Monastery* (Oxford, 2002)

Lichtheim, Miriam. *Late Egyptian wisdom in the international context* (Fribourg, 1983)

Lietzmann, Hans. *Das Leben des heiligen Symeon Stylites*, TU 32.4 (Leipzig, 1908)

Morard, Françoise-E. 'Monachos, moine. Histoire du terme grec jusqu'au IVe siècle', ZPT 20 (1973): 332–411

Murray, R. *Symbols of the church and kingdom* (Edinburgh, 2004^2)

Pargoire, J. 'Un mot sur les acémètes', *Échos d'Orient* 2 (1898–9): 304–8, 365–72

Patrich, Joseph. *Sabas, Leader of Palestinian monasticism. A comparative study in Eastern monasticism, fourth to seventh centuries* (Washington, DC, 1995)

Plested, Marcus. *The Macarian legacy: The place of Macarius-Symeon in the Eastern Christian tradition* (Oxford, 2004)

Regnault, Lucien. *Les pères du désert à travers leurs Apophthegmes* (Solesmes, 1987)

Rousseau, Philip. *Basil of Caesarea* (Berkeley, 1994)

Pachomius. The making of a community in fourth-century Egypt (Berkeley, 1999^2)

Rubenson, Samuel. 'The Egyptian relations of early Palestinian monasticism', in Anthony O'Mahoney, Göran Gunner and Kevork Hintlian, eds., *The Christian heritage in the Holy Land* (London, 1995), 35–46

The letters of St. Antony: Monasticism and the making of a saint (Minneapolis, 1995)

'Origen in the Egyptian monastic tradition of the fourth century', in W. A. Bienert and U. Kühneweg, eds., *Origeniana septima* (Louvain, 1999), 319–37

Silvas, Anna M. *The Asketikon of St Basil the Great* (Oxford, 2005)

Sion, O. 'The monasteries of the "Desert of the Jordan"', *Liber annus* 46 (1996): 245–64

Steppa, Jan-Eric. *John Rufus and the world vision of anti-Chalcedonian culture* (Piscataway, NJ, 2005^2)

Stewart, Columba. *"Working the earth of the heart": The Messalian heresy in history, texts, and language to A.D. 431* (Oxford, 1991)

Stroumsa, G. 'The Manichaean challenge to Egyptian Christianity', in B. A. Pearson and J. Goehring, eds., *The roots of Egyptian Christianity* (Philadelphia, 1986), 308–14

Veilleux, Armand, trans. *The Pachomian Koinonia* (Kalamazoo, MI, 1980–2)

Verheijen, L. *Saint Augustine's monasticism in the light of Acts 4:32–35* (Villanova, PA, 1979)

Vogüé, Adalbert de. *Histoire littéraire du mouvement monastique dans l'antiquité* (Paris, 1991–2005)

Vööbus, A. *History of asceticism in the Syrian Orient*, CSCO 184, 197, 500 (Louvain, 1958, 1960, 1988)

Wipszycka, Ewa. 'Le monachisme égyptien et les villes', *Travaux et mémoires* 12 (1994): 1–44

28

Asceticism and monasticism, II: Western

MARILYN DUNN

The beginnings of Western monasticism

Writing after the sack of Rome and the death of his friend, the Roman aristocrat and ascetic Marcella, in 410, Jerome attempted to describe the beginnings of Christian monasticism in the city over fifty years earlier:

> In those days, no highborn lady at Rome had made profession of the monastic life or had ventured – so strange and ignominious and degrading did it then seem – to call herself a nun. It was from some priests of Alexandria and from pope Athanasius and subsequently from Peter [sc., his successor as bishop of Alexandria] who to escape the persecution of the Arian heretics, had all fled for refuge to Rome . . . that Marcella heard of the life of the blessed Anthony, then still alive, and of the monasteries in the Thebaid founded by Pachomius and of the discipline laid down for virgins and for widows . . .[1]

While ascetic groups had existed in the West in the second and third centuries, the arrival of monasticism can be dated to the 340s when Bishop Eusebius of Vercelli, who had returned from exile in the East, imposed chastity and communal life on his clergy. From the 350s onwards, the *Life of Anthony* began to make an impression on Western readers. St Augustine recalls, in his *Confessions*, how his friend Ponticianus converted to the religious life when he came across an ascetic group at Trier and there read the *Life*. By the 370s, Ambrose, bishop of Milan, had introduced monastic life to his diocese as well as presiding over the public veiling of women who had dedicated themselves to a life of virginity. Knowledge of monasticism had already reached Gaul, when Hilary, bishop of Poitiers, returned from exile in the East.

The first male converts to the monastic life such as Ponticianus, Augustine himself and their influential contemporaries Jerome and Rufinus were intellectuals or civil servants rather than members of the highest social strata. The

---

1 Jerome, *Letter* 127; trans. NPNF 2, VI: 253–8.

reaches of the higher aristocracy were not initially touched by the earliest manifestations of monasticism in the West and the conversion of Marcella, a member of the *gens Caeonii*, in the mid 350s was, as Jerome indicates, something new and unheard-of. The initial response of the highest levels of Roman society to monasticism turned out to be a gendered one, as the first high-status Western ascetics were all female.

The most prominent members of the first generation of Roman aristocratic women who embraced the religious life were Marcella in the 350s and Paula and Melania the Elder in the 370s. What all three had in common when they took the decision to embrace a life of Christian asceticism was that they were widows. Within marriage the degree of autonomy allowed to a Roman wife was limited and, while she might in theory enjoy control over her own property, her husband usually administered it for her. For the numbers of widows produced by the Roman pattern of marriage between younger women and older men, re-marriage seems to have been the norm, whether to advance the interests of their birth-families or simply because it was more socially acceptable than remaining single. The example of Christian ascetics appears to have provided Roman women, for the first time, with the opportunity to break out of the cycle of marriage, widowhood and re-marriage.

Wealthy widows who chose a life of Christian asceticism might, like Marcella and, initially, Paula, turn their own households into a religious community where they could fast, pray, meditate and study. However, on being widowed, Melania the Elder left her son in the guardianship of the praetorian prefect and sailed for Egypt, where she made a tour of the most famous male ascetics of the day. (Later, Paula would similarly travel in both Egypt and the Holy Land.) Melania eventually settled in Jerusalem, where she and her teacher and spiritual adviser, Rufinus, lived in two adjoining religious communities, one for women, the other for men, which she built on the Mount of Olives, where it was believed the second coming of Christ would take place.

Viewed in the light of the heavy burden of family duties and obligations resting on the aristocratic Roman wife or widow, it is easy to see the attractions of Christian asceticism for these women. The wealth of Paula and in particular Melania, whose family originally hailed from Spain and whose estates could be found as far away as the British Isles, also enabled them to play the role of patroness to the church and to monasticism in particular. They gave away spectacular amounts of wealth. In his *Lausiac history* 10, Palladius reveals that later in life Melania was conscious that her motivation in her early years as an ascetic was partly tinged by that most worldly of sins, pride: expecting the thanks of the great Egyptian hermit Pambo for a donation to Nitria of three hundred pounds of silver in a silver coffer, she found herself rebuked for drawing attention to the magnificence of her gift.

The ascetic life also offered the opportunity for education and study far beyond what was normally expected of a Roman woman. Acting as tutor and adviser to Marcella and Paula from the 370s onwards, Jerome had to meet their exacting demands for translations and instruction. His letters praise the excellence of Paula's Hebrew and the depth of Marcella's learning, while Palladius not only extols Paula's abilities but claims that Melania turned night into day by perusing every line of the ancient commentators, including 3,000,000 lines of Origen . . .[2]

Such activities are the key to the whole early ascetic system. Following the Eastern example of an essentially Origenist programme of fasting, study and meditation, Roman ascetic women could hope to transcend what was popularly considered to be their physical and moral inferiority and achieve spiritual parity with men in the ultimate goal of the mind's union with God.

However, although this transformational asceticism and its associated benefits were attractive to Roman female aristocrats, the features which made it so appealing to them seem initially to have rendered it less so to their male counterparts. Early monasticism as exemplified by Anthony, the desert fathers and the Cappadocians tended to destabilise notions of gender difference as Origenism taught that – in theory – these were temporary and insignificant in the vast cycle of regeneration and renewal. Such notions of gender transcendence went against prevalent philosophical and scientific views of female inferiority or incompleteness. They also possessed the potential to subvert many of the *virtutes* that constituted the paradigms of Roman aristocratic masculinity – courage, military skill, dignity, prosperity and generosity. If, as has been suggested, this was also a period when Roman aristocrats no longer entered the military, eunuchs reached positions of importance and the father's control over the family was slightly diminished, then aristocratic males, clinging anxiously to traditional definitions of what constituted the masculine, were not likely to be attracted to monastic life in great numbers.[3] A second generation of Roman aristocratic ascetics consisted of young women such as Paula's daughter Eustochium and those recruited to a life of virginity by Bishop Ambrose of Milan in the 380s (to the fury of their families who saw marriage and property strategies undermined as the church went ahead with the consecration of virgins aged under forty). The few aristocratic males who embraced the

2 Palladius, *HL* 55; trans. Lowther Clarke.
3 See Mathew Kuefler, *The manly eunuch*.

ascetic life in the last years of the fourth century tended to be men such as Paulinus of Nola and Sulpicius Severus, who had experienced major crises or losses in their personal life – and the group of unnamed aristocrats who, according to Sulpicius, joined the hermit-group at Marmoutier founded by Martin, bishop of Tours (d. 397). Christianity had proved more attractive to Gallic than to Italian aristocrats and now the charisma of this decidedly un-aristocratic bishop, the first monk to reach episcopal rank in the West (in 371), was so great that he could inspire upper-class men to follow him. However, it is also the case that monastic life at Marmoutier was suited to the lifestyle of the aristocracy, as peasants carried out all heavy agricultural work needed to support the community, while the younger monks' labours were limited to the copying of manuscripts.[4]

What we know of Martin's foundation may indicate that the West was begin-ning to shape monasticism to its own perspectives and social structures at an early date. The same may be true of the monastic life created by Bishop Augus-tine of Hippo in North Africa. Augustine had converted both to Christianity and to asceticism while he was a teacher of rhetoric at Milan in the 380s. When, as a bishop, he came to compose the first Western monastic rule, its vision of asceticism was coloured not by an Origenist idea of self-transformation but by the gospel message of renunciation and also by his own experiences. It reflects Augustine's past, being strongly tinged both by his understanding of living in community with friends and by his former Neoplatonism, with its idea of the movement of the soul towards the One, 'to have one heart and soul seeking God'.[5] It also affirms the need for the grace of God in ascetic enterprise.

The achievements of Martin and Augustine in some respects foreshadowed what was to come. In the West, between the 380s and the 420s, ascetic and monastic ideology underwent a series of transformations that would ulti-mately also have the effect of rendering it more acceptable to males of the ruling class. The first change related in particular to women, as ideas of gen-der transcendence in religious life were increasingly overshadowed by a more traditional emphasis on female virginity and enclosure. Although as a young man he had experienced hermit life in Syria for two or three years and had been

---

4 M. R. Salzman, *The making of a Christian aristocracy*; Clare Stancliffe, *St Martin and his hagiographer*.
5 George Lawless, *Augustine of Hippo and his monastic rule*, 80–1; this work, which contains translations of the *Ordo monasterii* and *Praeceptum* as well as a study of Augustine's spiritual development, also reflects the significant contribution made to our understanding of the Augustinian *Rules* by Luc Verheijen over several decades. See also Sr. Mary Agatha et al., trans., *Saint Augustine: The monastic rules*.

a notable enthusiast for Origen's work, Jerome never seems fully to have come to terms with ideas of gender transcendence. In his notorious Letter 22, written in 384 and addressed to Paula's daughter Eustochium, Jerome counselled her to preserve her virginity by leading an enclosed religious life within her own household, indeed largely within her own chamber, shunning the society of married women and false religious and awaiting the arrival of Christ her Bridegroom. In this letter Jerome employed what for him would become a classic formulation of an individual's reward in the life after death: virgins would be rewarded one hundredfold, widows sixtyfold and the married only thirtyfold. Thus hierarchies of chastity on earth would be replicated in heaven in an afterlife that had nothing in common with the vast cyclical sweep of the soul's falling away from God and eventual reunion with him as envisaged by the Origenists.

Jerome's arrogant advocacy of the superiority of virginity could have sabotaged any possibility of the acceptance of asceticism in the West. The death of Eustochium's sister Blesilla – who had embraced the ascetic life as a young widow – as a result of overzealous fasting, was laid at his and her mother Paula's door: it is quite possible that she carried self-mortification too far in an effort to overcome the handicap of her perceived second-class status as widow, on which Jerome unfeelingly dwells in Letter 22. He, Paula and Eustochium were forced to leave Rome in 385 and they eventually settled in adjacent religious communities in Bethlehem. Jerome, though, did not remain silent. From Bethlehem, he added to his earlier imaginative venture into monastic hagiography, the *Life of Paul of Thebes*, a *Life of Hilarion*: both works would exert considerable influence over the ascetic imagination for centuries to come, as, too, would his *Life of Malchus*, with its promotion of the ideals of Christian chastity and virginity.[6] He kept up a stream of polemic against writers such as Helvidius, who denied the perpetual virginity of the mother of Christ, and Jovinian, who attempted to defend the position of the ordinary Christian as in no way inferior to the ascetic or virgin. Jerome's actions and writings had initially alarmed his Roman friends, who feared both the polarisation of their Christian community and the scorn of their pagan neighbours. However, he was part of a Western trend, also exemplified in the writings of Ambrose of Milan, which glorified virginity and identified the female virgin – or, at least her soul – as the Bride of Christ. Gradually, ideas of gender transcendence would become

---

6 All three *Lives* are translated by Carolinne White, *Early Christian Lives*, along with Athanasius' *Life of Anthony*, Sulpicius Severus' *Life of Martin of Tours* and Gregory the Great's *Life of Benedict* (= *Dialogues*, book II).

less prominent as an emphasis on female virginity and enclosure for religious women developed.[7]

Since the 370s, opposition within the church to Origenism itself had been growing. Origenist theology, speculative in nature and originally designed to counter the claims of Gnosticism, did not appeal to those in the post-Nicene church, such as Bishop Epiphanius of Salamis, who demanded certainty and hierarchy. Jerome's former friend, Rufinus, who had acted as spiritual adviser to Melania the Elder, returned to Italy from Bethlehem in 397 and began a programme of translation of works of Eastern spirituality into Latin: these included an early and incomplete version of Basil's *Long* and *Shorter Rules*, the *History of the monks in Egypt*, and probably the *Sententiae* for monks and virgins composed by Evagrius of Pontus. But neither this nor his Latin translation of Origen's *Peri archon* could halt the growth of opposition to Origenism.

The real crisis for Origenism in the West came in the second decade of the fifth century, when the theology of the British intellectual, Pelagius, who headed an ascetic group in Rome, caused a major sensation within Western Christendom. Pelagius held that a baptised Christian could live, if she or he so willed, without sin, by following all of God's commandments. To Jerome this was reminiscent of the Origenist concept of *apatheia* – and to achieve this, he scoffed, one had to be either God or a stone.[8] The most powerful opponent of the Pelagians, however, was Augustine of Hippo, who felt that they were guilty of denying the power of God's grace in the achievement of ascetic transformation. Augustine considered that he had experienced the grace of God himself when he had made his own conversions to Christianity and asceticism and his monastic rule had also acknowledged the need for God's grace. Now, in reply to the Pelagians, Augustine developed the belief not only in the need for the enabling grace of God but also for his co-operative grace, arguing not only that God's grace made possible human choices and actions, but also that its continuing help was necessary for any achievement. The evolution of this doctrine confronted those who practised transformational asceticism, as it implied that transformation could be achieved only with the co-operative grace of God. Transformational ascetics had not denied the need for God's grace: Evagrius had conceived of a joint operation of grace and free will. But the increasing precision of the Augustinian theology of grace could now make Origenism appear dangerously unfocused and blasphemous.

---

7 Jerome, *Against Helvidius* and *Against Jovinian*; see further David G. Hunter, 'Resistance to the virginal ideal' and 'Helvidius, Jovinian and the virginity of Mary'; Ambrose, *On virginity* and *Concerning virgins*.
8 See Jerome, *Letter* 133 ('To Ctesiphon'); trans. NPNF 2, VI: 272–80.

Western monastic ideology was re-fashioned along more acceptable lines by the work of John Cassian who, between about 420 and 430, composed two works on the monastic life, the *Institutes* and the *Conferences*. Cassian wrote for bishops and aristocrats in southern Gaul. Some of the former may have been influenced by Bishop Heros of Arles, a protégé of Martin of Tours, while the latter included Honoratus and Eucherius, the founders and guiding spirits of the island monastery of Lérins, opposite Cannes, which would become the most important community in fifth-century Gaul. Cassian himself (a native of Dacia or, perhaps, Gaul) had travelled in the East and settled at Marseille about 415, where he founded two monasteries, one for men, the other for women. His twenty-four *Conferences*, supposedly the discourses delivered by a number of desert fathers in the presence of Cassian and his friend Germanus, are not the entirely authentic teaching of Lower Egyptian monasticism but, rather, an elaborate construct in which Cassian seeks to present a palatable version of monastic life and its goals to the West. Thus he never once mentions Evagrius, the single most important influence on his theology, whom Jerome had attacked in 415.[9] He bases books 5 to 12 of his *Institutes* on the concept of Evagrius' eight 'evil thoughts' – but they are instead presented as the eight 'principal vices' (and would eventually become the Seven Deadly Sins). Elsewhere, the now controversial term *apatheia* is rendered by its less contentious alternative 'purity of heart'.[10] He tackles the issues raised by the Pelagian controversy: in *Conference* 13, he has Apa Chaeremon maintain that there is a delicate balance between grace and free will. This conference moves towards the Augustinian position on grace, emphasising the role of God in originating the will to do good, while in *Conference* 23 he effectively castigates the Pelagian idea of living without sin as a snare and delusion. And one of Cassian's most important legacies may be found in *Conference* 14. There, he uses the terms *praktike* and *theoretike* in relation to biblical study and contemplation and offers an attractive and attainable objective to Western elites, both religious and secular – the goal of a spiritual knowledge based on the reading of scripture. Cassian would soon be condemned by Prosper of Aquitaine, who did not consider he had moved far enough in the direction of Augustinian theories of grace. Yet although he was never happy about the Western tendencies to found monasteries on family estates, to avoid manual work and to multiply liturgies unnecessarily, he made a major contribution to the process by which monasticism became acceptable to Western elites.

9 For Cassian's relationship to Evagrius, S. Marsili's seminal *Giovanni Cassiano ed Evagrio Pontico* retains its value; see also C. Stewart, *Cassian the monk*.
10 See further B. Guevin, 'The beginning and end of purity of heart'.

Lérins, whose founders were among the dedicatees of the *Conferences*, became a flourishing aristocratic community notable for its learning. Many of its members went on to become bishops: Maximus and Faustus at Riez, Eucherius at Lyon, Lupus at Troyes and, at the beginning of the sixth century, Caesarius at Arles, to name only the best-known examples.

Styles of Western monasticism and asceticism

As the fifth century wore on, monasticism became an increasingly familiar fixture in Western society, reaching Ireland with the introduction of Christianity. The Council of Chalcedon (451) decreed that bishops were responsible for the monasteries of their diocese and should check that they were established on a sound financial basis. However, there were considerable divergences in the types of monastic life to be found within any one area of Western Europe in the fifth and sixth centuries. In Gaul, for instance, not all communities could afford or wished to embrace the aristocratic and learned lifestyle of Lérins. The *Lives of the Jura fathers*, composed at the end of the fifth century, portrays a community where monks carried out manual work. Though the 'fathers' – Romanus, Lupicinus and Eugendus – were of high rank, their *Lives* point out that they practised austerity and that their communities, Condat and Lausinne, took in poor as well as rich, followed the full common life and eventually instituted a communal dormitory.[11] In some dioceses on the fringes of Western Christendom, such as Noricum in the east and Dumio in the west, monasteries functioned as episcopal centres and mission-stations to pagans.

One of the most important developments in monastic life was brought about by the growing emphasis on the cult of saints. The removal of the relics of saints from extra-mural cemeteries and their housing in churches and basilicas from the late fourth century onwards led to the evolution of a basilical-style monasticism, where either clergy or monks from an associated monastery chanted a set liturgy in the basilica at regular hours of the day. (Here there is an element of contrast with the normal monastic practice of simply going through the 150 Psalms in order and, when the end of the psalter is reached, beginning again.) Rome housed a number of these institutions – Pope Leo the Great (*sed.* 440–61) founded the first of the three basilical monasteries that surrounded St Peter's. Another famous example of this type of monastery is St Maurice at Agaune (515), created at the burial place of martyrs of the Theban Legion, where monks carried out 'perpetual praise', *laus perennis*, based on

---

11 *Lives of the Jura fathers*, trans. Vivian et al.

the practice of the monastery of the 'Sleepless Ones' in Constantinople.[12] The monks were divided into a number of *turmae* or groups, which took it in turns to sing the liturgy so that it could be continued both by day and by night.

Soon after its foundation, Agaune received the body of its founder Sigismund and became an example of another important trend in monasticism. Despite Roman prohibitions against burial within cities, bishops, kings and aristocrats began to have themselves buried as near to the tombs of the saints as possible.[13] In the sixth century, the Frankish ruler Chlothar I built a church to the powerful intercessor St Médard at Soissons, while King Guntram was the patron of St Marcel at Chalon. In the seventh century Dagobert I would richly endow St Denis. The rulers buried in such basilicas hoped to ensure the intercession of the saints through the performance of the liturgy by the monks whose monasteries were attached to the churches: both St Marcel and St Denis would adopt the solemn perpetual chant of Agaune as a liturgy suitable for the burial place of kings. This was an age when it was believed that lesser sins would be purged from the souls of the dead at the end of time, immediately before the last judgment, so the system of regular or continual prayer carried out in the basilicas was intended to be maintained in perpetuity. Only royalty could generally afford to establish such powerhouses of prayer for themselves, although others might later aspire – and pay – to be buried there. The case of Bishop Caesarius of Arles (d. 542) demonstrates just how costly the business of establishing such a monastery could be. Caesarius created the nunnery of St Jean to serve as a centre of intercession both for his city of Arles and also for his own soul: both he himself and its nuns were to be buried in one of the churches attached to it. He obtained papal support for his ring-fencing of the income from a number of diocesan properties to establish and maintain this foundation and both the rule he compiled for the nuns and his testament display an overriding anxiety that his extraordinary arrangements might be dismantled by future bishops.

Caesarius' foundation of St Jean was exceptional in its size, housing over two hundred nuns on his death. The vast majority of monasteries were much smaller foundations, often house- or villa-monasteries such as those at Lulling-stone or Llandough in the British Isles where the community consisted of the founder's family and servants. Others were meant to be rather larger and more permanent institutions, but the letters of Pope Gregory I reveal that, in the case of late sixth-century Italy, many only had small or medium-sized

---

12 See the *Life of Alexander the Sleepless* (PO 6).
13 F. Masai, 'La "Vita patrum iurensium"'.

estates from which to support themselves. Hermits and recluses still formed part of the monastic scene – the writings of Bishop Gregory of Tours indicate the existence of a rich variety of ascetic experience in sixth-century Francia. However, they also suggest the nervousness of the epis-copate in relation to exotic experiment and a conviction that shrines and relics were, ultimately, easier to control than eccentric holy men and women.[14]

The development of monastic rules in the West

Rather than set down minutely detailed regulations, the earliest monastic rules frequently attempted to capture the essence of the spirit inspiring the groups from which they originated. In the fifth century, Latin versions of Basil of Caesarea's *Long* and *Short Rules* – Basil's replies to a number of questions on religious life – circulated in the West. Even Rufinus of Aquileia's translation of an early and incomplete set, which turned Basil's prefatory discourse to Christians living in the world into one aimed specifically at a monastic group, preserves the Gospel injunctions which Basil considered to be fundamental to Christian community: 'Love God with your whole heart and soul' and 'Love your neighbour as yourself.'

Another example of the attempt to capture the essence of community can be found in Augustine's monastic rule, the *Praeceptum* or *Regula tertia*, com-posed in the 390s, which would go on to become one of the most influential monastic rules of the middle ages, associated with the renewal of canonical life in the twelfth century and the Dominican order in the thirteenth.[15] Addressing community members, it declares: 'The chief motivation for your sharing life together is to live harmoniously in the house and to have one heart and soul seeking God.'[16] In highlighting these Gospel injunctions, both rules seek to express the spiritual bonds of community in which the boundaries between individuals are dissolved and conventional structures are rendered redundant. The setting down of written regulations together with the emphasis placed on the need for obedience to the superior in itself reflects a degree of institu-tionalisation of relationships, but it is still the case that neither rule elaborates very much in the way of structures and hierarchies. Augustine envisages that community members will mutually observe and correct each other. Basil

---

14 Gregory of Tours, *Life of the fathers*.
15 See n. 5, above.
16 Augustine, *Praeceptum* 1.2; trans. Lawless.

outlines the practice of confession to those with the gift of superior spiritual discernment, allowing that even the superior may be corrected (though, in the interests of good order, he adds, only by the older and more eminent brethren). Basil's *Rules* were used at the famous Gallic monastery of Lérins: their teachings on the monastery as a centre of service and charity for the Christian community at large fitted in well with the ethos of a house which would provide many aristocratic bishops for Gallic dioceses in the fifth century. This movement helped establish routes for the dissemination of Basil's *Rules* as far afield as Ireland by the sixth century.

Institutional structures are more prominent in the rule composed by Caesarius of Arles (d. 542) for his nunnery of St Jean of Arles.[17] Caesarius seems to have compiled his rule over a period of twenty years and although he excerpts Augustine's *Praeceptum* and the *Ordo monasterii*, they are now surrounded by much more detailed regulations. His use of Augustine reflects his admiration for the great bishop and theologian, but the latter's simple characterisation of a community united by bonds of love was hardly adequate to his needs. (In addition, Augustine's *Praeceptum* was used for men and women alike, while Caesarius' approach, as he states at the beginning of his work, is a gendered one.) Caesarius originally surrounded his selections from Augustine with an assortment of practical regulations governing admission and the day-to-day life of the community and later added a *Recapitulation* in which he re-stated or re-shaped many of his earlier prescriptions. The need to compose his *Rule for virgins* was forced upon Caesarius by the extent, the risks and, ultimately, the success and prestige of his undertaking in creating St Jean. That he was doing something new is indicated by the way in which the text has the air of a work in progress, encompassing additions, excisions and revisions.

In many respects Caesarius' *Rule* reflect the developments in communal monastic life since the fourth century. The notable size of the prestigious intercessory community of St Jean may not have been typical, but it does reflect the way in which communal monasticism had become an established part of society. This had led to the practice of placing children in monasteries, either for reasons of piety or frequently, in the case of girls, because their families would not provide dowries for them. The lack of vocation for the religious life on the part of many is reflected in the church councils' prescription of penalties for lapsed virgins who left their nunneries. Caesarius approaches this problem in a number of ways. He goes to great lengths to ensure that

17 Caesarius of Arles, *Rule for virgins*.

the nunnery is completely enclosed and separated from society: once a nun enters the house she can never leave again and she may only receive occasional visitors in the *salutatorium*, or monastic parlour, under surveillance. In church, the nuns are separated from the populace of Arles and heard, but not seen, as they sing their intercessory liturgy. But solutions to related questions were not always easily reached. Caesarius has difficulties in deciding what is to be done in the case of nuns who have been placed in the community as children and who can expect to inherit property on coming of age. His efforts to minimise social distinctions between the nuns by prescribing uniformity in clothing and limiting the height of headdresses are somewhat undermined by his inclusion of Augustine's teaching that the more delicately raised might be allowed better food and drink. In their attempts to capture the essence of community spirit, earlier monastic rules had undoubtedly understated many of the problems of communal life, but there can be little doubt that these were now thrown more sharply into relief by the way in which monasticism had become an accepted part of the social fabric. Caesarius effectively acknowledges the need for more structures to cope with these changes both by the way in which he constructs a hierarchy of command within the nunnery and also in his creation of the rule itself. Although he attempts to safeguard the essence of communal life by decreeing that the superior should normally dine with the community, she is now allowed to eat apart if she has business to transact; and there is a degree of distance between her and the nuns as she is assisted by a prioress, or second-in-command, together with a number of other officials with designated duties. However, the *Rule's* limitations in the face of social factors are revealed by the spectacular revolt of the nuns of Holy Cross, Poitiers, in 589–90. It had been imported to this prestigious nunnery by its founder, Queen Radegund, who died in 587, but proved inadequate to prevent a rebellion against the abbess Leubovera by over forty of her nuns. The revolt was led by two Merovingian princesses, who had been placed there against their will by the royal family and who, now that their charismatic kinswoman and her first appointee as abbess were dead, resented their subjection to a lower-class superior. In fairness to Caesarius, the social tensions that flourished at this royal foundation were probably extraordinary – and Abbess Leubovera did not help her own situation by breaching the spirit, if not quite the letter, of some of his regulations.[18]

A much more sophisticated and integrated attempt to deal with the potential problems confronting monastic communities is to be found in the *Rule* of

18 Gregory of Tours, *History of the Franks* 9.38–43 and 10.14–17, 20.

Benedict of Nursia,[19] composed in southern Italy – where Benedict is reputed to have founded the monastery of Monte Cassino in Campania – by the mid-550s. At first sight, its emergence is surprising: the best-known Italian monasteries in the sixth century were aristocratic foundations that carried on the identification of contemplation with reading and study. Eugippius' foundation of Lucullanum (Naples) in the 520s was a monastery with a scriptorium, from whence manuscripts, including a series of excerpts from Augustine's works, were dispatched to members of Eugippius' aristocratic circle. In the 550s, the prominent administrator Cassiodorus retired from public life to create the dual monastery – coenobium accompanied by hermitage – of Vivarium, on his family estates in Calabria and to compose the *Institutes of divine and human readings*, which prescribed both religious and secular study for his monks. In the 530s, he had planned to found a Christian university in Rome: now, in the wake of the Gothic Wars which ravaged Italy from the 530s to the 550s, he sent what remained of his original library, along with recently purchased books, to Vivarium, where the monastic scriptorium and library would, he hoped, contribute to halting the decline in the knowledge of letters and therefore of religious culture. (They eventually played a part in the diffusion of Christianity as a number of their exemplars were copied for Anglo-Saxon Northumbria in the seventh century.) But such enterprises were probably far removed from the experience of less prestigious communities, where there was not necessarily a scriptorium and where superiors struggled to keep order and discipline against a backdrop of warfare and plague. How were abbots to maintain their authority in communities where the original founders were no longer alive; or where the first flush of religious enthusiasm had cooled; or where a proportion of the inhabitants were child oblates with no real religious vocation? These were the questions that the Benedictine *Rule* set out to answer.

About Benedict himself, we know nothing except what we can deduce from the *Rule*: the *Dialogues* attributed to Pope Gregory the Great which contain a purported *Life* of the saint are inauthentic and date from the seventh century, while their presentation of Benedict's own monasticism is frequently at variance with his ideals and prescriptions. The *Dialogues* also paint a misleading picture of sixth-century Italian monasticism in general, creating a mythical landscape peopled by charismatic monastic leaders who were the heads of networks of monasteries and travelled about, preaching and teaching.[20] Benedict

---

19 *Rule of St Benedict* (SC 181–6); trans. in Fry, *RB 1980*.
20 Adalbert de Vogüé (SC 251, 260, 265) presents the *Dialogues* as authentically Gregorian. However, Francis Clark's *The pseudo-Gregorian dialogues* has exposed many problematic aspects of the text and its history, dating its emergence to the seventh century. See

confronts a more mundane but also more problematic reality, offering what is in effect a programme for the preservation of monasticism: the *Rule* is designed to be used by monasteries in a variety of situations and locations. Its genius lies in its identification of the potential dangers to community life of integration into society, instability and lack of discipline, and especially in its recognition that charismatic leadership may often be lacking. The *Rule* is particularly concerned with the authority of the community head and it attempts to create an *Amtscharisma*, a charisma of office, for the abbot, together with a stable hierarchy of officials to support him. Logically structured and highly organised (unlike Caesarius' *Rule for virgins*), it offered the first comprehensive blueprint for monastic life. Designed for rural monasteries, it presents concise directions on dress, diet and daily routine (although its liturgical instructions, which closely resemble what we know of the office of the major Roman basilicas, may possibly be a later interpolation).

The *Rule*, it might be said, represents the triumph of organisation and structure over the more spontaneous, immediate and personal ties of communal life highlighted in earlier monastic rules and writings. Yet these are not forgotten. It pays tribute to this tradition in its acknowledgment that eremitism is a higher form of monastic life than coenobitism and concludes by recommending the masters of monastic spirituality such as Cassian and Basil together with the desert tradition embodied in the *Lives of the fathers*. But Benedict also writes (chapter 73) that he is composing a 'little rule' for 'beginners' and, in order to establish stable structures, he focuses on rule, community, and above all on the figure of the superior or abbot. He states unequivocally that the strongest form of monastic life is community life under a rule and an abbot and condemns out of hand groups not headed by an abbot (*sarabaites*) and freeloaders who wander from monastery to monastery (gyrovagues). A monk who lives in community needs, according to Benedict, to embody the three cardinal monastic virtues of humility, silence (or restraint of speech) and obedience. The supreme authority in the Benedictine monastery is God; below him, there is the rule itself, which may not be infringed, and below this there is the abbot, characterised as the representative of God in the monastery. Chapter 2 of the *Rule* endows the abbot with very extensive powers (so extensive that it has to remind him not to abuse them). Chapter 3 shows that while the abbot

also Georg Jenal, *Italia ascetica atque monastica* I: 191–293, for the difficulties of placing the *Dialogues* in a sixth-century Italian context. For a view of the *Dialogues'* place of origin and purpose which differs from that of Clark, see Marilyn Dunn, *The emergence of monasticism*, chapters 6 and 9, and 'Gregory the Great, the vision of Fursey and the origins of purgatory'.

may assemble the monks to consult them on important matters, he is not obliged to take their advice. The sections setting out the powers of the abbot indicate that the Benedictine *Rule* was created to underpin the authority of superiors who did not necessarily possess the charisma of the great monastic founders and the fathers of early monasticism: for conformation of this thesis we need only look at the trepidation with which Benedict, in chapter 65, outlines the possibility of appointing a prior, who to him is a potential threat to, or subverter of, abbatial authority. Reluctantly conceding that a prior may be appointed by the abbot himself, Benedict prefers to maintain monastic discipline through the figures of the *decani* or deans, who exercise close supervision over groups of ten monks apiece. Benedict devotes considerable attention to discipline and, although he wishes the abbot to employ the traditional 'curative' approach to disobedient monks, the ultimate sanction is expulsion from the community.

Other key monastic officials are the cellarer, in charge of the monastery's property, and the porter or doorkeeper, who has the important task of regulating contacts between the monastery and the outside world. In Benedict's *Rule*, the relationship between the monastery and secular society is very carefully controlled: it is not envisaged that monks take orders, become priests or engage in pastoral care, and the abbot is enjoined to have only one monk ordained, to say mass for the community itself. Only the abbot and those to whom he has given permission may speak individually with visitors to the monastery and there is a separate kitchen for the abbot and for guests, who eat with him. When members of the community are allowed to go outside the monastery – for example, to sell any crafts that it might produce – they must report back to the abbot on what they have seen and heard. Artefacts are only to be sold at a reasonable price and there is no sense, as in Basil, that the monastery is there in part to serve society through donations of any profits to charity: on the contrary, it is treated throughout the *Rule* as a secluded and sequestered institution in an attempt to discourage too cosy a relationship with the world. The other major 'social' problem facing communities, the problem of child oblates with no vocation for the religious life, was possibly more acute in women's houses, but both piety and the desire to conserve family resources had also led to the placing of male children in monasteries. Benedict's answer to the problem was a simple if brutal one: children offered to monasteries by their parents were vowed for life, with no possibility of either being allowed to re-consider their position once they had reached the age of discretion (as recommended by Basil) or to cherish any hope of inheriting property (and therefore being able to contemplate a return to the outside world). He evidently thought that once these potential loopholes were closed, the oblate would be compelled to resign himself to the religious life.

The diffusion of Benedict's *Rule*

The traditional view of the diffusion of Benedict's *Rule* was that it was brought to Rome in the wake of the Lombard destruction of Monte Cassino in the 570/80s, was used by Pope Gregory I (*sed.* 590–604) in his own monastery on the Caelian Hill, and from Rome was then sent to England in 596 with Gregory's mission to the Anglo-Saxons. However, in the 1950s, the work of Hallinger and Ferrari[21] fundamentally challenged this scenario and it became clear that the *Rule* was not known in Rome until the eighth century. Gregory's letters, which frequently deal with monastic questions and problems, make no mention of either Benedict or his *Rule*. Had he been aware of the *Rule*, it is likely that he would have referred to it, as it would have been of considerable help to him in his struggles to maintain order, stability and discipline in Italian monastic life in the wake of the Lombard invasions. As it was, he had to find his own independent solutions. The *Rule* is mentioned in two works traditionally attributed to Gregory, the *Dialogues* and also the *Commentary on I Kings*, but the authenticity of the former has been questioned on a number of grounds (see above) and the latter is now revealed as the work of a twelfth-century abbot, Peter of Cava. Neither text can be taken as evidence of the early diffusion of the Benedictine *Rule*. For that, we need to turn to the history of Irish monasticism on the continent and in particular to the monasteries founded by Columbanus.

Columbanian monasticism and the Frankish aristocracy

Part of monasticism's contribution to the spread of Christianity in Ireland had lain in its development and administration of a distinctive penitential system. The traditional continental practice of penance had involved public confession, social stigma and civil disabilities: once the status of penitent was entered into, it lasted for the rest of the individual's life. Sporadic attempts by one or two prominent churchmen to make the system slightly less unattractive never

---

21 Guy Ferrari, *Early Roman monasteries*; Kassius Hallinger, 'Papst Gregor der Grosse und der heiliger Benedikt'; see also Ottorino Porcel, 'San Gregorio Magno y el monachato' and Adalbert de Vogüé, 'L'auteur du *Commentaire des Rois*'.

gained widespread currency and most people postponed confession of major sins until their deathbed. In Ireland, the process of Christianisation produced a new approach: the monastic practice of confession to a spiritual father, as advocated by Basil, was combined with the Irish legal custom of treating all misdemeanours as wrongs for which the law prescribed compensation to the injured party: thus a new system of tariffed, repeatable penance, with private confession and fixed penalties according to the seriousness of the offence, emerged. The earliest surviving Irish penitential is attributed to a famous monastic leader, Uuinniau or Finnian.

When the Irish monk Columbanus arrived in Francia, c. 590, as a *peregrinus pro Christo*, he preached repentance and this new form of penance with great success. He created the triple community of Luxeuil-Annegray-Fontaines on the borders of Austrasia and Burgundy and re-vitalised Christianity in eastern Francia, much to the alarm of the local episcopate, who saw him encroaching on their prerogatives. Despite their hostility and also despite the fact that he eventually fell out with a section of the Frankish royal family, Columbanus succeeded in gaining the support of some important local dynasties, whose children joined his community. Although he was forced to leave Francia in 612, taking a number of his followers with him, and died in Lombard Italy at his new monastery of Bobbio in 615, Columbanus had already laid the foundations for radical change in the pattern of Frankish monasticism.

Previously, Frankish communal monasticism had been identified largely with the basilicas established by royalty or with the senatorial aristocracy and the episcopate. Columbanus' forging of links with an aspirant Frankish aristocracy led many families to realise that the foundation of monasteries could be a valuable weapon in their struggle to establish themselves as a permanent elite in the early seventh century. Once a monastery was created, its lands became church land and therefore free from royal interference. The foundations of nunneries or double houses in particular gave the opportunity to keep daughters' inheritances (now permitted by law) out of the hands of the king and his supporters: the pious desire of a young woman to set up her own religious foundation on family lands could be offered as an excuse to prevent her being married off to a royal favourite and her inheritance for ever passing out of her family's control. All that was needed to keep a monastery or nunnery in family hands was a succession of willing relations who could be appointed as its abbot or abbess. Both male and female houses – including Rebais, St Wandrille, Romainmoutier, *Evoriacum* (Faremoutiers), les Andelys, Jouarre, Marchiennes, Nivelles, Laon, and Maubeuge – were established on this basis. Monasteries were thus ranked among the foundations of aristocratic landed power and helped lend an invaluable spiritual patina to an emergent aristocracy, in what has aptly been dubbed a process of 'self-sanctification'.

Charisma, authority and monastic rules *c.* 600

The *Amra Choluimb Cille*, a Gaelic praise-poem composed on the death of Columba (Colum Cille) of Iona in 597, indicates that the major influences on Irish monasticism at the end of the sixth century were Cassian, whose work had been particularly influential there, and the ascetic works of Basil. When Columbanus came to compose a rule of his own, the so-called *Monks' rule*,[22] it was probably at the request of the communities he left behind when he was expelled from Francia and – apart from instructions on diet and, in particular, liturgy – it contains little in the way of detail. Instead it distils aspects of Cassian's and Basil's teaching, beginning with the Gospel injunction which Basil considered as summing up the essence of community, to love God and then one's neighbour. In contrast to Caesarius and Benedict, Columbanus sets out no elaborate hierarchies of monastic officials or structures of command. Instead, he concentrates mainly on discussing the qualities which the individual monk should perfect – obedience; silence; poverty; the overcoming of greed and vanity; chastity; discretion, which enables the monk to weigh his actions in what Columbanus calls 'the scales of justice'; and mortification, the willingness to submit completely to the judgment of a senior. Such technologies of the self are not enlisted only in the service of the individual, but are related to communal life as a whole – for example, a monk who answers back is not only guilty of disobedience but is also, by setting a bad example to others, the 'destroyer of many'.

Columbanus also operated a tarriffed disciplinary system for his monks analogous to the *Penitential* which is attributed to him: this so-called *Communal rule* (which may have been set down in writing by his followers) lists a series of punishments for infringements of monastic decorum and discipline, ranging from the obligation to recite additional psalms for trivial faults to severe beatings for serious ones. Shortly after Columbanus' death at Bobbio, a number of the monks revolted against the alleged harshness of the monastic discipline administered by his chosen successor Attala, leaving the monastery to set up their own hermitages and small monastic communities. This revolt, which is said to have ended on the deaths of a number of its ringleaders, is important for

---

22 For Columbanus' *Rules* and *Penitential*, see *Sancti Columbani opera*, ed. Walker, 122–81.

our understanding, not only of the nature of monastic community, authority and rules at the end of late antiquity and the beginning of the early middle ages, but also of the transmission of the Benedictine *Rule*.

There was no strong organisation in the Columbanian *Monks' rule* to support the superior's authority against opposition, as Columbanus had relied on his own charisma to preserve the community. Attala now required to emphasise or to reinforce his own powers. To do this, he or his supporters created the *Rule of the Master*. Since the 1930s, attempts have been made to characterise this work as a pre-Benedictine monastic rule, from which Benedict of Nursia drew a substantial proportion of his material and ideas.[23] However, the *Rule of the Master* contains a number of important Columbanian symptoms in its liturgical instructions, its Trinitarian teaching, its dating of the equinoxes and its rituals for blessing food, while some of its technical terminology is drawn from Lombard Italy. It also demonstrates extensive knowledge of the Benedictine *Rule*, which appears to have arrived in northern Italy by the 600s. The *Rule of the Master* builds on Benedict's measures to strengthen the powers of the superior. It promotes the coenobitic life under a rule and abbot, elaborating at length on Benedict's castigation of *sarabaites* and gyrovagues, monks who are subject in practice to neither. It invests the abbot with a Benedictine *Amtscharisma*, going even further than Benedict himself by dispensing altogether with the potentially troublesome prior and counselling that the abbot should refrain from appointing a successor-designate until he is on his deathbed. It combines hierarchical structures with organisational ones, often giving even more minutely detailed instructions for the daily routine of the monastery than does Benedict. And it is supplemented by what appears to be a rule for smaller dependent monasteries or cells (currently edited as the *Regula Eugippii*) which developed a dual agricultural and pastoral role. Even though the *Rule's* debt to Benedict is an obvious one, it still attempts to create its own charisma: most chapters are in the form of replies to questions headed by the statement that 'The Lord replied through the Master.' Its companion rule for cells, while it quotes from the *Rule of the Master* itself, is prefaced by the Augustinian *Rules* and thus by a vibrant evocation of monastic communal

---

23 Arguments for pre-Benedictine origins can be found in Adalbert de Vogüé (SC 105–7) and *The Rule of the Master*, trans. Eberle and Philippi. Against this, Marilyn Dunn, 'Mastering Benedict'; see also Adalbert de Vogüé. 'The Master and St Benedict: A reply' and Marilyn Dunn, 'The Master and St Benedict: a rejoinder', along with '*Tánaise ríg*': The earliest evidence'. For the rule for Bobbio's cells, currently ascribed to Eugippius of Lucullanum, see Fernando Villegas and Adalbert de Vogüé (CSEL 87). For the origins of some of Bobbio's cells in the revolt against Attala, see Michele Tosi, 'I monaci colombaniani'.

spirit. The routinisation of monastic authority through the use of Benedict evidently had to be accomplished with a degree of circumspection at Bobbio.

However, this could be achieved a little more directly in monasteries founded as a result of the fusion of Columbanian inspiration with dynastic ambitions. The presence of the Benedictine *Rule* at Bobbio allowed it to be transmitted to the Frankish houses of the Columbanian congregation by the 620s. It may even have been used at Luxeuil itself, while its creation of order and authority was recognised as particularly useful in sustaining the new generation of aristocratic communities set up under Columbanian influence. Waldebert, who became Luxeuil's third abbot, employed it when composing his rule for the nunnery of Faremoutiers; later, Bishop Donatus of Besançon, a former monk of Luxeuil, would excerpt it along with Columbanus' *Monks' rule* and Caesarius of Arles' rule for nuns in the rule which he devised for his mother's nunnery of Jussamoutier. In both these works, Benedict provided the inspiration for defining the powers of the abbess and setting out a basic framework of monastic hierarchy. This would be the Benedictine *Rule*'s main function in other 'mixed' rules which emerged during the seventh century: the provision of support and structure for abbots or abbesses who were often aristocrats rather than charismatic religious leaders and who had, perhaps, comparatively limited experience of the religious life. In this period, the 'little rule' for 'beginners' would go on to play a vital part in the expansion of communal religious life in areas where monasticism (and, in the case of Anglo-Saxon England, Christianity itself) was a novel or unfamiliar phenomenon.

References

PRIMARY SOURCES

Ambrose. *Concerning virgins* (PL 16); trans. NPNF 2, x
    On virginity (PL 16); trans. Daniel Callam (Toronto, 1980)
Augustine. *Confessions*, trans. H. Chadwick (Oxford, 1991)
    Praeceptum. Sr Agatha Mary et al., trans., *Saint Augustine: The monastic rules* (Hyde Park, NY, 2004)
Basil of Caesarea. *Rule*, translated into Latin by Rufinus (CSEL 86)
Benedict. *Rule* (SC 181–6). Ed. Timothy Fry, *RB 1980: The rule of St. Benedict in Latin and English with notes* (Collegeville, MN, 1981)
Caesarius of Arles. *Rule for virgins* (in SC 345). Trans. Maria C. McCarthy, *The rule for nuns of Saint Caesarius of Arles: A translation with a critical introduction* (Washington, DC, 1960)
Cassiodorus. *Institutes*. Trans. James L. Halporn, *Institutions of divine and secular learning and on the soul* (Liverpool, 2004)
Columbanus. *Works*. Ed. G. S. M. Walker, *Sancti Columbani opera*, Scriptores Latini Hiberniae II (Dublin, 1957)

Eugippius of Lucullanum. *Rule* (CSEL 87)

Gregory the Great. *Dialogues* (SC 251, 260, 265)

Gregory of Tours. *History of the Franks* (MGH scr.mer. 1.1); trans. Lewis Thorpe (Harmondsworth, 1974)

Life of the fathers, trans. and ed. Edward James (Liverpool, 1985)

Jerome. *Against Jovinian* (PL 23); trans. NPNF 2, VI.

Letters (CSEL 54, 55, 56); trans. NPNF 2, VI

The perpetual virginity of Blessed Mary against Helvidius (PL 23); trans. NPNF 2, VI

John Cassian. *The conferences* (CSEL 13); trans. Boniface Ramsey (New York, 1997)

The monastic institutes, consisting of On the training of a monk and The Eight Deadly Sins (CSEL 17); trans. Jerome Bertram (London, 1999)

Life of Alexander the Sleepless (PO 6)

Lives of the Jura fathers (SC 142); trans. T. Vivian et al. (Kalamazoo, MI, 1989)

Palladius. *Historia Lausiaca* (*H.L.*). Ed. C. Butler, *The Lausiac history of Palladius, II. The Greek text edited with introduction and notes*, Texts and Studies 6.2 (Cambridge, 1904); see also G. J. M. Bartelink, ed., *Palladio. La storia Lausiaca* (Milan, 1974); trans. W. K. Lowther Clarke, *The Lausiac history of Palladius* (London, 1918)

The Rule of the Master (SC 105–7); trans. Luke Eberle and Charles Philippi (Kalamazoo, MI, 1977)

SECONDARY SOURCES

Clark, Elizabeth A. *Ascetic piety and women's faith* (Lewiston, 1986)

The Origenist Controversy: The cultural construction of an early Christian debate (Princeton, 1992)

Clark, Francis. *The pseudo-Gregorian dialogues* (Leiden, 1987)

Clarke, Howard B. and Mary Brennan, eds. *Columbanus and Merovingian monasticism* (Oxford, 1981)

Cloke, Gillian. *This female man of God* (London, 1995)

Dunn, Marilyn. *The emergence of monasticism. From the desert fathers to the early middle ages* (Oxford, 2003)

'Gregory the Great, the vision of Fursey and the origins of purgatory', *Peritia* 14 (2000): 238–54

'The Master and St Benedict: A rejoinder', *English historical review* 107 (1992): 104–11

'Mastering Benedict: Monastic rules and their authors in the early medieval West', *English historical review* 105 (1990): 567–94

'*Tánaise ríg*: The earliest evidence', *Peritia* 13 (1999): 249–54

Ferrari, Guy. *Early Roman monasteries. Notes for the history of the monasteries and convents at Rome from the V through the X century*, Studi di antichità cristiana 23 (Vatican, 1957)

Guevin, Benedict M. 'The beginning and end of purity of heart: From Cassian to the Master and Benedict', in Harriet Luckman and Linda Kulzer, eds., *Purity of heart in early ascetic and monastic literature* (Collegeville, MN, 1999): 197–214

Hallinger, Kassius. 'Papst Gregor der Grosse und der heiliger Benedikt', in B. Steidle ed., *Commentationes in Regula Sancti Benedicti*, SA 42 (Rome, 1957), 231–319

Hunter, David G. 'Helvidius, Jovinian and the virginity of Mary', *JECS* 1 (1993): 47–71

'Resistance to the virginal ideal in late fourth-century Rome: The case of Jovinian', *Theological studies* 48 (1987): 45–69

Jenal, Georg. *Italia ascetica atque monastica. Das Asketen- und Mönchtum in Italien von den Anfängen bis zur Zeit der Langobarden* (Stuttgart, 1995)

de Jong, Mayke. *In Samuel's image: Child oblation in the early medieval West* (Leiden, 1996)

Kelly, J. N. D. *Jerome. His life, writings and controversies* (London, 1975)

Klingshirn, W. *Caesarius of Arles* (Cambridge, 1994)

Kuefler, Mathew. *The manly eunuch. Masculinity, gender ambiguity and Christian ideology in late antiquity* (Chicago, 2001)

Lawless, George. *Augustine of Hippo and his monastic rule* (Oxford, 1987)

McNamara, Jo Ann. *The ordeal of community* (Toronto, 1993)

McNamara, Jo Ann and John Halborg. *Sainted women of the Dark Ages* (Durham, NC, 1994)

McNeill John T. and Helena Gamer. *Medieval handbooks of penance* (New York, 1990)

Marsili, Salvatore. *Giovanni Cassiano ed Evagrio Pontico*, SA 5 (Rome, 1936)

Masai, François. 'La "Vita patrum iurensium" et les débuts du monachisme à Saint-Maurice d'Agaune', in Johanne Autenrieth and Franz Brunhölzl, eds., *Festschrift Bernhard Bischoff, zu seinem 65 Geburtstag* (Stuttgart, 1971), 43–69

Muschiol, Gisela. *Famula Dei: Zur Liturgie in merowingischen Frauenklöstern* (Münster, 1994)

Porcel, Ottorino. 'San Gregorio Magno y el monachato. Cuestiones controvertidas', *Monastica*, Scripta et documenta 12 (Montserrat, 1960), 1–95

Prinz, Friedrich. *Frühes Mönchtum in Frankenreich* (Munich, 1988²)

Salisbury, Joyce. *Church fathers, independent virgins* (London, 1991)

Salzman, M. R. *The making of a Christian aristocracy: Social and religious change in the Western Roman empire* (Cambridge, MA, 2002)

Stancliffe, Clare. *St Martin and his hagiographer: History and miracle in Sulpicius Severus* (Oxford, 1983)

Stewart, Columba. *Cassian the monk* (New York, 1998)

Tosi, Michele. 'I monaci colombaniani del secolo VII portano un rinnovamente agricolo-religioso nella fascia littorale Ligure', *Archivum Bobiense* 14 (1992): 5–106

Vogüé, Adalbert de. 'L'auteur du *Commentaire des Rois* attribué à S. Grégoire: Un moine de Cava?,' *Revue bénédictine* 106 (1996): 319–31

'The Master and St Benedict: A reply', *English historical review* 107 (1992): 95–103

Wemple, Suzanne F. *Women in Frankish society: Marriage and the cloister 500 to 900* (Philadelphia, 1981)

White, Carolinne. *Early Christian Lives* (Harmondsworth, 1998)

29

Art and *Propaganda fide*: Christian art and architecture, 300–600

BEAT BRENK

Introduction: Art and the Church

Since Jesus declared poverty and humility to be the most important Christian virtues, the question inevitably arises as to why the church accepted architectural ornamentation and the public display of artistic pomp. Although the Church as institution never formally pronounced on this matter (e.g., at a council), it has traditionally used art and architecture to project a specific image and as an advertisement for itself. The first section of this essay discusses in a broader context the issue of the acceptance of the pictorial religious image in Christianity.

The cardinal rule of advertising is that it must offer its target audience benefits, or at least define benchmarks that are achievable for the consumer under the right circumstances. This then leads to the question as to which artistic media the church has used to instil faith in would-be converts. Hence, the second section discusses baptism and baptisteries, and poses the following question: Once a person had accepted Christ and been baptised, what impact did the church have on the believer through the medium of art and architecture?

The third section explores the following questions: How does the Church present its content? or, in modern parlance: How does the church market salvation to believers through the medium of art? If we wish to understand how art and architecture serve the interests of theology, the preaching of the Christian message, brotherly love, works of charity, the celebration of mass, and the cult of saints, we must turn not to texts but to actual works of ecclesiastical art and architecture.

Hence the fourth and final section of this essay is devoted to favourite subjects of Christian archaeology, i.e., catacombs, hypogea, sarcophagi, burial places, and mausoleums and their decorative accoutrements. The pivotal question here is: How does the church offer comfort to the dying, the dead and the bereaved through the medium of art and architecture?

The sweep of an epoch in the history of art is usually presented as a chrono-logical account and a systematically categorised list of its monuments. But this approach leaves the context and meaning of the monuments unexplained. It is important to show how the works became tools in late antique Christianity. Art and architecture are autonomous media that convey a message of their own by virtue of their peculiar quality. In other words, early Christian art and architecture are not mainly based on texts, on theological principles and conciliar decisions, although ecclesiastical art may sometimes reflect the con-tent of such texts. Thus, we find a latent tension between the function of art and architecture as a medium, on the one hand, and theological teaching and dogma, on the other hand – and this tension sometimes produces unexpected results.

We also find in art and architecture an inherently creative and often innova-tive, ultimately incalculable, energy. Art basically gives expression to ambition and desire, rather than to the way things are, and the visual arts have often revealed perspectives that were unavailable to the producers of texts. A work of art or architecture may well confront the viewer with creations, assertions and claims that reflect the patron's wishes in a more or less camouflaged or subtle manner. These assertions and claims are addressed not to the jurist or theologian, but rather to the visually adept observer. It is certainly wrong to assume that Christian art is a mere visual gloss on Christian doctrine

The acceptance of the religious image

How did it happen that religious images were accepted at some point, although every Christian knew that the Old Testament forbade the making of images (Exodus 20.4)? Unfortunately, we cannot reconstruct this departure from the letter of the law in detail, since most pre-Constantine Christian art (insofar as it existed at all) was either buried or destroyed during subsequent eras.[1] The Old Testament ban on the making of images was so absolute that nei-ther Jews nor Christians could possibly have ignored it, and any church doc-trine that sanctioned the making of images would have been tantamount to a violation of the second commandment.[2] The contradiction between the Mosaic ban on images and the figure of a bronze serpent (mentioned in Numbers 21.9) did not escape the notice of Christianity's adversaries. Justin Martyr and Tertullian sought to refute this contradiction by pointing

1 See M. C. Murray, 'Art in the Early Church'.
2 The decorations in both the church and the synagogue of Dura Europos should, however, be noted.

out that the symbolic nature of the bronze serpent constituted an image-like archetype of Christ's cross.[3] For these theologians, the decisive factor was that the image of the serpent referred to Christ and hence to something more exalted. The image was legitimised by typology.

At the beginning of the third century, Clement of Alexandria was faced with the problem of Christian art from a completely different standpoint. He advised newly baptised Christians, who customarily gave each other signet rings upon being baptised, to have a dove, a fish, a ship with billowing sails, a lyre or a ship's anchor engraved on the ring, adding, 'And if one of them is a fisherman, he will be reminded of the Apostle, as well as of the children that are pulled from the water [of baptism].'[4] Jesus said to Simon the fisherman that, having been baptised, 'from now on you will be a fisher of men' (Luke 5.10). Although the interpretation of the rings' images proposed by Clemens was non-doctrinal, it was nonetheless representative of the practice of a period of free association from motifs and meanings. This practice, together with that of citing typology and history of the salvation to justify the use of images, was gradually adopted by patrons of Christian buildings. However, the church was unable to formulate a conclusively coherent response to the issue of using images, and instead relied on ad hoc decisions; the impetus for the creation of Christian images had its origins outside the church.

The ubiquity of Greco-Roman art in the Mediterranean region forced Christians to take a position, although of course never a definitive one. Italy appears to have been the Mediterranean region that was the most receptive to the making of images. The increased prevalence of Christian motifs such as those found on Roman sarcophagi is nothing short of amazing in the period following the 'Edict of Milan' signed by Constantine and Licinius in 313 and the ensuing conversion to Christianity of the urban upper classes.

However, numerous sarcophagi were invisible because they were often buried. Perhaps the church was able to look the other way when it came to the 'invisible art' of the sarcophagi, which in any case were a product of private rather than church patronage. In other words, since funeral art was accessible only to survivors of the deceased, it did not belong to the public realm. We simply do not know how the church hierarchy dealt with images during the first quarter of the fourth century.[5] The Council of Elvira (a local synod held before 306, near modern Granada) prohibited paintings in churches, stating that anything in an image that was worshipped could not appear in a

---

3 Justin, *Dial.* 91.4; Tertullian, *Adv. Marc.* 2.18.7.

4 Clement of Alexandria (GCS Clem. Alex. 1), *Paed.* 3.11.59.2, 3.

5 Th. Klauser, 'Erwägungen zur Entstehung der altchristlichen Kunst'.

painting on the walls of any church.[6] Presumably, this prohibition was mainly aimed at images of Christ and God, which under no circumstances were to be worshipped. The church felt compelled to differentiate itself from the pagan practice of veneration of images of gods and emperors.

However, this rigorous distinction was destined to be short-lived. Already in the late fourth century, the Spanish poet Prudentius composed his *Dittochaeon*, which contained quatrains contrasting twenty-four scenes from the Old Testament with twenty-four from the New Testament. Prudentius apparently composed these verses for an existing series of typological church paintings.[7] The church needed to prove to its adherents that the Old Testament, as a de facto Jewish text and thus written in Hebrew, should be regarded as a book about Christ. All theologians and church fathers felt that it was essential to 'Christianise' the Old Testament. At about the same period Paulinus of Nola, a rich aristocrat, late antique *homme de lettres*, ascetic and eventually bishop, wrote the following in regard to his paintings in Cimitile: 'It may be asked how we arrived at this decision, to paint, a rare custom, images of living beings on the holy houses,' and answered his own question by saying:

> Listen, and I will attempt briefly to expound the causes . . . the majority of the crowd here, however, are peasant people, not devoid of religion but not able to read. These people, for long accustomed to profane cults, in which their belly was their God, are at last converted into proselytes for Christ while they admire the works of the saints in Christ open to everybody's gaze.[8]

The argument, 'He who cannot read should at least look,' was undoubtedly an ad hoc invention, imputing as it did a propagandistic persuasiveness to pictures that they did not always possess. If the power of paintings had been an issue at all within the church, suitable measures would have been taken to produce images whose meaning was accessible – although it is difficult to imagine how the church would have convinced artists to produce simple and readily understandable works. However, it appears that for the most part the church left it to the artists themselves to determine the composition and general style of their paintings. Mosaics such as those in the nave of S. Maria Maggiore in Rome (432–40) (installed at a height of 13 m), and especially mosaic in the church's triumphal arch (put up at a height of 17 m), could hardly be

---

6 Synod of Elvira, c. 36 (PL 84: 306).
7 Cf. Renate Pillinger, 'Die Tituli Historiarum'.
8 Paulinus, *Carm.* 27, ll. 542–51 (CSEL 30: 286), trans. Caecilia Davis-Weyer, *Early medieval art*, 19 (slightly altered).

deciphered at such distances. The scenes from Jacob's life in S. Maria Maggiore cannot be understood without a minute knowledge of the Bible, and the artistic subtlety of these images would have been over the heads of most observers. While the theological concepts underlying these mosaics indicate that they were designed by a *concepteur*[9] extremely well versed in theology and church doctrine, he allowed the mosaicists complete freedom to execute the work as they saw fit. Neither Paulinus of Nola nor Nilus of Ancyra[10] could have claimed that these mosaics were intended for the illiterate, since in fact they most assuredly were not. For example, what would an illiterate person have made of the two female figures on the inside of the façade wall at Rome's Church of S. Sabina (422–32)? The personifications are accompanied by inscriptions in large and clearly visible lettering, ECCLESIA EX GENTIBUS and ECCLESIA EX CIRCUMCISIONE, but the church doctrine underlying these two figures was the fifth-century equivalent of high-brow, i.e., only understandable to a select few faithful. The average Christian would only have vaguely understood that the women had something to do with a unified church made up of converted pagans and Jews.

It was only during the first half of the fifth century, and especially in the sixth century, that more readily understandable and programmatic church wall mosaics with clearer visual styles began to appear – but of course not because the church was actively propagating this trend. Examples of such works include the mosaics in the Baptistery of the Orthodox, at S. Vitale and at S. Apollinare Nuovo in Ravenna. Nevertheless, it was deemed necessary to identify ABEL and MELCHISEDEK at S. Vitale with inscriptions, since in the Bible neither character had offered their sacrifices on an altar. The altar was a purely Christian element that also added meaning to the image that led the observer to view Abel and Melchisedek more or less as priests performing a sacrifice. The content of the mosaic could only have been devised by a Christian *concepteur* with the intention of conveying a didactic message to the congregation.

On the other hand, the two imperial figures depicted in the apse mosaic at S. Vitale have no identifying inscriptions, presumably because, when the church was consecrated in 547, the portraits could have been of no one except Emperor Justinian I and Empress Theodora. The creator of the apse mosaic in the monastery church of St Catherine on Mt Sinai (548–65) achieved

---

9 On this notion see B. Brenk, 'Le texte et l'image dans la "Vie des Saints"'.
10 H. G. Thümmel, *Die Frühgeschichte der ostkirchlichen Bilderlehre.*

maximum clarity, since all of the figures of the Transfiguration except for Christ are accompanied by large inscriptions. Here too, an ecclesiastical *concepteur* probably made the decision to include these large inscriptions.

The apse mosaic commissioned by Pope Felix IV in S. Cosma e Damiano (526–30) on the Via Sacra in the Roman Forum clearly shows that no standards existed as to how the legibility and intelligibility of wall mosaics could be improved, since only the patron and one saint (Theodore) are identified by means of an inscription. Sts Peter and Paul are readily recognisable thanks to their iconographically standardised physiognomy, while Sts Cosmas and Damian require no identification as the patron saints of the church. St Theodore, who was from Asia Minor and was completely unknown in Rome, was undoubtedly included in the mosaic at the behest of King Theodoric. St Theodore was the patron of the king of Italy; without the king's permission a building site on the Roman Forum belonging to the state could not have been Christianised.

Despite the ardent wishes of early Christian authors such as Paulinus of Nola, Nilus of Ancyra, Gregory the Great and several others, ecclesiastical art failed to become a Bible for illiterate Christians, and was never able to be simply a visual rendering of textual content. It is doubtful whether visual art was created to served the church's purposes, and one often gets the impression that artists demanded recognition for their visions, which the church had no choice but to accept. During the fourth century, the church learned to accept the unavoidable fact of Christian images, but was unable to elaborate a suitable doctrine for this evolution.

However, there is some scholarly debate as to how quickly the church officially adopted a positive attitude toward Christian art in churches. No direct clues to programmatic frescoes and mosaics in Constantinian churches have survived, and it is surprising that comprehensive series of mosaics are found not in these churches, but rather in emperors' mausoleums and prestigious private rooms. The most significant examples are S. Costanza in Rome and the puzzling rotunda in the Villa Rustica at Centcelles near Tarragona.

The cupola of the S. Costanza[11] mausoleum for Constantina, Constantine's daughter who died in 354, presents a typological design for which Old and New Testament archetypes were selected. However, the scenes were depicted on an extremely small scale and are embedded in an aquatic and maritime setting that made their subject matter difficult to discern with the naked eye.

---

11 The cupola mosaics are preserved only in 16th-century drawings; H. Stern, 'Les mosaiques'.

Their very presence proclaimed the church's teaching that the promise of the Old Testament would find fulfilment in the New Testament.[12] In the scholarly literature, the two renowned throne scenes in the apses of the ambulatory at S. Costanza are always described as a later addition from the end of the fourth century, because the comparative iconographic method is regarded as the sole suitable one, i.e., it is believed that the two scenes echo the art of Christian apse decoration that has otherwise not survived. However, there is no evidence to support this claim. Why, following the death of Constantina, should anyone have been interested in or been authorised to decorate two apses that had heretofore been devoid of mosaics with a *traditio legis* (handing over of the law) and a *traditio clavis* (handing over of the keys)? Instead, these two apse mosaics should be regarded as an integral part of the overall decoration rather than as reflections of religious pictorial series that have not been preserved. The fact that Sts Peter and Paul are the main figures in the two mosaics indicates a keen interest on the part of members of the imperial family in matters pertaining to theology and the Roman papacy. In other words, financing the decoration of this mausoleum was their way of supporting the doctrines of the papal church, which itself did not yet dare to decorate its churches with images of Christ. It appears that the impetus for adorning churches with Christ's image came from private patrons.

The cupola mosaic in Centcelles (near Tarragona, Spain) is more difficult to assess since its function has not been conclusively established. There is little evidence to support the hypothesis that it was a funerary mosaic: no tomb or sarcophagus has ever been found. The edifice was undoubtedly a *villa rustica* with thermal baths and domed main rooms, one of whose domes is decorated with mosaics depicting Christian scenes as well as the villa's owner, who is depicted as the master of the hunt. The scenes from the Old and New Testament indicate that the owner was a Christian, but these decorations provide no insight into contemporaneous church decorations.[13]

During the first half of the fourth century, Christian art found far more fertile ground in the private and funerary sphere than in official ecclesiastical buildings, a fact that is borne out by the apse mosaics in both S. Pudenziana (Rome) and S. Aquilino (Milan). S. Pudenziana was built in the early fifth century in the private merchant's complex of a Roman named Pudens, while S. Aquilino may have been an imperial mausoleum from the late fourth century. The church shied away from any comparisons with temples and their

12 B. Brenk, *Spätantike und frühes Christentum*, 50.
13 Brenk, *Spätantike und frühes Christentum*, 50; Helmut Schlunk, *Die Mosaikkuppel von Centcelles*.

representations of gods and emperors, and appears to have avoided the use of images, particularly ones that depicted Christ only, because such images posed the risk that the faithful would not only look at the image of Christ during the mass, but would also worship it.

One prominent exception to this generalisation, however, is the silver *fastigium* (altar canopy) commissioned by Constantine in the church of S. Giovanni in Laterano. According to the *Liber pontificalis*, Constantine had the so-called *fastigium* erected as a screen-like, devotional structure that was meant to direct the viewer's gaze to Christ. Nearly life-sized silver statues of Christ with the twelve apostles, as well as Christ with four archangels, were installed on this arcade structure.[14] Silver sculptures were a traditional element of imperial statues and pagan temples, such as those of Artemis at Ephesus, whose god-like divine character was questioned by the apostle Paul because the statues were executed by human hands (Acts 19.23). Constantine also had silver statues of Christ and John the Baptist installed in the Lateran baptistery and serenely ignored suspicions that he favoured a pagan form of worship. However, silver statues inside the church did not go over well owing to the fact that, since the apologists of the second century, the church fathers had prohibited the worship of images of gods and emperors, causing Christians to spurn the silver statues because of their pagan character. A devotional Mithraic image in marble by a second-century Athenian sculptor named Criton was hacked to pieces at the Terme di Mitra in Ostia by Christians and hidden in a pit while the Christians were building a chapel in the baths.

Over the course of the fourth century, the church was forced gradually to distance itself from the concept of an aniconic church interior, although we unfortunately know nothing about the discourse that accompanied this evolution. Mosaics as a medium were immune from criticism since they had been a popular decorative medium in both profane and religious buildings during the late Roman period. They also had an advantage over sculpture in that they depicted an imaginary world and refrained from fully embodying the gods as sculpture did. Hence, three-dimensional silver and gold statues, as well as sculpture in general, were strongly associated with pagan worship and cult.[15]

It took the efforts of such high-ranking individuals as Ambrose of Milan and Paulinus of Nola to bring about the breakthrough that led to the use of mosaics in churches. According to Paulinus, Christian mosaics in churches

14 *Liber pontificalis* 33 (ed. Duchesne, I: 172); see S. De Blaauw, 'Das Fastigium der Lateran-basilika'.
15 T. Pekary, *Das römische Kaiserbildnis*, 66–80.

were a rarity, something the well-travelled Paulinus was in a position to know.[16] It seems that ecclesiastical ornamentation was mainly left to private persons until well into the fourth century. The decision on the part of the church to use mosaics and frescos as ornamentation should be seen against the backdrop of emperor worship and the worship of pagan deities and imperial statues: pagans anointed the statues of their deities with oil, dressed them, and adorned them with laurels. Imperial statues were installed in temples in which the devout worshipped the emperor and sang hymns in praise of him. Golden garments were draped over these statues, and the statues of both living and dead emperors were carried in processions. An empty chair was reserved for dead emperors at theatres. As the illustrations in the *Notitia dignitatum* ('Register of dignitaries') show, burnt offerings, torches, candles, lamps and candelabras were arrayed around the emperor's image, to which animals and wine were sacrificed.

At the beginning of the fourth century, the memory of the steadfast refusal of Christians to make sacrifices to the images of emperors and gods was still alive. During the era of Christian persecution, Christians were forced to stand in front of an image of the emperor and say, 'The emperor is the Lord [*Kyrios*],' although for Christians only Christ was Lord. They were also ordered to make sacrificial offerings to the emperor's guardian spirit – but the Christian martyrs remained steadfast. It is difficult, given these circumstances, to imagine how the church could have managed to accept the existence of three-dimensional images of Christ. The *fastigium* erected by Constantine in the Lateran church and the silver statue of Christ in the Lateran baptistery are the rare exception, not the rule. If the first Christian emperor decided to use the media of the imperial cult in the episcopal church in Rome, he is unlikely to have faced open criticism. We also do not know whether the visual cult of his own image that Constantine freely propagated found favour with church authorities – although extremely devout Christians must have been perplexed by the monumental statue of Constantine that had formerly been in the Maxentius basilica, and the bigger than life-size statue in the vestibule of the Lateran church.

Be that as it may, the practice of producing three-dimensional statues of emperors was continued. For fourth-century Christians, *proskynesis* (veneration) in the presence of the emperor's image was accepted unquestioningly. Representations of the emperor's likeness, as well as the institution of the emperor itself, began to lose ground in the fifth and sixth centuries, except

16 Paulinus, *Carm.* 27, l. 544 (trans. Davis-Weyer, *Early medieval art*, 18).

in Constantinople, where the emperor had his residence since the time of Constantine. It took decades before memories could fade of the sacrifices to statues of the emperor and of deities that pre-Constantine emperors had imposed on their subjects. A scene from the book of Daniel (3.6) found on fourth-century sarcophagi refers to the refusal to worship the image set up by King Nebuchadnezzar.[17] Around this same period, funerary art, which was predominantly produced in the private sphere, shows the three magi from the East gathered around the infant Jesus in a manner that depicts Jesus as the true king. Mary is sitting on a throne, and the magi sometimes offer Christ crowns which recall the imperial *aurum coronarium*. The three magi, who are dressed in Asian garb, look like submissive barbarians in the presence of an emperor, although Jesus' humanity is underscored by the fact that he is sitting on his mother's lap. Some of the iconography of emperor worship was absorbed amazingly quickly by Christian funerary art and, beginning in the fourth century, by official ecclesiastical art as well. But it must be realised that the context is wholly new and must be 'read' attentively. However, in church art, three-dimensional sculpture apparently fell into disrepute and, along with the pagan temples, was henceforth associated with demonic forces.

Propaganda fide as a spur to conversion, or: How to become a Christian

Although Christianity was not the only religion in antiquity that inducted new members by means of a consecration ceremony that committed them to purity and faith, it was the only religion with a separate (and, in some cases, externally identifiable) structure that was set aside exclusively for this specific ceremony – the baptistery. The baptism of Christ by John the Baptist with flowing water from the Jordan that is recounted in Mark was domesticated, so to speak, by the erection of a baptistery. Baptism connotes purity, washing and bathing, particularly washing away sins, the renunciation of Satan, and renewal through the bath of resurrection, as well as enlightenment and sealing (*sphragis*).[18] Although early regulations concerning baptism (e.g., in the *Didache*) provide some insight into the baptismal procedure, they are silent on the form of the baptistery and baptismal font and merely specify the procedure that should be followed during the rite. According to canon 19 of the 'Canons of Hippolytus', the baptistery was located near the church of the bishop because neophytes were

---

17 Guntram Koch, *Frühchristliche Sarkophage*, 148–51.
18 F. J. Dölger, *Sphragis*.

led to the church after baptism to celebrate the eucharist there.[19] The bishop awaited the neophyte in the church, where, by virtue of being baptised, he or she could now attend mass. In Jerusalem, the neophytes together with the bishop were first brought to the Church of the Holy Sepulchre. There a hymn was sung and the bishop said a prayer while standing in the latticework of the chapel in the rotunda (*anastasis*). Only after this ceremony was the neophyte allowed to attend mass in the five-nave basilica (*martyrium*).[20]

The Church did not find it necessary to issue rules for the architecture of baptisteries[21] and thus left decisions regarding baptistery design and ornamentation to the bishops and local builders. The Church also displayed a surprising degree of flexibility when it came to the act of baptismal immersion. The earliest surviving texts recommend full immersion, but stipulate that sprinkling (aspersion) is also acceptable if water is in short supply. Flowing water was not a mandatory requirement, a fact borne out by the oldest extant baptistery in a *domus ecclesiae* (232–3) in the East Syrian city of Dura Europos. The baptismal font, which was set in a shallow recess above the floor, had no water inlet and thus was only suitable for sprinkling ('aspersion'). It is striking that in this house Christian frescoes adorned the walls of the congregation's baptistery, but not its sanctuary. The local bishop was undoubtedly responsible for this, since he alone had the right to perform baptisms. Depictions of Christ performing miracles, Christ and the woman of Samaria (John 4), the resurrection, and two scenes from the Old Testament were meant to strengthen the faith of the neophyte. Since some of these subjects recur in Roman catacomb paintings, the draughtsman of the baptistery at Dura Europos must have been receptive to pictorial representations and must have come to some kind of agreement with a like-minded bishop. Thus began a momentous chapter in the history of Christian art, one that enabled pictorial representations to play a key role in Christian worship for centuries to come.

For a long period, the room in Dura Europos[22] remains our only example of a baptistery with figurative painting, and pictorial imagery did not begin appearing in baptisteries even in the period immediately following promulgation of the 'Edict of Milan' in 313. In their capacity as public and official ecclesiastical spaces, baptisteries probably remained as unadorned as the church sanctuaries themselves. This is exemplified by the baptistery of St Peter's in Rome, which was built in the northern transept of this church of the holy

---

19 PO 31.2: 382–3.
20 Egeria, *Travels* 38.1–2 (*SC* 296: 290–1).
21 A. Khatchatrian, *Les baptistères paléochrétiens*.
22 C. H. Kraeling, *The Christian building*.

martyr and whose existence is known only from literary sources. The first freestanding and monumental baptistery was constructed by the emperor Constantine at the same time as the Lateran basilica (Basilica Constantiniana) in Rome. The central-plan, circular baptistery was nearly 20m in diameter and had an approximately 1.7 metre-thick exterior wall with a baptismal font in the centre that Constantine decorated with the aforementioned silver statues of Jesus, John the Baptist and a lamb. Seven silver deer were also installed in the interior as spouts. This decorative programme does indeed constitute extreme artistic opulence. It also evokes associations with Psalm 42.1, which was later incorporated into the baptism liturgy – but the spectacle of the glinting silver sculptures would surely have precluded religious meditation! The Constantinian baptistery was built over an earlier thermal bath dating to the time of Septimius Severus so that the existing hydraulic system could be used. Water was piped in from the nearby Aqua Claudia aquaduct.

Although replaced a mere century later by Pope Sixtus III (see below), this baptistery – Rome's first – had by its very architecture let the public know that in this place people were formally converted to Christianity and baptised. Constantine's baptistery was an incunabulum that influenced the development of religious art and architecture in Italy, and particularly in Rome, for centuries to come.

Oddly, baptisteries were not always attached to episcopal churches. Aside from cathedrals, parish churches in big cities often had baptisteries, as did churches outside the city walls dedicated to the veneration of martyrs. Pope Damasus installed a baptistery in the *extra muros* martyr church of St Peter, having found a spring on the Vatican that was reputed to provide the *dona salutis* ('gifts of salvation'). The idea of ascribing a special power of salvation to baptisms performed in churches consecrated to a prominent martyr led to the establishment of baptisteries at numerous pilgrimage sites, including Abu Mena in Egypt and Kalat Seman in Syria. The inscription UNA SEDES PETRI, UNUM VERUMQUE LAVACRUM,[23] put up by Pope Damasus, underscores the fact that baptisms at St Peter's tomb were regarded as particularly salubrious, and suggests that St Peter's baptistery was thought to have outstripped its Lateran counterpart. The Damasus baptistery in St Peter's was devoid of pictorial ornamentation up to this point. In 403, the prefect of Rome had marble installed on the walls of the Vatican baptistery, prompting the poet Prudentius to compose a lyric tribute to the mosaic decoration and its depiction of a

---

23 Damasus, *Epigr.* 4 (ed. Ferrua, 94): 'There is one cathedra of Peter and one true cleansing bath.'

shepherd.[24] The shift from aniconic to figuratively ornamented sanctuaries that occurred *c.* 400 is impressively documented by inscriptions. If special powers of salvation could be ascribed to baptisms that were performed at a martyr's tomb, then the relics of these martyrs could also be stored in baptisteries. This practice is documented, for example, in the baptistery at Alahan Monastir in Isauria, as well as in the one at Albenga on the Ligurian coast, where a mosaic inscription refers to the individual relics.[25]

In Milan, Bishop Ambrose emulated Constantine by building martyrs' churches outside the city walls, as well as a freestanding baptistery adjacent to the city's cathedral. The baptistery has an octagonal central plan room with an interior diameter of 12.75 m and alternating semicircular and rectangular shallow niches. The centre of the baptistery was dominated by an octagonal, baptismal font, merely 80 cm deep, which was supplied with water by a lead pipe. The plinth of the structure was ornamented with *opus sectile* mosaics, and the cupola had gold mosaics. Each of the eight walls probably bore one of eight distiches composed by Ambrose that characterised the building as follows:

> The temple with its eight shallow niches (*octachorum templum*) was erected for sacred use. The spring is enclosed octagonally (*octagonus fons*), worthy of the sacred gift. It was necessary for the holy number eight to enclose the house of holy baptism, where true salvation returned to the nations (*populis vera salus rediit*), in the light of Christ who has risen victorious.[26]

For Ambrose, the number eight represented spiritual resurrection and rebirth.

Although Ambrose based his baptistery on the symbolism of the number eight, his was not the first baptistery to be built in this manner. Already in the middle of the fourth century, an octagonal plan had been selected for the baptistery in St Mary's in Ephesus, although not for reasons of symbolism but simply because rooms on an octagonal central plan with shallow niches were popular in late antiquity and served an extremely broad range of purposes. For example, a pagan building like the mausoleum in Diocletian's palace at Split is octagonal. The baptistery in Milan served as a model in Provence and northern Italy by virtue of Ambrose's having constructed it, rather than because of its symbolism.

The far smaller but exquisitely preserved fifth-century baptistery in Fréjus[27] gives us an impression of how the interior of an Ambrosian baptistery looked.

---

24 Prudentius, *Perist.* 12, ll. 39–44.

25 P.-A. Février, 'Baptistères, martyrs et reliques'.

26 *ILCV*, I: n. 1841.

27 N. Duval and J. Guyon, *Les premiers monuments chrétiens*, I: 158–64.

The corners of the octagon are decorated with re-used ancient columns and capitals. The space beneath the cupola is illuminated by a series of large tambour windows, and the walls were probably covered with whitewash rather than mosaics. In the mid-fifth century, baptisteries without mosaic decoration were still being constructed in Italy, the most outstanding example being the Lateran baptistery built by Pope Sixtus III in 432–40. This baptistery preserved eight porphyry columns from its predecessor, the Constantinian baptistery, although these columns themselves had been assembled from more ancient spolia. Sixtus chose an octagonal plan for this structure, whose marble-covered walls must have looked extremely opulent. Its most outstanding preserved features are the capitals and architrave, which selected with great care from classical buildings, the latter bearing an inscription by Pope Sixtus that emphasises the creation of a holy people (*gens sacranda*) by the rite of baptism and rejects heretical beliefs by saying 'one baptismal font, one spirit and one faith alone'.[28]

In view of the somewhat competitive relationship between the Lateran church and St Peter's, Sixtus' inscription may have been intended as a challenge issued by the Lateran baptistery to its counterpart. As at St Peter's, mosaics adorn the vestibule apse, which may have been used as a *consignatorium*.[29] The two shepherds and two sheep symbolise the acceptance of believers into the fold of the Christian congregation. The surviving mosaic is non-figurative. The zenith of the cupola portrays Christ as a lamb with four doves (the evangelists), as well as lilies (symbols of purity and innocence, but also of Christ) and roses. The main motif is an acanthus vine that curls upwards on a blue background and draws the viewer's gaze toward heaven and away from the earthly realm. This blue background is in the tradition of the mosaics decorating nymphaea. The draughtsman of this decorative programme camouflaged his message so that only initiates would understand it.

The mosaic programme at the Baptistery of Naples,[30] whose scenes can be 'read' effortlessly, stands in stark contrast to the symbol-laden Lateran decorations. This freestanding baptistery, which was constructed by Bishop Severus (*sed*. 362–408) within the bishop's palace (*intus episcopio*), is now located on the right side of the apse of the medieval church of S. Restituta. The structure, which is rectangular both inside and out, has a cupola on squinches. The fact that only the vault and squinches are decorated with mosaics is attributable to a centuries-old practice whereby only domed sections of public

---

28 *ILCV*, I: n. 1513c: 'Unus fons unus spiritus una fides'.
29 I.e., the room for the confirmation ceremony after baptism.
30 J.-L. Maier, *Le baptistère de Naples*.

baths and mausoleums were covered with mosaics. The four squinches were used for the four *zoas* (living creatures) mentioned in Ezekiel 1.5 and Apocalypse 4.6. Owing to the presence of windows in two of the tambour walls, only eight of the twelve apostles could be fitted in. The apostles are shown presenting Christ with laurel wreaths, a theme referring to the pagan-imperial *aurum coronarium*, which recurred in both Ravenna baptisteries in the fifth and sixth centuries. The cupola is divided radially. In the centre is a Chi-Rho sign (☧), with the hand of God against a starry background. Eight garlands of leaves lead from the eight corners of the tambour to the zenith of the cupola, thus creating eight trapezoidal fields, each of which is decorated with a scene from the New Testament. The following scenes are still recognisable today: the Samaritan woman at the well, the miracle at Cana, Christ giving the law to Peter and Paul (*traditio legis*), Jesus calling the fisherman Andrew, the parable of the miraculous draught (and possibly the holy women at the sepulchre).

The common element in nearly all the scenes is water depicted as a medium of salvation, but of course in widely differing ways. By depicting Jesus changing water into wine at Cana, the draughtsman created a rather superficial and pictorial association with baptismal water as such, whereas the parable of the fishing net and the calling are directly associated with the theme of conversion. The *traditio legis* bears the inscription DOMINUS LEGEM DAT. Christ appoints Peter as a medium of salvation for the church by handing over the scroll with the 'law' (*lex*), i.e., the new Christian way of life that the baptised are obliged to embrace. The idea of the law as a new Christian way of life could also be conveyed by appropriate baptismal gifts. For example, a bronze lamp left by Valerius Severus, perhaps urban prefect of 382 and father-in-law of Melania, in his aristocratic *domus* on the Coelian Hill in Rome, does not depict a *traditio legis*, but does contain the following inscription on the mast of the ship that Peter and Paul are sailing (and which thereby symbolises the church): DOMINUS LEGEM DAT VALERIO SEVERO EUTROPI VIVAS.[31] Although Peter cannot be regarded here as the recipient of the scroll, he is beyond doubt the pilot of the church in which the baptised neophyte Valerius Severus is a passenger. The *traditio legis* is occasionally found on the base of gold glass cups that were very likely baptismal gifts given to affluent upper-class Romans in the fourth century and which were also buried with the dead (see below). This signalled obedience to the teaching of the Roman church on the part of members of the

---

31 Brenk, *Die Christianisierung der spätrömischen Welt*, 113–21, 331 (fig. 178): 'God gives Valerius Severus Eutropius the Rule of Life. May ye live.'

upper class, who would have recognised in the figure of Peter the pope under whose authority baptisms were performed.[32]

Most early Christian baptisteries had adjoining rooms in which catechumens received instruction or the confirmation ceremony was performed. In the latter rite, which was held following the baptism itself, the bishop laid his hands on the neophyte (imposition of hands) and anointed the neophyte with consecrated oil·('chrism'). One *consignatorium* contained the following inscription: 'Here the hand of the supreme shepherd sealed the lambs, which were washed clean of all sin by the heavenly river.'[33] A preserved sixth-century baptistery in the large double church complex in the northwestern section of the 'new city' (*urbs nova*) in present-day Salona has an adjoining rectangular room on either side. The stone benches of the room on the right hand justify viewing it as a *katechumeneion*, a room to teach catechumens. The fact that the room on the left hand communicates with both baptistery doors via an archway may indicate that it served as a *consignatorium*. When the neophyte entered the room through the archway, he saw a floor mosaic of two deer drinking from a cantharus, and the accompanying inscription which said (Psalm 42.1): QUEMADMODUM DESIDERAT CERVUS AD FONTES AQUARUM: ITA DESIDERAT ANIMA MEA AD TE, DEUS.[34] These are words that the neophyte had just heard during the baptism rite. The bishop awaited the neophyte beside the priest's throne and anointed him with consecrated oil.

Although numerous baptisteries had adjoining rooms, in most cases the exact function of these spaces cannot be determined. They were used for confirmation, and in some cases exorcism was performed in them as well. Cyril of Jerusalem reported that the devil was renounced 'in the outside building', which was termed the 'vestibule of the baptistery'.[35]

Whereas the rites of baptism were undoubtedly performed on occasion at major pilgrimage sites, the prevalence of this practice remains unclear. We can only speculate as to how these conversions were realised without a lengthy period of catechetical instruction. Ad hoc conversions of pagans were apparently performed in the presence of Simeon Stylites on his pillar. The conversion business brooked no delays – a monumental baptistery with numerous adjoining rooms and its own church for celebration of the eucharist were erected 200 m outside of St Simeon's pilgrimage site at Kalat Seman. The

---

32 For the ideological background, see C. Piétri, '*Concordia apostolorum et renovatio urbis*'.

33 F. Dölger, 'Die Firmung in den Denkmälern', 16: 'Ubi pontifex consignat infantes: istic insontes caelesti flumine eotas pastoris summi dextera signat oves . . .'

34 Psalm 42.1: 'As a hind longs for the running streams, so do I long for thee, O God.'

35 Cyril, *Cat. myst.* 1.2 (PG 33: 1068).

east side of the octagonal baptistery contains a spacious apse and a small basin, the aspirants entering the building through a door in the north side and leaving it through a second door in the south side. This arrangement enabled candidates to be 'rushed through' the basin without entering the baptistery proper; once baptised, the neophyte could enter the church on the south end of the complex.[36]

The baptistery of the church of St Theodore (from 494) in Gerasa (Jerash in today's Jordan)[37] contained a mini-apse that could be traversed in a few strides. This appears to have been the first martyr's church in Gerasa (see below), but it is very much open to question whether or not the church attracted as many baptismal candidates as St Simeon's pilgrimage site at Kalat Seman. Moreover, the form of the church does not provide conclusive evidence as to its exact function. Only a few decades later, between 531 and 533, two prominent citizens of Gerasa financed construction of the church of St John, St Cosmas and St Damian. This tripartite church complex is only a stone's throw from St Theodore's to the east. The complex can in a sense be regarded as rivalling the cathedral complex since three churches rather than two had been assimilated into a single complex. One could see this as a kind of architectural 'one-upmanship'. The baptistery at the church of St John was intended to be a competitor for the baptistery at the church of Theodore, which had been constructed a mere three decades previously. We do not know if the new complex was ever used. But be that as it may, it should be regarded as the manifestation of exalted aspiration on the part of the city's *nouveau riche* private patrons, who built a species of 'private double cathedral' that they then enlarged into a 'triple cathedral'.

There are numerous reasons for the presence of multiple baptisteries in the same geographical location. Why would the Aegean island of Kos alone contain seven preserved early Christian baptisteries? The North African city of Leptis Magna was reported to have been the site of four baptisteries. And in the tiny agricultural settlement of Dar Qîta in northern Syria, two baptisteries were constructed within a period of only a few decades. The *chôrepiscopos*, who administered the rites of baptism on each Theophany (6 January) or on Easter Saturday, had to decide in which church the ceremony should be performed. But how did he decide? In the Latin West, it was customary to erect a single baptistery in agricultural villages. An outstanding example of a preserved rural baptistery is the sixth-century one in Riva S. Vitale in Ticino. The nearest cathedral city was 15 km away in Como, but the Riva S. Vitale congregation had its own baptistery thanks either to its own industriousness or an affluent local patron. The minuscule Negev settlement of Shivta (390 × 290 m) is unlikely to have had its own bishop, although the community was serviced by a chorepiscopos who made the rounds of the various settlements in the region. But the settlement did claim three churches and two baptisteries as its own. One baptistery was added to the narthex of the southern church, which had been built on the site of a *domus*, and in 607 another baptistery was added to the northern church, and community luminaries were interred there. It is at any rate clear that the house of worship in northern Shivta became more prestigious than the former mother church in the southern part of the settlement. Competition and the desire to gain the upper hand often provided the impetus for baptistery construction.

Two baptisteries could also represent two different Christian 'denominations', as for example in Ravenna,[38] where in the sixth century the Arian (Homoian) baptistery became the second baptismal space in the town, the first being the venerable Orthodox baptistery. Competition came into play here as well, since the Arians (Homoians) repeated the decoration programme of the cathedral baptistery for the cupola of their structure, albeit with some significant modifications. If the Arians (Homoians) had wished to distinguish themselves from an artistic standpoint, they could have devised their own iconographical programme. If the depictions of the baptism of Christ and the apostles presenting the laurel wreath (the *aurum coronarium*) to Jesus were good enough for the Orthodox, then they were good enough for the Arians (Homoians) too. However, the Arians (Homoians) did bow to contemporary fashion in depicting the sacred Jordan river not as a half-figure, as in the Orthodox version, but as a full figure that is conspicuously large on purely pictorial, narrative and compositional grounds.

The Orthodox baptistery in Ravenna, in which the mosaics were executed from 430 to 450, is by far the most opulently decorated early Christian baptistery. A marble wall covering up to eye level, a veritable carpet of mosaics ascending majestically to the zenith of the cupola, and stucco statues at window height – all combine to form one of the most figuratively complex decorative programmes in early Christendom. Here the neophyte's religious ardour was

---

38 F. W. Deichmann, *Ravenna. Geschichte und Monumente* and *Ravenna. Hauptstadt des spätantiken Abendlandes*.

aroused not only by images, but also by all the other artistic media as well. Only in isolated cases were pictorial programmes in early Christian baptisteries confined to baptism-related narratives, since their purpose was to encompass the entire spectrum of salvation history. Irrespective of whether a baptistery was a freestanding structure that was visible from afar or was integrated into the church itself, a great deal of effort and expense went into decorating the space with a view to sending an unmistakable message: art and architecture serve as a vehicle for converting non-believers to Christianity.

Post-conversion *propaganda fide*, or: How to keep the faith

Upon promulgation of the so-called Edict of Milan and Constantine's conversion to Christianity, the Church was faced with a new and wholly unforeseeable situation. Until that time, art and architecture had hardly ever been governed by church policies, and then only in isolated and marginal cases. Had the emperor not resolutely decided to support Christianity, the church would have been forced to continue being an essentially clandestine organisation with an improvised infrastructure. But the fact that Constantine forged ahead with church construction meant that henceforth the Church would benefit from governmental munificence. In fact, Constantine did not initiate his church building programme on his own, but worked together with Church leaders. The first Constantinian church was the cathedral of Rome, S. Giovanni in Laterano (Basilica Constantiniana).[39] Constantine then built churches over the burial places of the apostles Peter and Paul, in collaboration with Pope Sylvester, and constructed tributes to local saints such as Agnes, Lawrence, Marcellinus and Peter. Churches were also built at Constantine's behest in Ostia and Albano (near Rome), as well as in Capua and Naples. Constantine's construction programme included the new imperial capitals of Constantinople and Antioch, as well as the cities in the Holy Land most closely associated with Jesus (Jerusalem and Bethlehem). Thanks to Constantine's efforts, all of these cities were graced with new churches that were of architectural and artistic importance.

Did this astonishing achievement respond to a genuine need, or was it the mission of these new buildings to stake out claims and increase church attendance? In the early fourth century, there were far more Christians in

---

39 S. De Blaauw, *Cultus et decor*.

Rome than in Palestine, where it initially proved necessary to requisition certain *loca sancta* for Christianity. In this way, Palestine became an even more attractive destination, because the faithful were invited to visit the holy places associated with the various phases of Jesus' life and career in the Holy Land – even if the evidence presented to pilgrims may not always have been wholly persuasive.[40] The Church of the Holy Sepulchre took on central importance since it substantiated the creed's assertion of Christ's resurrection with the argument that Jesus' body was invisible. Pilgrims to Bethlehem were shown the grotto in which Mary had given birth to Jesus, and the Church of the Nativity 'proved' that Jesus had existed in the flesh on this earth. The churches that were built over the burial places of various apostles and martyrs were an innovation in that they promoted the desire on the part of the faithful to worship at graves, and made the physicality of the dead and their relics a matter of keen interest.[41]

Constantine's decision to construct a multi-nave basilica for the cathedral of Rome, as well as for the churches of St Peter and St Paul, had monumental repercussions. Already in the first century, Vitruvius had associated *dignitas* and *venustas* with the term 'basilica'.[42] The basilica, particularly the five-nave variant, employs the rhetoric of grandiloquence (*grandiloquus*). In addition, the work and expense necessitated by columns and capitals made the basilica a noticeably imposing and ornate structure. At the same time the ubiquitous marble, as well as the abundant silver religious statuary of Constantinian basilicas, generated positive publicity for imperial munificence and the concept of the House of God. The use of marble columns and capitals placed an extremely heavy financial and organisational burden on patrons. Imperial architects had a predilection for antique columns, which they commandeered from marble dumps and empty or ruined buildings. The carefully chosen construction materials gave rise to a new aesthetic consciousness that was based on the principle of variety (*varietas*). However, activation of the marble quarries in the eastern Mediterranean region resulted in the construction of numerous basilicas that contained only one type of building material, in accordance with the aesthetic principle of uniformity (*unitas*).

The process of adapting basilica architecture to the requirements of Christianity necessitated a strict separation between the area set aside for the altar and priest (presbytery) and the space occupied by the congregation. The presbytery was placed either within or in front of the apse; the entrance

40 See further ch. 21, above.
41 See further ch. 22, above.
42 Vitruvius, *On architecture* 5.1.6.

to the building on the narrow sides faced the presbytery. Anyone entering a Christian basilica had to cover a certain distance in order to reach the presbytery and the altar. The side aisles could serve to separate men and women, while the middle aisle was set aside for clerics, processions, festivals and official church meetings. Oftentimes the middle aisle contained a *solea*, a walled passageway used by the clerics as an entrance to the presbytery during processions. The middle aisles of Greek churches contained an *ambo* (pulpit). Separating the presbytery from the nave lent the Christian basilica a distinctly elongated shape that was an innovation in that the profane Roman basilica could never be transversed lengthways only. The decision to build multi-nave columned basilicas was not made on the grounds that this was a more suitable arrangement for religious purposes than, for example, an undivided space with columns. The basilica has always been regarded as a particularly ornate and sophisticated architectural form.

Constantine's construction programme had a far-reaching impact on his era. The basilica form he favoured was adopted throughout the Mediterranean region during the fourth century, including in relatively remote regions such as the Limestone Massif of northern Syria: Fafertin (372), Babiska Markianos Kyris church (390–407), the church of Julianos in Brad (390–402), Harâb Šams and Burĝ Heidar (mid-fourth century).[43] Although Christian basilicas in the region's small villages emulated basilica architecture, they were also extremely innovative since they were *ex novo* constructions that interpreted the aesthetic principle of *varietas* in a strikingly distinctive manner. Their most consequential feature was that the types of capitals used varied from one pair of columns to the next. For example, the Harâb Šams basilica contains an Ionic capital adjacent to a Tuscan capital with four leaves, followed by another Tuscan capital with volutes on all four corners. The Limestone Massif in northern Syria manifested more creativity with the basilica form than any other Mediterranean region.

The basilica was particularly favoured by bishops, although it was a popular choice among donors as well. This type of construction was the most successful in evoking *praestigium* (which in this context we can freely render as 'ambition') among the faithful. Of course, we do know of some exceptions to this rule, such as the double church complex with a baptistery in Aquileia that was constructed early in Constantine's reign. Both churches are devoid of apses, are rectangular, are divided into three naves by pillars and had a functional air in that their pillars were so far apart that only a wooden architrave or low clerestory were constructed above them. The richly coloured and in some cases

---

43 G. Tchalenko, *Les églises syriennes à Bêma*.

figurative floor mosaics are extremely unusual for the period. The decorative, non-Christian sections of the floor mosaics at Aquileia were selected and financed by various donors, whereas the church or the bishop (Theodorus) decided to install in the presbytery a depiction of the story of Jonah, which is ensconced in a large aquatic landscape and was chosen with a view to pictorialising the cardinal doctrine of the resurrection of the flesh.[44]

Ambrose was the 'Constantine' of Milan in the realm of church construction. Just as Constantine had erected the first episcopal church with a baptistery in Rome (S. Giovanni in Laterano) and a series of martyr's churches (St Peter's, St Paul's, S. Lorenzo, S. Agnese, SS. Marcellino e Pietro) outside the city walls, Ambrose likewise constructed the cathedral baptistery in S. Giovanni in Fonte as well as three martyrs' memorials (S. Nazaro, S. Ambrogio, S. Simpliciano) outside the city walls of Milan. Ambrose adopted Constantine's approach to church construction, except of course for the fact that Milan, like so many other cities and unlike Rome, lacked apostolic martyrs of its own and hence had no martyrs' burial places that had been prominent since before the reign of Constantine. Martyrs' relics were not discovered in Milan until the late fourth century; in fact, Ambrose was instrumental in locating them. The best-preserved early Christian martyrs' basilicas in Milan are the Basilica Apostolorum (S. Nazaro; 382) and S. Simpliciano. For these structures, Ambrose chose a cross-shaped plan whose space was not subdivided by columns, as was the case in privately financed buildings and above all the grand style of imperial architecture. The relics of the apostles (whose provenance is unknown) were placed in a silver reliquary at the crossing of the church, with St Nazarus' relics in the main apse. Four fifth-century bishops of Milan were honoured with cenotaphs near the apostles' relics. The apostles' church, which became a burial church for Milan's leading citizens, is architecturally unique, and has neither predecessors nor successors. Ambrose characterised the cruciform structure with the following epigram: FORMA CRUCIS TEMPLUM EST TEMPLUM VICTORIA CHRISTI.[45] Ambrose applies this interpretation to a church structure that was one of the earliest cruciform churches in Christian architecture. The architectural innovation here was that the church was not only cruciform inside, but visibly formed a cross from the outside as well.

Ambrose dotted the perimeter of Milan with four new structures that were placed on the four end points of an imaginary cross superimposed on the city. The Basilica Apostolorum at the southern end of Milan corresponded to

---

44 See further ch. 8, above.
45 *ILCV*, I: n. 1800: 'The church is in the shape of a cross, the (cruciform) cross signifies the victory of Christ.'

the Basilica Virginum (S. Simpliciano) in the north. Ambrose constructed the Basilica Martyrum (S. Ambrogio) on the west side of Milan and S. Dionisio on the east side. With a main hall that was 21.7 m across, the cruciform martyr's church S. Simpliciano counts as one of the largest early churches. In 386 Ambrose constructed the Basilica Ambrosiana for which he selected a conventional three-nave basilica with an apse at one end of the nave, rather than a cruciform plan. Together with Paulinus of Nola and other Italian bishops, Ambrose advocated the decoration of churches with biblical wall mosaics (see above).

As was initially the case in Milan, the imperial city of Ravenna also suffered from a shortage of martyrs' relics. The only local luminary who could be honoured there was the confessor-bishop Apollinaris, and although imported relics were available it was not until the sixth century that notable martyrs' churches like S. Apollinare in Classe were built. St Vitalis, on the other hand, had no connection to Ravenna. Ambrose of Milan promoted the cult of St Vitalis, but it was not until the fifth century that it arrived in Ravenna, where it was necessary to re-invent the legend of the saint. Both S. Apollinare in Classe (from 549) and S. Vitale (consecrated in 547) were erected with the financial backing of the banker Julianus Argentarius. S. Vitale was constructed inside rather than outside the city walls and was endowed with extremely lavish decoration.

The most architecturally and artistically notable early Christian churches were constructed at the behest of emperors and bishops. Edifices such as the monumental Hagia Sophia in Constantinople (with a space of 74.6 × 69.70m)[46] and the large pilgrimage church for St Simeon Stylites in Kalat Seman only make sense as imperial creations. The Christian emperors residing in Constantinople continued a tradition harking back to the first and second centuries, in creating for the decoration of their churches new types of capitals, architraves, friezes and so forth, invented and sculptured by workmen in the quarries of the island of Prokonnesos near Constantinople. From the end of the fourth century to the sixth century, Prokonnesian building material and liturgical furniture – such as chancel screens, altars and ambos – were exported to nearly all countries of the Mediterranean. Most of the churches (e.g., in Ravenna, the residence of the emperor from 402 onwards) were built with capitals, columns and chancel screens from the Prokonnesian quarries. For the church of Hagia Sophia, constructed by the emperor Justinian, many new and fancy types of capitals were invented, but the fanciest were restricted to the

---

46 R. Mainstone, *Hagia Sophia*; M. L. Fobelli, *Un tempio per Giustiniano*.

Megale Ekklesia, and have never been exported. This building, the cathedral and the stateroom of the emperor, is the largest church building ever built. Its ambitious design had no predecessor and was never copied by another church building, because it was meant to be incomparable and insuperable. As far as we know Hagia Sophia was not decorated with figural mosaics; its mosaic decoration was aniconic.

Churches not constructed at the behest of an emperor owe their existence to the support of affluent private citizens like Julianus Argentarius in Ravenna and local bishops. In Gerasa (see above), a series of donors' inscriptions provide precious insight into the relationships between bishops and private church patrons. The tripartite complex (mentioned above) consisting of the churches of St John and Sts Cosmas and Damian (531–3) was financed by two patrons, one of whom was a tribune named Dagistaeus. The patrons of the church of Bishop Elias (558–9), Beroios and Eulampia, were a member of the senatorial order and an official in the provincial administrative apparatus, respectively. The donor who financed the restoration of the city walls of Gerasa (440–1) was also a member of the nobility. The so-called Genesius Church (611) was financed by the goldsmith Johannes during the tenure of Bishop Genesius, while a veritable panoply of churches were erected under the aegis of Bishop Paul: the 'Procopius' Church (526), the Church of St George (529–30), the Church above the Synagogue (530–1), the Church of St John the Baptist (531), and the Church of Sts Cosmas and Damian (533). In contrast to the lavish churches in Constantinople, built mostly with Prokonnesian marble, the churches in Jordan re-used ancient building materials of the early imperial period.

In Rome,[47] private patronage financed the building of S. Pudenziana, S. Giovanni e Paolo and S. Stefano in the Via Latina, as well as S. Sabina on the Aventine. The latter was built, c. 422–3, on the property of the matron Sabina with funds provided by an Illyrian Christian named Petrus. The church is 53 m long and, with its twenty-four re-used ancient columns and capitals, its wall intarsia, wall mosaics and a carved cypress door, its rhetoric is that of bishops and popes rather than a private donor.

Although the Church never officially advocated sumptuous architecture in the grand manner, it certainly acted as though it had. As ecclesiastical archi- tecture spread not only to urban areas but also to villages, small settlements and even some remote mountainous or arid regions, it left an indelible and completely new kind of mark on the religious architecture of late antiquity. No other religion in antiquity was the equal of Christianity when it came to

---

47 R. Krautheimer, *Corpus basilicarum Christianarum Romae.*

propagating the architectural style of its houses of worship in such a multifarious and comprehensive manner.

Even though there was never any serious opposition to the sumptuousness of church and baptistery architecture, avowed opponents of pictorial representations emerged in all eras, including individuals such as Epiphanius of Salamis from Palestine. As a rule, figurative paintings and mosaics were used in moderation in fourth-century ecclesiastical spaces because the church was still dealing with the problem of religious images (see above). Hence it is not surprising that the *Liber pontificalis* ('The book of the popes'), which was composed in the sixth century, makes no mention of cycles of pictures in connection with early Christian churches. This book's sole reference to a decorated, coffered ceiling in gold occurs in the chapter on Pope Sylvester, in which it is twice mentioned that gold ornamentation was applied to the ceiling of the Lateran church at the behest of Constantine; the same statement is made about the ceiling in St Peter's.[48] The *Liber pontificalis* does not mention an apse mosaic at all; the apses of the Lateran church and of St Peter's were probably faced with marble. The earliest (accidentally) preserved figurative apse mosaic in a church is in S. Pudenziana (384–99) and depicts Christ and the apostles.[49] In the heavens, however, we see not God the Father but rather a bejewelled crucifix, placed on the hill of Golgotha, with the Tetramorphs of the Apocalypse. The depiction of the sole figure of Christ was deliberately eschewed in order to avoid criticism for making images of God. When Christ is depicted with the apostles, he is primarily portrayed in the role of teacher. But his golden tunica and pallium make him look like a king or an emperor.

The earliest preserved mosaic programme in a papal church is that in S. Maria Maggiore (432–40). In this mosaic, the discourse regarding the divine nature of Jesus and the Mother of God is realised with the aid of imperial iconography. In order to lend Mary credibility as the bearer of God (*theotokos*), she is clad in an imperial diadem, a bejewelled collar, and an embroidered *trabea* (the female toga). The infant Jesus is placed on the imperial throne. The actual birth of Jesus was not depicted since this event required no proof. In the mosaic, the Holy Family is received in Egypt like an imperial legation. This unprecedented and irreproducible iconography was not the product of an ecclesiastical decision but instead sprang from the mind of a theological 'maverick'. The uniqueness of the programme lies in the fact that a cycle on

48 *Liber pontificalis* 34 (ed. Duchesne, I: 172 and 176).
49 C. Ihm, *Die Programme der christlichen Apsismalerei*.

the life of the infant Jesus was displayed on the front apse wall in opposition to an extensive Old Testament cycle in the nave.

The entire programme at S. Maria Maggiore illustrates the underlying idea of Christ's prophecy that the covenant of the Old Testament would be fulfilled by the covenant of the New Testament. The forty-two scenes from the Old Testament in the nave of S. Maria Maggiore were not chosen for their content alone, but were meant to prefigure the salvation history of the New Testament scenes on the triumphal arch. This was in keeping with the general Christian desire to claim the Old Testament as a book about Christ. The underlying idea of the Old Testament cycle is to present God, Christ and the church as God's Holy People from the very beginning. Sarah, Rebecca, Rachel, Sephora and Rahab, all of whom are depicted in striking red-orange garments, are the female bearers of the idea of the pre-existing Church, and are led to the antitypes of Jesus: Abraham, Isaac, Jacob, Joseph, Moses and Joshua. The theologian who devised this 'highbrow' cycle was possibly criticised because the mosaics were unduly difficult to view and their theology insufficiently persuasive; there is no discernible sign that the mosaics from S. Maria Maggiore exercised influence elsewhere.[50]

The purpose of the apse paintings was entirely different from that of the nave mosaics, of whose existence most congregants were probably unaware. The nave mosaics were usually devoted to the earthly life of Christ and the saints. The fact that the apse was located behind the altar would almost automatically mean that its theme was associated with the act of worship. But appearances are deceptive. Apse pictures are not liturgical pictures even when they depict Christ as a particularly large and isolated figure, as is the case in S. Cosma e Damiano in Rome. Apse images were never worshipped, but they attracted notice, and in some cases they teach the believer how to approach the divine. Cult objects must somehow be accessible to and palpable for congregants, but apse pictures never were. Their function was to direct the congregation's gaze to the hereafter. The spherical curve of the apse was itself an image of the cosmos. Virtually all apse pictures portray Christ, Mary or the saints with stars, clouds and rainbows on a blue or gold background. Apse pictures were part of the presbytery, which was clearly separated from the congregation's area in the nave or side aisles. Apse images never tell a story, but instead provide congregants with a glimpse of the kingdom of heaven. Congregants would have found convincing the proposition that, once in heaven, the saints would intercede with Christ and Mary on their behalf. Apse mosaics and

---

50 B. Brenk, *Die frühchristlichen Mosaiken.*

their depictions of a Christian 'Olympus' were one of the most impressive innovations of Christian art.

Propaganda fide post mortem, or:
The consolation of art after death

Most of the catacombs in Rome were outgrowths of family crypts. In other words, the members of affluent families gradually converted to Christianity and then (mainly after 313) donated their crypts to the church. Thus, for example, elements of the original pagan hypogea from the second and third centuries can still be identified today in several catacombs, a particularly impressive example being the second-century hypogeum of the emperor Vespasian's niece Flavia in the Flavian family crypt in the Domitilla catacombs. Most such family crypts were decorated with conventional pagan funerary motifs that were unlikely to offend family members who were Christian converts. Pre-Constantinian Christian paintings are found there only rarely. The catacomb of Callistus originated in the early third century by connecting two formerly separated private hypogea with transversal corridors. The idea underlying this new burial area was revolutionary in that it was church-owned, and as such it is thought to have been used by all believers, the rich and the poor. While in antiquity only affluent people could afford a sarcophagus or a hypogeum, the catacomb administered by Callixtus was the first cemetery where rich and poor people were buried in the same way, that is to say, in *loculi* in the walls of the catacomb corridors. As a Church-owned burial place for the rich and the poor the catacombs were a truly Christian invention which had its effect up to the present time.

But the idea of humility and modesty underlying this creation was soon subverted when some affluent private and ecclesiastical people decided to have not only *loculi*, but also private cubicula, richly painted with scenes from the Old and New Testaments. Marble sarcophagi with Christian scenes were similarly located within the private cubicula. Even so, whereas pagan funeral inscriptions often inform us about the worldly success of the deceased in prolix detail, Christian funeral inscriptions are mostly laconic and tend to suppress individual accomplishments.

Catacombs proved to be a relatively short-lived phenomenon. Although pilgrims visited catacombs containing martyrs' tombs until early medieval times, from the fifth century onward, Christian congregants were increasingly buried in cemeteries above ground.

While the Church offered many believers, especially the poor, an honourable burial and tomb through the creation of the catacombs, affluent Christians continued to construct hypogea and mausoleums along the major roads outside the cities and decorated these with paintings and stucco. It is interesting to note that in Rome, where the production of pagan marble sarcophagi, richly decorated with reliefs, had since the second century been an important medium for the 'upper classes' to express their wishes and concerns about the after-life, sarcophagi were also chosen by wealthy Christians. Christian sarcophagi were mainly found in private mausoleums, or were placed beneath church floors, as was frequently the case. Burial in a church floor (such as in Sebastiano on the Via Appia, SS. Pietro e Marcellino, or S. Agnese) was available only to the rich. The idea was to secure the saint's intercession after resurrection. This explains, for example, why the sarcophagus of Junius Bassus, the prefect of Rome (d. 359), was found in a perfect state of conservation in 1595 in the presbyterium of Old St Peter's: the sarcophagus was never visible to the public at all; it was buried immediately after the death of the prefect.

Sarcophagi were primarily expressions of the wishes of wealthy individuals, who nonetheless must have made some kind of arrangements with the head of the sarcophagus workshop and with one ecclesiastical authority or another. We can only speculate as to the nature of these arrangements. However, the fact that one of the earliest Christian sarcophagi,[51] the bathtub sarcophagus in S. Maria Antiqua in Rome (250–70), depicts Jonah at rest alongside the baptism of Christ indicates that theology must have been a factor in choosing themes for sarcophagus ornamentation. At the same time, the scope of the Jonah scene is expanded here to a pastoral with grazing sheep, while two fishermen tinkering with a fish trap have been included in the aquatic scene that depicts Christ's baptism. The three central figures – the female *orans*, the teacher with the scroll, and the shepherd – are part and parcel of the traditional iconography of third-century pagan sarcophagi.

While Christian sarcophagi before Constantine were essentially one-of-a-kind creations, their evolution followed a radically different course after 313. From this point on, sarcophagi decorated with traditional pagan motifs faded into the background, while massive numbers of serially produced Christian sarcophagi began appearing on the market. Inasmuch as sarcophagi were ordered solely by members of the affluent upper class, it is safe to assume that

---

51 G. Bovini and H. Brandenburg, *Repertorium der christlichantiken Sarkophage*; J. Janssens, *Vita e morte del cristiano*; U. Volp, *Tod und Ritual*.

in the period following the 'Edict' the entire imperial entourage as well as all government officials began to orient themselves towards Christianity.

It is unlikely that buyers of sarcophagi had much to say in choosing the decorative programmes that accompanied them into the hereafter. Instead, the church, in the guise of art-friendly clerics, was probably asked *nolens volens* to express its views on the choice of scenes that were carved into sarcophagi. In their capacity as creators of the decorative programmes, the heads of sarcophagi workshops must have also played a role in determining the iconographic programme. We should therefore resist the temptation to regard the commercialisation of Christian sarcophagi as a sign of religious belief on the part of their purchasers. Burial in a marble sarcophagus decorated with figurative scenes occurred, from the purchaser's point of view, in a setting that was primarily societal and economic and had little to do with religion or the evolution of a distinct mentality.

Around the turn of the fourth century, figuratively decorated marble sarcophagi began to disappear from the repertoire of Roman Christian art. Sarcophagus ornamentation was an ephemeral phenomenon in the history of art, one that was displaced by the overriding concern on the part of affluent Christians to procure for themselves a burial place in close proximity to a martyr's tomb in a prominent martyr's church. This held true until medieval times. The late fourth-century *Apostolic constitutions* 6.30.2 encourages Christians to 'gather together without fear in the cemeteries to read from the Divine Scriptures and sing psalms for the martyrs who rest there, for all the saints and for your brothers who rest in the Lord'.

Since the church issued no regulations or prohibitions regarding the use of images, affluent private citizens were often buried with objects decorated with Christian scenes. Thus, for example, fragments of gold-glass bowls decorated with Christian scenes were found in the catacombs embedded in the mortar adjacent to the graves. They are demonstrably the vestiges of vessels and bowls that may well have been baptismal gifts for affluent citizens, who took these *memoria* of their conversion with them into the beyond. Fourth-century wooden boxes whose metal fittings are ornamented with Christian themes were found at Dunaujvaros (Intercisa) in Hungary. These were apparently jewellery boxes that belonged to prominent Christian women, who likewise carried these *memoria* of their affluence with them to the grave.

Wealthy Christians sought consolation not only in art but above all from martyrs and saints. In the early fourth century an affluent matron named Asclepia from Salona-Marusinac seems to have interred the relics of the martyr Anastasius in the lower level of her two-storey family mausoleum, thus privatising the practice of martyr worship.[52] On more than one occasion, women were instrumental in recovering martyrs' remains. According to an epigram by Pope Damasus, a woman named Lucilla, who was of course a member of the nobility, interred the mortal remains of Sts Peter and Marcellinus.[53] The sarcophagi of Asclepia and her husband, as well as the martyr's tomb, were placed in the vaulted first floor of Asclepia's hypogeum, which could only be accessed via a steep staircase. The two sarcophagi were separated from the martyr's tomb by a wall with a fenestella (small window) in it whose raison d'être was probably that during her lifetime Asclepia had been able to descend into this lower level to view the martyr's tomb. Or did Asclepia perhaps intend to maintain post-mortem visual and auditory contact with the martyr? The funeral repast to honour the deceased, as well as the mass on the martyr's anniversary, was held in the upper level of the mausoleum, which was fitted with an apse and stone benches. Following the collapse or destruction of the mausoleum, in the early fifth century the church perpetuated the cult of the martyr Anastasius by constructing two three-nave basilicas east of the site of the mausoleum. The martyr's remains were transferred to the east apse of the south basilica, where they could be available to all Christians. Only privileged citizens (i.e., the wealthy) received permission to be interred near the martyr's burial place, in the north basilica.

Manastirine,[54] an *extra muros* necropolis located on a road north of Salona, is one of the few Roman necropolises where it is possible to trace the paradigms of burial practices in antiquity from the first to the sixth centuries, as well as the advent and evolution of a martyr's tomb from the time it belonged to the private sphere until it was monumentalised by the church. Noteworthy here are the pagan and Christian burials side by side and the diversity of tomb types and burial paraphernalia, which, as at other burying grounds, bear witness to the gradual transition from cremation to interment. The elements that substantiate this evolution are first- and second-century stone urns, amphora tombs from the second to sixth centuries, tombs made of tegulae (flat, rectangular tiles), and masonry burial chambers, many of which feature massive barrel vaults and painting, or elaborately sculpted sarcophagi.

The martyr Domnio was buried in the predominantly pagan necropolis of Manastirine in the early fourth century. From approximately 320 to 420, upper-class citizens (i.e., bishops) were interred north of Domnio's tomb, above

---

52 For the following, see Brenk, *Die Christianisierung der spätrömischen Welt*, 103–4.
53 Damasus, *Epigr.* 28 (ed. Ferrua, 161).
54 N. Duval et al., eds., *Salona III*.

which an aedicule was probably constructed, whereas walls were built around bishops' graves. Monumentalisation was carried out on a more modest scale here. Just north of Domnio's burial place, an inscription was found containing the names of the five companions (Antiochianus, Gaianus, Telius, Paulinianus, Asterius) who suffered martyrdom with Domnio. Bishop Primus was likewise interred under the open sky, approximately 3 m west of Domnio's tomb, probably in 304, making his the first known *ad sanctos* burial (or burial 'near the saints'). Primus appears to have chosen a burial place on the basis of family ties, so as to be close to his uncle Domnio. Some years later, private circular mausoleums in the form of funeral apses, as well as a trapezoidal burial area, were erected, which indicates that wealthy members of the congregation gradually bought up the burial ground so that they could be buried near the saints. The consolation of being buried near the saints was reserved for the rich upper classes.

In 435, a 47.5 × 20.4m church was finally built over the cemetery but was likewise reserved for the last remains of the rich and powerful – although construction of the church did have the virtue of allowing the whole congregation to attend masses in the saints' honour. The transept containing the martyrs' and bishops' tombs was walled off from the nave by low marble walls, with the result that the transverse area in front of the apse was visible but not accessible from the nave.

Why did the church wait more than a century before constructing a church adjacent to or over these martyrs' tombs? Did the church have to wait before it could buy up the former pagan property to build on it? That the church lacked the financial resources for this is hard to believe. In any case, the prospect of being interred near the martyrs in a public cemetery must have appealed to members of the upper class.

A pinnacle of luxury and privilege (*omnibus impensis*, in the words of the consecration inscription) was achieved by Constantine's daughter Constantina (d. 354 in Bithynia). Probably between 338 and 350, she had a monumental mausoleum and church (S. Costanza) built adjacent to the tomb of St Agnes on Via Nomentana in Rome. The mausoleum – which is similar to the one in the Church of the Holy Sepulchre in Jerusalem in that it has a central-plan room with pilasters and a circular ambulatory – was fitted out with every decorative luxury that early Christendom could muster: innovative prestige architecture, uniform re-used columns and capitals, as well as marble covering for the vertical walls; mosaics in the domical vault, in the transverse apses, on the ceiling of the exedra above the sarcophagus, and in the cupola; and a porphyry sarcophagus imported from Egypt. Christian and explicitly theological themes are depicted only in the cupola mosaics in the two transverse apses, whereas the mosaics in the domical vault and the porphyry sarcophagus contain purely ornamental elements as well as Cupids harvesting and trampling grapes. Constantina's sarcophagus was placed in the exedra opposite the entrance, rather than in the middle of the central-plan room. Since Christian themes were rarely used as decorative elements on porphyry sarcophagi, one should avoid reading too much into the non-Christian ornamentation on Constantina's sarcophagus. The ram, peacock and Cupids trampling grapes were conventional symbols of good luck. The programmatic cupola decoration consisting of candelabras set on islets of a river landscape was entirely conventional. Twelve Old Testament scenes apparently corresponded to twelve New Testament scenes, but a cyclical narrative was not attempted. Instead, the decoration consisted solely of discrete items that were meant to be read as such – if they were visible at all, which is unlikely to have been the case. What sort of a rationale can be teased out of the mausoleum's succession of scenes from the books of Tobit, Joshua, Daniel and Moses? The determining factor was undoubtedly the desire to legitimise the Old Testament as pre-Christian doctrine, using a typology that was constantly referenced to aquatic themes. A playful river landscape extends along the base of the cupola, replete with putti frolicking and fishing, as well as birds, sea creatures and fishermen. These conventional images are meant to soften the viewer up for the Christian scenes, and the overall effect is indeed one of playfulness and intimacy. Somehow, one cannot avoid the impression that even biblical scenes were regarded as good luck charms. The images refer in a trivialising fashion to a kind of good luck to which the Old Testament already refers.

Viewed from this perspective, there is not all that much difference between the imperial mausoleum of S. Costanza and the minuscule early fourth-century mausoleum of the Julian family in the Vatican necropolis, which is only 14m from St Peter's tomb. In this mausoleum, Sol the sun god is depicted on a quadriga amongst grape vines with a shepherd, a fisherman and Jonah being swallowed by the whale. The unambiguously Christian but not necessarily theological iconography of Jonah is loosely associated with a fisherman, and this in turn is compatible with the symbols of the shepherd and sun, which act as additional pointers for achieving happiness in the hereafter. The fact that the Julian family mausoleum is so small that visitors must stoop to enter it means that it was not designed to be entered and that its mosaics were not meant to be viewed.

Afterword

At first glance, early Christian art appears to be a mere clone, or at best an identical twin, of its Greco-Roman counterpart, and there is indeed no denying the fact that early Christian art is based on the Greco-Roman artisan tradition and mindset. The ubiquity of Greco-Roman architecture emboldens us to categorise buildings such as Hagia Sophia in Constantinople or S. Vitale in Ravenna as 'classical' without giving the matter further thought. However, if we could take a time machine back to the sixth century, we would immediately be struck by the prevalent depopulation of ancient cities, where Christian edifices rose among ruined, empty and abandoned structures. Although the church had become a major property owner, it was unable to safeguard its holdings; this was all the more true of private property owners. The affluent were subject to a heavy tax burden, while foreign peoples were descending on the Roman empire from all sides. Faith in the economic and social viability of the Roman state was crumbling, a process that was hastened by the fact that in the fifth and sixth centuries the Church took over governmental functions such as building walls and roads, operating public baths and administering cities.[55] The educational level of the general population had declined steeply. The Church was increasingly intolerant of the whimsical approach to Greco-Roman myths, whose weakened hold on the minds of the populace left a vacuum that could not be filled by the legends of Christian saints and miracles.

The term 'classical' cannot be applied indiscriminately to all of early Christian art and architecture, for beginning in the third and fourth centuries the co-ordinates of the classical world began to undergo a fundamental shift. This was partially attributable to Christianity itself, which since 313 had acquired semi-official stature as an institution. Although a genuine state religion was not established until the reign of Justinian, the numerous ties that bound the Christian governing class to the Roman state led to continuity, as well as a new era in the realm of architecture and the visual arts. The collapse of centralised Roman authority, which worked to the advantage of the church under Constantine and Theodosius I, spawned increasing numbers of unique local artistic and architectural styles. A pilgrim who, for example, departed on a pilgrimage that took him from his native province of Noricum through Italy, North Africa, Egypt, Palestine, Syria, Asia Minor and Greece would have encountered a different form of worship and ecclesiastical architecture every

---

55 See further ch. 14, above.

100 km. This pilgrim would also have readily recognised the fact that, despite all this artistic, architectural and religious diversity, faith in one God reigned supreme everywhere he went – a faith that created a heretofore unprecedented commonality among Christians in the Mediterranean region.*

Bibliography

PRIMARY SOURCES

Apostolic constitutions (SC 320, 329, 336)
Canons of Hippolytus (PO 31)
Clement of Alexandria. *Paedagogus* (GCS Clemens Alexandrinus, 1)
Cyril of Jerusalem. *Catechesis* (PG 33)
Damasus. *Epigrammata*. Ed. A. Ferrua, *Epigrammata Damasiana* (Rome, 1942)
Egeria. *Travels* (SC 296)
Justin. *Dialogue with Trypho* (PTS 32)
Liber pontificalis, ed. L. Duchesne (Paris, 1886, 1892); supplementary volume, ed. C. Vogel (Paris, 1957)
Notitia dignitatum, ed. Otto Seeck (Berlin, 1876)
Paulinus. *Carmina* (CSEL 30)
Prudentius. *Peristefanon* (CCSL 126)
Synod of Elvira, canons (PL 84)
Tertullian. *Adversus Marcionem* (CCSL 1)
Vitruvius. *On architecture*; trans. F. Granger, LCL (London, 1931–4)

SECONDARY SOURCES

Blaauw, De, S. *Cultus et decor. Liturgia e architettura nella Roma tardoantica e medievale* (Vatican, 1994)
  'Das Fastigium der Lateranbasilika: Schöpferische Innovation, Unikat oder Paradigma?', in B. Brenk, ed., *Innovation in der Spätantike* (Wiesbaden, 1996), 53–64
Bovini, G. and H. Brandenburg. *Repertorium der christlich.antiken Sarkophage. Vol. 1: Rom und Ostia*, ed. F. W. Deichmann, (Wiesbaden, 1967)
Brenk, B. *Architettura e immagini del sacro nella tarda antichità* (Spoleto, 2005)
  Die Christianisierung der spätrömischen Welt (Wiesbaden, 2003)
  Die frühchristlichen Mosaiken von S. Maria Maggiore zu Rom (Wiesbaden, 1975)
  Spätantike und frühes Christentum, Propyläen-Kunstgeschichte, Suppl.-Bd. 1 (Frankfurt-am-Main, 1977)
  'Le texte et l'image dans la "Vie des Saints" au mogen âge: Rôle du concepteur et rôle du peintre', in *Texte et image: Actes du colloque international de Chantilly (13 au 15 octobre 1982)* (Paris, 1984), 31–9
Davis-Weyer, Caecilia. *Early medieval art 300–1150* (Englewood Cliffs, NJ, 1971)
Deichmann, F. W. *Ravenna. Geschichte und Monumente* (Wiesbaden, 1969)
  Ravenna. Hauptstadt des spätantiken Abendlandes. Kommentar 1.Teil (Wiesbaden, 1974)

---

* I express my warmest thanks to Herbert Kessler for reading and correcting my text (BB).

Dölger, F. J. 'Die Firmung in den Denkmälern des christlichen Altertums', *Römische Quartalschrift für christliche Altertumskunde und für Kirchengeschichte* 19 (1905): 1–41
   Sphragis. Eine altchristliche Taufbezeichnung (Paderborn, 1911)
Duval, N. and J. Guyon. *Les premiers monuments chrétiens de la France* (Paris, 1995)
Duval, N., E. Marin et al., eds. *Salona III. Manastirine, établissement préromain, nécropole et basilique paléochrétienne* (Rome, 2000)
Février, P.-A. 'Baptistères, martyrs et reliques', *Rivista di archeologia cristiana* 62 (1986): 109–38
Fobelli, M. L. *Un tempio per Giustiniano. Santa Sofia di Costantinopoli e la descrizione di Paolo Silenziario* (Rome, 2005)
Ihm, C. *Die Programme der christlichen Apsismalerei vom vierten Jahrhundert bis zur Mitte des achten Jahrhunderts* (Wiesbaden, 1960)
Janssens, J. *Vita e morte del cristiano negli epitaffi di Roma anteriori al sec. VII.* (Rome, 1981)
Khatchatrian, A. *Les baptistères paléochrétiens. Plans, notices et bibliographie* (Paris, 1962)
Klauser, Th. 'Erwägungen zur Entstehung der altchristlichen Kunst', *ZKG* 76 (1965): 1–11
Koch, Guntram. *Frühchristliche Sarkophage*, Handbuch der Archäologie (Munich, 2000)
Kraeling, C. H. *The Christian building. The excavation at Dura Europos. Final report* VIII/2 (New Haven, 1967)
Krautheimer, R. *Corpus Basilicarum Christianarum Romae* (Vatican 1937–77)
Lassus, J. *Sanctuaires chrétiens de Syrie* (Paris, 1947)
Maier, J.-L. *Le baptistère de Naples et ses mosaïques*, Paradosis XIX (Fribourg, 1964)
Mainstone, R. *Hagia Sophia. Architecture, structure and liturgy of Justinian's great church* (London, 1988)
Murray, M. C. 'Art in the early church', *JTS* 28 (1977): 303–45
Pekary, T. *Das römische Kaiserbildnis in Staat, Kult und Gesellschaft dargestellt anhand der Schriftquellen* (Berlin, 1985)
Piétri, C. 'Concordia apostolorum et renovatio urbis. Culte des martyrs et propaganda pontificale', *MEFRA* 73 (1961): 275–322
Pillinger, Renate. *Die Tituli Historiarum oder das sogenannte Dittochaeon des Prudentius. Versuch eines philologisch-archäologischen Kommentars* (Vienna, 1980)
Schlunk, Helmut. *Die Mosaikkuppel von Centcelles*, Bd. 1: Text, Bd. 2: Tafeln und Beilagen, Madrider Beiträge 13 (Mainz, 1988)
Stern, H. 'Les mosaiques de l'église de S. Constance à Rome', *DOP* 12 (1958): 157–233
Tchalenko, G. *Les églises syriennes à Bêma* (Paris, 1990)
Thümmel, H. G. *Die Frühgeschichte der ostkirchlichen Bilderlehre* (Berlin, 1999)
Volp, U. *Tod und Ritual in den christlichen Gemeinden der Antike* (Leiden, 2002)

Index